BIBLIOGRAPHY OF AMERICAN LITERATURE

VOLUME 5

BIBLIOGRAPHY OF

American Literature

COMPILED BY JACOB BLANCK

for the Bibliographical Society of America

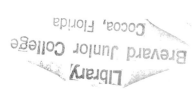

VOLUME FIVE

WASHINGTON IRVING to HENRY WADSWORTH LONGFELLOW

NEW HAVEN AND LONDON: *Yale University Press*

1969

The compilation of the manuscript of *Bibliography of American Literature* was made possible by a grant from the Lilly Endowment, Inc., of Indianapolis, Indiana, to the Bibliographical Society of America.

This fifth volume of

Bibliography of American Literature

is dedicated to the ever green memory of

JOSIAH KIRBY LILLY

1893–1966

His passing "leaves a lonesome place against the sky"

Contents

Authors in Volume Five

ILLUSTRATIONS

Acknowledgments

*They helped every one his neighbour; and every
one said to his brother, Be of good courage.*
—Isaiah, xxxxi:6

MANY—LIBRARIES and librarians, collectors, antiquarian booksellers, fellow-bibliographers and others—have, in one way or another, in large part or in small, contributed to this compilation. The list is long—far longer than that given here or of the sum total of the names published in the preceding volumes of the *Bibliography* under *Location Symbols* and *Acknowledgments*.

If it were practical, this list would include (with grateful thanks) the names of the anonymous catalogers, page-boys, deck attendants, and all those others who, methodically and efficiently, make modern libraries the remarkable instruments they are. To all these silent contributors the *Bibliography* is deeply grateful.

With each passing year (the *Bibliography* is now in its twenty-sixth year) the list—and the debt of gratitude—grows.

First and foremost the *Bibliography* is grateful to the Lilly Endowment, Inc., of Indianapolis, Indiana, whose continued support has brought the *Bibliography* this far;

The members of the *Bibliography's* Supervisory Committee (and the order of presentation is alphabetical): Frederick B. Adams, Jr., James T. Babb, C. Waller Barrett, William H. Bond, the late Clarence S. Brigham, the late William A. Jackson, David A. Randall, the late Carroll A. Wilson;

The editorial aides who assisted in bringing this volume to publication: James C. Armstrong, who resigned to make a more direct contribution to society; Kenneth E. Carpenter, an imaginative and stalwart assistant who resigned to become Associate in The Kress Library of Business and Economics, Harvard Business School; Susan Riddell, who continues to contribute to the project; and Jane Fulton Smith, who resigned to pursue bibliography in a less exacting area;

Messrs. Tin Shue Chin, Robert V. Gross and Merwin Phelps, all of The Library of Congress, who furnished copyright deposit dates and other information;

Messrs. Paul Goren and Perry O'Neil, tireless contributors of information relating to materials in The New York Public Library;

Messrs. Colin Clair and Simon Nowell-Smith, who furnished much precise information relating to British publication of our authors. The *Bibliography's* list of Henry James was vastly improved by Mr. Nowell-Smith's contributions;

Houghton Mifflin Company, surely a pillar of American literature, which generously permitted examination of its earlier manufacturing records;

And all these whose cooperation has been of immeasurable help:

John Eliot Alden, The Boston Public Library

Elizabeth Baer, Johns Hopkins University

James Belliveau, The Boston Athenæum

Mary E. Brown, The American Antiquarian Society

Roger Butterfield, New York City

Richard Cary, Colby College Library

Earle E. Coleman, Princeton University Library

Frank X. Cox, The Houghton Library

Thomas H. de Valcourt, The Longfellow House, Cambridge, Mass.

Donald C. Gallup, Yale University Library

Julia E. Harty, The Library of Congress

Christine D. Hathaway, Brown University Library

Parkman D. Howe, Needham, Mass.

Carolyn E. Jakeman, The Houghton Library

Dan H. Laurence, New York City

Edward N. MacConomy, Jr., The Library of Congress

Joseph P. McCarthy, The Houghton Library

Jocelyn J. Moss, The Alderman Library

David L. O'Neal, Milton, Mass.

William H. Runge, The Alderman Library

Marte Shaw, The Houghton Library

Anita Stanley, The Houghton Library

Joseph R. Sullivan, The Houghton Library

Lawrance R. Thompson, Princeton University

Neal B. Thornton, The Alderman Library

Roger J. Trienens, The Library of Congress

Robert L. Volz, Bowdoin College Library

And to all those libraries where the *Bibliography's* staff has been made welcome, is the project grateful. At risk of appearing partial, where partiality is not intended, let it again be recorded that the *Bibliography* is particularly grateful to The Houghton Library where, for so many years, the *Bibliography* has been a guest.

Certain notes (each identified) in the Jack London list are quoted from *Jack London: A Bibliography* (compiled by Hensley C. Woodbridge, John London and George H. Tweney), with the written permission of the publisher, The Talisman Press.

JB

General References

The following references are mentioned in the lists under the designations given.

Allibone	A Critical Dictionary of English Literature, and British and American Authors..., by S. Austin Allibone, 3 Vols.; two supplementary volumes compiled by John Foster Kirk, 1858–1891.
Am Cat	The American Catalogue..., 1880–1911.
Appleton	Appletons' Cyclopaedia of American Biography..., 1887–1901.
B A L	Bibliography of American Literature Compiled by Jacob Blanck for the Bibliographical Society of America, 1955–.
BMu Cat	The British Museum Catalogue of Printed Books, 1881–1905. And, British Museum General Catalogue of Printed Books ..., 1931– .
C H A L	The Cambridge History of American Literature..., 1917–1921.
D A B	Dictionary of American Biography..., 1928– .
D N B	The Dictionary of National Biography..., 1885– .
English Cat	The English Catalogue of Books...Issued in the United Kingdom..., 1864– .
Evans	American Bibliography..., by Charles Evans, 1903–1934. Continued by Clifford K. Shipton, 1955– .
Foley	American Authors 1795–1895 a Bibliography of First and Notable Editions..., by P. K. Foley, 1897.
Griffin	American Historical Association. Bibliography of American Historical Societies..., by Appleton Prentiss Griffin, 1896.
Johannsen	The House of Beadle and Adams and Its Dime and Nickel Novels..., by Albert Johannsen, 1950.
Johnson	American First Editions..., by Merle Johnson, 1929, 1932. And, editions of 1936, 1942, revised by Jacob Blanck.
Kaser	The Cost Book of Carey & Lea 1825–1838, edited by David Kaser ⟨1963⟩.
Kelly	See below under *Roorbach*.
L C Printed Cat	...A Catalog of Books Represented by Library of Congress Printed Cards..., 1942– .
Leon Brothers	Catalogue of First Editions of American Authors, Poets, Philosophers, Historians...Compiled...and for Sale by Leon & Brother, New York, 1885.

Livingston   The Chamberlain Bibliographies. A Bibliography of ... Henry
                   Wadsworth Longfellow ... by Luther S. Livingston, 1908.
Roorbach   Bibliotheca Americana. Catalogue of American Publications,
                   Including Reprints and Original Works ... Compiled and
                   Arranged by O. A. Roorbach, 1852–1861. Continued by
                   James Kelly, 1866–1871.
Sabin   A Dictionary of Books Relating to America, from its Discovery
                   to the Present Time, by Joseph Sabin; concluded by Wilber-
                   force Eames and R. W. G. Vail, 1868–1936.
Stone   First Editions of American Authors a Manual for Book-Lovers
                   ..., by Herbert Stuart Stone, 1893.
Thompson   American Literary Annuals & Gift Books 1825–1865, by Ralph
                   Thompson, 1936.
U S Cat   The United States Catalog ⟨of⟩ Books in Print ..., 1900–.
Wegelin   The bibliographical studies of Oscar Wegelin, pioneer worker
                   in the field of American literature, are cited by title within
                   the lists.
Wilson   Thirteen Author Collections of the Nineteenth Century and
                   Five Centuries of Familiar Quotations, edited by Jean C. S.
                   Wilson and David A. Randall, 1950.
Wright   American Fiction 1774–1850 a Contribution toward a Bibliog-
                   raphy, by Lyle H. Wright, 1939, 1948. *Or:* American Fiction
                   1851–1875 a Contribution toward a Bibliography, by Lyle
                   H. Wright, 1957. *Or:* American Fiction 1876–1900 a Con-
                   tribution toward a Bibliography, by Lyle H. Wright, 1966.

Principal Periodicals Consulted

A L B	Appleton's Literary Bulletin: A Monthly Record of New Books, English, French, German, and American (New York)
A L G	American Literary Gazette and Publishers' Circular (New York)
A M	Analectic Magazine (Philadelphia)
A Me	American Mercury (Hartford)
A Mi	American Minerva (New York)
A M M	American Monthly Magazine (New York)
A M R	American Monthly Review (Cambridge, Boston)
A P C	American Publishers' Circular and Literary Gazette (New York)
A Q R	American Quarterly Review (Philadelphia)
A R	Analytical Review; or, History of Literature, Domestic and Foreign (London)
Arc	Arcturus, a Journal of Books and Opinion (New York)
A R L J	The American Review and Literary Journal (New York)
Ath	Athenaeum; a Journal of Literature, Science, the Fine Arts, Music and the Drama (London)
A W R	American Review: A Whig Journal of Politics, Literature, Art and Science (New York)
B C	British Critic, and Quarterly Theological Review (London)
B F	Bibliographie de la France, ou Journal Général de l'Imprimerie et de la Librairie (Paris)
B J	Brother Jonathan (New York)
B Jl	Broadway Journal (New York)
Bkr	Bookseller (London)
B M	Bookseller's Medium and Publisher's Advertiser (New York)
B M L A	Bent's Monthly Literary Advertiser (London)
C	Critic; a Record of Literature, Art, Music, Science and the Drama (London)
C M	Canadian Monthly and National Review (Toronto)
C R	Critical Review; or, Annals of Literature (London)
C R N	Criterion, Literary and Critical Journal (New York)
E R	Eclectic Review (London)
G R R	General Repository and Review (Cambridge, Mass.)
H	The Harbinger (New York and Boston)
K	Knickerbocker, or New York Monthly Magazine (New York)
L A	Literary American (New York)
L G	Literary Gazette. A Weekly Journal of Literature, Science and the Fine Arts (London)

L G A A	Literary Gazette and American Athenaeum (New York)
L M	Literary Magazine and British Review (London)
L M A R	Literary Magazine, and American Register (Philadelphia)
L S R	Literary and Scientific Repository, and Critical Review (New York)
L W	Literary World (New York)
M A	Monthly Anthology, and Boston Review (Boston)
M M	The Monthly Magazine and American Review (New York)
M R	Monthly Review (London)
N & A	Nation and Athenaeum (London)
N A R	North American Review (Boston, New York)
N E	New Englander (New Haven, Conn.)
N E M	New-England Magazine (Boston)
N L A	Norton's Literary Advertiser (New York)
N L G	Norton's Literary Gazette and Publishers' Circular (New York)
N L R	New London Review (London)
N W	New World. A Weekly Family Journal of Popular Literature, Science, Art and News (New York)
N Y L G	New York Literary Gazette (New York), Sept. 1825–March, 1826. New York Literary Gazette and Journal of Belles Lettres, Arts, Sciences, &c., (New York), Sept. 1834–March, 1835. New York Literary Gazette (New York), Feb.–July, 1839.
N Y M	New-York Mirror: a Weekly Gazette of Literature and The Fine Arts (New York)
N Y R	New York Review (New York)
P	The Panoplist (Boston)
P C	Publishers' Circular and Booksellers' Record (London)
P F	Port Folio (Philadelphia)
P W	Publishers' Weekly (New York)
S L M	Southern Literary Messenger (Richmond, Va.)
S R	Southern Review (Charleston, S. C.)
S W M	Simm's Monthly Magazine, Southern and Western Monthly Magazine and Review (Charleston, S. C.)
T L S	Times Literary Supplement (London)
U A	Universal Asylum and Columbian Magazine (Philadelphia)
U S D R	United States Democratic Review (Washington, D. C.)
U S L A	United States Literary Advertiser, Publishers' Circular, and Monthly Register of Literature and Art (New York)
U S L G	United States Literary Gazette (Boston); United States Review and Literary Gazette (Boston, New York)
U S M D R	United States Magazine and Democratic Review (Washington, D. C., 1837–1840; New York, 1841–1851)
W M R	Western Monthly Review (Cincinnati, Ohio)
W P L N L	Wiley & Putnam's Literary News-Letter, and Monthly Register of New Books, Foreign and American (New York)
W T C	The Publishers' and Stationers' Weekly Trade Circular (New York)
W V	Wöchentliches Verzeichnis der erschienenen und der vorbereiteten Neuigkeiten des deutschen Buchhandels (Leipzig)

Location Symbols

A A S	American Antiquarian Society, Worcester, Mass.
A H	Mr. Arthur Amory Houghton, Jr., Queenstown, Maryland.
A L	Mr. Arthur Lovell, Chicago, Illinois.
A M	The Adirondack Museum, Blue Mountain Lake, N. Y.
A N C	Academy of the New Church Library, Bryn Athyn, Pa.
A W	Mr. Ames W. Williams, Alexandria, Va.
B	Brown University Library, Providence, R. I.
B A	Boston Athenæum, Boston, Mass.
B D	Bowdoin College, Brunswick, Maine.
B M L	Boston Medical Library, Boston, Mass.
B Mu	The British Museum, London.
B P L	Boston Public Library, Boston, Mass.
C	Cornell University Library, Ithaca, N. Y.
C A W	The late Carroll A. Wilson, New York, N. Y.
C C	The Century Association Library, New York, N. Y.
C F	Concord Free Public Library, Concord, Mass.
C H	Craigie-Longfellow House, Cambridge, Mass.
Ch H S	Chicago Historical Society, Chicago, Illinois.
C Ho	Mr. Charles Honce, New York, N. Y.
C H S	Connecticut Historical Society, Hartford, Conn.
CO	Colby College, Waterville, Maine.
C P	Cleveland Public Library, Cleveland, Ohio.
C P L	Cambridge Public Library, Cambridge, Mass.
C S S	Charles Scribner's Sons, New York, N. Y.
C U	Columbia University Libraries, New York, N. Y.
C U A	Catholic University of America Libraries, Washington, D. C.
C W B	Mr. Clifton Waller Barrett, Charlottesville, Virginia.
D	Dartmouth College Library, Hanover, N. H.
De V	Mr. Thomas H. de Valcourt, Cambridge, Mass.
D P L	Detroit Public Library, Detroit, Mich.
D U	Duke University Libraries, Durham, N. C.
E M	Edward Morrill & Son, Boston, Mass.
E M O R Y	Emory University Library, Atlanta, Ga.
F C W	The late Frank C. Willson, Melrose, Mass.
F H B	The late Francis Hyde Bangs, Ogunquit, Maine.
F L P	The Free Library of Philadelphia, Philadelphia, Pa.
F M	Rev. Frederick M. Meek, Chestnut Hill, Mass.
G	The Grosvenor Library, Buffalo, N. Y.

Gd	Goodspeed's Book Shop, Boston, Mass.
G E	The late Gabriel Engel, New York, N. Y.
Gi	Girard College Library, Philadelphia, Pa.
G M A	The late George Matthew Adams, New York, N. Y.
G O	Gilman's Old Books, Crompond, N. Y.
H	Harvard University Library, Cambridge, Mass.
HA	Haverford College Library, Haverford, Pa.
H C	Hamilton College Library, Clinton, N. Y.
H Cr	College of the Holy Cross, Dinand Memorial Library, Worcester, Mass.
H E H	Henry E. Huntington Library & Art Gallery, San Marino, Cal.
H M	Mr. Howard S. Mott, Sheffield, Mass.
H M L	Howard-Tilton Memorial Library, Tulane University, New Orleans, La.
H S P	The Historical Society of Pennsylvania, Philadelphia, Pa.
H U	Howard University Library, Washington, D. C.
H U C	Hebrew Union College Library, Cincinnati, Ohio.
I H S	Indiana State Historical Society, Indianapolis, Indiana.
I S L	Indiana State Library, Indianapolis, Indiana.
I U	Indiana University Library, Bloomington, Indiana.
J B	Mr. Jacob Blanck, Chestnut Hill, Mass.
J C	John Crerar Public Library, Chicago, Illinois.
J D G	Mr. John D. Gordan, New York, N. Y.
J F D	James F. Drake, Inc., New York, N. Y. *Note:* This distinguished firm of antiquarian booksellers ceased operation as of Dec. 31, 1965.
J H	Johns Hopkins University Libraries, Baltimore, Md.
J K L	The late J. K. Lilly, Indianapolis, Indiana.
J N	Mr. Jack Neiburg, Boston, Mass.
J N B	Mr. Jack N. Bartfield, New York, N. Y.
J S K	Mr. John S. Kebabian, New York, N. Y.
J T S	Jewish Theological Seminary of America Library, New York, N. Y.
J T W	Mr. John T. Winterich, Springfield, Mass.
J Z	Mr. Jacob Zeitlin, Los Angeles, Cal.
K	Kansas State Historical Society, Topeka, Kansas.
L B	Lever Brothers, Ltd., Port Sunlight, Cheshire, England.
L C	Library of Congress, Washington, D. C.
L C P	Library Company of Philadelphia, Philadelphia, Pa.
L S	Stanford University Libraries, Palo Alto, Cal.
Md H S	Maryland Historical Society, Baltimore, Md.
M F	Mr. Mason Foley, Hingham, Mass.
M H	Mr. Maxwell Hunley, Beverly Hills, Cal.
M H S	Massachusetts Historical Society Library, Boston, Mass.
M I C	Midwest Inter-Library Center, Chicago, Illinois.
Mi H S	Minnesota Historical Society, St. Paul, Minn.
M L	The Pierpont Morgan Library, New York, N. Y.
M S L	Massachusetts State Library, Boston, Mass.

N	Newberry Library, Chicago, Ill.
N H S L	New Hampshire State Library, Concord, N. H.
N J H	The New Jersey Historical Society, Newark, N. J.
N K	Mr. Norman Kane, Pottstown, Pa.
N L M	The National Library of Medicine, Washington, D. C.
N Y H S	The New-York Historical Society Library, New York, N. Y.
N Y P L	The New York Public Library, New York, N. Y.
N Y S	New York State Library, Albany, N. Y.
N Y S L	New York Society Library, New York, N. Y.
N Y U	New York University Libraries, New York, N. Y.
O	Oberlin College Library, Oberlin, Ohio.
O H S	The Ohio Historical Society, Columbus, Ohio.
O S	Ohio State University Libraries, Columbus, Ohio.
P	Princeton University Library, Princeton, N. J.
PB	Peabody Institute Library, Baltimore, Md.
P D H	Mr. Parkman D. Howe, Needham, Mass.
P H S L	Presbyterian Historical Society, Philadelphia, Pa.
P L	Portland Public Library, Portland, Me.
P P L	Providence Public Library, Providence, R. I.
P S U	Pennsylvania State University Library, University Park, Pa.
R	Rutgers University Library, New Brunswick, N. J.
R B	Mr. Robert K. Black, Upper Montclair, N. J.
R E S	Mr. Roger E. Stoddard, Concord, Mass.
R G	The late Rodman Gilder, New York, N. Y.
R I H	Rhode Island Historical Society Library, Providence, R. I.
R L	Redwood Library & Athenaeum, Newport, R. I.
R L W	Prof. Robert Lee Wolff, Cambridge, Mass.
S	Swarthmore College Library, Swarthmore, Pa.
S G	Seven Gables Bookshop, New York, N. Y.
S M	Smithsonian Institution Libraries, Washington, D. C.
S N S	Mr. Simon Nowell-Smith, Headington, Oxford, England.
S R L	Sondley Reference Library, Pack Memorial Public Library, Asheville, N. C.
S U I	State University of Iowa Libraries, Iowa City, Iowa.
S W J	The late Stuart W. Jackson, Gloucester, Va.
U C	University of Chicago Library, Chicago, Ill.
U C B	University of California, General Library, Berkeley, Cal.
U C L A	University of California at Los Angeles, University Library, Los Angeles, Cal.
U G	The University of Georgia Libraries, Athens, Ga.
U I	University of Illinois Library, Urbana, Illinois.
U K	University of Kentucky Libraries, Lexington, Ky.
U Mi	University of Michigan Library, Ann Arbor, Mich.
U Mn	University of Minnesota Library, Minneapolis, Minn.
U N B	University of New Brunswick Library, Fredericton, New Brunswick, Canada.
U N C	University of North Carolina Library, Chapel Hill, N. C.

U P	University of Pennsylvania Library, Philadelphia, Pa.
U R	University of Rochester Library, Rochester, N. Y.
U S C	University of Southern California Library, Los Angeles, Cal.
U S D A	United States Department of Agriculture Library, Washington, D. C.
U T	The University of Texas, Austin, Texas.
U Tn	University of Tennessee, James D. Hoskins Library, Knoxville, Tenn.
U V	University of Virginia, Alderman Library, Charlottesville, Va.
U W	University of Wisconsin, General Library, Madison, Wis.
V	Vassar College Library, Poughkeepsie, N. Y.
V P	The late Nathan Van Patten, Palo Alto, Cal.
V S L	Virginia State Library, Richmond, Va.
W	Wellesley College Library, Wellesley, Mass.
W C	Williams College Library, Williamstown, Mass.
W C L	Washington Cathedral Library, Washington, D. C.
W F P L	Worcester Free Public Library, Worcester, Mass.
Wh	Wheaton College Library, Norton, Mass.
W H C	Mr. Warder H. Cadbury, Albany, N. Y.
W L P	Mr. Walter L. Pforzheimer, Washington, D. C.
W M G	Mr. William M. Gibson, Upper Montclair, N. J.
W R	Western Reserve University Libraries, Cleveland, Ohio.
W S L	Washington University Libraries, St. Louis, Mo.
W U L	Wesleyan University, Olin Memorial Library, Middletown, Conn.
Y	Yale University Library, New Haven, Conn.

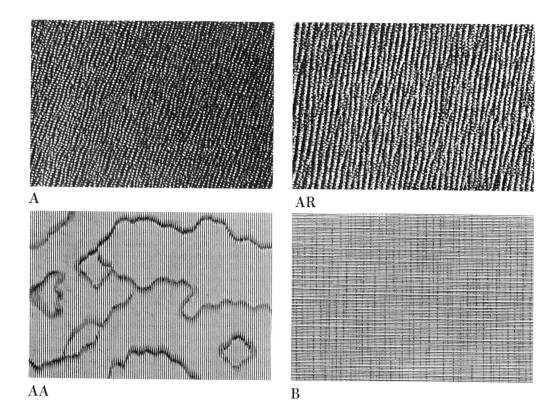

A

AR

AA

B

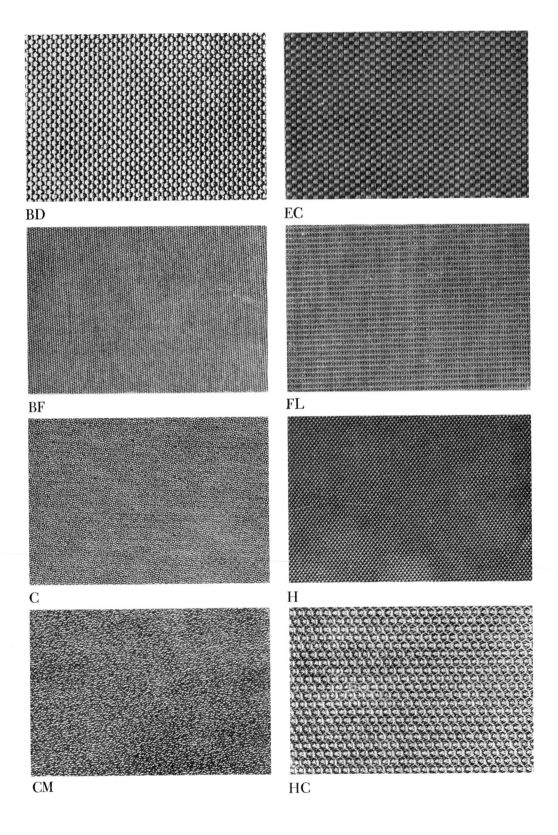

BD

EC

BF

FL

C

H

CM

HC

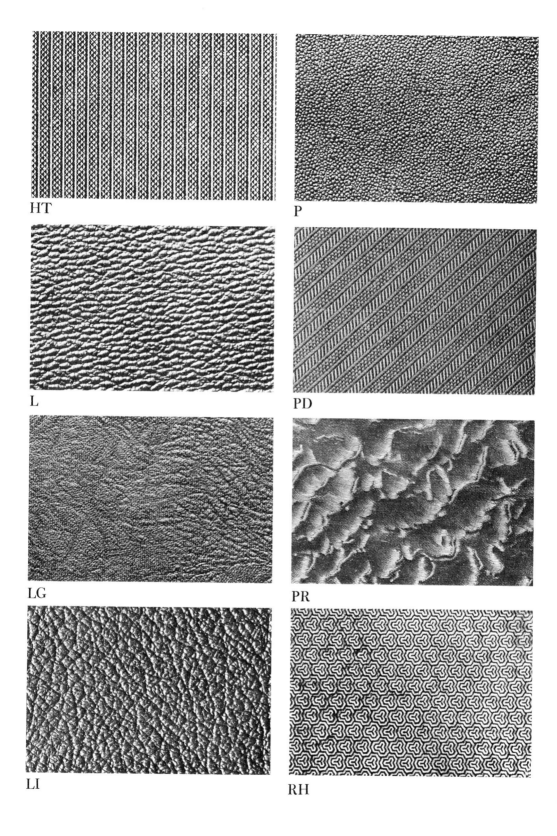

HT

P

L

PD

LG

PR

LI

RH

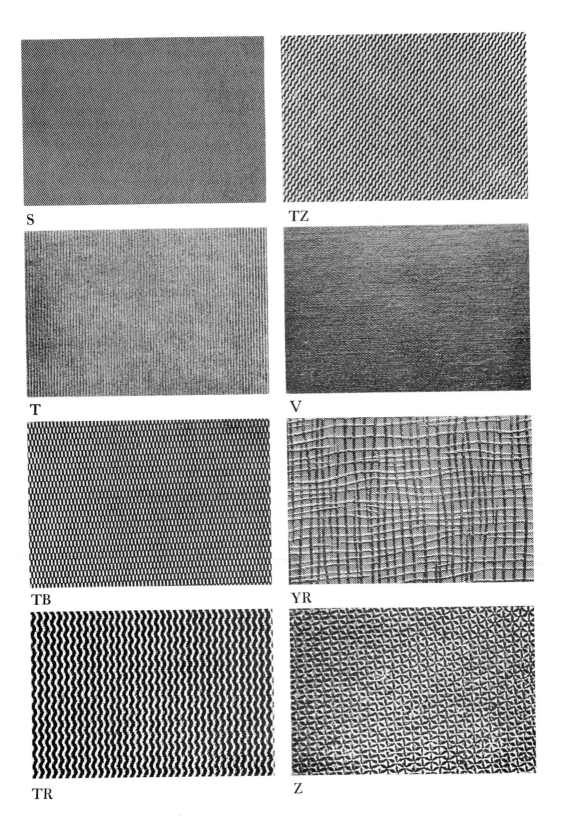

S

TZ

T

V

TB

YR

TR

Z

WASHINGTON IRVING

(Geoffrey Crayon, Diedrich Knickerbocker, Launcelot Langstaff, Jonathan Oldstyle)

1 7 8 3 – 1 8 5 9

For a comment on Irving's collaboration with John Howard Payne and others see entry No. 10222.

10095. ⟨Prospectus⟩ A Voyage to the Eastern Part of Terra Firma, or the Spanish Main, in South-America, during the Years 1801, 1802, 1803, and 1804 ... by F. Depons ... in Three Volumes ... Translated by an American Gentleman.

New-York: Printed by and for I Riley and Co. No. 1, City-Hotel, Broadway. 1806.

⟨i⟩-xxxii. 9⅛" x 5¾".

Printed pale tan paper wrapper.

"This work will be comprised in three large octavo volumes ... It will be printed on ⟨sic⟩ an entire new type ... and embellished with a handsome frontispiece and a large map ... and delivered to subscribers ... in handsome extra boards ... The three volumes are now translating by three gentlemen ... ready for delivery on the 10th of December next."—*From the front wrapper.*

Note: No copy of the published book (see next entry) has been seen with frontispiece as called for by the prospectus. For identification of the translators see next entry.

The prospectus comprises the first four gatherings of Vol. 1 as issued.

H

10096. A Voyage to the Eastern Part of Terra Firma, or the Spanish Main, in South-America, during the Years 1801, 1802, 1803, and 1804. Containing a Description of the Territory under the Jurisdiction of the Captain-General of Caraccas, Composed of the Provinces of Venezuela, Maracaibo, Varinas, Spanish Guiana, Cumana, and the Island of Margaretta; and Embracing Every Thing Relative to the Discovery, Conquest, Topography, Legislation, Commerce, Finance, Inhabitants and Productions of the Provinces, together with a View of the Manners and Customs of the Spaniards, and the Savage as Well as Civilized Indians. By F. Depons ... in Three Volumes ... with a Large Map of the Country, &c. Translated by an American Gentleman.

New-York: Printed by and for I. Riley and Co. No. 1, City-Hotel, Broadway. 1806.

Note: The title-page of Vol. 2 varies somewhat from the other title-pages in the matter of line endings and ornamentation. In some copies of Vol. 1 there is no period after the *I* in *I. Riley* in the imprint.

Vol. 1

⟨i⟩-xxxii, ⟨1⟩-⟨256⟩. Folded map inserted. 8⅜" scant x 5". Two settings have been noted of Sig. B; the sequence has not been established and the following designations are for identification only. The following notes are sufficient for identification:

Setting A	*Setting B*
P. x, line 15	
... *particu-/*	... *particularly/*
P. xi, line 13	
the subject as they have done./	ject as they have done./
P. xii, last line	
ven only of which are navigable./	only of which are navigable./

Some significance may attach to the fact that the prospectus (see preceding entry) is printed from *Setting A.*

1

Vol. 2

⟨1⟩-⟨370⟩.

Two states noted; the sequence presented is presumed correct:

A: p. 361 mispaged 359.

B: p. 361 so paged.

Vol. 3

⟨1⟩-⟨293⟩; blank, p. ⟨294⟩; advertisements, pp. ⟨295-296⟩.

According to the prospectus (see preceding entry) issued in "handsome extra boards"; no copy so bound has been located; seen only in contemporary leather or in relatively recent rebinding.

Translated by Irving in collaboration with his brother, Peter, and George Caines; see *The Life and Letters of Washington Irving,* by Pierre M. Irving, New York, 1862, Vol. 1, p. 219. The book, unidentified by Pierre M. Irving, was identified by Luther S. Livingston in "The First Books of Some American Authors," *The Bookman* (New York), Nov. 1898.

All examined copies of Vol. 1 have the error *Colnmbus* for *Columbus,* p. ⟨1⟩, line 8 from bottom.

At the end of each volume is a table of contents. In rebinding, these tables are frequently misbound at the front.

Title deposited Sept. 22, 1806. Noted as *in press* MA Sept. 1806. Noted for Dec. 10, 1806 (prospectus, see preceding entry). Noted as *in press* MA Dec. 1806. Listed MA April, 1807. The English edition was issued under the title *Travels in South America* . . . ; noted as *in the press* BMLA June, 1807; July, 1807; advertised as *now first published* BMLA Aug. 1807; reviewed ER Jan. 1808.

AAS H NYHS NYPL UV Y

10097. SALMAGUNDI, 1807–1808

This entry is a revision of "*Salmagundi* and its Publisher," by Jacob Blanck, in *The Papers of the Bibliographical Society of America,* Vol. 41, First Quarter, 1947; the reader is referred to it for supplementary material. To quote from that paper: This "is a reëxamination, and not a wholly new description, of *Salmagundi.* It is intended to be used in combination with Langfeld." In general, that statement continues applicable but is amended in an essential point: With all the respect due Messrs. Langfeld and Blackburn for their pioneer work the present entry, its shortcomings notwithstanding, may be

used independently. Since publication of the 1947 effort, other parts in original wrappered state (no great number), and other variants, have been found and are here described.

Parts bearing reprint notices (*Second Edition,* etc.) vary textually from earlier printings but for the purpose of this entry such marked reprints have been all but ignored and are neither listed nor described. Comparison with the *Third Edition* (so marked) of 1820, will probably reveal yet other textual variations; such study has not been made by BAL. For other editions see under 1814, 1824, 1835.

The parts were issued wholly untrimmed. Trimmed sheets in untrimmed wrappers must be viewed with suspicion. Such trimmed sheets have been removed from bound sets and dressed in wrappers to give the appearance of virginity.

Caution is urged in relating this collation to parts in binding. Certain parts (particularly those in binding) have been perfected or made whole by supplying leaves extracted from reprints. A superb example of this is an examined copy of Vol. 2 containing an imperfect *Part 11* perfected by supplying Sig. B from a copy of the *Second Edition* in which, while the pagination is the same as that of the first printing, the lining-off of the text is quite different. Hence, in the example cited the "Note," by William Wizard, Esq., appears on p. 228 and not (as in the first printing) on pp. 227-228. BAL has seen a copy of *Part 12* perfected by insertion of Sig. B from a *Second Edition;* (in the first printing there are but eight lines of text on p. 254; in the *Second Edition* there are twenty-eight lines of text). A bound volume has been seen with an 1807 title-page bound together with a table of contents taken from an 1808 printing. Unfortunately, the list of such frauds appears endless.

In view of the frequent occurrence of such perfected copies users of these notes are urged to check seeming unrecorded variants most carefully against known reprints, *i.e.,* copies bearing reprint notices.

However, it must be emphasized that perfected copies are sometimes found in contemporary, or near-contemporary, bindings which indicates that the perfecting may have been done not by latter-day sophisticators but, perhaps innocently enough, by the original publisher or his binders.

Certain intermediates were caused by stop-press alterations, use of mixed sheets or a combination of both.

In the earliest printings of *Parts 1-6* the part number is not present in the running heads. In *Parts 7-20,* the part number is present in the running heads on each recto.

In 1808 (?) Longworth had a stock of unsold parts and in order to make complete sets, reset and printed needed parts. These reprints (see

A
VOYAGE

TO THE

EASTERN PART OF TERRA FIRMA,

OR THE

SPANISH MAIN,

IN

SOUTH AMERICA,

During the years 1801, 1802, 1803, and 1804, containing a description of the Territory under the jurisdiction of the Captain-General of Caraccas, composed of the Provinces of Venezuela, Maracaibo, Varinas, Spanish Guiana, Cumana, and the Island of Margaretta ; and embracing every thing relative to the Discovery, Conquest, Topography, Legislation, Commerce, Finance, Inhabitants and Productions of the Provinces, together with a view of the manners and customs of the Spaniards, and the savage as well as civilized Indians, by F. DEPONS, late Agent of the French Government at Caraccas. In Three Volumes, with a large Map of the Country, &c.

THIS work will be comprised in three large octavo volumes, each containing between 400 and 500 pages. It will be printed on an entire new type and superfine medium paper, and embellished with a handsome frontispiece and a large map of the country, vignettes, &c. and delivered to subscribers at two dollars and a half per volume, in handsome extra boards. To non-subscribers, the price will be three dollars per volume in extra boards.

The three volumes are now translating by three gentlemen well skilled in the French and English languages, and fully competent to the task of translating, with ability and elegance, this important and interesting work.

This publication will be ready for delivery on the 10th of December next.

notes on *Parts 11-12*) are not signed or folded as individual parts but as parts of a larger whole.

Salmagundi was the joint production of Washington Irving, his brother William, and James Kirke Paulding. The authorship as here ascribed is based on Langfeld-Blackburn; a manuscript in the possession of the late Carroll A. Wilson; Paulding's annotated copy of Vol. 1 of the 1814 edition (in NYPL)*; and on Pierre M. Irving's *Life and Letters of Washington Irving*, New York, 1862–1864. There is some possibility that David Longworth, publisher of *Salmagundi,* was the author of certain of the pieces. Paulding's son, William, quotes his father as saying Longworth had "taken the liberty to add some of his nonsense occasionally" (*Literary Life of James K. Paulding*, N. Y., 1867, p. 39). However, William Paulding also (p. 38) failed to mention William Irving's co-authorship which casts doubt on the accuracy of his comments. Revived in 1819 by J. K. Paulding as *Salmagundi, Second Series.*

The work is so very badly printed that punctuation is often absent from the printed pages. This factor must be considered in checking the transcriptions.

No attempt has been made to record all the textual variations noted; those given below are sufficient for identification. For those who may wish a fuller record of the typographical changes see Langfeld-Blackburn, pp. 7-9, most of which bear up under reëxamination; a few are here reversed; some new ones added.

The final collation of *Salmagundi* has not been achieved. The following caution is no less appropriate than when originally published in Jacob Blanck's collation in PBSA, Vol. 41, 1947: *It would be nice to assert that this description is final and definitive; but with so comparatively few copies to work with ... anything remotely resembling finality is impossible. However, some progress toward that devoutly-to-be-wished end has been made.*

Part 1

SALMAGUNDI; OR, THE WHIM-WHAMS AND OPINIONS OF LAUNCELOT LANGSTAFF, ESQ. AND OTHERS ... ⟨The preceding, to this point, appears at the head of the first page of text of each of the parts, and therefore will not be repeated⟩

NO. I.] Saturday, January 24. 1807.

Caption-title. The above at head of p. ⟨3⟩.

⟨3⟩-20. $6\frac{7}{16}$ x $3\frac{3}{4}$". A single part (No. 19, in H) measures $6\frac{7}{16}$" x $4\frac{9}{16}$" but $6\frac{7}{16}$" x $3\frac{3}{4}$" is usual.

⟨A⟩⁹. *Signed:* ⟨A, A₁⟩, A₂₋₄, ⟨A₅₋₈⟩. A₄ inserted.

* For a description of this volume see PW, Nov. 28, 1936.

Imprint, p. 20, between horizontal rules: *New-York, Printed and Published by D. Longworth.*

⟨Introductory⟩, pp. ⟨3⟩-5. (Washington Irving, Paulding)

"Publisher's Notice," pp. 5-6.

"From the Elbow-Chair ... ," pp. 6-14 (Paulding)

"Theatrics," pp. 14-16 (Langfeld and Pierre Irving credit this to Washington Irving; annotated Vol. I to Paulding)

"New-York Assembly," pp. 17-20 (Washington Irving)

P. ⟨3⟩

First state	*Second state*
In Psalmanazar quotation: *folkesez*	In Psalmanazar quotation: *folksez*

P. 20, line 2

dress he! ...	dress! he ...

This part also occurs in a reprinting (without reprint notice) from an altered setting. In this reprinting the reading on p. ⟨3⟩ is *folksez;* the ... *dress! he* ... reading is present in the last line of p. 19; the imprint at the foot of p. 20 is printed below a double rule.

Part 2

NO. II.] Wednesday, February 4, 1807.

⟨21⟩-38.

⟨A⟩⁹. *Signed:* ⟨A, A₁⟩, A₂₋₄, ⟨A₅₋₈⟩. A₄ inserted.

No imprint on last page of text. Imprint present in *Second Edition.*

"From the Elbow-Chair ... ," pp. ⟨21⟩-27 (Washington Irving)

"Mr. Wilson's Concert," pp. 27-31 (Paulding)

Untitled piece beginning *Sitting late the other evening* ... , pp. 31-34 (Paulding)

"To Launcelot Langstaff, Esq.," pp. 35-37 (William Irving)

"Advertisement," pp. 37-38 (Langfeld and Pierre Irving credit to Washington Irving; annotated Vol. 1 to Paulding)

No textual variations noted.

Part 3

NO. III.] Friday, February 13, 1807.

⟨39⟩-56.

⟨A⟩⁹. *Signed:* ⟨A, A₁⟩, A₂₋₄, ⟨A₅₋₈⟩. A₄ inserted.

In the early printings, p. 56: ∴ *The second edition of No. I, is just published.* Longworth's imprint is not present. In later printings the statement regarding *No. I* is not present; Longworth's imprint is present.

"From My Elbow-Chair," pp. ⟨39⟩-42 (Washington Irving)

"Letter from Mustapha Rub-a-Dub Keli Khan ...," pp. 42-47. (Paulding; one paragraph by Washington Irving)

"Fashions," pp. 47-50 (Washington Irving)

Untitled piece beginning: *One of the greatest sources of amusement ...* , pp. 50-53 (Paulding)

" '——How now, mooncalf!'," pp. 53-54.

"Proclamation," pp. 54-56 (William Irving)

A reprint of No. 3 has been noted; done from a totally different setting although the pagination and signing are the same as in the first printings. The following is sufficient for ready identification:

First printings	*Reprint*
Last words, p. ⟨39⟩	
... *conversation with the/*	... *birds of passage,/*

Part 4

NO. IV.] Tuesday, February 24, 1807.

⟨57⟩-82

⟨A⟩⁹, A⁴. *Signed:* ⟨A₁₋₃⟩, A₄, A₄ ⟨*sic*⟩ inserted, ⟨A₅₋₈⟩, A⟨₁₋₄⟩.

Note: Signature mark A₄ (p. 65) occurs in two states of unknown sequence; either as *4*; or, *A4*.

Below text, p. 82: ⟨*double rule*⟩ / ⟨*three asterisks*⟩ *The second edition of No. II. is now in the* | *press and will be published in a few days.* | ⟨*rule*⟩ | *New-York, Printed and Published by D. Longworth* | ⟨*rule*⟩

"From My Elbow-Chair," pp. ⟨57⟩-60 (Washington Irving)

"Memorandums ...," pp. 61-67 (Paulding)

"From My Elbow-Chair," pp. 67-69

"Flummery ...," pp. 70-80

"General Remark" ⟨*sic*⟩, p. 80

"Notice," p. 81

"Card," pp. 81-82

Textual changes:

First state	*Second state*
P. 74, line 3	
... Toney (11	... Toney (11)
P. 74, line 7 up	
... (ro Lousy anee.)	... (or Lousy-anee.)

P. 76, line 4	
... steal/	... steal,/
P. 76, line 11 up	
... Doctors/	... Doctor's/
P. 77, line 8 up	
... Tony ...	... Toney ...
P. 79, line 7	
good man ...	good man, ...
P. 81, line 6	
... hertofore ...	... heretofore ...
P. 82, line 5	
... english, Will/	... english. Will/

Intermediates have been seen of this part.

Part 5

NO. V.] Saturday, March 7, 1807.

⟨83⟩-104.

⟨A⟩⁹, B². *Signed:* ⟨A, A₁⟩, A₂₋₄, ⟨A₅₋₈⟩, B⟨₁₋₂⟩. Leaf A₄ inserted.

At foot of p. 104: ⟨*rule*⟩ | *New-York, Printed and Published by D. Longworth.*

"From My Elbow-Chair," p. ⟨83⟩

"Letter from Mustapha Rub-a-Dub Keli Khan ...," pp. 84-94 (annotated Vol. 1 credits this to William Irving; Pierre Irving credits to Washington Irving)

"By Anthony Evergreen, Gent.," pp. 94-100 (Washington Irving)

"To the Ladies ...," pp. 101-104 (William Irving)

First state	*Second state*	*Third state*
	P. 99, line 4 up	
... have took ...	... have taken ...	... have taken ...
	P. 99, line 2 up	
... introducing/	... introducini-/	... introducing/
	P. 99, last line	
... unri-/	... unrg/	... unri-/

Part 6

NO. VI.] Friday, March 20, 1807.

⟨105⟩-124.

⟨A⟩⁹, B¹. *Signed:* ⟨A, A₁⟩, A₂₋₄, ⟨A₅₋₈⟩, B. Leaf A₄ inserted.

"From My Elbow-Chair," pp. ⟨105⟩-117 (Washington Irving)

"Theatrics," pp. 117-124 (Washington Irving)

Leaf B (pp. 123-124) was printed from two settings. It is presumed that these were used simultaneously.

Setting A

P. 123, line 7: . . . Philadelphian . . .

P. 123, line 12: . . . chance/

P. 123, line 13: he pappens . . .

P. 123, line 24: . . . vociferously! . . .

P. 123, line 11 up: they do is . . .

P. 123, line 4 up: . . . bull's . . . mortal / ⟨note the italic *s*⟩

P. 124, line 6: . . . such . . .

P. 124, line 12: . . . suspects that he . . .

P. 124, the imprint reads: ⟨rule⟩ | *New-York, Printed and Published by D. Longworth.*

Setting B (occurs in two states)
Setting B, State A

P. 123, line 7: . . . philadelphian . . .

P. 123, line 12: . . . chance he/

P. 123, line 13: happens . . .

P. 123, line 24: . . . vociferously; . . .

P. 123, line 11 up: they do, is . . .

P. 123, line 4 up: . . . bull's . . . mortal stab, /

P. 124, line 6: . . . suce . . .

P. 124, line 12: . . . suspects he that . . .

P. 124, the imprint reads: ⟨rule⟩ | *New-York, printed and published by D. Longworth.*

Setting B, State B

P. 123, line 7: . . . philadelphian . . .

P. 123, line 12: . . . chance he /

P. 123, line 13: happens . . .

P. 123, line 24: . . . vociferously; . . .

P. 123, line 11 up: they do, is . . .

P. 123, line 4 up: . . . bull's . . . mortal stab, /

P. 124, line 6: . . . suce . . .

P. 124, line 12: . . . suspects that he . . .

P. 124, the imprint reads: ⟨rule⟩ | *New-York, printed and published by D. Longworth.*

Part 7

NO. VII.] Saturday, April 4, 1807.

⟨125⟩-142.

⟨A⟩[9]. *Signed:* ⟨A, A₁⟩, A₂₋₄, ⟨A₅₋₈⟩. Leaf A₄ inserted.

Imprint at foot of p. 142: ⟨rule⟩ | *New-York, Printed and Published by D. Longworth.*

"Letter from Mustapha Rub-a-Dub Keli Khan . . . ," pp. ⟨125⟩-135 (Langfeld and Pierre Irving credit to Washington Irving; annotated Vol. 1 to William Irving)

"Note, by William Wizard, Esq.," pp. 130-131.

"From the Mill of Pindar Cockloft, Esq.," pp. 136-140 (William Irving)

"Notes, by William Wizard, Esq.," pp. 140-142 (Paulding)

First state	*Second state*
P. 129, line 11	
. . . excepting . . .	. . . except . . .

Part 8

NO. VIII.] Saturday, April 18, 1807.

⟨i-ii⟩, ⟨143⟩-162. Frontispiece portrait of Launcelot Langstaff, pp. ⟨i-ii⟩; see notes below regarding the portrait.

⟨A⟩[11]. *Signed:* ⟨-₁⟩, ⟨A, A₁⟩, A₂₋₄, ⟨A₅₋₉⟩. Leaf A₄ inserted.

No imprint on p. 162.

"By Anthony Evergreen, Gent.," pp. ⟨143⟩-151 (Langfeld credits to William Irving; annotated Vol. 1 to Washington Irving)

"On Style," pp. 152-159 (Washington Irving)

Untitled piece: *We have been considerably edified . . .* , pp. 159-162 (Washington Irving)

First state	*Second state*
P. 145, line 1	
straws . . .	straw's . . .
P. 146, line 19	
. . . publish, if . . .	. . . publish if . . .
P. 147, line 3 up	
. . . himself, and . . .	himself and . . .
P. 148, line 3	
stantial, house-keeping . . .	stantial house-keeping . . .
P. 148, line 4	
. . . poet, and . . .	. . . poet and . . .
P. 148, line 11	
lampooned, since . . .	lampooned since . . .

P. 148, line 29

... heroics, to make   ... heroics to make ...
...

P. 155, line 14

... at one time ad-   ... at one time, address ...   dress ...

P. 155, line 15

... at another, pass   ... at another pass ...
...

P. 155, line 7 up

... perseverance mere-   ... perseverance,
ly ...   merely ...

P. 155, line 2 up

... instance, have ...   ... instance have ...

P. 156, line 7

... hub-bub, but /   ... hub-bub but /

P. 156, line 18

... addition, which   ... addition which ...
...

P. 156, line 4 up

... money, but ...   ... money but ...

P. 156, line 3 up

... memorial of ...   ... memorial, of ...

P. 157, line 15

... started, the ...   ... started the ...

P. 157, line 10 up

... lodoiska ...   ... Lodoiska ...

P. 157, line 4 up

... *modesty, as* /   ... *modesty as* /

P. 160, line 9 up

... lord mayor, as ...   ... lord mayor as ...

P. 160, line 3 up

... word, the ...   ... word the ...

Intermediates of this part have been seen.

Part 9

NO. IX.] Saturday, April 25, 1807.

⟨163⟩-188.

⟨A⟩⁹, B⁴. *Signed:* ⟨A, A₁⟩, A₂₋₄, ⟨A₅₋₈⟩, B⟨₁₋₄⟩. Leaf A₄ inserted.

Imprint at foot of p. 188: ⟨rule⟩ / *New-York, Printed and Published by D. Longworth.* / ⟨rule⟩

"From My Elbow-Chair," pp. ⟨163⟩-170 (Washington Irving)

"From My Elbow-Chair," pp. 170-172

"Letter from Mustapha Rub-a-Dub Keli Kahn ⟨*sic*⟩ ... ," pp. 172-181 (William Irving according to annotated Vol. 1; Washington Irving according to Pierre Irving)

"From the Mill of Pindar Cockloft, Esq.," pp. 181-188 (William Irving)

No textual variations noted.

Part 10

NO. X.] SATURDAY, MAY 16, 1807.

⟨189⟩-206.

⟨A⟩⁹. *Signed:* ⟨A, A₁⟩, A₂₋₄, ⟨A₅₋₈⟩. Leaf A₄ inserted.

Imprint at foot of p. 206: ⟨*double rule*⟩ / *Printed & publised* ⟨*sic*⟩ *by D. Longworth,* / *at the Shakspeare-Gallery.*

"From My Elbow-Chair," pp. ⟨189⟩-191

"To Launcelot Langstaff, Esq.," pp. 191-198 (Paulding)

"The Stranger in Pennsylvania," pp. 198-206 (Washington Irving)

No textual variations noted; however in the presumed first state the error *publised* (for *published*) is present in the imprint, p. 206; in the presumed second the word is correctly spelled *published*.

Reprinted without change of date, with the following statement at head of p. ⟨189⟩: (*second edition, revised and corrected*) It is probable that the part was also reprinted without reprint notice; indeed, Langfeld (p. 9) so reports.

Part 11

NO. XI.] Tuesday, June 2, 1807. [NO. I. OF VOL. II.

⟨207⟩-228.

⟨A⁹, B²⟩. *Signed:* ⟨A, A₁⟩, A₂₋₄, ⟨A₅₋₈⟩, ⟨B₁₋₂⟩. Leaf A₄ inserted.

At foot of p. 228: ⟨*double rule*⟩ / *Printed & published by D. Longworth,* / *at the Shakspeare-Gallery.*

"Letter from Mustapha Rub-a-Dub Keli Khan ... ," pp. ⟨207⟩-218. (Washington Irving)

"... Mine Uncle John," pp. 219-227 (Paulding)

"Note, by William Wizard, Esq.," pp. 227-228.

First (?) *state*   *Second* (?) *state*

P. 214, line 5 up

... *beer barrels,* in-   ... *beer barrels* indeed ... (The read-   deed ... (The reading is thus in the   ing is thus in the 1814
printing marked   printing.)
Second Edition.)

This part was reprinted from a new setting and issued without reprint notice. Noted only as an integral part of a bound volume with 1808 general title-page and in all likelihood not issued thus as a separate part. Many typographic variations are present but the following is sufficient for ready identification: pp. ⟨207⟩-226. In the original 1807 printing the last word on p. ⟨207⟩ is: *slang-/* In the reset printing the word is: *state, /*

Part 12

NO. XII.] Saturday, June 27, 1807. [NO. II. OF VOL. II.

⟨229⟩-254.

⟨A⟩9, B4. *Signed:* ⟨A, A1⟩, A2-4, ⟨A5-8⟩, B⟨1-4⟩. Leaf A4 inserted.

"From My Elbow-Chair," pp. ⟨229⟩-238

"The Stranger at Home . . . ," pp. 239-248

"From My Elbow-Chair," pp. 249-250

"From the Mill of Pindar Cockloft, Esq.," pp. 250-254 (William Irving)

Imprint at foot of p. 254: ⟨*double rule*⟩ / *Printed by D. Longworth, at the Shakspeare-Gallery.*

No textual variations noted.

It is probable that this part was reprinted from a new setting without reprint notice.

Part 13

NO. XIII. Friday, August 14, 1807. NO. 3 OF VOL. 2.

⟨255⟩-280.

⟨A⟩9, B4. *Signed:* ⟨A, A1⟩, A2-4, ⟨A5-8⟩, B⟨1-4⟩. Leaf A4 inserted.

No imprint at foot of p. 280.

"From My Elbow-Chair," pp. ⟨255⟩-259

"Plans for Defending our Harbour," pp. 259-267

" . . . A Retrospect . . . ," pp. 268-279

"To Readers and Correspondents," pp. 279-280

No textual variations noted.

Reprinted from a new setting without notice of reprint. Noted only as an integral part of a bound volume with 1808 general title-page and in all likelihood not issued as a separate part. Many typographical variations present but the following is sufficient for identification: In the date line: NO. 13 and not NO. XIII as in the original separate printing.

Part 14

NO. 14] Saturday, Sept. 19, 1807. [NO. 4 OF VOL. 2.

⟨281⟩-306.

⟨A⟩9, B4. *Signed:* ⟨A, A1⟩, A2-4, ⟨A5-8⟩, B⟨1-4⟩. Leaf A4 inserted.

Imprint at foot of p. 306: ⟨*rule*⟩ / *Printed by D. Longworth, at the Shakspeare-Gallery.*

"From Mustapha Rub-a-Dub Keli Khan . . . ," pp. ⟨281⟩-291 (Langfeld credits to William Irving; Pierre Irving credits to Washington Irving)

"Cockloft Hall," pp. 292-302 (Washington Irving)

" . . . Theatrical Intelligence," pp. 302-306

No textual variations noted.

Reprinted from a new setting. Noted only as an integral part of a bound volume with 1808 general title-page. In all likelihood not issued as a separate. This reprint may be immediately identified by the presence of signature marks G and H.

Part 15

NO. 15] Thursday, Oct. 1, 1807. [NO. 5 OF VOL. 2.

⟨307⟩-324.

⟨A⟩9. *Signed:* ⟨A, A1⟩, A2-4, ⟨A5-8⟩. Leaf A4 inserted.

"Sketches from Nature," pp. ⟨307⟩-315

"On Greatness," pp. 315-324

First (?) state	*Second (?) state*
	P. 324
No imprint	The following imprint is present: ⟨*rule*⟩ / *New-York, Printed and Published by D. Longworth.*

Reprinted from a new setting. Noted only as an integral part of a bound volume with 1808 general title-page. In all likelihood not issued as a separate. This reprint may be immediately identified by the presence of signature marks I and K.

Part 16

NO 16] Thursday, Oct. 15, 1807 [NO. 6 OF VOL. 2.

⟨325⟩-342.

⟨A⟩9. *Signed:* ⟨A, A1⟩, A2-4, ⟨A5-8⟩. Leaf A4 inserted.

No imprint, p. 342.

"Style at Ballston," pp. ⟨325⟩-332

"From Mustapha Rub-a-Dub Keli Khan . . . ," pp. 333-342 (Washington Irving)

(Prefatory note by L. Langstaff, p. 332)

"Note, by William Wizard, Esq.," pp. 340-341

First state	Second state
	P. ⟨325⟩, line 4
. . . wits a . . .	. . . wits, a . . .
	P. 328, line 22
. . . couple who . . .	. . . couple, who . . .
	P. 330, line 1
transferred, bodily, to . . .	transferred bodily to . . .
	P. 331, line 13
losophy where . . .	losophy, where . . .
	P. 334, line 18
. . . **around;** /	. . . around, /
	P. 336, last line
. . . far from /	. . . Far from /

Intermediates have been noted.

Reprinted from a new setting. Noted only as an integral part of a bound volume with 1808 general title-page. In all likelihood not issued as a separate. This reprint may be immediately identified by the presence of signature marks K2, L, L2.

Part 17

NO. 17] Wednesday, Nov. 11, 1807 [NO. 7 OF VOL. 2.

⟨343⟩-360.

⟨A⟩⁹. *Signed:* ⟨A, A₁⟩, A₂₋₄, ⟨A₅₋₈⟩. Leaf A₄ inserted.

No imprint on p. 360.

"Autumnal Reflections," pp. ⟨343⟩-349

"By Launcelot Langstaff, Esq.," pp. 349-353

"Chap. CIX. of the Chronicles of . . . Gotham," pp. 354-360

First state	Second state
	P. 350, line 22
. . . ancsetors . . .	. . . ancestors . . .

Reprinted from a new setting. Noted only as an integral part of a bound volume with 1808 general title-page. In all likelihood not issued as a separate. This reprint may be immediately iden-

tified by the presence of signature marks M, M2, N.

Part 18

NO. 18] Tuesday, Nov. 24, 1807. [NO. 8 OF VOL. 2.

⟨361⟩-378.

⟨A⟩⁹. *Signed:* ⟨A, A₁⟩, A₂₋₄, ⟨A₅₋₈⟩. Leaf A₄ inserted.

Imprint at foot of p. 378: *New-York, printed and published by D. Longworth.* / ⟨rule⟩

"The Little Man in Black," pp. ⟨361⟩-370

"Letter from Mustapha Rub-a-Dub Keli Khan . . . ," pp. 371-378 (Paulding)

First state	Second state
	P. 373, line 3 up
. . . art . . .	. . . ar . . . ⟨Note: Absence of the *t* due to worn or broken type, not typographical error. It is probable the defect occurred during the earliest printing of this part.⟩
	P. 374, line 4
. . . and, so far . . .	. . . and so far . . .
	P. 374, line 7 up
. . . facinations . . .	. . . fascinations . . .

Intermediates have been seen.

Note: Leaf A₄ occurs in two states of uncertain sequence: Signed *A;* Signed *A₄.*

Reprinted from a new setting. Noted only as an integral part of a bound volume with 1808 general title-page. In all likelihood not issued as a separate. This reprint may be immediately identified by the presence of signature marks O and O2.

Part 19

NO. 19] Thursday, Dec 31 1807 [NO. 9 OF VOL. 2.

⟨379⟩-404.

⟨A⟩⁹, B⁴. *Signed:* ⟨A, A₁⟩, A₂₋₄, ⟨A₅₋₈⟩, B⟨₁₋₄⟩. Leaf A₄ inserted.

No imprint on p. 404.

"From My Elbow Chair," pp. ⟨379⟩-380

"Letter from Mustapha Rub-a-Dub Keli Khan . . . ," pp. 380-391 (Washington Irving)

"By Anthony Evergreen, Gent.," pp. 391-398

"Tea . . . ," pp. 399-404 (William Irving)

(Footnote by W. Wizard, p. 401)

No textual variations noted.

Reprinted from a new setting. Noted only as an integral part of a bound volume with 1808 general title-page. In all likelihood not issued as a separate. This reprint may be immediately identified by the presence of signature marks P, P2, Q, Q2; paged: ⟨379⟩-402.

Part 20

NO. 20] Monday, Jan. 25, 1808. [NO. X OF VOL. II.

⟨405⟩-430; plus: 4 pp., being the title-leaf and table of contents for Vol. II.

⟨A⟩⁹, B⁴; plus: ⟨-⟩². *Signed:* ⟨A, A₁⟩, A₂₋₄, ⟨A₅₋₈⟩, B⟨₁₋₄⟩; plus: ⟨-⟩². Leaf A₄ inserted.

No publisher's imprint at end of text. At foot of p. 430: ⟨*double rule*⟩ / END OF VOLUME II.

"From My Elbow-Chair," pp. ⟨405⟩-414 (Paulding)

"To the Ladies," pp. 415-422

" 'How hard it is' . . . ," pp. 423-430

First State	Second State
P. 417, line 2 up	
. . . exhibit . . .	. . . exhibits . . .

Reprinted from a new setting. Noted only as an integral part of a bound volume with 1808 general title-page. In all likelihood not issued as a separate. This reprint may be immediately identified by the presence of signature marks R and R2; paged ⟨403⟩-424.

THE FRONTISPIECE PORTRAIT

Part 8 contains a frontispiece portrait. The leaf on which it is printed is conjugate with pp. 161-162 and is not an insert as reported by Langfeld. The frontispiece has been noted in seven forms; the following sequence is probable:

Portrait 1

The portrait is uncaptioned. Noted in a copy of *Part 8,* first state; three copies of *Part 8,* intermediate state.

Portrait 2

The portrait is captioned: Launcelot Langstaff, esq. Noted in a copy of *Part 8,* first state; 4 copies of *Part 8,* intermediate state; 3 copies of Vol. 1 with 1807 title-page; 1 copy of Vol. 1, with 1808 title-page.

Portrait 3

The portrait is captioned: Launcelot Langstaff Noted only in a rebound set.

Portrait 4(?)

The portrait is captioned, between horizontal rules: LAUNCELOT LANGSTAFF Noted in a copy of *Part 8, Second Edition;* and, in rebound copies of known reprints.

Portrait 5(?)

The portrait is captioned: LAUNCELOT LANGSTAFF, ESQ. Noted only as a single leaf; no evidence it was ever conjugate with another leaf. Also noted in 2 bound volumes with 1808 title-page.

Portrait 6

The portrait is captioned: Launcelot Langstaff, esq. / FROM THE ORIGINAL DRAWING. Noted only in the edition of 1814.

Portrait 7

The portrait is captioned: LAUNCELOT LANGSTAFF, ESQ. / FROM THE ORIGINAL DRAWING. Printed on laid paper. Noted thus as an inserted frontispiece in the *Third Edition,* 1820.

TITLE-PAGE

No sequence has been determined and the following designations are for identification only. Any attempt to establish a sequence for the several forms of the front matter should be tempered with the realization that multiple setting (and consequent simultaneous printing) is a possibility.

Vol. I

The title-page and table of contents for Vol. I appear to have been issued separately and have not been found in any example of any part; they have been found in bound volumes only. Acting on the assumption that those title-pages dated 1807 preceded those dated 1808, the latter are here ignored.

Vol. II

The title-page and conjugate table of contents for Vol. II occur as the final leaves of *Part 20.*

Title-Page A, Vol. I

SALMAGUNDI; / OR, THE / WHIM-WHAMS AND OPINIONS / OF / LAUNCELOT LANGSTAFF, ESQ. / AND OTHERS. / ⟨double rule⟩ / ⟨3 lines of pidgin Latin⟩ / With baked, and broiled, and stewed, and toasted, / And fried, and boiled, and smoked, and roasted, / We treat the town. / ⟨double rule⟩ / VOL. I. / ⟨double rule⟩ / NEW-YORK: / PRINTED & PUBLISHED BY D. LONGWORTH, / At the Shakespeare-Gallery. / 1807

Note spelling of *broiled, stewed, boiled, smoked, Shakespeare.*

No copyright notice on verso.

Title-Page B, Vol. I

SALMAGUNDI; / OR, THE / WHIM-WHAMS AND OPIN-
IONS / OF / LAUNCELOT LANGSTAFF, ESQ. / AND
OTHERS. / ⟨double rule⟩ / ⟨3 lines of pidgin
Latin⟩ / With baked, and broiled, and stewed,
and toasted, / And fried, and boiled, and
smoked, and roasted, / We treat the town. /
⟨double rule⟩ / VOL. I. / ⟨double rule⟩ / NEW-
YORK: / PRINTED & PUBLISHED BY D. LONGWORTH, /
At the Shakspeare-Gallery. / ⟨dotted rule⟩ /
1807

Note spelling of *broiled, stewed, boiled, smoked,
Shakspeare.*

Copyright notice on verso: Salmagundi; or the
Whim-Whams and Opinions of / Launcelot
Langstaff, Esq. / ⟨double rule⟩ In some copies
the *f* in *of* is not present, in some copies the
hyphen in *Whim-Whams* is not present.

In table of contents:

Entry for p. 14: Theatrics . . .

Entry for p. 61, line 2: . . . Cockloft Travelling,
/ ⟨*Cockloft* is erroneous.⟩

Title-Page C, Vol. I

SALMAGUNDI; / OR, THE / WHIM-WHAMS AND OPIN-
IONS / OF / LAUNCELOT LANGSTAFF, ESQ. / AND
OTHERS. / ⟨double rule⟩ / ⟨3 lines of pidgin
Latin⟩ / With baked, and broil'd, and stew'd,
and toasted, / And fried, and boil'd, and smok'd
and roasted, / We treat the town. / ⟨double
rule⟩ / VOL. I. / ⟨double rule⟩ / NEW-YORK: /
PRINTED & PUBLISHED BY D. LONGWORTH, / At the
Shakspeare-Gallery. / ⟨dotted rule⟩ / 1807.

Note spelling of *broil'd, stew'd, boil'd, smok'd,
Shakspeare.*

Copyright notice on verso: Salmagundi; or the
Whim-Whams & Opinions of Laun- / celot,
⟨*sic*⟩ Langstaff, Esq. and others. / ⟨tapered
rule⟩

In table of contents:

Entry for p. 14: Theatrics . . .

Entry for p. 61, line 2: . . . Cockney Travel- /
⟨The reading is correct.⟩

Title-Page A, Vol. II

SALMAGUNDI; / OR, THE / WHIM-WHAMS AND OPIN-
IONS / OF / LAUNCELOT LANGSTAFF, ESQ. / AND
OTHERS. / ⟨double rule⟩ / ⟨3 lines of pidgin
Latin⟩ / With baked, and broiled, and stewed,
and toasted, / And fried, and boiled, and
smoked, and roasted, / We treat the town. /
⟨double rule⟩ / VOL. II. / ⟨double rule⟩ / NEW-
YORK: / PRINTED & PUBLISHED BY D. LONGWORTH, /
At the Shakspeare-Gallery. / 1808

Copyright notice on verso: Salmagundi; or the
Whim-Whams and Opinions of / Launcelot
Langstaff, esq. & others. / ⟨rule ornament consisting of tapered finials, two star-like ornaments,
five ⟨*sic*⟩ italic O's⟩

Noted in both states of *Part 20.*

Title-Page B, Vol. II

SALMAGUNDI; / OR THE / WHIM-WHAMS AND OPIN-
IONS / OF / LAUNCELOT LANGSTAFF, ESQ. / AND
OTHERS. / ⟨double rule⟩ / ⟨3 lines of pidgin
Latin⟩ / With baked, and broiled, and stewed,
and toasted, / And fried, and boiled, and
smoked, and roasted, / We treat the town. /
⟨double rule⟩ / VOL. II. / ⟨double rule⟩ / NEW-
YORK: / PRINTED & PUBLISHED BY D. LONGWORTH /
At the Shakspeare-Gallery. / 1808.

Copyright notice on verso: Salmagundi; or the
Whim Whams and Opinions of / Launcelot
Langstaff, esq. & others. / ⟨rule ornament consisting of tapered finials, two star-like ornaments, four ⟨*sic*⟩ italic O's⟩

Noted only in binding.

Title-Page C, Vol. II

SALMAGUNDI; / OR, THE / WHIM WHAMS AND OPIN-
IONS / OF / LAUNCELOT LANGSTAFF, ESQ. / AND
OTHERS. / ⟨double rule⟩ / ⟨3 lines of pidgin
Latin⟩ / With baked, and broiled, and stewed,
and toasted, / And fried, and boiled, and
smoked, and roasted, / We treat the town. /
⟨double rule⟩ / VOL II. / ⟨double rule⟩ / NEW-
YORK: / PRINTED AND PUBLISHED BY D. LONG-
WORTH, / At the Shakspeare-Gallery. / 1808.

Copyright notice on verso: Salmagundi; or the
Whim-Whams and Opinions of / Launcelot
Langstaff, esq & others. / ⟨rule ornament consisting of tapered finials separated by a tiny
cross-like ornament⟩

Noted only in the BA copy in binding, consisting (for the most part) of quite late printings.

THE WRAPPER

The wrappers occur in varying textures of paper
and shades of buff and yellow. Virtually all the
papers used are off-white with color applied to
the outer side, the inner side being uncolored.
A few noted are of pulp-dyed paper. Wrappers
other than those described below may exist; if
they do, they have not been seen (or recognized
as such) by BAL. It is indeed quite probable unknown variants or printings exist, but should a
seeming variant emerge it should be studied
with care since sophisticators have perfected not
only sheets but wrappers as well. BAL has seen
sophisticated wrappers which were skillful com-
binations of the front and back of two separate
wrappers. Close scrutiny of color variations and

of stab-marks is often a quite helpful guide in such cases. Also: Longworth's printing is of such poor quality that seeming variations on close examination sometimes prove to be nothing more than faulty press-work.

In the ideal set *Parts I-IV* inclusive would appear in *Wrapper A*. But examination of a number of copies indicates that wrappers were used *ad libitum* and that unrestored parts may occur in wrappers printed somewhat later than the sheets they enclose. The sad truth is that the rarity of *Salmagundi* in untouched state has caused a certain amount of restoration, which produces early parts in quite late wrappers. Nevertheless, this same condition *may* have been produced by the original binders who used any wrappers that came to hand. This original act, together with subsequent reconstruction, involves the problem. Examination of available wrappers has established, with fair certainty, the sequence here presented. In attempting the sequence BAL has leaned heavily on the evidence presented by the frequency with which certain wrappers appear on given parts. Study of the occurrence of the wrappers shows a fairly reasonable pattern of use by the binders. The presence of (for example) *Wrapper L* on a copy of *Part 2* suggests tampering and such a marked variation from the norm calls for careful examination.

THE OUTER FRONT WRAPPER

The outer front wrapper has been seen in the following six forms:

Form 1

⟨double rule⟩ / SALMAGUNDI, / OR, THE / WHIM-WHAMS AND OPINIONS / OF / LAUNCELOT LANG-STAFF, & OTHERS. / ⟨double rule⟩ / ⟨3 lines of pidgin Latin credited to Psalmanazar; 3 lines of doggerel⟩ / ⟨double rule⟩ / NEW-YORK: / PUB-LISHED BY DAVID LONGWORTH, / At the Shakspeare Gallery. / ⟨tapered rule⟩ / 1807

Note: There is a comma, not a semi-colon, at the end of SALMAGUNDI and, the spelling *folkesez*, not *folksez*, in the second line of the Psalmanazar quotation.

Form 2

⟨double rule⟩ / SALMAGUNDI; / OR, THE / WHIM-WHAMS AND OPINIONS / OF / LAUNCELOT LANG-STAFF, & OTHERS. / ⟨double rule⟩ / ⟨3 lines of pidgin Latin credited to Psalmanazar; 3 lines of doggerel⟩ / ⟨double rule⟩ / NEW-YORK: / PUB-LISHED BY DAVID LONGWORTH, / At the Shakspeare-Gallery. / ⟨tapered rule⟩ / 1807

Note: There is a semi-colon, not a comma, at the end of SALMAGUNDI and, the spelling *folkesez*, not *folksez*, in the second line of the Psalmana-

zar quotation. The hyphen in the imprint (*At the Shakspeare-Gallery*) is not present in all copies; in some copies it is present as a vestige only.

Form 3

It will be noted that there is no copyright notice on either *Form 1* or *Form 2*. *Form 3* varies considerably from the earlier forms, a distinguishing feature being the presence of a copyright notice dated "the sixth day of March, in the thirty-first year of the Independence." Note presence of the hyphen in the word *thirty-first*. The hyphen is found in progressive states of wear and finally disappears. The copyright date (*i.e.*, March 6, 1807) surely indicates that this form did not appear prior to *Part 5* which was issued under date March 7, 1807.

Double rule above the Psalmanazar quotation.

Tapered rule below the doggerel.

Imprint at foot, below a horizontal rule: NEW-YORK: PUBLISHED BY DAVID LONGWORTH. Note presence of the period.

Front wrappers 4, 5, 6 are basically the same as *Form 3; i.e.*, the copyright notice is present. However, certain features distinguish *Forms 4, 5, 6.*

Form 4

Double rule above the Psalmanazar quotation.

Tapered rule below the doggerel.

Imprint at foot, between horizontal rules: NEW-YORK: ⟨4 dots⟩ PUBLISHED BY DAVID LONGWORTH. Note presence of the period.

Form 5

Above the Psalmanazar quotation is a decorated rule consisting of two tapered rules divided by a minuscule Swiss cross.

Tapered rule below the doggerel.

Imprint at foot, between horizontal rules: NEW-YORK: ⟨4 dots⟩ PUBLISHED BY DAVID LONGWORTH ⟨note absence of period⟩

Form 6

Above the Psalmanazar quotation is a horizontal ornament, the central portion of which consists of five italic lower case *O*'s. A like ornament appears below the doggerel. Some significance may attach to the fact that this same ornament appears on the copyright page of the 1808 title-leaves; it does not appear on the reverse of the 1807 title-leaf.

Imprint at foot, between horizontal rules: NEW-YORK: ⟨4 dots⟩ PUBLISHED BY DAVID LONGWORTH ⟨note absence of period⟩

THE WRAPPERS

The wrappers have been noted in the following forms. See above for the varying forms of the front of the wrapper, here numbered *Forms 1-6*.

Wrapper A

Front: *Form 1*

Wrapper otherwise unprinted.

Noted on: 2 copies of *Part 1*, first state.

Wrapper B

Front: *Form 2*

Back: *... The Biography and Letters of ... Ninon de l'Enclos ...* <3 paragraphs: *Extract from the Preface*>

Noted on: *Part 1*, second edition; 4 copies of *Part 2*; 3 copies of *Part 3*.

Wrapper C

Front: *Form 2*

Back: *... Ninon de l'Enclos ...* <1 paragraph *Extract from the Preface*> *... Poems, by the Late R. B. Davis.*

Noted on: 4 copies of *Part 4*, second state.

Wrapper D

Front: *Form 3*

Back: *... Ninon de l'Enclos ...* <1 paragraph *Extract from the Preface*> *... Poems, by the Late R. B. Davis.*

Noted on: *Part 2*, second edition; 4 copies of *Part 3*, first printing; *Part 3*, second edition; *Part 4*, intermediate state; *Part 4*, second state; *Part 5*, states 1, 2, 3; *Part 6*, all three forms; 4 copies of *Part 7*; *Part 8*, intermediate state.

Wrapper E

Front: *Form 3*

Back: *Shakspeare's Plays ... April, 1807.*

Noted on: 2 copies, *Part 4*, second state; *Part 5*, first state; *Part 5*, second state; *Part 7*; *Part 8*, 1st state; 4 copies, *Part 8*, intermediate state; 6 copies, *Part 9*; *Part 10*, first state; 2 copies, *Part 10*, second state. Also noted on: 3 copies of *Part 1*, third edition; 2 copies of *Part 2*, second edition; *Part 3*, second edition.

Wrapper F

Front: *Form 3*

Back: *The Shakspeare Gallery is Now in Order to Admit Visitors ... The Curfew ... False Alarms ... Elegant Embost Visiting Cards ...*

Noted on: *Part 2*, second edition; *Part 3*, second edition; *Part 4*, second state; *Part 5*, second

state; *Part 6*, setting A; *Part 7*; 2 copies *Part 10*, first state; 2 copies *Part 10*, second state; *Part 11*, both states.

Wrapper G

Front: *Form 3*

Back: *Just Published, The Curfew ...*

Noted on: *Part 1*, second edition; *Part 1*, fourth edition; *Part 2*, second edition; *Part 2*, third edition; *Part 4*, second edition; 3 copies, *Part 12*; *Part 13*.

Wrapper H

Front: *Form 3*

Back: *... The Nun* <sic> *of St. Dominick ... Adrian and Orrila ... In the Press ––– The Rivals ... The Critic ... Elegant Embost Visiting Cards ...*

Noted on: 2 copies of *Part 13*.

Wrapper I

Front: *Form 4*

Back: *The Novice of St. Dominick ... Sully's painting-room is opened at No. 5 Gold-street ...*

Noted on: *Part 10*, second edition; 2 copies, *Part 13*; *Part 16*, first state; *Part 17*, first state; *Part 17*, second state.

Wrapper J

Front: *Form 3*

Inner wrapper (front and back): Imprinted with a list of *English and American Stage;* inner back wrapper ends with: *... Ethick Diversions ...*

Noted on: 4 copies of *Part 14*.

Wrapper K

Front: *Form 3*

Back: *Just Published ... Town and Country ... Adrian and Orrila ... Elegant Embost Visiting Cards ...* Inner wrapper blank.

Noted on: *Part 1*, fifth edition; *Part 11*, second state; *Part 13*; *Part 16*, first state; 2 copies, *Part 16*, intermediate state.

Wrapper L

Front: *Form 3*

Back: *Just published ... Town and Country ... Adrian and Orrila ... Elegant Embost Visiting Cards ...*

Inner front: *List of Plays ... Blue Beard ...* <to> *... Too Many Cooks.*

Inner back: <List continued> *Il Bondocani ...* <to> *... Douglas*

Noted on: 4 copies, *Part 15*, first state; 2 copies *Part 15*, second state; 3 copies, *Part 16*, first state.

Wrapper La

Same as *Wrapper L* but with the following variation: The inner back wrapper ends with *Adrian and Orrila*, not with *Douglas*.

Noted on: *Part 15*, first state; *Part 15*, second state.

Wrapper M

Front: *Form 4*

Back: *The Novice of St. Dominick ... Sully's painting-room is opened at the Theatre.*

Noted on: *Part 2*, fourth edition; *Part 10*, second edition; 4 copies of *Part 17*, second state.

Wrapper N

Front: *Form 4*

Back: *Subscriptions ... for ... Munroe & Francis' ... Shakspeare ... Just received, Mrs. Opie's Simple Tales ... Birds of Scotland ... In the press, Letters from England ...*

Noted on: 5 copies of *Part 18*, intermediate state; *Part 18*, second state.

Wrapper O

Front: *Form 4*

Back: *Subscriptions ... for ... Munroe & Francis' ... Shakspeare ... Just received, Mrs. Opie's Simple Tales ... Wild Irish Girl ... Birds of Scotland ... In the press, Letters from England ...*

Inner wrapper blank.

Noted on: *Part 13*; *Part 19*.

Wrapper P

Front: *Form 5*

Back: *Subscriptions ... for ... Munroe & Francis' ... Shakspeare ... Just received, Mrs. Opie's Simple Tales ... Wild Irish Girl ... Birds of Scotland ... In the press, Letters from England ...*

Inner front: *French and Spanish Books ... Contes des Feés ... Histoire de l'Expedition ... par Thomas Wilson*

Inner back: ⟨preceding list continued⟩ *Oeuvres ... de Demoustier ... Just received ... The Miseries of Human Life. Vol. II.*

Noted on: 3 copies of *Part 19*.

Wrapper Pa

Same as *Wrapper P* but the inner wrapper is blank.

Noted on: 2 copies of *Part 19*.

Wrapper Q

Front: *Form 6*

Back: *Just Published, a Second Volume of the Miseries of Human Life ... Power of Solitude ... Dominick ... Wild Irish Girl ... Lay of the Irish Harp ...*

Noted on: *Part 20*, second state.

Wrapper R

Front: *Form 6*

Back: *For sale by D. Longworth, at the Shakspeare-Gallery Just Published, a Second Volume of the Miseries of Human Life ...*

Noted on: *Part 20*, first state; *Part 20*, second state.

LOCATIONS

The entry is made on the basis of parts in the following collections: B, BA, H, IU, JFD, LC, NYPL, SM, UV, Y; a set in the collection of Mr. Alfred Rose, New York. Mr. David A. Randall, The Lilly Library, has made available his large personal collection of parts in both bound and original wrappered condition.

10098. A HISTORY OF NEW YORK, FROM THE BEGINNING OF THE WORLD TO THE END OF THE DUTCH DYNASTY ... BY DIEDRICH KNICKERBOCKER ... IN TWO VOLUMES ...

PUBLISHED BY INSKEEP & BRADFORD, NEW YORK; BRADFORD & INSKEEP, PHILADELPHIA; WM. M'IL-HENNEY, BOSTON; COALE & THOMAS, BALTIMORE; AND MORFORD, WILLINGTON, & CO. CHARLESTON. 1809.

1: ⟨i⟩-⟨xxiv⟩, ⟨1⟩-268. 7¾" scant x 4⅝". Inserted at the front is an engraved view of New Amsterdam. *Note:* The plate is inserted by one of two methods with no known priority, if any: Bound in by the right margin; or, the bottom edge so trimmed as to provide a stub for the binder. *Also note:* Forgeries of the plate have been seen. Comparison of the genuine with the forgery shows marked variations in detail. The genuine engraving shows the shading at the upper portion of the plate composed of sharply engraved horizontal lines; in the forgery the lines are liberally speckled.

2: ⟨i-ii⟩, ⟨1⟩-258; leaf excised or pasted under the end paper.

1: ⟨-⟩, A-I, K-U, X-Z⁶, Aa². 2: ⟨A⟩¹, B⁴, C-I, K-U, X-Z⁶; leaf Z₆ excised.

Laid blue paper boards, white paper shelfback. Flyleaves. On the spine is printed: 1 ⟨2⟩

According to Washington Irving's manuscript notebook (in H) 2000 copies were printed and bound.

For other editions see under 1812, 1848, 1886.

NYPL UV

10099. The Poetical Works of Thomas Campbell . . .

. . . 1810.

See note below. Issued in two formats as follows; sequence, if any, not determined.

Two-Volume Format

The Poetical Works of Thomas Campbell . . . to Which is Prefixed a Biographical Sketch of the Author, by a Gentleman of New-York. In Two Volumes . . .

Printed for Philip H. Nicklin & Co., Baltimore. Also, for D. W. Farrand and Green, Albany; D. Mallory and Co., Boston; Lyman and Hall, Portland; and E. Earle, Philadelphia. Fry and Kammerer, Printers. 1810.

Printed boards. "A Biographical Sketch of the Author," Vol. 1, pp. ‹vii›-xliii. The sketch is preceded by a divisional title-page with copyright notice on verso dated Aug. 16, 1810.

Also noted with the following imprint: Printed for D. W. Farrand & Green, Albany. Also, for E. Earle, Philadelphia; D. Mallory and Co. Boston; Lyman and Hall, Portland; and Philip H. Nickilin ‹sic; correctly spelled *Nicklin* in Vol. II› and Co., Baltimore. Fry and Kammerer, Printers. 1810.

It is probable that other variant imprints exist.

One-Volume Format

The Poetical Works of Thomas Campbell . . . to Which is Prefixed a Biographical Sketch of the Author, by a Gentleman of New-York.

Printed for D. W. Farrand & Green, Albany. Also, for E. Earle, Philadelphia; D. Mallory and Co. Boston; Lyman and Hall, Portland; and Philip H. Nicklin and Co., Baltimore. Fry and Kammerer, Printers. 1810.

Boards? "A Biographical Sketch of the Author," pp. ‹7›-41. Preceded by a divisional title-page with copyright notice on verso dated Aug. 16, 1810.

Also noted with the following imprint: Printed for Philip H. Nicklin & Co., Baltimore. Also, for D. W. Farrand and Green, Albany; D. Mallory and Co., Boston; Lyman and Hall, Portland; and E. Earle, Philadelphia. Fry and Kammerer, Printers. 1810.

Title-page deposited Aug. 16, 1810. Listed, as in 2 vols., under *new editions* in both MA and in P, Oct. 1810.

AAS (Vol. 1 only)   LC (Vols. 1-2, rebound; also a rebound copy of the one-volume format)   UV (Vol. 1 only)   Y (Vols. 1-2; also a rebound copy of the one-volume format)

NOTE

Biographical Sketch of Thomas Campbell

There were several printings and revisions of this sketch. The following have been noted. See entries under dates given.

1810

Two formats issued: As a 1-volume publication; as a 2-volume set. Sequence, if any, not determined.

1811

Reprints the sketch as in the preceding.

1815 and ‹1815›

A revised form of the sketch published herein. Two printings noted; sequence not established. Collected in *Spanish Papers*, Vol. 2, 1866.

1819

Williams & Edge (p. 98) state that the sketch appears in the following publication: *Specimens of the British Poets* ‹edited by Thomas Campbell›, *with Biographical and Critical Notices, and an Essay on English Poetry*, London: John Murray, 1819. Williams & Edge enter the title as not seen. Copies of this work in both NYPL and H do not contain the Irving sketch. Williams & Edge appear to be in error.

1821

Reprint.

1822

Williams & Edge (p. 98) state that the sketch appears in the following publication: *The Pleasures of Hope and Other Poems,* by Thomas Campbell, New York, 1822. No examined copy of this edition contains the sketch; all examined copies have vignette title-page dated 1820. Was there an 1820 printing? Williams & Edge appear to be in error.

1841 (Wiley & Putnam)

A revised form of the sketch appears herein.

1841 (Harper & Brothers)

Williams & Edge (p. 98) state that the sketch appears in *Life and Letters of Thomas Campbell,* by William Beattie, New York: Harper & Bro., 1841. Williams & Edge enter the title as not seen. Extended search has failed to produce a copy of the book. BAL suspects the book is a ghost and that Williams & Edge are in error.

1844

Reprint.

1845

Reprints the version of 1841 (Wiley & Putnam) but the final paragraph of the 1841 text is deleted and another substituted in square brackets. Final paragraph added by Irving?

1850

Life and Letters of Thomas Campbell, edited by William Beattie, New York: Harper & Brothers, 1850. Contains an introductory letter by Irving written for this edition. Not to be confused with the biographical sketch. Williams & Edge (p. 98) err in stating that this contains the biographical sketch.

1864

The Poetry and History of Wyoming: Containing Campbell's Gertrude, and the History of Wyoming . . . Third Edition, by William L. Stone, Albany, 1864. Sheets of the 1844 edition reissued with cancelled front matter and added index.

1866

Collected in *Spanish Papers . . . ,* by Washington Irving, New York, 1866. First collected publication of the 1815 version.

10100. A History of New-York . . . the Second Edition with Alterations. By Diedrich Knickerbocker . . . in Two Volumes . . .

New-York: Published by Inskeep and Bradford, and Bradford and Inskeep, Philadelphia. 1812.

Probably issued in paper boards.

For first edition see under 1809.

Title-page deposited June 3, 1812. Noted as *preparing* PF July, 1812. Reviewed by PF Oct. 1812.

AAS   BPL   H   NYHS   NYPL

10101. An Account of the Funeral Honours Bestowed on the Remains of Capt. Lawrence and Lieut. Ludlow, with the Eulogy Pronounced at Salem, on the Occasion, by Hon. Joseph Story . . . and Biographical and Poetical Notices . . .

Boston: Printed by Joshua Belcher. 1813.

Printed self-wrapper.

"Biography of Captain James Lawrence," credited to *Mr. Irvine,* pp. 17-32. Originally in AM Aug. 1813. Collected in *Spanish Papers . . . ,* Vol. 2, 1866.

Two states noted; the order is presumed correct:

State A

The letter of Aug. 18, 1813, p. 40, signed by Crowninshield, is addressed to a committee of three.

Tailpiece not present, p. 64.

State B

The letter of Aug. 18, 1813, p. 40, signed by Crowninshield, is addressed to a committee of seven.

Tailpiece present, p. 64.

Note: Intermediates have been seen, possibly produced by mixed sheets.

According to advertisements in *Boston Daily Advertiser* copies of the August issue of AM were available in Boston not later than Aug. 24, 1813. Title-page deposited for copyright Aug. 28, 1813. Advertised for *this day at 12 o'clock* in *Boston Daily Advertiser,* Sept. 3, 1813; Sept. 6, 1813. Advertised by J. Dabney at the Salem Bookstore as *just received, Salem Gazette,* Sept. 7, 1813.

BPL (B)   H (A, Intermediate)   LC (A, B)   NYPL (B)   UV (Intermediate)

10102. Salmagundi; or, the Whim-Whams and Opinions of Launcelot Langstaff, Esq. and Others . . . a New and Improved Edition . . .

New-York: Published by David Longworth, at the Shakspeare-Gallery. 1814.

2 Vols. Printed paper boards; and, unprinted blue-gray paper boards, white paper shelfback.

Revised ⟨by Irving?⟩. See above under 1807 for first edition.

Title-page deposited Jan. 21, 1814.

H   MHS

10103. A Compilation of Biographical Sketches of Distinguished Officers in the American Navy, with Other Interesting Matter . . . ⟨edited⟩ by Benjamin Folsom.

Newburyport: Published by the Compiler, and for Sale at the Newburyport-Bookstore, No. 13 Cornhill, and by Various Other Booksellers in the United States. Horatio G. Allen, Printer. 1814.

Printed paper boards sides, white paper shelfback.

Reprints (in abridged form) Irving's sketch of Lawrence; see above under 1813.

"Lieut. William Burrows," pp. 123-132. Collected in *Spanish Papers . . .* , Vol. 2, 1866.

"Com. Oliver Hazard Perry," pp. 132-147. For a fuller version see *Naval Biography . . .* , 1815, below. Collected in *Spanish Papers . . .* , Vol. 2, 1866.

Y

10104. The Poetical Works of Thomas Campbell

Contains a revised version of Irving's biographical sketch of Campbell; for the original version see above under 1810.

Two printings noted. The sequence has not been determined and the following designations are for identification only.

A

The Poetical Works of Thomas Campbell . . . to Which is Prefixed a Revised and Improved Biographical Sketch of the Author, by a Gentleman of New-York.

Philadelphia: Published by Edward Earle. William Fry, Printer. 1815.

⟨i⟩-⟨xxviii⟩, ⟨1⟩-234; blank, unpaged, leaf; ⟨235⟩-242. Does not contain an engraved, inserted, title-page. Noted only in trimmed state, bound in boards, leather shelfback; and, leather.

Occurs in two states: 1: P. 95 mispaged 59; 2: P. 95 correctly paged.

B

The Poetical Works of Thomas Campbell . . . to Which is Prefixed a Revised and Improved Biographical Sketch of the Author, by a Gentleman of New-York.

⟨Philadelphia: Published by Edward Earle. W. Fry, Printer, 1815⟩

⟨i⟩-⟨viii⟩, ⟨1⟩-261, blank leaf. Contains an inserted, engraved, title-page in addition to the typographic title-leaf.

Unprinted gray paper wrapper, white paper shelfback; and, unprinted gray paper boards, white paper shelfback.

Title-pages for both deposited March 17, 1815. The sketch (in the above revised form) first published in AM March, 1815. Noted as though published AM April, 1815.

UV (B)   Y (A: 1st, 2nd; B)

10105. Naval Biography; or Lives of the Most Distinguished American Naval Heroes of the Present Day.

Pittsburgh: Published by R. Patterson. S. Engles, Printer. 1815.

Marbled paper boards.

Reprint save for "Commodore O. H. Perry," pp. 70-95. Anonymous. Reprinted from AM. For an abbreviated printing of this sketch see above: *A Compilation . . .* , 1814. Collected in *Spanish Papers . . .* , Vol. 2, 1866.

LC

10106. THE SKETCH BOOK

Note

The Sketch Book, no less than *Salmagundi* (above 1807–1808), has been a particular darling of the sophisticators. Hence, caution is urged in relating this description to the book. Indeed, virtually all the sins of the sophisticators described in the entry for *Salmagundi* have been visited on *The Sketch Book.* The user of this entry may find the *Salmagundi* notes pertinent and useful.

BAL is convinced that the so-called intermediates were caused not by the printer but by the binder; and for 'binder' one may, if one chooses, read 'sophisticator' and more often than not be justified.

For the purposes of this entry BAL has all but ignored copies in binding.

Quite late in its study of *The Sketch Book* BAL became aware of the possibility that certain of the wrappers may have been printed from multiple settings; further investigation is indicated.

No attempt has been made by BAL to record the variant readings that occur in the reprints. For other editions see under 1820, 1824, 1848.

Part 1

THE SKETCH BOOK OF GEOFFREY CRAYON, GENT. NO. I . . .

NEW-YORK: PRINTED BY C. S. VAN WINKLE, NO. 101 GREENWICH-STREET. 1819.

⟨i⟩-iv, ⟨5⟩-94, blank leaf. 9¾₁₆″ x 5¾″ scant.

⟨1⟩-12⁴.

Printed tan paper wrapper. White end papers.

Title-page deposited May 15, 1819. Reviewed AM July, 1819.

There were at least two printings of this part, each from a different setting, before the date 1819 on the title-page was altered. The following variations are sufficient for identification:

1st Printing	*2nd Printing*

Pagination

⟨i⟩-iv, ⟨5⟩-94, blank leaf.	⟨i⟩-iv, ⟨5⟩-93; blank, p. ⟨94⟩; *Note*, p. 95; blank, p. ⟨96⟩. P. 95 mispaged 94.

Title-Page Imprint

/ No. 101 Greenwich-street. /	/ 101 Greenwich Street. /

Last line of copyright notice

"of designing . . .	"ving, and etching . . .

Part 2

THE SKETCH BOOK OF GEOFFREY CRAYON, GENT. NO. II . . .

NEW-YORK: PRINTED BY C. S. VAN WINKLE, 101 GREENWICH STREET. 1819.

⟨97⟩-169, blank leaf.

⟨13⟩, 14-15, ⟨16⟩, 17-19, ⟨20⟩-21⁴, ⟨22⟩².

Printed tan paper wrapper. Also: Chocolate brown paper wrapper. White end papers.

Note: The wrapper has been seen in the following forms; the sequence presented appears to be correct:

1: On the front is the statement: *Price 50 cents.*

2: On the front wrapper the price is altered by hand, in pen and ink, to 62½.

3: On the front wrapper the price is press-printed: 62½. Copies thus were printed on the blank reverse of the original *Price 50 cents* variety.

Inserted in the front matter of some copies is a notice (on a slip, approximately ¾″ x 5¼″) regarding unauthorized reprinting. The slip was printed from at least two different settings, perhaps simultaneously. No attempt has been made to record the typographic variations; examples may be seen in NYPL; textually the slips are identical.

Title-page deposited July 26, 1819. Listed and reviewed NAR Sept. 1819.

BAL has found no typographic or textual variations in *Part 2*.

"Part II also exists with p. (98) blank. Since this was a copyright entry ⟨*i.e.*, notice?⟩, it would seem that its omission was an oversight which was corrected in later copies of the book."—Langfeld-Blackburn, p. 16. No copy so distinguished has been seen by BAL.

Part 3

THE SKETCH BOOK OF GEOFFREY CRAYON, GENT. NO. III . . .

NEW-YORK: PRINTED BY C. S. VAN WINKLE, 101 GREENWICH STREET. 1819.

⟨171⟩-210, 203-242.

⟨23⟩-32⁴.

Printed tan paper wrapper. White end papers.

Note: The wrapper has been seen in the following forms; the sequence presented appears to be correct:

1: On the front wrapper the original price (press-printed) is 62½ but altered by hand in pen and ink to 75.

2: On the front wrapper the price is press-printed: 75. Wrappers thus usually occur printed on the reverse of the original 62½ variety.

Title-page deposited Aug. 11, 1819.

BAL has found no textual variations in *Part 3*. However, line 12, p. 240, occurs in two forms of unknown sequence; the designations are for identification only:

A: . . . ont he . . .

B: . . . on the . . .

Part 4

THE SKETCH BOOK OF GEOFFREY CRAYON, GENT. NO. IV . . .

NEW-YORK: PRINTED BY C. S. VAN WINKLE, 101 GREENWICH STREET. 1819.

⟨243⟩-⟨302⟩, ⟨i-ii⟩, ⟨303⟩-335.

⟨33⟩-44⁴.

Printed tan paper wrapper. White end papers.

Title-page deposited Oct. 12, 1819. Listed NAR Jan. 1820.

Inserted at the front of one examined copy (UV) is a single leaf of advertisements for M. Carey & Son, Philadelphia; presumably inserted by Carey and not by Van Winkle.

BAL has found no typographic or textual variations in *Part 4*.

Part 5

THE SKETCH BOOK OF GEOFFREY CRAYON, GENT. NO. V . . .

NEW-YORK: PRINTED BY C. S. VAN WINKLE, 101 GREENWICH STREET. 1819.

⟨337⟩-443.

⟨45⟩-46, ⟨47⟩-48, ⟨49⟩, 50-57⁴, 58².

Printed tan paper wrapper. Also: Printed gray paper wrapper. White end papers.

Title-page deposited Dec. 16, 1819. Listed AM Jan. 1820.

Inserted at the front of some copies is a leaf of advertisements for M. Thomas, Philadelphia; presumably inserted by Thomas and not by Van Winkle.

BAL has found no typographic or textual variations in *Part 5*.

Part 6

THE SKETCH BOOK OF GEOFFREY CRAYON, GENT. NO. VI . . .

NEW-YORK: PRINTED BY C. S. VAN WINKLE, 101 GREENWICH STREET. 1820.

⟨1⟩-120.

⟨1⟩-15⁴.

Printed tan paper wrapper. White end papers.

The wrapper carries the joint imprint of Haly and Thomas, New York; and, M. Thomas, Philadelphia. All examined copies of the wrapper are printed on salvage; concealed by the pastedown is the original printing with the imprint of C. S. Van Winkle.

Title-page deposited Feb. 10, 1820. Listed NAR April, 1820.

Two printings, from two different settings, have been noted. The following variations are sufficient for identification.

First Printing	Second Printing
P. 38, last line	
species . . .	order . . .
P. 93, line 8	
. . . his/	. . . histo- /
P. 105, line 9	
. . . la- /	. . . lamenta- /
P. 106, line 16	
. . . yeo- /	. . yeomen /
P. 106, line 17	
. . . has /	. . . ever /
P. 114, line 11	
. . . cast-iron /	. . . comb. /
P. 115, line 13	
. . . and /	. . . when /
P. 116, line 3	
. . . intelli- /	. . . intelligence /

the . . .   this . . .

Part 7

THE SKETCH BOOK OF GEOFFREY CRAYON, GENT. NO. VII . . .

NEW-YORK: PRINTED BY C. S. VAN WINKLE, 101 GREENWICH STREET. 1820.

⟨1⟩-123.

⟨1⟩-15⁴, 16².

Printed tan paper wrapper. White end papers.

Title-page deposited Aug. 12, 1820. *In the press and will be published in a few days -- New York Literary Journal*, Aug. 1820. *In press and will be published about the middle of the present month --* AM Sept. 1820. Listed LSR Oct. 1820.

Two printings, from two different settings, have been noted. The following variations are sufficient for identification.

First Printing	Second Printing
P. ⟨5⟩, line 2 of the preliminary poem	
. . . they . . .	. . . there . . .
P. 21, line 20	
. . . notes, and piling . . .	. . . notes, piling . . .
P. 33, line 6	
. . . which lavish, /	. . . that lavish, /
P. 33, line 18	
. . . placid air . . .	. . . placid demure . . .
P. 33, line 19	
. . . some shrew . . .	. . . some pestilent shrew . . .
P. 34	
22 lines of text	23 lines of text
P. 36, line 10	
. . . reccollections/	. . . recollections, /
P. 41, line 13	
. . . thick- /	. . . thicket, /
P. 45, line 3	
flowers. /	ers. The whole . . .
P. 46, last line	
tre of his cage. The scene . . .	tre of his cage. He had . . .

P. 64, last line

... royal /   favour. /

Note: Copies of both printings have been seen with a leaf of advertisements inserted at front; recto: ... *The Analectic Magazine* ... ; verso: *Books, Stationery and Fancy Articles. M. Thomas* ...

Locations

The present entry is made on the basis of copies in H, IU, LC, NYPL, SM, UV, Y.

10107. The Sketch Book of Geoffrey Crayon, Gent. ... ⟨Vol. I⟩

London: John Miller, Burlington Arcade. 1820.

Boards? See next entry for Vol. II. For first edition see under 1819–1820.

Reprint save for the author's "Advertisement," pp. ⟨v⟩-vi. Collected in *The Sketch Book ... Fourth American Edition,* 1824.

Noted as *preparing for publication* LG Oct. 19, 1819. Advertised by Miller in LG Jan. 15, 1820: *Preparing ... will appear early in February ... with alterations and additions by the author.* Unsold sheets were issued with cancel title-leaf as follows: ... *Second Edition. London: John Murray, Albemarle-Street. 1820.*

BPL   H

10108. The Sketch Book of Geoffrey Crayon, Gent. ... Vol. II.

London: John Murray, Albemarle-Street. 1820.

Boards? See preceding entry for Vol. I.

Revised; and extended by the addition of the following pieces:

"Traits of Indian Character," pp. ⟨213⟩-236.

"Philip of Pokanoket," pp. ⟨237⟩-272.

"L'Envoy," pp. ⟨415⟩-419.

For earliest located American publication of these three pieces see *The Sketch Book ... Fourth American Edition,* 1824.

Reviewed by ER Oct. 1820; listed ER Oct. 1820; reviewed MR Oct. 1820; reviewed BC Nov. 1820.

H   MHS

10109. BRACEBRIDGE HALL, OR THE HU-MOURISTS. A MEDLEY, BY GEOFFREY CRAYON, GENT. ... IN TWO VOLUMES ...

NEW-YORK: PRINTED BY C. S. VAN WINKLE, NO. 101 GREENWICH STREET. 1822.

Issued simultaneously with the London edition? See next two entries. For revised edition see under 1849.

1: ⟨1⟩-348. 9¼" x 5⅞".

2: ⟨1⟩-351.

1: ⟨1⟩-43⁴, 44².

2: ⟨1⟩-44⁴.

Drab brown paper boards, printed paper label on spine. Flyleaves.

Note: The only copies examined in original paper boards (BAL has seen but two) have the following statement on the spine labels: ... PUB-LISHED BY / M. & S. Thomas. / Philadelphia. All copies thus?

Title-page for Vol. 1 deposited April 5, 1822; for Vol. 2, May 9, 1822. Reviewed by LSR May, 1822.

NYPL   UV

10110. BRACEBRIDGE HALL; OR, THE HUMORISTS. BY GEOFFREY CRAYON, GENT. ... IN TWO VOLUMES ...

LONDON: JOHN MURRAY, ALBEMARLE-STREET. 1822.

Issued simultaneously with the New York edition? See preceding entry. Also see next entry.

1: ⟨i⟩-iv, ⟨1⟩-393; printer's imprint, p. ⟨394⟩; blank leaf. 9" x 5⅝".

2: ⟨i⟩-iv, ⟨1⟩-403; p. ⟨404⟩: blank save for printer's imprint; but see below.

1: ⟨A⟩², B-I, K-U, X-Z, AA-BB⁸, CC⁶.

2: ⟨A⟩², B-I, K-U, X-Z, AA-CC⁸, DD².

Two editions noted:

First Edition

As above. Text ends on p. 403, Vol. 2.

Second Edition

As above. Text extended by the insertion of added matter, pp. 402-403, Vol. 2, causing the text of Vol. 2 to end on p. 404. It is entirely possible that the addition was done during the course of printing but this is conjecture only.

Contains the following pieces which are not present in the first American edition: "The Author's Farewell," "Family Misfortune," "Lovers' Troubles," "The Rookery," "The Storm Ship." For first American book publication of these see next entry.

THE SHEETS

Printed from two settings. Certain pages (noted below) appear to have been done from three settings. Intermediates have been noted. These factors combine to produce copies of the book in many varieties. No ready argument emerges to support the primacy of any setting. The following selected variations are sufficient for identification.

BAL suggests that all copies issued by Murray under date 1822 be considered of equal primacy until evidence is produced to the contrary. In a letter to BAL, Dec. 2, 1964, the publisher reports: "4,000 copies printed made up of 3,000 plus a run-on of 1,000. No means of knowing the time interval between these printings but evidently very short and, in many cases, 'run-on' may mean that the whole lot were printed without a gap of time."

VOL. I

Setting A   *Setting B*

Title-page
The colon after LONDON is over:

Second A in ALBEMARLE   AR in ALBEMARLE

Verso of Title-page
Printer's name is spelled:

DAVSION   DAVISON

P. ⟨iii⟩
The rule is:

⅝" scant   ¾" scant

P. 14

Occurs in three settings. Sequence (if any) not known. The designations are for identification only and no sequence is suggested. The most readily apparent variation (as follows) is sufficient for identification. Reference is to the position of GEOFFREY CRAYON.

1: The G is set under a space and the *t* in *truly*

2: The G is set under the *in* in *Thine*

3: The G is set under the *ru* in *truly*

P. 24, line 7

ing, . . .   *when* . . .

P. 33

Occurs in three settings. Sequence (if any) not known. The designations are for identification only and no sequence is suggested. The most readily apparent variation (as follows) is sufficient for identification. Reference is to the position of signature mark D.

1: Appears below the *it* in *portrait*

2: Appears below the *a* in *portrait*

3: Appears below the final *t*, and space following, in *portrait*

P. 40, line 6
The period is over:

. . . *e* . . .   . . . *r* . . .

P. ⟨50⟩
The s in SONG is under:

. . . *an* . . .   ⟨space⟩

P. 55, last line

. . . *formed* | . . . *having* |

P. ⟨73⟩
The rules are:

13/16"   ⅞" full

P. 78, line 13

tyrannises . . .   *and* . . .

P. 80
BOOK OF HUNTING is set:

Partially under the word *purse*   To the right of the word *purse* which is set on the preceding line

Pp. 93-94

This leaf occurs as a cancel; and, as an integral leaf. No textual variations have been noted which leads to the conclusion that there are three forms of this leaf: *A*, with an error or other textual variation on either or both pages; postulated only, not seen. *B*, the altered cancel; *C*, the altered integral leaf. B and C were printed from two different settings; in the cancel the comma (line 4, p. 94) is set over *h* . . . ; in the integral the comma is set over ⟨*space*⟩*h* . . .

Note: Reported (but not seen by BAL save as a photographic reproduction) is a variation in the last line of p. 93; in one form *Mulligatawney-club* is set without spacing; in the other, spacing is present thus: *Mulligatawney club*. Significance not determined.

P. 96, line 8
The semi-colon is set over:

n . . .   ⟨space⟩

P. ⟨109⟩
The rule is:

13/16"   11/16" full

P. ⟨112⟩
The H in HAMLET

Set to the right of, and below, the quotation mark   Set under the quotation mark

P. 122, line 5

... whig; | ... Whig; |

P. ⟨134⟩
The heading reads:

... trees." | ... trees!" |

P. 144

Occurs in three settings. Sequence (if any) not
known. The designations are for identification
only and no sequence is suggested. The most
readily apparent variation (as follows) is sufficient for identification. Reference is to the period in the fifth line from the bottom of the
page.

1: Set over the *el* in *models*

2: Set over the *s* in *models*

3: Set over the *l* in *models*

P. 154, line 10

kissed ...   kiss'd ...

P. ⟨156⟩, line 2

... money ...   ... Money ...

P. 157, last line

... money ...   ... Money ...

P. 158, line 3

... Tibbets ...   ... Tibbetses ...

P. 162, line 7 up

... Tibbets ...   ... Tibbetses ...

P. 163, line 6 up

... money ...   ... Money ...

P. 180, line 7

when ...   were ...

P. 204, line 2

Remigius ...   Remegius ...

P. 210, line 2 up

The quotation mark is   The quotation mark is
set immediately below   set slightly to the left
the *k*   of the *k* above

P. 219, line 13

... Wyat, his ...   ... Wyat his ...

P. 237, line 4 up

have ...   I have ...

P. ⟨246⟩, line 3 up

renowned ...   nada ...

P. 248, line 14

was. | who ...

P. 259
Signature mark s2

The s is correctly set   The s is inverted

P. 270, line 3

... said he, wildly. | ... said he wildly. |

Sig. T, pp. 273-288

Printed from two settings but the variations are
too minute for ready description.

P. 304, line 9 up

... save him, but ...   ... save him but ...

P. 310, line 8 up

losophers' ...   losopher's ...

Sig. Y, pp. 321-336

Printed from two settings but the variations are
too minute for ready description.

P. 343, line 10 up

God, (that is ...   God (that is ...

P. 346, line 7 up

is ...   all ...

Sig. AA, pp. 353-368

Printed from two settings but the variations are
too minute for ready description.

P. 384, line 3 up

As she ...   ⟨As⟩ she ...

P. 387, line 2 up

... splendour. | ... splendor. |

P. 391
The rule is:

⅞" scant   ¾" scant

VOL. II
Imprint on verso of the title-page

The colon is set above   The colon is set above
a space   the letter N

P. ⟨iii⟩
The rule is:

⅝" scant   ¾"

P. 16, line 4 up

splendour ...   splendor ...

P. 42, line 13

... *goals* ... ‹for   ... *gaols* ... ‹correct-
gaols›   ly›

P. 60, line 2

... *money* /   ... *Money* /

P. 61, line 2 up

... *money* ...   ... *Money* ...

P. 65, line 5

... *money* ...   ... *Money* ...

P. 66, line 5 up

... *Ready-Money Jack*   ... *Ready Money Jack*
...   ...

P. 81, line 2

... *money* /   ... *Money* /

P. 106, last line

... *Cobbet* ...   ... *Cobbett* ...

P. 112, line 11 up

... *money* ...   ... *Money* ...

P. 113, line 5 up

... *money* ...   ... *Money* ...

P. 119, last line

The line is justified.   The line is not justi-
                             fied.

Sig. K, pp. 129-144

Printed from two settings but the variations are
too minute for ready description.

P. 144, line 5 up
The period is set over the letter:

s   *e*

Also occurs in yet another form, with the period
set over the letter *l*.

P. 162
The rule is:

⅝" full   ⅞"

P. 165

Occurs in three states (settings?). Sequence (if
any) not known. The designations are for identification only and no sequence is suggested.
The most readily apparent variation (as follows)
is sufficient for identification. Reference is to the
last line.

1: *money's jacket.* /
2: *Money's jacket.* /
3: *Ready-money's jacket.* /

P. ‹166›

DOCTOR MERRIE-MAN.   DOCTOR MERRIE-MAN,
1609.   1609.

P. 184, line 3

Milton: /   *by Milton:* /

P. 193
Sig. mark o is below:

‹space› *c*   *c*

P. ‹195›, line 6

... *Ready-money* ...   ... *Ready Money* ...

P. 196, line 6 up

... *Ready-money* ...   ... *Ready Money* ...

P. 223
Line 1 of the verses

... *called* ...   ... *call'd* ...

P. 225, line 1

... *Ready-money* ...   ... *Ready Money* ...

P. ‹231›
BOURNE'S ANTIQUITIES

Set in capital letters of   Set in large and small
uniform size   capital letters

P. 256, line 2

of a December ...   *a December* ...

Sig. S, pp. 257-272

Printed from two settings but the variations are
too minute for ready description.

P. 283, line 2 up

... *Knypper-* /   ... *Knipper-* /

P. 291, line 5 up

recollection. /   *rising.* /

P. 307, line 7

haunted house ...   *Haunted House* ...

P. ‹319›

Occurs in three states (settings?). Sequence (if
any) not known. The designations are for identification only and no sequence is suggested.
The most readily apparent variation (as follows)
is sufficient for identification. Reference is to the
rule at the head of text.

1: Measures 1⅛"
2: Measures ⅞"
3: Measures 11/16"

P. 321, line 8 up

was ...   — — was ...

P. 333
The rule is:

⅝″ full   ¾″

Note: Setting A occurs in two states; the order of presentation is probably correct: 1st: Mispaged at upper left corner: *281*; 2nd: correctly paged: *333*.

P. 350, line 2

bed ...   to bed ...

P. 354

Occurs in three states (settings?). Sequence (if any) not known. The designations are for identification only and no sequence is suggested. The most readily apparent variations (as follows) are sufficient for identification:

1: Line 6: ... *Spiegle* ...
   Line 8: ... *pro-* /

2: Line 6: ... *Speigle* ...
   Line 8: ... *pro-* /

3: Line 6: ... *Spiegel* ...
   Line 8: ... *the* /

P. 365, line 13

thee ...   of thee ...

P. ⟨375⟩
The rules are:

13⁄16″   1″

P. 380, line 5 up

money ...   Money ...

P. 386, line 4 up

... money /   ... Money /

P. 387, line 6 up

... money ...   ... Money ...

P. 391, line 3 up

... money ...   ... Money ...

P. 401, line 9

... *."   ... *?"

BINDING

The following bindings have been noted; sequence (if any) has not been determined and the designations are for identification only.

Binding A

Slate-blue paper boards sides, tan paper shelfback. Printed paper label on spine.

Binding B

Drab brown paper boards. Printed paper label on spine.

Binding C

Drab brown paper boards sides, green muslin shelfback. Printed paper label on spine.

Noted as *forthcoming* LG April 6, 1822. Noted as *issued* LG May 25, 1822. Reviewed by LG June 1, 1822; MR Aug. 1822; BC Sept. 1822.

The present entry made on the basis of copies (some being rebound) in:

BA H NYPL UV Y

10111. Bracebridge Hall, or the Humourists. A Medley, by Geoffrey Crayon, Gent. ... in Two Volumes ... ⟨Second American Edition⟩

New-York: Printed by C. S. Van Winkle, No. 101 Greenwich Street. 1822.

Boards? Leather?

See preceding two entries.

"... In the course of publication in England ... ⟨the author was⟩ enabled ... to make considerable alterations and additions; which will account for the material difference that will be perceived between the first and second editions ... published in America."—Vol. 1, p. ⟨iii⟩.

The following five pieces are here first collected in an American edition; each had prior publication in the London edition, above. "The Author's Farewell," "Family Misfortunes," "Lovers' Troubles," "The Rookery," "The Storm Ship." "True Gentlemen," so titled in the first edition, is here retitled "Gentility."

AAS BPL NYPL

10112. LETTERS OF JONATHAN OLD-STYLE, GENT. BY THE AUTHOR OF THE SKETCH BOOK. WITH A BIOGRAPHICAL NOTICE.

NEW-YORK: PUBLISHED BY WILLIAM H. CLAYTON. CLAYTON & VAN NORDEN, PRINTERS. 1824.

⟨i⟩-⟨xii⟩, ⟨5⟩-67. 9⅛″ x 5¹³⁄₁₆″.

⟨A⟩⁴, B², 2-9⁴.

Printed drab brown paper wrapper. White end papers. Flyleaf at front of some, not all, copies.

Title-page deposited Feb. 19, 1824. Listed NAR April, 1824. The London (Wilson) edition was advertised for *Monday* ⟨*i.e.,* April 12⟩ in LG April 10, 1824; listed LG April 17, 1824; listed BC April, 1824; a second edition advertised LG April 24, 1824; a third edition advertised LG May 22, 1824.

LC NYPL

10113. Salmagundi: Or, the Whim-Whams and Opinions of Launcelot Langstaff, Esq. and Others ... in Two Volumes ...

Paris: Printed by Jules Didot, Sen. for A. and W. Galignani, Rue Vivienne, No 18. M DCCC XXIV.

For first edition see under 1807. For first American publication of this revision see below under 1835.

Printed paper wrapper?

Also issued with the imprint: *Paris: Printed by Jules Didot, Sen. for Baudry, Rue du Coq. No 9. M DCCC XXIV.*

"The present edition has been submitted to the revision of one of the authors ⟨Irving⟩, who, at first, contemplated making essential alterations. On further consideration ... he contented himself with correcting merely a few ... glaring errors and flippancies ..."—p. vii.

"... I am sorry to see *Salmagundi* is published at London, with all its faults upon its head. I have corrected a copy for Galignani, whom I found bent upon putting it to press. My corrections consist almost entirely in expunging words, and here and there an offensive sentence ..."—Letter, Irving to Charles R. Leslie, Paris, Feb. 8, 1824, in: *The Life and Letters of Washington Irving,* Vol. 2, p. 186.

Listed BF March 20, 1824.

In the New York, 1860, edition of *Salmagundi,* p. xiv, the editor, E. A. Duyckinck, refers to an 1834 Paris, revised, edition. Langfeld-Blackburn, p. 10, appear to accept the 1834 date but caution: "We have not seen this." No separate 1834 edition is listed in either BF or *Catalogue Général des Livres Imprimés de la Bibliothèque Nationale, Auteurs;* both these sources list the 1824 edition. *Query:* Was Duyckinck referring to *The Complete Works of Washington Irving* ... , Paris, (Baudry), 1834, which reprints the Paris, 1824, edition of *Salmagundi.*

NYHS (Baudry)   UV (Galignani)

10114. Collection of English Literature. (Prospectus)

Paris: A. and W. Galignani, 18, Rue Vivienne; and, Jules Didot, Sen. 6, Rue du Pont-de-Lodi. 1824.

Not seen; not located. Entry on the basis of entries in BF, July 10, 1824 (entry No. 3654 in French, No. 3704 in English). It is probable that the 4-page prospectus found in some copies of Irving's *Tales of a Traveller, Part 3,* Philadelphia, 1824, is (more or less) a copy of the original Paris prospectus. Were copies of the original Paris prospectus bound in books issued by Galignani?

In-8° d'une demi-feuille.

"Sunday ⟨March⟩ 14 ⟨1824⟩. Write Prospectus & terms for Collection of British Literature— Galignani calls—& agrees to my terms—250 francs a vol. 2500 fr in advance—" —*Journal of Washington Irving (1823–1824),* edited by Stanley T. Williams, 1931, p. 148.

"This essay ⟨*Memoirs* (sic) *of the Life and Writings of Oliver Goldsmith*⟩ was written for the first volume of the series of English Classics ⟨published by Galignani, 1825⟩, and, as it happened, was the only one published. Irving never finished this task ..."—*ibid.,* p. 151, *fn.*

"Monday May 24 ⟨1824⟩—Galignani called on me—We signed agreement about the Collection of British Literature—At 10£ a volume for collating & correcting Biographies and notes &c. ..."—*ibid.,* p. 187.

"Mr. Irving is to select the authors and the parts of their works to be published. He is to collate and correct the Biographies and notes ... but it is expressly understood that he does not obligate himself to contribute any original matter. That is to be left entirely to his own discretion."—Extract from the agreement, Irving and Galignani, as given by Williams, *ibid.,* p. 187, *fn.*

"The last entry in his memorandum book, gives us a further allusion to Rogers, whose biography and that of Campbell he was intending to prepare for the collection of British Literature, for which Galignani had engaged his pen, though he never got beyond a brief life of Goldsmith, in an undertaking which soon fell to the ground."—*The Life and Letters of Washington Irving,* Vol. 2, 1862, p. 204.

For Irving's memoir of Goldsmith see below under 1825; *i.e.,* Oct. 1824.

10115. TALES OF A TRAVELLER. BY GEOFFREY CRAYON, GENT. ... IN TWO VOLUMES ...

LONDON: JOHN MURRAY, ALBEMARLE-STREET. 1824.

Contains five pieces which are not in the first American edition; see next entry. For other editions see under 1825, 1849.

1: ⟨i⟩-xvi, ⟨1⟩-364. 8⅞″ x 5⅝″. Wove paper watermarked *1824*.

2: ⟨i⟩-vi, ⟨1⟩-394; blank, p. ⟨395⟩, *but see note below;* printer's imprint, p. ⟨396⟩.

1: ⟨A⟩-I, K-U, X-Z⁸, AA⁴, BB².

2: ⟨A⟩², ⟨-⟩¹, B-I, K-U, X-Z, AA-BB⁸, CC⁶.

Tan paper boards sides, green muslin shelfback. Printed paper label on spine.

Caution: The present entry is tentative since it is based on examination of three rebound copies (BPL, LC, NYPL), a restored copy (Y), and an incomplete copy (UV) in original binding.

Two states noted; the sequence has not been determined and the designations are for identification only:

A

Vol. 2, p. ⟨395⟩ is blank.

B

Vol. 2, p. ⟨395⟩ is imprinted: *NOTICE. Several spurious Works have issued from the press, alleged to be by the Author Of The Sketch Book, but published without his knowledge or approbation. Among these is an incorrect Edition of Salmagundi* ...

Noted as *preparing* LG April 24, 1824. Advertised for Aug. 1 LG July 10, 17, 24, 1824. "We do not think that Mr. Washington Irving's new work will be published so early as was anticipated; perhaps a few weeks may elapse before it is completed."—LG Aug. 14, 1824. Advertised for Aug. 25 in LG Aug. 21, 1824. Advertised, reviewed, listed LG Aug. 28, 1824. Listed BC Aug. 1824. Other and later London printings: Murray, 1848; 1850; Routledge, 1850; Bohn, 1850; Simms & M'Intyre, 1850; Bell & Daldy, 1864; 1868.

BPL (rebound) LC (rebound) NYPL (rebound) UV (incomplete, in original boards) Y (restored)

10116. TALES OF A TRAVELLER ... BY GEOFFREY CRAYON, GENT. ...

PHILADELPHIA: H. C. CAREY & I. LEA, CHESNUT-STREET. 1824.

The London edition (see preceding entry) contains five pieces which are here omitted. For first American book publication of the omitted pieces see *Tales of a Traveller ... Second American Edition,* 1825, below.

Issued in 4 paper-covered parts.

Part *1*

⟨1⟩-165, blank leaf. 9⅛″ full x 5⅞″.

⟨1⟩², 2-21⁴, 22².

Two issues of the title-page have been noted:

1: With the publisher's name incorrectly given as: H. C. CARY & I. LEE

2: With the publisher's name correctly given as: H. C. CAREY & I. LEA

Printed tan paper wrapper. White end papers.

Two states of the wrapper have been noted; the sequence, if any, has not been determined and the designations are for identification only:

A

On the front the 8th line reads: ... NEW-YORK," &c. / ⟨Note presence of the comma.⟩

The publisher's name is given correctly: H. C. CAREY & I. LEA

B

On the front the 8th line reads: ... NEW-YORK." &c. / ⟨Note presence of the period after NEW-YORK.⟩

The publisher's name is given correctly: H. C. CAREY & I. LEA

Note: Two other forms of the wrappers were printed but BAL has not found these used as such:

Cancelled Wrapper A

On the front is the imprint of *C. S. Van Winkle*

Cancelled Wrapper B

On the front is the erroneous form of the publisher's name: *H. C. Cary & I. Lee*

These faulty wrappers were salvaged, and the blank side imprinted with the correct letterpress. The original, incorrect, letterpress is concealed by the white paper pastedowns. Salvage wrappers have been seen on Parts 1 and 4. (*Query:* Also used on Parts 2-3?) It is to be noted that not all copies of Parts 1 and 4 occur in salvage wrappers; some are printed on otherwise unprinted paper.

Part *2*

⟨1⟩-212.

⟨1⟩², 2-27⁴.

Two states have been noted; the order given is probable:

A: P. 99, line 13: ... *at housand* /

B: P. 99, line 13: ... *a thousand* /

Part *3*

⟨1⟩-135.

⟨1⟩², 2-17⁴, 18².

In some copies there is inserted at the front a

four-page *Prospectus of a Collection of English Literature, Edited by Washington Irving, Esq. . . .* Written by Irving? See entry No. 10114.

Note: The wrapper has been noted in two states; sequence, if any, not determined:

A: . . . CHESNUT-STREET . . .

B: . . . CHESNUT STREET . . .

Part 4

⟨1⟩-161, blank leaf.

⟨1⟩², 2-21⁴.

Part 1: Title-page deposited July 22, 1824. Reviewed in *Minerva* (N.Y.), Sept. 4, 1824. *Part 2:* Title-page deposited Aug. 14, 1824. Reviewed in *Minerva* (N. Y.), Sept. 18, 1824. *Part 3:* Title-page deposited Aug. 30, 1824. Listed in USLG Oct. 15, 1824. *Part 4:* Title-page deposited Aug. 30, 1824; reviewed in USLG Nov. 15, 1824.

The present entry made on the basis of copies in:

AAS   H   LC   NYPL   UV   Y

10117. The Sketch Book of Geoffrey Crayon, Gent. . . . Fourth American Edition. In Two Volumes . . .

New-York: Printed by C. S. Van Winkle, No. 2 Thames-street. 1824.

Boards, printed paper label on spine. For first edition see above under 1819.

Reprint save for the following which are here first collected in an American book:

a "Advertisement to the First English Edition"

b "L'Envoy"

b "Philip of Pokanoket"

b "Traits of Indian Character"

Key

a —Previously in *The Sketch Book . . .* ⟨Vol. 1⟩, London (Miller), 1820; see above.
b —Previously in *The Sketch Book . . .* Vol. 2, London (Murray), 1820; see above.

AAS

10118. The Miscellaneous Works of Oliver Goldsmith, with an Account of His Life and Writings. A New Edition, in Four Volumes. Edited by Washington Irving, Esq. . . .

Paris: Published by A. and W. Galignani, 18, Rue Vivienne; and Jules Didot, Sen. 6, Rue du Pont-de-Lodi. 1825.

Probably issued in printed wrapper.

"Memoirs ⟨sic⟩ of the Life and Writings of Oliver Goldsmith," Vol. 1, pp. ⟨i⟩-cxxviii.

Note: A rebound copy in H has on the title-page Vol. II *for* Vol. I. Status not known. Binder's error?

The memoir published as follows:

1825: As above. A Carey & Lea prospectus (found in some copies of Irving's *Tales of a Traveller*, Part 3, Philadelphia, 1824) indicates that the book was to be distributed in United States by Carey & Lea. No copy seen with the Carey & Lea imprint and presumably Carey & Lea abandoned the project. It was noted as *in press* NAR Oct. 1824; USLG March 15, 1825.

1830: Earliest located American publication: Philadelphia (Crissy & Grigg); see below under 1830. Reprint of the 1825 text. Numerous later printings from these plates.

1834: Paris (Baudry). Reprint.

1840: New York (Harper). Revised. See below under 1840.

1849: New York (Putnam). Further revised. See below under 1849.

See entry No. 10114.

Irving "has undertaken to edit 'a collection of English Literature,' to be published in Paris in monthly numbers"—*Minerva* (N.Y.), July 17, 1824. "Now publishing by subscription by Galignani and Didot, Paris, and Carey & Lea . . . two volumes monthly"—USLG Oct. 15, 1824. In this last notice the work is described as in three formats: *fine paper;* on *vellum paper with proof impression of the portrait;* and, *large super-fine vellum paper . . . etching on India paper . . . limited to 50 copies.* Listed BF Oct. 15, 1824 in the following formats: *papier fin; papier vélin carré; papier jésus-vélin.*

H   NYPL

10119. Tales of a Traveller. By Geoffrey Crayon, Gent. . . . Second American Edition. In Two Volumes . . .

New-York: Printed by C. S. Van Winkle, No. 2 Thames-street. 1825.

Paper boards, printed paper label on spine.

For first edition see above under 1824.

A revised and extended edition with some alteration of titles and the addition of the following pieces; each had prior publication in the London, 1824, edition:

"The Adventure of the German Student"

"The Belated Travellers"

"Notoriety"

"A Practical Philosopher"

"To the Reader"

Listed NAR April, 1825.

UV

10120. The Atlantic Souvenir; a Christmas and New Year's Offering. 1827.

Philadelphia: H. C. Carey & I. Lea. ⟨1826⟩

"On Passaic Falls. Written in the Year 1806," pp. 146-148. Collected in *Poems*, 1931.

For fuller entry see No. 614.

10121. The Literary Souvenir; or, Cabinet of Poetry and Romance. Edited by Alaric A. Watts ...

London: Longman, Rees, Orme, Brown, & Green; and John Andrews. 1827.

Cloth?

"A Contented Man," pp. ⟨1⟩-9. Collected in *Wolfert's Roost*, 1855.

Advertised for "early in November" LG Oct. 14, 1826. LG Oct. 14, 1826, noted: "... a limited number of copies on a larger size, with proofs of the plates on India paper, has been struck off ..." Advertised for *November* BMLA Oct. 1826. "... Reached us too late for a review this week"—LG Nov. 4, 1826. Reviewed LG Nov. 11, 1826, and advertised in same issue as *in a few days*. Advertised as *this day is published* LG Nov. 18, 1826. Described as *in press* BMLA Nov. 1826. Described as *now first published* BMLA Dec. 1826. Reviewed MR Dec. 1826.

H NYPL

10122. The Atlantic Souvenir; a Christmas and New Year's Offering. 1828.

Philadelphia: Carey, Lea & Carey. Sold in Boston by Hilliard, Gray, & Co. ⟨1827⟩

Printed paper boards.

"The Dull Lecture," p. 294. Collected in *Poems*, 1931.

Note: Also issued with the imprint: *Philadelphia: Carey, Lea & Carey.* ⟨1827⟩

Title-page deposited Aug. 27, 1827.

H

10123. A HISTORY OF THE LIFE AND VOYAGES OF CHRISTOPHER COLUMBUS ...

LONDON ... MDCCCXXVIII.

See next entry for American edition.

NOTE

Vols. 1-3

Printed by W. Clowes from two settings, with the exception of Sigs. B-X, Vol. 1, which were printed from a single setting.

Vol. 4

Printed by Thomas Davison from two settings.

In Vol. 1, Sig. ⟨A⟩ was printed from at least four settings; in Vol. 2, Sig. ⟨a⟩ was done from at least two settings; in Vol. 3, Sig. ⟨a⟩ was done from at least three settings; in Vol. 4, Sig. ⟨A⟩ was done from at least four settings. The settings for the title-pages (which occur in the gatherings cited) are essentially the same, and may be distinguished by the spacing. The variations are so very minuscule it is impracticable to describe them verbally. However, ready identification of at least two forms of the title-pages of Vols. 1-2 can be made on the basis of the presence, or absence, of the colon in the printer's imprint on the verso of the fly-title. Unfortunately about half the volumes examined lack the fly-title pages (removed in rebinding); hence BAL's inability to present a record of all possible varieties.

The above factors combine to produce copies of the book in an almost infinite variety. No ready argument emerges to support the primacy of any setting, if primacy there is. Certain stop-press alterations occurred and those discovered (and noted below) establish a sequence for certain of the gatherings within the setting from which they were printed. Copies made up of mixed sheets have been seen.

BAL suggests that all copies issued by Murray under date 1828 be considered of equal primacy until evidence is produced to the contrary.

Langfeld and Blackburn failed to recognize the multiple settings and offer three "issues" of the book; BAL suggests that the Langfeld-Blackburn description be disregarded.

A HISTORY OF THE LIFE AND VOYAGES OF CHRISTOPHER COLUMBUS ... IN FOUR VOLUMES ...

LONDON: JOHN MURRAY, ALBEMARLE-STREET. MDCCCXXVIII.

Issued with two folded, inserted, maps. These appear to have been inserted *ad libitum* and copies therefore have been seen with both maps inserted in Vol. 1; a single map in Vol. 1 and another in Vol. 2; etc., etc.

Vol. 1, Both Settings

⟨i-ii⟩, ⟨i⟩-viii; unpaged leaf; ⟨ix⟩-xii, ⟨1⟩-473;

blank, p. ⟨474⟩; Clowes imprint, p. ⟨475⟩; blank, p. ⟨476⟩. 8⅞″ x 5⅝″.

⟨A⟩², a⁴, b², B-I, K-U, X-Z, 2A-2G⁸, 2H⁶.

Vol. 2, Both Settings

⟨i-viii⟩, ⟨1⟩-490; Clowes imprint, p. ⟨491⟩; blank, p. ⟨492⟩.

⟨a⟩-b², B-I, K-U, X-Z, 2A-2H⁸, 2I⁶.

Vol. 3, Setting A

⟨i⟩-viii, ⟨1⟩-413; blank, p. ⟨414⟩; Clowes imprint, p. ⟨415⟩; blank, p. ⟨416⟩.

Vol. 3, Setting B

⟨i⟩-viii, ⟨1⟩-413; Clowes imprint, p. ⟨414⟩; blank, pp. ⟨415-416⟩.

Signature Collation, Vol. 3, Both Settings

⟨a⟩-b², B-I, K-U, X-Z, 2A-2D⁸.

Vol. 4, Both Settings

⟨i⟩-⟨viii⟩, ⟨1⟩-489; blank, pp. ⟨490-491⟩; Davison imprint, p. ⟨492⟩.

⟨A⟩⁴, B-I, K-U, X-Z, AA-HH⁸, II⁴, KK².

Tan paper boards; dark rose paper boards; printed paper label on spine. *Also:* Tan paper boards sides, purple muslin shelfback, printed paper label on spine. *Note:* A copy has been seen in fine-grained H cloth stamped in gold and blind. BAL has seen no other copies so bound. It is suggested that the binding be considered a publisher's secondary binding of a somewhat later period or a custom rebinding. The publisher's catalog for April, 1828 (in BPL) offers the book at two guineas only, the price given on the printed paper spine labels of the copies in paper boards.

The following record of typographic variations is sufficient to distinguish *Setting A* from *Setting B*. Sequence, if any (see notes at head of this entry), has not been determined and the designations are for identification only and no sequence is suggested or implied.

VOLUME ONE

Setting A	Setting B

Leaf a₁ recto

Sig. mark *a* under the letter *n*	Sig. mark *a* under the letter *w*

P. iv, line 8 up

... *manuscript,* /	... *manuscript* /

P. ⟨ix⟩
Entry for Ch. V

... *west* 52 /	... *West* 52 /

P. x, line 3 up

... *Cruize* ...	... *Cruise* ...

Signature D

Apparently printed from a single setting. The error *ont* for *out*, p. 34, line 3, is present in all examined copies.

Pp. 43-44

These pages have been noted in three forms. The sequence has not been determined and the designations are for identification only.

A

P. 43, line 1: *like Columbus* ...

P. 43, line 5: ... *strict* /

P. 43: The statement VOL. I. is not at the foot of the page. There is no asterisk below ⟨sic⟩ the footnote.

P. 44, line 11 of footnote: ... *Venet. 1606.*) ... (Note that the period is within the closing parenthesis)

P. 44, line 14 of footnote: ... *Derroto por Tofino* ... (Which is correct) The leaf is a cancel.

B

P. 43, line 1: *to the coast* ...

P. 43, line 4: ... *strict* /

P. 43: The statement VOL. I. is present at foot of the page. Also at foot of the page an asterisk is present *below* the footnote and is set under the *N* in *N. Mundo.*

P. 44, line 11 of footnote: ... *Venet. 1606.*) ... (Note that the period is within the closing parenthesis)

P. 44, line 14 of footnote: ... *Terroto por Cofino* ... (Which is erroneous)

The leaf is a cancel.

C

P. 43, line 1: *to the coast* ...

P. 43, line 4: ... *eco-* /

P. 43: The statement VOL. I. is present at foot of the page. Also at foot of the page an asterisk is present *below* the footnote and is set under the word *del.*

P. 44, line 11 of footnote: ... *Venet. 1606*). ... (Note that the period is outside the closing parenthesis, not within)

P. 44, line 14 of footnote: ... *Terroto por Cofino* ... (Which is erroneous)

The leaf is probably a cancel; inability to locate an example of this form of the leaf in original boards as issued prevents making a positive statement.

P. 92
Lines 6-7 of the footnote

1st: ... from / from ...

2nd: ... Hope, / from ...

This appears to be a stop-press correction and but a single setting is involved.

Signature I

Apparently printed from a single setting. The following errors are common to all examined copies:

P. 100, line 11: *1476* for *1486*

P. 113, running head: *Portugal* for *Castile*

P. 115, running head: *Portugal* for *Castile*

P. 117, last line: ... *confided* ... for ... *confined* ...

P. 121, line 1: *stitutiou* ... for *stitution* ...

P. 122, line 7 up: ... *eclesiastical* ... for ... *ecclesiastical* ...

P. 127, lines 12-13: ... *ima- / mined* ... for ... *ima- / gined* ...

Signature O

Apparently printed from a single setting. The following errors are common to all examined copies:

P. 200, line 4 of the footnote: *1803* for *1503*

P. 200, line 3 up of the footnote: *Alexander VII* for *Alexander VI*

Signature P

Apparently printed from a single setting. The following errors are common to all examined copies:

P. 211, line 4 up: ... *west*.* / for ... *east*.* /

P. 222, line 6: ... *were* ... for ... *where* ...

Signature S

Apparently from a single setting. The following error is common to all examined copies:

P. 261, line 1: ... *where* ... for ... *were* ...

Signature T

Apparently from a single setting. The following error is common to all examined copies:

P. 286, line 10 up: ... *at the* / for ... *of the* /

P. 321, line 15

... *ca-* /   ... *grand* /

P. 322

Mispaged 232   Paged 322

P. 333

All examined copies have the error *collection* for *collation,* line 10.

P. 337, line 2

... *exulta-* /   ... *exultation,* /

P. 338, line 3 up

ble jewel*. /   *jewel*.* /

P. 352, footnote

... *Colon.,* ...   ... *Colon,* ...

P. 353, line 3 up

anything ...   *than any* ...

P. 375, line 8 up

... *Yañes* ...   ... *Yanes* ...

P. 381, line 7

... *to think, that* ...   ... *to think that,* ...

P. 385, line 4 up

rope; ...   *rope:* ...

P. 386, line 3 up

vailed ...   *prevailed* ...

Note: All examined copies have the error *1492* for *1493,* p. 386.

P. 401, line 7

... *ensued* ...   ... *ensued,* ...

P. 402, line 5 up

... *Still, the king* ...   ... *Still the King* ...

P. 417, line 6

... *pronounced* /   ... *pronounced a* /

P. 418, line 9 up

... *dispositions at* /   ... *dispositions* /

P. 433, line 7

the king ...   *"whom the king* ...

P. 436, line 4 up

... *seize upon,* ...   ... *seize upon* ...

P. 455, line 9

... *extolled* /   ... *ex-* /

P. 456, line 7 up

... *possession of* /   ... *possession* /

P. 465, line 12

... *prin-* | ... *the* |

P. 471, line 14

... *west,* | ... *west;* |

P. 472, footnote

... *Vasconcelos* ...   ... *Vasconceles* ...

VOLUME TWO

P. ⟨v⟩
The rule under CONTENTS

1¼″ scant   13⁄16″

P. ⟨vi⟩
Entry for Ch. VII

... *Hispani-* | ... *Hispaniola,* |

P. 2, line 9 up

... *as* | ... *as de-* |

P. 3, line 5

... *sunrise the whole* | ... *sunrise the* |

P. 19, line 10

... *commanded, that,* ... *commanded that,*
...   ...

P. 20, line 1

... *every thing* ...   ... *everything* ...

P. 34, line 3 up

... *and* ...   ... *aud* ...

P. 37, line 3

... *exertions, but* | ... *exertions; but* |

P. 50, line 3
The comma is set over:

The *f* in *of* and a space   The *h* in *him*

Two states of *Setting B* noted; sequence, if any,
has not been determined; designations are for
identification only:

  a: In the heading: [*Book VI* |
    Line 7 up: ... *Escobido* |

  b: In the heading: [*Book VI.* |
    Line 7 up: ... *Escobido,* |

P. 51, line 5

... *arrived with* ...   ... *arrived, with* ...

P. 65, line 5

... *countrymen*   ... *countrymen,*
were ...   *were* ...

P. 66, line 3 up

... *natives* | ... *natives,* |

P. 67, line 1

... *cacique who* | ... *cacique, who* |

P. 82, line 2

... *most perni-* | ... *most per-* |

P. 83, last line

... *persons of credi-* | ... *persons of* |

P. 97, line 4

... *extended as* | ... *extended* |

P. 98, line 1

... *inspired a min-* | ... *inspired a* |

P. 113, Sig. mark I

under *ma*   under *m*

P. 114, line 8 up

... *caciques* ...   ... *cicaques* ...

P. 129, line 6

... *which he* | ... *which* |

P. 134, line 1

corn but ...   *ing corn* ...

P. ⟨147⟩, line 1

... *from the* | ... *from* |

P. 154

The rule is ⅝″ scant   The rule is ¾″ scant

P. 161, line 9 up

... *hid him-* | ... *hid* |

P. 177, line 8

... *in the midst* | ... *in the* |

P. 178, line 1

alone ...   *dress alone* ...

P. 193, line 2

... *clusters of is-* | ... *clusters of* |

P. 194, line 1

at wide ...   *precarious and at* ...

P. 209, line 8 up

... *island,* | ... *island* |

P. 210, line 4

... *adverse, be-* | ... *adverse,* |

P. ⟨215⟩

Rule measures ½″   Rule measures 9⁄16″ full

P. 225, line 5

... *sister* | ... *sister,* |

P. 227, line 2

... *followers,* /   ... *follow-* /

P. 230, line 7 up

where ...   *were* ...

P. 241, last line

prevented. /   *vented.* /

P. 242, synopsis, line 2

... OF OJEDA TO /   ... OF OJEDA /

P. 257, line 3

... *weapons and* ...   ... *weapons, and* ...

P. 260, line 7 up

maravedies for ...   *maravedies, for* ...

P. 262, line 7

... *He* /   ... *He re-* /

P. 275, line 7

... *made* ...   ... *make* ...

P. 278, line 1

bella ...   *Isabella* ...

Pp. 288-289

In all examined copies, both settings, a hiatus in the text causes the following reading: ... *under the supervision of the admiral, or,* / *absence, in presence of those in authority* ...

P. 292, line 7

... *East* ...   ... *east* ...

P. 293, line 6 up

... *persons* /   ... *persons re-* /

P. 309, line 9 up

... *to be ex-* /   ... *to be* /

P. 310, line 1

return to ...   *don her* ...

P. 321, line 6 up

... *natives of* /   ... *natives* /

P. 322, line 1

the sympathy ...   *won the sympathy* ...

P. 337, line 12

... *cavarels* ...   ... *caravels* ...

P. 352, line 11 up

lestations ...   *molestations* ...

P. 353, line 8

.. *already enume-* /   ... *already* /

P. 354, line 3

to the Catholic ...   *the Catholic* ...

P. 367, line 9

... *justify* /   ... *jnstify* /

P. 369, line 5

... *him as* /   ... *him as a* /

P. 372, line 2 up

glasses ...   *ing-glasses* ...

P. 394, line 1

... *when once* /   ... *when* /

P. 398, last line

some Spaniard ...   *only have fallen* ...

P. 402, line 5

... *unknown to* /   ... *unknown* /

P. 403, line 8

Saviour will ...   *viour will* ...

P. 417, last line

... *serious* ...   ... *seious* ...

P. 428, line 11

... *fellow-caciques* ...   ... *follow-caciques* ...

P. 433, line 5

... *posts thus* ...   ... *posts, thus* ...

P. 437, line 11

... *to their su-* /   ... *to their* /

P. 440, at head

[*Book XI.*   [*Book IX.*

P. 449, line 11 up

.. *to the ves-* /   ... *to the* /

P. 454, line 7

lic works ...   *public works* ...

P. 466, line 2 up

... *in tri-* /   ... *in* /

P. 479, line 8

determined ...   *he determined* ...

P. 481, line 11 up

... *in the fast-* /   ... *in the* /

P. 482, line 5 up

and flames of ...   *flames of* ...

P. 490

Paged 490 | Early copies mispaged *460;* later copies correctly paged *490*

VOLUME THREE

P. ⟨v⟩

The word *page* at the head of the column of page reference numbers is set in:

Capital initial, otherwise in lower case. | Set in capital letters only.

P. vi
Reference to p. 131

... *Colum-* / | ... *Columbus* /

P. ⟨1⟩, line 5

... *sweets of* / | ... *sweets* /

P. 12, line 5

... *such* / | ... *such se-* /

P. 17, line 7

... *Sovereigns* ... | ... *sovereigns* ...

P. 18, line 1

... *Majes-* / | ... *majes-* /

P. 34, line 6

... *or* / | ... *or de-* /

P. 37, line 5 up

... *of its so-* / | ... *of its* /

P. 49, last line

... *circumstances obliged* / | ... *circum-* /

P. 50, line 1

Columbus ... | *stances* ...

P. 60

Page number 60 present or absent. Sequence? | Page number 60 present in all examined copies.

P. 66, line 6 up

serted; ... | *serted,* ...

P. 67, line 10

... *trust him-* / | ... *trust* /

P. 78

Mispaged *87* | Paged *78*

P. ⟨85⟩
First line of synopsis

... COLUM- / | ... COLUMBUS. /

P. 88, line 8

... *disor-* / | ... *disorderly* /

P. 97, line 2

... *"admi-* / | ... *"admiral* /

P. 98, line 9

fall; ... | *fal;* ...

P. 117, line 8 up

... *private; and* / | ... *private;* /

P. 118, line 4

... *precaution to sub-* / | ... *precaution to* /

P. 130, line 9

... *respect and as-* / | ... *respect and* /

P. 143, line 8

... *westward* / | .. *west-* /

P. 145, line 12

... *reaching Xa-* / | ... *reaching* /

P. 158, line 13

... *they* / | ... *they in-* /

P. 162, line 6 up

... *were* ... | ... *where* ...

P. 163, line 3

... *ascertained* ... | ... *sustained* ...

P. 179, line 5

... *his enthu-* / | ... *his en-* /

P. 186, line 14

... *to appre-* / | ... *to ap-* /

P. 193, line 7

... *im-* / | ... *impa-* /

P. 206, line 11

... *and hide-* / | ... *and* /

P. 210, line 3

... *of va-* / | ... *of* /

P. 213, line 4 up

... *Spaniards* / | ... *Spa-* /

P. 227, line 8

... *and sea* / | ... *and sea-* /

P. 232, line 3 up

.. *for European* / | ... *for* /

P. 243, lines 7-8

... *too | shallow* ...   ... *be | toos hal-low* ...

P. 250, line 2

... *the dominions of |*   ... *the dominions |*

P. 257, line 5 up

... *penetrate as |*   ... *penetrate as a |*

P. 266, line 6

... *ascertain his |*   ... *ascertain |*

P. 274, line 12

... *barba- |*   ... *bar- |*

P. 279, line 5

... *to be con- |*   ... *to be |*

P. 289, line 2 up

... *unfortu- |*   ... *unfortunate |*

P. 292, line 2

... *ne- |*   .. *neces- |*

P. 305, line 11

... *life in peril |*   .. *life in|*

P. 308, line 7

... *fourteenth |*   ... *four- |*

P. 328, last line

... *By scru- |*   ... *By |*

P. 329, line 1

pulous ...   *scrupulous* ...

P. 339, line 10 up

... *immedi- |*   ... *imme- |*

P. 342, line 6

... *Columbus him- |*   ... *Columbus |*

P. 356, line 9

... *them, and* ...   ... *them; and* ...

P. 359, line 2

... *from their pur- |*   ... *from their |*

P. 371, line 2 up

... *thousand |*   ... *thou- |*

P. 372, line 5

... *persons and|*   ... *persons and the |*

P. 390, line 5

... *and lived at |*   ... *and lived |*

P. 391, last line

horror and ...   *ror and* ...

P. 404, line 3 up

and loss ...   *anguish and* ...

P. 405, line 3

... *their death |*   ... *their death be |*

Printer's imprint

On p. ⟨415⟩   On p. ⟨414⟩

VOLUME FOUR

P. 5, line 1

... *of all transac- |*   ... *of all trans- |*

P. 6, line 1

ble massacre ...   *massacre* ...

P. 17, line 11 up

... *Jamaica, might,* ...   ... *Jamaica might,* ...

P. 18, line 10

... *Morales |*   ... *Morales, |*

P. 33, line 3 up

... *last will of his |*   ... *last will |*

P. 36, line 4

All examined copies, both settings: *wave* for *waive*

P. 38, heading

[Book XVIII.   [Book XVIII

P. 51, line 7 up

... *might af- |*   ... *might |*

P. 52, line 10 up

... *their se- |*   ... *their sedi- |*

P. ⟨65⟩

Rule between text and heading

1″ full   15/16″

P. 72, line 11

... *and all |*   ... *and all the |*

P. 77, line 1

that it was ...   *that is was* ...

P. 81

The running head

Set 1 13/16″ wide   Set 1 3/4″ wide

P. 82
The running head

Set 1¾₂″ wide   Set 1½₂″ wide

P. 100, line 11

... *1825* ...   ... *1525* ...

P. ⟨111⟩, line 9
The tilde in *de Zuñiga* is:

A short horizontal dash   The conventional
curved character

P. 113, line 3 up
The tilde in *de Zuñiga* is:

A short horizontal dash   The conventional
curved character

P. 114, footnote

... *Anales* ...   ... *Annales* ...

P. 129, the folio

The numerals are uni-   The figure *9* drops be-
form size   low the line of *12*

P. 130, line 7

other ...   *another* ...

P. ⟨145⟩

The heading is set 2⅛″   The heading is set 2″
wide   scant wide

P. 146, last line

... *cor-* | ... *corsair,* |

P. 161, line 2

The comma is set over   The comma is set over
a space   the letter *t*

P. 162, line 11

be terra ...   *to be terra* ...

P. 185, last line

... *extre-* | ... *ex-* |

P. 186, line 1

mity ...   *tremity* ...

P. 196, line 9 up

... *teconding* ...   ... *seconding* ...

P. ⟨197⟩
First line of synopsis

... DIED IN | ... DIED IN THE |

P. 209
Signature mark P set below:

at   *of*

P. 210, line 11

inserted into ...   *inserted in* ...

P. 235, line 9 up

... *decades* ...   ... *Decades* ...

P. 236, line 2 up

... *Pinazas,* | ... *Pinezas,* |

P. 241

Running head set 1⅜″   Running head set 1⅜″
full   scant

P. 242, line 9 up

... *whereas,* ...   ... *whereas* ...

P. 257

Running head set 1⁷⁄₁₆″   Running head set 1⁵⁄₁₆″
scant   full

P. 258, line 8

... *port* ...   ... *Port* ...

P. ⟨273⟩
First line of synopsis

... MENTIONED | ... MENTIONED IN |

P. 274, line 2

Semicolon set over let-   Semicolon set over letter *i*   ter *n*

P. 289, line 16

and, ...   *and* ...

P. 290, line 2

Set flush at right   Not set flush at right

P. ⟨313⟩, line 7

... *him a de-* | ... *him a* |

P. 318, line 7

the time ...   *of the time* ...

P. 322
The heading: THE IMAGINARY ISLAND

Set 1½″ full wide   Set 1½″ scant wide

P. 325, line 9

... *testified,*   ... *testified having* ...
having ...

P. ⟨333⟩, heading

... SEVEN CITIES. | ... SEVEN CITIES |

P. ⟨337⟩, heading

Set 2¹³⁄₁₆″ scant wide   Set 2½″ wide

P. 343, line 11

... *country* /   ... *country,* ... /

P. 345, line 4

ward III. ...   *ward III.,* ...

P. 351, line 4

... *licenses* ...   ... *licences* ...

P. 354, line 8 up

with a ...   *with the* ...

P. 360, line 3

... *ne-* /   ... *neg-* /

P. 369, line 2 up

... *reluc-* /   ... *reluct-* /

P. 376, line 10

mation ...   *formation* ...

P. 379, line 6 up

... *World* ...   ... *World,* ...

P. ⟨381⟩
The rule in the heading measures:

1" full wide   ¾" wide

P. ⟨383⟩
The rule in the heading measures:

1" full wide   ¾" wide

P. 385, line 3 up

cation, ...   *cation* ...

P. ⟨387⟩, line 1

Set flush at the left   Indented

P. ⟨393⟩
The chapter heading

Setting A occurs in two   No. XXXII.
states, probably in the
order given:

1: XXXII.

2: No. XXXII.

P. 405, line 10

... *dis-* /   ... *di-* /

P. 406, line 7

it ...   *of* ...

P. 414, running head

ON THE SITUATION OF,   ON THE SITUATION, &c.
&c.

P. ⟨415⟩
WILL OF COLUMBUS.

Set 1⅜" full wide   Set 1¼" scant

P. 421, line 10

... *inherit this* ...   ... *inherit his* ...

P. 428

Paged *428*   Mispaged *423*

P. 435, line 7

... *Diego, my son* ...   ... *Diego my son* ...

P. ⟨437⟩

The rule measures   The rule measures
1¹⁄₁₆"   ¹⁵⁄₁₆" scant

P. 442, line 4 up

of Columbus ...   *mains of Columbus* ...

P. 448, line 2

the mountains ...   *of the mountains* ...

P. 450, line 9 up

bus' indignation ...   *bus's indignation* ...

P. 457, last line

steers along the ...   *along the* ...

P. 464, line 2

of his ...   *claims* ...

P. 469, line 11 up

... *introduced to* ...   ... *introduced
                              into* ...

P. 476, line 10

Macham ..   *Machan* ...

P. 481, line 6 up

... *voyage,* /   ... *voyage, ii.* /

P. 482, line 6

Pigeons, Wood ...   *Pigeons, wood* ...

P. 489, line 16

... *a desert,* /   ... *a desert* /

Note: According to the publisher's *Memoirs* (Vol. 2, p. 258) *"Columbus, had been published in America before* ... ⟨*it*⟩ *appeared in England."* The publisher was in error.

Letter from the publisher to BAL, Dec. 2, 1964: "... two printers were used. The first movement out of the stock book is dated 28 February 1828. There was a printing of 4,000 copies which consisted of 3,000 plus a run-on printing of 1,000 which might, in these days, be called a reprint even though the type was not taken off the machine . . ."

Prematurely advertised as *nearly ready* BMLA Nov. 1827; and, Jan. 1828. Noted as *nearly ready* LG Feb. 2, 1828. Reviewed LG Feb. 2, 1828: *This work will appear ‹sic› in the course of the ensuing month.* Announced for Feb. 11 LG Feb. 9, 1828. Listed Ath Feb. 12, 1828. Reviewed Ath Feb. 12, 19, 26, 1828. Listed LG Feb. 15, 1828. Noted for *the present month* BMLA Feb. 1828. Listed MR March, 1828. Reviewed ER March, 1828. Noted as *just published* BMLA March, 1828. Announced for *this day* Ath April 1, 1828, *but* with extracts from reviews. Reviewed MR April, 1828. Listed as a *February* publication BMLA April, 1828. PC March, 1850, reported that "the MS, being purchased in this country for a very large sum, and published prior to its appearance in America . . ." See next entry.

The present entry made on the basis of copies in the possession of: BPL; *Mr. Donald C. Gallup*; H; HM; NYPL; *Mr. Rollin G. Osterweis*; UV; Y.

10124. A HISTORY OF THE LIFE AND VOYAGES OF CHRISTOPHER COLUMBUS . . . IN THREE VOLUMES . . .

G. & C. CARVILL, 108 BROADWAY, NEW-YORK. 1828.

See preceding entry for first London edition. For revised editions see under 1831, 1848. For abridged editions see under 1829.

1: ‹i›-xvi, ‹1›-399. Folded map inserted. 9¹⁄₁₆" x 5¾".

2: ‹i›-viii, ‹9›-367.

3: ‹i›-viii, ‹13›-420. *Note:* Folio *420* occurs as follows; sequence not determined and the designations are for identification only: A: Folio *420* present; B: Folio not present; C: Only the numeral *o* present.

1: ‹A›-B, 1-50⁴. Sig. mark 6 (p. 41) not present in some copies.

2: ‹1›-46⁴.

3: ‹-›, 1-51⁴.

Brown paper boards sides, brown muslin shelfback; brown paper boards sides, purple muslin shelfback. Flyleaves. Printed paper label on spine.

Title-page deposited Jan. 24, 1828; no further record found in the Copyright Office. *Evening Post* (N.Y.), Feb. 20, 1828: *In the press and will shortly be published;* with the same notice repeated in the issues of March 3-8, 1828, inclusive. No further notices found. Reviewed AQR March, 1828. In the John Murray archives,

London, there is an affidavit sworn to by Ebenezer Irving, Sept. 1850, in which Irving swears that the New York edition of the book was published March 15, 1828. (The affidavit was required at the time Murray sued Bohn for infringement.)

BA NYPL UV

10125. A CHRONICLE OF THE CONQUEST OF GRANADA. BY FRAY ANTONIO AGAPIDA. IN TWO VOLUMES . . .

PHILADELPHIA: CAREY, LEA & CAREY—CHESNUT-STREET. 1829.

See next entry.

Small Paper Format

1: ‹1›-2, ‹iii›-xii, ‹13›-311; plus: publisher's catalogue, 4 pp. 7¾" x 4⅝".

2: ‹i›-vi, ‹7›-319.

1: ‹A›-I, K-U, X-Z, Aa-Cc⁶; plus: A². *Also signed:* ‹1-2›, 3-39⁴; plus: A².

2: ‹A›-I, K-U, X-Z, Aa-Cc⁶, Dd⁴. *Also signed:* ‹1›-28, 30, 30-35, 33, 37-40⁴.

Drab paper boards sides, rose-purple muslin shelfback. Printed paper label on spine. Flyleaves.

Large Paper Format

Pagination: As above. Leaf size: 9⅛" x 5¾".

1: ‹1-2›, 3-39⁴; plus: ‹-›². *Also signed:* ‹A›-I, K-U, X-Z, Aa-Cc⁶; ‹-›².

2: ‹1›-28, 30, 30-35, 33, 37-40⁴. *Also signed:* ‹A›-I, K-U, X-Z, Aa-Cc⁶, Dd⁴.

Drab paper boards sides, brown muslin shelfback; also, purple muslin shelfback. Printed paper label on spine. Flyleaves.

According to Kaser there were 3000 copies printed of the small paper format; 500 copies of the large paper format.

Title-page deposited March 6, 1829. Reviewed AQR March, 1829. Described as *lately published* AMM April, 1829. See under 1850 for revised edition.

B (Small Paper) H (Small Paper) NYPL (Both formats) UV (Large Paper)

10126. A Chronicle of the Conquest of Granada. From the Mss. of Fray Antonio Agapida . . . in Two Volumes . . .

London: John Murray, Albemarle-Street. MDCCCXXIX.

For first edition see preceding entry. The text

of this first English edition varies from that of the first American edition.

Paper boards, printed paper label on spine. Also: Paper boards, cloth shelfback, printed paper label on spine.

Advertised as published on *April 14*, in LG Aug. 1, 1829; the statement is erroneous. Advertised for publication *in a few days* LG Feb. 21, 28; March 7, 14, 21, 1829. Noted for publication *in little more than a fortnight*, LG March 28, 1829. Advertised for *publication in the course of the next six weeks* LG April 4, 11, 18, 25, 1829. Reviewed LG May 23, 1829. Listed Ath May 29, 1829, and advertised for *this day*, same issue. Listed LG May 30, 1829; ER June, 1829.

BPL   LC   UV   Y

10127. The Life and Voyages of Christopher Columbus, by Washington Irving. (Abridged by the Same.) . . .

Stereotyped by James Conner, for G. & C. & H. Carvill, 108 Broadway, New-York. 1829.

An abridgement of the 1828 edition, above. "Advertisement," by Irving, pp. <3>-4.

Noted only in publisher's leather.

Title deposited April 4, 1829. Reviewed *Critic* (N.Y.), June 13, 1829.

Several later printings and editions were issued. The following have been noted by BAL and on the basis of reasonably full comparison are here classified as either revised (or extended) editions; and, as reprints. The list is probably far from complete.

London: John Murray, Albemarle-Street. MD-CCCXXX.
Somewhat revised. Reviewed LG Feb. 27, 1830. Listed Ath March 6, 1830. See entry No. 10128. *Note:* Williams-Edge (p. 69) report a Murray edition of 1829 but note the entry as *not seen.* Williams-Edge appear to be in error; no such 1829 edition has been traced by BAL.

Paris: Baudry & Galignani, 1830.
Not seen. A reprint of the London, 1830, revision? Listed BF Dec. 4, 1830.

Stereotyped by James Conner, for G. & C. & H. Carvill, 108 Broadway, New-York. 1830.
Reprint.

Stereotyped by James Conner, for G. & C. & H. Carvill, 108 Broadway, New-York. 1831.
First American printing of the London, 1830, version. See entry No. 10130.

London: John Murray, Albemarle-Street. MD-CCCXXXI.
Reprint.

<*New York*> *Printed by J. & J. Harper, 82 Cliff-Street. 1833.*
Reprint.

<*New York*> *N. & J. White. Printed by J. & J. Harper, 82 Cliff-Street. 1833.*
Reprint.

New York: Published by N. & J. White, 108 Pearl-Street. 1834.
Basically the text of the London, 1830, edition but somewhat altered. Did Irving do the alterations? See entry No. 10137.

New York: Published by N. and J. White, 108 Pearl-Street. 1835.
Reprint.

Boston: Marsh, Capen, Lyon, and Webb. 1839.
Reprint save for a note (by Irving?), pp. v-vi; and, a glossary contributed by the anonymous editor, Joseph W. Ingraham. See entry No. 10152.

New-York: Published by Collins, Keese & Co., No. 254 Pearl Street. 1839.
Reprint.

London: Printed for Thomas Tegg, 73, Cheapside. 1841.
Reprint.

Bath, N. Y. R. L. Underhill & Co. 1844.
Reprint.

New York: Harper & Brothers, Publishers, 329 & 331 Pearl Street, Franklin Square. 1855.
Reprint.

– – – –. *1856.*
Reprint.

London: William Tegg, 1866.
Not seen. Presumably a reprint. Advertised PC May 15, June 1, 1866; listed PC June 15, 1866.

AAS   BPL   H   LC   NYHS   NYPL   Y

10128. The Life and Voyages of Christopher Columbus. By Washington Irving. (Abridged by the Same.)

London: John Murray, Albemarle-Street. MD-CCCXXX.

For comment see note under preceding entry.

Y

10129. The Miscellaneous Works of Oliver Goldsmith, with an Account of His Life and Writings. Stereotyped from the Paris Edition, Edited by Washington Irving . . .

Philadelphia: Published by J. Crissy and J. Grigg. 1830

Probably issued in paper boards, printed paper label on spine.

For an earlier printing see above under 1825.

"Memoirs of the Life and Writings of Oliver Goldsmith," pp. ⟨7⟩-56.

Listed NAR Oct. 1830.

Many reprintings including the following:

Philadelphia: Crissy, 1833, 1835, 1836, 1837, 1841.

Philadelphia: Crissy & Markley, n.d.

AAS   BPL   H   NYPL

10130. The Life and Voyages of Christopher Columbus, by Washington Irving. (Abridged by the Same.) ... A New Edition, with Additions and Improvements, by the Author.

> Stereotyped by James Conner, for G. & C. & H. Carvill, 108 Broadway, New-York. 1831.

Cloth, leather label on spine.

For comment see entry No. 10127.

Title deposited March 9, 1831.

H

10131. History of the Life and Voyages of Christopher Columbus ... a New Edition Revised and Corrected by the Author. In Two Volumes ...

> G. & C. & H. Carvill, No. 108 Broadway, New-York. 1831.

Probably issued in paper boards, cloth shelf-back, printed paper label on spine.

A revised edition. See above under 1828 for the first edition.

AAS   LC   Y

10132. VOYAGES AND DISCOVERIES OF THE COMPANIONS OF COLUMBUS ...

LONDON: JOHN MURRAY, ALBEMARLE STREET. MDCCCXXXI.

For first American edition see next entry.

⟨i⟩-xviii, ⟨1⟩-337; advertisements, p. ⟨338⟩. Inserted: Frontispiece, 1 plate, folded map; other illustrations in text. 6⅛″ x 3⅞″.

⟨-⟩⁸, c¹, B-I, K-U, X-Y⁸, ⟨Z⟩¹.

Two bindings noted; sequence (if any) not determined and the designations are for identification only:

A

T cloth: brown. Sides stamped in blind with a double-rule frame enclosing a filigree. Spine lettered in gold. Yellow-coated end papers. The binding does not identify the book as part of *The Family Library* series. Williams-Edge (but without presentation of evidence) state that this binding is the earlier.

B

Tan muslin, printed in black only. Identified on the binding as No. XVIII in *The Family Library* series. Inserted at front: Publisher's catalogue dated *December, MDCCCXXX.*

All examined copies have the error *council* for *counsel,* p. 267, line 2.

Noted as *in the press* MR Dec. 1830. Advertised for Jan. 1, 1831, in LG Jan. 1, 1831; and as *published this day* Ath Jan. 1, 1831. Reviewed in LG Jan. 1, 8, 22, 1831; Ath Jan. 1, 22, 1831; MR Feb. 1831. Reprinted and reissued by Tegg (London), 1861, 1866; noted in PC July 15, 1861; Ath July 20, 1861; PC May 15, June 1, 1866; listed PC June 15, 1866.

H (A)   Y (an incomplete B)

10133. VOYAGES AND DISCOVERIES OF THE COMPANIONS OF COLUMBUS ...

PHILADELPHIA: CAREY AND LEA—CHESNUT STREET. 1831.

For prior London publication see preceding entry.

⟨1⟩-350; 2 pp. advertisements. 9³⁄₁₆″ x 5¾″.

⟨1⟩-44⁴.

Drab brown paper boards sides, purple muslin shelfback, printed paper label on spine. Flyleaves. Inserted at the front of some copies is a 4-page advertisement for *The Encyclopaedia Americana,* dated Feb. 1830.

According to Kaser 3000 copies were printed.

Title-page deposited Dec. 31, 1830. Reviewed AQR March, 1831. For revised edition see below under 1848–1849.

H   NYSL   UV

10134. Poems by William Cullen Bryant, an American. Edited by Washington Irving.

> London: J. Andrews, 167, New Bond Street. M. DCCC. XXXII.

The dedication to Samuel Rogers, pp. ⟨iii⟩-vi, by Irving.

Paper boards, cloth shelfback, printed paper label.

Reviewed LG March 3, 1832. Listed LG March 10, 1832. Advertised as *this day published* Ath March 10, 17, 1832.

H

10135. THE ALHAMBRA. BY GEOFFREY CRAYON ... IN TWO VOLUMES ...

LONDON: HENRY COLBURN AND RICHARD BENTLEY, NEW BURLINGTON STREET. 1832.

For first American edition see next entry.

1: ⟨i⟩-viii, ⟨1⟩-333; blank leaf. Laid paper. *Note:* Also occurs on mixed laid and wove papers. 8⅞″ x 5⅝″.

2: ⟨i-viii⟩, ⟨1⟩-299; printer's imprint, p. ⟨300⟩; advertisements, pp. ⟨301-304⟩.

1: ⟨A⟩⁴, B-I, K-U, X-Y⁸.

2: ⟨A⟩⁴, B-I, K-U⁸.

Drab paper boards, printed paper label on spine. The label has been noted as follows; sequence, if any, not known; the designations are for identification only:

Label A

⟨*double rule*⟩ / THE / ALHAMBRA. / BY / GEOFFREY CRAYON / ⟨*rule*⟩ / VOL. I. ⟨II.⟩ / ⟨*double rule*⟩ Noted on the first printing only.

Label B

⟨*double rule*⟩ / THE / ALHAMBRA. / BY / GEOFFREY CRAYON. / ⟨*rule*⟩ / IN TWO VOLS. / VOL. I. ⟨II.⟩ / ⟨*double rule*⟩ The label thus has been seen on both the first and the "new and cheaper" printings. *See below.*

Advertised for May 1 Ath April 14, 1832. Reviewed LG April 28, 1832. Advertised as *just published* and listed LG May 5, 1832. Reviewed and listed Ath May 5, 1832.

Note: Also issued in a "new and cheaper" edition; advertised thus and listed Ath July 28, 1832. *Pagination:* Vol. 1: ⟨i⟩-viii, ⟨1⟩-312; Vol. 2: ⟨i-iv⟩, ⟨1⟩-295; blank, p. ⟨296⟩; advertisements, pp. ⟨297-300⟩. Reprinted and reissued in one volume as No. 49 in Bentley's *Standard Novels and Romances* series; advertised for *immediate publication* LG Nov. 14, 1835; reviewed LG April 9, 1836.

LC (First)   Y (First; also, "new and cheaper")

10136. THE ALHAMBRA: A SERIES OF TALES AND SKETCHES OF THE MOORS AND SPANIARDS. BY THE AUTHOR OF THE SKETCH BOOK. IN TWO VOLUMES ...

PHILADELPHIA: CAREY & LEA. 1832.

In imprint of Vol. 2: *Philadelphla* for *Philadelphia.*

For prior publication in London see preceding entry. Also see under 1851.

1: ⟨i⟩-iv, ⟨13⟩-⟨235⟩. 7¹³⁄₁₆″ x 4⅝″ full.

2: ⟨1⟩-236; blank, pp. ⟨237-244⟩. *See note below regarding terminal blank leaves.*

1: ⟨1⟩², 2-19⁶, 20-21².

2: ⟨1⟩², 2-21⁶. *See note below regarding Sig. 21.*

Note: Two binding variants of Vol. 2 have been seen. Sequence, if any, not determined; the designations are for identification only:

Binding Variant A

Leaves 21₃₋₄ present as blanks.

Leaf 21₅ used as a pastedown.

21₆ either excised or pasted under 21₅.

Binding Variant B

Leaves 21₃₋₄ excised.

Leaves 21₅₋₆ present as blanks.

True binder's flyleaf and end paper at back.

Tan paper boards, purple muslin shelfback, printed paper label on spine. In some copies: Flyleaves; but see note above regarding binding variants. Terminal catalog, 36 pp., inserted in some copies of Vol. 1.

Copyright notice in Vol. 1 only.

A copy in LC (*Binding Variant A*; not a deposit copy) inscribed by early owner June 15, 1832. Noted as *recently published* NEM July, 1832.

AAS (A)   H (A,B)   LC (A)   NYHS (A)   NYPL (A,B)

10137. The Life and Voyages of Christopher Columbus, by Washington Irving. Abridged and Arranged by the Author, Expressly for the Use of Schools.

New York: Published by N. and J. White, 108 Pearl-Street. 1834.

For comment see entry No. 10127.

Printed boards sides, leather shelfback. See below for comment on other bindings.

Noted in the following printings:

1

Copyright notice only on verso of title-leaf. Copyright notice dated *one thousand eight hundred and thirty-one.* Noted only in printed paper boards, leather shelfback.

2

On verso of title-leaf is the copyright notice; and, *James Van Norden, Printer, 49 William-street.* / Copyright notice dated *one thousand eight hundred and thirty-one.* Noted only in publisher's leather.

3

On verso of title-leaf is the copyright notice; and, *James Van Norden, Printer, 49 William-street.* | Copyright notice is dated *one thousand eight hundred and thirty-four.* Noted only in publisher's leather.

4

On verso of the title-leaf is the copyright notice; and, *James Van Norden, Printer,* | *49 William-street.* | Copyright notice is dated *one thousand eight hundred and thirty-four.* Noted only in printed paper boards, leather shelfback.

Deposited Sept. 19, 1834.

AAS (2nd)   UV (3rd, 4th)   Y (1st, 2nd)

10138. History of the Rise and Progress of the Arts of Design in the United States. By William Dunlap ...

New-York: George P. Scott and Co. Printers, 33 Ann Street. 1834.

According to the prepublication prospectus issued for the above (in LC) Irving contributed to this publication; the extent of his contribution is not known. Irving is known to have contributed a long letter on Gilbert Stuart Newton which appears in Vol. 2, pp. 302-304.

For a fuller description see entry No. 5026.

10139. A TOUR ON THE PRAIRIES. BY THE AUTHOR OF "THE SKETCH-BOOK."

LONDON: JOHN MURRAY, ALBEMARLE STREET. MDCCCXXXV.

The above preceded by a general title-page for the series:

Miscellanies. By the Author of "The Sketch-Book." No I. Containing A Tour on the Prairies. London: John Murray, Albemarle Street. MDCCCXXXV.

For first American edition see next entry.

On the basis of but five copies examined the following appears to be an accurate statement; it must be noted, however, that comparison of additional copies may show that yet other gatherings were done from more than a single setting.

Through p. 144 (*i.e.,* up to and including Sig. G, but exclusive of the front matter), printed from two settings.

The inner forme of Sig. H printed from two settings; the outer forme printed from but one.

From p. 169 to end (*i.e.,* Sigs. I-P) printed from a single setting. Note, however, that certain minor typographic variations suggest that the formes may have been reimposed for the printing of additional copies.

The sequence, *if any,* of the two settings has not been established and BAL theorizes that after running off through Sig. G (and the types distributed) the print order was increased which required resetting of the text through p. 144.

The front matter occurs in two distinct states, with slight variations. The folding of the sheets (see the signature collations) may be sufficient for identification. Sequence, *if any,* for the front matter has not been determined.

The following notes are sufficient for identification. The designations are completely arbitrary and are not intended to suggest a sequence.

SETTING A

⟨i⟩-⟨xiv⟩, ⟨1⟩-335; printer's imprint, p. ⟨336⟩. Laid paper. 7^{15}/₁₆″ x 4⅞″.

⟨a-b², c-d¹⟩, a¹, B-I, K-P¹². *Signed:* ⟨A⟩⁶, a¹, B-I, K-P¹².

SETTING B

⟨i⟩-⟨xiv⟩, ⟨1⟩-335; printer's imprint, p. ⟨336⟩. Laid paper. 7^{15}/₁₆″ x 4⅞″.

⟨A⟩⁶, a¹, B-I, K-P¹².

Drab brown paper boards, printed paper label on spine. *Also:* H cloth, blue-black, printed paper label on spine. *Also:* P cloth, green, printed paper label on spine. The spine label has been noted in two states; sequence, if any, has not been determined and the designations are for identification only:

Label A: There is no hyphen in SKETCH BOOK

Label B: A hyphen present thus in SKETCH-BOOK

Setting A	Setting B
P. xi, last line	
... 22⟨0⟩	... 220
P. xii	
The first chapter heading is:	
XXVI ⟨correctly⟩	XXIV ⟨incorrectly⟩
P. ⟨1⟩	
Signature mark B	
Appears under a comma and space	Appears under a space
P. 21	
Mispaged 12	Paged 21
P. 25, line 7	
dation ...	*tion* ...

P. 26, line 8

being ...   ing ...

P. 49, last line

keep ...   word. |

P. 50, line 3

... halt, | ... halt |

P. 95, line 15

... vainglorious ...   ... vain-glorious ...

P. 96, line 10

The period is set   The period is set al-
slightly to the left of   most directly over the
the comma below.   comma below.

P. 97
Sig. mark F

Set below the *h* in *the*   Set below a space

P. 99
Sig. mark F2

The *F* is set under the   The *F* is set under a
word *on*   space

P. 119, line 6 up
The semi-colon

Set over the *t* in *the*   Set over a space

P. 122, line 5 up

... chief ...   ... Chief ...

P. 144
At top of page

Folio and running-   Folio only present
head present

P. 146, line 6 up

... burdens ...   ... burthens ...

P. 172, line 5

The gathering in which this page occurs (Sig.
I) may have been removed from the press and
then reimposed. Certain minor variations (note
the varying position of signature mark *I*, for
example) suggest the possibility. The following
alteration however was not caused by reim-
position; nor has BAL determined which state
preceded the other. The designations are for
identification only.

State a: ... "far West" |

State b: ... far West |

Pp. 193-216

But a single setting noted.

Pp. 217-240

But a single setting noted. Certain minor variations suggest the forme may have been reimposed.

P. 222

No signature mark   Signature mark *L3*
present.   present.

P. 227
The *L* in signature mark *L6*

Set under the *in* in   Set under a space
amusing

Advertised for March 2 in Ath Feb. 21, 28,
1835. Advertised for publication *in a few days*
BMLA Feb. 1835. Advertised for *this day* LG
March 7, 1835; Ath March 7, 1835. Reviewed
and listed LG March 7, 1835. Reviewed Ath
March 7, 1835. Listed Ath March 21, 1835.

NYPL UV Y

10140. A TOUR ON THE PRAIRIES. BY
THE AUTHOR OF THE SKETCH BOOK.

PHILADELPHIA: CAREY, LEA, & BLANCHARD. 1835.

The above is preceded by a general title-page
for the series: *The Crayon Miscellany. By the
Author of the Sketch Book. No. 1. Containing
a Tour on the Prairies. Philadelphia: Carey,
Lea, & Blanchard. 1835.*

For prior London publication see preceding
entry.

⟨i⟩-⟨xvi⟩, ⟨17⟩-274; blank leaf; plus: Publisher's
catalog. 7$\frac{1}{16}$" x 4$\frac{7}{16}$".

⟨1⟩-23⁶; plus: Publisher's catalog.

Two states (printings?) noted:

1

Sheets bulk (exclusive of the catalog) $\frac{9}{16}$". P.
247, last line of synopsis: *binger of dawn.* |

2

Sheets bulk (exclusive of the catalog) 1$\frac{1}{16}$". P.
247, last line of synopsis: *harbinger of dawn.* |

Muslin, both blue and green noted. Printed paper label on spine. Flyleaves. The label has been
seen in two states; sequence, if any, not determined, and the designations are for identification only:

Label A: The statement *No. I* is not present.

Label B: The statement *No. I* is present.

The inserted terminal catalog has been seen in
five forms; no sequence has been established
and the designations are for identification only:

Catalog A: 24 pages. P. ‹3›: . . . *The Wondrous Tale of Alroy* . . .

Catalog B: 24 pages. P. ‹3›: . . . *The Headsman* . . .

Catalog C: 36 pages. P. ‹25›: *Just Published . . . Private Memoirs of Napoleon Bonaparte* . . .

Catalog D: 12 pages.

Catalog E: 36 pages. P. ‹25›: *The National School Manual* . . .

According to Kaser 5000 copies were printed.

BA copy received April 18, 1835. Reviewed by K April, 1835, prior to publication: *will be published early in the present month.* Reviewed (again) by K May, 1835: *has . . . been published.* Reviewed NEM May, 1835. For a revised edition see *The Crayon Miscellany,* 1849.

B   BA   BPL   H   LC   NYPL   Y

10141. ABBOTSFORD, AND NEWSTEAD ABBEY. BY THE AUTHOR OF "THE SKETCH-BOOK."

LONDON: JOHN MURRAY, ALBEMARLE STREET. MDCCCXXXV.

The above preceded by a general title-page for the series: *Miscellanies. By the Author of "The Sketch-Book." No II. Containing Abbotsford, and Newstead Abbey. London: John Murray, Albemarle Street. MDCCCXXXV.*

For first American edition see next entry.

‹i-viii›, ‹1›-290; blank, pp. ‹291-292›; *but see note below.* 7⅞″ x 4⅞″. All examined copies are printed on mixed papers, both laid and wove papers being used.

‹A›⁴, B-I, K-N¹², O².

Note: P. ‹291› has been noted in two states; sequence not determined and the following designations are for identification only. Further study is indicated.

A: P. ‹291› blank.

B: P. ‹291› imprinted: *Lately was published . . . A Tour on the Prairies* . . .

Drab brown boards, printed paper label on spine. *Also:* Drab brown boards, decorated cloth shelfback, printed paper label on spine. *Also:* Drab brown boards, green T cloth shelfback, printed paper label on spine.

Letter (in H), April 9, 1835, John Murray to Col. Aspinwall: "I will give Mr Washington Irving for the Copyright of The Crayon Miscellany Six Hundred Pound ‹sic› payable in the following manner *viz* £ 400 at 6 & 9 months after the day of publication and £ 200 at 6 & 9 months after the day of the publication of a

second Edition ––– the first Edition to consist of 3,000 copies." Advertised for *this day* LG May 9, 1835; Ath May 9, 1835. Reviewed and listed LG May 9, 1835; Ath May 9, 1835. Advertised as *just published* BMLA May, 1835. Listed BMLA May, 1835.

LC (A)   NYPL (imperfect B)   Y (imperfect B)

10142. ABBOTSFORD AND NEWSTEAD ABBEY. BY THE AUTHOR OF THE SKETCH BOOK.

PHILADELPHIA: CAREY, LEA & BLANCHARD. 1835.

The above is preceded by a general title-page for the series: *The Crayon Miscellany. By the Author of the Sketch Book. No. 2. Containing Abbotsford and Newstead Abbey. Philadelphia: Carey, Lea, and Blanchard. 1835.*

For prior London publication see preceding entry.

‹1›-230; blank leaf; plus publisher's catalog. 7³⁄₁₆″ x 4⁵⁄₁₆″.

‹1›-19⁶, 20²; plus publisher's catalog.

Two printings noted:

1: As above. Copyright notice on both pp. ‹2› and ‹4›.

2: ‹1›-230; 10 pp. advertisements; plus: 12 pp. advertisements. Copyright notice on p. ‹2›; p. ‹4› blank. ‹1›-20⁶; plus: ‹21›⁶.

Note: The inserted terminal catalog has been noted in three forms; sequence not determined; the designations are for identification only.

Catalog A: 32 pages.

Catalog B: 36 pages. ‹1⁴, 2-3⁶, 4²›.

Catalog C: 36 pages. ‹1⁴, 2², 3-4⁶›.

Blue muslin; green muslin. Printed paper label on spine; *see note below.* Flyleaves.

Two states of the label have been noted; sequence, if any, not determined and the designations are for identification only:

Label A: In the last line *Sketch Book* is printed in bold-face roman.

Label B: In the last line *Sketch Book* is printed in italic.

According to Kaser 5000 copies printed. Noted as *ready* K June, 1835. For a revised edition see *The Crayon Miscellany,* 1849.

AAS   B   BA   LC   NYHS   NYPL   UV   Y

10143. The Conquest of Florida, by Hernando de Soto. By Theodore Irving . . . in Two Volumes . . .

Philadelphia: Carey, Lea & Blanchard. 1835.

"... Written at your ⟨*i.e.*, Washington Irving's⟩ suggestion, and the materials of which they are composed were moulded into their present form and feature under your affectionate and judicious advice." –– From the dedication to Washington Irving.

Reviewed AMM June, 1835; K June, 1835. The London (Carey & Kennett) edition reviewed Ath Aug. 15, 1835. The London (Churton) edition listed Ath Sept. 19, 1835; reviewed Ath Sept. 26, 1835. The London (Bohn) edition advertised for *August* Ath July 27, 1850.

UV

10144. LEGENDS OF THE CONQUEST OF SPAIN. BY THE AUTHOR OF THE SKETCH BOOK.

PHILADELPHIA: CAREY, LEA & BLANCHARD. 1835.

The above is preceded by a general title-page for the series: *The Crayon Miscellany. By the Author of the Sketch Book. No. 3. Containing Legends of the Conquest of Spain. Philadelphia: Carey, Lea & Blanchard. 1835.*

⟨i-iv⟩, ⟨i⟩-⟨x⟩, ⟨11⟩-276; plus: Publisher's catalog, pp. ⟨1⟩-8. 7$\frac{1}{16}$" x 4$\frac{1}{4}$" full.

⟨-⟩², ⟨1⟩-23⁶; plus: ⟨24⟩⁴.

Note: In the front matter is a note regarding *Beauties of Washington Irving* which occurs in two settings with no known sequence:

Setting A: The last line of the first paragraph begins: *advertised* . . .

Setting B: The last line of the first paragraph begins: *vertised* . . .

It is to be noted that the note appears on either ⟨-⟩$_{1v}$ or on ⟨-⟩$_{2v}$. This variation could have been caused at the bindery and presumably no sequence is involved.

Green muslin. Printed paper label on spine. Flyleaves.

According to Kaser 5000 copies printed. A copy in LC (not a deposit copy) inscribed by early owner Oct. 12, 1835. Listed NAR Jan. 1836.

BA LC NYPL UV Y

10145. Heath's Book of Beauty. 1836 . . . Edited by the Countess of Blessington.

London: Longman, Rees, Orme, Brown, Green, and Longman, Paternoster Row; Rittner & Goupil, Paris; and A. Asher, Berlin. ⟨n.d., 1835⟩

Cloth?

"The Haunted Ship," pp. ⟨253⟩-257, here credited to "the author of *The Sketch-Book.*" See *Friendship's Offering* . . . , 1849, below.

Reviewed Ath Dec. 5, 1835, which remarks that Irving contributed "an old-fashioned legend."

NYPL

10146. The Gift: A Christmas and New Year's Present for 1836. Edited by Miss Leslie.

Philadelphia: E. L. Carey & A. Hart. ⟨n.d., 1835⟩

Leather.

"An Unwritten Drama of Lord Byron," pp. 166-171. For separate publication see below under 1925.

To be published ere long –– K Aug. 1835. Listed NAR Jan. 1836.

UV

10147. Salmagundi; or, the Whim-Whams and Opinions of Launcelot Langstaff . . . a New Edition, Corrected by the Authors.

New-York: Harper & Brothers 82 Cliff-Street. 1835.

2 Vols. Issued as Vols. 1-2 of J. K. Paulding's works.

Two states (probably printings) noted:

1

Vol. 1: The sheets bulk ⅝".

Vol. 2: The sheets bulk 11⁄16". Copyright notice not present.

2

Vol. 1: The sheets bulk ½".

Vol. 2: The sheets bulk 9⁄16". Copyright notice present.

For first edition see above under 1807-1808. First American publication of the Paris, 1824, edition, with alterations by J. K. Paulding.

Noted as *forthcoming* K Feb. 1835. Vol. 1 deposited June 24, 1835. Reviewed (from advance sheets?) K July, 1835. Vol. 2 deposited (belatedly?) Sept. 11, 1835.

BA (2nd) H (1st)

10148. ASTORIA, OR ANECDOTES OF AN ENTERPRISE BEYOND THE ROCKY MOUNTAINS . . . IN TWO VOLUMES . . .

PHILADELPHIA: CAREY, LEA, & BLANCHARD. 1836.

1: ⟨1⟩-6, ⟨vii⟩-xii, ⟨13⟩-285; blank leaf. 8$\frac{11}{16}$" x 5$\frac{7}{16}$".

2: ⟨i⟩-viii, ⟨9⟩-279; plus: 8 pp. advertisements.

Note: A folded map showing the routes of Hunt and Stuart inserted in one volume or the other.

1: ⟨1⟩-24⁶.

2: ⟨1⟩-23⁶, 24²; plus: ⟨25⟩⁴.

Two states noted:

1

As above.

Vol. 1, verso of the title-leaf has present a copyright notice and the imprint of *Henry W. Rees, Stereotyper.*

Vol. 2, p. 239, the following garbled footnote present: *Bra6.db ury. P. 6 | *Breckenridge.

First page of terminal advertisements: BOOKS PUBLISHED ... The terminal advertisements are not boxed.

2

Pagination and signature collation as above.

Verso of the title-leaf, Vol. 1, wholly blank.

Vol. 2, p. 239, the "footnote" is not present.

First page of terminal advertisements: New Works ... ⟨*i.e.*, in upper and lower case⟩ The terminal advertisements are boxed.

Noted in a variety of cloths; presumably used simultaneously. The following designations are for identification only.

Cloth A

Purplish old rose embossed with a pattern of snake-like tracks. Flyleaves.

Cloth B

V-like cloth (blue; green; purple) embossed with an arrangement of heavy dots. Flyleaves.

Cloth C

Brown T-like cloth embossed with a floral pattern. Flyleaves.

Cloth D

S-like cloth (blue; purple; tan) damasked with a floral pattern. Flyleaves.

Cloth E

Coarse CM cloth: blue; slate. Flyleaves.

Cloth F

Coarse T cloth: purple. Flyleaves.

Cloth G

Dark blue-green cloth embossed with a pattern of cross-like stars. Flyleaves.

Cloth H

Blue P-like cloth embossed with a branch-like pattern. Flyleaves.

Cloth I

C-like cloth (brown) embossed with a pattern of stars, dots, and ornaments composed of four elongated tulip-like units. Flyleaves.

Cloth J

Purple cloth embossed with a pattern of dots and hollow diamonds. Flyleaves.

Copies of the second state have been seen in one or another of the above; and, purple and blue S-like cloths.

According to Kaser 4000 copies printed Oct. 18, 1836. Deposited Oct. 19, 1836. Noted as *published* K Nov. 1836. For a revised edition see under 1849.

AAS (1st, 2nd)   NYPL (1st)   UV (1st)   Y (1st)

10149. The Magnolia for 1837. Edited by Henry William Herbert.

> New-York: Bancroft & Holley, 8, Astor House, Broadway ... Boston ... New-Orleans. ⟨1836⟩

"The Widow's Ordeal, or a Judicial Trial by Combat," pp. ⟨257⟩-274.

"The Creole Village. A Sketch from a Steamboat," pp. ⟨315⟩-326.

Both collected in *Wolfert's Roost,* 1855.

For comment see entry No. 986.

10150. Adventures of Captain Bonneville, or Scenes beyond the Rocky Mountains of the Far West ... in Three Volumes ...

> London: Richard Bentley, New Burlington Street. 1837.

For first American edition, and for a comment on Irving's part in the authorship of this publication, see next entry.

1: ⟨i-iv⟩, ⟨1⟩-303. 7¾" x 4¾".

2: ⟨i-iv⟩, ⟨1⟩-292.

3: ⟨i-iv⟩, ⟨1⟩-302.

Boards, printed paper label on spine. Also, paper boards sides, cloth shelfback, printed paper label on spine.

Advertised as *new ... immediately* LG April 29, 1837. Noted as *will immediately publish* LG May 6, 1837. Noted as *just published* LG May 13, 27, 1837. Listed and reviewed LG May 13, 1837. Listed and reviewed Ath May 13, 1837. Listed BMLA May, 1837. A *second edition* advertised as *now ready* LG July 29, 1837. The Paris (Galignani) edition listed BF Aug. 26, 1837; the Baudry edition listed BF Sept. 9, 1837.

UV (Vol. 1 misbound)   Y

10151. The Rocky Mountains: Or, Scenes, Incidents, and Adventures in the Far West; Digested from the Journal of Captain B. L. E. Bonneville, of the Army of the United States, and Illustrated from Various Other Sources, by Washington Irving. In Two Volumes ...

Philadelphia. Carey, Lea, & Blanchard. 1837.

For prior English publication see preceding entry. For revised edition see under 1849.

1: ⟨1⟩-⟨10⟩, ⟨xi⟩-xvi, ⟨17⟩-248. Folded map inserted. 7⅝" x 4½".

2: ⟨i⟩-⟨viii⟩, ⟨9⟩-248. Folded map inserted.

Cloth, printed paper label on spine. Flyleaves.

Some copies of Vol. 1 have a 12-page catalog inserted at the back, thus producing the following binding variants; the designations are for identification only and no sequence is suggested:

A: No catalog present.

B: On p. 2 of the catalog *Astoria* is given a 2-line entry.

C: Pp. ⟨1-7⟩ of the catalog, paged ⟨2⟩-6, vii, xi, are devoted to *Astoria*.

According to Kaser 5000 copies printed.

Based on the journals of Benjamin Louis Eulalie de Bonneville (1796–1878). Bonneville's "manuscript has formed the staple of the following work. I have occasionally interwoven facts and details, gathered from various sources, especially from the conversations and journals of some of the captain's contemporaries, who were actors in the scenes he describes. I have also given it a tone and coloring drawn from my own observation ... However, the work is substantially the narrative of the worthy captain ..." ---p. 8.

BA copy received July 5, 1837. Reviewed AMM Aug. 1837.

BA H NYHS NYPL UV Y

10152. The Life and Voyages of Christopher Columbus. By Washington Irving. (Abridged by the Same.) Including the Author's Visit to Palos ...

Boston: Marsh, Capen, Lyon, and Webb. 1839.

Cloth, leather shelfback; also: cloth, leather shelfback and corners.

Issued as *The School Library*, Vol. 1.

For comment see entry No. 10127.

Deposited March 23, 1840. Reviewed NAR April, 1840.

AAS H Y

10153. The Romancist, and Novelist's Library: The Best Works of the Best Authors ...

London: Printed by C. Reynell, Little Pulteney Street. J. Clements, Nos. 21 and 22 Little Pulteney Street, Regent Street. MDCCCXXXIX. ⟨-MDCCCXL.⟩

A collection of weekly story papers issued under the above title. 4 Vols. On Vols. 3-4: *Edited by William Hazlitt.*

Vols. 1-2 dated MDCCCXXXIX; vols. 3-4 dated MDCCCXL.

Reprint save for:

"The Enchanted Island; or, the Adelantado ⟨*sic*⟩ of the Seven Cities," Vol. 2, pp. ⟨346⟩-348. Collected in *Wolfert's Roost*, 1855, as "The Phantom Island."

"The Abencerrage; or, Recollections of the Alhambra," Vol. 3, pp. ⟨223⟩-224. Collected in *Wolfert's Roost*, 1855.

H

10154. Tales of the Grotesque and Arabesque. By Edgar A. Poe ... in Two Volumes ...

Philadelphia: Lea and Blanchard. 1840.

Cloth, printed paper label.

Comment, Vol. 2, p. ⟨i⟩.

Note: Some copies of Vol. 2, p. *213* is mispaged *231*.

Deposited Nov. 27, 1839.

H NYPL

10155. The Rough-Hewer, Devoted to the Support of the Democratic Principles of Jefferson.

Albany, N. Y. February 20, 1840 ...

Caption-title.

An occasional newspaper issued during the presidential campaign. Complete in 38 numbers, Feb. 20, 1840 to Oct. 30, 1840; a final number (No. 39) issued under date Dec. 24, 1840; and, an undated *Extra*, issued October(?). Continuous pagination; the *Extra* separately paged.

"A Time of Unexampled Prosperity," No. 9, April 16, 1840, p. 67. Collected in *Wolfert's Roost*, 1855.

H

10156. The Life of Oliver Goldsmith, with Selections from His Writings. By Washington Irving. In Two Volumes ...

New-York: Harper & Brothers, 82 Cliff-Street. 1840.

1: ⟨v⟩-viii, ⟨9⟩-323. 6" x 3¾". Frontispiece inserted.

2: ⟨i-iv⟩, ⟨i⟩-⟨vi⟩, ⟨7⟩-313, blank leaf.

Two bindings noted; the order is probable:

A: CM cloth: black. Stamped in gold. Flyleaves.

B: Tan muslin. Printed in black.

Two printings of Vol. 2 have been noted; the order is probable:

A: Sig. CC in 8. Superfluous signature mark DD on p. 313.

B: Sig. CC in 6; DD in 2.

Issued as Harper's *Family Library*, Nos. 121-122.

"Biography of Oliver Goldsmith," Vol. 1, pp. ⟨9⟩-186. For another version see *The Miscellaneous Works of Oliver Goldsmith* ... , 1825.

In press K Nov. 1840. Listed Arc Dec. 1840. As part of *The School District Library* reviewed NYR Jan. 1841. As part of the *Family Library* reviewed *The New-Yorker*, Feb. 6, 1841.

AAS (Binding A, Sheets B) NYHS (Binding B, Sheets B) UV (Binding A, Sheets A) Y (Binding B, Sheets B)

10157. The Family Visitor. ⟨Edited⟩ by John Hayward ...

Boston: Weeks, Jordan, and Company. New York: Tanner and Disturnell. Philadelphia: William Marshall and Company. Baltimore: Cushing and Brothers. 1840.

Reprint with the exception of: "The Birds of Spring," pp. 110-114. Collected in *Wolfert's Roost*, 1855.

EM

10158. The Poetry and History of Wyoming: Containing Campbell's Gertrude, with a Biographical Sketch of the Author, by Washington Irving, and the History of Wyoming ... by William L. Stone.

New-York & London: Wiley and Putnam. 1841.

"A Biographical Sketch of Thomas Campbell," pp. ⟨ix⟩-xxiv. A revised and extended version of an earlier sketch. For comment see under *Biographical Sketch of Thomas Campbell*, 1810, above.

Deposited March 31, 1841.

AAS H MHS NYHS

10159. BIOGRAPHY AND POETICAL REMAINS OF THE LATE MARGARET MILLER DAVIDSON ...

PHILADELPHIA: LEA AND BLANCHARD. 1841.

⟨i⟩-⟨viii⟩, ⟨9⟩-359; plus: 8 pp. advertisements. 7¹¹⁄₁₆" x 4¾".

⟨1⟩⁴, 2-10, ⟨11⟩-23⁸; plus: ⟨-⟩⁴.

Coarse T cloth: black. Yellow-coated on white end papers. Triple flyleaves.

Irving's biography appears on pp. ⟨9⟩-152.

Deposited June 10, 1841. BA copy received June 22, 1841. Listed USMDR July, 1841. The earliest English edition noted was advertised by Wiley & Putnam as the *third edition* Ath May 14, 1842. Other London editions: Tilt & Bogue, listed PC Oct. 1, 1842, Ath Oct. 8, 1842, LG Oct. 8, 1842; under the title *Life and Recollections* ... advertised by Tegg, and by Aylott & Jones, LG Oct. 28, 1848; a Bogue (successor to Tilt & Bogue) edition advertised in Ath Dec. 14, 1850; a Knight & Son edition listed Ath Oct. 14, 1854.

AAS UV

10160. Harvey's Scenes of the Primitive Forest of America, at the Four Periods of the Year, Spring, Summer, Autumn & Winter, Engraved from His Original Paintings, Accompanied with Descriptive Letter-Press ...

New-York: Published by George Harvey, Office 8, Fulton Street, Printed by Charles Vinten, 63, Vesey Street, near Greenwich. 1841.

Edited by Irving.

One part only published. Printed paper boards, leather shelfback.

Cover imprint: New York ... George Harvey ... Messrs. Ackermann & Co. Strand, London. 1841. Johnson & Co. Printers, 10, Brooke Street, Holborn. *Also occurs with cover imprint:* London: Published by George Harvey, 16, Foley Place, Great Portland Street, and Messrs. Ackermann & Co. Strand. 1841. Johnson & Co. Printers, 10, Brooke Street, Holborn.

Note: Johnson appears to have printed the covers only; the sheets bear the imprint of *Vinten, New York.*

According to the prospectus (a copy in UV) the work was to be issued in "8 numbers, to be issued every 3 months; each number to consist of 5 Views, and accompanied with a sheet of Letterpress, descriptive of the scene and effect, edited by Washington Irving, Esq."

"... Being ... less practiced with the pen than with the pencil, I have obtained the promise of my friend Washington Irving, Esq., to revise my manuscript." -- From Harvey's preface.

κ March, 1841: "Mr. George Harvey ... has issued proposals for publishing, for subscribers only ... forty ... views of American scenery ... in eight numbers, one to be issued every three months. Each number will consist of five views ... with a sheet of letter-press ... revised by Mr. Washington Irving."

Deposited March 8, 1842. "A volume, containing the first four engravings of the series is on our table ..." -- κ Dec. 1842.

Note: Contemporary notices (see above) call for five plates; the work was issued with but four.

UV

10161. The Poetical Works of Thomas Campbell, Complete: With a Memoir of the Author by Washington Irving ...

Philadelphia: Lea and Blanchard. 1845.

"Memoir of Thomas Campbell," pp. ⟨v⟩-xv. For comment see under *Biographical Sketch of Thomas Campbell*, 1810, above. The present (*i.e.*, 1845) version is a reprint of the version of 1841, *q.v.*, but with the final paragraph omitted and another, in square brackets, substituted. *Query:* Did Irving write this final paragraph of 1845?

For publication note see entry No. 6662.

10162. The Knickerbocker Sketch-Book ... Edited by Lewis Gaylord Clark ...

New-York: Burgess, Stringer and Company. 1845.

Printed paper wrapper.

"Note to the Editor," p. iv. Incorporated in the editor's "Preface."

"The First Locomotive Again," pp. ⟨27⟩-29.

"The Early Experiences of Ralph Ringwood," pp. ⟨41⟩-83.

"Guests from Gibbet-Island. A Legend of Communipaw," pp. ⟨117⟩-132.

"Mountjoy ...," pp. ⟨165⟩-218.

The preceding three pieces collected in *Wolfert's Roost*, 1855.

Note: All examined copies are mispaged: ⟨i⟩-vi, ⟨9⟩-46; unpaged leaf; ⟨41⟩-243.

A copy in NYPL inscribed by Duyckinck May 22, 1845. Listed as *new* BJl May 31, 1845. Noted as *published* κ May, 1845. Reviewed BJl June 7,

1845; NYM June 14, 1845. Listed WPLNL July, 1845.

NYPL   UV

10163. ⟨Broadside. Printed on both sides. At head of the first page:⟩ For the satisfaction of those who take an interest in the question of the retention here of the Collection of the Works of the Old Masters, and of the accompanying Collection of Engravings, now at the Lyceum Gallery, the following extracts from letters, and from various publications, are collected together as testimony of their value ...

⟨n.p., n.d., New York: George F. Nesbitt, 1848⟩

Imprint below text, on verso.

Single cut sheet. Blue-gray paper.

On verso (together with comments by others) is an "Extract from a Letter of Washington Irving, Esq., respecting the same Painting," *i.e.*, Murillo's "The Flight into Egypt."

Issued after Sept. 8, 1848, that being the date of one of the notes here published.

HM

THE WORKS

According to the publisher's catalog (see those inserted in the volumes of the set) the set was available in cloth; half calf; half morocco; full calf.

The volumes were reprinted several, perhaps many, times; those issued under altered dates are readily recognized for what they are: Reprints. However, certain of the reprints were issued without title-page but with general title-page only; and since some bear the statement *New Edition, Revised*, they are apt to be mistaken for revised editions which in fact they are not, but simply reprints.

Vols. 1-15 (as here described) were issued 1848-1851.

Although not so designated (in the earlier printings) *Wolfert's Roost*, 1855, was considered Vol. 16 but was first issued without a general title-page so identifying it. However, some copies of the early printings were issued with the statement *Irving's Works* stamped on the spine. BAL has not determined when a general title-page was first used identifying *Wolfert's Roost* as Vol. 16 but the printing of 1861 does carry such a feature.

10164. A History of New-York

Issued as Vol. 1 of *The Works*. See note

above. For first edition see under 1809. Also see under 1849.

Two printings noted:

1

A / HISTORY OF NEW-YORK, / FROM THE / BEGIN-
NING OF THE WORLD TO THE END OF / THE DUTCH
DYNASTY; / CONTAINING, / AMONG MANY SURPRIS-
ING AND CURIOUS MATTERS, / ⟨*etc., etc.*⟩ / BY /
Diedrich Knickerbocker. / ⟨*rule*⟩ / ⟨*2 lines in
Dutch*⟩ / ⟨*rule*⟩ / THE AUTHOR'S REVISED EDI-
TION. / COMPLETE IN ONE VOLUME. / NEW-YORK:
/ GEORGE P. PUTNAM, 155 BROADWAY / And 142
Strand, London. / 1848.

⟨i⟩-xvi, ⟨13⟩-452. In the front matter: P. ⟨xiv⟩
not paged.

⟨-⟩², ⟨1⟩-⟨4⟩, 5-18¹², 19⁶, ⟨20⟩⁴.

2

A / HISTORY OF NEW-YORK, / FROM THE / BEGIN-
NING OF THE WORLD TO THE END OF / THE DUTCH
DYNASTY; / CONTAINING, AMONG MANY SURPRIS-
ING AND CURIOUS MATTERS, THE UNUTTERABLE /
⟨*etc., etc.*⟩ / BY / Diedrich Knickerbocker. /
⟨*rule*⟩ / ⟨*2 lines in Dutch*⟩ / ⟨*rule*⟩ / THE
AUTHOR'S REVISED EDITION. / COMPLETE IN ONE
VOLUME. / NEW-YORK: / GEORGE P. PUTNAM, 155
BROADWAY, / And 142 Strand, London. / 1848.

⟨i⟩-xvi, ⟨13⟩-452. In the front matter: P. xiv
so paged.

⟨-⟩⁸, 1*⁴, ⟨*⟩², 2-3, ⟨4⟩, 5-18¹², 19⁸, ⟨20⟩².

In some copies of the second printing there is
an inserted terminal catalog dated *Sept., 1848.*

"The Author's Apology," dated 1848, pp. ⟨xi⟩-
⟨xiv⟩. See comment above regarding the paging
of p. ⟨xiv⟩.

Advertised for Sept. 1 LW Aug. 19, 1848. Listed
LW Aug. 26, 1848. A second edition advertised
LW Sept. 30, 1848. *Murray* (PC April 16, 1849)
advertised an edition; noted as *nearly ready* PC
May 1, 1849; *to be ready in May* PC May 15,
1849; then, no further notices; project aban-
doned. Other British editions: *Routledge*, listed
Ath June 1, 1850; *Simms & M'Intyre*, listed PC
June 15, 1850; *Bohn*, listed Ath June 29, 1850;
W. S. Orr, and *Ingram, Cooke & Co.*, listed PC
June 1, 1854.

AAS (2nd)   BA (1st)   UV (2nd)

10165. The Sketch Book of Geoffrey Crayon,
      Gent. The Author's Revised Edition . . .

    New-York: George P. Putnam, 155 Broadway,
    and 142 Strand, London 1848.

Issued as Vol. 2 of *The Works.* See note preceding entry No. 10164. For first edition see above
under 1819–1820.

Contains the following material here first in
book form:

"Preface to the Revised Edition," pp. ⟨vii⟩-xii.

"A Sunday in London," pp. ⟨141⟩-143.

"London Antiques," pp. ⟨299⟩-305.

Note: Not illustrated; text not enclosed by a
single rule frame.

Advertised LW Sept. 30, 1848. Listed LW Oct.
7, 1848. Advertised for *this day* LW Oct. 7, 1848.
The *illustrated edition* (Darley illustrations)
advertised for *Oct. 16* LW Oct. 7, 1848; noted as
just published LW Oct. 28, 1848. USMDR in re-
viewing the *unillustrated* edition, issue of Nov.
1848, commented that the publisher "has . . . in
press an illustrated" edition.

British Editions

Murray: Listed by both Ath and LG Feb. 10,
1849.

Simms & M'Intyre: Listed Ath April 27, 1850.

Routledge: Listed Ath May 4, 1850; PC May 15,
1850.

Bohn: Listed Ath May 11, 1850, as No. 7 of
Bohn's Shilling Series. A *new edition* listed PC
Dec. 6, 1854.

Charles Daly: Advertised PC July 15, 1850; Jan.
16, 1851; July 16, 1851; Aug. 1, 1851.

Tegg: Advertised as a volume in the "reissue of
The Family Library, Second Series" PC July 15,
1861; Ath July 20, 1861.

Longman: Announced in Ath Dec. 20, 1852.
No further word found.

Bell & Daldy: Various editions advertised and
noted during the period 1863–1869: in *Bell &
Daldy's Pocket Volumes Series, The Artist's Edition, The Elzevir Edition;* all issued well after
the earliest London appearances.

Routledge: Listed PC Oct. 1, 1867.

Nimmo: Listed Bkr June, 1875.

H   UV

10166. The Life and Voyages of Christopher
      Columbus; to Which Are Added Those of
      His Companions . . . Author's Revised Edi-
      tion . . .

    New-York: George P. Putnam, 155 Broadway,
    and 142 Strand, London. 1848.

Vol. 1 dated 1848; Vols. 2-3 dated 1849.

Issued as Vols. 3-5 of *The Works.* See note preceding entry No. 10164. For prior editions see
above under years 1828, 1831.

Leaf: 7⁷⁄₁₆″ x 5¹⁄₁₆″. The *Octavo Edition* (leaf 9¼″ x 5⅝″), each volume dated *1849*, is a reprint. See publication notes below.

VOL. 1

Two printings have been noted:

1

On the title-page: A period is present after *London* in the imprint.

Sig. 19 in 6.

P. ⟨439⟩ dated *November, 1848*.

Inserted at the front is a slip: *The Maps belonging to the Life and Voyages of Columbus will be given in Vol. II., to be published on the first of January, 1849.*

The terminal catalog (the final leaves of Sig. 19) paged: 1-4.

2

On the title-page: Period not present after *London* in the imprint.

Sig. 19 in 12.

P. ⟨439⟩ dated *November, 1848*.

Inserted slip at front, as described above.

The terminal catalog (the final leaves of Sig. 19) paged: 1-6, 1-9.

Note: Langfeld-Blackburn (p. 27) state: "... in the first issue ... the advertisements at the back are dated November, 1848. Later issues ... the advertisements are undated ..." BAL has failed to locate such an undated catalog.

VOL. 2

Three printings have been noted:

1

P. ⟨495⟩ dated *November, 1848*.

The terminal catalog (the final leaves of Sig. 21) paged 1-6, 1-4.

Some copies have inserted at front a "Publisher's Notice": *The present volume containing ... 100 pages more than was originally estimated ... the price is necessarily increased to $1 50. The next volume will comprise the whole of the "Companions of Columbus" ...*

2

P. ⟨495⟩ undated.

The terminal catalog (the final leaves of Sig. 21) paged 3-12.

3

P. ⟨495⟩ undated.

The terminal catalog (the final leaves of Sig. 21) paged 2-11.

VOL. 3

Three printings have been noted:

1

Sig. 21 is in 12.

P. ⟨493⟩ dated *November, 1848*.

The terminal catalog (the final leaves of Sig. 21) paged 1-6, 1-6.

2

Sig. 21 is in 12.

P. ⟨493⟩ undated.

The terminal catalog (the final leaves of Sig. 21) paged 3-14.

3

Sig. 21 is in 6.

No terminal catalog.

Vol. 1: Advertised for Nov. 1 in LW Oct. 28, 1848. A copy of the first printing in Y inscribed by early owner Nov. 10, 1848. Listed LW Nov. 11, 1848. Reviewed LW Nov. 11, 1848. A second edition advertised for *next week* LW Dec. 2, 1848. A copy of the second printing in Y inscribed by early owner Feb. 5, 1849.

Vol. 2: Advertised for Jan. 1, 1849, LW Dec. 9, 1848. Advertised as *recently published* LW Jan. 6, 1849. Listed LW Jan. 13, 1849.

Vol. 3: Advertised for Feb. 1, 1849, LW Jan. 13, 1849.

Octavo Edition

Each volume dated 1849. Leaf 9¼″ x 5⅝″. Advertised LW March 24, 1849. Advertised LW April 21, 1849, as published April 16, 1849.

H (*Vol. 1:* 1st, 2nd; *Vol. 2:* 1st, 2nd, 3rd; *Vol. 3:* 1st, 2nd, 3rd) HM (Octavo Edition) NYPL (*Vol. 1:* 2nd) Y (*Vol. 1:* 1st, 2nd)

10167. Bracebridge Hall, or the Humorists ... by Geoffrey Crayon, Gentn. ... Author's Revised Edition ...

New-York: George P. Putnam, 155 Broadway, and 142 Strand, London. 1849.

Issued as Vol. 6 of *The Works*. See note preceding entry No. 10164. For first edition see under 1822.

Advertised LW Dec. 2, 1848. Advertised as *published this week* LW Dec. 9, 1848. Deposited Dec. 15, 1848. Listed LW Dec. 16, 1848.

H NYPL UV

10168. Tales of a Traveller. By Geoffrey Crayon, Gentn. ... Author's Revised Edition ...

New-York: George P. Putnam, 155 Broadway, and 142 Strand, London. 1849.

Issued as Vol. 7 of *The Works*. See note preceding entry No. 10164. For first edition see under 1824.

Noted as *published this week* LW March 10, 1849. Listed LW March 17, 1849. A copy in Y inscribed by early owner April 4, 1849. Deposited May 7, 1849.

AAS NYHS UV Y

10169. Astoria ... Author's Revised Edition ...

New-York: George P. Putnam, 155 Broadway. And 142 Strand, London 1849.

Issued as Vol. 8 of *The Works*. See note preceding entry No. 10164. For first edition see under 1836.

Advertised for April 18, 1849, LW April 21, 1849. Listed LW April 28, 1849. Deposited May 5, 1849.

Note: Usually occurs with unprinted cream-white paper end papers; a copy in LC (inscribed *Executive Mansion 1850*) has end papers imprinted with publisher's advertisements. Significance, if any, not determined.

BPL LC UV Y

10170. A Book of the Hudson. Collected from the Various Works of Diedrich Knickerbocker. Edited by Geoffrey Crayon.

New York: G. P. Putnam, 155 Broadway. 1849.

FIRST PRINTING

⟨i-ii⟩, ⟨i⟩-viii, ⟨11⟩-215; blank, p. ⟨216⟩; plus: publisher's catalog, pp. ⟨1⟩-⟨16⟩. P. ⟨1⟩ of catalog dated *March, 1849;* p. ⟨16⟩ of catalog dated *November, 1848.* 6¹⁄₁₆″ x 4³⁄₁₆″. *Not illustrated.*

Reprint save for:

"Introduction," 2 pp.; one page being from "Letter to the Editor of *The Knickerbocker,* on Commencing His Monthly Contributions" which was collected in *Spanish Papers,* 1866, Vol. 2; the other page apparently written for *A Book of the Hudson.*

"Communipaw." Originally in K Sept. 1839. The K version collected in *Spanish Papers,* 1866, Vol. 2. The version in *A Book of the Hudson* is so extensively revised that it may well be called a totally different piece.

"Guests from Gibbet Island." Earlier in *The Knickerbocker Sketch-Book,* 1845.

TB cloth: green. Sides wholly blindstamped with a vignette of Rip van Winkle, dog, etc., in an oval frame; the whole in a triple-rule box, an ornament at each inner corner. Edges plain. Title on spine: *Book of the Hudson*

Note: Also noted in printed gray paper wrapper, no terminal catalog; imprint on front of wrapper: *New York: Published, by Arrangement with the Proprietors, by S. Colman, 55 William St. Wholesale Agent and Publisher. 1849.* On outer back wrapper is an advertisement for Irving's works, with Vols. 11-15 noted as: ... *not yet ready, June, 1849.* Since the book was first issued in April (see publication notes below) this format is presumed late.

SECOND PRINTING

The second printing was done from a new setting. Pagination: ⟨i⟩-viii, ⟨9⟩-283; blank, pp. ⟨284-286⟩. Vignette title-page and three plates inserted.

The *second* printing has been seen in the following bindings; the designations are completely arbitrary and no sequence is implied. The following variations are sufficient for identification.

Binding A

TB cloth: green.

Front: Goldstamped with a vignette of Rip van Winkle.

Back: Blindstamped with a vignette of Rip van Winkle.

Edges: Plain.

Title on spine: *Book of the Hudson*

Binding B

T cloth: blue.

Front: Goldstamped with a vignette of Rip van Winkle.

Back: Goldstamped with a vignette of Rip van Winkle.

Edges: Gilt.

Title on spine: *Book of the Hudson*

Binding C

A cloth: green.

Front: Blindstamped with a vignette of Rip van Winkle.

Back: Blindstamped with a vignette of Rip van Winkle.

Edges: Plain.

Title on spine: *Book of the Hudson*

Binding D

A cloth: green; slate.

Front: Goldstamped with a vignette of Rip van Winkle.

Back: Goldstamped with a vignette of Rip van Winkle.

Edges: Gilt.

Title on spine: *Tales of the Hudson*

Binding E

A cloth: blue. T cloth: brown.

Front: Goldstamped with a vignette of Rip van Winkle.

Back: Blindstamped with a vignette of Rip van Winkle.

Edges: Plain.

Title on spine: *Tales of the Hudson*

Binding F

T cloth: slate.

Front: Blindstamped with a vignette of Rip van Winkle.

Back: Blindstamped with a vignette of Rip van Winkle.

Edges: Plain.

Title on spine: *Tales of the Hudson*

Advertised LW April 14, 1849. Published April 14 according to an advertisement in LW April 21, 1849. Reviewed LW April 21, 1849. Deposited May 7, 1849. Reviewed K May, 1849. A "new edition . . . with four illustrations" advertised in certain of the catalogs issued by Putnam in 1850.

AAS (1st; 2nd in F binding)   B (2nd in E binding)   BA (1st)   BPL (2nd in C binding)   H (2nd in A binding)   LC (2nd in C binding)   NYHS (1st)   NYPL (1st; 2nd in B binding; 2nd in E binding)   UV (1st in cloth; 1st in paper; 2nd in D binding)   Y (1st; 2nd in D binding)

10171. The Crayon Miscellany . . . Author's Revised Edition . . .

New-York: George P. Putnam, 155 Broadway, and 142 Strand, London. 1849.

Issued as Vol. 9 of *The Works.* See note preceding entry No. 10164. For first edition see *Abbotsford and Newstead Abbey,* 1835; and, *A Tour on the Prairies,* 1835.

Note: In all examined copies the divisional title-page for *Abbotsford and Newstead Abbey* appears incorrectly on p. ⟨200⟩. Do any copies

dated 1849 have the divisional title-page on (as it should be) p. ⟨199⟩?

Deposited May 7, 1849. Listed LW May 12, 1849.

H   LC   UV   Y

10172. The Adventures of Captain Bonneville, U.S.A., in the Rocky Mountains and the Far West . . . Author's Revised Edition . . .

New-York: George P. Putnam, 155 Broadway, and 142 Strand, London. 1849.

Issued as Vol. 10 of *The Works.* See note preceding entry No. 10164. For first edition see under 1837.

Advertised for June 4, 1849, LW June 2, 1849. Listed LW June 23, 1849. The following notes relating to the British editions are based on contemporary notices: *Bohn:* Listed Ath July 15, 1850; *Routledge:* Listed Ath June 29, 1850; a *new edition* listed PC June 1, 1855; *Maxwell:* Listed Ath Nov. 21, 1885.

AAS   UV   Y

10173. Oliver Goldsmith: A Biography . . .

New-York: George P. Putnam, 155 Broadway. London: John Murray. 1849.

Issued as Vol. 11 of *The Works.* See note preceding entry No. 10164. For earlier, shorter, versions of this biography see *The Miscellaneous Works of Oliver Goldsmith,* 1825, 1830; and, *The Life of Oliver Goldsmith,* 1840.

Trade edition: 7⅞₁₆″ x 5″. *Illustrated edition:* 8⁷⁄₁₆″ x 5¹⁵⁄₁₆″. Examination of typewear indicates that the trade edition was printed prior to the illustrated edition.

"Preface," pp. ⟨xv⟩-xvi (trade edition); pp. ⟨3-4⟩ (illustrated edition).

Three forms of the inserted terminal catalog have been noted in the trade edition; sequence, if any, not known.

A: Pp. 16. Paged 25-36, ⟨37-40⟩. P. ⟨37⟩ dated *July, 1849.*

B: Pp. 24. Paged 1-24. P. 1 dated *July, 1849.*

C: Pp. 36. P. 1 dated *July, 1849.*

Trade edition listed LW Sept. 1, 1849; reviewed LW Sept. 1, 1849. The illustrated edition listed LW Dec. 1, 1849: "A complete printed copy . . . was brought to London by the last mail from New York. The work will appear simultaneously in America and this country; but the name of the London publisher is, we believe, as yet unknown."—Ath Aug. 25, 1849. LG Oct. 6, 1849: "published in New York above a month ago."

The earliest British edition (Murray) was advertised for Nov. 1, 1849, in LG Oct. 6, 20, 1849; listed Ath Oct. 27, 1849. The Clarke (London) edition listed PC Dec. 15, 1849. The Routledge (London) edition listed PC Jan. 15, 1850. The Bohn (London) edition listed Ath April 27, 1850.

AAS   H   NYPL

10174. A History of New-York ... by Diedrich Knickerbocker ... The Author's Revised Edition ... ⟨Second Edition⟩

New-York: George P. Putnam, 155 Broadway, and 142 Strand, London. 1849.

Pp. 454. For first edition of this revision see above under 1848.

Extended by the addition of text, pp. 222-223.

H

10175. MAHOMET AND HIS SUCCESSORS ... IN TWO VOLUMES ...

NEW-YORK: GEORGE P. PUTNAM, 155 BROADWAY. M.DCCC.L.

Issued as Vols. 12-13 of *The Works.* See note preceding entry No. 10164.

1: ⟨i-iv⟩, ⟨i⟩-⟨xii⟩, ⟨13⟩-373; plus: 36 pp. publisher's catalog. 7½″ x 5⅛″.

2: ⟨i-iv⟩, ⟨i⟩-xii, ⟨13⟩-500.

1: ⟨-⟩², ⟨1⟩-15¹², 16², ⟨17⟩¹, ⟨18⟩⁴; plus: ⟨19¹², 20⁶⟩. *Note:* further study may show that 16 is a singleton; ⟨17⟩ is in 2.

2: ⟨-⟩², 1-20¹², 21¹⁰.

Three printings of Vol. 1 have been noted:

1

As above.

P. 1 of the terminal catalog dated *July, 1849.*

P. 15 of the terminal catalog lists Irving's *Works* as in *XV* volumes, with Vol. XV described only as *A new volume;* Vols. XI-XV described as *not yet ready, June, 1849.*

The general title-page reads: ... MAHOMET AND HIS SUCCESSORS. / VOL. XII. / ...

2

⟨i-iv⟩, ⟨i⟩-⟨xii⟩, ⟨13⟩-373; blank, p. ⟨374⟩; 6 pp. advertisements, paged 16, 15, 19, 20, 22, 7; plus: Publisher's catalog, pp. 1-36.

⟨-⟩², ⟨1⟩-15¹², 16¹⁰; plus: ⟨17¹², 18⁶⟩.

P. 1 of the inserted catalog is dated *July, 1849,* and is otherwise the same as the catalog inserted in the first printing described above.

The general title-page reads: ... MAHOMET AND HIS SUCCESSORS. / VOL. XII. / ...

3

⟨i-iv⟩, ⟨i⟩-⟨xii⟩, ⟨13⟩-373; blank, p. ⟨374⟩; 2 pp. advertisements, paged 7-8.

⟨-⟩², ⟨1⟩-15¹², 16⁸.

Inserted at back is a publisher's catalog paged: 1-13, 13A, 14-17, 17A, 18-⟨45⟩; blank, p. ⟨46⟩. P. 1 of catalog undated. Also noted with inserted catalog paged: 1-17, 17A, 18-23, 23-⟨45⟩; blank, p. ⟨46⟩.

The general title-page reads: ... VOL. XII. / MAHOMET AND HIS SUCCESSORS. / ...

TB cloth: green. End papers of cream, off-white, buff, noted. Flyleaves.

Vol. 1: Noted for *this week* LW Dec. 15, 1849. Reviewed and listed LW Dec. 22, 1849. *Vol. 2:* Advertised for April 1 LW March 9, 1850. Noted for *this week* LW April 6, 1850. Listed LW April 13, 1850.

AAS (1st)   H (2nd)   NYPL (1st)   UV (3rd)

10176. Friendship's Offering: A Christmas, New Year and Birthday Present, for MDCCCXLIX.

Boston: Published by Phillips & Sampson. 1849.

Leather.

"The Haunted Ship," pp. ⟨326⟩-330. Previously in *Heath's Book of Beauty. 1836 ... ,* London ⟨n.d., 1835⟩, above.

For a discussion of the disputed authorship of "The Haunted Ship" see Thompson, p. 122; and, *American Literature,* Jan. 1934, Jan. 1935, Nov. 1939. In this last is published a letter from Irving which makes clear that Irving not only wrote the piece but in May, 1835, offered it for publication.

NYPL

10177. Chronicle of the Conquest of Granada ...

New-York: George P. Putnam, 155 Broadway. London: John Murray. 1850.

Issued as Vol. 14 of *The Works.* See note preceding entry No. 10164. For first edition see under 1829.

"Note to the Revised Edition," pp. xv-xix.

Deposited Aug. 2, 1850. Noted for *this week* LW Aug. 3, 1850. Listed LW Aug. 24, 1850. *Note:* A Routledge (London) edition listed Ath May 4, 1850; a Bohn (London) edition listed Ath May 18, 1850. Since both these latter were issued prior to the revised New York edition (neither has been located for examination) it is plausible to assume that they are reprints of the earlier, unrevised, text.

H NYPL

10178. Life and Letters of Thomas Campbell. Edited by William Beattie ... in Two Volumes ...

New York: Harper & Brothers, Publishers, 82 Cliff Street. 1850.

Cloth?

Introductory letter, pp. xi-xvi. Not to be confused with Irving's earlier (1810, 1841, 1845) biographical sketches of Campbell. Collected in *Spanish Papers,* 1866. The letter does not appear in the London, 1849, edition of Campbell and was written for this Harper, 1850, edition at the request of the publishers.

H

10179. Strictly Confidential. Memorandum: The following are selected from letters placed before the State Department, recommending ‹John Howard Payne› ... to office under the present administration ...

‹n.p., n.d., probably Washington, D. C., 1850›

The above at head of p. ‹1›.

Single cut sheet folded to 4 pages. Text on pp. ‹1›-3; p. ‹4› blank.

Letter, April 4, 1849, recommending John Howard Payne, p. 3.

H

10180. The Alhambra ... Author's Revised Edition.

New-York: George P. Putnam, 155 Broadway. M.DCCC.LI.

Issued as Vol. 15 of *The Works.* See note preceding entry No. 10164. For first edition see under 1832.

Not illustrated. See next entry.

Will publish immediately—LW April 19, 1851. Listed LW May 3, 1851.

AAS H UV

10181. The Alhambra   Author's Revised Edition. With Illustrations by Felix O. C. Darley ...

New-York: George P. Putnam, 155 Broadway. M.DCCC.LI.

Illustrated. Printed from the plates of the preceding entry but contains Irving's "Preface to the Revised Edition," pp. ‹9›-10; dated at end *Sunnyside, 1851.*

Advertised NLA Sept. 15, 1851, for *September* in the following bindings: "dark cloth, extra gilt, $3.50; extra blue, gilt edges, $4; morocco extra, very elegant richly gilt edges, $6." Bolton (*American Book Illustrators*) reports fifty copies on large paper.

NYPL

10182. Bertie: Or, Life in the Old Field. A Humorous Novel. By Capt. Gregory Seaworthy ‹pseud. for George Higby Throop› ... with a Letter to the Author from Washington Irving.

Philadelphia: A. Hart, Late Carey and Hart. 126 Chestnut Street. 1851.

Cloth?

Letter, Sunnyside, Sept. 17, 1850, pp. ‹vii›-viii.

Deposited March(?) 13, 1851. Reviewed SLM Sept. 1851.

LC

10183. The Home Book of the Picturesque ...

New-York: G. P. Putnam, 155 Broadway. MDCCCLII.

"The Catskill Mountains," pp. ‹71›-78. Collected in *Spanish Papers,* 1866.

For comment see entry No. 1648.

10184. Memorial of James Fenimore Cooper

New York G P Putnam 1852

Letters, pp. ‹7›, 12; remarks, p. 23.

For comment see entry No. 6953.

10185. A Reply to Messrs. G. & C. Merriam's Attack upon the Character of Dr. Worcester and His Dictionaries.

Boston: Jenks, Hickling and Swan. 1854.

Cover-title. Printed self wrapper.

Letter, June 25, 1851, p. 30.

Note: Reprinted and reissued with the imprint: *Boston: Hickling, Swan and Brown. 1854.*

AAS (2nd) H (1st)

10186. The Knickerbocker Gallery: A Testimonial to the Editor of the Knickerbocker Magazine from Its Contributors ...

New-York: Samuel Hueston, 348 Broadway. MDCCCLV.

"Conversations with Talma. From Rough Notes in a Common-Place Book," pp. ⟨15⟩-22. Collected in *Spanish Papers*, 1866.

For comment see entry No. 1033.

10187. CHRONICLES OF WOLFERT'S ROOST AND OTHER PAPERS ... AUTHOR'S EDITION.

EDINBURGH: THOMAS CONSTABLE AND CO. S. LOW, SON, & CO.; HAMILTON, ADAMS, & CO., LONDON. JAMES M'GLASHAN, DUBLIN. MDCCCLV.

For first American edition see next entry.

⟨1⟩-⟨6⟩, ⟨i⟩-vi, ⟨1⟩-351; printer's imprint, p. ⟨352⟩; plus: Publisher's catalog, 4 pp. 7" scant x $4^{11}/_{16}$".

⟨-⟩6, A-I, K-U, X-Y8; plus: ⟨Z⟩2.

Two printings noted:

1

As above. Leaves ⟨-⟩$_{1-2}$ imprinted with an advertisement for *Constable's Miscellany of Foreign Literature*. Leaf ⟨-⟩$_{3r}$: *In the Press ... Volume V ...*

2

The only located copy appears to be imperfect and repaired, hence these notes on the second printing are tentative. However, a distinguishing feature is the announcement in the front matter which, in this later printing, reads: *In the Press ... Volume VII ...*

Issued as *Constable's Miscellany of Foreign Literature,* Vol. IV.

T cloth: tan. Yellow-coated end-papers.

Announced PC Dec. 6, 1854. "... By arrangement with the author ... to issue simultaneously with the American edition" –– Ath Jan. 13, PC Jan. 16, 1855. Advertised for Jan. 15, Ath Jan. 13, PC Jan. 16, 1855. Advertised as *just published* Ath Jan. 20, 1855. Listed Ath Jan. 20, 1855; PC Feb. 1, 1855. Second edition advertised as *ready* PC March 15, 1855; listed PC March 15, 1855. The Routledge edition listed PC March 15, 1855.

Y (1st, 2nd)

10188. WOLFERT'S ROOST AND OTHER PAPERS, NOW FIRST COLLECTED ...

NEW YORK: G. P. PUTNAM & CO., 12 PARK PLACE. 1855.

For prior London publication see preceding entry.

⟨1⟩-383; plus: Publisher's catalog dated *Feb'y., 1855.*, pp. ⟨1⟩-12. Frontispiece and vignette title-page (a single cut sheet folded to 4 pp.) pasted to the stub of excised leaf ⟨1⟩$_2$. $7^5/_{16}$" x $4^{15}/_{16}$" full.

⟨1⟩-16¹²; plus: ⟨-⟩6. Leaf ⟨1⟩$_2$ excised.

There were at least six printings before alteration of the date, 1855, in the imprint.

First Printing

As above.

Second Printing

Imprint as above.

⟨5⟩-383; plus: Publisher's catalog dated *Feb'y., 1855.*, pp. ⟨1⟩-12. Frontispiece and vignette title-page inserted.

⟨1⟩¹⁰, 2-16¹²; plus: ⟨-⟩6.

Later 1855 Printings

No attempt has been made to establish a sequence for the later printings which may be distinguished by alteration of the imprint. In the first two printings the publisher's address is *12 Park Place;* in later printings the address is *10 Park Place.*

TZ cloth: slate-green. Edges plain, not gilded. Yellow end papers. Flyleaves. At center of the front is a goldstamped vignette, front cover bordered by a blindstamped rococo frame. Not seen with the statement *Irving's Works* on the spine but such copies may yet be found on first printing sheets. Reprints with the statement *Irving's Works* were prepared as Vol. 16 of *The Works* although not so designated on the sheets. See note preceding entry No. 10164.

BINDING NOTE

Reprints have been seen in the above binding. Reprints have also been seen in variant bindings, the following features being sufficient for ready recognition. The designations are virtually arbitrary and no sequence is suggested.

Binding Variant A

TZ cloth: slate-green. Publisher's monogram (not a vignette) blindstamped at center of the sides. Edges plain.

Binding Variant B

TZ cloth: black. Goldstamped vignette on front cover within a blindstamped oval frame, the whole on a field of blindstamped rectangular ornaments. On spine: *Irving's Works*. Edges plain.

Binding Variant C

Same as *Binding Variant B* but the statement *Irving's Works* is not present on the spine.

Binding Variant D

A cloth: red. No vignette on the front. Front cover goldstamped with a leafy frame. Edges gilded.

Note: The error *tho* for *the*, p. 383, line 3 from bottom of page, occurs in all examined copies of the 1855 and 1856 printings.

Deposited Feb. 6, 1855. Listed as having been published *since February 1* NLG Feb. 15, 1855.

AAS (1st) BA (1st) H (1st) NYHS (1st) NYPL (1st, 2nd) UV (1st, 2nd) Reprints have been seen at B, H, IU, NYPL, UV.

10189. Cyclopædia of American Literature; Embracing Personal and Critical Notices of Authors ... by Evert A. Duyckinck and George L. Duyckinck. In Two Volumes ...

New York: Charles Scribner. 1855.

"To Mr. Washington Irving we are indebted for a special act of courtesy, in his contribution to the notice of Allston of an interesting series of personal reminiscences." —— Vol. 1, p. ix. See Vol. 2, pp. 14-16.

AAS BPL H UV Y

10190. Books Published by Chas. Scribner. An Important National Work. Cyclopedia of American Literature ...

⟨n.p., n.d., New York, 1855?⟩

4-page leaflet. P. ⟨1⟩ blank. The above at head of p. ⟨2⟩.

"From Washington Irving, Esq.," an 8-line testimonial, p. ⟨2⟩.

NYPL

10191. ⟨Testimonial: Allibone's *A Critical Dictionary of English Literature*⟩

Irving's testimonial is in the form of a letter dated *Sunnyside, Aug. 23d, 1855*: "Messrs. Childs & Peterson: Gentlemen:—Accept my thanks for the specimen you have sent me of Mr. Allibone's Critical Dictionary of English Literature. The undertaking does honor to that gentleman's enterprise; and the manner in which, from the specimen before me, (464 pages) he appears to execute it ..."

In all likelihood the testimonial was published in many forms. It has, however, been seen only printed together with other like testimonials. It has been located in the following two forms; other forms probably exist. It is doubtful that a publication sequence can be established and the following designations are for identification only.

A

In: Single cut sheet, printed on recto only. 10" x 6⅝". At head of sheet: *Testimonials To Allibone's Critical Dictionary of English Literature ...* ; imprinted: *Published by Childs & Peterson, No. 124 Arch Street, Philadelphia ...* ⟨n.d., 1855?⟩

B

In: *A Critical Dictionary Of English Literature, And British And American Authors ... By S. Austin Allibone ...* , Philadelphia: Childs & Peterson, 1856. Printed self-wrapper. 16 pp.

H (B)   JB (A)

10192. THE LIFE OF GEORGE WASHINGTON, 1855–1859

The publication history of this work is involved; a chronology is essential. The publisher's advertisements, and frequently trade listings and notices, are unclear and often fail to identify the format. On the basis of such listings and notices the following chronology has been prepared. Detailed publication notes are given under the individual volumes as described below. For general publication notes see below.

Originally announced in three volumes. With publication of Vol. 3 the publishers announced that the work would be completed in five volumes.

The work was issued in six formats as follows:

OCTAVO EDITION

Leaf 9⁵⁄₁₆" tall. According to APC Nov. 24, 1855, available in cloth; sheep; half calf; calf. Vols. 1-3 first published in United States in this format. Vols. 1-2 appear to have been issued simultaneously in New York (Putnam) and in London (Bohn). Vols. 4-5 issued simultaneously with the *Twelvemo Edition* described below. Also referred to in notices as *Subscribers' Library Edition* and *Subscribers' Edition.* See *Mount Vernon Edition* below.

TWELVEMO EDITION

Sometimes referred to as
THE POPULAR EDITION

Leaf 7⅜" scant tall. Vols. 1-3 are reprints. Vols. 4-5 issued simultaneously with the *Octavo Edition.* Noted in the following bindings of unknown sequence, if any:

A: BD cloth: gray-green. TB cloth: green. Sides blindstamped with an ornate (zigzag within rules) border enclosing a double rule box.

B: TB cloth: gray-green. Sides blindstamped with a rule border, publisher's monogram at center.

C: TB cloth: gray-green. Sides blindstamped with a rule border. Front goldstamped with face and reverse of Washington medal. Back blindstamped with publisher's monogram.

ILLUSTRATED EDITION

Leaf 10¾″ tall. Not to be confused with extra-illustrated copies of the *Octavo Edition* (leaf 9⁵⁄₁₆″ tall). On the basis of trade notices and advertisements, published after both the *Octavo Edition* and the *Twelvemo Edition*.

Issued in semi-monthly paper-covered parts. At head of front of the wrapper: *Illustrated Edition of Irving's Washington*. During the course of publication this was changed to *Irving's Washington Illustrated*. Precise date of change not determined. Advertised APC Dec. 11, 1858, as available in cloth; cloth gilt extra; half morocco, extra; half morocco, gilt; full morocco, extra.

On the title-page is the statement *Illustrated Edition*.

The dating of the several title-pages is on the basis of sets, some being incomplete, some being reprints. It is possible BAL has not seen a full set of the earliest printing.

Parts 1-14: Comprise Vol. 1. Vignette title-page dated 1856; typographic title-page dated 1856.

Parts 15-28: Comprise Vol. 2. Issued in 11 sections. Typographic title-page dated 1857. Issued without vignette title-page?

Parts 29-42: Comprise Vol. 3. Issued in 7 sections. Vignette title-page dated 1859; typographic title-page dated 1858.

Parts 43-56: Comprise Vol. 4. Issued in 7 sections. Vignette title-page dated 1859; typographic title-page dated 1858.

Parts 57-68: Comprise Vol. 5. Issued in 5 sections. Typographic title-page dated 1859. Issued without vignette title-page?

LARGE PAPER EDITION

Sometimes referred to as
QUARTO EDITION

Leaf 12³⁄₁₆″ tall. Limited to 110 numbered sets. Described in APC Dec. 11, 1858, as "the Magnificent Quarto Edition ... superfine paper ... plates on India Paper ..."

Reprint.

SUNNYSIDE EDITION

Leaf 7½″ tall. The only examined set is in three-quarters leather. Each volume dated 1859. According to an advertisement inserted at back of Vol. 5, *Twelvemo Edition*, the *Sunnyside Edition* was *in press* and was to be available in cloth; and, four styles of leather.

Reprint.

MOUNT VERNON EDITION

Not seen. Advertised as though published APC Aug. 27, 1859. The advertisement suggests that this may have been made up of sheets of the *Octavo Edition* with 95 inserted steel engravings and 50 woodcut illustrations. See *Octavo Edition* above.

GENERAL PUBLICATION NOTES

For detailed publication information see under the individual volumes as described below.

NLG March 15, 1855:

"G. P. Putnam ... have in press *George Washington, a Biography,* by Washington Irving, in 12mo., uniform with Irving's other works. Also an octavo edition ... The work is expected to be completed in three volumes ––– the first volume to be ready in May; the second in August; and the third in the Autumn ..."

NLG April 2, 1855:

Advertised by Putnam as *in press,* both the 12mo and the 8vo editions. The advertisement repeats the publication schedule as above.

NLG May 15, 1855:

C. T. Evans, New York, advertises for agents to sell the book. "For Specimen Copies, which will be forwarded free of postage, on receipt of price, $2, Subscription Books ‹*i.e.,* prospectuses› and full particulars, apply to the General Agent ..." Under *Literary Intelligence* it is stated that the first edition is to be in 8vo, that it will be sold to subscribers, and that the first volume is nearly ready. The same advertisement repeated NLG June 1 and 15, 1855.

APC Sept. 1, 1855:

Life of Washington, 3 Vols., under *List of Announcements.* Also advertised as *in press, The Subscribers' Library Edition.* One statement or the other, or both, repeated in issues of APC through Nov. 17, 1855.

APC Aug. 28, 1858:

The *Twelvemo Edition* offered by Putnam in a *new issue* available in sheep; half calf extra; or half calf antique. The *Octavo Edition* offered in sheep; half calf extra; or full calf.

VOL. 1 OCTAVO EDITION

LIFE OF GEORGE WASHINGTON . . . IN THREE VOLS. VOL. I.

NEW YORK: G. P. PUTNAM & CO., 10 PARK PLACE. 1855.

⟨i⟩-xvi, ⟨1⟩-504. Inserted: Frontispiece, 2 one-page maps, 1 two-page map. 9⁵⁄₁₆″ x 6″.

⟨-⟩⁸, ⟨1⟩-31⁸, 32⁴.

Three printings noted in the following possible sequence:

First(?) Printing

As above.

John F. Trow imprint on copyright page.

Second(?) Printing

As above.

R. Craighead imprint on the copyright page. A copyright deposit copy thus.

Third(?) Printing

As above.

No printer's imprint on the copyright page.

Note: In Vol. 2, p. ⟨519⟩, there is an erratum notice: "In the early editions ⟨sic⟩ of the first volume . . . (p. 137), it is stated that . . . Major Stobo was excepted . . . The name should have been Muse instead of Stobo . . ." The *Stobo* reading is present in all examined copies, all printings, of the above. The correction has been seen in an 1856 printing.

T cloth: blue-black; dull purple; purple-black; slate. Buff end papers; yellow end papers; white end papers. Flyleaves. The following variations have been noted in the spine stamping; no sequence may be involved and BAL gives the variations for the record only:

Spine A: The volume number is an arabic 1. No period after WASHINGTON

Spine B: The volume number is a roman I. No period after WASHINGTON

Spine C: The volume number is a roman I. Period present after WASHINGTON

BOHN EDITION

LIFE OF GEORGE WASHINGTON. BY WASHINGTON IRVING. IN THREE VOLUMES. VOL. I. COMPRISING HIS EARLY LIFE, EXPEDITIONS, AND CAMPAIGNS.

LONDON: HENRY G. BOHN, YORK STREET, COVENT GARDEN. 1855.

Note: Collation tentative; based on examination of a single, repaired, copy.

⟨i⟩-xvi, ⟨1⟩-348, 2 blank leaves. Frontispiece portrait of Washington inserted. 7⅛″ x 4⁷⁄₁₆″.

⟨A⟩-I, K-U, X-Z⁸.

Printed green paper boards. Outer back cover dated *June 1, 1855.* End papers printed in blue with publisher's advertisements. Inserted at front: 2 pp. publisher's advertisements, printed in blue; at back: 4 pp. publisher's advertisements, printed in blue.

Note: In another, and almost certainly later printing, the title-page reads:

Life of George Washington. By Washington Irving. Vol. I. Early Life, Expeditions, and Campaigns.

> *London: Henry G. Bohn, York Street, Covent Garden. 1855.*

Other variations are present within the volume but the title-page is sufficient for ready identification.

The New York (Putnam) and London (Bohn) editions appear to have been issued simultaneously:

Bohn: Advertised as *in a few days* Ath April 28, 1855.

Bohn: Advertised as *in a few days* PC May 1, 1855.

Murray: Advertised as *next week* Ath May 12, 1855.

Murray: Advertised as *immediately* PC May 15, 1855.

Murray: Noted as *next week* PC May 15, 1855.

Murray: Noted as *in a few days* Ath May 19, 1855.

Putnam: Reviewed NLG June 1, 1855.

Bohn: Listed PC June 1, 1855.

Bohn: Listed Ath June 2, 1855.

Putnam: Listed NLG June 15, 1855.

Bohn: Reviewed LG June 16, 1855.

Murray: Listed PC July 17, 1855.

Putnam: Deposited (*Octavo Edition*) Aug. 16, 1855.

Putnam: Twelvemo edition listed APC Aug. 9, 1856.

Putnam: Twelvemo edition advertised as *now ready* APC Sept. 20, 1856.

Tauchnitz: Issued in Leipzig as No. 342 in the *Collection of British Authors* series under date 1856. Further information wanting.

AAS (2nd)   H (1st)   NYHS (3rd)   NYPL (1st; 2nd; 1st Bohn)   UV (1st; 2nd Bohn)

VOL. 2 OCTAVO EDITION

LIFE OF GEORGE WASHINGTON ... IN THREE VOLS. VOL. II.

NEW YORK: G. P. PUTNAM & CO., 10 PARK PLACE. 1855.

⟨i⟩-xii, ⟨1⟩-⟨519⟩. Inserted: Frontispiece, 2 one-page maps, 1 two-page map. 9⁵⁄₁₆″ x 5¹³⁄₁₆″.

⟨-⟩⁶, 1-32⁸, 33², ⟨34⟩².

T cloth: blue-black; dull purple; purple-black; slate. Buff end papers; yellow end papers; white end papers. Flyleaves.

In the first printing the *Map of Westchester County* ... is listed on p. xii as at p. 226. The map has been seen variously inserted at pp. 236, 270, 276. An uncollated copy (rebound) lists the map as at p. 276. Was the correction made during the run of the first printing? In an 1857 printing the position of the map is given as at p. 270.

BOHN EDITION

LIFE OF GEORGE WASHINGTON. BY WASHINGTON IRVING. IN THREE VOLUMES. VOL. II. THE AMERICAN WAR, INVASION OF CANADA, &C.

LONDON: HENRY G. BOHN, YORK STREET, COVENT GARDEN. 1856.

Note: Collation tentative; based on examination of a single, repaired, copy.

⟨i⟩-⟨xii⟩, 349-715; printer's imprint, p. ⟨716⟩. 7⅛″ x 4⁷⁄₁₆″.

⟨-⟩⁶, 2A-2I, 2K-2U, 2X-2Z⁸.

Printed green paper boards. End papers printed in blue with publisher's advertisements; leaves (number not known) of publisher's advertisements, printed in blue, inserted at front and at back.

Query: Reprinted without the statement IN THREE VOLUMES on the title-page?

The New York (Putnam) and London (Bohn) editions appear to have been issued simultaneously:

Putnam: Advertised as *in a few days* APC Nov. 24, 1855; and: *The cheaper edition in 12mo. will be issued as soon as the whole work is complete.* This advertisement repeated in APC Dec. 1, 8, 15, 1855.

Putnam: Advertised for *next week* APC Dec. 22, 29, 1855.

Bohn: Listed PC Feb. 1, 1856; Ath Feb. 2, 1856.

Putnam: Deposited Feb. 16, 1856.

Murray: Listed PC April 1, 1856.

Putnam: Twelvemo edition advertised for Sept. 1 in APC Aug. 16, 1856.

Putnam: Twelvemo edition listed APC Sept. 6, 1856.

Putnam: Twelvemo edition advertised as *now ready* APC Sept. 20, 1856.

Tauchnitz: Issued in Leipzig as No. 349 in the *Collection of British Authors* series. Further information wanting.

AAS (Putnam) H (Putnam) NYHS (Putnam) NYPL (Bohn)

VOL. 3 OCTAVO EDITION

LIFE OF GEORGE WASHINGTON ... VOL. III.

NEW YORK: G. P. PUTNAM & CO., 321 BROADWAY. 1856.

⟨i-ii⟩, ⟨i⟩-xiv, ⟨1⟩-523. Inserted: Frontispiece, 4 one-page plates, 1 two-page plate; other illustrations in text. 9⁵⁄₁₆″ x 5¹³⁄₁₆″.

⟨-⟩⁸, 1-3, 3, 5-32⁸, 33⁶.

T cloth: blue-black; dull purple; purple-black; slate. Buff end papers; yellow end papers; white end papers. Flyleaves.

Inserted opposite p. ⟨524⟩ is a *Publisher's Advertisement* (6″ x 4⅝″): "... No subscriber will regret the Author's extension of his plan ⟨to increase the number of volumes in the work⟩ ... New title-pages, with the number of volumes correctly stated, will be furnished with the concluding volume." Below the preceding is a 7-line notice addressed *To Correspondents*, dated *Sunnyside, June, 1856,* and signed *W. I.*

Two states (printings?) noted:

1: P. 248, line 6 up: ... *near, Fishkill,* ...

2: P. 248, line 6 up: ... *near Fishkill,* ...
Note: The later reading has been seen only in a rebound copy. Second state? Second printing?

Putnam: Clearly the *Octavo Edition* advertised APC June 14, 1856: *will be delivered ... between the 15th and 20th inst.*

Putnam: Octavo Edition. Listed APC June 21, 1856.

Putnam: Octavo Edition. Deposited July 5, 1856.

Putnam: Octavo Edition. Advertised APC July 5, 1856, as though published.

Putnam: Twelvemo Edition. Described as *The Popular Edition* advertised APC July 5, 1856, for Aug. 1. The advertisement repeated in issues of July 12, 19, 26, Aug. 2, 9, 1856.

Bohn: Listed PC Aug. 1, 1856; Ath Aug. 2, 1856.

Putnam: Twelvemo Edition. Advertised for Oct. 1 in APC Aug. 16, 1856.

Murray: Listed PC Sept. 15, 1856.

Putnam: Twelvemo Edition. Advertised as *now ready* APC Sept. 20, 1856.

Putnam: Twelvemo Edition. Listed APC Oct. 4, 1856.

Tauchnitz: Issued as No. 368 in *Collection of British Authors* series; further information wanting.

AAS　H　NYHS　UV

VOL. 4 OCTAVO EDITION

LIFE OF GEORGE WASHINGTON ... VOL. IV.

NEW YORK: G. P. PUTNAM & CO., 321 BROADWAY. 1857.

Two printings of undetermined sequence (if any) have been noted. The order of presentation is completely arbitrary:

Printing A

⟨i-ii⟩, ⟨i⟩-x, ⟨1⟩-518, blank leaf. Inserted: Frontispiece, 3 plates. $9\frac{5}{16}$" x $5\frac{13}{16}$". In some copies the final leaf (the blank) is excised.

⟨-⟩^{6}, 1-32^8, 33^4. In some copies leaf 33$_4$ is excised.

Printing B

⟨i-ii⟩, ⟨1⟩-4, ⟨i⟩-x, ⟨1⟩-518; 10 pp. advertisements, paged: ⟨i-ii⟩, 30, 13, 14, 15, 21, 12, 20, 23. Inserted: Frontispiece, 3 plates.

⟨-⟩^{8}, 1-33^8.

Leaves ⟨-⟩$_{2-3}$ and 33$_{4-8}$ imprinted with publisher's advertisements.

Ba

Sheets of *Printing B* with leaves ⟨-⟩$_{2-3}$ and 33$_{4-8}$ excised.

T cloth: blue-black; dull purple; purple-black; slate. Buff end papers; yellow end papers; white end papers. Flyleaves.

VOL. 4 TWELVEMO EDITION

LIFE OF GEORGE WASHINGTON. BY WASHINGTON IRVING. IN FOUR VOLS. VOL. IV.

NEW YORK: G. P. PUTNAM & CO., 321 BROADWAY. 1857.

Note: The title-leaf is integral and bears the statement: IN FOUR VOLS. The statement being erroneous the title-leaf was cancelled; hence, copies occur with cancelled title-leaf on which the statement is not present.

⟨i⟩-⟨xii⟩, ⟨1⟩-479. Frontispiece inserted. $7\frac{3}{8}$" x $4\frac{1}{8}$".

⟨-⟩^{6}, 1-20^{12}. See note above regarding leaf ⟨-⟩$_2$ (the title-leaf).

Three bindings noted; sequence (if any) not determined. The following features are sufficient for ready identification:

Binding A

BD cloth: gray-green. TB cloth: green. Sides blindstamped with an ornate (zig-zag within rules) border enclosing a double rule box. Yellow end papers. Flyleaves.

Binding B

TB cloth: gray-green. Sides blindstamped with a rule border, publisher's monogram at center. Yellow end papers. Flyleaves.

Binding C

TB cloth: gray-green. Sides blindstamped with a rule border. Front goldstamped with face and reverse of Washington medal. Back blindstamped with publisher's monogram. Yellow end papers. Flyleaves.

APC March 7, 1857, in a somewhat startling report commented that "the *ms.* of the fourth volume ... has just been put in the printer's hands, and is expected to be issued in a few ⟨sic⟩ days ..." Advertised APC, April 18, 1857, both formats, for *about the first week in May;* same advertisement repeated APC April 25, May 2, 1857. Both formats advertised APC May 9, 1857: *will issue, in a few days;* same advertisement repeated in issue of May 16, 1857. APC May 23, 1857, prints an extract from a review; and, carries an advertisement stating that both formats *will issue, in a few days.* Listed (prematurely?) APC May 30, 1857; but the listing is erroneous which suggests the listing may have been done on the basis of publisher's misinformation, rather than on actual receipt of the books. APC May 30, 1857 (same issue as erroneous listing) carries an advertisement in which the publisher continues to announce *will issue, in a few days.* APC June 6, 1857, reports receipt of the book, but fails to identify format; same issue continues Putnam's advertisement in which the book *will issue, in a few days.* Deposited for copyright July 8, 1857. The Bohn (London) edition listed PC Aug. 1, 1857. APC Aug. 8, 1857, carries an advertisement in which (for the first time) the book appears to be published. No listings found for a Murray (London) edition; presumably not published in London by Murray. The Tauchnitz (Leipzig) edition issued as No. 406, *Collection of British Authors* series; publication information wanting.

The present entry made on the basis of copies at AAS, B, BA, BPL, H, NYHS, NYPL, UV, Y.

VOL. 5 OCTAVO EDITION

LIFE OF GEORGE WASHINGTON ... VOL. V.

NEW YORK: G. P. PUTNAM, 115 NASSAU STREET. 1859.

⟨i-iv⟩, ⟨i⟩-xii, ⟨1⟩-456. Inserted: Frontispiece, 1 plate, 1 two-page facsimile. 9⁵⁄₁₆″ x 5¹³⁄₁₆″. The first leaf excised or pasted under the end paper.

⟨-⟩⁸, 1-21, 3², 23-28⁸, 29⁴. Leaf ⟨-⟩₁ excised or pasted under the end paper.

Two states (printings?) noted:

1: Signature 22 mis-signed 32.

2: Signature 22 correctly signed.

T cloth: blue-black; dull purple; purple-black; slate. Buff end papers; yellow end papers; white end papers. Flyleaf at back.

VOL. 5 TWELVEMO EDITION

LIFE OF GEORGE WASHINGTON ... VOL. V.

NEW YORK: G. P. PUTNAM, 115 NASSAU STREET. M.DCCC.LIX.

⟨i⟩-xii, ⟨1⟩-434. Inserted: Frontispiece and 1 plate. 7½″ scant x 5″.

⟨-⟩⁶, 1-17¹², 12¹², 19¹.

Two states (printings?) noted:

1: Signature 18 mis-signed 12.

2: Signature 18 correctly signed.

Three bindings noted; for description of these see above under *Vol. 4, Twelvemo Edition.* In some copies there is inserted at the back a publisher's catalog, 8 pp.

APC Oct. 30, 1858, reported Irving "engaged upon the fifth and concluding volume of his Life of Washington." Putnam advertised both formats APC March 12, 1859, for *early in April;* advertisement repeated issue of March 19, 1859. Advertisement APC April 23, 1859: Vol. 5 "being unavoidably delayed, in the press, ... publication is deferred until the 10th May ...'"; repeated APC April 30, 1859. Both formats advertised APC May 7, 1859: "will publish, May 10th." Both formats listed APC May 14, 1859. Putnam advertisement, APC May 21, 1859: "The publisher regrets that many orders from the Trade should remain so long unsupplied. During the unexpected delay in the publication, the orders accumulated largely, and the first large edition was exhausted by the eager demand before the second was through the press.

A full supply is expected next week ..." *The Illustrated Edition* advertised for July, APC May 21, 1859. Both formats advertised as *now ready* APC June 18, 1859. The Bohn (London) edition listed Ath July 2, 1859; PC July 16, 1859; Bkr July, 1859. Putnam edition deposited for copyright Aug. 9, 1859. No listings found for a Murray (London) edition; presumably not published in London by Murray. The Tauchnitz (Leipzig) edition issued as No. 484, *Collection of British Authors* series; publication information wanting.

AAS (12mo 2nd)   H (12mo 2nd)   NYHS (8vo 2nd; 12mo 1st)   NYPL (8vo 1st; 8vo 2nd)   UV (8vo 1st)   Y (8vo 1st)

ILLUSTRATIONS TO IRVING'S LIFE OF WASHINGTON

The publishers offered for sale plates for insertion in *The Octavo Edition.*

The earliest notice found by BAL for these illustrations appeared in APC July 5, 1856, which stated that the illustrations were *nearly ready* and were "sold separately to bind in or accompany the octavo edition"; and, the illustrations also appeared in "a New Edition of the work in Monthly Nos. ...."

According to an advertisement in APC Dec. 11, 1858, the plates were also to be had "neatly put up in a box, ready to be inserted."

As a cloth-bound volume, uniform with *The Octavo Edition,* issued with title-page as follows; earlier dating not seen or reported:

Illustrations to Irving's Life of Washington. To His Inauguration as President. Comprising 87 Engravings on Steel, and 45 Wood-Cuts.

New York: G. P. Putnam, (for the Proprietor,) 506 Broadway. 1859.

Two forms of the above have been seen; the following variations are sufficient for ready identification:

1st

In the list of illustrations each entry has, at the left, an identifying roman numeral. On p. ⟨v⟩ is an entry for *Washington at Fort Necessity.* The list is for Vols. 1-4 only.

2nd

In the list of illustrations the identifying roman numerals are not present. On p. ⟨v⟩ there is no entry for *Washington at Fort Necessity.* The list is for Vols. 1-5. In this form the number of illustrations has been increased although the title-page reading, *87 Engravings on Steel, and 45 Wood-Cuts,* remains unchanged.

The plates were also offered for sale in the terminal advertisements of *Life and Letters*, Vol. 1, 1862: "... 102 steel plates, proof-impressions on India Paper ... quarto, in portfolio, $25.00. Any plate may be had separately, price .40. ... to match the 8vo edition, 1 vol., cloth, 6.00."

LC (1st)   UV (both)

LIFE OF GEORGE WASHINGTON ... VOL. III.

NEW YORK ... 1856.

See entry No. 10192.

10193. An Appeal To The People Of The United States In Behalf Of Lamartine. We have heard with the liveliest fellow-feeling, that the illustrious Alphonse De Lamartine calls across the Atlantic to the lovers of Literature in the United States, to take part with him in his struggle with the evil days on which he has fallen ...

⟨New York: D. Appleton & Co., 1856⟩

Single cut sheet folded to make four pages. Caption-title. The above at head of p. ⟨1⟩.

Signed by Irving and others.

An appeal on behalf of Lamartine, proposing publication of his *Familiar Course of Literature*.

UV

10194. ... The (Old) Farmer's Almanack ... for the Year of Our Lord 1857 ... by Robert B. Thomas ...

Boston: Published by Hickling, Swan & Brown ... 1856 ...

Printed paper wrapper. At head of title: Number Sixty-Five.

Testimonial for Worcester's dictionaries, dated *October 3, 1855*, on inner front wrapper. *Note:* There is every likelihood this testimonial was published in other forms but no other publication has been found by BAL. Not to be confused with Irving's letter in *A Reply ...*, Boston, 1854, described above.

H   NYPL

LIFE OF GEORGE WASHINGTON ... VOL. IV.

NEW YORK ... 1857.

See entry No. 10192.

10195. The following is a perfect fac-simile of the letter that / Washington Irving did write to the author of / "Sartaroe." / ⟨in facsimile:⟩

Sunnyside Dec 12' 1857. / Dear Sir: / I have repeatedly, through the / press, given a general apology for a / want of promptness in replying to my / almost innumerable correspondents. / ⟨etc., etc.⟩ / I read your work with interest ...

⟨n.p., n.d., presumably Philadelphia, 1857? 1858?⟩

Single cut sheet of paper folded to four pages; text on pp. ⟨1-2⟩; pp. ⟨3-4⟩ blank. Page: 8 3/16" x 5 1/4".

A letter addressed to James A. Maitland, author of *Sartaroe*. See next entry.

HM

10196. Sartaroe: A Tale of Norway. By James A. Maitland ...

Philadelphia: T. B. Peterson & Brothers, No. 306 Chestnut Street. ⟨1858⟩

Letter, Irving to Maitland, *Sunnyside, Irvington, Nov. 1st, 1857*, printed on both the title-page and on p. xvii, *i.e.,* ⟨1⟩1r. Not the same letter as that addressed to Maitland, Dec. 12, 1857; see preceding entry.

AAS   Y

LIFE OF GEORGE WASHINGTON ... VOL. V.

NEW YORK ... 1859.

See entry No. 10192.

10197. To the Literature of the Language What a Dictionary of Words Is to the Language Itself. Allibone's Dictionary of Authors ...

Childs & Peterson, 602 Arch Street, Philadelphia. ⟨1859⟩

Printed self-wrapper. Cover-title.

Letter, Aug. 23, 1855, p. 4; here reprinted. For prior publication see entry No. 10191.

Letter, Jan. 12, 1859, p. 4.

NYPL

10198. LIFE AND LETTERS, 1862–1864

The publication history of this book is involved. The publisher's advertisements, and frequently the trade listings and notices, are unclear and often fail to identify the format. On the basis of such listings and notices the following entry has been prepared. A detailed publication statement is given below.

Lacking the precise information required for establishment of a chronology BAL is obliged, reluctantly, to give equal status to the five formats here described.

SUNNYSIDE EDITION

Printed on wove paper. Leaf 7¾" tall. At foot of spine: SUNNYSIDE EDIT. Bound in TR cloth: blue; green; slate.

NATIONAL EDITION

Printed on laid paper. Leaf 8" tall. At foot of spine: *National Edition* Bound in polished green V cloth.

NATIONAL EDITION (SUPERFINE)

Printed on wove paper. Leaf 7⅝" full tall. At foot of spine: *National Edition* Bound in green TR cloth.

LARGE PAPER EDITION

Printed on laid paper. Leaf 8⅛" tall. Edition not identified on spine. Bound in green BD cloth; green TR cloth; green Z cloth.

Advertised APC Dec. 1, 1862, as "only 100 copies printed in this style"; however, an advertisement in APC for March 18, 1863, gives the figure as 250 copies.

ILLUSTRATED EDITION

Not seen. Description taken from publisher's advertisement APC March 18, 1863: "A few copies ⟨of the *Large Paper Edition*⟩ ... with extra engravings on steel, elegantly bound in morocco, gilt edges."

PUBLICATION DATES

Vol. 1

Sunnyside: Advertised APC Feb. 1862, for *about the 1st April.*

Bentley (London): Announced as *shortly to be published* Ath March 15, 29, 1862.

Sunnyside: Advertised APC March, 1862, for *next month.*

National (Superfine): Duyckinck's copy in NYPL inscribed by him April 3, 1862.

Bentley (London): Advertised Ath April 5, 1862, as *immediately.*

Bentley (London): Advertised as *ready* Ath April 12, 1862.

Bentley (London): Listed Ath April 19, 1862.

Bentley (London): Reviewed Ath April 26, 1862.

Bentley (London): Listed PC May 1, 1862.

Sunnyside: Listed (this format?) APC May, 1862.

Bohn (London): Listed Ath July 12, 1862; PC July 17, 1862.

Large Paper: Advertised APC Sept. 1, 1862.

Large Paper: Advertised APC Dec. 1, 1862, as *now ready.*

National: Advertised APC Dec. 1, 1862, as *now ready.*

National (Superfine): Advertised APC Dec. 1, 1862, as *now ready.*

Note: In 1864 Bell & Daldy, London, reissued the Bohn edition.

Vol. 2

National (Superfine): Oscar Irving's copy in NYPL inscribed Aug. 27, 1862.

Sunnyside: Advertised APC Sept. 1, 1862, as *now ready. Note:* APC did not publish an August issue.

Bentley (London): Advertised as *new* Ath Sept. 6, 1862.

Bentley (London): Advertised as *ready* Ath Sept. 13, 1862.

Bentley (London): Listed Ath Sept. 13, 1862.

Bentley (London): Reviewed Ath Sept. 13, 1862.

Bentley (London): Listed PC Sept. 15, 1862.

Bohn (London): Listed Ath Sept. 27, 1862; PC Oct. 15, 1862.

Unknown Putnam format: Reviewed NAR Oct. 1862.

Sunnyside: Advertised APC Dec. 1, 1862, as *now ready.*

National: Advertised APC Dec. 1, 1862, as *now ready.*

National (Superfine): Advertised APC Dec. 1, 1862, as *now ready.*

Large Paper: Advertised APC Dec. 1, 1862, as *now ready.*

Note: In 1864 Bell & Daldy, London, reissued the Bohn edition.

Vol. 3

Sunnyside: Advertised APC May 1, 1863, as *ready in May.*

Large Paper: Advertised APC May 1, 1863, as *ready in May.*

National: Advertised APC May 1, 1863, as *ready in May.*

Sunnyside: Listed (this format?) APC June 1, 1863. The listing may refer to the *National Edition.*

Bentley (London): Listed Ath June 20, 1863. *Note:* Contains some material added by the British publisher. For a comment see ALG Nov.

16, 1863, pp. 40-41, whence the following: "... we find that the third volume ... has been interpolated on page 314, and two new chapters inserted (xxiii. and xxiv.), eighty-one pages in all, without the slightest reasonable excuse, and in defiance of all the requirements of ordinary courtesy ... bad taste ... moral insensibility ... flagrant ..."

Bohn (London): Listed Ath June 27, 1863.

Bentley (London): Listed PC July 1, 1863.

Bohn (London): Listed PC July 15, 1863.

Note: In 1864 Bell & Daldy, London, reissued the Bohn edition.

Vol. 4

Sunnyside: Advertised APC Sept. 15, 1863, as *in press.*

Large Paper: Advertised APC Sept. 15, 1863, for *September.*

Sunnyside: Listed ALG Dec. 1, 1863.

National (Superfine): Advertised ALG Dec. 1, 1863.

Sunnyside: Advertised ALG Dec. 1, 1863, as *completed;* and, listed.

National: Advertised ALG Dec. 1, 1863.

Bentley (London): Listed Ath Jan. 16, 1864; PC Jan. 16, 1864; reviewed Ath Jan. 23, 1864; listed Bkr Jan. 30, 1864.

Bohn (London): Listed Bkr March 31, 1864; PC April 1, 1864; Ath April 2, 1864.

Note: In 1864 Bell & Daldy, London, reissued the Bohn edition.

SUNNYSIDE EDITION
Vol. 1

THE LIFE AND LETTERS OF WASHINGTON IRVING. BY ... PIERRE M. IRVING. VOLUME I.

NEW YORK: G. P. PUTNAM, 532 BROADWAY. 1862.

$\langle 1 \rangle$-463; blank, p. $\langle 464 \rangle$; advertisements, pp. $\langle 1 \rangle$-$\langle 16 \rangle$. Frontispiece and 1 plate inserted. $7\frac{3}{4}''$ x $5\frac{1}{8}''$ scant. Printed on wove paper.

$\langle 1 \rangle$-3, 3, 5-20^{12}. *Also signed (with the signature marks in parentheses):* $\langle 1 \rangle$-30^8.

TR cloth: blue; green. At foot of spine: SUNNYSIDE EDIT. Brown-coated on white end papers. Flyleaves.

H NYPL

Vol. 2

THE LIFE AND LETTERS OF WASHINGTON IRVING. BY ... PIERRE M. IRVING. VOLUME II.

NEW YORK: G. P. PUTNAM, 532 BROADWAY. 1862.

$\langle 1 \rangle$-492. Frontispiece inserted. $7\frac{5}{8}''$ x $5\frac{1}{8}''$ scant. Printed on wove paper.

$\langle 1 \rangle$-20^{12}, 21^6. *Also signed (with the signature marks in parentheses):* $\langle 1 \rangle$-30^8, 31^6.

TR cloth: blue. At foot of spine: SUNNYSIDE EDIT. Brown-coated on white end papers. Flyleaves.

H

Vol. 3

THE LIFE AND LETTERS OF WASHINGTON IRVING. BY ... PIERRE M. IRVING. VOLUME III.

NEW YORK: G. P. PUTNAM, 441 BROADWAY. 1863.

$\langle$i-ii$\rangle$, $\langle 1 \rangle$-$\langle 10 \rangle$, $\langle 13 \rangle$-403. Frontispiece inserted. $7\frac{5}{8}''$ scant x $5\frac{5}{16}''$. Printed on wove paper.

$\langle 1 \rangle$-16^{12}, 17^{10}. *Also signed (with the signature marks in parentheses):* $\langle 1 \rangle$-25^8, 26^2.

TR cloth: blue; slate. At foot of spine: SUNNYSIDE EDIT. Brown-coated on white end papers. Flyleaves.

H Y

Vol. 4

THE LIFE AND LETTERS OF WASHINGTON IRVING. BY ... PIERRE M. IRVING. VOLUME IV.

NEW YORK: G. P. PUTNAM, 441 BROADWAY. 1864.

$\langle 1 \rangle$-450, blank leaf. Frontispiece inserted. $7\frac{9}{16}''$ x $5\frac{1}{8}''$ scant. Printed on wove paper.

$\langle 1 \rangle$-18^{12}, 19^{10}. *Also signed (with the signature marks in parentheses):* $\langle 1 \rangle$-27^8, 28^{10}.

TR cloth: blue; green. At foot of spine: SUNNYSIDE EDIT. Brown-coated on white end papers. Flyleaves.

H NYPL

NATIONAL EDITION
Vol. 1

THE LIFE AND LETTERS OF WASHINGTON IRVING. BY ... PIERRE M. IRVING. VOLUME I.

NEW YORK: G. P. PUTNAM, 532 BROADWAY. 1862.

$\langle 1 \rangle$-463. Frontispiece and 1 plate inserted. $8''$ x $5\frac{5}{16}''$. Printed on laid paper.

$\langle 1 \rangle$-29^8. The preceding signature marks are set within parentheses. *Also signed:* $\langle 1 \rangle$-3, 3, 5-19^{12}, 20^4.

Polished V cloth: green. At foot of spine: Marbled end papers. Laid paper flyleaves.
National Edition

AAS

Vol. 2

THE LIFE AND LETTERS OF WASHING-
TON IRVING. BY ... PIERRE M. IRVING.
VOLUME II.

NEW YORK: G. P. PUTNAM, 532 BROADWAY. 1862.

$\langle 1 \rangle$-486; $\langle i$-iv$\rangle$; 487-492. Frontispiece inserted. *See note below.* 8" x 5$\frac{1}{16}$". Printed on laid paper.

$\langle 1 \rangle$-31^8. The preceding signature marks are set within parentheses. *Also signed:* $\langle 1 \rangle$-20^{12}, 21^8. *See note below.*

Note: Leaves 31$_{4-5}$ are blanks due to faulty imposition; the text is not affected. It is possible that these blank leaves are not present in all copies since they could have been removed at the bindery without trace.

Polished V cloth: green. At foot of spine: National Edition   Marbled end papers.

AAS

Vol. 3

THE LIFE AND LETTERS OF WASHING-
TON IRVING. BY ... PIERRE M. IRVING.
VOLUME III.

NEW YORK: G. P. PUTNAM, 441 BROADWAY. 1863.

$\langle i$-ii$\rangle$, $\langle 1 \rangle$-$\langle 10 \rangle$, $\langle 13 \rangle$-403. Frontispiece inserted. 7$\frac{7}{8}$" scant x 5$\frac{3}{8}$". Printed on laid paper.

$\langle 1 \rangle$-16^{12}, 17^{10}. *Also signed (with the signature marks in parentheses):* $\langle 1 \rangle$-25^8, 26^2.

Polished V cloth: green. At foot of spine: National Edition   Marbled end papers (probable).

AAS

Vol. 4

THE LIFE AND LETTERS OF WASHING-
TON IRVING. BY ... PIERRE M. IRVING.
VOLUME IV.

NEW YORK: G. P. PUTNAM, 441 BROADWAY. 1864.

$\langle 1 \rangle$-450, blank leaf. Frontispiece inserted. 7$\frac{7}{8}$" x 5$\frac{1}{2}$". Printed on laid paper.

$\langle 1 \rangle$-18^{12}, 19^{10}. *Also signed (with the signature marks in parentheses):* $\langle 1 \rangle$-27^8, 28^{10}.

Polished V cloth: green. At foot of spine: National Edition   Marbled end papers.

AAS

NATIONAL EDITION (SUPERFINE)

Vol. 1

THE LIFE AND LETTERS OF WASHING-
TON IRVING. BY ... PIERRE M. IRVING.
VOLUME I.

NEW YORK: G. P. PUTNAM, 532 BROADWAY. 1862.

$\langle 1 \rangle$-463. Frontispiece and 1 plate inserted. 7$\frac{5}{8}$" full x 5$\frac{5}{16}$". Printed on wove paper.

$\langle 1 \rangle$-29^8. The preceding signature marks are set within parentheses. *Also signed:* $\langle 1 \rangle$-3, 3, 5-19^{12}, 20^4.

TR cloth: green. At foot of spine: National Edition   Marbled end papers. Flyleaves.

H   NYPL

Vol. 2

THE LIFE AND LETTERS OF WASHING-
TON IRVING. BY ... PIERRE M. IRVING.
VOLUME II.

NEW YORK: G. P. PUTNAM, 532 BROADWAY. 1862.

$\langle 1 \rangle$-492. Frontispiece inserted. 7$\frac{5}{8}$" x 5$\frac{1}{4}$". Printed on wove paper.

$\langle 1 \rangle$-30^8, 31^6. The preceding signature marks are set within parentheses. *Also signed:* $\langle 1 \rangle$-20^{12}, 21^6.

TR cloth: green. At foot of spine: National Edition   Marbled end papers. Flyleaves in some copies.

H   NYPL

Vol. 3

THE LIFE AND LETTERS OF WASHING-
TON IRVING. BY ... PIERRE M. IRVING.
VOLUME III.

NEW YORK: G. P. PUTNAM, 441 BROADWAY. 1863.

$\langle i$-ii$\rangle$, $\langle 1 \rangle$-$\langle 10 \rangle$, $\langle 13 \rangle$-403. Frontispiece inserted. 7$\frac{5}{8}$" x 5$\frac{5}{16}$". Printed on wove paper.

$\langle 1 \rangle$-16^{12}, 17^{10}. *Also signed (with the signature marks in parentheses):* $\langle 1 \rangle$-25^8, 26^2.

TR cloth: green. At foot of spine: National Edition   Marbled end papers; also, brown-coated on white end papers. Flyleaves in some copies.

H   NYPL

Vol. 4

THE LIFE AND LETTERS OF WASHING-
TON IRVING. BY ... PIERRE M. IRVING.
VOLUME IV.

NEW YORK: G. P. PUTNAM, 441 BROADWAY. 1864.

$\langle 1 \rangle$-450, blank leaf. Frontispiece inserted. 7$\frac{5}{8}$" x 5$\frac{5}{16}$". Printed on wove paper.

‹1›-18¹², 19¹⁰. *Also signed (with the signature marks in parentheses):* ‹1›-27⁸, 28¹⁰.

TR cloth: green. At foot of spine: National Edition   Brown-coated on white end papers. Flyleaves.

NYPL   UV

LARGE PAPER EDITION
Vol. 1

THE LIFE AND LETTERS OF WASHINGTON IRVING. BY ... PIERRE M. IRVING. VOLUME I.

NEW YORK: G. P. PUTNAM, 532 BROADWAY. 1862.

‹1›-463. Frontispiece and 1 plate inserted. 8⅞" x 6⁵⁄₁₆". Printed on laid paper.

‹1›-29⁸. The preceding signature marks are set within parentheses. *Also signed:* ‹1›-3, 3, 5-19¹², 20⁴.

BD cloth: green. Brown-coated on white end papers. Laid paper flyleaves.

NYPL   Y

Vol. 2

THE LIFE AND LETTERS OF WASHINGTON IRVING. BY ... PIERRE M. IRVING. VOLUME II.

NEW YORK: G. P. PUTNAM, 532 BROADWAY. 1862.

‹1›-492. Frontispiece inserted. 8⅞" x 6⁵⁄₁₆". Printed on laid paper.

‹1›-30⁸, 31⁶. The preceding signature marks are set within parentheses. *Also signed:* ‹1›-20¹², 21⁶.

BD cloth: green. Brown-coated on white end papers. Laid paper flyleaves.

NYPL   Y

Vol. 3

THE LIFE AND LETTERS OF WASHINGTON IRVING. BY ... PIERRE M. IRVING. VOLUME III.

NEW YORK: G. P. PUTNAM, 441 BROADWAY. 1863.

‹i-ii›, ‹1›-‹10›, ‹13›-403. Frontispiece inserted. 8¹⁵⁄₁₆" x 6⁵⁄₁₆". Printed on laid paper.

‹1›-25⁸, 26². The preceding signature marks are set within parentheses. *Also signed:* ‹1›-16¹², 17¹⁰.

TR cloth: green. Z cloth: green. Brown-coated on white end papers. Laid paper flyleaves.

BPL   NYPL   Y

Vol. 4

THE LIFE AND LETTERS OF WASHINGTON IRVING. BY ... PIERRE M. IRVING. VOLUME IV.

NEW YORK: G. P. PUTNAM, 441 BROADWAY. 1864.

‹1›-450, blank leaf. Frontispiece inserted. 8⅞" x 6⁵⁄₁₆". Printed on laid paper.

‹1›-28⁸, ‹29›². The preceding signature marks are set within parentheses. *Also signed:* ‹1›-18¹², 19¹⁰.

TR cloth: green. Brown-coated on white end papers. Laid paper flyleaves.

BPL   NYPL   Y

THE LIFE AND LETTERS ...

NEW YORK ... 1863.

See entry No. 10198.

10199. Dream Life ... by Ik. Marvel ‹*i.e.*, Donald Grant Mitchell› ... a New Edition.

New York: Charles Scribner, 124 Grand Street. 1863.

Letter to Mitchell, Nov. 1851, pp. ‹iii›-iv.

Listed (as in cloth; and, morocco) ALG Nov. 16, 1863. Deposited Dec. 16, 1863. Distributed in London by Trübner; listed under American books PC Dec. 8, 1863.

H (cloth)

THE LIFE AND LETTERS ...

NEW YORK ... 1864.

See entry No. 10198.

10200. The Spirit of the Fair ...

New York, April 5–9, 11–16, 18–23, 1864.

"The Story of Pelayo," No. 11, p. 126; No. 12, pp. 138-139. Collected in *Spanish Papers*, 1866.

For comment see entry No. 413.

10201. SPANISH PAPERS AND OTHER MISCELLANIES, HITHERTO UNPUBLISHED OR UNCOLLECTED ... ARRANGED AND EDITED BY PIERRE M. IRVING. IN TWO VOLUMES ...

NEW YORK: G. P. PUTNAM; HURD AND HOUGHTON. 1866.

1: ‹i›-‹xvi›, ‹1›-466, blank leaf. Portrait frontispiece inserted. 7⁷⁄₁₆" x 4⅞".

2: ‹i-vi›, 11-487.

1: ⟨1⟩-20¹², 21².

2: ⟨1⟩-20¹², 21².

TR cloth: slate. TZ cloth: slate. Yellow-coated on white end papers. Flyleaves. The spine is stamped: IRVING'S / WORKS / ⟨rule⟩ / SPANISH / PAPERS / ⟨rule⟩ / VOL. I. ⟨II.⟩ / ⟨rule⟩ ⟨All the preceding, save for the final rule, within a floriated three-sided frame⟩

Also noted in a variant (remainder?) binding: Purple-slate P cloth. The spine is stamped: ⟨double rule⟩ / IRVING'S / WORKS / ⟨horizontal ornament composed of two lozenges connected by a small circle⟩ / SPANISH / PAPERS / ⟨rule⟩ / VOL. I. ⟨II.⟩ / ⟨the preceding seven lines in a shield⟩ / ⟨WI monogram⟩ / ⟨double rule⟩ Yellow-coated on white end papers. Flyleaves?

Note: No located copy, in either of the above bindings, has the publisher's name imprinted on the spine. Langfeld-Blackburn (p. 46) report copies with the spine imprint of J. B. Lippincott. However, *J. B. Lippincott & Co.'s Catalogue of Publications and Importations . . .* , Philadelphia, Feb. 1871, contains the following notice on p. 28: *Having made arrangements for the exclusive publication of Irving's Works, we have the pleasure of announcing them . . .*

Advertised for Sept. 1, 1866, in ALG Sept. 1, 1866. BA copy received Sept. 18, 1866. Listed ALG Oct. 1, 1866. The London (Low) edition listed Ath Oct. 20, 1866; Bkr Oct. 31, 1866; PC Nov. 1, 1866.

AAS   MHS   NYPL   UV (variant binding)

10202. The Life and Writings of John Howard Payne . . . by Gabriel Harrison.

Albany, N. Y.   Joel Munsell. 1875.

Letter to Payne, April 30, 1821, pp. 83-84.

"Song," *Oh, turn, cruel, fair one . . .* , p. 397.

"Signs of the Times," p. 398.

Both the preceding collected in *Poems*, 1931.

Two formats issued:

Quarto Edition; leaf 12″ tall. Issued in cloth?

Octavo Edition; leaf 10⅞″ tall. Issued in cloth.

"Published By Subscription, A Limited Edition Of Two Hundred And Fifty Octavos, And Fifteen Quartos."—Certificate of issue.

H (both)   NYPL (Octavo)

10203. A History of New-York . . . by Diedrich Knickerbocker . . . a New Edition, Containing Unpublished Corrections . . . in Two Volumes . . .

New-York   Printed for the Grolier Club MDCCCLXXXVI

Printed paper boards. 175 copies on Holland paper, 2 copies on vellum. For first edition see above under 1809.

Note: The title-page for Vol. 1 has an error in the quotation: *flaarheid* for *klaarheid*. A corrected title-page was inserted at the back of Vol. 2, together with instructions to the binder, to cancel the offending title-leaf and insert the corrected title-leaf.

H   NYHS   NYPL   Y

10204. LETTERS FROM WASHINGTON IRVING TO MRS. WILLIAM RENWICK, AND TO HER SON, JAMES RENWICK . . . WRITTEN BETWEEN SEPTEMBER 10th, 1811 AND APRIL 5th, 1816. PRINTED FOR PRIVATE DISTRIBUTION.

⟨n.p., n.d., New York, 1915⟩

Cover-title.

3-34. 8½″ x 5½″.

⟨-⟩¹⁶.

Printed gray-blue linen-weave paper wrapper.

Published after January, 1915, before July 14, 1915.

NYHS   NYPL   UV   Y

10205. THE LETTERS OF WASHINGTON IRVING TO HENRY BREVOORT EDITED . . . BY GEORGE S. HELLMAN . . . IN TWO VOLUMES . . .

NEW YORK   G. P. PUTNAM'S SONS   THE KNICKERBOCKER PRESS   1915

Title-page in black and red.

1: ⟨i-ii⟩, ⟨i⟩-⟨lviii⟩, 1-198, blank leaf. Laid paper. Inserted: Certificate of issue, frontispiece, folded facsimile. 9⁵⁄₁₆″ x 5¾″.

2: ⟨i-ii⟩, ⟨i⟩-⟨x⟩, 1-248. Inserted: Certificate of issue, frontispiece, folded facsimile.

1: ⟨a⟩⁶, ⟨b-d⟩⁸, 1-12⁸, 13⁴.

2: ⟨a⟩⁶, 1-15⁸, 16⁴.

Gray cartridge paper boards; sides goldstamped; goldstamped leather label on spine. Buff end papers. Double flyleaf at back of Vol. 2.

". . . Limited to Two Hundred and Fifty-five sets . . . This is No. . . . October, 1915."—Certificate of issue.

Trade edition issued in 1918.

A companion publication was issued in the same format: *Letters of Henry Brevoort to*

Washington Irving together with Other Un-published Brevoort Papers, edited by George S. Hellman, New York: G. P. Putnam's Sons, 1916; 2 Vols., limited to 310 numbered sets.

Deposited Oct. 28, 1915. H copy received Nov. 1, 1915. Listed PW Nov. 6, 1915.

BA H NYHS

10206. THE JOURNALS OF WASHINGTON IRVING (HITHERTO UNPUBLISHED) EDITED BY WILLIAM P. TRENT AND GEORGE S. HELLMAN PRINTED FOR MEMBERS ONLY

THE BIBLIOPHILE SOCIETY BOSTON MCMXIX

1: ⟨i-ii⟩, vii-⟨xxvi⟩, ⟨1⟩-225. Paper watermarked *Old Stratford.* Inserted: Certificate of issue, 2 frontispieces, title-page, 9 plates; other illustrations in text. 9¹⁄₁₆″ x 6¼″.

2: ⟨i-ii⟩, 7-199. Inserted: Certificate of issue, frontispiece, title-page, 1 plate.

3: ⟨i-ii⟩, 1-220, blank leaf. Inserted: Certificate of issue, title-page, 2 frontispieces, 3 plates; other illustrations in text.

1: ⟨1-15⁸, 16⁴⟩.

2: ⟨1-11⁸, 12¹⁰⟩.

3: ⟨1-14⁸⟩.

Tan paper boards sides, tan C-like cloth shelf-back. End papers and double flyleaves of book stock. Top edges gilt.

"... 430 Copies ..."—Certificate of issue.

See *The Western Journals ...* , 1944, below.

Deposited Jan. 24, 1920.

Hellman Printing

The Journals of Washington Irving (from July, 1815, to July, 1842) Edited by William P. Trent and George S. Hellman

Boston MCMXIX

3 Vols. Printed paper boards.

"... The Bibliophile Society, after printing an edition for its members, has issued a few copies to Mr. George S. Hellman for private distribution, of which this is one ..."—Certificate of issue.

H (both) NYHS (both) NYPL (Bibliophile)

10207. NOTES AND JOURNAL OF TRAVEL IN EUROPE 1804–1805 ... WITH AN INTRODUCTION BY WILLIAM P. TRENT ... IN THREE VOLUMES ...

NEW YORK THE GROLIER CLUB 1921

1: ⟨i⟩-xliv, ⟨1⟩-167. Vignette title-page and 1 plate inserted. 6¹³⁄₁₆″ x 4⁵⁄₁₆″.

2: ⟨i-viii⟩, ⟨1⟩-188. Vignette title-page and 1 plate inserted.

3: ⟨i-viii⟩, ⟨1⟩-199; colophon, p. ⟨200⟩. Vignette title-page and 1 plate inserted.

Note: The vignette title-pages are dated *1920.*

1: ⟨1-12⁸, 13⁴, 14⁶⟩.

2: ⟨1-11⁸, 12⁴, 13⁶⟩.

3: ⟨1-13⁸⟩.

Mottled T-like cloth: blue. Top edges gilt.

"... Two hundred and fifty-seven sets on rag paper ... and three sets on Japanese vellum ... printed ... September, 1921"—Colophon.

Deposited Feb. 4, 1922.

H NYPL

10208. From Pinafores to Politics by Mrs. J. Borden Harriman

New York Henry Holt and Company 1923

"The Lay of the Sunnyside Ducks," pp. 22-23. Collected in *Poems, 1931.*

On copyright page: *First printing, October, 1923*

Deposited Nov. 22, 1923.

H

10209. ABU HASSAN ... (HITHERTO UNPUBLISHED) WITH AN INTRODUCTION BY GEORGE S. HELLMAN PRINTED EXCLUSIVELY FOR MEMBERS OF THE BIBLIOPHILE SOCIETY

BOSTON MCMXXIV

Title-page in black, blue and orange.

⟨3⟩-83, blank leaf. Laid paper watermarked *Deckle d'Aigle.* 9⁷⁄₁₆″ x 6⁵⁄₁₆″. Inserted: Certificate of issue, 2 four-page facsimiles, 2 two-page facsimiles.

⟨1-4⁸, 5¹⁰⟩.

Green B cloth sides, white vellum shelfback. End papers of bookstock. Double flyleaves. Top edges gilt.

"... 455 copies ..."—Certificate of issue.

Deposited Nov. 17, 1924.

AAS H NYHS NYPL

10210. The Wild Huntsman ... (Hitherto Unpublished) with an Introduction by George S. Hellman Printed Exclusively for Members of the Bibliophile Society

Boston MCMXXIV

⟨3⟩-113. Laid paper watermarked *Deckle d'Aigle.* 9½″ x 6⅜″. Inserted: Certificate of issue, 4 two-page facsimiles, 1 four-page facsimile. *Note:* A surviving copyright deposit copy is printed on wove paper watermarked *Van Gelder Zonen Holland.* Issued on both types of paper? Cloth, vellum shelfback.

Irving's adaptation of Friedrich Kind's *Der Freischütz.* For a comment on Irving's hand in another adaptation of the same work see *Trial without Jury* ... , 1940, below.

" ... 455 copies ..."—Certificate of issue.

Deposited Nov. 17, 1924.

BA H LC NYPL

10211. AN UNWRITTEN DRAMA OF LORD BYRON ... WITH AN INTRODUCTION BY THOMAS OLLIVE MABBOTT ...

CHARLES F. HEARTMAN METUCHEN, NEW JERSEY 1925

⟨1-13⟩; blank leaf. Laid paper, some copies displaying the watermark: *Fabriano (Italy).* 9⅜″ x 6⁵⁄₁₆″.

⟨-⟩⁸.

Mottled green paper boards, printed paper label on front.

51 numbered copies only.

Previously in *The Gift ... for 1836,* Philadelphia ⟨n.d., 1835⟩, described above.

BPL H NYHS NYPL

10212. WASHINGTON IRVING DIARY SPAIN 1828–1829 EDITED FROM THE MANUSCRIPT IN THE LIBRARY OF THE SOCIETY BY CLARA LOUISA PENNEY ...

THE HISPANIC SOCIETY OF AMERICA NEW YORK 1926

⟨i⟩-xviii, ⟨1⟩-142. Frontispiece and 6 plates inserted. 6⁷⁄₁₆″ x 4⁹⁄₁₆″.

⟨1-10⁸⟩.

V cloth: tan. Cream end papers imprinted with the society's seal, etc., and *Hispanic Catalogues Series* and *Hispanic Society of America.* Edges red. Rounded corners, both cover and leaves.

Deposited May 17, 1926. Reviewed TLS Sept. 30, 1926.

BA H NYPL

10213. NOTES WHILE PREPARING SKETCH BOOK ... 1817 ... EDITED WITH A CRITICAL INTRODUCTION BY STANLEY T. WILLIAMS

NEW HAVEN YALE UNIVERSITY PRESS MDCCCC-XXVII

⟨i-xii⟩, ⟨1⟩-97; blank, p. ⟨98⟩; colophon, p. ⟨99⟩. Frontispiece (tipped to stub of excised pp. ⟨iii-iv⟩); 1 two-page facsimile inserted. 8″ scant x 5″.

⟨1-7⁸⟩. Leaf ⟨1⟩₂ excised.

Blue paper boards sides, black V cloth shelfback. White end papers, some bearing the watermark *Vidalon.* Double flyleaves, some displaying an armorial device watermark. Top edges gilt.

"Five hundred and twenty-five copies ... printed ... October, 1927 ... No. ...."—Colophon.

Deposited Dec. 12, 1927.

BA H NYPL

10214. TOUR IN SCOTLAND 1817 AND OTHER MANUSCRIPT NOTES ... EDITED WITH A CRITICAL INTRO-DUCTION BY STANLEY T. WILLIAMS

NEW HAVEN YALE UNIVERSITY PRESS MDCCC-CXXVII

⟨i-xii⟩, ⟨1⟩-146; colophon, p. ⟨147⟩. Frontispiece (a 2-page map) tipped to stub of excised pp. ⟨iii-iv⟩; 5 inserted plates. 8″ x 5″. Watermarked with a shield and crown device.

⟨1-10⁸⟩. Leaf ⟨1⟩₂ excised.

Blue paper boards sides, black V cloth shelfback. White end papers; in some copies the watermark *Vidalon* is present. Double flyleaves. Top edges gilt.

"Five hundred and twenty-five copies ... printed ... October, 1927 ... No. ...."—Colophon.

Deposited Dec. 12, 1927.

H NYPL Y

10215. LETTERS FROM SUNNYSIDE AND SPAIN ... EDITED BY STANLEY T. WIL-LIAMS

NEW HAVEN YALE UNIVERSITY PRESS LONDON HUMPHREY MILFORD OXFORD UNIVERSITY PRESS 1928

⟨i⟩-⟨viii⟩, ⟨1⟩-80. Frontispiece and 2 plates inserted. 8⅝″ x 5⅝″ scant.

⟨1-4⁸, 5⁴, 6⁸⟩.

Blue-green linen; the deposit copies thus. Also noted in a variant (remainder?) binding of maroon V cloth.

Deposited Oct. 25, 1928.

H (linen) NYPL (linen) UV (V cloth)

10216. JOURNAL OF WASHINGTON IRV-
ING (1823–1824) EDITED BY STANLEY T.
WILLIAMS

CAMBRIDGE HARVARD UNIVERSITY PRESS 1931

⟨i⟩-⟨xviii⟩, ⟨1⟩-132; ⟨xix-xx⟩; 133-278, blank
leaf. Frontispiece inserted. Pp. ⟨xix-xx⟩ bear
an illustration. Paper watermarked *Flemish
Book.* 7¹³⁄₁₆″ x 5¹⁄₁₆″.

⟨1-14⁸, 15⁶, 16-19⁸⟩.

B cloth: maroon. Sides blindstamped with a
rule frame. Top edges gilt. Deposit copies thus.
Also noted in two variant (remainder?) bindings:

Variant A

B cloth: maroon. Sides unstamped. Top edges
plain.

Variant B

S cloth: blue. Sides unstamped. Top edges plain.

Deposited Feb. 24, 1931.

AAS (Variant A) H NYHS (Variant B) NYPL
Y

10217. The Poems of Washington Irving
Brought together from Various Sources by
William R. Langfeld

New York The New York Public Library
1931

Printed paper wrapper. 400 copies printed.

"Of this edition, twenty-eight copies were spe-
cially bound for presentation by the compiler."
—Langfeld-Blackburn, p. 52. Not located by
BAL.

AAS H NYPL

10218. WASHINGTON IRVING AND THE
STORROWS LETTERS FROM ENG-
LAND AND THE CONTINENT 1821–1828
EDITED BY STANLEY T. WILLIAMS

CAMBRIDGE, MASSACHUSETTS HARVARD UNIVER-
SITY PRESS MCMXXXIII

⟨i⟩-⟨x⟩, ⟨1⟩-136, blank leaf. Frontispiece and 2
plates inserted. 8″ x 5⁵⁄₁₆″.

⟨1-7⁸, 8¹⁰, 9⁸⟩.

Red balloon cloth. Top edges gilt.

Note: The caption on the portrait frontispiece
miscredits ownership of the original to Edward
C. Storrow; and, misdates Gilbert Stuart Newton: *c. 1803.* In some copies the errors are corrected by means of an errata slip.

NYPL copy received June 12, 1933. Deposited
June 19, 1933.

AAS H NYHS NYPL

10219. JOURNAL, 1803 . . . EDITED BY
STANLEY T. WILLIAMS

OXFORD UNIVERSITY PRESS LONDON AND NEW
YORK 1934

⟨i-ii⟩, ⟨i⟩-⟨xii⟩, ⟨1⟩-48, blank leaf. Laid paper
watermarked *Strathmore Emissary Text.* Frontispiece and 1 plate inserted. 6¹¹⁄₁₆″ x 4¼″.

⟨1-8⁴⟩.

Marbled paper boards sides, blue V cloth shelfback and corners. Printed paper label on front.
Top edges gilt. End papers of bookstock.

On copyright page: *First Edition* Deposited
Dec. 17, 1934.

AAS NYPL

10220. FACSIMILE OF A LETTER FROM
WASHINGTON IRVING TO JESSE MER-
WIN, PROTOTYPE OF "ICHABOD
CRANE." PRESENTED TO THE MEM-
BERS OF THE SAINT NICHOLAS SOCI-
ETY ON THE OCCASION OF ITS CEN-
TENNIAL DINNER, THROUGH THE
GENEROSITY OF MR. SEYMOUR VAN
SANTVOORD.

⟨n.p., n.d., presumably New York, 1935⟩

Cover-title. The above, in blue, printed on the
face of an envelope, 4⅜″ full x 5⅝″. The facsimile enclosed is printed on a single leaf folded
to make four pages. Page: 10⅜″ x 8¼″.

*Sunnyside Feb 12th 1851 You must excuse me,
my good friend Merwin, for suffering your letter
to remain so long unanswered . . .*

UV

10221. JOURNAL OF WASHINGTON IRV-
ING 1828 AND MISCELLANEOUS NOTES
ON MOORISH LEGEND AND HISTORY
EDITED BY STANLEY T. WILLIAMS

NEW YORK AMERICAN BOOK COMPANY
MCMXXXVII

⟨i⟩-⟨xvi⟩, 1-80. Inserted: A two-page map and
4 plates. 7⅞″ x 5³⁄₁₆″.

⟨1-6⁸⟩.

B cloth: blue.

On the copyright page of the first printing:
W.P.I

Deposited Nov. 5, 1937.

H NYPL

10222. Trial without Jury & Other Plays by John Howard Payne   Edited by Codman Hislop and W. R. Richardson

Princeton   New Jersey   Princeton University Press   1940

America's Lost Plays series, Vol. 5.

"Mazeppa; or, the Wild Horse of Tartary," pp. ‹163›-204. "*Mazeppa* . . . was probably never performed . . . written in 1825, when its source, Léopold and Cuvelier's *Mazeppa; ou, le Cheval Tartare*, was produced . . . and published in Paris. Payne's manuscript is dated November 12 of that year, but the play was practically complete by October 2; for at that time Irving, returning it with revisions, advised Payne . . ." —p. ‹165›.

"The Spanish Husband; or, First and Last Love," pp. ‹205›-264. Sometimes titled "The Spanish Hero," "The Painter of His Own Dishonor" and "The Spanish Grandee." The following references to the play are taken from Irving's *Journals*, Vol. 2, 1919, pp. 81 and 83 respectively: Jan. 14, 1825: ". . . *correcting Payne's play of Span[ish] Hero* . . ."; Jan. 19, 1825: ". . . *corrected Payne's play* . . .".

Deposited Sept. 17, 1940.

Note: The contemporary evidence of Irving's letters and journals shows that he assisted Payne and others. Williams (*Life* . . . , 1935, Vol. 1, p. 461) states: "Other plays for which he made suggestions were: *'Twas I, Red Riding Hood, Mazeppa, Peter Smink, Norah, or the Girl of Erin.*" The following notes are pertinent.

Azendai, by John Howard Payne. No record of publication found. For Irving's comments see *Journal*, 1931, pp. 54, 55, 56, 57, 72, 73, 74, 76.

Charles the Second; or, the Merry Monarch . . . , by John Howard Payne, London, 1824. Letter, Irving to his brother Peter, London, May 31, 1824: ". . . I shall assist Payne in pruning the piece to-day, and I have no doubt it will have a good run. Payne intends putting it to press immediately . . ."—*Life and Letters of Washington Irving*, Vol. 2, 1862, p. 194. For other comments see Irving's *Journal*, 1931, pp. 62, 63, 64. The earliest located American edition of *Charles the Second* was issued by Neal & Mackenzie, Philadelphia, 1829.

The Freyschütz; or, the Wild Huntsman of Bohemia . . . , altered from the German of Friedrich Kind, by Barham Livius; music by Carl Maria von Weber, London, 1824. ". . . Wrote hints for Livius' introduction to *Freischütz*—

called on Livius . . ."; ". . . Went to Livius'— worked over one act and preface of *Freischütz* . . ."—*Journals*, 1919, entries for Oct. 6, 8, 1824. For other references see Irving's *Journals*, Vol. 1, 1919, pp. 156, 208, 209. For Irving's version see *The Wild Huntsman*, 1924, above. Williams (*Journal*, 1931, p. 57) errs in stating that Payne did a translation of *The Freyschütz*.

Leocadri, translated from the original French of Eugène Scribe and Mélesville (pseud. of Duveurier, Anne Honoré Joseph, baron). Translated in collaboration with Barham Livius. Presumably unpublished. For Irving's comments see *Journals*, Vol. 2, 1919, pp. 62, 63, 65, 66, 80. Music by Daniel François Auber.

Married and Single, by John Howard Payne. No record of publication. For Irving's comments see *Journal*, 1931, pp. 43, 44.

Norah; or, the Girl of Erin, by John Howard Payne. No record of publication.

Peter Smink; or, the Armistice, a Comic Drama in One Act, adapted from the French by John Howard Payne. According to the front matter "first performed at the Royal Surrey Theatre, July, 1822." No contemporary publication found. A copy in H (London: Thomas Hailes Lacy, n.d.) was issued not before 1857. BAL has found no evidence that Irving worked on this play as early as 1822. Is the *ca.* 1857 printing the one on which Irving worked?

Red Riding Hood, by John Howard Payne. No record of publication.

Richelieu: A Domestic Tragedy, by John Howard Payne, New York, 1826. "In the little comedy of Charles the Second I have referred to the assistance you gave me, without venturing to violate your injunction with regard to the concealment of your name. But that aid has been repeated to such an extent in the present matter, as to render it imperative upon me to offer you my thanks publicly . . ."—from Payne's dedicatory epistle addressed to Irving, p. 4. Many references to Irving's part in the writing of this play are in the *Journal*, 1931, for the period Aug. 29, 1823 to Oct. 23, 1825.

'Twas I; or, the Truth a Lie, a Farce in Two Acts, by John Howard Payne, New York, 1827. The London editions of Thomas Hailes Lacy, issued without date, were published not prior to 1849.

A Year in Spain, by a Young American ‹Alexander Slidell Mackenzie›, 2 Vols., London, 1831. "I send a copy of Slidell's *Year in Spain*, which I corrected for the press, and got Murray to publish . . ."—letter, Irving to Ebenezer Irving, Feb. 22, 1830, *Life and Letters,* Vol. 2, 1862, p. 450. Irving appears to have had no connection with the original edition, Boston, 1829.

H NYPL Y

10223. The Western Journals of Washington Irving Edited and Annotated by John Francis McDermott

Norman   University of Oklahoma Press
MCMXLIV

On copyright page: *First Edition*

American Exploration and Travel Series, Vol. 8.

A newly edited edition of *The Journals . . . ,* Boston, 1919.

"In preparing the text I have made use of a microfilm of the originals and the Trent-Hellman edition published by the Bibliophile Society of Boston in 1919."—P. ix.

Deposited Nov. 26, 1944. Published Nov. 27, 1944 (date taken from an advance copy).

H NYPL

10224. WASHINGTON IRVING IN SPAIN: UNPUBLISHED LETTERS CHIEFLY TO MRS. HENRY O'SHEA, 1844–1854 . . .

⟨n.p., n.d., New York: The New York Public Library, 1958⟩

Cover-title.

⟨1⟩-36, 2 blank leaves. 10" x 7" scant. Pale cream-white paper. Inserted (by wrapping around leaves 2 and 19) is a cut sheet of white calendered paper; on the preliminary leaf of which is printed two halftone portraits, one on the recto, the other on the verso; the conjugate leaf is blank.

⟨-⟩20. *Note:* Signature 2 appears on p. 5, signature mark 3 on p. 13; these, apparently, for use in imposing the *Bulletin.*

On the title-page: *Preprints from the Bulletin of The New York Public Library Volume LXII (December 1958) and Volume LXIII (January 1959)*

Edited by Clara L. Penney.

UV

IN THIS SECTION the following classifications are listed: Reprints issued under Irving's name; and, separate editions, *i.e.,* pieces reprinted from Irving's own books. See *Section III* for a list of books by authors other than Irving containing reprints of Irving material. The list of posthumous reprints is representative, not all-inclusive.

Note: Certain other reprints of Irving's own books are noted in the publication information given in the *Section I* entries.

10225. Salmagundi; or, the Whim-Whams and Opinions of Launcelot Langstaff, Esq., and Others . . . Reprinted from the American Edition, with an Introductory Essay and Explanatory Notes, by John Lambert . . .

London: Printed for J. M. Richardson, 23, Cornhill, opposite the Royal Exchange. 1811.

2 Vols. Boards, printed paper label on spine.

A cursory examination indicates that in spite of certain minor textual variations (by the British editor?) this is, as the title-page states, "reprinted from the American edition."

Also issued two volumes in one, cloth; the style of binding suggests publication *ca.* 1840.

10226. A History of New York . . . the Third Edition. By Diedrich Knickerbocker . . . in Two Volumes . . .

Philadelphia: Published by M. Thomas. J. Maxwell, Printer. <Wm. Fry, Printer.> 1819.

Boards, printed paper label on spine. Title-page deposited March 5, 1819. Listed NAR Sept. 1819.

10227. A History of New York . . . by Diedrich Knickerbocker . . . a New Edition . . .

London: John Murray, Albemarle-Street. 1820.

Boards?

10228. A Humourous History of New York . . . a New Edition. By Diedrich Knickerbocker . . .

London: Printed for W. Wright, 46, Fleet-Street. 1820.

Boards?

10229. Salmagundi; or, the Whim-Whams and Opinions of Launcelot Langstaff, Esq. and Others . . . Third Edition . . .

New-York: Published by Thomas Longworth and Co. 1820.

2 Vols. Vol. 2 imprinted: *New-York: Published by Thomas Longworth and Co. J. Seymour, Printer. 1820.*

Noted only as a single cloth-bound volume, printed paper label on spine; presumably a remainder issued *ca.* 1850.

10230. A History of New York . . . by Diedrich Knickerbocker . . . a New Edition . . .

London: John Murray, Albemarle Street. 1821.

2 Vols. Issued in boards?

10231. A History of New York . . . by Diedrich Knickerbocker . . . a New Edition.

Glasgow: Printed for John Wylie & Co. By Robert Chapman. 1821.

Boards?

10232. The Sketch Book of Geoffrey Crayon . . . a New Edition. In Two Volumes . . .

London: John Murray, Albemarle Street. 1821.

Boards?

10233. The Sketch Book of Geoffrey Crayon . . . New Edition. In Two Volumes . . .

London: John Murray, Albemarle-Street. 1822.

Boards?

10234. Bracebridge Hall; or the Humorists. By Geoffrey Crayon . . . A New Edition. In Two Volumes . . .

London: John Murray, Albemarle Street. 1823.

Boards?

10235. The Sketch Book of Geoffrey Crayon . . .
New Edition. In Two Volumes . . .

London: John Murray, Albemarle Street.
1823.

Boards?

10236. The Sketch Book of Geoffrey Crayon . . .
New Edition. In Two Volumes . . .

Paris: Published by Baudry, 9, Rue du Coq;
and Jules Didot, Senior, 6, Rue du Pont-de-
Lodi. M DCCC XXIII.

Printed paper wrapper?

10237. The Sketch Book of Geoffrey Crayon,
Gent. With the Last Corrections of the Author . . . Eighth Edition . . .

Dresden: Printed for the Editor A. Montucci
LL. D. Sold by Him No. 8. Alt-Markt—
And Friedrich Fleischer, Bookseller, in Leip-
sic. MDCCCXXIII.

Printed paper wrapper?

10238. A History of New York . . . in Two Volumes. Fourth American Edition. By Diedrich
Knickerbocker . . .

New-York: Printed by C. S. Van Winkle, No.
2 Thames-Street. 1824.

Boards? Reviewed by *Minerva* (N.Y.), Aug. 21,
1824, which is quite certain Irving is not the
author and enjoins the author, whoever he is,
"to proceed in the career he has begun" but
hopes that he will "aim at more originality . . .
for the imitation of any writer . . . is an un-
worthy pursuit."

10239. Tales of a Traveller. By Geoffrey Crayon
. . . in Two Volumes . . .

Paris: Published by L. Baudry, at the English,
French, Italian, German, and Spanish Library,
Rue du Coq Saint-Honoré, 1824.

Printed paper wrapper? Listed BF Oct. 30, 1824.

10240. Bracebridge Hall; or the Humorists. By
Geoffrey Crayon . . . a New Edition. In Two
Volumes . . .

London: John Murray, Albemarle Street.
MDCCCXXIV.

Boards?

10241. A History of New-York . . . by Diedrich
Knickerbocker.

London: Printed for Thomas Tegg, 73,

Cheapside; Rodwell and Martin, Bond Street:
Also, R. Griffin and Co. Glasgow. 1824.

Boards?

10242. A History of New-York . . . in Two Volumes. By Diedrich Knickerbocker . . .

Paris: Printed by Jules Didot, Sen. for A. and
W. Galignani, No 18, Rue Vivienne.
M DCCC XXIV.

Printed paper wrapper?

10243. Salmagundi: Or, the Whim-Whams and
Opinions of Launcelot Langstaff, Esq. And
Others. By the Author of Knickerbocker's
History of New York . . .

London: Printed by T. Davison, Whitefriars;
for Thomas Tegg, 73, Cheapside; Rodwell
and Martin, Bond-Street: Also R. Griffin and
Co. Glasgow. 1824.

Boards, printed paper label on spine.

Langfeld-Blackburn (pp. 10-11) state that "the
text differs from that of all preceding editions."
However, the sense of the "Publisher's Notice,"
p. v, indicates that this is a reprint of the Paris,
1824, edition: "The present edition is printed
from one which has been submitted to the revision of one of the authors, who, at first, contemplated making essential alterations . . ." See
the entry (in *Section I*) for the Paris, 1824 (Galignani), edition.

Three forms of the title-page have been seen;
the sequence has not been determined and the
designations are wholly arbitrary:

A: Without the statement *New Edition*.

B: With the statement: *New Edition*.

C: With the statement: *New Edition, Corrected
and Revised by the Author*.

10244. Salmagundi: Or, the Whim-Whams and
Opinions of Launcelot Langstaff, Esq. and
Others . . .

London: Printed and Published by J. Lim-
bird, 143, Strand, (Near Somerset House.)
1824.

Printed paper wrapper?

10245. *Entry cancelled.*

10246. The Sketch Book of Geoffrey Crayon . . .
New Edition. In Two Volumes . . .

Paris: Published by A. and W. Galignani, at

the English, French, Italian, German and Spanish Library, 18, Rue Vivienne. 1824.

Printed paper wrapper?

10247. The Beauties of Washington Irving . . .

Glasgow: Printed for Richard Griffin & Co. 75, Hutcheson Street. MDCCCXXV.

Printed boards. Also issued with the imprint: *London: Printed for John Bumpus, 85, Newgate Street. MDCCCXXV.* See below under 1835.

10248. Bracebridge Hall; or, the Humorists. By Geoffrey Crayon . . . a New Edition. In Two Volumes . . .

London: John Murray, Albemarle Street. MDCCCXXV.

Boards?

10249. A History of New-York . . . by Diedrich Knickerbocker.

London: John Bumpus, 85, Newgate Street; and R. Griffin & Co., Glasgow. 1825.

Boards?

10250. A History of New York . . . by Diedrich Knickerbocker . . .

London. William Charlton Wright, 65, Pater Noster Row. 1825 . . .

Printed boards.

10251. Salmagundi: Or, the Whim-Whams and Opinions of Launcelot Langstaff, Esq. and Others . . .

London: John Bumpus, 85, Newgate Street. 1825.

Boards, printed paper label on spine. Exhibits some textual variations, presumably introduced by the British editor.

10252. The Sketch Book of Geoffrey Crayon . . . A New Edition. In Two Volumes . . .

Paris: Published by L. Baudry . . . 1825.

Printed paper wrapper?

10253. Tales of a Traveller. By Geoffrey Crayon . . . New Edition. In Two Volumes . . .

London: John Murray, Albemarle-Street. 1825.

Boards?

10254. Bracebridge Hall, or the Humourists. A Medley, by Geoffrey Crayon . . . Third American Edition. In Two Volumes . . .

New-York: Printed by C. S. Van Winkle, No. 48 Pine-Street. 1826.

Boards?

10255. The Sketch Book of Geoffrey Crayon . . . New Edition. In Two Volumes . . .

London: John Murray, Albemarle-Street. MDCCCXXVI.

Boards, cloth shelfback, printed paper label on spine.

10256. The Sketch Book of Geoffrey Crayon . . . Fifth American Edition. In Two Volumes . . .

New-York: Printed by C. S. Van Winkle, No. 48 Pine-Street. 1826.

Boards, printed paper label on spine. In this edition "Christmas Day" is broken down into two separate sketches and appears as "Christmas Day" and "Christmas Dinner."

10257. Bracebridge Hall; or the Humorists. By Geoffrey Crayon . . . a New Edition. In Two Volumes . . .

Paris: Published by A. and W. Galignani, at the English, French, Italian, German, and Spanish Library, No 18, Rue Vivienne. 1827.

Printed paper wrapper?

10258. A History of the Life and Voyages of Christopher Columbus . . . In Four Volumes . . .

Paris: Baudry, at the Foreign Library, No 9, Rue du Coq-Saint-Honoré. 1828.

Printed paper wrapper. Also issued with the imprint: *Paris: Published by A. and W. Galignani, at the English, French, Italian, German, and Spanish Library, No 18, Rue Vivienne. 1828.* Both the Baudry and Galignani imprints listed BF March 22, 1828.

10259. A History of New York . . . by Diedrich Knickerbocker.

London: Robert Thurston, Fleet Street. 1828.

Boards?

10260. A Chronicle of the Conquest of Granada . . .

Paris: Published by A. and W. Galignani . . . 1829.

Printed paper wrapper? Listed BF July 4, 1829. Again listed BF July 11, 1829 with the Baudry and Galignani imprints, the Baudry imprint having been erroneously omitted from the July 4 listing.

10261. A History of New-York ... in Two Volumes. Sixth American Edition. By Diedrich Knickerbocker ...

Philadelphia: Carey, Lea & Carey. Chesnut-Street. 1829.

Boards?

10262. The Sketch-Book of Geoffrey Crayon ... in Two Volumes ... Seventh American Edition.

Philadelphia: Carey, Lea & Carey Chesnut-Street. 1829.

Boards, printed paper label on spine. For other so-called "seventh American" editions see under 1830, 1831.

10263. The Devil and Tom Walker: Together with Deacon Grubb and the Old Nick.

Woodstock, Vt. Printed and Published by R. & A. Colton. 1830.

Anonymous. Unprinted blue paper wrapper. "The Devil and Tom Walker" previously in *Tales of a Traveller,* 1824. Authorship of "Deacon Grubb and the Old Nick" unknown.

10264. A History of New-York ... in Two Volumes. Seventh American Edition. By Diedrich Knickerbocker ...

Philadelphia: Carey & Lea Chesnut-Street. 1830.

Boards? Vol. 2 dated 1831. For other so-called "seventh American" editions see below under 1832, 1834, 1835.

10265. The Life and Voyages of Christopher Columbus, by Washington Irving. (Abridged by the Same.) ...

Paris: Baudry and Galignani, 1830.

Not seen. Title and imprint postulated. For comment see entry No. 10127.

10266. The Life and Voyages of Christopher Columbus, by Washington Irving. (Abridged by the Same.) ...

Stereotyped by James Conner, for G. & C. & H. Carvill, 108 Broadway, New-York. 1830.

Leather. For comment see entry No. 10127.

10267. The Sketch-Book of Geoffrey Crayon ... in Two Volumes ... Seventh American Edition.

Philadelphia: Carey & Lea Chesnut-Street. 1830.

Boards, printed paper label on spine. For other so-called "seventh American" editions see under 1829, 1831.

10268. Voyages of the Companions of Columbus ...

Paris: Published by A. and W. Galignani, at the English, French, Italian, German, and Spanish Library, No 18, Rue Vivienne. 1831.

Printed paper wrapper? Listed BF Feb. 26, 1831.

10269. Voyages and Discoveries of the Companions of Columbus ...

Paris, Baudry, Bookseller in Foreign Languages, 9, Rue du Coq-Saint-Honoré; 1831.

Printed paper wrapper? Listed BF March 26, 1831.

10270. Bracebridge Hall: Or, the Humourists. A Medley. By Geoffrey Crayon ... in Two Volumes ... Fourth American Edition.

Philadelphia: Carey & Lea Chesnut-Street. 1831.

Boards, printed paper label on spine. For another so-called "fourth American" edition see below under 1835.

10271. The Life and Voyages of Christopher Columbus. By Washington Irving. (Abridged by the Same.)

London: John Murray, Albemarle-Street. MDCCCXXXI.

Cloth? See entry No. 10127.

10272. The Sketch-Book of Geoffrey Crayon ... in Two Volumes ... Seventh American Edition ...

Philadelphia: Carey & Lea Chesnut-Street. 1831.

Boards, printed paper label on spine. For other so-called "seventh American" editions see under 1829, 1830.

10273. The Alhambra; or the New Sketch Book ...

Paris: Published by A. and W. Galignani, at the English, French, Italian, German, and Spanish Library, No 18, Rue Vivienne. 1832.

Printed yellow paper wrapper pasted over white inner wrapper. Listed BF May 26, 1832.

10274. A History of New-York ... in Two Volumes. Seventh American Edition. By Diedrich Knickerbocker ...

Philadelphia: Carey & Lea   Chesnut-Street. 1832.

Boards, printed paper label on spine? For other so-called "seventh American" editions see under 1830, 1834, 1835.

10275. The Sketch-Book of Geoffrey Crayon ... in Two Volumes ...

Philadelphia: Carey & Lea   Chesnut-Street. 1832.

Boards?

10276. Tales of a Traveller. By Geoffrey Crayon ... Third American Edition. In Two Volumes ...

Philadelphia: Carey & Lea. Chestnut Street. 1832.

Boards, printed paper label on spine.

10277. A History of New York ... by Diedrich Knickerbocker.

London: Printed for T. T. & J. Tegg, 73, Cheapside; and Richard Griffin and Co., Glasgow. MDCCCXXXIII.

Cloth, printed paper label on spine.

10278. The Life and Voyages of Christopher Columbus by Washington Irving. (Abridged by the Same.) ... A New Edition, with Additions and Improvements, by the Author.

⟨New York⟩ Printed by J. & J. Harper, 82 Cliff-Street. 1833.

Noted only in publisher's leather. For comment see entry No. 10127.

10279. The Life and Voyages of Christopher Columbus by Washington Irving. (Abridged by the Same.) ... a New Edition, with Additions and Improvements, by the Author.

⟨New York⟩ N. & J. White. Printed by J. & J. Harper, 82 Cliff-Street. 1833.

Leather? For comment see entry No. 10127.

10280. The Complete Works of Washington Irving in One Volume, with a Memoir of the Author.

Paris, Baudry's European Library ... 1834.

Issued in four paper parts. The individual parts listed BF, 1-4 respectively, as follows: Aug. 23,

1834; Sept. 27, 1834; Oct. 18, 1834; Nov. 8, 1834.

10281. A History of New-York ... in Two Volumes. Seventh American Edition. By Diedrich Knickerbocker ...

Philadelphia: Carey & Lea   Chesnut-Street. 1834.

Boards, printed paper label on spine? For other so-called "seventh American" editions see under 1830, 1832, 1835.

10282. The Sketch-Book of Geoffrey Crayon, Esq. A New Edition. In Two Volumes ...

London: John Murray, Albemarle Street. MDCCCXXXIV.

Cloth?

10283. A Tour on the Prairies ...

Paris: Published by A. and W. Galignani and Co, Rue Vivienne, No 18. 1835.

Printed paper wrapper? A Baudry 12mo printing listed BF March 21, 1835; a Baudry 18mo printing listed BF March 28, 1835. The Galignani printing listed BF March 28, 1835.

10284. Abbotsford and Newstead Abbey ...

Paris. Baudry's European Library ... 1835.

Printed paper wrapper? A 12mo printing listed BF May 16, 1835; a 16mo printing listed BF May 23, 1835. A *Galignani* printing, 12mo, listed BF May 23, 1835.

10285. The Beauties of Washington Irving ...

Philadelphia: Carey, Lea, & Blanchard. 1835.

Pp. 270. In some copies the copyright notice in the name of Washington Irving is pasted to the verso of the title-leaf; the pasted notice conceals no printing.

According to Kaser 1000 copies printed Aug. 31, 1835.

Listed NAR Oct. 1835. Reviewed NEM Nov. 1835. For prior British publication see above under 1825.

"The selection bearing the foregoing title was not made by Mr. Irving. It originally appeared in England ⟨in 1825⟩, and was the piratical act of some English bookseller. A copy was stereotyped by some American publisher, and was about to be put to press in this country, when he was informed that he would be liable to prosecution for infringing the copyrights of the works selected from. Mr. I. purchased the plates to destroy them. He was afterwards in-duced to permit us to issue an edition for our own benefit. The copyright was taken out and advertised by Mr. Irving's agent, without his knowledge.

"This explanation is due to Mr. I., that he may not stand chargeable with the indelicacy of selecting and pointing out any portions of his writings as 'beauties'."—Publisher's note, front matter of Irving's *Legends of the Conquest of Spain,* Philadelphia, 1835.

10286. The Beauties of Washington Irving ... the Fourth Edition.

London: Printed for Thomas Tegg and Son, Cheapside; R. Griffin and Co. Glasgow; and Tegg, Wise, and Co. Dublin. 1835.

Advertised LG Dec. 19, 26, 1835.

10287. Legends of the Conquest of Spain. By the Author of "The Sketch-Book."

London: John Murray, Albemarle Street. MDCCCXXXV.

Boards, cloth shelfback, printed paper label on spine.

Advertised Ath Dec. 5, 1835, as *published this day.* Reviewed Ath Dec. 12, 1835; LG Dec. 12, 19, 1835. Listed LG Dec. 19, 1835; Ath Dec. 26, 1835. The Galignani and Baudry (Paris) editions listed BF Jan. 25, 1836.

10288. Bracebridge Hall: Or, the Humourists. A Medley. By Geoffrey Crayon ... in Two Volumes ... Fourth American Edition.

Philadelphia: Carey & Lea Chesnut-Street. 1835.

Boards, printed paper label on spine. For another so-called "fourth American" edition see above under 1831.

10289. Bracebridge Hall: Or, the Humourists. A Medley. By Geoffrey Crayon ... in Two Volumes ... a New Edition.

Philadelphia: Carey, Lea, & Blanchard. 1835.

Boards, printed paper label on spine. Imprint dated *1835;* copyright notice dated *1836.*

10290. The History of New York ... by Diedrich Knickerbocker.

London: Printed for T. T. & J. Tegg, 73, Cheapside; and Richard Griffin and Co., Glasgow. MDCCCXXXV.

10291. A History of New-York ... in Two Volumes. Seventh American Edition. By Diedrich Knickerbocker ...

Philadelphia: Carey & Lea Chesnut-Street. 1835.

Boards, printed paper label on spine. For other so-called "seventh American" editions see above under 1830, 1832, 1834.

10292. The History of Rip Van Winkle ...

Edinburgh: Printed for Oliver & Boyd, Tweedale-Court. Price Twopence. ⟨n.d., *ca.* 1835⟩

Printed paper wrapper. Anonymous.

10293. The Life and Voyages of Christopher Columbus, by Washington Irving. Abridged and Arranged by the Author, Expressly for the Use of Schools.

New York: Published by N. and J. White, 108 Pearl-Street. 1835.

Printed paper boards sides, leather shelfback. For comment see entry No. 10127.

10294. The Sketch-Book of Geoffrey Crayon ... in Two Volumes ... a New Edition.

Philadelphia: Carey, Lea, & Blanchard. 1835.

Cloth, printed paper label on spine. Also: Boards, printed paper label on spine.

10295. The Sketch-Book of Geoffrey Crayon ...

Paris, Baudry's European Library ... 1836.

Printed paper wrapper? Listed BF March 12, 1836.

10296. Astoria ...

London: Richard Bentley, New Burlington Street. 1836.

3 Vols. Boards? Announced as *just ready* Ath Oct. 15, 1836; as *now ready* Ath Oct. 22, 1836. Listed Ath Oct. 22, 1836. Reviewed LG Oct. 22, 1836; Ath Oct. 22, 29, 1836. A *second edition* advertised LG Feb. 4, 1837; Ath Feb. 4, 1837. Reissued, 1838, as Vol. 2 of *Standard Library of Popular Modern Literature.* Advertised PC Nov. 15, 1848, under the title *Adventures beyond the Rocky Mountains.* A *Routledge* edition listed LG July 13, 1850; Ath July 13, 1850; PC Aug. 1, 1850. A *Bohn* edition listed Ath Sept. 7, 1850, PC Sept. 16, 1850.

10297. A History of New-York ... in Two Volumes. A New Edition. By Diedrich Knickerbocker ...

Philadelphia: Carey, Lea, & Blanchard. 1836.

Boards, printed paper label on spine. Also: Cloth, printed paper label on spine.

Two states (printings?) of Vol. 1 have been noted: A: The copyright notice is in 26 lines; B: The copyright notice is in 3 lines.

Noted as *already issued* K Oct. 1836.

10298. Astoria; or, Enterprise beyond the Rocky Mountains . . .

Paris, Published by A. and W. Galignani and Co., Rue Vivienne, No 18. 1836.

Printed paper wrapper? Listed BF Nov. 26, 1836. Also issued with the imprint of *Baudry's European Library,* listed BF Nov. 26, 1836.

10299. The Alhambra . . . by the Author of "The Sketch Book." In Two Volumes . . . a New Edition.

Philadelphia: Carey, Lea and Blanchard. 1836.

Boards, printed paper label on spine?

10300. Bracebridge Hall . . . by Geoffrey Crayon . . . in Two Volumes . . . a New Edition.

Philadelphia: Carey, Lea, & Blanchard. 1836.

Cloth, printed paper label on spine.

10301. A History of New-York . . . by Diedrich Knickerbocker.

London: Printed for Thomas Tegg and Son, 73, Cheapside. MDCCCXXXVI.

10302. The Sketch-Book of Geoffrey Crayon . . . in Two Volumes . . . a New Edition.

Philadelphia: Carey, Lea, & Blanchard. 1836.

Cloth, printed paper label on spine.

10303. Tales of a Traveller, by Geoffrey Crayon . . . in Two Volumes . . . a New Edition.

Philadelphia: Carey, Lea, & Blanchard. 1836.

Cloth?

10304. The Beauties of Washington Irving . . .

Philadelphia: Carey, Lea, & Blanchard. 1837.

10305. A Chronicle of the Conquest of Granada. By Fray Antonio Agapida. In Two Volumes . . . a New Edition.

Philadelphia: Carey, Lea, & Blanchard. 1837.

Cloth?

10306. Essays and Sketches . . .

London: Charles Tilt, Fleet Street. MDCCC-XXXVII.

Listed Ath July 1, 1837.

10307. A History of New-York, from the Beginning of the World to the End of the Dutch Dynasty . . . in Two Volumes. A New Edition. By Diedrich Knickerbocker . . .

Philadelphia: Carey, Lea, & Blanchard. 1837.

Cloth, printed paper label on spine.

10308. The Sketch-Book of Geoffrey Crayon . . . in Two Volumes . . . a New Edition.

Philadelphia: Carey, Lea, & Blanchard 1837.

Cloth?

10309. Tales of a Traveller, by Geoffrey Crayon . . . in Two Volumes . . . a New Edition.

Philadelphia: Carey, Lea, & Blanchard. 1837.

Cloth?

10310. The Beauties of Washington Irving . . .

Philadelphia: Carey, Lea, & Blanchard. 1838.

10311. The Beauties of Washington Irving . . .

Philadelphia: Carey, Lea & Blanchard, for George W. Gorton. 1838.

Leather.

10312. Bracebridge Hall: Or, the Humourists. A Medley. By Geoffrey Crayon . . . in Two Volumes . . . a New Edition.

Philadelphia: Carey, Lea, & Blanchard. 1838.

Cloth, printed paper label on spine.

10313. A Chronicle of the Conquest of Granada. By Fray Antonio Agapida. In Two Volumes . . . a New Edition.

Philadelphia: Carey, Lea, & Blanchard. 1838.

Cloth, printed paper label on spine.

10314. The Beauties of Washington Irving . . .

Philadelphia: Lea & Blanchard, Successors to Carey & Co. 1839.

10315. Bracebridge Hall: Or, the Humourists. A Medley. By Geoffrey Crayon . . . in Two Volumes . . . a New Edition.

Philadelphia: Lea & Blanchard, Successors to Carey & Co. 1839.

Cloth, printed paper label on spine.

10316. The History of New York . . . by Diedrich Knickerbocker.

⟨Smith's Standard Library ... London: William Smith, 113, Fleet Street ... MDCCCXXXIX ...⟩

Printed paper wrapper; imprint from wrapper.

10317. A History of New York ... by Diedrich Knickerbocker. A New Edition.

London: Printed for Thomas Tegg, 73, Cheapside; Tegg and Co., Dublin; R. Griffin and Co., Glasgow; also, J. and S. A. Tegg, Sydney and Hobart Town. MDCCCXXXIX.

Cloth?

10318. The Life and Voyages of Christopher Columbus ... Abridged ... by the Author ...

New-York: Published by Collins, Keese & Co., No. 254 Pearl Street. 1839.

Cloth? For comment see entry No. 10127.

10319. Salmagundi: Or, the Whim-Whams and Opinions of Launcelot Langstaff, Esq. and Others. By the Author of "Knickerbocker's History of New York," ... New Edition, Corrected and Revised by the Author.

London: Printed for Thomas Tegg, 73, Cheapside; Tegg and Co., Dublin; R. Griffin and Co., Glasgow; also, J. and S. A. Tegg, Sydney and Hobart Town. MDCCCXXXIX.

10320. The Sketch-Book of Geoffrey Crayon ... in Two Volumes ... a New Edition.

Philadelphia: Lea & Blanchard, Successors to Carey & Co. 1839.

Cloth, printed paper label on spine.

10321. The Gentleman in Black, and Tales of Other Days. With Illustrations by George Cruikshank and Others.

London: Printed for Charles Daly, 19, Red Lion Square. 1840.

Cloth?

10322. Tales of the Alhambra; to Which are Added Legends of the Conquest of Spain ...

Paris: Baudry's European Library ... 1840.

Printed paper wrapper?

10323. The Works of Washington Irving ... in Two Volumes. With a Portrait of the Author ...

Philadelphia: Lea and Blanchard. 1840.

Listed NAR July, 1840. Reviewed K July, 1840.

10324. The Beauties of Washington Irving ...

Philadelphia: Lea & Blanchard. 1841.

10325. Bracebridge Hall: Or, the Humourists. A Medley. By Geoffrey Crayon ... in Two Volumes ... a New Edition.

Philadelphia: Lea & Blanchard. 1841.

Cloth?

10326. The Life and Voyages of Christopher Columbus. By Washington Irving, (Abridged by the Same.) Second Edition.

London: Printed for Thomas Tegg, 73, Cheapside. 1841.

Cloth? For comment see entry No. 10127.

10327. Salmagundi; or the Whim-Whams and Opinions of Launcelot Langstaff, Esq. ...

London: Published by C. Daly, Red Lion Square. 1841.

Cloth?

10328. Tales of a Traveller. By Geoffrey Crayon ... in Two Volumes ... a New Edition.

Philadelphia: Lea & Blanchard. 1841.

Cloth, printed paper label on spine.

10329. A History of New-York ... in Two Volumes. A New Edition. By Diedrich Knickerbocker ...

Philadelphia: Lea & Blanchard. 1842.

Cloth, printed paper label on spine.

10330. Biography and Poetical Remains of the Late Margaret Miller Davidson. By Washington Irving ... a New Edition, Revised.

Philadelphia: Lea and Blanchard. 1843.

Printed paper wrapper.

10331. Essays and Sketches ...

London: David Bogue, Fleet Street. MDCCCXLIV.

10332. ... Sands of Gold, (Sifted from the Flood of Fugitive Literature,) Number One: Containing ... The Wife, by Washington Irving ...

New York: Morris & Willis, Publishers, Office of The New Mirror No. 4 Ann-Street. 1844.

Printed paper wrapper. Cover-title. At head of title: Price] Double Extra of The New Mirror. [25 Cents.

Issued as *The Mirror Library*, No. 15.

10333. The Life and Voyages of Christopher Columbus, by Washington Irving. Abridged and Arranged by the Author, Expressly for the Use of Schools.

Bath, N. Y. R. L. Underhill & Co. 1844.

Leather? For comment see entry No. 10127.

10334. Voyages and Discoveries of the Companions of Columbus, by Washington Irving ⟨sic⟩. With a Complete Vocabulary Compiled by Dr. E. Amthor. Revised Edition.

Leipzig, Published by Renger. 1846.

Printed paper wrapper?

10335. The Scenery of the Catskill Mountains as Described by Irving, Cooper, Bryant, Willis Gaylord Clark, N. P. Willis ... Park Benjamin ... and Other Eminent Writers.

New-York: Published by D. Fanshaw, 575 Broadway, Printing-Office, 35 Ann, Corner of Nassau-St. Price 12½ Cents. ⟨n.d., 1847?⟩

Cover-title. Printed paper wrapper.

Five editions of this publication have been noted:

1

Pp. 39. Imprint as above. On p. ⟨1⟩ the "Note by the Compiler" comprises 7 lines. Copy in B.

2

Pp. 39. Imprint: *New-York: D. Fanshaw, Publisher, and Book and Job Printer, Corner of Ann and Nassau-streets. ⟨n.d.⟩.* The "Notice" by the compiler, p. ⟨1⟩, comprises 10 lines. Copy in H.

3

Pp. 49. Imprint: *New-York: D. Fanshaw, Publisher, and Book and Job Printer, Corner of Ann and Nassau-streets. ⟨n.d.⟩.* The "Notice" by the compiler, p. ⟨1⟩, comprises 13 lines. Copy in H inscribed by early owner July 9, 1862.

4

Pp. 49. Imprint: *Catskill   Joseph Joesbury, Printer, "Journal Office." 1864.* Copy in CU.

5

Pp. 49. Imprint: *Catskill: J. B. Hall & Son, Recorder Office, 1872.* Copy in H.

10335A. Illustrations of Rip Van Winkle ... by Felix O C Darley ...

⟨New York⟩ The American Art-Union MDCCC-XLVIII.

Printed paper wrapper. The Cundall (London) edition advertised as *just published* Ath April 13, 1850.

10335B. A History of the Earth and Animated Nature, by Oliver Goldsmith. With ... a Life of the Author, by Washington Irving ... in Two Volumes ...

London, Edinburgh, and Dublin. A. Fullarton and Co. 1848.

Cloth? Advertised (prematurely?) Ath March 20, 1847, as *just published;* but no record of 1847 publication found in PC's annual catalog of 1847. A presumed reprint listed PC Jan. 1, 1850; and a printing, almost certainly Fullarton's, listed PC Oct. 1, 1850; Ath Dec. 14, 1850. Another⟨?⟩ edition (London: Orr) listed PC Jan. 1, 1851.

10336. Tales of a Traveller. By Geoffrey Crayon ... New Edition.

London: John Murray, Albemarle Street. 1848.

Cloth?

10337. The Crayon Reading Book: Comprising Selections from the Various Writings of Washington Irving. Prepared for the Use of Schools.

New-York: Geo. P. Putnam, 155 Broadway. 1849.

Cloth, leather shelfback. Listed LW Aug. 18, 1849. Deposited Feb. 2, 1850.

10338. Oliver Goldsmith: A Biography ...

London: John Murray, Albemarle Street. 1849.

Listed Ath Oct. 27, 1849; PC Nov. 1, 1849. A Routledge (London) edition listed PC Oct. 1, 1851. For further comment see in Sec. I: *The Miscellaneous Works of Oliver Goldsmith ...,* 1825.

10339. The Life and Voyages of Christopher Columbus; together with the Voyages of His Companions ... a New and Revised Edition. In Three Volumes ...

London: John Murray, Albemarle Street. 1849.

Advertised Ath April 28, 1849, as *nearly ready.* Advertised under *forthcoming books* PC Oct. 15, 1849; Ath Nov. 3, 1849. Advertised as *forthcoming* Ath Nov. 17, 1849; for *December* Ath Nov. 10 and Dec. 1, 1849. Advertised as *ready* Ath Dec. 8, 1849. Listed Ath and PC Dec. 15, 1849. The *Bohn* (London) edition issued in

1850; see below. Other London editions: *Routledge*, listed Ath May 11, 1850; PC June 1, 1850; *Bickers & Son*, listed Bkr Dec. 2, 1876; *Cassell & Co.*, listed Ath Oct. 3, 1885.

10340. Illustrations of the Legend of Sleepy Hollow ... by Felix O C Darley ...

⟨New York⟩ The American Art-Union MDCCC-XLIX

Printed paper wrapper.

10341. Lives of Mahomet and His Successors ... in Two Volumes ...

London: John Murray, Albemarle Street. 1850.

Vol. 1, p. ⟨iii⟩: *Life of Mahomet* ... Vol. 2, p. ⟨i⟩: *Lives of the Successors of Mahomet* ...

Vol. 1: Advertised for *January,* Ath Dec. 29, 1849; as *shortly* PC Jan. 1, 1850; for Jan. 21, Ath Jan. 5, 1850; for *next week* Ath Jan. 12, 1850; for *next week* PC Jan. 15, 1850. Reviewed LG Jan. 26, 1850. Listed PC Feb. 1, 1850; Ath and LG Feb. 2, 1850.

Vol. 2: Advertised for *next week* PC Feb. 15, 1850; Ath Feb. 16, 1850; for March 20, PC March 15, 1850; Ath March 16, 1850. Listed Ath and LG April 6, 1850. Reviewed LG April 13, 1850. Listed PC April 15, 1850.

10342. Life of Mahomet ...

London: Henry G. Bohn, York Street, Covent Garden. 1850.

Cloth? "... This volume ... was published at New York in December last, imported and sold here in January, more than a fortnight before any English edition appeared ..."—From the publisher's preliminary advertisement, dated Feb. 21, 1850.

Advertised as *now ready* Ath Feb. 23, 1850; PC March 1, 1850. Listed Ath and LG Feb. 23, 1850. This, together with *Lives of the Successors of Mahomet,* issued as a single volume; listed PC May 15, 1850.

10343. The Life of Mahomet ...

London   George Routledge & Co., Soho Square. 1850.

Listed PC March 15, 1850, *boards* only. Advertised as both cloth; and, boards, Ath March 23, 1850.

10344. Lives of the Successors of Mahomet ...

London: Henry G. Bohn, York Street, Covent Garden. 1850.

Cloth? Listed Ath April 20, 1850; PC May 1, 1850. This, together with *Life of Mahomet,* issued as a single volume; listed PC May 15, 1850.

10345. Lives of Mahomet and His Successors ...

London: George Routledge & Co., Soho Square. 1850.

Printed paper boards; and, cloth.

Advertised as *now ready* (both bindings) Ath April 13, 1850. Listed (boards only) PC May 1, 1850. Reviewed LG May 4, 1850. Reprinted together with *The Life of Mahomet,* 1850, two volumes in one, and listed PC June 15, 1850. A *new edition* advertised Ath Dec. 6, 1851, as in cloth, edges plain; and, cloth, edges gilded. Reprinted and reissued under the revised title *Lives of the Successors of Mahomet.*

10346. Lives of Mahomet and His Successors ...

Paris, Baudry's European Library, A. and W. Galignani and Co. ... 1850

Printed paper wrapper? Listed BF May 4, 1850.

10347. The Voyages and Discoveries of the Companions of Columbus ... Author's Revised Edition ...

London: Henry G. Bohn, York Street, Covent Garden. 1850.

Printed paper boards. Issued as a double volume in *Bohn's Shilling Series.* Listed Ath and LG June 29, 1850; PC July 15, 1850. As separate volumes (not seen by BAL) Vol. 1 listed by Ath June 1, 1850; Vol. 2 listed by Ath June 15, 1850.

10348. Astoria ... Author's Revised Edition ...

London: Henry G. Bohn, York Street, Covent Garden. 1850.

Printed paper boards, leather shelfback. Issued as a double volume in *Bohn's Shilling Series.* Advertised for *September* Ath Aug. 31, 1850. Listed Ath Sept. 7, 1850; PC Sept. 16, 1850.

10349. Bracebridge Hall; or, the Humorists. A Medley. By Geoffrey Crayon ... Author's Revised Edition.

London: Henry G. Bohn, York Street, Covent Garden. 1850.

Printed paper boards? Issued as a double volume in *Bohn's Shilling Series.* Advertised for *September* Ath Aug. 31, 1850. Listed Ath Sept. 7, 1850; PC Sept. 16, 1850.

10350. The Life of Mahomet . . .

Leipzig   Bernh. Tauchnitz Jun. 1850.

Printed paper wrapper. Issued as No. 191 of *Collection of British Authors Series.* Reprinted and reissued not before 1859 with the publisher's later style of imprint: *Leipzig Bernhard Tauchnitz 1850.*

10351. Lives of the Successors of Mahomet . . .

Leipzig   Bernh. Tauchnitz Jun. 1850.

Printed paper wrapper. Issued as No. 192 of *Collection of British Authors Series.* Reprinted and reissued with the publisher's later style of imprint: *Leipzig Bernhard Tauchnitz 1850.*

10352. Tales of the Alhambra . . . Revised and Corrected by the Author.

London: Richard Bentley, New Burlington Street; and Bell & Bradfute, Edinburgh. 1850.

Cloth? Other London editions (noted but not seen): *Routledge:* Listed Ath July 6, 1850; PC July 15, 1850; *Bohn:* Listed Ath and LG July 13, 1850.

10353. Illustrations of Washington Irving's Dolph Heyliger Designed and Etched by John W Ehninger

New-York   George P Putnam   155 Broadway
M DCCC LI

Advertised as *now ready* LW Dec. 14, 1850; for *Saturday* LW Dec. 21, 1850; as *now ready* LW Dec. 28, 1850. Distributed in London by Chapman; listed PC April 15, 1851. An Addey edition advertised for *immediate publication* PC Dec. 1, 1851; advertised as *just ready* Ath Dec. 13, 1851.

10354. Oliver Goldsmith's Works: Poems, Comedies, Essays, Vicar of Wakefield: With Life by Washington Irving . . .

London: Charles Daly, Greville Street, Hatton Garden. ⟨n.d., 1851⟩

"The *Life* . . . has been epitomised . . . Stripped of all the superfluous matter . . ."—Editorial note, p. lxiv.

Advertised (but not as a new book) PC Jan. 16, 1851, as in cloth; and, leather.

10355. Abbotsford, and Newstead Abbey . . . with an Appendix, Peculiar to the Present Edition.

London: Henry G. Bohn, York Street, Covent Garden. 1853.

Cloth?

10356. A History of the Earth and Animated Nature, by Oliver Goldsmith. With . . . a Life of the Author, by Washington Irving . . . in Two Volumes . . .

London, Edinburgh, and Dublin: A. Fullarton and Co. 1853.

Cloth?

10357. Sketch of William Roscoe . . .

Liverpool: Printed by Harris and Company. ⟨1853⟩

Printed paper wrapper.

10358. Home Authors and Home Artists; or, American Scenery, Art, and Literature. Comprising a Series of Essays by Washington Irving, W. C. Bryant, Fenimore Cooper Miss Cooper, N. P. Willis, Bayard Taylor, H. T. Tuckerman . . .

New York: Leavitt and Allen, 27 Dey Street. ⟨n.d., 1854⟩

Sheets of *The Home Book of the Picturesque,* 1852 (BAL No. 1648), reissued with cancel title-leaf. Issued in cloth; and, leather.

Advertised for Sept. 20, in NLG Sept. 15, 1854; as *published* NLG Oct. 16, 1854.

10359. The Life and Voyages of Christopher Columbus. By Washington Irving. (Abridged by the Same.) . . .

New York: Harper & Brothers, Publishers, 329 & 331 Pearl Street, Franklin Square. 1855.

Reprinted and reissued under date 1856. For comment see entry No. 10127.

10360. Wolfert's Roost and Other Tales . . .

London: Henry G. Bohn, York Street, Covent Garden. 1855.

Advertised Ath March 10, 1855; PC March 15, 1855. Listed Ath March 10, 1855; PC March 15, 1855. According to contemporary notices issued in boards and in a "fine edition." Noted only in rebound state.

10361. The Battle of Bunker Hill, June 17, 1775 . . .

. . . Oak Hall   Nos. 32 & 34 North Street, Boston, Mass. ⟨n.d., ca. 1855⟩

Single cut sheet. Wove paper. Printed in three columns on the recto only. Title at head. Imprint taken from illustration at center of sheet. 18¾″ x 9⁄16″. Reprinted from *Life of Washington,* Vol. 1, Chap. 41.

10362. Selections from the Works of Washington Irving . . .

Leipzig: F. A. Brockhaus. 1856.

Printed paper wrapper.

10363. Wolfert Webber; or, Golden Dreams . . .

London: Henry Lea, Warwick Lane. 1856

Printed paper wrapper. Issued as *The Fireside Library*, Vol. 9.

"Wolfert Webber" previously in *Tales of a Traveller*, 1824. Also contains "The Patriot Slave"; by Irving?

10364. The Gentleman in Black, and Tales of Other Days. With Illustrations by George Cruikshank. And Others.

St. Louis   Edwards & Bushell   1857.

Anonymous. Cloth?

10365. Irving Vignettes. Vignette Illustrations of the Writings of Washington Irving . . .

New York: G. P. Putnam, No. 321 Broadway. 1857.

Vignette title-page dated 1858. Reprinted and reissued as *Illustrated Beauties of Irving*, 1858.

10366. Salmagundi; or, the Whim-Whams and Opinions of Launcelot Langstaff, Esq., and Others . . .

New York: G. P. Putnam & Co., 321 Broadway. 1857.

Putnam's Railway Classics series. Two states (printings?) noted; the sequence has not been determined and the following designations are for identification only: A: p. ⟨244⟩ blank; B: p. ⟨244⟩ imprinted with notes.

10367. Illustrated Beauties of Irving. Vignette Illustrations of the Writings of Washington Irving . . .

Philadelphia: Childs & Peterson, 602, Arch Street, 1858.

Reprint of *Irving Vignettes*, 1857, above.

10368. Irving Vignettes. Vignette Illustrations of the Writings of Washington Irving . . .

New York: G. P. Putnam, No. 321 Broadway. 1858.

Cloth; and, leather. Issued in two formats: *small paper*, 7⅟₁₆″ x 4⅛″; *large paper*, 8⅟₁₆″ x 6⅛″. For an earlier printing see above under 1857.

10369. Salmagundi . . . by William Irving, James Kirke Paulding and Washington Irving . . . Printed from the Original Edition, with a Preface and Notes by Evert A. Duyckinck.

New York: G. P. Putnam, 115 Nassau Street, 1860.

Noted as *received* BM May 15, 1860. Advertised for May 12 BM May 15, 1860. Listed BM June 1, 1860.

Issued in three formats:

National Edition: Leaf 7⅝″ full x 5¼″. Covers bevelled. At foot of spine: *National Edition.* Sheets bulk 1⅛″. Noted in A cloth.

Trade Edition: Leaf 7⅝″ x 5″. Covers not bevelled. Format not identified on spine. Sheets bulk ⅞″. Noted in BD cloth.

Large Paper Edition: Leaf 8⅝″ x 6⅛″ (or larger?). Sheets bulk 1⅛″ full. Noted only in ⟨publisher's?⟩ three-quarter leather.

10370. Irving Gems. Selected from the Works of Washington Irving. By J.H.B.

Buffalo: Breed, Butler & Co. 1861.

Deposited Sept. 22, 1862. BAL has not checked the text of this miniature but assumes that it is, as the title-page indicates, all reprint. Reissued not before 1866 imprinted: *Buffalo: Breed, Lent & Co. ⟨1861⟩*

10371. The Hudson Legends . . .

New York: G. P. Putnam, 441 Broadway. MDCCCLXIV.

Sheets of the 1864 (Putnam) printings of "Rip Van Winkle" and "Legend of Sleepy Hollow" issued as a single volume with general title-page as above.

Advertised APC Sept. 15, 1863. Advertised for Nov. 10 ALG Nov. 2, 1863. Listed ALG Nov. 16, 1863.

10372. Legend of Sleepy Hollow . . .

New York: G. P. Putnam, 441 Broadway. MDCCCLXIV.

Printed paper boards, printed paper label on front. Advertised APC Sept. 15, 1863. Listed ALG Nov. 16, 1863.

10373. Rip Van Winkle . . .

New York: G. P. Putnam, 441 Broadway. MDCCCLXIV.

Printed paper boards, printed paper label on front. Advertised APC Sept. 15, 1863. Listed ALG Nov. 16, 1863.

10374. ... "A Time of Unexampled Prosperity" ...

New-York   Office of the Rebellion Record 1864

Printed paper wrapper? At head of title: *Reading on the Rail*. Reprinted from *Wolfert's Roost*, 1855. Noticed ALG Aug. 1, 1864.

10375. Sketch Book of Geoffrey Crayon Gent. Artist's Edition ...

New York: G. P. Putnam, 441 Broadway. M DCCC LXIV.

Noted only in publisher's leather.

10376. The Life and Voyages of Christopher Columbus. By Washington Irving. (Abridged by the Same.) ...

London: William Tegg, 1866.

Not seen. Title and imprint postulated. Presumably a reprint. Entry from advertisements in PC May 15, June 1, 1866; listed PC June 15, 1866. For comment see entry No. 10127.

10377. Wolfert's Roost and Other Papers, Now First Collected ... Author's Revised Edition.

New York: G. P. Putnam; Hurd and Houghton. Cleveland: Ingham and Bragg. 1866.

Cloth?

10378. Biographies and Miscellaneous Papers ... Collected and Arranged by Pierre Irving

London Bell and Daldy York Street Covent Garden 1867

Listed Ath Oct 19; PC Nov. 1, 1867.

10379. Christmas in England. Papers from the "Sketch-Book" ...

New York: G. P. Putnam; Hurd and Houghton. Riverside Press. 1867.

10380. Spanish Papers and Other Miscellanies, Hitherto Unpublished or Uncollected ... in Two Volumes ...

New York: G. P. Putnam and Son, 661 Broadway. Opposite Bond Street. 1867.

"One hundred copies printed on large paper" —Certificate of issue. Leaf: 8¼″ x 5¹³⁄₁₆″. Also a small paper printing of this date?

10381. The Life and Voyages of Christopher Columbus; to Which are Added Those of His Companions ... Author's Revised Edition ...

New York G. P. Putnam's Sons 27 and 29 West 23d Street <1868; *i.e., ca.* 1887>

3 Vols. *People's Edition.* Vol. 1 dated <1868>; Vols. 2-3 dated 1887.

10382. Biographies and Miscellanies ... Edited by ... Pierre M. Irving.

New York: G. P. Putnam and Son, 661 Broadway, opposite Bond Street. 1869.

Cloth?

10383. Rip   A Legend of the Kaatskill Mountains ...

New York: G. P. Putnam and Sons, Publishers ... Henry L. Hinton, Publisher, 680 Broadway. 1870 ...

Printed paper wrapper; and, cloth. See next two entries.

10384. Rip Van Winkle. A Legend of the Kaatskill Mountains ...

New York: G. P. Putnam and Sons ... H. L. Hinton, Publisher, 680 Broadway. 1870.

Printed paper wrapper. Inserted in some copies is a 4-page leaflet advertising Hinton's publications. See preceding entry; see next entry.

10385. Rip Van Winkle. A Legend of the Kaatskill Mountains ...

New York: G. P. Putnam and Son, <*sic*> 661 Broadway. Opposite Bond Street. 1870.

Jefferson Edition. See preceding two entries.

10386. ... The Moor's Legacy ...

Winning, Hill & Ware 389 St. Paul Street Montreal <1870>

Printed paper wrapper. At head of title: Carratraca Mineral Springs Co. of North Plantagenet Ontario

10387. The Sunnyside Book ... <by> Bryant, Curtis, Stedman, Bayard Taylor, Howells, <Richard Henry> Stoddard ... Wm. Allan <*sic*> Butler ... Irving ...

New York G. P. Putnam & Sons Association Building, 23d Street 1871

Cloth; and, morocco. Certain of the Irving pieces herein have titles assigned by the editor.

Advertised for Nov. 15 ALG Nov. 1, 1870. Listed ALG Dec. 1870; PC Dec. 31, 1870.

10388. The Crayon Reader: Comprising Selections from the Various Writings of Washington Irving. For the Use of Schools and Classes.

New York: G. P. Putnam's Sons, 4th Ave. and 23d Street. 1871.

10389. The Scenery of the Catskill Mountains, as Described by Irving, Cooper, Bryant, Willis Gaylord Clark, N. P. Willis . . . Park Benjamin . . . Bayard Taylor.

Catskill: J. B. Hall & Son, Recorder Office, 1872.

Printed paper wrapper. See entry No. 10335.

10390. Biographies and Miscellanies . . . Edited by . . . Pierre M. Irving.

Philadelphia: J. B. Lippincott & Co. 1873.

10391. Shakespeare's Home; Visited and Described by Washington Irving and F. W. Fairholt . . .

New York: J. Sabin & Sons, 84 Nassau Street. 1877.

Large paper edition, leaf 9½″ tall; small paper edition, leaf 7⅝″ tall.

10392. American Prose Hawthorne: Irving: Longfellow: Whittier: Holmes: Lowell: Thoreau: Emerson With Introductions and Notes by the Editor of "American Poems" ⟨Horace E. Scudder⟩

Boston Houghton, Osgood and Company The Riverside Press, Cambridge 1880

10393. Rip Van Winkle and Other Sketches . . .

New York The Useful Knowledge Publishing Company 1882

Listed PW June 17, 1882.

10394. The Crayon Papers . . .

New York: John W. Lovell Company, 14 & 16 Vesey Street, ⟨sic⟩ ⟨1883⟩

Printed paper wrapper. Issued under date Oct. 17, 1883. Also issued in cloth.

10395. The Mutability of Literature A Colloquy in Westminster Abbey . . .

New York Arthur Hinds, Publisher 3 West 3d Street 1885

10396. The Pride of the Village, and Other Tales . . .

Philadelphia: J. B. Lippincott Company. London: 15 Russell Street, Covent Garden. ⟨1886⟩

Deposited July 24, 1886.

10397. Knickerbocker Sketches from "A History of New York." . . .

Philadelphia: J. B. Lippincott Company. 1886.

10398. The Angler . . .

Boston Samuel E Cassino MDCCCXCII

Leaf: 6¹³⁄₁₆″ x 5¼″. Also issued in an *Edition de Luxe:* The separate leaves, printed on recto only, mounted on stiff paper leaves (9⅞″ x 7⅞″); tied, in a portfolio. Another printing was issued by A.S.W. Rosenbach, 1931, 150 numbered copies only; yet another issued in 1933, by The Harbor Press, New York.

10399. Stories and Legends from Washington Irving . . .

New York & London G. P. Putnam's Sons ⟨1896⟩

Listed PW Oct. 24, 1896. Cloth?

10400. Christmas Day . . .

London At the de la More Press 298 Regent Street W 1902

Printed paper wrapper over flexible boards.

10401. The Fur Traders of the Columbia River and the Rocky Mountains as Described by Washington Irving in His Account of "Astoria," and the Record of "The Adventures of Captain Bonneville" with Some Additions by the Editor ⟨Frank Lincoln Olmsted⟩

G. P. Putnam's Sons New York and London The Knickerbocker Press 1903

On copyright page: *Published, May, 1903*

10402. Christmas at Bracebridge Hall . . .

London. Ernest Nister. New York. E. P. Dutton & Co. . . . ⟨n.d., 1905⟩

Received at BMU Dec. 22, 1905. Pictorial boards.

10403. The Keeping of Christmas at Bracebridge Hall . . . Illustrations by C. E. Brock

1906 Lond. J. M. Dent & Co. New York. E. P. Dutton & Co.

10404. Legends of the Alhambra . . .

Philadelphia & London J. B. Lippincott Company 1909

On copyright page: *Published October, 1909* Listed PW Nov. 20, 1909.

10405. Bachelors and a Bachelor's Confessions ...

... E. P. Dutton and Co. New York MCMIX

Pictorial boards.

10406. Christmas Eve ...

London. Hodder & Stoughton ⟨n.d., 1910⟩

10407. Washington Irving Travels in Missouri and the South   Reprint from the Missouri Historical Review, October, 1910 Notes by F. A. Sampson

Columbia, Missouri, 1910

Cover-title. Printed paper wrapper.

10408. New-Year Civilities ... an Excerpt from Salmagundi ...

New York   Privately Printed   Christmas 1912

Printed paper boards. "Of this book two hundred copies have been printed for Thomas Nast Fairbanks at the Village Press, in December, 1912." Text extracted from "From My Elbow-Chair," *Salmagundi,* Part 20; probably written by J. K. Paulding.

10409. Letters of Washington Irving to Henry Brevoort Edited ... by George S. Hellman ...

New York G. P. Putnam's Sons The Knickerbocker Press 1918

See under year 1915 in *Sec. I.*

10410. The Bold Dragoon and Other Ghostly Tales ... Selected ... by Anne Carroll Moore ...

Alfred A. Knopf. New Amsterdam 1930

WASHINGTON IRVING

SECTION III

IN THIS SECTION are listed books by authors other than Irving which contain material by him reprinted from earlier books. See *Section Two* for reprints issued under Irving's name.

Travels through Lower Canada, and the United States of North America, in the Years 1806, 1807, and 1808 . . . by John Lambert . . .

London: Printed for Richard Phillips, Bridge-Street, Blackfriars. 1810. By T. Gillet, Crown-Court, Fleet-Street.

3 Vols. Probably issued in paper boards. In Vols. 2-3 the word *Printer* is present after the name *Gillet* in the imprint.

Extracts from *Salmagundi,* Vol. 2, pp. 234-394; *i.e.,* pp. 234-349.

Lambert was much impressed by *Salmagundi*. "Many of the young men . . . whose minds have not been wholly absorbed by pounds, shillings, and pence, have shewn that they possess literary qualifications and talents, that would, if their time and fortune permitted, rank them among some of the distinguished authors of Europe. The most prominent of their late productions is the *Salmagundi* . . . This little work has been deservedly a great favourite with the public, and bids fair to be handed down with honour to posterity. It possesses more of the broad humour of Rabelais and Swift, than the elegant morality of Addison and Steele, and therefore less likely to become a classical work; but as a correct picture of the people of New York, and other parts of the country, though somewhat heightened by caricature, and as a humourous representation of their manners, habits, and customs, it will always be read with interest by a native of the United States."—Vol. 2, p. 203.

The Poetical Works of Thomas Campbell . . . to Which is Prefixed a Biographical Sketch of the Author, by a Gentleman of New-York. Second American Edition.

Baltimore: Published by Philip H. Nicklin . . . Fry and Kammerer, Printers. 1811.

Boards?

Biography of James Lawrence, Esq. Late a Captain in the Navy of The United States: together with a Collection of the Most Interesting Papers, Relative to the Action between the Chesapeake and Shannon . . .

New-Brunswick: Printed and Published by L. Deare, at Washington's Head. 1813.

Printed paper boards. Title-page deposited Sept. 28, 1813.

American Naval Biography. Compiled by Isaac Bailey . . .

Providence, (R.I.) Published by Isaac Bailey, near the Turk's Head. H. Mann & Co. Printers. 1815.

Leather?

The Poetical Works of Thomas Campbell. To Which Is Prefixed, a Biographical Sketch of the Author. First Complete American Edition.

Philadelphia: Published by Edward Parker. William Brown, Printer. 1821.

Leather?

The Literary Coronal for 1822. Edited by John Mennons.

Glasgow, 1822.

Not seen. Reprint?

". . . Made up wholly of selections from Irving."—Fred Lewis Pattee: "Anthologies of American Literature before 1861," in: *The Colophon* . . . , Part 16, New York, 1934.

"Mr. Lawson seems early to have taken an interest in American letters; for in 1821 we find him in correspondence with Mr. John Mennons, editor of the Greenock Advertiser, who was then engaged in publishing a miscellaneous collection of prose and verse, entitled the Literary Coronal. Mr. Mennons desired to introduce specimens of American authors, then a novelty to the British public, into his book, and Mr. Lawson supplied him with the materials."—From the biographical sketch of James Lawson in Duyckinck's *Cyclopædia of American Literature,* 1855, Vol. 2, p. 280.

The Class Book of American Literature ... by John Frost.

> Boston ... 1826.
>
> For comment see BAL, Vol. 1, p. 136.

The Classical Reader ... by Rev. F. W. P. Greenwood and G. B. Emerson ...

> Boston ... 1826.
>
> For fuller entry see BAL, Vol. 4, p. 187.
>
> "Description of Roscoe," pp. 42-45; extracted from "Roscoe," *Sketch Book,* 1819–1820. "Visit to the Grave of Shakespeare," pp. 45-48; extracted from "Stratford-on-Avon," *Sketch Book,* 1819–1820.

The National Reader ... ⟨Edited⟩ by John Pierpont ...

> Boston ... 1827.
>
> For fuller comment see entry No. 1593.

The American Common-Place Book of Prose ...

> Boston ... MDCCCXXVIII.
>
> For fuller comment see entry No. 619.
>
> Contains several pieces, by Irving here reprinted under their original titles. "Scenery in the Highlands on the River Hudson," pp. 346-350, is a title assigned to an extract from "Dolph Heyliger," *Bracebridge Hall,* 1822.

The Cypress Wreath, or Mourner's Friend ...

> Greenfield, Mass. Printed and Published by Phelps & Clark. 1828.
>
> "The Spirits of the Departed," pp. 86-88, is an extract from "St. Mark's Eve," *Bracebridge Hall,* 1822.

Specimens of American Poetry ... in Three Volumes. By Samuel Kettell ...

> Boston ... MDCCCXXIX.
>
> For comment see entry No. 3251.
>
> "The Falls of the Passaic," Vol. 2, pp. 173-174; otherwise: "On Passaic Falls ... ," truncated and somewhat altered textually. See entry No. 10120.

The Lady's Cabinet Album ...

> New-York ... MDCCCXXXII.
>
> For fuller entry see No. 6793.

The Premium ...

> Philadelphia ... 1833.
>
> For fuller entry see No. 5689.

"The Rainy Sunday," pp. 58-61; extracted from "The Stout Gentleman," *Bracebridge Hall,* 1822. "Reception of Columbus on His Return to Spain," pp. 192-195; extracted from *A History of the Life and Voyages of Christopher Columbus,* 1828. "The Adventure of the Mason," pp. 257-261, previously in *The Alhambra,* 1832.

The Western Reader ... Selected ... by James Hall.

> Cincinnati ... 1833.
>
> For fuller entry see No. 3261.

The Lady's Cabinet Album ...

> New-York: Published by Peabody and Co. MDCCCXXXIV.
>
> Cloth? Reissued as *The Lady's Album,* 1835; and, *The Moss Rose,* n.d., *ca.* 1845.

Selections from the American Poets ...

> Dublin ... 1834.
>
> For comment see BAL, Vol. 2, p. 397.

The Intelligent Reader: Designed as a Sequel to the Child's Guide ...

> Springfield: Published by G. and C. Merriam. 1835.
>
> Printed paper boards, leather shelfback. "The Sage Decision of the Renowned Governor van Twiller," pp. 159-161, is an extract from *A History of New York ...* , 1809.

The Young Lady's Gift, a Common-Place Book of Prose and Poetry.

> Providence: B. Cranston & Co. 1836.

The New-York Book of Poetry ...

> New-York ... 1837.
>
> For fuller entry see No. 3272.

The Lady's Cabinet Album ...

> New-York: E. Sands. MDCCCXXXVII.
>
> Cloth? Reissued as *The Moss Rose,* n.d., *ca.* 1845.

The Mourner's Gift. Edited by Mrs. M. A. Patrick ...

> New York: Van Nostrand & Dwight. MDCCCXXXVII.
>
> "Strewing Flowers upon Graves," 190-192; extracted from "Rural Funerals," *Sketch Book,* 1819–1820.

The Lady's Cabinet Album ...

New-York, Published for the Booksellers ⟨1839⟩

Not seen. Entry from Williams-Edge, p. 12.

Presumably a reprint of *The Lady's Cabinet Album* ..., New York, 1832.

The Southern First Class Book ... Selected ... by M. M. Mason ...

Macon ... 1839.

"The Character of Columbus," p. 137; extracted from the final chapter of *Life and Voyages of Christopher Columbus,* 1828. For fuller entry see BAL, Vol. 1, p. 371.

The Gems of American Poetry, by Distinguished Authors.

New-York: A. & C. B. Edwards. 1840.

The Poets of America ... Edited by John Keese.

New York ... 1840.

For comment see BAL, Vol. 1, pp. 232-233.

American Melodies ... Compiled by George P. Morris ...

New-York ... 1841.

For comment see entry No. 997.

Every Body's Book: Or Something for All ... First Series.

New-York: Wiley and Putnam, 161 Broadway. 1841.

Reviewed K Aug. 1841. Listed NAR Oct. 1841.

The Family Christian Almanac for the United States ... for ... 1843 ...

Published by the American Tract Society; and Sold, Wholesale and Retail, at 150 Nassau-Street, New-York ... ⟨n.d., 1842?⟩

Printed paper wrapper. "The Bride," p. 25, extracted from "The Wedding," *Bracebridge Hall,* 1822.

The Christian Family Annual 1844. By Rev. Daniel Newell.

New York   Office of the Christian Family Magazine. 132 Nassau-Street ... ⟨n.d., 1843⟩

A periodical bound as an annual. Cloth?

The Christian Family Annual. Vol. 3. Edited and Published by Rev. Daniel Newell.

New York: No. 126 Nassau-Street ... ⟨n.d., 1844⟩

A periodical bound as an annual. Cloth?

"Feathered Songsters," pp. 396-399, is a truncated version of "The Birds of Spring"; see *The Family Visitor,* 1840, in Sec. 1.

The Poetry and History of Wyoming: Containing Campbell's Gertrude, and the History of Wyoming ... by William L. Stone ... Second Edition, Enlarged.

New York: Mark H. Newman. 1844.

Deposited April 3, 1844. *Note:* Unsold sheets were reissued under date 1864 by J. Munsell, Albany, New York, as the *Third Edition* (so stated on the title-page). In the 1864 issue the original front matter has been cancelled and Munsell's front matter inserted.

The Moss Rose, or an Annual Gift ...

New-York: Published by Nafis & Cornish. ⟨n.d., *ca.* 1845⟩

Leather?

The District School Reader; or, Exercises in Reading and Speaking; Designed for the Highest Class in Public and Private Schools. By William D. Swan ...

Boston: Charles C. Little and James Brown. 1845.

Noted only in leather.

Contains "Voyage to Europe," pp. 58-65, reprinted from "The Voyage," *Sketch Book,* 1819–1820; "Life on the Prairies," pp. 131-135; "A Bee-Hunt," pp. 184-187, the preceding two pieces extracted from *A Tour on the Prairies,* 1835; "Shakspeare's Tomb," pp. 322-325, reprinted from "Stratford-on-Avon," *Sketch Book,* 1819–1820; "The Broken Heart," reprinted from *Sketch Book,* 1819–1820.

The Parlor Annual and Christian Family Casket. 1846. Edited by an Association of Clergymen.

Published by J. E. D. Comstock, 126 Nassau-Street. N-York ⟨n.d., 1845? 1846?⟩

Sheets of a periodical bound as an annual.

"The Widow and Her Son," pp. 192-195; reprinted from *Sketch Book,* 1819–1820. "The Grave," pp. 216-217; extracted from "Rural Funerals," *Sketch Book,* 1819–1820.

A Library of the Prose and Poetry of Europe and America ... Compiled by G. P. Morris and N. P. Willis. Complete in One Volume.

New-York: Paine and Burgess. 1846.

The Family Circle, and Parlor Annual. 1848. Edited and Published by Rev. D. Newell.

New-York: 126 Nassau-Street ... ⟨n.d., 1847⟩

Sheets of a periodical bound as an annual.

"The Graves of Those We Love," pp. 142-144; extracted from "Rural Funerals," *Sketch Book,* 1819–1820.

The Prose Writers of America ... by Rufus Wilmot Griswold ...

Philadelphia ... 1847.

For comment see entry No. 6676.

The Marriage Offering: A Compilation of Prose and Poetry. ⟨Edited by Abiel A. Livermore⟩

Boston: Wm. Crosby and H. P. Nichols, 111 Washington Street. 1848.

"A Testimony," p. 186; reprinted from *Sketch Book,* 1819–1820.

... The (Old) Farmer's Almanack ... for the Year of Our Lord 1852 ... by Robert B. Thomas ...

Boston: Published by Jenks, Hickling & Swan ... 1851 ...

Printed paper wrapper. At head of title: Number Sixty.

"Ready-Money Jack and His Farm-House," p. 39; extracted from *Bracebridge Hall,* 1822.

Garden Walks with the Poets. By Mrs. C. M. Kirkland.

New-York ... 1852.

For comment see entry No. 1379.

The Humorous Speaker: Being a Choice Collection of Amusing Pieces, Both in Prose and Verse ... Selected ... by Oliver Oldham ...

New York: Newman & Ivison, 178 Fulton Street. Cincinnati: Moore, Anderson & Co. Chicago: S. C. Griggs & Co. Auburn: J. C. Ivison & Co. Detroit: A. M'Farren 1853.

Cloth, leather shelfback.

"Knickerbocker's New-England Farmer," pp. 290-291; extracted from *A History of New York,* 1809.

The Wheat-Sheaf ...

Philadelphia ... 1853.

For comment see entry No. 3176.

The Wedding Dress. Edited by a Lady ...

Boston: Thos. O. Walker. 1854.

The White Veil ... Edited by Mrs. Sarah Josepha Hale ...

Philadelphia ... 1854.

For comment see entry No. 6883.

Lilies and Violets ... by Rosalie Bell ...

New York ... 1855.

For comment see entry No. 1658.

The Wheat-Sheaf ...

Philadelphia ... ⟨1856⟩

For fuller entry see in Longfellow list, *Section IV.*

The Angel Visitor; or, the Voices of the Heart. Edited by Frances E. Percival ...

Boston: L. P. Crown & Company. Toronto: C. W. Bostwick & Barnard. Philadelphia: J. W. Bradley. Providence: O. W. Potter. 1857.

Note: Reprinted and reissued by Crown & Emery, Boston, 1857.

"Remembrance of the Dead," pp. 157-160; extracted from "Rural Funerals," *Sketch Book,* 1819–1820.

The Atlantic Souvenir, for 1859 ...

New York: Derby & Jackson, 119 Nassau Street. 1859.

Leather.

... The Constellation.

New York, 1859 ...

For fuller description see No. 1034.

The American Reader ... by Augustus DeKalb Tarr ...

Philadelphia ... 1860.

For fuller entry see BAL, Vol. 3, p. 338.

The Mosaic. Edited by J.H.B.

Buffalo: Breed, Butler & Co. 1861.

Extract, pp. 56-57, taken from "Rural Life in England," *Sketch Book,* 1819–1820. Reprinted and reissued by Breed, Lent & Co., Buffalo ⟨1861; *i.e.,* not before 1866⟩

The Poetry and History of Wyoming: Containing Campbell's Gertrude, and the History of Wyoming from its Discovery to the Beginning of the Present Century. By William L. Stone ... Third Edition ...

Albany: J. Munsell, 78 State Street. 1864.

Reissue of the 1844 (Newman) sheets with the original front matter cancelled, new front matter inserted, and an index added.

Lyra Elegantiarum ... Edited by Frederick Locker ...

London: Edward Moxon & Co., Dover Street. 1867.

"Album Verses," pp. 276-277, had prior publication in *The Life and Letters* ... , Vol. 2, 1862, pp. 85-86, under the title "Written in the Deep Dene Album."

Tom Hood's Comic Readings in Prose and Verse ...

London ... ⟨n.d., 1869⟩

For comment see entry No. 1546.

Vers de Société Selected ... by Charles H. Jones ...

New York ... 1875

For comment see BAL, Vol. 1, p. 73. "Album Verses," pp. 265-266. See *Lyra Elegantiarum* ... , 1867, above.

... Burlesque.

Boston ... 1875.

For fuller entry see No. 4765. "An Account of the Golden Age of New York," pp. 148-162; extracted from *A History of New York*, 1809.

Essays from the North American Review. Edited by Allen Thorndike Rice.

New York ... 1879.

For comment see entry No. 679.

Gems for the Fireside ... ⟨Compiled by⟩ Rev. O. H. Tiffany ...

Boston ... 1881.

For fuller entry see in Longfellow *Section IV*.

Gems for the Fireside ... ⟨Compiled by⟩ Rev. O. H. Tiffany ...

Springfield ... ⟨1883⟩

For fuller entry see in Longfellow *Section IV*.

Brilliant Diamonds of Poetry and Prose ... ⟨Compiled by⟩ Rev. O. H. Tiffany ...

... ⟨n.p., 1883⟩

For fuller entry see in Longfellow *Section IV*.

Mountain, Lake, and River ... by N. P. Willis ...

Boston ... 1884.

For comment see BAL, Vol. 3, p. 253.

Opening Addresses Edited by Laurence Hutton

New-York ... 1887

For comment see entry No. 1045.

Mark Twain's Library of Humor ...

New York ... 1888

For comment see entry No. 9636.

Half-Hours with the Best Humorous Authors. Selected ... by Charles Morris ... American.

Philadelphia ... 1889.

For comment see entry No. 3813.

Modern Eloquence ... ⟨Edited by⟩ Thomas B. Reed ...

... Philadelphia ⟨1900; i.e., 1901⟩

For comment see entry No. 3467.

REFERENCES AND ANA

... The Literary Picture Gallery, and Admonitory Epistles, to the Visitors of Ballston-Spa. By Simeon Senex, Esquire.

Ballston-Spa: Printed by Miller & Riggs. 1808.

Cover-title. Issued in four(?) parts. At head of title: No. II. ⟨III.⟩ ... Printed self-wrapper.

BAL has seen *Parts 2-3* only.

Sometimes ascribed to Irving. Williams and Edge, p. 160, state: "almost certainly ... ⟨not⟩ written by" Irving.

Fragment of a Journal of a Sentimental Philosopher, during His Residence in the City of New-York. To Which Is Added, a Discourse upon ... Eloquence As a Science ...

New-York: Published by E. Sargeant, No. 39 Wall-Street. 1809.

Anonymous. Printed paper wrapper. Sometimes ascribed to Irving. Williams and Edge, p. 160: "... Irving may have contributed ⟨to this⟩ ... probably written by Rodman." See *Life and Letters*, 1862, Vol. 1, p. 125. Also see next entry.

Listed MA April, 1809, without mention of authorship.

The New-York Review; or, Critical Journal. To Be Continued As Occasion Requires. March 1809. Containing Strictures on a Pamphlet Entitled "Fragments of the Journal of a Sentimental Philosopher." ...

New-York: Published by Inskeep & Bradford, No. 128, Broadway.

Cover-title? Self-wrapper? Paged ⟨101⟩-119. Published thus? All published? See preceding entry.

A Word in Season, Touching the Present Misunderstanding in the Episcopal Church. By a Layman . . .

New-York: Printed by D. & G. Bruce, Slote-Lane. 1811.

Issued in printed paper wrapper? Sometimes attributed to Irving. Langfeld-Blackburn (p. 66), state: "not generally accepted as having been written" by Irving. Williams and Edge (p. 160), state "almost certainly" not by Irving.

Brief Remarks on the "Wife" of Washington Irving . . . ⟨by Egbert Benson⟩

New-York: Printed by Grattan and Banks, Corner of Nassau & Spruce Streets. 1819.

Cover-title? Printed paper wrapper? Two printings noted: 1: Pp. ⟨1⟩-18, list of errata at foot of p. 18; 2: Pp. ⟨1⟩-16.

Listed NAR April, 1820.

The Spectre Bridegroom; or, a Ghost in Spite of Himself. A Farce. In Two Acts. Founded on a Story of the Same Name, in the Sketch Book. By W. T. Moncrieff . . . [As Performed at the New-York Theatre.]

New-York: Published by E. Murden, Circulating Library and Dramatic Repository, No. 4 Chamber-Street. Dec. 1821.

Cover-title? Printed paper wrapper?

The Manuscript of Diedrich Knickerbocker, Jun. . . .

New-York: Published by E. Bliss and E. White. J. Seymour, Printer. 1824.

Also issued with the imprint: *New-York:— 1824.*

Printed paper wrapper? Cover-title?

"I can state positively that . . . ⟨this⟩ was not written by Washington Irving. It was one of a considerable number of imitations . . . it was reviewed in the *United States Literary Gazette* . . . ⟨Oct. 1, 1824⟩ I cannot name the author."—Letter, Stanley T. Williams, March 13, 1932, in NYPL.

Friendship's Offering. A Literary Album. Edited by Thomas K. Hervey . . .

London: Lupton Relfe, 13, Cornhill. 1826.

Noted in leather (small paper edition; leaf 5¼" x 3¼"); and paper boards, printed label on front (large paper edition; 7⅞" x 5⅛").

"Marian Seaforth. A Tale of America," pp. ⟨318⟩-346. Anonymous.

"Reichter and His Staghounds. A Tale," pp. ⟨369⟩-386. Anonymous.

Noted in MR Feb. 1826, which commented that the above anonymous tales "bear, unless we much mistake, many of the features of Geoffrey Crayon, in his moods of pathos and humour respectively." Did Irving write these stories? On p. vii Hervey acknowledges assistance received from Irving; and, on pp. ix-x: "The Editor has only to add, that there are a few individuals who have afforded him the use of their talents, withholding, (from particular circumstances, which will not operate next year,) that of their names. They are fully included in his acknowledgments of obligation; and would, in one or two instances, be entitled to more particular notice, if the absence of their names did not prevent individual mention."

The Anniversary; or, Poetry and Prose for M DCCC XXIX. Edited by Allan Cunningham.

London: Published by John Sharpe, Duke Street, Piccadilly. 1829. ⟨i.e., 1828⟩

Small paper edition (in silk): 7¾" x 4¾" full; large paper format (in three quarters leather and silk): 10" x 6¼". The small paper format has also been seen with the following imprint: *London: Published by John Sharpe, Duke Street, Piccadilly; and Thomas Wardle, Philadelphia. 1829.*

"Abbotsford Described, by a Distinguished American," pp. 81-100; sometimes attributed to Irving. The text indicates that the piece was written in 1825; and, further, that the author was "amply provided with letters of introduction" including one to Sir Walter Scott. Since Irving first met Scott in 1817 (see Irving's letter to Peter Irving, Sept. 1, 1817, in *Life and Letters*) it becomes clear that Irving was not the author of the description.

Forget Me Not   A New Years Gift.

Published by Judah Dobson   No. 108 Chesnut Strt. Philadelphia. 1828

"Ellen," pp. 300-302. "Sometimes ascribed to Irving."—Williams and Edge, p. 165.

Cloth?

A History of the Life and Voyages of Christopher Columbus . . .

New York, 1829

Not seen. Not located. Entry on the basis of the following statement in Langfeld-Blackburn, p. 27: "The second American edition, published in 1829, contained additional matter." Not to be confused with the abridged edition of 1829. Did Langfeld-Blackburn confuse the abridged edition with the full?

Novelas Españolas. El Serrano de las Alpujarras; y el Cuadro Misterioso. ⟨Edited by Henry Wadsworth Longfellow⟩

Brunswick . . . 1830.

"The stories are adaptations in Spanish from Washington Irving's *Rip Van Winkle* and *The Young Italian.*"—*LC Printed Cat.*

For a fuller description see entry No. 12044.

. . . Rip Van Winkle; or, the Demons of the Catskill Mountains!!! A National Drama, in Two Acts by John Kerr . . .

Phliadelphia ⟨*sic*⟩: Published by R. H. Lenfestey, No. 53 North Sixth Street. ⟨n.d., *ca.* 1829–1834⟩

At head of title: Lenfestey's Edition. Cover-title? Issued in printed paper wrapper?

LG Oct. 6, 1832, contains a review of *Rip Van Winkle: A Comedy;* author's name not given.

Legendary History of Mahomet.

London: John Murray, 1831.

Advertised as *in the press* LG Sept. 10, 17, Oct. 1, 1831. Another advertisement LG Sept. 17, 1831, identifies the book as one in *The Family Library* series, *in the press.* Announced as *forthcoming* Ath Sept. 17, 1831. Advertised LG Oct. 1, 1831. Murray did not include the title in his list of Irving's works advertised in Ath Dec. 31, 1831. Finally published, 1850, as *Mahomet and His Successors;* see Williams's *Life . . . ,* 1935, Vol. 2, pp. 21-23.

Salmagundi . . .

Paris, 1834.

See entry No. 10113.

Spain Revisited. By the Author of "A Year in Spain.' . . . In Two Volumes . . .

New-York: Harper & Brothers, Cliff-St. 1836.

Sometimes misattributed to Irving. The author was Alexander Slidell Mackenzie. For Irving's comment on this book see his letter to Pierre Irving, Feb. 6, 1832, in *Life and Letters,* Vol. 2, 1862, pp. 470-471.

The Moorish Drum   Sung by Miss Sheriff, in the Musical Romance of the Moorish Captive. Written by Washington Irving, Esq. Composed by George Perry.

New York   Published by Hewitt & Jaques 239 Broadway. ⟨n.d., 1837–1841⟩

Sheet music. The above at head of p. ⟨1⟩. *By Irving?* Text otherwise unlocated.

Ahmed al Kamel: Or, the Pilgrim of Love. The Libretto, (Founded on a Tale by Washington Irving,) by the Late Henry J. Finn . . . Performed at the New National Opera House on Monday, 12th October, 1840 . . .

New-York: M. C. Martin, Print., 113 Fulton Street. 1840.

Cover-title. Printed self-wrapper. Based on "Legend of Prince Ahmed al Kamel," *Alhambra,* 1832.

Prospectus of the International Art-Union 1849.

Oliver & Brother, Printers, New-York   ⟨1849⟩

Cover-title. Printed paper wrapper. Irving listed, p. ⟨3⟩, as one of a Committee of Reference. Noted as *received* SLM Feb. 1849.

⟨First⟩ Annual Report of the Trustees of the Astor Library of the City of New-York. Made to the Legislature, January 29, 1850.

Albany: Weed, Parsons & Co., Public Printers. 1850.

Cover-title. Printed paper wrapper. As president of the Board of Trustees Irving participated in the preparation of the report. He also participated in preparing the following succeeding reports: 2nd, 1851; 5th, 1854; 6th, 1855; 7th, 1856; 8th, 1857; 9th, 1858; 10th, 1859. Irving appears not to have participated in preparation of the third and fourth reports.

The Present, or a Gift for the Times. Edited by F. A. Moore . . .

Manchester, N. H.   Robert Moore. 1850.

"Woman and Marriage," pp. 127-131. Not found elsewhere. *By Irving?*

The Irving Offering: A Token of Affection, for 1851.

New-York: Leavitt and Company, No. 191 Broadway. 1851.

Contains nothing by Irving. For fuller description see entry No. 3171.

Supreme Court. Jean de Nottbeck, and Cecilia, His Wife: *vs.* William B. Astor, Washington

Irving, Daniel Lord, James Gallatin, and John Jacob Astor, Jr., Executors of the Last Will and Testament of John Jacob Astor, Deceased. Record of Bill of Exceptions. On Appeal ...

> New-York: Sibell & Mott, Stationers and Printers. 20 Wall Street, Corner of Nassau. ⟨n.d., 1851?⟩
>
> Cover-title? Printed paper wrapper?

The Irving Offering. A Token of Affection, for 1852.

> New-York: Leavitt and Company, 12 Vesey-Street. 1852.
>
> The sense of the "Preface" indicates that this book contains nothing by Irving, nevertheless the very first story herein is a reprint of his "The Stout Gentleman." Possibly a reprint of a British collection under an altered title. The signed pieces are simply enough disposed of; the unsigned pieces do not appear to be Irving's.

The Irving Gift ...

> Buffalo: Published by Phinney & Co. 1853.
>
> "... Will be published in about three weeks ..."—LW Nov. 6, 1852.

Rip Van Winkle: An Original, American, Grand Opera, in Three Acts. Music by Geo. F. Bristow. The Libretto by J. H. Wainwright. As Originally Produced in America by the Pyne and Harrison Troupe, at Niblo's Garden, New York, on Thursday, September 27, 1855.

> New York: Published by Wardle Corbyn, at William Hall & Son's Music Store, No. 239 Broadway. 1855
>
> Printed paper wrapper.

Tributes to Washington Irving, on the Publication of Wolfert's Roost.

> ⟨n.p., n.d., New York, 1855?⟩
>
> Cover-title. Printed paper wrapper.

... Rip Van Winkle; a Legend of the Catskills. A Romantic Drama, in Two Acts. Adapted ... by Charles Burke ...

> New York: Samuel French, 122 Nassau Street, (Up Stairs.) ⟨n.d., not before 1857⟩
>
> At head of title: French's Standard Drama. The Acting Edition. No. CLXXIV. Probably issued in printed paper wrapper. A reprint bears the publisher's later (ca. 1880) address: *38 East 14 Street, New York.*

The Death of Washington Irving; a Discourse Delivered in the Second Reformed Dutch Church, of Tarrytown, New-York, on ... Dec. 11, 1859, by ... Rev. John A. Todd ...

> New York: Isaac J. Oliver, Steam Book and Job Printer, 32 Beekman Street. 1859.
>
> Printed paper wrapper.

Sermons on the Occasion of the Death of the Late Washington Irving, Preached in Christ Church, Tarrytown, by the Rev. William Creighton ... and the Rev. J. Selden Spencer ...

> New-York: Pudney & Russell, Printers, No. 79 John-Street. 1859.
>
> Cover-title? Printed paper wrapper?

A Discourse on the Life, Character and Genius of Washington Irving ... by William Cullen Bryant.

> New York: G. P. Putnam, 115 Nassau Street, 1860.
>
> For fuller description see entry No. 1668.

Irvingiana: A Memorial of Washington Irving ...

> New York: Charles B. Richardson. 1860.
>
> For fuller description see entry No. 656; and to which add the following information: Also issued in a large paper edition, limited to 110 copies, unprinted boards; leaf size: 11¾" x 9⅛".

Obituary Notice of Washington Irving. By Henry Coppée. Read before the American Philosophical Society, in Philadelphia, September 21st, 1860.

> C. Sherman & Son, Printers, Seventh and Cherry Sts., Philada. ⟨1860⟩
>
> Cover-title. Printed paper wrapper.

The Pilgrim of Love! A Fairy Romance, in One Act. By Henry James Byron ...

> Thomas Hailes Lacy, 89, Strand, (Opposite Southampton Street, Covent Garden Market), London. ⟨n.d., 1860?⟩
>
> Printed paper wrapper? "First performed at the Theatre Royal Haymarket ... Monday, April 9th, 1860 ... Founded on one of Washington Irving's *Legends of the Alhambra* ..." —p. 2.

Washington Irving. Mr. Bryant's Address on His Life and Genius ...

> New York: G. P. Putnam. 1860.
>
> For comment see note under entry No. 8796.

Washington Irving and Cotemporaries ... Edited by William Watson Waldron ...

New York: W. H. Kelley & Co., 653 Broadway. ⟨n.d., 1863?⟩

Memoir of Washington Irving. With Selections from His Works, and Criticisms. By Charles Adams ...

New York: Carlton & Lanahan. San Francisco: E. Thomas. Cincinnati: Hitchcock & Walden. Sunday-School Department. ⟨1870⟩

Anselmo Bertini. A Poem, by Arobine Elizabeth Hilton.

Quincy, Ill: Herald Printing Company. 1871.

Printed paper wrapper. A rhymed version of Irving's "The Story of the Young Italian," *Tales of a Traveller*, 1824.

Studies of Irving by Charles Dudley Warner, William Cullen Bryant ⟨and⟩ George Palmer Putnam

New York   G. P. Putnam's Sons   182 Fifth Avenue   1880

Listed PW April 10, 1880.

... Washington Irving. By Charles Dudley Warner.

Boston: Houghton, Mifflin and Company. The Riverside Press, Cambridge. 1881.

At head of title: American Men of Letters. Deposited Nov. 18, 1881; listed PW Dec. 10, 1881.

Washington Irving   Commemoration of the One Hundredth Anniversary of His Birth by the Washington Irving Association at Tarrytown-on-Hudson Tuesday Evening, April 3, 1883 ...

G. P. Putnam's Sons   New York: 27 & 29 West 23d Street   London: 25 Henrietta Street, Covent Garden   1884

Belford's Annual 1886–7. Edited by Thomas W. Handford ...

Chicago and New York: Belford Clarke & Co. ⟨1886⟩

Boards, printed in imitation of tree calf.

"The Days of Childhood," p. 128. Not located elsewhere. *By Irving?*

Washington Irving   A Sketch by George William Curtis

New-York   The Grolier Club   MDCCCXCI

For fuller description see entry No. 4390.

The Work of Washington Irving by Charles Dudley Warner ...

New York   Harper & Brothers Publishers 1893

Deposited Aug. 2, 1893; listed PW Aug. 5, 1893.

A Stray Leaf from the Correspondence of Washington Irving and Charles Dickens by William Loring Andrews

Printed at the De Vinne Press New-York, 1894 and Embellished with Engravings on Copper and Zinc

"... Seventy-seven ⟨numbered⟩ copies, all of which were printed on Japan paper ... The first fifteen copies, numbered 1 to 15, contain proofs of three states of the copperplate engraving of the steamship *Britannia*."—Certificate of issue.

Washington Irving by Henry W. Boynton

Boston and New York   Houghton, Mifflin and Company   The Riverside Press, Cambridge 1901

On copyright page: *Published October, 1901*

A Short Sketch of Washington Irving and His Writings, by Geo. Washington Sandell ...

Southampton: "Southampton Times" Steam Printing Works, 70, above Bar. 1903

Printed paper wrapper.

Letters of Henry Brevoort to Washington Irving together with Other Unpublished Brevoort Papers Edited ... by George S. Hellman ...

New York   G. P. Putnam's Sons   The Knickerbocker Press   1916

2 Vols. Printed paper boards, leather label on spine. "... Limited to Three Hundred and Ten ⟨numbered⟩ sets ..."

Washington Irving Esquire ... by George S. Hellman ...

New York: Alfred A Knopf   MCMXXV

On copyright page: *Published, April, 1925*

The Hellman Collection of Irvingiana ... by R. W. G. Vail ...

New York   The New York Public Library 1929

Printed paper wrapper. Three hundred copies reprinted from the *Bulletin of the New York Public Library*, April, 1929.

Washington Irving   A Bibliography Compiled by William R. Langfeld with the Bibliographic

Assistance of Philip C. Blackburn

New York   The New York Public Library
1933

"Reprinted with Additions and Revisions from
the *Bulletin of the New York Public Library*
of June–December 1932 in an Edition of Four
Hundred and Fifty Copies . . . September
1933"—Colophon.

Washington Irving   Representative Selections,
with Introduction, Bibliography, and Notes by
Henry A. Pochmann . . .

American Book Company   New York . .
⟨1934⟩

The earliest printing has the symbol *W.P.I.*
on the copyright page.

The Life of Washington Irving by Stanley T.
Williams . . .

New York   Oxford University Press   London:
Humphrey Milford   1935

2 Vols. On copyright page: *First Edition*

A Bibliography of the Writings of Washington
Irving   A Check List Compiled by Stanley T.
Williams and Mary Allen Edge

New York   Oxford University Press   1936

Washington Irving on the Prairie . . . by Henry
Leavitt Ellsworth Edited by Stanley T. Williams
and Barbara D. Simison

New York   American Book Company   MCM-
XXXVII

The earliest printing has the symbol *W.P.I.*
on the copyright page. Deposited Nov. 5,
1937.

Letters to Sarah Storrow from Spain by Washington Irving Edited by Barbara D. Simison . . .

⟨n.p., n.d., New Haven, 1938⟩

Caption-title. The above at head of first page
of text. Paged: ⟨187⟩-237. Printed self-
wrapper.

Offprint from: *Papers in Honor of Andrew
Keogh Librarian of Yale University by the
Staff of the Library 30 June 1938,* New Haven,
1938.

The Spanish Adventures of Washington Irving
⟨by⟩ Claude G. Bowers

1940 . . . Houghton Mifflin Company   Boston
The Riverside Press   Cambridge

Letters of Jonathan Oldstyle . . . Reproduced
in Facsimile from the Edition of 1824 with an
Introduction by Stanley T. Williams

Published for the Facsimile Text Society by
Columbia University Press   New York: MCM-
XLI

Published Feb. 18, 1941 (publisher's statement). Deposited March 5, 1941.

. . . A Tour on the Prairies Edited . . . by John
Francis McDermott

University of Oklahoma Press: Norman ⟨1956⟩

At head of title: Washington Irving

HELEN MARIA FISKE HUNT JACKSON

(H.H., Saxe Holm)

1 8 3 0 – 1 8 8 5

The birthdate frequently is given as 1831. Ruth Odell (*Helen Hunt Jackson* ... , 1939, p. 12) gives the birthdate as Oct. 15, 1830; baptismal date May 8, 1831; the dates being those in the records of the Church of Christ in Amherst College.

Born Helen Maria Fiske. On Oct. 28, 1852, she married Edward Bissell Hunt. Hence those publications issued under the initials *H.H.* prior to that date, sometimes offered as hers, may be dismissed as not of her authorship. Among these publications are: *Old Times, with Other Familiar Sketches, in Prose and Verse: For Young People,* by M. H. and H. H., Lowell, 1846; and, *The Soldier-Cap; or, I'll Be a General,* Philadelphia, 1851, with a preface signed *H.H.*

10411. The Drum Beat

Published by the Brooklyn and Long Island Fair, for the Benefit of the U. S. Sanitary Commission ... Brooklyn ... 1864 ...

"A Charade," No. 8, p. 3; signed *H. H.;* presumed to be by Mrs. Jackson.

For fuller comment see entry No. 148.

10412. Bathmendi: A Persian Tale. Translated for the Children, from the French of Florian by H. H.

Loring, Publisher, 319 Washington Street, Boston: 1867.

⟨1⟩-23. Laid paper. 6⁷⁄₁₆″ x 4¾″. Printed tan paper wrapper.

Y

10413. VERSES. BY H. H.

BOSTON: FIELDS, OSGOOD, & CO. 1870.

Title-page in black and red. For extended editions see under 1871, 1874.

⟨i⟩-⟨viii⟩, ⟨9⟩-100. 5¹³⁄₁₆″ x 4⅛″.

⟨1², 2-7⁸⟩.

C cloth: brown; green; purple. Brown-coated on white end papers. Green-coated on white end papers. Flyleaves. Edges stained red.

According to the publisher's records 948 copies printed Nov. 25, 1870; 494 copies bound Dec. 7, 1870; 445 copies bound Feb. 16, 1871. BPL copy inscribed by early owner Dec. 7, 1870. Listed ALG Jan. 2, 1871.

AAS   B   BPL   H   NYPL   Y

10414. Balloon Post ...

Boston, Mass., April ... 1871 ...

"Greenough's Statue of Grief," No. 3, p. ⟨1⟩.

An occasional newspaper. 6 numbers. For fuller comment see entry No. 4038.

10415. Verses. By H. H. ⟨Second Edition⟩

Boston: James R. Osgood and Company, Late Ticknor & Fields, and Fields, Osgood, & Co. 1871.

Extended edition. Contains the following poems not present in the 1870 edition:

"Christmas Night in St. Peter's"
"Light on the Mountain-Tops"
"Love's Rich and Poor"
"The Sign of the Daisy"
"Vintage"
"Welcome"

According to the publisher's records, 500 copies were printed on June 3, 1871. H copy inscribed by early owner July 10, 1871. For another edition see under 1874.

H   UV

10416. BITS OF TRAVEL. BY H. H.

LONDON, 1871.

Not located. Entry on the basis of listing in PC Dec. 8, 1871, where the book is described as a 16mo, pp. 171 and priced at 7s.

Erroneous entry? Perhaps a copyright printing?

For first American edition see entry No. 10418.

10417. The Christmas Locket   A Holiday Number of Old & New

    Boston: Roberts Brothers, 143 Washington Street. 1871.

Cover-title. Printed paper wrapper.

"The Bethlehem Poem," pp. 47-49; collected in *Verses*, 1874, as "Two Loves."

Dated Dec. 25, 1871 on p. ⟨1⟩.

AAS

10418. BITS OF TRAVEL. BY H. H.

    BOSTON: JAMES R. OSGOOD AND COMPANY, LATE TICKNOR & FIELDS, AND FIELDS, OSGOOD, & CO. 1872.

For possible prior publication see this title above under 1871. For an altered edition see below under 1873.

⟨i-iv⟩, ⟨1⟩-304. 5⅛″ x 4³⁄₁₆″.

⟨-⟩², A-S⁸. *Also signed:* ⟨-⟩², 1-12¹², 13⁸.

Moiréd T cloth: blue; green. V cloth: blue. Brown-coated on white end papers. Flyleaves in some copies. Edges stained red.

According to the publisher's records there were four printings dated 1872:

1: Jan. 23, 1872. 1412 copies printed by Welch, Bigelow on paper weighing 70 lbs. per ream. Bound during the period Jan. 30–March 26, 1872.

2: May 1, 1872. 514 copies printed by Welch, Bigelow on paper weighing 54 lbs. per ream. Bound during the period May 14–22, 1872.

3: June 7, 1872. 1000 copies printed by Welch, Bigelow on paper weighing 54 lbs. per ream. Bound during the period June 12–July 3, 1872.

4: Aug. 15, 1872. 825 copies printed by Rand, Avery on paper weighing 54 lbs. per ream. Bound during the period Aug. 23–Oct. 4, 1872.

BAL has been unable to distinguish four printings, but the publisher's records confirm the following sequence:

1

Sheets bulk ¾″ (or a trifle more). Welch, Bigelow imprint on copyright page and p. 304.

2 and 3

Sheets bulk ⅝″ scant. Welch, Bigelow imprint on copyright page and p. 304.

4

In the only located copy (rebound, hence not collatable) the sheets bulk 11⁄₁₆″. Printer's imprint not present on copyright page nor on p. 304.

Listed for January publication WTC Jan. 18, 1872. Listed WTC Feb. 15, 1872.

H (1)   NYPL (1, 4)   Y (1, 2 and 3)

10419. BITS OF TALK ABOUT HOME MATTERS. BY H. H. . . .

    BOSTON: ROBERTS BROTHERS. 1873.

⟨i⟩-viii, ⟨9⟩-239. 5¹³⁄₁₆″ x 4¼″ scant.

⟨1⟩-15⁸.

P cloth: blue; green; purple; terra-cotta. Brown-coated on white end papers. Laid or wove paper flyleaves. Edges stained red.

Noted *will issue in February* PW Jan. 24, 1873. BPL copy inscribed by early owner March 5, 1873. Listed PW March 15, 1873. London (Sampson Low) edition listed Ath May 17, 1873. An edition with the imprint of Adam, Stevenson & Co., (Toronto) was reviewed by Bkr July, 1873.

BA   BPL   H

10420. Bits of Travel. By H. H.

    Boston: James R. Osgood and Company, Late Ticknor & Fields, and Fields, Osgood, & Co. 1873.

For first edition see under 1872.

Contains a "Prefatory Note," dated May 7, 1873, written for this edition. Somewhat revised.

Note: An earlier printing, also issued under date 1873, is of the earlier text and does not contain the new "Prefatory Note."

Advertised (as a revised edition) PW July 5, 1873.

H   NYPL   Y

10421. SAXE HOLM'S STORIES

    NEW YORK   SCRIBNER, ARMSTRONG, & COMPANY 1874

⟨i-iv⟩, ⟨1⟩-350, 4 pp. advertisements, blank leaf. Laid paper. 7³⁄₁₆″ x 5⅛″.

⟨1², 2-15¹², 16¹⁰⟩. *Signed:* ⟨-⟩², 1-21⁸, 22¹⁰.

BATHMENDI:

𝔄 Persian Tale.

TRANSLATED FOR THE CHILDREN,

FROM

THE FRENCH OF FLORIAN.

BY

H. H.

LORING, PUBLISHER,

319 WASHINGTON STREET, BOSTON.

1867.

PRICE, 25 CENTS.

C cloth: green; terra-cotta. FL cloth: green. H-like cloth: terra-cotta. Brown-coated on white end papers. Wove or laid paper flyleaf at front. *Note:* According to an advertisement in PW Jan. 31, 1874, the book was available in *plain* binding ($1.50); and, *extra gilt* ($1.75). BAL has traced no copy in *extra gilt*.

Advertised for *Nov. 20* PW Nov. 15, 1873. Listed PW Nov. 22, 1873. BA copy received Nov. 29, 1873. Low importation advertised PC Dec. 31, 1873.

UV Y

10422. VERSES. BY H. H. . . . ‹NEW AND ENLARGED EDITION›

BOSTON: ROBERTS BROTHERS. 1874.

Title-page in black and red. A much extended edition. For other editions see under 1870, 1871.

‹i-ii›, ‹i›-viii, ‹9›-191. 5¾″ full x 4³⁄₁₆″.

‹1⁹, 2-12⁸›. Leaf ‹1›₂ inserted.

S cloth: blue; brown; green; purple. Brown-coated on white end papers. Flyleaves. Edges stained red.

Two states of the binding noted. The sequence is probable.

A: Three daisy-like flowers goldstamped on front cover.

B: The front cover does not have three gold-stamped daisy-like flowers. Also thus on the 1875 printing.

Note: According to the publisher's advertisement PW Jan. 3, 1874, the first edition was sold out within a week and a new printing made. BAL suggests that the binding may hold a clue to identification of the first and the second printings.

On copyright page: *New and Enlarged Edition.* Contains 41 poems first collected herein.

Advertised as *ready December 10* PW Nov. 22, 1873. Listed PW Dec. 13, 1873. Noticed Ath Feb. 7, 1874. Reviewed Bkr March, 1874.

AAS (A)   B (A)   H (A, B)   UV (B)   Y (A)

10423. The Hospital Bazaar . . .

Chicago . . . 1874 . . .

"The Coin of the Realm. A Song Dedicated to All Lovers," No. 6, p. 84.

For comment see entry No. 7274.

10424. THE STORY OF BOON. BY H. H.

BOSTON: ROBERTS BROTHERS. 1874.

‹1›-28. 6⅞″ x 5⁷⁄₁₆″.

‹-›¹⁴.

Printed white laid paper wrapper pasted to white wove end papers. *Also:* Printed mottled blue-gray wove paper wrapper pasted to white wove end papers.

Advertised for *Dec. 15* PW Dec. 5, 1874. BPL copy received Dec. 15, 1874. Listed PW Dec. 19, 1874. Second edition advertised as *nearly ready* PW Jan. 2, 1875.

AAS B BPL H Y

10425. Laurel Leaves. Original Poems, Stories, and Essays . . .

Boston: William F. Gill and Company, 309 Washington Street. 1876.

"Fretting," pp. 131-135.

For comment see entry No. 116.

10426. Golden Treasures of Poetry, Romance, and Art by Eminent Poets, Novelists, and Essayists . . .

Boston   William F. Gill and Company   309 Washington Street   1876

"New Year's Morning," pp. 13-14, signed *H. H.*; collected in *Sonnets and Lyrics*, 1886.

For comment see entry No. 1749.

10427. . . . MERCY PHILBRICK'S CHOICE.

BOSTON: ROBERTS BROTHERS. 1876.

At head of title: NO NAME SERIES . . .

Anonymous.

‹i-vi›, ‹1›-296, blank leaf. 6⁹⁄₁₆″ x 4⅜″ scant.

‹1-19⁸›. *Signed:* ‹-›³, 1-12¹², 13⁵. *Also signed:* ‹-›³, A-R⁸, S⁵.

V cloth: black. Pale buff end papers imprinted with publisher's advertisements. Flyleaves.

Note: There may be two or more unidentified printings dated 1876. The fourth thousand advertised PW Oct. 28, 1876. Odell, pp. 141-142, states: "Helen confessed to Conway that she was deeply hurt in spite of a wave of adulation from inferior sources and the fact that the book had sold over eight thousand copies in four months . . . Thomas Niles of Roberts Brothers was, however, more interested in financial returns than in critical estimates, and the eight thousand sales reassured him . . ."

Query: Issued simultaneously in London by Sampson Low?

Announced for *Sept. 20* PW Sept. 16, 1876.
Listed PW Sept. 16, 1876. The fourth thousand
advertised PW Oct. 28, 1876. The London (Sampson Low) edition advertised as *ready* PC Sept. 16,
1876; listed Ath Sept. 23, 1876; listed PC Oct. 1,
1876. A printing was announced by Ward, Lock
& Tyler (London) but was not published; see
their letter in Ath July 28, 1877.

AAS   USC

10428. BITS OF TALK, IN VERSE AND
PROSE, FOR YOUNG FOLKS. BY H. H. . . .

BOSTON: ROBERTS BROTHERS. 1876.

⟨i⟩-vi, 7-244; 8 pp. advertisements. Frontispiece
and 3 plates inserted. 5¾″ x 4³⁄₁₆″.

⟨1⟩-13, ⟨14⟩, 15⁸, 16⁶.

S cloth: green; purple; terra-cotta. Blue-coated
on white end papers. Brown-coated on white
end papers. Green-coated on white end papers.
Flyleaves. Edges stained red.

Advertised for *Oct. 15* PW Sept. 16, 1876. Listed
PW Nov. 11, 1876.

B   H

10429. Poems of Places Edited by Henry W.
Longfellow . . . Italy. Vol. I.

Boston: James R. Osgood and Company, Late
Ticknor & Fields, and Fields, Osgood, & Co.
1877.

"Vino Santo," pp. 177-178.

For comment see entry No. 12184.

10430. Poems of Places Edited by Henry W.
Longfellow . . . Italy. Vol. III.

Boston: James R. Osgood and Company, Late
Ticknor & Fields, and Fields, Osgood, & Co.
1877.

"Torcello," p. 122.

For comment see entry No. 12186.

10431. . . . HETTY'S STRANGE HISTORY.
BY THE AUTHOR OF "MERCY PHIL-
BRICK'S CHOICE."

BOSTON: ROBERTS BROTHERS. 1877.

At head of title: NO NAME SERIES . . .

⟨i-ii⟩, ⟨1⟩-291; blank, p. ⟨292⟩; advertisements,
pp. ⟨293-294⟩. 6⁹⁄₁₆″ x 4⁵⁄₁₆″.

⟨1², 2-19⁸, 20²⟩. *Signed:* ⟨-⟩¹, ⟨1⟩-18⁸, 19³.

V cloth: black. Cream-white end papers imprinted with publisher's advertisements. Flyleaves.

Two printings noted:

1

As above.

2

⟨1⟩-291; blank, p. ⟨292⟩; advertisements, pp.
⟨293-296⟩.

⟨1⟩-18⁸, 19⁴.

Listed PW July 14, 1877. BA copy received July
21, 1877. Advertised as *ready July 21st* PW July
28, 1877. Noticed Ath Oct. 13, 1877.

AAS (2nd)   H (1st)   LC (1st)   NYPL (1st)

10432. Star Selections, 1876. A Fresh Collection
of Patriotic Readings, in Prose and Poetry. By
Professor J. E. Goodrich.

New York: Sheldon & Company, No. 8 Murray Street. 1877.

Printed boards, cloth shelfback.

"Freedom," p. 45; collected in *Sonnets and
Lyrics*, 1886.

H

10433. Charlotte Cushman: Her Letters and
Memories of Her Life. Edited by . . . Emma
Stebbins . . .

Boston: Houghton, Osgood and Company.
The Riverside Press, Cambridge. 1878.

"Charlotte Cushman," pp. 302-303. Collected in
Sonnets and Lyrics, 1886.

For comment see entry No. 1471.

10434. BITS OF TRAVEL AT HOME. BY
H. H. . . .

BOSTON: ROBERTS BROTHERS. 1878.

Two printings noted. The order of presentation
is presumed correct:

1

⟨i⟩-vi, ⟨1⟩-413; blank, p. ⟨414⟩; 4 pp. advertisements. Frontispiece inserted. 5¹¹⁄₁₆″ x 4³⁄₁₆″.

⟨1-26⁸, 27⁴⟩. *Signed:* ⟨1⟩¹¹, 2-25⁸, 26⁹.

A deposit copy thus. A copy at AAS is inscribed
by the publisher June 7, 1878.

2

⟨i-ii⟩, ⟨i⟩-vi, ⟨1⟩-413; blank, p. ⟨414⟩; 2 pp.
advertisements. Frontispiece inserted. 5¾″ x 4⅛″.

⟨-⟩⁴, ⟨1⟩-9, ⟨10-11⟩, 12-26⁸.

P cloth: brown; green; terra-cotta. Green-coated
on white end papers. Greenish-black coated on
white end papers. Mottled blue-gray end papers

printed in mauve with a floral pattern (noted on second printing sheets). Edges stained red.

Noted as *just ready* PW May 4, 1878. *Roberts Brothers are now ready to receive advance orders* ...—PW May 11, 1878. Listed PW June 1, 1878.

AAS (1st)   H (1st, 2nd)

10435. SAXE HOLM'S STORIES SECOND SERIES.

NEW YORK: CHARLES SCRIBNER'S SONS, SUCCESSORS TO SCRIBNER, ARMSTRONG & CO. 1878.

⟨i-viii⟩, ⟨1⟩-384; plus: 4 pp. advertisements. Laid paper. 7³⁄₁₆″ x 5″ scant.

⟨1⁴, 2-17¹²; plus: 18²⟩. *Signed:* ⟨-⟩⁴, 1, ⟨2⟩, 3-6, ⟨7⟩, 8-24⁸; plus: ⟨25⟩².

S cloth: blue; red. Brown-coated on white end papers. Single or double flyleaves of laid paper.

According to the records of the printer, H. O. Houghton, there were two printings without change of date: 1st, July 8, 1878, 1350 copies; 2nd, Sept. 18, 1878, 500 copies. Further study indicated.

Listed PW July 20, 1878.

AAS H Y

10436. NELLY'S SILVER MINE. A STORY OF COLORADO LIFE. BY H. H. ...

BOSTON: ROBERTS BROTHERS. 1878.

⟨1⟩-379; blank, p. ⟨380⟩; 4 pp. advertisements. Frontispiece and 3 plates inserted. 6⅝″ scant x 4⅜″.

⟨1⟩-24⁸.

C cloth: blue; brown; green; orange; terra-cotta. Brown-coated on white end papers. Flyleaves.

Listed PW Oct. 12, 1878.

AAS BA H

10437. ... A Masque of Poets. Including Guy Vernon, a Novelette in Verse.

Boston: Roberts Brothers. 1878.

"Horizon," p. 159. Uncollected.

"Quatrains," pp. 48-49. Collected in *Sonnets and Lyrics,* 1886.

"A Woman's Death Wound," p. 74. Collected in *Sonnets and Lyrics,* 1886.

For fuller entry see No. 118.

10438. Letters from a Cat. Published by Her Mistress for the Benefit of All Cats and the

Amusement of Little Children. ⟨Edited⟩ By H. H. ...

Boston: Roberts Brothers. 1879.

"Introduction," pp. ⟨5⟩-26.

The letters were written by Mrs. Jackson's mother, Deborah Waterman Vinal Fiske. See Odell, pp. 152, 230 (footnote 29). Mrs. Jackson's "Introduction" sets forth the origin of the letters and establishes the authorship.

Advertised for *November 1* PW Oct. 25, 1879. Listed PW Nov. 15, 1879.

AAS H

10439. Papyrus Leaves ... Edited by William Fearing Gill ...

New York: R. Worthington. 1880.

Reprint save for "The Genius of Common Sense," pp. 315-318.

Deposited Dec. 26, 1879. For fuller comment see entry No. 2477.

10440. The Atlantic Monthly Supplement. The Holmes Breakfast ...

⟨n.p., n.d., Boston, February, 1880⟩

Self-wrapper. Caption-title. Pp. ⟨1⟩-24.

"To Oliver Wendell Holmes, on His Seventieth Birthday," pp. 9-10.

Issued as a supplement to *Atlantic Monthly,* Feb. 1880. *Not noted as a separate;* seen *only* as an integral part of the issue cited. *Query:* Was this ever issued as a separate?

H NYPL

10441. The Art Autograph ... ⟨May, 1880⟩

... The Art Interchange, 140 Nassau Street, New York ... Copyright: 1880; by Wm. Whitlock.

"The Relief Ship at Twilight," p. ⟨10⟩.

For comment see BAL, Vol. 3, p. 157.

10442. ... The Reading Club and Handy Speaker ... Edited by George M. Baker. No. 8.

Boston: Lee and Shepard, Publishers. New York: Charles T. Dillingham. 1880.

"Two Dreams," pp. 13-14.

For comment see entry No. 7316.

10443. Warne's Illustrated International Annual ... Edited by Joseph Hatton

London   Frederick Warne and Co.   Bedford Street, Strand 1880 (All Rights Reserved)

Cloth?

"Hide-and-Seek Town," pp. 36-46.

NYPL

10444. A CENTURY OF DISHONOR   A SKETCH OF THE UNITED STATES GOVERNMENT'S DEALINGS WITH SOME OF THE INDIAN TRIBES BY H. H. . . .

NEW YORK   HARPER & BROTHERS, FRANKLIN SQUARE   1881

⟨i-ii⟩, ⟨i⟩-x, ⟨1⟩-457; blank, p. ⟨458⟩; advertisements, pp. ⟨1⟩-6. 7⁵⁄₁₆″ x 4⅞″.

⟨-⟩¹⁰, 1-19¹².

S cloth: brown. Brown-coated on white end papers. Flyleaves.

NYPL copy inscribed by the author Jan. 25, 1881. Listed PW Jan. 29, 1881. The London, Chatto & Windus edition (American sheets with cancel title-page) advertised Ath Feb. 12, 26, 1881. Listed Ath Feb. 26, 1881; PC March 15, 1881. See *Report on the Condition and Needs of the Mission Indians* . . . , 1883, below.

AAS   H   MHS

10445. Harper's Cyclopædia of British and American Poetry Edited by Epes Sargent

New York   Harper & Brothers, Franklin Square   1881

Reprint save for "October," p. 844. Collected as "October's Bright Blue Weather" in *Sonnets and Lyrics*, 1886.

For comment see entry No. 4336.

10446. MAMMY TITTLEBACK AND HER FAMILY. A TRUE STORY OF SEVENTEEN CATS. BY H. H. . . .

BOSTON: ROBERTS BROTHERS. 1881.

⟨1⟩-101, blank leaf. Frontispiece and 8 plates inserted. 7¼″ full x 5¹³⁄₁₆″.

⟨1⟩-6⁸, 7⁴.

C cloth: blue. S cloth: brown; green. Gray-coated on white end papers printed in brown with a floral pattern. White end papers printed in brown with a floral pattern. White end papers printed in green with a floral pattern. Flyleaves.

Two printings noted:

1

As above.

P. 55, running head: MAMY YTITTLEBACK

2

⟨1⟩-101. 7 integral plates not reckoned in the printed pagination. Frontispiece and 1 plate inserted.

⟨1-2⁸, 3⁶, 4-7⁸, 8⁴⟩. *Signed:* ⟨1⟩¹⁰, 2⁸, 3¹⁰, 4-6⁹, 7³.

P. 55, running head: MAMMY TITTLEBACK

Deposited Sept. 12, 1881. Listed PW Oct. 15, 1881. The London (Bogue) edition advertised Ath Oct. 1, 1881 and Nov. 19, 1881; listed Ath Dec. 3, 1881.

BPL (2nd)   H (1st)   NYPL (1st)   UV (1st)

10447. Christmas Carols and Midsummer Songs. By American Poets . . .

Boston: D. Lothrop & Company, Franklin Street. ⟨1881⟩

"A Baby Show," pp. ⟨49⟩-52.

For comment see entry No. 6297.

10448. In Memoriam. James A. Garfield . . . Compiled by Henry J. Cookinham . . .

Utica, N. Y.   Curtiss & Childs, Publishers, 167 Genesee Street. MDCCCLXXXI.

"Flowers on a Grave," pp. 60-62. Collected in *Sonnets and Lyrics*, 1886.

Deposited Nov. 21, 1881.

BA

10449. Indian Summer   Autumn   Poems and Sketches ⟨Compiled by⟩ L. Clarkson . . .

New York   E. P. Dutton & Company   713 Broadway   1881. Copyright, 1880, by E. P. Dutton & Co.

Reprint save for "September," p. 12. Collected in *Sonnets and Lyrics*, 1886.

"A Red Rose in September," p. 8, otherwise "A Wild Rose in September," *Verses*, 1874.

CH   H

10450. THE TRAINING OF CHILDREN. BY H. H.

N. Y. & BROOKLYN PUBLISHING CO., LIMITED. NEW YORK, 1882.

⟨1⟩-35. 6¼″ full x 4⅞″.

⟨-⟩¹⁸.

Printed pale buff wrapper.

Deposited Dec. 16, 1881. Listed PW May 13, 1882.

AAS LC

10451. The Cambridge Book of Poetry and Song ... by Charlotte Fiske Bates ...

New York: Thomas Y. Crowell & Co., No. 13 Astor Place. ⟨1882⟩

Reprint save for:

"July," p. 831. Collected in *Sonnets and Lyrics*, 1886.

"March," p. 831. Collected in *Sonnets and Lyrics, 1886*.

"My Nasturtiums," p. 832. Uncollected.

Reprinted and reissued in 2 Vols., imprinted: *New York: 46 East 14th Street ... Boston: 100 Purchase Street ⟨1882; i.e., not before 1890⟩*

For fuller comment see entry No. 7887.

10452. A Memorial of Josiah Gilbert Holland Discourses and Tributes Called forth by His Death, October 12, 1881

Printed, Not Published ⟨n.d., 1882?⟩

Printed paper wrapper.

"The Last Words," pp. 93-94, consisting of two sonnets: *We may not choose! Ah, if we might ...* ; and, *We may not choose; but if we did ...*

H LC NYPL

10453. REPORT ON THE CONDITION AND NEEDS OF THE MISSION INDIANS OF CALIFORNIA, MADE BY SPECIAL AGENTS HELEN JACKSON AND ABBOT KINNEY, TO THE COMMISSIONER OF INDIAN AFFAIRS.

WASHINGTON: GOVERNMENT PRINTING OFFICE. 1883. 5690 M I

⟨1⟩-35. 9¾" x 6¹⁄₁₆".

⟨1⟩-2⁸, 3².

Printed greenish-gray paper wrapper.

Reprinted in the 1885 edition of *A Century of Dishonor ...* ; see in *Section II*.

An abbreviated version was issued in Boston, 1887; see in *Section II*.

The following is a result of Mrs. Jackson's report:

... Message from the President of the United States, Transmitting a Communication of the 11th Instant, from the Secretary of the Interior, Submitting a Draft of Bill "for the Relief of the Mission Indians in the State of California." January 14, 1884 ...

⟨n.p., Washington, D. C., Government Printing Office, 1884⟩

Caption-title. The above on p. ⟨1⟩. Printed self-wrapper. At head of title: 48th Congress, 1st Session. Senate. Ex. Doc. No. 49.

"From January until April ⟨1880⟩ Helen gave her entire mind, strength, heart, and soul to the Indian cause. A whirlwind of industry, she circulated petitions and tracts and bombarded with stinging protest and rebukes prominent editors, Army officers, ministers of the gospel, college presidents, and Congressmen." -- Odell, p. 164. If certain of these polemics were written by Mrs. Jackson and issued in separate form, they have not come to the attention of BAL.

H LC NYPL UV

10454. The Elocutionist's Annual Number 12 ... Compiled by Mrs. J. W. Shoemaker.

Publication Department, National School of Elocution and Oratory. Philadelphia. 1884.

Cloth; and, printed paper wrapper.

"The Newsboy's Debt," pp. 141-145.

Deposited July 26, 1884.

LC

10455. THE HUNTER CATS OF CONNOR-LOA ...

BOSTON: ROBERTS BROTHERS. 1884.

Two printings noted. The sequence is probable.

A

⟨5⟩-156; advertisements, pp. ⟨157-160⟩; plus: 4 pp. advertisements. Frontispiece and 6 plates inserted. 7⁵⁄₁₆" x 5¾" full.

⟨1-9⁸, 10⁶; plus: 11²⟩. *Signed:* ⟨1⟩⁶, 2-7, ⟨8⟩, 9-10⁸; plus: ⟨11⟩².

Tailpiece, p. 156: Uncaptioned engraving of an Indian.

P. ⟨160⟩: *Messrs. Roberts Brothers' Publications. Bits of Travel at Home ...*

S cloth: brown; green; red. White end papers printed in olive with a leafy decoration. Flyleaves.

B

Pagination and collation as above.

Tailpiece, p. 156: Illustration captioned: *Mats Made by Ysidro. -- Page. 126.*

P. ⟨160⟩: *Books of Travel* . . .

C cloth: blue. White end papers printed in olive with a leafy decoration. Flyleaves.

Deposited Sept. 20, 1884. Noted as *just ready* PW Oct. 4, 1884. Listed PW Oct. 4, 1884.

AAS (A, B)   BA (A)   H (A)   HEH (A)   LC (A)

10456. RAMONA. A STORY . . .

BOSTON: ROBERTS BROTHERS. 1884.

⟨i-ii⟩, ⟨1⟩-490; 4 pp. advertisements. 7¼″ x 4⅞″.

1-31⁸. *Note:* The signature marks appear on the recto of the second leaf of each gathering.

S cloth: gray; mustard; light olive-green; red. White end papers printed in green or tan-green with an all-over floral decoration. Flyleaves.

Listed PW Nov. 8, 1884. The London (Macmillan) edition announced PC Oct. 1, 1884; advertised for *in a few days* PC Nov. 15, 1884; listed Ath Nov. 22, 1884.

H   NYPL   Y

10457. EASTER BELLS   AN ORIGINAL POEM . . . WITH DESIGNS . . . BY SUSIE B. SKELDING . . .

NEW YORK   WHITE, STOKES, & ALLEN PUBLISHERS ⟨1884⟩

⟨1⟩-22, blank leaf; laid paper. Four leaves of illustrations (wove paper) inserted and reckoned in the printed pagination. 9″ x 8⅛″.

⟨-⟩⁸.

Pictorial wrapper, tied with ribbon, or, possibly, cord. *Also:* Pictorial silver boards with silver silk floss fringe. (Issued in a variety of pictorial board bindings?)

Deposited Dec. 31, 1884. Listed PW March 14, 1885.

LC   Y

10458. Pansies and Orchids . . . Arranged and Illustrated by Susie B. Skelding . . .

New York   White, Stokes, & Allen   1884

Illuminated paper wrapper. Unpaged.

Reprint save for "The Orchid."

FCW

10459. We Young Folks   Original Stories for Boys and Girls by Harriet Beecher Stowe . . . Mary E. Wilkins . . . Sarah O. Jewett and Others . . .

Boston   D. Lothrop and Company   Franklin and Hawley Streets. ⟨1886, *i.e.,* 1885⟩

Contains "Mr. Any-Time the Spaniard."

For comment see entry No. 6308.

10460. ZEPH. A POSTHUMOUS STORY . . .

BOSTON: ROBERTS BROTHERS. 1885.

⟨1⟩-253; blank, p. ⟨254⟩; 2 pp. advertisements. 7¹⁄₁₆″ x 4¾″.

⟨1⟩-16⁸.

S cloth: green; mustard; red. Stamped in black and gold; or, brown and gold. Gray-coated on white end papers; also: Olive-coated on white end papers; also: Gray-coated on white end papers printed in green with a leafy pattern. Flyleaves. Leaf of advertisements, 6⅝″ x 4¹⁵⁄₁₆″, inserted at front.

Noted for January 25 PW Jan. 23, 1886. Listed PW Jan. 23, 1886. BA copy received Jan. 26, 1886. The Edinburgh (Douglas) edition (consisting of American sheets, according to BMU) advertised as *nearly ready* Ath Feb. 13, 1886; listed Ath Feb. 27, 1886.

B   H   NYPL   Y

We Young Folks   Original Stories for Boys and Girls by Harriet Beecher Stowe . . . Mary E. Wilkins . . . Sarah O. Jewett and Others . . .

Boston . . . ⟨1886; *i.e.,* 1885⟩

See above under 1885.

10461. February Edited by Oscar Fay Adams . . .

Boston   D. Lothrop and Company   Franklin and Hawley Streets   ⟨1886⟩

"February," p. 88. Collected in *Sonnets and Lyrics,* 1886.

For comment see entry No. 59.

10462. GLIMPSES OF THREE COASTS . . .

BOSTON: ROBERTS BROTHERS. 1886.

⟨i-iv⟩, ⟨1⟩-418; 2 pp. advertisements. 7³⁄₁₆″ x 4¹³⁄₁₆″.

⟨1-26⁸, 27⁴⟩. *Signed:* ⟨-⟩², ⟨1⟩-26⁸, 27².

S cloth: gray; green; red; terra-cotta; yellow. Front cover stamped in black or brown. White end papers printed in gold-yellow with a leafy pattern. White end papers printed in green with a leafy pattern. Flyleaves.

Noted for *April 15* PW April 10, 1886. Deposited April 12, 1886. Advertised for *this week* PW April 17, 1886. A copy at BA received April 20, 1886. Listed PW April 24, 1886.

AAS   H   UV

10463. April Edited by Oscar Fay Adams . . .

Boston D. Lothrop and Company Franklin and Hawley Streets ⟨1886⟩

Reprint save for "April," p. 82. Collected in *Sonnets and Lyrics*, 1886.

For comment see entry No. 61.

10464. A Visit to the Mission Indians of Southern California, and Other Western Tribes. By Prof. C. C. Painter . . .

Office of the Indian Rights Association, No. 1316 Filbert Street, Philadelphia. 1886.

Printed paper wrapper.

"Acquainted with Grief," p. 11. Only four stanzas herein. The complete poem collected in *Sonnets and Lyrics*, 1886.

Published after April 14, 1886 (the pamphlet is dated thus at end) but before May 13, 1886. A letter of C. C. Painter, dated May 13, 1886 (in HSP) encloses an undated clipping mentioning the publication of this pamphlet.

H

10465. August Edited by Oscar Fay Adams . . .

Boston D. Lothrop and Company Franklin and Hawley Streets ⟨1886⟩

Reprint save for "August," p. 15. Collected in *Sonnets and Lyrics*, 1886.

For comment see entry No. 66.

10466. September Edited by Oscar Fay Adams . . .

Boston D. Lothrop and Company Franklin and Hawley Streets ⟨1886⟩

Reprint save for:

"September Woods," pp. 95-97.

"September," pp. 131-132.

Both collected in *Sonnets and Lyrics*, 1886.

For comment see entry No. 67.

10467. Belford's Annual 1886-7. Edited by Thomas W. Handford . . .

Chicago and New York: Belford Clarke & Co. ⟨1886⟩

Boards printed in imitation of tree calf.

"One Day at a Time," p. 78. Also in *Belford's Chatterbox December, 1886;* see next entry.

Title deposited Sept. 23, 1886. Copies deposited Oct. 11, 1886.

H

10468. Belford's Chatterbox December, 1886. Edited by Thomas W. Handford . . .

Chicago and New York: Belford Clarke & Co. ⟨1886⟩

Printed paper boards. *Not* a periodical in spite of the title-page.

"One Day at a Time," p. 78. Also in *Belford's Annual 1886-7;* see preceding entry.

Deposited Oct. 11, 1886.

LC

10469. October Edited by Oscar Fay Adams . . .

Boston D. Lothrop and Company Franklin and Hawley Streets ⟨1886⟩

Reprint save for "October," p. 40. Collected in *Sonnets and Lyrics*, 1886.

For comment see entry No. 68.

10470. SONNETS AND LYRICS . . .

BOSTON ROBERTS BROTHERS 1886

Title-page in black and orange. For another edition see under 1889.

⟨i⟩-x, ⟨7⟩-135. Laid paper. 5¾" x 4¹⁄₁₆".

⟨-⟩², ⟨1⟩-8⁸, 9⁴.

S cloth: blue-green; gray; green; mustard. Gray-coated on white end papers. White end papers printed in brown with a leafy pattern. Laid paper flyleaves. Edges stained red. Also noted in extra-gilt bindings: White V cloth, white laid paper end papers and flyleaves, edges gilt.

Probably edited by Sarah Chauncey Woolsey (Susan Coolidge, *pseud.*), a reader at Roberts Brothers and a well-known author in her own right. However, BAL has been unable to find any positive evidence to support the probability.

Note: Sheets have been seen bound together with Jackson's *Verses*, Boston, 1887; binder's title: *Helen Jackson's Poems.*

Advertised as though published PW Nov. 20/27, 1886. Deposited Nov. 20, 1886. BA copy received Nov. 23, 1886. Listed PW Dec. 4, 1886.

B BA BPL H NYPL Y

10471. BETWEEN WHILES . . .

BOSTON: ROBERTS BROTHERS. 1887.

⟨1⟩-304. 6¹⁵⁄₁₆" x 4⅝".

⟨1⟩-19⁸.

S cloth: mustard; red. White end papers printed in greenish-brown with leafy pattern. Flyleaves.

Deposited May 5, 1887. H copy received May 10, 1887. Listed PW May 14, 1887.

AAS H NYPL

10472. Rhymes of the Rockies; or, What the Poets Have Found to Say of the Beautiful Scenery on the Denver & Rio Grande Railroad, the Scenic Line of the World.

Copyright, 1887, by S. K. Hooper. Chicago: Poole Bros., Printers and Engravers.

Pictorial wrapper; and, pictorial paper boards.

"Twin Lakes. The Yacht Dauntless," pp. 41-42.

NYPL Y

10473. The Leisure Hour Library ... F. M. Lupton ... April 7, 1888 ... New York ... Special Number. Vol. III. No. 185. The Mammoth Christmas Budget ...

⟨New York: F. M. Lupton, 1888⟩

Printed paper wrapper. Cover-title. Unpaged.

Contains "How the Parson Broke the Sabbath".

HM

10474. Belford's Annual. 1888–9. Edited by Thomas W. Handford ...

Chicago, New York and San Francisco. Belford Clarke & Co. ⟨1888⟩

"Home," p. 58.

For comment see entry No. 5735.

10475. A Memoir of T. Buchanan Read ...

Printed for Private Circulation Philadelphia 1889

"American Celebrities Abroad. Thomas Buchanan Read," pp. 38-39.

For comment see entry No. 1231.

10476. Boys' and Girls' New Pictorial Library of Prose, Poetry and Art ... by ... Eminent Authors ... with an Introduction by ... Rev. W. H. Milburn ...

Chicago and New York: R. S. Peale & Company. 1889.

"We Runned Away," pp. 83-84.

For comment see entry No. 6319.

10477. Sonnets and Lyrics ... ⟨Second Edition⟩

Boston Roberts Brothers 1889

For first edition see under 1886.

Reprint save for "With Them That Do Rejoice" and "Cheyenne Mountain."

Note: Not located as a separate volume; seen only bound with *Verses,* 1890, issued with binder's title: *Helen Jackson's Poems.*

H

10478. Wide Awake Pleasure Book Gems of Literature and Art by American Authors and Artists

Boston D Lothrop Company Washington Street opposite Bromfield ⟨1889⟩

"That Things Are No Worse, Sire." Uncollected.

"Popsy's Table Cloths." Collected in *Pansy Billings and Popsy* ... ⟨1898⟩.

For comment see entry No. 6320.

10479. Young Folks Golden Treasury of Travel and Adventure Short Sketches by the Best Writers Including ... Helen Jackson ... and Others ...

Boston D Lothrop Company Washington Street opposite Bromfield ⟨1890⟩

"Popsy's Grand Journey," pp. ⟨177⟩-183. Collected in *Pansy Billings and Popsy* ... ⟨1898⟩.

NK

10480. Selections from the Youth's Companion for Supplementary Reading. Number 12. In the Southwest ...

... 1897. Perry Mason & Company, Boston, Mass.

Printed paper wrapper.

"The Oldest American Houses," pp. ⟨50⟩-54.

Deposited Sept. 23, 1897.

LC

10481. Selections from the Youth's Companion for Supplementary Reading. Number 13. On the Plains ...

... 1897. Perry Mason & Company, Boston, Mass.

Printed paper wrapper.

"Ranch Life," pp. ⟨25⟩-29.

Deposited Sept. 23, 1897.

LC

10482. PANSY BILLINGS AND POPSY TWO STORIES OF GIRL LIFE ...

BOSTON   LOTHROP PUBLISHING COMPANY ⟨1898⟩

Two printings noted. The sequence is probable.

A

⟨i-ii⟩, ⟨1⟩-107, blank leaf. Frontispiece and 1 plate inserted. 7½″ scant x 5½″.

⟨1-7⟩⁸.

T cloth: green. Front stamped in blue and blue-black.

B

⟨i-ii⟩, ⟨1⟩-68, ⟨iii-iv⟩, 69-107. Illustrated. 7¼″ x 4¹³⁄₁₆″.

⟨1-7⟩⁸.

V cloth: olive-gray; tan. Front lithographed in gold, black and colors.

AAS (B)   HEH (B)   Y (A)

10483. Our Holidays   Their Meaning and Spirit Retold from St. Nicholas

Published by the Century Co.   New York MCMV

"A Chinese New Year's in California," pp. 82-84.

For comment see entry No. 5171A.

Collections of reprinted material issued under Mrs. Jackson's name; separate editions (*i.e.,* pieces reprinted from Mrs. Jackson's books and issued in separate form). For a list of books by authors other than Mrs. Jackson containing reprinted material by her, see *Section III.*

Mrs. Jackson's *Verses* and *Sonnets and Lyrics* were frequently issued bound together as single volumes. Simultaneously with the separate works? According to contemporary advertisements these omnibus volumes were available in the following bindings: Cloth; cloth, edges gilt; padded calf; padded morocco; kinnikinnick. (See PW Sept. 24, 1887; Oct. 22, 1887; Nov. 17/24, 1888.)

10484. Verses. By H. H.

Boston: James R. Osgood and Company, Late Ticknor & Fields, and Fields, Osgood, & Co. 1872.

According to the publisher's records, 470 copies were printed May 13, 1872.

10485. Draxy Miller's Dowry and the Elder's Wife. By Saxe Holm.

London: Sampson Low, Marston, Low, & Searle, Crown Buildings, 188, Fleet Street. 1875.

Advertised as *nearly ready* PC Feb. 16, 1875. Listed Ath Feb. 13, 1875.

10486. Verses. By H. H. . . .

Boston: Roberts Brothers. 1875.

On copyright page: *New and Enlarged Edition.*

10487. Verses. By H. H. . . .

Boston: Roberts Brothers. 1877.

On copyright page: *New and Enlarged Edition.*

10488. Verses. By H. H. . . .

Boston: Roberts Brothers. 1879.

On copyright page: *New and Enlarged Edition.*

10489. Letters from a Cat. Published by Her Mistress . . .

London: David Bogue, 3, St. Martin's Place, W. C. ⟨n.d., 1880⟩

Anonymous. Cloth? Listed Ath March 13, 1880; PC and Bkr April 2, 1880. In PC Feb. 1, 1883, W. H. Allen & Co. advertised they had taken over this title from Bogue.

10490. Spinning by H. H. Drawn by I. M. P. By Permission of Roberts Brothers.

Coates Brothers Publishers. Cliftondale, Mass. ⟨n.d., *ca.* 1880⟩

6 chromolithographs printed on one side of leaf only; tied with ribbon in stiff paper boards; Christmas card pasted to front. Presumably issued as a Christmas token. *Note:* An edition advertised by Lothrop in PW Sept. 24, 1887. Same sheets?

10491. Verses. By H. H. . . .

Boston: Roberts Brothers. 1882.

On copyright page: *New and Enlarged Edition.*

10492. Colorado Springs. By H. H. Reprinted from "Bits of Travel at Home."

Boston: Roberts Brothers. 1883.

Printed gray-tan paper wrapper.

10493. Cat Stories . . . Letters from a Cat. Mammy Tittleback and Her Family. The Hunter Cats of Connorloa . . .

Boston: Little, Brown, and Company. ⟨1884⟩

Another printing (dated 1886?) advertised for Oct. 1 in PW Sept. 26, 1885.

10494. Seventeen Cats: A True Story of Mammy Tittleback and Her Family . . .

London: Cassell & Co., 1884.

Not seen. Title and imprint postulated. Entry on the basis of trade notices.

Presumably a reprint of *Mammy Tittleback and Her Family* . . . , Boston, 1881.

Listed PC Sept. 15, 1884. Advertised PC Oct. 1, 1884. Reviewed PC Dec. 6, 1884.

10495. Verses. By H. H. . . .

Boston: Roberts Brothers. 1884.

On copyright page: *New and Enlarged Edition*

10496. A Century of Dishonor . . . New Edition, Enlarged by the Addition of the Report of the Needs of the Mission Indians of California

Boston   Roberts Brothers   1885

Advertised for Sept. 19 PW Sept. 12, 1885. Deposited Sept. 26, 1885. Listed PW Oct. 3, 1885. Reprints *A Century of Dishonor*, 1881, and *Report on the Condition and Needs of the Mission Indians of California*, 1883.

10497. Verses. By H. H. . . .

Boston: Roberts Brothers. 1885.

On copyright page: *New and Enlarged Edition.*

10498. The Procession of Flowers in Colorado . . .

Boston: Roberts Brothers. 1886.

100 numbered copies only signed by the illustrator. Listed PW Dec. 4, 1886; and Dec. 3, 1887.

10499. Verses. By H. H. . . .

Boston: Roberts Brothers. 1886.

On copyright page: *New and Enlarged Edition.*

10500. Helen Jackson's Poems

⟨Boston: Roberts Brothers, 1887⟩

Cover-title. Sheets of *Verses*, 1887; and, *Sonnets and Lyrics*, 1886; or, 1887, bound together and issued as a single volume. Advertised for Oct. 25 in PW Oct. 22, 1887. Listed PW Oct. 29, 1887, as in: cloth; cloth, gilt extra; flexible morocco; flexible morocco, gilt extra; calf.

10501. Report of Mrs. Helen Hunt Jackson and Abbot Kinney on the Mission Indians in 1883. Abbreviated.

Boston: Press of Stanley and Usher, 171 Devonshire Street. 1887.

Cover-title. Printed paper wrapper.

10502. Sonnets and Lyrics . . .

Boston   Roberts Brothers   1887

10503. Best. By Helen Hunt . . .

⟨n.p., n.d., 1887?⟩

Heavy white card. About 1/16″ thick. Edges bevelled and gilded. Corners rounded. 6⅞″ x 3⁵⁄₁₆″. Printed on recto only. *Note:* Dated on the basis of a like publication of one of Longfellow's poems which could not have been issued before May 7, 1887. Reprinted from *Verses*, 1870.

10504. Helen Jackson's Poems

⟨Boston: Roberts Brothers, 1888⟩

Cover-title. Sheets of *Verses*, 1888; and, *Sonnets and Lyrics*, 1888, bound together and issued as a single volume.

10505. My Legacy . . .

Boston: H. H. Carter & Karrick. 1888.

Printed paper wrapper. Tied with cord. Reprinted from *Verses*, 1870.

10506. Helen Jackson's Poems

⟨Boston: Roberts Brothers, 1890⟩

Cover-title. Sheets of *Verses*, 1890; and, *Sonnets and Lyrics*, 1889, bound together and issued as a single volume. See *Sonnets and Lyrics*, 1889, entry No. 10477.

10507. Helen Jackson's Poems

⟨Boston: Roberts Brothers, 1890⟩

Cover-title. Sheets of *Verses*, 1890; and, *Sonnets and Lyrics*, 1890, bound together and issued as a single volume.

10508. A Calendar of Sonnets . . .

Boston: Roberts Brothers Publishers   Somerset Street   1891

Advertised for Oct. 17 PW Oct. 10, 1891. Noted as *just ready* PW Oct. 17, 1891. Listed PW Oct. 24, 1891.

10509. Sonnets and Lyrics . . .

Boston   Roberts Brothers   1891

10510. Zeph . . . Author's Edition

Edinburgh   David Douglas, Castle Street   1892

Printed paper wrapper. Advertised as *nearly ready* Ath Feb. 13, 1892. Listed Ath and PC March 5; and Bkr March, 1892.

10511. Poems . . .

Roberts Brothers Boston   1892

Occurs in two forms: TRADE: Laid paper; all edges gilded; 7⁵⁄₁₆″ x 4⅞″; title-page in black. LIMITED: Wove paper watermarked *L L Brown*

Paper Company; top edges gilded, otherwise untrimmed; 8¾" x 5¾"; title-page in black and red; limited to 250 copies. Deposited Sept. 30, 1892 (Limited ed.). Advertised as *ready Oct. 14* PW Oct. 8, 1892. Listed PW Dec. 10, 1892.

10512. Helen Jackson's Poems

⟨Boston: Roberts Brothers, 1892⟩

Cover-title. Sheets of *Verses,* 1892; and, *Sonnets and Lyrics,* 1892, bound together and issued as a single volume.

10513. Sonnets and Lyrics ...

Boston   Roberts Brothers   1892

10514. Poems ...

Boston   Roberts Brothers   1893

Note: The title-leaf is a cancel. Sheets of an earlier printing with cancel title-page?

10515. Verses. By H. H. ...

Boston: Roberts Brothers. 1893.

On copyright page: *New and Enlarged Edition.*

10516. The Helen Jackson Year-Book Selections by Harriet T. Perry

Boston: Roberts Bros. 1895

Deposited Oct. 4, 1895. Listed PW Oct. 26, 1895.

10517. Sonnets and Lyrics ...

Boston   Roberts Brothers   1895

10518. Verses. By H. H. ...

Boston: Roberts Brothers. 1895.

10519. I Wonder What the Clover Thinks. By Saxe Holm.

Boston: L. Prang & Company, 1896.

Not located. Title and imprint postulated.

"L. Prang & Co. have prepared for the coming holiday season an unusually large number of new booklets, calendars, and art novelties. Foremost among these ... *I Wonder What the Clover Thinks* ... by Saxe Holm, accompanied by six full-page illustrations of red and white clover in full colors by Bessie Gray ... These booklets are all tied with silk ribbons and put up in boxes ..."—PW, Nov. 14, 1896, p. 835.

Presumably a separate printing of "A Song of Clover" in *Saxe Holm's Stories,* first series, New York, 1874.

10520. The Procession of Flowers in Colorado ...

Boston: Roberts Brothers. 1897.

Printed paper wrapper. In *The Colorado Series.* Deposited Sept. 24, 1897. See under 1886 for an earlier printing.

10521. Poems ...

Boston   Roberts Brothers   1897

10522. Glimpses of California and the Missions ...

Boston   Little, Brown, & Company   1902

Deposited April 17, 1902. Noted as *just published* PW Sept. 6, 1902.

10523. Father Junipero and the Mission Indians of California ...

Boston   Little, Brown, & Company   1902

Deposited June 11, 1902.

10524. ... The Fir-Tree and the Brook (8 Part Chorus) ⟨by⟩ Bertram Shapleigh, Op. 54 ...

London   W. Breitkopf & Härtel   54 Great Marlborough Street ⟨1908⟩

Cover-title. Sheet music. At head of title: *Breitkopf & Härtel's Choruses* ... Plate number L.185.

10525. The Cahuilla Reservation   Reprint from the Appendix to ... "A Century of Dishonor." ... Copyright by Roberts Bros., 1885 ... Boston ...

⟨n.p., n.d., *ca.* 1920⟩

Single cut sheet folded to make 4 pages. The above at head of p. ⟨1⟩.

10526. St. Christopher   The Text by Helen Hunt Jackson   The Music by William Y. Webbe ...

New York   The H. W. Gray Company   Sole Agents for Novello & Co., Ltd. ⟨1921⟩

Printed paper wrapper. Cover-title. Otherwise "The Parable of St. Christopher," in *Bits of Talk ... for Young Folks,* 1876.

10527. ... My Day in the Wilderness ...

Published for Its Members by the Book Club of California December 1939

At head of title: *Six California Tales: Number Six*   Printed paper wrapper. Limited to 650 copies. Reprinted from *Bits of Travel at Home,* 1878.

In this section are listed books by authors other than Jackson which contain material by her reprinted from earlier books. See *Section II* for a list of collections of reprinted material issued under Jackson's name and separate editions.

Songs of Home Selected from Many Sources . . .

New York: Charles Scribner and Company. 1871.

Illustrated Library of Favorite Song . . . Edited by J. G. Holland . . .

New York . . . ⟨1873⟩

For comment see entry No. 2853.

The Poet's Gift of Consolation to Sorrowing Mothers.

A. S. Barnes & Co. New York. ⟨n.d., 1873⟩

Songs of Nature . . .

New York . . . 1873.

For comment see entry No. 4760.

Sea and Shore . . .

Boston . . . 1874.

For comment see entry No. 4043.

The Chamber of Peace . . .

New York . . . ⟨1874⟩

For comment see entry No. 425.

Parnassus Edited by Ralph Waldo Emerson . . .

Boston . . . 1875.

For fuller information see entry No. 5269.

The Ark . . .

Boston . . . 1875 . . .

For comment see entry No. 281.

The Echo. A Journal of the Fair . . .

New York . . . 1875 . . .

For comment see entry No. 1744.

Songs of Three Centuries. Edited by John Greenleaf Whittier.

Boston . . . 1876.

For comment see entry No. 11341.

The Mountains . . .

Boston . . . 1876.

For comment see entry No. 1239.

Autumn Leaves.

⟨n.p., n.d., 1876?⟩

For comment see entry No. 11344. "Not As I Will," pp. 17-18; also in (reprinted from?) *Verses*, 1874.

The Reading Club and Handy Speaker . . . Edited by George M. Baker. No. 4.

Boston . . . 1877.

For comment see entry No. 8303.

Poems of Places Edited by Henry W. Longfellow . . . Italy. Vol. II.

Boston . . . 1877.

For comment see entry No. 12185.

Poems of Places Edited by Henry W. Longfellow . . . Switzerland and Austria.

Boston . . . 1877.

For comment see entry No. 12190.

One Hundred Choice Selections No. 14 . . .

. . . Philadelphia . . . 1877.

For comment see BAL, Vol. 2, p. 104. "A Courteous Mother," pp. 75-78; otherwise "A Day with a Courteous Mother," in *Bits of Talk About Home Matters*, 1873.

Poems of Places Edited by Henry W. Longfellow . . . Greece, and Turkey in Europe.

Boston . . . 1878.

For comment see entry No. 12198.

Folded Hands . . .

. . . New York ⟨1878⟩

Deposited April 15, 1878. For fuller entry see No. 2922.

Golden Thoughts on Mother, Home and Heaven ... with an Introduction by Rev. Theo. L. Cuyler ...

New-York: E. B. Treat, 757 Broadway ... ⟨1878⟩

"A Mother's Love," p. 34; otherwise "The Love of God," in *Saxe Holm's Stories*, 1874.

A subscription book and as such issued with variant imprints; also, presumably, issued in a variety of bindings. Deposited Dec. 2, 1878.

Garnered Treasures from the Poets ...

Philadelphia ... 1878.

For fuller entry see No. 4772.

Poetry of America ... ⟨Edited⟩ by W. J. Linton.

London ... 1878.

For fuller entry see No. 7872.

Tears for the Little Ones. A Collection of Poems and Passages Inspired by the Loss of Children. Edited by Helen Kendrick Johnson ...

Boston: James R. Osgood and Company, Late Ticknor & Fields and Fields, Osgood, & Co. 1878.

Introduction dated June, 1877. Copyright notice dated 1877.

The Children's Book of Poetry ... Selected ... by Henry T. Coates ...

Porter & Coates. Philadelphia. ⟨1879⟩

At the Beautiful Gate ...

New York ... 1880.

" 'Blind Spinner'," pp. 60-62; otherwise "Spinning," *Verses*, 1870.

For comment see BAL, Vol. 2, pp. 104-105.

Selections in Verse ⟨Edited by Rachel J. A. Haldeman⟩ ...

Philadelphia: J. B. Lippincott & Co. 1881.

A copy in H inscribed by the editor July 25, 1881. A letter (in H) from the editor to Longfellow identifies the editor.

Wide Awake Pleasure Book. ⟨Vol. 13⟩

Boston ... ⟨1881⟩

For comment see entry No. 6298.

Favorite Poems ...

New York ... ⟨n.d., after May 1, 1881⟩

For fuller entry see under Lucy Larcom, *Section 3*.

Purple and Gold Arranged by Kate Sanborn ...

Boston ... 1882 ...

For comment see BAL, Vol. 1, p. 379.

Tender and True. Poems of Love Selected by the Editor of "Quiet Hours," "Sunshine in the Soul," Etc. ⟨Mary Wilder Foote Tileston⟩

Boston: George H. Ellis, 141 Franklin Street. 1882.

Copyright notice dated 1881. Reprinted with an 1883 imprint and copyright notice dated 1882.

The Poet and the Children ... Edited by Matthew Henry Lothrop ...

Boston ... ⟨1882⟩

For comment see entry No. 3788.

... Selections for School Exhibitions and Private Reading ... Nos. 1, 2, 3 ...

Boston ... 1882.

For comment see BAL, Vol. 2, p. 472.

A Handful of Blossoms ... Arranged and Illustrated by Susie B. Skelding

New York   White, Stokes, & Allen   1883

Fringed pictorial boards. Unpaged. Deposited Sept. 6, 1883.

Flowers from Hill and Dale   Poems Arranged ... by Susie Barstow Skelding ...

New York ... 1883

For fuller entry see No. 11363.

Flowers from Glade and Garden   Poems Arranged ... by Susie Barstow Skelding ...

New York ... 1884

For comment see BAL, Vol. 2, p. 39.

Roses and Forget-Me-Nots   A Valentine ... Arranged ... by Susie B. Skelding

New York   White, Stokes, & Allen   1884

Pictorial wrapper.

Flowers for Winter Days ... Arranged ... by Susie Barstow Skelding ...

New York ... 1885

For fuller entry see BAL, Vol. 4, p. 444.

Spring Blossoms ... Poems by Prominent Authors Arranged ... by Susie Barstow Skelding ...

New York   White, Stokes, & Allen   1885

Tied. Color print pasted to front. Deposited Aug. 3, 1885.

Flowers from Sunlight and Shade ... Arranged and Illustrated by Susie Barstow Skelding ...

New York   White, Stokes, & Allen   1885

Deposited Aug. 15, 1885.

Flowers from Here and There   Poems Arranged by ... Susie Barstow Skelding ...

New York   White, Stokes, & Allen   1885

March Edited by Oscar Fay Adams ...

Boston ... ‹1886›

For comment see entry No. 60.

May Edited by Oscar Fay Adams ...

Boston ... ‹1886›

For comment see entry No. 63.

July Edited by Oscar Fay Adams ...

Boston ... ‹1886›

For comment see entry No. 65.

Familiar Birds and What the Poets Sing of Them ... Edited by Susie Barstow Skelding ...

New York ... 1886

For comment see BAL, Vol. 1, p. 86.

Songs of Birds Edited by Susie Barstow Skelding ...

New York   White, Stokes, & Allen   1886

Unprinted flexible paper boards. Tied to front is a pictorial label printed on celluloid. Unpaged. Tied.

The Two Voices   Poems ... Selected by John W. Chadwick ...

Troy ... 1886

For fuller entry see Lucy Larcom list, Section Three.

Birds and Blossoms and What the Poets Sing of Them ... Edited by Susie Barstow Skelding ...

New York   Frederick A. Stokes Successor to White, Stokes, & Allen   1887

Deposited July 29, 1887.

No. 17. Standard Recitations ... Compiled ... by Frances P. Sullivan ... September, 1887 ...

... N. Y. ... ‹1887›

For comment see entry No. 9009.

Wide Awake Pleasure Book   Gems of Literature and Art by American Authors and Artists

Boston   D Lothrop Company   Franklin and Hawley Streets ‹1887›

Pictorial boards, cloth shelfback. Unpaged.

Bits of Distant Land and Sea. Edited ... by Susie Barstow Skelding ...

New York   Copyright, 1888, by Frederick A. Stokes & Brother 1888

Deposited Aug. 4, 1888.

Sea Vistas in Many Climes Edited ... by Susie Barstow Skelding ...

New York   Copyright, 1888, by Frederick A. Stokes & Brother 1888

Deposited Aug. 4, 1888.

Franklin Square Song Collection ... No. 5. Selected by J. P. McCaskey ...

New York ... ‹1888›

"The Birds Must Know," p. 85; otherwise "The Way to Sing," *Verses*, 1870. For fuller entry see BAL, Vol. 4, p. 333.

Mother Songs Selected by Esther T. Housh ...

Brattleboro, Vt. ... 1888.

For comment see entry No. 11502.

Love Songs Selected by Esther T. Housh ...

Brattleboro, Vt.: Frank E. Housh & Co., Publishers. 1888.

Printed paper wrapper.

American Sonnets. Selected ... by William Sharp.

London ... ‹n.d., 1889›

For comment see BAL, Vol. 3, p. 101.

... Harper's Fifth Reader   American Authors

New York ... 1889

"The Sheep-Shearing," pp. 294-303, extracted from *Ramona*, 1884. For comment see entry No. 7917.

Belford's Annual. 1889–90. Edited by Thomas W. Handford ...

Chicago. New York and. San Francisco. Belford Clarke & Co. ⟨1889⟩

Printed paper boards, cloth shelfback. Deposited Oct. 10, 1889. Reprints "Lifted Over," p. 178. "An Ideal Happy Home," p. 106 is extracted from "Wanted – – a Home" in *Bits of Talk About Home Matters,* 1873.

Buds and Blossoms Illustrated

Philadelphia Peterson Magazine Co. 1889

The Poets' Year ... Edited by Oscar Fay Adams ...

Boston ... ⟨1890⟩

For comment see entry No. 80.

American Sonnets Selected ... by T. W. Higginson and E. H. Bigelow

Boston ... 1890

For comment see entry No. 8373.

Representative Sonnets by American Poets ... by Charles H. Crandall

Boston ... 1890

For comment see entry No. 8374.

No. 30. Standard Recitations by Best Authors ... Compiled ... by Frances P. Sullivan ... December 1890 ...

M. J. Ivers & Co., Publishers, 86 Nassau Street, N. Y. ... ⟨1890⟩

Printed paper wrapper. Deposited Feb. 21, 1891. Reprinted and reissued with the publisher's later address: *379 Pearl Street.*

No. 31. Standard Recitations by Best Authors ... Compiled ... by Frances P. Sullivan ... March 1891 ...

... N. Y. ... ⟨1891⟩

For comment see BAL, Vol. 2, p. 275.

Out of the Heart Poems for Lovers Young and Old Selected by John White Chadwick ... and Annie Hathaway Chadwick ...

Troy, N. Y. Nims and Knight 1891

Various styles of binding. Listed PW Nov. 14, 1891. Reissued by Joseph Knight Company, Boston ⟨1891; *i.e.,* 1893⟩; advertised as *just published* PW May 27, 1893.

The Lover's Year-Book of Poetry ... ⟨Compiled⟩ by Horace Parker Chandler Vol. I. January to June

Boston ... 1891

For comment see entry No. 4015.

Younger American Poets 1830–1890 Edited by Douglas Sladen ...

... London ... 1891

For fuller entry see No. 6557.

Younger American Poets 1830–1890 Edited by Douglas Sladen ...

... New York 1891

For fuller entry see No. 6558.

Holidays at Home for Winter and Summer ...

Boston ... ⟨1892⟩

For comment see BAL, Vol. 2, p. 116.

Franklin Square Song Collection ... No. 8. Selected by J. P. McCaskey ...

New York ... 1892

For fuller entry see BAL, Vol. 1, p. 381.

The Lover's Year-Book of Poetry ... ⟨Compiled⟩ by Horace Parker Chandler Vol. II. July to December

Boston ... 1892

For fuller entry see BAL, Vol. 4, p. 61.

Sun Prints in Sky Tints ... by Irene E. Jerome

Boston ... 1893

Reprints "Down to Sleep," p. 77. "White Clover," p. 27, is extracted from "A Road-Side," *Bits of Travel at Home,* 1878. For fuller entry see BAL, Vol. 2, p. 452.

Random Rhymes. ⟨Edited by Roland R. Conklin⟩

⟨n.p., Kansas City, Mo., 1893⟩

The Lover's Year-Book of Poetry ⟨Second Series⟩ ... Married-Life and Child-Life ⟨Compiled⟩ by Horace Parker Chandler ...

Boston ... 1893

For comment see entry No. 10903.

Autumn Leaves ... Edited by Daphne Dale.

⟨n.p.⟩ 1893. National Book Mart.

For fuller entry see No. 6336A.

Evenings with Colorado Poets. A Compilation of Selections ... Compiled ... by Francis S. Kinder, and F. Clarence Spencer.

Denver, Colo.: The Chain & Hardy Co. 1894.

Later American Poems Edited by J. E. Wetherell . . .

    Toronto: The Copp, Clark Company, Limited. 1896.

The Lover's Year-Book of Poetry   A Collection of Love Poems for Every Day in the Year   The Other Life by Horace Parker Chandler   Vol. I. January to June

    Boston   Roberts Brothers   1896

The Treasury of American Sacred Song . . . Edited by W. Garrett Horder . . .

    London . . . 1896

    For fuller entry see under Lucy Larcom, *Section 3.*

Library of the World's Best Literature Ancient and Modern   Charles Dudley Warner Editor . . . Thirty Volumes Vol. XIV

    New York . . . ⟨1897⟩

    For fuller entry see No. 10624. Deposited July 27, 1897.

Voices of Doubt and Trust Selected by Volney Streamer

    New York   Brentano's   1897

    Deposited Sept. 2, 1897.

. . . Our Country: West.

    1897: Perry Mason & Company, Boston, Mass.

    At head of title: The Companion Series.

    Deposited Nov. 12, 1897.

Fireside Treasures . . .

    Boston . . . ⟨1898⟩

    For comment see BAL, Vol. 2, p. 116.

Dew Drops and Diamonds . . .

    . . . 1898 . . . Chicago . . .

    For comment see BAL, Vol. 1, p. 77.

The International Library of Famous Literature . . . Compiled . . . by Nathan Haskell Dole, Forrest Morgan and Caroline Ticknor . . .

    New York   Merrill and Baker   Publishers ⟨1898⟩

    For fuller entry see in Sarah Orne Jewett reprints.

The International Library of Famous Literature . . . Edited by Dr. Richard Garnett . . . in Twenty Volumes . . .

London   Issued by The Standard 1899

    For comment see entry No. 10638.

. . . Industries of To-day Edited by M. A. L. Lane.

    Boston, U.S.A.   Ginn & Company, Publishers   The Athenaeum Press   1904

    At head of title: Youth's Companion Series

    Deposited Feb. 2, 1904.

Through Italy with the Poets   Compiled by Robert Haven Schauffler . . .

    New York . . . 1908

    For comment see BAL, Vol. 4, p. 446.

Pathway to Western Literature ⟨Edited⟩ by Nettie S. Gaines . . .

    Stockton, California   Nettie S. Gaines   All Rights Reserved ⟨1910⟩

The Pike's Peak Region in Song and Myth by Elijah Clarence Hills

    ⟨Colorado Springs, Colorado, January, 1913⟩

    Printed paper wrapper. *Colorado College Publication General Series No. 66 Language Series Vol. II., No. 29,* pp. 165-220.

A Collection of Verse by California Poets from 1849 to 1915 Compiled by Augustin S. Macdonald . . .

    A. M. Robertson   San Francisco   1914

    Erratum slip, pp. 34-35. Printed paper boards.

Golden Songs of the Golden State Selected by Marguerite Wilkinson

    Chicago   A. C. McClurg & Co.   1917

    On copyright page: *Published November, 1917*

Literary California . . . ⟨Compiled⟩ by Ella Sterling Mighels . . .

    . . . San Francisco . . . 1918

    For comment see BAL, Vol. 1, p. 226.

St. Nicholas Book of Verse Edited by Mary Budd Skinner and Joseph Osmun Skinner . . .

    . . . New York . . . MCMXXIII

    For comment see entry No. 818.

Songs and Stories Selected . . . by Edwin Markham . . .

    Powell Publishing Company   San Francisco   Los Angeles   Chicago ⟨1931⟩

The Californians: Writings of Their Past and Present Edited by Robert Pearsall ⟨and⟩ Ursula Spier Erickson ...

San Francisco Hesperian House ⟨1961⟩

2 Vols. All Jackson material herein reprinted from other books. "Outdoor Industries," Vol. 1, pp. 331-337, extracted from *Glimpses of Three Coasts*, 1886.

REFERENCES AND ANA

In Memoriam. Hugh A. Pue, Esq. Died November 24th, 1867, Aged 55 Years, 5 Months.

⟨n.p., n.d., Philadelphia, 1867⟩

Cover-title. Printed paper wrapper. "Wreck," p. ⟨2⟩, signed *H.H.* By Helen Hunt Jackson? By Henry Holt?

Nathan the Wise A Dramatic Poem by Gotthold Ephraim Lessing Translated by Ellen Frothingham ...

New York: Leypoldt & Holt. 1868.

The "Sketch of Lessing," pp. ⟨v⟩-xxiii, signed *H.H.* is not by Helen Hunt Jackson, but by Henry Holt. In a note to the Library of Congress (original in LC) dated Oct. 30, 1917, Henry Holt acknowledges authorship of the "Sketch."

In Memoriam Helen Hunt Jackson (H.H.)

⟨Denver, Colo., Frank S. Thayer, 1886⟩

Anonymous. Cover-title. Printed paper wrapper. Four pages of text. An extended edition (six pages of text) was issued with the statement "revised edition" added to the copyright notice; extended by the addition of a biographical sketch by Louis Swinburne.

Ramona, a Play in Five Acts, Adapted from Helen Hunt Jackson's Indian Novel by Ina Dillaye ...

Syracuse, N.Y.: Printed by F. LeC. Dillaye, 81 & 82 Wieting Block ... 1887 ...

Printed paper wrapper.

Fifty-Two Stories for Girlhood and Youth ... Edited by Alfred H. Miles ...

London ... ⟨1893⟩

"Miss Lapham's Japanese Silk," pp. 397-408, signed *H.H.* By Mrs. Jackson? For comment see entry No. 6336.

The Genesis of the Story of Ramona Why the Book Was Written, Explanatory Text of Points of Interest Mentioned in the Story ... by A. C. Vroman and T. F. Barnes

1899 Press of Kingsley-Barnes & Neuner Company Los Angeles, Cal.

Cloth? Wrapper?

The Real Ramona of Helen Hunt Jackson's Famous Novel by D. A. Hufford

D. A. Hufford & Co., Publishers 226 West Sixth Street Los Angeles, Cal. ⟨1900⟩

Printed paper wrapper. *Note:* The earliest copy examined has the statement *Third Edition* on the copyright page.

The True Story of "Ramona" Its Facts and Fictions, Inspiration and Purpose by Carlyle Channing Davis ... and William A. Alderson ...

New York Dodge Publishing Company 220 East 23d Street ⟨1914⟩

Helen Hunt Jackson (H. H.) by Ruth Odell

D. Appleton-Century Company Incorporated New York 1939 London

At end of index, p. 326, is the symbol (*1*), indicating *first printing*.

10528. Balloon Post . . .

Boston, Mass., April . . . 1871 . . .

An occasional newspaper. 6 numbers. For comment see entry No. 4038.

"Still Waters," No. 2, pp. 8-10. Reprinted in *The Dial of the Old South Clock,* an occasional newspaper published by The Old South Church, Boston, 1879. Collected in *The Complete Plays* ⟨1949⟩.

10529. A PASSIONATE PILGRIM, AND OTHER TALES . . .

BOSTON: JAMES R. OSGOOD AND COMPANY, LATE TICKNOR & FIELDS, AND FIELDS, OSGOOD, & CO. 1875.

⟨1⟩-496. 7½″ x 4¾″.

⟨1², 2-21¹², 22⁶⟩. *Signed:* ⟨A⟩-Z, AA-EE⁸. *Also signed:* ⟨1⟩-20¹², 21⁸.

C cloth: green. FL cloth: purple; terra-cotta. Covers bevelled. Brown-coated on white end papers. Flyleaves. Spine imprint: J. R. OSGOOD & CO

Note: The publisher's records show there was but one printing of this date: 1510 copies printed Jan. 27, 1875. Copies were being bound as late as 1882. Copies of the first printing were later issued in binding with spine imprint: HOUGHTON, OSGOOD & CO.; and, even later: HOUGHTON, MIFFLIN & CO.

Published Jan. 31, 1875 (publisher's records). Deposited Feb. 2, 1875. Listed PW Feb. 6, 1875. Noted (as a Trübner importation) Ath March 16, 1875.

CO (1st) H (1st; Houghton, Osgood) LC (Houghton, Mifflin) NYPL (1st) Y (Houghton, Mifflin)

10530. TRANSATLANTIC SKETCHES . . .

BOSTON: JAMES R. OSGOOD AND COMPANY, LATE TICKNOR & FIELDS, AND FIELDS, OSGOOD, & CO. 1875.

⟨i⟩-vi, ⟨7⟩-401, blank leaf. 7⁷⁄₁₆″ x 4¾″.

⟨1⟩-16¹², 17¹⁰. *Also signed:* ⟨A⟩-Y⁸, ⟨Z⟩².

C cloth: green. FL cloth: purple; terra-cotta. Covers bevelled. Brown-coated on white end papers. Flyleaves. Spine imprint: J. R. OSGOOD & CO

Note: The publisher's records show there was but one printing of this date: 1578 copies printed April 21, 1875. Copies were being bound as late as 1882. Copies of the first printing were later issued in binding with spine imprint: HOUGHTON MIFFLIN & CO. *Query:* Also bound with the *Houghton, Osgood & Company* spine imprint?

Note: Sheets occur either conventionally sewn with thread; or, stapled. BAL suspects that stapled copies represent a later binding order; a surviving copyright deposit copy is sewn; a copy with the *Houghton Mifflin* stamping (in UV) is stapled.

Printed April 21, 1875. A copy in H received from the publisher April 27, 1875. Deposited May 1, 1875. Listed PW May 1, 1875. Noted (as a Trübner importation) Ath June 26, 1875. See *Foreign Parts,* 1883, below.

AAS B CO H LC UV (also *Houghton Mifflin*)

10531. RODERICK HUDSON . . .

BOSTON: JAMES R. OSGOOD AND COMPANY, LATE TICKNOR & FIELDS, AND FIELDS, OSGOOD, & CO. 1876.

For other editions see under 1879, 1882.

⟨i-iv⟩, ⟨1⟩-482, blank leaf. 7⅜″ scant x 4¹³⁄₁₆″.

⟨1², 2-21¹², 22²⟩. *Signed:* ⟨-⟩², 1-30⁸, 31².

C cloth: green. FL cloth: terra-cotta. Covers bevelled. Brown-coated on white end papers. Flyleaves. Spine imprint: J. R. OSGOOD & CO.

Note: The publisher's records show but one printing of this date; and, copies were being bound as late as 1882. Copies of the first printing were later issued in binding with the spine imprint: HOUGHTON, MIFFLIN & CO. *Query:* Also bound with the *Houghton, Osgood & Company* spine imprint?

The following readings are common to all examined copies:

P. 12, line 6: . . . *illustratd*
P. 16, line 3: *to her* . . .
P. 447, line 11: . . . *Casamassina* . . .

The publisher's records: 1572 copies printed Nov. 10, 1875; bound during the period Nov. 17, 1875–Jan. 28, 1882. Plates melted May 23, 1894.

Noted as *just ready* pw Nov. 20, 1875. Deposited Nov. 24, 1875. Listed pw Dec. 4, 1875. Noted (as a Trübner importation) Ath Feb. 12, 1876.

AAS   H   JSK (Houghton Mifflin binding)   UV

10532. THE AMERICAN . . .

> BOSTON: JAMES R. OSGOOD AND COMPANY, LATE TICKNOR & FIELDS, AND FIELDS, OSGOOD, & CO. 1877.

⟨1⟩-473; 2 blank leaves; leaf excised or pasted under the end paper. $7\frac{3}{8}''$ x $4\frac{3}{4}''$.

⟨1-20⟩^{12}. Leaf ⟨20⟩$_{12}$ excised or pasted under the end paper. *Signed:* ⟨1⟩-30^8.

Note: The publisher's records show three printings as follows: April 30, 1877, 1008 copies; May 18, 1877, 514 copies; Aug. 29, 1877, 504 copies. Copies were being bound as late as Sept. 11, 1878, by which time the firm name had changed from *James R. Osgood & Co.,* to *Houghton, Osgood & Co.,* which accounts for the variant binding noted below. BAL has been unable to discover any variations in the sheets that might distinguish one printing from another but it seems reasonable to assume that copies in the later binding are of the third printing. There is a possibility that the copies first printed do not have a period following the co in the title-page imprint but positive proof of this is lacking and further study is indicated.

FL cloth: green; terra-cotta. Bevelled covers. Brown-coated on white end papers. Flyleaf at front.

Note: Two binding issues noted:

1: Spine imprint: J. R. OSGOOD & CO.

2: Spine imprint: HOUGHTON, OSGOOD & CO.

Noted for *immediate publication* pw April 28, 1877. Title deposited May 4, 1877. BA copy received May 5, 1877. Deposited May 11, 1877. Listed pw May 12, 1877. Reviewed (Boston edition) Ath July 7, 1877. The Ward, Lock (London) edition listed pc Dec. 18, 1877. Macmillan (London) edition listed Ath March 8, 1879. Ward, Lock & Bowden (London) edition listed pc May 5, 1894. *See next entry.*

H   JSK (Houghton, Osgood)   LC   NYPL   UV

10533. The American . . . Authorized Edition. In Two Volumes . . .

Leipzig   Bernhard Tauchnitz   1878.

2 Vols. Printed paper wrapper. Issued as Nos. 1713-1714 of *Collection of British Authors* series.

For first edition see preceding entry.

Reprint save for a brief 3-line note, Vol. 1, p. ⟨5⟩: *The present edition . . . is published with my full assent . . . Paris, Dec. 1877.*

The earliest copy noted is dated *January 1878* on outer back wrapper.

Listed wv Feb. 7, 1878.

LC   Y

10534. FRENCH POETS AND NOVELISTS . . .

> LONDON: MACMILLAN AND CO. 1878. [THE RIGHT OF TRANSLATION AND REPRODUCTION IS RESERVED.]

⟨i-viii⟩, ⟨1⟩-439; printer's imprint, p. ⟨440⟩. $7\frac{1}{2}''$ x 5''.

⟨A⟩^{4}, B-I, K-U, X-Z, AA-EE^8, FF^4.

V cloth: greenish-black.

Note: In all examined copies the figure 2 in folio *280* is lacking.

Announced Ath Oct. 13, 1877. Noted as *new* pc Oct. 16, 1877. Advertised as *this day* Ath Feb. 23, 1878. Listed Ath Feb. 23, 1878. Advertised as *this day* pc and Bkr March 1, 1878. Listed pc and Bkr March 1, 1878. Listed pw March 16, 1878. Again listed (erroneously described as an American book) pc April 16, 1878.

Note: Two copies were deposited for copyright in Washington; each bears receipt date of *1877;* an obvious error. In one copy the date has been corrected, by hand, to *1878.* The Copyright Office is unable to account for the 1877 date and reports that the copies were received from Macmillan on March 7, 1878.

CO   LC   Y

10535. WATCH AND WARD . . .

> BOSTON: HOUGHTON, OSGOOD AND COMPANY. THE RIVERSIDE PRESS, CAMBRIDGE. 1878.

Two printings noted:

1

⟨1⟩-219; blank leaf; leaf excised or pasted under the end paper. $5\frac{13}{16}''$ x $4\frac{1}{4}''$ scant.

⟨1-14⟩^{8}. Leaf ⟨14⟩$_8$ excised or pasted under the end paper.

1000 copies printed May, 1878 (publisher's records).

HENRY JAMES
Entry Nos. 10560 and 10529
Much Reduced
(Harvard University Library, Yale University Library)

2

⟨1⟩-219.

⟨1-13⁸, 14⁶⟩.

280 copies printed July 15, 1878 (publisher's records).

S cloth: green; terra-cotta. Tan-coated on white end papers; green-coated on white end papers. Flyleaf at front. Edges stained red.

Printed May, 1878. Noted for *May 29* PW May 25, 1878. Deposited May 31, 1878. BA copy (first printing) received June 5, 1878. Listed PW June 8, 1878. Second printing done July 15, 1878. Reviewed Ath Aug. 10, 1878.

BA (1st)   LC (1st, being a deposit copy)   UV (1st, 2nd)

10536. THE EUROPEANS. A SKETCH ... IN TWO VOLUMES ...

LONDON: MACMILLAN AND CO. 1878.

Note: The publisher's records (see below) indicate three printings dated 1878; the fourth printing dated 1879. BAL offers the present entry not as final but as a contribution to the final solution. For first American edition see next entry.

1: ⟨i-iv⟩, ⟨1⟩-255. 7⁵⁄₁₆″ x 5″.

2: ⟨i-iv⟩, ⟨1⟩-272.

1: ⟨A⟩², B-I, K-R⁸.

2: ⟨A⟩², B-I, K-S⁸.

C cloth: blue. Brown-coated on white end papers. Inserted at back of Vol. 1: Publisher's catalog, pp. 40, dated *June 1878*.

VOL. 1, FIRST (?) PRINTING

P. 24, last line ends: ... *drawing,* |

P. 77, last line ends: ... *say* |

P. 83, last line ends: ... *door way.* |

P. 137, last line ends: ... *peculiar influences.* |

P. 156, last line ends: ... *indiscriminately* |

Pp. 171, 173, 175: The chapter number in the running heads is erroneously printed IV for V. In all copies examined by BAL the I has been erased.

Pp. 177-191, rectos only: The chapter number in the running heads is correctly printed V.

Pp. 195, 213: The chapter number is correctly printed V.

VOL. 1, SECOND (?) PRINTING

Not seen by BAL? Unrecognized by BAL?

Mr. Simon Nowell-Smith reports that his copy, and a copy in the London Library, have the following readings. Mixed sheets? Second printing?

P. 24, last line ends: ... *drawing,* |

P. 77, last line ends: ... *say.* |

P. 83, last line ends: ... *doorway.* |

P. 137, last line ends: ... *peculiar influences.* |

P. 156, last line ends: ... *indiscriminately,* |

Pp. 171-191, rectos only: The chapter number in the running heads is IV for V throughout. This feature also reported by Edel-Laurence, pp. 37-38.

Pp. 195, 213: The chapter number is correctly printed V.

VOL. 1, THIRD (?) PRINTING

Noted only as a two-volumes-in-one production; not as part of a two-volume set.

P. 24, last line ends: ... *drawing* |

P. 77, last line ends: ... *say.* |

P. 83, last line ends: ... *doorway.* |

P. 137, last line ends: ... *peculiar influence!* |

P. 156, last line ends: ... *indiscriminately,* |

Pp. 171, 173, 175: The chapter number in the running heads is correctly printed V.

Pp. 177-191, rectos only: The chapter number in the running heads is erroneously printed IV.

Pp. 195, 213: The chapter number in the running heads is erroneously Y for V.

VOL. 2, FIRST (?) PRINTING

P. 46, last line: *this* ...

P. 101, last line ends: ... *moment,* |

P. 272: Four lines of text present.

P. 272, printer's imprint: CLAY AND TAYLOR, PRINTERS, BUNGAY.

VOL. 2, SECOND (?) PRINTING

P. 46, last line: *this* ...

P. 101, last line ends: ... *moment,* |

P. 272: Five lines of text present.

P. 272, printer's imprint: CLAY AND TAYLOR, PRINTERS, BUNGAY.

VOL. 2, THIRD (?) PRINTING

Noted only as a two-volumes-in-one production; not as part of a two-volume set.

P. 46, last line: *his* ...

P. 101, last line ends: ... *moment* |

P. 272: Five lines of text present.

P. 272, printer's imprint: ⟨rule⟩ / BUNGAY: CLAY AND TAYLOR, PRINTERS.

First printed, 2 Vols., Sept. 1878 (publisher's records). Advertised PC Sept. 16, 1878, as *just ready*. Advertised, 2 Vols., as *this day* Ath Sept. 21, 1878. Listed, 2 Vols., Ath Sept. 21, 1878. Second printing, 2 Vols., Oct. 1878 (publisher's records). Reviewed, 2 Vols., Ath Oct. 5, 1878. The "second edition" (*i.e.*, second printing) advertised Ath Oct. 19, 1878. Third printing (presumably issued two-volumes-in-one) printed Nov. 1878 (publisher's records). Listed PC Nov. 2, 1878. Advertised, with reviews, 2 Vols., Ath Nov. 9, 1878. A one-volume edition (*i.e.*, the 6/-reprint) advertised for *next week* Ath April 19, 1879; listed Ath April 26, 1879; PC May 16, 1879.

The present entry made on the basis of copies in:

AAS   CO   H   LC   UV   Y

10537. THE EUROPEANS. A SKETCH ...

BOSTON: HOUGHTON, OSGOOD AND COMPANY. THE RIVERSIDE PRESS, CAMBRIDGE. 1879.

For prior London publication see preceding entry.

⟨i-iv⟩, ⟨1⟩-281, blank leaf. 7⁷⁄₁₆" x 4¾".

⟨1², 2-12¹², 13¹⁰⟩. *Signed:* ⟨-⟩², 1-17⁸, 18⁶.

Note: According to the publisher's records (see below) there were at least three printings issued under date 1879. The following printings have been recognized; but it must be noted that one of the following may represent two printings.

1st (and 2nd?) Printing

Pagination and signature collation as given above.

2nd (3rd?) Printing

⟨i-ii⟩, ⟨1⟩-281; blank leaf; leaf excised or pasted under the end paper.

⟨1-12⟩¹². Leaf ⟨12⟩₁₂ excised or pasted under the end paper. *Signed:* ⟨-⟩¹, 1-17⁸, 18⁷. *Note:* In the only examined copy of this printing the title-leaf (⟨1⟩₁) appears to be a singleton and is not conjugate with ⟨1⟩₁₂. Further investigation indicated.

FL cloth: green (both Kelly green and dark green noted); terra-cotta. Brown-coated on white end papers. The flyleaves have been noted in the following forms; sequence, if any, not determined: *A:* Single laid paper flyleaf at front, single wove paper flyleaf at back; *B:* Two wove paper flyleaves at front, two wove paper flyleaves at back; *C:* Two laid paper flyleaves at front, two laid paper flyleaves at back; *D:*

Single wove paper flyleaf at front, single wove paper flyleaf at back; *E:* Two laid paper flyleaves at front, two wove paper flyleaves at back. Covers bevelled.

Printing Record

Oct. 7, 1878: 1558 copies printed. Bound during the period Oct. 9-21, 1878.

Dec. 24, 1878. *Second printing.* 286 copies. Bound during the period Jan. 2-March 19, 1879.

April 21, 1879. *Third printing.* 282 copies. Bound during the period April 30-Dec. 1, 1879.

Noted for Oct. 12 PW Oct. 5, 1878. Deposited Oct. 16, 1878. Listed PW Oct. 19, 1878. The Leipzig (Tauchnitz) edition listed WV Dec. 12, 1878.

BPL (2nd ⟨3rd?⟩)   CO (1st ⟨2nd?⟩)   H (1st ⟨2nd?⟩)   NYPL (1st ⟨2nd?⟩)

10538. DAISY MILLER A STUDY ...

NEW YORK   HARPER & BROTHERS, PUBLISHERS FRANKLIN SQUARE 1879

Issued as *Harper's Half-Hour Series*, No. 82.

⟨1⟩-116; 12 pp. advertisements. 4¹³⁄₁₆" x 3³⁄₁₆" (paper); 4¹¹⁄₁₆" x 3⅛" (cloth).

⟨1⟩-88.

Printed tan-gray paper wrapper; also, green S cloth, drab tan end papers.

Noted as *just ready* PW Nov. 2, 1878. Listed PW Nov. 9, 1878, as in wrapper. The Leipzig (Tauchnitz) edition listed WV June 12, 1879. For London and Leipzig editions see below under 1879.

AAS   CO   UV   Y

10539. AN INTERNATIONAL EPISODE ...

NEW YORK   HARPER & BROTHERS, PUBLISHERS FRANKLIN SQUARE 1879

Issued as *Harper's Half-Hour Series*, No. 91.

⟨1⟩-136; 8 pp. advertisements. 4¹³⁄₁₆" x 3³⁄₁₆" (paper); 4¹¹⁄₁₆" x 3⅛" (cloth).

⟨A⟩-I⁸.

Printed gray paper wrapper; also, green S cloth, drab tan end papers.

Two states (printings?) noted:

1

P. 44, last line: *blue* ...

P. 45, first line: *blue* ...

P. ⟨137⟩: *By Virginia W. Johnson* ...

Noted in both cloth; and, printed paper wrapper.

2

P. 44, last line: *blue* ...

P. 45, first line: *beth* ...

P. ⟨137⟩: *Bulwer's Works* ...

Noted in printed paper wrapper only.

Note: Edel-Laurence (p. 41) report "two states of advertisements in the first-issue copies, one having advertisements of Bulwer's works on p. ⟨137⟩ ... the other advertising the works of Virginia L. ⟨sic⟩ Johnson on p. ⟨137⟩ ..." Intensive checking by BAL has failed to locate a copy of the first state (printing?) with the Bulwer advertisement on p. ⟨137⟩.

The CO copy (1st, cloth) inscribed by early owner Jan. 15, 1879. The UV copy (1st, wrapper) inscribed by early owner Jan. 25, 1879. Listed PW Feb. 1, 1879, as in wrapper.

CO (1st) H (1st) IU (1st, 2nd) LC (1st) NYPL (1st) UV (1st)

10540. Daisy Miller: A Study. An International Episode. Four Meetings ... in Two Volumes ...

London: Macmillan and Co. 1879. [Right of Translation Is Reserved.]

For prior publication of *Daisy Miller* see above under 1879; also see preceding and next entries.

2 Vols. Reprint save for "Four Meetings," Vol. 2, pp. ⟨175⟩-263. First American book publication: *The Author of Beltraffio* ... , Boston, 1885.

Two states (printings?) of Vol. 2 noted:

1: P. 144 mispaged 145.

2: P. 144 correctly paged 144.

Printed Feb. 1879 (publisher's records). Advertised as *this day* Ath Feb. 15, 22, 1879. Listed Ath Feb. 22, 1879. Advertised as *this day* Bkr March 1, 1879, PC March 1, 1879. Reviewed Ath March 1, 1879. Reprinted March, 1879 (publisher's records). Reprinted in one volume Aug. 1879 (publisher's records). Reprinted in one volume Dec. 1879 (publisher's records); this printing, presumably, is the one described as a *new edition* and listed Ath Jan. 10, 1880, PC Jan. 17, 1880.

H (2nd) LC (2nd) Y (1st)

10541. Daisy Miller: A Study. An International Episode. Four Meetings ... Authorized Edition.

Leipzig   Bernhard Tauchnitz   1879.

Caution: Entry tentative, being based on two imperfect examples and a copy lacking the wrapper.

Printed paper wrapper. Issued as No. 1819 in *Collection of British Authors* series.

Reprint save for a 4-line note on p. ⟨2⟩, dated at end *April 1879.* For prior publication of the stories see preceding three entries.

Outer back wrapper dated *April 1879;* inserted terminal catalog dated *June 1879.*

Listed WV June 12, 1879.

LC UV Y

10542. Roderick Hudson ... in Three Volumes ... Revised Edition.

London: Macmillan and Co. 1879.

See under 1876 for first edition.

"Note. *Roderick Hudson* was originally published in Boston ... It has now been minutely revised, and has received a large number of verbal alterations. Several passages have been rewritten."—Vol. 1, p. ⟨iii⟩. For first American publication of this text see No. 10555.

Two binding variants have been noted; the sequence (if any) has not been determined and the designations are for identification only:

A: Leaf measures 7⁵⁄₁₆″ x 4⅞″. The inner panel on the front cover is (overall) 6⅛″ full tall.

B: Leaf measures 7⅛″ x 4⅞″. The inner panel on the front cover is (overall) 6⅛″ scant tall.

Common to both bindings: Publisher's catalog dated *May 1879* inserted in Vol. 1.

Listed Ath June 14, 1879. Advertised as *just ready* PC June 17, 1879; as *now ready* Ath June 21, 1879. Listed PC July 1, 1879. The Leipzig (Tauchnitz) edition listed WV Sept. 11, 1879. A new printing in one volume listed Ath May 8, 1880; PC May 15, 1880.

H (A,B) LC (A)

10543. THE MADONNA OF THE FUTURE AND OTHER TALES ... IN TWO VOLUMES ...

LONDON: MACMILLAN AND CO. 1879.   THE RIGHT OF TRANSLATION IS RESERVED.

1: ⟨i-viii⟩, ⟨1⟩-288. 7⁷⁄₁₆″ x 4¹⁵⁄₁₆″.

2: ⟨i-viii⟩, ⟨1⟩-245; printer's imprint, p. ⟨246⟩; 2 pp. advertisements.

1: ⟨A⟩⁴, B-I, K-T⁸.

2: ⟨A⟩⁴, B-I, K-Q⁸, R⁴.

BF cloth: blue. Brown-coated on white end papers.

Reprint save for:

"Benvolio" and "Longstaff's Marriage." For first American book publication see entry No. 10707.

"The Diary of a Man of Fifty." For first American book publication see entry No. 10550.

Listed Ath Oct. 11, 1879. Advertised for *this day* Ath Oct. 11, 1879; PC Oct. 17, 1879; Ath Oct. 18, 1879. Listed PC Nov. 3, 1879. Reprinted in one volume 1880 (publisher's records). The one volume reprint listed Ath April 17, 1880; PC May 1, 1880. The Leipzig (Tauchnitz) edition listed WV March 4, 1880.

H   NYPL

10544. HAWTHORNE ...

    LONDON   MACMILLAN AND CO   1879   THE RIGHT OF TRANSLATION AND REPRODUCTION IS RESERVED

⟨i⟩-⟨viii⟩, ⟨1⟩-183; printer's imprint, p. ⟨184⟩; plus: Publisher's catalog, 4 pp; see below for comment on the catalog. 7⅝" scant x 5⅛" (untrimmed); 7¼" x 4¹⁵⁄₁₆" (trimmed).

⟨A⟩⁴, B-I, K-M⁸, N⁴.

Note: Folio *19* occurs with the figure *9* either present or absent; no sequence has been established. Similarly, signature mark *C* is either present or absent.

The book has been noted as follows; the sequence is uncertain and the designations are for identification only:

Binding Variant A

Cloth: Unbleached linen, front cover unstamped, printed paper label on spine.

End papers: White wove

Leaves: Untrimmed

Publisher's catalog: 4 pp., inserted at back. Two variants have been noted:

    (a): Printed on paper appreciably thinner than that used in the body of the book. On p. 2 four titles listed as though published, together with a list of 13 titles under the heading *In preparation.*

    (b): Printed on paper somewhat thicker than that used in the body of the book. On p. 2 five titles are listed as though published (with extracts from reviews); 4 titles listed as though either published or about to be published; 8 titles listed under the heading *In preparation.*

Binding Variant B

Cloth: Orange V

Front cover: The first line of stamping reads: HAWTHORNE

End papers: Blue-coated on white

Leaves: Trimmed

Publisher's catalog: 4 pp., inserted at back. Printed on paper appreciably thinner than that used in the body of the book.

P. 2 of catalog: 4 titles listed as though published, together with a list of 13 titles under the heading *In preparation.*

Binding Variant C

Cloth: Red V

Front cover: The first line of stamping reads: ENGLISH MEN OF LETTERS

End papers: Blue-coated on white

Leaves: Trimmed

Publisher's catalog: 4 pp., inserted at back. Two variants have been noted:

    (a): Printed on paper appreciably thinner than that used in the body of the book. On p. 2 four titles are listed as though published, together with a list of 13 titles under the heading *In preparation.*

    (b): Printed on paper similar to that used in the body of the book. On p. 2 eight titles are listed as though published.

Note: The errors *express* (for *express*), p. 47, line 4 from bottom; and, *Blithdale* (for *Blithedale*), p. 137, line 1, are present in all examined copies of this date.

Advertised as *immediately* Ath Dec. 6, 1879. Listed Ath Dec. 13, 1879. Advertised as *this day* PC Dec. 18, 1879. Listed PC Dec. 31, 1879. For New York edition see below under 1880.

BPL (Ca)   CO (Aa; B; Ca; Cb)   H (Aa)   LC (Ca) NYPL (Ca)   SNS (Ab)   UV (Aa; Ca; Cb)   Y (Ca)

10545. Roderick Hudson ... Authorized Edition. In Two Volumes ...

    Leipzig   Bernhard Tauchnitz   1879.

Printed paper wrapper. Issued as Nos. 1842-1843 in *Collection of British Authors* series.

Reprint save for a 4-line note, p. ⟨5⟩, Vol. 1, dated at end *London, Aug. 1879.* Outer back wrapper of each volume dated *August 1879.*

See under 1876 for first edition. Listed WV Sept. 11, 1879.

LC

10546. CONFIDENCE ... IN TWO VOLUMES ...

LONDON   CHATTO & WINDUS, PICCADILLY   1880
ALL RIGHTS RESERVED

For first American edition see below under
1880 (February).

1: ⟨i-iv⟩, ⟨1⟩-309; blank, p. ⟨310⟩; device, p.
⟨311⟩. 7⁵⁄₁₆″ x 4⅞″.

2: ⟨i-iv⟩, ⟨1⟩-253; blank, p. ⟨254⟩; device, p.
⟨255⟩.

1: ⟨A⟩², B-I, K-U⁸, X⁴.

2: ⟨A⟩², B-I, K-R⁸.

V cloth: green; olive-brown. White paper end
papers printed in blue with a floral pattern.
Publisher's catalog inserted at back of Vol. 2,
pp. 32, dated *December, 1879*.

Advertised for Dec. 10 Bkr Dec. 2, 1879. Advertised as *now ready* Ath Dec. 13, 1879. Listed
Ath Dec. 13, 1879. CO copy inscribed by James
Dec. 14, 1879. Advertised as *now ready* (with
extract from a review) Ath Dec. 27, 1879. Listed
PC Dec. 31, 1879. A *second edition* advertised
Bkr Feb. 1880; Ath March 6, 1880. A 1-volume
printing listed Ath June 26, 1880; PC July 15,
1880. As a volume in the *Piccadilly Novels* series
listed Ath Nov. 13, 1880; PC Nov. 15, 1880; Bkr
Dec. 1, 1880.

CO H LC UV

10547. HAWTHORNE . . .

NEW YORK   HARPER & BROTHERS, PUBLISHERS
FRANKLIN SQUARE   1880

For prior British publication see above under
1879.

⟨i⟩-viii, ⟨1⟩-177; blank, p. ⟨178⟩; 6 pp. advertisements. 7⁵⁄₁₆″ x 4⅛″.

⟨1⟩-8¹².

V cloth: Dark green (*i.e.*, faded black?). Brown-
coated end papers. Flyleaves.

Listed PW Jan. 10, 1880. Deposited Jan. 17,
1880.

Note: A reprint was issued imprinted: *New York
Harper & Brothers, Publishers Franklin Square
⟨1879⟩*, in the printed paper wrapper of *Harper's
Handy Series*, dated May 27, 1887.

H UV

10548. A BUNDLE OF LETTERS . . . (RE-
PRINTED FROM THE PARISIAN.)

LORING, PUBLISHER, CORNER BROMFIELD & WASH-
INGTON STREETS, BOSTON. ⟨n.d., 1880⟩

⟨1⟩-64. 6¾″ full x 5⅜″.

⟨1-4⟩⁸.

Printed stiff paper wrapper: blue; cream; pink;
printed with a plaid-like pattern in blue and
red, lettered in black. The wrapper has been
noted in the following forms; sequence, if any,
not determined and the designations are for
identification only. Other variations are present;
the following are sufficient to distinguish. The
possibility of multiple simultaneous printing
may not be ignored.

A

Both inner and outer wrapper decorated with
plaid-like rules. On the front cover the space
between *Letters* and BY is ¹¹⁄₁₆″. A comma is
present at end of line: HENRY JAMES, JR.,

B

Both inner and outer wrapper decorated with
plaid-like rules. On the front cover the space
between *Letters* and BY is 1″ scant. The comma
noted above is not present.

C

The plaid-like rules are present on outer
wrapper only. On the front cover the space between *Letters* and BY is ⅞″. The comma noted
above is not present. The line HENRY JAMES, JR.
is set 2″ wide.

D

The plaid-like rules are present on the outer
wrapper only. On the front cover the space
between *Letters* and BY is ⅞″. The comma
noted above is not present. The line HENRY
JAMES, JR. is set 1¹⁵⁄₁₆″ wide.

A copy in UV (in Wrapper A) inscribed by early
owner Jan. 1880. Listed PW Feb. 7, 1880.

AAS (B)   B (D)   BA (B,D)   H (A,B,C,D)   LC (D)
UV (A,B,C,D)   Y (B,C)

10549. CONFIDENCE . . .

BOSTON: HOUGHTON, OSGOOD AND COMPANY.
THE RIVERSIDE PRESS, CAMBRIDGE.   1880.

For prior London publication see above under
1880, *i.e.*, Dec. 1879. Also see below under
1962.

⟨1⟩-347. 7⁷⁄₁₆″ x 4⅞″.

⟨1-14¹², 15⁶⟩. *Signed:* ⟨1⟩-21⁸, 22⁶.

Note: The publisher's records show the following printings: 1st printing, 1500 copies, Feb.
6, 1880; 2nd printing, 1000 copies, Feb. 28,
1880; 3rd printing, 1000 copies, March 9, 1880.
BAL has been unable to discover any variations
that might distinguish the printings. It is reasonable to suppose that copies in the later binding
(see below) are of a later printing.

C cloth: green; terra-cotta. Covers bevelled. Brown-coated on white end papers. Flyleaves. Edel-Laurence (p. 44) describe the book as in "fine-cross-ribbed cloth"; no copy so bound has been traced by BAL.

Two binding issues noted:

1: Spine imprint: HOUGHTON, OSGOOD & CO.

2: Spine imprint: HOUGHTON, MIFFLIN & CO.

The following errors are present in all examined copies of this date:

P. 171, line 9: *like me call* (for *like me to call*)

P. ⟨323⟩, line 7: *to place, as* (for *to place it, as*)

P. 345, line 1: *chance* (for *change*)

Advertised for Feb. 18 in PW Feb. 14, 1880. BA copy received Feb. 19, 1880. Deposited Feb. 23, 1880. Listed PW Feb. 28, 1880. "When the first edition of 1500 copies . . . was published a fortnight ago, the orders had reached 2100, and a new edition was started at once."—PW March 6, 1880. Listed Bkr April, 1880. The Leipzig (Tauchnitz) edition listed WV June 3, 1880.

CO   H (also 2nd binding)   UV

10550. THE DIARY OF A MAN OF FIFTY AND A BUNDLE OF LETTERS . . .

NEW YORK   HARPER & BROTHERS, PUBLISHERS   FRANKLIN SQUARE   1880

Issued as *Harper's Half-Hour Series,* No. 135.

For prior London publication of "The Diary of a Man of Fifty" see *The Madonna of the Future . . . ,* London, 1879, above. "A Bundle of Letters" had prior American publication; see above under 1880.

⟨1⟩-135; blank, p. ⟨136⟩; 8 pp. advertisements. 4¾" full x 3³⁄₁₆" (paper); 4¹¹⁄₁₆" x 3⅛" (cloth).

⟨1⟩-9⁸.

Printed tan paper wrapper. Green S cloth, ecru end papers.

Note: Edel-Laurence (p. 50) report the "cloth issue appears in three distinct binding states. In the first, lettering is red-brown, with titles of both tales on spine. In the second, both titles are lettered in black on spine. In the third, lettering is in orange-red, with only *The Diary of a Man of Fifty* imprinted on spine. No priority has been established." BAL has failed to locate the three reported varieties and has seen only the following; sequence, if any, not known:

Cloth Binding A

Spine lettered in black: THE DIARY OF A MAN OF FIFTY AND A BUNDLE OF LETTERS

Cloth Binding B

Spine lettered in black: THE DIARY OF A MAN OF FIFTY

Deposited April 9, 1880. BA copy (in wrapper) received April 16, 1880. Listed PW April 17, 1880, as in paper. Advertised PW April 17, 1880, as both in cloth and in paper.

BA (wrapper)   BPL (cloth binding A)   CO (cloth bindings A, B)   H (cloth binding A)   NYPL (wrapper)   UV (wrapper)   Y (wrapper)

10551. WASHINGTON SQUARE . . .

NEW YORK   HARPER & BROTHERS, FRANKLIN SQUARE   1881

⟨1⟩-266; 6 pp. advertisements. Illustrated. 6⅝" full x 4⅝".

⟨1⟩-17⁸.

S cloth: dark olive-green. Brown-coated on white; tan-coated on white; tan; end papers.

Deposited Dec. 1, 1880. BA copy received Dec. 9, 1880. Listed PW Dec. 11, 1880. *See next entry.*

H   NYPL   UV

10552. Washington Square   The Pension Beaurepas   A Bundle of Letters . . .

London   Macmillan and Co. 1881

2 Vols.

Reprint save for "The Pension Beaurepas," for first American book publication of which see *The Siege of London . . . ,* Boston, 1883.

Two printings of Vol. 2 have been noted:

1: Paged: ⟨i-iv⟩, ⟨1⟩-267, 368-371.

2: Paged: ⟨i-iv⟩, ⟨1⟩-271.

Two bindings noted; the following variations are sufficient for identification:

1

BF cloth: blue. Author's name on spine thus: H. JAMES JR

2

C cloth: terra-cotta. Author's name on spine thus: HENRY JAMES, JUN. In some copies leaf ⟨T⟩₂ excised (Vol. 1). Noted on second printing only.

Printed Jan. 1881 (publisher's records). Advertised as *immediately* Ath Jan. 15, 1881. Listed Ath Jan. 29, 1881; PC Feb. 1, 1881. Advertised with extracts from reviews Ath Feb. 12, 1881. Reprinted March, 1881 (publisher's records). Advertised with extracts from reviews PC March

1, 1881. Reprinted in one volume Aug. 1881 (publisher's records). One-volume edition listed Ath Aug. 13, 1881; listed PC Sept. 1, 1881.

CO (1st, 2nd)   H (2nd)   LC (2nd)   UV (2nd)

10553. THE PORTRAIT OF A LADY ... IN THREE VOLUMES ...

LONDON: MACMILLAN AND CO. 1881. THE RIGHT OF TRANSLATION AND REPRODUCTION IS RESERVED.

For first American edition see next entry.

Note: The three title-pages vary slightly in punctuation and capitalization.

1: ⟨i-iv⟩, ⟨1⟩-266, blank leaf. 7½" x 4⅞".

2: ⟨i-iv⟩, ⟨1⟩-253; printer's imprint, p. ⟨254⟩; blank leaf.

3: ⟨i-iv⟩, ⟨1⟩-248.

1: ⟨A⟩², B-I, K-R⁸, S⁶.

2: ⟨A⟩², B-I, K-R⁸.

3: ⟨A⟩², B-I, K-Q⁸, R⁴.

BF cloth: blue. Brown-coated on white end papers. Publisher's catalog inserted at back of Vol. 3, noted in the following printings: *A:* Dated *January, 1881; B:* Dated *April, 1881.* A copy has been reported (not seen by BAL) with catalog dated *December, 1881.*

Printed 1881 (publisher's records). Advertised for Nov. 4 in Ath Oct. 29, 1881; PC Nov. 1, 1881. Advertised as *now ready* Ath Nov. 5, 1881. Listed Ath Nov. 12, 1881; PC Nov. 15, 1881. Advertised as *now ready* PC Nov. 15, 1881. Reprinted Jan. 1882 (publisher's records). Reprinted in one volume June, 1882 (publisher's records).

H   NYPL   UV

10554. THE PORTRAIT OF A LADY ...

BOSTON: HOUGHTON, MIFFLIN AND COMPANY. NEW YORK: 11 EAST SEVENTEENTH STREET. THE RIVERSIDE PRESS, CAMBRIDGE. 1882.

For prior London publication see preceding entry.

According to the publisher's records (see below) there were five printings during the period Oct. 27, 1881–March 7, 1882. The sixth printing, Aug. 26, 1882, was issued with an alteration on the title-page; see publishing record below. BAL has been unable to identify these printings but on the basis of the publisher's records, and examination of a number of copies of the book, BAL offers the following tentative statement.

FIRST PRINTING, FIRST ISSUE, FIRST STATE

Not located; not seen; postulated only.

⟨1¹, 2-22¹², 23⁸⟩.

Signature ⟨20⟩ misimposed and a consequent irregularity present in pp. 433-456.

FIRST PRINTING, FIRST ISSUE, SECOND STATE

⟨i-ii⟩, ⟨1⟩-520. 7⁷⁄₁₆" x 4¾".

⟨1¹, 2-19¹², 20¹⁰, 21-22¹, 23-24¹², 25⁸⟩. *Signed:* ⟨A⟩¹, B-I, K-U, X-Z, AA-II, KK⁸, LL⁴.

The error caused by misimposition corrected at the bindery.

Locations: H

FIRST PRINTING, SECOND ISSUE

⟨i-ii⟩, ⟨1⟩-520.

⟨1¹, 2-22¹², 23⁸⟩. *Signed:* ⟨A⟩¹, B-I, K-U, X-Z, AA-II, KK⁸, LL⁴.

The error caused by misimposition corrected in press.

Locations: AAS   Y

S cloth: green. (Also brown?). Brown-coated on white end papers. Flyleaves. The fillet carrying the title on the front cover is decorated with but the merest suggestion of a maze-like pattern. Known late printings have been noted in both green and brown S cloths, some with brown-coated end papers, some with white paper end papers printed in yellow with a floral pattern. Also on late printings the fillet carrying the title on the front cover is decorated with a sharply defined, clearly visible, maze-like pattern. However, further study is indicated.

LATER PRINTINGS

A distinguishing feature of all later printings seen, dated 1882, is the title-leaf which occurs as ⟨1⟩₁, conjugate with ⟨1⟩₁₂.

PRINTING RECORD

First Printing: Oct. 27, 1881. 1520 copies. Bound during the period Nov. 15–23, 1881. On Nov. 11, 1881, 18 copies were sewn. Incorporated in this entry is a charge for composition and electrotyping of a title-page. Under date Nov. 2, 1881 is a charge for composition and electrotyping of the copyright page; and, charge for printing 1500 copies of the title-leaf.

Second Printing: Nov. 21 (22?), 1881. 1012 copies. Bound during the period Nov. 23–Dec. 12, 1881. *Note:* Under date of Nov. 22, 1881, there is a charge for correcting plates, one half hour. The alteration has not been found by BAL.

Third Printing: Dec. 9, 1881. 1020 copies. Bound during the period Dec. 12, 1881–Jan. 14, 1882.

Fourth Printing: Jan. 24, 1882. 1005 copies.

Fifth Printing: March 7, 1882. 1020 copies.

Sixth Printing: Aug. 26, 1882. 516 copies. Included in the record is a charge for altering the title-page; insertion of a reprint notice?

Seventh Printing: Feb. 24, 1883. 500 copies. The entry includes a charge for alteration of the title-page; date 1882 altered to 1883?

Advertised for Nov. 16, 1881, PW Nov. 12, 1881. Deposited Nov. 21, 1881. Listed PW Dec. 10, 1881. The Leipzig (Tauchnitz) edition, three volumes, listed WV March 9, 1882.

The present entry made on the basis of copies in AAS, BPL, CO, H, LC, NYPL, UV, Y.

10555. Roderick Hudson ... Revised Edition.

Boston: Houghton, Mifflin and Company. New York: 11 East Seventeenth Street. The Riverside Press, Cambridge. 1882.

For first edition see above under 1876.

First American publication of the revised London, 1879, text. Made up of sheets of the London, 1-volume, 1880, printing with cancel title-leaf as above. The Riverside Press records show 250 title-leaves printed April 28, 1882.

Advertised for May 10, 1882, PW May 6, 1882. Deposited May 16, 1882.

LC   NYPL

10556. DAISY MILLER A COMEDY ... NOT PUBLISHED

⟨n.p., LONDON⟩ 1882

⟨i-iv⟩, ⟨1⟩-139. 7⁷⁄₁₆″ x 4¹⁵⁄₁₆″.

⟨A⟩², B-I⁸, K⁴, L².

Printed paper wrapper.

Two printings noted; the sequence has not been established and the following designations are for identification only. According to the records the first printing (six copies) was done on June 6, 1882. On June 10, 1882, Macmillan reported to the printers that "Mr. James is much pleased"; and on July 3, 1882, "twelve more copies" were ordered.

A

Printed on laid paper. The printed wrapper is of mottled gray paper.

B

Printed on wove paper. The printed wrapper is of mottled pale buff paper.

No record of deposit in either Copyright Office or in BMU.

Intermediates have been seen: Printed on laid paper save for the final gathering which is printed on wove; mottled gray paper wrapper.

For published edition see below under 1883.

CO (A)   H (B; intermediate)   NYPL (intermediate)

10557. THE POINT OF VIEW ... NOT PUBLISHED

⟨n.p., LONDON⟩ 1882

For published edition see next entry.

⟨i-iv⟩, ⟨1⟩-59. 7½″ x 5¹⁄₁₆″.

⟨A⟩², B-D⁸, E⁴, ⟨F⟩².

Printed gray paper wrapper.

No record of receipt in Copyright Office or BMU.

According to the Macmillan records copy was sent to the printer July 4, 1882, with a request for six proof copies; types distributed Oct. 1882.

CO

10558. THE SIEGE OF LONDON, THE PENSION BEAUREPAS, AND THE POINT OF VIEW ...

BOSTON: JAMES R. OSGOOD AND COMPANY. 1883.

For prior publication of "The Pension Beaurepas" see *Washington Square ...* , London, 1881. See preceding entry for prior printing of "The Point of View."

⟨i-vi⟩, ⟨1⟩-294. 7⅜″ x 4¾″.

⟨1-25⁶⟩. *Signed:* ⟨-⟩³, ⟨1⟩-12¹², 13³.

C cloth: terra-cotta. S cloth: blue; brown; green; mottled purple. V cloth: green. White laid paper, white wove paper, end papers. Publisher's monogram at foot of spine. Edel-Laurence (p. 57) report "copies of the first impression, bound in 1888 and later, have the Houghton Mifflin & Co. imprint on spine"; no copy thus traced by BAL.

1528 copies printed Jan. 19, 1883; bound during the period Jan. 29–Feb. 27, 1883. The second printing (with the statement *Second Edition* on the title-page), 1038 copies, printed March 12, 1883. Unsold sheets of the second printing were acquired by Houghton, Mifflin & Co., April 11, 1889.

Noted as *just ready* PW Feb. 24, 1883. A copy in H received Feb. 27, 1883. BA copy received Feb. 28, 1883. Deposited March 2, 1883. Listed PW March 3, 1883.

H   NYPL   UV

10559. Foreign Parts ...

Leipzig Bernhard Tauchnitz 1883.

Printed paper wrapper. Issued as No. 2164 *Collection of British Authors* series.

"Note," written for this edition, p. ⟨5⟩. A revised edition of *Transatlantic Sketches*, 1875.

Noted both with and without inserted terminal catalog dated *July 1883*. The earliest copies noted have the outer back wrapper dated *July 1883*.

Listed wv Aug. 2, 1883.

AAS   LC   UV

10560. ... DAISY MILLER   A COMEDY IN THREE ACTS

BOSTON   JAMES R. OSGOOD AND COMPANY   1883

At head of title: HENRY JAMES

For prior appearance see above under 1882.

⟨i-ii⟩, ⟨1⟩-189. Laid paper. 7⁷⁄₁₆″ x 4¾″.

⟨1-16⁶⟩. *Signed:* ⟨-⟩¹, ⟨1⟩-11⁸, 12⁷.

S cloth: blue; blue-green; brown; green; purple; red. White laid end papers. JRO monogram at foot of spine.

Later Bindings

Copies with the *Ticknor & Company* monogram at the foot of spine were bound March 30, 1888. The records indicate 130 copies so bound.

Sheets were acquired by *Houghton, Mifflin & Company* April 11, 1889, and bound with their spine imprint not before Dec. 3, 1889.

First printing: 1016 copies, Aug. 17, 1883. The first copies were bound Aug. 22, 1883.

Advertised as though published PW Sept. 8, 1883. BA copy received Sept. 10, 1883. Deposited Sept. 13, 1883. Listed PW Sept. 29, 1883.

BA   H (1st; Ticknor binding; Houghton Mifflin binding)   UV

10561. French Poets and Novelists ... Authorized Edition.

Leipzig   Bernhard Tauchnitz   1883.

Printed paper wrapper. Issued as No. 2181 *Collection of British Authors* series.

Reprint save for the few words added to the prefatory "Note." For first edition see above under 1878.

Listed wv Sept. 20, 1883.

LC

10562. PORTRAITS OF PLACES ...

LONDON   MACMILLAN AND CO. 1883

For first American edition see next entry.

⟨i⟩-⟨viii⟩, ⟨1⟩-376. 7⁷⁄₁₆″ x 5″.

⟨A⟩⁴, B-I, K-U, X-Z, 2A⁸, 2B⁴.

V cloth: blue-green. *Two states of the binding noted;* the sequence has not been determined and the designations are for identification only:

Binding A

On the spine the name JAMES is stamped from letters of uniform size; the M in MACMILLAN is larger than the other letters in the publisher's name.

Binding B

On the spine the name JAMES is stamped from letters of uniform size; the name MACMILLAN is stamped from letters of uniform size.

Note: The spine also occurs as follows: The J in JAMES is larger than the other letters in the name; the M in MACMILLAN is larger than the other letters in the name. *Not seen by BAL.* For a photographic reproduction of this unlocated variety see plate opposite p. 132, *Points 1874-1930 ...*, by Percy H. Muir, London, 1931.

Announced PC Oct. 1, 1883. Advertised as though published Ath Dec. 15, 1883. Listed Ath Dec. 15, 1883. Advertised as though published PC Dec. 18, 1883. Listed PC Dec. 31, 1883.

CO(binding B)   H(binding A)   NYPL(binding A)   UV(binding A)

10563. ... PORTRAITS OF PLACES

BOSTON   JAMES R. OSGOOD AND COMPANY 1884

At head of title: HENRY JAMES

For prior publication see preceding entry.

⟨i-viii⟩, ⟨1⟩-376. 7⅜″ x 4⅞″.

⟨1-32⁶⟩. *Signed:* ⟨A⟩⁴, B-I, ⟨K⟩-U, X-Z, 2A⁸, 2B⁴.

C cloth: green-blue; mustard. P cloth: mustard. S cloth: brown; gray-blue. White laid end papers.

1500 copies printed Jan. 3, 1884. Deposited Feb. 2, 1884. Noted as *ready* PW Feb. 2, 1884. BA copy received Feb. 5, 1884. A copy in H received Feb. 8, 1884. Listed PW Feb. 16, 1884.

H

10564. Nana: A Realistic Novel. By Émile Zola. Translated without Abridgment from the 127th French Edition ...

London: Vizetelly & Co., 42 Catherine Street, Strand. 1884.

"Mr. Henry James on *Nana*," pp. ⟨xiv⟩-xv. Truncated; for printing in full see *The Future of the Novel*, 1956, below.

Two bindings noted; sequence, if any, not known. The designations are for identification only:

A

V cloth: blue. Stamped in gold, maroon, black and blind.

B

S cloth: tan. Printed paper label on spine.

Listed Ath March 29, 1884.

H (both)

10565. The Siege of London; The Point of View; A Passionate Pilgrim ... Authorized Edition.

Leipzig Bernhard Tauchnitz 1884.

Printed paper wrapper. Issued as No. 2234 *Collection of British Authors* series.

Reprint save for the note on p. ⟨5⟩; and the note on p. ⟨6⟩: *It is proper to state that the last of the three tales ⟨"A Passionate Pilgrim"⟩ contained in this volume ... has been, in the matter of language, much altered and amended for reproduction here ... December 1883.*

Noted with inserted terminal catalog dated *March 1884.*

Listed wv April 17, 1884.

LC

10566. NOTES (NO. 15 OF SERIES) ... ON A COLLECTION OF DRAWINGS BY MR. GEORGE DU MAURIER EXHIBITED AT THE FINE ART SOCIETY'S 148 NEW BOND STREET 1884

⟨LONDON, 1884⟩

Three editions noted; the sequence has not been determined and the designations are for identification only.

A

⟨1⟩-64. Frontispiece. 8¼" x 5¼".

⟨A⟩-D⁸.

At foot of p. 64: PRINTED BY J. S. VIRTUE AND CO., LIMITED, CITY ROAD, LONDON.

B

⟨1⟩-66. Frontispiece. 8⅜" scant x 5⅜".

⟨A⟩-D⁸, E¹.

At foot of p. 66: PRINTED BY J. S. VIRTUE AND CO., LIMITED, CITY ROAD, LONDON.

C

⟨1⟩-66. Frontispiece. 8⅜" x 5¼".

⟨A⟩-D⁸, E¹. *Signature collation probable.*

At foot of p. 66: LONDON: PRINTED BY J. S. VIRTUE AND CO., LIMITED, CITY ROAD.

A cursory examination shows no variations in the James text; many variations occur in the catalog proper, pp. ⟨19⟩ to end.

Printed blue-gray paper wrapper.

According to Ath June 21, 1884, the exhibition was opened to private view June 21, 1884; public view June 23, 1884.

BPL (C) H (C) LC (A,B)

10567. Stories by American Authors V ...

New York Charles Scribner's Sons 1884

"A Light Man," pp. ⟨5⟩-53. Collected in *Stories Revived*, London, 1885; and, *Master Eustace*, New York, 1920.

Two bindings noted:

1: Yellow V cloth, stamped in black. Top edges plain. A surviving copyright deposit copy thus.

2: Mustard V cloth sides, dark olive V cloth shelfback, stamped in gold. Top edges gilt. Issued thus during the period 1886–1889.

Deposited July 26, 1884. BA copy (rebound) received July 28, 1884. Listed PW Aug. 2, 1884.

H NYPL UV Y

10568. Portraits of Places ... Authorized Edition.

Leipzig Bernhard Tauchnitz 1884.

Caution: Entry tentative; made on the basis of a copy with outer back wrapper dated *September 1900;* and, a copy lacking wrapper.

Printed paper wrapper. Issued as No. 2276 *Collection of British Authors* series.

Reprint save for a 2-line note, p. ⟨5⟩, dated at end: *Paris, Feb. 14th, 1884.*

Listed wv Aug. 28, 1884.

LC Y

10569. ... TALES OF THREE CITIES

BOSTON JAMES R. OSGOOD AND COMPANY 1884

At head of title: HENRY JAMES

⟨i-iv⟩, ⟨1⟩-359. 7⅜" x 4¹³⁄₁₆".

⟨1², 2-31⁶⟩. *Signed:* ⟨-⟩², ⟨1⟩-4, ⟨5⟩-16, ⟨17⟩-22⁸, 23⁴.

S cloth: blue; brown; green; mustard. Publisher's monogram at foot of spine. Also noted in a later binding with the spine imprint of *Houghton Mifflin & Co.*

Note: A curious copy, status unknown, is at AAS; quite possibly a set of sheets put into binding by a private collector: S cloth: dark purple-brown. Unstamped save for the spine which is goldstamped: TALES / OF THREE / CITIES / ⟨*dash*⟩ / HENRY JAMES

The lettering is from a face unlike that used by either Osgood or Houghton, Mifflin & Co. Leaf: 7¾″ scant x 5″. Top edges gilt. Brown-coated on white end papers printed in black with a crown and fleur-de-lis pattern.

1500 copies printed June 29, (24?) 1884. On April 11, 1889 Houghton, Mifflin & Company received 400 copies (in sheets) from Ticknor & Company which were bound during the period beginning May 19, 1890. The records indicate that no copies were bound by Ticknor & Company.

Noted for *next week* PW Oct. 18, 1884. Deposited Oct. 20, 1884. Listed PW Oct. 25, 1884. The London (Macmillan) edition noted for *next week* Ath Nov. 15, 1884; listed Ath Nov. 22, 1884, PC Dec. 6, 1884, Bkr Dec. 13, 1884.

Edel-Laurence (p. 67) err in their statement regarding the copyright printing of this work. The publisher's records show printing for purposes of copyright as follows:

Sept. 4, 1883. "Impressions of a Cousin," 12 copies printed. A title-page was entered for copyright Aug. 30, 1883.

Jan. 5, 1884. "Lady Barberina," chapters 1-4, 12 copies printed.

Jan. 17, 1884. "Lady Barberina," concluded, 12 copies printed.

March 17 (7?), 1884. "A New England Winter," 12 copies printed.

None of the above copyright printings located.

H   NYPL   UV (Houghton Mifflin binding)

10570. ... A LITTLE TOUR IN FRANCE

BOSTON   JAMES R. OSGOOD AND COMPANY   1885

At head of title: HENRY JAMES

⟨i-iv⟩, ⟨1⟩-255. Laid paper. 7⅜″ x 4⅞″.

⟨1-20⁶, 21¹⁰⟩. *Signed:* ⟨-⟩², 1-16⁸.

C cloth: terra-cotta. S cloth: blue; brown; green; purple-brown. White laid end papers. Publisher's monogram at foot of spine.

Note: Also noted in the following later bindings; the sequence (if any) is not known and the

designations are for identification only; other variations are present but the following is sufficient for identification:

A: Spine imprint: HOUGHTON / MIFFLIN & CO.

B: Spine imprint: HOUGHTON / MIFFLIN ⟨*dot*⟩ & ⟨*dot*⟩ CO

Also note: Edel-Laurence (p. 64) state: "Some copies lack the border and frame in blind on covers; some lack binder's fly-leaves at front and back." All copies of the Osgood binding examined by BAL have a blindstamped double-rule frame on the sides; do not have flyleaves.

Aug. 14, 1884: 1500 copies printed.

April 10, 1888: Fifty copies bound by Ticknor & Company. Not seen in the Ticknor binding.

April 11, 1889: Unsold copies (in sheets) acquired by Houghton, Mifflin & Company; about 350 copies.

Sept. 13, 1889 to Dec. 24, 1891: 192 copies put in binding by Houghton, Mifflin & Company.

Oct. 26, 1890: 175 copies pulped.

Sept. 25, 1891: 62 copies of a four-page cancel printed. New title-page with altered imprint?

Noted for *this week* PW Sept. 6, 1884. Deposited Sept. 10, 1884. A copy in H received Sept. 12, 1884. Listed PW Sept. 13, 1884. Reviewed Ath April 25, 1885. For revised edition see under 1900.

AAS   CO   H(B)   LC(A)   NYPL

10571. ... THE AUTHOR OF BELTRAFFIO PANDORA   GEORGINA'S REASONS THE PATH OF DUTY   FOUR MEETINGS

BOSTON   JAMES R. OSGOOD AND COMPANY   1885

At head of title: HENRY JAMES

⟨i-ii⟩, ⟨1⟩-362. 7⅜″ x 4¹³⁄₁₆″.

⟨1-30⁶, 31²⟩. *Signed:* ⟨-⟩¹, ⟨1⟩-22⁸, 23⁵.

S cloth: brown; gold; green. Publisher's monogram at foot of spine.

Jan. 28, 1885: 1500 copies printed.

Jan. 30, 1885: On this date the last lot to be bound by Osgood.

April 11, 1889: 700 copies (in sheets) delivered to Houghton, Mifflin & Company.

Feb. 11, 1890 to Oct. 21, 1898: During this period 192 copies were put in binding by Houghton, Mifflin & Company, presumably with their spine imprint; no copy thus distinguished located.

Oct. 26, 1890: 500 copies (in sheets) pulped by Houghton, Mifflin & Co.

BA copy received Feb. 9, 1885. Deposited Feb. 11, 1885. Listed PW Feb. 14, 1885.

AAS   B   CO   UV

10572. ... THE ART OF FICTION

BOSTON   CUPPLES, UPHAM AND COMPANY   1885

At head of title: WALTER BESANT

⟨1⟩-85; blank, p. ⟨86⟩; advertisements, pp. ⟨87-91⟩. 6¾" x 4⅞".

⟨1-5⁸, 6⁶⟩.

V cloth: yellow.

"The Art of Fiction," by Besant, pp. 3-48; James's "The Art of Fiction," pp. 51-85. James's name on p. ⟨49⟩; not on title-page.

Note: All copies traced by BAL have p. ⟨92⟩ blank. Edel-Laurence (p. 68) call for advertisements on p. ⟨92⟩; no copy thus seen by BAL.

P. ⟨87⟩ dated *October, 1884. The Art of Fiction* is listed as in paper, p. ⟨87⟩; reference is to the prior publication of Besant's piece as a separate, not to the publication here collated. The Besant separate was listed PW Aug. 30, 1884.

The enlarged "second edition" (*i.e.,* the publication here collated) advertised PW Nov. 22/29, 1884, as though published. UV copy inscribed by early owner March 23, 1885. Reprinted not before 1889 by Cupples & Hurd, The Algonquin Press, Boston.

AAS   BA   NYPL   UV

10573. STORIES REVIVED IN THREE VOL-UMES ...

LONDON   MACMILLAN AND CO.   1885

1: ... THE AUTHOR OF 'BELTRAFFIO.' PANDORA. THE PATH OF DUTY. A DAY OF DAYS. A LIGHT MAN ...

2: ... GEORGINA'S REASONS. A PASSIONATE PILGRIM. A LANDSCAPE-PAINTER. ROSE-AGATHE ...

3: ... POOR RICHARD. THE LAST OF THE VALERII. MASTER EUSTACE. THE ROMANCE OF CERTAIN OLD CLOTHES. A MOST EXTRAORDINARY CASE ...

1: ⟨i-viii⟩, ⟨1⟩-280. 7½" x 5" scant.

2: ⟨i-viii⟩, ⟨1⟩-280.

3: ⟨i-viii⟩, ⟨1⟩-269; blank, p. ⟨270⟩; 2 pp. advertisements.

1: ⟨A⟩⁴, B-I, K-S⁸, T⁴.

2: ⟨A⟩⁴, B-I, K-S⁸, T⁴.

3: ⟨A⟩⁴, B-I, K-S⁸.

Three styles of binding have been noted; the order of presentation is all but arbitrary and the designations are for identification only:

Binding A

BF cloth: blue. Brown-coated end papers. On the spine VOL is stamped from letters of uniform size.

Binding B

S cloth: green. White end papers printed in blue with a mosaic pattern. On the spine the V in VOL is larger than the letters OL.

Binding C

C cloth: green. White end papers printed in blue with a mosaic pattern. On the spine the V in VOL is larger than the letters OL.

Noted as *nearly ready* PC April 15, 1885. Printed May, 1885 (publisher's records). Noted as *nearly ready* PC May 1, 1885. Advertised as though ready PC May 15, 1885. Listed Ath May 16, 1885. *The two-volume reprint:* Advertised as new PC Oct. 15, 1885; printed Nov. 1885 (publisher's records); listed PC Dec. 18, 1885.

AAS (C)   H (A,B)   NYPL (A)

10574. A Little Tour in France ... Authorized Edition.

Leipzig   Bernhard Tauchnitz   1885.

Caution: Entry tentative; made on the basis of incomplete copies and known reprints.

Printed paper wrapper. Issued as No. 2334 *Collection of British Authors* series.

Reprint save for a note, p. ⟨4⟩, dated at end *London: May, 1885.* For first edition see above under 1885.

Listed WV June 11, 1885.

H   LC   NYPL   UV

10575. THE BOSTONIANS   A NOVEL ... IN THREE VOLUMES ...

LONDON   MACMILLAN AND CO. 1886

For first American edition see next entry.

On the title-pages: 1, no period after the word VOL; 2, 3, period present after the word VOL.

1: ⟨i-iv⟩, ⟨1⟩-244. 7⁹⁄₁₆" x 5".

2: ⟨i-iv⟩, ⟨1⟩-226, 2 pp. advertisements.

3: ⟨i-iv⟩, ⟨1⟩-232; plus: 4 pp. advertisements.

1: ⟨A⟩², B-I, K-Q⁸, R².

2: ⟨A⟩², B-I, K-P⁸, Q².

3: ⟨A⟩², B-I, K-P⁸, Q⁴; plus: ⟨R⟩².

BF cloth: blue. Brown-coated on white end papers.

Note: The publisher's records show two printings of the work in three volumes: 1st printing, Feb. 1886; 2nd printing, March, 1886. BAL has been unable to distinguish two printings. A possible mark of identification could be the running head, Vol. 1, p. 31, where, in some copies, the chapter number appears (correctly) III; in some copies it appears (incorrectly) II. Also, some slight variations have been noted in the depth of the type pages. Further investigation required.

Announced PC Oct. 1, 1885. Noted as *immediately* PC Jan. 15, 1886. Printed Feb. 1886 (publisher's records). Noted as *immediately* PC Feb. 1, 1886; as *next week* Ath Feb. 6, 13, 1886. Listed Ath Feb. 13, 1886. Noted as *new* PC Feb. 15, 1886, Ath Feb. 20, 1886. Reprinted March, 1886 (publisher's records). Reviewed Ath March 6, 1886. *One-volume printing* (first American edition; first one-volume British reprint) printed Feb. 1886 (publisher's records); advertised as *new* Ath, PC May 15, 1886; listed Ath May 22, 1886; and, Bkr and PC June 1, 1886.

AAS   H   NYPL

10576. THE BOSTONIANS A NOVEL ...

LONDON AND NEW YORK   MACMILLAN AND CO. 1886

First American edition. For prior publication see preceding entry.

⟨i-iv⟩, ⟨1⟩-449; blank, p. ⟨450⟩; advertisements, pp. ⟨451-452⟩. 7⅜″ x 4⅞″.

⟨A⟩², B-I, K-U, X-Z, 2A-2F⁸, ⟨2G⟩².

Orange V cloth sides, maroon V cloth shelf-back (probable first binding); blue-black-coated on white end papers. Blue-black BF cloth (probable second binding) with either blue-black-coated end papers; or, white wove end papers.

Printed in Edinburgh by R. & R. Clark, in Feb. 1886. The first American edition and the first one-volume London printing (see preceding entry) are of a single printing. It is presumed that copies with leaf ⟨2G⟩₂ excised were intended for British distribution; those with leaf ⟨2G⟩₂ present were distributed in United States.

Printed Feb. 1886 (publisher's records). Deposited March 13, 1886. Listed PW April 3, 1886.

H   LC   UV   Y

10577. THE PRINCESS CASAMASSIMA A NOVEL ... IN THREE VOLUMES ...

LONDON   MACMILLAN AND CO. AND NEW YORK 1886

For first American edition see next entry.

1: ⟨i-iv⟩, ⟨1⟩-252. 7½″ full x 5″.

2: ⟨i-iv⟩, ⟨1⟩-257; blank, p. ⟨258⟩; 2 pp. advertisements.

3: ⟨i-iv⟩, ⟨1⟩-242, 2 pp. advertisements.

1: ⟨A⟩², B-I, K-Q⁸, R⁶.

2: ⟨A⟩², B-I, K-R⁸, S².

3: ⟨A⟩², B-I, K-Q⁸, R².

BF cloth: blue. Brown-coated on white end papers; green-coated on white end papers.

Two states of the binding noted; the sequence (if any) has not been determined and the designations are for identification only:

A

In the spine imprint the letters ACMILLAN are stamped from a face ³⁄₃₂″ tall. The *o* in *Co* is set above a short dash. Brown-coated on white end papers. James's personal copy (in H) is in this form.

B

In the spine imprint the letters ACMILLAN are stamped from a face ⅛″ tall. The *o* in *Co* is set above a dot. Green-coated on white end papers.

Printed Oct. 1886 (publisher's records). Listed (prematurely?) PC Oct. 1, 1886. Advertised for *next week* Ath Oct. 9, 1886; as though ready PC Oct. 15, 1886. Listed Ath Oct. 16, 1886. Advertised for *next week* Ath Oct. 16, 1886; as though ready Ath Oct. 23, 1886. Listed (again) PC Nov. 1, 1886. Reviewed Bkr, PC Nov. 1, 1886; Ath Nov. 6, 1886.

A *one-volume* printing was done in Oct. 1886 (publisher's records). In this format the sheets were exported to United States as the first American edition; see next entry. And, distributed in Great Britain as the first one-volume British edition; listed Ath July 9, 1887. Mr. Simon Nowell-Smith informs BAL that these last were issued with a cancel title-leaf dated 1887.

H (A,B)   LC (A)   UV (A)

10578. THE PRINCESS CASAMASSIMA A NOVEL ...

LONDON   MACMILLAN AND CO. AND NEW YORK 1886

First American edition. For prior publication see preceding entry.

⟨i-iv⟩, ⟨1⟩-596. 7⁹⁄₁₆″ full x 4⅞″.

⟨A⟩², B-I, K-U, X-Z, 2A-2I, 2K-2P⁸, 2Q².

S cloth: blue-green. White wove end papers. No inserted catalog.

Later bindings noted:

Later Binding A

BF cloth: blue-black. Inserted terminal catalog dated *September, 1887.*

Later Binding B

BF cloth: blue-black. Inserted terminal catalog dated *20.5.97 (i.e.,* May 20, 1897).

Deposited Nov. 1, 1886. A copy in BA (now rebound) received Nov. 2, 1886. Listed PW Nov. 13, 1886. Printed October, 1886; see publication notes under preceding entry.

AAS   BA(B)   H   LC(A)   NYPL

10579. A Catalogue of the Drawings by Mr. Edwin A. Abbey for "She Stoops to Conquer." A Comedy by Dr. Oliver Goldsmith

⟨Gilliss Brothers & Turnure, Art Age Press, 75-79 Fulton Street, New York, n.d., 1886⟩

Cover-title. Printed self-wrapper.

Also occurs with the following imprint on the front: *Grolier Club December Fifteenth to Twenty-second, Eighteen Hundred and Eighty-Six New York* A copy thus in the Grolier Club, New York. *Query:* Also issued with other imprints as required?

"Edwin A. Abbey," pp. 3-7. Collected in *Picture and Text,* 1893.

H   Y

10580. What American Authors Think about International Copyright

New-York   American Copyright League   1888

Extract from a letter, originally in *The Critic* (N.Y.), Dec. 10, 1887, p. 12.

For comment see entry No. 218.

10581. PARTIAL PORTRAITS ...

LONDON   MACMILLAN AND CO. AND NEW YORK 1888   ALL RIGHTS RESERVED

Imprint of R. and R. Clark, Edinburgh, below text, p. 408.

⟨i-xii⟩, ⟨1⟩-408; plus: 4 pp. advertisements. 7 1/16″ x 4 3/4″. *Note:* In some copies pp. ⟨i-ii⟩ excised.

⟨A⟩⁶, B-I, K-U, X-Z, 2A-2C⁸, 2D⁴; plus: ⟨-⟩². In some copies ⟨A⟩₁ excised.

V cloth: blue-green.

The publisher's records show but one printing in 1888; distributed in both Great Britain and the United States. Edel-Laurence, p. 78, state that in copies distributed in the United States

the terminal advertisements are priced in dollars; no such copy traced by BAL which has seen only copies with British prices.

Under the title *Half-Length Portraits* announced Ath Feb. 4, 1888. As *Partial Portraits* advertised PC May 1, 1888. Advertised for *next week* Ath May 5, 1888. Listed Ath May 12, 1888. Advertised as though published Ath May 12, 1888. Listed PC May 15, 1888. BA copy received May 21, 1888. Deposited (U.S.) May 25, 1888. Listed (but no copy received) PW June 16, 1888.

AAS   CO   H   LC   NYPL   UV   Y

10582. THE REVERBERATOR ... IN TWO VOLUMES ...

LONDON   MACMILLAN AND CO. AND NEW YORK 1888   ALL RIGHTS RESERVED

For first American edition see next entry.

1: ⟨i-iv⟩, ⟨1⟩-190; 2 pp. advertisements. 7 1/8″ x 4 13/16″.

2: ⟨i-iv⟩, ⟨1⟩-207; printer's imprint, p. ⟨208⟩.

1: ⟨A⟩², B-I, K-N⁸.

2: ⟨A⟩², B-I, K-O⁸.

V cloth: blue; greenish-blue. Black-coated on white end papers.

Printed May, 1888 (publisher's records). Advertised as *just ready* PC May 15, 1888; as *next week* Ath May 19, 26, 1888; as *at all libraries* PC May 26, June 1, 1888. Listed PC June 1, Ath June 9, 1888. A copy in CO inscribed by James June 7, 1888. Reprinted in one volume (the first one-volume British printing) Aug. 1888 (publisher's records); listed Ath Sept. 1; PC Sept. 15, 1888.

AAS   CO   H   NYPL

10583. THE REVERBERATOR ...

LONDON   MACMILLAN AND CO. AND NEW YORK 1888   THE RIGHT OF TRANSLATION AND REPRODUCTION IS RESERVED

First American edition. For prior London publication see preceding entry.

⟨i-iv⟩, ⟨1⟩-229; printer's imprint, p. ⟨230⟩; blank leaf. 7 5/16″ x 4 7/8″. *Also:* 6 7/8″ x 4 11/16″. *Query:* Does the variation in size represent two binding orders separated by time?

⟨A⟩², B-I, K-P⁸, Q⁴.

S cloth: blue. Blue-black coated on white end papers.

Note: P. ⟨iv⟩ bears only the following: Copyright, / 1888, / By HENRY JAMES Not to be confused with the first London one-volume edition which has the following statement on p. ⟨iv⟩: *Copyright, 1888 ... First Edition ... June 1888. New Edition ... August 1888.*

Deposited June 14, 1888. BA copy received June 26, 1888. Listed PW June 30, 1888.

H   LC   UV   Y

10584. THE ASPERN PAPERS LOUISA PALLANT THE MODERN WARNING ... IN TWO VOLUMES ...

LONDON   MACMILLAN AND CO. AND NEW YORK
1888   ALL RIGHTS RESERVED

For first American edition see next entry.

1: ⟨i-viii⟩, ⟨1⟩-239. 7⅛″ x 4¹³⁄₁₆″.

2: ⟨i-viii⟩, ⟨1⟩-258, 6 pp. advertisements.

1: ⟨A⟩⁴, B-I, K-Q⁸.

2: ⟨A⟩⁴, B-I, K-R⁸, S⁴.

V cloth: blue. Black-coated on white end papers. *Note:* Edel-Laurence (p. 80) report: "Library of Congress copy contains white end-papers." The copy cited has been sophisticated and may therefore be ignored.

Advertised as *immediately* Ath Sept. 29, 1888. Announced PC Oct. 1, 1888. Advertised for *next week* Ath Oct. 6, 1888; for *Oct. 16th* Ath Oct. 13, 1888; as though published PC Oct. 15, 1888. Listed PC Oct. 15, 1888.

AAS   CO   H

10585. THE ASPERN PAPERS LOUISA PALLANT THE MODERN WARNING ...

LONDON   MACMILLAN AND CO. AND NEW YORK
1888   ALL RIGHTS RESERVED

First American edition. For prior publication see preceding entry.

⟨i-viii⟩, ⟨1⟩-290, blank leaf. 7⅜″ x 4⅞″.

⟨A⟩⁴, B-I, K-T⁸, U².

S cloth: blue. Black-coated end papers.

Deposited Nov. 1, 1888. Listed PW Nov. 10, 1888.

H   UV

10586. A LONDON LIFE THE PATAGONIA THE LIAR MRS. TEMPERLY ... IN TWO VOLUMES ...

LONDON   MACMILLAN AND CO. AND NEW YORK
1889   ALL RIGHTS RESERVED

For first American edition see next entry.

1: ⟨i-viii⟩, ⟨1⟩-281; blank, p. ⟨282⟩; 2 pp. advertisements. 7⅛″ full x 4¾″.

2: ⟨i-viii⟩, ⟨1⟩-361; blank, p. ⟨362⟩; 2 pp. advertisements.

1: ⟨A⟩⁴, B-I, K-S⁸, T⁴, ⟨U⟩².

2: ⟨A⟩⁴, B-I, K-U, X-Z⁸, 2A⁴, ⟨2B⟩².

V cloth: greenish-blue. Black-coated end papers.

Advertised as *just ready* PC Feb. 15, 1889. Printed March, 1889 (publisher's records). Advertised as *just ready* PC March 1, 1889; Bkr March 1, 1889. Listed (prematurely?) PC March 1, 1889. Advertised as *immediately* Ath April 6, 1889; PC April 15, 1889; Ath April 20, 1889. Advertised for *next week* Ath April 27, 1889. Listed Ath April 27, 1889. Advertised as though published PC May 1, 1889; Ath May 4, 1889. Listed (again) PC May 15, 1889. *The one volume edition (i.e., the first one volume British edition)* printed June, 1889; listed Ath June 8, 1889; advertised as though published PC June 15, 1889; listed PC June 15, 1889.

CO   UV

10587. A LONDON LIFE THE PATAGONIA THE LIAR MRS. TEMPERLY ...

LONDON   MACMILLAN AND CO. AND NEW YORK
1889   ALL RIGHTS RESERVED

First American edition. For prior publication see preceding entry.

⟨i-viii⟩, ⟨1⟩-366; 2 pp. advertisements (priced in U. S. currency). 7⁵⁄₁₆″ x 4⅞″ full.

⟨A⟩⁴, B-I, K-U, X-Z, 2A⁸.

S cloth: blue. Black-coated end papers.

Deposited for copyright May 1, 1889. Listed PW May 11, 1889.

BA   H

10588. The Odd Number Thirteen Tales by Guy de Maupassant The Translation by Jonathan Sturges An Introduction by Henry James

New York   Harper & Brothers, Franklin Square   1889

"Introduction. Guy de Maupassant," pp. ⟨vii⟩-xvii.

Deposited Oct. 30, 1889. The London (Osgood, McIlvaine) edition advertised as *published this day* Ath Oct. 3, 1891; listed PC Oct. 10, 1891.

AAS   H   UV

10589. The Art of Authorship ... Compiled ... by George Bainton.

London: James Clarke & Co., 13 & 14, Fleet Street. 1890.

Contribution, pp. 207-208.

For comment see entry No. 1271.

10590. THE TRAGIC MUSE ... IN TWO
VOLUMES ...

BOSTON AND NEW YORK   HOUGHTON, MIFFLIN
AND COMPANY   THE RIVERSIDE PRESS, CAMBRIDGE
1890

1: ⟨i-iv⟩, ⟨1⟩-422, blank leaf. 7" x 4¹¹⁄₁₆".

2: ⟨i-iv⟩, ⟨423⟩-882.

1: ⟨1², 2-27⁸, 28⁴⟩.

2: ⟨1², 2-29⁸, 30⁶⟩.

Two printings noted:

1

As above.

2

1: ⟨i-iv⟩, ⟨1⟩-422, blank leaf.

2: ⟨i-ii⟩, ⟨423⟩-882, blank leaf.

1: ⟨1-26⁸, 27⁶⟩.

2: ⟨1-29⁸⟩.

V cloth: green; red. White laid end papers. Flyleaf at front of Vol. 1; flyleaf at back of Vol. 2.

Printed June 3, 1890 (Vol. 1: 1014 copies; Vol.
2: 1020 copies). Bound during the period June
4 to July 2, 1890. Noted for June 7 PW May
31, 1890. Deposited June 9, 1890. BA copy received June 10, 1890. Listed PW June 21, 1890.
Second printing (278 copies) Nov. 8, 1890.

AAS (2nd)   H   NYPL   UV

10591. The Art of Authorship ... Compiled ...
by George Bainton

New York   D. Appleton and Company   1890

Contribution, pp. 207-208.

For comment see entry No. 1272.

10592. ... Port Tarascon   The Last Adventures
of the Illustrious Tartarin Translated by
Henry James ...

New York   Harper & Brothers, Franklin
Square   1891

At head of title: Alphonse Daudet

⟨i-vi⟩, ⟨1⟩-359; blank, p. ⟨360⟩; 4 pp. advertisements. Illustrated. 9" x 6⅛".

"Translator's Preface," pp. ⟨1⟩-8.

*Noted in the following bindings; the sequence
is presumed correct:*

Binding A

S cloth: blue. Stamped in gold and silver. **Top
edges gilt.** A principal feature of the fillet at the
foot of spine is a fretwork rule. The frontispiece
is a portrait of Daudet; the head faces left.

Binding B

S cloth: blue. Stamped in gold and silver. **Top
edges gilt.** A principal feature of the fillet at the
foot of spine is a fretwork rule. The frontispiece
is a portrait of Daudet; the head faces the
reader.

Binding C

S cloth: blue. Stamped in gold and silver. **Top
edges plain.** A fretwork rule not present in the
fillet at foot of spine. The frontispiece is a
portrait of Daudet; the head faces the reader.

Binding D (E?)

V cloth: orange. Stamped in black only. **Top
edges plain.** A fretwork rule not present in the
fillet at foot of spine. The frontispiece is a
portrait of Daudet; the head faces left.

Binding E (D?)

V cloth: cream. Stamped in black only. **Top
edges plain.** A fretwork rule not present in the
fillet at foot of spine. The frontispiece is a portrait of Daudet; the head faces the reader.

Deposited Oct. 30, 1890. Listed PW Nov. 8, 1890.

AAS (A)   CO (A)   H (D,E)   NYPL (A)   Y (A,B,C)

10593. CATALOGUE OF A COLLECTION
OF DRAWINGS BY ALFRED PARSONS,
R.I. WITH A PREFATORY NOTE BY
HENRY JAMES. EXHIBITED AT THE
FINE ART SOCIETY'S.

148, NEW BOND STREET, W., LONDON. 1891.

⟨1⟩-15. 8⅜" x 5½" scant.

⟨-⟩⁸.

Printed gray-blue paper wrapper.

Collected in *Picture and Text*, 1893.

The exhibition was opened to the public March
9, 1891.

CO   UV   Y

10594. Mine Own People by Rudyard Kipling
... with a Critical Introduction by Henry
James ...

New York   United States Book Company Successors to John W. Lovell Company   150
Worth St., Cor. Mission Place ⟨1891⟩

"Introduction," pp. ⟨vii⟩-xxvi. Collected in
Views and Reviews, 1908.

Deposited for copyright March 9, 1891. Listed PW May 23, 1891

Noted in the following bindings; sequence, if any, not determined. The designations are for identification only.

Binding A

V cloth: maroon. Goldstamped. Covers bevelled. A copy in H inscribed by early owner April 14, 1891; another in NYPL inscribed by early owner April, 1891. *Note:* Last line of text, p. 33, reads: *I know that |*

Binding B

V cloth: tan. Stamped in brown. Covers not bevelled. On front: INDIAN TALES—IV. a feature not present on *Binding A.* A copy in H inscribed by early owner *Xmas. 1891. Note:* Last line of text, p. 33, reads: *I know that |*

OTHER PRINTINGS NOTED

The following are presumed reprints. In each of the following the last line, p. 33, has been repaired and reads: *I know that breed. |* No attempt has been made to present a firm sequence of these later printings and the designations are for identification only.

REPRINT A

New York   United States Book Company Successors To John W. Lovell Company   150 Worth St., Cor. Mission Place ⟨1891⟩

At head of title: *Lovell's International Series, No. 153*

Issued under date March 9, 1891; but such dates are notoriously unreliable; see BAL, Vol. 1, p. xvi, for comment.

The James introduction called for by the title-page is not present.

Issued in printed paper wrapper. The inner back wrapper imprinted with a list of *Lovell's International Series,* Nos. 90-154 (listed as though published); Nos. 155-163 under the heading *Will Shortly Appear.*

Locations: H

REPRINT B

Same as *Reprint A* save for the following variations:

James's introduction is present.

Inner back wrapper lists Nos. 104-180 in *Lovell's International Series* as though published.

A copy thus deposited for copyright July 23, 1892.

Locations: LC

REPRINT C

New York   Lovell, Coryell & Company   310-318 Sixth Avenue ⟨1891⟩

Issued *ca.* 1894.

Locations: H

REPRINT D

Chicago   W. B. Conkey Company ⟨1891⟩

Issued late 19th century or early 20th.

Locations: H

REPRINT E

New York   International Book Company   17 and 19 Waverley Place ⟨n.d.⟩

Noted only in the printed paper wrapper of *The Fireside Series,* No. 141; issued under date Nov. 1891, by J. S. Ogilvie, Publisher, New York.

Locations: H

REPRINT F

New York: George Munro's Sons, Publishers, 17 to 27 Vandewater Street. ⟨n.d.⟩

Issued in printed paper wrapper as *Munro's Library of Popular Novels,* No. 190, under date May 13, 1896.

Locations: H

REPRINT G

R. F. Fenno & Company Publishers   9 & 11 E. Sixteenth Street New York City 1899

Printed paper wrapper.

Locations: H

REPRINT H

New York   Frank F. Lovell Company   23 Duane Street ⟨n.d., 1899⟩

Printed paper wrapper. Issued under date (on wrapper) Sept. 1, 1899, as *The Lotus Series,* No. 1. A later printing from the same plates was issued by *Manhattan Press, New York, n.d.*

Locations: LC (both)

Reported, not seen: *The Seaside Library,* No. 1909; printed paper wrapper. Listed PW Dec. 26, 1891.

H (First printing, *Binding A, Binding B*)   NYPL (First printing, *Binding A*)

10595. THE AMERICAN   A COMEDY IN FOUR ACTS . . .

LONDON   WILLIAM   HEINEMANN   1891   [ALL RIGHTS RESERVED]

Privately printed for use of the author and the players.

⟨i-iv⟩, ⟨1⟩-191. 7¼″ scant x 4¾″.

⟨-⟩², A-I, K-M⁸.

Printed blue-gray paper wrapper.

Two printings noted:

1

Wrapper and title-page: THE AMERICAN / A COMEDY IN FOUR ACTS / ⟨etc.⟩

P. 49, Valentin's second speech: *What can she mean itbut ⟨sic⟩ for . . .*

P. 56: The folio is correct; *i.e.,* 56. Running head: TBE AMERICAN

P. 81, the stage direction for Claire's second speech: *. . . with a deliberate movement of his own . . .*

2

Wrapper and title-page: THE AMERICAN / IN FOUR ACTS / ⟨etc.⟩

P. 49, Valentin's second speech: *What can she mean it for but . . .*

P. 56: Incorrectly paged 65. The running head reads (correctly): THE AMERICAN

P. 81, the stage direction for Claire's second speech: *. . . with a deliberate movement of her own . . .*

Interleaved copies of the second printing have been seen.

The play was produced in London Oct. 1891; a review appeared in Ath Oct. 3, 1891. Collected in *Complete Plays* ⟨1949⟩.

CO (1st)   H (1st; interleaved 2nd)

10596. THE LESSON OF THE MASTER THE MARRIAGES THE PUPIL BROOKSMITH THE SOLUTION SIR EDMUND ORME . . .

NEW YORK   MACMILLAN AND CO. AND LONDON 1892   ALL RIGHTS RESERVED

⟨i⟩-⟨vi⟩, 1-302; 12 pp. advertisements. 7⁷⁄₁₆″ x 5″.

⟨1-20⁸⟩. *Signed:* ⟨-⟩³, A-I, K-T⁸, ⟨U⟩⁵.

V cloth: gray-blue.

Deposited Feb. 4, 1892. BA copy received Feb. 23, 1892. Listed PW Feb. 27, 1892.

LONDON EDITION

THE LESSON OF THE MASTER   THE MARRIAGES   THE PUPIL BROOKSMITH THE SOLUTION   SIR EDMUND ORME . . .

LONDON   MACMILLAN AND CO. AND NEW YORK 1892   ALL RIGHTS RESERVED

Issued simultaneously with the New York edition? Imprints of J. S. Cushing & Co., Boston; and, Berwick & Smith, Boston, on copyright page.

⟨i-ii⟩, ⟨i⟩-⟨vi⟩, 1-302, blank leaf. 7⅜″ x 5″.

⟨-⟩⁴, A-I, K-T⁸.

H cloth: blue. Gray-green coated on white end papers. Inserted at back is a publisher's catalog, pp. 44, dated *December, 1891.* In some copies there is an additional catalog of 4 pages, dated at foot of p. ⟨4⟩, 20.2.92.

Listed Ath Feb. 27, 1892. Advertised as *now ready* Ath, PC Feb. 27, 1892. Listed PC March 5, 1892.

AAS (New York)   CO (New York)   H (Both) NYPL (New York)   UV (London)   Y (London)

10597. The Average Woman by Wolcott Balestier with a Biographical Sketch by Henry James

Leipzig   Heinemann and Balestier Limited, London   1892

Printed paper wrapper. Issued as No. 100 in *The English Library* series.

"Wolcott Balestier," pp. ⟨vii⟩-xxxi. Collected in *The American Essays,* 1956.

The only located copy has the back wrapper dated *March 1892.* If the date is to be accepted then the Leipzig edition preceded the American edition; see next entry.

The London (Heinemann) edition was advertised as *in preparation* Ath April 30, 1892; as for *May 30* PC May 14, 1892. Noted as *in a few days* PC June 18, 1892. Listed Ath June 18, PC June 25, 1892.

LC

10598. The Average Woman by Wolcott Balestier with a Preface by Henry James

New York   United States Book Company   5 and 7 East Sixteenth Street   Chicago: 266 & 268 Wabash Ave. ⟨1892⟩

See preceding entry for prior publication.

"Wolcott Balestier," pp. ⟨11⟩-34.

Listed PW July 2, 1892. H copy received July 2, 1892.

BA   H   UV   Y

10599. The Great Streets of the World by Richard Harding Davis . . . Henry James . . . ⟨and Others⟩

New York   Charles Scribner's Sons   1892

"The Grand Canal," pp. <143>-172. Collected in *Italian Hours,* 1909.

Deposited Oct. 28, 1892. Noted as *just ready* PW Oct. 29, 1892. Listed PW Nov. 5, 1892. The London (American sheets with cancel title-leaf of Osgood, McIlvaine) edition listed Ath Dec. 17, 1892. *Note:* Copies with the Harper spine imprint were issued *ca.* 1897.

AAS BA UV Y

10600. THE REAL THING AND OTHER TALES . . .

NEW YORK   MACMILLAN AND CO. AND LONDON 1893   ALL RIGHTS RESERVED

<i>-<x>, 1-275; blank, p. <276>; 2 pp. advertisements. 7⅜" full x 5".

<1-18⁸>.

V cloth: gray-blue.

Two issues noted:

1

The title-leaf is an integral part of its gathering. Copyright notice dated 1892.

2

The title-leaf is a cancel. Copyright notice dated 1893. With a single exception all copies examined, including both deposit copies, are thus. The book was deposited March 8, 1893, which accounts for the altered copyright notice; *i.e.,* the date 1892 was erroneous. BAL presumes the alteration was made prior to publication and that all copies were supposed to have the correction. Sheets issued in London (see below) have the 1892 copyright notice and the title-leaf is integral.

Deposited March 8, 1893. The publisher's records indicate that both the London and the New York editions were to be issued simultaneously, on March 10, 1893. Noted as *just ready* PW March 18, 1893. Listed PW March 18, 1893.

LONDON EDITION

THE REAL THING AND OTHER TALES . . .

LONDON   MACMILLAN AND CO. AND NEW YORK 1893   ALL RIGHTS RESERVED

<i-x>, 1-275, blank leaf. 7⅜" x 4¹⁵⁄₁₆". The title-leaf is integral, the copyright notice dated 1892.

<1-18⁸>.

BF cloth: blue. Green-coated end papers. Publisher's catalog, pp. 47, inserted at back, dated *January, 1893.*

Issued simultaneously with the New York edition? Printed at the same time and place (The Norwood Press, U.S.A.) as the New York edition. Listed Ath March 18, 1893; advertised as though published Ath March 25, 1893; listed PC April 1, 1893; advertised as though published PC April 1, 1893. Also issued in *Macmillan's Colonial Library* series; date of publication not determined; identified on both the binding and title-page as part of the series.

AAS (New York, 1893)   CO (New York, 1892)   H (New York, 1893)   LC (London)   NYPL (London)   UV (London)

10601. PICTURE AND TEXT . . .

NEW YORK   HARPER AND BROTHERS   MDCCCXCIII

Title-page in black, orange and buff.

<i-xii>, <1>-175. Frontispiece. Printed protective tissue inserted. 7 plates inserted. 5⅞" full x 3⅝" (in white V); 5¹⁵⁄₁₆" x 3½" (in green V).

<a>⁶, 1-11⁸. *Note:* Sig. <a> consists of a gathering of 4 leaves of bookstock, plus an insert on coated paper consisting of a single cut sheet folded to 4 pages comprising the frontispiece and the title-leaf.

V cloth: green; white. Stamped in gold. White laid end papers. Copies in white V cloth have the top edges gilded; copies in green V cloth have the top edges plain.

Note: Noted also in remainder binding: Red V cloth, stamped in black, top edges plain. Edel-Laurence (p. 92) report other remainder bindings: "green cloth, lettering in red and ornaments blocked in grey . . . grey cloth, lettering and ornaments in black . . ."

Deposited (green V, goldstamped) June 3, 1893. BA copy (green V, goldstamped) received June 6, 1893. Listed PW June 10, 1893.

BA BPL (red V remainder) CO H

10602. THE PRIVATE LIFE   THE WHEEL OF TIME   LORD BEAUPRE   THE VISITS   COLLABORATION   OWEN WINGRAVE . . .

LONDON   JAMES R. OSGOOD, McILVAINE & CO. 45, ALBEMARLE STREET, W. 1893

For first American edition see below under 1893 (August); 1893 (Sept.).

<i-viii>, <1>-331; printer's imprint, p. <332>. Laid paper. 7½" x 5".

A⁴, B-I, K-U, X⁸, Y⁶.

T cloth: blue. White laid end papers.

Advertised as *ready this day* Ath June 3, 1893.

Listed Ath June 3, 1893; PC June 10, 1893. Advertised as *just out* PC June 17, 1893.

AAS   CO   H

10603. ESSAYS IN LONDON AND ELSEWHERE . . .

LONDON   JAMES R. OSGOOD, McILVAINE & CO. 45 ALBEMARLE STREET, W.   MDCCCXCIII   ALL RIGHTS RESERVED

For first American edition see below under 1893 (Sept.).

⟨i-viii⟩, ⟨1⟩-320. Laid paper. 8″ x 5¼″.

⟨A⟩⁴, B-I, K-U, X⁸

T cloth: salmon. White laid end papers.

Advertised as *new* PC June 17, 1893. Listed Ath June 17, 1893. A copy in CO inscribed by James to Edmund Gosse, June 20, 1893. Listed PC June 24, 1893. Reviewed PC June 24, 1893.

B   CO   Y

10604. THE PRIVATE LIFE   LORD BEAUPRÉ   THE VISITS . . .

NEW YORK   HARPER & BROTHERS PUBLISHERS 1893

For prior publication of these three tales see *The Private Life* . . . , above, under 1893 (June).

⟨i-vi⟩, ⟨1⟩-232, 4 pp. advertisements. 6⅞″ x 4⁷⁄₁₆″.

⟨a⟩², ⟨b⟩¹, ⟨1⟩-14⁸, 15⁶.

Six bindings noted; the sequence has not been established but *Bindings D-F* are almost surely remainder bindings.

Binding A

S cloth: green.
Front: Stamped in gold and silver.
Spine: Stamped in gold and silver.
Top edges: Gilt.
End papers: White laid paper.

Binding B

V cloth: gray-blue.
Front: Stamped in gold and silver.
Spine: Stamped in gold and silver.
Top edges: Stained light yellow.
End papers: White laid paper.

Binding C

V cloth: blue.
Front: Stamped in gold and silver.

Spine: Stamped in gold and silver.
Top edges: Plain.
End papers: White laid paper.

Binding D

V cloth: gray.
Front: Stamped in black.
Spine: Stamped in black.
Top edges: Plain.
End papers: White laid paper.

Binding E

T cloth: maroon.
Front: Unstamped.
Spine: Stamped in gold and blind.
Top edges: Plain.
End papers: White laid paper.

Binding F

V cloth: tan.
Front: Stamped in black.
Spine: Stamped in black.
Top edges: Plain.
End papers: White laid paper.

Advertised for Aug. 15 PW Aug. 12, 1893. Deposited Aug. 16, 1893. Listed PW Aug. 19, 1893.

AAS (A)   BA (B)   CO (B,E,F)   H (C,D)   NYPL (B)

10605. ESSAYS IN LONDON AND ELSEWHERE . . .

NEW YORK   HARPER & BROTHERS PUBLISHERS 1893

For prior publication see above under 1893 (June).

⟨i-viii⟩, ⟨1⟩-305; blank, p. ⟨306⟩; 6 pp. advertisements. 7⁹⁄₁₆″ x 5″.

⟨-⟩⁴, 1-19⁸, ⟨20⟩⁴.

S cloth: blue. White laid end papers.

Noted as *at once* PW Sept. 9, 1893. Deposited Sept. 12, 1893. Listed PW Sept. 16, 1893. BA copy received Sept. 16, 1893.

H   NYPL

10606. THE WHEEL OF TIME   COLLABORATION   OWEN WINGRAVE . . .

NEW YORK   HARPER & BROTHERS PUBLISHERS 1893

For prior publication see above, *The Private Life* . . . , 1893 (June).

⟨i-iv⟩, ⟨1⟩-220. 6¹³⁄₁₆″ full x 4⁷⁄₁₆″.

⟨-⟩², ⟨1⟩-6, ⟨7⟩-9, ⟨10⟩-13⁸, 14⁶.

V cloth: blue-green. Stamped in gold and silver. White laid end papers. Top edges stained yellow. A surviving copyright deposit copy thus. Also noted in the following remainder bindings; the designations are arbitrary:

Variant A

V cloth: green. Sides unstamped. Spine stamped in red and in blind. Top edges plain.

Variant B

C cloth: maroon. Sides unstamped. Spine stamped in gold and in blind. Top edges plain.

Note: Edel-Laurence (p. 97) report a "secondary binding" of red cloth, stamped in gold and blind on front cover and spine, top edges plain; no copy thus traced by BAL.

Noted as *nearly ready* PW Aug. 26, 1893. Deposited Sept. 26, 1893. Listed PW Oct. 7, 1893.

AAS (Variant A)   H (1st. Variant B)   NYPL (1st. Variant A)

10607. THEATRICALS   TWO COMEDIES   TENANTS DISENGAGED . . .

LONDON   OSGOOD, McILVAINE & CO.   45 ALBEMARLE STREET 1894   ALL RIGHTS RESERVED

For first American edition see next entry.

⟨i⟩-⟨viii⟩, ⟨1⟩-325; blank, p. ⟨326⟩; advertisements, p. ⟨327⟩. 7⅝″ x 5″.

⟨A⟩⁴, B-I, K-U, X⁸, Y⁴.

Green linen. White laid end papers.

Advertised for *next week* Ath May 26, 1894. Listed Ath June 9, 1894; PC June 16, 1894. Reviewed PC June 16, 1894.

H   Y

10608. THEATRICALS   TWO COMEDIES   TENANTS DISENGAGED . . .

NEW YORK   HARPER & BROTHERS, PUBLISHERS   1894   ALL RIGHTS RESERVED

For prior(?) publication see preceding entry.

⟨i⟩-⟨viii⟩, ⟨1⟩-325; blank leaf. 7⅝″ x 5″.

⟨A⟩⁴, B-I, K-U, X⁸, Y⁴.

Green linen. White laid end papers.

Clark (Edinburgh) imprint at foot of p. 325.

Listed PW June 16, 1894. No record of copyright deposit found.

AAS   H   LC   NYPL

10609. . . . GUY   DOMVILLE   PLAY   IN   THREE ACTS . . .

LONDON: PRINTED BY J. MILES & CO., 195, WARDOUR STREET, OXFORD STREET, W. 1894.

At head of title: PRINTED AS MANUSCRIPT FOR PRIVATE CIRCULATION ONLY.

⟨1⟩-79. 7³⁄₁₆″ x 4¹³⁄₁₆″.

⟨A⟩-E⁸.

Printed blue paper wrapper.

Privately printed; not published. Ath Aug. 18, 1894, noted that the play was "to be produced." "In October 1894 a few acting copies of the play were printed 'in intense secrecy, for use in the theatre.' "—*Complete Plays* ⟨1949⟩, p. 467; information derived from James's letter to William James, Oct. 27, 1894, *ibid.*, p. 833. Ath Dec. 29, 1894, reported the play as forthcoming. "To-night witnesses the reopening of the St. James's with *Guy Domville*"—Ath Jan. 5, 1895. Reviewed (and pronounced a failure) Ath Jan. 12, 1895. Collected in *Complete Plays* ⟨1949⟩ but extracts had prior publication in *The George Alexander Birthday Book*, 1903; and, *The Drama Birthday Book*, 1895. Information regarding this last from Edel-Laurence.

CO   H   UV

10610. THEATRICALS   SECOND SERIES   THE ALBUM   THE REPROBATE . . .

LONDON   OSGOOD, McILVAINE & CO.   45 ALBEMARLE STREET   1895   ALL RIGHTS RESERVED.

For first American edition see next entry.

⟨i⟩-⟨xvi⟩, ⟨1⟩-416; plus: 2 pp. advertisements. 7⁹⁄₁₆″ x 5″ full.

⟨A⟩-I, K-U, X-Z, 2A-2D⁸; plus: ⟨-⟩¹.

Green linen. White laid end papers.

Listed Ath Dec. 1, 1894; PC Dec. 8, 1894. Advertised as *just published* Ath Dec. 8, 1894.

H   UV

10611. THEATRICALS   SECOND SERIES   THE ALBUM   THE REPROBATE . . .

NEW YORK   HARPER & BROTHERS, PUBLISHERS   1895   ALL RIGHTS RESERVED.

For prior publication see preceding entry.

⟨i⟩-⟨xvi⟩, ⟨1⟩-416. 7⁹⁄₁₆″ x 5″.

⟨A⟩-I, K-U, X-Z, 2A-2D⁸.

Green linen. White laid end papers.

Clark (Edinburgh) imprint at foot of p. 416.

A copy in H received Dec. 14, 1894. Noted as

just issued PW Dec. 15, 1894. Listed PW Dec. 22, 1894.

H NYPL

10612. THE QUEST OF THE HOLY GRAIL

Notes describing a series of fifteen paintings by Edwin Austin Abbey written by Mrs. Abbey with some assistance from James. Contemporary evidence indicates that James's assistance may have been limited to the first five paintings only.

"The great frieze for the Boston Public Library, painted by Eadwin⟨*sic*⟩ A. Abbey, is now in place, and Mr. Abbey has been going over the pictures very carefully to make sure they are quite perfect before the paint becomes dry. The pictures are to be reproduced in a small volume of popular character, giving an account of the work, its meaning and origin, to be written by Mr. and Mrs. Abbey, with the valuable assistance of Henry James."—PW April 27, 1895, p. 690.

"In the end the story was told in fifteen scenes, the period decided upon being the twelfth century. In the first scene—and in this summary use has been made of the catalogue of the exhibition of the second part of the series, in the Guildhall in 1901, which was a composite work of Henry James and Mrs. Abbey ..."— E. V. Lucas: *Edwin Austin Abbey,* London, 1921, Vol. 1, p. 232.

"... The description of this panel ⟨*i.e.,* the fifth⟩ is from the pen of Henry James ..."— *ibid.,* p. 233.

Undated letter from James to Mrs. Abbey: "Why, this is most awfully, charmingly, troublingly graceful. My 'help' [referring to the preface for the 'Grail' exhibition brochure] last winter wasn't worth any kind of recognition— it was help most lame and inadequate. But the spirit that moves you is noble ..."—*ibid.,* Vol. 2, p. 278.

Note: BAL has been unable to find any convincing evidence to support a common assertion that the Boston Public Library printed 30 copies of the text in 1895. However, it may be that such a printing was done; see entry No. 363, sale catalog of the Tannahill and Carstairs collections, American Art Association-Anderson Galleries, Inc., New York, 1933, catalog No. 4069. In this the title is given as: *The Quest and Achievement of the Holy Grail: Wall Paintings in the Delivery Room ...* ; dated (by the cataloger) [*Boston, 1895*]; and described thus: *An Outline of this version of the Legend of Henry James. Printed in 15 numbered paragraphs on one side of two folio sheets; laid in original wrappers, with cloth back and paper*

label ... but 30 copies were printed for the use of the Boston Public Library. Since the full suite of fifteen paintings was not completed until 1901 the cataloger appears to have erred in the dating.

A

First Edition

"THE QUEST OF THE HOLY GRAIL." THE FIRST PORTION OF A SERIES OF PAINT-INGS TO BE DONE FOR THE DECORA-TION OF THE PUBLIC LIBRARY OF BOSTON, U.S.A. BY EDWIN A. ABBEY. NOW SHOWN FOR A LIMITED PERIOD AT THE GALLERIES 9, CONDUIT ST., W. DAILY FROM 10 A.M. TO 6 P.M.

⟨London⟩ JANUARY 1895.

Anonymous. Written by Mrs. Edwin A. Abbey with some assistance from James.

Cover-title.

⟨1⟩-7. Laid paper watermarked with the Van Gelder device. $7\frac{1}{2}$" x $4^{15}\!/_{16}$".

⟨-⟩^{4}.

Printed self-wrapper.

The notes describe the first five paintings only.

Locations: UV

B

First American Edition

THE QUEST OF THE HOLY GRAIL A SERIES OF PAINTINGS DONE FOR THE DECORATION OF THE DELIVERY ROOM IN THE PUBLIC LIBRARY OF THE CITY OF BOSTON BY EDWIN A. ABBEY

R H RVSSELL AND SON PVBLISHERS N Y MDCCCXCV

Anonymous. Written by Mrs. Edwin A. Abbey with some assistance from James.

⟨1-16⟩. Illustrated. $9\frac{1}{8}$" x $11\frac{3}{4}$".

⟨1^4, 2-3^2⟩.

Printed cream paper boards, white V cloth shelf-back. Top edges gilt.

The notes (here somewhat revised) describe the first five paintings only.

Advertised as though ready PW June 1, 1895. Listed PW June 29, 1895.

Locations: H

C

Second English Edition

... Exhibition at the Guildhall Art Gallery of the Series of Paintings Presenting "The Quest of the Holy Grail." Executed for the Decoration of the Public Library of Boston, U.S.A. by Edwin A. Abbey ... from Monday, 28th October, to Tuesday, 19th November, 1901 ...

‹London, 1901›

Anonymous. At head of title: The Corporation of London.

Printed paper wrapper. The notes are on pp. ‹7›-16 and are for the entire series of fifteen paintings.

Locations: *Not seen.* Entry on the basis of a photographic copy of the original in The Guildhall, London.

D

Second American Edition

Exhibition at the American Art Galleries   Madison Square South   Of the Second Half of the Series of Paintings Presenting "The Quest of the Holy Grail" Done for the Decoration of the Public Library of Boston by Edwin A. Abbey, R.A. Open Daily 9 A.M. to 6 P.M., from Monday, December 9th to Saturday, December 21st, inclusive

American Art Association, Managers   New York   1901

Anonymous.

‹1›-14, blank leaf. 8⅝″ x 5¾″.

‹-›⁸.

Printed mottled blue-gray paper wrapper.

The notes are for the entire series of fifteen paintings.

Locations: UV

Later Printings Noted

E

Monthly Bulletin of Books Added to the Public Library of the City of Boston. Vol. VII. No. 3. March, 1902.

   Boston. Published by the Trustees. 1902.

Cover-title. Printed self-wrapper.

Text, anonymous, covering all fifteen paintings, pp. 127-131. Printed in relatively narrow measure, the lines being 3″ wide.

Heading, p. 127: BOSTON PUBLIC LIBRARY. / ‹decorated rule› / THE QUEST AND ACHIEVEMENT OF / THE HOLY GRAIL. / Paintings by Edwin A. Abbey, R.A. / ‹text›

Locations: BPL   H(received March 10, 1902)

F

A card, estimated size. 11″ x 8″, printed on both sides, in two columns, printed from the setting used in the preceding.

Not seen.

BAL theorizes that such a printing (printings?) was prepared in 1902 for the use of the public in viewing the paintings in The Boston Public Library. Current printings of the note in this form, bear James's name as author and are provided by The Boston Public Library for use of the public; it is probable that the earliest printing (or printings) was issued anonymously. Known reprints were done on Aug. 9, 1943 (600 copies); March 16, 1951 (100 copies); information on the basis of printer's marks on the cards examined in BPL. H has an example of the 1951 reprinting.

G

Fiftieth Annual Report of the Trustees of the Public Library of the City of Boston 1901-1902.

   Boston   Municipal Printing Office   1902

Printed paper wrapper. Some copies have an inserted presentation slip reading: *With the Compliments of the Trustees* ...

"The Quest and Achievement of the Holy Grail," pp. 104-108; anonymous.

Issued after May 16, 1902.

Locations: BPL   H

Note

At some unknown time BPL issued a series of annotated postcard reproductions of the paintings; fifteen cards in an envelope. The text is by an unknown author.

10613. TERMINATIONS   THE DEATH OF THE LION   THE COXON FUND   THE MIDDLE YEARS   THE ALTAR OF THE DEAD ...

   NEW YORK   HARPER & BROTHERS PUBLISHERS   1895

Printed for copyright purposes only; for published editions see next two entries.

‹i›-‹vi›, ‹1›-242. 7⅛″ x 4⅞″.

‹1-15⁸, 16⁴›. *Signed:* ‹-›³, ‹1›-15⁸, 16¹.

S cloth: blue. Printed white paper label on spine. Flyleaves.

Deposited May 15, 1895.

LC

10614. TERMINATIONS   THE DEATH OF THE LION   THE COXON FUND   THE MIDDLE YEARS   THE ALTAR OF THE DEAD ...

LONDON: WILLIAM HEINEMANN MDCCCXCV

Title-page printed in black and red-orange.

First published edition. For a copyright printing see preceding entry; for first American edition see next entry.

⟨i-viii⟩, ⟨1⟩-260. Laid paper. 7½″ x 5″.

⟨-⟩⁴, A-I, K-Q⁸, R².

S cloth: blue. White laid end papers. Publisher's catalog, 16 pp., inserted at back. The earliest form of the binding has four irises blindstamped on the front; a later form of the binding is blindstamped on the front with an arrangement of tulips.

In addition to the printing described above (designed for distribution in England) there was also a colonial edition printed on wove (not laid) paper, title-page printed in black (not black and red-orange), the date in the imprint in arabic (not roman) numerals; date of publication not determined. Hybrid copies have been seen made up of mixed laid and wove papers.

Advertised as *forthcoming* PC April 27, 1895. Advertised for *May* Ath April 27, 1895. Noted for *Wednesday next* (*i.e.*, May 15) PC May 11, 1895. A copy in CO presented by James to Mrs. Humphry Ward May 17, 1895. Listed Ath May 18, 1895; PC May 18, 1895.

CO UV

10615. TERMINATIONS THE DEATH OF THE LION THE COXON FUND THE MIDDLE YEARS THE ALTAR OF THE DEAD . . .

NEW YORK   HARPER & BROTHERS PUBLISHERS 1895

First published American edition; see preceding two entries.

⟨i-viii⟩, ⟨1⟩-242, 6 pp. advertisements. 7⁵⁄₁₆″ full x 4⅞″.

⟨-⟩⁴, 1-15⁸, 16⁴.

S cloth: green. V cloth: green. White laid end papers. *Note:* All copies examined by BAL have two ornaments on the spine. Edel-Laurence (p. 103) report a "secondary binding" a principal feature of which is "elimination of ornament on spine"; no copy thus traced by BAL.

Noted as *published on the 18th* PW June 22, 1895. Listed PW June 22, 1895.

AAS BA H NYPL

10616. EMBARRASSMENTS . . .

NEW YORK   THE MACMILLAN COMPANY   LONDON: MACMILLAN & CO., LTD. 1896   ALL RIGHTS RESERVED

Printed for copyright purposes only; for published editions see next two entries.

⟨i⟩-⟨vi⟩, ⟨1⟩-320, blank leaf. Printed on *wove* paper. 7¾″ x 5¼″.

⟨1-20⁸, 21⁴⟩. *Signed:* ⟨A⟩³, ⟨B⟩-I, K-U, X⁸, ⟨Y⟩¹.

Maroon linen. Sides blindstamped with a single rule border. Spine goldstamped: EMBARRASS-MENTS / ⟨*rule*⟩ / HENRY JAMES / MACMILLAN & Cᵒ Top edges gilded. White wove end papers.

Deposited June 10, 1896.

LC

10617. EMBARRASSMENTS   THE FIGURE IN THE CARPET   GLASSES   THE NEXT TIME   THE WAY IT CAME . . .

LONDON: WILLIAM HEINEMANN MDCCCXCVI

Title-page printed in black and red-orange.

First published edition. For a copyright printing see preceding entry; for first American edition see next entry.

⟨i-viii⟩, ⟨1⟩-263. Laid paper. 7⁹⁄₁₆″ scant x 5″.

⟨-⟩⁴, A-I, K-Q⁸, R⁴.

S cloth: blue. White laid end papers. Publisher's catalog, 32 pp., inserted at back. The earliest form of the binding has four irises blindstamped on the front; a later form of the binding is blindstamped on the front with an arrangement of tulips.

In addition to the printing described above (designed for publication in England) there was also a colonial edition printed on wove (not laid) paper, the title-page printed in black (not black and red-orange), the date in the imprint in arabic (not roman) numerals; date of publication not determined. Hybrid copies have been seen made up of mixed laid and wove papers.

Advertised as *forthcoming* PC May 9, 1896. Published June 12, 1896 (publisher's records). Listed Ath June 20, 1896; PC June 20, 1896.

LC UV

10618. EMBARRASSMENTS . . .

NEW YORK   THE MACMILLAN COMPANY   LON-DON: MACMILLAN & CO., LTD. 1896   ALL RIGHTS RESERVED

First published American edition; see preceding two entries.

⟨i⟩-⟨vi⟩, ⟨1⟩-320, 2 pp. advertisements. *Laid* paper. 7¾″ x 5³⁄₁₆″.

⟨1-20⁸, 21⁴⟩. *Signed:* ⟨A⟩³, ⟨B⟩-I, K-U, X⁸, ⟨Y⟩¹.

Two bindings noted; sequence, if any, not determined. The designations are for identification only.

Binding A

EC cloth: maroon. Also: maroon linen. Sides blindstamped with a single rule border. Spine goldstamped: EMBARRASSMENTS / ⟨rule⟩ / HENRY JAMES / MACMILLAN & C⁰. White laid end papers. No flyleaves. Top edges gilt.

Binding B

Maroon linen. Sides blindstamped with a single rule border. Spine goldstamped: EMBARRASS-MENTS / ⟨rule⟩ / HENRY JAMES / THE MACMILLAN / COMPANY White laid end papers. Flyleaf at front. Top edges gilt.

Noted as *nearly ready* PW June 6, 1896; as *just ready* PW June 20, 1896. BA copy (Binding B) received July 2, 1896. Listed PW July 4, 1896. AAS (Binding A) BA (Binding B) H (both) NYPL (Binding B) UV (Binding B)

10619. THE OTHER HOUSE ...

NEW YORK THE MACMILLAN COMPANY LONDON: MACMILLAN & CO., LTD. 1896 ALL RIGHTS RESERVED

Printed for copyright purposes only; for published editions see next two entries.

8 parts, each with fly-title page, title-page, copyright notice dated 1896. Laid paper. 7¼″ x 5″.

Part 1

⟨i-iv⟩, ⟨1⟩-81, 86-87, 84-85, 82-83, 88. Note incorrect imposition.

⟨1², 2-12⁴⟩. *Signed:* ⟨A⟩², ⟨B⟩-F⁸, G⁴.

Deposited June 22, 1896.

Part 2

⟨i-iv⟩, ⟨1⟩-35.

⟨1-5⁴⟩. Unsigned.

Deposited July 10, 1896.

Part 3

⟨i-iv⟩, 35-95, blank leaf.

⟨1², 2-9⁴⟩. Unsigned.

Deposited: No record of deposit found.

Part 4

⟨i-iv⟩, 95-122.

⟨1², 2-4⁴, 5²⟩. Unsigned.

Deposited Aug. 5, 1896.

Part 5

⟨i-iv⟩, 211⟨sic⟩-233.

⟨1², 2-4⁴⟩. *Signed:* ⟨-⟩¹, ⟨P⟩⁸, Q⁵.

Deposited Aug. 13, 1896.

Part 6

⟨i-iv⟩, ⟨233⟩⟨sic⟩-293, blank leaf.

⟨1², 2-9⁴⟩. *Signed:* ⟨-⟩⁶, R-T⁸, U⁴.

Deposited Aug. 28, 1896.

Part 7

⟨i-iv⟩, ⟨293⟩⟨sic⟩-356.

⟨1², 2-9⁴⟩. *Signed:* ⟨-⟩⁸, X-Z⁸, 2A².

Deposited Sept. 8, 1896.

Part 8

⟨i-iv⟩, 357-388.

⟨1-2¹, 3-10²⟩. *Signed:* ⟨-⟩⁸, 2B⁸, 2C².

Deposited Sept. 22, 1896.

Printed blue-gray laid paper wrappers.

CO LC(lacking Part 3) UV(Parts 4-6).

10620. THE OTHER HOUSE ... IN TWO VOLUMES ...

LONDON WILLIAM HEINEMANN 1896

See preceding entry.

Issued simultaneously with first American edition (next entry)? A letter from Henry James to Houghton, Mifflin & Co., original in H, Sept. 21, 1896, indicates that the London and the New York editions were issued simultaneously. Contemporary trade notices suggest that the London edition may have issued a few days prior to the New York.

1: ⟨i-iv⟩, ⟨1⟩-206, blank leaf. Laid paper. 7⁵⁄₁₆″ x 4⅞″.

2: ⟨i-iv⟩, ⟨1⟩-202, blank leaf.

1: ⟨-⟩², A-I, K-N⁸.

2: ⟨-⟩², A-I, K-M⁸, N⁶.

S cloth: blue. White laid end papers. Publisher's catalog inserted at back of each volume:

Vol. 1: Pp. 32. P. ⟨1⟩: *The Manxman* ... *Note:* This catalog is sometimes found at the back of both volumes.

Vol. 2: Pp. 32. P. ⟨1⟩ dated *August 1896*.

Note: Edel-Laurence (p. 106) state: "Some copies lack the circular ornament in blind on front cover." No copy thus traced by BAL. All copies examined by BAL have a blindstamped circular ornament at left of title on the front cover.

Published Oct. 1, 1896 (publisher's records). Advertised for Oct. 1 Ath Sept. 26, 1896. UV copy presented to Mrs. Humphry Ward by James Oct. 2, 1896. Listed Ath Oct. 3, 1896; PC Oct. 3, 1896; Bkr Oct. 9, 1896. Relisted PC Oct. 10, 1896. A 1-volume edition listed Ath July 10, 1897; PC July 24, 1897. As a volume in *Heinemann's Colonial Library of Popular Fiction* published June 16, 1897 (publisher's records).

H UV

10621. THE OTHER HOUSE ...

NEW YORK THE MACMILLAN COMPANY LONDON: MACMILLAN & CO., LTD. 1896 ALL RIGHTS RESERVED

First published American edition. See preceding two entries.

⟨i-iv⟩, ⟨1⟩-388; advertisements, pp. ⟨389-391⟩; blank, p. ⟨392⟩. Laid paper. 7½" full x 5" full.

⟨1-24⁸, 25⁶⟩. *Signed:* ⟨A⟩², ⟨B⟩-I, K-U, X-Z, 2A-2B⁸, 2C⁴.

Red, also maroon, linen. White wove end papers. Top edges gilt. Spine goldstamped: THE / ⟨*rule*⟩ / OTHER / ⟨*rule*⟩ / HOUSE / ⟨*rule*⟩ / HENRY JAMES / THE MACMILLAN / COMPANY

Note: The copyright deposit copies are in a variant (trial?) binding; Spine goldstamped: THE / ⟨*rule*⟩ / OTHER HOUSE / ⟨*rule*⟩ / HENRY JAMES / THE MACMILLAN / COMPANY White laid end papers, top edges gilt.

Advertised (prematurely) as *new* PW Sept. 26, 1896. Deposited (advance copies?) Oct. 7, 1896. H copy received Oct. 26, 1896. Listed PW Oct. 31, 1896.

AAS LC (variant) Y

Library of the World's Best Literature ...

New York ... ⟨1896-1899⟩

See entry No. 10624.

10622. THE SPOILS OF POYNTON ...

LONDON: WILLIAM HEINEMANN MDCCCXCVII

Title-page printed in black and red-orange.

Issued simultaneously with the first American edition? See next entry.

⟨i-iv⟩, ⟨1⟩-286; advertisement, p. ⟨287⟩. Laid paper. 7½" x 4¹⁵⁄₁₆". *Note:* Edel-Laurence (p. 108) state "some copies ... contain a blank leaf, pp. ⟨287-288⟩, in place of advertisements"; BAL has seen no copy thus.

⟨A⟩², B-I, K-T⁸.

S cloth: blue. Publisher's catalog, 32 pp., inserted at back. White laid end papers. The

earliest form of the binding has four irises blindstamped on the front; a later form of the binding is blindstamped on the front with an arrangement of tulips.

In addition to the printing described above (designed for publication in England) there was also a colonial edition printed on wove (not laid) paper, title-page printed in black (not black and red-orange), the date in the imprint in arabic (not roman) numerals; date of publication not determined. Hybrid copies have been seen made up of mixed laid and wove papers.

Advertised for Feb. 6, PC Jan. 9, 1897. Noted as *published today* PC Feb. 6, 1897. Advertised as though published Ath Feb. 6, 1897. Listed PC Feb. 6, 1897. A copy in NYPL inscribed by James Feb. 11, 1897. Listed Ath Feb. 13, 1897.

CO H NYPL

10623. THE SPOILS OF POYNTON ...

BOSTON AND NEW YORK HOUGHTON, MIFFLIN AND COMPANY THE RIVERSIDE PRESS, CAMBRIDGE 1897

Issued simultaneously with the London edition? See preceding entry.

⟨i-iv⟩, ⟨1⟩-323. Laid paper. 7⁷⁄₁₆" x 4¹⁵⁄₁₆".

⟨1-20⁸, 21⁴⟩.

T cloth: brown; green. White laid end papers. Laid paper flyleaves.

According to the publisher's records the first printing, Jan. 21, 1897, consisted of 1554 copies, put in binding during the period Feb. 5-24, 1897. A second printing, 508 copies, was done March 9, 1897, put in binding during the period March 26, 1897-March 14, 1904. BAL has been unable to distinguish the first from the second printing.

Printed Jan. 21, 1897. Deposited Feb. 8, 1897. Listed PW Feb. 20, 1897. Reprinted March 9, 1897.

BA NYPL UV

10624. Library of the World's Best Literature Ancient and Modern Charles Dudley Warner Editor ... Thirty ⟨Thirty-One⟩ Volumes ...

New York R. S. Peale and J. A. Hill Publishers ⟨1896-1899⟩

Vols. 1-2 dated ⟨1896⟩; Vols. 3-27 dated ⟨1897⟩; Vols. 28-30 dated ⟨1898⟩. An *Index-Guide* was issued as Vol. 31 under date ⟨1899⟩.

There were several printings issued under varying imprints, including an edition in 45 volumes with the imprint of *The International Society*, New York. Subscription books were issued under curious circumstances and the record of publication is seldom, if ever, clear. It is possible two or more formats were issued simultaneously.

The following contributions by James were written for this publication:

"Nathaniel Hawthorne," Vol. 12, pp. 7053-7061. Deposited May 29, 1897. Collected in *The American Essays*, 1956.

"James Russell Lowell," Vol. 16, pp. 9229-9237. Deposited Aug. 9, 1897. Collected in *The American Essays*, 1956.

"Ivan Turgeneff," Vol. 25, pp. 15057-15062. Deposited Jan. 31, 1898. Collected in *The Art of Fiction* . . . , 1948.

H

10625. WHAT MAISIE KNEW . . .

LONDON: WILLIAM HEINEMANN MDCCCXCVIII ⟨*i.e.*, 1897⟩

Title-page printed in black and red-orange.

For first American edition see below under 1897 (Nov.).

⟨i-iv⟩, ⟨1⟩-304. Laid paper. 7⁹⁄₁₆″ x 5″.

⟨-⟩², A-I, K-T⁸.

S cloth: blue. White laid end papers. Publisher's catalog, 32 pp., inserted at back. The earliest form of the binding has four irises blindstamped on the front; a later form of the binding is blindstamped on the front with an arrangement of tulips.

For a comment on the printing distributed in the colonies, dated (in arabic) 1897, see below.

Note: A set of sheets, trimmed to 7³⁄₁₆″ x 4⅞″ scant, lacking the catalog, and bound in blue L-like cloth, was in the collection of C. Bacon Collamore, Nov. 1946; sides blindstamped with an ornamental frame of Victorian flavor. The binding otherwise varies considerably from the norm. It has been asserted that the binding is a publisher's variant but BAL has been unable to find any evidence to support the assertion and suspects that the binding was privately done for an early owner.

Advertised as though published Ath Sept. 18, 1897. Listed Ath Sept. 18, 1897. Listed PC Sept. 25, 1897. NYPL copy inscribed by James Sept. 27, 1897.

"The publishers report that the copies of this book sent to reviewers had the title-page printed in black only, without ornament, and dated 1897 in arabic numerals. No advertisements were inserted at back of book."—I. R. Brussel: *Anglo-*

American First Editions Part Two: West to East 1786–1930, 1936, p. 79. *See note following.*

"Brussel records the colonial issue sheets in the third standard binding (the title-page of which he reproduces in a special plate) as advance review copies, citing the publisher as source of information. The Heinemann records, however, show that there was only one title-leaf printed for the first impression, and that the title-page Brussel cites is of the colonial issue. Despite an 1897 imprint (printed August 1897), it ⟨the colonial issue⟩ was not published until March 1898."—Edel-Laurence, p. 110.

It is entirely possible that the publishers distributed copies of the colonial issue for review, rather than copies of the printing dated MDCCCXCVIII. The listing in Ath (Sept. 18, 1897) is without comment which may be significant since Ath often made acid comment whenever the title-page of a book was postdated.

H NYPL Y

10626. Last Studies by Hubert Crackanthorpe . . . with . . . an Appreciation by Henry James

London   William Heinemann   1897

"Hubert Crackanthorpe," pp. xi-xxiii.

Advertised Ath Oct. 9, 1897. Advertised as *shortly* Ath Oct. 23, 1897. Advertised as though published Ath Oct. 30, 1897. Listed Ath Oct. 30, 1897; PC Nov. 6, 1897.

H LC UV Y

10627. WHAT MAISIE KNEW . . .

HERBERT S. STONE & CO.   CHICAGO & NEW YORK M DCCC XCVII

Title-page in black and orange. For prior British publication see above under 1897 (Sept.).

⟨i-iv⟩, ⟨1⟩-470; printer's device, p. ⟨471⟩. Laid paper; see below for a comment. 7½″ x 4¾″ full.

⟨-⟩², ⟨1⟩-29⁸, 30⁴.

Note: Printed on paper watermarked *Stone & Kimball / New York* displaying the SK device; and, on paper watermarked *H. S. Stone & Company / Chicago / The Chap Book* Herbert S. Stone & Company, publishers of *What Maisie Knew,* succeeded Stone & Kimball in 1896.

Note: A *second edition* was advertised in PW Oct. 27, 1897. Does the watermark (see above) distinguish the first from the second printing?

V cloth: slate. End papers and double flyleaves of bookstock. Top edges gilt.

Listed PW Nov. 6, 1897.

H   LC   Y

10628. JOHN DELAVOY ...

> NEW YORK THE MACMILLAN COMPANY LON-
> DON: MACMILLAN & CO., LTD. 1897 ALL RIGHTS
> RESERVED

Printed for copyright purposes only.

⟨i-iv⟩, ⟨1⟩-74, blank leaf. 7¼″ x 4⅞″.

⟨1-10⁴⟩. *Signed:* ⟨A⟩², ⟨B⟩-E⁸, F⁶. *Signature collation tentative.*

Printed gray-green laid paper wrapper.

Deposited Dec. 4, 1897. Collected in *The Soft Side,* 1900.

LC

WHAT MAISIE KNEW ...

> LONDON ... MDCCCXCVIII ⟨*i.e.,* 1897⟩

See above under 1897 (Sept.).

10629. THE TURN OF THE SCREW ...

> LONDON: WILLIAM HEINEMANN ALL RIGHTS
> RESERVED MDCCCXCVIII

Printed for copyright purposes only. Title-page printed in black only. *Not seen;* entry on the basis of a photographic copy of the title-page and on correspondence. Contains *The Turn of the Screw* only.

⟨i-ii⟩, ⟨1⟩-169, 3 blank leaves. 7⅛″ x 4½″.

⟨A⟩-I, K-L⁸.

Unprinted pale blue paper wrapper.

Deposited BMU Jan. 27, 1898. Collected in *The Two Magics ...,* 1898 (Oct.), below.

BMU

Library of the World's Best Literature Ancient and Modern ...

> New York ... ⟨1898⟩

See entry No. 10624.

10630. IN THE CAGE ...

> HERBERT S. STONE & COMPANY CHICAGO & NEW
> YORK MDCCCXCVIII

Title-page in black and orange. *See next entry.*

⟨i-viii⟩, 1-229; blank, p. ⟨230⟩; printer's imprint, p. ⟨231⟩. Laid paper watermarked *H. S. Stone & Company Chicago The Chap Book* 7½″ scant x 4¾″.

⟨1⁴, 2-15⁸, 16⁴⟩.

V cloth: slate. End papers of bookstock; double flyleaf of bookstock at back. Top edges gilt.

Deposited Aug. 8, 1898. Announced for *September* PW Sept. 24, 1898. Noted as *now ready* PW Oct. 1, 1898. A copy in H received Oct. 5, 1898. Listed PW Oct. 8, 1898.

BA H NYPL UV

10631. IN THE CAGE ...

> LONDON DUCKWORTH AND CO. 3 HENRIETTA
> STREET, W.C. 1898

Issued simultaneously with American edition? See preceding entry.

Two printings ⟨of Sig. M only?⟩ noted:

1

⟨i-iv⟩, ⟨1⟩-187; blank, p. ⟨188⟩; 4 pp. advertisements; plus: 12 pages advertisements. 7⅜″ full x 5″. Wholly untrimmed.

⟨-⟩², A-I, K-M⁸; plus: N⁶.

Coarse unbleached linen. White laid end papers. *Note:* All examined copies have the publisher's device stamped in black on the back cover. Edel-Laurence (p. 112) report "some copies lack publisher's device on back cover"; no copy thus seen by BAL.

2

⟨i-iv⟩, ⟨1⟩-187. 7⁵⁄₁₆″ x 4¹³⁄₁₆″. Trimmed.

⟨-⟩², A-I, K-L⁸, M⁶.

Noted only in the blackstamped blue V cloth binding of The Times Book Club. Issued thus not before 1905.

Noted as *at once* Ath April 23, 1898. Advertised PC May 14, 1898. Noted for *early next month* PC July 23, 1898. Published Aug. 8, 1898 (publisher's records). Listed Ath Aug. 13, 1898; PC Aug. 20, 1898.

CO H UV (second)

10632. THE TWO MAGICS THE TURN OF THE SCREW COVERING END ...

> NEW YORK THE MACMILLAN COMPANY LON-
> DON: MACMILLAN & CO., LTD. 1898 ALL RIGHTS
> RESERVED

Prepared for copyright purposes. For prior printing of "The Turn of the Screw" see above under 1898 (Jan.). For published editions see next two entries.

⟨i-iv⟩, ⟨1⟩-393, blank leaf. Laid paper. 7½″ full x 5⅛″.

⟨1-25⁸⟩. *Signed:* ⟨A⟩², ⟨B⟩-I, K-U, X-Z, 2A-2B⁸, 2C⁶.

Red linen. Publisher's spine imprint stamped from large and small capitals. Top edges gilt.

Deposited Sept. 30, 1898.

LC

10633. THE TWO MAGICS THE TURN OF
THE SCREW COVERING END . . .

LONDON: WILLIAM HEINEMANN MDCCCXCVIII

Title-page printed in black and red-orange. See
preceding entry; see next entry. Also see *The
Turn of the Screw*, 1898 (Jan.), above.

⟨i-iv⟩, ⟨1⟩-310; blank leaf. Laid paper. 7½"
x 5".

⟨-⟩², A-I, K-T⁸, U⁴.

S cloth: blue. White laid end papers. Publisher's
catalog, pp. 32, inserted at back. The earliest
form of the binding has four irises blindstamped
on the front; a later form of the binding is
blindstamped on the front with an arrangement
of tulips.

In addition to the printing described above (designed for publication in England) there was
also a colonial edition printed on wove (not
laid) paper, title-page printed in black (not
black and red-orange), the date in the imprint
in arabic (not roman) numerals; date of publication not determined. Hybrid copies have been
seen made up of mixed laid and wove papers.

Announced PC Oct. 1, 1898. Advertised for
Wednesday (*i.e.*, Oct. 5) in Ath Oct. 1, 1898.
Listed PC Oct. 8, 1898; Ath Oct. 15, 1898. Ad-
vertised Ath Oct. 15, 1898, with extract from a
review. Again listed PC Oct. 15, 1898. Reviewed
Ath Oct. 22, 1898; PC Oct. 22, 1898.

LC

10634. THE TWO MAGICS THE TURN OF
THE SCREW COVERING END . . .

NEW YORK THE MACMILLAN COMPANY LON-
DON: MACMILLAN & CO., LTD. 1898 ALL RIGHTS
RESERVED

First published American edition. See preceding
two entries; also see *The Turn of the Screw*,
1898 (Jan.), above.

⟨i-iv⟩, ⟨1⟩-393; blank, p. ⟨394⟩; 2 pp. advertisements; plus: 1 p. advertisements. Laid paper.
7½" x 5⅛". *See note below.*

⟨1-25⁸; plus: 26¹⟩. *Signed:* ⟨A⟩², ⟨B⟩-I, K-U,
X-Z, 2A-2B⁸, 2C⁶; plus ⟨2D⟩¹. *See note below.*

Red linen. Top edges gilt.

Note: Three binder's variants of undetermined
sequence noted; the designations are for identification only:

A: Spine imprint in large and small capitals.
3 pp. terminal advts. ⟨2D⟩ present.

B: Spine imprint in capitals of uniform size.
3 pp. terminal advts. ⟨2D⟩ present.

C: Spine imprint in capitals of uniform size.
2 pp. terminal advts. ⟨2D⟩ not present.

Noted as *just . . . out* PW Oct. 15, 1898. Listed
PW Oct. 22, 1898.

CO (A)   NYPL (B)   UV (A,C)   Y (A,C)

10635. Impressions by Pierre Loti with an Introduction by Henry James

Archibald Constable and Co. Westminster
MDCCCXCVIII.

"Pierre Loti," pp. ⟨1⟩-21. For New York edition
see under 1900, below.

Four bindings noted; the order of presentation
is presumed correct:

A: Green V cloth sides, white vellum shelfback.
Stamped in black and gold.

B: Green V cloth sides, white vellum shelfback.
Stamped in green only.

C: Green V cloth. Spine imprint: Constable/
Westminster/

D: Green V cloth. Spine imprint: Constable/
London./

Noted (Constable "are publishing it") PC April
30, 1898. Advertised without comment Ath Oct.
8, 1898. Listed Ath Nov. 12, 1898; PC Nov. 12,
1898. Advertised with reviews PC Dec. 3, 1898.

LC (D)   NYPL (A)   UV (A,B)   Y (A,B,C)

10636. THE AWKWARD AGE A NOVEL . . .

HARPER & BROTHERS PUBLISHERS   NEW YORK
AND LONDON 1899

Issued simultaneously with the first London edition? See next entry.

⟨i-iv⟩, ⟨1⟩-⟨457⟩; blank, p. ⟨458⟩; 2 pp. advertisements. 7⁹⁄₁₆" x 4¹³⁄₁₆".

⟨-⟩², ⟨A⟩-F, ⟨G⟩-H, ⟨J⟩-U, X-Z, 2A-2E⁸, 2F⁶.

T cloth: brown. White laid end papers.

Note: The book occurs on two weights of paper,
perhaps representing two printings. The sequence, if any, has not been determined and
the designations are for identification only:

A: Sheets bulk 1⅜". Publisher's spine imprint
stamped in upper and lower case roman.

B: Sheets bulk 1⅛". Publisher's spine imprint
stamped in upper and lower case roman save
for the *s* in *Harpers* which is italic.

Deposited April 25, 1899. Listed PW May 20,
1899.

H (A,B)   LC (A, being a deposit copy)   Y (A,B)

10637. THE AWKWARD AGE ...

LONDON: WILLIAM HEINEMANN   MDCCCXCIX

Title-page printed in black and red-orange. Issued simultaneously with the New York edition? See preceding entry.

⟨i-ii⟩, ⟨i⟩-vi, ⟨1⟩-414, 2 pp. advertisements. Laid paper. 7½″ x 5″.

⟨-⟩⁴, A-I, K-U, X-Z, 2A-2C⁸.

S cloth: blue. White laid end papers. The earliest form of the binding has four irises blindstamped on the front; a later form of the binding is blindstamped on the front with an arrangement of tulips. *Note:* Edel-Laurence (p. 115) state "some copies lack publisher's device in blind on back cover"; no copy thus traced by BAL.

Inserted at back: Publisher's catalog, pp. 32. Two forms of the catalog have been seen; sequence, if any, not determined; the designations are for identification only. The following variation is sufficient for identification:

Catalog A, last page: *The Nigger of the 'Narcissus'* ...

Catalog B, last page: *The Latest Fiction* ...

Note: In addition to the printing described above (designed for publication in England) there was also a colonial edition printed on wove (not laid) paper, title-page printed in black (not black and red-orange), the date in the imprint in arabic (not roman) numerals; date of publication not determined. Hybrid copies have been seen made up of mixed laid and wove papers.

Noted as *in the press* Ath March 18, 1899. Published April 25, 1899 (publisher's records). Listed Ath April 29, 1899.

AAS   CO   Y

10638. The International Library of Famous Literature Selections from the World's Great Writers ... Edited by Dr. Richard Garnett ... in Association with M. Leon Vallée ... Dr. Alois Brandl ... Donald G. Mitchell ... in Twenty Volumes ...

London   Issued by the Standard   1899

A subscription book and as such issued in a variety of bindings.

"The Future of the Novel," Vol. 14, pp. ⟨xi⟩-xxii. Collected in *The Future of the Novel*, 1956. For American publication see *The Universal Anthology* ... ⟨1899; i.e., 1901⟩, below.

Advertised in *Bookman* (London), Jan. 1900. Deposited BMu Feb. 14, 1900.

H

... The Universal Anthology ...

... ⟨1899⟩

See below under 1901.

10639. THE SOFT SIDE ...

NEW YORK   THE MACMILLAN COMPANY   LONDON: MACMILLAN & CO., LTD. 1900   ALL RIGHTS RESERVED

Issued simultaneously with the first London edition? See next entry.

⟨i⟩-⟨vi⟩, 1-326; advertisements, pp. ⟨327-329⟩. Laid paper. 7⁹⁄₁₆″ x 5⅛″.

⟨1-21⁸⟩. *Signed:* ⟨A⟩³, B-I, K-U, X⁸, Y⁵.

Maroon buckram. Top edges gilt. *Note:* In some copies there is a blindstamped rule at top and at bottom of spine.

Deposited Aug. 23, 1900 (perhaps a no longer extant advance printing?). A copy presented by James to Edmund Gosse, Sept. 30, 1900, in CO. Listed PW Oct. 6, 1900.

CO   H   NYPL   UV

10640. THE SOFT SIDE ...

METHUEN & CO.   36 ESSEX STREET W. C.   LONDON   1900

See preceding entry.

⟨i-viii⟩, ⟨1⟩-391; printer's imprint, p. ⟨392⟩. Laid paper. 7½″ x 5″.

⟨-⟩⁴, A-I, K-U, X-Z, 2A⁸, 2B⁴.

T cloth: red. White laid end papers. Noted both with and without inserted terminal catalog. The catalog occurs with the following dates: *August 1900; October 1900;* and, *November 1900.*

Noted as *shortly* PC July 28, 1900; as *immediately* PC Aug. 25, 1900; as *just ... published* Ath Aug. 25, 1900. Published Aug. 30, 1900 (publisher's records). Listed Ath Sept. 8, 1900. A copy in UV inscribed by James Sept. 13, 1900.

NYPL   UV   Y

10641. ... The Vicar of Wakefield ... by Oliver Goldsmith ... with an Introduction by Henry James

New York   The Century Co.   MCM

At head of title: The Century Classics

"Introduction," pp. xi-xx.

Deposited Oct. 18, 1900.

H   LC   UV   Y

10642. A Little Tour in France ...

Boston and New York   Houghton, Mifflin and Company   The Riverside Press, Cambridge   M DCCCC

For first edition see under 1885.

Revised edition. Contains a "Preface," pp. ⟨iii⟩-vii, written for this edition.

Referred to in the publisher's records as *The Holiday Edition.*

Printed Oct. 18, 1900 (2030 copies). Three copies bound in paper, Oct. 19, 1900. Put in binding during the period Oct. 24, 1900 to May 28, 1901. Deposited Oct. 26, 1900. Noted for *middle of next week* PW Oct. 27, 1900. Listed PW Nov. 3, 1900. BA copy received Nov. 6, 1900. 25 copies bound in "½ p. mor." on Nov. 9, 1900. 5 copies rebound in half morocco June 22, 1901.

Also issued in a large paper edition limited to 250 numbered copies; boards, cloth shelfback, printed paper label on spine. Imprinted: *Cambridge   Printed at the Riverside Press* MDCCCC 265 copies printed Nov. 19, 1900. 2 copies bound for copyright purposes, Nov. 21, 1900. Received at Copyright Office Nov. 22, 1900. Bound during the period Nov. 21 to Dec. 1, 1900. (By Nov. 21, 1900, 1218 copies of the trade edition were in binding.)

Issued in London by Heinemann; two formats advertised for *next week* Ath Oct. 20, 1900; for *Monday (i.e.,* Oct. 29) Ath Oct. 27, 1900. Listed Ath Nov. 3, 1900; PC Nov. 10, 1900.

H (trade) LC (large paper) NYPL (trade) Y (both)

10643. Impressions by Pierre Loti with an Introduction by Henry James

New York: Brentano's: MDCCCC.

For prior British publication see above under 1898.

"Pierre Loti," pp. ⟨1⟩-21.

Sheets of the London edition with cancel title-page. At foot of spine: *Brentano's*

Listed PW Sept. 29, 1900.

P

10644. THE SACRED FOUNT ...

NEW YORK   CHARLES SCRIBNER'S SONS   1901

Two printings noted:

First Printing

⟨i-iv⟩, 1-319. 7⅝" x 5³⁄₁₆".

⟨1², 2-21⁸⟩.

Nail heads present in the gutters of pp. 40-41, 120-121, 184-185, 248-249, 312-313.

Note: In some copies a divisional title-leaf is inserted between Sigs. ⟨1⟩ and ⟨2⟩.

Second Printing

⟨i-viii⟩, 1-319.

⟨1⁴, 2-21⁸⟩.

Nail heads noted above not present.

Old rose (usually faded to tan) sateen. Stamped in gold. Top edges gilt. Copies of the second printing have been noted in the rose sateen binding; and, in blue T cloth with the front stamped in white and black, the spine stamped in gold; top edges plain.

Deposited Feb. 7, 1901. Published Feb. 8, 1901, in a printing of 3000 copies (publisher's records). Noted for Feb. 9 PW Jan. 26, 1901. Listed PW Feb. 16, 1901.

AAS (1st)   BA (1st)   H (1st; 2nd)   LC (1st, being a deposit copy; 2nd)   UV (1st; 2nd)   Y (1st)

10645. The May Book   Compiled by Mrs. Aria in Aid of Charing Cross Hospital ...

London   Macmillan & Co. Limited   1901

Trade edition: Title-page printed in black only. *Limited edition:* Title-page printed in black and brown.

Trade Edition

Two bindings noted; sequence, if any, not determined. The designations are for identification only. The following features are sufficient for identification:

A: A principal feature of the front cover stamping is a steeple silhouetted against the sky. Bound in cloth.

B: A principal feature of the front cover stamping is the figure of a woman. Bound in cloth.

Limited Edition

On p. ⟨ii⟩: *Only One Hundred Copies of this Edition have been Printed.* Bound in gold-stamped vellum.

"The Saint's Afternoon," pp. 1-10. Collected in *Italian Hours,* 1909.

Listed Ath May 18, 1901; PC May 18, 1901.

H (limited; trade binding A)   UV (trade binding B)

10646. ... The Universal Anthology   A Collection of the Best Literature ... Edited by Richard Garnett ... Leon Vallée ... Alois Brandl ...

Published by The Clarke Company, Limited, London Merrill & Baker, New York Emile Terquem, Paris Bibliothek Verlag, Berlin ⟨1899; *i.e.,* 1901⟩

33 Vols. At head of title: Westminster Edition

Earliest located American book publication of "The Future of the Novel," Vol. 28, pp. xiii-xxiv. For prior British publication see entry No. 10638. Collected in *The Future of the Novel,* 1956.

A subscription set and as such published in a variety of formats. For a comment on the problem presented by this type of publication see *The International Library of Famous Literature* ... ⟨1898⟩, in the Sarah Orne Jewett list of reprints.

The set (*Westminster Edition*) was deposited for copyright (U.S.) during the period Dec. 1, 1899 to June 28, 1902. *Westminster Edition,* Vol. 28, deposited August 13, 1901; listed PW Dec. 21, 1901. *The Garnett Memorial Edition* issued not before 1906.

LC NYPL

... "The Quest of the Holy Grail" ...

... 1901

See above under 1895.

10647. THE WINGS OF THE DOVE ...

NEW YORK   CHARLES SCRIBNER'S SONS   1902

2 Vols.

1: ⟨i-iv⟩, ⟨1⟩-329, blank leaf. Laid paper. 7⁹⁄₁₆" x 4¹⁵⁄₁₆".

2: ⟨i-iv⟩, ⟨1⟩-439, 2 blank leaves. *Note:* In some copies the final blank is excised.

1: ⟨-⟩², ⟨1⟩-7, ⟨8⟩-14, ⟨15⟩-20⁸, 21⁶.

2: ⟨-⟩², ⟨1⟩-21, ⟨22⟩-27⁸, 28⁶. *Note:* In some copies 28₆ is excised.

Sateen: old rose; olive-tan; tan; the variations in color may have been caused by fading. Top edges gilt. Noted with wove end papers; and, laid end papers. Flyleaves have been noted as follows:

Vol. 1: No flyleaves.

Vol. 1: Laid paper flyleaf at front; none at back.

Vol. 1: 2 laid paper flyleaves at front; none at back.

Vol. 2: No flyleaves.

Vol. 2: Laid paper flyleaf at front; none at back.

Vol. 2: A laid paper flyleaf at front and at back.

Also noted in a secondary binding (Tabard Inn?) of maroon T cloth; see BAL, Vol. 1, p. xxxii.

On copyright page: *Published, August, 1902* Deposited Aug. 22, 1902. 3000 copies printed; published Aug. 29, 1902 (publisher's records). Listed PW Sept. 6, 1902.

AAS (Tabard binding) BA (Tabard binding) BPL H NYPL UV (also Tabard binding)

10648. Madame Bovary Translated from the French of Gustave Flaubert with a Critical Introduction by Henry James

London: William Heinemann: Mcmii

"Gustave Flaubert," pp. v-xliii. Collected in *Notes on Novelists,* 1914. For American publication see below under 1902 (Dec.).

In the *A Century of French Romance* series.

Announced Ath Sept. 21, 1901. Advertised for *next week* Ath May 3, 1902. Advertised as though published Ath May 10, 1902. Listed Ath May 24, 1902.

LC UV Y

10649. The Two Young Brides Translated from the French of Honoré de Balzac by the Lady Mary Loyd with a Critical Introduction by Henry James ...

New York   D. Appleton & Co. ⟨1902⟩

"Honoré de Balzac," pp. v-xliii. Collected in *Notes on Novelists,* 1914.

Issued in a variety of formats; see below. The copyright deposit copy has general title-page as follows: *Parisian Edition   A Century of French Romance   Edited by Edmund Gosse ... Limited to One Thousand sets of which this is No. ...*

Deposited Aug. 28, 1902. The London (Heinemann) edition listed Ath Oct. 4, 1902. Appleton edition listed PW Dec. 27, 1902, as available in the following formats: *Parisian Edition; Versailles Edition; Grand Format Edition; Grand Prix Edition.* Reprinted and reissued by P. F. Collier & Son, New York ⟨1902; *i.e.,* 1903⟩. *Query:* Was the New York edition issued prior to the London?

LC

10650. Madame Bovary Translated from the French of Gustave Flaubert by W. G. Blaydes with a Critical Introduction by Henry James ...

New York   D. Appleton & Co. ⟨1902⟩

Not seen; entry from Edel-Laurence, p. 231; and

pw listing. For prior British publication see above under 1902 (May).

Contains James's "Gustave Flaubert."

Listed pw Dec. 27, 1902, in the following formats: *Parisian Edition, Versailles Edition, Grand Format Edition, Grand Prix Edition*. Reprinted and reissued by P. F. Collier & Son, New York ⟨1902⟩.

The Quest of the Holy Grail

1902

See above under 1895.

10651. THE AMBASSADORS ...

LONDON AND NEW YORK   HARPER & BROTHERS PUBLISHERS ...

Prepared for copyright purposes only. For published editions see below under 1903.

Not seen. Entry on the basis of correspondence and photographic copies.

9 paper-covered parts. Received for copyright on the dates given at University Library, Cambridge, England.

1: Dated *1902*. 23 pp. Received March 3, 1903.

2: Dated *1903*. Pp. 24-48. Received April 6, 1903.

3: Dated *1903*. Pp. 49-70. Received May 11, 1903.

4: Dated *1903*. Pp. 71-93. Received May 16, 1903.

5: Dated *1903*. Pp. 94-118. Received June 10, 1903.

6: Dated *1903*. Pp. 119-143. Received June 25, 1903.

7: Dated *1903*. Pp. 144-166. Received July 23, 1903.

8: Dated *1903*. Pp. 167-190. Received Aug. 29, 1903.

9: Dated *1903*. Pp. 191-215. Received Oct. 12, 1903.

Note: At the foot of each title-page is a copyright notice in the name of Harper & Brothers, dated 1902. For a comment on the texts of this novel see "Henry James: Some Bibliographical and Textual Matters," by Brian Birch, in *The Library*, June, 1965.

10652. THE BETTER SORT

Issued simultaneously in New York and London.

New York

THE BETTER SORT ...

NEW YORK   CHARLES SCRIBNER'S SONS 1903

⟨i-viii⟩, 1-⟨429⟩, blank leaf. Laid paper. 7⁹⁄₁₆" x 4¹⁵⁄₁₆".

⟨1⁴, 2-28⁸⟩.

Sateen: old rose; tan; the variations in color may have been caused by fading. White laid end papers. Top edges gilt. The publisher's spine imprint occurs in two forms of unknown sequence, if any; the designations are purely arbitrary; A: Stamped from a face ⅛" plus tall; B: Stamped from a face ⅛" scant tall. Also noted in a secondary (Tabard Inn?) binding of maroon T cloth; see BAL, Vol. 1, p. xxxii.

On copyright page: *Published, February, 1903* Deposited Feb. 26, 1903. BA copy received March 3, 1903. Listed pw March 7, 1903.

H   JB(Tabard)   NYPL   UV   Y

London

THE BETTER SORT ...

METHUEN & CO.   36 ESSEX STREET W.C. LONDON 1903

⟨i-viii⟩, ⟨1⟩-312. 7½" x 5".

⟨A⟩⁴, B-I, K-U⁸, X⁴.

T cloth: red. Publisher's catalog, pp. 40, dated on p. ⟨1⟩: *February 1903*, inserted at back. Also noted in a variant (remainder?) binding: Blue S-like cloth; no terminal catalog.

Advertised for Feb. 26 in Ath Jan. 17, 1903. Listed Ath March 7, 1903.

AAS(variant)   B   H(variant)   UV(variant)   Y

10653. THE AMBASSADORS ...

METHUEN & CO.   36 ESSEX STREET W.C. LONDON 1903

For prior printing see above under 1902; for American edition see below under 1903 (Nov.).

⟨i-iv⟩, ⟨1⟩-458; printer's imprint, p. ⟨459⟩. 7½" x 4⅞" full.

⟨A⟩², B-I, K-U, X-Z, 2A-2F⁸, 2G⁶.

T cloth: red. Publisher's catalog, pp. 38, dated *July 1903*, inserted at back.

Published Sept. 24, 1903 (publisher's records). Listed Bkr Nov. 6, 1903. Reviewed Ath Nov. 28, 1903.

H   UV

10654. The Novels and Stories of Iván Turgénieff   Memoirs of a Sportsman ... Translated ... by Isabel F. Hapgood with an Introduction by Henry James

New York   Charles Scribner's Sons   1903

Issued as Vol. 1 of a sixteen volume set.

"Iván Turgénieff," pp. v-xxxix. For prior publication see *Partial Portraits*, London, 1888.

Deposited Sept. 28, 1903. BA copy received Jan. 8, 1904. Listed PW Jan. 30, 1904, as in both cloth and in half levant. Distributed in London by Dent; the earliest announcement noted being in Ath Sept. 9, 1905; advertised as *in preparation* Ath Oct. 14, 1905; reviewed Ath Jan. 20, 1906.

BA

10655. WILLIAM WETMORE STORY AND HIS FRIENDS ...

Issued simultaneously in Boston and Great Britain. Sheets imported by Houghton, Mifflin & Company; see publication notes below.

Boston (Houghton, Mifflin & Co.)

WILLIAM WETMORE STORY AND HIS FRIENDS FROM LETTERS, DIARIES, AND RECOLLECTIONS ... IN TWO VOLUMES ...

HOUGHTON, MIFFLIN & CO. BOSTON 1903 ALL RIGHTS RESERVED

1: ⟨i-viii⟩, ⟨1⟩-371. Frontispiece inserted. 7¹⁵⁄₁₆" x 5¼".

2: ⟨i-viii⟩, ⟨1⟩-345, blank leaf. Frontispiece inserted.

1: ⟨-⟩⁴, ⟨A⟩-I, K-U, X-Z⁸, 2A².

2: ⟨-⟩⁴, ⟨A⟩-I, K-U, X⁸, Y⁶.

V cloth: green. White laid end papers. Flyleaf at back of Vol. 1. Top edges gilt. *Note:* A copy has been seen (in LC, not a copyright deposit copy) which varies from the preceding: White wove paper end papers, no flyleaf at back of Vol. 1.

Edinburgh and London (Blackwood)

WILLIAM WETMORE STORY AND HIS FRIENDS FROM LETTERS, DIARIES, AND RECOLLECTIONS ... IN TWO VOLUMES ...

WILLIAM BLACKWOOD AND SONS EDINBURGH AND LONDON MCMIII ALL RIGHTS RESERVED

1: ⟨i-viii⟩, ⟨1⟩-371. Frontispiece inserted. 8¹⁄₁₆" x 5¼".

2: ⟨i-viii⟩, ⟨1⟩-345, blank leaf. Frontispiece inserted.

1: ⟨-⟩⁴, ⟨A⟩-I, K-U, X-Z⁸, 2A².

2: ⟨-⟩⁴, ⟨A⟩-I, K-U, X⁸, Y⁶.

Blue-gray V-like cloth.

Note

Signatures ⟨A⟩-Q, Vol. 1, were printed from two settings. Issued simultaneously? There is probably significance in the fact that Setting B has also been seen in a copy of the Houghton, Mifflin & Company issue dated 1904.

Setting A	*Setting B*
P. 7, line 11	
Question mark above the letter *I*	Question mark above space
P. 16, last line	
v of *vanished* beneath *m* of *come*	*v* of *vanished* beneath *om* of *come*
P. 23, line 10	
... *work of his* |	... *work of* |
P. 24, line 2 up	
... *to* |	... *held* |
P. 47, line 3 up	
Exclamation mark over *u* of *quite*	Exclamation mark over *i* of *quite*
P. 48, line 14	
Period under *iv* of *receiving*	Period under *ei* of *receiving*
P. 53, line 12	
Period after *audiences* is to the right of the period on line 11	Period after *audiences* is to the left of the period on line 11
P. 55, line 12	
... *Long-wharf* ...	... *Long - wharf* ...
P. 73, line 9	
... *say* |	... *couldn't* |
P. 74, line 8	
... *just* |	... *has* |
P. 86, last line	
Last dot beneath *w* of *how*	Last dot beneath *o* of *how*
P. ⟨93⟩, line 15	
Period over space	Period over *r* of *whatever*
P. 99, line 19	
... *spring - time* |	... *spring-time* |
P. 104, line 4	
... *field-driver* ...	... *field - driver* ...
P. 114, line 7	
... *dis-* |	... *of* |
P. 125, line 3	
Period over first *s* in *unless*	Period over second *s* in *unless*
P. 134, line 4 up	
Semi-colon over *re* in *were*	Semi-colon over the second *e* in *were*
P. 141, line 11	
be of *be-braided* beneath *ate* of *gates,*	*be* of *be-braided* beneath *es,* of *gates,*
P. 157, line 14	
... *American sub-* |	... *American* |
P. 158, line 3	
tremly ...	*tremely* ...

P. 161, foot of page

VOL. beneath *La Principessa*   VOL. beneath *Principessa*

P. 170, line 9 up

Period beneath space   Period beneath *o* of *who*

P. 177, line 20

Period beneath space   Period beneath terminal *t* of *that*

P. 179, line 12

. . . *a-fortnight,* | . . . *a fortnight,* |

P. 198, line 3 up

as beneath *fes* of *confessed*   *as* beneath *nfe* of *confessed*

P. 201, line 15

sumer . . .   *mer* . . .

P. 221, line 10 up

Semi-colon over quotation marks   Semi-colon over space

P. 223, line 18

is beneath ⟨space⟩ *h*   *is* beneath *t* ⟨space⟩

P. 231, line 12

Period beneath second *c* of *character*   Period beneath second *a* of *character*

P. 236, line 3

Dot beneath *or* of *for*   Dot beneath *o* of *for*

P. 242, line 3 up

Comma over *pe* of *perched*   Comma over space

P. 252, line 4

Exclamation point beneath *s* of *shall*   Exclamation point beneath space

Publication Notes

Edel-Laurence (p. 127) report "five subsequent issues, up to September 1905 . . . lacking any imprint to distinguish them from first issue." The statement is faulty. Copies of the American issue have been seen with the imprint date altered to 1904; a copy thus at NYPL was acquired May 27, 1904. It is nevertheless possible that the earliest reprints were issued under date 1903 without notice of reprint.

Sept. 1903: Blackwood's records show 1260 copies printed. *First printing.*

Sept. 5, 1903: Under invoice of this date Houghton, Mifflin & Company received 520 sets of sheets. No record of American copyright deposit found.

Sept. 26, 1903: A single copy bound in paper by Houghton, Mifflin & Company.

Sept. 29, 1903: A single copy bound in cloth by Houghton, Mifflin & Company. Presumably a trial binding.

Sept. 29, 1903: Under this date James presented a copy of the Edinburgh issue to Edmund Gosse; now in CO. Setting A.

Sept. 30, 1903: Five copies bound in cloth by Houghton, Mifflin & Company.

Oct. 1, 1903: 492 copies put in binding by Houghton, Mifflin & Company.

Oct. 3, 1903: PW of this date carried an advertisement (Houghton, Mifflin & Company) announcing the book for Oct. 7 publication.

Oct. 3, 1903: PW of this date commented editorially that the book was to be published Oct. 7, 1903.

Oct. 10, 1903: Blackwood issue listed PC of this date.

Oct. 10, 1903: Blackwood issue listed Ath of this date.

Oct. 10, 1903: Blackwood issue advertised as though published Ath of this date.

Oct. 10, 1903: Houghton, Mifflin & Company issue listed PW of this date.

Oct. 16, 1903: Under invoice of this date Houghton, Mifflin & Company received 250 sets of sheets

Oct. 23, 1903: Blackwood issue reviewed TLS of this date.

Nov. 5, 1903: Under invoice of this date Houghton, Mifflin & Company received 150 sets of sheets.

Nov. 7, 1903: Blackwood issue reviewed Ath of this date.

Nov. 9, 1903: By this date all copies of the original (Sept. 5) shipment were in binding.

Nov. 11, 1903: Under invoice of this date Houghton, Mifflin & Company received 100 sets of sheets.

Nov. 11, 1903: Under this date the Houghton, Mifflin & Company records show a charge for the composition and printing (four hours) of 25 copies of a four-page cancel. Further information wanting.

Nov. 1903: According to Blackwood's records a *second printing*, 230 copies, was done during this month. The records suggest some resetting of the types; signatures ⟨A⟩-Q?

Dec. 1903: According to Blackwood's records a *third printing*, 378 copies, was done during this month. 250 of these were done with the Houghton, Mifflin & Company imprint.

Dec. 29, 1903: Under invoice of this date Houghton, Mifflin & Company received 250 sets of sheets; *see preceding note.*

Feb. 1904: According to Blackwood's records a *fourth printing*, 150 copies, was done during this month.

Aug. 1905: According to Blackwood's records a *fifth printing*, 200 copies, was done during this month.

During the years 1904–1905 Houghton, Mifflin & Company received 510 additional sets of sheets.

BA (Boston issue, setting B)   BPL (Boston issue, setting A)   H (Boston issue, settings A and B; Edinburgh issue, setting A)   NYPL (Edinburgh issue, setting A)   Y (Edinburgh issue, setting A)

10656. THE AMBASSADORS A NOVEL ...

NEW YORK AND LONDON   HARPER & BROTHERS PUBLISHERS MCMIII

Title-page in black and orange. For prior printing see above under 1902; for prior publication see above under 1903 (Sept.).

⟨i-ii⟩, ⟨1⟩-⟨432⟩. 8¼″ scant x 5⅜″ full.

⟨-⟩¹, ⟨1⟩-27⁸.

Gray-blue paper boards embossed with a linen weave. White laid end papers. Top edges gilt. Issued in a protective wrapper of blue S cloth, stamped in gold. Edel-Laurence (p. 124) report a remainder binding "in dust jacket bound over boards"; not located by BAL.

On copyright page: *Published November, 1903.* Announced PW Sept. 26, 1903. Advertised as *new* PW Oct. 24, 1903. Deposited Nov. 6, 1903. Listed PW Nov. 14, 1903. *Note:* A thoroughly sophisticated copy has been seen (LC) with an inscription dated *June 1903*.

AAS   CO   H

10657. The George Alexander Birthday Book

Printed & Published by John Lane   Vigo Street, London, & New York. 1903

Extracts from *Guy Domville* (printed as manuscript, 1894, above) pp. 10, 14, 58, 62, 68, 96, 110, 130, 148.

H

10658. American Literary Criticism Selected and Edited, with an Introductory Essay by William Morton Payne ...

Longmans, Green, and Co. 91 and 93 Fifth Avenue, New York London and Bombay 1904

"Sainte-Beuve," pp. 299-318.

Deposited Sept. 19, 1904. Listed PW Oct. 15, 1904.

H

10659. THE GOLDEN BOWL ...

NEW YORK   CHARLES SCRIBNER'S SONS   1904

2 Vols.

1: ⟨i-iv⟩, ⟨1⟩-412. Laid paper. 7½″ full x 4⅞″.

2: ⟨i-iv⟩, ⟨1⟩-377, blank leaf.

1: ⟨-⟩², ⟨1⟩-25⁸, 26⁶.

2: ⟨1-24⁸⟩. *Signed:* ⟨-⟩², ⟨1⟩-23⁸, 24⁶.

Tan sateen (faded old rose?). White laid end papers. Top edges gilt.

On copyright page: *Published, November, 1904* Announced PW Sept. 24, 1904. Noted for *about October 1* PW Sept. 24, 1904. Deposited Nov. 10, 1904. Published Nov. 12, 1904, in a printing of 2000 copies (publisher's records). Listed PW Nov. 19, 1904. Sheets of the Scribner printing deposited at the Bodleian by Methuen (London) Dec. 3, 1904. The Methuen (London) edition advertised as *just published* Ath Feb. 11, 1905; listed Ath Feb. 18, 1905.

H   NYPL   Y

10660. THE QUESTION OF OUR SPEECH   THE LESSON OF BALZAC   TWO LECTURES ...

BOSTON AND NEW YORK   HOUGHTON, MIFFLIN AND COMPANY   THE RIVERSIDE PRESS, CAMBRIDGE 1905

Title-page in black and sepia.

⟨i-vi⟩, ⟨1⟩-⟨116⟩; blank, p. ⟨117⟩; printer's imprint, p. ⟨118⟩. Laid paper. 7⁷⁄₁₆″ x 4½″ (trade edition); 7⅝″ x 4½″ (limited edition).

⟨1¹⁰, 2-7⁸, 8⁴⟩. ⟨1⟩₂₋₃ is a single cut sheet folded and inserted.

Trade Format

V cloth: blue; greenish-black; maroon. White laid end papers. Flyleaf at front. Top edges gilt.

Limited Format

Gray paper boards, straw-colored V cloth shelf-back, printed paper label on spine. On copyright page: *Of The First Edition Three Hundred Copies Have Been Printed And Bound Entirely Uncut With Paper Label*

Note: The publisher's records show that there were two printings in 1905; BAL has been unable to discover any feature that might distinguish the first printing from the second. *Query:* Was the second printing dated 1906? Or, more probably, ⟨1905⟩?

On copyright page: *Published October 1905* Printed (both formats) Sept. 16, 1905: 314 untrimmed copies, 1721 trade copies. *Trade format* bound during the period Sept. 27–Dec. 16, 1905. Deposited Sept. 29, 1905. Announced PW Sept. 30, 1905. *Untrimmed format* bound Oct. 5, 1905. Noted for *to-day* PW Oct. 7, 1905. An H copy (trade format) received Oct. 13, 1905. Trade format listed PW Oct. 21, 1905. The publisher's records for Dec. 19, 1905, show a charge for alteration of the plates: Change in date on title-page? Change in the preliminary advertisements? Both? Second printing recorded by the publishers Dec. 20, 1905.

AAS   CO   H

10661. English Hours . . .

London   William Heinemann   1905

For first American edition see next entry.

Reprint save for a "Note," dated 1905; "Winchelsea, Rye and 'Denis Duval'," and "Old Suffolk." Also contains some revisions.

Gray V cloth. Unsold sheets issued *ca.* 1915 in green V cloth with green linen shelfback. Edel-Laurence (p. 130) report a "'gift binding' in red half calf, red linen-grain cloth boards"; not seen by BAL.

On copyright page: *Published October 1905* Announced Ath Sept. 30, 1905. Published Oct. 18, 1905 (publisher's records). Advertised as though published Ath Oct. 21, 1905. A copy in CO presented by James to Edmund Gosse Oct. 22, 1905. Reviewed Ath Oct. 28, 1905. Listed Ath Oct. 28, 1905.

CO (both)   UV (remainder)   Y (remainder)

10662. English Hours . . .

First American edition. See preceding entry for prior publication and comment.

Holiday Edition

English Hours . . .

Boston and New York   Houghton, Mifflin and Company   The Riverside Press, Cambridge   MDCCCCV

This is the trade edition. The designation *Holiday Edition* does not appear in the book but is used in the publisher's records and in advertisements. Bound in cloth; but see below for comment on copies in half morocco.

On copyright page: *Published October 1905* Announced PW Sept. 30, 1905. 2034 copies printed Oct. 20, 1905. Bound during the period Oct. 20, 1905–Jan. 17, 1906. Advertised for *next Saturday* ⟨*i.e.,* Oct. 28⟩ PW Oct. 21, 1905. Noted for Oct. 28 PW Oct. 21, 1905. Deposited Oct. 23, 1905. A copy in NYPL received Oct. 28, 1905.

During the period Nov. 6, 1905–Jan. 17, 1906, 37 copies were bound in half morocco. Listed PW Nov. 18, 1905.

H   NYPL   UV

Large Paper Edition

English Hours . . .

Cambridge   Printed at the Riverside Press mdccccv

Green paper boards sides, white linen shelfback and corners. Printed paper label on spine.

On copyright page: *Published October 1905* 421 copies printed Oct. 9, 1905. Two copies bound for copyright purposes on Nov. 1, 1905; on same date 7 copies bound for office use. All copies bound during the period Nov. 1–14, 1905. Deposited Nov. 6, 1905.

UV   Y

10663. THE AMERICAN SCENE

1907

According to the publisher's records issued simultaneously in London and the British colonies. The New York edition appears to have been issued simultaneously as well but it may have issued a few days after the British issues. Sec. VII of the final chapter (British editions), pp. 460-465, does not appear in the New York edition.

London Edition

THE AMERICAN SCENE . . .

LONDON   CHAPMAN AND HALL, LTD   1907

⟨i⟩-⟨viii⟩, ⟨1⟩-465; printer's imprint, p. ⟨466⟩; advertisements, pp. ⟨467-472⟩. 8⅝″ scant x 5⁹⁄₁₆″.

⟨-⟩⁴, 1-29⁸, 30⁴.

Maroon buckram. A feature of the stamping is a double rule frame blindstamped on the front cover. Top edges gilt. Edel-Laurence (p. 133) report a remainder binding of "red cross-grain cloth . . . a single-rule border in blind on front cover"; no copy traced by BAL.

Noted for Jan. 30 Ath Jan. 26, 1907. A copy in UV presented by James to Edmund Gosse Jan. 29, 1907. Listed Ath Feb. 2, 1907.

Colonial Edition

THE AMERICAN SCENE . . .

LONDON   GEORGE BELL & SONS AND BOMBAY 1907

⟨i⟩-⟨viii⟩, ⟨1⟩-465; printer's imprint, p. ⟨466⟩. 8¾″ x 5⅝″.

⟨-⟩⁴, 1-29⁸, 30¹.

T cloth: red.

P. ⟨i⟩: *Bell's Indian and Colonial Library* . . .

P. ⟨ii⟩: *This Edition is issued for Circulation in India and the Colonies only.*

New York Edition

THE AMERICAN SCENE . . .

HARPER & BROTHERS PUBLISHERS   NEW YORK AND LONDON MCMVII

⟨i-ii⟩, ⟨i⟩-⟨viii⟩, 1-⟨443⟩, blank leaf. 8³⁄₁₆″ x 5⅜″.

⟨-⟩⁴, ⟨1⟩-28⁸.

T cloth: blue. Stamped in gold, top edges gilt. Also noted in a remainder binding: Blue V cloth, stamped in black, top edges plain.

On copyright page: *Published February, 1907.* Deposited Jan. 30, 1907. A copy received by NYPL Feb. 7, 1907. Listed PW Feb. 16, 1907.

AAS (colonial) BA (New York) BPL (New York remainder) H (New York; New York remainder) NYPL (New York) Y (London)

10664. . . . The Tempest with a Special Introduction by Henry James . . .

New York George D. Sproul 1907

At head of title: The Complete Works of William Shakespeare with Annotations and a General Introduction by Sidney Lee Volume XVI

Paper boards, cloth shelfback, printed paper label on spine.

The University Press Shakespeare, Renaissance Edition.

"Introduction," pp. ix-xxxii.

Listed (presumably the above) PW March 2, 1907. The above deposited for copyright Oct. 21, 1907.

Note: As a subscription book probably issued in a variety of formats with varying imprints. The following imprints have been seen:

The Renaissance Press MCMVII

New York George D. Sproul MCMVII

New York Harper & Brothers Publishers ⟨1907, i.e., ca. 1910⟩

Boston The Jefferson Press New York ⟨1908⟩

The earliest London printing traced, on the basis of contemporary trade notices, was issued 1910–1911.

BPL (Sproul 1907; Harper) NYPL (Jefferson; Renaissance) UV (Sproul MCMVII)

10665. The Novels and Tales of Henry James New York Edition . . .

New York Charles Scribner's Sons . . .

26 Vols. Issued in cloth; and, half leather. Revised text; some volumes, as indicated below, contain a preface written for this edition.

Note: Also issued in a large paper edition limited to 156 numbered copies. Although the trade and the large paper editions presumably were issued simultaneously, Vols. 3-6 of the large paper edition were antedated 1907.

Also note: Some sheets of *The Letters of Henry James* . . . , 1920, were bound uniform with the *New York Edition* and offered as Vols. 27-28.

1: *Roderick Hudson.* Dated 1907. "Preface," pp. v-⟨xx⟩. Deposited Dec. 14, 1907. Listed PW Dec. 28, 1907.

2: *The American.* Dated 1907. "Preface," pp. v-⟨xxiii⟩. Deposited Dec. 16, 1907. Listed PW Feb. 2, 1908.

3-4: *The Portrait of a Lady.* Dated 1908. "Preface," Vol. 1, pp. v-⟨xxi⟩. Deposited Jan. 20, 1908. Listed PW March 7, 1908.

5-6: *The Princess Casamassima.* Dated 1908. "Preface," Vol. 1, pp. v-⟨xxiii⟩. Deposited Feb. 14, 1908. Listed PW March 7, 1908.

7-8: *The Tragic Muse.* Dated 1908. "Preface," Vol. 1, pp. v-⟨xxii⟩. Deposited March 27, 1908. Listed PW April 18, 1908.

9: *The Awkward Age.* Dated 1908. "Preface," pp. v-⟨xxiv⟩. Deposited May 16, 1908. Listed PW Dec. 5, 1908.

10: *The Spoils of Poynton. A London Life. The Chaperon.* Dated 1908. "Preface," pp. v-⟨xxiv⟩. Deposited May 16, 1908. Listed PW Dec. 5, 1908.

11: *What Maisie Knew. In the Cage. The Pupil.* Dated 1908. "Preface," pp. v-⟨xxii⟩. Deposited July 14, 1908. Listed PW Dec. 5, 1908.

12: *The Aspern Papers. The Turn of the Screw. The Liar. The Two Faces.* Dated 1908. "Preface," pp. v-⟨xxiv⟩. Deposited July 14, 1908. Listed PW Dec. 5, 1908.

13: *The Reverberator. Madame de Mauves. A Passionate Pilgrim and Other Tales.* Dated 1908. "Preface," pp. v-⟨xxi⟩. Deposited Dec. 3, 1908. Listed PW Feb. 6, 1909.

14: *Lady Barbarina. The Siege of London. An International Episode and Other Tales.* Dated 1908. "Preface," pp. v-⟨xxii⟩. Deposited Dec. 3, 1908. Listed PW Feb. 6, 1909.

15: *The Lesson of the Master. The Death of the Lion. The Next Time and Other Tales.* Dated 1909. "Preface," pp. v-⟨xviii⟩. Deposited March 20, 1909. Listed PW April 13, 1909.

16: *The Author of Beltraffio. The Middle Years. Greville Fane and Other Tales.* Dated 1909.

"Preface," pp. v-⟨xii⟩. Also contains here first in book form "Fordham Castle." Deposited March 20, 1909. Listed PW April 13, 1909.

17: *The Altar of the Dead. The Beast in the Jungle. The Birthplace and Other Tales.* Dated 1909. "Preface," pp. v-⟨xxix⟩. Also contains here first in book form "The Jolly Corner" and "Julia Bride." Deposited April 14, 1909. Listed PW May 1, 1909.

18: *Daisy Miller. Pandora. The Patagonia and Other Tales.* Dated 1909. "Preface," pp. v-⟨xxiv⟩. Deposited April 14, 1909. Listed PW May 1, 1909.

19-20: *The Wings of the Dove.* Dated 1909. "Preface," Vol. 1, pp. v-⟨xxiii⟩. Deposited April 22, 1909. Listed PW June 19, 1909.

21-22: *The Ambassadors.* Dated 1909. "Preface," Vol. 1, pp. v-⟨xxiii⟩. Deposited June 10, 1909. Listed PW June 19, 1909.

23-24: *The Golden Bowl.* Dated 1909. "Preface," Vol. 1, pp. v-⟨xxv⟩. Deposited Aug. 3, 1909. Listed PW Aug. 21, 1909.

25: *The Ivory Tower.* Dated 1917. Issued simultaneously with the trade edition?

26: *The Sense of the Past.* Dated 1917. Issued simultaneously with the trade edition?

The London (Macmillan) edition was first announced in Ath Sept. 26, 1908; the work was promised in fortnightly volumes. PC Oct. 3, 1908: "The handsome edition of the novels and tales of Mr. Henry James, in twenty-three octavo volumes, is to be issued fortnightly by Messrs. Macmillan & Co. The first volume, *Roderick Hudson,* was published on September 29th."

NYPL

10666. VIEWS AND REVIEWS ... NOW FIRST COLLECTED   INTRODUCTION BY LE ROY PHILLIPS ...

BOSTON   THE BALL PUBLISHING COMPANY   1908

⟨i⟩-⟨xiv⟩, 1-241. *Limited edition:* Laid paper, 7¹¹⁄₁₆″ x 5³⁄₁₆″. *Trade edition:* Wove paper, 7½″ x 5⅛″.

⟨1-16⁸⟩.

Limited Edition

Goldstamped white imitation vellum folded over flexible boards, black leather label on spine. White laid end papers. Certificate of issue, p. ⟨iv⟩: *This edition is limited to one hundred and sixty copies, of which this is No. ...*

Trade Edition

T cloth: olive. White laid or wove end papers. Top edges gilt.

Deposited (trade format) May 15, 1908. A copy of the trade edition received by BA June 3, 1908. Both formats listed PW June 6, 1908.

B (trade)   BA (trade)   H (both)   Y (limited)

10667. The Whole Family   A Novel by Twelve Authors ...

New York and London   Harper & Brothers Publishers   MCMVIII

"The Married Son," pp. 144-⟨184⟩.

For comment see entry No. 9790.

10668. ITALIAN HOURS ...

LONDON   WILLIAM HEINEMANN   1909

Title-page in black and brown. For first American edition see next entry.

⟨i⟩-⟨xii⟩, ⟨1⟩-376. Laid paper. Frontispiece and 31 plates in color tipped to inserted leaves, each with printed protective tissue; and, 32 inserted plates printed in monotone. 10½″ x 8″.

⟨a⟩⁴, b², A-I, K-U, X-Z⁸, 2A⁴.

Green buckram. Publisher's device blindstamped on back cover. White laid end papers. Top edges gilt. *Note:* Edel-Laurence report (p. 143) a 1916 remainder binding which may be distinguished by the presence of a blindstamped "medallion" on back cover (in place of the Heinemann device) and the top edges "blue-grey-stained"; not traced by BAL.

Noted for *next Thursday ⟨i.e.,* Oct. 7⟩ Ath Oct. 2, 1909. Noted as *shortly* Bkr Oct. 8, 1909; *next week* Ath Oct. 16, and Bkr Oct. 22, 1909. Listed Bkr Nov. 5, 1909.

CO   H

10669. ITALIAN HOURS ...

BOSTON AND NEW YORK   HOUGHTON MIFFLIN COMPANY   MDCCCCIX

Title-page in black and orange. See preceding entry for prior publication.

⟨i-ii⟩, ⟨i⟩-⟨x⟩, ⟨1⟩-⟨505⟩; printer's imprint, p. ⟨506⟩. Frontispiece and 31 plates inserted. Laid paper. 10⅝″ x 8″.

⟨1⁵, 2¹, 3-33⁸, 34⁴, 35¹⟩. ⟨1⟩₃ inserted.

V cloth: terra-cotta. White laid end papers. Flyleaf at back. Top edges gilt.

On copyright page: *Published November 1909* Printed Nov. 9, 1909; 1530 copies; bound during the period Nov. 9, 1909–Dec. 21, 1909. Deposited Nov. 24, 1909. Noted for Nov. 20 PW Nov. 13, 1909. Advertised for *November* PW Nov. 13, 1909. Listed PW Dec. 4, 1909.

"A second impression, December 1909, consisted of 500 copies, lacking any imprint to distinguish them from first issue."—Edel-Laurence, p. 144. The statement is erroneous. The publisher's records show that 504 copies were printed, December 18, 1909, and that the statement *Second Impression* is present; a copy thus in NYPL.

Note: The publisher's records show that on Nov. 30, 1909, a charge was made for three hours of corrections to the plates. And, under date Dec. 23, 1909, is recorded the printing of 68 copies of a four-page cancel although the printing order was for but 25 copies. Further information wanting.

AAS   CO   H

10670. In After Days   Thoughts on the Future Life by W. D. Howells ... Julia Ward Howe ... ⟨and Others⟩

Harper & Brothers Publishers   New York and London   MCMX

"Is There a Life after Death?," pp. 199-⟨233⟩.

For comment see entry No. 8498.

10671. THE FINER GRAIN ...

NEW YORK   CHARLES SCRIBNER'S SONS   1910

⟨i-viii⟩, ⟨1⟩-312. Laid paper. 7½″ x 4⅞″.

⟨1-20⁸⟩.

Greenish-brown sateen. White laid end papers. Top edges gilt.

On copyright page: *Published October, 1910* Published Oct. 6, 1910 (publisher's records). PW Oct. 8, 1910, commented: "fast making ⟨its⟩ way to popularity." Deposited Oct. 12, 1910. A copy in Y inscribed by early owner Oct. 14, 1910. Listed PW Oct. 15, 1910.

CO   H   NYPL   UV

10672. The Henry James Year Book Selected and Arranged by Evelyn Garnaut Smalley with an Introduction by Henry James and William Dean Howells

Richard G. Badger   The Gorham Press   Boston ⟨1911⟩

"The Author to the Public," p. ⟨9⟩.

Note: Edel-Laurence, pp. 146-147, report a printing with the following imprint: *Richard G. Badger: Boston ⟨1911⟩* No copy thus traced by BAL. A surviving copyright deposit copy is imprinted as above.

Cloth over flexible boards, red ribbon marker; also, flexible leather, red ribbon marker. For fuller comment see entry No. 9816.

10673. THE OUTCRY ...

METHUEN & CO. LTD.   36 ESSEX STREET W.C. LONDON ⟨1911⟩

For American edition see next entry.

⟨i-iv⟩, 1-311; printer's imprint, p. ⟨312⟩. 7⁹⁄₁₆″ x 5″.

a², 1-19⁸, 20⁴.

B-like cloth: green. Publisher's catalog, pp. ⟨1⟩-⟨32⟩ inserted at back. The catalog has been noted with the following dates: *March 1911; August 1911; September 1911.*

On reverse of title-leaf: *First published in 1911* Noted for *next week* Bkr Sept. 29, 1911. Noted for Oct. 5, Ath Sept. 30, 1911. Listed Bkr Oct. 6, 1911. Reviewed Ath Oct. 7, 1911.

H   UV   Y

10674. THE OUTCRY ...

NEW YORK   CHARLES SCRIBNER'S SONS   1911

For prior publication see preceding entry.

⟨i-vi⟩, ⟨1⟩-261. 7½″ x 4⅞″.

⟨1-16⁸, 17⁶⟩.

Greenish-brown sateen. Top edges gilt.

On copyright page: *Published September, 1911* BA copy received Oct. 10, 1911. Deposited Oct. 14, 1911. Listed PW Oct. 14, 1911.

H   NYPL   UV   Y

10675. ... BROWNING'S CENTENARY ED-MUND GOSSE   SIR ARTHUR PINERO HENRY JAMES   TUESDAY, MAY 7th, 1912 (REPRINTED FROM 'TRANSACTIONS R.S.L.,' VOL. XXXI, PART IV.)

LONDON   ASHER AND CO.   14, BEDFORD STREET, W.C. 1912.

At head of title: ROYAL SOCIETY OF LITERATURE THE ACADEMIC COMMITTEE

⟨1⟩-50. 8½″ x 5½″.

⟨1⟩-3⁸, 4¹.

Printed mottled blue-gray paper wrapper.

"The Novel in *The Ring and the Book*," pp. 21-50. Collected in *Notes on Novelists,* 1914.

Listed Ath Nov. 16, 1912.

H   UV

10676. The Days of a Year by M. D. Ashley Dodd with an Appreciation by Henry James ...

Herbert Jenkins Limited   12 Arundel Place Haymarket   London SW   MCMXIII

Cloth; and, leather.

"Foreword," pp. v-vii, being a letter written by James, Sept. 30, 1907, "which the author received ... when the book first appeared" in **1907.**

Noted as *in preparation* Bkr Oct. 4, 1912. Listed Ath Oct. 26, 1912; Bkr Nov. 1, 1912.

UV

10677. A SMALL BOY AND OTHERS

1913

Issued simultaneously in London and New York?

New York Edition

A SMALL BOY AND OTHERS ...

NEW YORK   CHARLES SCRIBNER'S SONS   1913

⟨i-viii⟩, 1-419. Frontispiece inserted. 8³⁄₁₆" x 5½" full.

⟨1-26⁸, 27⁶⟩.

Two issues noted:

First Issue

Leaf ⟨1⟩₁ is not a cancel. On the verso: Publisher's advertisement in 11 lines.

Second Issue

Leaf ⟨1⟩₁ is a cancel. On the verso: Publisher's advertisement in 4 lines, the two final lines reading: In preparation / NOTES OF A SON AND BROTHER

Greenish-brown sateen. Top edges gilt.

On copyright page: *Published March, 1913* Announced PW Feb. 15, 1913. BA copy received April 1, 1913. Deposited April 2, 1913. Listed PW April 5, 1913.

London Edition

A SMALL BOY AND OTHERS ...

MACMILLAN AND CO., LIMITED   ST. MARTIN'S STREET, LONDON   1913

⟨i-iv⟩, 1-436; advertisements, pp. ⟨437-438⟩; blank leaf. Frontispiece inserted. 8⅞" x 5⅝".

⟨A⟩², B-I, K-U, X-Z, 2A-2E⁸, 2F⁴. See note below *in re* 2F.

V cloth: blue.

According to the publisher's records the printer, on April 7, 1913, was ordered to prepare a single leaf announcement for James's *Notes of a Son and Brother.* The leaf is inserted in 2F of some copies; Mr. Simon Nowell-Smith reports a copy thus in his collection.

Shortly—Bkr March 14, 1913. *Immediately after Easter* ⟨i.e., March 23⟩—Ath March 15, 1913. Noted for April 1, Ath March 29, 1913. Published April 1, 1913 (publisher's records). Advertised as though published Bkr April 4, 1913. Listed Bkr April 11, 1913.

H (New York, 1st and 2nd)   LC (New York, 1st, being a deposit copy)   UV (New York, 1st; London)

10678. 21, CARLYLE MANSIONS CHEYNE WALK, S.W. APRIL 21st, 1913 DEAR FRIENDS ALL ...

⟨LONDON, 1913⟩

⟨1-4⟩. Laid paper watermarked W KING / ALTON MILL and a device, monogram, and the statement: ENGLISH HAND MADE Since the piece is printed on a cut sheet the complete watermark may, or may not, be present. 10⅞" x 8⁹⁄₁₆".

Single cut sheet folded to make 4 pages.

On p. ⟨1⟩ is the text of a letter acknowledging a birthday testimonial letter dated April 15, 1913, requesting James to sit for a portrait by John Singer Sargent. A list of the subscribers to the portrait fund on pp. ⟨2-4⟩. At foot of p. ⟨4⟩: LONDON: CHISWICK PRESS. Collected in *The Letters of Henry James,* 1920.

CO   H   UV

10679. NOTES OF A SON AND BROTHER ...

NEW YORK   CHARLES SCRIBNER'S SONS   1914

⟨i-x⟩, 1-515, blank leaf. Frontispiece and 5 plates inserted. 8³⁄₁₆" x 5½".

⟨1-33⁸⟩.

Greenish-brown sateen. Top edges gilt.

On copyright page: *Published March, 1914* Published March 7, 1914, in a printing of 3000 copies (publisher's records). BA copy received March 10, 1914. Deposited March 13, 1914. Advertised as *just published* PW March 14, 1914. Listed PW March 14, 1914.

H   NYPL

10680. NOTES ON NOVELISTS WITH SOME OTHER NOTES ...

MCMXIV   J. M. DENT & SONS LTD.   ALDINE HOUSE, BEDFORD ST., W.C.

Title-page in black and red. For first American printing see next entry. Contains a brief preface omitted from the New York edition.

⟨i⟩-⟨viii⟩, ⟨1⟩-360. 8¼" x 6".

⟨A⟩-I, K-U, X-Z⁸.

Coarse B cloth: green. Top edges stained dull gray-green. Also noted with top edges stained dull brown; *i.e.*, faded green?

Noted as *shortly* Ath Oct. 10, 1914. Listed Ath Oct. 10, 1914. Published Oct. 13, 1914 (publisher's records). A copy in NYPL inscribed by James Oct. 14, 1914. Noted as *just published* Bkr Oct. 16, 1914.

AAS CO NYPL

10681. NOTES ON NOVELISTS WITH SOME OTHER NOTES . . .

NEW YORK CHARLES SCRIBNER'S SONS 1914

See preceding entry.

⟨i⟩-⟨viii⟩, 1-455. 8¾₁₆″ x 5½″ full.

⟨1-29⁸⟩.

Noted in various shades (result of fading?) of brown, green, pink-brown sateen. Top edges gilt.

On copyright page: *Published October, 1914* Published Oct. 14, 1914, in a printing of 1950 copies (publisher's records). A copy in NYPL received Oct. 21, 1914. Listed PW Oct. 24, 1914.

H

10682. The Oxford Book of American Essays Chosen by Brander Matthews . . .

New York Oxford University Press . . . London . . . 1914 . . .

"The Théâtre Français," pp. 368-393. Earliest located American book publication. For prior publication see *French Poets and Novelists*, London, 1878.

For fuller description see BAL, Vol. 4, p. 446.

10683. THE AMERICAN VOLUNTEER MOTOR-AMBULANCE CORPS IN FRANCE A LETTER TO THE EDITOR OF AN AMERICAN JOURNAL . . .

MACMILLAN AND CO., LIMITED ST. MARTIN'S STREET, LONDON 1914 PRICE ONE PENNY

Cover-title.

1-12. 8½″ x 5½″.

⟨-⟩⁶.

Printed blue paper wrapper. Also noted in printed gray (faded blue?) paper wrapper.

Collected in *Within the Rim* ⟨1918; *i.e.*, 1919⟩

Dated at end *November 25th, 1914*. Advertised as though published Ath Dec. 19, 1914. Listed Bkr Dec. 25, 1914.

BA H NYPL Y

10684. Sixty American Opinions on the War

London: T. Fisher Unwin, Ltd. 1 Adelphi Terrace W.C. ⟨1915⟩

Contribution, p. 92.

For comment see entry No. 9833.

10685. ENGLAND AT WAR: AN ESSAY THE QUESTION OF THE MIND . . .

ISSUED BY THE CENTRAL COMMITTEE FOR NATIONAL PATRIOTIC ORGANISATIONS C. P. BUILDING, 62 CHARING CROSS, LONDON, W.C. PRICE ONE PENNY. ⟨n.d., 1915⟩

Cover-title.

⟨1⟩-20. Laid paper watermarked with a windmill and the figures *1590*. 8⁹₁₆″ x 5⁹₁₆″.

⟨-⟩¹⁰.

Printed self-wrapper.

"The Question of the Mind," by James, pp. 3-12.

Deposited BMU July 14, 1915.

CO H NYPL UV Y

10686. The Book of France In Aid of the French Parliamentary Committee's Fund for the Relief of the Invaded Departments Edited by Winifred Stephens . . .

Macmillan and Co., Limited St. Martin's Street, London Édouard Champion, Paris 1915

"France," pp. 1-8. Collected in *Within the Rim* ⟨1918, *i.e.*, 1919⟩

"The Saints of France," pp. 176-182; translated from the French of Maurice Barrès.

Bkr July 2, 1915, reported that an edition was to be issued simultaneously by Édouard Champion, Paris; noted by BAL only as described above. Noted for July 14, 1915, Bkr July 2, 1915. Listed Ath July 17, 1915. Noted as *just published* Bkr July 23, 1915.

AAS H NYPL

10687. . . . Art and the Actor by Constant Coquelin Translated by Abby Langdon Alger with an Introduction by Henry James

Printed for the Dramatic Museum of Columbia University in the City of New York MCMXV

At head of title: Papers on Acting II

Boards, printed paper label.

"Introduction," pp. 1-36. For another version see "Coquelin," in *The American Theatre* . . . ⟨1934⟩, below.

"Of this book three hundred and thirty-three copies were printed ... September, MCMXV"—Colophon.

Deposited Nov. 6, 1915.

BA H LC

10688. The Book of the Homeless (Le Livre des Sans-Foyer) Edited by Edith Wharton ...

New York Charles Scribner's Sons MDCCCCXVI

"The Long Wards," pp. 115-125. Collected in *Within the Rim* ⟨1918, *i.e.,* 1919⟩.

For comment see entry No. 9836.

10689. Letters from America by Rupert Brooke. With a Preface by Henry James

New York: Charles Scribner's Sons 597-599 Fifth Avenue. 1916

"Rupert Brooke," pp. ix-xlii.

The publisher's records show three printings as follows: Jan. 21, 1916, 2075 copies; Feb. 21, 2000 copies; Oct. 20, 1000 copies. BAL has been unable to distinguish the first but it is possible that the presence of broken type on p. xv (last line), p. xvii (last line), p. 153 (last line), p. 161 (running head) indicates later printing. It will be observed that copies occur on two weights of paper and that the sheets therefore bulk either 1" or ¾"; further study indicated.

On copyright page: *Published January, 1916* Deposited Jan. 31, 1916. Listed PW Feb. 5, 1916.

BA H LC

10690. LETTERS TO AN EDITOR ...

⟨LONDON, 1916⟩

⟨i-ii⟩, ⟨1⟩-16, blank leaf. 9" full x 7⁵⁄₁₆". Watermarked *Raleigh Fine*.

⟨-⟩¹⁰.

Printed flexible purple boards mounted on book stock, tied with black cord.

"... Hitherto unpublished letters by Henry James, twenty-five copies only ... privately printed by Clement Shorter ... London, April 1st, 1916."—p. ⟨2⟩.

See Edel-Laurence, pp. 257-258, for an interesting comment regarding the number of copies allegedly printed.

H LC

10691. Glasses ...

London: Martin Secker Number Five John Street Adelphi ⟨1916⟩

In *Uniform Edition of the Tales* series. For American edition see below under 1916.

"*Glasses* is not included in the *Definitive Edition;* it first appeared in ... *Embarrassments* ... The text was revised by the author for this edition very shortly before his death."—p. ⟨4⟩.

Listed PC Sept. 30, 1916.

UMi

10692. Pictures and Other Passages from Henry James Selected by Ruth Head

London Chatto & Windus MCMXVI

For American edition see below under 1917.

Marbled paper boards sides, cloth shelfback, printed paper label on spine.

A selection from James's published books. Embodied in the editor's preface is a letter from James to the editor.

Listed Bkr Oct. 1916; Ath Nov. 1916.

LC UV Y

10693. Glasses ...

Le Roy Phillips Boston ⟨1916, *i.e.,* 1917⟩

For London edition, and comment, see above under 1916 (Sept.).

No trade notices found, nor record of copyright deposit. Edel-Laurence (pp. 155-156) report copies first prepared in May, 1917 were "lost at sea ... Replacement copies were issued ... December 1917 ..."

AAS H Y

10694. THE IVORY TOWER ...

LONDON: 48 PALL MALL W. COLLINS SONS & CO. LTD. GLASGOW MELBOURNE AUCKLAND ⟨1917⟩

Edited by Percy Lubbock. For American edition see below under 1917 (Oct.).

⟨i⟩-⟨viii⟩, 1-⟨348⟩. Frontispiece inserted. 7¹¹⁄₁₆" x 5³⁄₁₆".

⟨-⟩⁴, A-I, K-U, X⁸, Y⁶.

V cloth: blue.

Advertised for Sept. 6, 1917, Ath Sept. 1917. Published Sept. 6, 1917 (publisher's records). Listed Bkr Sept. 1917.

UV Y

10695. THE SENSE OF THE PAST ...

LONDON: 48 PALL MALL W. COLLINS SONS & CO. LTD. GLASGOW MELBOURNE AUCKLAND ⟨1917⟩

Edited by Percy Lubbock. For American edition see below under 1917 (Oct.).

⟨i⟩-⟨viii⟩, 1-⟨351⟩. Portrait frontispiece inserted. 7¾″ scant x 5³⁄₁₆″.

⟨-⟩⁴, A-I, K-U, X-Y⁸.

V cloth: blue.

Advertised for Sept. 6, 1917, Ath Sept. 1917. Published Sept. 6, 1917 (publisher's records). Noted as *received* Bkr Sept. 1917. Listed Bkr Oct. 1917.

NYPL UV Y

10696. Pictures and Other Passages from Henry James Selected by Ruth Head

New York Frederick A. Stokes Company Publishers ⟨n.d., 1917⟩

For prior publication and comment see above under 1916.

Marbled paper boards sides, cloth shelfback, printed paper label on spine. Made up of the London sheets with cancel title-leaf.

Listed PW Oct. 6, 1917.

BPL LC UV

10697. THE IVORY TOWER ...

NEW YORK CHARLES SCRIBNER'S SONS 1917

Edited by Percy Lubbock. For prior publication see above under 1917 (Sept.).

⟨i-ii⟩, ⟨i⟩-⟨viii⟩, 1-357. 7⁷⁄₁₆″ x 4⅞″.

⟨1-23⁸⟩.

Greenish-brown sateen. Top edges gilt.

On copyright page: *Published October, 1917* Published Oct. 26, 1917, in a printing of 1500 copies (publisher's records). Deposited Nov. 2, 1917. Listed PW Nov. 3, 1917.

Note: Also issued (simultaneously?) as Vol. 25 of *The Novels and Tales of Henry James;* see entry No. 10665.

H NYPL UV

10698. THE SENSE OF THE PAST ...

NEW YORK CHARLES SCRIBNER'S SONS 1917

Edited by Percy Lubbock. For prior publication see above under 1917 (Sept.).

⟨i-x⟩, 1-358. 7⁷⁄₁₆″ x 4⅞″.

⟨1-23⁸⟩.

Greenish-brown sateen. Top edges gilt. Also noted in a variant (remainder?) binding: Brown V cloth, top edges plain.

On copyright page: *Published October, 1917* Published Oct. 26, 1917, in a printing of 1500

copies (publisher's records). Deposited Oct. 31, 1917. Listed PW Nov. 3, 1917.

Note: Also issued (simultaneously?) as Vol. 26 of *The Novels and Tales of Henry James;* see entry No. 10665.

AAS CO Y (variant)

10699. THE MIDDLE YEARS ...

LONDON: 48 PALL MALL W. COLLINS SONS & CO. LTD. GLASGOW MELBOURNE AUCKLAND ⟨1917⟩

Edited by Percy Lubbock. For first American edition see next entry.

⟨i-viii⟩, 1-⟨118⟩, blank leaf. Frontispiece inserted. 7¹¹⁄₁₆″ x 5³⁄₁₆″.

⟨-⟩⁴, A-G⁸, H⁴.

V cloth: blue.

Announced Ath Sept. 1917. Published Oct. 18, 1917 (publisher's records). Reviewed TLS Oct. 18, 1917. Listed Bkr Nov. 1917. The second impression (so marked) advertised Bkr Nov. 1917.

UV

10700. THE MIDDLE YEARS ...

NEW YORK CHARLES SCRIBNER'S SONS 1917

Edited by Percy Lubbock. For prior publication see preceding entry.

⟨i-viii⟩, 1-119. Frontispiece inserted. 8¼″ x 5½″.

⟨1-8⁸⟩.

Brown sateen.

On copyright page: *Published November, 1917* Published Nov. 23, 1917, in a printing of 1275 copies (publisher's records). Deposited Nov. 27, 1917. A copy received by H Nov. 28, 1917. Listed PW Dec. 1, 1917.

H NYPL UV

10701. GABRIELLE DE BERGERAC ...

NEW YORK BONI AND LIVERIGHT 1918

Edited by Albert Mordell.

⟨1⟩-153, blank leaf. 7⅜″ x 4⅝″.

⟨1-9⁸, 10⁶⟩.

Printed green paper boards sides, white V cloth shelfback.

Listed PW Dec. 7, 1918. Deposited Jan. 3, 1919.

AAS H LC UV Y

10702. WITHIN THE RIM AND OTHER ESSAYS 1914-15 ...

LONDON: 48 PALL MALL   W. COLLINS SONS &
CO. LTD.   GLASGOW   MELBOURNE   AUCKLAND
⟨1918; *i.e.*, 1919⟩

⟨1⟩-⟨119⟩. 7¾″ x 5⅛″.

⟨A⟩-G⁸, H⁴.

V cloth: blue.

Deposited BMU March 19, 1919. Listed PC March
22, 1919. Noted as *recently published* Bkr March,
1919. See entry No. 10712.

BA   H   NYPL

10703. TRAVELLING COMPANIONS . . .

BONI AND LIVERIGHT   NEW YORK   1919

Edited by Albert Mordell.

⟨i⟩-⟨x⟩, 1-309. 7⁵⁄₁₆″ full x 4¹⁵⁄₁₆″.

⟨1-20⁸⟩.

V cloth: green. *Note:* The publisher's spine imprint has been noted in two forms, the following order is presumed correct:

A: LIVERIGHT measures ¾″ wide.

B: LIVERIGHT measures 1″ wide.

Listed PW May 3, 1919. No record of copyright
deposit found.

CO (A)   H (A)   LC (B)

10704. A LANDSCAPE PAINTER . . .

NEW YORK   SCOTT AND SELTZER   1919

Edited by Albert Mordell.

⟨i-vi⟩, 1-287, blank leaf. *Limited edition:* 7¾″ x
5¼″ (untrimmed). *Trade edition:* 7¼″ full x 5″
(trimmed).

⟨1-17⁸, 18⁴, 19⁸⟩.

Limited Edition

V cloth: blue. Printed paper label on spine:
*. . . Special Issue of the First Edition Limited
to 250 copies . . .*

Trade Edition

T cloth: green. Stamped in gold and blind.

Trade edition deposited Dec. 22, 1919. Trade
edition listed PW Jan. 3, 1920. Published Jan.
2, 1920, according to an advertisement in PW
Jan. 31, 1920.

AAS (limited)   CO (limited)   H (trade)   NYPL
(trade)

10705. THE LETTERS OF HENRY JAMES
SELECTED AND EDITED BY PERCY
LUBBOCK . . .

MACMILLAN AND CO., LIMITED   ST. MARTIN'S
STREET, LONDON   1920

2 Vols. For first American edition see next
entry.

1: ⟨i⟩-⟨xxxii⟩, ⟨1⟩-441; *End of Vol. I . . .* , p.
⟨442⟩; blank leaf. Frontispiece inserted. 8⅞″ x
5¾″ scant.

2: ⟨i⟩-⟨xii⟩, ⟨1⟩-529, blank leaf. Frontispiece
and 1 folded plate inserted.

1: ⟨a⟩-b, A-I, K-U, X-Z, 2A-2D⁸, ⟨2E⟩⁶.

2: ⟨a⟩⁶, A-I, K-U, X-Z, 2A-2I⁸, 2K¹⁰.

V cloth: blue.

Published April 8, 1920 (publisher's records).
Advertised for April 8, 1920 Bkr March, 1920.
Advertised and reviewed TLS April 8, 1920.
Reviewed, advertised and listed Ath April 23,
1920.

NYPL   Y

10706. THE LETTERS OF HENRY JAMES
SELECTED AND EDITED BY PERCY
LUBBOCK . . .

NEW YORK   CHARLES SCRIBNER'S SONS   1920

2 Vols. For prior London publication see preceding entry.

1: ⟨i⟩-⟨xxxiv⟩, 1-434. Frontispiece inserted.
8¹¹⁄₁₆″ scant x 5¹³⁄₁₆″.

2: ⟨i⟩-⟨xiv⟩, 1-511, blank leaf. Frontispiece and
1 folded plate inserted.

1: ⟨1-28⁸, 29¹⁰⟩.

2: ⟨1-33⁸⟩.

V cloth: greenish-black. *Note:* Some sheets were
bound uniform with *The New York Edition;*
see entry No. 10665.

Published April 9, 1920, in a printing of 3000
copies (publisher's records). Listed PW April 10,
1920. MHS copy received April 13, 1920. Deposited April 20, 1920.

H   MHS   UV

10707. MASTER EUSTACE . . .

NEW YORK   THOMAS SELTZER   1920

⟨i-vi⟩, 1-280, blank leaf. 7⁵⁄₁₆″ x 4¹⁵⁄₁₆″. Paper
watermarked *Suede Finish.*

⟨1-18⁸⟩.

T cloth: green.

Note: Also issued in a so-called large paper
edition; apparently sheets of the trade printing
issued untrimmed; size of leaf: 7¹¹⁄₁₆″ x 5⅛″.
Bound in blue V cloth, printed paper label on

spine. A copy in LC inscribed in an unidentified hand: *300 copies.*

BA copy received Nov. 11, 1920. Listed PW Nov. 20, 1920.

BA   H   LC (untrimmed)   NYPL   UV

10708. NOTES AND REVIEWS ... WITH A PREFACE BY PIERRE DE CHAIGNON LA ROSE   A SERIES OF TWENTY-FIVE PAPERS HITHERTO UNPUBLISHED IN BOOK FORM

DUNSTER HOUSE   CAMBRIDGE, MASSACHUSETTS M D CCCC XXI

Title-page in black and orange.

Trade Edition

⟨i⟩-xx, 1-227. Wove paper watermarked *Albion Text.* 8¾″ x 6″.

⟨1-14⁸, 15⁴, 16⁸⟩.

Printed blue paper boards, blue V cloth shelfback. Tan end papers.

Limited Edition

⟨i⟩-xx, 1-227. Unwatermarked wove paper. 8¾″ x 5¹⁵⁄₁₆″.

⟨1-14⁸, 15⁴, 16⁸⟩.

Printed tan Fabriano paper boards, tan V cloth shelfback. Tan end papers. Flyleaves of bookstock.

On copyright page: *Of this Edition Thirty Copies have been printed on Normandy Vellum, of which this is Number ...*

Announced for April 25, 1921 (prospectus; copy in UV). Trade edition deposited May 23, 1921. Trade copy received by BA June 20, 1921. Listed Ath June 25, 1921; PW July 2, 1921. Listed Bkr Dec. 1921, as distributed in Great Britain by Jackson (London); issued with Jackson imprint?

AAS (trade)   CO (trade)   H (trade)   LC (limited) UV (limited)

10709. A LETTER FROM HENRY JAMES TO MRS. LINTON

PRIVATELY PRINTED ⟨n.p., n.d., CAMBRIDGE, MASS., 1921⟩

Edited and issued by George Parker Winship.

⟨1-13⟩; blank, p. ⟨14⟩; colophon, p. ⟨15⟩. Printed on *Glaslan* laid paper. 6⅛″ x 4¾″ full.

⟨-⟩⁸.

Issued in a variety of colored, hand-blocked, papers. In some copies the first and last leaves are used as pastedowns.

This letter has been put into type on the fifty-first anniversary of the inception of a great novelist's happiest romance   At the Sign of The George—p. ⟨15⟩.

Published Dec. 1921.

H   NYPL   UV

10710. "A MOST UNHOLY TRADE" BEING LETTERS ON THE DRAMA BY HENRY JAMES

⟨CAMBRIDGE, MASS.⟩ THE SCARAB PRESS PRIVATELY PRINTED MCMXXIII

⟨i-ii⟩, ⟨1⟩-⟨18⟩; colophon, p. ⟨19⟩; 3 blank leaves. Frontispiece tipped to p. ⟨2⟩. 6″ x 4½″.

⟨1-2⁴, 3², 4⁴⟩.

Printed paper wrapper pasted over flexible boards, brown V cloth shelfback. End papers of bookstock.

"... One hundred copies are for sale ..."—p. ⟨19⟩.

Note: The colophon, p. ⟨19⟩, occurs in two states:

A: The colophon is in 14 lines, the last line being: *Copy Number*

B: The colophon is in 13 lines, the line *Copy Number* not present.

The above order is presumed correct. BAL assumes that copies without the statement, *Copy Number,* were printed in addition to the specified hundred copies.

Deposited Sept. 6, 1923. Listed PW Jan. 5, 1924.

BA (A)   BPL (B)   H (B)   LC (B, being a deposit copy)   NYPL (B)   UV (B)   Y (B)

10711. THREE LETTERS FROM HENRY JAMES TO JOSEPH CONRAD

⟨LONDON: THE FIRST EDITION CLUB, 1926⟩

Cover-title.

Edited by G. Jean-Aubry.

⟨1-10⟩, blank leaf. Pale gray-blue laid paper. 8⅝″ x 6⅞″.

⟨-⟩⁶.

"220 copies ... printed ..."—p. ⟨2⟩.

Printed self-wrapper.

Issued as one of a group of eleven pamphlets under the general title *Twenty Letters to Joseph Conrad,* London, 1926.

H   Y

10712. Harper Essays Edited by Henry Seidel Canby ...

New York and London   Harper & Brothers Publishers MCMXXVII

Boards, cloth shelfback, printed paper label on front.

"Within the Rim," pp. 221-234. First located American book publication; for prior publication see *Within the Rim*, London ‹1918, *i.e.,* 1919›.

On copyright page *First Edition;* and, code letters *H-B,* signifying *printed Aug. 1927.* Deposited Oct. 6, 1927. Listed PW Oct. 8, 1927; Bkr Dec. 1927.

H   LC NYPL UV

10713. LETTERS OF HENRY JAMES TO WALTER BERRY

THE BLACK SUN PRESS ÉDITIONS NARCISSE RUE CARDINALE PARIS MCMXXVIII

Title-page in black and orange.

‹1-72›. Laid Van Gelder paper. Facsimile letter inserted. 10⅝" x 9⅛". Also copies on Japan vellum: Leaf 10⅝" full x 9" full; facsimile letter inserted; also inserted is an original Henry James letter.

‹1-9›⁴.

Printed paper vellum wrapper folded over ‹1›₁ and ‹9›₄.

"This first edition ... printed ... Paris October 1928 ... is strictly limited to 16 copies on Japan Paper each copy supplemented by one of the original letters, and 100 numbered copies on Hollande Van Gelder Zonen ..."—colophon.

CO (paper)   UV(both)

10714. ... LETTERS TO A. C. BENSON AND AUGUSTE MONOD; NOW FIRST PUBLISHED, AND EDITED WITH AN INTRODUCTION BY E. F. BENSON

1930 LONDON: ELKIN MATHEWS & MARROT NEW YORK: CHARLES SCRIBNER'S SONS

At head of title: HENRY JAMES:

‹i-iv›, ‹i›-‹xii›, ‹1›-118, blank leaf. Laid paper watermarked *Glastonbury.* 8¾" scant x 5¹¹⁄₁₆".

‹-›⁸, A-G⁸, H⁴.

Rough V cloth: green. Cream laid end papers. Top edges stained green.

"... Limited to 1050 copies ... This is number ..."—Certificate of issue.

Note: Mr. Simon Nowell-Smith informs BAL "that there were four copies printed and bound before it was discovered that the printer's imprint on the title-verso was lacking." A copy thus is in Mr. Nowell-Smith's collection. All copies examined by BAL have the *University Press, Glasgow,* imprint on the verso of the title-leaf.

Announced for *early autumn* TLS July 31, 1930. Noted for *Sept. 11* PC Sept. 6, 1930. BA copy received Nov. 15, 1930. Reviewed TLS Nov. 25, 1930.

H   Y

10715. THEATRE AND FRIENDSHIP SOME HENRY JAMES LETTERS WITH A COMMENTARY BY ELIZABETH ROBINS

LONDON   JONATHAN CAPE   BEDFORD SQUARE ‹1932›

For American edition see below under 1932 (Sept.).

‹1›-311. Frontispiece and 3 plates inserted. 7⅞" x 5⁵⁄₁₆".

‹A›-I, K-T⁸, U⁴.

Green linen. Top edges stained green.

On copyright page: *First Published 1932* Advertised for July 18 Bkr June 24, 1932. Listed Bkr July 22, 1932. BA copy received Aug. 3, 1932. Deposited (this printing) for U.S. copyright Aug. 16, 1932.

BA   H   NYPL

10716. Reading, Writing and Remembering A Literary Record by E. V. Lucas ...

Methuen & Co. Ltd. 36 Essex Street W.C. London ‹1932›

For American edition see below under 1932 (Oct.).

"... Description of ... *The Finer Grain* ... prepared for the publishers ...," pp. 184-185.

On reverse of title-leaf: *First Published in 1932* Published Sept. 22, 1932 (publisher's records). Listed *Publisher & Bookseller,* Sept. 23, 1932; PC Oct. 1, 1932.

H

10717. THEATRE AND FRIENDSHIP SOME HENRY JAMES LETTERS WITH A COMMENTARY BY ELIZABETH ROBINS

NEW YORK   G. P. PUTNAM'S SONS   1932

For prior publication see above under 1932 (July).

‹1›-303. Laid paper. Frontispiece and 5 plates inserted. 8¼" x 5½".

‹1-19›⁸.

V cloth: maroon, stamped in gold. Top edges stained maroon. Also noted in a variant (remainder?) binding: Rough-toothed mauve V cloth, stamped in yellow, top edges plain.

Listed PW Sept. 24, 1932. Deposited Sept. 26, 1932.

AAS   NYPL   UV (variant)

10718. Reading, Writing and Remembering A Literary Record by E. V. Lucas ...

Harper & Brothers Publishers   New York and London 1932

For prior publication see above under 1932 (Sept.).

"... Description of ... *The Finer Grain* ... prepared for the publishers ..."—p. 184.

On copyright page: *First Edition;* and, code letters *H-G,* signifying *printed August 1932.*

Deposited Oct. 6, 1932. Listed PW Oct. 8, 1932.

H

10719. The American Theatre As Seen by Its Critics 1752–1934 Edited by Montrose J. Moses and John Mason Brown

W. W. Norton & Company, Inc. New York ⟨1934⟩

"Some Notes on the Theatre," pp. 122-126. "Salvini's Othello," pp. 126-128. "Coquelin," pp. 128-132; for another version of this see the introduction to *Art and the Actor,* by Constant Coquelin, 1915, above.

On copyright page: *First Edition*

H

10720. The Shock of Recognition   The Development of Literature in the United States Recorded by the Men Who Made It   Edited by Edmund Wilson

Doubleday, Doran and Company, Inc.   Garden City   New York 1943

Reprint save for "William Dean Howells," pp. 570-579.

"... Published in *Harper's Weekly* of June 19, 1886, and ... never reprinted by James in any of his volumes of criticism ..."—p. 566. Collected in *The American Essays,* 1956.

On copyright page: *First Edition*

BA

10721. The American Novels and Stories of Henry James Edited ... by F. O. Matthiessen

1947   New York: Alfred A. Knopf

Reprint save for "The Story of a Year," pp. 3-36. See next entry.

On copyright page: *First Edition* Deposited Jan. 24, 1947.

H   LC   NYPL   UV

10722. ... HENRY JAMES' NOTES FOR THE IVORY TOWER ...

⟨n.p., n.d., NEW YORK⟩ ALFRED A. KNOPF, INC. ⟨1947⟩

At head: EDITOR'S AND PUBLISHER'S NOTE FOR THE AMERICAN NOVELS AND STORIES OF HENRY JAMES

Cover-title.

⟨993⟩-1036, 2 blank leaves. 8¼" x 5½".

⟨-⟩²⁴.

Printed self-wrapper.

Prepared for insertion in copies of *The American Novels ...* , 1947; see preceding entry.

"... Unintentionally omitted from our first edition ..."—p. ⟨993⟩.

UV

10723. THE NOTEBOOKS OF HENRY JAMES EDITED BY F. O. MATTHIESSEN AND KENNETH B. MURDOCK

NEW YORK   OXFORD UNIVERSITY PRESS   1947

⟨i⟩-xxviii, ⟨1⟩-425, blank leaf. Frontispiece. 9³⁄₁₆" x 6⅛".

⟨1-13¹⁶, 14⁴, 15¹⁶⟩.

V cloth: blue.

Deposited Oct. 7, 1947. H copy received Oct. 29, 1947. Listed PW Nov. 1, 1947.

H   NYPL

10724. The Art of Fiction and Other Essays ... with an Introduction by Morris Roberts

New York   Oxford University Press   1948

All the material herein, save for "Ivan Turgénieff," had prior publication in James's own books. "Ivan Turgénieff" here first collected; for prior book publication see entry No. 10624.

Received (*sic*) at PW March 8, 1948. Deposited March 24, 1948. Published April 22, 1948 (publisher's statement).

H   LC   NYPL

10725. ... THE SCENIC ART   NOTES ON ACTING & THE DRAMA: 1872–1901 EDITED ... BY ALLAN WADE

NEW BRUNSWICK RUTGERS UNIVERSITY PRESS 1948

At head of title: HENRY JAMES

⟨i-ii⟩, ⟨i⟩-⟨xxvi⟩, ⟨1⟩-384, 2 blank leaves. 8 pages of illustrations on four inserted leaves. 8³⁄₁₆″ x 5¼″.

⟨1-13¹⁶⟩.

V cloth: green. Top edges stained green.

Published May 3, 1948 (publisher's statement). Listed PW May 8, 1948. Deposited June 21, 1948. The London (Hart-Davis) edition, dated 1949, reviewed by TLS Jan. 6, 1950.

H NYPL

10726. Henry James and Robert Louis Stevenson A Record of Friendship and Criticism Edited ... by Janet Adam Smith

Rupert Hart-Davis: London 1948

Reprint with the exception of the "fragment of a letter," pp. 228-231.

Published Oct. 29, 1948 (publisher's records).

BA H UV Y

10727. The Ghostly Tales of Henry James Edited ... by Leon Edel

New Brunswick Rutgers University Press 1948 ⟨i.e., 1949⟩

Reprint save for "The Ghostly Rental," pp. 105-140.

Note: All examined copies, including a copyright deposit copy, have the title-page dated 1948, the copyright notice dated 1949.

Deposited March 21, 1949.

BA UV Y

10728. THE COMPLETE PLAYS OF HENRY JAMES EDITED BY LEON EDEL

J. B. LIPPINCOTT COMPANY PHILADELPHIA AND NEW YORK ⟨1949⟩

⟨1⟩-846, blank leaf. Frontispiece and 11 plates inserted. Facsimiles in text. 9³⁄₁₆″ x 6⅛″.

⟨1-2¹⁶, 3⁸, 4-27¹⁶⟩.

Note: In all examined copies the title-leaf is a cancel. Regarding this the publishers stated (letter to BAL, Nov. 29, 1949): "The entire edition has the tipped-in title page which you noticed ... The reason for the cancel was that at the time we went to press we did not have complete copy for the wording of the copyright page on hand, and rather than delay the books beyond the point of meeting our retail publica-

tion date, we printed the entire American and English editions without these two pages. We later printed them on a small press and tipped them into each copy of the book while the sheets were being folded in the bindery. Therefore, there are naturally no copies in existence with any previous title page."

Brown V cloth sides, tan buckram shelfback. Top edges stained red-brown.

On copyright page: *First Edition* Deposited Aug. 25, 1949. A copy received ⟨sic⟩ by PW Aug. 31, 1949. Published Oct. 12, 1949 (publisher's statement). Listed PW Oct. 15, 1949. The London (Hart-Davis) edition, American printed, issued in Dec. 1949, according to *The English Catalogue* ... ; reviewed TLS Jan. 6, 1950.

H

10729. EIGHT UNCOLLECTED TALES OF HENRY JAMES EDITED WITH AN INTRODUCTION BY EDNA KENTON

RUTGERS UNIVERSITY PRESS NEW BRUNSWICK, N. J. 1950

⟨i-vi⟩, ⟨1⟩-314. 8⁵⁄₁₆″ x 5½″ scant.

⟨1-10¹⁶⟩.

V cloth: green.

Note: Of the eight tales herein five are here first in book form; the remaining three ("The Story of a Year," "Gabrielle de Bergerac" and "The Ghostly Rental") had prior American book publication.

Deposited Sept. 26, 1950.

B H

10730. Thomas Sergeant Perry: A Biography and Letters to Perry from William, Henry, and Garth Wilkinson James by Virginia Harlow

1950 Durham, N. C. Duke University Press

"Letters to Perry from William, Henry, and Garth Wilkinson James," pp. 239-350.

"These letters, addressed to Perry, have been transcribed from original manuscripts and from copies ..."—p. ⟨238⟩.

Deposited Dec. 26, 1950. Listed PW Jan. 6, 1951. BA copy received April 3, 1951. Issued in Great Britain by Cambridge University Press, May, 1951.

BA

10731. Literary Opinion in America Essays Illustrating the Status, Methods, and Problems of Criticism in the United States in the Twentieth Century Edited by Morton Dauwen Zabel   Revised Edition

Harper & Brothers   New York ⟨1951⟩

Reprint save for "The Question of the Opportunities," pp. 51-55; and, "The Great Form," pp. 56-57. The James material does not appear in the first edition, 1937.

On copyright page: Code letters *B-A,* signifying *printed Feb. 1951.* Deposited March 16, 1951.

H   LC

10732. The Portable Henry James Edited ... by Morton Dauwen Zabel

New York   1951   The Viking Press

Reprint save for "Henry James to H. G. Wells," pp. 482-489, which comprises two of James's letters, both collected in *Henry James and H. G. Wells* ... , 1958.

On copyright page: *Published in August 1951* Deposited Aug. 24, 1951.

LC   Y

10733. Daumier Caricaturist ...

⟨Emmaus, Pennsylvania⟩   Miniature Books Rodale Press ⟨1954⟩

Printed paper boards, cloth shelfback.

First book printing of the original text as published in *Century Magazine,* Jan. 1890. In revised form the article published in *Picture and Text,* 1893.

On copyright page: *First Published In This Edition 1954 By The Rodale Press, Emmaus, Pennsylvania   Printed In England*

On copyright page of the British issue: *First Published In This Edition 1954 By The Rodale Press, 123 New Bond Street, London   Printed In England At The Chiswick Press*

According to *English Catalogue* the British issue was published April 9, 1954. Publication date for American edition not determined.

LC (British)   UV (American)

10734. THE   SELECTED   LETTERS   OF HENRY JAMES EDITED ... BY LEON EDEL

NEW YORK   FARRAR, STRAUS AND CUDAHY ⟨1955⟩

⟨i⟩-xxxiv, ⟨1⟩-235; blank leaf. 8³⁄₁₆″ x 5½″.

⟨1-7¹⁶, 8⁸, 9¹⁶⟩.

V cloth: orange.

"In this volume are printed some hundred and

twenty of the thousands of letters written by Henry James. One half of those given here appear for the first time ..."—p. vii.

On copyright page: *First Printing, 1955* BA copy received Dec. 6, 1955. Deposited Dec. 9, 1955. The London (Hart-Davis) edition issued Jan. 1956, according to *British National Bibliography.*

BA   UV

10735. Tales of the Criminous   A Selection from the Works of William Roughead Made and Edited by W. N. Roughead together with Fourteen Letters to the Author from Henry James

Cassell and Company Ltd   London ⟨1956⟩

"Letters from Henry James to William Roughead 1913–1915," pp. 251-266.

"Of the fourteen letters, four (III, V, VIII and IX) were included by Mr. Percy Lubbock in his ... *The Letters of Henry James* ... and one of them (X) has been used by Mr. Leon Edel in his *Selected Letters of Henry James* ... Except for the quotations in 'Enjoyment of Murder,' none of the others has ever been published before." —p. 250.

Deposited for U. S. copyright Aug. 16, 1956. Reviewed TLS Aug. 31, 1956.

BA   H   LC

10736. ... THE AMERICAN ESSAYS EDITED ... BY LEON EDEL

VINTAGE BOOKS NEW YORK   1956

At head of title: HENRY JAMES

⟨i-ii⟩, ⟨i⟩-xx, ⟨1⟩-288; ⟨i⟩-⟨x⟩. 7¼″ x 4¼″.

So-called perfect binding.

Printed stiff white paper wrapper.

Issued as No. K-40 of *Vintage Books* series.

"In this volume I have collected all of Henry James's essays on American letters together with certain of his miscellaneous writings on American subjects. The material was widely scattered, and almost half of it appears here for the first time in book form ..."—p. ⟨v⟩.

On copyright page: *First Edition* Deposited Aug. 30, 1956.

LC

10737. .... The Future of the Novel   Essays on the Art of Fiction Edited ... by Leon Edel

Vintage Books   New York   1956

At head of title: Henry James

Printed paper wrapper.

Reprint save for:

"George Eliot's *Middlemarch*," pp. 80-89.

"Nana," pp. 89-96. For prior publication of a portion of this see above: *Nana* ... , 1884.

On copyright page: *First Edition*   Deposited Aug. 30, 1956.

Y

10738. "A TRAGEDY OF ERROR": JAMES'S FIRST STORY WITH A PREFATORY NOTE BY LEON EDEL

⟨REPRINTED FROM THE NEW ENGLAND QUARTERLY, VOL. XXIX, NO. 3. SEPT., 1956⟩

Cover-title.

291-317. Printed on mixed papers, both laid and wove being used. $9\frac{5}{16}$" x $6\frac{1}{16}$".

14 single leaves. Stapled.

Collected in *The Complete Tales*, Vol. 1, 1962.

Printed green paper wrapper.

UV

10739. THE PAINTER'S EYE NOTES AND ESSAYS ON THE PICTORIAL ARTS BY HENRY JAMES SELECTED AND EDITED WITH AN INTRODUCTION BY JOHN L. SWEENEY

LONDON   RUPERT HART-DAVIS 1956

For first American edition see next entry. Portions had prior publication in *Picture and Text*, 1893.

⟨1⟩-274; blank leaf. Frontispiece inserted. 8" x $5\frac{1}{8}$".

⟨A⟩-I, K-Q⁸, R¹⁰.

Unfinished brown-orange V cloth. Top edges stained brown-orange.

Listed Bkr Oct. 27, 1956 as published on Oct. 11, 1956. A copy received at LC Oct. 25, 1956.

LC Y

10740. THE PAINTER'S EYE NOTES AND ESSAYS ON THE PICTORIAL ARTS BY HENRY JAMES SELECTED AND EDITED WITH AN INTRODUCTION BY JOHN L. SWEENEY

HARVARD UNIVERSITY PRESS   CAMBRIDGE, MASSACHUSETTS 1956

For prior publication see preceding entry. Portions had prior publication in *Picture and Text*, 1893.

⟨1⟩-274, blank leaf. Frontispiece inserted. 8" x $5\frac{1}{8}$".

⟨A⟩-I, K-Q⁸, R¹⁰.

Unfinished brown-orange V cloth. Top edges stained brown-orange.

BA copy received Nov. 20, 1956. Published Nov. 21, 1956 (publisher's records).

B BA

10741. AUTOBIOGRAPHY IN FICTION: AN UNPUBLISHED REVIEW BY HENRY JAMES ⟨edited⟩ BY LEON EDEL OFFPRINT FROM HARVARD LIBRARY BULLETIN VOLUME XI, NUMBER 2

⟨CAMBRIDGE, MASS., HARVARD LIBRARY BULLETIN⟩ SPRING 1957

Cover-title.

245-257. Wove paper watermarked *Warren's Olde Style*. $10\frac{1}{4}$" x $6\frac{13}{16}$". Two facsimiles (printed on a single leaf, verso and recto) inserted.

⟨a², b-f¹⟩.

Printed stiff gray paper wrapper.

UV copy inscribed by Edel Aug. 21, 1957.

UV

10742. ... PARISIAN SKETCHES LETTERS TO THE NEW YORK TRIBUNE 1875–1876 EDITED ... BY LEON EDEL AND ILSE DUSOIR LIND

NEW YORK UNIVERSITY PRESS   WASHINGTON SQUARE 1957

At head of title: HENRY JAMES

⟨i⟩-⟨xxxviii⟩, ⟨1⟩-262, 2 blank leaves. Frontispiece inserted. $7\frac{15}{16}$" x $5\frac{3}{8}$".

⟨1-8¹⁶, 9⁸, 10¹⁶⟩.

V cloth: blue.

"Henry James's Paris letters to the New York *Tribune* of almost eighty years ago have been collected in this volume for the first time. Three of the letters were reprinted by James during his lifetime, the remainder were allowed to linger in the crumbling newspaper files ... In recent years extracts ... were included in Allan Wade's ... *The Scenic Art;* and certain passages ... were incorporated by John L. Sweeney in ... *The Painter's Eye*. The majority of the letters ... remained uncollected ..."—P. v.

Deposited Oct. 18, 1957.

B BA Y

10743. The House of Fiction Essays on the Novel by Henry James Edited ... by Leon Edel

London Rupert Hart-Davis 1957

⟨1⟩-286; blank leaf. 8″ scant x 5⅛″ scant.

Reprint save for "Far from the Madding Crowd." The rest of the material herein had prior publication in James's own books; or, is here first collected, having had prior publication as contributions to the works of other authors or editors.

Reviewed in *The Times,* Oct. 24, 1957.

B

10744. LITERARY REVIEWS AND ESSAYS ... ON AMERICAN, ENGLISH, AND FRENCH LITERATURE EDITED BY ALBERT MORDELL

TWAYNE PUBLISHERS NEW YORK ⟨1957⟩

⟨1⟩-409, 3 blank leaves. 8⅞″ x 6″ full.

⟨1-13⟩¹⁶.

Blue buckram.

Listed PW Dec. 30, 1957. Deposited Jan. 2, 1958. Reissued as No. E-116 in the *Evergreen Book* series by Grove Press, Inc., New York ⟨1957; *i.e.,* 1958⟩; printed paper wrapper; listed PW Sept. 8, 1958. Edel-Laurence (p. 196) report "a second impression carries the imprint of Vista House"; not seen by BAL.

B LC

10745. Henry James and H. G. Wells A Record of Their Friendship, Their Debate on the Art of Fiction, and Their Quarrel Edited ... by Leon Edel & Gordon N. Ray

London Rupert Hart-Davis 1958

For American publication see next entry.

Contains some material by James here first in book form.

Listed Bkr Feb. 22, 1958.

LC

10746. Henry James and H. G. Wells A Record of Their Friendship, Their Debate on the Art of Fiction, and Their Quarrel Edited ... by Leon Edel & Gordon N. Ray

University of Illinois Press Urbana, 1958

For prior London publication and comment see preceding entry.

Deposited March 31, 1958.

BA LC UV

10747. HOWELLS AND JAMES: A DOUBLE BILLING NOVEL-WRITING AND NOVEL-READING ...

NEW YORK   THE NEW YORK PUBLIC LIBRARY 1958

For comment see entry No. 9879.

10748. FRENCH WRITERS AND AMERICAN WOMEN   ESSAYS BY HENRY JAMES EDITED ... BY PETER BUITENHUIS

THE COMPASS PUBLISHING COMPANY, BRANFORD, CONNECTICUT 1960

⟨i-iv⟩, i-x, 1-81. 9¾″ x 6⅞″.

⟨1-24⟩².

Printed white paper wrapper.

H

10749. ... Confidence ... Now First Edited from the Manuscript. With Notes, Introduction, and Bibliography by Herbert Ruhm. With Contemporary Reviews, and Excerpts from the Notebooks ...

The Universal Library Grosset & Dunlap New York ⟨1962⟩

Pictorial paper wrapper. For first edition see above under 1880.

On copyright page: *Universal Library. First Edition, October 1962.*

LC

Reprints of James's own books; and, books containing reprinted James material but with James's name on the title-page. For certain European printings not found in this section see publication notes in *Section One*.

10750. The Europeans ... Authorized Edition.

Leipzig Bernhard Tauchnitz 1878.

Printed paper wrapper. Issued as No. 1792 of the series. Outer back wrapper dated *November 1878*.

Hawthorne ...

New York ... ⟨1879; *i.e.*, 1887⟩

See below under 1887.

10751. The Madonna of the Future. Longstaff's Marriage. Madame de Mauves ... Authorized Edition.

Leipzig Bernhard Tauchnitz 1880.

Printed paper wrapper. Issued as No. 1881 of the series. The earliest located copy has outer back wrapper dated *August 1884*.

10752. Eugene Pickering. The Diary of a Man of Fifty. Benvolio ... Authorized Edition.

Leipzig Bernhard Tauchnitz 1880.

Printed paper wrapper. Issued as No. 1888 of the series. Listed wv April 8, 1880.

10753. ... Sweet Nelly, My Heart's Delight. By Walter Besant and James Rice. And A Bundle of Letters. By Henry James, Jr. ...

⟨At head of title:⟩ The Seaside Library ... George Munro, Publisher ... New York ... February 23, 1880.

Caption-title. The above at head of p. ⟨1⟩. Printed self-wrapper. Vol. xxxiv, No. 702, of the series. If the date given (Feb. 23, 1880) is to be accepted then this is a reprint. It must be noted, however, that the dating of publications such as this is notoriously misleading; more often than not such publications were antedated rather than postdated which seems to be so in this case. Deposited for copyright July 27, 1880.

10754. Roderick Hudson ... New Edition.

London: Macmillan and Co. 1880.

10755. Washington Square The Pension Beaurepas A Bundle of Letters ... in Two Volumes ...

Leipzig Bernhard Tauchnitz 1881.

Printed paper wrapper. Issued as Nos. 1977-1978 of the series. Listed wv June 9, 1881.

10756. ... Daisy Miller: A Study; and Other Stories ...

Published by Harper & Brothers, New York ... ⟨1883⟩

Printed paper wrapper. Cover-title. At head of title: Harper's Franklin Square Library. Number 303 ... Issued under date of March 30, 1883. Deposited March 31, 1883. Listed pw April 7, 1883.

10757. ⟨Novels and Tales of Henry James⟩

London Macmillan and Co. 1883

The order of listing here is alphabetical:

The American ... in Two Volumes ...

Confidence ...

Daisy Miller: A Study Four Meetings Longstaff's Marriage Benvolio ...

The Europeans ...

An International Episode The Pension Beaurepas The Point of View ...

The Madonna of the Future: A Bundle of Letters: The Diary of a Man of Fifty: Eugene Pickering ...

The Portrait of a Lady ... in Three Volumes ...

Roderick Hudson ... in Two Volumes ...

The Siege of London Madame de Mauves ...

Washington Square ...

Internal evidence indicates that certain, perhaps all, of the volumes went into two or more printings.

Noted in the following styles of binding; the designations are wholly arbitrary:

A: Blue V cloth, stamped in gold. The sheets occur either conventionally sewn; or, stapled.

B: Printed paper wrapper.

C: Orange V cloth, stamped in brown.

Note: Edel-Laurence report copies in "flexible cloth boards in varying colours (salmon, ochre, cream, green, etc.) . . ." and, reportedly, "as bound two volumes in one in uniform secondary binding."

Advertised Bkr Oct. 4, 1883, as *Novels and Tales by Henry James, nearly ready.* Again advertised Bkr Nov. 3, 1883. The entire set published Nov. 13, 1883 (publisher's records). Listed PC Dec. 6, 1883, as in cloth; and, printed paper wrapper. Listed Bkr Dec. 11, 1883.

Advertised under varying titles: *Novels and Tales by Henry James; Works by Henry James; Popular Edition of Novels and Tales; Pocket Edition of Mr. Henry James's Novels and Tales.* Edel-Laurence (pp. 58-60) refer to the set as the *Collective Edition of 1883.*

10758. French Poets and Novelists . . .

London   Macmillan and Co. 1884

10759. Stories Revived   First Series . . .

London   Macmillan and Co. 1885

At end of text: *End of Vol. I.*

10760. Stories Revived   Second Series . . .

London   Macmillan and Co. 1885

10761. Hawthorne . . .

New York   Harper & Brothers, Publishers Franklin Square ⟨1879; *i.e.,* 1887⟩

Printed paper wrapper. Issued under date May 27, 1887, as No. 133 in *Harper's Handy Series.*

Deposited May 28, 1887. Stripped of the dated wrapper this may well be mistaken for an 1879 publication.

10762. The Madonna of the Future: A Bundle of Letters: The Diary of a Man of Fifty: Eugene Pickering . . .

London   Macmillan and Co. 1887

10763. The Reverberator . . .

London   Macmillan and Co. And New York 1888   The Right of Translation and Reproduction is Reserved

1 Vol. Pp. 229. On copyright page: *Copyright, 1888, by Henry James. First Edition (2 vols.*

Globe 8vo) June 1888. New Edition 1 vol. Crown 8vo, August 1888.

Blue BF cloth stamped in gold, black and blind. Inserted at back: Publisher's catalog dated *April, 1888.*

Unsold sheets were issued, not before 1905, in the orange V cloth binding of The Times Book Club.

10764. The Tragic Muse . . . in Three Volumes . . .

London: Macmillan and Co. And New York 1890   The Right of Translation and Reproduction is Reserved

No precise date of publication established but the publisher's files (correspondence with the printer) indicate that publication was almost certainly during the last week in June, 1890. Advertised as *nearly ready* Bkr June 1, 1890; PC June 2, 1890. Listed (prematurely) PC June 2, 1890. Advertised for *the present month* Ath June 7, 1890; as *shortly* Ath June 14, 1890; as *shortly* PC June 16, 1890; as though published Ath June 28, 1890. Listed Ath July 5, 1890. Advertised (with reviews) Ath July 19, 1890. Reviewed Ath July 26, 1890. Listed PC Nov. 15, 1890; Bkr Dec. 13, 1890. *The one-volume edition,* dated 1891, advertised as *forthcoming* Ath Feb. 7, 1891; listed Ath Feb. 14, 1891; Bkr March 5, 1891.

10765. Soldiers Three . . . with Other Stories by Rudyard Kipling with a Critical Introduction by Henry James . . .

Leipzig   Heinemann and Balestier Limited, London   1891

Printed paper wrapper. Issued as No. 59 in *The English Library* series. Back wrapper dated *October, 1891.*

10766. . . . Port Tarascon . . . Translated by Henry James . . .

London   Sampson Low, Marston, Searle & Rivington Limited   St. Dunstan's House, Fetter Lane. 1891 . . .

At head of title: *Alphonse Daudet.* Advertised for *November* Ath Sept. 27, 1890. Advertised as *at all libraries* Ath Nov. 22, 1890. Listed Ath Nov. 29, 1890. Advertised as though published PC Dec. 1, 1890. Listed Bkr Dec. 13, 1890; PC Dec. 15, 1890.

10767. The Lesson of the Master   The Marriages   The Pupil   Brooksmith   The Solution   Sir Edmunde Orme . . .

Leipzig   Heinemann and Balestier (Ltd. London) 1892

Printed paper wrapper. Back wrapper dated *Aug. 1892.* Issued as No. 135 of *The English Library* series.

10768. Daisy Miller & An International Episode . . . Illustrated . . . by Harry W. McVickar

Harper & Brothers New York MDCCCXCII

Trade edition (in cloth); and, a de luxe format (in vellum) limited to 250 numbered copies. Trade edition deposited Nov. 3, 1892.

10769. Mine Own People by Rudyard Kipling with a Critical Introduction by Henry James

New York Frank F. Lovell Company 23 Duane Street ⟨n.d., 1899⟩

Printed paper wrapper. Wrapper dated Sept. 1, 1899. Issued as No. 1 of *The Lotus Series.* Reprinted and reissued: *New York Manhattan Press 474 West Broadway* ⟨n.d.⟩. See entry No. 10594.

10770. . . . Nathaniel Hawthorne . . .

New York Doubleday & McClure Company 1899

At head of title: *The Warner Classics* . . . Issued as Vol. 2 of *The Warner Classics.* Deposited Sept. 2, 1899.

10771. The Sacred Fount . . .

Methuen & Co. 36 Essex Street W.C. London 1901

Advertised as *ready* Ath Feb. 23, 1901. Listed Ath Feb. 23, 1901. Reviewed Ath March 2, 1901.

10772. The Wings of the Dove . . .

Westminster Archibald Constable and Co., Ltd. 2 Whitehall Gardens, S.W. 1902

Published this day—Ath Aug. 30, 1902. Listed Ath Sept. 6, 1902.

10773. Roderick Hudson . . .

Boston and New York Houghton, Mifflin and Company The Riverside Press, Cambridge 1902

10774. . . . Madame Bovary Translated from the French by W. Blaydes with a Critical Introduction by Henry James . . .

P. F. Collier & Son New York ⟨1902⟩

At head of title: *Gustave Flaubert* In *The French Classical Romances* series.

10775. . . . The Two Young Brides Translated from the French by the Lady Mary Loyd with a Critical Introduction by Henry James . . .

P. F. Collier & Son New York ⟨1902; *i.e.,* 1903⟩

At head of title: *Honoré de Balzac* Deposited Feb. 6, 1903.

10776. A Passionate Pilgrim and Other Tales . . .

Boston Houghton, Mifflin and Company New York: 85 Fifth Avenue The Riverside Press, Cambridge ⟨1903⟩

Sheets of an earlier printing with cancel title-leaf. Prepared for copyright renewal purposes. Three title-leaves printed Jan. 24, 1903; publisher's records. Deposited Jan. 30, 1903. *Location:* LC.

10777. Transatlantic Sketches . . .

Boston and New York Houghton, Mifflin and Company The Riverside Press, Cambridge ⟨1903⟩

Sheets of an earlier printing with cancel title-leaf. Prepared for copyright renewal purposes. Three title-leaves printed Jan. 24, 1903; publisher's records. Deposited Jan. 30, 1903. *Location:* LC.

10778. The Diary of a Man of Fifty . . .

New York Harper & Brothers Publishers Franklin Square Copyright, 1880, 1908, by Henry James

Cover-title. Printed paper wrapper. Prepared for copyright renewal purposes only. 61 leaves, printed on rectos only, paged ⟨8⟩-68. Deposited March 25, 1908.

10779. A Bundle of Letters . . .

New York Harper & Brothers Publishers Franklin Square Copyright, 1880, 1908, by Henry James

Cover-title. Printed paper wrapper. Prepared for copyright renewal purposes only. 66 leaves, printed on rectos only, paged ⟨70⟩-135.

10780. Julia Bride . . .

New York and London Harper & Brothers Publishers MCMIX

Red S cloth, stamped in gold and blind, top edges gilt. Also noted in the following variant (remainder?) bindings; the designations are for identification only and are not intended to suggest a sequence:

Variant A: Tan V cloth, lettered in black, top edges gilt. Front cover decorated with a lily.

Variant B: Purple V cloth, lettered in black, top edges gilt. Front cover is not decorated with a lily.

Variant C: Tan V cloth, lettered in black, top edges plain.

Variant D: Tan paper boards, red V cloth shelf-back, lettered in black, top edges plain.

Variant E: Tan paper boards, lettered in black, top edges plain.

On copyright page: *Published September, 1909.* For prior publication see *The Novels and Tales,* Vol. 17, deposited April 14, 1909. As a separate publication *Julia Bride* was received at NYPL Sept. 23, 1909; deposited Sept. 25, 1909; noted as *at once* PW Oct. 2, 1909; listed PW Oct. 9, 1909.

10781. The Finer Grain ...

    Methuen & Co. Ltd. 36 Essex Street W.C. London ⟨1910⟩

On copyright page: *First Published in 1910* Copy in Y inscribed by early owner Oct. 8, 1910. Published Oct. 13, 1910 (publisher's records). Listed Ath Oct. 15, 1910. Noted as though published Ath Oct. 15, 1910.

10782. The Henry James Year Book   Selected and Arranged by Evelyn Garnaut Smalley with an Introduction by Henry James and William Dean Howells

    London   J. M. Dent & Sons, Ltd. Covent Garden ⟨n.d., 1912⟩

For comment see entry No. 9816.

10783. Notes of a Son & Brother ...

    Macmillan and Co., Limited St. Martin's Street, London 1914

Noted as *shortly* Bkr Feb. 6, 1914. Noted as *immediately* Bkr March 6, 1914; PC March 7, 1914. UV copy inscribed by James March 13, 1914. Advertised as though published Ath March 14, 1914. *Just published*—Bkr March 20, 1914. Listed Bkr March 20, 1914; PC March 21, 1914.

10784. The Beast in the Jungle ...

    London: Martin Secker   Number Five John Street Adelphi ⟨1915⟩

10785. The Coxon Fund ...

    London: Martin Secker   Number Five John Street Adelphi ⟨1915⟩

10786. The Death of the Lion ...

    London: Martin Secker   Number Five John Street Adelphi ⟨1915⟩

10787. The Altar of the Dead ...

    London: Martin Secker   Number Five John Street Adelphi ⟨1915; *i.e.,* 1916⟩

Occurs with the date *1915* on reverse of title-leaf (copies first printed); and, with date 1916 on reverse of title-leaf. Printed in 1915 but not published until 1916. Listed PC Sept. 30, 1916. Received by BMU Dec. 12, 1916.

10788. The Figure in the Carpet ...

    Le Roy Phillips Boston ⟨1916⟩

Also issued by Secker (London); listed PC Sept. 30, 1916.

10789. Letters from America by Rupert Brooke. With a Preface by Henry James

    London: Sidgwick & Jackson, Ltd. 3 Adam Street, Adelphi, W. C. 1916

Cloth, printed paper label on spine. Two states of the label have been seen: A: Date in the last line is *1915,* altered to *1916;* B: Date in last line is *1916.* A review copy has been seen with the *1916* variety of label.

Published March 8, 1916 (date from a review copy in UV). Advertised as though published Ath March, 1916. Listed Ath March 1916; Bkr April 1916. Bkr Aug. 1916 reported that a "second impression" had been issued.

10790. The Pupil ...

    London: Martin Secker   Number Five John Street Adelphi ⟨1916⟩

Listed PC Sept. 30, 1916.

10791. The Pupil ...

    Le Roy Phillips Boston   ⟨1916⟩

10792. Roderick Hudson ...

    Boston and New York   Houghton Mifflin Company   The Riverside Press   Cambridge 1917

Reprinted from the plates of *The New York Edition,* 1907.

10793. The Jolly Corner ...

    London: Martin Secker   Number Five John Street Adelphi ⟨1918⟩

10794. Refugees in Chelsea ...

Chelsea, at the Ashendene Press ⟨1920⟩

Printed paper boards, cloth shelfback. "Printed ... April ... 1920. 50 copies on paper and 6 copies on vellum. For private circulation only." —Colophon.

10795. ⟨The Novels and Stories of Henry James. New and Complete Edition. Edited by Percy Lubbock⟩

Macmillan and Co., Limited   St. Martin's Street, London   1921 ⟨-1923⟩

35 Vols. The volume numbers are not present on the several volumes; nor are the volumes so marked as to indicate they are part of a set.

Issued in two formats: *Crown 8vo* (leaf 7⁹⁄₁₆″ x 5″); and, foolscap 8vo *Pocket Edition* (leaf 6¾″ x 4⅜″).

1: *Roderick Hudson*, 1921.

2: *The American*, 1921.

3: *The Europeans*, 1921.

4: *Confidence*, 1921.

5: *Washington Square*, 1921.

6-7: *The Portrait of a Lady*, 1921.

8-9: *The Bostonians*, 1921.

10-11: *The Princess Casamassima*, 1921.

12-13: *The Tragic Muse*, 1921.

14: *The Awkward Age*, 1922.

15: *The Spoils of Poynton, A London Life, The Chaperon*, 1922.

16: *What Maisie Knew, In the Cage, The Pupil*, 1922.

17: *The Aspern Papers, The Turn of the Screw, The Liar, The Two Faces*, 1922.

18: *The Reverberator, Madame de Mauves, A Passionate Pilgrim, and Other Tales*, 1922.

19: *Lady Barbarina, The Siege of London, An International Episode, and Other Tales*, 1922.

20: *The Lesson of the Master, The Death of the Lion, The Next Time, and Other Tales*, 1922.

21: *The Author of Beltraffio, The Middle Years, Greville Fane, and Other Tales*, 1922.

22: *The Altar of the Dead, The Beast in the Jungle, The Birthplace, and Other Tales*, 1922.

23: *Daisy Miller Pandora The Patagonia and Other Tales*, 1922.

24: *Watch and Ward, Longstaff's Marriage, Eugene Pickering, and Other Tales*, 1923.

25: *The Diary of a Man of Fifty, A New England Winter, The Path of Duty, and Other Tales*, 1923.

26: *The Last of the Valerii, Master Eustace, The Romance of Certain Old Clothes, and Other Tales*, 1923.

27: *Lord Beaupré, The Visits, The Wheel of Time, and Other Tales*, 1923.

28: *Maud-Evelyn, The Special Type, The Papers, and Other Tales*, 1923.

29: *The Sacred Fount*, 1923.

30-31: *The Wings of the Dove*, 1923.

32-33: *The Ambassadors*, 1923.

34-35: *The Golden Bowl*, 1923.

Bkr Jan. 1921, noted that publication of the set was to begin during the current month.

10796. ... La Curée   Translated ... by Alexander Teixeira de Mattos with an Essay by Henry James

Published in New York by Boni and Liveright, 1924

At head of title: *Émile Zola*   Cloth, printed paper label on spine. 2050 copies only.

10797. ... Queer People and a Damning Passion (De Grey: A Romance) ...

Haldeman-Julius Publications Girard, Kansas ⟨n.d., 1931⟩

At head of title: Little Blue Book No. 1671 Edited by E. Haldeman-Julius   Printed paper wrapper.

10798. ... The Sweetheart of M. Briseux ...

Haldeman-Julius Publications Girard, Kansas ⟨1931⟩

At head of title: Little Blue Book No. 1672 Edited by E. Haldeman-Julius   Printed paper wrapper.

10799. ... The Runaway Wife ...

Haldeman-Julius Publications Girard, Kansas ⟨n.d., 1931⟩

At head of title: Little Blue Book No. 1673 Edited by E. Haldeman-Julius   Printed paper wrapper.

10800. ... Spiritual Magnetism ...

Haldeman-Julius Publications Girard, Kansas ⟨1931⟩

At head of title: Little Blue Book No. 1674 Edited by E. Haldeman-Julius   Printed paper wrapper.

10801. ... The Mad Lovers and the Emperor's Topaz (Adina) ...

Haldeman-Julius Publications Girard, Kansas ⟨1931⟩

At head of title: Little Blue Book No. 1675 Edited by E. Haldeman-Julius   Printed paper wrapper.

10802. The Art of the Novel   Critical Prefaces ... with an Introduction by Richard P. Blackmur

Charles Scribner's Sons   New York   London MCMXXXIV

Code letter *A* on copyright page. Deposited Nov. 9, 1934.

10803. ... Representative Selections, with Introduction, Bibliography, and Notes by Lyon N. Richardson ...

American Book Company New York   Cincinnati Chicago Boston Atlanta ⟨1941⟩

At head of title: Henry James   On copyright page of the first printing is the symbol: *E.P.I.* Deposited Sept. 9, 1941.

10804. The Great Short Novels of Henry James Edited ... by Philip Rahv

Dial Press Inc. New York ⟨1944⟩

Deposited Nov. 17, 1944.

10805. ... Stories of Writers & Artists Edited with an Introduction by F. O. Matthiessen

A New Directions Book ⟨New York, 1875–1903; *i.e.*, 1944⟩

At head of title: Henry James Bound in cloth. Also occurs with the word *And* instead of the ampersand on the title-page; bound in paper boards, black V cloth shelfback. Sequence not determined.

10806. The Short Stories of Henry James ... Edited ... by Clifton Fadiman

Random House New York ⟨1945⟩

On copyright page: *First Printing* Deposited Oct. 7, 1945.

10807. The American Scene   Together with Three Essays from "Portraits of Places" ... Edited ... by W. H. Auden

New York Charles Scribner's Sons   1946

On copyright page is the code letter: *A*. Deposited Nov. 8, 1946.

10808. Fourteen Stories by Henry James Selected by David Garnett

London Rupert Hart-Davis 1946

10809. Selected Tales of Henry James

London The Richards Press 8 Charles Street St. James's Square ⟨1947⟩

Cloth?

10810. The Spoils of Poynton with A London Life The Chaperon ...

⟨London⟩ John Lehmann MCMXLVII

10811. The Lesson of the Master and Other Stories ...

⟨London⟩ John Lehmann MCMXLVIII

10812. ... Portraits of Places with an Essay on James as a Traveller by George Alvin Finch

Lear Publishers New York ⟨1948⟩

At head of title: Henry James

10813. The Short Stories of Henry James Selected ... by Clifton Fadiman

The Modern Library New York ⟨1948⟩

On copyright page: *First Modern Library Giant Edition 1948*

10814. Ten Short Stories of Henry James Selected, with an Introduction, by Michael Swan

⟨London⟩ John Lehmann MCMXLVIII

10815. ... Selected Short Stories Edited ... by Quentin Anderson

New York   Rinehart & Co., Inc. Toronto ⟨1950⟩

Printed paper wrapper. Deposited Aug. 11, 1950.

10816. ... Selected Fiction Edited ... by Leon Edel

New York E. P. Dutton & Co., Inc. 1953

At head of title: Henry James Deposited May 21, 1953.

10817. ... Autobiography Edited ... by Frederick W. Dupee ...

Criterion Books New York ⟨1956⟩

At head of title: Henry James

BA copy received April 24, 1956. Deposited May 3, 1956. Issued in London by W. H. Allen; according to *English Catalogue* issued Dec. 1956.

10818. ... Selected Short Stories Edited ... by Quentin Anderson Revised

New York Rinehart & Co., Inc. Toronto ⟨1957⟩

At head of title: Henry James Printed paper wrapper. Issued as No. 31 in the *Rinehart Editions* series. Deposited Sept. 16, 1957.

10819. ... Selected Stories Chosen with an Introduction by Gerard Hopkins

London Oxford University Press ⟨1957⟩

At head of title: Henry James   Reviewed in *The Times*, Oct. 24, 1957. In *The World's Classics* series.

10820. The Art of Travel Scenes and Journeys in America, England, France and Italy from the Travel Writings of Henry James Edited ... by Morton Dauwen Zabel

Doubleday Anchor Books Doubleday & Company, Inc., Garden City, New York 1958

On copyright page: *First Edition*   Published June 19, 1958 (publisher's statement). Deposited June 25, 1958.

10821. In the Cage & Other Tales ... Edited ... by Morton Dauwen Zabel

Doubleday Anchor Books Doubleday & Company, Inc. Garden City, New York 1958

Printed paper wrapper. No. A 131 of the series. On copyright page: *First Edition*

10822. ... Guy Domville Play in Three Acts ... ⟨Edited⟩ by Leon Edel

J. B. Lippincott Company Philadelphia & New York ⟨1960⟩

On copyright page: *First Edition*

10823. ... English Hours Edited ... by Alma Louise Lowe ...

The Orion Press New York ⟨1960⟩

At head of title: Henry James

10824. ... Seven Stories and Studies

New York Appleton-Century-Crofts, Inc. ⟨1961⟩

At head of title: Edward Stone ... Editor ... Printed paper wrapper. On copyright page: *621-1* Deposited April 7, 1961.

10825. ... Lady Barberina ⟨sic⟩ and Other Tales ... with Variants, Notes, Introduction and Bibliography by Herbert Ruhm

The Universal Library Grosset & Dunlap New York ⟨1961⟩

At head of title: Henry James Printed paper wrapper. No. UL 116 in *Grosset's Universal Library*. On copyright page: *First Edition, October 1961* See next entry.

10826. ... Lady Barberina ⟨sic⟩ and Other Tales ... with Variants, Notes, Introduction and Bibliography by Herbert Ruhm

The Vanguard Press, Inc. New York ⟨1961⟩

At head of title: Henry James Issued in cloth. On copyright page: *First Edition, October 1961* See preceding entry.

10827. Short Novels of Henry James ... Introduction by E. Hudson Long

Dodd, Mead & Company New York ⟨1961⟩

Deposited Dec. 5, 1961.

10828. Guy Domville A Play in Three Acts ... Comments by Bernard Shaw H. G. Wells Arnold Bennett Preceded by Biographical Chapters ... by Leon Edel

London Rupert Hart-Davis 1961

10829. The Madonna of the Future and Other Early Stories ... Foreword by Willard Thorp

A Signet Classic Published by The New American Library ⟨1962⟩

Printed paper wrapper. On copyright page: *First Printing, March, 1962*

10830. The Complete Tales of Henry James Edited with an Introduction by Leon Edel ...

Rupert Hart-Davis Soho Square London 1962 ⟨–1964⟩

1: *1864–1868*. Imprint dated 1962. Deposited for U. S. copyright (this printing) July 25, 1962.

2: *1868–1872*. Imprint dated 1962. Deposited for U. S. copyright (this printing) July 25, 1962.

3: *1873–1875*. Imprint dated 1962. Deposited for U. S. copyright (this printing) Nov. 9, 1962.

4: *1876–1882*. Imprint dated 1962. Deposited for U. S. copyright (this printing) Nov. 9, 1962.

5: *1883–1884*. Imprint dated 1963. Deposited for U. S. copyright (this printing) Aug. 5, 1963.

6: *1884–1888*. Imprint dated 1963. Deposited for U. S. copyright (this printing) Aug. 5, 1963.

7: *1888–1891*. Imprint dated 1963. Deposited for U. S. copyright (this printing) Oct. 7, 1963.

8: *1891–1892*. Imprint dated 1963. Deposited for U. S. copyright (this printing) Oct. 7, 1963.

9: *1892–1898*. Imprint dated 1964. Deposited for U. S. copyright (this printing) Aug. 27, 1964.

10: *1898–1899*. Imprint dated 1964. Deposited for U. S. copyright (this printing) Aug. 27, 1964.

11: *1900–1903*. Imprint dated 1964. No record of copyright deposit found.

12: *1903–1910*. Imprint dated 1964. No record of copyright deposit found.

10831. The Complete Tales of Henry James Edited with an Introduction by Leon Edel ...

J. B. Lippincott Company Philadelphia and New York ⟨1962⟩ (–⟨1964⟩)

1: *1864–1868*. Imprint dated ⟨1962⟩. Deposited Feb. 8, 1963.

2: *1868–1872*. Imprint dated ⟨1962⟩. Deposited March 4, 1963.

3: *1873–1875*. Imprint dated ⟨1962⟩. Deposited Dec. 17, 1962.

4: *1876–1882*. Imprint dated ⟨1962⟩. Deposited Dec. 17, 1962.

5: *1883–1884*. Imprint dated ⟨1963⟩. Deposited Aug. 8, 1963.

6: *1884–1888*. Imprint dated ⟨1963⟩. Deposited Aug. 8, 1963.

7: *1888–1891*. Imprint dated ⟨1963⟩. Deposited Feb. 17, 1964.

8: *1891–1892*. Imprint dated ⟨1963⟩. Deposited Feb. 17, 1964.

9: *1892–1898*. Imprint dated ⟨1964⟩. Deposited Jan. 7, 1965.

10: *1898–1899*. Imprint dated ⟨1964⟩. Deposited Jan. 7, 1965.

11: *1900–1903*. Imprint dated ⟨1964⟩. Deposited Sept. 28, 1965.

12: *1903–1910*. Imprint dated ⟨1964⟩. Deposited Sept. 28, 1965.

IN THIS SECTION are listed books by authors other than Henry James which contain material by him reprinted from earlier books. See *Section II* for a list of reprints issued under James's name.

Fame's Tribute to Children . . .

Chicago . . . 1892

For comment see BAL, Vol. 1, p. 76.

The Warner Classics Selected from the Introductory Studies Included in Charles Dudley Warner's Library of the World's Best Literature.

New York, Harper's Weekly Club, 93 Fifth Avenue, 1897.

4 Vols. Deposited Oct. 30, 1897.

The International Library of Famous Literature . . . Compiled . . . by Nathan Haskell Dole, Forrest Morgan and Caroline Ticknor . . .

New York   Merrill and Baker   Publishers ⟨1898⟩

For fuller entry see in Sarah Orne Jewett reprints.

Mine Own People by Rudyard Kipling

R. F. Fenno & Company Publishers   9 & 11 E. Sixteenth Street   New York City   1899

. . . The Story of a Child Translated from the French of Pierre Loti by Caroline F. Smith . . .

C. C. Birchard & Company   221 Columbus Avenue   Boston, Mass. ⟨n.d., 1901?⟩

At head: The narrative surpasses in retrospective reach all other records of childish experience. James Sully.

Single cut sheet of laid paper folded to make four pages. Issued as an advertisement.

On p. ⟨2⟩ is a brief extract (in mangled form) from James's "Pierre Loti" in *Essays in London and Elsewhere*, N. Y., 1893, p. 161.

The Library of Oratory Ancient and Modern . . . Chauncey M. Depew . . . Editor-in-Chief . . . in Fifteen Volumes   Volume XV . . .

New York: The Globe Publishing Company 1902

A subscription book and as such probably issued in a variety of bindings and with variant imprints. Also noted with the following imprint: *A. L. Fowle   New York* ⟨*1902*⟩ Deposited (Globe imprint) May 21, 1902.

Short Story Classics (American) . . . Edited by William Patten . . .

. . . New York ⟨1905⟩

5 Vols. For comment see entry No. 6378.

Mine Own People   The Works of Rudyard Kipling

The Nottingham Society   New York   Philadelphia   Chicago ⟨1909⟩

A subscription set; probably issued in a variety of bindings and with varying imprints.

Une Vie by Guy de Maupassant

Boni and Liveright, Inc. Publishers   New York ⟨n.d., 1918⟩

Imitation leather binding. Reprinted and reissued with the imprint: *The Modern Library Publishers New York* ⟨*n.d.*⟩

The Great Modern American Stories . . . Edited . . . by William Dean Howells

New York . . . 1920

For comment see entry No. 6479.

A Book of Long Stories . . . Edited by Arthur H. Nethercot . . .

New York   The Macmillan Company   1927 All Rights Reserved

On copyright page: *Published October, 1927.* Deposited Oct. 6, 1927.

Constance Fenimore Woolson . . . Being Scattered Chapters from the History of the Cooper, Pomeroy, Woolson and Benedict Families, with Extracts from Their Letters and Journals, As Well As Articles and Poems by Constance Fenimore Woolson, Arranged and Edited by Clare Benedict.

London: Ellis, 29, New Bond Street, W. 1. ⟨1930⟩

500 numbered copies only. A reprint (so noted on p. ⟨vi⟩) issued under date ⟨1930⟩ with abbreviated title as follows: *Constance Fenimore Woolson Arranged and Edited by Clare Benedict.*

The Yellow Book   A Selection Compiled by Norman Denny

The Bodley Head   London   The Viking Press New York ⟨1950⟩

SELECTED REFERENCES AND ANA

Another Chapter of "The Bostonians." By Henrietta James ⟨pseud. for ?⟩

Bloomfield, N. J.: S. Morris Hulin, Publisher. 1887.

Printed paper wrapper.

The Novels of Henry James   A Study by Elisabeth Luther Cary with a Bibliography by Frederick A. King

G. P. Putnam's Sons   New York and London The Knickerbocker Press   1905

Bibliography, pp. 189-215.

A Bibliography of the Writings of Henry James by Le Roy Phillips

Boston and New York   Houghton, Mifflin and Company   The Riverside Press, Cambridge MDCCCCVI

250 numbered copies only. Boards, cloth shelfback, paper label on spine. See under 1930 for revised edition.

Henry James   A Critical Study by Ford Madox Hueffer

London   Martin Secker   Number Five John Street Adelphi MCMXIII

Henry James by Rebecca West

London   Nisbet & Co. Ltd. 22 Berners Street, W. ⟨1916⟩

Issued in United States with the imprint: *New York   Henry Holt and Company ⟨1916⟩*

The Method of Henry James by Joseph Warren Beach . . .

New Haven   Yale University Press   London: Humphrey Milford Oxford University Press MDCCCCXVIII

On copyright page: *First published, January, 1918*

Commemorative Tribute to Henry James by Bliss Perry Prepared for the American Academy of Arts and Letters 1921

⟨New York⟩ American Academy of Arts and Letters 1922

Printed paper wrapper.

Henry James at Work by Theodora Bosanquet

Printed and Published by Leonard and Virginia Woolf at The Hogarth Press, 52 Tavistock Square, London. 1924

Printed paper wrapper.

The Pilgrimage of Henry James by Van Wyck Brooks . . .

New York   E. P. Dutton & Company   681 Fifth Avenue ⟨1925⟩

The Tragic Muse   A Play in Three Acts by Hubert Griffith Adapted from the Novel . . . by Henry James

London   George Allen & Unwin Ltd. Museum Street ⟨1927⟩

Paper boards, cloth shelfback, printed paper labels. On copyright page: *First published in 1927*

Berkeley Square   A Play in Three Acts by John L. Balderston (The Plot Suggested by Henry James's Posthumous Fragment, "The Sense of the Past." . . .

New York   The Macmillan Company   1929

On copyright page: *Published November, 1929.*

Henry James's Criticism by Morris Roberts

Cambridge   Harvard University Press   1929

Boards, cloth shelfback.

A Bibliography of the Writings of Henry James by LeRoy Phillips

New York   Coward McCann   1930

Boards, cloth shelfback, printed paper label on spine. 525 numbered copies only. See above under 1906 for first edition of this pioneer work.

. . . The Prefaces of Henry James

Paris Jouve et Cie, Éditeurs 15, Rue Racine, 15   1931

At head of title: Leon Edel . . .   Printed paper wrapper.

The Three Jameses   A Family of Minds . . . by C. Hartley Grattan . . .

Longmans, Green and Co.   London   New York Toronto 1932

On copyright page: *First Edition*

The Modern Fables of Henry James by Edwin Marion Snell

    Cambridge Massachusetts 1935 Harvard University Press

    Printed paper wrapper. *Harvard Honors Theses in English Number 8.*

. . . Criticism in American Periodicals of the Works of Henry James from 1866 to 1916 A Dissertation . . . by Richard Nicholas Foley

    The Catholic University of America Press Washington, D.C. 1944

    At head of title: The Catholic University of America   Printed paper wrapper.

Henry James   The Major Phase by F. O. Matthiessen

    Oxford University Press London New York Toronto 1944

The Question of Henry James   A Collection of Critical Essays Edited by F. W. Dupee

    New York: Henry Holt and Company ⟨1945⟩

    On copyright page: *First Printing*

The James Family Including Selections . . . by F. O. Matthiessen

    New York Alfred A. Knopf 1947

The Legend of the Master Compiled by Simon Nowell-Smith . . .

    Constable London ⟨1947⟩

    On copyright page: *First published 1947* See next entry.

The Legend of the Master Compiled by Simon Nowell-Smith . . .

    New York Charles Scribner's Sons 1948

    On copyright page of first printing: *A* See preceding entry. "Pen-portraits and anecdotes of James are here assembled from upwards of a hundred and fifty contemporary sources, and are so arranged as to illustrate the different manifestations of . . . James . . ."—From the dust jacket.

The Heiress   A Play by Ruth and Augustus Goetz   Suggested by the Henry James Novel Washington Square

    Dramatists Play Service Inc.   New York ⟨1948⟩

The Innocents   A New Play by William Archibald Based on The Turn of the Screw by Henry James . . .

    Coward-McCann, Inc.   New York ⟨1950⟩

    Deposited June 8, 1950.

Henry James 1843–1870   The Untried Years ⟨by⟩ Leon Edel

    J. B. Lippincott Company   Philadelphia New York ⟨1953⟩

    On copyright page: *First Edition   Note:* An ambiguous entry in the *English Catalogue* causes this biography to appear as a work by Henry James titled *The Untried Years.*

A Bibliography of Henry James ⟨by⟩ Leon Edel and Dan H. Laurence

    Rupert Hart-Davis   Soho Square   London 1957

    See below under 1961 for a revised edition.

Child of Fortune by Guy Bolton   Adapted from "Wings of the Dove" by Henry James   A Play in Three Acts

    Dramatists Play Service Inc. ⟨1957⟩

    Printed paper wrapper. Deposited May 13, 1957.

A Bibliography of Henry James ⟨by⟩ Leon Edel and Dan H. Laurence ⟨Second Edition, Revised⟩

    Rupert Hart-Davis   Soho Square   London 1961

    For first edition see above under 1957.

Discovery of a Genius   William Dean Howells and Henry James Compiled and Edited by Albert Mordell . . .

    Twayne Publishers New York ⟨1961⟩

    For comment see entry No. 9882B.

Henry James 1870–1881   The Conquest of London ⟨by⟩ Leon Edel

    J. B. Lippincott Company   Philadelphia New York ⟨1962⟩

    On copyright page: *First Edition*

Henry James 1882–1895   The Middle Years ⟨by⟩ Leon Edel

    J. B. Lippincott Company   Philadelphia New York ⟨1962⟩

    On copyright page: *First Edition*

THOMAS ALLIBONE JANVIER

1 8 4 9 – 1 9 1 3

10832. Stories by American Authors ⟨Vol.⟩ x . . .

New York   Charles Scribner's Sons   1885

"Pancha: A Story of Monterey," pp. ⟨5⟩-44. Collected in *Stories of Old New Spain*, 1891.

Two bindings noted; for comment see entry No. 10567. Also see entry No. 1256.

10833. COLOR STUDIES . . .

NEW YORK   CHARLES SCRIBNER'S SONS   1885

⟨i-vi⟩, ⟨1⟩-227; blank, p. ⟨228⟩; advertisements, pp. ⟨229-233⟩. Laid paper. 6⅞" x 4¹⁵⁄₁₆".

⟨1-15⟩⁸. *Signed:* ⟨-⟩³, ⟨1⟩-11, ⟨12-14⁸, 15⁵⟩.

V cloth: gray; slate-green; tan. White laid end papers. Flyleaves. Top edges stained yellow; or, yellow-orange. *Note:* The spine imprint occurs stamped in blue; or, in brown.

Published Sept. 19, 1885, 1000 copies (publisher's records). Deposited Sept. 26, 1885. Listed PW Oct. 3, 1885. The London (Bickers) edition listed Ath March 27, 1886. Reprinted, 1891, with the addition of "A Mexican Campaign," under the title *Color Studies and a Mexican Campaign;* see below.

H   NYPL

10834. THE MEXICAN GUIDE . . .

NEW YORK   CHARLES SCRIBNER'S SONS   1886

⟨i⟩-⟨x⟩, ⟨1⟩-310. 6¾" x 4⅜".

⟨1-20⟩⁸. *Signed:* ⟨-⟩⁵, ⟨1⟩-2, ⟨3-4⟩, 5-18⁸, 19¹¹.

Leather: black; green. Pale yellow end papers. Flyleaves. Inserted into a pocket of each inner cover is a map. Edges marbled. Four pages of advertisements inserted at front.

Deposited March 8, 1886. For other editions and reprints see under 1887, 1888, 1889, 1890, and 1895.

AAS   Y

10835. The Mexican Guide . . . New Edition ⟨*i.e.,* Second Edition⟩

New York   Charles Scribner's Sons   1887

Leather. One map inserted in flap in each cover. "Preface ⟨for this edition⟩," pp. ⟨iii⟩-v, dated at end *January 1, 1887.*

"In the present edition . . . the greater part of the material, fully two-thirds, is new. The work has been recast . . ."—p. ⟨iii⟩.

Advertised for *to-day* PW Jan. 15, 1887. Deposited Jan. 20, 1887. Listed PW Jan. 22, 1887; Ath April 23, 1887. For comment see preceding entry.

UV

10836. The Mexican Guide . . . Third Edition

New York   Charles Scribner's Sons   1888

Leather. Three maps inserted in covers.

"The Mexican Guide. Supplement for the Year 1888," pp. ⟨xv⟩-xxviii.

Advertised as *just ready* PW Jan. 7, 1888. Deposited Jan. 9, 1888. Listed PW Jan. 21, 1888. For other editions and reprints see under 1886, 1887, 1889, 1890, and 1895.

UV

10837. The Mexican Guide . . . Fourth Edition

New York   Charles Scribner's Sons   1889

"Preface ⟨to the Fourth Edition⟩" p. ⟨iii⟩, dated at end *January, 1889.*

Advertised for Feb. 16 in PW Feb. 16, 1889. Listed PW March 2, 1889. For other editions and reprints see under 1886, 1887, 1888, 1890, and 1895.

UV

10838. . . . A Romance of Tompkins Square . . .

⟨New York: Harper & Brothers, 1889⟩

Caption-title. Title preceded by a captioned illustration.

Supplement to *Harper's Weekly,* April 20, 1889. Issued as a separate? Noted only as part of the magazine.

Janvier's "A Romance of Tompkins Square,"
pp. ⟨313⟩-316. Collected in *The Uncle of an
Angel* . . . , 1891.

H NYPL

10839. The Mexican Guide . . . Fifth Edition

New York   Charles Scribner's Sons   1890

"Supplement for the Year 1890," pp. ⟨xiii⟩-xvi.

Deposited Jan. 18, 1890. Reprinted under date
1891 and 1893. Sheets of a late printing of this
edition also issued with a cancel title-leaf dated
1895. For other editions see under 1886, 1887,
1888, and 1889.

AAS

10840. Jorge Isaacs   María   A South American
Romance . . . Translation by Rollo Ogden . . .
Introduction by Thomas A. Janvier

New York   Harper & Brothers, Franklin
Square   1890

"Introduction," pp. ⟨v⟩-xi, dated *February 5,
1890.*

Listed PW March 15, 1890; PC April 15, 1890.

AAS   H   Y

10841. THE AZTEC TREASURE-HOUSE
A ROMANCE OF CONTEMPORANEOUS
ANTIQUITY . . .

NEW YORK   HARPER & BROTHERS, FRANKLIN
SQUARE   1890

⟨i⟩-⟨xii⟩, ⟨13⟩-446, 2 pp. advertisements. Frontispiece and 18 plates inserted. 7⅜" x 4¹⁵⁄₁₆".

⟨1⟩-28⁸.

V cloth: olive-green. Wove paper end papers.
Also laid paper end papers? Flyleaves.

A copy in H presented by Janvier to his wife,
the dedicatee, July 1, 1890. Listed PW July 5,
1890. The London (Sampson Low) edition announced Ath Sept. 27, 1890; listed Ath Nov. 1,
1890.

H NYPL

10842. STORIES OF OLD NEW SPAIN . . .

NEW YORK   D. APPLETON AND COMPANY   1891

CLOTH

⟨1⟩-326; 10 pp. advertisements. Printed on
mixed laid and wove papers. Frontispiece inserted. 7¹⁄₁₆" x 4¾".

⟨1⟩-21⁸.

V cloth: greenish-gray; tan. Green-coated on
white end papers. Tan-coated on white end papers. Laid; or, wove paper flyleaves.

PAPER WRAPPER

Pagination and collation as above. Printed on
mixed laid and wove papers. No frontispiece.
7" x 4¾".

Printed terra-cotta paper wrapper. Issued under
date April 15, 1891, as No. 71 of *Appletons'
Town and Country Library.*

Advertised as a new publication (in cloth and
wrapper) PW April 18, 1891. Copy in wrapper
deposited April 24, 1891. A copy at BA, in cloth,
received April 29, 1891. Listed (in cloth and
wrapper) PW May 2, 1891. The London (Osgood,
McIlvaine) edition advertised as *in the press* PC
April 25, 1891; listed Ath June 20, 1891.

UV (cloth; wrapper)   Y (cloth)

10843. COLOR STUDIES AND A MEXICAN
CAMPAIGN . . .

NEW YORK   CHARLES SCRIBNER'S SONS   1891

Reprint of "Color Studies;" see under 1885.
First edition for "A Mexican Campaign," pp.
⟨231⟩-391. *Note:* In all examined copies the
title-leaf is a cancel.

CLOTH

⟨i-vi⟩, ⟨1⟩-391, blank leaf. Wove paper. 7⅜" x
4⅞".

⟨1-25⟩⁸. *Signed:* ⟨-⟩³, ⟨1⟩-11, ⟨12-15⟩, 16-24⁸,
25⁵.

Two bindings noted; the sequence presented is
probable.

A

Tan V cloth shelfback, gray linen sides printed
with an arrangement of squares and florets in
maroon, blue, gray-blue, and gold. The cloth,
probably hand-blocked, varies in pattern. The
front cover (on the tan V cloth) lettered in blue
outlined in red. The dedication copy (at H)
inscribed June 4, 1891, thus. Another copy at
H received June 11, 1891, thus. Top edges plain.

B

Leaf measures 6¹⁵⁄₁₆" scant x 4⅞". Red V cloth
shelfback, mottled pink V cloth sides. The front
cover (on the mottled pink V cloth) lettered in
silver outlined in red. Top edges stained yellow.
A copy thus at Y inscribed by Janvier April 7,
1893.

PAPER WRAPPER

Pagination and collation as above. Printed on
laid paper. Leaf: 7⅝" full x 4¹⁵⁄₁₆" scant.

Printed yellow paper wrapper.

A copy in cloth deposited June 4, 1891. A copy
in H (Binding A) presented by Janvier to his

wife, the dedicatee, June 4, 1891. Noted as *just issued* PW June 6, 1891. Advertised (in cloth and in wrapper) PW June 6, 1891. A copy in H (Binding A) received June 11, 1891. Listed (in cloth and in wrapper) PW June 13, 1891.

AAS (Binding A)   H (Binding A)   UV (Binding B; wrapper)   Y (Bindings A, B)

10844. THE UNCLE OF AN ANGEL AND OTHER STORIES ...

NEW YORK   HARPER & BROTHERS, FRANKLIN SQUARE 1891

<i-x>, <1>-287; blank, p. <288>; 4 pp. advertisements. Frontispiece and 14 plates inserted; all reckoned in the printed pagination. Other illustrations in the text. 7³⁄₁₆″ x 4¹³⁄₁₆″.

<->⁴, <1>-16⁸, 17⁴.

S cloth: pinkish-brown; tan. White laid end papers.

A copy in H presented by Janvier to his wife, the dedicatee, July 24, 1891. Deposited July 24, 1891. Noted as *nearly ready* PW July 25, 1891. A copy at BA received July 27, 1891. Listed PW Aug. 1, 1891. The London edition (not seen; possibly an import distributed by Brentano) announced for *immediate publication* PC Oct. 31, 1891. An edition (sewed, 2/6) listed Ath Oct. 24, 1891.

Reissued as No. 707 in *Harper's Franklin Square Library*, under date *August, 1891*. Deposited Aug. 26, 1891. Noted as added to the *Franklin Square Library* PW Aug. 29, 1891. Printed blue paper wrapper.

AAS H NYPL

10845. Flower o' the Vine   Romantic Ballads and Sospiri di Roma   By William Sharp With Introduction by Thomas A. Janvier

Charles L. Webster and Company Publishers New York MDCCCXCII

"Introduction," pp. v-xii, dated *April 7, 1892*.

Advertised as *published today* PW May 7, 1892. Deposited May 11, 1892. Listed PW May 14, 1892.

AAS H LC NYPL Y

10846. The Armies of To-Day   A Description of the Armies of the   Leading Nations at the Present Time ...

New York   Harper & Brothers Publishers 1893

"The Mexican Army," pp. <361>-396.

Deposited Nov. 16, 1892. Listed PW Dec. 3, 1892.

H

10847. AN EMBASSY TO PROVENCE ...

NEW YORK   THE CENTURY CO.   1893

<i-xii>, 1-132. Pp. <v-vi> excised and frontispiece tipped to stub. 7⁹⁄₁₆″ x 5⅛″.

<->⁶, <1>-8⁸, 9². Leaf <->₃ excised and frontispiece tipped to stub.

Four forms of the binding have been noted. The sequence (if any) is not known and the designations are for identification only.

A

White V cloth. Stamped in gold only. Top edges gilded. Leaf <->₃ excised and frontispiece tipped to stub. A copy in H presented by Janvier to his wife, the dedicatee, Sept. 6, 1893.

B

Orange V cloth. Stamped in gold and green. Top edges gilded. Leaf <->₃ excised and frontispiece tipped to stub. The deposit copies thus; also a copy at BA received Oct. 17, 1893.

C

Orange V cloth. Stamped in gold and green. Top edges gilded. Leaf <->₃ present. Frontispiece inserted.

D

Orange V cloth. Stamped in gold and green. Top edges plain. Leaf <->₃ present. Frontispiece inserted.

Note: The London (Unwin) issue (American sheets with altered imprint) is in brown-orange cloth, otherwise as Binding C.

Noted as *in preparation* PW July 1, 1893. A copy in H (Binding A) presented by Janvier to his wife, the dedicatee, Sept. 6, 1893. Deposited (Binding B) Sept. 26, 1893. A copy in BA (Binding B) received Oct. 17, 1893. Listed PW Oct. 21, 1893. The London (Unwin) edition (American sheets) announced PC Oct. 14, 1893; listed Bkr Dec. 15, 1893.

AAS (B)   BA (B)   H (A, B, D)   LC (B, being a deposit copy)   NYPL (C)   UV (C)   Y (B, D)

10848. THE WOMEN'S CONQUEST OF NEW-YORK BY A MEMBER OF THE COMMITTEE OF SAFETY OF 1908 ...

NEW YORK   HARPER & BROTHERS PUBLISHERS 1953 <*i.e.,* 1894>

<i-iv>, <1>-84. 7⁵⁄₁₆″ scant x 4⅞″.

<->², 1-5⁸, 6².

Printed white paper wrapper.

Harper's Franklin Square Library No. 750. Extra. June, 1894 . . .—p. ⟨i⟩.

A copy at NYPL inscribed by Janvier July 6, 1894. Deposited July 7, 1894. Listed PW July 21, 1894.

LC

10849. IN OLD NEW YORK . . .

NEW YORK   HARPER & BROTHERS PUBLISHERS 1894

⟨i⟩-⟨xii⟩, ⟨1⟩-285; blank, p. ⟨286⟩; 2 pp. advertisements. Illustrated. Six 2-page maps inserted. 7¼″ x 4⅞″.

⟨-⟩⁶, 1-⟨2⟩, 3-4, ⟨5⟩, 6, ⟨7⟩, 8-9, ⟨10-12⟩, 13, ⟨14⟩, 15-18⁸.

V cloth: brown. White laid end papers.

Noted as *nearly ready* PW Aug. 25, 1894. Deposited Aug. 25, 1894. A copy at BA received Aug. 30, 1894. Listed PW Sept. 1, 1894.

AAS   BA   H   NYPL

10850. Saint Antonio of the Gardens . . . with a Translation into Provençal by Miss Mary Girard . . .

Avignon   House of J. Roumanille, Publisher 19, Saint Agricol Street 1895

Text in English and Provençal on opposing pages; the English text reprinted from *Stories of Old New Spain,* 1891.

Printed paper wrapper.

Limited to 10 numbered copies *sus papié d'Oulando* and 150 copies *sus papié tencha.*

A copy at Y inscribed by Catharine Janvier Christmas, 1895.

H (tencha) NYPL (tencha) UV (Oulando) Y (tencha)

10851. The Mexican Guide . . . Sixth Edition

New York   Charles Scribner's Sons 1895

Reprint.

Sheets of a printing of the *Fifth Edition* issued with cancel title-leaf. See under 1890 for first printing of *Fifth Edition.* For other editions see under 1886, 1887, 1888, 1889.

FLP

10852. The Reds of the Midi   An Episode of the French Revolution Translated from the Provençal of Félix Gras by Catharine A. Janvier with an Introduction by Thomas A. Janvier

New York   D. Appleton and Company   1896

"Introduction," pp. v-xvii.

Noted as *shortly* PW Jan. 11, 1896. Advertised as *ready on Monday* ⟨April 4⟩ PW April 4, 1896. A copy in H received April 8, 1896. A copy in BA received April 15, 1896. Listed PW April 18, 1896.

AAS   H   Y

10853. Library of the World's Best Literature Ancient and Modern Charles Dudley Warner Editor . . . Thirty Volumes . . .

New York   R. S. Peale and J. A. Hill Publishers ⟨1896–1899⟩

Reprint save for "The Episode of the Marques de Valdeflores," Vol. 14, pp. 8118-8143. Collected in *At the Casa Napoleon,* 1914.

Vol. 14 deposited July 27, 1897. For comment see entry No. 10624.

10854. IN THE SARGASSO SEA   A NOVEL
Issued simultaneously in New York and in London?

NEW YORK

IN THE SARGASSO SEA   A NOVEL . . .

NEW YORK AND LONDON   HARPER & BROTHERS PUBLISHERS 1898

⟨i⟩-⟨viii⟩, 1-⟨293⟩; blank, p. ⟨294⟩; 2 pp. advertisements. 7³⁄₁₆″ x 4⅞″.

⟨-⟩⁴, A-I, K-L, ⟨M⟩, N-S⁸, T⁴.

EC cloth: red. White laid end papers.

Note: A variant has been seen; bound in green V cloth; p. v not paged. The page is numbered in all examined copies in red EC cloth, and in a surviving (now rebound) copyright deposit copy. The folio is not present in the 1899 printing. Further study indicated.

LONDON

IN THE SARGASSO SEA   A NOVEL . . .

LONDON AND NEW YORK   HARPER & BROTHERS PUBLISHERS 1898

⟨i-viii⟩, 1-⟨293⟩; blank, p. ⟨294⟩; pp. ⟨295-296⟩ excised. 7⅜″ x 5″.

⟨-⟩⁴, A-I, K-L, ⟨M⟩, N-S⁸, T⁴. Leaf T₄ excised.

V cloth: blue; green. Top edges gilt.

Printed from the American setting. On p. ⟨ii⟩: *Printed in New York, U.S.A.*

London: Listed Ath July 9, 1898. Advertised for *next week* Ath July 9, 1898. A copy in H presented by Janvier to Mrs. Janvier (the dedicatee), July 16, 1898; another (also in H) presented by Janvier to Charles E. Dana, July 16, 1898. Advertised as though published Ath July 16, 1898.

New York: Deposited July 15, 1898. BA copy received July 19, 1898. Listed PW July 23, 1898.

AAS (N.Y.) H (N.Y., London) NYPL (N.Y.) Y (variant N. Y.)

10855. Fifty-Two Stories of Heroism in Life and Action for Boys ... Edited by Alfred H. Miles ...

London   Hutchinson & Co. Paternoster Row, E. C.   ⟨1899⟩

Not seen.

"The Polidore Lot," pp. 336-344.

Issued in October according to *English Catalogue*. BMU copy received Nov. 28, 1899.

10856. THE PASSING OF THOMAS   IN THE ST. PETER'S SET   AT THE GRAND HÔTEL DU PARADIS   THE FISH OF MONSIEUR QUISSARD   LE BON ONCLE D'AMÉRIQUE   FIVE STORIES ...

NEW YORK AND LONDON   HARPER & BROTHERS, PUBLISHERS 1900

⟨i-xii⟩, ⟨1⟩-⟨181⟩; blank, p. ⟨182⟩; advertisements, pp. ⟨183-184⟩. Frontispiece and 6 plates inserted; other illustrations in text. 7³⁄₁₆″ full x 4⅞″.

⟨-⟩⁶, ⟨A⟩-I, K-L⁸, M⁴.

V cloth: blue-gray. White laid end papers.

Deposited June 1, 1900. A copy at H received June 2, 1900. Listed PW June 9, 1900.

AAS   H

10857. IN GREAT WATERS   FOUR STORIES ...

NEW YORK AND LONDON   HARPER & BROTHERS PUBLISHERS 1901

Title-page in black and orange.

⟨i-viii⟩, ⟨1⟩-⟨223⟩. Laid paper. Frontispiece and 7 plates inserted. 7⅜″ x 4⅞″ scant.

⟨-⟩⁴, ⟨A⟩-I, K-O⁸.

C cloth: green. H cloth: green. White laid end papers.

On copyright page: *November, 1901.* Deposited Nov. 8, 1901. A copy in H presented by Janvier to his wife, the dedicatee, Nov. 8, 1901. A copy

in AAS inscribed by early owner Nov. 15, 1901. Listed PW Nov. 16, 1901.

AAS   BA   H   NYPL   Y

10858. THE CHRISTMAS KALENDS OF PROVENCE AND SOME OTHER PROVENÇAL FESTIVALS ...

HARPER & BROTHERS PUBLISHERS   NEW YORK AND LONDON   1902

Title-page in black and orange.

⟨i⟩-⟨viii⟩, ⟨1⟩-⟨262⟩, blank leaf. Frontispiece and 15 plates inserted. 7⅜″ x 4⅞″.

⟨-⟩⁴, ⟨1⟩-12, ⟨13⟩, 14-16⁸, 17⁴.

T cloth: green. White laid end papers.

On copyright page: *Published November, 1902.* Deposited Nov. 7, 1902. A copy in H presented by Janvier to his wife, the dedicatee, Nov. 8, 1902. A copy in BA received Nov. 11, 1902. Listed PW Nov. 15, 1902. London (Harper, 1903) edition advertised for Oct. 14 in Ath Oct. 10, 1903; listed Ath Oct. 24, 1903; advertised Ath Nov. 7, 1903. *Note:* BAL has found no evidence to support the listing in *The English Catalogue* which describes the book as a Dec. 1902, publication.

AAS   H   Y

10859. THE DUTCH FOUNDING OF NEW YORK ...

NEW YORK AND LONDON   HARPER & BROTHERS PUBLISHERS 1903

Title-page in black and red.

⟨i-ii⟩, ⟨i⟩-⟨vi⟩, 1-⟨218⟩, blank leaf. Frontispiece with printed tissue and 11 plates inserted. 8¹¹⁄₁₆″ x 5¹³⁄₁₆″.

⟨-⟩⁴, ⟨1⟩-13⁸, 14⁶.

Three bindings noted; the following sequence is probable:

A

S cloth: blue. Brown leather shelfback. White label on front. Stamped in gold. Top edges gilt. White laid end papers. A copy thus in BA received Oct. 13, 1903. A copy in H presented by Janvier to his wife, Nov. 1903.

B (C?)

S cloth: blue. Stamped in gold and blind. Top edges gilt. White laid end papers.

C (B?)

V cloth: green. Unstamped. Paper label on spine printed in red. Top edges plain. White laid end papers.

On copyright page: *Published October, 1903.*
Announced PW Sept. 26, 1903. Deposited Oct.
2, 1903. Advertised as *new* PW Oct. 3, 1903. A
copy at BA (Binding A) received Oct. 13, 1903.
Listed PW Dec. 5, 1903.

AAS (B)   BA (A)   H (A,B,C)   UV (C)

10860. Mark Twain's Library of Humor
Women and Things . . .

Harper & Brothers Publishers New York and
London MCMVI

"Santa Fé Charley's Kindergarten," pp. ⟨47⟩-
81. Collected in *Santa Fé's Partner,* 1907.

For comment see entry No. 3667.

10861. Under the Sunset Harper's Novelettes
Edited by William Dean Howells and Henry
Mills Alden

Harper & Brothers Publishers New York and
London 1906

"The Sage-brush Hen," pp. ⟨18⟩-42. Collected
in *Santa Fé's Partner,* 1907.

For comment see entry No. 9770.

10862. Mark Twain's Library of Humor A
Little Nonsense . . .

Harper & Brothers Publishers New York and
London MCMVI

"Maternal Instinct," pp. ⟨38⟩-47.

For comment see entry No. 3669.

10863. Fifty-Two Pioneer Stories All round the
Compass. Stories of Travellers . . . Edited by
Alfred H. Miles . . .

London: Hutchinson & Co., 34, Paternoster
Row. ⟨1906⟩

Not seen.

"The Discovery of America," pp. 45-53.

BMU copy received Nov. 23, 1906.

10864. SANTA FÉ'S PARTNER BEING
SOME MEMORIALS OF EVENTS IN A
NEW-MEXICAN TRACK-END TOWN . . .

NEW YORK AND LONDON   HARPER & BROTHERS
PUBLISHERS 1907

Title-page in black and orange.

⟨i-x⟩, 1-⟨237⟩. Frontispiece and 7 plates inserted. 7⅜″ x 5″.

⟨-⟩⁴, ⟨1⟩-15⁸.

Two states noted:

1: As above. Leaf ⟨-⟩₄ not a cancel. First illustration listed on p. ⟨vii⟩: *Her Left Hand* . . .

2: As above but leaf ⟨-⟩₄ is a cancel. First illustration listed on p. ⟨vii⟩: *Look! Look!* . . .

V cloth: blue.

On copyright page: *Published September, 1907.*
Deposited Sept. 11, 1907. A copy in H presented
by Janvier to his wife, the dedicatee, Sept. 12,
1907. BA copy received Sept. 18, 1907. Listed
PW Sept. 21, 1907. The London (Harper) edition
advertised as *shortly* Ath Oct. 5, 1907; listed Ath
Nov. 23, 1907.

AAS (2nd)   BA (2nd)   H (1st)   LC (1st)   NYPL
(2nd)   UV (2nd)   Y (2nd)

10865. HENRY HUDSON A BRIEF STATE-
MENT OF HIS AIMS AND HIS ACHIEVE-
MENTS . . . TO WHICH IS ADDED A
NEWLY-DISCOVERED PARTIAL REC-
ORD NOW FIRST PUBLISHED OF THE
TRIAL OF THE MUTINEERS BY WHOM
HE AND OTHERS WERE ABANDONED
TO THEIR DEATH

NEW YORK AND LONDON   HARPER & BROTHERS
PUBLISHERS 1909

⟨i-ii⟩, ⟨i⟩-⟨xvi⟩, 1-⟨148⟩. Frontispiece inserted.
9 plates in text not considered in the printed
pagination. 6⅞″ scant x 4⁷⁄₁₆″.

⟨-⟩⁴, ⟨1⟩-9, ⟨10⟩-11⁸.

V cloth: blue. Stamped in white and blue.
Illustration pasted to front.

Note: Also noted in a variant (remainder?) binding of red V cloth stamped in black. In some
copies leaf ⟨-⟩₁ excised.

On copyright page: *Published August, 1909.* A
copy in H presented by Janvier to his wife, the
dedicatee, Aug. 19, 1909. NYPL copy received
Aug. 19, 1909. Deposited Aug. 20, 1909. Listed
PW Aug. 28, 1909. The London (Harper) edition
advertised as *new and forthcoming* Ath Sept.
11, 1909; listed Ath Sept. 11, 1909.

AAS (variant)   BA   H   UV (variant)   Y

10866. LEGENDS OF THE CITY OF MEX-
ICO . . .

HARPER & BROTHERS PUBLISHERS   NEW YORK
AND LONDON MCMX

Title-page in black and orange.

⟨i⟩-⟨xxii⟩, 1-⟨165⟩; 2 blank leaves. Frontispiece,
title-page (not considered in the pagination),
and 12 plates inserted. Frontispiece and title-
leaf are conjugates. Printed on uncalendered
paper save for the title-leaf, frontispiece, and

the inserted illustrations, all of which are on calendered paper. $8\frac{11}{16}$" x $5\frac{13}{16}$".

⟨-⟩, 1-9, ⟨10⟩-11⁸.

V cloth: green. Lettering in gold.

Note: Also noted in a variant (remainder?) binding of yellow V cloth, lettering in black.

On copyright page: *Published January, 1910.* NYPL copy received Jan. 14, 1910. A copy in H presented by Janvier to his wife, the dedicatee, Jan. 15, 1910. Listed PW Jan. 22, 1910. The London (Harper) edition listed Bkr April 1, 1910.

AAS BA H (both) NYPL

10867. FROM THE SOUTH OF FRANCE THE ROSES OF MONSIEUR ALPHONSE THE POODLE OF MONSIEUR GÁILLARD THE RECRUDESCENCE OF MADAME VIC MADAME JOLICOEUR'S CAT A CONSOLATE GIANTESS ...

HARPER & BROTHERS PUBLISHERS NEW YORK AND LONDON MCMXII

⟨i-xii⟩, ⟨1⟩-⟨235⟩. Frontispiece. 7 plates inserted. $7\frac{5}{16}$" x $4\frac{7}{8}$".

⟨1⟩¹¹, 2-15⁸, 16¹. *Note:* Sig. ⟨1⟩ consists of a gathering of 8 leaves of bookstock, extended to 11 leaves by the insertion of 3 leaves on coated paper; *i.e.*, the frontispiece and title-leaf, which are conjugates, and the inserted dedication leaf.

V cloth: blue. Goldstamped.

Note: Two variant (remainder?) bindings have been noted. No sequence has been determined, and the designations are for identification only.

Variant A

V cloth: green. Stamped in black only.

Variant B

Flexible V cloth: red. Stamped in black only.

On copyright page: *Published May, 1912* A copy at H presented by Janvier to his wife, the dedicatee, May 1, 1912. Deposited May 11, 1912. A copy at NYPL inscribed by Janvier May 12, 1912. Listed PW May 18, 1912. The London (Harper) edition listed Bkr June 7, 1912.

AAS (Variant A) BA H NYPL UV (Variant B) Y

10868. AT THE CASA NAPOLEON ...

HARPER & BROTHERS PUBLISHERS NEW YORK AND LONDON MCMXIV

⟨iii⟩-⟨xvi⟩, 1-⟨226⟩. Frontispiece and 8 plates inserted. $7\frac{5}{16}$" x $4\frac{7}{8}$".

⟨1⟩-15⁸.

V cloth: blue. Goldstamped. *Note:* Also noted in a variant (remainder?) binding of blue-gray V cloth, blackstamped.

On copyright page: *Published June, 1914* and code letters: *E-O* (signifying printed May, 1914). Deposited June 8, 1914. A copy at BA received June 9, 1914. Listed PW June 20, 1914. The London (Harper) edition listed Bkr July 3, 1914.

BA H (trade; variant) NYPL Y (variant)

10869. The Second St. Nicholas Anthology Edited by Henry Steele Commager

Random House New York ⟨1950⟩

"The Bilged Midshipman," pp. 264-271.

For comment see entry No. 821b.

REPRINTS

The following publication contains material by Janvier reprinted from an earlier book.

Short Story Classics (American) ... Edited by William Patten ...

... New York ⟨1905⟩

5 Vols. For comment see entry No. 6378.

ANA

1877 Evening Bulletin Carrier's Annual Address.

⟨n.p., Philadelphia Evening Bulletin, 1877⟩

Anonymous. Single cut sheet of unwatermarked gray wove paper, folded to make four pages. Printed throughout in blue; a gold frame on each page. $8\frac{1}{4}$" x $6\frac{7}{8}$". The above on p. ⟨1⟩; text, pp. ⟨3-4⟩.

By Janvier? A copy was located in Janvier's collection of his own publications (in H).

Letter, *The Evening and Sunday Bulletin* (Philadelphia), Feb. 2, 1965, to BAL: "Thomas Allibone Janvier was on the *Bulletin* staff about 1877 and may have written the Carrier's Address, but we have no confirmation of this."

THOMAS A. JANVIER
Entry No. 10866
Much Reduced
(Harvard University Library)

SARAH ORNE JEWETT

(Alice C. Eliot)

1 8 4 9 – 1 9 0 9

Caution: Do not confuse Sarah Orne Jewett with Mrs. Sophia Orne Johnson, author of *The New York Fashion Book of Etiquette, a Compendium of Social Knowledge,* New York ⟨1887⟩, and author of several pieces on flowers and gardening which were published in *The Independent* (New York). Certain of her pieces were signed with the initials *S.O.J.*

10870. The Tonic ...

⟨Portland, Maine, 1873⟩

"Birds' Nests." In issue of June 11, 1873.

"Doctors and Patients." In issue of June 12, 1873.

"Protoplasm and House-Cleaning." In issue of June 17, 1873.

For comment see entry No. 8885.

10871. DEEPHAVEN ...

BOSTON: JAMES R. OSGOOD AND COMPANY, LATE TICKNOR & FIELDS, AND FIELDS, OSGOOD, & CO. 1877.

Title-page in black and red.

According to the publisher's records there were five printings in 1877: 1st, March 1, 1877, 1280 copies; 2nd, May 9, 1877, 500 copies; 3rd, June 12, 1877, 500 copies; 4th, marked *Fourth Edition,* Aug. 1, 1877, 500 copies; 5th, marked *Fifth Edition,* Sept. 3, 1877, 500 copies.

First (also Second?) Printing

⟨i-ii⟩, ⟨1⟩-255, blank leaf. 5⅞″ scant x 4¹⁄₁₆″.

⟨1²⟩, 2-17⁸⟩. *Signed:* ⟨-⟩¹, ⟨1⟩-10¹², 11⁹. *Also signed:* ⟨-⟩¹, ⟨A⟩-P⁸, ⟨Q⟩¹.

P. 65, line 16: ... *was/*

Third (also Second?) Printing

Pagination and collation as above.

P. 65, line 16: ... *so /*

S cloth: green; mauve. Blue-black-coated on white end papers. Green-coated on white end papers. Edges stained red.

Advertised as *in a few days* PW April 7, 1877. Listed PW April 14, 1877.

AAS (*was* reading) BPL (*so* reading) H (*was* reading) NYPL (*was* reading)

10872. Happy Days for Boys and Girls ... Contributions by Louisa M. Alcott, Alice and Phoebe Carey ... and Others.

Philadelphia: Porter & Coates, 822 Chestnut Street. ⟨1877⟩

"The Orchard's Grand-mother," pp. 9-17.

For comment see entry No. 2859.

10873. The Home Budget ... Vol. 1. No. 3.

Portsmouth, N. H., July 17, 1878 ...

Caption-title. The above at head of p. ⟨1⟩.

An occasional newspaper. *Not seen.* Entry on the basis of a photographic copy. A copy of the original is in New Hampshire Historical Society, Concord, New Hampshire.

Contains Jewett's "Boat Song." For separate publication as sheet music see below under 1879. Collected in *Verses,* 1916.

10874. PLAY DAYS. A BOOK OF STORIES FOR CHILDREN ...

BOSTON: HOUGHTON, OSGOOD AND COMPANY. THE RIVERSIDE PRESS, CAMBRIDGE. 1878.

⟨1⟩-213, blank leaf. 6¾″ full x 5⅜″.

⟨1⟩-13⁸, 14⁴.

S cloth: brown; red. Brown-coated on white end papers. Flyleaves.

According to the publisher's records, 1684 copies printed Oct. 18, 1878. Noted for *this week* PW Oct. 26, 1878. Listed PW Nov. 2, 1878.

H NYPL

10875. Boat Song ... Music by Richd. Hoffman ...

New-York, G. Schirmer ... 1879 ...

Sheet music. Cover-title. Plate number 2146.

See *The Home Budget,* 1878, above.

"Mrs. Fields has just written me that you, I mean *The Atlantic,* took the boat song away to be printed. I'm afraid you wont ⟨*sic*⟩ want it, for it is already in print. I gave it to a little paper that was published at a fair in Portsmouth, and Hoffman the New York pianist saw it by chance and set it to music and it was afterward published by some music publishers. I am very sorry, for I wish it could be in the *Atlantic* and this all puts it out of the question, doesn't it? I wrote it for the *Atlantic* to begin with, strangely enough. Mr. Howells sent to me for some verses at the time when he had a musical department in the magazine, but he didn't like my boat song though I have always been fond of it myself ... —Letter, Jewett to Thomas Bailey Aldrich, Feb. 20, ⟨1888?⟩; original in H.

Deposited April 9, 1879.

LC

10876. OLD FRIENDS AND NEW ...

BOSTON: HOUGHTON, OSGOOD AND COMPANY. THE RIVERSIDE PRESS, CAMBRIDGE. 1879.

⟨i-iv⟩, ⟨1⟩-269. 5¹³⁄₁₆″ x 4¼″.

⟨1⁹, 2-17⁸⟩. Leaf ⟨1⟩₁ excised; ⟨1⟩₃ (title-leaf) inserted.

Two printings noted:

1

As above. On Sept. 13, 1879, 1000 copies printed (publisher's records). The author's copy (in H) inscribed Oct. 13, 1879, thus. A copy thus at AAS inscribed by an early owner Oct. 25, 1879.

2

⟨i-ii⟩, ⟨1⟩-269.

⟨1-17⟩⁸.

500 copies printed Oct. 31, 1879 (publisher's records).

S cloth: blue; brown; green. Black-coated on white end papers. Green-coated on white end papers. Flyleaves. Edges stained red.

Printed Sept. 13, 1879. Advertised for October

11 PW Sept. 27, 1879. Author's own copy at H inscribed Oct. 13, 1879. Listed PW Oct. 18, 1879.

AAS (1st) H (1st) LC (2nd) UV (1st; 2nd)

10877. The New England Story-Book. Stories by Famous New England Authors: Mrs. A. D. Whitney ... Sarah O. Jewett ... Elizabeth Stuart Phelps, Celia Thaxter ... E. L. Bynner ... Louise Chandler Moulton ... Etc.

Boston: D. Lothrop and Company, Franklin Street, Corner of Hawley. ⟨1880⟩

Unpaged.

Contains "Cake Crumbs." Also in (reprinted from?) *Wide Awake Pleasure Book* ⟨Vol. 10⟩, Boston ⟨1880⟩. For a comment on *The Wide Awake Pleasure Books* see BAL, Vol. 1, p. 73.

Listed PW Nov. 13, 1880.

UV Y

10878. COUNTRY BY-WAYS ...

BOSTON HOUGHTON, MIFFLIN AND COMPANY THE RIVERSIDE PRESS, CAMBRIDGE 1881

Title-page in black and red.

⟨i-viii⟩, ⟨1⟩-249. 5⅞″ full x 4¼″ full.

⟨a-b⟩¹, ⟨c⟩², 1-15⁸, 10⁴ ⟨*sic*⟩, ⟨17⟩¹.

S cloth: blue; green. V cloth: blue. Black-coated on white end papers. Blue-coated on white end papers. Flyleaves. Covers bevelled. Top edges gilded.

According to the publisher's records, 2000 copies printed Oct. 12, 1881. Advertised for Oct. 19 PW Oct. 15, 1881. The author's own copy (in H) inscribed Oct. 20, 1881. A copy at BA received Oct. 24, 1881. Listed PW Oct. 29, 1881. Deposited Nov. 21, 1881. The London (Trübner) edition (American sheets?) noted as received Ath Jan. 21, 1882.

AAS H

10879. The Sword and the Pen ...

Boston ... 1881 ...

"At Waking," No. 7, p. ⟨1⟩.

An occasional newspaper. For comment see entry No. 123.

10880. Katy's Birthday by Sara ⟨*sic*⟩ O. Jewett. With Other Stories by Famous Authors

Boston D. Lothrop and Company 32 Franklin Street ⟨1883⟩

Contains "Katy's Birthday."

Deposited Oct. 24, 1883. For comment see entry No. 3792.

10881. THE MATE OF THE DAYLIGHT AND FRIENDS ASHORE . . .

BOSTON   HOUGHTON, MIFFLIN AND COMPANY NEW YORK: 11 EAST SEVENTEENTH STREET   THE RIVERSIDE PRESS, CAMBRIDGE 1884

Title-page in black and red.

⟨i-viii⟩, ⟨1⟩-254. Laid paper. 6″ x 4⁵⁄₁₆″.

⟨1², 2-17⁸, 18¹⟩. *Signed:* ⟨-⟩⁴, 1-13, ⟨14⟩-15⁸, 16⁷.

Green S cloth sides, brown V cloth shelfback. Green-coated on white end papers. Flyleaves of bookstock. Top edges gilded.

According to the publisher's records, 1500 copies printed Nov. 17, 1883. A copy at H received Nov. 22, 1883. Deposited Nov. 24, 1883. Listed PW Dec. 15, 1883. Noticed by Ath July 12, 1884.

H NYPL

10882. A COUNTRY DOCTOR . . .

BOSTON   HOUGHTON, MIFFLIN AND COMPANY NEW YORK: 11 EAST SEVENTEENTH STREET   THE RIVERSIDE PRESS, CAMBRIDGE 1884

⟨i-viii⟩, ⟨1⟩-351; plus: 12 pp. advertisements. Laid paper. 7″ x 4⁹⁄₁₆″.

⟨-⟩⁴, ⟨1-14¹², 15⁸, plus: 16⁶⟩. *Signed:* ⟨-⟩⁴, 1-22⁸; plus: ⟨23⟩⁶.

S cloth: green. Gray-coated on white end papers. Laid paper flyleaf at back of some copies.

According to publisher's records, 1500 copies printed June 5, 1884. Advertised for *next week* PW June 7, 1884. Listed PW June 21, 1884. Reviewed Ath Aug. 30, 1884.

H NYPL

10883. Baby World Stories, Rhymes, and Pictures for Little Folks Compiled from St. Nicholas by Mary Mapes Dodge

The Century Co. New-York ⟨1884⟩

"Perseverance," p. 258.

For comment see entry No. 4778.

10884. . . . Plucky Boys by the Author of John Halifax, Gentleman, ⟨*i.e.*, Mrs. Dinah Maria Mulock Craik⟩ and Other Authors . . .

Boston D. Lothrop and Company Franklin Street ⟨1884⟩

At head of title: Business Boys' Library.—III.

"The Church Mouse," pp. 187-212.

Listed PW Oct. 11, 1884. Deposited Oct. 29, 1884.

H LC UV

10885. A MARSH ISLAND . . .

BOSTON   HOUGHTON, MIFFLIN AND COMPANY NEW YORK: 11 EAST SEVENTEENTH STREET   THE RIVERSIDE PRESS, CAMBRIDGE 1885

Three printings noted:

1

⟨i-ii⟩, ⟨1⟩-292; inserted blank leaf; 12 pp. advertisements. Laid paper. 7¹⁄₁₆″ x 4⅝″.

⟨1¹³, 2-12¹², 13⁹⟩. Leaves ⟨1⟩₂ and ⟨13⟩₃ inserted. *Signed:* ⟨1⟩⁹, 2-18⁸, 19⁹.

Publisher's New York street address present in the imprint.

On p. ⟨ii⟩: *By the same Author* . . . ⟨6 titles⟩.

On p. 8 of the terminal advertisements *A Marsh Island* is described as *In press*.

2500 copies printed May 14, 1885 (publisher's records). The author's own copy (in H) inscribed May 14, 1885, thus; also a copy at Y inscribed by the author May 20, 1885.

2

⟨i-ii⟩, ⟨1⟩-292; blank leaf; 12 pp. advertisements; blank leaf. Laid paper.

⟨1¹³, 2-12¹², 13¹⁰⟩. Leaf ⟨1⟩₂ inserted. *Signed:* ⟨1⟩⁹, 2-18⁸, 19¹⁰.

Publisher's New York street address present in the imprint.

On p. ⟨ii⟩: *By the same Author* . . . ⟨6 titles⟩.

On p. 8 of the terminal advertisements *A Marsh Island* is priced at $1.25.

1000 copies printed May 22, 1885 (publisher's records).

3

⟨i-ii⟩, ⟨1⟩-292; blank leaf; 12 pp. advertisements; 2 blank leaves. Laid paper.

⟨1-13⟩¹². *Note:* The title-leaf is not an insert. *Signed:* ⟨-⟩¹, ⟨1⟩-19⁸, ⟨20⟩³.

Publisher's New York street address not in the imprint. The publisher's records show that the imprint was altered for this printing.

On p. ⟨ii⟩: *Writings of Sarah Orne Jewett* . . . ⟨7 titles⟩.

On p. 8 of the terminal advertisements *A Marsh Island* is priced at $1.25.

500 copies printed Aug. 26, 1885 (publisher's records).

Dark green V cloth sides, olive-green V cloth shelfback. White laid end papers. Flyleaves of laid or wove paper.

Advertised for May 16 PW May 9, 1885. Printed May 14, 1885. Author's own copy in H inscribed May 14, 1885. Deposited May 20, 1885. Y copy inscribed by author May 20, 1885. Listed PW May 23, 1885. Reviewed PC Sept. 15, 1885.

AAS (1st)   H (1st, 3rd)   NYPL (2nd)   Y (1st, 3rd)

10886. Chautauqua Young Folks' Annual Eight Series of Articles in One Volume ...

Boston: D. Lothrop and Company. Franklin and Hawley Streets. ⟨1886; *i.e.*, 1885⟩

"Town Clerks," pp. 13-15.

For comment see entry No. 56.

10887. A WHITE HERON AND OTHER STORIES ...

BOSTON AND NEW YORK   HOUGHTON, MIFFLIN AND COMPANY   THE RIVERSIDE PRESS, CAMBRIDGE 1886

Two printings noted:

First Printing

⟨i-x⟩, ⟨1⟩-254, blank leaf; plus: 6 pp. advertisements, blank leaf. 6" x 4⅝₁₆".

⟨1¹, 2⁴, 3-18⁸; plus: 19⁴⟩. *Note:* In some copies leaf ⟨19⟩₃ is excised.

P. ⟨ii⟩: *A White Heron* described as a *16mo.*

First printing, Sept. 3, 1886, 1500 copies (publisher's records).

Two issues of the first printing noted:

First Printing, First Issue

Pp. 174-175: Missing text causes reading: ... *and servile crea-* | *panionship* ...

First Printing, Second Issue

Pp. 174-175 read: ... *not happen again,* | *and he felt* ...

Note: Pp. 174-175 (leaves ⟨13⟩₇₋₈) are cancels. The publisher's records show that on Sept. 20, 1886, the plates were altered (1 hour) and 500 copies of two cancel leaves printed.

Second Printing

⟨i-x⟩, ⟨1⟩-254; blank leaf; 4 pp. advertisements; blank leaf.

⟨1-17⟩⁸.

P. ⟨ii⟩: *A White Heron* described as an *18mo.*

Pp. 174-175 correctly read: ... *not happen again,* | *and he felt* ...

Second printing, Sept. 24, 1886, 500 copies (publisher's records).

White V cloth sides, green V cloth shelfback. Front stamped in green. White laid end papers. Flyleaf at front. Top edges gilded. *Note:* Also issued in a variant (experimental?) binding: Green S cloth sides, brown V cloth shelfback; front stamped in brown; gray-coated on white end papers; top edges gilded; noted only on the author's own copy in H.

Advertised for Sept. 11 PW Sept. 4, 1886. Deposited Sept. 13, 1886. Listed PW Sept. 25, 1886.

H (1st printing, 1st issue; 1st printing, 2nd issue; 2nd printing)   UV (1st printing, 1st issue)   Y (1st printing, 1st issue)

10888. ... THE STORY OF THE NORMANS TOLD CHIEFLY IN RELATION TO THEIR CONQUEST OF ENGLAND ...

NEW YORK AND LONDON   G. P. PUTNAM'S SONS THE KNICKERBOCKER PRESS 1887

At head of title: THE STORY OF THE NATIONS

⟨i-ii⟩, ⟨i⟩-⟨xvi⟩, 1-373; blank, p. ⟨374⟩; 2 pp. advertisements. Illustrated. Folded map inserted. 7⁹₁₆" x 5³₁₆".

⟨1¹, 2⁸, 3-17¹², 18-19⁴⟩.

V cloth: gray-green. Gray end papers.

Deposited Jan. 29, 1887. BA copy received Feb. 1, 1887. Listed PW Feb. 12, 1887.

AAS   BA   H

10889. Ballads of Romance and History by Susan Coolidge ... Sarah O Jewett ... ⟨and Others⟩

Boston   D Lothrop Company   ⟨1887⟩

"York Garrison 1640," pp. 29-32. See below under 1888.

Note: Weber gives as the imprint for this book: *Boston, D. Lothrop & Co., 1887.* No copy so imprinted has been seen by BAL. The firm became *D. Lothrop Company* on Feb. 26, 1887, some six months prior to publication of the book.

Note: All examined copies have the error *Berwick and Smiih* for *Berwick and Smith* on copyright page.

Listed PW Oct. 22, 1887.

NYPL   UV

10890. THE KING OF FOLLY ISLAND AND OTHER PEOPLE ...

BOSTON AND NEW YORK   HOUGHTON, MIFFLIN AND COMPANY   THE RIVERSIDE PRESS, CAMBRIDGE 1888

⟨i-x⟩, ⟨1⟩-339; blank, p. ⟨340⟩; 12 pp. advertisements. 6¹⁵₁₆" full x 4⅝₁₆" full.

⟨1¹, 2⁴, 3-24⁸⟩.

Green V cloth sides, gray-green V cloth shelf-back. White laid end papers. Flyleaves.

According to the publisher's records, 2000 copies printed May 22, 1888. Deposited May 24, 1888. Author's own copy in H inscribed May 27, 1888. Noted as *just ready* PW June 2, 1888. Listed PW June 9, 1888. Earliest noted English edition: London (Duckworth) advertised for June 12, 1903 Ath June 6, 1903.

H   NYPL

10891. The Poets of Maine ... Compiled by George Bancroft Griffith

Portland, Maine   Elwell, Pickard & Company Transcript Job Print   Edward Small, Binder 1888

"The Eagle Trees," pp. 740-742.

"A Child's Grave," pp. 742-743. Collected in *Verses*, 1916.

Listed PW June 23, 1888.

H   NYPL   UV

10892. The Fête ...

Published by Eliot Library Association. Eliot, Maine, August 21–22, 1888. Vol. I. No. 1.

Cover-title.

An occasional newspaper. 8 pp. All published? Issued in printed gray paper wrapper.

"A Plea for Front Yards," p. ⟨2⟩. Elsewhere unlocated.

H

10893. York Garrison 1640 ...

⟨n.p., n.d., Boston: D. Lothrop Company(?), not before 1888⟩

Cover-title. Pp. ⟨25⟩-32. 10¼″ x 8¼″ scant. Printed paper boards; see below.

A curious production of unknown status. The sheets may have been extracted from *Ballads of Romance and History* ⟨1887⟩, see above; or, printed from the plates used in the production of that book.

Amateurishly bound in boards. Pasted to the front is a pictorial color print with title, name of author, and: *A Merrie Christmas To You.*

On the back cover is a list of Lothrop publications (Lothrop's name is not present however) one of which is *My Uncle Florimond*, by Henry Harland, which was published in Sept. 1888.

Y

10894. Wide Awake Pleasure Book   Gems of Literature and Art by American Authors and Artists

Boston   D Lothrop Company   Washington Street opposite Bromfield   ⟨1889⟩

Contains "A Christmas Guest."

For comment see entry No. 6320.

10895. BETTY LEICESTER   A STORY FOR GIRLS ...

BOSTON AND NEW YORK   HOUGHTON, MIFFLIN AND COMPANY   THE RIVERSIDE PRESS, CAMBRIDGE 1890

⟨i-viii⟩, ⟨1⟩-287. 6″ scant x 4⅜″.

⟨1⁴, 2-19⁸⟩.

White V cloth sides, red S cloth shelfback. White laid end papers. Flyleaves. Top edges gilt.

Note: According to the publisher's records there were six printings during 1889 and 1890, as follows; issued under date 1890: *First printing*, Nov. 9, 1889, 1500 copies; *Second printing*, Nov. 25, 1889, 1000 copies; *Third printing*, Dec. 16, 1889, 500 copies; *Fourth printing*, Dec. 17, 1889, 1000 copies; *Fifth printing*, Dec. 21, 1889, 1000 copies; *Sixth printing*, Aug. 11, 1890, 1018 copies. BAL has been able to distinguish but three printings:

First (and later?) Printing
Collation: As above.

10 titles listed in the advertisement opposite the title-page.

The author's own copy (in H), inscribed Nov. 11, 1889, thus. The surviving copyright deposit copy, received Nov. 14, 1889, thus.

Reprints, Prior to 6th Printing
Collation: ⟨1-18⁸, 19⁴⟩.

10 titles listed in advertisement opposite the title-page.

Sixth Printing
Collation: ⟨1-18⁸, 19⁴⟩.

11 titles listed in the advertisement opposite the title-page. The added title is *Tales of New England*, which was listed PW May 10, 1890.

Note: Johnson reports copies on large paper; no large paper copies have been traced by BAL and no record of such format has been found in the publisher's files.

Printed Nov. 9, 1889. Author's own copy in H inscribed Nov. 11, 1889. Deposited Nov. 14, 1889. Listed PW Dec. 7, 1889.

AAS (reprint) BA (6th) H (1st) LC (1st) UV (1st, 6th) Y (1st)

10896. The Art of Authorship . . . Compiled . . . by George Bainton.

  London: James Clarke & Co., 13 & 14, Fleet Street. 1890.

Contribution, pp. 177-178.

For comment see entry No. 1271.

10897. The Art of Authorship . . . Compiled . . . by George Bainton

  New York D. Appleton and Company 1890

Contribution, pp. 177-178.

For comment see entry No. 1272.

10898. STRANGERS AND WAYFARERS . . .

  BOSTON AND NEW YORK HOUGHTON, MIFFLIN AND COMPANY THE RIVERSIDE PRESS, CAMBRIDGE 1890

⟨i-viii⟩, ⟨1⟩-279. $6^{15}/_{16}$″ x $4^{5}/_{8}$″ full.

⟨1⁴, 2-18⁸, 19⁴⟩.

White V cloth sides; salmon, or green silk shelf-back. White laid end papers. Flyleaves; or flyleaf at front only.

Printed Nov. 14, 1890, 1568 copies (publisher's records). Deposited Nov. 17, 1890. According to the publisher's records all copies of the first printing were in binding by Nov. 19, 1890. Noted for Nov. 19 PW Nov. 15, 1890. A second printing (date altered to 1891?) was done Nov. 25, 1890, 1022 copies; bound during the period Dec. 2, 1890–Jan. 26, 1891 (publisher's records). Listed PW Dec. 6, 1890. The London (Osgood, McIlvaine) edition noted as *in the press* PC April 25, 1891; advertised for *this day* Ath and PC May 30, 1891; listed Ath and PC June 6, 1891.

H Y

10899. A Memorial of the One Hundredth Anniversary of the Founding of Berwick Academy South Berwick, Maine July First, 1891

  Printed at the Riverside Press Cambridge ⟨n.d., 1892⟩

Printed paper wrapper.

Edited by Jewett.

"Preface," pp. ⟨iii⟩-viii.

According to the printer's records, 1000 copies printed April 13, 1892. MHS copy received May 12, 1892.

Note: According to the printer's records, on March 16, 1892, 10 copies of an address by Dr.

John Lord were printed, the bill for which was paid by Sarah Orne Jewett. The address is possibly the one which appears in *A Memorial of the One Hundredth Anniversary* . . . ⟨n.d., 1892⟩. Does it contain a prefatory note by Jewett? Edited by Jewett?

H MHS NYPL Y

10900. Lothrop's Annual by the Best American Authors and the Best American Artists.

  Boston D. Lothrop Company Washington Street opposite Bromfield ⟨1892⟩

"Peg's Little Chair," pp. 126-137.

Deposited Sept. 12, 1892.

LC

10901. Fame's Tribute to Children . . . ⟨Edited by Martha S. Hill⟩

  Chicago A. C. McClurg and Company 1892

Statement, p. 73.

For fuller entry see BAL, Vol. 1, p. 76.

LC

10902. A NATIVE OF WINBY AND OTHER TALES . . .

  BOSTON AND NEW YORK HOUGHTON, MIFFLIN AND COMPANY THE RIVERSIDE PRESS, CAMBRIDGE 1893

⟨i-viii⟩, ⟨1⟩-309; blank, p. ⟨310⟩; 2 pp. advertisements. $6^{15}/_{16}$″ x $4^{5}/_{8}$″.

⟨1-20⟩⁸. *Note:* Inserted at back of some copies is a single cut sheet folded to make 4 pages, devoted to publisher's advertisements.

V cloth: green. Maroon-coated on white end papers. Flyleaves.

According to the publisher's records, 2000 copies printed on Oct. 13, 1893. Deposited Oct. 18, 1893. Noted as *just issued* PW Oct. 21, 1893. Author's own copy in H inscribed Oct. 24, 1893. Listed PW Oct. 28, 1893.

H NYPL UV

10903. The Lover's Year-Book of Poetry ⟨Second Series⟩ . . . Married-Life and Child-Life ⟨Compiled⟩ by Horace Parker Chandler . . .

  Boston Roberts Brothers 1893

2 Vols.

"Together," vol. 1, pp. 206-207. Collected in *Verses*, 1916.

Listed PW Dec. 2, 1893.

H

10904. Deephaven . . . Illustrated by Charles and Marcia Woodbury

For first edition see above under 1877.

Large-Paper Edition

Imprint: Cambridge   Printed at the Riverside Press M DCCC XCIV

On reverse of title-leaf: *Two Hundred and Fifty Copies Printed. Number*

"Preface," pp. ⟨1⟩-8, dated at end: *October, 1893.*

262 copies printed Oct. 27, 1893 (publisher's records). Bound Nov. 7–Dec. 1, 1893.

Note: All examined copies have the error *geeen* for *green,* p. 167, line 5.

Holiday Edition

Imprint: Boston and New York   Houghton, Mifflin and Company   The Riverside Press, Cambridge M DCCC XCIV

Referred to as *Holiday Edition* in the publisher's records.

Two printings noted:

1

P. 167, line 5: *geeen* for *green.*

2560 copies printed Oct. 30(?), 1893 (publisher's records). Bound Oct. 26 ⟨*sic*⟩–Dec. 27, 1893. Of this printing 262 copies sent to Osgood, McIlvaine & Co., London, Oct. 27, 1893.

2

P. 167, line 5: *green* is correctly spelled.

According to the publisher's records, the plate was corrected on Dec. 18, 1893. The second printing, 516 copies, Jan. 16, 1894.

Note: The trade edition has the front stamped in silver. Reprints have been noted with the front stamped in either gold or silver. A copy of the second printing (at BA) is bound in publisher's imitation leather.

Trade format deposited Nov. 4, 1893. Author's own copy of trade format at H inscribed Nov. 4, 1893. Trade and large paper formats listed PW Nov. 11, 1893. Large paper format deposited Nov. 20, 1893. The London (Osgood, McIlvaine; American sheets) edition listed Ath Dec. 2, 1893.

AAS (trade, 1st)   BA (trade, 2nd)   H (large paper; trade, 1st and 2nd)   LC (large paper; trade, 1st)   Y (large paper; trade, 2nd)

10905. BETTY LEICESTER'S ENGLISH XMAS A NEW CHAPTER OF AN OLD STORY . . .

PRIVATELY PRINTED FOR THE BRYN MAWR SCHOOL BALTIMORE EXMAS ⟨*sic*⟩, 1894

⟨1⟩-81. Laid paper. 7½″ x 5″. Printed on recto only save for title-leaf.

⟨1-10⁸, 11¹⟩.

V cloth: white. White laid end papers. Top edges gilded.

Deposited Dec. 28, 1894. For a revised edition see under 1899.

AAS   H

10906. THE LIFE OF NANCY . . .

BOSTON AND NEW YORK   HOUGHTON, MIFFLIN AND COMPANY   THE RIVERSIDE PRESS, CAMBRIDGE 1895

⟨i-vi⟩, ⟨1⟩-322. 6¹⁵⁄₁₆″ scant x 4½″.

⟨1-20⁸, 21⁴⟩.

V cloth: blue; green. White laid end papers. Flyleaves.

According to the publisher's records, 2500 copies printed Oct. 1, 1895. Deposited Oct. 8, 1895. Noted as *just ready* PW Oct. 12, 1895. H copy inscribed by author Oct. 13, 1895. Another H copy inscribed by author Oct. 15, 1895. Listed PW Oct. 19, 1895. The London (Longmans) edition listed Ath Jan. 25, 1896. The Houghton, Mifflin records show that the Longmans edition was printed (520 copies) Nov. 4, 1895, and constituted the 2nd printing.

BA   H   NYPL

10907. Stories and Poems for Children by Celia Thaxter

Boston and New York   Houghton, Mifflin and Company   The Riverside Press, Cambridge 1895

Edited by Jewett.

Note, p. ⟨iii⟩, signed at end: *S.O.J.*

The publisher's records show 2560 copies printed, Oct. 25, 1895; bound during the period Nov. 5, 1895 to July 14, 1898 (1899?). Many variations in the binding are probable; BAL has noted the following; the sequence is probable:

A: Publisher's spine imprint measures (both lines included) ³⁄₁₆″ high. Jewett's personal copy (in H) thus.

B: Publisher's spine imprint measures (both lines included) ¼″ high.

Note: The publisher's records show that on Dec. 3, 1895, 25 copies were bound untrimmed, printed paper label on spine. Unlocated by BAL.

Printed Oct. 25, 1895. Deposited Nov. 8, 1895. Noted for Nov. 15 PW Nov. 9, 1895. Listed PW Nov. 16, 1895.

B (B)   H (A)

10908. Human Documents   Portraits and Biographies of Eminent Men ...

New York   S. S. McClure, Limited   30 Lafayette Place   1895

Printed paper wrapper; also, cloth.

"Introduction," pp. ⟨v⟩-vi.

NYPL   UV

10908A. ... A VILLAGE PATRIOT ...

⟨n.p., NEW YORK⟩ [COPYRIGHT, 1896, BY THE BACHELLER SYNDICATE.] ...

Prepared for subscribers to The Bacheller Syndicate. For comment see *Note* at end of this list.

Single sheet. Printed on recto only.   Estimated size 22" x 16".   Printed together with other material which has been trimmed away from the only located example.

At head of title: (*For Publication July 4.*)

Uncollected.

H

10909. The Poems of Celia Thaxter

Boston and New York   Houghton, Mifflin and Company   The Riverside Press, Cambridge 1896

Edited by Jewett.

"Introduction," pp. ⟨v⟩-viii.

Issued simultaneously in three styles of binding; the designations are for identification only:

A

V cloth: green. Sides blindstamped with a rule border, spine stamped in gold. A copy thus (in H) inscribed by Jewett: *First copy. September 1896.*

B

Green sateen. Front cover and spine stamped in gold. On front: *Appledore Edition.*

C

Cloth, printed paper label on spine. *Not located;* entry on the basis of the publisher's records which report 198 untrimmed copies bound Aug. 15, 1896.

Note: On p. ⟨i⟩: *Appledore Edition* ... ; on p. ⟨ii⟩: *This is a copy from the first edition of this*

book   These statements appear in both styles A and B. Also in C?

Printed Aug. 4, 1896, 1541 copies. Bound during the period Aug. 11–Dec. 21, 1896. Deposited Aug. 15, 1896. Noted as *just ready* PW Oct. 3, 1896. Listed PW Oct. 10, 1896.

H (A,B)

10910. THE COUNTRY OF THE POINTED FIRS ...

BOSTON AND NEW YORK   HOUGHTON MIFFLIN AND COMPANY   THE RIVERSIDE PRESS   CAMBRIDGE   MDCCCXCVI

Title-page in black and orange.

⟨i-viii⟩, ⟨1⟩-213; blank, p. ⟨214⟩; 2 pp. advertisements. Laid paper. 6¹⁵⁄₁₆" scant x 4½".

⟨1-14⟩⁸. ⟨1⟩₂₋₃ are inserted conjugates.

Two printings noted:

1

As above. The author's own copy (in H) inscribed Oct. 27, 1896, thus. A copy deposited Oct. 28, 1896, thus.

According to the publisher's records 2524 copies printed Oct. 27, 1896, of which 6 copies were prepared with the London imprint of A. P. Watt & Son (for British copyright?) and 105 copies with the London imprint of T. Fisher Unwin. All copies of the American issue were in binding by Nov. 28, 1896.

2

⟨i-viii⟩, ⟨1⟩-213; blank, p. ⟨214⟩; 2 pp. advertisements; blank leaf.

⟨1⁹, 2-14⁸⟩. ⟨1⟩₂ inserted.

According to the publisher's records 984 copies printed Dec. 5, 1896; bound during the period Dec. 7 to 11, 1896.

V cloth: green. Laid end papers. Wove paper; or, laid paper flyleaves. *Second printing sheets* occur in green V cloth, laid end papers, laid paper flyleaf at front, no flyleaf at back. *Second printing sheets* also occur in green sateen, laid end papers, laid paper flyleaf at front, no flyleaf at back. *Note:* In the advertisement, p. ⟨2⟩, the present title is described as with "gilt top"; no copy examined by BAL is so distinguished.

Advertised for Oct. 31, PW Oct. 24, 1896. Deposited Oct. 28, 1896. Listed PW Nov. 7, 1896. The London edition (Unwin) advertised for *next week* Ath Nov. 28, 1896; listed Ath Nov. 28, 1896; Bkr Dec. 11, 1896.

AAS (1st)   H (1st, 2nd)   LC (1st)   NYPL (1st, 2nd)   UV (2nd)

10911. Little Men and Women   Edited by Charles Stuart Pratt   and Ella Farman Pratt . . .

Boston   Alpha Publishing Company   1896

"The Little Top-Knot Hen," pp. ⟨346⟩-348.

For comment see entry No. 6345.

10912. Betty Leicester's Christmas . . .

Boston and New York   Houghton, Mifflin and Company   The Riverside Press, Cambridge   1899

Revised reissue of *Betty Leicester's English Xmas,* 1894.

Deposited Oct. 17, 1899.

AAS BA H LC Y

10913. THE QUEEN'S TWIN AND OTHER STORIES . . .

BOSTON AND NEW YORK   HOUGHTON, MIFFLIN AND COMPANY   THE RIVERSIDE PRESS, CAMBRIDGE M DCCC XCIX

Title-page in black and orange.

⟨i-xii⟩, ⟨1⟩-232; blank, p. ⟨233⟩; printer's imprint, p. ⟨234⟩; blank leaf. Laid paper. 6$\frac{15}{16}$" x 4½". Pp. ⟨xi-xii⟩ excised.

⟨1^6, 2-15^8, 16^6⟩. ⟨1⟩$_6$ excised; leaves ⟨1⟩$_{2-3}$ conjugate; leaves ⟨1⟩$_{4-5}$ conjugate.

V cloth: blue; green; slate; yellow. Stamped in either gold or in silver. White laid end papers.

The publisher's records (which are somewhat contradictory regarding this publication) indicate 3020 copies printed, Nov. 1899; bound during the period Nov. 21–Dec. 19, 1899; *second printing* (date altered to 1900) consisted of 1007 copies, printed Dec. 21, 1899.

Deposited Nov. 18, 1899. Author's own copy (in H) inscribed Nov. 22, 1899. BA copy received Dec. 5, 1899. Listed PW Dec. 9, 1899. The London (Smith, Elder; American sheets) edition advertised as *just published* Ath Feb. 24, 1900; listed Ath Feb. 24, 1900.

H NYPL

10914. THE TORY LOVER . . .

BOSTON AND NEW YORK   HOUGHTON, MIFFLIN AND COMPANY   THE RIVERSIDE PRESS, CAMBRIDGE 1901

According to the publisher's records there were five printings dated 1901:

1st: Aug. 30 ⟨sic⟩ 1901, 5058 copies printed. Bound during the period Aug. 27–Sept. 21, 1901.

2nd: Sept. 20, 1901, the plates were altered, and 2500 copies printed. Bound during the period Sept. 21–Sept. 25, 1901.

3rd: Sept. 24, 1901, 2000 copies printed. Bound during the period Sept. 25–Sept. 28, 1901.

4th: Sept. 27, 1901, 2500 copies printed. Bound during the period Sept. 28–Nov. 1, 1901. The records indicate that the plates were altered for this printing; further information wanting.

5th: Nov. 14, 1901, 2016 copies printed. The records indicate that the plates were altered for this printing; further information wanting.

Note: In a letter to the publisher (original in H), Nov. 22 ⟨1901⟩, Miss Jewett requested several alterations; all but one have been noted in an undated reprint. These alterations may have first appeared in the unlocated sixth printing (Dec. 16, 1901) which, according to the publisher's records, was issued under date 1902.

BAL has been unable to identify all five printings, but has identified the first printing. Note that the publisher's records show that the plates were altered for the second printing.

First Printing

⟨i-ii⟩, ⟨i⟩-⟨viii⟩, ⟨1⟩-405; printer's imprint, p. ⟨406⟩; blank leaf. Frontispiece and 3 plates inserted. 7$\frac{11}{16}$" x 4$\frac{15}{16}$" full.

⟨1^1, 2^4, 3-26^8, 29^{12}⟩.

Published September, 1901 on copyright page.

Quotation, in chapter heading, p. ⟨278⟩ reads: *"Lackynge, my love, I goe from place to place."*

P. 154: 34 lines of text.

Reprints

⟨i-ii⟩, ⟨i⟩-⟨viii⟩, ⟨1⟩-405; printer's imprint, p. ⟨406⟩. Frontispiece and 3 plates inserted.

⟨1-26⟩^{8}.

Publication notice does not appear on copyright page.

Quotation, p. ⟨278⟩ reads: *"Lackyng my love, I goe from place to place."*

P. 154: 33 lines of text.

Green V cloth. Rough maroon V cloth. Smooth red V cloth. Author's name stamped on front cover. White laid end papers. Flyleaf at front.

Note: Reprints have been seen in maroon T cloth with variant stamping, a principal feature of which is the absence of the author's name from the front cover. Prepared for The Tabard Inn Library? See BAL, Vol. 1, pp. xxxii-xxxiii. Copy in H.

Deposited Aug. 28, 1901. UV copy (first printing) inscribed by Jewett Sept. 10, 1901. Listed PW Oct. 5, 1901. The London (Smith, Elder) edition, which has the textual peculiarities of the first American printing, advertised for Nov. 12 Ath Nov. 2, 1901; listed Ath Nov. 23, 1901.

AAS (reprint) H (1st; reprint) NYPL (1st; reprint) UV (1st) Y (1st)

10915. ... THE GREEN BOWL

BOSTON   SMALL, MAYNARD & COMPANY   1901

Cover-title. At head of title: A HOUSE PARTY

Anonymous.

⟨1⟩-29, blank leaf. 7¼″ x 4⅝″.

⟨1-2⁸⟩.

Printed paper wrapper.

Jewett's contribution to *A House Party*, 1901 (see next entry), prepared for copyright purposes; not issued in this form.

Deposited Nov. 4, 1901.

H

10916. A House Party   An Account of the Stories Told at a Gathering of Famous American Authors ... ⟨Edited⟩ by Paul Leicester Ford

Boston   Small, Maynard & Company   1901

"The Green Bowl," pp. 208-235; anonymous.

For a copyright printing see preceding entry.

For comment see entry No. 6229.

10917. Songs of Nature Edited by John Burroughs

New York   McClure Phillips & Co MCMI ...

"A Caged Bird," pp. 175-176. Collected in *Verses*, 1916.

For comment see entry No. 2169.

10918. Twentieth-Century Ladies' Reciter Compiled and Edited by Ernest Pertwee ...

London   George Routledge & Sons, Ltd Broadway House, Ludgate Hill, E.C.   1904

Not seen.

"Sheltered," pp. 24-31.

BMU

10919. AN EMPTY PURSE   A CHRISTMAS STORY ...

BOSTON   PRIVATELY PRINTED   1905

⟨1⟩-⟨16⟩. 7⁵⁄₁₆″ x 4½″.

⟨-⟩⁸.

Printed gray cartridge paper wrapper.

BA H NYPL

10920. Letters of Sarah Wyman Whitman

Cambridge   Printed at the Riverside Press 1907

Boards, leather shelfback; and, full morocco.

Edited by Jewett, according to Matthiessen, p. 123.

"Editorial Note," pp. v-⟨viii⟩; unsigned.

H

10921. Stories and Tales.

Boston and New York   Houghton Mifflin Company   The Riverside Press   Cambridge ⟨1884–1910; *i.e.,* 1910⟩

Note: For the most part printed from plates used in the production of earlier, separate, volumes. No volume is identified as part of a set. The designation *Stories and Tales* is taken from contemporary notices and advertisements.

Cloth; and, leather.

The order of presentation is alphabetical.

A Country Doctor ... ⟨1884; *i.e.,* 1910⟩
  Reprint

The Country of the Pointed Firs ... ⟨1910⟩
  Reprint save for "William's Wedding."

Deephaven ... ⟨1905; *i.e.,* 1910⟩
  Reprint

The Life of Nancy ... ⟨1895; *i.e.,* 1910⟩
  Reprint

A Native of Winby and Other Tales ... ⟨1893; *i.e.,* 1910⟩
  Reprint

The Queen's Twin and Other Stories ... ⟨1899; *i.e.,* 1910⟩
  Reprint

Tales of New England ... ⟨1907; *i.e.,* 1910⟩
  Reprint

Issued in maroon V cloth, sides unstamped; a deposit copy thus. Also issued in flexible maroon skiver, a principal feature of the stamping being the author's signature in facsimile on the front cover.

Advertised as *today* PW Oct. 1, 1910. "A hitherto unpublished story of Miss Jewett's is included

A HOUSE PARTY

The Green Bowl

S. O. J.

SCIRE
QVOD
SCIENDVM

BOSTON
Small, Maynard & Company
1901

in the last volume of the set."—PW Nov. 12, 1910; presumably reference is to "William's Wedding," in *The Country of the Pointed Firs*. Listed PW Dec. 3, 1910. Distributed in London by Constable; listed Bkr Feb. 24, 1911; yet, advertised as *just published* Bkr Oct. 6, 1911.

H

10922. LETTERS OF SARAH ORNE JEWETT EDITED BY ANNIE FIELDS

BOSTON AND NEW YORK HOUGHTON MIFFLIN COMPANY THE RIVERSIDE PRESS CAMBRIDGE 1911

⟨i-vi⟩, ⟨1⟩-259; printer's imprint, p. ⟨260⟩; blank leaf. Frontispiece and 3 plates inserted. 7¹¹⁄₁₆″ x 5⅝″.

⟨1⁶, 2-17⁸⟩.

V cloth: green. Top edges gilded.

According to the publisher's records there were two printings without alteration. *First printing:* Sept. 19, 1911, 1624 copies printed. Bound Sept. 21–Dec. 4, 1911. On Oct. 5, 1911, 250 title-pages were prepared with the Constable (London) imprint. *Second printing:* Dec. 8, 1911. 1042 copies printed. *Third printing:* Printed Dec. 11, 1911; date removed from the title-page and the statement *Third Impression* added to copyright page.

On copyright page: *Published October 1911* Advertised as *published today* PW Oct. 7, 1911. NYPL copy received Oct. 7, 1911. Deposited Oct. 12, 1911. Listed PW Oct. 14, 1911. The London (Constable) edition announced Bkr Feb. 2, 1912; listed Bkr Feb. 9, 1912.

H NYPL

10923. **1912.** SOCIETY FOR THE PROTECTION OF NATIVE PLANTS. LEAFLET NO. 22. ⟨14 lines in facsimile autograph beginning: *I am most heartily in sympathy with the plan for protecting our wild flowers* ...⟩

FOR MORE LEAFLETS APPLY TO MISS M. E. CARTER, BOSTON SOCIETY OF NATURAL HISTORY, BOSTON.

Single leaf. Printed on recto only. 8⁵⁄₁₆″ x 5⅜″ full.

H

10924. VERSES ...

BOSTON PRINTED FOR HER FRIENDS 1916

Edited by M. A. DeWolfe Howe.

⟨i-iv⟩, ⟨i⟩-⟨viii⟩, 1-33, blank leaf. 7⁷⁄₁₆″ x 5¼″ scant.

⟨1-6⁴⟩.

Bluish-gray cartridge paper boards sides, olive-drab T or V cloth shelfback. Printed paper label on spine. Flyleaves.

H copy inscribed by Mary Jewett July 18, 1916.

AAS B BA H NYPL UV

10925. American Local-Color Stories Edited ... by Harry R. Warfel ... and G. Harrison Orians ...

New York American Book Company ... ⟨1941⟩

Reprint save for "The Gray Mills of Farley," pp. 363-382.

First printing has symbol *E.P.1* on copyright page.

H copy received Oct. 27, 1941.

H

10926. LETTERS OF SARAH ORNE JEWETT NOW IN THE COLBY COLLEGE LIBRARY WITH EXPLANATORY NOTES BY CARL J. WEBER

WATERVILLE, MAINE COLBY COLLEGE PRESS 1947

Title-page in black and orange.

⟨i-ii⟩, ⟨1⟩-75; blank, p. ⟨76⟩; colophon, p. ⟨77⟩. Paper watermarked *Ragston S-N*. 7¹⁄₁₆″ x 4¾″ scant.

⟨1-5⁸⟩.

Marbled paper boards, white V cloth shelfback.

Colophon: ... *Two hundred and twenty-five copies ... printed ... August, 1947 ... this copy is Number* ...

Deposited Nov. 3, 1947.

AAS BA LC

10927. Youth's Companion Edited by Lovell Thompson with Three Former Companion Editors, M. A. DeWolfe Howe, Arthur Stanwood Pier, and Harford Powel ...

Houghton Mifflin Company Boston The Riverside Press Cambridge 1954

"The Stage Tavern," pp. 342-351.

"Looking Back on Girlhood," pp. 416-421.

Deposited Oct. 11, 1954.

H

10928. SARAH ORNE JEWETT LETTERS EDITED WITH AN INTRODUCTION AND NOTES BY RICHARD CARY

WATERVILLE, MAINE COLBY COLLEGE PRESS 1956

Title-page in black and orange.

‹1›-88, ‹i-ii›, 89-117. Two illustrations on a single leaf, printed on both sides, inserted; one page facsimile in text (here designated ‹i-ii›), not reckoned in printed pagination. 10″ x 7″.

‹1⁸, 2⁴, 3-8⁸›

V cloth: blue.

P. ‹7›: ... *Ninety-four letters in this volume ... More than half appear in print for the first time* ...

Deposited Nov. 26, 1956.

BA Y

10929. The World of Dunnet Landing A Sarah Orne Jewett Collection Edited by David Bonnell Green

University of Nebraska Press Lincoln ‹1962›

Printed paper wrapper.

Reprint save for "The Foreigner," pp. ‹250›-291. *"The Foreigner* is reprinted from the *Atlantic Monthly* for August, 1900 ..."—pp. 418-419.

LC

SARAH ORNE JEWETT

SECTION II

Collections of reprinted material issued under Jewett's name; separate editions (*i.e.*, pieces reprinted from Jewett's books and issued in separate form). For a list of books by authors other than Jewett containing reprinted Jewett material see *Section III*.

10930. We Young Folks Original Stories for Boys and Girls by Harriet Beecher Stowe ... Mary E. Wilkins ... Sarah O. Jewett and Others ...

Boston D. Lothrop and Company Franklin and Hawley Streets. ⟨1886, *i.e.*, 1885⟩

For comment see entry No. 6308.

10931. The Mate of the Daylight and Friends Ashore ... Third Edition.

Boston Houghton, Mifflin and Company New York: 11 East Seventeenth Street The Riverside Press, Cambridge 1885

10932. The New England Story-Book. Stories by Famous New England Authors: Mrs. A. D. Whitney ... Sarah O. Jewett ... Elizabeth Stuart Phelps, Celia Thaxter ... E. L. Bynner ... Louise Chandler Moulton, Etc, ⟨*sic*⟩ Etc.

Boston: D. Lothrop and Company, Franklin Street, Corner of Hawley. ⟨1886⟩

Pictorial paper boards. Unpaged. Deposited July 23, 1886.

10933. The Favorite Story-Book Stories by Famous Authors Mrs. A. D. T. Whitney ... Sarah O. Jewett ... Etc.

Boston D Lothrop Company Washington Street opposite Bromfield ⟨1889⟩

Pictorial paper boards. Unpaged.

10934. ... Tales of New England ...

Boston and New York Houghton, Mifflin and Company The Riverside Press, Cambridge 1890

At head of title: The Riverside Aldine Series

Two formats issued: Blue V cloth, goldstamped, edges trimmed; and, red V cloth, printed paper label on spine, edges untrimmed. *Note:* Johnson (1942, p. 295) states: "The first printing ... has no mention of this title in the advertisements"; all copies located by BAL have the title listed in the front matter card; the Johnson note, presumably, refers to the terminal advertisements. Johnson also states: "Reissued in 1912 with one added story"; no such printing located by BAL.

Listed PW May 10, 1890. The London (Osgood, McIlvaine) edition, 1893, advertised as *shortly* Ath June 17, 1893; listed Ath July 29, 1893; listed and reviewed PC Aug. 5, 1893; second edition listed PC Oct. 14, 1893.

10935. Old Friends and New. By S. O. Jewitt ⟨*sic*⟩ ...

London: William Nicholson and Sons, 20, Warwick Square, Paternoster Row, E.C., and Albion Works, Wakefield. ⟨n.d., 1890⟩

All known Jewett material herein is reprint. Also contains two short pieces of doubtful authorship not found in any of Jewett's books: "A Brave Boy" and "Little Jimmy." Issued as *Victoria Series*, No. 8. Publication date on the basis of London directories. In the possession of Everett D. Jewett, Rowley, Mass., July, 1966.

10936. Tales of New England ...

Boston and New York Houghton, Mifflin and Company The Riverside Press, Cambridge 1894

10937. Tales of New England ...

Boston and New York Houghton, Mifflin and Company The Riverside Press, Cambridge 1895

10938. ... Tales of New England ...

Boston, New York, and Chicago Houghton, Mifflin & Company The Riverside Press, Cambridge ⟨1896⟩

At head of title: The Riverside School Library

Cloth, leather shelfback. Deposited Oct. 14, 1896.

10939. ... The Normans ...

New York   G. P. Putnam's Sons   London:
T. Fisher Unwin   1898

At head of title: The Story of the Nations

Cloth, leather shelfback; also, cloth. Reprint of
The Story of the Normans, 1887.

10940. ... The Normans ...

New York   G. P. Putnam's Sons   London:
T. Fisher Unwin   1901

At head of title: The Story of the Nations

Reprint of *The Story of the Normans,* 1887.

10941. The Dulham Ladies ...

Boston and New York   Houghton Mifflin and
Company   The Riverside Press   Cambridge
MCMIV

Printed paper wrapper. Reprinted from *A
White Heron* ... , 1886.

10942. Deephaven ...

Boston and New York   Houghton, Mifflin and
Company   The Riverside Press, Cambridge
⟨1905⟩

Deposited Jan. 5, 1905. Sheets of an unidentified
printing, with cancel title-leaf, prepared for
copyright renewal purposes. The publisher's records show two title-pages printed Jan. 3, 1905.

10943. Old Friends and New ...

Boston and New York   Houghton, Mifflin
and Company   The Riverside Press, Cambridge ⟨1907⟩

Sheets of an unidentified earlier printing with
cancel title-leaf as above. Prepared for copyright renewal purposes. The publisher's records
show two title-leaves printed July 1, 1907. Deposited July 8, 1907.

10944. ... The Night before Thanksgiving   A
White Heron   and   Selected Stories ...
⟨Edited⟩ by Katharine H. Shute ...

Boston   New York   Chicago   Houghton Mifflin Company   The Riverside Press   Cambridge ⟨1911⟩

At head of title: The Riverside Literature Series

Issued in printed paper wrapper as No. 202 of
the series; also, cloth. Also reprinted with later
copyright dates. Listed PW Jan. 28, 1911 (in
cloth). Deposited Feb. 14, 1911.

10945. ... Play Day Stories ... Edited by Katharine H. Shute ...

Boston   New York   Chicago   Houghton Mifflin Company   The Riverside Press   Cambridge ⟨1914⟩

At head of title: The Riverside Literature Series

10946. ... The Best Stories of Sarah Orne
Jewett Selected and Arranged with a Preface
by Willa Cather ...

Boston and New York   Houghton Mifflin
Company   The Riverside Press   Cambridge
1925

2 vols. At head of title: The Mayflower Edition

Listed PW March 28, 1925.

10947. The Only Rose and Other Tales ...
with an Introduction by Rebecca West

London   Jonathan Cape   30 Bedford Square
⟨1937⟩

10948. Verses ... Centennial Edition ...

American Weave Press, Cleveland   1949

Printed paper wrapper.

10949. Lady Ferry ... with an Introduction by
Annie E. Mower

Waterville, Maine   Colby College Press   1950

Boards, cloth shelfback. Reprinted from *Old
Friends and New,* 1879. Deposited April 24,
1950.

SECTION III

In this section are listed books by authors other than Jewett which contain material by her reprinted from earlier books. See *Section II* for a list of collections of reprinted material issued under Jewett's name and separate editions.

The Children's Book of Poetry ... Selected ... by Henry T. Coates ...

   Porter & Coates. Philadelphia. ⟨1879⟩

Dick's Recitations and Readings No. 10 ... Edited by Wm. B. Dick ...

   New York ... ⟨1879⟩

   "The Discontented Buttercup," pp. 37-38; otherwise, "Discontent" in *Play Days*, 1878.

   For comment see entry No. 5538.

Grandma's Garden ... Arranged by Kate Sanborn ...

   Boston ... 1883

   "The Gardens of the Puritan Grandmother," p. 25; extracted from "From a Mournful Villager" in *Country By-Ways*, 1881. For comment see entry No. 3791.

Golden Years   Original and Instructive Stories by Margaret Sidney ... Mary E. Wilkins ...

   Boston   D Lothrop and Company   Franklin and Hawley Streets   ⟨1886⟩

   Pictorial paper boards. Deposited Aug. 24, 1886.

Boys and Girls' Annual   1887 ... Edited by William Blair Perkins ...

   Boston ... ⟨1886⟩

   For comment see BAL, Vol. 3, p. 242.

Wide Awake Pleasure Book   Gems of Literature and Art ...

   Boston ... ⟨1887⟩

   For fuller entry see under Helen Hunt Jackson, *Section Three*.

Young Folks Story Book ...

   New York ... ⟨1888⟩

For comment see BAL, Vol. 2, p. 115.

A Library of American Literature ... Edited by Edmund Clarence Stedman and Ellen Mackay Hutchinson ...

   New-York ... 1888–1890.

   For comment see entry No. 1350.

Tennyson's Fairies and Other Stories ...

   Boston   D Lothrop Company   Washington Street opposite Bromfield   ⟨1889⟩

   Compiled by Karl H. Goodwin, according to LC catalogue. Deposited April 29, 1889. Noted as issued *this week* PW June 29, 1889. Listed PW Aug. 3, 1889.

Our Boys and Girls for 1890 ...

   Boston ... ⟨1889⟩

   For comment see BAL, Vol. 2, p. 115.

Golden Lays for Youthful Days ...

   ... Chicago ... 1889.

   For comment see entry No. 7899A.

Our Boys' and Girls' Story Book ...

   Boston ... ⟨1890⟩

   For comment see BAL, Vol. 2, p. 116.

The Youth's Companion at Home and School. Edited by Mrs. Grace Townsend.

   Chicago, Philadelphia, and Stockton, California: L. P. Miller & Company, 1891.

   Not seen. Entry from Weber, p. 52.

Werner's Readings and Recitations No. 15 Compiled ... by Caroline Earnest Dickenson

   New York ... 1896 ...

   For comment see BAL, Vol. 3, p. 139.

Library of the World's Best Literature Ancient and Modern   Charles Dudley Warner Editor ... Thirty Volumes ...

   New York ... ⟨1896–1899⟩

   For comment see entry No. 10624.

Wide Awake Story Book for Our Boys and Girls . . .

Boston Lothrop Publishing Company ⟨1897⟩

Pictorial boards, cloth shelfback. Unpaged. Deposited May 29, 1897.

The International Library of Famous Literature Selections from the World's Great Writers . . . with Biographical and Explanatory Notes and with Introductions by Donald G. Mitchell . . . and Andrew Lang Compiled and Arranged by Nathan Haskell Dole, Forrest Morgan and Caroline Ticknor . . .

New York   Merrill and Baker Publishers ⟨1898⟩

20 Vols. Deposited Oct. 6, 1898.

Note: Subscription sets such as this present a special, sometimes insoluble, problem. They were customarily issued in a variety of formats, often with variations in title or imprint or both; with each format issued under a fanciful designation. Usually the typographic variations were limited to the front matter, with copyright date left unaltered. Hence reprints, the copyright date retained, often were issued years after first publication. Lacking positive evidence, copyright dates in subscription books should not be related to year of actual publication.

The present set was deposited for copyright Oct. 6, 1898, with title and imprint as given above. BAL has noted the set in a so-called *Imperial Edition de Luxe,* limited to 1000 numbered copies, imprinted *New York International Library Company* . . . ⟨1898⟩; The Library of Congress reports a reprint issued in 1904 under the title *The Bibliophile Library of Literature.* In 1899 the set was issued in London, with some additional text, and with editorship credited to Richard Garnett, Leon Vallée, Alois Brandl and Donald G. Mitchell. The New York edition was issued as though edited by Nathan Haskell Dole, Forrest Morgan, Caroline Ticknor, and with introductions by Donald G. Mitchell and Andrew Lang. It is entirely probable the editing was done by anonymous editors and that those named as editors merely lent their names to the undertaking. In the case of the present work, *The International Library,* The Library of Congress reports that Nathan Haskell Dole, one of the alleged editors, repudiated "the use of his name in connection with this publication."

Lothrop's Annual . . .

Boston Lothrop Publishing Company ⟨1899⟩

Pictorial boards, cloth shelfback. Unpaged. Deposited April 12, 1899.

Best Things from American Literature Edited by Irving Bacheller . . .

New York . . . 1899

For comment see entry No. 4086.

The International Library of Famous Literature . . . Edited by Dr. Richard Garnett . . . in Twenty Volumes . . .

London Issued by The Standard 1899

For comment see entry No. 10638.

Winter Tales for Fireside Reading . . .

Boston Lothrop Publishing Company ⟨1902⟩

Pictorial boards, cloth shelfback. Unpaged. Deposited March 19, 1902.

The Children's Hour ⟨Vol. 10⟩ Modern Stories Selected & Arranged by Eva March Tappan

⟨n.p., Boston and New York⟩ Houghton Mifflin & Company 1907 . . .

. . . Short Stories Selected and Edited by Leonard B. Moulton . . .

Boston New York Chicago Houghton Mifflin Company The Riverside Press Cambridge ⟨1915⟩

At head of title: The Riverside Literature Series

Deposited June 1, 1915.

The Promise of Country Life   Descriptions Narrations without Plot Short Stories Edited by James Cloyd Bowman . . .

D. C. Heath & Co., Publishers Boston New York Chicago ⟨1916⟩

Deposited May 24, 1916.

A Little Book of Friends by Harriet Prescott Spofford

Boston Little, Brown, and Company 1916

The verses on pp. 77-79 had prior publication in *Verses,* 1916, under the title "Star Island." Also reprints "The Gloucester Mother," pp. 41-42. On copyright page: *Published, Septem-*

ber, 1916 Deposited Sept. 29, 1916. Listed PW Sept. 30, 1916.

The Great Modern American Stories ... Edited ... by William Dean Howells

New York ... 1920

For comment see entry No. 6479.

The World's One Hundred Best Short Stories ‹in Ten Volumes› Grant Overton Editor-in-Chief Volume Six Courage

Funk & Wagnalls Company New York and London ‹1927›

Deposited Oct. 1, 1927.

Prose and Poetry of America Including a History of American Literature Edited by H. Ward McGraw ...

The L W Singer Company Syracuse Chicago Dallas ‹1934›

Atlantic Harvest Memoirs of *The Atlantic* ... Compiled by Ellery Sedgwick ...

Little, Brown and Company Boston 1947

Published Sept. 24, 1947.

REFERENCES AND ANA

Fiftieth Annual Report of the Trustees of the Public Library of the City of Boston 1901–1902.

Boston Municipal Printing Office 1902

Printed paper wrapper. That portion of the report beginning: "The Committee on Books suggest the need of extra assistants in the Children's Reading-room," pp. 55-56, written in large part by Jewett as a member of the Examining Committee during the period 1900–1902. The original typescript, signed by Jewett, is in the Jewett archive at H.

Sarah Orne Jewett by Francis Otto Matthiessen ...

Boston and New York Houghton Mifflin Company The Riverside Press Cambridge 1929

Printed paper label on spine.

A Bibliography of the Published Writings of Sarah Orne Jewett Compiled by Clara Carter Weber and Carl J. Weber

Waterville, Maine Colby College Press 1949

300 copies only. Colophon: "... Printed and bound ... July 1949 ..."

Sarah Orne Jewett by Richard Cary ...

Twayne Publishers, Inc. ,: New York ‹1962›

Printed boards. *Note:* Imprint transcribed as it occurs. Richard Cary confirms all copies thus.

NOTE

"A Dark Night," "An Empty Purse, a New England Christmas Tale," "In a Country Practice," "Little French Mary," "The Night before Thanksgiving," "A Pinch of Salt," "Told in the Tavern," "A Village Patriot."

According to David Bonnell Green (*The Papers of the Bibliographical Society of America*, Vol. 53, Fourth Quarter, 1959, pp. 331-334), the above stories were syndicated by The Bacheller Syndicate, New York. If the syndicate followed usual procedure, each story was put in type and distributed to subscribers; such printings may have been in either galley or broadsheet form. No such printings have been seen or reported. Green also calls attention to S. S. McClure's statement (*My Autobiography*, New York ‹1914›, p. 182): "... Miss Sarah Orne Jewett ... wrote for the ‹McClure› syndicate" which suggests that The McClure Syndicate may have issued like printings.

Nota bene: After the above was put in type an example was located; see entry No. 10908A.

Of the above stories only the following have been located in book form: "An Empty Purse, a New England Christmas Tale," issued as a separate book, Boston, 1905; "Little French Mary," in *The Life of Nancy*, 1895; and, "The Night before Thanksgiving," in *The Queen's Twin*, 1899. Of "A Dark Night" Green says: "seems evidently to be a preliminary sketch for chapters 42 through 44 of *The Tory Lover* ..."

RICHARD MALCOLM JOHNSTON

1 8 2 2 – 1 8 9 8

Caution: Do not confuse Richard Malcolm Johnston with Robert Matteson Johnston, 1867–1920, author of *The Holy Christian Church* ... , Boston, Houghton Mifflin Company, 1912.

NOTE

" ... After a brief stay in the employment of the ⟨United States⟩ Commissioner of Labor and on the preparation of the *Blue Book,* I was placed in the Bureau of Education, with a salary of twelve hundred dollars. There I have been since the first of January, 1896, going back and forth ⟨from Baltimore⟩ every week day ... The first ten weeks of my time in the Bureau were given to assisting in editing and indexing the papers of the Commissioner. About the middle of March the latter suggested that I write a paper ⟨see entry No. 10981⟩ on early educational life in my native region, middle Georgia, beginning with the rural schools known as *Old Field.* I was to tell of the sort of teachers, the schoolhouses, text-books, manner of teaching, the sports and games of school children, of holidays, turnouts, etc. To this end I read quite a number of books of school life, and upon children's sports in England, Japan, etc. This was printed in the Commissioner's report, and was followed by another paper of about equal length in which were told first of boys and girls out of school, the rise of academies, the effort to maintain a manual labor school, ending with a sketch of the State University."—*Autobiography,* pp. 92-94.

No attempt has been made to trace all the materials on which Johnston may have worked while in the employment of the Commissioner of Labor. See entries 10981, 10985 for two such publications.

10950. THE ENGLISH CLASSICS: A HISTORICAL SKETCH OF THE LITERATURE OF ENGLAND FROM THE EARLIEST TIMES TO THE ACCESSION OF KING GEORGE III ...

PHILADELPHIA: J. B. LIPPINCOTT & CO.   1860.

⟨i⟩-viii, 9-275. 7⅜″ x 4¾″.

⟨1⟩-5, ⟨6-7⟩, 8-23⁶.

BD cloth: purple. Unprinted pale buff end papers; also pale buff end papers printed with publisher's advertisements. Flyleaves.

Deposited March 31, 1860. For an enlarged edition see *English Literature* ... , 1873.

AAS LC UV Y

10951. The Southern Field and Fireside Novelette, No. 1. Containing "Myra Bruce, or True Love Running Roughly," ... "Riverlands," ... "Five Chapters of a History: A Georgia Court, Forty Years Ago."

... James Gardner, Augusta, Ga. ⟨1863⟩

Printed paper wrapper. Cover-title.

"Five Chapters of a History: A Georgia Court, Forty Years Ago," pp. ⟨1⟩-19; anonymous. Collected in *Georgia Sketches,* 1864, as "Judge Mike and His Court, or, Five Chapters of a Georgia History." Collected, with revisions, in *Dukesborough Tales,* 1871, as "Judge Mike's Court."

Note: This publication contains three short stories, each separately paged. Johnston's contribution is the third.

UNC

10952. GEORGIA SKETCHES; CONTAINING MR. ISRAEL MEADOWS AND HIS SCHOOL. JUDGE MIKE AND HIS COURT. HOW BILL WILLIAMS TOOK THE RESPONSIBILITY MISS PEA, MISS SPOUTER AND THE YANKEE. FROM RECOLLECTIONS OF AN OLD MAN. BY PHILEMON PERCH ...

⟨AUGUSTA, GA.⟩   PUBLISHED BY STOCKTON & CO. SOUTHERN FIELD AND FIRESIDE OFFICE, 1864.

Cover-title.

⟨3⟩-114. 7¾″ scant x 5½″. *Note:* P. 16 mispaged 6; space for 1 present.

⟨1-3⁸, 4-5¹⁶⟩

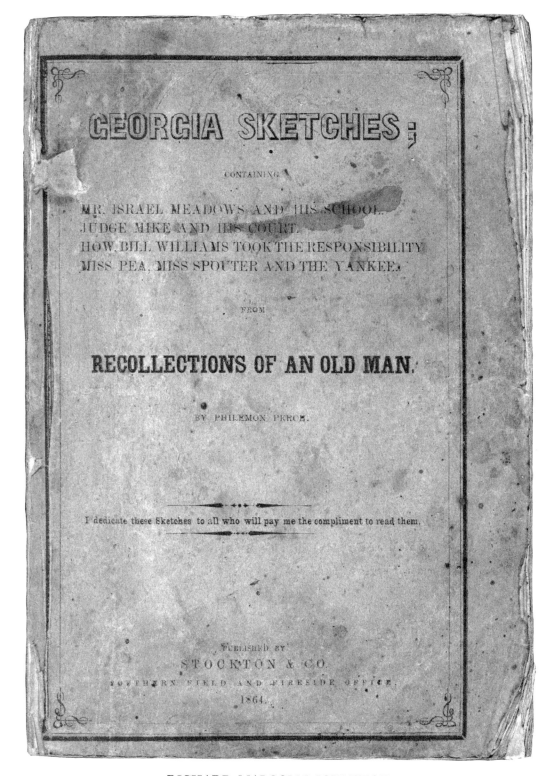

GEORGIA SKETCHES;

CONTAINING

MR. ISRAEL MEADOWS AND HIS SCHOOL.
JUDGE MIKE AND HIS COURT.
HOW BILL WILLIAMS TOOK THE RESPONSIBILITY
MISS PEA, MISS SPOUTER AND THE YANKEE.

FROM

RECOLLECTIONS OF AN OLD MAN.

BY PHILEMON PERCH.

I dedicate these Sketches to all who will pay me the compliment to read them.

PUBLISHED BY
STOCKTON & CO.
SOUTHERN FIELD AND FIRESIDE OFFICE.
1864.

RICHARD MALCOLM JOHNSTON
Entry No. 10952
(Yale University Library)

Printed tan paper wrapper.

Y

10953. ADDRESS, SPOKEN AT THE GEOR-
GIA ACADEMY OF THE BLIND, JUNE
27th, 1867 ...

BALTIMORE: THE SUN BOOK AND JOB PRINTING
ESTABLISHMENT 1867.

⟨1⟩-15. 9″ full x 5¹¹⁄₁₆″.

⟨1-2⟩⁴.

Printed yellow paper wrapper.

Issued after Aug. 1, 1867.

UG

10954. ADDRESS SPOKEN BEFORE THE
PHI KAPPA AND DEMOSTHENIAN SOCI-
ETIES OF THE UNIVERSITY OF GEOR-
GIA, ON COMMENCEMENT DAY, AU-
GUST 2d, 1869, ON THE DEAD OF
GEORGIA ...

⟨ATHENS, GA., 1869⟩

⟨1⟩-29; blank, p. ⟨30⟩; blank leaf. 8¹⁵⁄₁₆″ scant x
5½″ scant.

⟨1⟩-4⁴.

Printed paper wrapper.

Issued after Aug. 16, 1869.

EMORY

10955. DUKESBOROUGH TALES BY PHILE-
MON PERCH.

BALTIMORE: TURNBULL BROTHERS. 1871.

⟨i-viii⟩, ⟨1⟩-232. 7⅝″ full x 5⁹⁄₁₆″.

⟨-⟩⁴, 1-29⁴.

C cloth: green. P cloth: green. Brown-coated on
white end papers. Flyleaves. Covers bevelled.

BA copy received Aug. 28, 1871. For earlier versions of certain of the tales herein see *Georgia
Sketches* ... , 1864, above. For other editions see
under 1874, 1883, and 1892.

AAS   BA

10956. ENGLISH LITERATURE. A HISTOR-
ICAL SKETCH OF ENGLISH LITERA-
TURE FROM THE EARLIEST TIMES. BY
RICHARD MALCOLM JOHNSTON AND
WILLIAM HAND BROWNE.

UNIVERSITY PUBLISHING COMPANY, NEW YORK
AND BALTIMORE. 1873.

An extensively enlarged edition of *English Classics* ... , 1860.

⟨1⟩-395. 7¼″ full x 4⅞″ full.

⟨1⟩-16¹², 17⁶.

P-like cloth: brown. Flyleaves. Edges sprinkled
brown.

Two issues of the binding noted. The sequence,
if any, is not known, and the designations are for
identification only.

A

Sides blindstamped with a rule frame; at center
of each side a panel with rounded corners
stamped in blind from a dotted rule tool. No
fillets stamped on spine. A copy (at Y) presented
by the authors, inscribed (by the recipient?) Aug.
1872. Olive-coated on white end papers.

B

Sides blindstamped with a rules frame, the inner
rule curved at the corners, and the corners decorated. A fillet, stamped in blind, at top and at
bottom of spine. Brown-coated on white end papers.

Listed WTC Sept. 19, 1872.

Y (A,B)

10957. Dukesborough Tales by Philemon Perch.
Second Enlarged Edition.

Baltimore: Turnbull Brothers. 1874.

For other editions see under 1871, 1883, and
1892.

Sheets of the 1871 edition reissued with cancel
title-leaf; and, bound in at the back: "Old
Friends and New," paged ⟨1⟩-98. The pagination suggests that "Old Friends and New" may
have been issued as a separate pamphlet, but no
such publication has been found.

UV

10958. SCHOOL AND COLLEGE DISCI-
PLINE: AN ADDRESS DELIVERED BE-
FORE THE PHILOMATHEAN SOCIETY,
OF ST. JOHN'S COLLEGE, ANNAPOLIS,
MARYLAND, ON DECEMBER 11th, 1873
...

BALTIMORE: CHARLES HARVEY & CO., PRINTERS,
NO. 3 POST OFFICE AVENUE. 1874.

⟨1⟩-15. 8¾″ x 5¾″.

⟨-⟩⁸.

Printed gray paper wrapper.

AAS

10959. LIFE OF ALEXANDER H. STEPHENS.
BY RICHARD MALCOLM JOHNSTON
AND WILLIAM HAND BROWNE.

PHILADELPHIA: J. B. LIPPINCOTT & CO. 1878.

⟨1⟩-619. 2 frontispieces inserted. 8¾″ full x 5¾″.

⟨1⟩-33, 35 ⟨sic⟩, 35-388, 396.

S cloth: blue; mauve; terra-cotta. Brown-coated on white end papers. Flyleaves. Bevelled covers.

Listed PW Aug. 31, 1878. NYPL copy received Sept. 19, 1878. Reviewed Ath June 21, 1879. For other editions see under 1883 and 1884.

AAS Y

10960. . . . The Baltimore Christmas Magazine. Edited by Geo. Edwin Dorsey.

1880 Baltimore News Company, Agents.

Printed paper wrapper. Cover-title. At head of title: Price 35 cts.

"Intermingling of the Serious and the Sportive in the Merchant of Venice and in Falstaff," pp. 19-25.

Not a periodical, the name notwithstanding.

JH

10961. . . . Dukesborough Tales . . .

⟨New York: Harper & Brothers, 1883⟩

Self-wrapper. Cover-title. At head of title: Harper's Franklin Square Library. Number 290 . . . January 12, 1883 . . .

Extended by the addition of seven stories. For other editions see under 1871, 1874, and 1892.

Issued under date of Jan. 12, 1883. Listed PW Jan. 20, 1883.

NYPL UCB

10962. ⟨A circular letter regarding Life of Alexander H. Stephens⟩

⟨Philadelphia, J. B. Lippincott & Co., 1883⟩

Not seen. Issued as a separate?

"J. B. Lippincott & Co. publish a circular letter from R. M. Johnston and William Hand Browne, protesting against the publication of the unauthorized and unreliable biographies of the late A. H. Stephens. The biography prepared by them and published by Messrs. Lippincott, was gotten up with the consent of Mr. Stephens, received his approval, and was declared by him to be entirely in consonance with the facts of his history."—PW April 7, 1883, p. 421.

10963. Life of Alexander H. Stephens. By Richard Malcolm Johnston and William Hand Browne. New and Revised Edition.

Philadelphia: J. B. Lippincott & Co. 1883.

For first edition see under 1878; also see under 1884.

Pp. 635.

Deposited May 21, 1883. Listed PW June 16, 1883.

LC

10964. OLD MARK LANGSTON A TALE OF DUKE'S CREEK . . .

NEW YORK   HARPER & BROTHERS, FRANKLIN SQUARE 1884

⟨i-ii⟩, ⟨1⟩-338; 10 pp. advertisements. 6¹¹⁄₁₆″ scant x 4⁹⁄₁₆″.

⟨-⟩², ⟨1⟩⁷, 2-21⁸, 22⁶. ⟨1⟩₂.₅.₆ inserted; ⟨1⟩₁.₇ and ⟨1⟩₃.₄ conjugates.

S cloth: gray-blue. Tan-coated on white end papers. White end papers printed in pale yellow with a leafy decoration. Flyleaves.

Deposited Jan. 23, 1884. Listed PW Jan. 26, 1884. The London (Sampson Low) edition listed Ath Jan. 26, 1884.

AAS H

10965. History of Philadelphia. 1609–1884. By J. Thomas Scharf and Thompson Westcott . . .

Philadelphia: L. H. Everts & Co. 1884.

3 Vols.

"Authors and Literature of Philadelphia," Vol. 2, pp. 1099-1173; anonymous. Authorship on basis of Preface, p. v.

Vols. 1-3 deposited May 14, 1884. H copy received June 7, 1884.

H

10966. Life of Alexander H. Stephens . . . New and Revised Edition.

Philadelphia: J. B. Lippincott & Co. 1884.

See above under 1878 and 1883 for other editions.

Pp. 709. Extended by the addition of "Appendix F, Funeral Ceremonies . . . ," pp. 630-703.

H UV

10967. TWO GRAY TOURISTS: FROM PAPERS OF MR. PHILEMON PERCH. EDITED BY RICHARD MALCOLM JOHNSTON . . .

BALTIMORE: THE BALTIMORE PUBLISHING CO. NO. 174 WEST BALTIMORE STREET. ⟨1885⟩

⟨1⟩-3, iv, 5, vi-viii, ⟨1⟩-276. 7¼″ x 4⅞″.

⟨-⟩⁴, ⟨1⟩-23⁶.

S cloth: blue; green; red; yellow. Brown-coated on white end papers. Flyleaves.

Two states of the binding noted. The sequence is not known, and the designations are for identification only.

A: The author's name erroneously spelled on spine: JOHNSON.

B: The author's name correctly spelled on spine: JOHNSTON. Copyright deposit copy thus.

Deposited Nov. 4, 1885.

AAS (Binding A)   H (Binding A)   LC (Binding B)   UV (Binding A)

10968. MR. ABSALOM BILLINGSLEA AND OTHER GEORGIA FOLK ...

NEW YORK   HARPER & BROTHERS, FRANKLIN SQUARE   1888

⟨i⟩-viii, ⟨1⟩-414; 6 pp. advertisements. Frontispiece and 10 plates (reckoned in the printed pagination) inserted. 6⅝″ x 4⁹⁄₁₆″.

⟨1⟩-25⁸, 26⁴.

V cloth: mustard-brown. Flyleaves.

Advertised for January 10 PW Jan. 7, 1888. BA copy received Jan. 17, 1888. Listed PW Jan. 21, 1888.

AAS   BA   H   NYPL

10969. OGEECHEE CROSS-FIRINGS A NOVEL ...

NEW YORK   HARPER & BROTHERS, FRANKLIN SQUARE   1889

⟨i-viii⟩, ⟨1⟩-149; blank, p. ⟨150⟩; 2 pp. advertisements. Illustrated. 8″ x 5⅝″.

⟨-⟩⁴, 1-9⁸, 10⁴.

Printed blue paper wrapper. Issued under date Sept. 1889 as No. 656 of *Harper's Franklin Square Library, New Series.*

Deposited Sept. 7, 1889. Listed PW Sept. 28, 1889.

AAS   LC   Y

10970. WIDOW GUTHRIE A NOVEL ...

NEW YORK   D. APPLETON AND COMPANY   1890

Title-page in black and orange.

⟨i-iv⟩, ⟨1⟩-⟨vi⟩, ⟨7⟩-309; blank, p. ⟨310⟩; 10 pp. advertisements. Laid paper. Frontispiece and 5 plates inserted. 7⅜″ x 4¹⁵⁄₁₆″.

⟨-⟩², 1-20⁸.

CM-like cloth: blue. Light brown-coated on white end papers. Laid paper flyleaves.

BA copy received Dec. 2, 1890. Listed PW Dec. 6, 1890. Deposited Dec. 11, 1890.

BA   H   NYPL

10971. THE PRIMES AND THEIR NEIGHBORS

Issued in three formats: *Town and Country Library* edition, in printed paper wrapper, unillustrated; *Town and Country Library* edition, in cloth, unillustrated; and, *illustrated edition.*

TOWN AND COUNTRY LIBRARY, WRAPPER FORMAT

Advertised PW March 21, 1891. This format deposited April 1, 1891.

THE PRIMES AND THEIR NEIGHBORS TEN TALES OF MIDDLE GEORGIA BY RICHARD MALCOLM JOHNSTON AUTHOR OF WIDOW GUTHRIE, DUKESBOROUGH TALES, MARK LANGSTON, ETC. ⟨4 lines of verse⟩

NEW YORK   D. APPLETON AND COMPANY   1891

⟨1⟩-310; 10 pp. advertisements. Laid paper. 7¹⁄₁₆″ x 4¾″.

⟨1⟩-20⁸.

Printed terra-cotta paper wrapper. Issued under date March 15, 1891, as *Appletons' Town and Country Library*, No. 69.

TOWN AND COUNTRY LIBRARY, CLOTH FORMAT

No publication information found. Presumably issued simultaneously with the other formats.

Title-page as above.

⟨1⟩-310; 10 pp. advertisements. Laid paper. 7″ full x 4¾″.

⟨1⟩-20⁸.

V cloth: blue. Flyleaves.

ILLUSTRATED EDITION

BA copy received March 17, 1891. Advertised PW March 21, 1891. Listed PW March 28, 1891.

THE PRIMES AND THEIR NEIGHBORS TEN TALES OF MIDDLE GEORGIA BY RICHARD MALCOLM JOHNSTON AUTHOR OF WIDOW GUTHRIE, DUKESBOROUGH TALES, MARK LANGSTON, ETC. WITH ILLUSTRATIONS BY E. W. KEMBLE, A. B. FROST, AND OTHERS ⟨4 lines of verse⟩

NEW YORK   D. APPLETON AND COMPANY   1891

⟨i-ii⟩, ⟨1⟩-6, ⟨iii-iv⟩, ⟨7⟩-310; advertisements, pp. ⟨311-316⟩. Frontispiece and 19 plates inserted. Laid paper. 7⅜″ x 5″.

⟨1⟩-20⁸.

CM-like cloth: blue. Buff-coated on white end papers. Laid paper flyleaves.

AAS (wrapper) H (cloth) NYPL (wrapper) UV (wrapper; and, illustrated) Y (illustrated)

10972. STUDIES, LITERARY AND SOCIAL ... FIRST SERIES.

INDIANAPOLIS: THE BOWEN-MERRILL CO. 1891.

⟨i-vi⟩, 1-241. 6⅝″ x 4¹¹⁄₁₆″.

⟨a⟩², ⟨b⟩¹, ⟨1-3⟩, 4-⟨5⟩, 6-8, ⟨9⟩, 10-15⁸, ⟨16⟩¹.

Two states of the binding noted. The sequence, if any, is not known, and the designations are for identification only.

A

V cloth: blue. Stamped in gold and silver. Flyleaves.

B

FL-like cloth: dark chocolate brown. S cloth: blue. V cloth: blue. Goldstamped only. Flyleaves. *Note:* Was this less elaborate binding used on copies intended as school textbooks?

Was the book issued in both a trade and a school edition?

Noted as *just issued* PW Oct. 24, 1891. Listed PW Oct. 31, 1891. Deposited Jan. 4, 1893 ⟨sic⟩. See under 1892 for *Second Series.*

H (A) LC (B) NYPL (A) UV (B) Y (B)

10973. Santa Claus Entirely New Stories for Boys and Girls ... ⟨by⟩ ... Richard Malcolm Johnston ... Harriet Prescott Spofford ... ⟨and Others⟩

  Brodix Publishing Company Washington, D.C. ⟨1891⟩

Pictorial paper boards, cloth shelfback.

"The Two Woollys," pp. 137-138, 161-162, 170-172. Collected in *Little Ike Templin,* 1894.

EM

10974. Dukesborough Tales The Chronicles of Mr. Bill Williams ...

  New York D. Appleton and Company 1892

Issued in cloth; and, printed paper wrapper, under date of April 15, 1892, as No. 93 of *Appletons' Town and Country Library.*

The author has "carefully revised and now submits six stories selected from the original sixteen ..."—"Preface," p. ⟨vii⟩, dated May 5, 1892. For other editions see under 1871, 1874, and 1883.

Deposited (wrapper) May 26, 1892. Listed PW June 11, 1892, as in cloth; and, paper. *Note:* The wrapper format is another example of the unreliable nature of publisher's dates on this sort of serial publication. The wrapper was issued under date of April 15, 1892; the "Preface" is dated May 5, 1892; and the wrapper format was deposited May 26, 1892.

H (cloth) LC (wrapper) UV (cloth) Y (cloth; wrapper)

10975. MR. FORTNER'S MARITAL CLAIMS AND OTHER STORIES ...

  NEW YORK D. APPLETON AND COMPANY 1892

⟨i-vi⟩, 1-182; 4 pp. advertisements. 6½″ x 4⁵⁄₁₆″.

⟨1⟩-12⁸.

Printed white paper boards. White end papers and edges printed in green with a floral pattern. Flyleaves.

Deposited Aug. 31, 1892. BA copy received Sept. 6, 1892. Listed PW Sept. 17, 1892. Ath Oct. 1, 1892: *Will shortly publish;* but no British edition recorded; Ath may have been referring to an importation.

H NYPL UV

10976. MR. BILLY DOWNS AND HIS LIKES ...

  NEW YORK CHARLES L. WEBSTER & CO. 1892

⟨i⟩-⟨x⟩, 11-232, blank leaf; 6 pp. advertisements; plus: 2 pp. advertisements. Frontispiece inserted. 7⅛″ x 4¾″.

⟨1-15⁸; plus: 16¹⟩.

S cloth: green. Flyleaves.

Deposited Nov. 21, 1892. BA copy received Nov. 29, 1892. Listed PW Dec. 3, 1892.

AAS BA H

10977. Pearce Amerson's Will ...

  Philadelphia: J. B. Lippincott Company. ⟨1892⟩

See below under 1898 for trade edition.

Lippincott's Monthly Magazine for December, 1892, with title-page as above.

Printed paper wrapper. Also boards, cloth shelfback?

LC Y

10978. STUDIES, LITERARY AND SOCIAL ... SECOND SERIES.

  INDIANAPOLIS: THE BOWEN-MERRILL CO. 1892.

⟨i-viii⟩, 1-240. 6⅝″ x 4¹¹⁄₁₆″.

⟨1⁴, 2-16⁸⟩.

Two states of the binding noted. The sequence, if any, is not known, and the designations are for identification only.

A

V cloth: blue. Stamped in gold and silver. Flyleaves.

B

H cloth: blue-green; green. Goldstamped only. Flyleaves. Was this less elaborate binding used on copies intended as school textbooks? Was the book issued in both a trade and a school edition?

Deposited Dec. 23, 1892. Listed PW Dec. 24, 1892. For *First Series* see under 1891.

H (A)   LC (B)   NYPL (A)   UV (B)   Y (B)

10979. LITTLE IKE TEMPLIN AND OTHER STORIES ...

BOSTON   LOTHROP PUBLISHING COMPANY   1894

⟨i-xii⟩, 1-259; blank, p. ⟨260⟩; 2 pp. advertisements. Frontispiece inserted; also, 5 inserted plates, reckoned in the printed pagination. 7⁹⁄₁₆″ x 5″.

⟨1-16⁸, 17⁴⟩.

S cloth: gray; tan. V cloth: gray-tan.

Advertised as *in press* PW May 26, 1894. Deposited Sept. 1, 1894. Listed PW Oct. 6, 1894.

H Y

10980. Addresses and Letters Read at the Memorial Meeting in Honor of Brother Azarias ...

Washington, D. C. St. John's College. 1894.

"Brother Azarias As a Literary Artist," pp. 42-47.

Issued after May 17, 1894. Y copy inscribed by Charles Warren Stoddard Dec. 1894.

Y

10980A. Great Men and Famous Women A Series of Pen and Pencil Sketches ... Copyright, 1894 ... Edited by Charles F. Horne

New-York: Selmar Hess Publisher

8 Vols. Noted only in three quarters leather, cloth sides. Presumably a subscription book and if so probably issued in a variety of formats.

"Thomas Chatterton," Vol. 7, pp. 107–111.

H

10981. ... EARLY EDUCATION IN MIDDLE GEORGIA. ⟨Part I⟩ THE ATLANTA EXPOSITION. ENGLISH TEACHING OF AMERICAN HISTORY.

WASHINGTON: GOVERNMENT PRINTING OFFICE. 1896.

At head of title: UNITED STATES BUREAU OF EDUCATION. CHAPTERS FROM THE REPORT OF THE COMMISSIONER OF EDUCATION FOR 1894-95.

⟨i-ii⟩, 1699-1787. 9¹⁄₁₆″ x 5⅝″ full.

Leaves extracted from *Report of the Commissioner of Education for the Year 1894-95*, Vol. 2, Washington, 1896, with inserted title-leaf as above.

Printed gray paper wrapper.

"Early Educational Life in Middle Georgia ⟨Part I⟩," pp. 1699-1733; pp. 1735 to end: Material by authors other than Johnston. For Part 2 see entry No. 10985.

H

10982. OLD TIMES IN MIDDLE GEORGIA ...

NEW YORK   THE MACMILLAN COMPANY   LONDON: MACMILLAN & CO., LTD. 1897   ALL RIGHTS RESERVED

⟨i⟩-vi, ⟨1⟩-249; blank, p. ⟨250⟩; plus: 4 pp. advertisements. Laid paper. 7⅜″ x 4¹⁵⁄₁₆″.

⟨1-16⁸; plus: 17²⟩. *Signed:* ⟨A⟩³, ⟨B⟩-G, ⟨H⟩, I, K-Q⁸, R⁷.

V cloth: green. White laid end papers. White wove end papers.

Noted *will publish shortly* PW June 5, 1897. Deposited July 10, 1897. Listed PW July 31, 1897 (as not received); again (as received) PW Aug. 7, 1897. The London (Macmillan) edition listed Ath Aug. 28, 1897.

BA   H   NYPL   Y

10983. ... LECTURES ON LITERATURE ENGLISH, FRENCH AND SPANISH ...

AKRON, O.   D. H. McBRIDE & CO. 1897

At head of title: CATHOLIC SUMMER AND WINTER SCHOOL LIBRARY

⟨i-iv⟩, ⟨1⟩-269, blank leaf. Laid paper. 6⅛″ x 3⅝″.

⟨1⟩¹⁰, 2-17⁸.

S cloth: maroon. Laid end papers.

AAS   Y

10984. Ninety-First Anniversary Celebration of the New England Society in the City of New

York at the Waldorf, 5th Ave. and 33rd St Tuesday, December 22, 1896

⟨n.p., n.d., New York, The New England Society in the City of New York, 1897⟩

Printed paper wrapper.

"Speech . . . ," pp. 50-55.

Y

10985. . . . EARLY EDUCATIONAL LIFE IN MIDDLE GEORGIA. ⟨Part II⟩

WASHINGTON: GOVERNMENT PRINTING OFFICE. 1897.

At head of title: UNITED STATES BUREAU OF EDUCATION. CHAPTER XVI FROM REPORT OF THE COMMISSIONER OF EDUCATION FOR 1895–96.

⟨837⟩-886. 9″ full x 5¾″.

Leaves extracted from *Report of the Commissioner of Education for the Year 1895–96*, Vol. 1, Washington, 1897, with inserted title-leaf, as above. For Part 1 see entry No. 10981.

Printed gray paper wrapper.

UG

10986. PEARCE AMERSON'S WILL . . .

CHICAGO WAY AND WILLIAMS 1898

See under 1892.

Title-page in black and orange.

⟨i-x⟩, 1-275; blank, p. ⟨276⟩; printer's imprint, p. ⟨277⟩. Laid paper. Frontispiece and 2 plates inserted. 6¹¹⁄₁₆″ x 4⁹⁄₁₆″.

⟨1⁴, 2-18⁸, 19⁴⟩. *Signed:* ⟨-⟩⁵, 1-17⁸, 18³.

V cloth: blue. White laid end papers. Top edges gilded.

Listed PW June 4, 1898.

AAS H

10987. Studies Literary and Social . . . First and Second Series

Indianapolis The Bowen-Merrill Company 1899

Cloth, printed paper label on spine.

Reprint.

B

10988. AUTOBIOGRAPHY OF COL. RICHARD MALCOLM JOHNSTON

WASHINGTON THE NEALE COMPANY M C M

⟨1⟩-190, blank leaf. Laid paper. Frontispiece in-

serted. 7¹³⁄₁₆″ x 5¼″.

⟨1-12⟩⁸.

S cloth: orange. Laid end papers.

AAS B H

REPRINTS

The following publications contain material by Johnston reprinted from other books.

The Southern Student's Hand-Book of Selections for Reading and Oratory. By John G. James . . .

A. S. Barnes & Co., New York, Chicago and New Orleans. 1879.

"The Georgia Leaders after the War," pp. 101-103; extracted from *Address Spoken before the Phi Kappa and Demosthenian Societies* . . . ⟨1869⟩, pp. 6-8.

Oddities in Southern Life and Character Edited by Henry Watterson . . .

Boston . . . 1883

For fuller entry see No. 574.

Humorous Masterpieces from American Literature Edited by Edward T. Mason

New York . . . 1886

For comment see entry No. 4624A.

Mark Twain's Library of Humor . . .

New York . . . 1888

For comment see entry No. 9636.

Stories by the Hearth . . .

Boston . . . ⟨1895⟩

For comment see entry No. 88.

Famous Story Book by the Best American Authors . . .

Boston . . . ⟨1896⟩

For comment see BAL, Vol. 1, p. 19.

Library of the World's Best Literature Ancient and Modern Charles Dudley Warner Editor . . . Thirty Volumes Vol. XIV

New York . . . ⟨1897⟩

For comment see entry No. 10624. Deposited July 27, 1897.

Story Land in Prose and Verse . . .

Boston . . . ⟨1900⟩

For comment see BAL, Vol. 3, p. 317.

... The World's Best Literature Editors John W. Cunliffe Ashley H. Thorndike ...

New York   Printed at The Knickerbocker Press for the Warner Library Company Toronto: Glasgow, Brook & Company 1917

At head of title: *University Edition   The Warner Library in Thirty Volumes   Volume 14* Probably issued in a variety of formats and with varying imprints. Vol. 14 deposited Dec. 3, 1917.

REFERENCES AND ANA

The "Southern Rights" and "Union" Parties in Maryland Contrasted.

Baltimore: Printed by W. M. Innes, Adams Express Building. 1863.

Printed paper wrapper. Anonymous. Sometimes attributed to Johnston. Both Library of Congress and Yale University Library credit authorship to John Fulton, 1834–1907.

Literary Estimate and Bibliography of Richard Malcolm Johnston by Edmund Clarence Stedman, Stephen B. Weeks ...

Printed by Harrisburg Publishing Co. Harrisburg, Pa.: 1898.

Printed paper wrapper.

NOTE

Address on Female Education, Delivered at Cuthbert, Ga., in 1856.

Address on Education at a Baptist College.

Neither of the above located. Entries on the basis of Stephen B. Weeks's bibliography in *Literary Estimate and Bibliography of Richard Malcolm Johnston,* by Edmund Clarence Stedman and Stephen B. Weeks, 1898, pp. 325, 327. In his entries the bibliographer states *no copy ⟨copies⟩ seen, but known to have been printed.* In book form?

JOHN BEAUCHAMP JONES

(Luke Shortfield, A Squatter)

1 8 1 0 — 1 8 6 6

Note: Sabin (Part 9, p. 323) erroneously credits Jones with the authorship of *Major Jones's Courtship, Major Jones's Sketches of Travel* and *Chronicles of Pineville.* These were written by William Tappan Thompson and are so listed in Sabin, Part 146, pp. 160-161.

10989. WILD WESTERN SCENES; A NAR-RATIVE OF ADVENTURES IN THE WESTERN WILDERNESS, FORTY YEARS AGO; WHEREIN THE CONDUCT OF DANIEL BOONE, THE GREAT AMERI-CAN PIONEER, IS PARTICULARLY DE-SCRIBED. ALSO, MINUTE ACCOUNTS ARE GIVEN OF BEAR HUNTS—DEER AND BUFFALO HUNTS—DESPERATE CONFLICTS WITH THE SAVAGES—WOLF HUNTS—FISHING AND FOWL-ING ADVENTURES—ENCOUNTERS WITH SERPENTS, ETC. ETC. . . . ‹FIRST SERIES›

NEW YORK: SAMUEL COLMAN, 14, JOHN ST. BAL-TIMORE: N. HICKMAN, 86, BALTIMORE ST. SHER-WOOD & CO., PRINTERS, BALTIMORE. 1841.

Pp. 248.

For other editions see under 1849, 1852, 1856. For *Second Series* see under 1856.

Issued in paper-covered parts. *No complete set in parts has been located and the present entry therefore is completely tentative.* The inner back of the wrapper of part 2 states: " . . . Will be issued in numbers simultaneously in Balti-more, New York, Philadelphia and Boston. The work will be completed in not less than six nor more than seven numbers." Following is a de-scription of Part 2, the only part seen in a wrapper:

45-84. 8^{15}⁄$_{16}$" x 5⅝". Illustrated.

7-11^4.

Printed pinkish-white paper wrapper.

LC (in binding, lacking wrappers)   UV (Part 2)

10990. THE BOOK OF VISIONS: BEING A TRANSCRIPT OF THE RECORD OF THE SECRET THOUGHTS OF A VARIETY OF INDIVIDUALS WHILE ATTENDING CHURCH . . .

PHILADELPHIA: PUBLISHED BY J. W. MOORE. 1847.

Anonymous.

‹v›-xii, ‹13›-135. 7⅜" scant x 4⁹⁄$_{16}$".

‹1›^{4}, 2-11^6, 12^2.

P cloth: blue. Flyleaves.

Title-page entered July 29, 1847; no record of deposit of book. Noticed LW Oct. 30, 1847. Listed LW Nov. 6, 1847.

LC

10991. RURAL SPORTS; A TALE. IN FOUR PARTS . . .

PHILADELPHIA: CHARLES MARSHALL, 148 CHEST-NUT STREET. 1849.

‹i›-vi, ‹7›-43; blank, p. ‹44›; 4 pp. advertise-ments. 7⅜" scant x 4¾".

‹1›-4^6.

Printed tan paper wrapper.

Deposited April 11, 1849. Reviewed SLM June, 1849.

H   LC

10992. THE WESTERN MERCHANT. A NARRATIVE. CONTAINING USEFUL IN-STRUCTION FOR THE WESTERN MAN OF BUSINESS WHO MAKES HIS PUR-CHASES IN THE EAST; ALSO, INFORMA-TION FOR THE EASTERN MAN WHOSE CUSTOMERS ARE IN THE WEST: LIKE-WISE, HINTS FOR THOSE WHO DE-SIGN EMIGRATING TO THE WEST. DE-

DUCED FROM ACTUAL EXPERIENCE. BY LUKE SHORTFIELD.

PHILADELPHIA: GRIGG, ELLIOT & CO., NO 14 NORTH FOURTH STREET. 1849.

<i>-<viii>, <13>-268. 7⁷⁄₁₆″ x 4½″.

<1>⁴, 2-22⁶, 23².

Two states of the binding noted. The sequence, if any, has not been determined and the designations are for identification only.

A

T cloth: brown. Sides blindstamped with a frame, a filigree at top and at bottom. Yellow end papers. Flyleaves. No inserted catalog.

B

T cloth: black. Sides blindstamped with a frame, a filigree at center of sides. Yellow end papers. Flyleaves. Grigg, Elliot & Company's catalog inserted.

Note: Copies have been seen with Lippincott, Grambo & Company's inserted catalog; issued not before Jan. 1, 1850. Since copies thus are in library rebinding BAL is unable to comment on the original binding; *i.e.,* whether *State A* or *State B.*

Copyright notice dated 1848, but no record of copyright found. Advertised LW June 2, 1849, as *lately published.*

AAS (B)   UV (A)   Y (A)

10993. Wild Western Scenes: A Narrative of Adventures in the Western Wilderness ... by Luke Shortfield ...

Philadelphia: Grigg, Elliot and Co. 14 North Fourth Street. 1849.

For other editions see under 1841, 1852, 1856.

Two states of the binding noted. The sequence, if any, has not been determined and the designations are for identification only.

A

H cloth: black. T cloth: slate-blue. Sides blindstamped with a frame, a filigree at top and at bottom. Cream end papers. Flyleaves.

B

A cloth: brown. T cloth: black. Sides blindstamped with a frame, a filigree at the center of the sides. Cream end papers. Flyleaves.

Advertised as *this day published* LW June 2, 1849. Issued in London as *Life in the Far West: A Narrative of Adventure,* by Luke Shortfield; not seen. Also issued as: *Life in the Far West: A Narrative of Adventures in the West-* *ern Wilderness,* by Luke Shortfield, Dublin: James M'Glashan, MDCCCL; copy in H.

AAS (B)   H (B)   NYPL (A)   Y (A)

10994. THE CITY MERCHANT; OR, THE MYSTERIOUS FAILURE ...

PHILADELPHIA: LIPPINCOTT, GRAMBO & CO., SUCCESSORS TO GRIGG, ELLIOT & CO. 1851.

<i-iv>, <13>-235. Frontispiece and 9 plates inserted. 7¼″ x 4⁷⁄₁₆″.

<1>², 2-19⁶, 20⁴.

Note: Located only in what is undoubtedly a remainder format, bound together with *The Milliner and the Millionaire,* by Mrs. Dr. Hicks, Philadelphia: Lippincott, Grambo & Co., 1852. Cloth. Spine title: SELECT NOVELS.

Noted as *in press* LW Feb. 8, 1851. Advertised as *just published* LW March 1, 1851.

AAS   B

10995. ADVENTURES OF COL. GRACCHUS VANDERBOMB, OF SLOUGHCREEK, IN PURSUIT OF THE PRESIDENCY: ALSO, THE EXPLOITS OF MR. NUMERIUS PLUTARCH KIPPS, HIS PRIVATE SECRETARY ...

PHILADELPHIA: A. HART, LATE CAREY & HART. 1852.

<1>-5, vi-viii, 19-202; plus 24 pp. advertisements paged 1-14, 16-17, 21-28. 7¹¹⁄₁₆″ x 4½″.

<1>-16⁶; plus: <17>¹².

Printed white paper wrapper.

Listed NLG March 15, 1852. Deposited May 1, 1852. Reviewed LW May 1, 1852. Listed LW May 15, 1852.

Note: According to the wrapper, issued as a volume in *Library of Humorous American Works, with Illustrations by Darley.* The book is not illustrated, save for front of the wrapper.

H   LC   NYPL

10996. THE SPANGLERS AND TINGLES; OR, THE RIVAL BELLES. A TALE, UNVEILING SOME OF THE MYSTERIES OF SOCIETY AND POLITICS AS THEY EXIST AT THE PRESENT TIME IN THE UNITED STATES ...

PHILADELPHIA: A. HART, LATE CAREY & HART. 1852.

<1>-<4>, <15>-270. 7⅜″ full x 4½″ scant (a trimmed example).

<1>-21⁶, 22⁴.

Pictorial tan paper wrapper. Publisher's catalog, pp. 1-14, 16-17, 21-28, inserted at back.

Listed and reviewed LW April 10, 1852. Deposited April 19, 1852.

Note: According to the wrapper, issued as a volume in *Library of Humorous American Works, with Illustrations by Darley.* The book is not illustrated, save for front of the wrapper.

LC

10997. Wild Western Scenes . . . New Stereotype Edition, Revised and Corrected . . .

Philadelphia: Lippincott, Grambo & Co. 1852.

Note: Vignette title-page dated 1851. Copyright notice dated 1852.

Printed paper wrapper.

"Preface," p. 4, dated 1852.

For other editions see under 1841, 1849, and 1856.

NYPL

10998. THE MONARCHIST: AN HISTORI- CAL NOVEL, EMBRACING REAL CHAR- ACTERS AND ROMANTIC ADVEN- TURES . . .

PHILADELPHIA: A. HART, LATE CAREY & HART, NO. 126 CHESTNUT STREET. 1853.

⟨1⟩-336; plus: in some copies, 24 pp. advertise- ments. 7½″ x 4⅝″. A set of untrimmed sheets (UV) measures: 8⅛″ x 4¹¹⁄₁₆″.

⟨1⟩-28⁶; plus: in some copies, ⟨29⟩¹².

A cloth: black; slate. Pale yellow end papers. Flyleaves. *Note:* According to Roorbach issued in both cloth; and, printed paper wrapper. Seen only in cloth.

Deposited April 7, 1853. Listed LW April 9, 1853. Listed NLG April 15, 1853.

AAS UV Y

10999. LIFE AND ADVENTURES OF A COUNTRY MERCHANT. A NARRATIVE OF HIS EXPLOITS AT HOME, DURING HIS TRAVELS, AND IN THE CITIES. DE- SIGNED TO AMUSE AND INSTRUCT . . .

PHILADELPHIA: LIPPINCOTT, GRAMBO & CO. 1854.

Not a reprint of *The Western Merchant.* See next entry for *Second Edition.*

⟨1⟩-396. Frontispiece and vignette title-page in- serted. 7⅜″ full x 4¾″. *See binding note below.*

⟨1⟩-26, ⟨27⟩, 28-33⁶. *See binding note below.*

Two states of the binding noted. The sequence, if any, not known; the designations are for iden- tification only.

A

T cloth: purple. Publisher's monogram stamped on sides. Yellow end papers. Flyleaves. Leaves ⟨1⟩₁₋₂ excised.

B

T cloth: green. Publisher's monogram not stamped on sides. Yellow end papers. Flyleaves. Leaf ⟨1⟩₂ excised.

Note: Neither of the above noted with inserted publisher's catalog. A rebound copy at NYPL contains an inserted publisher's catalog, pp. 36, at back.

Lately published—NLG April 1, 1854. *Published since April 1*—NLG April 15, 1854. Listed as an American book PC May 15, 1854.

LC (A)   Y (B)

11000. Life and Adventures of a Country Mer- chant. A Narrative . . . ⟨Second Edition⟩

Philadelphia: Lippincott, Grambo & Co. 1854.

"Preface to the Second Edition," p. 7.

For first edition see preceding entry.

AAS

11001. FREAKS OF FORTUNE: OR, THE HISTORY AND ADVENTURES OF NED LORN . . .

PHILADELPHIA: T. B. PETERSON, NO. 102 CHEST- NUT STREET.   ⟨1854⟩

⟨5⟩-401; 11 pp. advertisements, paged 2-12. Dou- ble frontispiece and 1 plate inserted. 7¹¹⁄₁₆″ x 4⁹⁄₁₆″.

⟨1-17⟩¹². *Signed:* ⟨1⟩-33, ⟨34⟩⁶.

A cloth: blue; brown; purple. T cloth: purple; slate. Yellow end papers. Flyleaves.

Listed NLG Oct. 2, 1854. Listed as an American book PC Nov. 15, 1854.

H LC NYPL Y

11002. THE WINKLES; OR, THE MERRY MONOMANIACS. AN AMERICAN PIC- TURE WITH PORTRAITS OF THE NA- TIVES. BY THE AUTHOR OF "WILD WESTERN SCENES," ETC.

NEW YORK: D. APPLETON AND COMPANY, 346 & 348 BROADWAY. LONDON: 16 LITTLE BRITAIN. 1855.

CLOTH

⟨i⟩-xii, ⟨1⟩-424; 8 pp. advertisements. 7⅝" full x
4¹⁵⁄₁₆".

⟨-⟩⁶, 1-18¹².

T cloth: brown; purple. End papers noted:
blue-coated on white; brown-coated on white;
green-coated on white; pink-coated on white;
rose-coated on white. Flyleaves.

WRAPPER

2 Vols. Title-page in Vol. 1 only.

1: ⟨i⟩-xii, ⟨1⟩-216. 7⅞" x 5".

2: 217-424; 8 pp. advertisements.

1: ⟨-⟩⁶, 1-9¹².

2: 10-18¹².

Printed tan paper wrapper.

Three states (printings?) noted. The sequence
has not been established, and the designations
are for identification only. Reference is to the
terminal advertisements.

A: P. ⟨6⟩: . . . Capt. Canot . . .

B: P. ⟨6⟩: . . . Mile Stones in Our Life Journey . . .

C: P. ⟨6⟩: . . . Memoirs of Napoleon . . .

Deposited June 14, 1855. Listed NLG July 1,
1855. H copy received July 5, 1855. Listed as an
American book PC Oct. 15, 1855.

AAS (A, wrapper)   B (A, cloth)   LC (C, cloth)   Y
(B, cloth)

11003. WILD WESTERN SCENES.-SECOND
SERIES. THE WAR-PATH: A NARRA-
TIVE OF ADVENTURES IN THE WIL-
DERNESS: WITH MINUTE DETAILS OF
THE CAPTIVITY OF SUNDRY PERSONS;
AMUSING AND PERILOUS INCIDENTS
DURING THEIR ABODE IN THE WILD
WOODS; FEARFUL BATTLES WITH
THE INDIANS . . .

PHILADELPHIA: J. B. LIPPINCOTT & CO. 1856.

For *First Series* see above under 1841.

⟨1⟩-335. Frontispiece and 7 plates inserted. 7½"
scant x 4⁹⁄₁₆".

⟨1⟩-28⁶.

Two bindings noted. The sequence, if any, not
determined. The designations are for identification only.

A

A cloth: light green. Sides blindstamped with a
frame, enclosing a circular ornament. Yellow
end papers. Flyleaves.

B

A cloth: blue. Sides blindstamped with a frame
enclosing a grolieresque ornament. Yellow end
papers. Flyleaves.

Advertised as *just published* CRN June 7, 1856.
Advertised as *to be issued in July and August*
CRN July 5, 1856. Advertised as a Trübner importation Ath Aug. 9, 1856. Listed as an American book PC Aug. 15, 1856. Deposited Oct. 21,
1856.

Note: According to Roorbach also issued in paper wrapper; not seen.

NYPL (A)   UV (B)

11004. Wild Western Scenes: A Narrative of
Adventures in the Western Wilderness . . .
New Stereotype Edition, Altered, Revised, and
Corrected . . .

Philadelphia: J. B. Lippincott & Co.   1856.

For other editions see under 1841, 1849, and
1852.

Printed paper wrapper.

"Preface" ⟨for this edition⟩ pp. 3-4, dated at
end *March, 1856.*

Deposited Dec. 2, 1856.

LC

11005. BORDER WAR; A TALE OF DIS-
UNION . . .

NEW YORK: RUDD & CARLETON, 130 GRAND
STREET, (BROOKS BUILDING, COR. OF BROADWAY.)
MDCCCLIX.

⟨i⟩-x, ⟨11⟩-502, blank leaf. 7⁵⁄₁₆" x 4⅞".

⟨1⟩-21¹². *Note:* In all examined copies p. 465 is
erroneously signed 20 (rather than 20*) and p.
473 has the superfluous signature mark 20*.

BD cloth: brown; purple. Brown-coated on
white end papers. Green-coated on white end
papers. Flyleaves. Publisher's catalog, pp. ⟨i-ii⟩,
⟨1⟩-6, inserted at back.

Listed BM April 15, 1859.

BA   H   UV

11006. WILD WESTERN SCENES; OR, THE
WHITE SPIRIT OF THE WILDERNESS.
BEING A NARRATIVE OF ADVEN-
TURES, EMBRACING THE SAME CHAR-
ACTERS PORTRAYED IN THE ORIGI-
NAL "WILD WESTERN SCENES," OVER
ONE HUNDRED EDITIONS OF WHICH
HAVE BEEN SOLD IN EUROPE AND
AMERICA . . . [NEW SERIES.]

RICHMOND: M. A. MALSBY, PUBLISHER.   1863.

⟨i⟩-iv, ⟨1⟩-123; Note, p. ⟨124⟩. 7⁹⁄₁₆″ x 4½″ full.

⟨-⟩², ⟨1⟩-5¹², 6².

Printed tan paper wrapper.

"NOTE.—Owing to the destruction, by fire, of the Bath Paper Mills near Hamburg, S. C., the Publisher has been disappointed in getting such a quantity of book paper as would justify in publishing the entire work at this time, and therefore, has been compelled to issue it in two volumes, the second of which is now in press . . ." —p. ⟨124⟩. Vol. 2 appears not to have been published.

BA   UV   Y

11007. LOVE AND MONEY . . .

> PHILADELPHIA: T. B. PETERSON & BROTHERS, 306 CHESTNUT STREET. ⟨1865⟩

⟨17⟩-407; blank, p. ⟨408⟩; 8 pp. advertisements. 7⁵⁄₁₆″ x 4⅛″.

⟨1⟩-25⁸.

HC cloth: purple. Yellow end papers. Flyleaves. Also printed wrapper?

Advertised as *just out,* in paper and cloth, ALG Sept. 15, 1865.

Gd

11008. A REBEL WAR CLERK'S DIARY AT THE CONFEDERATE STATES CAPITAL . . .

> PHILADELPHIA: J. B. LIPPINCOTT & CO. 1866.

2 Vols.

1: ⟨i⟩-xii, 13-392. 8¹⁄₁₆″ x 5³⁄₁₆″.

2: ⟨1⟩-480.

1: ⟨1⟩-32⁶, 33⁴.

2: ⟨1⟩-40⁶.

Four bindings noted. The sequence of *Bindings A-C* has not been determined and the designations are for identification only.

Binding A

C cloth: plum. Yellow end papers. Flyleaves. Spine imprint: J.B.L.&C° A copy thus received at MHS April 14, 1866.

Binding B

S cloth: terra-cotta. Brown-coated end papers. Flyleaves. Spine imprint: J.B.LIPPINCOTT & CO.

Binding C

C cloth: black. Peach end papers. Flyleaves. No spine imprint.

Binding D

S cloth: orange. Brown-coated end papers. Flyleaves. Spine imprint: J.B.LIPPINCOTT CO. Not before March, 1885, in which month J. B. Lippincott & Company became J. B. Lippincott Company.

Deposited April 4, 1866. BA copy (now rebound) received April 13, 1866. MHS copy (*Binding A*) received April 14, 1866. Reviewed ALG April 16, 1866. Listed ALG May 1, 1866. As a Trübner importation advertised Ath May 19, 1866; Bkr May 31, 1866; listed Bkr May 31, 1866; PC June 1, 1866; reviewed Ath July 14, 1866.

AAS (*Binding C*)   MHS (*Binding A*)   NYPL (*Bindings A,B,D*)

The following are reprints of Jones's own books.

11009. Wild Western Scenes: A Narrative of Adventures in the Western Wilderness, Forty Years Ago . . . By a Squatter.

Philadelphia: E. Ferrett & Co. 68 South Fourth Street. 1845.

Printed paper wrapper? Reprint of the 1841 printing.

11010. Life in the Far West: A Narrative of Adventures in the Western Wilderness. By Luke Shortfield.

Dublin: Published by James M'Glashan, 21, D'Olier Street. MDCCCL.

Reprint of *Wild Western Scenes* . . . , 1849.

11011. Wild Southern Scenes. A Tale of Disunion! and Border War! . . .

Philadelphia: T. B. Peterson & Brothers, 306 Chestnut Street. ⟨1859⟩

Reprint of *Border War* . . . , 1859. Listed APC Nov. 19, 1859.

11012. Secession, Coercion, and Civil War. The Story of 1861 . . .

Philadelphia: T. B. Peterson and Brothers, 306 Chestnut Street. ⟨1861⟩

Anonymous. Reprint of *Border War* . . . , 1859.

11013. The War-Path; or, Wild Western Scenes . . .

Halifax: Milner and Sowerby. 1861.

Reprint of *Wild Western Scenes. Second Series. The War-Path* . . . , 1856.

11014. The Rival Belles; or, Life in Washington . . .

Philadelphia: T. B. Peterson and Brothers, 306 Chestnut Street. ⟨1864⟩

Reprint of *The Spanglers and Tingles* . . . , 1852. According to Kelly issued in both cloth; and, printed paper wrapper. Announced ALG

Aug. 15, 1864. Listed (both cloth and paper wrapper) ALG Oct. 1, 1864.

11015. The Rival Belles; or, Life in Washington . . .

Philadelphia: T. B. Peterson & Brothers; 306 Chestnut Street. ⟨1878⟩

Reprint of *The Spanglers and Tingles* . . . , 1852.

REFERENCES AND ANA

Thoughts on the Literary Prospects of America. An Essay: By J. Jones.

Baltimore: Printed by John Murphy. MDCCCXXXIX.

⟨1⟩-16. 8⅝″ scant x 5⅜″. ⟨1⟩-2⁴. Printed paper wrapper? Self-wrapper?

By the subject of this list? Attributed to John Beauchamp Jones by Sabin (note under entry No. 36537) and by Foley. BAL has found no supporting evidence. A copy of the publication is in LC. By Joshua Jones of Baltimore? Josiah Jones of Baltimore?

Life and Adventure in the South Pacific. By a Roving Printer.

New York: Harper & Brothers, Publishers, Franklin Square. 1861.

Attributed to John Beauchamp Jones by Cushing (*Initials and Pseudonyms*, N. Y., 1885); to John B. Jones in *A Collection of Books . . . Illustrating the Whale Fishery . . . in the Free Public Library*, New Bedford, Mass., 1920 (on the basis of Cushing?). BAL has found no evidence to support the attribution.

Elementary Arithmetic, in Cherokee and English, Designed for Beginners. By John B. Jones. Prepared by Authority of the Cherokee National Council.

Cherokee National Press: Tahlequah, Cherokee Nation . . . 1870.

Boards, cloth corners and shelfback. Not by John Beauchamp Jones, but by John Buttrick Jones. See Pilling, *Indian Languages* . . . , p. 94.

A Rebel War Clerk's Diary at the Confederate States Capital ... A New and Enlarged Edition Edited with an Introduction and Historical Notes by Howard Swiggett ... in Two Volumes ...

New York Old Hickory Bookshop 1935

Deposited April 1, 1935.

... A Rebel War Clerk's Diary Condensed, Edited, and Annotated by Earl Schenck Miers ...

Sagamore Press, Inc. Publishers New York <1958>

At head of title: John B. Jones

SAMUEL BENJAMIN HELBERT JUDAH

(Terentius Phlogobombos)

1 8 0 4 – 1 8 7 6

Judah's birthdate is frequently given as 1799 and *ca.* 1799; his third name as *Herbert* rather than *Helbert*. The date 1804 and the name *Helbert* are confirmed by the records of Congregation Shearith Israel, New York; and by documents in the Mayor's Court Records of the Hall of Records, New York City. Also see *Americans of Jewish Descent, A Compendium of Genealogy*, compiled by Malcolm H. Stern, Cincinnati ⟨1960⟩, p. 101.

11016. THE MOUNTAIN TORRENT, A GRAND MELO-DRAMA, INTERSPERSED WITH SONGS, CHORUSES, &C. IN TWO ACTS ...

NEW-YORK: PUBLISHED BY THOMAS LONGWORTH, AT THE DRAMATIC REPOSITORY, SHAKSPEARE-GALLERY. 1820.

Cover-title.

⟨i⟩-⟨vi⟩, ⟨7⟩-54. 6⅜″ x 4″.

⟨A⟩-C⁶, D⁹. D₅ (signed D₄) is an insert.

Self-wrapper.

Preface dated April 12, 1820. No copyright notice.

AAS   B   H   NYHS   NYPL

11017. ODOFRIEDE; THE OUTCAST; A DRAMATIC POEM ...

NEW-YORK: WILEY AND HALSTED, WALL-STREET. M DCCC XXII.

⟨1⟩-⟨95⟩. 9⅛″ x 5¾″ scant.

⟨1⟩-12⁴. *Note:* Signature mark 6 (p. 41) not present in some copies.

Printed tan paper wrapper. White paper pastedowns.

Title deposited Dec. 20, 1821. Reviewed PF March 1822. Listed NAR April 1822.

11018. THE ROSE OF ARRAGON; OR, THE VIGIL OF ST. MARK: A MELO-DRAMA, IN TWO ACTS ...

NEW-YORK: PRINTED AND PUBLISHED BY S. KING. 386 BROADWAY. 1822.

Note: Copies occur with the statement *Second Edition* on the title-page. BAL suspects that all copies are of a single printing and that the statement, *Second Edition*, represents nothing more than a stop-press alteration designed to suggest popularity of the publication.

⟨1⟩-38. 7″ x 4⅜″.

⟨1⟩⁹, 2⁹, ⟨3⟩¹. Leaves ⟨1⟩₅ and 2₅ inserted.

Printed drab tan paper wrapper. *Note: Two forms of the wrapper have been noted.* The sequence, *if any,* has not been determined and the designations are for identification only.

A: *Rose of Arragon* is set in solid face. *Second Edition* also thus.

B: *Rose of Arragon* is set in hollow face. *Second Edition* also thus.

Note: The possibility of simultaneous printing from multiple settings may not be ignored. Other variations are present but the above is sufficient for ready identification.

Title deposited May 7, 1822.

AAS (A)   H (B)   NYHS (A)   Y (B)

11019. A TALE OF LEXINGTON: A NATIONAL COMEDY, FOUNDED ON THE OPENING OF THE REVOLUTION. IN THREE ACTS ...

NEW-YORK: PUBLISHED AT THE DRAMATIC REPOSITORY, 208 BROADWAY. H. SAGE'S BOOK AND MUSIC STORE. 1823.

Cover-title.

⟨i⟩-⟨vi⟩, ⟨7⟩-60. 6¼″ x 4″.

B

⟨1⟩-4⁶, 5², 6¹, 7², 8¹.

Self-wrapper.

Title deposited April 7, 1823. Reviewed as an American book LG Jan. 24, 1824.

AAS B H LC NYHS UV

11020. GOTHAM AND THE GOTHAMITES, A MEDLEY ...

NEW-YORK: PUBLISHED FOR THE AUTHOR, AND SOLD BY S. KING, 136 WILLIAM-STREET. 1823.

Anonymous.

⟨i⟩-lvi, ⟨1⟩-93; *An After Thought*, p. ⟨94⟩; blank leaf. 5⅞″ x 3¼″.

⟨1⟩-5, 4 ⟨*sic*⟩¹², 7⁴.

Printed tan boards. Flyleaves.

The Grand Jury ... has found a bill against Judah, the author ... of ⟨this⟩ scurrilous book—Minerva (New York) July 19, 1823.

"Immediately upon the publication of the book ⟨*Gotham and the Gothamites*⟩ he ⟨Judah⟩ caused handbills to be posted up throughout the city, offering a reward for the discovery of the author, and wrote anonymous letters to a considerable number of persons he had mentioned in it, which ... informed them generally that the work had appeared ..."—Charles Patrick Daly: *The Settlement of the Jews in North America*, New York, 1893, p. 142. BAL has not found a copy of the handbill.

AAS LC NYPL UV Y

11021. THE BUCCANEERS; A ROMANCE OF OUR OWN COUNTRY, IN ITS ANCIENT DAY ... CAREFULLY COLLATED FROM THE LABORIOUS RESEARCHES, AND MINUTE INVESTIGATIONS, OF THAT EXCELLENT ANTIQUARY AND SUBLIME PHILOSOPHER, YCLEPT TERENTIUS PHLOGOBOMBOS ...

BOSTON: MUNROE & FRANCIS, 128 WASHINGTON-STREET. NEW-YORK: CHARLES S. FRANCIS, 252 BROADWAY. 1827.

2 Vols.

1: ⟨i⟩-⟨xxviii⟩, ⟨29⟩-263. 7¾″ x 4¾″. *Note:* DAB correctly reports that "certain ... passages ⟨in the preface⟩ were cut after the book had been printed." The reference is to pp. xix-xxiv (leaves 2₄₋₆). In all examined copies the three leaves comprising pp. xix-xxiv are excised and replaced by a single leaf cancel paged xix-xx. The resultant faulty pagination notwithstanding, there is no textual hiatus. The revised text on pp. xix-xx (the inserted cancel) is from a setting unlike that in the rest of the preface.

2: ⟨1⟩-384.

1: ⟨1⟩-22⁶. Leaves 2₄₋₆ excised; see note above.

2: ⟨1⟩-32⁶. In all examined copies (all forms) p. 101 signed 9 for 9*.

Blue-gray paper boards, pink muslin shelfback. Also, blue-gray paper boards, white paper shelfback. Printed label on spine.

Three forms of the book have been noted. There is a possibility that but a single printing is involved; and that the variations are of the title-leaves only.

First Printing

Title-leaves, both volumes, are integral parts of their respective gatherings; neither is a cancel. Imprint as given above. Collation as given above. Two states of Vol. 1 noted; the order given is probable.

A: Vol. 1, p. 263, line 1: ... *the/*

B: Vol. 1, p. 263, line 1: ... ⟨*t*⟩*he/*

Second Edition (so-called)

The title-pages are from an altered setting. In addition to the resetting of certain lines, in some of which the type faces are changed, there is present the statement: SECOND EDITION. Leaves 2₄₋₆ (Vol. 1) excised. The cancel (pp. xix-xx) present in some copies. The title-leaf, Vol. 1, is an integral part of its gathering. The title-leaf for Vol. 2 is a cancel. Imprint as in the *First Printing*.

Second Issue (?)

Issued with cancelled title-leaves (both volumes) imprinted: THE IMPRINT WHEREOF IS AT NEW-YORK. A. D. 1827. Leaves 2₄₋₆ (Vol. 1) excised. The cancel (pp. xix-xx) present. The title-page for Vol. 1 (Vol. 1 only) has been noted in two states; the sequence is presumed correct:

Second Issue (?), Title-leaf A

... *Settlement of the Niew Nederlandts* ...

Second Issue (?), Title-leaf B

... *Settlement of the Nieuw Nederlandts* ...

Title deposited June 9, 1827. Listed NAR Jan. 1828.

AAS (Second Issue, title-leaf A) H (Second Edition) NYHS (Second Edition) UV (First Printing) Y (Second Issue, title-leaf B)

ANA

Richelieu: A Domestic Tragedy, Founded on Fact ... by John Howard Payne ...

New-York: Published by E. M. Murden ... 1826.

Sometimes misattributed to Judah (as in Wegelin's *Early American Plays ...* , 1900; error corrected by Wegelin in his revised edition of 1905). Probably issued in printed paper wrapper.

ATTRIBUTED WORKS

BAL has been unable to find any evidence that the following anonymous publications, sometimes attributed to Judah, were written by him.

The Maid of Midian, a Tragedy, in Four Acts; Founded on the Massacre of the Midian Captives, by Order of Moses: As Recorded in the Thirty-First Chapter of the Book of Numbers ...

Philadelphia, Published by A. E. Armstrong, No. 45, North Second Street. 1833.

Printed paper wrapper. "This piece is generally attributed to S. B. H. Judah."—A. S. W. Rosenbach, *An American Jewish Bibliography* ⟨1926⟩, p. 288.

David and Uriah. A Drama, in Five Acts; Founded on the Exploits of the Man after God's Own Heart ...

Philadelphia: Published by the Author. 1835.

Cover-title? Printed paper wrapper? Self-wrapper? The final paragraph of the "To the Reader" indicates that the author of *David and Uriah* was also the author of *The Maid of Midian:* "The avidity with which another small publication of a similar kind ⟨*The Maid of Midian*⟩ has been purchased and perused, has given the writer confidence in the belief that what is now offered to the public, will meet with an equally favourable reception ..."

Edwin Wolf, 2d, in "Some Unrecorded American Judaica Printed before 1851," in *Essays in American Jewish History to Commemorate the Tenth Anniversary of the Founding of the American Jewish Archives ...* , Cincinnati, 1958, p. 217, attributes *David and Uriah* to Judah.

The Maid of Midian: A Tragedy. In Four Acts. Founded on the Massacre of the Midian Captives by Order of Moses ... Third Edition with Improvements.

Philadelphia. Published by the Author. 1836.

Printed paper wrapper? For first edition see above. No copy of the *Second Edition* (if such there is) has been located.

Spirit of Fanaticism: A Poetical Rhapsody ...

New-York: Published at the "Beacon" Office, 94 Roosevelt-Street. 1842.

Printed paper wrapper.

Attributed to Judah by NYPL and by Edwin Wolf, 2d, in "Some Unrecorded American Judaica Printed before 1851," in *Essays in American Jewish History to Commemorate the Tenth Anniversary of the Founding of the American Jewish Archives ...* , Cincinnati, 1958, p. 225. In a letter to BAL (Aug. 11, 1965) Mr. Wolf states that he "does not now know upon what authority he attributed the work to Judah."

The Battles of Joshua; a New Version, with Notes; Offered to the Consideration of Commentators.

Philadelphia: Printed & Sold by H. Young, Corner of Passyunk Rd. & Shippen St. and for Sale at No. 94 Rosevelt ⟨*sic*⟩ St. New York. 1843.

Cover-title? Printed paper wrapper? Self-wrapper? Attributed to Judah by NYPL.

The Mystical Craft, the Most Crafty of All Crafts. And the Most Delusive of All Delusions, As Exemplified by Our Modern Mercuries, or Missionaries, and Others Engaged in the Great Measures for Proselyting the World, and for Hastening on the Glorious Millenium of Ecclesiastical Supremacy in This Favoured Land of Liberty.

New York: Published by G. Vale, at the Beacon Office, No. 94 Rosevelt ⟨*sic*⟩ Street, also by H. Young, Corner of Passyunk Road and Shippen Street, Philadelphia. 1844.

Printed paper wrapper. Attributed to Judah by NYPL.

SYLVESTER JUDD

1813 – 1853

Caution: Do not confuse Sylvester Judd, 1813–1853, with Sylvester Judd, 1789–1860, author of *Thomas Judd and His Descendants,* Northampton, 1856; and, *History of Hadley ...,* Northampton, 1863.

11022. ... A YOUNG MAN'S ACCOUNT OF HIS CONVERSION FROM CALVINISM. A STATEMENT OF FACTS.

PRINTED FOR THE AMERICAN UNITARIAN ASSOCIATION. BOSTON: JAMES MUNROE & CO. 134 WASHINGTON STREET. MARCH, 1838 ...

Anonymous.

Cover-title. At head of title: 1ST SERIES. NO. 128.

⟨1⟩-34, blank leaf. Also has supplementary pagination for the series: ⟨207⟩-240, blank leaf. 8" x 5⅝" scant.

⟨1⟩-3⁶.

Self-wrapper.

An entry for this title in LC catalog indicates that there is also an undated printing issued *ca. 184-?* Further information wanting. A printing dated 1855 (in BPL) has Judd's name on the title-page.

H LC

11023. ... THE LITTLE COAT: A SERMON ...

⟨AMERICAN REFORM TRACT AND BOOK SOCIETY, n.d., *ca.* 1840⟩

Caption-title. Imprint at foot of p. 8. At head of title: NO. 9.

⟨1⟩-8. 6¹⁵⁄₁₆" full x 4⁵⁄₁₆".

⟨-⟩⁴.

Printed self-wrapper?

Reprinted in the Unitarian Sunday-School Society's *Tract Series,* No. 14 ⟨n.d., 1911?⟩.

Y

11024. THE BEAUTIFUL ZION. A SERMON ... PREACHED JULY 4, 1841.

AUGUSTA: SEVERANCE AND DORR, PRINTERS. 1841.

Cover-title?

⟨1⟩-27. 8" x 5" full.

⟨1⟩-2⁶, 3².

Probably issued in self-wrapper.

AAS H

11025. A MORAL REVIEW OF THE REVOLUTIONARY WAR, OR SOME OF THE EVILS OF THAT EVENT CONSIDERED. A DISCOURSE DELIVERED AT THE UNITARIAN CHURCH, AUGUSTA, SABBATH EVENING, MARCH 13TH, 1842. WITH AN INTRODUCTORY ADDRESS, AND NOTES ...

HALLOWELL: GLAZIER, MASTERS & SMITH, PRINTERS. 1842.

⟨1⟩-48. 8¹⁵⁄₁₆" full x 5⅝".

⟨1⟩-6⁴.

Printed paper wrapper: blue-gray; brown.

Listed NAR July, 1842.

H LC NYPL

11026. A DISCOURSE TOUCHING THE CAUSES AND REMEDIES OF INTEMPERANCE. PREACHED FEBRUARY 2, 1845 ...

AUGUSTA: WM. T. JOHNSON, PRINTER. 1845.

Cover-title?

⟨1⟩-40. 9³⁄₁₆" x 5⅝".

⟨1⟩-5⁴.

Possibly issued in unprinted buff; or, gray paper wrapper.

H MHS

11027. MARGARET. A TALE OF THE REAL AND IDEAL, BLIGHT AND BLOOM; INCLUDING SKETCHES OF A PLACE NOT BEFORE DESCRIBED, CALLED MONS CHRISTI ...

BOSTON: JORDAN AND WILEY. SOLD BY C. S. FRANCIS, BURGESS AND STRINGER, AND W. TAYLOR, NEW YORK; G. B. ZIEBER AND CO., PHILADELPHIA; SHURTZ AND TAYLOR, BALTIMORE; A. HEAD, CHARLESTON, S. C.; AND TAYLOR AND CO., WASHINGTON, D. C. M DCCC XLV.

Anonymous. For a revised edition see under 1851.

⟨i-iv⟩, ⟨1⟩-460. $7^{13}/_{16}$″ x $4^{7}/_{8}$″.

⟨-⟩², 1-38⁶, 39².

T cloth: black. Pale buff end papers. Flyleaves.

Note: Two binding issues noted:

1(?): Publisher's spine imprint not present.

2(?): Publisher's imprint on spine: MUNROE & CO.

Note: In all examined copies, p. 6 is mispaged 9, p. 9 is mispaged 6; p. 168, line 1: *fuffy* for *fluffy.*

Title deposited June 30, 1845. Reviewed H Sept. 6, 1845. Noted as *recently published* K Oct. 1845. Wiley & Putnam importation listed PC Oct. 1, 1845.

AAS (1st)   UV (2nd)

11028. Sermons on Christian Communion, Designed to Promote the Growth of the Religious Affections, by Living Ministers ... Edited by T. R. Sullivan.

Boston: Wm. Crosby and H. P. Nichols, 111 Washington Street. 1848.

"Worth of the Soul," pp. ⟨23⟩-37.

For comment see entry No. 1367.

11029. PHILO: AN EVANGELIAD. BY THE AUTHOR OF 'MARGARET; A TALE OF THE REAL AND IDEAL.'

BOSTON: PHILLIPS, SAMPSON, AND COMPANY. 1850.

⟨1⟩-244, 4 pp. advertisements; plus: 2 pp. advertisements, blank leaf. $7^{5}/_{16}$″ x $4^{11}/_{16}$″ (gilt binding). $7^{1}/_{4}$″ scant x $4^{5}/_{8}$″ (extra-gilt binding).

⟨1⟩-20⁶, 21⁴; plus: ⟨22⟩².

Gilt Binding

T cloth: black. Stamped in gold and in blind. Yellow end papers. Flyleaves. Edges plain.

Extra-Gilt Binding

T cloth: red. Stamped in gold only. Cream end papers. Flyleaves. Edges gilt.

Noted for *immediate publication* LW Nov. 17, 1849. Deposited Dec. 28, 1849. Listed LW Jan. 19, 1850. Reviewed LW Jan. 26, 1850. Chapman importation listed PC Feb. 15, 1850. Davidson importation advertised Ath Feb. 23, 1850; PC March 1, 1850; listed PC June 1, 1850.

B (gilt) BA (gilt) BPL (extra-gilt) H (gilt) LC (gilt, being a deposit copy)

11030. THE TRUE DIGNITY OF POLITICS. A SERMON ... PREACHED IN CHRIST CHURCH, AUGUSTA, MAY 26, 1850.

AUGUSTA: WILLIAM T. JOHNSON, PRINTER TO THE STATE. 1850.

⟨1⟩-21; order to print, p. ⟨22⟩; blank leaf. 9″ scant x $5^{1}/_{2}$″ full.

⟨1⟩-3⁴.

Printed blue, faun, or pink paper wrapper.

"... May 30, 1850. Ordered, That 1,000 copies ... be printed ..."—p. ⟨22⟩.

AAS   B   H

11031. RICHARD EDNEY AND THE GOVERNOR'S FAMILY. A RUS-URBAN TALE, SIMPLE AND POPULAR, YET CULTURED AND NOBLE, OF MORALS, SENTIMENT, AND LIFE, PRACTICALLY TREATED AND PLEASANTLY ILLUSTRATED ... BY THE AUTHOR OF "MARGARET," AND "PHILO." ...

BOSTON: PHILLIPS, SAMPSON & COMPANY. 1850.

⟨i⟩-vi, ⟨7⟩-468. $7^{1}/_{4}$″ full x $4^{9}/_{16}$″.

⟨1⟩-39⁶.

T cloth: black. White; or, yellow end papers. Flyleaves.

Advertised as *recently published* LW Nov. 30, 1850. Deposited Dec. 4, 1850. Reviewed LW Dec. 7, 1850. The Chapman importation advertised Ath Jan. 11, 1851; listed PC Jan. 16, 1851; reviewed Ath Jan. 18, 1851.

AAS   MHS

11032. Margaret: A Tale of the Real and the Ideal ... Revised Edition ... by the Author of "Philo," ...

Boston: Phillips, Sampson, and Company. 1851.

2 Vols. For first edition see above under 1845.

"Author's Note," Vol. 1, pp. ⟨iii⟩-v, dated at end May 12, 1851.

Two bindings noted. The sequence (if any) has not been determined and the designations are for identification only.

A

T cloth: black; tan. Spine stamped in gold: MARGARET / ⟨lozenge rule⟩ / VOL. I. ⟨II.⟩ / A copy thus at AAS inscribed by early owner Oct. 6, 1851.

B

T cloth: black. Spine stamped in gold: MARGARET: / A TALE OF THE / REAL AND IDEAL / BLIGHT AND BLOOM / ⟨rule⟩ / VOL. I. ⟨II.⟩ / BOSTON. /

Note: Other binding variations are present but the above is sufficient for identification.

A copy in AAS (Binding A) inscribed by early owner Oct. 6, 1851. Listed NLA Oct. 15, 1851; LW Oct. 18, 1851. The London (Chapman importation?) listed PC Nov. 1, 1851. Listed Ath and LG Oct. 25, 1851.

Note: The Boston issue dated 1857 appears to be sheets of the 1851 printing with cancel title-leaf.

AAS (A)   UV (A,B)

11033. THE BIRTHRIGHT CHURCH: A DISCOURSE ... DESIGNED FOR "THURSDAY LECTURE" IN BOSTON, JAN. 6, 1853 ...

BOSTON: CROSBY, NICHOLS, & COMPANY, 111, WASHINGTON STREET. 1853.

Edited by Joseph H. Williams.

⟨1⟩-49. 9 3/16″ x 5 7/8″.

⟨1⟩-6⁴, 7¹.

Printed tan paper wrapper.

Prefatory note dated April 18, 1853. Listed NLG June 15, 1853. Reprinted Augusta, Me., under date 1854.

AAS   H   MHS

11034. THE CHURCH: IN A SERIES OF DIS-COURSES ...

BOSTON: CROSBY, NICHOLS, AND COMPANY, 111 WASHINGTON STREET. 1854.

Edited by Joseph H. Williams.

⟨i-ii⟩, ⟨i⟩-⟨x⟩, ⟨1⟩-274, blank leaf. 7 5/8″ x 4 3/4″ full.

⟨a⟩⁶, 1-21, ⟨22⟩-23⁶, *Note:* Signature mark 3 lacking in some copies.

T cloth: black. Yellow end papers. Flyleaves.

Listed NLG April 15, 1854.

AAS   BA   NYPL   Y

11035. Richard Edney and the Governor's Family ...

Boston: Roberts Brothers, 1880.

Reprint. See above under 1850.

Advertised for *this week* PW March 20, 1880. Noted for *this week* PW March 27, 1880. Listed PW April 3, 1880.

NYPL

REPRINTS

The following books contain material by Judd reprinted from earlier books.

The Harp and the Cross ... Compiled by Stephen G. Bulfinch ...

Boston ... 1857.

"Hymn to Jesus," pp. 80-81, and "Love, Hope, and Faith," pp. 133-134 are both extracted from *Philo* ..., 1850. For comment see BAL, Vol. V, p. 599.

Children's Praise. A Book of Prayers and Hymns for the Children of the Church ...

Boston: Ticknor and Fields. M DCCC LVIII.

Untitled poem, *O Son of God! Thy children we* ..., p. 108; extracted from *Philo* ..., 1850.

The Atlantic Almanac 1873 ...

Boston: James R. Osgood and Company. Late Ticknor & Fields, and Fields, Osgood, & Co. Office of the Atlantic Monthly. [Entered According to Act of Congress ... 1872 ...

Printed wrapper. "The Stage-Driver," p. 59; extracted from *Richard Edney* ..., 1850.

The Sword and the Pen ...

Boston ... 1881 ...

Two paragraphs of prose, No. 1, p. 6; extracted from *Margaret* ..., 1845. For comment see entry No. 123.

... Harper's Fifth Reader   American Authors New York ... 1889

"Lost in the Woods," pp. 244-254; extracted from *Margaret* ..., 1845.

For comment see entry No. 7917.

Proceedings of the Class of 1836 at Their First General Meeting.

<New Haven, 1839>

Cover-title. Printed wrapper. On pp. 10-11 is a brief report on Judd's post-college activities; presumably based on a report prepared by Judd.

... A Sermon Preached at Park Street Church, Portland, Sunday, Jan. 30, 1853, by Rev. R. P. Cutler. Occasioned by the Death of Rev. Sylvester Judd.

Portland: Published by H. J. Little & Co. Foster and Gerrish, Printers. 1853.

Printed wrapper. At head of title: "How is the strong staff broken ...

Life and Character of the Rev. Sylvester Judd. <By Arethusa Hall>

Boston: Crosby, Nichols, and Company. New York: C. S. Francis and Co. 1854.

Advertised as *now ready* NLG Oct. 2, 1854. Listed NLG Nov. 1, 1854. Reviewed NLG Nov. 15, 1854. Deposited March 22, 1855.

Compositions in Outline by Felix O. C. Darley from Judd's Margaret ...

Redfield, 34 Beekman St. New York ... 1856 ...

Printed paper boards. Reissued after Nov. 1, 1860, imprinted *Widdleton, 27 Howard St. New York ... 1856* ...

Sylvester Judd ... Novelist of Transcendentalism by Philip Judd Brockway

Printed at the University Press Orono, Maine 1941

Printed wrapper. Issued as University of Maine Studies, Second Series, No. 53. (*The Maine Bulletin*, Vol. XLIII, No. 12, April 1941).

JOHN PENDLETON KENNEDY

(Mr. Ambrose, Paul Ambrose, A Citizen of Maryland, A Man of the Times, Mark Littleton, A Member of the Twenty-Seventh Congress, Mephistopheles, Solomon Secondthoughts, A Southern Man)

1 7 9 5 - 1 8 7 0

As a member of the Congress, and later as Secretary of the Navy, Kennedy's name is attached to many official publications. No attempt has been made to locate and to describe such material but a representative selection will be found at the end of this list. Kennedy's own copies of many of these, with notes indicating his authorship (in whole or in part), are in The Peabody Institute, Baltimore, Maryland.

11036. THE RED BOOK

A periodical publication written wholly by Kennedy and Peter Hoffman Cruse. Anonymous. Issued in printed paper wrappers.

Note: This entry is all but tentative. BAL has been unable to locate a sufficient number of copies on which to base a satisfactory collation. There is a possibility that some parts, perhaps all, went into two or more printings but information is lacking; *Part One* was indeed issued in a second edition; see below.

For a discussion of this publication see *"The Red Book, 1819–1821, a Satire on Baltimore Society,"* by Charles H. Bohner, in *Maryland Historical Magazine, a Quarterly,* Sept. 1956, pp. 175-187. In his opening paragraph Bohner states that "within two months" of publication "a third edition" of the first number "was called for." But since (as Bohner makes amply clear) the publisher was something of a promoter, the "call" may well have been inspired by him, rather than the public, and the "third edition" nothing more tangible than a product of the publisher's imagination.

... THE RED BOOK ...

> BALTIMORE: PRINTED BY J. ROBINSON, CIRCULATING LIBRARY, CORNER OF MARKET AND BELVIDERE-STREETS. OPPOSITE THE FRANKLIN BANK. ⟨1819–1821⟩

Leaf: 6³⁄₁₆″ x 3⅞″.

Title-page of Part 1 as above. At head of title: NO. I. PRICE 25 CENTS.

Part 1

⟨1⟩-36.

⟨1⟩-3⁶.

Dated on p. ⟨1⟩: *October 23, 1819.*

Part 2

⟨37⟩-88.

4-7⁶, 8².

Dated on p. ⟨37⟩: *Nov. 5, 1819.*

Part 3

⟨89⟩-132.

10-12⁶, 13⁴.

Dated on p. ⟨89⟩: *Nov. 18, 1819.*

Part 4

⟨133⟩-171; blank, p. ⟨172⟩.

14-16⁶, 17².

Dated on p. ⟨133⟩: *Dec. 6, 1819.*

Part 5

⟨173⟩-212.

18-20⁶, 21².

Dated on p. ⟨173⟩: *Dec. 24, 1819.*

Part 6

⟨213⟩-262; *Advertisement,* p. ⟨263⟩; blank, p. ⟨264⟩. P. 252 mispaged 262.

22-⟨23⟩, 24-25⁶, 26².

Dated on p. ⟨213⟩: *Jan. 22, 1820.*

Copies occur with, and without, the statement *No. 6* and signature mark *26* on p. ⟨261⟩; sequence not established.

Part 7

⟨1⟩-42.

1-3⁶, 4², 5¹.

Dated on p. ⟨1⟩: *March 3, 1820.*

Copies occur as follows, the sequence presented is presumed correct:

A: At foot of p. ⟨1⟩: VOL. I

B: At foot of p. ⟨1⟩: VOL. II

Part 8

⟨43⟩-87, blank leaf.

6-9⁶.

Sheets undated. Wrapper dated *April 12, 1820.*

Part 9

⟨89⟩-130.

10-12⁶, 13², 14¹.

Sheets undated. *Date on wrapper?*

Part 10

⟨131⟩-174.

15-17⁶, 18⁴.

Sheets undated. Wrapper dated *March 16, 1821.*

This entry made on the basis of copies, complete and otherwise, in B, LC, MdHS, PB, UV, Y.

11037. The Red Book ... Second Edition ...

Baltimore: Printed by J. Robinson, Circulating Library, Corner of Market & Belvidere-Streets, Opposite the Franklin Bank. 1820.

2 Vols. Vol. 2 imprinted:

Baltimore: Printed by J. Robinson, Circulating Library, Market & Belvidere-Streets, Opposite the Franklin Bank. 1821.

For first edition see preceding entry. Anonymous.

Printed paper boards?

Quite possibly made up of unsold sheets of the earlier printing (printings?) save for *Part 1.* In this second edition "Journal of a Day" and "From Our Note Book," both of which appear in *Part 1,* first printing, are replaced by "Preface to the Second Edition of the First Volume" and "An Olde Prophecie."

Title deposited Oct. 22, 1820.

The present entry made on the basis of copies, complete and otherwise, in MdHS, PB, UV, Y.

11038. ADDRESS DELIVERED ON BEHALF OF THE FACULTY OF ARTS AND SCIENCES, ON THE OCCASION OF THE OPENING OF THE COLLEGIATE DEPARTMENT IN THE UNIVERSITY OF MARYLAND, ON THE 3d OF JANUARY, 1831 ...

BALTIMORE: PRINTED BY JOHN D. TOY, CORNER OF MARKET AND ST. PAUL STREETS. 1831.

Cover-title.

⟨1⟩-26, blank leaf. 9″ x 5⅝″.

⟨1⟩-3⁴, 4².

Printed self-wrapper.

AAS   H   NYPL

11039. ADDRESS OF THE FRIENDS OF DOMESTIC INDUSTRY, ASSEMBLED IN CONVENTION, AT NEW-YORK, OCTOBER 26, 1831, TO THE PEOPLE OF THE UNITED STATES.

PUBLISHED BY ORDER OF THE CONVENTION. BALTIMORE, NOVEMBER 10, 1831.

Cover-title? Anonymous.

⟨1⟩-44. 8⅝″ x 5⁷⁄₁₆″. *Note:* The measurement is that of a trimmed example.

⟨1⟩-5⁴, 6².

Printed self-wrapper? Printed wrapper?

Kennedy's own copy (in PB) is annotated by him and identifies his co-authors as Warren Dutton, Charles J. Ingersol ⟨or: Ingersoll⟩. The annotations further indicate that Kennedy wrote the following passages:

Pp. 10-14: *We may pursue ... ⟨to⟩ ... hope and joy.*

Pp. 16-18: *It is an error to suppose ... ⟨to⟩ ... innumerable blessings.*

Pp. 24-28: *A reference to our own experience ... ⟨to⟩ ... class of the community.*

Pp. 29-30: *Mistaken opinions ... ⟨to⟩ ... applied our cotton.*

Pp. 32-33: *Whilst we assert ... ⟨to⟩ ... competition of domestic labour.*

The *Address* is signed at end by the officers of the convention; Kennedy's name is not present.

PB

11040. SWALLOW BARN, OR A SOJOURN IN THE OLD DOMINION. IN TWO VOLUMES ...

PHILADELPHIA: CAREY & LEA, CHESTNUT STREET. 1832.

Dedication, "Preface" and "Introductory Epistle," signed *Mark Littleton.* For revised edition see below under 1851.

1: ⟨i-ii⟩, ⟨i⟩-x, ⟨1⟩-312. 7¾″ x 4⅝″.

2: ⟨i⟩-iv, ⟨1⟩-320.

1: ⟨-⟩⁶, 1-26⁶.

2: ⟨-⟩², 1-26⁶, 27⁴.

Drab brown paper boards, rose AR cloth shelf-back; also purple muslin shelfback. Printed paper label on spine. Flyleaves. 36 page catalog inserted in some copies of Vol. 2.

Copyright notice not present in Vol. 2; six lines of errata, Vol. 2, p. iv.

2000 copies printed May 10, 1832 (Kaser, p. 114). Letter from H. C. Carey to Kennedy, May 19, 1832 (original in PB): "It will be published . . . in a day or two." Noted as *recently published* NEM July, 1832. The London (Newman) edition noted as *this day* Ath Aug. 11, 1832; advertised as though published LG Aug. 11, 1832; reviewed LG Aug. 18, 1832; advertised as *now first published* BMLA Aug. 1832; listed LG and Ath Sept. 1, 1832.

B NYPL UV

11041. ADDRESS DELIVERED BEFORE THE HORTICULTURAL SOCIETY OF MARYLAND, AT ITS FIRST ANNUAL EXHIBITION, JUNE 12, 1833 . . .

BALTIMORE: JOHN D. TOY, PRINTER. 1833.

⟨1⟩-33, blank leaf. 9⅟₁₆″ x 5⁹⁄₁₆″.

⟨1⟩², 2-5⁴.

Printed paper wrapper: blue-gray, tan.

Reviewed NEM Oct. 1833.

BPL H LC NYPL

11042. ADDRESS . . . OCTOBER 17, 1833

Two printings have been noted; sequence not determined. The designations are for identification only.

Printing A

AN ADDRESS DELIVERED BEFORE THE AMERICAN INSTITUTE, AT CHATHAM-STREET CHAPEL IN THE CITY OF NEW-YORK, OCTOBER 17, 1833 . . .

NEW-YORK: GEORGE F. HOPKINS & SON, NO. 44 NASSAU-STREET. 1833.

⟨1⟩-34. 8⅞″ x 5½″.

⟨1⟩-4⁴, 5¹.

Printed blue paper wrapper.

Printing B

AN ADDRESS DELIVERED BEFORE THE AMERICAN INSTITUTE, AT CHATHAM

STREET CHAPEL, IN THE CITY OF NEW-YORK, OCTOBER 17th, 1833 . . . TOGETHER WITH A DETAILED ACCOUNT OF THE ARTICLES EXHIBITED AT THE SIXTH ANNUAL FAIR.

NEW-YORK: D. K. MINOR, NO. 35 WALL STREET. MDCCCXXXIII.

Cover-title?

⟨1⟩-24. 9⅞″ scant x 6½″ scant. Illustrated.

⟨A⟩⁸, B⁴.

Printed self-wrapper? Printed paper wrapper?

"Address," pp. ⟨3⟩-15.

Deposited Oct. 31, 1833, according to the copyright notice (both printings).

AAS (A) BPL (B) MHS (A) NYPL (A)

11043. A DISCOURSE ON THE LIFE AND CHARACTER OF WILLIAM WIRT, LATE ATTORNEY GENERAL OF THE UNITED STATES; PRONOUNCED AT THE REQUEST OF THE BALTIMORE BAR BEFORE THE CITIZENS OF BALTIMORE, ON THE 20th OF MAY, 1834 . . .

BALTIMORE: WILLIAM & JOSEPH NEAL. 1834.

⟨i-ii⟩, ⟨i⟩-⟨vi⟩, ⟨5⟩-63. 8⅝″ x 5¼″.

⟨1⟩-8⁴, 9².

Printed buff paper wrapper.

Deposited June 5, 1834.

LC NYPL

11044. HORSE SHOE ROBINSON; A TALE OF THE TORY ASCENDENCY. BY THE AUTHOR OF 'SWALLOW BARN.' . . . IN TWO VOLUMES . . .

PHILADELPHIA: CAREY, LEA & BLANCHARD. 1835.

Note: The statement IN TWO VOLUMES not present on the title-page of Vol. 2.

"To the Reader" signed at end *Mark Littleton*.

See next entry. For revised editions see below under 1836, 1852.

1: ⟨i-ii⟩, ⟨i⟩-⟨vi⟩, ⟨13⟩-325, blank leaf. 7⁹⁄₁₆″ x 4⅜″.

2: ⟨1⟩-298, blank leaf.

1: ⟨1⟩⁴, 2-27⁶, ⟨28⟩².

2: ⟨1⟩-25⁶.

Purple muslin, printed paper label on spine. Flyleaves. Publisher's catalog, 8 pp., inserted at front of Vol. 2.

Kaser (p. 172) reports a letter from the publisher to the printer, Jan. 8, 1835, "indicating that the first 1500 copies ... would be the first edition and the remaining 1500 copies would be the 'second edition' ..." The only copy located by BAL bearing the statement SECOND EDITION is almost certainly not of the same printing as the first; note, for example, the variations in the signature marks. Further investigation is indicated.

3000 copies printed June, 1835 (Kaser, p. 172). Deposited June 2, 1835. A copy in UV inscribed by Kennedy June 10, 1835. Reviewed K July, 1835.

H

11045. Horse-Shoe Robinson. By the Author of "Swallow Barn." ... In Three Volumes ...

London: Richard Bentley, New Burlington Street. (Successor to Henry Colburn.) 1835.

According to contemporary notices issued in paper boards.

See preceding entry for prior publication.

Dedicated to Samuel Rogers under date May 16, 1835; the dedication in the American edition is to Washington Irving, dated May 1, 1835. Contains a preface written for this London edition, apparently written by Kennedy; letter, Kennedy to Bentley (in PB), April 8, 1835, mentions a proposed preface for the London edition "which I design to send you."

In press—LG April 18, 1835. *Immediately*—Ath April 18, 1835. *Shortly*—Ath May 2, 1835. *Just published*—LG May 16, 1835. *Just ready*—Ath May 23, 1835. Advertised as *just published* LG May 23, 1835; May 30, 1835; June 6, 1835. *Will publish immediately*—Ath June 6, 1835. *Will publish during the present month*—Ath June 13, 1835. Listed LG June 20, 1835; Ath June 20, 1835. *Just published*—Ath June 20, 1835. Reviewed LG June 27, 1835; Ath July 11, 1835. Listed BMLA July, 1835, as though issued during the period June 8–July 8, 1835.

Letter, Bentley to Kennedy (in PB) London, June 29, 1835: "On Saturday last ⟨*i.e.*, June 27⟩ Mr Miller of Henrietta Street called upon me in consequence of a communication from Messrs Carey & Lee ⟨*sic*⟩, intimating a desire on their part that I would keep back the publication ... till the autumn. Unfortunately I had delivered my edition three days before ⟨*i.e.*, June 24⟩ ... A copy of the English edition accompanies this note ..."

HSP   PB

11046. Horse Shoe Robinson. A Tale of the Tory Ascendency. By the Author of "Swallow Barn." ... Third Edition. In Two Volumes ...

Philadelphia: Carey, Lea & Blanchard. 1836.

2 Vols. Cloth, printed paper label on spine.

"... The reader will ... discover in this edition some few corrections ..."—From the "Advertisement to the Third Edition," Vol. 1, p. ⟨vi⟩.

For first edition, and a note on the *Second Edition*, see above under 1835. The publisher's records (according to Kaser, p. 190) indicate that of the three thousand copies printed, 1500 were issued with the statement *Third Edition* on the title-page; and, 1500 copies issued with the statement *Fourth Edition* on the title-page. Further study required. The front matter of each "edition" was printed from a different setting. Study may show that the *Third Edition* and the *Fourth Edition* are two separate printings.

AAS (3rd, 4th)   Y (3rd)

11047. ROB OF THE BOWL: A LEGEND OF ST. INIGOE'S. BY THE AUTHOR OF "SWALLOW BARN," "HORSE-SHOE ROBINSON," &C. ... IN TWO VOLUMES ...

PHILADELPHIA: LEA & BLANCHARD. SUCCESSORS TO CAREY & CO. 1838.

For revised edition see below under 1854.

1: ⟨i-iv⟩, ⟨13⟩-270, blank leaf. 7⅜" scant x 4⁷⁄₁₆".

2: ⟨1⟩-275.

1: ⟨1⟩², 2-22⁶, 23⁴.

2: ⟨1⟩-23⁶.

Muslin: green; purple. Printed paper label on spine. Flyleaves. Publisher's catalog, 16 pp., inserted at back of Vol. 1.

Published Dec. 15, 1838 (letter in PB, from Lea & Blanchard to Kennedy, Dec. 14, 1838: "It will be published tomorrow ..."). Deposited Dec. 15, 1838. Reviewed K Feb. 1839. The London (Bentley) edition advertised as *just ready* LG Dec. 22, 1838; as *just published* LG Jan. 5, 1839; listed Ath Jan. 5, 1839, LG Jan. 5, 1839; reviewed LG Jan. 12, 1839; listed PC Jan. 15, 1839; reviewed Ath Jan. 19, 1839. Also issued in London in *The Novel Newspaper*, as Nos. 48-51; published under date 1839; precise publication information wanting, but presumably issued after the Bentley edition.

NYPL   UV

11048. The Dedication of Green Mount Cemetery. July 13th, 1839.

Baltimore: Printed by Woods & Crane. 1839.

Printed paper wrapper.

"Address," pp. ⟨17⟩-35. Collected in *Occasional Addresses* ... , 1872.

H   MHS

11049. Tales of the Grotesque and Arabesque. By Edgar A. Poe ... in Two Volumes ...

Philadelphia: Lea and Blanchard. 1840.

Cloth, printed paper label on spine.

Comment on the book, Vol. 2, p. ⟨i⟩.

Note: Vol. 2 occurs in two states of undetermined sequence; the designations are for identification only:

A: P. 213 mispaged 231.

B: P. 213 so paged.

Deposited Nov. 27, 1839.

H (B)   NYPL (A, B)

11050. QUODLIBET: CONTAINING SOME ANNALS THEREOF, WITH AN AUTHENTIC ACCOUNT OF THE ORIGIN AND GROWTH OF THE BOROUGH AND THE SAYINGS AND DOINGS OF SUNDRY OF THE TOWNSPEOPLE ... EDITED BY SOLOMON SECONDTHOUGHTS, SCHOOLMASTER, FROM ORIGINAL MSS. INDITED BY HIM ...

PHILADELPHIA: LEA & BLANCHARD. 1840.

For *Second Edition* see under 1860.

⟨i⟩-xxiv, ⟨25⟩-250, blank leaf. P. 250 mispaged 350. 7¾″ x 4¾″.

⟨1⟩-21⁶.

H cloth: black; brown; tan. Flyleaves.

Published Sept. 18, 1840 (letter, Lea & Blanchard to Kennedy, Sept. 18, 1840, in PB). Deposited (unbound sheets) Sept. 21, 1840. Listed NAR Oct. 1840.

AAS   NYPL   UV

11051. DEFENCE OF THE WHIGS. BY A MEMBER OF THE TWENTY-SEVENTH CONGRESS.

NEW-YORK: HARPER & BROTHERS, 82 CLIFF-ST. 1844.

⟨1⟩-152; advertisements, pp. 1-4; plus: 5-28. 7″ x 4⅛″.

⟨A⟩-B, ⟨C⟩-I, K-N; plus: ⟨O-P⟩⁶. *Note:* Sigs. ⟨O-P⟩ signed ⟨A⟩⁴, B⁶, C².

Printed blue paper wrapper.

Note: In all copies examined (save one) the copyright notice is, more or less, at the center of p. ⟨2⟩. In the exception (the Toner copy in LC) the notice appears about 1½″ from the top of the page. BAL has been unable to determine the significance of this feature.

Deposited March 14, 1844.

LC   NYPL   Y

11052. DISCOURSE ON THE LIFE AND CHARACTER OF GEORGE CALVERT, THE FIRST LORD BALTIMORE: MADE BY JOHN P. KENNEDY, BEFORE THE MARYLAND HISTORICAL SOCIETY, DECEMBER 9, 1845 ...

BALTIMORE: PRINTED FOR THE SOCIETY BY J. MURPHY, 178 BALTIMORE STREET. MDCCCXLV.

Title-page in black and red. Also issued with the imprint: BALTIMORE: PRINTED AND PUBLISHED BY J. MURPHY, 178 BALTIMORE STREET. MDCCCXLV.

⟨1⟩-50, blank leaf. 8¹⁵⁄₁₆″ x 5¹¹⁄₁₆″.

⟨1⟩-6⁴, 7².

Printed tan paper wrapper, white end papers.

Deposited Jan. 4, 1846. UV copy inscribed by Kennedy Jan. 10, 1846.

AAS   H   UV   Y

11053. SOME PASSAGES IN THE LIFE OF WILLIAM THOM: A LECTURE DELIVERED FEBRUARY 4, 1846, BEFORE THE ASBURY SABBATH SCHOOL ...

⟨n.p., BALTIMORE?⟩ 1846.

⟨1⟩-24. 7⅜″ scant x 4¾″ scant.

⟨-⟩¹².

Printed paper wrapper: yellow; white.

H   LC   NYPL   PB   Y

11054. REPLY OF J. P. KENNEDY TO THE REVIEW OF HIS DISCOURSE ON THE LIFE AND CHARACTER OF CALVERT, PUBLISHED IN THE UNITED STATES CATHOLIC MAGAZINE, APRIL, 1846.

BALTIMORE: PRINTED BY JOHN MURPHY, 178 MARKET STREET. MDCCCXLVI.

⟨1⟩-32. 9¼″ scant x 5¾″ scant.

⟨1⟩-4⁴.

Printed paper wrapper: green; tan.

Dated at end *May 15th, 1846.* Noted NAR Oct. 1846.

H   LC   NYPL

11055. Dinner to the Hon. Daniel Webster, of Massachusetts: By the Merchants, and Other Citizens of Philadelphia, December 2, 1846, with Mr. Webster's Speech.

Philadelphia: Crissy & Markley, Printers, No. 4 Minor Street. 1847.

Printed paper wrapper.

Toast, p. 76.

H NYPL

11056. MEMOIRS OF THE LIFE OF WIL-
LIAM WIRT, ATTORNEY GENERAL OF
THE UNITED STATES ... IN TWO VOL-
UMES ...

PHILADELPHIA: LEA AND BLANCHARD. 1849.

For revised edition see next entry.

1: ⟨1⟩-417, blank leaf. Frontispiece inserted. 9"
x 5$\frac{11}{16}$".

2: ⟨1⟩-450; *Errata*, p. ⟨451⟩. Folded facsimile
inserted as a frontispiece.

1: ⟨1⟩-35⁶.

2: ⟨1⟩⁴, 2-38⁶.

T cloth: black. Flyleaves. Inserted at back of
Vol. 1: *Illustrated Scientific Books*, pp. 1-4; *Catalogue of Lea & Blanchard's Publications*, pp.
⟨1⟩-16; *Catalogue of Lea & Blanchard's Publications*, pp. ⟨1-32⟩.

Advertised as *just published* LW Oct. 6, 1849.
Under date Oct. 27, 1849, the publishers wrote
Kennedy that copies had been shipped him;
original letter in PB. Listed and reviewed LW
Oct. 27, 1849. Deposited (unbound sheets) Oct.
31, 1849. BA copy received Nov. 14, 1849. Dis-
tributed in Great Britain by Davidson for John
Wiley; advertised as *recent* Ath Feb. 23, 1850, PC
March 1, 1850; reviewed LG Feb. 23, 1850.

AAS   BA   H   MHS

11057. Memoirs of the Life of William Wirt ...
a New and Revised Edition. In Two Volumes ...

Philadelphia: Lea and Blanchard. 1850.

For first edition see preceding entry.

Issued in a large paper format (leaf 8$\frac{13}{16}$" full x
5$\frac{5}{8}$"); and, a small paper format (7$\frac{5}{8}$" x 4$\frac{7}{8}$").
But see below.

"Preface to the New Edition," dated *December,
1849*, on recto of leaf following the dedication.

"In the preparation of the present edition, I
have found necessity and opportunity for a revision of my work, which has enabled me to
make some emendations; to correct some errors,
both of the printer and my own ..."—From
the preface.

Small paper edition advertised as *just ready* LW
Jan. 5, 1850. Letter, Lea & Blanchard to Kennedy, Jan. 11, 1850 (original in PB): "At length
we are fairly out with the revised edition & full

supplies are with your Booksellers with copies
freely distributed to Editors ... The octavo ⟨*i.e.*,
large paper⟩ Ed will be ready in 5 or 6 days
when copies shall be sent ...". Small paper edition advertised for Jan. 12, LW Jan. 12, 1850.
Letter, Lea & Blanchard to Kennedy, Jan. 28,
1850 (original in PB): "... By Adams Express we
send ... four copies folded & two in cloth of the
new 8vo ⟨*i.e.*, large paper⟩ Ed. It will soon follow the Cheap Ed. ⟨*i.e.*, small paper⟩ to all
Booksellers." Small paper edition listed LW Feb.
2, 1850. Both formats advertised LW March 2,
1850.

AAS (small paper)   H (small paper)   LC (small
paper)   MHS (small paper)   Y (small paper,
large paper)

11058. Swallow Barn, or a Sojourn in the Old
Dominion ... Revised Edition ...

New-York: George P. Putnam. 1851.

For first edition see above under 1832.

"A Word in Advance, from the Author to the
Reader," pp. ⟨7⟩-11.

Two issues (printings?) of undetermined sequence noted; the designations are for identification only:

A: John F. Trow imprint on copyright page.

B: John F. Trow imprint not present.

The list of illustrations in both is printed on an
inserted leaf.

Noted as *in a few days* LW Aug. 2, 1851. Advertised as *ready* NLA Sept. 15, 1851. Published
Sept. 18, 1851, according to a letter (in PB), Putnam to Kennedy Sept. 15, 1851. Listed LW Sept.
27, 1851. The Chapman importation advertised
as *now ready* PC Oct. 1, 1851; listed PC Oct. 1,
1851; LG Oct. 4, 1851. Deposited Nov. 18, 1851.

AAS (A)   BA (A)   LC (A)   NYPL (A)   PB (A)   UV
(A,B)   Y (B)

11059. ADDRESS DELIVERED BEFORE THE
MARYLAND INSTITUTE FOR THE PRO-
MOTION OF THE MECHANIC ARTS, ON
THE OCCASION OF THE OPENING OF
THE FOURTH ANNUAL EXHIBITION,
ON THE 21st OCTOBER, 1851, BEING
THE FIRST EXHIBITION IN THE NEW
HALL OF THE INSTITUTE ...

BALTIMORE: PRINTED BY JOHN MURPHY & CO.
NO. 178 MARKET STREET. 1851.

⟨1⟩-29, blank leaf. 9$\frac{1}{4}$" x 5$\frac{3}{4}$" full. Folded plate
and frontispiece inserted.

⟨1⟩-4⁴.

Printed paper wrapper: blue; brown; green; pink.

Note: Also seen in what is presumably a presentation binding: Red A cloth, stamped in gold, yellow end papers, edges sprinkled red-brown. The only located copies (2) are inscribed by Kennedy. Leaf: 8¹³⁄₁₆″ x 5⁹⁄₁₆″.

An extended edition, enlarged by the addition of an appendix, has been reported; further information wanting.

UV copy (in cloth) inscribed by Kennedy Feb. 12, 1852. Listed LW Feb. 14, 1852, 29 pp.; binding not mentioned. Listed NLG Feb. 15, 1852, 29 pp., as a pamphlet.

H   LC   MHS   PB   UV (cloth)   Y (cloth)

11060. Horse-Shoe Robinson: A Tale of the Tory Ascendency ... Revised Edition.

New York: George P. Putnam, 10 Park Place. 1852.

For first edition see above under 1835.

Issued in one volume; see publication notes below for comment on a two-volume format.

"Introduction," dated at end April 12, 1852, pp. ⟨v⟩-xii.

Letter, publisher to Kennedy (original in PB), April 26, 1852: "*Horse-Shoe Robinson* is at last recd from the bindery ... It is somewhat too large a book to sell for $1.50 ..."

Letter, publisher to Kennedy (original in Pц), May 4, 1852: "... Your suggestion touching the 2 Vol. edition ... will be attended to. New Titles are printing and copies in 2 Vols will be bound, in a few days ..." One-volume edition advertised for *this week* LW May 8, 1852; listed as in one volume LW May 15, 1852; NLG May 15, 1852. Both formats advertised NLG May 15, 1852; LW May 29, 1852.

AAS (1 vol.)   NYPL (1 vol.)   PB (2 vols.)   Y (1 vol.)

11061. Rob of the Bowl. A Legend of St. Inigoe's ... Revised Edition.

New York: G. P. Putnam & Co., 10 Park Place. M.DCCC.LIV.

For first edition see above under 1838.

Letter, Kennedy to Putnam, Jan. 22, 1854 (copy in the Kennedy letter books at PB): " ... As to the publication of *Rob of the Bowl*, I am quite content you should defer it until the time you propose. It will suit my convenience to have the proofs sent to me in the month of May. Take

care of the copy I have sent you. So many of the corrections are made in pencil that they may become illegible if not carefully handled ..." First printing, 1000 copies, was done in Feb. 1854 (Kennedy archive at PB). Letter, Putnam to Kennedy, March 14, 1854 (original in PB): "... We shall send you some copies ... in a day, or two ...". Listed NLG April 15, 1854. Letter, Putnam to Kennedy, June 26, 1854 (original in PB), informs Kennedy that a new portrait has been prepared. Second printing, 500 copies, was done in Sept. 1854 (Kennedy archive at PB). Third printing, 500 copies, was done in Nov. 1855 (Kennedy archive at PB) by which time, presumably, the date in the imprint was altered.

The publication notes (above) indicate that the first and the second printings may have been issued under date M.DCCC.LIV. If so, BAL has been unable to distinguish the first from the second printing; a clue may be the reengraved portrait referred to in Putnam's letter of June 26, 1854, cited above.

AAS   NYPL   Y

11062. Inauguration of the Statue of Warren, by the Bunker Hill Monument Association, June 17, 1857.

Boston: By Authority of the Committee. 1858.

"Speech of Mr. Kennedy," pp. 72-75.

H   NYPL

11063. To the Literature of the Language What a Dictionary of Words Is to the Language Itself. Allibone's Dictionary of Authors ...

Childs & Peterson, 602 Arch Street, Philadelphia. ⟨1859⟩

Printed self-wrapper. Cover-title.

Letter, Jan. 31, 1859, p. 8.

NYPL

11064. Quodlibet: Containing Some Annals Thereof ... by Solomon Secondthoughts ... Second Edition.

Philadelphia: J. B. Lippincott & Co., 1860.

For first edition see above under 1840.

"A Word from the Author," pp. v-viii.

According to a statement of account (in Kennedy archive, PB), sent Kennedy by the publisher Jan. 26, 1861, 1000 copies were printed Sept. 4, 1860. Listed ALG Oct. 13, 1860. BA copy received Oct. 16, 1860.

B   LC

11065. THE BORDER STATES, THEIR POWER AND DUTY IN THE PRESENT DISORDERED CONDITION OF THE COUNTRY.

⟨n.p., BALTIMORE?, 1860⟩

Anonymous.

⟨1⟩-46, blank leaf. 9″ x 5¹³⁄₁₆″.

⟨1⟩-6⁴.

Printed tan paper wrapper.

Dated at end: *Maryland, December 17, 1860.* 1-line erratum p. 46.

Note: Reprinted with Kennedy named as author, and issued with the imprint: *Philadelphia: J. B. Lippincott & Co. 1861.* Copies in AAS, NYPL, PB, Y. Deposited Jan. 7, 1861; a copy in AAS inscribed by early owner Feb. 16, 1861. Letter, Lippincott to Kennedy, Dec. 29, 1860 (original in PB): "... The pamphlet did not reach me until last evening. I gave it a cursory examination was pleased with it have put it to press ... " Letter, Lippincott to Kennedy, Jan. 1, 1861 (original in PB): "... We send you this day ... Fifty Copies of your pamphlet on the Border States, and you may rest assured that we will use all the facilities of our house to have it generally circulated ... "

H LC NYPL PB

11066. THE GREAT DRAMA; AN APPEAL TO MARYLAND ...

JOHN D. TOY, PRINTER, BALTIMORE. ⟨1861⟩

Cover-title.

⟨1⟩-16. 9⅛″ scant x 5⅞″.

⟨-⟩⁸.

Printed self-wrapper.

Dated at end: *Baltimore, May 9, 1861.*

H LC MHS NYPL PB

11067. THE PRIVILEGE OF THE WRIT OF HABEAS CORPUS UNDER THE CONSTITUTION OF THE UNITED STATES. IN WHAT IT CONSISTS. HOW IT IS ALLOWED. HOW IT IS SUSPENDED. IT IS THE REGULATION OF THE LAW, NOT THE AUTHORIZATION OF AN EXERCISE OF LEGISLATIVE POWER.

PHILADELPHIA. 1862.

Anonymous.

⟨1⟩-16. 9⅛″ x 5¾″.

⟨1⟩-2⁴.

Printed green paper wrapper.

Issued after April 4, 1862.

BA NYPL

11068. SLAVERY THE MERE PRETEXT FOR THE REBELLION; NOT ITS CAUSE. ANDREW JACKSON'S PROPHECY IN 1833. HIS LAST WILL AND TESTAMENT IN 1843. BEQUESTS OF HIS THREE SWORDS: HIS SOLEMN INJUNCTION TO WIELD THEM "IN SUPPORT OF OUR GLORIOUS UNION" AGAINST ALL ASSAILANTS, WHETHER "FOREIGN ENEMIES OR DOMESTIC TRAITORS." PICTURE OF THE CONSPIRACY. DRAWN IN 1863, BY A SOUTHERN MAN.

PHILADELPHIA: C. SHERMAN, SON & CO., PRINTERS. 1863.

Cover-title.

Signed at end: *Paul Ambrose.*

1-16. 9⅛″ x 5⅞″.

⟨-⟩⁸.

Printed tan paper wrapper.

Reprinted from *The National Intelligencer,* Washington, D. C., March, 1863. Collected as "Letter VI" in *Mr. Ambrose's Letters* ..., 1865.

AAS H LC MHS PB Y

11069. Address of the Union State Central Committee, with the Proceedings of the Meeting, at Temperance Temple, August 26, 1863. With the Resolutions of the State Convention.

Baltimore: Printed by Bull & Tuttle, Clipper Office. 1863.

Printed self-wrapper. Cover-title.

"Address ..," pp. ⟨2⟩-9, signed at end by Kennedy and others.

Y

11070. Autograph Leaves of Our Country's Authors. ⟨Compiled by John Pendleton Kennedy and Alexander Bliss⟩

Baltimore, Cushings & Bailey 1864.

For fuller entry see No. 2418.

Note: The editors, Kennedy and Bliss, under date of Feb. 5, 1864, issued a printed letter asking "the Authors of America, to contribute ... one or more pages in his own handwriting ... to be lithographed and to form a volume, which shall be published and sold for the exclusive benefit of the Sanitary and Christian Commissions." A copy of the appeal is in H.

11071. BALTIMORE LONG AGO.

⟨n.p., n.d., BALTIMORE: PRINTED BY JOHN D. TOY, 1864⟩

Anonymous.

⟨1⟩-30, blank leaf. 7½″ x 4½″.

⟨1⟩², 2-3⁶, ⟨4⟩².

Printed pink paper wrapper.

Offprint ⟨preprint?⟩ from *Our Country, in its Relations to the Past, Present and Future. A National Book* ..., edited by Mrs. Lincoln Phelps, Baltimore: Printed by John D. Toy, 1864. Copy in Maryland Historical Society, Baltimore, Md.

MdHS PB

11072. LETTER OF MR. PAUL AMBROSE, ON THE GREAT REBELLION IN THE UNITED STATES ...

⟨n.p., n.d., probably 1864⟩

Caption-title. The above at head of p. ⟨1⟩.

⟨1-4⟩. Laid paper. 10⁵⁄₁₆″ x 9⁹⁄₁₆″.

⟨-⟩².

Single cut sheet folded to four pages.

The letter is dated *January, 1864*. Collected as "Letter VII" in *Mr. Ambrose's Letters* ..., 1865.

LC NYPL

11073. MR. AMBROSE'S LETTERS ON THE REBELLION ...

NEW YORK: PUBLISHED BY HURD AND HOUGHTON. BALTIMORE: JAMES S. WATERS. 1865.

⟨i⟩-⟨viii⟩, ⟨1⟩-246, blank leaf. Laid paper. 6¾″ x 4⁹⁄₁₆″ (cloth). 7″ scant x 4⁹⁄₁₆″ (wrapper).

⟨-⟩⁴, ⟨1⟩-15⁸, 16⁴.

C cloth: purple-brown. Brown-coated end papers. Flyleaves of bookstock. Edges stained red. Also: Printed tan (laid?) paper wrapper, white laid end papers.

Advertised as *nearly ready* ALG Nov. 1, 1865. Letter, Nov. 10, 1865, Hurd & Houghton to Kennedy (original in PB): "... The Copy of *Ambrose* was sent to Prof Goldwin Smith as you desired ... We had already sent a copy to Mr Tuckerman and he has written a good notice of it in the *Boston Transcript* ..." H copy received Nov. 13, 1865. Listed (both cloth; and, wrapper) ALG Nov. 15, 1865. Deposited Dec. 2, 1865. Reviewed Ath Jan. 6, 1866.

BA H NYPL UV

11074. The Peabody Institute of the City of Baltimore. The Founder's Letters and the Papers Relating to Its Dedication and Its History up to the 1st January, 1868.

Baltimore: Printed by William K. Boyle. 1868.

Printed paper wrapper. Irregular pagination. Note the style of imprint. Not illustrated. Leaf: 8⅝″ full x 5½″.

Made up of a series of pamphlets and other ephemera including *Letter from George Peabody, Esq. to the Trustees for the Establishment of an Institute in the City of Baltimore*, Baltimore, 1857; with added material including Kennedy's "Address of the Trustees." Kennedy's address is prefaced by the following comment: "... Prepared by ... John P. Kennedy, to be delivered at the Inauguration of the Institute which was expected to take place in the month of May, 1866. In accordance with the expressed wish of Mr. Peabody, the Inauguration was postponed until the 25th October, 1866. In the meantime events occurred to render it necessary to modify certain portions of Mr. Kennedy's original address. His absence in Europe prevented him from delivering it in person on the day last named, when it was read by George W. Dobbin, Esq., on behalf of The Trustees, modified ..."

The above material, including Kennedy's address, was formally published in *The Peabody Institute of the City of Baltimore. The Founder's Letters and the Papers Relating to Its Dedication and Its History, up to the 1st January, 1868;* imprinted: *Baltimore: Steam Press of William K. Boyle, Corner of Baltimore and St. Paul Streets. 1868*. Bound in cloth; regular pagination (pp. ⟨1⟩-146); illustrations (photographs) inserted; leaf: 9⅛″ scant x 5¾″.

Collected in *Occasional Addresses* ..., New York, 1872.

H (both)

11075. PEABODY INSTITUTE. ADDRESS OF THE PRESIDENT TO THE BOARD OF TRUSTEES, ON THE ORGANIZATION AND GOVERNMENT OF THE INSTITUTE. FEBRUARY 12, 1870.

⟨BALTIMORE, 1870⟩

⟨1⟩-33, blank leaf. 8⅝″ scant x 5½″.

⟨1⟩-4⁴, ⟨5⟩².

Printed salmon paper wrapper.

BPL H

11076. COLLECTED WORKS

Note: Not a true set; made up of separately issued volumes. In the H set (as an example)

Rob of the Bowl is a copy of the 1866 printing. 10 Volumes.

Occasional Addresses; and the Letters of Mr. Ambrose on the Rebellion . . .

New York: G. P. Putnam & Sons, Association Building. 1872.

Reprint with the exception of:

"The Spirit of the Age; False and True Progress. A Lecture Delivered before the Mechanics' Institute, Baltimore, February 7th, 1854." Also contains material here first collected.

Memoirs of the Life of William Wirt . . . a New and Revised Edition . . .

New York: G. P. Putnam and Sons, Association Building, 4th Avenue and 23d St. 1872.

2 Vols. Reprint.

Political and Official Papers . . .

New York: G. P. Putnam & Sons. Association Building. 1872.

See entry No. 11077.

Quodlibet: Containing Some Annals Thereof . . . by Solomon Secondthoughts . . . Third Edition.

New York: G. P. Putnam and Sons, Association Building, 4th Avenue and 23d St. 1872.

Reprint.

Rob of the Bowl. A Legend of St. Inigoe's . . .

New York: G. P. Putnam and Sons, Association Building, 4th Avenue and 23d St. 1872.

Reprint.

At Home and Abroad: A Series of Essays . . .

G. P. Putnam & Sons. Association Building, Twenty-Third Street, 1872.

See entry No. 11078.

Horse-Shoe Robinson . . . Revised Edition.

New York: G. P. Putnam and Sons, Association Building, 4th Avenue and 23d St. 1872.

Reprint.

Swallow Barn; or, a Sojourn in the Old Dominion . . . Revised Edition . . .

New York: G. P. Putnam and Sons, Association Building, 4th Avenue and 23d St. 1872.

Reprint.

The Life of John Pendleton Kennedy. By Henry T. Tuckerman.

New York: G. P. Putnam & Sons, Association Building. 1871.

The present entry made on the basis of sets (some incomplete) at AAS BA H MHS NYPL PB UV Y

11077. Political and Official Papers . . .

New York: G. P. Putnam & Sons. Association Building. 1872.

A gathering together of previously published writings.

Listed WTC April 25, 1872. BA copy received April 25, 1872.

AAS BA NYPL UV Y

11078. AT HOME AND ABROAD: A SERIES OF ESSAYS: WITH A JOURNAL IN EUROPE IN 1867–8 . . .

G. P. PUTNAM & SONS. ASSOCIATION BUILDING, TWENTY-THIRD STREET, 1872.

⟨1⟩-415; blank, p. ⟨416⟩; 4 pp. advertisements paged 6-7, 9-10. 7½" x 4⅞".

⟨1⟩-17¹², 18⁶.

C cloth: brown. Brown-coated on white end papers. Flyleaves.

Listed PW March 28, 1872.

AAS BA NYPL

11079. Occasional Addresses; and the Letters of Mr. Ambrose on the Rebellion . . .

New York: G. P. Putnam & Sons, Association Building. 1872.

Reprint save for "The Spirit of the Age; False and True Progress. A Lecture Delivered before the Mechanics' Institute, Baltimore, February 7th, 1854." Also contains material here first collected.

BA BPL NYPL UV Y

POLITICAL, OFFICIAL and LIKE PUBLICATIONS

As a member of the Congress, and later as Secretary of the Navy, Kennedy's name is attached to many official publications. No attempt has been made to locate and to describe such material. The following is a representative selection. Kennedy's own copies of many of these, with notes indicating his authorship (in whole or in part), are in The Peabody Institute, Baltimore, Maryland. For a comment on "off-subject" publications see BAL, Vol. 1, p. xviii.

A Review of Mr. Cambreleng's Report from the Committee of Commerce, in the House of

Representatives, at the First Session of the Twenty First Congress. By Mephistopheles ...

Baltimore: Printed by Wm. Ogden Niles. 1830.

Cover-title. Printed self-wrapper. Pp. 72.

H   MHS   UV

The Memorial of the Permanent Committee of the New-York Convention of the Friends of Domestic Industry, to the Senate and House of Representatives of the United States.

⟨Philadelphia⟩ January 22, 1833.

See next entry for another printing; sequence not determined.

Cover-title. Printed self-wrapper. Pp. 28. Signed at end by Thomas Ellicott, as *Chairman pro. tem.;* and by Kennedy, as *Secretary.*

H   Y

The Memorial of the Permanent Committee of the New-York Convention of the Friends of Domestic Industry, to the Senate and House of Representatives of the United States.

⟨Philadelphia⟩ January 22, 1833.

See preceding entry for another printing.

Cover-title. Printed self-wrapper. Pp. 28. Signed at end by Hezekiah Niles, as *Chairman;* and by Kennedy, as *Secretary.*

PB

The Address of the City of Baltimore to the Citizens of Maryland; Made in Pursuance of Resolutions Passed in Town Meeting, on the 6th Inst. Inviting the Citizens of Maryland, Friendly to Internal Improvement to Send Delegates to the Convention on the Second of May, to be Held in the City of Baltimore ...

⟨Baltimore, April 12, 1836⟩

Caption-title. Printed self-wrapper? The above on p. ⟨1⟩. Pp. 8. At end of text: *Samuel Smith* (as though author). Kennedy's personal copy (in PB) inscribed by Kennedy: *by J.P.K.*

PB

Journal of the Proceedings of the Convention on Internal Improvements of Maryland, Held in Baltimore, May 2, 1836.

Baltimore: John D. Toy, Printer, Corner of Market and St. Paul Streets. 1836.

Cover-title? Printed wrapper? Self-wrapper? Kennedy participated in the convention.

PB

Letters of a Man of the Times, to the Citizens of Baltimore. [Originally Published in the American.]

Baltimore: Printed by Sands & Neilson, N. E. Corner Charles & Market-Sts. 1836.

Printed yellow paper wrapper. Pp. 24. Anonymous. Presumably by Kennedy. A copy was bound by Kennedy with pamphlets known to have been written by him; in PB. Attributed to Kennedy by LC.

BPL   LC

Strictures on the Letter of Charles J. Ingersoll, Esq. Touching the Right of a Legislature to Repeal a Charter. With an Appendix, Containing the Letters of Mr. Ingersoll, of Mr. Dallas, of Mr. Forward, and of Mr. Biddle, in Illustration of the Subject Discussed. By a Citizen of Maryland ...

Baltimore: Joseph Neal, 174 Market Street, 1836.

Printed paper wrapper. Pp. 104. Presumably by Kennedy. A copy was bound by Kennedy with pamphlets known to have been written by him; in PB.

Susquehanna Canal ...

⟨n.p., n.d., 1836⟩

Caption-title. The above at head of p. ⟨1⟩. Printed paper wrapper? Printed self-wrapper? Signed at end by Howes Goldsborough and others; Kennedy's name not present. Pp. 8.

"At a meeting of sundry citizens of Harford county, held at Havre de Grace on the 25th day of January, 1836, to consider the Report made by a committee of the citizens of Port Deposite, in relation to the proposed Canal from Columbia to tide, which report was published in the Cecil Whig, on the 26th of December last, it was resolved, that a committee of five persons be appointed to prepare a statement in reply to said report:

"Whereupon the said committee being appointed, and having given careful consideration to the said report of the committee of the citizens of Port Deposite, presented the following statement ..."—P. ⟨1⟩.

According to a pencilled note in Kennedy's hand, in Kennedy's personal copy of this publication, the statement published herein was written by Kennedy; in PB.

Speech ... Delivered in the House of Representatives, on the 22d and 23d June, 1838, in the Debate on the Sub Treasury Bill.

Baltimore: Printed by John D. Toy, Corner of Market and St. Paul Streets. 1838.

Pp. 32. Printed self-wrapper. Cover-title.

BA   MHS   Y

Speech ... on the Bill Making Appropriations for the Civil and Diplomatic Service for the Year 1839. Delivered in the House of Representatives, February 19, 1839.

Washington: Printed by Gales and Seaton. 1839.

Pp. 38, blank leaf. Printed self-wrapper. Cover-title.

BA   H   LC   MHS

Report of the Select Committee of the Baltimore and Ohio Rail Road Company, Appointed to Prepare an Exposition in Reference to So Much of the Governor's Message of January 2, 1840, as Relates to the Affairs of That Company. Report Made by the Committee, January 13, 1840.

Baltimore: Printed by John Murphy, 146 Market Street. 1840.

Pp. 26. Cover-title? Printed paper wrapper?

Signed at end by Wm. H. Marriott, as chairman of the committee; and, others; Kennedy's name not present. Kennedy's personal copy (in PB) is inscribed by Kennedy on the title-page: *By J.P.K.*

PB

By the Whig Members of Congress ...

⟨n.p., n.d., 1841⟩

Pp. 7. Single cut sheet folded to make 8 pp. Caption-title, the above at head of p. ⟨1⟩.

Signed at end by Kennedy and others.

"At a meeting of the Whig members of the Senate and House of Representatives of the 27th Congress of the United States, held in the City of Washington on the 11th of September, 1841 ... ⟨it was⟩ Resolved, That it is expedient for the Whigs of the Senate and House of Representatives ... to publish an Address to the People of the United States, containing a succinct exposition ..."—p. ⟨1⟩.

PB   WR

... Plan of Finance. [To Accompany Bill H.R. No. 206.] February 17, 1842. Mr. Cushing, from the Select Committee Appointed on So Much of the President's Message as Relates to a Plan of Finance, Made the Following Report ...

⟨Washington, D. C., 1842⟩

Pp. 78, blank leaf. Caption-title. The above at head of p. ⟨1⟩. At head of title: *27th Congress, 2d Session. Rep. No. 244. Ho. of Reps.* Probably self-wrapper.

"Report of Mr. John P. Kennedy," pp. 52-62.

PB

... Commerce and Navigation. May 28, 1842. Read, and Laid upon the Table. Mr. J. P. Kennedy, from the Committee on Commerce, Made the Following Report ...

⟨Washington, D. C., 1842⟩

Pp. 63. Folded plate inserted. Caption-title. The above at head of p. ⟨1⟩. At head of title: *27th Congress, 2d Session. Rep. No. 835. Ho. of Reps.* Printed paper wrapper?

MHS   PB

Letter of J. P. Kennedy to His Constituents, Citizens of the Fourth Congressional District in the State of Maryland, on the Principles and Value of the Protective System.

⟨Baltimore, 1842⟩

Pp. 32. Self-wrapper. Cover-title. Dated at end *October 25, 1842.* Listed NAR Jan. 1843.

AAS   LC   MHS   NYPL   PB

... Warehouse System. [To Accompany Bill H. R. No. 730.] January 26, 1843. Mr. Kennedy, from the Committee on Commerce, Made the Following Report ...

⟨Washington, D. C., 1843⟩

Pp. 17. Caption-title. The above at head of p. ⟨1⟩. At head of title: *27th Congress, 3d Session. Rep. No. 103. Ho. of Reps.* Probably printed self-wrapper.

PB

... Report of Mr. Kennedy, of Maryland, from the Committee on Commerce of the House of Representatives of the United States, on the Memorial of the Friends of African Colonization, Assembled in Convention in the City of Washington, May, 1842 ...

Washington: Printed by Gales and Seaton. 1843.

Pp. 1088. Cover-title? At head of title: *27th Congress, 3d Session, Rep. No. 283. Ho. of Reps. African Colonization—Slave Trade—Commerce.*

Dated Feb. 28, 1843. Reviewed NAR Oct. 1843.

H   MHS   NYPL

Letter of J. P. Kennedy, of the House of Representatives, in the Congress of the United States, on the Proposition to Transfer the Stock Held by the Federal Government in the Chesapeake and Ohio Canal, to the State of Maryland. Addressed to the Hon. the President of the Senate, and the Hon. the Speaker of the House of Delegates, in the General Assembly of Maryland, December, 1844.

Washington: J. and G. S. Gideon, Printers. 1844.

Pp. 20. Printed paper wrapper. Dated at end *Dec. 25, 1844.*

BA   NYPL   UV

To the Mechanics and Workingmen of the City of Baltimore, of Both Political Parties . . .

⟨n.p., n.d., 1844?⟩

Pp. 8. Caption-title. The above at head of p. ⟨1⟩. Printed self-wrapper?

"The correspondence between Mr. Legrand and myself, recently published, will show that I have been invited by him, at the instance of his political friends, to meet him in public, to discuss the questions involved in the pending election . . ."—p. ⟨1⟩.

PB

To the Whigs of Baltimore . . .

⟨n.p., Jan. 25, 1844⟩

Pp. 6, blank leaf. Caption-title. The above at head of p. ⟨1⟩. Dated at end *Jan. 25, 1844.* Printed self-wrapper?

"Fellow Citizens: The Convention of the Fourth Congressional District has just done me the honor to nominate me as your candidate, for a seat in the House of Representatives, for this District . . ."—p. ⟨1⟩.

MHS   PB   UV

. . . Duties on Coffee Imported from the Netherlands. [To Accompany Joint Resolution H. R. No. 78.] March 3, 1845. Mr. J. P. Kennedy, from the Committee on Commerce, Submitted the Following Report . . .

⟨Washington, D. C.⟩ Blair & Rives, Print. ⟨1845⟩

Pp. 9. Caption-title. The above on p. ⟨1⟩. At head of title: *28th Congress, 2d Session. Rep. No. 188. Ho. of Reps.* Probably self-wrapper.

PB

. . . Marine Hospitals. [To Accompany Bill H. R. No. 608.] February 14, 1845. Mr. J. P. Ken-

nedy, from the Committee on Commerce, Made the Following Report . . .

⟨Washington, D. C.⟩ Blair & Rives, Print. ⟨1845⟩

Pp. 19. Caption-title. The above on p. ⟨1⟩. At head of title: *28th Congress, 2d Session. Rep. No. 124. Ho. of Reps.* Probably self-wrapper.

PB

Proceedings of a Meeting of the Stockholders of the Baltimore & Ohio Rail Road Company, Held in the City of Baltimore, on the 12th July, 1845, to Consider the Act of the General Assembly of Virginia, Passed February 19, 1845. To Which is Appended the Report Made to the Meeting, by the Chief Engineer.

⟨n.p., n.d., 1845⟩

Cover-title. Preamble and resolutions by Kennedy, pp. 4-7.

PB

Speech . . . on the Annexation of Texas. Delivered in the House of Representatives, U. S., January 11, 1845 . . .

⟨n.p., Washington, D. C.⟩ J. & G. S. Gideon, Printers ⟨n.d., 1845⟩

Pp. 16. P. ⟨1⟩ as above. Printed self-wrapper.

BA   H   MHS   NYPL   UV   Y

To the Mechanics, Manufacturers, and Working Men of the City of Baltimore.

Baltimore: Printed by Samuel Sands, N. E. Corner of Charles & Baltimore Streets. 1845.

Pp. 16. Cover-title. Printed self-wrapper.

BA   PB   UV

Letters . . . to the Citizens of the District . . .

⟨n.p., n.d., Baltimore, 1847?⟩

Pp. 16. Caption-title. The above at head of p. ⟨1⟩. Printed self-wrapper?

PB   UV

Report of the Committee Composing the Delegation, Appointed by the Citizens of Baltimore, to the Susquehanna Railroad Convention, Held at Sunbury, Pennsylvania, May 20th, 1851: Now Republished, with a Map . . .

Baltimore: "The Printing Office," Sun Iron Building. 1852.

A revised edition of an unlocated report issued "in the latter part of last spring." Probably issued in printed paper wrapper. "To the Citizens of Baltimore," p. ⟨3⟩.

LC   PB

Notes on the Acts of Congress Touching the Retirement of Naval Officers . . .

⟨Nice, France: Printed by Caisson & Mignon, 1867⟩

Pp. 14; printer's imprint, p. ⟨15⟩. Caption-title. The above at head of p. ⟨3⟩. Unprinted white paper wrapper.

AAS   BA   Y

REPRINTS

The following publications contain material by Kennedy reprinted from earlier books.

Half-Hours with the Best Humorous Authors. Selected . . . by Charles Morris . . . American.

Philadelphia . . . 1889.

"Suspension of Specie Payments," Vol. 2, pp. 309-318, is an extract from *The Annals of Quodlibet*.

For fuller entry see No. 3813.

. . . Harper's Fifth Reader   American Authors

New York . . . 1889

Pp. 139-150, extract from *Horse Shoe Robinson*, Chap. XXII.

For fuller entry see No. 7917.

REFERENCES AND ANA

A Review, on the Article in the Southern Review, for 1830, on the Several Speeches Made during the Debate on Mr. Foote's Resolution, by Mr. Hayne of South Carolina, and Mr. Webster of Massachusetts. By Lucius Falkland . . .

Baltimore: Printed by Sands & Neilson, N. W. Corner of Gay and Market-Streets. 1830.

Cover-title? Printed wrapper? Sometimes attributed to Kennedy. BAL has found no evidence to support the attribution.

The Premium . . .

Philadelphia . . . 1833.

"The Mother's Injunction, on Presenting Her Son with a Bible," pp. 276-277; credited merely to *Kennedy*. BAL cannot believe John Pendleton Kennedy the author.

For fuller entry see No. 5689.

Review of the Hon. John P. Kennedy's Discourse on the Life and Character of George Calvert . . .

Baltimore: Printed by John Murphy, 178 Market Street, MDCCCXLVI.

Printed paper wrapper. Anonymous. By Bernard U. Campbell. Listed NAR July, 1846.

Remarks of the United States Catholic Magazine on the Discussion between the Hon. J. P. Kennedy and His Reviewer.

⟨n.p., n.d., probably Baltimore, 1846⟩

Caption-title. The above at head of p. ⟨1⟩. 8 pp. Printed self-wrapper.

The Blackwater Chronicle   A Narrative of an Expedition into the Land of Canaan, in Randolph County, Virginia . . . by "The Clerke of Oxenforde." . . .

Redfield   110 and 112 Nassau Street, New York. 1853.

Sometimes attributed to John Pendleton Kennedy. The author was Pendleton Kennedy, a brother of John Pendleton Kennedy. Published in Great Britain under the title: *Narrative of an Expedition of Five Americans into a Country of Wild Animals . . . without Any Aid of Government* . . .

Reviewed LW Nov. 10, 1853. Deposited Nov. 29, 1853. Listed PC Jan. 2, 1854.

. . . Horseshoe Robinson; or, the Battle of King's Mountain. A Legendary Patriotic Drama, in Three Acts. By Clifton W. Tayleure . . .

. . . 1858 . . . New York: Samuel French, 122 Nassau Street, (Up Stairs.)

At head of title: *French's Standard Drama. The Acting Edition. No. CCXIII.* Printed paper wrapper.

. . . The Virginians   A Tale of the Last Century by W. M. Thackeray . . .

London: Bradbury and Evans, 11, Bouverie Street. 1857.

24 paper-covered parts. For comment see *A Thackeray Library . . .*, by Henry Sayre van Duzer, New York, 1919, pp. 133-141.

For a comment on Kennedy's contribution to this book see extract from his journal, Paris, Sept. 26, 1858, as published in *The Life of John Pendleton Kennedy*, by Henry T. Tuckerman, New York, 1871. p. 296. Also see: "Thackeray and Virginia" by Jay B. Hubbell, in *The Virginia Quarterly Review*, Jan. 1927; and, *The Letters and Private Papers of Wil-*

liam Makepeace Thackeray, edited by Gordon
N. Ray, 1946, Vol. 4, p. 111.

Jewels from the Quarry of the Mind . . . Edited
by James H. Head . . .

> Boston . . . 1862.
>
> "Long Life," p. 68, credited to *Kennedy.* BAL
> cannot believe John Pendleton Kennedy the
> author.
>
> For comment see entry No. 1036.

The Spirit of the Fair . . .

> New York, April 5-9, 11-16, 18-23, 1864.
>
> According to a notice in No. 5 (issue of April
> 9, 1864), p. 52, Kennedy contributed to this
> publication. Nothing identified as Kennedy's
> found.
>
> For comment see entry No. 11186.

Proceedings of the Board of Trustees of the
Peabody Institute of the City of Baltimore, on
the Announcement of the Death of Hon. John
Pendleton Kennedy . . .

> ⟨Baltimore, 1870⟩
>
> Caption-title. Preceding at the head of p. ⟨1⟩.
> Printed paper wrapper.

Tributes to the Memory of Hon. John Pendleton Kennedy.

> Reprinted ⟨*i.e.,* preprinted⟩ from the Pro-
> ceedings of the Massachusetts Historical So-
> ciety. ⟨n.p., Boston, 1870⟩
>
> Cover-title. Printed paper wrapper.

The Life of John Pendleton Kennedy. By Henry
T. Tuckerman.

New York: G. P. Putnam & Sons, Association
Building. 1871.

Rob, the Hermit; or, the Black Chapel of Maryland. A Romantic Drama, in Four Acts, Dramatized from J. P. Kennedy's Novel of "Rob of the
Bowl," by Charles Frederick Adams . . .

> New York: Happy Hours Company, No. 5
> Beekman Street. ⟨1879⟩
>
> Printed paper wrapper. Issued as No. 101 of
> *The Acting Drama* series. *Note:* Also occurs
> with the imprint of Harold Roorbach, Pub-
> lisher, New York.

Swallow Barn or a Sojourn in the Old Dominion
. . . Edited . . . by Jay B. Hubbell

> Harcourt, Brace and Company   New York
> ⟨1929⟩
>
> Deposited April 12, 1929.

John Pendleton Kennedy by Edward M. Gwath-
mey

> Thomas Nelson and Sons   New York   1931

Horse-Shoe Robinson . . . Edited . . . by Ernest
E. Leisy . . .

> American Book Company   New York . . .
> ⟨1937⟩
>
> Deposited March 15, 1937. The symbol *E.P.1*
> present on the copyright page of the first
> printing.

John Pendleton Kennedy   Gentleman from Baltimore ⟨by⟩ Charles H. Bohner

> The Johns Hopkins Press: Baltimore ⟨1961⟩

FRANCIS SCOTT KEY

1 7 7 9 – 1 8 4 3

Key was an attorney and as such prepared, or had prepared for his signature, legal documents. A list (presumably incomplete) of these follows the main section of this list. Similar material may be found in the published reports of the United States Congress.

11080. ORATION, FEBRUARY 22, 1814

Two printings noted. The sequence has not been established and the designations are for identification only.

Printing A

AN ORATION, DELIVERED BY FRANCIS S. KEY, ESQ. BEFORE THE WASHINGTON SOCIETY OF ALEXANDRIA. AT A MEETING OF THE WASHINGTON SOCIETY OF ALEXANDRIA, ON TUESDAY THE 22d OF FEBRUARY, 1814. ON MOTION ... FRANCIS S. KEY ... BE REQUESTED TO FURNISH A COPY ... FOR PUBLICATION ...

⟨n.p., n.d., ALEXANDRIA, VA., 1814⟩

Caption-title. The above at head of p. ⟨1⟩.

⟨1⟩-15. 8¹⁄₁₆″ x 5″.

⟨A⟩-B⁴.

So issued? Printed paper wrapper? Self-wrapper?

Printing B

AN ORATION DELIVERED BY FRANCIS S. KEY, ESQ. AT A MEETING OF THE WASHINGTON SOCIETY OF ALEXANDRIA, CA. ⟨*sic*⟩ ON TUESDAY THE 22d OF MARCH, 1814 ...

⟨n.p., n.d., 1814?⟩

Caption-title. The above at head of p. ⟨1⟩.

⟨1⟩-20. 7⅝″ scant x 4¹⁵⁄₁₆″ full.

⟨1-2⁴, 3²⟩.

So issued? Issued in wrapper?

Note: The only located copy has the date *March, 1814,* altered by hand in pen and ink to *February, 1814.*

AAS (B) LC (A)

11081. THE STAR SPANGLED BANNER

There have been several attempts to present an account of the first publication of "The Star Spangled Banner" in handbill form and as sheet music, but none is based on provable evidence. Indeed, hearsay evidence rather than fact is present more often than not. Here listed are those printings seen by BAL which have claim to primacy.

The earliest known appearances of the poem *of ascertainable date* were anonymous and under the title "Defence of Fort M'Henry" (see below in *Section One*). It therefore appears safe to assume that any printing under the title "The Star Spangled Banner" is a later printing. And when both the later title and Key's name are present the evidence of late printing is even stronger. BAL has been unable to establish a sequence on the basis of textual variations; known later printings often are of the original, unrevised, text.

No study of the early appearances of the poem can be attempted without reference to *The Star Spangled Banner,* by Oscar G. T. Sonneck, Washington, 1914; *The Star Spangled Banner ... an Annotated Bibliographical List ...,* by Joseph Muller, New York, 1935; and, *Early American Sheet Music ...,* by Harry Dichter and Elliott Shapiro, New York, 1941.

In the following list BAL has ignored all printings dated 1815 or later; these are clearly reprints. The list is broken down into four sections as follows: *Section One:* dated periodical appearances; *Section Two:* separate printings, exclusive of sheet music; *Section Three:* book appearances; *Section Four:* sheet music.

SECTION ONE

Dated periodical appearances. In each the title is given as "Defence of Fort M'Henry." In each the poem appears anonymously.

A

Baltimore Patriot and Evening Advertiser, Sept. 20, 1814.

B

Baltimore American and Commercial Daily Advertiser, Sept. 21, 1814.

C

National Intelligencer, Washington, D. C., Sept. 27, 1814.

D

Independent Chronicle, Boston, Oct. 3, 1814.

E

Maryland Gazette, and Political Intelligencer, Annapolis, Md., Oct. 13, 1814.

F

Federal Gazette & Baltimore Daily Advertiser, Oct. 14, 1814.

G

Analectic Magazine, Philadelphia, Nov. 1814.

H

Providence Patriot. Columbian Phenix, Providence, R. I., Dec. 10, 1814.

SECTION TWO

Separate Printings (Sheet Music Excluded)

Note: Printings B, C, D, have the appearance of having been done, not at the time of the battle but later, perhaps as commemorative publications. Printings Da, E, F, G are reprints.

A

DEFENCE OF FORT M'HENRY. / ⟨note, 14 lines: *The annexed song was composed under the following circumstances ...* ⟩ / Tune—ANACREON IN HEAVEN. / ⟨text: 4 stanzas⟩ / ⟨n.p., n.d.⟩

Single leaf. 8⅛″ x 6⅜″. Measurement approximated.

Printed on recto only. Anonymous.

Dated 1814 by both Sonneck and Library of Congress but BAL has found no evidence to support the dating save the title and lack of Key's name.

In the earliest located *dated* publication (*Baltimore Patriot ...*, Sept. 20, 1814) the text is preceded by an editorial note stating in part that the poem had "already been extensively circulated." The reference, presumably, is to a separate printing. On the basis of title, and the

absence of Key's name, this handbill may logically be considered the earliest known handbill printing, but BAL has found no evidence to support the assumption that it is the presumed handbill referred to in the editorial note. Sonneck's acceptance (p. 88) of this printing as such is less than convincing. Indeed, Sonneck's ascription is (to quote him) based on "absence of proof to the contrary." If the account of Samuel Sands, who claims to have first set the type of "The Star Spangled Banner" is to be credited, the first separate printing was done from the setting of *The Baltimore American.* See J. Thomas Scharf's *The Chronicles of Baltimore ...* , Baltimore, 1874, p. 352; and letter (original in LC), Samuel Sands to Brantz Mayer, Baltimore, Jan. 1, 1877.

Location: LC

B

DEFENCE OF FORT M'HENRY. / ⟨double rule⟩ / ⟨note, 19 lines: *The annexed song was composed under the following circumstances ...* ⟩ / ⟨rule⟩ / Tune—ANACREON IN HEAVEN. / ⟨text: 4 stanzas⟩ / ⟨n.p., n.d.⟩ / ⟨all the preceding in a frame of type ornaments⟩

Single leaf. 9¹¹⁄₁₆″ scant x 4¾″ full. Unwatermarked laid paper.

Printed on recto only. Not anonymous; Key's name present in the editorial note. After 1814?

Location: IU

C

THE STAR SPANGLED / BANNER. / ⟨decorated rule⟩ / ⟨text⟩ / ⟨lozenge rule⟩ / Written by F. Key, Esq. during the conflict between / Fort M'Henry, and the British Fleet, in 1814. / ⟨all the preceding in an oval frame of type ornaments; surrounding the frame is⟩ BOMBARDMENT OF FORT M'HENRY ⟨ornament⟩ Each letter of this last is surrounded by a ring of stars. The whole within a greek fret frame, at the lower right of the frame (*i.e.,* within the frame itself) is: SWAIN, typ. At each inner upper corner of the greek fret frame is a spreadeagle; at each lower inner corner is a decoration of rays. Perhaps printed by E. C. Swain, Baltimore.

Printed on the recto of a piece of white satin. The statement *written ... in 1814* surely suggests post-1814 publication.

Two printings seen; the designations are for identification only:

a: Printed in red and black. 10³⁄₁₆″ x 7⅝″.

b: Printed in black only. 15″ scant x 10½″.

Locations: LC (b) UV (a)

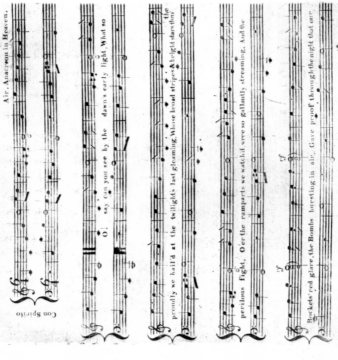

D

THE STAR SPANGLED / BANNER. / ‹decorated rule› / ‹text› / ‹lozenge rule› / Written by Francis S. Key, Esq. of Georgetown, / (D.C.) in 1814. / ‹ornament: 4-pointed star› / ‹all the preceding in an oval frame; surrounding the frame is:› BOMBARDMENT OF FORT M'HENRY. Each letter of this last is enclosed by a ring of stars. The whole within a frame composed of stylized leaves. Within the outer frame: At upper left, a 3-masted ship under sail; at upper right: an American eagle; at each inner lower corner: rays.

Printed on the recto of a piece of white satin. 14⅞″ x 11¹¹⁄₁₆″.

The statement *written ... in 1814* surely suggests post-1814 publication.

Location: B

Da

‹spreadeagle› / Bombardment of Fort M'Henry. / ‹rule› / ‹text› / ‹all the preceding in a frame of ornaments› / John D. Toy, printer, corner of St. Paul's lane and Market street. / ‹n.d., not before Aug. 1823›

Single leaf. Printed on recto only. 7½″ full x 5⅞″.

Anonymous.

Reprint.

Location: MdHS

E

Begone Dull Care. / Star Spangled Banner. / AND / BRIGHT PHOEBUS / ‹text, printed in two columns› / ‹rule› / Printed and Sold Wholesale and Retail, by C. Brown 211 Water-st. N.Y. / ‹n.d., not before 1825›

Single leaf. 9⅝″ x 7⅜″ (a trimmed example).

Printed on recto only. Anonymous.

Reprint.

Location: B

F

‹spreadeagle› / Star-spangled Banner. / ‹rule› / ‹text of The Star Spangled Banner› / ‹double rule› / Mellow Horn. The Drum. / ‹text of the two preceding, printed in two columns› / ‹the whole within a frame of type ornaments consisting of circular units and florets› / ‹n.p., n.d., ca. 1835›

Single leaf. 10¼″ x 4¹⁵⁄₁₆″.

Printed on recto only. Anonymous.

Reprint.

Location: LC

G

THE STAR-SPANGLED BANNER. ‹blue› / ‹text, printed in red in the form of 7 stripes; at upper left, field printed in blue with 34 white stars; at left, blue-printed staff; in short, the text, with field, is set in the form of the American flag› / ‹n.p., n.d., not before 1867›

Single leaf. 12⅞″ x 11¾″.

Printed on recto only. Anonymous.

Reprint.

Location: LC

Note: The Maryland Historical Society reports possession of two printings on silk similar to, but not the same as, printings C and D. Each carries the statement *written by Francis S. Key ... in 1814* which BAL very strongly suspects is indication of quite late printing. Another broadside printing (on silk?), present location not known, is reproduced in *The Seventh Star. Facts and Figures about the State of Maryland ... Published by the Board of Public Works for the Louisiana Purchase Exposition,* Baltimore, 1904, p. ‹22›, where it is described as a "fac-simile of 'broadside' as the song first appeared in print." The claim of primacy may be dismissed.

Query: The frequency of these elaborate printings on silk suggests that they may have been done for a national celebration; perhaps the semi-centennial of American Independence.

SECTION THREE

Appearances in books; sequence undetermined; arranged alphabetically by title of book. The designations are for identification only. First collected in Key's *Poems,* New York, 1857. The earliest publication as a separate book known to BAL is the edition illustrated by F. O. C. Darley, New York: James G. Gregory, 1861; cover-title; printed paper wrapper; pp. 12.

A

The American Muse: Or, Songster's Companion.

New-York: Printed and Sold by Smith & Forman, at the Franklin Juvenile Bookstores, 195 and 213 Greenwich-Street. 1814.

Cover-title? Issued in wrapper?

"Defence of Fort M'Henry," pp. 187-188. Anonymous. Pp. 216. For an extended edition of this book see *The Columbian Harmonist,* below.

Location: B

B

American Patriotic and Comic Modern Songs. Commemorative of Naval Victories, &c.

Newburyport, Printed and Sold by W. & J. Gilman, at Their Miscellaneous Book-Store, No. 2, Middle-Street. Sold also by Booksellers in the United States. 1814.

Printed paper wrapper.

"The Star-Spangled Banner; or, the Defence of Fort M'Henry," pp. 36-37. Anonymous.

Locations: B IU

C

The Columbian Harmonist, or Songster's Repository: Being a Selection of the Most Approved Sentimental, Patriotic, and Other Songs.

New-York: Printed and Sold by Smith & Forman, at the Franklin Juvenile Bookstores, 195 and 213 Greenwich-Street. 1814.

Cover-title? Issued in wrapper?

"Defence of Fort M'Henry," pp. 187-188. Anonymous. Pp. 288. This is an extended edition of *The American Muse,* above. *Reprint.*

Locations: B H

D

National Songster; or, a Collection of the Most Admired Patriotic Songs, on the Brilliant Victories, Achieved by the Naval and Military Heroes of the United States of America, over Equal and Superior Forces of the British. From the Best American Authors. First Hagers-Town Edition.

Hagers-Town: Printed by John Gruber and Daniel May. 1814.

Unprinted gray paper wrapper.

"Defence of Fort M'Henry," pp. 30-31. Anonymous.

Locations: AAS IU UV Y

SECTION FOUR

Sheet Music

It is almost universally accepted, but definite proof is lacking, that as sheet music the poem was first published by Carrs Music Store, Baltimore, Maryland.

The popular setting was probably composed by John Stafford Smith (1740–1836). For an account of the melody, a popular 18th century song, see "The Melody of *The Star Spangled Banner* in the United States before 1820," by Richard S. Hill, in *Essays Honoring Lawrence C. Wroth,* Portland, Maine, 1951. A setting by James Hewitt (1770–1827) was issued *ca.* 1815.

The following entries are arranged alphabetically by place of publication; under place alphabetically by publisher.

A

THE / STAR SPANGLED BANNER / A PARIOTIC ⟨sic⟩ SONG. / Baltimore. Printed and Sold at CARRS Music Store 36 Baltimore Street. / Air. Anacreon in Heaven. / ⟨text and music⟩ / ⟨n.d.⟩

The above on p. ⟨2⟩.

Text and music on pp. ⟨2-3⟩; pp. ⟨1⟩ and ⟨4⟩ blank. Plate numbers: (*Tssb.*) (*Pl. 1.*) on p. ⟨2⟩; (*Tssb.*) (*Pl. 2.*) on p. ⟨3⟩.

At foot of pp. ⟨2-3⟩: (*Adap^d & Arr^d by T.C.*) T.C., *i.e.,* Thomas Carr.

Dated 1814 by the Library of Congress but BAL has found no evidence to support the dating. Carr was at the address given 1814–1819.

Locations: IU LC

B

A Celebrated PATRIOTIC SONG, / THE / STAR SPANGLED BANNER / Written (during the Bombardment of FORT McHenry, on the 12th & 13th Septr 1814,) by / B. ⟨sic⟩ KEY Esqr / Baltimore. Printed and Sold at CARRS Music Store 36 Baltimore Street. / Air. Anacreon in Heaven. / ⟨text and music⟩ / ⟨n.d.⟩

The above on p. ⟨2⟩.

Printed from the altered plates of *Printing A.*

Text and music on pp. ⟨2-3⟩; pp. ⟨1⟩ and ⟨4⟩ blank. Plate numbers: (*Tssb.*) (*Pl. 1.*) on p. ⟨2⟩; (*Tssb.*) (*Pl. 2.*) on p. ⟨3⟩.

At foot of pp. ⟨2-3⟩: (*Adap^d & Arr^d by T.C.*) T. C., *i.e.,* Thomas Carr.

Dated by Library of Congress ⟨1814?⟩.

Location: LC

C

Star Spangled Banner. / ⟨flag and clouds⟩ / PHILADELPHIA / Published by A. Bacon & Co. S. 4th. St. / ⟨text and music⟩ / ⟨n.d.⟩

The above on p. ⟨2⟩.

Text and music on pp. ⟨2-3⟩; pp. ⟨1⟩ and ⟨4⟩ blank.

Dated *ca.* 1815 by Library of Congress. Dated ⟨1816?⟩ by Richard J. Wolfe in *Secular Music in America . . . ,* entry No. 8345.

Note: The earliest located copy is printed on laid paper, watermarked with a device; unpaged; no plate numbers. A later printing is on unwatermarked wove paper; page numbers 2-3 present; plate number 17 present. Reissued *ca.* 1823 by J. G. Klemm, Philadelphia, n.d.

Location: LC (all 3)

D

THE / BATTLE OF THE WABASH: / A PA-TRIOTIC SONG, / Written by Joseph Hutton, / To the favourite Air of / Anacreon in Heaven. / ⟨row of stars⟩ / PHILADELPHIA. Published by G. E. Blake. / ⟨n.d.⟩

The above at head of p. ⟨1⟩.

No plate numbers.

"The Battle of the Wabash," pp. ⟨1-2⟩. On p. ⟨3⟩, text only: FORT Mc.HENRY. / OR, THE STAR SPANGLED BANNER, / Sung with great applause by Mr. Hardinge, at the Theatre Baltimore. / AIR, ANACREON IN HEAVEN. / ⟨text: 4 numbered stanzas⟩ / ⟨rule composed of lazy S's and stars.⟩

Dated ⟨1814?⟩ by Library of Congress. On the basis of seemingly sound evidence dated by Muller as not before Oct. 19, 1814.

Locations: IU LC

E

WASHINGTON GUARDS. Philadelphia: Published and Sold at G. Willig's Music Store ⟨1814⟩.

Not seen. Entry from Dichter and Shapiro, pp. 36-37. "Fort McHenry; or, the Star Spangled Banner," p. 4.

REPRINTS

The following *undated* appearances as sheet music are arranged alphabetically by place of publication; alphabetically by publisher under place. Excluded are obvious reprints such as those decorated with Civil War motifs and the like; and, arrangements for mixed voices. The Smith and Hewitt settings are not indicated.

The following entries are made on the basis of copies in AAS, B, BA, BPL, H, LC, NYPL, Y. The dating (for the most part) is that ascribed by the Library of Congress.

BALTIMORE

The Star Spangled Banner. F. D. Benteen, n.d., 1844.

—————. J. E. Boswell, n.d., not before 1843.

—————. Marked: *New Edition.* T. Carr, n.d., 1821.

—————. John Cole, n.d., 1825.

—————. Geo. Willig, n.d., *ca.* 1824.

—————. Geo. Willig, Jr., n.d., 1843?

BOSTON

—————. C. Bradlee, 107 Washington Street, n.d., *ca.* 1835.

—————. E. H. Wade, 197 Washington Street, n.d., 1849.

CINCINNATI

—————. John Church, Jr., 66 West 4th St., n.d., 1859?

LOUISVILLE

—————. David P. Faulds, Main Street, n.d., *ca.* 1850.

NEW YORK

—————. Atwill, 201 Broadway, n.d., *ca.* 1835.

—————. Firth & Hall, 1 Franklin Square, n.d., *ca.* 1830.

—————. Firth, Pond & Co., 1 Franklin Square, n.d., 1851?

—————. J. A. & W. Geib, 23 Maiden Lane, n.d., *ca.* 1820.

—————. Geib & Co., 23 Maiden Lane, n.d., 1816?

—————. Geib & Walker, 23 Maiden Lane, n.d., 1829.

—————. William Hall & Son, 239 Broadway, n.d., 1848?

—————. William Hall & Son, 543 Broadway, n.d., 1859?

—————. E. H. Harding, 229 Bowery, n.d., *ca.* 1870.

—————. J. Hewitt, 156½ William Street, n.d., *ca.* 1815. The earliest located Hewitt setting.

—————. Hewitt & Jaques, 239 Broadway, n.d., *ca.* 1839.

—————. Millets Music Saloon, 329 Broadway, n.d., *ca.* 1840.

—————. William A. Pond & Co., n.d., *ca.* 1860.

—————. E. Riley, 29 Chatham Street, n.d., *ca.* 1820.

PHILADELPHIA

—————. A. Fiot, n.d., *ca.* 1840.

—————. J. E. Gould, n.d., after 1850.

—————. J. G. Klemm, 3 S. 3rd Street, n.d., 1823?

—————. W. R. Smith, 135 N. 8th Street, n.d., 1865?

Yankee Doodle & Star Spangled Banner. J. C. Smith, 213 Chestnut Street, n.d., *ca.* 1846.

Hail Columbia, with Yankee Doodle & Star Spangled Banner. Osbourn's Music Saloon, 30 S. 4th Street, n.d., 1838.

11082. Church Poetry: Being Portions of the Psalms in Verse, and Hymns Suited to the

Festivals and Fasts, and Various Occasions of the Church. Selected and Altered from Various Authors. By Wm. Augustus Muhlenberg ...

Philadelphia: Published by S. Potter & Co. J. Maxwell, Printer. 1823.

Cloth? Inserted errata slip, 17 lines.

Hymn, *Lord, with glowing heart I'd praise thee,* pp. 208-209. Collected in *Poems,* 1857.

Note: A Dictionary of Hymnology ... , by John Julian, London, 1915, reports that varying versions of the hymn appear in the Unitarian *Hymns for the Church of Christ,* Boston, 1853; and, *Manual of Praise,* Oberlin, Ohio, 1880.

LC

11083. A DISCOURSE ON EDUCATION, DELIVERED IN ST. ANNE'S CHURCH, ANNAPOLIS, AFTER THE COMMENCEMENT OF ST. JOHN'S COLLEGE FEBRUARY 22d, 1827 ...

OFFICE OF THE MARYLAND GAZETTE, ANNAPOLIS. J. GREEN, PRINT. 1827.

<1>-26, <i>-xviii. 8⅛" full x 5³⁄₁₆".

<1>-5⁴, 6².

Printed paper wrapper? Cover-title?

Listed USLG Sept. 1827; NAR Oct. 1827.

AAS   LC

11084. American Colonization Society. The Proceedings of a Public Meeting, Held in the Middle Dutch Church. Together with Addresses Delivered on that Occasion, by the Rev. Mr. Gallaudet ... Captain Stockton ... Francis S. Key ...

New-York: Printed at the Protestant Episcopal Press, No. 46 Lumber-Street, 1829.

Printed paper wrapper.

"Address of Francis S. Key, Esq.," pp. 23-28.

BPL   NYPL

11085. The Christian Lyre. By Joshua Leavitt ...

New York: Published by Jona. Leavitt, at the Theological Bookstore, 182 Broadway. Sleight & Robinson Printers. 1830.

Cloth, leather label on spine.

"If Life's Pleasures Charm Thee," p. 108. Anonymous. Collected in *Poems,* 1857, under the title "Life."

B

11086. ORATION DELIVERED ... IN THE ROTUNDO OF THE CAPITOL OF THE U. STATES, ON THE 4th OF JULY, 1831 ...

<n.p., n.d., 1831?>

Caption-title. The above at head of p. <1>.

<1>-16. 9¾" x 5¾" full.

<1-2>⁴.

Issued in printed wrapper?

LC   UV (incomplete)

11087. The Home of the Soul ... <Music by Henry R. Bishop>

Philadelphia, Miller & Osbourn   35 Nᵗʰ Fourth Sᵗ Copy Right Secured. <n.d., 1832>

Sheet music. The above at head of p. 16. Paged 16-17. Plate number 7 at foot of pp. 16-17. Dated <1832> by LC.

Issued as part of a series? Removed from a larger work? At foot of pp. 16-17: *First Number.*

Collected in *Poems,* 1857.

LC

11088. THE POWER OF LITERATURE AND ITS CONNEXION WITH RELIGION: AN ORATION, DELIVERED AT BRISTOL COLLEGE, JULY 23, 1834, BEFORE THE PHILOLOGIAN SOCIETY ...

<BRISTOL, PENNA.> PUBLISHED BY ORDER OF THE SOCIETY. BRISTOL COLLEGE PRESS. MDCCCXXXIV.

<1>-19. 9⁹⁄₁₆" x 5¾".

<A>-B⁴, C².

Printed blue paper wrapper.

B   NYPL   Y

11089. A COLLECTION OF FACTS IN REGARD TO LIBERIA, BY JUDGE PAINE, OF VERMONT: TO WHICH IS ADDED THE CORRESPONDENCE OF THE REV. BENJAMIN TAPPAN, OF MAINE, AND FRANCIS S. KEY, ESQUIRE, OF THE DISTRICT OF COLUMBIA.

WOODSTOCK, VT: PRINTED BY AUGUSTUS PALMER. 1839.

<1>-36. 8⅜" x 4¹¹⁄₁₆".

<1>-3⁶.

Printed paper wrapper, both white and tan noted.

AAS   LC

11090. Proceedings of a National Convention for the Promotion of Education in the United

States, Held at the City Hall, in the City of Washington, May 6, 7, 8, 1840.

Washington: P. Force, Printer. 1840.

Cover-title? Issued in printed paper wrapper?

Resolutions, pp. 9, 11.

H

11091. SPEECH ... BEFORE THE COLONIZATION CONVENTION, MAY 9, 1842.

⟨n.p., n.d., Washington, D. C., 1842⟩ ALEXANDER & BARNARD, PRINTERS.

Cover-title.

⟨3⟩-17. 8⅞″ x 5⅞″ scant.

⟨1⟩⁴, 2*⁴.

Printed white paper wrapper.

Offprint from: *Proceedings of a Convention of the Friends of African Colonization, Held in Washington City, May 4, 1842*, Washington, 1842, pp. 34-49. Copy in LC.

LC Y

11092. ... NARRATIVE OF MR DANIEL MURRAY. IN A LETTER OF THE LATE HON. FRANCIS S. KEY, OF GEORGETOWN, DISTRICT OF COLUMBIA ...

PUBLISHED BY THE AMERICAN TRACT SOCIETY. ⟨n.p., n.d., Boston? New York? 1843⟩

At head of title: NO. 441

Title at head of p. ⟨1⟩; imprint at foot of p. 4.

Single cut sheet folded to make 4 pages.

⟨1⟩-4. Also paged ⟨97⟩-100. 7⁵⁄₁₆″ x 4⅜″ scant.

Issued prior to Nov. 6, 1843, on which date H received a copy of the *Twenty-Ninth Annual Report of the American Tract Society, Boston ...*, Boston, 1843, wherein (p. 73) the Key tract is listed.

Note: Under the title *Daniel Murray, Late Lieutenant in the American Navy. Extract from a Letter Written by a Pious Lawyer ...*, issued n.p., n.d., Raleigh, N. C., as a Civil War tract. Place and dating from *Confederate Imprints ...*, by Marjorie Lyle Crandall, Boston, 1955, Vol. 2, p. 796.

BA (reprint) Y

11092A. Cyclopædia of American Literature; Embracing Personal and Critical Notices of Authors ... by Evert A. Duyckinck and George L. Duyckinck. In Two Volumes ...

New York: Charles Scribner. 1855.

"Song," Vol. 1, p. 663 (*When the warrior returns ...*).

"Hymn for the Fourth of July," Vol. 1, p. 664.

Both collected in *Poems*, 1857.

Advertised APC Dec. 29, 1855, as in cloth; half calf; half calf extra; half morocco extra; calf extra; morocco extra.

H

11093. POEMS ... WITH AN INTRODUCTORY LETTER BY CHIEF JUSTICE TANEY.

NEW YORK: ROBERT CARTER & BROTHERS, NO. 530 BROADWAY. 1857

Edited by Henry V. D. Johns.

⟨i⟩-⟨xii⟩, ⟨13⟩-203; plus: Publisher's catalogue, pp. ⟨1⟩-12. See below for leaf sizes.

⟨1-8¹², 9⁶; plus: 10⁶⟩. Signed: ⟨1-2⟩, 3-14, 16, 16, ⟨17⟩⁶; plus: ⟨18⟩⁶.

Three bindings noted; sequence, if any, not determined.

A

A cloth: blue. Both sides stamped in gold with a triple rule frame enclosing an arrangement of filigrees, a vertical filigree ornament at the center. Edges gilt. Yellow end papers. Flyleaves. Leaf size: 6½″ full x 4¼″.

B

T cloth: black. Both sides stamped in blind with a triple rule frame enclosing a filigree frame, the center of the sides unstamped. Edges plain. Yellow end papers. Flyleaves. Leaf size: 6½″ full x 4⅜″ scant.

C

T cloth: black; purple. Sides blindstamped with a triple rule frame. At center of sides, also blindstamped, a vertical filigree ornament. Edges plain. Yellow end papers. Flyleaves. Leaf size: 6⅝″ scant x 4⅜″ full.

Note: Allibone reports imprint as *Baltimore, 1857;* no such imprint traced by BAL.

Deposited Nov. 7, 1856. A rebound copy at NYPL inscribed by early owner Nov. 27, 1856.

AAS (C)   B (A)   H (B)   NYPL (C)   UV (A)   Y (C)

LEGAL AND LIKE PUBLICATIONS

As an attorney Key's name is attached to certain legal and like documents. The following have been seen by BAL; the list is presumed incomplete. For a comment on "off-subject" publications see BAL, Vol. 1, p. xviii.

Supreme Court. Appellant's Statement. Mayor, Aldermen, & Common Council of the City of Washington, for the Use of James H. Blake, and Others, *vs.* Moses Young. Error from the Circuit Court of the District of Columbia for the County of Washington ...

⟨n.p., n.d., Washington, D. C., 1819⟩

Caption-title. Printed self-wrapper. At end: *Ashton & Key, for Appellants.* Pp. 13.

UV

Speech of Francis S. Key, Esq. Counsel for Gen. Samuel Houston, on His Trial before the House of Representatives for a Breach of Privilege.

City of Washington: Printed at the Globe Office by F. P. Blair. 1832.

Cover-title? Printed paper wrapper? 16 pp.

NYPL UV

Claim of the Legal Representatives of Nimrod Farrow and Richard Harris, before the Committee of Claims of the House of Representatives, Twenty-Fourth Congress, First Session.

Washington: Printed by Gales and Seaton. 1836.

Printed paper wrapper? Signed at p. 47 by Key and W. Jones. Pp. 52. Errata slip inserted.

LC

A Part of a Speech Pronounced by Francis S. Key, Esq. on the Trial of Reuben Crandall, M. D. before the Circuit Court of the District of Columbia, at the March Term Thereof, 1836, on an Indictment for Publishing Libels with Intent to Excite Sedition and Insurrection among the Slaves and Free Coloured People of Said District. [From the African Repository for November 1836.]

Washington: 1836.

Cover-title. Printed self-wrapper. Pp. 15.

B H Y

Mexican Treaty ...

⟨n.p., n.d., 1842?⟩

Caption-title. The above at head of p. ⟨1⟩. Single cut sheet folded to make 4 pages. Signed at end by Key and others.

According to the provisions of the act for carrying into effect the Convention with Mexico, the certificates of the awards of the Commissioners are to be issued when the commission shall be completed and closed ...

LC LCP

... Report of Mr. Kennedy, of Maryland, from the Committee on Commerce of the House of Representatives ...

Washington ... 1843.

Remarks, pp. 51–66. For fuller entry see in John Pendleton Kennedy list.

REPRINTS

The following publications contain material by Key reprinted from earlier books. Not listed are the uncounted thousands of reprintings of "The Star Spangled Banner" issued 1815 and later.

The Family Circle, and Parlor Annual. 1848. Edited and Published by Rev. D. Newell.

New-York: 126 Nassau-Street ... ⟨n.d., 1847⟩

Sheets of a periodical bound as an annual. "The Home of the Soul," p. 18, had prior publication as sheet music; see in main list under 1832.

Lyra Americana ... Selected ... by the Rev. George T. Rider ...

New York ... 1865.

For comment see entry No. 2827. "The Sacrifice of Praise," pp. 181–182; otherwise "Hymn," *Poems,* 1857, pp. ⟨171⟩-172.

Lyra Americana: Hymns of Praise and Faith, from American Poets.

London: The Religious Tract Society ... 1865.

Listed PC Oct. 2, 1865; Ath Oct. 7, 1865.

Lyra Sacra Americana: Or, Gems from American Sacred Poetry. Selected ... by Charles Dexter Cleveland ...

New York: Charles Scribner and Company. London: Sampson Low, Son, and Marston. 1868.

Christian Lyrics: Chiefly Selected from Modern Authors ... ⟨Compiled by Lucy Fletcher Massey⟩

London: Frederick Warne and Co. Bedford Street, Covent Garden. New York: Scribner, Welford, & Co. ⟨n.d., 1871⟩

Cloth?

Belford's Annual. 1889–90 ...

Chicago ... ⟨1889⟩

For comment see in list of Jackson reprints. "The Silk Worm's Song," p. 20; otherwise "The Worm's Death-Song," *Poems,* 1857.

Songs of the South ... Edited by Jennie Thornley Clarke ...

Philadelphia ... 1896

For comment see in Lanier list, Sec. III.

300 Years The Poets and Poetry of Maryland Edited by Loker Raley

Henry Harrison Poetry Publisher New York ⟨1937⟩

Youth's Companion Edited by Lovell Thompson ...

... Boston ... 1954

For comment see entry No. 10927. "The Butterfly's Hope," pp. 965-966; otherwise "The Worm's Death-Song," *Poems*, 1857.

REFERENCES AND ANA

Supplement to the Boston Gazette, for Thursday, April 28, 1808. Truth Reason Argument Eloquence. Mr. Key's Speech ...

⟨Boston, 1808⟩

Caption-title. The above at head of single sheet. Laid paper. 19⅜″ x 13⅛″. Printed on recto only. Text in five columns.

Not by Francis Scott Key but by his uncle, Philip Barton Key (1757–1815), member of Congress, 1807–1813.

Poems by the Late Doctor John Shaw. To Which is Prefixed a Biographical Sketch of the Author.

Published by Edward Earle, Philadelphia, and by Edward J. Coale, Baltimore. Fry and Kammerer, Printers. 1810.

Edited, anonymously, by John Elihu Hall. Paper boards.

"Of the earlier years of ... ⟨Shaw's⟩ life, the writer of these memoirs ⟨Hall⟩ is acquainted with little but what has been gathered from the information of others. He is particularly indebted to ..." Francis Scott Key.—P. ⟨1⟩.

A Sketch of the Character of the Late Francis Scott Key ... by the Rev. John T. Brooke ...

Cincinnati: Published by Wilson & Drake, West Fourth Street. Kendall and Barnard, Printers. 1843.

Printed paper wrapper?

... The Mission of Francis Scott Key to Alabama in 1833 by Thomas Chalmers McCorvey [From the Transactions 1899–1903, Vol. IV]

Montgomery, Alabama 1904

Printed paper wrapper. Cover-title. At head of title: The Alabama Historical Society Montgomery Reprint No. 6

A Sketch of Francis Scott Key, with a Glimpse of His Ancestors ⟨by⟩ F. S. Key Smith ...

[Reprinted from the Records of the Columbia Historical Society, Washington, D. C. Vol. 11, 1909.]

Printed paper wrapper. Cover-title.

Francis Scott Key Author of the Star Spangled Banner ... by F. S. Key-Smith ...

Published by Key-Smith and Company Evans Building, Washington, D. C. ⟨1911⟩

... "The Star Spangled Banner" (Revised and Enlarged from the "Report" on the Above and Other Airs, Issued in 1909) by Oscar George Theodore Sonneck ...

Washington   Government Printing Office 1914

At head of title: Library of Congress

The Star Spangled Banner Words and Music Issued between 1814–1864 An Annotated Bibliographical List ... Compiled by Joseph Muller ...

G. A. Baker & Co., Inc. New York, 1935.

500 copies only. Printed label on spine.

Spangled Banner The Story of Francis Scott Key ⟨by⟩ Victor Weybright

Farrar & Rinehart Inc.   On Murray Hill New York ⟨1935⟩

The first printing has the publisher's device on the copyright page.

Francis Scott Key Life and Times by Edward S. Delaplaine ...

Biography Press 38 Halsey Street, Brooklyn New York 1937

On copyright page: *First Edition*

500 copies, numbered, signed by the author.

Freedom's Flag The Story of Francis Scott Key by Rupert Sargent Holland

Macrae Smith Company Philadelphia ⟨1943⟩

The First Book Edition of the Star-Spangled Banner ... with an Introduction by Richard B. Morris ...

Franklin Watts, Inc.   575 Lexington Ave. New York 22 ⟨1961⟩

On copyright page: *First Printing*

11094. Delta Upsilon Songs Brought under One Cover by William Otto Miller ...

Published by the Executive Council in the Year of the Fraternity the Seventy-Second ... ⟨1906⟩

"Down among the Dead Men," pp. 20-21. Collected in *Memories of My Son* ... ⟨1920⟩.

UV

11095. The Younger Choir with an Introduction by Edwin Markham

Moods Publishing Company New York 1910

Printed boards.

"Ballade of My Lady's Beauty," pp. 51-52.

"George Meredith," p. 53.

Both collected in *Summer of Love*, 1911.

". . . 500 copies . . . printed . . . numbers 1 through 50 have been autographed . . ."

Listed PW April 23, 1910. Deposited April 27, 1910.

H NYPL UV

11096. SUMMER OF LOVE ...

NEW YORK THE BAKER & TAYLOR COMPANY 1911

⟨i-xii⟩, 1-92. 7⁹⁄₁₆" x 5¼" scant.

⟨1-6⁸, 7⁴⟩.

V cloth: blue-gray. Goldstamped. Top edges gilt. Spine imprint: THE / BAKER / AND / TAYLOR / COMPANY

Also noted in a variant binding of undetermined status: V cloth: brown-orange. Unstamped. Pasted to the front cover as a label is a trimmed title-page. Top edges plain. Remainder?

Note: Copies have been reported with the Doubleday, Page spine imprint; not seen by BAL. PW Jan. 6, 1912 noted: "The Baker & Taylor Co. have arranged with Doubleday, Page & Co. to take over their list of publications . . ."

A copy at UV inscribed by Kilmer Sept. 22, 1911. Deposited Sept. 25, 1911. Listed PW Oct. 21, 1911.

AAS B H (variant) NYPL UV Y (both)

11097. The Lyric Year One Hundred Poems Edited by Ferdinand Earle

New York Mitchell Kennerley 1912

"Martin," pp. 141-142. Collected in *Trees* ... ⟨1914⟩.

For comment see entry No. 2284.

11098. Gifts of Shee ... Music by Annie Kilburn-Kilmer ...

London ... The Star Music Publishing Co. Ltd. ... ⟨1912⟩

Sheet music. Cover-title.

Not seen. Entry from *Whimsical Whimsies* ... , by Annie Kilburn-Kilmer ⟨1927⟩.

Reprinted from *Summer of Love*, 1911.

11099. A Lullaby for a Baby Fairy ... Music by Annie Kilburn-Kilmer ...

London ... The Star Music Publishing Co. Ltd. ... ⟨1912⟩

Sheet music. Cover-title.

Not seen. Entry from *Whimsical Whimsies* ... , by Annie Kilburn-Kilmer ⟨1927⟩.

Reprinted from *Summer of Love*, 1911.

11100. The Song of Terre d'Amour ... Music by Annie Kilburn-Kilmer ...

London ... The Star Music Publishing Co. Ltd. ... ⟨1912⟩

Sheet music. Cover-title.

Not seen. Entry from *Whimsical Whimsies* ... , by Annie Kilburn-Kilmer ⟨1927⟩.

Earliest located book publication: *Memories of My Son* ... ⟨1920⟩, below.

11101. Anthology of Magazine Verse for 1913 ... by William Stanley Braithwaite ...

Issued by W.S.B. Cambridge, Massachusetts ⟨1913⟩

"Trees," p. 7. Collected in *Trees* ... ⟨1914⟩.

For comment see entry No. 3037.

11102. Pierre de Coulevain

⟨n.p., n.d., 1913⟩

Cover-title? Printed self-wrapper? Printed paper wrapper?

"Sur la Branche. ('Pierre de Coulevain,' Died Aug. 21, 1913.)," p. ⟨7⟩.

NYPL

11103. The Yellow Gown. Song. Words by Joyce Kilmer and Annie Kilburn-Kilmer. Music by Annie Kilburn-Kilmer ...

London ... The Star Music Publishing Co. Ltd. ... ⟨1913⟩

Sheet music. Cover-title.

Not seen. Entry from *Whimsical Whimsies* ..., by Annie Kilburn-Kilmer ⟨1927⟩.

Earliest located book publication: *Memories of My Son* ... ⟨1920⟩, below.

11104. TREES AND OTHER POEMS ...

NEW YORK   GEORGE H DORAN COMPANY ⟨1914⟩

⟨i-iv⟩, ⟨1⟩-75; plus: 4 blank leaves. 7¹³/₁₆″ x 5⅜″ scant.

⟨1-5⁸, plus: 6⁴⟩

Tan-gray laid paper boards. Top edges gilded. Printed paper labels.

Note: There may have been more than one printing in the form described above. Hence, the description may well be of the first *printings* rather than of the first *printing*. Quite late printings may be recognized by the statement on the copyright page: *Printed in the United States of America.*

It is generally accepted that the following features occur only on later printings: Tan laid paper boards, edges plain; terminal gathering of 4 blank leaves not present. BAL concurs although recognizing the danger of basing sequence of sheets on the binding.

An undoubted reprint, at Y, collates:

⟨i-viii⟩, ⟨1⟩-75, 2 blank leaves. ⟨1-5⁸, 6⁴⟩. Tan laid paper boards, edges plain.

Also note: P. 22: *Cortez* for *Cortes* occurs in all early printings examined.

A copy in GD inscribed by Kilmer Oct. 8, 1914. Listed PW Oct. 17, 1914.

AAS H   UV   Y

11105. A Valentine ... Music by Annie Kilburn-Kilmer ...

London ... The Star Music Publishing Co. Ltd. ... ⟨1914⟩

Sheet music. Cover-title.

Not seen. Entry from *Whimsical Whimsies* ..., by Annie Kilburn-Kilmer ⟨1927⟩.

Collected in *Joyce Kilmer* ... ⟨1918⟩.

11106. Little Verses and Big Names

New York   MCMXV   George H. Doran Company

"Supposed Meditations of an Infant of Eighteen Months Concerning Gramercy Park," by Aline and Joyce Kilmer, p. 14.

For comment see entry No. 482.

11107. Anthology of Magazine Verse for 1915 ... Edited by William Stanley Braithwaite

New York   Gomme & Marshall   1915

Boards, cloth shelfback; printed paper label on spine.

"The White Ships and the Red," pp. 134-137. Collected in *Main Street* ... ⟨1917⟩.

Listed PW Dec. 18, 1915.

H

11108. THE CIRCUS AND OTHER ESSAYS ...

NEW YORK   LAURENCE J. GOMME   1916

⟨i-viii⟩, ⟨1⟩-79. 6⅝″ x 4⁵/₁₆″.

⟨1-5⁸, 6⁴⟩.

Tan laid paper boards, brown T cloth shelfback.

Note: The remainder was taken over by Mitchell Kennerley (New York) who issued the book with a slip, pasted to the front pastedown, imprinted as follows: *This book is now published by Mitchell Kennerley.*

A copy at UV inscribed by Kilmer Nov. 24, 1916. Deposited Nov. 28, 1916. Listed PW Dec. 16, 1916. For an enlarged edition see under 1921.

AAS UV   Y

11109. In the Day of Battle   Poems of the Great War Selected by Carrie Ellen Holman

Toronto William Briggs 1916

Paper boards, cloth shelfback, printed paper label on front and on spine.

"The New School," pp. 40-42. Collected in *Main Street* . . . ⟨1917⟩.

Registered for copyright Nov. 28, 1916.

EM

11110. Verses by Hilaire Belloc with an Introduction by Joyce Kilmer

New York Laurence J. Gomme 1916

Cloth?

"Introduction," pp. xi-xxvii.

Deposited Dec. 4, 1916.

NYPL

11111. LITERATURE IN THE MAKING BY SOME OF ITS MAKERS PRESENTED BY JOYCE KILMER

HARPER & BROTHERS NEW YORK AND LONDON ⟨1917⟩

⟨i-xvi⟩, ⟨1⟩-⟨319⟩. 7¼" full x 4⅞".

⟨-⟩⁸, ⟨1-3⟩, 4-8, ⟨9⟩, 10-20⁸.

S cloth: brown.

Note: Sheets also occur in a variant (remainder?) binding of tan paper boards; variant in Y.

On copyright page: *Published April, 1917*; and, code letters D-R (signifying *printed April, 1917*). Deposited May 5, 1917. A copy at NYPL received May 9, 1917. Listed PW May 12, 1917.

AAS BA H NYPL

11112. The Mayor of Casterbridge by Thomas Hardy Introduction by Joyce Kilmer

Boni and Liveright, Inc. Publishers New York ⟨n.d., 1917⟩

Imitation leather. Issued in *The Modern Library*.

"Introduction," pp. xi-xiv.

Listed PW July 21, 1917.

H

11113. THE COURAGE OF ENLIGHTEN-MENT AN ADDRESS DELIVERED IN CAMPION COLLEGE PRAIRIE DU CHIEN, WIS., TO THE MEMBERS OF THE GRADUATING CLASS JUNE FIFTEENTH NINETEEN HUNDRED SEVENTEEN

⟨n.p., n.d., 1917⟩

⟨1⟩-14, blank leaf. Paper watermarked *Dresden Pamphlet*. 7⅝" x 4⅞".

⟨-⟩⁸.

Printed buff laid paper wrapper.

H (received July 30, 1917)

11114. MAIN STREET AND OTHER POEMS . . .

NEW YORK GEORGE H DORAN COMPANY ⟨1917⟩

⟨i-ii⟩, ⟨1⟩-78. 7¹³⁄₁₆" x 5³⁄₁₆".

⟨1-5⟩⁸.

Brown laid paper boards; printed paper label on front and on spine. Top edges gilded.

Note: There were probably several printings in the form described above. Although recognizing the danger of basing sequence of sheets on the binding, BAL suggests that the following bindings occur only on later printings: tan laid paper boards, top edges plain; green cloth.

A copy at H received Oct. 4, 1917. Listed PW Oct. 13, 1917. Deposited Oct. 16, 1917.

AAS BA NYPL UV

11115. Dreams and Images An Anthology of Catholic Poets Edited by Joyce Kilmer

Boni and Liveright New York 1917

"Acknowledgment," p. ⟨iii⟩.

"Introduction," pp. vii-viii.

A copy at BA received Jan. 2, 1918. Listed PW Jan. 12, 1918. Deposited Feb. 25, 1918.

BA Y

11116. Trees . . . Music by Carl Hahn . . .

The John Church Company Cincinnati New York London . . . ⟨1918⟩

Sheet music. Cover-title. Plate number: 18048-4.

Two printings noted:

1

On back cover: Advertisement for "Sleepy-Town," copyrighted 1914.

2

On back cover: Advertisement for "The Little Woman in Gray," copyrighted 1921.

Reprinted from *Trees* . . . ⟨1914⟩.

Deposited Oct. 10, 1918.

Other settings:

Music by Annie Kilburn-Kilmer. London: The Star Music Publishing Co., Ltd. ⟨1920⟩

Music by Oscar Rasbach. New York: G. Schirmer, Inc. ⟨1922⟩. This is the setting most often heard.

B (Hahn setting, both printings)

11117. Yanks   A Book of A.E.F. Verse

⟨Paris⟩ Published in France by the Stars and Stripes the Official Newspaper of the American Expeditionary Forces 1918 . . .

Unpaged. Edited by John T. Winterich and Hudson Hawley. Printed tan paper wrapper.

Published Nov. 27, 1918. See notes below.

Contains "The Wood Called Rouge-Bouquet." Collected in *Joyce Kilmer . . .* , New York ⟨1918⟩ (Dec.) under the title "Rouge Bouquet."

"While we had hoped to make the first deliveries of *Yanks . . .* by November 15, certain unforeseen circumstances, such as a formidable document signed on the dotted line by a number of Germanic emissaries and the celebrations consequent thereupon, coupled with the difficulties attendant on getting a book out on time by a Yankee editor whose knowledge of French would hardly qualify him for acceptance by the Forty Immortals, prevented, unfortunately, the issuance of the precious volume until the day before Thanksgiving.

"Now, however, we are going strong, with the first edition all bespoken, and the second, or Victory Edition, proudly slipping down the ways.

"There will be more editions to follow, to judge from the way our kind and admiring friends are sandbagging, sniping and grenading us in order to obtain copies to send home as a keepsake of the war. Just give us a little time in which to negotiate, through the medium of three interpreters, the delivery of more copies, and a little more time before we can put the official *bon à tirer* on the revised proofs for the later editions, and a little more time to shake hands with our French printing compatriots, and we'll kick through with all the *Yanks* you desire."—*The Stars and Stripes*, Dec. 6, 1918, p. 4.

On verso of the title-page: *First Edition*. Reprints occur with one, or both, of the following added statements: *Victory Edition* and *Peace Edition*. Commenting on this Col. Winterich wrote BAL on Oct. 7, 1963: "I was not bibliographically minded in 1918 and had nothing to do with that *First Edition* slug (but Pvt. Hudson Hawley and I did select the contents). I don't think our commanding officer, Capt. Guy T. Viskniskki, was bibliographically minded either, but I think he was responsible for both the *First Edition* and the *Victory Edition* slugs. The earliest copies were in smooth tan wrappers, supposed to be an approximation of the olive drab uniform. Later printings, some of them anyway, were in a light blue pebbled paper. Odd that one should know so little about something one helped create and saw through the press . . . The Linotype operator was Pvt. Robert E. Lee."

NYPL   UV

11118. JOYCE KILMER   EDITED WITH A MEMOIR BY ROBERT CORTES HOLLIDAY . . .

NEW YORK   GEORGE H. DORAN COMPANY   ⟨1918⟩

2 Vols.

1: . . . MEMOIR AND POEMS

2: . . . PROSE WORKS

1: ⟨i⟩-⟨xvi⟩, 17-271. Frontispiece, one plate, and one folded facsimile inserted. 8⁵⁄₁₆" x 5½".

2: ⟨i-ii⟩, ⟨i⟩-⟨x⟩, 11-290, 2 blank leaves. Frontispiece and 2 plates inserted. *Note:* In some copies the last blank leaf is used as the pastedown.

1: ⟨1-17⟩⁸.

2: ⟨1-18⁸, 19⁴⟩. *Note:* In some copies ⟨19⟩₄ is used as the pastedown.

Gray-green laid paper boards, green V, or, green T cloth shelfback. Printed paper label on spine.

Note: In the earliest printing (printings?) the verso of each fly-title-leaf is blank; in a known later printing the versos bear a list of books.

Deposited Dec. 21, 1918. Listed PW Jan. 25, 1919. The London (Hodder & Stoughton) edition listed Bkr Sept. 1919; issued as *Poems, Essays, and Letters*.

B   BA   H   NYPL

11119. THE PEACEMAKER . . .

⟨n.p.⟩ . . . 1918. HENRY T. BAILEY

Printed in black and red. Single card. Printed on recto only. Issued as a Christmas card. 9⅛" scant x 6⁵⁄₁₆" scant.

Also in (reprinted from?) *Joyce Kilmer . . .* ⟨1918⟩. For publication as sheet music see below under 1922.

B

11120. Father Duffy's Story . . . by Francis P. Duffy . . . with an Historical Appendix by Joyce Kilmer

New York   George H. Doran Company ⟨1919⟩

"Historical Appendix," pp. 331-353.

Deposited Dec. 19, 1919.

AAS   H   Y

11121. Memories of My Son Sergeant Joyce Kilmer by Annie Kilburn Kilmer with Numerous Unpublished Poems and Letters ...

New York Brentano's ⟨1920⟩

"Only Limited Edition Printed from Type and the Type Is Distributed"—p. ⟨iii⟩.

Deposited June 5, 1920. Listed PW June 12, 1920.

B   H   UV   Y

11122. THE CIRCUS AND OTHER ESSAYS AND FUGITIVE PIECES ... EDITED WITH INTRODUCTION BY ROBERT CORTES HOLLIDAY

NEW YORK   GEORGE H. DORAN COMPANY ⟨1921⟩

For first edition see under 1916. "Fugitive Pieces," pp. 137-311, here first collected.

⟨i-iv⟩, ⟨i⟩-⟨xii⟩, 13-311, 2 blank leaves. 8″ full x 5½″.

⟨1-20⟩⁸.

Tan-white boards, green T, or, green V cloth shelfback. Printed paper label on spine. Extra label tipped in at back.

Listed PW April 16, 1921. BA copy received April 26, 1921. Deposited April 27, 1921.

BA   H   NYPL

11123. The Peacemaker ... Music by Burt G. Wilder

Printed for the Composer by John Worley Company, Boston 1922 Copyright of the Words, George H. Doran Company, Boston ⟨sic⟩

Sheet music. Cover-title. See under 1918 for prior separate printing.

Reprinted from Joyce Kilmer ... ⟨1918⟩.

B   H   MHS   Y

11124. Memorial Day ... Music by Frank Patterson ...

Hinds, Hayden & Eldredge, Inc. Publishers New York ⟨1923⟩

Sheet music. Cover-title. Plate number: 652-8.

Reprinted from Trees ... ⟨1914⟩.

Deposited Feb. 6, 1923.

LC

11125. The House with Nobody in It ...

⟨n.p.⟩ Privately Printed 1923

Boards, paper label.

Reprinted from Trees ... ⟨1914⟩. For publication as sheet music see below under ⟨1933⟩.

One hundred numbered copies printed for I. A. Brauerman; and, presumably, 200 copies for George F. Trenholm.

AAS   NYPL

11126. Song Slender Your Hands ... Music by Alexander MacFadyen ...

Boston: Oliver Ditson Company ... ⟨1925⟩

Sheet music. Cover-title. Plate number (high voice): 74680-3. Also issued for medium voice; not seen.

Reprinted from Summer of Love ... , 1911.

Deposited March 23, 1925.

B

11127. Trees ... Decorated by E. MacKinstry

George H. Doran Company New York ⟨1925⟩

Pictorial paper boards sides, cloth shelfback.

Reprinted from Trees ... ⟨1914⟩.

First (only?) printing has the publisher's monogram on copyright page.

Deposited April 29, 1925.

B   Y

11128. Leaves from My Life by Annie Kilburn Kilmer ...

Frye Publishing Co. 15 West 107th Street New York City ⟨1925⟩

Material by Kilmer, pp. 133-152, some of which had prior publication in Memories of My Son ... ⟨1920⟩.

Deposited July 14, 1925. A copy at NYPL received Aug. 19, 1925.

B   NYPL   Y

11129. Dreams and Images An Anthology of Catholic Poets Edited by Joyce Kilmer with Supplementary Poems Edited by Shaemas O'Sheel

Boni and Liveright New York MCMXXVI

Reprint. For first edition see under 1917.

LC

11130. The Catholic Anthology by Thomas Walsh ...

New York The Macmillan Company 1927 . . .

Reprint save for "Daw's Dinner," p. 421.

Deposited Sept. 14, 1927.

NYPL

11131. The Constant Lamp . . . Music by Marion Atwood . . .

G. Schirmer (Inc.), New York . . . ⟨1931⟩

Sheet music. Cover-title. Plate number: 35473.

Otherwise "Citizen of the World" in *Trees* . . . ⟨1914⟩.

B

11132. . . . The Night Our Lady Came . . .

The Boston Music Co. 116 Boylston Street, Boston, Mass. ⟨1932⟩

Sheet music. Cover-title. At head of title: The Boston Music Company Octavo Church Music Christmas Carols . . . Plate number: B.M.Co. 8861-2.

Music by Florence N. Wilson.

Otherwise "Gates and Doors" in *Main Street* . . . ⟨1917⟩.

Deposited Dec. 27, 1932.

LC

11133. . . . The House with Nobody in It . . . Music by Lee Montgomery . . .

Chappell-Harms Inc. 62 West 45th St. New York, N. Y. Chappell & Co, Ltd. London-Sydney Made in U.S.A. ⟨1933⟩

Sheet music. Cover-title. At head of title: No. 1 in C . . . No. 2 in E . . . Plate number: 8326-5.

Reprinted from *Trees* . . . ⟨1914⟩. See under 1923 for another printing of the text.

Deposited Aug. 4, 1933.

B LC

11134. . . . A Ballad of Christmas Eve Christmas Anthem for Mixed Chorus, with Soprano Solo . . . ⟨Music by⟩ L. Camilieri

New York: The H. W. Gray Co., Sole Agents for Novello & Co., Limited: London . . . 1934 . . .

Music. Pp. ⟨1⟩-11; advertisement, p. ⟨12⟩. The above on p. ⟨1⟩. At head of title: No. 1294 Church Music Review Price 15 Cents

Otherwise "Gates and Doors," *Main Street* . . . ⟨1917⟩. See entry No. 11132.

Deposited Oct. 16, 1934.

B LC

11135. The Smart Set Anthology Edited by Burton Rascoe and Groff Conklin

Reynal & Hitchcock New York ⟨1934⟩

"Whitemail," pp. 214-221.

Two states of the binding noted; the order of presentation is presumed correct:

A: On spine: *Roscoe* for *Rascoe*. A copy thus at H received Dec. 4, 1934.

B: On spine: *Rascoe* correctly spelled. A copy thus at NYPL received Dec. 10, 1934.

Deposited Nov. 30, 1934.

H NYPL

11136. Christmas Eve A Joyful Song . . . Music by Richard Hageman . . .

Galaxy Music Corporation 17 West 46th Street New York, N. Y. ⟨1936⟩

Sheet music. Cover-title. Plate number: G.M. 733-6.

Otherwise "Gates and Doors," in *Main Street* . . . ⟨1917⟩. See *The Night Our Lady Came* ⟨1932⟩ for an earlier printing as sheet music.

Deposited Nov. 19, 1936.

LC

11137. Joyce Kilmer's Anthology of Catholic Poets

Liveright Publishing Corporation New York ⟨1937⟩

A reprint of *Dreams and Images,* 1917.

A copy at BA received Oct. 26, 1937. Deposited Dec. 7, 1937.

Note: There were several later printings and editions; none contains any first edition material by Kilmer. Among these later publications:

Liveright Publishing Corporation New York ⟨1939⟩

Halcyon House New York ⟨1940⟩

Halcyon House Garden City, New York ⟨1947⟩

Doubleday & Company, Inc. Garden City, New York ⟨1955⟩. Printed paper wrapper.

BA H LC

11138. Roofs . . . Music by Robert MacGimsey . . .

Carl Fischer Inc. New York . . . ⟨1939⟩

Sheet music. Cover-title. Plate number: 28545-7.

Reprinted from *Main Street* . . . ⟨1917⟩.

B

REPRINTS

The following publications contain material by Kilmer reprinted from earlier books.

Anthology of Magazine Verse for 1914 ... by William Stanley Braithwaite

   ... Cambridge ... ⟨1914⟩

For fuller entry see No. 3045.

Poems of the Great War Selected by J. W. Cunliffe ...

   New York The Macmillan Company 1916 ...

   On copyright page: *Published November, 1916.*

Anthology of Magazine Verse for 1917 ... Edited by William Stanley Braithwaite

   Boston Small, Maynard & Company Publishers ⟨1917⟩

   Boards, cloth shelfback, paper label on spine. Listed PW Dec. 29, 1917.

"Remember the Lusitania" A Sermon Preached in the Church of the Advent, Boston by the Rector Rev. William Harman van Allen ... May 7, 1917 (Being the Second Anniversary of the Sinking of the Lusitania) ...

   ⟨n.p., Boston, 1917?⟩

   Printed self-wrapper. Cover-title. "The Scarlet Ship," pp. 4-6, otherwise "The White Ships and the Red," previously in *Anthology of Magazine Verse for 1915* ... , 1915.

The Bellman Book of Verse 1906–1919 Chosen and Edited by William C. Edgar ...

   Minneapolis, Minn., U.S.A. The Bellman Company 1919

The Great War in Verse and Prose Selected and Edited by J. E. Wetherell ...

   Toronto Printed and Published by A. T. Wilgress, Printer to the King's Most Excellent Majesty 1919

   Cloth?

The Second Book of Modern Verse ... Edited by Jessie B. Rittenhouse

   Boston and New York Houghton Mifflin Company The Riverside Press Cambridge 1919

A Treasury of War Poetry ... Second Series

Edited, with Introduction and Notes, by George Herbert Clarke ...

   Boston and New York Houghton Mifflin Company The Riverside Press Cambridge 1919

Yanks A.E.F. Verse Originally Published in "The Stars and Stripes" the Official Newspaper of the American Expeditionary Forces ⟨Edited by John T. Winterich and Hudson Hawley⟩

   G. P. Putnam's Sons New York and London The Knickerbocker Press 1919

   Deposited Jan. 17, 1920.

Modern Essays Selected by Christopher Morley

   New York Harcourt, Brace and Company 1921

   Two states noted: 1: P. 50, last line ends: *... is now* / 2: P. 50, last line ends: *... is not* / Advertised as *Published November 23rd* PW Nov. 26, 1921. Listed PW Dec. 10, 1921.

The Jester Book of Columbia Light Verse Edited by Otto v. St. Whitelock ...

   New York ... 1922

   For fuller entry see No. 815.

Second Contemporary Verse Anthology Selected from the Magazine "Contemporary Verse" 1920–1923 by the Editor Charles Wharton Stork

   New York E. P. Dutton & Company 681 Fifth Avenue ⟨1923⟩

   Paper labels. "This first edition is limited to 1500 copies."

The Soul of the City ... Compiled by Garland Greever and Joseph M. Bachelor

   Boston ... 1923

   For comment see BAL, Vol. 3, p. 288.

Columbia Verse ... Edited by Cargill Sprietsma ...

   New York ... 1924 ...

   For comment see entry No. 820.

The Joy of Life An Anthology of Lyrics Drawn Chiefly from the Works of Living Poets by E. V. Lucas ...

   Methuen & Co. Ltd. 36 Essex Street W. C. London ⟨1927⟩

   Issued in a trade edition (cloth); and, a limited edition in boards, cloth shelfback, label on spine, 250 copies, numbered and signed. Both formats listed Bkr Oct. 28, 1927.

Tree Feelings

⟨Appalachee Camps, Boothbay Harbor, Maine, n.d., *ca.* 1930⟩

Boothbay Folder No. 4. Single leaf folded to four pages.

Five Interviews with William Dean Howells Edited by George Arms ... and William M. Gibson ...

Reprinted from Vol. xxxvii, No. 2, April, 1943, of "Americana," ...

Printed paper wrapper. Cover-title.

Whimsical Whimsies Little Pictures of People and Things by Annie Kilburn-Kilmer ...

The Avondale Press Incorporated New York ⟨1927⟩

Cloth, portrait of the author pasted to front cover. Contains six poems by Kilmer (here reprinted) set to music.

Kilmer and Campion

Campion Jesuit High School Prairie du Chien, Wisconsin ⟨1937⟩

Leather-grained flexible paper boards, plastic shelfback.

CAROLINE MATILDA STANSBURY KIRKLAND

(Mrs. Mary Clavers)

1 8 0 1 – 1 8 6 4

Caution: Do not confuse this author with her granddaughter, Caroline Kirkland, author of *Some African Highways: A Journey of Two American Women to Uganda and the Transvaal,* Boston ⟨1908⟩; and, compiler of *Chicago Yesterdays,* Chicago, 1919.

11139. A NEW HOME—WHO'LL FOLLOW? OR, GLIMPSES OF WESTERN LIFE. BY MRS. MARY CLAVERS ...

NEW-YORK: C. S. FRANCIS, 252 BROADWAY. BOSTON; J. H. FRANCIS, NO. 128 WASHINGTON-STREET. 1839.

⟨i⟩-vi, ⟨7⟩-317; blank, p. ⟨318⟩; 2 pp. advertisements. 7⅝" x 4½".

⟨1⟩-26⁶, 27⁴.

Note: In all examined copies Chap. XXII misnumbered X.

H cloth: black. T cloth: black; blue; brown; purple. Flyleaves.

Deposited Sept. 13, 1839. Listed Ath Oct. 26, 1839. Reviewed K Nov. 1839. As a Wiley & Putnam importation listed BMLA Nov. 1839; PC Nov. 1, 1839; announced for *this day* Ath Nov. 2, 1839; reviewed LG Nov. 9, 1839. For other editions see under 1840, 1850.

AAS NYPL

11140. Montacute: Or a New Home—Who'll Follow? By Mrs. Mary Clavers ...

London: E. Churton, 26, Holles Street. 1840.

Reprint of *A New Home* ... , 1839.

2 Vols. Cloth?

Advertised Ath Jan. 25, 1840. Listed Ath Feb. 8, 1840. Listed LG and PC Feb. 15, 1840. Also reprinted in London under the title *A New Home: Who'll Follow? Or, Glimpses of Western Life. Published in London under the Title of "Montacute." By Mrs. Mary Clavers ...* , London: John Cunningham, 1840; in *The Novel Newspaper* series; printed paper wrapper?

H

11141. A New Home—Who'll Follow? Or, Glimpses of Western Life. By Mrs. Mary Clavers ... Second Edition.

New-York: C. S. Francis, 252 Broadway. Boston: J. H. Francis, No. 128 Washington Street. 1840.

For first edition see under 1839.

From a new setting. A cursory comparison with the first edition indicates a few minor alterations.

No American listings found. Advertised by Wiley & Putnam PC Sept. 15, 1840: "... 2d Edition ... the original edition, and half the price of the London edition." Listed Ath Sept. 19, 1840; PC Oct. 1, 1840. A third edition listed PC Aug. 1, 1842.

AAS   B   LC

11142. The Gift: A Christmas and New Year's Present for 1842.

Philadelphia: Carey & Hart. ⟨1841⟩

"The Bee-Tree," pp. 47-71. Collected in *Western Clearings,* 1845.

For comment see entry No. 1002.

11143. FOREST LIFE. BY THE AUTHOR OF "A NEW HOME." ... IN TWO VOLUMES ...

NEW YORK: C. S. FRANCIS & CO., 252 BROADWAY. BOSTON: J. H. FRANCIS, 128 WASHINGTON ST. 1842.

Two printings noted.

First Printing

1: ⟨1⟩-250, blank leaf. 7⁵⁄₁₆" x 4⅝".

2: ⟨1⟩-234; advertisements, pp. ⟨235-236⟩; plus: Publisher's 12-page catalog; see note below.

1: ⟨1⟩-21⁶.

2: ⟨1⟩-19⁶, 20⁴; plus: ⟨21⟩⁶.

Vol. 1, p. 14: Lines 2-3 from the bottom are set off as though extracted from a poem.

Vol. 2, p. 61: The final line of text is *Newyork. | ⟨sic⟩*

Vol. 2, pp. ⟨235-236⟩: Imprinted with an advertisement for Scott's works.

T cloth: black; blue. Printed paper label on spine; the statement *Second Edition* not present on label. Inserted at front of either volume is a single cut sheet folded to four pages; blank save for p. ⟨4⟩ which is imprinted with an advertisement for *A New Home ... Third Edition*; and, *Forest Life.*

Note: It will be observed that in the third line of the copyright notice, Vol. 2, the final word, *of,* occurs either with or without the *f.* In the only examined copy of the second printing (see below) the *f* is lacking.

Note: The 12-page catalog inserted in Vol. 2 of the first printing occurs as follows. The designations are for identification only and no sequence (if sequence there is) is either implied or suggested. Each catalog is printed from the same setting (plates?) and the variation may be the result of either imposition, or (most probably), a lapse in the bindery. The following is sufficient for ready recognition:

Catalog State A: P. ⟨1⟩ devoted to *The Popular Poems of Sir Walter Scott.*

Catalog State B: P. ⟨1⟩ devoted to a list of *Medical* books.

Second Printing

1: ⟨1⟩-250, blank leaf.

2: ⟨1⟩-234; blank, pp. ⟨235-236⟩; plus: Publisher's 11-page catalog.

1: ⟨1⟩-21⁶.

2: ⟨1⟩-19⁶, 20⁴; plus: ⟨21⟩⁶.

Vol. 1, p. 14: Set solid; the final lines not set off as though extracted from a poem.

Vol. 2, p. 61: The final line of text is: *New York. | ⟨sic⟩*

Vol. 2, pp. ⟨235-236⟩: Blank.

T cloth: tan. Printed paper label on spine including the statement: *Second Edition.* Inserted at front of Vol. 1 is a single cut sheet folded to four pages; blank save for p. ⟨4⟩ which is imprinted with an advertisement for *A New Home ... Third Edition*; and, *Forest Life.*

Will be issued ... on or near the 1st of June, K June, 1842. Reviewed BJ July 2, 1842; K Aug. 1842; USMDR Aug. 1842; NAR Oct. 1842. The London (Longman) edition announced as *in press* PC July 1, 1842; advertised for July 28 LG July 23, 1842; listed Ath and LG July 30, 1842; PC Aug. 1, 1842; reviewed Ath Aug. 6, 1842. Other London editions: *William Tegg,* listed by Ath and LG Nov. 11, 1848; PC Nov. 15, 1848; *Knight & Son,* listed PC Jan. 1, 1853.

AAS (1st; 2nd)   BPL (1st)   UV (1st)

11144. The Principles of Morality, and the Private and Political Rights and Obligations of Mankind. By Jonathan Dymond. Abridged, and Provided with Questions, for the Use of Schools and of Young Persons Generally. By Caroline M. Kirkland.

New York: C. S. Francis & Co., 252 Broadway. Boston: J. H. Francis, 128 Washington St. 1842.

Cloth, leather shelfback.

"Preface," pp. ⟨5⟩-8.

Deposited July 21, 1842. Reviewed BJ July 30; K Oct. 1842.

H

11145. The Gift: A Christmas and New Year's Present. MDCCCXLIII.

Philadelphia: Carey and Hart. ⟨1842⟩

"Chances and Changes, or, a Clerical Wooing," pp. 20-44.

"Idle People," pp. 154-162.

Both collected in *Western Clearings,* 1845.

For comment see entry No. 8069.

11146. The Gift: A Christmas and New Year's Present. MDCCCXLIV.

Philadelphia: Carey and Hart. 1844.

"Ambuscades and Sorties," pp. ⟨9⟩-36.

"Half-Lengths from Life," pp. ⟨97⟩-121.

Both collected in *Western Clearings,* 1845.

For comment see entry No. 4021.

11147. The Gift: A Christmas, New Year, and Birthday Present. MDCCCXLV.

Philadelphia: Carey and Hart. 1845.

Cloth; and, leather.

"The Schoolmaster's Progress," pp. ⟨10⟩-25.

Collected in *Western Clearings,* 1845.

For comment see entry No. 4024.

11148. A Plea for Woman: Being a Vindication of the Importance and Extent of Her Natural Sphere of Action ... by Mrs. Hugo Reid ... with an Introduction, by Mrs. C. M. Kirkland ...

New York: Farmer & Daggers, xxx Ann Street. 1845.

Cloth?

"Introduction by the American Editor," pp. ⟨v⟩-xxv.

Reviewed BJl Feb. 15, 1845.

LC

11149. WESTERN CLEARINGS ...

NEW YORK: WILEY AND PUTNAM, 161 BROADWAY. 1845.

⟨i-iv⟩, ⟨i⟩-viii, ⟨1⟩-238, blank leaf. 7⁷⁄₁₆″ x 5⅛″.

⟨1⟩⁶, 2-8, ⟨9⟩, 10-12, ⟨13⟩, 14-16⁸. *Note:* A superfluous signature mark 10 is on p. 125.

Printed pale buff paper wrapper. Issued as No. VII in *Wiley and Putnam's Library of American Books. Note:* Also issued in slate-blue T cloth bound with James Hall's *The Wilderness and the War Path,* 1846; advertised thus WPLNL April 1846.

Advertised as *in press* WPLNL Nov. 1845. Listed WPLNL Dec. 1845. The London (Wiley & Putnam, 1846) edition (presumably sheets of the American printing dated 1846, with cancel title-leaf) listed Ath and LG Jan. 17, 1846; listed and advertised PC Feb. 2, 1846. Reviewed LG March 7, 1846. *Life in the Woods,* presumably the same book, advertised as *already published* Ath and LG Sept. 12, 1846; PC Sept. 15, 1846. A Routledge edition listed Ath Oct. 19, 1850.

NYPL (with *The Wilderness*)   UV (wrapper)

11150. The Settler's New Home; or, Glimpses of Western Life. By Mrs. Mary Clavers ...

London: T. Allman, 42, Holborn Hill. 1845.

Reprint of *A New Home* ... , 1839.

B

11151. The Liberty Bell. By Friends of Freedom ...

Boston: Massachusetts Anti-Slavery Fair. MDCCCXLVI.

"Recollections of Anti-Slavery at the West," pp. 195-203.

"... This twelfth Anti-Slavery Bazaar will commence on Tuesday, Dec. 23d ... *The Liberty Bell* will be published on the first morning of

the Bazaar ..."—*Daily Evening Transcript* (Boston) Dec. 23, 1845. Contemporary inscriptions also indicate that the book was issued on Dec. 23, 1845.

For fuller entry see No. 6495.

11152. The Fountain. A Gift: "To Stir up the Pure Mind by Way of Remembrance." ... Edited by H. Hastings Weld.

Philadelphia: William Sloanaker. 1847.

"Agnes. A Story of Revolutionary Times," pp. 54-78.

For comment see entry No. 9296.

11153. Spenser and the Faëry Queen. ⟨Rendered into modern English⟩ by Mrs. C. M. Kirkland.

New York and London: Wiley and Putnam. 1847.

⟨i⟩-⟨viii⟩, ⟨1⟩-246; publisher's catalog: ⟨i⟩-⟨x⟩. 7¼″ x 4¾″. Issued in printed paper wrapper as No. xxv of *Wiley and Putnam's Library of American Books.* Sheets also occur bound in cloth together with *Selections from the Poetical Works of Geoffrey Chaucer,* edited by Charles H. Deshler, New York & London (Wiley & Putnam), 1847.

"Preface," pp. ⟨v⟩-vii. Biographical sketch of Spenser, pp. ⟨1⟩-41.

Announced as *in preparation* WPLNL April, 1846. Deposited (in wrapper) Jan. 9, 1847. Noted as *just ready* WPLNL Jan. 1847. Listed LW Feb. 6, 1847. The London (Wiley & Putnam) issue (American sheets with cancel title-leaf) advertised as *nearly ready* PC March 1, 1847; listed PC May 15, 1847; Ath May 29, 1847; LG May 29, 1847.

LC (wrapper)   NYPL (cloth, with Deshler)

11154. Woman, Her Education and Influence. By Mrs. Hugo Reid. With a General Introduction, by Mrs. C. M. Kirkland ...

New York: Fowlers and Wells, Phrenological Cabinet, 131 Nassau Street, and by Booksellers Generally. 1847.

Printed paper wrapper?

Reprint. For an earlier appearance of this introduction see *A Plea for Woman,* 1845.

Listed LW July 10, 1847. Reissued ⟨n.d., not before 1854⟩ with the publisher's later address, 308 Broadway, in the imprint.

LC

11155. The Ladies' Wreath, a Magazine Devoted to Literature, Industry and Religion. Edited by Mrs. S. T. Martyn.

New York: J. H. Martyn, 162 Nassau-Street. 1847.

Cloth; also, leather.

"A Noble Charity," pp. 9-11.

Listed LW April 10, 1847.

For fuller entry see BAL Vol. 3, p. 273.

11156. Powers' Statue of the Greek Slave.

New York: R. Craighead, Printer, 112 Fulton Street. 1847.

Printed paper wrapper.

"From the Pen of Mrs. Kirkland," pp. 29-30.

AAS H

11157. The Odd-Fellows' Offering, for 1848: Edited by James L. Ridgely and Paschal Donaldson.

New York: Published by Edward Walker, 114 Fulton Street. M DCCC XLVIII.

"Rustic Hospitality," pp. 99-107. Collected as "Western Traits," in *Autumn Hours* . . . , 1854.

Title deposited April 22, 1847.

H

11158. Dahcotah; or, Life and Legends of the Sioux around Fort Snelling. By Mrs. Mary Eastman, with Preface by Mrs. C. M. Kirkland . . .

New York: John Wiley, 161 Broadway. 1849.

"Preface," pp. ⟨v⟩-xi, dated at end: *New York, March, 1849.*

Advertised *published on April 28, 1849;* and, noted as *just published* LW May 5, 1849. Deposited May 7, 1849. Listed LW May 12, 1849. The Wiley importation listed PC June 1, 1849; advertised for June 4, PC June 1, 1849. The Chapman importation advertised as *just imported* Ath June 30 and July 21, 1849. *Note:* A photographic facsimile edition was published by Ross & Haines, Inc., Minneapolis, Minn., 1962.

B

11159. HOLIDAYS ABROAD; OR EUROPE FROM THE WEST . . .

NEW YORK: BAKER AND SCRIBNER, 145 NASSAU STREET AND 36 PARK ROW. 1849.

2 Vols.

1: ⟨i-iv⟩, ⟨i⟩-viii, ⟨9⟩-303; blank leaf; leaf excised or pasted under the end paper. 7⅜" x 4¹⁵⁄₁₆".

2: ⟨i⟩-iv, ⟨5⟩-332; advertisements, pp. ⟨333-336⟩.

1: ⟨-⟩², ⟨1⟩-12¹², 13¹⁰. 13₁₀ excised or pasted under the end paper.

2: ⟨1⟩-14¹².

TB cloth: black. Pale yellow end papers. In some copies of Vol. 1: flyleaf at front. Single flyleaves in Vol. 2. In some copies of Vol. 1: 4 pp. advertisements inserted at front.

Deposited May 16, 1849 (publisher's records). Deposited May 22, 1849 (copyright office records). Listed LW May 26, 1849. Chapman importation advertised PC June 15, 1849; listed Ath June 23, 1849; LG June 23, 1849; PC July 2, 1849. Wiley importation advertised Ath July 21, 1849, as *just received.*

B BA

11160. The Odd-Fellows' Offering, for 1850 . . . Contributed Chiefly by Members of the Order.

New York: Published by Edward Walker, 114 Fulton Street. M DCCC L.

"The Orphan's Funeral," pp. 123-135.

Reviewed K Dec. 1849. Listed LW Dec. 1, 1849.

H

11161. A New Home—Who'll Follow? Or, Glimpses of Western Life. By Mrs. Mary Clavers . . . Fourth Edition. Revised by the Author . . .

New York: C. S. Francis & Co., 252 Broadway. Boston: J. H. Francis, 128 Washington Street. 1850.

"Preface to the Fourth Edition," p. ⟨5⟩. See under 1839 for first edition.

Advertised as *in press* LW Aug. 25, 1850.

Noted in green cloth grained with a pattern of fine, vertical, chain-like ribs. Sides blindstamped with a triple rule frame, a filigree at each inner corner, a wreath at the center. Location: UV.

Also noted in green TB cloth, the sides blindstamped with an ornate frame. Copies in AAS, UV.

AAS UV

11162. The Fountain and the Bottle; Comprising Thrilling Examples of the Opposite Effects of Temperance and Intemperance. Edited by a Son of Temperance.

Boston: Published by Horace Wentworth, 86 Washington Street, 1850.

"John Hinchley," pp. 166-176. Collected, with the omission of the first three paragraphs and the final paragraph, in *A Book for the Home Circle* ... , 1853, as "Steps to Ruin ...".

H

11163. The Gem of the Season: A Souvenir for MDCCCLI ...

New-York: Leavitt and Company, 191 Broadway. MDCCCLI.

Leather.

"A Love of a Singing-Master," pp. ⟨203⟩-210. Collected in *The Evening Book* ... , 1852, pp. 294-300, as part of "The Singing School."

Advertised as *just ready* LW July 13, 1850.

NYPL   P

11164. The Odd-Fellows' Offering, for 1851 ...

New York: Published by Edward Walker, 114 Fulton-Street. M DCCC LI.

Leather.

"Making Love Scientifically," pp. 92-100. Collected in *Autumn Hours* ... , 1854.

H

11165. The Dew-Drop: A Tribute of Affection. For MDCCCLII.

Philadelphia: Lippincott, Grambo & Co. 1852.

"English and American Manners," pp. ⟨132⟩-146. For another version see "What Shall We Be," in *The Evening Book* ... , 1852, below.

For comment see entry No. 1188.

11166. THE EVENING BOOK: OR, FIRESIDE TALK ON MORALS AND MANNERS, WITH SKETCHES OF WESTERN LIFE ...

NEW YORK: CHARLES SCRIBNER, 145 NASSAU STREET. 1852.

⟨i⟩-⟨xii⟩, ⟨13⟩-312. Frontispiece, vignette title-page, and 5 plates inserted. 8⁷⁄₁₆" scant x 6⅛".

⟨1-19⁸, 20⁴⟩. *Signed:* ⟨1⟩-⟨3⟩, 4-5, ⟨6⟩-⟨10⟩, 11, ⟨12⟩, 13¹².

A cloth: blue; green; plum. Yellow-coated on white end papers. White end papers. Flyleaves. Edges gilded. Also in morocco according to contemporary notices.

Advertised as *in press and will publish immediately* NLA Sept. 15, 1851. Advertised as in cloth; and, morocco, NLA Nov. 15, 1851. Listed NLA

Nov. 15, 1851, as in cloth; and, morocco. Advertised for *this week* LW Nov. 29, 1851. Listed as in cloth; and, morocco, LW Nov. 29, 1851. Reviewed LW Nov. 29, 1851. Deposited Feb. 7, 1852. Distributed in London by Chapman; advertised Ath Feb. 14, 1852; LG March 27, 1852.

H   Y

11167. THE BOOK OF HOME BEAUTY ...

NEW-YORK: G. P. PUTNAM, 155 BROADWAY. MDCCCLII.

Large Paper

⟨1⟩-6, ⟨1⟩-145. Vignette title-page and 12 plates inserted. 18¾" x 12½".

⟨a⟩², ⟨b⟩¹, 1-23, ⟨24-25⟩, 26-30, ⟨31⟩, 32-35, ⟨36⟩², ⟨37⟩¹.

Leather. Also, A cloth: blue. Yellow end papers. Flyleaves. Edges gilded. *Note:* In all likelihood the book was issued in several styles of cloth and leather.

Small Paper

⟨1⟩-6, ⟨1⟩-145. Vignette title-page and 12 plates inserted. 12½" scant x 9⅜".

⟨a⟩¹, ⟨b⟩², ⟨1⟩-12, ⟨13⟩, 14-15, ⟨16⟩, 17-18⁴, ⟨19⟩¹.

A cloth: blue. Covers bevelled. Yellow end papers. Flyleaves. Edges gilt. Also in leather according to contemporary notices.

Announced NLA Oct. 15, 1851. Advertised as *now ready,* LW Nov. 8, 1851: small paper format in cloth; and, leather; also large paper format, binding not given. Small paper format, in cloth; and, morocco, listed NLA Nov. 15, 1851. Advertised NLA Nov. 15, 1851: small paper format in cloth; and, leather; also large paper format, binding not given. Listed (small paper format) LW Nov. 22, 1851. Reviewed LW Nov. 22, 1851.

London Publication

Listed, name of importer not given, LG Nov. 15, 1851. Reviewed Ath Nov. 22, 1851; LG Dec. 27, 1851. *Chapman* importation advertised Ath Nov. 15, Dec. 6, Dec. 27, 1851. *Delf* importation listed PC Dec. 1, 1851. *Low* importation advertised as *just imported* Ath Dec. 4, 1852, *new issue;* advertised for *Christmas* PC Dec. 3, 1852; listed LG Dec. 11, 1852; PC Jan. 1, 1853.

AAS (small paper)   BA (small paper)   H (large paper in cloth; and, leather)

11168. The Odd-Fellows' Offering, for 1852 ...

New York: Published by Edward Walker, 114 Fulton-Street. M DCCC LII.

Leather.

THE LOG SCHOOL HOUSE.

CAROLINE M. KIRKLAND
Entry No. 11166
Illustration from *The Evening Book...*, 1852
(Harvard University Library)

"Lessons in the Forest," pp. 130-142.

H

11169. Garden Walks with the Poets. ⟨Edited⟩ by Mrs. C. M. Kirkland.

New-York: G. P. Putnam & Company, 10 Park Place. 1852.

For comment see entry No. 1379.

11170. A BOOK FOR THE HOME CIRCLE; OR, FAMILIAR THOUGHTS ON VARIOUS TOPICS, LITERARY, MORAL AND SOCIAL. A COMPANION FOR THE EVENING BOOK . . .

NEW YORK: CHARLES SCRIBNER, 145 NASSAU STREET. 1853.

⟨i⟩-⟨xii⟩, ⟨13⟩-312. Frontispiece, vignette title-page, and 6 plates inserted. 8¼" x 6¹⁄₁₆" (cloth). 8⅛" full x 6" full (leather).

⟨1-19⁸, 20⁴⟩. *Signed:* ⟨1⟩-2, 4⟨*sic*⟩, ⟨4⟩, 5-6, ⟨7-13⟩¹².

A cloth: purple. Yellow-coated on white end papers. Flyleaves? (The only copy seen in cloth has been repaired.) Edges gilded. Also: leather, edges gilded.

Title deposited Oct. 26, 1852. Noted LW Nov. 13, 1852. Listed NLG Nov. 15, 1852. Listed and reviewed LW Dec. 25, 1852.

B (leather)   Y (cloth)

11171. Homes of American Authors; Comprising Anecdotical, Personal, and Descriptive Sketches, by Various Writers . . .

New-York: G. P. Putnam and Co., 10 Park Place. M.DCCC.LIII.

Contains "Bryant," pp. ⟨65⟩-81; anonymous, but Mrs. Kirkland is listed as a contributor on p. vi. See under 1896 for separate publication under Mrs. Kirkland's name.

For comment see entry No. 1345.

11172. Autographs for Freedom. ⟨Edited by Julia Griffiths⟩

Boston: John P. Jewett and Company. Cleveland, Ohio: Jewett, Proctor, and Worthington. London: Low and Company. 1853.

"Momma Charlotte," pp. 13-17.

Listed NLG Feb. 15, 1853. Deposited Feb. 26, 1853. Listed LW March 5, 1853. Listed as an American book PC March 15, 1853.

H

11173. THE HELPING HAND: COMPRISING AN ACCOUNT OF THE HOME, FOR DISCHARGED FEMALE CONVICTS, AND AN APPEAL IN BEHALF OF THAT INSTITUTION . . . (SOLD FOR THE BENEFIT OF THE INSTITUTION.)

NEW YORK: CHARLES SCRIBNER, 145 NASSAU STREET. 1853.

⟨1⟩-⟨144⟩. Frontispiece inserted. 8³⁄₁₆" x 6⅛". Pp. ⟨1-2⟩, ⟨143-144⟩, are excised or pasted under the end papers.

⟨1-2⟩, 3-5, ⟨6⟩, 7-8, ⟨9⟩⁸. ⟨1⟩₁ and ⟨9⟩₈ excised or pasted under end paper.

Blue; or, green flexible boards. Yellow end papers. Yellow-coated on white end papers. Edges gilded.

Listed NLG June 15, 1853. Listed as an American book PC July 16, 1853.

NYPL   Y

11174. The Family Fire-Side Book; or, Monuments of Temperance . . . Edited by a Most Worthy Patriarch of the Sons of Temperance . . .

Philadelphia: Leary & Getz, Publishers, 1853.

Leather. Precise publication date not determined.

"Comfort," pp. 264-280. Also in (reprinted from?) *A Book for the Home Circle*, 1853, above. *Note:* Also appears in *The American Temperance Offering, and Sons and Daughters of Temperance Gift for 1852*, New York, 1852, a periodical issued with title-page to give the appearance of a gift book or an annual.

HM

11175. AUTUMN HOURS, AND FIRESIDE READING . . .

NEW YORK: CHARLES SCRIBNER, 145 NASSAU STREET. 1854.

⟨i⟩-x, ⟨11⟩-311. Vignette title-page, frontispiece, and 3 plates inserted. 8⁵⁄₁₆" x 6⅛".

⟨1-2⟩, 3-19⁸, 20⁴. Leaf ⟨1⟩₄ (the list of illustrations) is a cancel. Signature mark 2 appears incorrectly on p. 25.

A cloth: red. T cloth: gray-green. Cream-coated on white end papers. Flyleaves. All edges gilded. Also leather?

"Search after Pleasure," pp. ⟨35⟩-203, is a revised reprint of *The Book of Home Beauty*, 1852.

"Western Traits," pp. ⟨232⟩-239, had previous publication in *The Odd-Fellows' Offering, for 1848,* under the title "Rustic Hospitality."

"Making Love Scientifically," pp. ⟨265⟩-273, had prior publication in *The Odd-Fellows' Offering, for 1851.*

Listed NLG Nov. 15, 1853. Advertised NLG Nov. 15, 1853, as in cloth; and, morocco.

AAS Y

11176. Homes of American Statesmen . . .

New-York: G. P. Putnam and Co., 10 Park Place. London: Sampson Low, Son and Co. M.DCCC.LIV.

"Washington," pp. ⟨3⟩-61.

Listed NLG Jan. 1, 1854.

For further comment see entry No. 1347.

11177. Autographs for Freedom. Edited by Julia Griffiths . . .

Auburn: Alden, Beardsley & Co. Rochester: Wanzer, Beardsley & Co. 1854.

"A Wish," p. ⟨209⟩; listed in table of contents as at p. 207.

For comment see entry No. 5224.

11178. Leaflets of Memory: An Illuminated Annual for MDCCCLV.

Philadelphia: Published by E. H. Butler & Co. 1855.

Leather.

"Mahomet," pp. 206-223.

Title deposited Aug. 17, 1854; no record of book deposit.

H

11179. Pictures and Readings from American Authors, Being the Choice Volume of Putnam's Magazine.

New York: Leavitt and Allen. 1855.

Cloth, printed paper label on spine. Irregular pagination.

An omnibus volume made up of the following issues of *Putnam's Monthly:* March, May, July, August, Sept., Oct. 1853; May, 1854. Issued with title-page as above.

"Educational Institutions of New-York," pp. ⟨1⟩-16, July, 1853.

IU

11180. MEMOIRS OF WASHINGTON . . .

NEW YORK: D. APPLETON & CO., 346 & 348 BROADWAY. LONDON: 16 LITTLE BRITAIN. 1857.

⟨i⟩-xii, ⟨1⟩-516. Frontispiece and 8 plates inserted. 7⅝" x 5 1/16".

⟨-⟩⁶, ⟨1⟩-13, ⟨14⟩, 15-21¹², ⟨22⟩⁶. Superfluous signature mark 2 appears at p. 9.

T cloth: brown; purple; slate. Blue-coated on white end papers. Brown-coated on white end papers. Green-coated on white end papers. Flyleaves.

Deposited Dec. 13, 1856. A copy at BA received Dec. 22, 1856. A copy at NYPL inscribed by Duyckinck, Christmas, 1856.

Note: According to Sabin and Roorbach also issued as a school book without plates.

BA H MHS

11181. Tales and Sketches for the Fire-Side, by the Best American Authors. Selected from Putnam's Magazine.

New York: A. Dowling, 36 Beekman Street 1857.

"Watering-Place Worries," in the issue of Nov. 1854.

For comment see entry No. 8239.

11182. Gifts of Genius: A Miscellany of Prose and Poetry, by American Authors.

New York: Printed for C. A. Davenport. ⟨1859⟩

"June Twenty-Ninth, Eighteen Fifty-Nine," pp. 253-258.

For comment see entry No. 3717.

11183. Only Once. Original Papers, by Various Contributors.

Published for the Benefit of the New York Infirmary for Women and Children, No. 126 Second Avenue. 1862 . . .

Printed paper wrapper.

"Potato Days," pp. 4-5.

Title deposited Feb. 27, 1862. Issued without plates (at 25¢); with 4 plates (at 50¢).

H

11184. The School-Girl's Garland. A Selection of Poetry, in Four Parts. By Mrs. C. M. Kirkland. First Series. Parts First and Second.

New York: Charles Scribner, 124 Grand Street. 1864.

For *Second Series* (Parts 3-4) see next entry.

"Preface," pp. ⟨3⟩-5.

For fuller entry see No. 4837.

11185. The School-Girl's Garland. A Selection of Poetry, in Four Parts. By Mrs. C. M. Kirkland. Second Series. Parts Third and Fourth.

New York: Charles Scribner, 124 Grand Street. 1864.

For *First Series* (Parts 1-2) see preceding entry.

Deposited April 2, 1864. Listed ALG April 15, 1864.

B   Y

11186. The Spirit of the Fair . . .

New York, April 5-9, 11-16, 18-23, 1864.

An occasional magazine issued by the Metropolitan Fair for the benefit of the U. S. Sanitary Commission. 17 numbers.

"Later . . . the . . . plates were purchased by John F. Trow. A general title . . . and a leaf, *Publisher's Notice,* were prefixed, and the whole issued in one volume, bound in boards. The covers of the numbers were not included, so that there is a gap of four pages between each two numbers. A *Report of the Treasurer* . . . is bound in at the end."—*A Bibliography of . . . James Russell Lowell,* by Luther S. Livingston, New York, 1914, p. 67.

"Who's Been at the Fair?" No. 17, pp. 201-202.

H   NYPL

11187. Patriotic Eloquence: Being Selections from One Hundred Years of National Literature. Compiled for the Use of Schools in Reading and Speaking. By Mrs. C. M. Kirkland.

New York: Charles Scribner & Co., 654 Broadway. Ingham & Bragg, Cleveland, Ohio. 1866.

Cloth?

"Introduction," pp. ⟨iii⟩-vi, dated at end: *July, 1860.*

Below the end of the introduction is a note, dated at end *November, 1865:* "NOTE.—This work not having been brought by Mrs. Kirkland beyond the beginning of the Rebellion, it has been thought best to give additional value to the collection by introducing some specimens of the oratory and poetry which have been called forth by the events of the past four years. It is proper also to mention that the notes, which formed a part of the compiler's original plan, have been added by another hand."

Copyright notice dated 1865. Advertised for April publication ALG April 2, 1866. Noted as *just ready* ALG May 1, 1866. Listed PC May 1, 1866. Deposited May 5, 1866. Listed ALG May 15, 1866.

LC   Y

11188. The Garland of Poetry for the Young. A Selection in Four Parts . . . Two Volumes in One.

New York: Charles Scribner & Company. 1868.

A reissue of *The School-Girl's Garland,* (First and Second Series), 1864.

Advertised for Oct. 17 ALG Oct. 1, 1868.

AAS   H   NYPL

11189. Our New Home in the West; or Glimpses of Life among the Early Settlers. By Mrs. Mary Clavers. (Mrs. C. M. Kirkland.) . . .

New York: James Miller, Publisher, 647 Broadway. 1872.

Reprinted from the plates of *A New Home . . . Fourth Edition,* 1850, with the omission of Mrs. Kirkland's "Preface to the Fourth Edition."

BA

11190. Poetry of the Flowers Selected by Mrs. C. M. Kirtland ⟨sic⟩

New York: Thomas Y. Crowell & Co., No. 13 Astor Place. ⟨n.d., not before Nov. 1880⟩

Reprinted from *Garden Walks with the Poets,* 1852.

Also reprinted with the following imprints:

New York   John W. Lovell Company   150 Worth Street, Corner Mission Place ⟨n.d., *ca.* 1890⟩

New York   American Publishers Corporation 310-318 Sixth Avenue ⟨n.d., 1896–1897⟩

H (Lovell)   NYPL (American)   UV (Crowell)

11191. . . . Little Journeys to the Homes of American Authors   Bryant by Caroline H. ⟨sic⟩ Kirkland

February, 1896   New York and London: G. P. Putnam's Sons   New Rochelle, N. Y. The Knickerbocker Press.

Self-wrapper. Cover-title. At head of title: Vol. II. No. 2. . . .

First separate edition. Originally in *Homes of American Authors,* 1853.

Deposited Feb. 12, 1896. Listed PW Feb. 15, 1896.

B   LC   Y

REPRINTS

The following publications contain material by Mrs. Kirkland reprinted from earlier books.

The Prose Writers of America ... by Rufus Wilmot Griswold ...

Philadelphia ... 1847.

For comment see entry No. 6676.

Thrilling Scenes in Cottage Life; or the Opposite Effects of Vice and Virtue. Edited by a Son of Temperance.

Hartford: Published by Case, Tiffany & Co. 1854.

The Gem Annual: A Christmas, New-Year, and Birthday Gift, for MDCCCLV.

Philadelphia ... 1855.

"Sunday in the Country," pp. 255-260, extracted from "The Log Schoolhouse," in *The Evening Book*, 1852. For comment see entry No. 3179.

Cyclopædia of American Literature ... by Evert A. Duyckinck and George L. Duyckinck. In Two Volumes ...

New York ... 1855.

"Meeting of the 'Female Beneficent Society'," Vol. 2, pp. 563-565, extracted from *A New Home* ..., 1839. "Hospitality," Vol. 2, pp. 565-566, extracted from "A Chapter on Hospitality," *The Evening Book*, 1852. For fuller entry see No. 11092A.

The Adopted Daughter. By Alice Carey. And Other Tales.

Philadelphia: J. B. Smith & Co., 610 Chestnut St. 1859.

Half-Hours with the Best Humorous Authors. Selected ... by Charles Morris ... American.

Philadelphia ... 1889.

"Mr. and Mrs. Doubleday," Vol. 1, pp. 484-489; extracted from *A New Home* ..., 1839, pp. 116-122. For comment see entry No. 3813.

REFERENCES AND ANA

The Classical Reader; A Selection of Lessons in Prose and Verse. From the Most Esteemed English and American Writers ... by Rev. F. W. P. Greenwood and G. B. Emerson ...

Boston: Printed and Published by Lincoln &

Edmands, No. 59 Washington-Street, (Cornhill.) 1826.

Cloth? Leather? "The Baneful Effects of Intemperance," pp. 311-315, attributed to *Kirkland;* extracted from John T. Kirkland's *A Sermon Delivered before the Massachusetts Society for the Suppression of Intemperance at Their Annual Meeting ... May 27, 1814 ...,* Boston: Printed by John Eliot, 1814.

The American Common-Place Book of Prose ... ⟨Edited by George B. Cheever⟩

Boston ... MDCCCXXVIII.

"Character of Fisher Ames," pp. 88-94, attributed to *Kirkland,* is by John Thornton Kirkland and was previously published in *Works of Fisher Ames* (Boston: Wait & Co., 1809). For fuller description see entry No. 619.

Western Border Life; or, What Fanny Hunter Saw and Heard in Kanzas and Missouri.

New York: Derby & Jackson, 119 Nassau Street. Cincinnati: H. W. Derby & Co. 1856.

Anonymous. Credited to Mrs. Kirkland by a card in the National Union Catalog, but BAL doubts the ascription. The printed LC catalog does not ascribe this to Mrs. Kirkland. Wright does not identify the author. Further support for doubting Mrs. Kirkland's authorship is lent by the dedication: "With ... love and gratitude ... dear Father ... I dedicate this, my first ⟨*sic*⟩ book, to you ..." Reprinted ⟨1863⟩ by John E. Potter & Co., Philadelphia.

Address at the Funeral of Mrs. Caroline M. Kirkland, at All-Souls' Church, New York, on Sunday, April 10, 1864, by S. K. Lothrop, of Brattle-Street Church, Boston ...

⟨n.p., n.d., 1864⟩

Single cut sheet folded to make four pages. The above at head of p. ⟨1⟩. Text on pp. ⟨1⟩-3; p. ⟨4⟩ blank. A copy at H received June 6, 1864.

The Destiny of Our Country. By Charles P. Kirkland.

New York: Published by Anson D. F. Randolph, No. 770 Broadway. 1864.

Printed paper wrapper. Attributed erroneously to Mrs. Kirkland by Appleton.

A New Home or Life in the Clearings ... Edited ... by John Nerber

G. P. Putnam's Sons New York ⟨1953⟩

Decorated paper boards, cloth shelfback. "This editing of *A New Home,* and those portions of *Forest Life* which by substance belong to the earlier narrative, is not meant ... to be definitive. It is designed only as an introduction for the modern reader ..."—p. 16.

Deposited Oct. 5, 1953.

JOSEPH KIRKLAND

1 8 3 0 - 1 8 9 4

11192. Pictures and Readings from American Authors, Being the Choice Volume of Putnam's Magazine.

New York: Leavitt and Allen. 1855.

"Rejected MSS," pp. 180-182, Aug. 1853.

For comment see entry No. 11179.

11193. Fenno's Favorites. 100 Choice Pieces for Reading and Speaking ... ⟨Compiled⟩ by Frank H. Fenno ...

Philadelphia: John E. Potter & Company, 1111 and 1113 Market Street. ⟨1884⟩

Printed paper wrapper. On wrapper: *No. 1* ...

"The Lady or the Tiger," pp. 188-192.

EM

11194. ZURY: THE MEANEST MAN IN SPRING COUNTY A NOVEL OF WESTERN LIFE ...

BOSTON AND NEW YORK   HOUGHTON, MIFFLIN AND COMPANY   THE RIVERSIDE PRESS, CAMBRIDGE 1887

⟨i⟩-vi, ⟨1⟩-538, blank leaf; advertisements, pp. ⟨1⟩-6; plus: 7-12, blank leaf. Frontispiece inserted. Pp. ⟨iii-iv⟩ excised. 7½" full x 4^{15}⁄$_{16}$".

⟨1-23^{12}; plus: 24^4⟩. Leaf ⟨1⟩$_2$ (presumably a blank) excised.

V cloth: brown; olive-gray; yellow. Gray-coated on white end papers. Flyleaf at front.

April 25, 1887, 1500 copies printed (publisher's records). Deposited April 30, 1887. Listed PW May 7, 1887. See next entry for revised edition.

H NYPL

11195. Zury: The Meanest Man in Spring County A Novel of Western Life ... ⟨Revised⟩

Boston and New York Houghton, Mifflin and Company The Riverside Press, Cambridge 1888

Revised. For first edition see preceding entry. "Preface," p. ⟨iii⟩.

270 copies, dated 1888, printed Dec. 16, 1887 (publisher's records).

BA

11196. THE McVEYS (AN EPISODE) ...

BOSTON AND NEW YORK   HOUGHTON, MIFFLIN AND COMPANY   THE RIVERSIDE PRESS, CAMBRIDGE 1888

⟨i-iv⟩, ⟨i⟩-iv, ⟨1⟩-468, blank leaf; advertisements, pp. ⟨1⟩-4; plus: 5-12. 6^{15}⁄$_{16}$" x 4⅝".

⟨1^9, 2-30^8; plus: 31^4⟩. ⟨1⟩$_2$ inserted.

V cloth: brown; gray; green; mustard. Gray-coated on white end papers. Flyleaf at back.

Two states of the binding noted. The sequence, if any, is not known, and the designations are for identification only.

A

The illustration on the front cover depicts surveyors at work against a mountain background.

B

The illustration on the front cover depicts surveyors at work on a prairie ⟨riverbank?⟩. Noted only on a repaired, incomplete copy, which presumably collates as above.

Note: The publisher's records show that this book was bound from Sept. 18, 1888 to March 31, 1903; and that on Oct. 6, 1888, 23 copies were put in special binding. *Query:* Does this account for *Bindings A and B?*

Sept. 15, 1888, 1500 copies printed (publisher's records). A copy at AAS (Binding A) inscribed by early owner Sept. 22, 1888. Deposited Sept. 24, 1888. A rebound copy at H received Sept. 29, 1888. A copy at BA (Binding A) received Oct. 2, 1888. Listed PW Oct. 13, 1888.

AAS (both)   BA (A)   NYPL (A)

11197. "Uncle Dick" Wootton ... by Howard Louis Conard with an Introduction by Maj. Joseph Kirkland

Chicago W. E. Dibble & Co 1890

"Introduction," pp. ⟨13⟩-16.

Listed PW March 1, 1890, as a subscription book available in cloth; half morocco; full morocco.

H

11198. ... THE CAPTAIN OF COMPANY K ...

CHICAGO: DIBBLE PUBLISHING COMPANY, 260 CLARK STREET. 1891.

At head of title: "DETROIT FREE-PRESS" COMPETITION, FIRST-PRIZE STORY.

⟨1⟩-351; advertisements, p. 252 (sic). Frontispiece inserted. Other illustrations in text. Laid paper. 8³⁄₁₆″ x 5⁹⁄₁₆″.

⟨1⟩-10, 11a (the a inverted), 11, 13-22⁸.

S cloth: blue. Coarse wove end papers printed in blue-gray with a stylized floral pattern. Quadruple flyleaves of bookstock. Also issued in printed paper wrapper? See publication notes below.

Note: In all copies seen by BAL p. 296 ends: *... tamper with Faith.* Two lines of text are missing; the omission supplied by a pasted slip ending: *... I remimber thim fallen* ⟨sic⟩

Deposited Sept. 18, 1891. Listed PW Oct. 17, 1891, as in cloth; and, in printed paper wrapper, identified as No. 10 in the *Optimus Series*. The listing suggests that the book was distributed by Donohue, Henneberry & Co., Chicago. Not seen in the *Optimus Series* format.

AAS H UV

11199. THE STORY OF CHICAGO ...

CHICAGO DIBBLE PUBLISHING COMPANY 1892

See under 1894 for Vol. 2. Also see next entry.

⟨i⟩-⟨xxiv⟩, ⟨1⟩-470; advertisements, pp. 471-488. Inserted: 1 folded chart; 10 full-page plates printed on 5 leaves; 1 full-page plate printed on recto only opposite p. 268. Other illustrations in text. 10⁷⁄₁₆″ x 7¹³⁄₁₆″.

⟨1⁸, 2⁴, 3-32⁸, 33⁴⟩.

Note: The full-page plate opposite p. 268 carries the following note: *Omitted in first edition, to appear in its place ⟨i⟩n subsequent editions.* In some copies the word *in* is wholly absent. Although it appears likely that copies first issued did not have the inserted plate, all copies examined by BAL, including the copyright deposit copies, have the plate present.

S cloth: olive-brown. Tan ⟨oxidized white?⟩ end papers printed in brown with a floral pattern. Flyleaf at back. As a subscription book probably issued in a variety of styles, cloth and leather.

Deposited Feb. 1, 1892. Listed PW March 5, 1892.

AAS

11200. The Story of Chicago ... ⟨Second Edition⟩

Chicago Dibble Publishing Company 1892

For first edition see preceding entry.

Cloth; and, leather.

"Preface to the Second Edition," p. ⟨v⟩, dated *April 1, 1892.* Contains material not present in the first edition.

B H

11201. Lily Pearl and the Mistress of Rosedale by Ida Glenwood, "The Blind Bard of Michigan." ... Edited by Major Joseph Kirkland.

Chicago: Dibble Publishing Co. 1892.

"Editor's Preface," p. 9.

Ida Glenwood is a pseudonym for Mrs. C. M. R. Gorton.

Deposited July 18, 1892.

B LC

11202. The Chicago Massacre of 1812 with Illustrations and Historical Documents ...

Chicago The Dibble Publishing Company 334 Dearborn Street 1893

Cloth; and, printed paper wrapper. See next entry.

Essentially a compilation (rather than an original work) of material by others and selections from Kirkland's previous publications.

Deposited in wrapper June 24, 1893. Listed PW Aug. 5, 1893 in cloth; and, wrapper. Reissued with the imprint: *Chicago: Alhambra Book Co* ⟨1893; i.e., 1895?⟩

AAS (wrapper) H (cloth) LC (wrapper) NYPL (cloth)

11203. The First Book of the Authors Club Liber Scriptorum ...

New York Published by the Authors Club M DCCC XCIII

"Jean Baptiste Pointe de Saible," pp. ⟨328⟩-335. For prior publication in slightly varying form see preceding entry, *The Chicago Mass-*

acre of 1812 . . . , wherein this appears as "Appendix A," pp. 133-141; at p. 141 the following statement is present: *From "Liber Scriptorum," published by the Authors' ⟨sic⟩ Club, New York.* This suggests earlier publication in *The First Book of the Authors Club* but the publication sequence is clear; *The Chicago Massacre of 1812* . . . , was deposited June 24, 1893; the editors' preface in *The First Book of the Authors Club* is dated Sept. 4, 1893. For yet another slightly revised text see below *History of Chicago* . . . , Vol. 1, 1895, pp. 27-30.

For fuller entry see No. 1283.

11204. THE STORY OF CHICAGO BY JOSEPH KIRKLAND AND CAROLINE KIRKLAND VOL. II

CHICAGO DIBBLE PUBLISHING COMPANY 1894

For Vol. 1 see above under 1892.

⟨i⟩-xv, 16-512; plus: 2 pp. advertisements, paged 513-514. Illustrated. 10⁷⁄₁₆″ x 7¾″.

⟨1-32⁸; plus: 33¹⟩

Completed by Kirkland's daughter, Caroline. "As my father used few notes and made no general plan for this second volume it is due to him to say that his work ends with the eighteenth chapter, except for the main portion of the history of the Public Library; the responsibility for the remainder rests with me."—from the "Preface," p. ⟨v⟩.

Brown morocco. T-grained end papers printed in gold (on deep purple) with a scroll-floret pattern. Flyleaves. Edges gilded. *Note:* As a subscription book probably issued in a variety of cloth and leather bindings. Contemporary notices offer the book in cloth; half morocco; and morocco.

Deposited Dec. 21, 1894. A copy at H inscribed by early owner Jan. 1, 1895. Listed PW April 27, 1895.

AAS H

11205. The Poor in Great Cities Their Problems and What Is Doing ⟨sic⟩ to Solve Them by Robert A. Woods . . . Joseph Kirkland . . . ⟨and Others⟩

New York Charles Scribner's Sons 1895

"Among the Poor of Chicago," pp. ⟨195⟩-239.

Deposited Nov. 23, 1895. Listed PW Dec. 7, 1895.

B H LC UV

11206. . . . History of Chicago Illinois ⟨Edited by John⟩ Moses. ⟨and Joseph⟩ Kirkland.

Aided by Eminent Local Writers . . .

Chicago & New York: Munsell & Co., Publishers. 1895.

2 Vols. At head of title: Aboriginal to Metropolitan.

"Up to the Fort Dearborn Massacre of 1812," Vol. 1, pp. ⟨3⟩-62. Incorporated in Chap. III is Kirkland's "Jean Baptiste Pointe de Saible" which, with textual variations, had prior publication in entries 11202-11203.

"Joseph Kirkland," Vol. 1, pp. 704-706, incorporates Kirkland's autobiographical sketch in *The Story of Chicago,* Vol. 2, 1894.

"The Bench and Bar," Vol. 2, pp. 152-189.

Deposited Jan. 29, 1896.

NYPL Y

11207. Tales from McClure's The West . . .

New York Doubleday & McClure Co. 1897

Cloth; and, flexible leather.

"The Surgeon's Miracle," pp. 115-136.

H

REPRINTS

The following publications contain material by Joseph Kirkland reprinted from earlier books.

Tales and Sketches for the Fire-Side, by the Best American Authors. Selected from Putnam's Magazine.

New York . . . 1857.

For comment see entry No. 8239.

No. 21. Standard Comic Recitations by Best Authors . . . Compiled . . . by Frances P. Sullivan . . . September, 1888 . . .

M. J. Ivers & Co., Publishers, 86 Nassau Street, N. Y. . . . ⟨1888⟩

Printed paper wrapper. Deposited Oct. 10, 1888. Reprinted with the publisher's later address, *379 Pearl Street,* in the imprint.

Fame's Tribute to Children . . .

Chicago . . . 1892

Extract from *Zury,* p. 111.

For comment see BAL, Vol. 1, p. 76.

REFERENCES AND ANA

The Married Flirt

A dramatization in collaboration with James

B. Runnion. ". . . A five-act dramatization of Daudet's novel *Sidonie*. The play was produced, with the subtitle *The Married Flirt*, at McVicker's Theater in Chicago and ran for a fortnight in December, 1877 . . . *Sidonie* was the name given the American translation of *Fromont jeune et Risler aîné*, which appeared in 1874."—"Joseph Kirkland, Pioneer Realist," by John T. Flanagan, in *American Literature*, Vol. XI, No. 3, Nov. 1939, p. 279.

No record of publication found. For an account of the translation see Henson, pp. 72-75; and, Kirkland's "An Experiment in Play Writing," in *The Atlantic Monthly*, Vol. 44, No. 262, pp. 149-155.

In Memoriam Joseph Kirkland   Born January 7, 1830   Died April 29, 1894

Chicago Literary Club   1894

Printed paper wrapper.

Joseph Kirkland by Clyde E. Henson . . .

Twayne Publishers, Inc.   New York   ⟨1962⟩

MELVILLE DE LANCEY LANDON

(Eli Perkins, Lan)

1 8 3 9 – 1 9 1 0

11208. THE FRANCO-PRUSSIAN WAR IN A NUTSHELL. A DAILY DIARY OF DIPLOMACY, BATTLES, AND WAR LITERATURE . . . FROM OFFICIAL FRENCH AND PRUSSIAN FIELD SURVEYS . . .

NEW YORK: G. W. CARLETON & CO., PUBLISHERS, MADISON SQUARE. LONDON: S. LOW, SON & CO. M.DCCC.LXXI.

⟨i⟩-x, ⟨11⟩-486; advertisements, pp. ⟨3⟩-8. Frontispiece; 1 plate; 3 2-page maps; 10 1-page maps inserted. 7⅛″ x 4¹³⁄₁₆″.

⟨1-2⟩, 3-20¹², 21⁶.

C cloth: green; purple. Purple end papers. Flyleaves.

The error *plyaing* for *playing,* p. 298, line 9 up, is present in all examined copies.

Listed PW March 1, 1871.

HA UP

11209. SARATOGA IN 1901. BY ELI PERKINS . . .

NEW YORK. 1872. SHELDON & COMPANY.

⟨i⟩-⟨viii⟩, 1-249; vignette, p. ⟨250⟩; 2 blank leaves; leaf excised or pasted under end paper. Illustrated. 7⅞″ scant x 5⁵⁄₁₆″.

⟨-⟩⁴, A-P⁸.

C cloth: orange. F cloth: blue. FL cloth: brown. Yellow end papers. Flyleaf at front.

A copy at BA received Aug. 21, 1872. Listed WTC Aug. 22, 1872.

B H

11210. Th: Nast's Illustrated Almanac for 1873 . . .

. . . 1872 . . . Harper & Brothers . . . ⟨New York⟩

"New-Year's Calls," pp. 17-21. Collected in *Eli Perkins (At Large)* . . . , 1875.

For comment see entry No. 3346.

11211. The Hospital Bazaar . . .

Chicago . . . 1874 . . .

"Eli in Love," together with an introductory anecdote, No. 2, p. 23. Collected in *Eli Perkins (At Large)* . . . , 1875.

An occasional newspaper. For comment see entry No. 7274.

11212. Artemus Ward: His Works, Complete . . . and a Biographical Sketch by Melville D. Landon . . .

New York: G. W. Carleton & Co., Publishers. London: J. C. Hotten. M.DCCC.LXXV.

"Chas. Farrar Browne, 'Artemus Ward,'" pp. ⟨11⟩-24.

Listed PW June 26, 1875.

AAS BA H

11213. ELI PERKINS (AT LARGE): HIS SAYINGS AND DOINGS . . .

NEW YORK: J. B. FORD & COMPANY. 1875.

⟨i⟩-viii, 9-248; advertisements, pp. ⟨1⟩-16; plus: 17-18. Frontispiece inserted; other illustrations in text. 7⁵⁄₁₆″ x 4⅞″.

⟨A⟩-C, ⟨D-E⟩, F-I, K-L¹²; plus: ⟨M⟩¹.

Cream linen. C cloth: brown. S cloth: blue; brown; green. Yellow end papers. Flyleaves.

Note: P. 171, last line, period lacking in all copies examined.

Listed PW Aug. 28, 1875. According to PW Sept. 22, 1877, the plates and 164 remainder copies were sold to Lippincott, Sept. 18, 1877. Toronto (Belford) edition listed CM April 1877.

B H NYPL

11214. Journal of the Fair for the New St. Patrick's Cathedral ...

New York ... October 23, 1878 ... ⟨to⟩ December 5, 1878 ...

An occasional newspaper issued for the benefit of St. Patrick's Cathedral, New York. Complete in 31 numbers.

Reprint save for "Animate and Inanimate Nature," No. 4, p. 2, October 26, 1878. "Written expressly for the *Journal*" but compare with "Animate Nature," in *Eli Perkins (At Large)* ... , 1875, p. 183. Also compare with "Animate and Inanimate Nature" in *Wit and Humor of the Age* ... , 1883, pp. 125-126.

H

11215. For Our Boys A Collection of Original Literary Offerings by Popular Writers at Home and Abroad. Published and Sold for the Benefit of the "Youths' Directory," of San Francisco, a Benevolent Institution for Friendless Boys. Edited by Ambrose P. Dietz ...

San Francisco: A. L. Bancroft and Company. 1879.

"Modern Love-Story," pp. 104-107. A version of "Eli in Love," in *Eli Perkins (At Large)* ... , 1875. Yet another version appears in *Wit And Humor of the Age* ... , 1883, as "Eli Perkins' Love Story."

Reviewed in *New York Mail*, Feb. 14, 1879.

UV

11216. Edison and His Inventions ... Edited by J. B. McClure.

Chicago: Rhodes & McClure, Publishers. 1879.

Cloth; and, printed paper wrapper.

"Eli Perkins and Mr. Edison," pp. 117-118. Collected in *Wit and Humor of the Age* ... , 1883. For another version see "Eli on Fire-Proof Houses" in *Eli Perkins (At Large)* ... , 1875.

Title deposited Feb. 17, 1879. Preface dated May 21, 1879. Deposited Feb. 24, 1881 ⟨sic⟩.

H NYPL

11217. ELI PERKINS, HIS LAST JOKES. INDIVIDUALIZED BY HIS INIMITABLE WIT, PATHOS AND HUMOR.

NEW YORK: A. J. FISHER, PUBLISHER, NO. 24 VESEY STREET. (ASTOR HOUSE BLOCK.) ⟨n.d., 1879? 1880?⟩

⟨1⟩-60; advertisements, pp. ⟨61-64⟩. 6⁵⁄₁₆″ x 4″. ⟨1-2⟩¹⁶.

Printed bluish-gray paper wrapper.

A collection of squibs and short sketches; some reprinted from *Eli Perkins (At Large)* ... , 1875; others appear in *Wit and Humor of the Age* ... , 1883; and, *Wit, Humor and Pathos*, 1883; some otherwise unlocated.

H

11218. Biographical Sketch of the Class of 1861 of Union College Schenectady, N. Y.

⟨W. O. Bunn, Book and Job Printer, Homer, N. Y., n.d., 1882⟩

Landon's account of the "Decennial Meeting of the Class ... 1871 ... ," pp. 6-7, dated Dec. 12, 1881. Also contains, pp. 68-72, a biographical (autobiographical?) sketch.

Union College Library, Schenectady, N. Y.

11219. Eli Perkins Wit, Humor and Pathos ...

Chicago: Belford, Clarke & Co., 1883.

Reprint save for 17 pieces. *Note:* Printed in part from the plates of *Eli Perkins (At Large)* ... , 1875. Certain other pieces are present in altered form.

Advertised for March 1 PW Feb. 24, 1883, as in cloth; and, paper. Listed PW April 14, 1883.

LC

11220. Wit and Humor of the Age ... by Mark Twain, Robt. J. Burdette, Josh Billings, Alex. Sweet, Eli Perkins. With the Philosophy of Wit and Humor, by Melville D. Landon ...

Chicago: Western Publishing House. 1883.

Contains a number of short skits, conundrums, mots, etc., by Landon. BAL has not determined which of these occur here first in book form, nor how many are revisions of pieces which had prior book publication. BAL is aware that some of these pieces are here present under altered titles and are revised, but a definitive list of these cannot be offered short of doing an exhaustive concordance of Landon's writings.

Reprinted with the following imprints: *Chicago Star Publishing Company;* and, *Star Publishing Company, Chicago.*

Title deposited Sept. 2, 1883. Books deposited on either March 17, 1884; or, April 28, 1884; the record is not clear.

H

11221. Third Annual St. Jacobs Oil Family Calendar 1885 and Book of Health and Humor
for the Million Containing Original Humorous Articles & Illustrations by the Leading
Humorists of America.

The Charles A. Vogeler Company Baltimore,
Maryland, U.S.A. Copyright. ‹1884›

Printed paper wrapper. Cover-title.

"What Drove Me to a Lunatic Asylum," p. 5.
"Written for the St. Jacobs Oil Family Calendar ..."

AAS

11222. Second Crop. Pickings from Puck. Being a Choice Collection of ... Pieces, Poems
and Pictures from Puck ...

New York: Keppler & Schwarzmann. ‹1885›

"What Reformed Eli Perkins," p. 7.

For comment see entry No. 691.

11223. Beecher Memorial Contemporaneous
Tributes to the Memory of Henry Ward
Beecher Compiled and Edited by Edward W.
Bok

Privately Printed Brooklyn, New York 1887

Contribution, pp. 105-106.

For comment see entry No. 2148.

11224. ... Some Famous Pseudonyms. Well-
Known Authors Tell the Stories of Their
Nom de Plumes ... ‹Edited by Edward W.
Bok›

... Copyrighted ... 1889, by the Bok Syndicate Press of New York ...

The above at head of first column. At head of
sheet: This Article Is Furnished by the Bok
Syndicate Press ...

Single cut sheet. Printed in five columns.
Printed on recto only. Prepared for the use
of Bok Syndicate subscribers.

Contains an autobiographical statement by Landon.

H

11225. ... Kings of the Platform and Pulpit
‹Compiled› by Melville D. Landon ...

Chicago F. C. Smedley & Co., Publishers.
1890

For fuller entry see BAL, Vol. 2, 249. Also
see *American Lecturers* ..., below, under *ca.*
1898.

Y

11226. ... THIRTY YEARS OF WIT AND
REMINISCENCES OF WITTY, WISE AND
ELOQUENT MEN ...

NEW YORK CASSELL PUBLISHING COMPANY, 104
& 106 FOURTH AVENUE, NEW YORK. ‹1891›

At head of title: ELI PERKINS

‹i›-‹xii›, 1-305; blank leaf, excised or pasted
under end paper in some copies. Frontispiece
inserted; facsimiles in text. 7¼" full x 4¹⁵⁄₁₆".

‹1-20›⁸. ‹20›₈ excised or pasted under end paper in some copies.

V cloth: brown; gray; green. Flyleaf at front of
some copies.

Advertised PW Sept. 19/26, 1891, as *forthcoming*,
in cloth. Deposited (cloth) Sept. 25, 1891. Listed
(cloth) PW Oct. 10, 1891. Also advertised as in
cloth PW Oct. 17, 1891; Jan. 30, 1892. Issued as
No. 114 in *Cassell's Sunshine Series* under date
May 30, 1892. Advertised PW May 28, 1892 as a
recent issue in *Cassell's Sunshine Series*, in cloth;
and, wrapper. The London (Cassell) edition
listed Ath Nov. 7, 1891.

B H LC NYSL Y

American Lecturers and Humorists ...

... Akron ... New York ‹1893; *i.e., ca.* 1898›

See below under 1898.

11227. MONEY GOLD, SILVER OR BIMET-
ALLISM ...

CHICAGO CHARLES H. KERR & COMPANY 1895

‹1›-157, 3 pp. advertisements. Illustrated. 7⁹⁄₁₆"
x 5⁵⁄₁₆".

‹1-10›⁸.

Printed yellow-coated on white paper wrapper.

On copyright page: *American Politics, No. 2.* ...
June, 1895. Deposited July 5, 1895. Listed PW
July 20, 1895.

LC NYPL Y

11228. American Lecturers and Humorists by
Melville D. Landon ...

The Saalfield Publishing Company Akron,
Ohio New York ‹1893; *i.e., ca.* 1898›

Reprint of *Kings of the Platform and Pulpit*,
1890, with the omission of "Professor David
Swing," pp. 479-490; and, the insertion of "David
Harum," pp. 479-490.

Could not have been issued prior to March 31,
1898, the date of Edward Noyes Westcott's
death, a fact recorded herein on p. 479.

Reissued by Werner, 1900, under the original title, *Kings of the Platform and Pulpit*.

G

11229. Bohemia   Official Publication of the International League of Press Clubs for the Building and Endowment of the Journalists' Home ... Vol. I. Alexander K. McClure, Editor-in-Chief ...

... The International League of Press Clubs James S. McCartney Treasurer   Journalists' Home Fund   Philadelphia 1904.

"Funny Dialects," pp. 269-272.

For comment see entry No. 8697.

11230. What's Next or Shall a Man Live Again? ... Compiled by Clara Spalding Ellis ...

Boston   Richard G. Badger   The Gorham Press   1906

Statement, pp. 82-83.

EM

IN THIS SECTION are listed collections of reprinted material issued under Landon's name.

11231. ... American Fun for Grave and Gay. The Best Things from ... Eli Perkins ⟨and Others⟩ ...

F. M. Lupton, Publisher, 27 Park Place, New York. ⟨n.d., 1883–1886⟩

Cover-title. At head of title: *Price Twenty-Five Cents*. Printed paper wrapper.

11232. ... Wit, Humor and Pathos ...

New York: Frank F. Lovell & Company, 83 Elm Street. ⟨n.d., 1887⟩

At head of title: Eli Perkins Printed paper wrapper. Issued under date March 30, 1887, as No. 42 in *Lovell's Household Library*.

11233. ... Wit, Humor and Pathos ...

Chicago: Donohue, Henneberry & Co. 407-425 Dearborn Street 1890

At head of title: Eli Perkins On binding: *Caxton Edition*

11234. The Complete Works of Artemus Ward, (Charles Farrar Browne.) With a Biographical Sketch (by Melville D. Landon, "Eli Perkins,") ...

New York: G. W. Dillingham Co., Publishers. MDCCCXCVIII.

11235. ... Thirty Years of Wit and Reminiscences of Witty Wise and Eloquent Men ...

1899 The Werner Company New York Akron, Ohio Chicago

At head of title: Eli Perkins

11236. Comical Hits by Famous Wits ... with the Philosophy of Wit and Humor by Melville D. Landon ...

Copyright 1900 by Robert W. Patton ... Chicago Thompson & Thomas 267 Wabash Ave.

Deposited Dec. 10, 1900. Reprint of *Wit and Humor of the Age* ... , 1883.

11236A. Kings of the Platform and Pulpit ...

Chicago ... The Werner Company 1900

11237. Library of Wit and Humor ... with "Philosophy of Wit and Humor" ...

1901 ... Chicago M. A. Donohue & Co. 407-429 Dearborn St.

Reprint of the first portion of *Wit and Humor of the Age* ... , 1883.

11238. Library of Wit and Humor ... with "Philosophy of Wit and Humor" ...

Copyright 1901 ... Chicago Thompson & Thomas 262 Wabash Avenue

Reprint of the first portion of *Wit and Humor of the Age* ... , 1883.

11239. Masters of Mirth and Eloquence ...

The Golden West Publishing Company Seattle, Washington ⟨1906⟩

11240. American Lecturers and Humorists ...

The Saalfield Publishing Company Akron, Ohio New York ⟨1906⟩

Cloth, portrait of Mark Twain pasted to front cover. Reprint of *Kings of the Platform and Pulpit*.

In this section are listed books by authors other than Landon which contain material by him reprinted from earlier books.

One Hundred Choice Selections No. 29 ...

  ... Philadelphia ... 1889.

For comment see BAL, Vol. 3, p. 64.

No. 26. Standard Recitations ... by Frances P. Sullivan ...

  ... N. Y. ... ⟨1890⟩

For comment see entry No. 134.

... Masterpieces of Wit and Humor with ... Introduction by Robert J. Burdette ...

  ⟨n.p.⟩ Copyright, 1902, by E. J. Long

"Champion Mean Men," pp. 360-361; otherwise "Eli Perkins on Mean Men" in *Wit and Humor of the Age* ... , 1883. For comment see entry No. 2013.

Mark Twain's Library of Humor The Primrose Way ...

  ... New York ... MCMVI

"On Preventing Fires," pp. ⟨178⟩-179; otherwise "Eli Perkins and Mr. Edison," in *Edison and His Inventions* ... , 1879. For fuller entry see No. 3668.

ANA

No. 17. Standard Recitations ... Compiled ... by Frances P. Sullivan ...

  ... N. Y. ... ⟨1887⟩

" 'Kissing Mother'," p. 9, credited to *Eli Perkins*. However, the piece had prior publication in Landon's *Wit and Humor of the Age* ... , 1883, where it is credited to George Peck. For comment see entry No. 9009.

Landon's lecture manager, Harrison Downes (sometimes spelled Downs), New York, issued a series of newspaper-like publicity pieces designed to promote the Eli Perkins lectures. Those examined (6 examples at H) are each of four pages, 21″ x 14″, and devoted to extracts from Landon's lectures and writings, blurbs, announcements, etc. The H copies are variously dated 1887–'8 to 1901–'02. The announcements were available, at a low rate, to the various organizations sponsoring the lectures, and the headlines were altered to fit the time and place.

SIDNEY CLOPTON LANIER

1 8 4 2 – 1 8 8 1

11241. TIGER-LILIES. A NOVEL . . .

NEW YORK: PUBLISHED BY HURD AND HOUGH-TON, 459 BROOME STREET. 1867.

⟨i-ii⟩, ⟨i⟩-⟨vi⟩, ⟨1⟩-252. Laid paper. 7⅛″ x 4¹¹⁄₁₆″.

⟨-⟩⁴, 1-15⁸, 16⁶.

C cloth: green; purple; terra-cotta. Cream-coated on white end papers; pale peach-coated on white end papers. Laid paper flyleaves. *Note:* All examined copies have the error *Lillies* for *Lilies* on the spine.

Two states noted; the sequence is presumed correct:

A: The title-leaf is a cancel. A surviving deposit copy thus.

B: The title-leaf is an integral part of its gathering.

Presumably the above were preceded by an as yet unlocated form of the title-leaf. For a discussion of this book see John S. Mayfield's study *Sidney Lanier's Tiger-Lilies: A Bibliographical Mystery,* Syracuse University Library Associates, 1964.

Announced ALG Sept. 2, 1867. Announced as *ready in October* ALG Sept. 16, 1867. Deposited Nov. 23, 1867. Listed ALG Dec. 2, 1867.

AAS (B)   H (A)   UV (A,B)

11242. FOR THE GOLDEN WEDDING OF STERLING AND SARAH LANIER   SEPTEMBER 27th, 1868.   BY THE ELDEST GRANDSON.

⟨n.p., 1868⟩

Not seen. Entry on the basis of a photographic copy in JH.

Cover-title. Single cut sheet folded to make 4 pages. 8⁵⁄₁₆″ x 5½″. Text on pp. ⟨2-3⟩.

Collected in *Poems,* 1884.

11243. Little Ella   A Beautiful Ballad Dedicated to Ella S. Montgomery by Her Friend S. C. Lanier   May 10. 1866 ⟨*sic*⟩ . . .

Montgomery, Ala.   R. W. Offutt & Co. . . . 1868 . . .

Sheet music. Cover-title. Both text and music by Lanier.

Collected in *Centennial Edition,* Vol. 1.

JH

11244. Catalogue of the Trustees, Faculty, Alumnae and Students of Furlow Masonic Female College, Americus, Ga., 1868–1869.

Macon, Georgia: J. W. Burke & Co., Stationers, Printers and Binders, 1869.

Not located. Entry on the basis of "A Commencement Address by Sidney Lanier," by Jay B. Hubbell, in *American Literature,* Vol. 2, No. 4, Jan. 1931; and, footnote, p. 247, of *Centennial Edition* of Lanier's works, Vol. 5.

Contains "Annual Address before the Furlow Masonic Female College, Delivered June 30th, 1869," pp. 19-30.

11245. The Living Writers of the South. By James Wood Davidson . . .

New York: Carleton, Publisher, Madison Square. London: S. Low, Son, & Co. MDCCCLXIX.

"Barnacles," p. 322. Collected in *Poems,* 1884.

"The Tournament," p. 322. The three stanzas printed here are collected as part of "The Tournament. Joust First," in *Poems,* 1884.

Note: In all examined copies the text on p. 328 is erroneously duplicated on p. 323.

H   NYPL

11246. Martha Washington Court Journal. First Edition.

Baltimore, February 22, 1875 . . .

SIDNEY LANIER
Entry No. 11243
Much Reduced
(Johns Hopkins University Libraries)

tions. The following list is presented in what is presumed the correct sequence. It must be noted that other printings may exist.

A

. . . The Centennial Meditation of Columbia. A Cantata for the Inaugural Ceremonies at Philadelphia, May 10, 1876. Poem by Sidney Lanier . . . Music by Dudley Buck . . .

New York: G. Schirmer, 701 Broadway. ⟨1876⟩

Printed boards, cloth shelfback. At head of title: 1776–1876. By Appointment of the U. S. Centennial Commission.

"The Centennial Meditation of Columbia," pp. ⟨3⟩-4.

Probably printed in March 1876. ". . . I have received a copy of the piano-score of the Cantata . . . This piano-score is only written for the purpose of drilling the chorus . . ."—Letter, Sidney Lanier, Baltimore, March 18, 1876, to Mary Day Lanier, in *Centennial Edition*, Vol. 9, p. 338. Noticed as *just published New-York Daily Tribune*, March 31, 1876. ". . . The first gun has already been fired by the *Tribune* man in a notice of the Cantata,—which he had no right to *notice* at all, it having been printed (*not* published) solely for the purpose of drilling the Chorus . . ."—Letter, Sidney Lanier, Baltimore, April 4, 1876, to Robert S. Lanier, in *Centennial Edition*, Vol. 9, p. 351.

". . . In view of the fact that the poem is now printed with the piano-score and is liable at any time to be copied—and copied badly by other papers, would it not be well for me if it were printed by the *Tribune*, properly? . . ."—Letter, Sidney Lanier, Baltimore, April 8, 1876, to Bayard Taylor, in *Centennial Edition*, Vol. 9, p. 354. The poem is printed in full in the *New-York Daily Tribune*, April 12, 1876 with the statement "printed copies are now in the hands of 800 singers."

B

1776. 1876. International Exhibition of 1876. Opening Ceremonies. Order of Exercises. Fairmount Park, Philadelphia, May 10th, 1876 . . .

⟨n.p., n.d., Philadelphia, 1876⟩

Single cut sheet folded to four pages. "Cantata" on p. ⟨2⟩. Page: 11" x 8⁷⁄₁₆". Issued as a program.

C

Prayer, Hymn, Cantata, and Speeches in the Opening Ceremonies of the International Exposition. Not to Be Published Until after the Ceremonies Have Taken Place . . .

⟨n.p., n.d., Philadelphia, 1876⟩

Single leaf. Printed on one side only. Issued a press release.

D

The New Century for Woman. No. 1.

Philadelphia, Saturday, May 13, 1876 . . .

Caption-title. The above at head of p. ⟨1⟩. An occasional newspaper, 8 pp., "published by the Women's Centennial Committee, Woman's Building, International Exhibition, Philadelphia."

"Cantata," p. 8. Anonymous.

E

Tribune Extra, No. 32.

New York, 1876.

Not located. Presumably contains the "Cantata." "The large extra edition of *The Daily Tribune* of May 10 . . . having been entirely exhausted, orders for it will in future be filled with *The Tribune Extra No. 32*, which contains, in addition to the matter given in *The Daily*, a full account of the opening ceremonies . . ."—*New-York Daily Tribune*, May 20, 1876, p. 6.

F (G?)

The Centennial Liberty Bell . . . by Jos. S. Longshore . . . and Benjamin L. Knowles . . .

Philadelphia: Claxton, Remsen & Haffelfinger. 624, 626, 628 Market St. 1876.

Cloth?

"Cantata," pp. 142-143.

Title entered March 13, 1876; again, Sept. 27, 1876. Copies of the book deposited Sept. 27, 1876.

G (F?)

The Illustrated History of the Centennial Exhibition . . . a Concise History of the Origin and Success of the Exhibition . . . by James D. McCabe . . .

Published by the National Publishing Co., Philadelphia, Pa.; Chicago, Ill.; St. Louis, Mo., and Columbus, Ohio. ⟨1876⟩

Noted in three-quarters leather. As a subscription book probably issued in a variety of bindings and with varying imprints. Preface dated at end *August 1st, 1876*. A copy at AAS inscribed by early owner Oct. 1876.

"Centennial Cantata," pp. 287-288.

AAS (A,B,G) BPL (F) CAW (C) H (A) JH (D) UV (A, B) Y (B)

Caption-title. The above at head of p. ‹1›. An occasional newspaper, 4 pp., "issued for the Ladies of the Martha Washington Tea Party."

"Martha Washington," p. ‹1›. Collected in *Poems*, 1884.

JH

Florida ...

Philadelphia ... ‹1875›

See next entry.

11247. FLORIDA: ITS SCENERY, CLIMATE, AND HISTORY. WITH AN ACCOUNT OF CHARLESTON, SAVANNAH, AUGUSTA, AND AIKEN; A CHAPTER FOR CONSUMPTIVES; VARIOUS PAPERS ON FRUIT-CULTURE; AND A COMPLETE HAND-BOOK AND GUIDE ...

PHILADELPHIA: J. B. LIPPINCOTT & CO. 1876.

‹1›-336; plus: advertisements, pp. i-ix, blank leaf. Illustrated. 7½" scant x 4¾".

‹1-3›, 4-9, ‹10›, 11-28⁶; plus: ‹29›⁶. *Also signed:* ‹A-B›, C-I, K-O¹²; plus: ‹P›⁶.

C cloth: green. S cloth: brown; green; mauve; purple; terra-cotta. Brown-coated on white end papers. Flyleaves.

Noted in the following forms; the order of presentation in the *Centennial Edition*, Vol. 6, is incorrect.

First Edition

Title-page: As above. Date *1876* present. Title-page contains the statement: *Various Papers on Fruit-Culture.*

Pagination: As above.

Pp. 52-53: No footnote.

P. 70, line 5: *The Metropolitan Hotel, a quarter of a mile ...*

P. 130: No footnote.

P. 213: No footnote.

P. 217: 21 lines of text.

P. 235, line 1: *One of the ...*

P. ix of terminal advertisements: *Advertiser. Abstract ... The Season of 1875-6 ...*

Noted in cloth only.

Deposited Nov. 30, 1875. Listed, cloth only, PW Dec. 11, 1875; PC Jan. 18, 1876.

Note: A *second edition* ‹*i.e.,* printing› advertised PW, cloth only, Jan. 22, 1876. If (as this advertisement indicates) there were two print-

ings of the first edition, BAL has been unable to distinguish them.

Second Edition

This appears to be textually the same as the first edition but does not contain the "various papers on fruit-culture" which were contributed by authors other than Sidney Lanier.

Title-page: The date *1876* is not present, nor is the statement: *Various Papers on Fruit-Culture.*

Pagination: ‹1›-268; advertisements: i-ix; blank, pp. ‹x-xii›. Illustrated.

Pp. 52-53: No footnote.

P. 70, line 5: *The Metropolitan Hotel, a quarter of a mile ...*

P. 130: No footnote.

P. 213: No footnote.

P. 217: 21 lines of text.

P. 235, line 1: *One of the ...*

P. ix of terminal advertisements: *Advertiser. Abstract ... The Season of 1877 ...*

Noted in printed paper wrapper only.

Listed PW Feb. 17, 1877, *stiff cover* only.

Revised Edition

Title-page: The date *1876* is not present, nor is the statement: *Various Papers on Fruit-Culture.*

Pagination: ‹1›-266. Illustrated.

Pp. 52-53: Footnote present: *The Indians were released in May, 1878 ...*

P. 70, line 5: *The St. Marks Hotel, formerly known as the Metro- |*

P. 130: Footnote present: *Since the first edition of this book ...*

P. 213: Footnote present.

P. 217: 28 lines of text.

P. 235, line 1: *Perhaps the ...*

P. 263: *General Itinerary ... On or about January 1, 1881 ...*

Advertised as *just published,* in both cloth and paper, PW March 19, 1881. Listed PW March 26, 1881, in both cloth and paper.

AAS (1st; 2nd; revised) H (1st; revised) LC (1st) UV (1st; revised) Y (1st; revised)

11248. THE CENTENNIAL MEDITATION OF COLUMBIA

Lanier's "Cantata" written for the opening ceremonies of the Centennial Exposition in Philadelphia, 1876, appeared in numerous publica-

The Poems of Bartholomew Griffin ...

   ... 1876

See below under 1881.

11249. POEMS ...

   PHILADELPHIA   J. B. LIPPINCOTT & CO. LONDON:
   16 SOUTHAMPTON ST., COVENT GARDEN. 1877

⟨1⟩-94, blank leaf. 6⅞″ scant x 4½″.

⟨A⟩-F⁸. *Also signed:* ⟨1⟩-8⁶.

C cloth: green; purple; terra-cotta. S cloth:
brown; green; purple. Brown-coated on white
end papers. Flyleaves. Covers bevelled.

Two states of the binding noted. The sequence,
if any, is not known and the designations are for
identification only:

A: Circular device blindstamped on the back
cover. A surviving deposit copy thus.

B: Device not present on back cover.

Advertised PW Oct. 28, 1876, as *in a few days.*
Listed PW Nov. 11, 1876.

AAS (A)   B (A)   BA (A)   BPL (A)   H (A)   LC (A)
NYPL (A, B)   UV (A)

11250. Sketch of the Life of J.F.D. Lanier.
(Printed for the Use of His Family Only.)
Second Edition.

   ⟨n.p.⟩ 1877.

Letter to J.F.D. Lanier, dated July 6, 1877, pp.
75-87; not in the earlier editions of 1870 and
1871. See below under 1879.

AAS   UV   Y

11251. The Dial of the Old South Clock ...

   ... Boston, December 5, 1877 ... ⟨to⟩ December 15, 1877 ...

An occasional newspaper. Complete in 10 numbers.

"A Weather-Vane," No. 5, Dec. 10, 1877, p. 7.
Collected in the *Centennial Edition,* Vol. 1. For
a comment see "A Humorous Quatrain by
Lanier," by John Howard Birss, in *American
Literature,* Nov. 1933.

BA

11252. Every Saturday   Devoted to Literature,
Music, Art, Science and General Information
Christmas Supplement.

   Baltimore, December 22, 1877 ...

Not seen. Entry on the basis of a photostatic
copy in JH.

Caption-title. The above at head of p. ⟨1⟩.

"The Hard Times in Elfland. A Story of Christmas Eve," p. ⟨1⟩. Under the title "The Hard
Times in Elfland, a Christmas-Eve Story for Children," appears in the *Centennial Edition,* Vol. 1.
First collected in *Poems,* 1884.

11253. Charlotte Cushman: Her Letters and
Memories of Her Life. Edited by ... Emma
Stebbins ...

   Boston: Houghton, Osgood and Company.
The Riverside Press, Cambridge. 1878.

Reprint save for "To Miss Charlotte Cushman,"
p. 268. Collected in *Centennial Edition,* Vol. 1.

For comment see entry No. 1471.

11254. SYLLABUS. SHAKSPERE COURSE:
LECTURES I, II, III. MR. LANIER. COM-
MENCING SATURDAY, NOVEMBER 2d,
12 O'CLOCK, AT THE PEABODY INSTI-
TUTE ...

   ⟨n.p., n.d., BALTIMORE, 1878⟩

Caption-title. The above on p. ⟨1⟩.

⟨1⟩-8. 9³⁄₁₆″ x 5⅞″ scant.

⟨-⟩⁴.

Printed self-wrapper.

JH

11255. ... A Masque of Poets. Including Guy
Vernon, a Novelette in Verse.

   Boston: Roberts Brothers. 1878.

"The Marshes of Glynn," pp. 88-94. Collected as
"Hymns of the Marshes: Part IV. The Marshes
of Glynn" in *Poems,* 1884.

For fuller entry see No. 118.

11256. The Southern Student's Hand-Book of
Selections for Reading and Oratory. By John
G. James ...

   A. S. Barnes & Co., New York, Chicago and
New Orleans. 1879.

Cloth?

Reprint save for "The Power of Prayer; or, the
First Steamboat up the Alabama," in collaboration with Clifford Lanier, pp. 355-358. Collected
in *Poems,* 1884.

JH (Inscribed by the editor March 25, 1879)

11257. The Boy's Froissart   Being Sir John
Froissart's Chronicles ... Edited for Boys ...
by Sidney Lanier ...

   New-York   Charles Scribner's Sons   743 & 745
Broadway   1879

"Introduction," pp. v-xv.

Two states (probably printings) noted:

1

On title-page: *Boy's*

Printer's imprint not present on copyright page.

2

On title-page: *Boys'*

Rand, Avery, & Company imprint on copyright page.

Note: The printings of 1882, 1884, 1895, 1907, and later, revert to the *Boy's* form of title-page.

Advertised for Nov. 13th in PW Nov. 8, 1879. Published Nov. 13, 1879 (publisher's records). Listed PW Nov. 29, 1879. The London edition (Sampson Low) noted as *just ready* Ath Nov. 29, 1879; listed Ath Dec. 6, 1879.

AAS (2nd)   H (2nd)   JH (1st: inscribed by Lanier Nov. 1879; 2nd: inscribed by early owner Christmas 1879)   LC (1st; being a deposit copy)   UV (2nd)   Y (2nd)

11258. ⟨Supplement to *Sketch of the Life of J.F.D. Lanier* . . . , 1877, Second Edition⟩

⟨n.p., 1879⟩

Pp. ⟨89⟩-106. 8¹¹/₁₆″ x 5⅞″.

⟨-⟩¹⁰.

This supplement consists of a letter, Baltimore, Md., April 2, 1879, addressed to *My Dear Sir* (*i.e.,* J.F.D. Lanier) supplementing Sidney Lanier's earlier such letter of July 6, 1877, and designed for insertion in *Sketch of the Life of J.F.D. Lanier* . . . , 1877, Second Edition, q.v.

JH

11259. THE SCIENCE OF ENGLISH VERSE . . .

NEW YORK   CHARLES SCRIBNER'S SONS   743 AND 745 BROADWAY   1880

Noted in the following forms; BAL suspects there was but a single printing and the variations, therefore, were produced at the bindery. No firm sequence has been established and the order of presentation is all but arbitrary; the designations are for identification only.

Note: The plaid-like stamping referred to below was not applied by the binder but is an original feature of the binder's cloth.

Also note: The single inserted leaf which occurs as either a fly-title-page or as a divisional title-page in the front matter is not present in the publisher's file copy (now in NYPL); however,

the book is in deplorable condition and absence of the leaf may mean nothing more than extraction and loss since leaving the bindery.

Binder's Variant A

⟨i-vi⟩ (pp. ⟨i-ii⟩ excised or pasted under the end paper), ⟨i⟩-⟨xxiv⟩, 21-315; blank, p. ⟨316⟩; advertisements, pp. ⟨317-322⟩; 3 blank leaves, the third being excised or pasted under the end paper. 8″ scant x 5″. Laid paper.

⟨1⁴, 2¹³, 3-14¹², 15⁸⟩. Leaves ⟨1⟩₁ and ⟨15⟩₈ excised or pasted under the end paper. Leaf ⟨2⟩₁₁ (the divisional title-page) inserted.

Noted in *Binding Variant A, Binding Variant B;* see below. The surviving copyright deposit copy (*Binding Variant A*) thus. Copies thus in *Binding Variant A, Binding Variant B,* have been seen inscribed by Lanier *May, 1880.*

Binder's Variant B

⟨i-vi⟩ (pp. ⟨i-ii⟩ excised or pasted under the end paper), ⟨i⟩-⟨xxiv⟩, 21-315; blank, p. ⟨316⟩; advertisements, pp. ⟨317-322⟩; 3 blank leaves, the last two being excised or pasted under the end paper. 8″ scant x 5″. Laid paper.

⟨1⁴, 2¹³, 3-14¹², 15⁸⟩. Leaves ⟨1⟩₁ and ⟨15⟩₇₋₈ excised or pasted under the end paper. Leaf ⟨2⟩₁₁ (the divisional title-page) inserted.

Noted in *Binding Variant B;* see below.

Binder's Variant C

⟨i-vi⟩ (excised); ⟨i⟩-⟨xxiv⟩, 21-315; blank, p. ⟨316⟩; advertisements, pp. ⟨317-322⟩; 3 blank leaves, the third being excised or pasted under the end paper. 7⅞″ full x 5″. Laid paper.

⟨1⁴, 2¹³, 3-14¹², 15⁸⟩. Leaves ⟨1⟩₁₋₃ excised. Leaf ⟨2⟩₁₁ (the divisional title-page) inserted. Leaf ⟨15⟩₈ excised or pasted under the end paper.

Noted in *Binding Variant C;* see below.

Binder's Variant D

⟨i-ii⟩ (inserted fly-title-page); ⟨i-vi⟩ (excised); ⟨i⟩-xxii, 21-315; blank, p. ⟨316⟩; advertisements, pp. ⟨317-322⟩; 3 blank leaves, the last of which is excised or pasted under the end paper. 8″ scant x 5″. Laid paper.

⟨1¹, 2⁴, 3-15¹², 16⁸⟩. Leaves ⟨2⟩₁₋₃ excised. Leaf ⟨16⟩₈ excised or pasted under the end paper. ⟨1⟩ is the fly-title-page.

Noted in *Binding Variant D;* see below.

Binding Variant A

V cloth: brown; green. Stamped in blind with a plaid-like pattern. Gray-coated end papers. No flyleaves. Covers bevelled.

Noted on *Binder's Variant A* sheets; copies have been seen inscribed *May, 1880.*

Binding Variant B

S cloth: purple. Not stamped in blind with a plaid-like pattern. Gray-coated end papers. No flyleaves. Covers bevelled.

Noted on *Binder's Variant A* sheets; *Binder's Variant B* sheets. A copy (*Binder's Variant A* sheets) has been seen inscribed by Lanier *May, 1880.*

Binding Variant C

V cloth: olive-brown. Stamped in blind with a plaid-like pattern. Brown-coated end papers. Two flyleaves (wove paper) at front. Covers bevelled.

Noted on *Binder's Variant C* sheets.

Binding Variant D

V cloth: green. Stamped in blind with a plaid-like pattern. Brown-coated end papers. Wove paper flyleaf at front. Covers bevelled.

Noted on *Binder's Variant D* sheets.

Note: All examined copies of this date have the following reading, p. 164, line 4: *... with an arsis...* In an 1897 reprint the reading is: *... with anacrusis ...*

Published May 13, 1880 (publisher's records). Listed PW May 22, 1880.

Locations

Binder's Variant A sheets, *Binding Variant A:*
H   LC (being a deposit copy)   NYPL

Binder's Variant A sheets, *Binding Variant B:*
AAS   H   Y

Binder's Variant B sheets, *Binding Variant B:*
H

Binder's Variant C sheets, *Binding Variant C:*
B   Y

Binder's Variant D sheets, *Binding Variant D:*
H   LC (not a deposit copy)

11260. The Art Autograph ... ⟨May, 1880⟩

... The Art Interchange, 140 Nassau Street, New York ... Copyright: 1880; by Wm. Whitlock.

Poem, beginning: *Heartsome Ireland, winsome Ireland,* p. ⟨10⟩. Collected as "Ireland" in *Poems,* 1884.

For comment see BAL, Vol. 3, p. 157.

NYPL

11261. The Boy's King Arthur   Being Sir Thomas Malory's History of King Arthur and His Knights of the Round Table Edited for Boys with an Introduction by Sidney Lanier ...

New York   Charles Scribner's Sons   743 and 745 Broadway   1880

"Introduction," pp. iii-xxiii, dated at end October, 1880.

Advertised for Nov. 9 PW Nov. 6, 1880. A copy at JH inscribed by Lanier Nov. 11, 1880. Published Nov. 12, 1880 (publisher's records). Listed PW Nov. 13, 1880. The London (Sampson Low) edition listed Ath Dec. 4, 1880.

AAS   B   H   JH   NYPL   UV   Y

11262. ... The Baltimore Christmas Magazine. Edited by Geo. Edwin Dorsey.

1880   Baltimore News Company, Agents.

Printed paper wrapper. Cover-title. At head of title: *Price 35 cts.*

Not a periodical, the name notwithstanding.

"Ode to Johns Hopkins University," pp. 59-61. Collected in *Poems,* 1884.

JH

11263. SUNRISE ...

⟨BALTIMORE, DECEMBER, 1880.⟩

Single cut sheet folded to make four pages. Page: 8⅟₁₆″ x 5⅟₁₆″. P. ⟨1⟩ as above. Text on pp. ⟨1-4⟩. At end of text: *Baltimore, December, 1880.*

Collected in *Poems,* 1884.

JH

11264. Supplements to the Sixteen Volumes of the American Cyclopædia, Containing New Articles and Continuations of Subjects Treated in the Body of the Work.

New York: D. Appleton and Company, 1, 3, and 5 Bond Street. London: 16 Little Britain. 1881.

Paged ⟨809⟩-826; ⟨801⟩-808; ⟨801⟩-804; etc., etc., with each supplement identified as to the appropriate volume.

"Johns Hopkins University," supplement to Vol. 9, pp. 858-861; anonymous. Collected in *Centennial Edition,* Vol. 3.

Note: The entry for this in the *Centennial Edition* is erroneous.

AAS (Inscribed by the publisher March 16, 1881)

Florida . . .

Philadelphia . . . ⟨1875; *i.e.,* 1881⟩

See entry No. 11247.

11265. Harper's Cyclopædia of British and American Poetry Edited by Epes Sargent

New York   Harper & Brothers, Franklin Square   1881

"A Rose-Moral," p. 916; otherwise "White," being the second of two "Rose-Morals," the other being titled "Red." Previously in *Poems,* 1877, but here in revised form.

Also contains the following poems; collected in *Poems,* 1884.

"Evening Song," pp. 916-917.

"The Harlequin of Dreams," p. 917.

"From the Flats," p. 917.

For comment see entry No. 4336.

11266. The Boy's Mabinogion   Being the Earliest Welsh Tales of King Arthur in the Famous Red Book of Hergest   Edited for Boys with an Introduction by Sidney Lanier . . .

New York   Charles Scribner's Sons   743 and 745 Broadway   1881

"Introduction," pp. iii-xx.

Advertised for Nov. 5 PW Nov. 5, 1881. Published Nov. 5, 1881 (publisher's records). Deposited Nov. 11, 1881. Listed PW Nov. 12, 1881. The London (Sampson Low) edition advertised as *shortly* Ath Nov. 12, 1881; listed Ath Nov. 26, 1881.

AAS   B   BPL   NYPL   UV   Y

11267. The Poems of Bartholomew Griffin . . . Edited . . . by . . . Alexander B. Grosart . . .

⟨Manchester, England⟩ Printed for the Subscribers. 1876. ⟨*i.e., ca.* 1881⟩

Printed paper wrapper.

"A Forgotten English Poet," pp. 71-84; also paged 15-28. *Note:* Pp. 71-84 printed not before 1881 and inserted in the 1876 publication.

". . . Rigidly limited to Fifty ⟨numbered⟩ Copies . . ."—p. ⟨iii⟩.

H   LC

11268. The Boy's Percy   Being Old Ballads of War, Adventure and Love from Bishop Thomas Percy's Reliques of Ancient English Poetry . . . Edited for Boys with an Introduction by Sidney Lanier . . .

New York   Charles Scribner's Sons   1882

"Introduction," pp. ⟨vii⟩-xxxi.

Issued in two formats; the sequence is presumed correct:

A

Leaf: 7¾″ x 5⁹⁄₁₆″. Binding does not carry the statement: *The Boy's Library of Legend and Chivalry*

B

Leaf: 7⅝″ x 5⁵⁄₁₆″. Binding carries the statement: *The Boy's Library of Legend and Chivalry Note:* The printings of 1884, 1893, and 1909 thus.

Advertised for Nov. 2 PW Nov. 4, 1882. Deposited Nov. 11, 1882. Listed PW Dec. 2, 1882. The London (Sampson Low) edition noted as *shortly* PC Dec. 18, 1882; listed Ath Jan. 20, 1883.

AAS (A)   B (both)   UV (both)

11269. THE ENGLISH NOVEL AND THE PRINCIPLE OF ITS DEVELOPMENT . . .

NEW YORK   CHARLES SCRIBNER'S SONS   1883

Edited by William Hand Browne.

⟨i-viii⟩, ⟨1⟩-293; blank, p. ⟨294⟩; 10 pp. advertisements. Laid paper. 7¹⁵⁄₁₆″ x 5¹⁄₁₆″.

⟨-⟩⁴, 1-12¹², 13⁸. *Note:* A superfluous signature mark 2 appears on p. 25.

V cloth, embossed with a plaid-like pattern: brown; green; olive. Covers bevelled. Brown-coated on white end papers. Laid paper flyleaf at back.

Published May 5, 1883 (publisher's records). Deposited May 8, 1883. A copy in BA received May 9, 1883. Listed PW May 12, 1883. For a revised edition see below under 1897.

AAS   B

11270. POEMS OF SIDNEY LANIER EDITED BY HIS WIFE WITH A MEMORIAL BY WILLIAM HAYES WARD . . .

NEW YORK   CHARLES SCRIBNER'S SONS   1884

⟨i-vi⟩, ⟨i⟩-⟨xlii⟩, ⟨1⟩-252, 2 blank leaves. *See signature collation below.* Frontispiece inserted. 7⅝″ full x 5³⁄₁₆″.

⟨1-19⟩⁸. Leaves ⟨1⟩₁ and ⟨19⟩₈ excised or pasted under the end papers. *Signed:* ⟨A-B⟩, ⟨1⟩-10¹², ⟨11⟩⁸.

S cloth: gray; V cloth: green. Covers bevelled. Top edges gilt. Errata slip inserted at p. ⟨xlii⟩; or, at p. ⟨xi⟩.

Published Nov. 25, 1884, in a printing of 1000 copies (publisher's records). Deposited Dec. 3, 1884. Listed PW Dec. 6, 1884. For other editions see under 1891, 1916.

AAS NYPL Y

11271. San Antonio de Bexar   A Guide and History Compiled and Edited by William Corner . . .

San Antonio, Texas   Bainbridge & Corner Christmas, 1890

"San Antonio de Bexar," pp. <68>-94. Collected in *Retrospects and Prospects*, 1899.

Deposited Jan. 9, 1891.

H JH LC Y

11272. WATER LILIES. A FAIRY SONG

<BOSTON: L. PRANG & CO., 1890>

Cover-title.

<1-8>. 3½″ x 8¼″. Pp. <2-3, 6-7> blank. Printed in gold and colors.

<->⁴.

Collected in *Centennial Edition*, Vol. 1.

JH

11273. Poems of Sidney Lanier Edited by His Wife . . . New Edition

New York   Charles Scribner's Sons   1891.

Reprint save for the following:

"Control." "Control" appears in the *Centennial Edition*, Vol. 1, as one of the "Poem Outlines."

"Marsh Hymns. Between Dawn and Sunrise."

"On a Palmetto."

"Struggle."

"A Sunrise Song."

"Thou and I."

"To J. D. H." Appears in the *Centennial Edition*, Vol. 1, with two additional stanzas as "To Captain James DeWitt Hankins."

Deposited Sept. 17, 1891. The London (Gay & Bird) edition advertised as though published Ath April 30, 1892; listed PC April 23, 1892. For other editions see under 1884, 1916.

AAS B Y

11274. . . . Sidney Lanier. By William Malone Baskervill . . .

Barbee & Smith, Agents, Nashville, Tenn. <1896>

Cover-title. At head of title: *Nos. 4, 5, and 6. Thirty Cents* . . .

Printed paper wrapper.

In addition to extracts from letters, etc., contains two poems:

Untitled, 5 lines, *I was the earliest bird awake* . . . , p. 226. Collected as No. 184 of "Poem Outlines" in *Centennial Edition*, Vol. 1.

Untitled, 12 lines, *O Lord, if thou wert needy as I* . . . , p. 190. Collected as No. 135 of "Poem Outlines" in *Centennial Edition*, Vol. 1.

Issued as the Oct.–Dec., 1896, number of the *Southern Writers* series.

H Y

11275. The English Novel   A Study in the Development of Personality . . . Revised Edition

New York   Charles Scribner's Sons   1897

See under 1883 for the first edition.

Edited by Mary Day Lanier.

Published Jan. 23, 1897 (publisher's records). Deposited Jan. 25, 1897.

H NYPL

11276. MUSIC AND POETRY   ESSAYS UP-ON SOME ASPECTS AND INTER-RELA-TIONS OF THE TWO ARTS . . .

NEW YORK   CHARLES SCRIBNER'S SONS   1898

Edited by Henry Wysham Lanier.

<i-viii>, <1>-248. 7¹⁵⁄₁₆″ x 5¼″.

<1-16>⁸. *Signed:* <->⁴, 1-15⁸, 16⁴.

Note: Also issued with a "Prefatory Note," dated at end *October, 1898,* inserted between <1>₄₋₅.

S-like cloth: green.

Advertised as *in press* PW Sept. 24, 1898. Published Dec. 3, 1898 (publisher's records). A copy at BA received Dec. 6, 1898. Listed PW Dec. 10, 1898.

AAS BA H JH Y

11277. RETROSPECTS AND PROSPECTS DESCRIPTIVE AND HISTORICAL ESSAYS . . .

NEW YORK   CHARLES SCRIBNER'S SONS   1899

Edited by Henry Wysham Lanier.

<i>-<x>, <1>-228, blank leaf. 8″ x 5¼″.

<1-15>⁸. *Signed:* <->⁵, 1-14⁸, 15³.

S-like cloth: green.

Noted PW March 11, 1899. Deposited April 14, 1899. Advertised as *ready to-day* PW April 15, 1899. Published April 15, 1899 (publisher's records). A copy at NYPL received April 15, 1899. A copy at BA received April 20, 1899. Listed PW April 22, 1899.

BA   H   NYPL

11278. LETTERS OF SIDNEY LANIER   SE-LECTIONS FROM HIS CORRESPOND-ENCE 1866–1881 . . .

NEW YORK   CHARLES SCRIBNER'S SONS   1899

Edited by Henry Wysham Lanier.

⟨i⟩-⟨xiv⟩, ⟨1⟩-245. Frontispiece, 1 plate and a 2-page facsimile inserted. $7^{15}\!/_{16}''$ x $5\frac{1}{4}''$.

⟨1-16⁸, 17²⟩. *Signed:* ⟨-⟩⁷, ⟨1⟩-15⁸, 16³.

S-like cloth: green.

Advertised as *will publish in September* PW Aug. 26, 1899. Deposited Oct. 14, 1899. A copy at BA received Oct. 17, 1899. Listed PW Oct. 21, 1899.

AAS   B   BA   H

11279. BOB   THE STORY OF OUR MOCK-ING-BIRD . . .

CHARLES SCRIBNER'S SONS   NEW YORK,   MDCCC-XCIX

Title-page in black and green.

⟨i-xiv⟩, 1-⟨69⟩; blank, p. ⟨70⟩; imprint of Merrymount Press, p. ⟨71⟩; blank leaf. 16 color plates inserted. $8\frac{1}{2}''$ x $5\frac{7}{8}''$.

⟨1-5⁸, 6⁴⟩.

Printed paper boards. Top edges stained yellow.

Deposited Nov. 25, 1899. Published Nov. 25, 1899 (publisher's records). Listed PW Dec. 9, 1899.

AAS   Y

11280. SHAKSPERE AND HIS FORERUN-NERS   STUDIES IN ELIZABETHAN POETRY AND ITS DEVELOPMENT FROM EARLY ENGLISH . . .

NEW YORK   DOUBLEDAY, PAGE & CO. 1902.

Title-page in black and orange.

Edited by Henry Wysham Lanier.

2 Vols.

TRADE EDITION

1: ⟨i⟩-xxiv, ⟨1⟩-324; 2 blank leaves. Frontispiece and 42 plates inserted. Laid paper. $9\frac{3}{4}''$ x $6^{9}\!/_{16}''$.

2: ⟨i⟩-⟨xx⟩, ⟨1⟩-329, blank leaf. Frontispiece and 52 plates inserted. *Note:* The plate opposite p. 124 is not listed.

1: ⟨1-22⟩⁸.

2: ⟨1-22⟩⁸.

T cloth: red. Red-coated on white end papers. Flyleaves in some copies. Top edges gilded.

LIMITED EDITION

1: Pagination and collation as above, save for: Certificate of issue inserted before p. ⟨i⟩; facsimile of a page of Lanier manuscript inserted, in some copies, at pp. xiv-xv. Van Gelder paper. $10\frac{3}{4}''$ x $7\frac{1}{8}''$.

2: Pagination and collation as above, save for certificate of issue inserted before p. ⟨i⟩.

Certificate of issue: "This . . . is one of an edition of one hundred and two, printed on Van Gelder . . . This is No . . ."

Gray paper boards; printed gray paper label on spine. Gray end papers, lined with a sheet of Van Gelder. Van Gelder flyleaves.

Limited edition deposited Dec. 1, 1902. A copy of trade edition at BA received Dec. 9, 1902. Both formats listed PW Dec. 13, 1902, where the trade edition is listed as also available in three-quarters morocco. The London (Heinemann) edition advertised as though published Ath Feb. 21, 1903; listed Ath Feb. 21, 1903.

AAS (large paper)   BA (trade)   H (trade)   NYPL (large paper)   UV (trade)

11281. The Lanier Book   Selections in Prose and Verse from the Writings of Sidney Lanier   Edited by Mary E. Burt . . .

New York   Charles Scribner's Sons   1904

Reprint save for the following:

"The Story of a Proverb," pp. 3-19.

"The Story of King Arthur," pp. 23-35.

"Fame," p. 49.

Note: A copy at NYPL (inscribed by Mary Day Lanier, Christmas, 1904) has some handwritten corrections. In all examined copies of the 1904 printing the errors are present; some of the corrections were incorporated in a printing dated 1914.

Deposited Aug. 26, 1904. Published Aug. 26, 1904 (publisher's records). Listed PW Nov. 12, 1904.

B   LC   NYPL

11282. Some Reminiscences and Early Letters of Sidney Lanier by George Herbert Clarke . . .

Macon, Georgia   The J. W. Burke Company
1907

Printed paper wrapper; and, cloth.

In addition to letters, contains "To G. H.," pp.
17-18. Collected in *Centennial Edition,* Vol. 1.

Reprinted and reissued without imprint on title-
page.

Listed PW Oct. 19, 1907, in both cloth and
paper. Deposited April 29, 1908.

B   H   NYPL   Y

11283. POEM OUTLINES ...

NEW YORK   CHARLES SCRIBNER'S SONS   MDCC-
CCVIII

⟨i⟩-⟨viii⟩, 1-120. 7½" x 5¼".

⟨1-8⟩⁸.

V cloth: green. Top edges gilded. Ribbon
marker.

On copyright page: *Published September, 1908*
Noted for *next week* PW Sept. 19, 1908. Deposited Sept. 23, 1908. A copy at NYPL received
Sept. 25, 1908. Published Sept. 26, 1908 (publisher's records). Listed PW Oct. 3, 1908.

AAS   B   BA   H   NYPL

11284. Poems of Sidney Lanier Edited by His
Wife ... New Edition

New York   Charles Scribner's Sons   1916

Reprint save for:

"Our Hills," p. 222.

"Laughter in the Senate," p. 223.

First Issue

The table of contents printed from the unaltered plates of an earlier edition. "Our Hills"
and "Laughter in the Senate" not listed. Pp.
vii-⟨x⟩ (leaves ⟨1⟩₅₋₆) integral parts of gathering ⟨1⟩; not cancels. *Not seen; postulated only.*

Second Issue

Table of contents printed from the altered
plates of an earlier edition. "Our Hills" and
"Laughter in the Senate" listed on p. viii. Pp.
vii-⟨x⟩ (leaves ⟨1⟩₅₋₆) present as singleton cancels. The only located copy is bound in green
V cloth with a floral decoration goldstamped
on the front cover. This same style of binding
also on certain printings issued prior to this
extended edition of 1916.

Third Issue

Table of contents printed from the altered
plates of an earlier edition. "Our Hills" and

"Laughter in the Senate" listed on p. viii. Pp.
⟨iii⟩-⟨x⟩ (leaves ⟨1⟩₅₋₆ and their conjugates are
cancels, printed on paper somewhat different
from that in the rest of the book. Bound
in green T cloth, the front cover goldstamped
SIDNEY / LANIER within a goldstamped wreath.
Perhaps bound at some time after first publication of this extended edition of 1916. Two
copies received by H on April 5, 1918. This same
binding noted on the printings issued 1918,
1920, 1925.

Reprints were issued under date 1918, 1920,
1925. For earlier editions see under 1884, 1891.

AAS (3d)   H (2d, 3d)   JH (3d)

11285. Stratford on the Potomac by Ethel Armes
and Address on Robert E. Lee by Sidney
Lanier

Publishers William Alexander Jr. Chapter
United Daughters of the Confederacy Greenwich, Connecticut   MCMXXVIII

Printed paper wrapper; halftone illustration
pasted to front.

"Robert E. Lee in Memoriam," pp. 5-8. Collected in *Centennial Edition,* Vol. 5.

Deposited Nov. 15, 1928.

H   JH   NYPL   UV

11286. A Lost Occasional Poem by Sidney
Lanier by Charles Francis Bopes   Reprinted
from American Literature, Vol. 5, No. 3, November 1933

⟨n.p., Durham, N. C., 1933⟩

Cover-title. Single leaf folded to make four
pages.

Contains "To Lillian." Collected as No. 39 of
"Poem Outlines" in *Centennial Edition,* Vol. 1.

Y

11287. Father Tabb   Poet   Priest   Soldier   Wit
Memories and Impressions of a Personal
Friend ⟨by⟩ Gordon Blair

Richmond, Virginia   The Press of Whittet &
Shepperson   MCMXL

Boards, cloth shelfback, paper label on spine.

"Letters from Sidney Lanier," pp. 55-65.

H   NYPL

11288. LETTERS   SIDNEY LANIER TO
COL. JOHN G. JAMES

THE MIRIAM LUTCHER STARK LIBRARY   THE
UNIVERSITY OF TEXAS AUSTIN, TEXAS   1942

Title-page in black and green.

Edited by Margaret Lee Wiley.

⟨i-iv⟩, ⟨i⟩-⟨xviii⟩, 1-15; blank, p. ⟨16⟩; colophon, p. ⟨17⟩; 4 blank leaves. Half-tone portrait tipped to p. ⟨v⟩; facsimile letter inserted, the blank conjugate being between pp. ⟨18-19⟩; other illustrations in text. Laid paper. 8$\frac{7}{16}$" x 5$\frac{3}{16}$".

⟨1-2⟩^{12}.

Flexible boards pasted to ⟨1⟩$_1$ and ⟨2⟩$_{12}$. Printed green laid paper wrapper.

"One hundred and sixty-five copies . . ."—Colophon.

H   UV   Y

11289. ⟨Works⟩ Centennial Edition . . .

   Baltimore   The Johns Hopkins Press   1945

10 Vols. Contains much material here first collected or published.

1: Poems and Poem Outlines Edited by Charles R. Anderson

2: The Science of English Verse and Essays on Music Edited by Paull Franklin Baum

3: Shakspere and His Forerunners Edited by Kemp Malone

4: The English Novel and Essays on Literature Edited by Clarence Gohdes and Kemp Malone

5: Tiger-Lilies and Southern Prose Edited by Garland Greever Assisted by Cecil Abernethy

6: Florida and Miscellaneous Prose Bibliography Edited by Philip Graham

7: Letters 1857–1868 Edited by Charles R. Anderson and Aubrey H. Starke

8: Letters 1869–1873 Edited by Charles R. Anderson and Aubrey H. Starke

9: Letters 1874–1877 Edited by Charles R. Anderson and Aubrey H. Starke

10: Letters 1878–1881 Appendices, Calendar, and Index Edited by Charles R. Anderson and Aubrey H. Starke

All volumes deposited May 3, 1946.

B   H   LC

SIDNEY CLOPTON LANIER

SECTION II

Collections of reprinted material issued under Lanier's name; separate editions (*i.e.,* pieces reprinted from Lanier's own books). For sheet music (with text reprinted from Lanier's own books) see *Section III*. For a list of books by authors other than Lanier containing reprinted Lanier material see *Section IV*.

11290. Some Highways and Byways of American Travel. By Edward Strahan, Sidney Lanier, Edward A. Pollard, and Others . . .

Philadelphia J. B. Lippincott & Co. 1878.

Contains two extracts from *Florida . . .* , 1876. Listed as an American publication PC Dec. 31, 1877; advertised by Trübner as an importation Bkr July, 1878.

11291. Knightly Legends of Wales or the Boy's Mabinogion . . . Edited . . . by Sidney Lanier . . .

New York Charles Scribner's Sons 1884

Reprint of *The Boy's Mabinogion,* 1881. Deposited for copyright Oct. 13, 1884. Listed PW Dec. 20, 1884.

11292. Poems of Sidney Lanier Edited by His Wife . . . New Edition

New York Charles Scribner's Sons 1894

Apparently a reprint of the 1891 edition. The following are reprints: 1896, 1897, 1899, 1900, 1903, 1904, 1908, 1910, 1912, 1913. The 1912 "printing" has been seen with cancel title-leaf only; presumably the sheets of an earlier printing with altered title-page. The "new edition" issued under the imprint of Arthur F. Bird, London, 1906, is a reprint.

11293. Select Poems . . . Edited with an Introduction, Notes, and Bibliography by Morgan Callaway, Jr. . . .

New York Charles Scribner's Sons 1895

Deposited Jan. 22, 1895. Published Jan. 22, 1895 (publisher's records). Reprinted and reissued under date ⟨1895⟩.

11294. Select Poems of Sidney Lanier Edited . . . by Morgan Callaway, Jr. . . .

New York Charles Scribner's Sons 1906

Reprint of the preceding. Here listed only for the record since this 1906 printing is listed in the bibliography of the *Centennial Edition,* 1945, Vol. 6, p. 380.

11295. Hymns of the Marshes . . .

Charles Scribner's Sons New York MCMVII

Advertised PW Sept. 28, 1907. Deposited Nov. 13, 1907. Noted as *just ready* PW Nov. 16, 1907. Listed PW Dec. 7, 1907.

11296. Selections from Sidney Lanier Prose and Verse . . . Edited by Henry W. Lanier

Charles Scribner's Sons New York Chicago Boston ⟨1916⟩

The first printing has code letter *A* on the copyright page. Deposited March 3, 1916.

11297. Selected Poems . . . with a Preface by Stark Young

Charles Scribner's Sons, New York . . . London 1947

The first printing has code letter *A* on the copyright page. Deposited Nov. 14, 1947.

11298. The Marshes of Glynn . . . a Photographic Interpretation by Mose Daniels

Duell, Sloan and Pearce New York ⟨1949⟩

Published Nov. 18, 1949 (publisher's statement). Deposited Nov. 30, 1949.

11299. The Marshes of Glynn . . .

Darien, Georgia The Ashantilly Press 1957

Printed paper wrapper. Deposited Dec. 4, 1957.

SIDNEY CLOPTON LANIER

SECTION III

Sheet Music

Text reprinted from Lanier's books. For musical compositions by Lanier see in list of *References and Ana,* below. See entry No. 11243.

A Ballad of Trees and the Master ... Music by Francis Urban ...

Baltimore. Otto Sutro & Co. 207 W. Baltimore St. ... 1886 ...

Cover-title. Reprinted from *Poems,* 1884. Two states (printings?) noted; 1: No permission notice at foot of p. 3; 2: At foot of p. 3 is the following notice: *By Permission of the Publishers of Sidney Lanier's Poems.*

Other and later settings noted:

Music by G. W. Chadwick, 1899.

----- Janie Alexander Patterson, 1917.

----- H. Alexander Matthews, 1921.

----- H. W. Dyckman, 1924.

Also issued under the title "Into the Woods My Master Went"; the following settings noted:

Music by Daniel Protheroe, 1908

----- David E. Roberts, 1918.

----- George B. Nevin, 1926.

----- T. Tertius Noble, 1926.

----- Carrie B. Adams, 1931.

----- Arthur Shepherd, 1935.

----- Frances McCollin, 1940.

----- Harry Rowe Shelley, 1940.

... A Sunset Song ... Music by Grace Worcester Root.

Chicago ... Clayton F. Summy. 174-176 Wabash Ave. ... 1891 ...

Cover-title. At head of title: *To Eleanor Smith.* Plate number: CFS 101. Otherwise "Evening Song," *Poems,* 1884.

Also issued under the title "Evening Song," the following noted:

Music by Eleanor Everest Freer, 1907.

----- Henry Hadley, 1911.

----- Maurice B. DePackh, 1927.

Also issued under the title "Look off, Dear Love," the following noted:

Music by James H. Rogers, 1899.

----- Gladys Pettit Bumstead, 1927.

Also issued under the title "A Love Song," music by Reginald de Koven, 1896.

3 Songs ... Set to Music by K. Hill.

Riga, P. Neldner. ⟨n.d., 1891?⟩

Cover-title. Plate numbers P.N. 50. R; P.N. 51. R; P.N. 52. R. "Marie," pp. 9-11; otherwise "Song for *The Jacquerie,*" beginning *May the maiden ... , Poems,* 1884. For another setting see below under 1897.

... A Love Song ...

New York ... ⟨1896⟩

See "A Sunset Song," 1891, above.

... May the Maiden ...

... 1897 ... New York G. Schirmer

Cover-title. At head of title: *Reginald de Koven* Plate number 13241. Otherwise "Song for *The Jacquerie,*" beginning *May the maiden ... , Poems,* 1884. For an earlier setting see 3 *Songs ... ,* n.d., 1891?, above.

Another setting, by John A. Carpenter, published 1912.

Look off, Dear Love ...

... New York ... ⟨1899⟩

See "A Sunset Song," 1891, above.

... Rose Moral No 1 ⟨*i.e.,* No. 2⟩ ... Music by Harriet Ware ...

⟨n.p., New York⟩ ... MCMI ... T. B. Harms & Co. ...

The above on p. 2. At head of title: *Dedicated to Mr. Edward W. Strong.* Deposited for copyright April 5, 1901. Reprinted from *Poems,* 1877. See next two entries.

... Rose Moral No 2 ⟨*i.e.,* No. 1⟩ ... Music by Harriet Ware ...

⟨n.p., New York⟩ ... MCMI ... T. B. Harms & Co. ...

The above on p. 2. At head of title: *Dedicated to Mrs. Amelia Calkins.* Deposited for copyright April 5, 1901. Reprinted from *Poems,* 1877. See preceding entry; see next entry.

... Rose Morals ...

Boston, C. W. Thompson & Co. 13 West St. ⟨1903⟩

Cover-title. At head of title: *Songs ⟨by⟩ Harriet Priscilla Sawyer* ... Plate number 977-3. Deposited for copyright Aug. 1, 1903. Reprinted from *Poems,* 1877. See preceding two entries.

... Thou and I ... Music by Willis H. Alling ...

The William Maxwell Music Co. 8 East Sixteenth Street, New York. ⟨1902⟩

Cover-title. At head of title: 2 clefs. Plate number (in key of G printing) 519-3. Also issued in key of B; plate number 518-3. De-

posited (key of B) Oct. 23, 1902. Reprinted from *Poems,* 1891.

Also a setting by Clara Bell Palmer, New York ⟨1902⟩.

...Evening Song ...

... Milwaukee ... ⟨1907⟩

See "A Sunset Song," 1891, above.

... Into the Woods My Master Went ...

... 1908 ...

See "A Ballad of Trees and the Master," 1886, above.

...A Song of the Future for Double Chorus ... Music by Philip James

New York: The H. W. Gray Co., Sole Agents for Novello & Co., Limited: London ... 1923 ...

At head of title: *N° 254 Modern Series* ...

Reprinted from *Poems,* 1884.

SIDNEY CLOPTON LANIER

SECTION IV

IN THIS SECTION are listed books by authors other than Lanier which contain material by him reprinted from earlier books. See *Section II* for collections of reprinted material issued under Lanier's name; and, separate editions.

Star Selections, 1876 ... by Professor J. E. Goodrich.

New York ... 1877.

For comment see entry No. 10432.

Poems of Places Edited by Henry W. Longfellow ... Southern States.

Boston ... 1879.

For comment see entry No. 12213.

The Cambridge Book of Poetry and Song ... by Charlotte Fiske Bates ...

New York ... ‹1882›

For comment see entry No. 7887.

Poems of American Patriotism Chosen by J. Brander Matthews

New-York Charles Scribner's Sons 1882

A copy in H received Nov. 25, 1882. Listed PW Dec. 2, 1882.

Bugle-Echoes ... Edited by Francis F. Browne

New York ... MDCCCLXXXVI

For comment see BAL, Vol. 1, p. 75. "The Tournament," pp. 328-329 extracted from "Psalm of the West," *Poems,* 1877.

Poems of Wild Life ... Edited by Charles G. D. Roberts ...

London ... 1888

For comment see BAL, Vol. 1, p. 380.

American Sonnets. Selected ... by William Sharp.

London ... ‹n.d., 1889›

For comment see BAL, Vol. 3, p. 101.

... Harper's Fifth Reader American Authors

New York ... 1889

For comment see entry No. 7917.

Franklin Square Song Collection ... No. 6 ...

New York ... ‹1889›

For comment see entry No. 9019. "The Trees and the Master," p. 15; otherwise "A Ballad of Trees and the Master," *Poems,* 1884.

American Sonnets Selected ... by T. W. Higginson and E. H. Bigelow

Boston ... 1890

For comment see entry No. 8373.

Representative Sonnets by American Poets ... by Charles H. Crandall

Boston ... 1890

For comment see entry No. 8374.

Younger American Poets ... Edited by Douglas Sladen ...

... London ... 1891

For comment see entry No. 6557.

Younger American Poets ... Edited by Douglas Sladen ...

... New York 1891

For comment see entry No. 6558.

Werner's Readings and Recitations. No. 5 ... Compiled ... by Sara Sigourney Rice.

New York ... 1891.

For comment see entry No. 3433.

Christopher Columbus and His Monument Columbia ... Compiled by J. M. Dickey.

Chicago ... 1892.

For fuller entry see BAL, Vol. 2, p. 391.

The Lover's Year-Book of Poetry ‹Second Series› ... Married-Life and Child-Life ‹Compiled› by Horace Parker Chandler ...

Boston ... 1893

For comment see entry No. 10903. "With a Rose," Vol. 2, p. 63; otherwise "To ———, with a Rose," *Poems,* 1877.

Through Love to Light   A Selection ... by John White Chadwick and Annie Hathaway Chadwick

> Boston ... 1896
>
> For comment see entry No. 2633.

Songs of the South   Choice Selections from Southern Poets ... Edited by Jennie Thornley Clarke ... Introduction by Joel Chandler Harris ...

> Philadelphia   J. B. Lippincott Company 1896
>
> Two formats issued: *Trade edition:* Top edges plain. Leaf $7^{11}/_{16}''$ x $4^{7}/_{8}''$. *Limited edition:* Top edges gilded. Leaf $7^{15}/_{16}''$ x $5^{1}/_{8}''$. Limited to 250 copies. Listed (presumably the trade edition) PW Dec. 5, 1896; PC Dec. 26, 1896.

Later American Poems Edited by J. E. Wetherell ...

> Toronto: The Copp, Clark Company, Limited. 1896.

The Treasury of American Sacred Song ... Edited by W. Garrett Horder ...

> London ... 1896
>
> For fuller entry see in Larcom, Section 3.

The International Library of Famous Literature ... Compiled ... by Nathan Haskell Dole, Forrest Morgan and Caroline Ticknor ... in Twenty Volumes ...

> New York   Merrill and Baker Publishers ⟨1898⟩
>
> For comment see in Sarah Orne Jewett reprints.

The International Library of Famous Literature ... Edited by Dr. Richard Garnett ... in Twenty Volumes ...

> London   Issued by The Standard   1899
>
> For comment see entry No. 10638.

Poets of the South   A Series of Biographical and Critical Studies with Typical Poems, Annotated by F. V. N. Painter ...

> New York   Cincinnati   Chicago   American Book Company ⟨1903⟩
>
> On copyright page of first printing *W. P. 1*

Three Centuries of Southern Poetry ... ⟨by⟩ Carl Holliday ...

Nashville ... ⟨1908⟩

> For fuller entry see BAL, Vol. 1, p. 101.

The Two Hundred and Sixty-Ninth Annual Record of the Ancient and Honorable Artillery Company of Massachusetts 1906–1907   Sermon by Rev. Thomas Van Ness of Boston

> 1908   The Mudge Press, Printers   55 Franklin St., Boston
>
> Printed paper wrapper. Untitled, ten lines, *Bring old Renown ...*, p. 32; extracted from "Ode to the Johns Hopkins University" in *Poems*, 1884.

Masterpieces of the Southern Poets by Walter Neale ...

> New York   The Neale Publishing Company 1912

One Hundred Choice Selections Number 40 ... Edited by Henry Gaines Hawn

> Philadelphia ... 1914
>
> For comment see BAL, Vol. 1, p. 77.

A Roycroft Anthology ... Edited by John T. Hoyle ...

> ... East Aurora, N.Y. MCMXVII
>
> For comment see entry No. 4099 (where this publication is misdated MCMVII).

American Mystical Verse ... Selected by Irene Hunter ...

> D. Appleton and Company   New York MCMXXV

The Joy of Life   An Anthology ... by E. V. Lucas ...

> ... London ⟨1927⟩
>
> For comment see in Joyce Kilmer reprints.

The Catholic Anthology by Thomas Walsh ...

> New York   The Macmillan Company 1927 ...
>
> Deposited Sept. 14, 1927.

300 Years   The Poets and Poetry of Maryland Edited by Loker Raley

> Henry Harrison   Poetry Publisher   New York ⟨1937⟩

The St. Nicholas Anthology Edited by Henry Steele Commager ...

Random House   New York ⟨1948⟩

Listed PW Nov. 20, 1948.

Gentlemen, Scholars and Scoundrels   A Treasury of the Best of Harper's Magazine from 1850 to the Present Edited by Horace Knowles

Harper & Brothers   New York ⟨1959⟩

REFERENCES AND ANA

Sidney Lanier.

⟨n.p., n.d., probably Baltimore, Md., 1881⟩

Cover-title. Printed self-wrapper. Pp. 15. Inserted in some copies of *Sketch of the Life of J. F. D. Lanier ... Second Edition,* 1877. Report of a memorial meeting held at Johns Hopkins University, Oct. 22, 1881.

Il Balen (from Il Trovatore.) Air and Variation for Flute, with Piano Accompaniment, by the Late Sidney Lanier ...

Copyright 1883 by A. G. Badger.

Sheet music. Cover-title.

... Love That Hath Us in the Net. Words by Tennyson. Music by ... Sidney Lanier ...

New Orleans: Published by A. E. Blackmar & Co. 220 Camp St. ⟨1884⟩

Sheet music. Cover-title. At head of title: *A Little Song Gem.* Plate No. 1435.2. *Not seen.* Entry on basis of photostatic copy in JH.

Sidney Lanier. A Paper by ... Merrill E. Gates ...

From the Presbyterian Review for October, 1887.

Cover-title. Printed paper wrapper.

The Forty-Sixth Birthday of Sidney Lanier ...

Publication Agency of the Johns Hopkins University Baltimore 1888

Cover-title: A Memorial of Sidney Lanier

Printed paper wrapper.

A Brief Sketch of the Life and Writings of Sidney Lanier. By Charles N. West ...

Savannah, Ga. Townsend, Printer and Binder. 1888.

Printed paper wrapper.

From Dixie. Original Articles ... ⟨Edited by Kate Pleasants Mimor⟩

Richmond, Va. ... MDCCCXCIII.

For comment see entry No. 458. "To Lucie," p. ⟨39⟩ is not by Lanier. In Mrs. Lanier's copy (at JH) is the following note in her hand: "The verses *To Lucie* were contributed under a misapprehension ..." The poem was written by Frances Litchfield Turnbull.

Sidney Lanier by Edwin Mims ...

Boston and New York   Houghton, Mifflin and Company   The Riverside Press, Cambridge 1905

Two formats issued: *Trade edition:* Cloth, goldstamped; top edges gilded, otherwise rough trimmed. Leaf: 7⅜″ x 5″. *Limited edition:* Cloth, printed paper label on spine. Wholly untrimmed. Leaf: 7⅝″ x 5″ full. ".. One Hundred and Fifty Copies ... Wholly Uncut with Paper Label."—Certificate of issue.

... Sidney Lanier by Henry Nelson Snyder

New York: Eaton & Mains   Cincinnati: Jennings & Graham ⟨1906⟩

At head of title: Modern Poets and Christian Teaching   "This volume is not to be received as a biography of Sidney Lanier. It is rather an attempt to interpret ... the message of the man and his works ..."—p. 7.

Sidney Lanier at Rockingham Springs   Where and How the "Science of English Verse" Was Written ... by John W. Wayland ...

Ruebush-Elkins Co.   Dayton, Va.   1912

Fifteen Minutes with Sidney Lanier   A Paper Read Feb. 10, 1903, on the Occasion of Unveiling a Bust of the Poet at Tulane University, New Orleans by Gustaf R. Westfeldt

⟨New Orleans, 1915⟩

Printed paper wrapper.

Sidney Lanier   Musician, Poet   Soldier by E. Dorothy Blount Lamar

Published at Macon, Georgia by the J. W. Burke Company   Nineteen Hundred and Twenty-Two

Printed paper wrapper.

Sidney Lanier   A Study in Personality ... by Thomas Edwin Spencer

Printed for the Author   1930   Saint Louis, Missouri

Printed paper wrapper. "... Prepared for the Schoolmasters' Club, of St. Louis, in 1911 ..." —p. ⟨ii⟩. 100 numbered copies.

A Commencement Address by Sidney Lanier by Jay B. Hubbell

Reprinted from American Literature, Vol. II, No. 4, January, 1931

Cover-title. Printed paper wrapper. For an earlier printing of the address here discussed and reprinted see above: *Catalogue of the Trustees, Faculty, Alumnae and Students of Furlow Masonic Female College* ... , 1869.

Poems of Trees A Sidney Lanier Memorial ⟨Vol. 1⟩ ⟨Edited by Wightman F. Melton⟩

Banner Press Emory University Georgia ⟨1932⟩

Boards, cloth shelfback. Seven succeeding volumes (with varying imprints) were issued 1933–1939.

A collection of poems, by various authors, issued as a memorial.

Sidney Lanier in Texas by John S. Mayfield With an Introductory Note by the Late George Edward Woodberry

Dallas: The Boyd Press MCMXXXII

Black leather-grained boards folded over stiff black inner paper covers; printed label on front. 119 copies only.

A Humorous Quatrain by Lanier by John Howard Birss

Reprinted from American Literature, Vol. 5, No. 3, November 1933

Cover-title. Single leaf folded to make four pages. Reprints "A Weather-Vane." See *The Dial of the Old South Clock* ... , 1877, above.

Sidney Lanier A Biographical and Critical Study by Aubrey Harrison Starke ...

Chapel Hill The University of North Carolina Press 1933

Sidney Lanier's Immoral Bird by John S. Mayfield

H. E. Pickersgill Perth Amboy, N. J. 1935

Cover-title. Printed paper wrapper. "... First published in the May–June, 1935 issue of *The American Book Collector* ... Thirty-five separate reprints have been made. This is number --"—Certificate of issue.

Some New Facts Concerning Sidney Lanier in Florida by John S. Mayfield

Reprinted from The Johns Hopkins Alumni Magazine Vol. XXIV, No. 1, November, 1935

Cover-title. Printed paper wrapper.

The Life of Sidney Lanier by Lincoln Lorenz

1935 Coward-McCann, Inc. New York

Contains the first appearance of "To Mrs. S. C. Bird," p. 208. Collected in *Centennial Edition,* Vol. 1.

An Uncollected Sonnet by Lanier by Aubrey Starke

Reprinted from American Literature, Vol. 7, No. 4, January, 1936

Cover-title. Printed self-wrapper. Reprints a "Sonnet," anonymous, from the *Southern Literary Messenger* of May, 1862. For a comment, casting doubt on the ascription to Lanier, see *Centennial Edition,* Vol. 1, pp. lxxxix-xc.

Sidney Lanier at Oglethorpe University by Leola Selman Beeson ...

Macon, Georgia The J. W. Burke Company 1936

150 copies only.

Sidney Lanier by William Lyon Phelps ...

John S. Mayfield Washington, District of Columbia MCMXXXVII

Printed paper wrapper.

A Concordance to the Poems of Sidney Lanier Including the Poem Outlines and Certain Uncollected Items ⟨by⟩ Philip Graham and Joseph Jones

The University of Texas Press Austin 1939

Sidney Lanier Poet and Prosodist ⟨by⟩ Richard Webb and Edwin R. Coulson

Athens The University of Georgia Press 1941

... Florida and Miscellaneous Prose Bibliography Edited by Philip Graham

Baltimore The Johns Hopkins Press 1945

At head of title: Centennial Edition Volume VI ...

Bibliography, pp. 379-412.

See entry No. 11289.

The Hall of Fame for Great Americans on the Campus of New York University Unveiling of the Bust and Tablet for Sidney Lanier in the Auditorium of the Library of the University University Heights, New York City October 3, 1946 ...

‹New York: The Marchbanks Press, 1946›

Cover-title. Printed self-wrapper. Issued as a program.

Sidney Lanier   The Poet of the South by Allen P. Tankersley   Prepared Especially for the School Children of Georgia Who Will Participate in the U.D.C. Historical Essay Contest in 1954.

‹Athens, Ga.: Speering Printing Co., 1954›

Caption-title. Printed self-wrapper.

Sidney Lanier's *Tiger-Lilies:* A Bibliographical Mystery by John S. Mayfield . . .

Syracuse University Library Associates   1964

Printed paper wrapper.

LUCY LARCOM

1 8 2 4 — 1 8 9 3

11300. Oh Why Art Thou Roaming ... Worbs ⟨*sic*⟩ by Miss Lucy Larcom. Music by Louis Strack

Boston ... Oliver Ditson 115 Washington St. ... 1847 ...

Sheet music. The above on p. ⟨1⟩. Plate number: 1268. Printed on a single sheet, folded to 4 pp. Outer side blank. Words and music on inner side, paged ⟨1⟩-2.

AAS B

11301. The Female Poets of America. By Rufus Wilmot Griswold ...

Philadelphia: Carey and Hart, Chesnut Street. MDCCCXLIX.

"Elisha and the Angels," p. 360; "The Burning Prairie," p. 361.

For fuller comment see entry No. 6681.

11302. SIMILITUDES ...

BOSTON: JOHN P. JEWETT AND COMPANY. CLEVELAND, OHIO: JEWETT, PROCTOR, AND WORTHINGTON. 1854.

⟨1⟩-103; blank leaf; leaf excised or pasted under the end paper. Illustrated. 6½″ x 4⅜″.

⟨1-2⟩, 3-6⁸, 7², ⟨8⟩⁴. Leaf ⟨8⟩₄ excised or pasted under the end paper. *Note:* It is probable that 7 is in fact 2 singletons.

Two styles of binding have been noted. The sequence (if any) has not been determined and the designations are for identification only.

A

A cloth: red. T cloth: blue; green; red. Sides blindstamped with a triple rule frame; within the frame, also blindstamped, at top and bottom, an ornament composed of ribbons and florets. Note that the ornaments do not touch the cartouche. Goldstamped at center is a cartouche enclosing the goldstamped title: SIMILITUDES. All the preceding save for the lettering, which is not present, repeated in blind on the back cover. All edges plain. Also, all edges gilded. Off-white end papers. Flyleaf at front.

B

T cloth: blue. Sides blindstamped with a triple rule frame; within the frame, also blindstamped, at top and at bottom, an ornament composed of rococo arcs, leaves, florets. The ornaments virtually touch the cartouche. Goldstamped at center is a cartouche enclosing the goldstamped title: SIMILITUDES. All the preceding, save for the lettering which is not present, repeated in blind on the back cover. All edges plain. Off-white end papers. Flyleaf at front.

Listed NLG Nov. 15, 1853. AAS copy (Binding A) inscribed by the publisher Nov. 1853. The London (Low) importation listed PC Feb. 1, 1854.

Reprinted from the original plates and issued with the imprint: Boston: Henry Hoyt, No. 9 Cornhill. ⟨n.d.⟩.

AAS (A) B (A) BA (B) H (A) NYPL (A) Y (A)

11303. CALL TO KANSAS.

According to a note in *Printing A,* dated March 13, 1855, Lucy Larcom was awarded a prize "for the best Song suited for Kanzas Immigrants" in a contest sponsored by the New England Emigrant Aid Co. Her "Call to Kanzas" was published in various forms by several publishers. The following have been noted, and it is reasonable to suppose that the following list is incomplete. BAL has been unable to determine a sequence. The designations are for identification only.

A

THE KANZAS PRIZE SONG ... CALL TO KANZAS ...

⟨BOSTON: NEW ENGLAND EMIGRANT AID CO., 1855⟩

Single leaf. Printed on recto only. 8½″ full x 5⅜″. Preceding the text is a note, *March 13th, 1855,* signed *Thomas H. Webb, Sec'y N. E. Emigrant Aid Co. No. 3 Winter Street.*

B

The Kansas Call . . . Music by E. Ives Jr. . . .

New-York . . . S. T. Gordon, 297 Broadway . . . 1855 . . .

Not seen.

Sheet music. Cover-title. At head of p. 3: *The Kansa's Call* ⟨sic⟩ On cover: LARCON *for* LARCOM.

C

Kanzas Prize Song . . . Music by E. Norman, Jr.

Boston: Published by C. C. Mead, 91 Washington Street . . . 1855 . . .

Sheet music. Cover-title.

D

. . . Kanzas Prize Song . . .

Entered . . . 1855, by G. Adams, in the Clerk's Office of the District Court of the District of Massachusetts.

Not seen.

At head of title: . . . Music by E. Norman, Jr.

Printed on cloth. Printed on recto only. "They ⟨Lucy Larcom's words⟩ were printed, with the appropriate music of Mr. E. Norman, on cotton handkerchiefs, which were given away by the thousand."—Addison, p. 62.

Deposited May 1, 1855.

E

Lays of the Emigrants, as Sung by the Parties for Kanzas, on the Days of Their Departure from Boston, during the Spring of 1855.

Boston: Alfred Mudge & Son, Printers, 1855.

Single cut sheet folded to make four pages. P. ⟨1⟩ as above.

Three editions noted. The sequence is not known and the designations are for identification only.

Ea

"Call to Kanzas," by Larcom, pp. 2-3; "Stand by the Right! . . ." by J. R. Orton, p. 4.

Eb

"Call to Kanzas," by Larcom, pp. ⟨2⟩-3; "Rallying Song for Kanzas Emigrants," anonymous, pp. 3-4; "Kanzas Rally," anonymous, p. 4.

Ec

"Call to Kanzas," by Larcom, pp. 2-3; "The Kanzas Emigrant's Song," anonymous, pp. 3-4.

B (C) EM (Ea, Eb, Ec) H (A) K (B, D) Y (Ec)

11304. The Ladies' Wreath and Parlor Annual.

New York: Burdick and Scovill, No. 8 Spruce Street. ⟨n.d., 1856⟩

Cloth. Also issued in leather? Printed from the altered plates of *The Ladies' Wreath*, New York, a monthly magazine.

"Bethany," pp. 217-218.

"Elijah in the Desert," pp. 272-273.

"Our Father's House," pp. 281-282.

H

11305. The Ladies' Wreath and Parlor Annual.

New York: Burdick and Scovill, No. 8 Spruce Street. ⟨n.d., 1856? 1857?⟩

Cloth. Also issued in leather? Printed from the altered plates of *The Ladies' Wreath*, New York, a monthly magazine. The volume retains the original pagination of the periodical printing: ⟨9⟩-⟨220⟩; ⟨9⟩-220.

"The Mists and the Mountain. An Allegory," pp. ⟨128⟩-130.

"Three Sonnets," p. 162.

"Expostulation," p. 38 of the 2nd part.

"To My Thoughts," p. 76 of the 2nd part.

"Hand in Hand with Angels," pp. 157-158 of the 2nd part. Also appears in *The Psalms of Life* . . . ⟨1857⟩; see next entry. Collected in *Poems*, 1869.

"The Mullen," pp. 217-218 of the 2nd part.

B

11306. The Psalms of Life: A Compilation of Psalms, Hymns, Chants, Anthems, &c. . . . ⟨Compiled⟩ by John S. Adams . . .

Boston: Published by Oliver Ditson & Co. New York . . . Philadelphia . . . Cincinnati . . . ⟨1857⟩

"Hand in Hand with Angels," p. 155. Also in (reprinted from?) *The Ladies' Wreath and Parlor Annual* ⟨1856? 1857?⟩; see preceding entry. Collected in *Poems*, 1869.

Listed (as a Ditson publication) APC Feb. 7, 1857. Also issued (reissued?) with the imprint: *Boston: Published by Bela Marsh, 15 Franklin Street.* ⟨*1857*⟩

H

THE KANZAS PRIZE SONG.

To Miss Lucy Larcom, of Beverly, was awarded, for the subjoined production, the premium of Fifty Dollars, which one of our liberal minded fellow citizens authorized me to offer for the best Song suited for Kanzas Immigrants.

There were eighty-eight competitors; and as some of their productions are very acceptable, they will from time to time be published, as successive Parties leave for the Territory.

THOMAS H. WEBB,
SEC'Y N. E. EMIGRANT AID Co.

MARCH 13th, 1855.

No. 3 Winter Street.

CALL TO KANZAS.

BY LUCY LARCOM.

(Air,— *Nelly Bly.*)

Yoemen strong, hither throng!
  Nature's honest men,
We will make the wilderness
  Bud and bloom again.
Bring the sickle, speed the plough,
  Turn the ready soil!
Freedom is the noblest pay
  For the true man's toil.
Ho! brothers! come, brothers!
  Hasten all with me,
We'll sing upon the Kanzas plains
  A song of Liberty!

Father, haste! o'er the waste
  Lies a pleasant land,
There your fire-side altar stones
  Fixed in truth shall stand.
There your sons, brave and good,
  Shall to freemen grow,
Clad in triple mail of Right,
  Wrong to overthrow
Ho! brothers! come, brothers!
  Hasten all with me,
We'll sing upon the Kanzas plains
  A song of Liberty.

Mother, come! here's a home
  In the waiting West.
Bring the seeds of love and peace
  You who sow them best.
Faithful hearts, holy prayers,
  Keep from taint the air,

Soil a mother's tears have wet,
  Golden crops shall bear.
Come, mother! fond mother,
  List! we call to thee,
We'll sing upon the Kanzas plains,
  A song of Liberty.

Brother brave, stem the wave!
  Firm the prairies tread!
Up the dark Missouri flood
  Be your canvas spread.
Sister true, join us too
  Where the Kanzas flows.
Let the Northern lily bloom
  With the Southern rose.
Brave brother, true sister,
  List! we call to thee,
We'll sing upon the Kanzas plains,
  A song of Liberty.

One and all, hear our call
  Echo through the land!
Aid us with the willing heart
  And the strong right hand!
Feed the spark, the Pilgrims struck
  On old Plymouth Rock!
To the watch-fires of the free
  Millions glad shall flock.
Ho! brothers! come, brothers!
  Hasten all with me,
We'll sing upon the Kanzas plains,
  A song of Liberty.

11307. The Ladies' Wreath and Parlor Annual.

New York: Burdick and Scovill, No. 8 Spruce Street ⟨n.d., 1857⟩

Cloth? Leather? Printed from the altered plates of *The Ladies' Wreath*, New York, a monthly magazine. The volume retains the original pagination of the periodical printing: 220; 214. Also occurs (reissue?) with the following imprint: *New York: John F. Scovill, No. 8 Spruce Street ⟨n.d.⟩*.

"Living and Loving," p. ⟨12⟩.

NYPL

11308. The Ladies' Wreath and Parlor Annual.

New York: Burdick and Scovill, No. 8 Spruce Street ⟨n.d., 1857?⟩

Cloth. Also issued in leather? Printed from the altered plates of *The Ladies' Wreath*, New York, a monthly magazine.

"Is All Vanity?," p. 64.

"The Bird of Hope," p. 85.

"The Three Gifts," pp. ⟨127⟩-128. Collected in *Ships in the Mist* ⟨1860⟩.

"Angel Guardianship," pp. 416-417.

H

11309. LOTTIE'S THOUGHT-BOOK.

PHILADELPHIA: AMERICAN SUNDAY-SCHOOL UN-ION, NO. 1122 CHESTNUT STREET. NEW YORK NO. 375 BROADWAY. ⟨1858⟩

Anonymous.

⟨1⟩-118, blank leaf. Frontispiece inserted. 6½" scant x 4⁵⁄₁₆".

⟨1⟩⁴, 2-10⁶, 11².

BD cloth: black. Pale yellow end papers. Flyleaves.

"Her next little book, *Lottie's Thought-Book*, was published by the American Sunday School Union, Philadelphia, in 1858 ..."—Addison, p. 62.

H (Inscribed by early owner, Dec. 25, 1858)

11310. Hannah's at the Window Binding Shoes ... Composed by Asa B. Hutchinson ...

Boston ... Oliver Ditson & Co 277 Washington St ... 1859 ...

Sheet music. Cover-title. Plate number: 19770.

Two printings noted:

1

At head of music, p. 3: *Words and Melody by Asa B. Hutchinson.*

2

At head of music, p. 3: *Words by Lucy Larcone ⟨sic⟩.*

Note: The earliest printing (printings?) of *Printing 1* have the figure 3½ (*i.e.*, 35¢) on front cover; later printings: Figure 4 (*i.e.*, 40¢). *Also note:* The earliest printings are from engraved plates; a quite late printing is printed from types, with typographic, not engraved, cover.

Earliest located book appearance: *Folk Songs ...*, 1861; see below. Collected in *Poems*, 1869.

AAS (1st, 2nd)   B (1st, 2nd)   H (1st, 2nd)

11311. SHIPS IN THE MIST; AND OTHER STORIES ...

BOSTON: HENRY HOYT, NO. 9 CORNHILL. ⟨1860⟩

⟨1⟩-48. Frontispiece inserted. 5¾" x 3¾".

⟨1⟩-3⁸.

BD cloth: red. T cloth: dull purple. Yellow end papers. Flyleaves.

Note: Misdated 1859 by Foley.

Listed APC and BM Dec. 15, 1860.

AAS   LC   Y

11312. Folk Songs Selected and Edited by John Williamson Palmer ...

New York: Charles Scribner, 124 Grand Street. London: Sampson Low, Son and Company. M DCCC LXI.

Noted in publisher's leather only.

"Hannah Binding Shoes," pp. 126-128. For publication as sheet music see above under 1859. Collected in *Poems*, 1869.

A copy in CH inscribed by early owner Nov. 1, 1860. Listed APC Nov. 3, 1860. Advertised APC Nov. 10, 1860, as in turkey morocco, antique morocco, morocco elegant; apparently not issued in cloth.

CH   H

11313. War Songs of the American Union ...

Boston: William V. Spencer, 94 Washington Street. ⟨1861⟩

"The Nineteenth of April, 1861," pp. 65-66. Collected in *Poems*, 1869.

For comment see entry No. 8804.

11314. LEILA AMONG THE MOUNTAINS.

BOSTON: HENRY HOYT, NO. 9 CORNHILL. ⟨1861⟩

Anonymous. Attributed to Larcom on the basis of an entry in *American Catalogue ...* , 1880; and, Foley. By Larcom?

⟨1⟩-153; 2 blank leaves; leaf excised or pasted under the end paper. Frontispiece inserted; other illustrations in text. 6⁹⁄₁₆″ x 4³⁄₁₆″.

⟨1-9⁸, 10-11⁴⟩. ⟨11⟩₄ excised or pasted under the end paper.

C cloth: purple. Peach end papers. Flyleaf at front.

Listed, as anonymous, APC May 11, 1861. A new printing listed, as anonymous, PW Oct. 24, 1874.

NYPL

11315. Songs for War Time. German Airs with English Words, for the Army, the Family and the School.

Boston: Gould and Lincoln, 59 Washington Street. 1863.

"Memorial of the Slain," pp. 12-13, a translation.

"Freedom's Morning," p. 17.

For comment see entry No. 1680.

11316. Lyrics of Loyalty Arranged and Edited by Frank Moore

New York   George P. Putnam   1864

"Christmas and New Year, 1862-3," pp. 289-291.

For comment see entry No. 1203.

11317. Over-Songs

⟨n.p., Taunton, Mass.⟩ M DCCC LXIV

"Invocation," pp. 22-23.

According to Harvard College Library catalog, edited by Abijah M. Ide.

For comment see entry No. 4289.

11318. Hymns of the Ages. Third Series.

Boston: Ticknor and Fields. 1865.

Edited by Mrs. Caroline Snowden Whitmarsh Guild and Mrs. Anne E. Guild; preface signed: *C.S.W.* and *A.E.G.*

"As Strangers and Pilgrims," pp. 138-139. Collected in *Poems,* 1869.

Announced ALG Sept. 15, 1864. Advertised as *nearly ready* ALG Nov. 1, 1864. A copy at H received from the publisher Nov. 28, 1864. Listed ALG Dec. 15, 1864.

H

11319. The Flower of Liberty.   Edited and Illustrated by Julia A. M. Furbish.

Boston: Ticknor and Fields. 1866.

"The Flag," pp. 77-78. Collected in *Poems,* 1869.

For comment see entry No. 1424.

11320. Poetry Lyrical, Narrative, and Satirical of the Civil War Selected and Edited by Richard Grant White

New York   The American News Company 119 & 121 Nassau Street   1866

"Out in the Cold," pp. 25-27.

For comment see entry No. 4604.

11321. Breathings of the Better Life. Edited by Lucy Larcom.

Boston: Ticknor and Fields. 1867.

"Prefatory," pp. ⟨iii⟩-vi.

Announced ALG May 1, 1866. Noted for December in ALG Sept. 15, 1866. Dec. 11, 1866, 2066 copies printed (publisher's records). A copy at H received from the publisher Dec. 22, 1866. Listed ALG Jan. 1, 1867. Second printing, Sept. 13, 1871. For another edition see under 1879.

AAS   B   H   Y

11322. Household Reading: Selections from The Congregationalist. 1849–1866.

Boston: Galen James & Co., 15 Cornhill. 1867.

"My Angel-Dress," pp. 86-87. Collected in *Poems,* 1869.

"What Are You Thinking About?," pp. 161-162.

"Monica and Augustine," pp. 359-361. Collected in *Poems,* 1869.

H

11323. Two Hundredth Anniversary of the First Parish, Beverly.

⟨n.p., n.d., Beverly, Mass., 1867⟩

Single cut sheet folded to make four pages. P. ⟨1⟩ as above. Issued as a program.

Untitled hymn, *The sea made music to the shore,* p. ⟨4⟩. Reprinted in *An Address Delivered in the First Parish, Beverly, October 2, 1867 ...* , by Christopher T. Thayer, Boston, 1868. Collected in the unillustrated ⟨sic⟩ edition of *The Poetical Works,* 1885, as "Hymn ... for the Two Hundredth Anniversary of the Old South Church, Beverly, Mass."

BA

11324. Brown University in the Civil War. A Memorial. ⟨Edited by Henry Sweetser Burrage⟩

Providence. 1868.

"Charles Louis Harrington. Class of 1864," pp. ⟨263⟩-267.

MHS (Inscribed by early owner March 17, 1868)

11325. Chimes for Childhood. A Collection of Songs for Little Ones. ⟨Edited by Dana Estes⟩ ...

Boston: Lee and Shepard. ⟨1868⟩

"If I Were a Sunbeam," pp. 24-25.

"The Rivulet," pp. 135-136.

Both collected in *Childhood Songs*, 1875.

Listed ALG Oct. 15, 1868.

H

11326. The National Peace Jubilee, and Musical Reporter.

Boston ... May 15, 1869 ... ⟨to⟩ July 24, 1869 ...

"Across the River," issue of July 17, 1869, p. 20. Collected in *Poems*, 1869.

For comment see entry No. 8869.

11327. POEMS ...

BOSTON: FIELDS, OSGOOD, & CO., SUCCESSORS TO TICKNOR AND FIELDS. 1869.

⟨i-ii⟩, ⟨i⟩-x, ⟨1⟩-275. Laid paper. 7" x 4½".

⟨-⟩⁶, ⟨1⟩-7, ⟨8⟩, 9-11¹², 12⁶. *Also signed:* ⟨-⟩⁶, ⟨A⟩-Q⁸, R².

C cloth: blue; brown; green; purple; purplish-brown. Brown-coated on white end papers. Laid paper flyleaves. Spine imprint: FIELDS, OSGOOD & CO. A known reprint has been seen with the FO monogram at foot of spine.

Note: Copies of the fourth printing bound after 1870 have the spine imprint: JAMES R. OSGOOD & CO.; wove paper flyleaves; or, laid paper flyleaf at front, wove paper flyleaf at back.

Also note: The period after POEMS on the title-page is lacking in all examined copies with the JAMES R. OSGOOD & CO. spine imprint.

According to the publisher's records, there were four printings dated 1869:

1st: Nov. 4, 1868, 1524 copies, bound by Nov. 13, 1868.

2nd: Dec. 23, 1868, 522 copies, bound between Dec. 29, 1868 and Jan. 4, 1869.

3rd: Jan. 28, 1869, 426 copies, bound on Feb. 6, 1869. Prior to this printing seven hours were spent correcting the plates.

4th: Aug. 11, 1869, 514 copies, bound between Oct. 14, 1869 and April 28, 1876.

BAL has been able to distinguish the following printings:

Printings 1 and 2

P. 113, line 11: *As Asgard's ...*

Printings 3 and 4

P. 113, line 11: *As at the ...* See binding notes above.

A copy of what must be the first printing presented by Larcom to Thomas Wentworth Higginson, Nov. 16, 1868; in BPL. Deposited Nov. 17, 1868. Listed ALG Dec. 1, 1868. Listed PC (but with date given as *1868*) Jan. 16, 1869.

The present entry made on the basis of copies in: AAS, BPL, H, NYPL, UV, Y.

11328. ... Berrying Song

Boston, G. D. Russell & Company   126 Tremont, opp. Park St. ... 1870 ...

Sheet music. Cover-title. At head of title: *Our Young Folks 6 Little Songs by F. Boott. Originally Published in Our Young Folks ...*

Plate number: 1964.

Collected in *Childhood Songs*, 1875.

B

11329. Ever New, and Never Old, or Twice Told Stories, by the Best Authors.

Boston: Joseph H. Allen, 1870.

"How Different Persons See the Ocean," pp. ⟨119⟩-124.

H

11330. ... Swing away ...

Boston, G. D. Russell & Company   126 Tremont, opp. Park St. ... 1870 ...

Sheet music. Cover-title. At head of title: *Our Young Folks 6 Little Songs by F. Boott. Originally Published in Our Young Folks ...*

Plate number: 1963.

Collected in *Childhood Songs*, 1875.

B

11331. The Lady's Almanac for 1872

Published by George A. Coolidge, Office of the "Old and New," 143 Washington St. Boston. ⟨1871⟩

"On the Stairway," pp. 95-96. Collected in *Childhood Songs*, 1875.

H

11332. Child Life: A Collection of Poems, Edited by John Greenleaf Whittier ...

Boston: James R. Osgood and Company, Late Ticknor & Fields, and Fields, Osgood & Co. 1872.

Cloth; and, leather.

"It is but just to acknowledge ... obligations to kind friends whose valuable suggestions have materially aided ... and, in an especial manner ... indebtedness to Lucy Larcom ... who has given ... the benefit of her cultivated taste ..." —"Preface," p. <vii>.

"In 1872, she did her first work of collaboration with Mr. Whittier. Conceiving the plan of printing a volume of poems dealing with the life of children, he secured her aid, and *Child-Life* was the first book which they produced in this way. He deferred to her judgment in the selection of the material, and, when doubtful, he always accepted her opinion ..."—Addison, pp. 175-176.

"... *Child Life* (poetry) which was the first Mr. Whittier and I compiled together ..."—From a letter, Larcom to Houghton, Mifflin & Co., Nov. 1, 1892; letter in H.

For further comment on Larcom's share in the production of this compilation see Thomas Franklin Currier's *A Bibliography of John Greenleaf Whittier,* 1937, p. 118.

Larcom's poems included herein had prior book publication. "Grace and Her Friends," pp. 48-50, had prior publication in *Poems,* 1869, under the title "Blue-Eyed Grace."

Note: The publisher's records indicate two printings were issued under date 1872; the first printed by *The Aldine Press, James Sutton & Co., New York;* the second printing done by *Welch, Bigelow & Co., Cambridge.* All copies examined by BAL have (on the copyright page) the imprint of *The Aldine Press.* Query: Do copies occur without a printer's imprint? Or, with the imprint of Welch, Bigelow & Company?

Printed Oct. 1871, 4500 copies; bound during the period Nov. 11, 1871 to March 14, 1872 (publisher's records). Also according to the publisher's records copies were bound in cloth; morocco; half calf. Deposited Nov. 17, 1871. Listed ALG Dec. 1871; PC Dec. 8, 1871. Second printing, April 10, 1872, 1010 copies (publisher's records). Third printing, Oct. 14, 1872, issued with altered date on the title-page. The London (Nisbet) edition listed Ath Dec. 6, 1873.

H

11333. Fawn Footed Nannie Composed by H. R. Palmer,

Published by John Church & Co., Cincinnati.

New-York: Wm. A. Pond & Co. Geo. F. Root & Sons, Chicago. Boston: O. Ditson & Co. <1873>

Sheet music. Cover-title.

Collected in *Childhood Songs,* 1875.

B

11334. Child Life in Prose. Edited by John Greenleaf Whittier ...

Boston: James R. Osgood and Company, Late Ticknor & Fields, and Fields, Osgood, & Co. 1874.

"How Margery Wondered," pp. 145-148.

The publisher's records show that although Whittier was paid a royalty for this book, Lucy Larcom was also paid $500 for *preparing copy.*

3520 copies printed Oct. 22, 1873 (publisher's records); bound during the period Oct. 23, 1873–Feb. 13, 1874. Listed PW Oct. 25, 1873. Deposited Oct. 29, 1873. The date on the title-page was altered for the second printing, Oct. 8, 1874 (publisher's records). The London (Book Society) edition listed Ath Jan. 31, 1880.

H   NYPL   UV

11335. CHILDHOOD SONGS ...

BOSTON: JAMES R. OSGOOD AND COMPANY, LATE TICKNOR & FIELDS, AND FIELDS, OSGOOD, & CO. 1875.

<i>-<xviii>, <19>-202, blank leaf. Illustrated. 7⅜" x 5¼" full.

<1-12⁸, 13⁴, 14²>.

FL-like cloth: brown; green; terra-cotta. S cloth: brown. Moiréd T cloth: brown. Covers bevelled. Brown-coated on white end papers. Dark green-coated on white end papers. Flyleaves. Edges gilded.

Note: The publisher's records show that 480 cancel title-pages were printed Dec. 12, 1878 and that copies on hand were issued with the altered title-leaf. The nature of the alteration has not been determined.

Printed Nov. 17, 1874 in an edition of 3000 copies (publisher's records). On Nov. 25, 1874, Whittier acknowledged receipt of a copy (Addison, p. 176). Listed PW Nov. 28, 1874.

B   BA   H   Y

11336. The Ark ...

Boston ... 1875 ...

"The Car-Horse," Vol. 1, No. 2, p. <1>.

An occasional newspaper. For comment see entry No. 281.

11337. AN IDYL OF WORK . . .

BOSTON: JAMES R. OSGOOD AND COMPANY, LATE
TICKNOR & FIELDS, AND FIELDS, OSGOOD, & CO.
1875.

⟨i⟩-⟨x⟩, ⟨11⟩-183. 6¹³⁄₁₆″ x 4½″.

⟨1-7¹², 8⁸⟩.

C cloth: green. FL-like cloth: purple. S cloth:
brown. Brown-coated on white end papers. Flyleaves.

May 29, 1875, 950 copies printed (publisher's
records). Bound June 3–Sept. 25, 1875. BPL copy
received June 5, 1875. Listed PW June 12, 1875.
The London (Trübner) importation noticed
Ath Aug. 7, 1875. Feb. 14, 1876, 280 copies
printed, presumably dated 1876.

AAS   B   BA   BPL   H   NYPL   Y

11338. Our Greeting.

June 30, Wheaton Female Seminary, Norton,
Mass. 1875.

Caption-title. The above at head of p. ⟨3⟩.
Printed self-wrapper.

An occasional newspaper. Presumably all published.

"Response of the Past to the Present," p. ⟨6⟩.
Collected as "At Norton Again" in the unillustrated ⟨sic⟩ edition of The Poetical Works,
1885.

wh

11339. Sheets for the Cradle . . .

Boston . . . 1875 . . .

"What Shall We Wrap the Baby in," Vol. 1,
No. 1, p. ⟨1⟩. Collected in the unillustrated
⟨sic⟩ edition of The Poetical Works, 1885.

An occasional newspaper. For comment see
entry No. 4048.

11340. Silhouettes and Songs Illustrative of the
Months. Twelve Designs by Helen Maria
Hinds. Edited by Edward E. Hale . . . and
Poems by John G. Whittier . . . Lucy Larcom
. . . ⟨and Others⟩

Boston: Lockwood, Brooks, & Co. 1876.

Unpaged.

Contains Larcom's "February."

For comment see entry No. 9130.

11341. Songs of Three Centuries. Edited by
John Greenleaf Whittier.

Boston: James R. Osgood and Company, Late
Ticknor & Fields, and Fields, Osgood, & Co.
1876.

Reprint save for "A Strip of Blue," pp. 274-275.
Collected in Wild Roses . . . , 1881.

Co-edited by Lucy Larcom. "It only remains for
me to acknowledge the valuable suggestions and
aid I have received . . . especially the essential
assistance I have had from Lucy Larcom . . ."
—From Whittier's "Preface," p. vi. For further
comment on Larcom's co-editorship see Thomas
Franklin Currier's A Bibliography of John
Greenleaf Whittier, 1937, pp. 131-132.

Two formats issued. The books do not bear the
following designations but are thus referred to
in contemporary listings.

HOUSEHOLD EDITION

Title-page printed in black only. Top edges
plain. Leaf: 7⅜″ x 4¾″.

According to the publisher's records there were
two printings issued under date 1876: 1st, Dec.
3, 1875, 4080 copies; 2nd, Jan. 15, 1876, 2028
copies. BAL has not identified the first printing.

HOLIDAY EDITION

Title-page printed in black and red. Top edges
gilt. Leaf: 8″ x 5⁹⁄₁₆″.

According to the publisher's records there were
two printings issued under date 1876: 1st, Nov.
29, 1875, 1416 copies; 2nd, Dec. 27, 1875, 1140
copies. BAL has not identified the first printing.

H copy (Household Edition) received Dec. 8,
1875. Holiday Edition deposited Dec. 9, 1875.
Both formats listed PW Dec. 11, 1875. See under
1890 for an extended edition.

H (both)

11342. . . . Semi-Centennial of the First Congregational Church, Lowell, Mass., Tuesday,
June 6th, 1876.

Lowell, Mass.: Stone, Huse & Co., Book and
Job Printers, No. 130 Central Street. 1876.

At head of title: 1826. 1876. . . .

Printed paper wrapper.

". . . The following ⟨untitled⟩ Hymn, written
for the occasion . . . ," As oft we came in earlier
days, p. 38. Collected in the unillustrated ⟨sic⟩
edition of The Poetical Works, 1885, as "Hymn.
For the Semi-Centennial Celebration at the
First Congregational Church, Lowell, Mass."

B

11343. Roadside Poems for Summer Travellers.
Edited by Lucy Larcom.

Boston: James R. Osgood and Company, (Late Ticknor & Fields, and Fields, Osgood, & Co.) 1876.

"Preface," pp. 5-6.

Larcom's poems are reprint save for "White Everlasting Flowers," pp. 138-141. Collected in *Wild Roses . . .* , 1881.

"Veiled," pp. 246-248 appeared untitled in *An Idyl of Work,* 1875. In the unillustrated ⟨*sic*⟩ edition of *The Poetical Works,* 1885, it appears under the title "A Mountain-Resurrection."

Two printings noted:

1

⟨1⟩-263. P. ⟨2⟩ blank.

⟨-⟩², ⟨1⟩⁶, 2-16⁸, 17⁴.

Noted only with the spine imprint of James R. Osgood & Co.

Printed June 5, 1876, 1000 copies (publisher's records). Bound June 6–10, 1876.

2

⟨1⟩-263. P. ⟨2⟩ imprinted with a boxed advertisement headed: *Miss Larcom's Writings.*

⟨1⁴, 2-17⁸⟩. *Signed:* ⟨1⟩-16⁸, 17⁴.

Noted with the spine imprint of James R. Osgood & Co.; and, the spine imprint of Houghton, Mifflin & Co.

Printed Aug. 5, 1876, 500 copies (publisher's records). Bound Aug. 15, 1876–May 28, 1895.

Noted for *immediate publication* PW June 10, 1876. Y copy of first printing inscribed by Larcom June 14, 1876. Listed PW June 17, 1876.

AAS (1st)   H (1st)   MHS (2nd)   NYPL (2nd)   Y (1st)

11344. Autumn Leaves. ⟨Edited by L. R. Swain?⟩

⟨n.p., n.d., 1876?⟩

Reprint save for "Sylvia," pp. 100-104. Collected in *Wild Roses . . .* , 1881.

Copy in the possession of JB inscribed by early owner Jan. 1, 1877.

H   JB

11345. Hillside and Seaside in Poetry   A Companion to "Roadside Poems"   Edited by Lucy Larcom

Boston   James R. Osgood and Company (Late Ticknor & Fields, and Fields, Osgood, & Co.) 1877

Reprint save for the "Preface," pp. 3-4.

According to the publisher's records, 1000 copies printed June 6, 1877. Listed PW June 30, 1877.

AAS   H   LC   NYPL   Y

11346. Poems of Places Edited by Henry W. Longfellow . . . America. New England. Vol. II.

Boston: Houghton, Osgood and Company. The Riverside Press, Cambridge. 1879.

Reprint save for "In a Cloud Rift," pp. 270-272. Collected in *Wild Roses . . .* , 1881.

For comment see entry No. 12209.

11347. Re-Dedication of Seminary Hall Wheaton Seminary, ⟨Norton, Mass.⟩ Wednesday, Jan. 15th, 1879.

⟨n.p., n.d., Norton, Mass., 1879⟩

Single cut sheet folded to make four pages. Title on p. ⟨1⟩. At foot of p. ⟨4⟩: *Beacon Press: Thomas Todd, 1 Somerset St., Boston.* Issued as a program.

"Original Hymn," *Life is growth, and growth is change,* p. ⟨4⟩. Collected in *At the Beautiful Gate,* 1892.

H

11348. Poems of Places Edited by Henry W. Longfellow . . . America. Western States.

Boston: Houghton, Osgood and Company. The Riverside Press, Cambridge. 1879.

Reprint save for "A Prairie Nest," pp. 177-179. Collected in *Wild Roses . . .* , 1881.

For comment see entry No. 12214.

11349. Poems of Places Edited by Henry W. Longfellow . . . Oceanica . . . Miscellaneous Seas and Islands.

Boston: Houghton, Osgood and Company. The Riverside Press, Cambridge. 1879.

"Bermoothes," pp. ⟨261⟩-265. Collected in *Wild Roses . . .* , 1881.

For comment see entry No. 12216.

11350. Breathings of the Better Life. Edited by Lucy Larcom. Third Edition, Revised.

Boston: Houghton, Osgood, and Company. The Riverside Press, Cambridge. 1879.

Not seen. Title and imprint postulated. Issued under date 1880? Entry on the basis of publisher's records and located reprints.

For first edition see under 1867.

"Preface to Third Edition," pp. ⟨vii⟩-viii, dated at end: *Boston, 1879.*

"The present edition has been enlarged by the addition of some verses from the compiler's pen, and also from other sources."—From the "Preface," p. viii. It seems certain that those anonymous additions printed herein *within* quotation marks were not written by Larcom; those anonymous additions printed *without* quotation marks were written by Larcom. This method of identification was used by Larcom in *Beckonings for Every Day,* 1886. The following anonymous pieces are by Larcom:

P. 14. Extract from "A Thanksgiving," *Poems,* 1869.

P. 20. Extract from "Hints," *Poems,* 1869.

P. ⟨52⟩. Untitled, 3 six-line stanzas. Collected in *Wild Roses . . . ,* 1881, as part of "Show Me Thy Way."

P. 56. Extract from "The Still Hour," *Poems,* 1869.

P. 68. Untitled, 2 six-line stanzas. Collected in *Wild Roses . . . ,* 1881, as part of "Praying Always."

P. ⟨70⟩. Untitled, 2 six-line stanzas. Collected in *Wild Roses . . . ,* 1881, as part of "Foretaste."

P. 77. Untitled, 2 lines beginning: *Only the souls in tune with theirs the angels' secret guess . . .* Elsewhere unlocated.

P. 88. Untitled, 3 4-line stanzas. Collected in *Wild Roses . . . ,* 1881, as part of "Yet Onward."

P. ⟨108⟩. Untitled, 3 four-line stanzas. Collected in *Wild Roses . . . ,* 1881, as part of "The Heart of God."

P. ⟨128⟩. Untitled, 4 four-line stanzas. Collected in *Wild Roses . . . ,* 1881, as part of "Daily Bread."

P. ⟨154⟩. Extract from "Hand in Hand with Angels," *Poems,* 1869.

P. 170. Untitled, 6 lines. Collected in *Wild Roses . . . ,* 1881, as part of "The Ladder of Angels."

P. 183. Untitled, 3 verses beginning: *"Peace I leave with you . . .* Elsewhere unlocated.

P. ⟨196⟩. "My Cup Runneth Over." Collected in *Wild Roses . . . ,* 1881.

P. 201. Extract from "At the Beautiful Gate," *Poems,* 1869.

P. 209. Extract from "A Thanksgiving," *Poems,* 1869.

P. 224. Extract from "More Life," *Poems,* 1869.

P. 228. Untitled, 8 lines. Collected in *Wild Roses . . . ,* 1881, as part of "Drawing Nearer."

P. 256. Extract from "Near Shore," *Poems,* 1869.

According to the publisher's records, 286 copies printed June 26, 1879. Advertised for *Sept.* 27 in PW Sept. 20, 1879. Advertised as *today* PW Oct. 4, 1879.

REPRINTS

Third Edition, Revised. Boston, 1880. *Query:* Is this a reprint? Or, perhaps, the first printing of the *Third Edition, Revised?*

Third Edition, Revised. Boston, 1881.

Sixth Edition, Revised. Boston, 1886. On Aug. 8, 1883 (letter in H) Lucy Larcom wrote the publishers and requested certain corrections. The corrections consisted, for the most part, of the addition of names of authors to those pieces which, in the earlier printings, were anonymous. The alterations first appear in this printing.

Other reprints, according to the publishers records: Jan. 1889; Sept. 1892; April 1895.

11351. Home Life in Song with the Poets of To-Day . . . ⟨Compiled by A. D. F. Randolph⟩

New York: Anson D. F. Randolph & Company, 900 Broadway, Cor. 20th Street. ⟨1879⟩

Reprint save for "They Said," p. 175. Collected in the unillustrated ⟨*sic*⟩ edition of *The Poetical Works,* 1885.

For comment see entry No. 432.

11352. Landscape in American Poetry. ⟨Compiled⟩ by Lucy Larcom . . .

New York: D. Appleton and Company. 549 & 551 Broadway. ⟨1879⟩

Cloth; and, leather.

Selections from a number of poets with connecting comment by Larcom.

Note: Reissued, not before Feb. 1880, with the publisher's Bond Street address in the imprint.

Advertised for *November 29* in PW Nov. 29, 1879. Listed PW Dec. 20, 1879.

AAS B H Y

11353. The Children's Book of Poetry: Carefully Selected . . . by Henry T. Coates . . .

Porter & Coates. Philadelphia. ⟨1879⟩

"Little Bridget's Country Week," pp. 392-393. Collected in the unillustrated ⟨*sic*⟩ edition of *The Poetical Works,* 1885.

CH

Breathings of the Better Life. Edited by Lucy Larcom. Third Edition, Revised.

Boston: Houghton, Osgood, and Company. The Riverside Press, Cambridge. 1880.

Reprint? For comment see entry No. 11350.

Copyright notice dated 1866. "Preface to the Third Edition," pp. ⟨vii⟩-viii, dated at end *Boston, 1879.*

BPL

11354. *Entry cancelled.*

11355. The Fifth Half Century of the Arrival of John Winthrop at Salem, Massachusetts. Commemorative Exercises by the Essex Institute, June 22, 1880. [From the Historical Collections of the Essex Institute.]

Salem: Printed for the Essex Institute. 1880.

Printed paper wrapper.

"The Lady Arbella," pp. 29-31. Collected in *Wild Roses . . . ,* 1881.

Note: Appears also in *Essex Institute Historical Collections,* Vol. 17, Salem, 1880, pp. 221-223.

B

11356. Worth Keeping: Selected from The Congregationalist and Boston Recorder, 1870–1879.

Boston: W. L. Greene & Co. Congregational House, Corner Beacon and Somerset Streets, 1880.

"Our Christ," p. 28. Collected in *Wild Roses . . . ,* 1881.

JN copy inscribed by early owner Sept. 1, 1880.

JN

11357. SNOW BLOOM AND OTHER POEMS . . .

⟨NEWTON, MASS., MRS. N. V. WALKER, n.d., after Oct. 23, 1880, before 1882⟩

⟨1⟩-22; printer's imprint, p. ⟨23⟩. 7¼" x 6¼". ⟨-⟩¹².

Printed stiff white paper wrapper.

These Poems Are Published By Permission Of, And By Arrangement With, Miss Larcom And Her Publishers, Houghton, Mifflin & Co. Mrs. N. V. Walker, Newton, Mass.—P. ⟨4⟩.

Reprint with the possible exception of the following four poems which appear also in *Wild Roses . . . ,* 1881:

"His Birthday"

"Immortal Years"

"Snow Bloom"

"A White World"

Also contains the following two poems, here in their earliest located book appearance; both in the unillustrated ⟨sic⟩ edition of *The Poetical Works,* 1885:

"A Christmas Thought"

"Woman's Christmas"

B UI

11358. WILD ROSES OF CAPE ANN, AND OTHER POEMS . . .

BOSTON: HOUGHTON, MIFFLIN AND COMPANY. THE RIVERSIDE PRESS, CAMBRIDGE. 1881.

⟨i-ii⟩, ⟨i⟩-vi, ⟨7⟩-272, blank leaf. 7³⁄₁₆" x 4⅝".

⟨1-23⟩⁶. *Signed:* ⟨-⟩¹, ⟨1⟩-9, ⟨10⟩-13, ⟨14⟩-17⁸, ⟨18⟩¹.

S cloth: blue; brown; green; purple; terra-cotta. V cloth: blue; brown. Gray-coated on white end papers. Grayish-green-coated on white end papers. White laid end papers. Flyleaves. Top edges gilded.

Note: According to the publisher's records there were two printings without alteration of the title-page: 1st, Oct. 27, 1880, 1000 copies; 2nd, Dec. 13, 1880, 150 copies. The records also show that the plates were altered prior to the second printing. BAL has been unable to distinguish two printings. The error *Freind* for *Friend,* 17th entry, p. iv, is present in all examined copies including a copy of the *Third Edition* (so marked on the title-page).

Advertised for Nov. 17 PW Nov. 6, 1880. Listed PW Dec. 4, 1880.

AAS BA H NYPL

11359. The Sword and the Pen . . .

Boston . . . 1881 . . .

"Surrender. April 10, 1865," No. 3, p. 2.

" 'He Died for Me'," No. 7, p. 4.

An occasional newspaper. For comment see entry No. 123.

11360. The Thirty-Second Annual Report of the Executive Committee of the Children's Mission to the Children of the Destitute, in the City of Boston; with an Account of the Proceedings at the Annual Meeting, May 25, 1881 . . .

Boston: Rooms of the Children's Mission, 277 Tremont Street, opposite Common Street. 1881.

Cover-title. Printed paper wrapper.

"Original Hymn," *We are the children of one Father,* pp. 11-12.

H

11361. In Memoriam.

⟨Beacon Press: Thomas Todd, Printer, 1 Somerset St., Boston, n.d., 1882?⟩

Printed paper wrapper.

"In Memoriam. A.E.C.," pp. ⟨15⟩-20.

A memorial of Ann E. Carter, d. March 4, 1882.

wh

11362. Grandma's Garden   With Many Original Poems Suggested and Arranged by Kate Sanborn ...

Boston   James R. Osgood and Company 1883

"Our Lady-of-the-Lilies," pp. 8-10. Collected in the unillustrated ⟨sic⟩ edition of *The Poetical Works,* 1885.

For comment see entry No. 3791.

11363. Flowers from Hill and Dale   Poems Arranged and Illustrated by Susie Barstow Skelding ...

New York   White, Stokes, and Allen   1883

Reprint save for "Wood-Fringe," p. ⟨29⟩.

Note: An omnibus volume, issued with title-page as above, containing the following three separate books edited by Skelding: *A Handful of Blossoms, Maple Leaves and Golden Rod* and *Songs of Flowers.* Each of the separate publications, and the omnibus volume, listed in PW Oct. 13, 1883. See next entry.

NYPL

11364. Songs of Flowers ... Arranged and Illustrated by Susie B. Skelding

New York   White, Stokes, & Allen   1883

Flexible pictorial boards, fringed cover. Unpaged.

Contains "Wood-Fringe."   See preceding entry.

Deposited Sept. 6, 1883.

LC

11365. Our Famous Women. Comprising the Lives and Deeds of American Women ... by ... Harriet Beecher Stowe. Rose Terry Cooke. Harriet Prescott Spofford. Elizabeth Stuart

Phelps ... Louise Chandler Moulton. Lucy Larcom. Julia Ward Howe ...

Hartford, Conn.: A. D. Worthington and Company. Chicago: A. G. Nettleton & Co. Cleveland: C. C. Wick & Co. 1883.

A subscription book and as such probably issued with varying imprints.

"Clara Barton," pp. 94-116.

Also contains a biographical sketch of Lucy Larcom by Mrs. A.D.T. Whitney, pp. 415-436.

Note: Addison (p. 239) refers to this publication as though issued under the title *American Women of Note.* Further information wanting.

Deposited Oct. 22, 1883. BA copy received Dec. 19, 1883. Listed PW Jan. 12, 1884, in three bindings: Cloth (at $3.50 and at $4.00); and, leather; the two prices for the cloth binding probably indicate cloth, gold stamping; and, cloth, gold stamping, edges gilt.

BA

11366. Baby World   Stories, Rhymes, and Pictures for Little Folks Compiled from St. Nicholas by Mary Mapes Dodge

The Century Co.   New-York ⟨1884⟩

"Happy Fields of Summer," p. 95. Collected in the unillustrated ⟨sic⟩ edition of *The Poetical Works,* 1885.

For comment see entry No. 4778.

The Poetical Works ...

Boston ... ⟨1884; *i.e.,* not before 1885⟩

See below in *Section II* under 1885.

11367. The Whittier Calendar with Selections for Every Day in the Year ⟨1885⟩

Copyright 1884 by Houghton, Mifflin & Co. Boston.

Not seen. Title and imprint postulated. Possibly the same format as *The Holmes Calendar;* see entry No. 9171.

"Yours of the 21st is received. I should enjoy preparing the Whittier Calendar, and will put other things aside, to do it ..."—From a letter, Larcom to Mr. Garrison of Houghton, Mifflin & Co., Feb. 23, 1884; letter in H.

"... Thanks for the Whittier Calendars, which are promised ..."—From a letter, Larcom to Mr. Houghton of Houghton, Mifflin & Co., Nov. 11, 1884. From the postscript: "The Calendars have arrived and seem to me very nice, simple, and pretty ..."; letter in H.

11368. THE POETICAL WORKS ... HOUSE-HOLD EDITION

BOSTON   HOUGHTON, MIFFLIN AND COMPANY
NEW YORK: 11 EAST SEVENTEENTH STREET   THE
RIVERSIDE PRESS, CAMBRIDGE   1885

Note: Contains a portrait frontispiece, otherwise not illustrated. Not to be confused with the *Household Edition with Illustrations,* 1885; see in *Section II* for this last.

⟨i-iv⟩, ⟨i⟩-viii, ⟨1⟩-318; publisher's catalog, pp. ⟨1⟩-6, plus: pp. 7-16, blank leaf. Portrait frontispiece inserted. 7⅜″ x 4⅞″.

⟨1-28⁶, plus: 29⁶⟩. *Signed:* ⟨-⟩⁶, 1-6, ⟨7⟩-9, ⟨10⟩-13, 17 ⟨*sic*⟩, ⟨15⟩-16, ⟨17⟩-20, ⟨21⟩⁸.

BF cloth: blue. H cloth: blue; brown. Olive-gray-coated on white end papers. Also issued in half calf, morocco, tree calf according to the advertisement, p. ⟨iv⟩.

Two issues of the binding noted:

1: Front cover and spine goldstamped: LARCOM'S POEMS

2: Front cover and spine goldstamped: LUCY LARCOM'S POEMS

Concerning the stamping, Lucy Larcom wrote the publishers, Nov. 11, 1884 (letter in H): "I wrote ... yesterday, expressing regret that only the word ⟨*sic*⟩ Larcom was used on the cover of my new edition. I do hope it can be changed, for I think it in bad taste. It seems to class me among 'them literary fellows';—but I do not want to be a 'fellow' at all. It strikes me so unpleasantly, as it stands, I do not want to give the book to my friends."

Note: The frontispiece occurs in two forms:

A: The portrait is printed from an engraved block; the book published thus.

B: The portrait is a photographic print. Noted only in presentation copies. Lucy Larcom did not like the engraved portrait and presumably had a photographic portrait prepared for presentation copies. On Nov. 11, 1884, she wrote the publishers (letter in H): "I mentioned the portrait, also, as not being quite so satisfactory as in the catalogue. The white spot in the eyeball seems to be the chief trouble. Mr. Closson said that could be filled up—'plugged' I believe was the word. I think the darker impressions are much the best, in expression. Cannot all future copies be so? ..." All examined copies of the engraved portrait in the unillustrated edition show a white spot on each eye. In the illustrated *Household Edition* the spots are not present.

Of the 284 poems herein about 65 are either here first collected or here first in book form.

Certain of the poems are present under altered titles, some being revised as well.

Printed Oct. 27, 1884, 1010 copies (publisher's records). Bound during the period Nov. 3, 1884–March 19, 1885. Deposited Nov. 8, 1884. Listed PW Nov. 15, 1884.

AAS (1st binding)   BPL (1st binding)   LC (1st binding, being a deposit copy)   NYPL (2nd binding, photographic frontispiece portrait, presented by Larcom to Elizabeth Stuart Phelps, Dec. 1884)   UV (2nd binding, photographic frontispiece portrait, presented by Larcom to Miss A. H. Johnson, March 26, 1885)

11369. Ossipee Mountain Park ...

⟨n.p., n.d., probably New Hampshire, 1885⟩

Caption-title. The above at head of p. ⟨1⟩. A 15-page pamphlet issued as promotional material; a series of extracts from periodicals extolling the virtues of Ossipee Park. Date on the basis of an extract herein from *Lowell Morning Mail* of July 14, 1885.

"Letter from Lucy Larcom," Ossipee Park, N. H., October 13, 1884, pp. 6-7.

B

11370. Fiftieth Anniversary of Wheaton Female Seminary. June 30th and July 1st, 1885. Commemorative Exercises. Addresses and Poem.

⟨Printed by Lane Brothers, Norton, Mass., n.d., 1885?⟩

Printed paper wrapper. Two-line errata slip inserted.

"The Old Scholars," pp. ⟨59⟩-65.

H   WH

11371. WHEATON SEMINARY; A SEMI-CENTENNIAL SKETCH ...

CAMBRIDGE: PRINTED AT THE RIVERSIDE PRESS. 1885.

⟨i-iv⟩, ⟨1⟩-94. Laid paper. Frontispiece and 6 plates inserted. 8⁹⁄₁₆″ x 5¾″.

⟨1-6⁸, 7¹⟩. *Signed:* ⟨-⟩², ⟨1⟩-5⁸, 6⁷.

S cloth: dark olive-brown. V cloth: gray; olive-green. Gray-green-coated on white end papers. Flyleaves. Top edges gilt.

Two issues noted:

1

Pp. 23-24, 91-92 are not cancels.

P. 23, line 3: ... *Illinois*/

P. 92, line 10: *This Seminary* ...

2

Pp. 23-24, 91-92 are cancels.

P. 23, line 3: ... *Indiana/*

P. 92, line 10: *It is more ...*

According to the printer's records 1000 copies printed on June 26, 1885. On Aug. 6, 1885, 500 copies of each cancel printed.

AAS (1st)   B (1st)   BPL (2nd)   H (1st)   NYPL (1st)

11372. St. Nicholas Songs ... ⟨Edited by Waldo Selden Pratt⟩

The Century Co. New-York ⟨1885⟩

Reprint save for "Childhood's Gold," pp. 102-103.

For comment see entry No. 3800.

11373. EASTER MESSENGERS   A NEW POEM OF THE FLOWERS ...

NEW YORK   COPYRIGHT, 1886, BY WHITE, STOKES, & ALLEN   1886

⟨1⟩-24. Text on laid paper. 8¹³⁄₁₆″ x 7⅞″ scant. Illustrated with 4 full-page plates in color. *Note:* Text and plates reckoned in the printed pagination; plates printed on wove paper.

12 leaves, punched and tied with white ribbon.

Printed paper cover, tied to sheets. Edges silvered.

Also a de luxe format. Leaf: 9″ x 8⅛″. The leaves are not singletons but comprise an 8vo gathering with the plates inserted. Punched and tied with ribbon. Bound in printed satin. Label on front cover. White paper pastedowns.

De luxe format deposited Feb. 5, 1886.

B (trade)   LC (de luxe)   Y (de luxe)

11374. Beckonings for Every Day   A Calendar of Thought   Arranged by Lucy Larcom

Boston and New York   Houghton, Mifflin and Company   The Riverside Press, Cambridge 1886

"Introductory," pp. ⟨1⟩-3.

"The compiler has connected these groups of thought by a thread of her own, from month to month; but credit has been given for everything not original by quotation-marks where unknown, or by the names of known authors."—From the "Introductory," p. 3.

The following poems, according to this statement, are by Larcom. Except as noted, they are elsewhere unlocated.

P. ⟨4⟩. "The New Year."

P. ⟨39⟩. "Spring."

P. ⟨94⟩. "Summer."

P. 128. Untitled, 4 lines. Collected in *Easter Gleams*, 1890, as part of "The Word."

Pp. 140-141. Untitled, 8 lines beginning: *O great befriending natures ...*

P. ⟨147⟩. "Autumn."

P. 164. Untitled, 4 lines beginning: *Three humble friends of His, in lofty light ...*

P. 166. Untitled, 4 lines beginning: *If I truly love The One ...*

P. 181. Untitled, 2 4-line stanzas beginning: *They are alive, who seemed to die ...*

P. 192. Extract from "At the Beautiful Gate," *Poems*, 1869.

P. ⟨201⟩. "Winter."

Pp. 217-218. Untitled, 9 lines beginning: *When Christmas comes, we hear again the word ...*

Sept. 16, 1886, 786 copies printed (publisher's records). Deposited Oct. 16, 1886. Listed PW Nov. 13, 1886. The London (Ward, Lock) edition listed Ath Nov. 6, 1886; received at BMU Nov. 22, 1886. Reissued ca. 1891 as *The Golden Calendar* by Ward, Lock, Bowden.

AAS   NYPL   Y

11375. Breathings of the Better Life. Edited by Lucy Larcom. Sixth Edition, Revised.

Boston: Houghton, Mifflin and Company. New York: 11 East Seventeenth Street. The Riverside Press, Cambridge. 1886.

This printing contains some corrections. For fuller comment see *Breathings of the Better Life*, 1879.

B

11376. Beecher Memorial   Contemporaneous Tributes to the Memory of Henry Ward Beecher   Compiled and Edited by Edward W. Bok

Privately Printed   Brooklyn, New York   1887

"Henry Ward Beecher. A Memory of a Sermon," pp. 36-37.

For comment see entry No. 2148.

11377. Ballads of Romance and History by Susan Coolidge ⟨and Others⟩ ...

Boston   D Lothrop Company   ⟨1887⟩

"A Ballad of the Hemlock Tree," pp. 91-94.

For publication as a separate see below under *1888?*.

For comment see entry No. 10889.

11378. The Cross and the Grail. By Lucy Larcom. With Selections from the Poets Shakespeare, Longfellow, Whittier and Phoebe and Alice Cary ...

1887. Woman's Temperance Pub'n Association Chicago.

Printed celluloid wrapper; and, cloth.

Unpaged.

Reprint save for "The Cross and the Grail."

H

11379. Dedication of the Norton Public Library, Norton, Mass. Wednesday, February 1, 1888 ...

Norton, Mass. Issued by the Board of Directors. Press of Lane Brothers. 1888.

Printed paper wrapper.

"Good Books. Written for the Opening of the Norton Public Library," pp. ⟨33⟩-34.

In a letter to BAL from Mrs. Philip Stepanek, Acting Librarian of the Norton Public Library, at a meeting of the directors of the library, April 9, 1888, "... the edition ordered printed was 650 ..." At the same meeting the "bill for printing the dedication pamphlet approved." The report of the May 14, 1888 directors meeting "states that a copy of the dedication ⟨pamphlet⟩ had been sent to the State House Librarian."

B   H

11380. THE HEMLOCK TREE   A MERRIE CHRISTMAS TO YOV ...

⟨n.p., n.d., probably Boston: D. Lothrop Company, 1888?⟩

Cover-title, printed in colors.

⟨87⟩-94. Illustrated. 10¼" x 8".

⟨-⟩⁴.

White paper boards. Label (as above) pasted to front.

Previously in *Ballads of Romance and History*, by Susan Coolidge ⟨and others⟩, Boston ⟨1887⟩, above.

Publisher's list printed on back cover; one of the books offered is Henry Harland's *My Uncle Florimond* which was published by Lothrop in Sept. 1888.

B

11381. A NEW ENGLAND GIRLHOOD OUTLINED FROM MEMORY ...

BOSTON AND NEW YORK   HOUGHTON, MIFFLIN AND COMPANY   THE RIVERSIDE PRESS, CAMBRIDGE 1889

⟨i-iv⟩, ⟨1⟩-274; blank leaf; 2 pp. advertisements, blank leaf. 6⅝" x 4³⁄₁₆".

⟨1², 2-18⁸, 19⁴⟩.

V cloth: blue. White laid end papers. Issued as No. 6 of *The Riverside Library for Young People* series.

Printed Nov. 29, 1889, 1500 copies (publisher's records). H copy received Dec. 2, 1889. Deposited Dec. 2, 1889. Noted for Dec. 13 PW Dec. 7, 1889. Listed PW Dec. 14, 1889.

AAS   H

11382. EASTER GLEAMS ...

BOSTON AND NEW YORK   HOUGHTON, MIFFLIN AND COMPANY   THE RIVERSIDE PRESS, CAMBRIDGE 1890

⟨1⟩-45; four-line extract, p. ⟨46⟩; advertisements, pp. ⟨47-48⟩. Laid paper watermarked *John Dickinson & Co.* 6" x 4½" scant.

⟨1-6⟩⁴.

Printed paper vellum wrapper folded over stiff laid paper end papers. Laid paper flyleaves.

1042 copies printed March 11, 1890; bound during the period March 11-31, 1890 (publisher's records). Deposited March 15, 1890. Listed PW March 29, 1890.

AAS   B   UV

11383. THE GOVERNOR'S TREE.   ORIGINAL POEM ... ARBOR DAY, 1890 ...

⟨n.p., 1890⟩

Caption-title. The above at head of p. ⟨1⟩. Single cut sheet of white laid paper folded to make 4 pages. Size of page: 7¹³⁄₁₆" x 4⅝". Printed throughout in dark blue.

AAS   B   Y

11384. Songs of Three Centuries Edited by John Greenleaf Whittier ...

Boston and New York   Houghton, Mifflin and Company   The Riverside Press, Cambridge 1890

See under 1876 for first edition.

Enlarged edition. According to Addison (p. 259) edited by Larcom, but further information is lacking.

H

11385. AS IT IS IN HEAVEN ...

BOSTON AND NEW YORK   HOUGHTON, MIFFLIN
AND COMPANY THE RIVERSIDE PRESS, CAMBRIDGE
1891

Two editions noted:

1

⟨i⟩-⟨viii⟩, ⟨9⟩-157; blank leaf. 6⁹⁄₁₆″ x 4¼″ scant.

⟨1-10⟩⁸.

Printed March 2, 1891, 1016 copies (publisher's
records). Bound March 5–12, save for 15 copies
bound in flexible morocco March 21, 1891.

2

⟨i⟩-⟨viii⟩, ⟨9⟩-156.

⟨1-9⁸, 10⁶⟩.

Printed March 12, 1891, 516 copies (publisher's
records). Bound March 16–June 11, 1891; three
copies bound June 11, 1891, in white morocco.

Two issues of the binding noted:

1

V cloth: blue. White laid end papers. Flyleaf at
front. Top edges gilded. Front cover not lettered.

2

V cloth: blue; white. White laid end papers.
Flyleaves; or, flyleaf at front only. Top edges
gilded. Title present on front cover.

Noted for March publication PW Feb. 14, 1891.
Deposited March 9, 1891. Noted for March 11
PW March 7, 1891. Listed PW March 21, 1891.

AAS (2nd edition, 2nd binding) B (1st edition,
1st binding) H (2nd edition, 2nd binding) LC
(1st edition, 1st binding) NYPL (2nd edition,
2nd binding) UV (1st edition, 2nd binding) Y
(2nd edition, 2nd binding)

11386. THE UNSEEN FRIEND ...

BOSTON AND NEW YORK   HOUGHTON, MIFFLIN
AND COMPANY THE RIVERSIDE PRESS, CAMBRIDGE
1892

⟨i-ii⟩, ⟨i⟩-⟨xiv⟩, ⟨1⟩-217, blank leaf. 6⁹⁄₁₆″ x 4¼″
scant.

⟨1-14⁸, 15⁶⟩.

S cloth: gray. V cloth: white. White laid end
papers. Flyleaf at front. Top edges gilded. Also
issued in flexible morocco according to contemporary notices.

Printed March 23, 1892, 1500 copies (publisher's
records). Deposited March 28, 1892. Listed PW
April 9, 1892, as in cloth; and, flexible morocco.

The London (Gay & Bird) importation listed
Ath June 24, 1893.

B BA H NYPL Y

11387. Fourth Annual Reunion of the Association of Working Girls' Clubs at Tremont
Temple, Wednesday, April 20, 1892 ... Programme ...

Single cut sheet folded twice to make six pages.
Printed in blue throughout. Issued as a program.

Contains Larcom's "The Work of the World."
For a separate printing see below under *1893?*.

BA

11388. No. 37.   Standard Recitations by Best
Authors ... Compiled ... by Frances P. Sullivan ... September 1892 ...

M. J. Ivers & Co., Publishers, 379 Pearl Street,
N. Y. .... ⟨1892⟩

"God in Christ," p. 33. If we accept the Sept.
1892 date (which may or may not be accurate;
see BAL, Vol. 1, p. xvi), the poem is here published prior to collection in *At the Beautiful
Gate*, 1892; see next entry.

For comment see entry No. 1996.

11389. AT THE BEAUTIFUL GATE AND
OTHER SONGS OF FAITH ...

BOSTON AND NEW YORK   HOUGHTON, MIFFLIN
AND COMPANY THE RIVERSIDE PRESS, CAMBRIDGE
1892

Two printings noted:

1

⟨i-iv⟩, ⟨i⟩-⟨xii⟩, ⟨1⟩-117, blank leaf. 6⁹⁄₁₆″ x 4¼″.

⟨1-8⁸, 9⁴⟩.

The *Dedication* has no punctuation save for a
comma at end of the 6th line.

P. 114: The poem "Transfigured" comprises 5
stanzas.

2

⟨i-ii⟩, ⟨i⟩-⟨xii⟩, ⟨1⟩-117.

⟨1-8⁸, 9²⟩.

The *Dedication* has been improved by the addition of commas at end of lines 2 and 4.

P. 114: The poem "Transfigured" extended;
comprises 6 stanzas.

Confirmation of the above sequence may be
found in Lucy Larcom's letter to the publisher,
Oct. 21, 1892; letter in H.

S cloth: green. V cloth: white. White laid end
papers. Top edges gilt.

"The suggestion by friends, that such of the writer's lyrics as are of an especially serious and devotional character should be brought together in a small volume, has led to the following collection. Many of these—more than a third, perhaps—have been written since the complete (Household) edition ... was published, about ten years ago, and are not included in that edition. Others are now for the first time in print ..."—"Prefatory Note," p. ⟨v⟩.

1540 copies printed Oct. 13, 1892; bound Oct. 17–31, 1892; publisher's records. Noted for Oct. 22 in PW Oct. 8, 1892. Deposited Oct. 24, 1892. Listed PW Oct. 29, 1892. Second printing, 1022 copies, Nov. 25, 1892; bound Nov. 29–Dec. 23, 1892; publisher's records. For the third printing (Dec. 23, 1892) the date in the imprint was altered to 1893.

AAS (1st)   BA (1st)   H (1st, 2nd)   LC (1st, being a deposit copy)   NYPL (1st)   Y (1st, 2nd)

11390. Werner's Readings and Recitations No. 10 America's Recitation Book Compiled and Arranged by Caroline B. Le Row

Edgar S. Werner & Company   New York ... Copyright, 1892 ...

Printed paper wrapper?

"The Nineteenth of April, 1861," and a specially written introduction to the poem, p. 235. The poem was previously in *Poems*, 1869, but is here somewhat revised.

NYPL

11391. Memorial to John Greenleaf Whittier, by the Citizens of Amesbury. December 17, 1892.

Amesbury: Fred A. Brown, Publisher, 1893.

Printed paper wrapper.

"John Greenleaf Whittier, a Citizen of Amesbury," p. 35.

H   NYPL

11392. The National Exposition Souvenir What America Owes to Women Edited by Lydia Hoyt Farmer with an Introduction by Julia Ward Howe

Buffalo   Chicago   New York   Charles Wells Moulton   1893

"The Lady Arbella" is here reprinted, but with a specially prepared introduction, "Arbella Johnson," pp. ⟨40⟩-41.

For comment see entry No. 9485.

11393. THE WORK OF THE WORLD. WRITTEN FOR THE MASS. ASSOCIATION OF WORKING GIRLS' CLUBS ...

⟨n.p., n.d., 1893?⟩

Single leaf. Printed on recto only. 7⅞" x 4¾".

Issued not before April 17, 1893.

For prior publication in a program see above under 1892.

B

11394. LUCY LARCOM   LIFE, LETTERS, AND DIARY BY DANIEL DULANY ADDISON

BOSTON AND NEW YORK   HOUGHTON, MIFFLIN AND COMPANY   THE RIVERSIDE PRESS, CAMBRIDGE 1894

⟨i-ii⟩, ⟨i⟩-⟨x⟩, ⟨1⟩-295. Frontispiece inserted. 7" x 4¹¹⁄₁₆".

⟨1-19⁸, 20²⟩.

V cloth: green; maroon. Gray-coated on white end papers. Flyleaves. Top edges gilt.

Printed Oct. 13, 1894; 1002 copies. Bound during the period Oct. 18–Nov. 19, 1894. Deposited Oct. 19, 1894. Listed PW Oct. 27, 1894. Second printing, for which the date was altered to 1895, Dec. 11, 1894. (Publisher's records.)

AAS   H

11395. The Rushlight   Special Number in Memory of Lucy Larcom Issued by the Trustees of Wheaton Seminary, Norton, Mass. Edited by Susan Hayes Ward

Boston   Geo. H. Ellis, Printer, 141 Franklin Street   1894

Printed paper wrapper.

Reprint save for:

"Written in a Wheaton Girl's Album," p. ⟨4⟩.

"Dreaming and Waking," pp. 48-49.

"This Beautiful Year. (Written for the Class of 1891.)," pp. 116-117.

Also contains a selection of letters written by Larcom.

BPL

11395A. Three Minute Readings for College Girls   Selected and Edited by Harry Cassell Davis ...

Copyright, 1897 ... Hinds & Noble, Publishers   4-5-13-14 Cooper Institute   New York City

"Who Plants a Tree?," pp. 180-181. The poem also appears in *The Hamilton Declamation Quarterly Edited by Professors Oren Root and Brainard G. Smith . . . ,* Vol. 1, No. 1, April, 1895, Syracuse, 1895.

H

11396. Loom and Spindle or Life among the Early Mill Girls with a Sketch of "The Lowell Offering" and Some of Its Contributors by Harriet H. Robinson . . .

New York: 46 East 14th Street   Thomas Y. Crowell & Company   Boston: 100 Purchase Street ⟨1898⟩

"Harriet Jane Hanson," pp. 157-163. Also autobiographical comment, etc., pp. 164-185.

H

11397. Thoughts and Experiences in and out of School by John B. Peaslee . . . accompanied by Letters from Longfellow, Whittier, Holmes, and Other American Authors

Printed for the Author by Curts & Jennings, Cincinnati, Ohio   1900

Letter, April 17, 1883, pp. 319-320.

H copy received Jan. 30, 1900. Listed PW March 31, 1900.

H

11398. Our Holidays   Their Meaning and Spirit Retold from St. Nicholas

Published by The Century Co.   New York MCMV

"Longfellow and the Children," pp. 125-138.

For comment see entry No. 5171A.

11399. . . . The Lowell Offering.   October, 1845 . . .

⟨Boston: The Directors of the Old South Work, n.d., *ca.* 1905⟩

Caption-title. The above at head of p. ⟨1⟩. At head of title: *Old South Leaflets. No. 157.* Printed self-wrapper. Double pagination: ⟨1⟩-24; and, 129-152.

Contains some material by Larcom reprinted from *The Lowell Offering.* For a comment on *The Lowell Offering* see *Mind amongst the Spindles,* 1844, in list of references below.

H

11400. HER GARDEN   A MEMORIAL POEM . . . (HITHERTO UNPUBLISHED)

CAMBRIDGE   PRINTED BY LOUIS FOSTER WESTON 1909

⟨1-15⟩. 8 3/16″ x 6 1/8″. Printed in brown. Pale buff paper. Illustrated.

⟨-⟩⁸.

Printed french-folded tan paper wrapper watermarked *Florentine (Italy).*

Deposited June 4, 1909.

B   H

11401. Poems of Country Life   A Modern Anthology by George S. Bryan . . .

New York   Sturgis & Walton Company   1912

"A Mountain Pastoral," pp. 30-31.

For comment see entry No. 7906.

11402. The Beverly Beacon   A Woman's Newspaper

Beverly, November First, Nineteen-Thirteen . . .

An occasional publication. All issued?

"Prospect Hill," p. 7.

H

11403. LETTERS OF LUCY LARCOM TO THE WHITTIERS   GRACE F. SHEPARD [REPRINTS FROM THE NEW ENGLAND QUARTERLY, VOLUME III, NUMBER 3, 1930]

COPYRIGHT 1930 BY THE SOUTHWORTH PRESS ⟨PORTLAND, MAINE⟩

⟨499⟩-518, 2 blank leaves. 9 1/4″ full x 5 7/8″. Watermarked *Flemish Book*

⟨-⟩¹².

Printed green paper wrapper.

H

11404. Youth's Companion   Edited by Lovell Thompson with Three Former Companion Editors, M. A. DeWolfe Howe, Arthur Stanwood Pier, and Harford Powel . . .

Houghton Mifflin Company   Boston   The Riverside Press   Cambridge   1954

Reprint save for "Looking back on Girlhood," pp. 410-415.

Deposited Oct. 11, 1954.

H

LUCY LARCOM

SECTION II

COLLECTIONS of reprinted material issued under Larcom's name; separate editions (*i.e.,* pieces reprinted from Larcom's books and issued in separate form). For a list of books by authors other than Larcom containing reprinted Larcom material see *Section III*.

11405. Poor Lone Hannah ... Music by F. Boott ...

Boston. Oliver Ditson & Co. 277 Washington St. ... 1869 ...

Sheet music. Cover-title. Plate number 25655. For an earlier setting see *Hannah's at the Window Binding Shoes*, 1859.

11406. The Old Barn Window, John ... Music by Violetta ...

Boston ... John F. Perry & Co 538 Washn St. ... 1876

Sheet music. Cover-title. Copyright notice on cover dated 1876; on p. 3: 1875. Reprint of "The Barn Window" from *Childhood Songs*, 1875.

11407. Hannah Binding Shoes ...

Forbes Co. Boston ‹n.d., *ca.* 1880›

A lithographed trade card, 2⅝" x 4¾" full. Text of "Hannah Binding Shoes" on verso. On recto, in colors, a seascape with mackerel in foreground. Issued as an advertisement: *Ask Your Grocer For "Deep Sea" Mess Mackerel. Fat, Juicy, Fine Flavored.* Publisher's imprint at lower right. Previously published as sheet music in 1859 and in *Poems*, 1869.

11408. A Year in Heaven.

‹n.p., n.d., *ca.* 1880.›

Cover-title. First and final leaves pasted to thin paper boards, over which is folded a printed white paper vellum wrapper. Author's name at end of text. Printed throughout in gold. Reprinted from *Poems*, 1869.

11409. The Poetical Works ... Household Edition with Illustrations

Boston Houghton, Mifflin and Company New York: 11 East Seventeenth Street The Riverside Press, Cambridge 1885

Reprint of the unillustrated ‹sic› edition of *The Poetical Works*, 1885. According to the publisher's records, 510 copies printed May 22, 1885. Advertised PW Sept. 26, 1885. Of the illustrated edition there were 16 printings during the period May, 1885–January, 1900. Certain of these reprints were issued under date of original copyright (‹1884›), others were issued with the title-page bearing the date of actual issue.

11410. The Old Barn Window, John ... Music by Violetta ...

Boston Oliver Ditson & Co. 451 Washington St. ... ‹1885›

Sheet music. Cover-title. Plate number 468-5. For an earlier printing see entry No. 11406.

11411. How Best to Minister ...

‹n.p., n.d., *ca.* 1885›

Printed on a card, corners rounded, 2⅛" x 4⅛". Mounted on a piece of blue satin ribbon. Reprinted from "Ye Did It unto Me," *Wild Roses* ... , 1881.

11412. Autumn Leaves: A Pictorial Library of Prose, Poetry and Art, by ... Eminent Authors ... Celia Thaxter ... Lucy Larcom ... and Many Others ... Edited by Daphne Dale.

‹n.p.› 1893. National Book Mart

"Jack-in-the-Swamp," pp. 185-186; otherwise "Jack-in-the-Pulpit," *Poetical Works*, 1885.

11413. ... The Golden Calendar A Birthday Book and Diary of Beautiful Thoughts. Arranged by Lucy Larcom ...

Ward, Lock, Bowden, and Co., London: Warwick House, Salisbury Square, E. C. New York: East 12th Street. Melbourne: St. James's Street. Sydney: York Street. ‹after *ca.* Sept. 1891; before *ca.* April 1893›

At head of title: *"A text may find him who a sermon flies."—George Herbert.* Pictorial wooden boards sides, cloth shelfback. Issued in Boston as *Beckonings for Every Day* . . . , 1886.

11414. Childhood's Sunny Days . . . ⟨by⟩ Lucy Larcom . . . and Others . . .

   . . . 1895 . . . Chicago . . .

For comment see entry No. 4747. "Life's Stairway" is extracted from "On the Stairway," *Childhood Songs,* 1875. "I Said It in the Moun-

tain Path;" otherwise "Shared," *Wild Roses* . . . , 1881.

11415. The Joys of the Years . . .

   ⟨n.p., n.d., *ca.* 1900.⟩

Card. 9⅛″ x 6⅛″ full. Printed on recto only. Otherwise "Growing Old," *Wild Roses* . . . , 1881.

LUCY LARCOM

SECTION III

IN THIS SECTION are listed books by authors other than Larcom which contain material by her reprinted from earlier books. See *Section II* for a list of collections of reprinted material issued under Larcom's name and separate editions.

The Harp of Freedom ... by Geo. W. Clark ...

New-York: Miller, Orton & Mulligan, 25 Park Row. Boston ... Rochester, N.Y. 1856.

"Ho! for Kansas," pp. 59-61 is a reprint of "Call to Kanzas"; see above under 1855.

Poems of Old Age ...

Boston: George Coolidge, 13 Tremont Row. 1861.

Title deposited Dec. 12, 1860. No further record in Copyright Office.

Chimes of Freedom and Union. A Collection of Poems ... by Various Authors ...

Boston ... MDCCCLXI.

For fuller entry see No. 8808.

The Rebellion Record: A Diary of American Events ... Edited by Frank Moore ... First Volume ...

New York: G. P. Putnam. C. T. Evans, General Agent. 1861.

For comment see entry No. 11531.

Home Ballads by Our Home Poets ... ⟨Second Edition⟩

New York ... 1865.

For comment see BAL, Vol. 1, p. 248.

Household Reading: Selections from The Congregationalist. 1849–1867.

Boston: W. L. Greene & Co., 15 Cornhill. 1868.

Light at Eventide. A Compilation of Choice Religious Hymns and Poems. By the Editor of "Chimes for Childhood," "Echoes from Home," Etc.

Boston: Lee and Shepard, Publishers. New York: Lee, Shepard and Dillingham. ⟨1870⟩

Edited by Dana Estes.

Declamations and Dialogues for the Sunday-School. By Prof. J. H. Gilmore ...

Boston: Henry A. Young & Co. No. 24 Cornhill. ⟨1871⟩

Reissued with the imprint: Boston: Young & Bartlett, 26 School Street. ⟨1871, *i.e.*, 1874–1877⟩

Songs of Home Selected from Many Sources ...

New York: Charles Scribner and Company. 1871.

American Poems. Selected and Edited by William Michael Rossetti ...

London: E. Moxon, Son, & Co., Dover Street, and 1 Amen Corner, Paternoster Row. ⟨n.d., after Nov. 1872⟩

Cloth?

Hymns for Mothers and Children. Second Series ...

Boston ... 1872.

For fuller entry see BAL, Vol. 4, p. 215.

The Poets of the Nineteenth Century. Selected and Edited by ... Robert Aris Willmott ... with English and American Additions, Arranged by Evert A. Duyckinck ...

New York: Harper & Brothers, Publishers, Franklin Square. 1872.

CH copy inscribed by early owner Christmas, 1871.

Public and Parlor Readings: Prose and Poetry for the Use of Reading Clubs and for Public and Social Entertainment. Miscellaneous. Edited by Lewis B. Monroe.

Boston: Lee and Shepard, Publishers. New York: Lee, Shepard, and Dillingham. 1872.

H copy received Feb. 16, 1872.

Illustrated Library of Favorite Song ... Edited by J. G. Holland ...

    New York ... ‹1873›

    For comment see entry No. 2853.

One Hundred Choice Selections No. 8 ...

    ... Philadelphia ... 1874.

    For fuller entry see BAL, Vol. 1, p. 84.

Sea and Shore ...

    Boston ... 1874.

    For comment see entry No. 4043.

One Hundred Choice Selections No. 9 ...

    ... Philadelphia ... 1874.

    For comment see BAL, Vol. 2, p. 168.

Hymns of Praise and Prayer. Collected and Edited by James Martineau ...

    London: Longmans, Green, Reader and Dyer. 1874.

    Hymn No. 543; otherwise, "Across the River," reprinted from *Poems,* 1869.

... The Quarterly Elocutionist ... Edited ... by Mrs. Anna Randall-Diehl ... January, 1875 ...

    ... New York ... 1875.

    For fuller entry see No. 4729.

The Elocutionist's Annual Number 2 ...

    Philadelphia ... 1875.

    For comment see BAL, Vol. 2, p. 247.

Poets and Poetry of Printerdom ... Edited by Oscar H. Harpel ...

    Cincinnati ... 1875.

    For comment see BAL, Vol. 3, p. 370.

The Sunny Side ... by Chas. W. Wendté and H. S. Perkins ...

    New York ... ‹1875›

    For fuller entry see No. 178.

Dick's Recitations and Readings No. 2 ...

    New York ... ‹1876›

    For comment see entry No. 285.

The Mountains ...

    Boston ... 1876.

    For comment see entry No. 1239.

Poems of the Life beyond and within ... Edited ... by Giles B. Stebbins ...

    Boston ... 1877.

    For fuller entry see No. 9451. Reprints "Hand in Hand with Angels." "Not Lost," pp. 168-169 is an extract from "Across the River," *Poems,* 1869.

The Elocutionist's Annual Number 6 ...

    Philadelphia ... 1878.

    For comment see BAL, Vol. 2, p. 248.

Garnered Treasures from the Poets ...

    Philadelphia ... 1878.

    For fuller entry see No. 4772.

Poetry of America ... ‹Edited› by W. J. Linton.

    London ... 1878.

    For fuller entry see No. 7872. All Larcom material herein reprinted from earlier books. "The Curtain of the Dark," p. 272, is extracted from "Hints," *Poems,* 1869.

Poems of Places Edited by Henry W. Longfellow ... New England. Vol. I.

    Boston ... 1879.

    For comment see entry No. 12208.

At the Beautiful Gate ... Compiled by ... ‹Anson D. F. Randolph›

    New York ... 1880.

    For comment see BAL, Vol. 2, pp. 104-105.

Unto the Desired Haven, and Other Religious Poems. Compiled by the Editor of "The Changed Cross;" ‹A.D.F. Randolph› ...

    New York: Anson D. F. Randolph & Company, 900 Broadway, Cor. 20th Street. 1880.

    Advertised for *October* PW Sept. 6, 1879. Advertised in PW Nov. 1, 1879, as in cloth gilt; cloth gilt with hand-painted binding. Listed PW Nov. 8, 1879. Also occurs as part of an omnibus volume, bound together with *At the Beautiful Gate* and *The Palace of the King;* the omnibus advertised in PW April 3, 1880.

The Elocutionist's Annual Number 7 ...

    Philadelphia ... 1880.

    For comment see BAL, Vol. 1, p. 74.

White Mountain Vistas. The Pemigewasset Valley ...

    Boston: L. Prang & Co. ‹n.d., *ca.* 1880›

Cover-title. Printed paper wrapper. "Franconia Notch from the Pemigewasset," p. ⟨5⟩; otherwise "My Mountain," *Poems,* 1869.

Harper's Cyclopædia of British and American Poetry Edited by Epes Sargent

New York . . . 1881

For comment see entry No. 4336.

Favorite Poems, Selected from English and American Authors.

New York: Thomas Y. Crowell & Co., No. 13 Astor Place. ⟨n.d., after May 1, 1881⟩

Marbled paper boards sides, leather shelfback; cloth. Also issued in a red line edition.

Purple and Gold Arranged by Kate Sanborn . . .

Boston . . . 1882 . . .

For comment see BAL, Vol. 1, p. 379.

The Lincoln Memorial . . . Edited by Osborn H. Oldroyd . . .

New York . . . MDCCCLXXXII

For comment see entry No. 1092.

The Cambridge Book of Poetry and Song . . . by Charlotte Fiske Bates . . .

New York . . . ⟨1882⟩

For comment see entry No. 7887.

. . . Selections for School Exhibitions and Private Reading . . . Nos. 1, 2, 3 . . .

Boston . . . 1882.

For comment see BAL, Vol. 2, p. 472.

Maple Leaves and Golden Rod . . . Arranged . . . by Susie B. Skelding

New York White, Stokes, & Allen 1883

Pictorial boards. Unpaged.

Surf and Wave: The Sea as Sung by the Poets. Edited by Anna L. Ward . . .

New York: Thomas Y. Crowell & Co. 13 Astor Place. ⟨1883⟩

Mountain, Lake, and River . . . by N. P. Willis . . .

Boston . . . 1884.

For comment see BAL, Vol. 3, p. 253.

Flowers from Glade and Garden Poems Arranged . . . by Susie Barstow Skelding . . .

New York . . . 1884

For comment see BAL, Vol. 2, p. 39.

Belford's Chatterbox. December, 1884. Edited by Elmo. ⟨*i.e.,* Thomas W. Handford?⟩ . . .

Chicago and New York: Belford, Clarke & Co. 1884.

Pictorial paper boards sides, cloth shelfback. Deposited Oct. 13, 1884. "I Thank Thee, O My God!," p. 16; otherwise "A Thanksgiving," *Poems,* 1869.

Songs of Flowers . . . Arranged and Illustrated by Susie B. Skelding

New York White, Stokes, & Allen 1884

Pictorial boards, silk fringe. Tied. Deposited Jan. 30, 1885.

An Old Scrap-Book. With Additions . . .

⟨Cambridge⟩ February 8, 1884.

For comment see entry No. 7763.

No. 6. Standard Recitations by Best Authors . . . Compiled . . . by Frances P. Sullivan . . . December, 1884 . . .

. . . N. Y. . . . ⟨1884⟩

For fuller entry see BAL, Vol. 3, p. 370.

January Edited by Oscar Fay Adams . . .

Boston . . . ⟨1885⟩

For comment see entry No. 58.

No. 8. Standard Recitations by Best Authors . . . Compiled . . . by Frances P. Sullivan . . . June, 1885 . . .

. . . N.Y. . . . ⟨1885⟩

For fuller entry see BAL, Vol. 3, p. 81.

Midsummer Flowers . . . Poems by Prominent Authors Arranged and Illustrated by Susie Barstow Skelding . . .

New York White, Stokes, & Allen 1885

Silk, color print pasted to front cover. Tied. Deposited Aug. 3, 1885.

The Eureka Collection of Recitations and Readings, Number One . . . Edited by Mrs. Anna Randall Diehl . . .

New York: J. S. Ogilvie & Company, 31 Rose Street. ⟨1885⟩

Printed paper wrapper. Deposited Sept. 26, 1885.

Flowers from Here and There   Poems Arranged and Illustrated by Susie Barstow Skelding ...

New York   White, Stokes, & Allen   1885

From Moor and Glen ... Poems ... Arranged ... by Susie B. Skelding ...

New York   White, Stokes, & Allen   1885

Unpaged. Cloth, tied, pictorial label pasted to front.

Childhood's Happy Days ... Edited by Edward Everett Hale.

New York ... ⟨n.d., *ca.* 1885⟩

For comment see BAL, Vol. 4, p. 381.

February Edited by Oscar Fay Adams ...

Boston ... ⟨1886⟩

For comment see entry No. 59.

March Edited by Oscar Fay Adams ...

Boston ... ⟨1886⟩

For comment see entry No. 60.

Bugle-Echoes ... Edited by Francis F. Browne

New York ... MDCCCLXXXVI

For comment see BAL, Vol. 1, p. 75.

Representative Poems of Living Poets ...

... New York   1886

For comment see entry No. 436.

May Edited by Oscar Fay Adams ...

Boston ... ⟨1886⟩

For comment see entry No. 63.

June Edited by Oscar Fay Adams ...

Boston ... ⟨1886⟩

For comment see entry No. 64.

July Edited by Oscar Fay Adams ...

Boston ... ⟨1886⟩

For comment see entry No. 65. "In Young July," p. 1; otherwise, "Thirty-Five," *Poems,* 1869.

September Edited by Oscar Fay Adams ...

Boston ... ⟨1886⟩

For comment see entry No. 67.

Belford's Annual 1886–7. Edited by Thomas W. Handford ...

Chicago ... ⟨1886⟩

For comment see entry No. 10467. Reprints "Hand in Hand with Angels"; and, "July," which is otherwise "Thirty-Five," *Poems,* 1869. See next entry.

Belford's Chatterbox December, 1886. Edited by Thomas W. Handford ...

Chicago ... ⟨1886⟩

For comment see entry No. 10468. Reprints "Hand in Hand with Angels"; and, "July" which is otherwise "Thirty-Five," *Poems,* 1869. See preceding entry.

October Edited by Oscar Fay Adams ...

Boston ... ⟨1886⟩

For comment see entry No. 68.

Familiar Birds and What the Poets Sing of Them ... Edited by Susie Barstow Skelding ...

New York ... 1886

For comment see BAL, Vol. 1, p. 86.

November Edited by Oscar Fay Adams ...

Boston ... ⟨1886⟩

For comment see entry No. 69.

Songsters of the Branches Edited by Susie Barstow Skelding ...

New York   White, Stokes, & Allen   1886

Pictorial stiff paper wrapper. Unpaged. Tied.

A Temperance Souvenir Compiled by Mrs. G. S. Hunt ...

Chicago   Woman's Temperance Publication Association   MDCCCLXXXVI

Printed paper wrapper. Unpaged. Contains fifteen lines (*Wherefore drink with me ...*); otherwise "My Cup Runneth Over," *Wild Roses,* 1881.

The Two Voices   Poems of the Mountains and the Sea Selected by John W. Chadwick ...

Troy, N. Y.   H. B. Nims & Company   1886

Reprinted with the imprint: *Boston   Joseph Knight Company Publishers* ⟨1886⟩

Flowers from Field and Woodland ... Edited by Josephine Pollard

New York   Frederick A. Stokes & Brother   1888

Deposited Aug. 4, 1888.

Belford's Annual. 1888–9. Edited by Thomas W. Handford ...

Chicago ... ⟨1888⟩

For comment see entry No. 5735.

Golden Milestones Illustrated by L. K. Harlow.

L. Prang & Co. Boston. Copyright 1888 by L. Prang & Co. Boston.

Hand painted wrapper. Contains an untitled extract from "Growing Old," *Wild Roses*, 1881.

A Memorial of the Rev. Charles H. Wheeler, Late Pastor of the Church of the Unity, Winchendon, Mass.

Boston: Damrell & Upham, Old Corner Bookstore. 1888.

Printed wrapper.

Boys' and Girls' New Pictorial Library ... Introduction by ... Rev. W. H. Milburn ...

Chicago ... 1889.

For comment see entry No. 6319. "Jack-in-the-Swamp," pp. 185-186; otherwise, "Jack-in-the-Pulpit," *The Poetical Works*, 1885.

Buds and Blossoms ...

Philadelphia Peterson Magazine Co. 1889

Golden Lays for Youthful Days. Selected Poems from the Best Poets ...

... Chicago ... 1889.

For comment see entry No. 7899A. "Little Bridget's Christmas Flowers," pp. 179-181; otherwise, "Little Bridget's Country Week," *The Poetical Works*, 1885.

... Harper's Fifth Reader American Authors

New York ... 1889

For comment see entry No. 7917.

Hymns of Faith and Life. Collected and Edited by the Rev. John Hunter.

Glasgow: J. Maclehose & Sons, 1889.

Not seen. "A friend gave me your *Hymns of Faith and Life,* in the winter, telling me she had found one or two of mine in it. On looking it over, I find five, not all of which are credited to me, though all are included in the *Household Edition* of my poems ..."—From a letter, Larcom to John Hunter, July 10, 1890, as published in Addison, p. 197.

The Poets of Essex County. Massachusetts. By Sidney Perley ...

Salem, Mass.: Sidney Perley. 1889.

White Mountain Vistas The Crystal Hills Illustrated by F. Schuyler Mathews

L Prang & Co Boston ... 1889 ...

Cover-title. Printed self-wrapper. Unpaged. All Larcom material herein reprinted from earlier books. "Mt. Adams from Mt. Washington" and "The Mt. Washington Railway" extracted from "In a Cloud Rift," *Wild Roses*, 1881.

The Poets' Year ... Edited by Oscar Fay Adams ...

Boston ... ⟨1890⟩

For comment see entry No. 80.

American Sonnets Selected ... by T. W. Higginson and E. H. Bigelow

Boston ... 1890

For comment see entry No. 8373.

Representative Sonnets by American Poets ... by Charles H. Crandall

Boston ... 1890

For comment see entry No. 8374.

Local and National Poets of America ... Edited ... ⟨by⟩ Thos. W. Herringshaw ...

Chicago ... 1890.

For fuller entry see BAL, Vol. 2, p. 391.

The Speakers' Library ... Edited by Daphne Dale.

1890 ... Chicago ...

For comment see entry No. 6324.

No. 39. Standard Recitations by Best Authors ... Compiled ... by Frances P. Sullivan ... March 1893 ...

... N. Y. ... 1893

For fuller entry see BAL, Vol. 3, p. 139. "A Death and a Life," pp. 38-39, is a combined version of "Hannah Binding Shoes" and "Skipper Ben," both reprinted from *Poems*, 1869.

Sun Prints in Sky Tints ... by Irene E. Jerome

Boston ... 1893

For fuller entry see BAL, Vol. 2, p. 452.

Fifty-Two Stories for Children. Told in the Twilight, Told in the Nursery, Told in the Holidays, Told at Odd Times. Edited by Alfred H. Miles . . .

London: Hutchinson & Co., 34, Paternoster Row. ⟨1893⟩

Not seen. Issued in Nov. 1893 according to *The English Catalogue of Books.* Received by BMU Jan. 16, 1894.

The Lover's Year-Book of Poetry ⟨Second Series⟩ . . . Married-Life and Child-Life ⟨Compiled⟩ by Horace Parker Chandler . . .

Boston . . . 1893

For comment see entry No. 10903.

Quaker Poems A Collection of Verse Relating to the Society of Friends. Compiled by Charles Francis Jenkins.

Philadelphia: John C. Winston & Co. 1893.

"John G. Whittier," pp. 127-128; otherwise, "J.G.W.," *Wild Roses,* 1881.

Hymns. Supplemental to Existing Collections. Selected and Edited by W. Garrett Horder . . .

London: Elliot Stock, 62, Paternoster Row, E.C. ⟨n.d., 1894⟩

Received BMU Feb. 5, 1894. All Larcom material herein reprinted from other books. The untitled poem, hymn No. 1147, is otherwise "Dawn," *Easter Gleams,* 1890.

Through Love to Light A Selection . . . by John White Chadwick and Annie Hathaway Chadwick

Boston . . . 1896

For comment see entry No. 2633.

Platform Pearls for Temperance Workers and Other Reformers A Collection of Recitations . . . Compiled by Lilian M. Heath

New York Funk & Wagnalls Company London and Toronto 1896

The Treasury of American Sacred Song . . . Selected and Edited by W. Garrett Horder . . .

London Henry Frowde Oxford University Press Warehouse Amen Corner, E. C. New York: 91 & 93 Fifth Avenue 1896

Cloth, vellum shelfback.

Dew Drops and Diamonds A . . . Collection . . . for Boys and Girls . . .

. . . 1898 . . . Chicago . . .

For comment see BAL, Vol. 1, p. 77. Contains reprinted material. "Causes for Thankfulness" is an extract from "A Thanksgiving," *Poems,* 1869.

Songs of Nature Edited by John Burroughs

New York . . . MCMI . . .

For comment see entry No. 2169.

The Young Folks' Library . . .

. . . Boston ⟨1901–1902⟩

For comment see entry No. 391.

St. Nicholas Book of Verse Edited by Mary Budd Skinner and Joseph Osmun Skinner . . .

. . . New York . . . MCMXXIII

For comment see entry No. 818.

The Soul of the City . . . Compiled by Garland Greever and Joseph M. Bachelor

Boston . . . 1923

For comment see BAL, Vol. 3, p. 288.

American Mystical Verse An Anthology Selected by Irene Hunter . . .

D. Appleton and Company New York MCMXXV

Rushlight Centennial Edition 1835–1935 An Anthology

Wheaton College   Norton, Massachusetts Wheaton College Press ⟨n.d., 1935?⟩

Printed boards, cloth shelfback.

REFERENCES AND ANA

. . . Lights and Shadows of Factory Life in New England. By a Factory Girl . . .

. . . J. Winchester . . . New York . . . 1843

Caption-title. At head of title: The New World . . . Extra Series . . . Number 51 . . . February, 1843 . . .

Sometimes erroneously credited to Lucy Larcom. The author was Eliza Jane Cate (1812–1884). See *Loom and Spindle or Life among the Early Mill Girls . . .* , by Harriet H. Robinson, New York ⟨1898⟩, p. 119.

Mind amongst the Spindles: A Selection from The Lowell Offering, a Miscellany Wholly Composed by the Factory Girls of an American City. With an Introduction, by the English Editor.

London: Charles Knight & Co., Ludgate Street. 1844.

Cloth? Selections from *The Lowell Offering* to which periodical Larcom contributed. This book, however, contains nothing identified as by Larcom. See next entry.

Mind amongst the Spindles. A Miscellany, Wholly Composed by the Factory Girls. Selected from The Lowell Offering. With an Introduction by the English Editor, and a Letter from Harriet Martineau.

Boston: Jordan, Swift & Wiley. 1845.

Noticed in *Daily Evening Transcript* (Boston), Nov. 14, 1844, as *to be issued this afternoon.* See the London (1844) edition above. Also see following note.

THE FACTORY OPERATIVES' MAGAZINE
(and related publications)

"The two magazines published by the mill-girls, the *Lowell Offering* and the *Operatives' Magazine,* originated with literary meetings in the vestry of two religious societies, the first in the Universalist Church, the second in the First Congregational, to which my sister and I belonged.

"On account of our belonging there, our contributions were given to the *Operatives' Magazine,* the first periodical for which I ever wrote, issued by the literary society of which our minister took charge . . ."—*A New England Girlhood,* pp. 209-210.

". . . After a while the assertion was circulated, through some distant newspaper, that our magazine was not written by ourselves at all, but by 'Lowell lawyers.' This seemed almost too foolish a suggestion to contradict, but the editor of the *Offering* thought it best to give the name and occupation of some of the writers by way of refutation. It was for this reason (much against my own wish) that my real name was first attached to anything I wrote . . . After I began to read and love Wordsworth, my favorite *nom de plume* was *Rotha.* In the later numbers of the magazine, the editor more frequently made use of my initials."—*ibid.,* pp. 223-224.

The Factory Operatives' Magazine

Commenced publication April, 1841. Under this title but one number issued. With publication of the second number the title was altered to:

The Operatives' Magazine

Absorbed in 1842 by *The Lowell Offering, New Series,* which started publication as:

The Lowell Offering

This periodical commenced in Oct. 1840, suspended March, 1841, and was revived as:

The Lowell Offering, New Series

Commenced April, 1841, suspended Dec. 1845. According to Harriet H. Robinson (*Loom and Spindle . . . ,* New York ⟨1898⟩, p. 104), the publication was revived as:

The New England Offering

A single number issued Sept. 1847; revived April, 1848; suspended March, 1850.

Predecessors of the above were "two or three little fortnightly papers, ⟨presumably circulated in *ms* only⟩ to which the ⟨factory⟩ girls contributed. Each ran a troubled existence of a few months, and then gave place to its successor, bearing a new name. *The Casket,* for a time, held their jewels of thought; then *The Bouquet* gathered their full-blown ideas into a more pretentious collection. The most permanent of these literary productions was one that started with the intention of being very profound,—it was called *The Diving Bell . . .*"—*Lucy Larcom Life, Letters and Diary,* 1894, p. 9.

"Our little sheet was called *The Diving Bell,* probably from the sea-associations of the name. We kept our secrets of authorship very close from everybody except the editor, who had to decipher the handwriting and copy the pieces . . . Our little home-journal went bravely on through twelve numbers. Its yellow manuscript pages occasionally meet my eyes . . ."—*A New England Girlhood,* pp. 170, 174.

Wheaton Female Seminary, July 11th, 1855. Parting Hymn. [Original.] . . .

⟨n.p., presumably Norton, Mass., 1855⟩

Single cut sheet folded to make four pages. The above on p. ⟨1⟩. Six four-line stanzas beginning: *Father, God of light and power . . .* Anonymous. By Larcom? The only copies located (Wheaton College, Norton, Mass.) have penciled notations ascribing authorship to Larcom.

The Sunbeam and Other Stories.

Boston, 1860.

Not seen; not located. Entry from Foley, p. 166. Ghost?

Intensive search has failed to produce such a book. A book so titled was listed without author, as a Henry Hoyt (Boston) publication, in *The Uniform Trade List Circular* (Phila. ⟨1867⟩), p. 151 and, *Publishers' Uniform Trade List Directory* (Phila., 1868), p. 171. A "new edition", with authorship credited to Lucy Larcom, listed in *The American Catalogue* ... , 1880, with a note indicating that the "new edition" was an 1872 reprint of a book first issued in 1860.

The only 1860 publication of similar title located by BAL is the anonymous *The Sunbeam,* Boston (Hoyt), but this is a reissue (with some curious alterations by the binder, and insertion of Hoyt's cancel title-leaf) of sheets published by John P. Jewett & Co., Boston, 1855; the Hoyt title-page is dated 1860. The only located book bearing the title *The Sunbeam and Other Stories,* anonymous, was copyrighted 1863 and issued by the Presbyterian Board of Publication, Philadelphia.

An Address in Memory of Lucy Larcom, Delivered on Sunday, April 30, 1893, in St. Peter's Church, Beverly, Massachusetts, by Rev. Daniel Dulany Addison ...

> Boston: Damrell & Upham, the Old Corner Bookstore, 283 Washington Street. ⟨n.d., 1893?⟩

> Printed paper wrapper.

Lucy Larcom   Life, Letters, and Diary by Daniel Dulany Addison

> Boston ... 1894

> Referred to in the above list as *Addison.* For fuller entry see No. 11394.

Loom and Spindle or Life among the Early Mill Girls with a Sketch of "The Lowell Offering" and Some of Its Contributors by Harriet H. Robinson ...

> New York: 46 East 14th Street   Thomas Y. Crowell & Company   Boston: 100 Purchase Street ⟨1898⟩

GEORGE PARSONS LATHROP

1 8 5 1 – 1 8 9 8

Note: As secretary of the American Copyright League, Lathrop's name appears on certain of the printed documents issued by this organization in 1883–1885. BAL has all but ignored such official ephemera but see entry Nos. 11446, 11454.

11416. ROSE AND ROOF-TREE: POEMS ...

BOSTON   JAMES R. OSGOOD AND COMPANY   1875

⟨i⟩-⟨xii⟩, ⟨13⟩-126, blank leaf. Frontispiece inserted. 6¾″ x 4½″ full.

⟨1-5¹², 6⁴⟩. *Signed:* ⟨1-2⟩, 3-6, ⟨7⟩, 8⁸.

C cloth: green; terra-cotta. FL cloth: purple; terra-cotta. Brown-coated on white end papers.

500 copies printed Oct. 29, 1875 (publisher's records). A copy at BPL received Nov. 19, 1875. Listed PW Nov. 20, 1875. Noticed (as a Trübner importation) Ath March 4, 1876.

AAS   B   BPL   H   NYPL   UV

11417. ... The Cambridge of 1776 ... Edited for the Ladies Centennial Committee by A. G. ⟨i.e., Arthur Gilman⟩ ...

Cambridge: Printed on the Site of Fort Number One: Over against the Town of Brighton, on the River's Side. To Be Sold in Boston by Lockwood, Brooks, and Company, on Washington and Bromfield Streets. M D CCC LXX VI.

At head of title: Theatrum Majorum.

"Praise of the Past," pp. ⟨117⟩-118.

Two editions noted:

First Edition

Copyright notice in name of *Mary Williams Greely.*

Leaf 2₁ (pp. 17-⟨18⟩), in all examined copies, is a cancel. All issued thus?

Noted in the following styles of binding. The sequence, if any, has not been determined and the designations are for identification only.

A: S cloth: green; terra-cotta. Front lettered in gold. Blackstamped tree, without background, on front; tree repeated on back in blind.

B: S cloth: green; mauve. Front lettered in gold. Blackstamped tree, with background, on front.

C: Printed gray paper wrapper, with the following imprint on the wrapper:

Cambridge: The Ladies' Centennial Committee. Boston: Lockwood, Brooks, & Co.   381 Washington Street.   New York: Hurd & Houghton. 1876.

Second Edition

Copyright notice in name of *Lockwood, Brooks, & Co.*

Leaf 2₁ (pp. 17-⟨18⟩), is not a cancel.

Inserted in the front matter is a leaf imprinted with a note to the second edition headed: *Ad Suum Cuique Reddendum.*

Noted in green S cloth. Front stamped wholly in gold; the tree shows the background. Tree vignette blindstamped on back cover.

Note: The present entry is revised and supersedes entry No. 9570.

Soon PW Dec. 11, 1875. Gd copy (first, Binding A) presented Jan. 4, 1876, by Alice M. Longfellow, chairman of the publication committee, to Mary Williams Greely, the copyright claimant. Listed and advertised (both paper and cloth) PW Jan. 29, 1876. Deposited May 7, 1877.

AAS (1st, binding B)   B (1st, binding A)   BA (1st, binding A)   BPL (1st, binding A)   H (1st, binding B; binding C)   NYPL (1st, binding A; 2nd)   Y (1st, binding A; binding B)

11418. A STUDY OF HAWTHORNE ...

BOSTON: JAMES R. OSGOOD AND COMPANY, LATE TICKNOR & FIELDS, AND FIELDS, OSGOOD, & CO. 1876.

Title-page in black and red.

⟨i⟩-vi, ⟨7⟩-350; advertisement, p. ⟨351⟩. 5⅞″ x 4⅛″.

⟨1², 2-22⁸, 23⁶⟩. *Signed:* ⟨A⟩-R, ⟨S-U⟩, V⁸. *Also signed:* ⟨1⟩-9, ⟨10⟩-12, ⟨13⟩-14¹², 15⁸.

S cloth: green; terra-cotta. Green-coated on white end papers. Flyleaves. Edges stained red.

Two binding issues noted:

1: Spine imprint: JAMES R. OSGOOD & CO.

2: Spine imprint: HOUGHTON, MIFFLIN & CO.

Printed May 29, 1876, 2000 copies; bound during the period June 6, 1876–Aug. 12, 1887 (publisher's records). Noted as *just ready* PW June 10, 1876. Listed PW June 17, 1876.

B (1st)   NYPL (1st, 2nd).

11419. The Sunshine of Thine Eyes ... Music by Geo. L. Osgood ...

Boston   G. D. Russell & Company   126 Tremont St ... 1876 ...

Sheet music. Cover-title. Plate number: 3838-3. (alto). Also issued for soprano; plate number: 3831-3.

Reprinted from *Rose and Roof-Tree*, 1875.

Reprinted and reissued by Oliver Ditson & Co.

B

11420. ... AFTERGLOW.

BOSTON: ROBERTS BROTHERS.   1877.

Anonymous. At head of title: NO NAME SERIES. "IS THE GENTLEMAN ANONYMOUS? IS HE A GREAT UNKNOWN?" DANIEL DERONDA.

⟨1⟩-316, 4 pp. advertisements. 6⁹⁄₁₆″ x 4⁵⁄₁₆″.

⟨1⟩-20⁸.

V cloth: black. Cream end papers imprinted with advertisements. Flyleaves.

Two varieties of the advertisements on the end papers noted, apparently used at random, and copies of the book occur with either or both:

A

P. ⟨ii⟩: ... *A Modern Mephistopheles* ...

P. ⟨iii⟩: ... *"Is That All?"* ...

B

P. ⟨ii⟩: ... *Kismet* ...

P. ⟨iii⟩: ... *Deirdrè* ...

Note: In some copies is inserted a printed slip of blue paper, 1⅝″ x 3¹⁵⁄₁₆″, reading: *Publishers' Notice. Editors and all others reprinting ... poems or extracts ... are requested to give credit ...*

Noted for *next week* PW June 2, 1877. Adver-

tised for June 10 PW June 9, 1877. Listed PW June 9, 1877. Reviewed Ath July 7, 1877.

AAS   H   NYPL   UV

11421. ODE

The following printings noted. Sequence not established. The designations are for identification only.

A

ODE. WORDS BY G. P. LATHROP. MUSIC BY EDWARD M. DOW ...

⟨n.p., n.d., 1878?⟩

Single leaf. 8⅞″ x 5″. Music not present.

Note: On NYPL copy the composer's name is crossed out and the name Julius Eichberg is substituted.

Written on the NYPL copy: "Sung at 240th Annual Celebration of the Ancient & Honorable Artillery Co.   June 3, 1878."

B

Order of Exercises at the Two Hundred and Fortieth Anniversary of the Ancient & Honorable Artillery Co., Monday, June 3, 1878 ... at the Hollis Street Church.

⟨n.p., 1878⟩

Single cut sheet folded to make four pages. Issued as a program.

"Ode," p. ⟨2⟩.

Reprinted in: *The Two Hundred and Fortieth Annual Record of the Ancient and Honorable Artillery Co. of Massachusetts. 1877–78 ...* , Boston, 1878; printed paper wrapper.

H (B)   NYPL (A)

11422. SOMEBODY ELSE ...

BOSTON: ROBERTS BROTHERS.   1878.

⟨i-viii⟩, ⟨1⟩-342, 2 pp. advertisements. 5¾″ x 4³⁄₁₆″ scant.

⟨1-22⟩⁸. *Signed:* ⟨-⟩⁴, 1-21⁸, 22⁴.

S cloth: green; mauve; purple; red; rust. Gray-coated on white end papers. Flyleaves. Edges stained red.

"... Will issue by the 1st of July"—Advertisement, PW June 29, 1878. BPL copy received July 5, 1878. Listed PW July 6, 1878.

AAS   B   H   NYPL   Y

11423. ... A Masque of Poets. Including Guy Vernon, a Novelette in Verse.

Boston: Roberts Brothers.   1878.

Edited by Lathrop; contains the following po-ems by him:

"The Bride of War," pp. 104-113. Collected in *Dreams and Days*, 1892.

"Don't Overdo It," pp. 68-69.

"Immortal Clouds," p. 167.

"Love and Fate," p. 32.

"The Rhone Cradle," pp. 129-130.

"Yachting," p. 66.

For fuller entry see No. 118.

11424. Poems of Places Edited by Henry W. Longfellow . . . America. New England. Vol. II.

Boston: Houghton, Osgood and Company. The Riverside Press, Cambridge. 1879.

"Bride Brook," pp. 236-239. Collected in *Dreams and Days*, 1892.

For comment see entry No. 12209.

11425. Home Life in Song with the Poets of To-Day . . . ⟨Compiled by A.D.F. Randolph⟩

New York: Anson D. F. Randolph & Com-pany, 900 Broadway, Cor. 20th Street. ⟨1879⟩

"Thanksgiving Turkey," p. 122. Collected in *Dreams and Days*, 1892.

For comment see entry No. 432.

11426. Papyrus Leaves . . . Edited by William Fearing Gill . . .

New York: R. Worthington. 1880.

"The Too Soon Dead," pp. 151-163.

"Shamrock and Laurel," p. 281.

Deposited Dec. 26, 1879. For fuller comment see entry No. 2477.

11427. . . . PRESIDENTIAL PILLS BEING A VADEMECUM OF MATTERS IN PARTIC-ULAR CONCERNING GENERALS HAN-FIELD AND GARCOCK . . .

BOSTON   A. WILLIAMS & CO. PUBLISHERS   283 WASHINGTON STREET   1880

At head of title: "SOMETHING NO VOTER SHOULD BE WITHOUT"—THE AUTHOR

⟨1⟩-22, 2 pp. advertisements. Six integral plates not reckoned in the printed pagination. 5⅞" x 4¼".

⟨1-2⁸, 3²⟩.

Printed blue-green paper wrapper.

Listed PW Sept. 25, 1880.

AAS   Y

11428. Indian Summer   Autumn   Poems and Sketches ⟨Compiled by⟩ L. Clarkson . . .

New York   E. P. Dutton & Company   713 Broadway   1881. Copyright, 1880, by E. P. Dutton & Co.

"October Snow. To Longfellow on His Seven-tieth Birthday," p. 52.

CH   H

11429. In Memoriam. Gems of Poetry and Song on James A. Garfield . . .

Columbus, O⟨hio⟩. J. C. McClenahan & Company. 1881.

"Garfield, President of the People. Died Sep-tember 19, 1881," pp. 59-60.

For comment see entry No. 122.

11430. IN THE DISTANCE. AN AMERICAN STORY . . . IN TWO VOLUMES . . .

LONDON: SAMPSON LOW, MARSTON, SEARLE, & RIVINGTON, CROWN BUILDINGS, 188, FLEET STREET. 1882. [ALL RIGHTS RESERVED.]

For first American edition see next entry.

Warning: The only copy examined has been re-bound. The pagination and collation tentative.

1: ⟨i⟩-iv, ⟨1⟩-323; printer's imprint, p. ⟨324⟩. 7³⁄₁₆" scant x 4¾".

2: ⟨i⟩-iv, ⟨1⟩-308.

1: ⟨A⟩², B-I, K-U, X⁸, Y².

2: ⟨A⟩², B-I, K-T, U⁸, X².

Cloth?

Listed PC March 1, 1882; Ath March 4, 1882. Noted *will be published almost immediately* Ath March 4, 1882. Reviewed Ath April 8, 1882.

Y

11431. IN THE DISTANCE   A NOVEL . . .

BOSTON   JAMES R. OSGOOD AND COMPANY   1882

For prior London publication see preceding en-try.

⟨i⟩-vi, ⟨7⟩-374; publisher's catalog, pp. ⟨1⟩-10, dated on p. ⟨1⟩: *February, 1882*. 6¹¹⁄₁₆" x 4¹¹⁄₁₆".

⟨1⟩-24⁸.

S cloth: brown; yellow. Yellow end papers.

According to the publisher's records, 1520 copies printed Feb. 21, 1882. Bound during the period

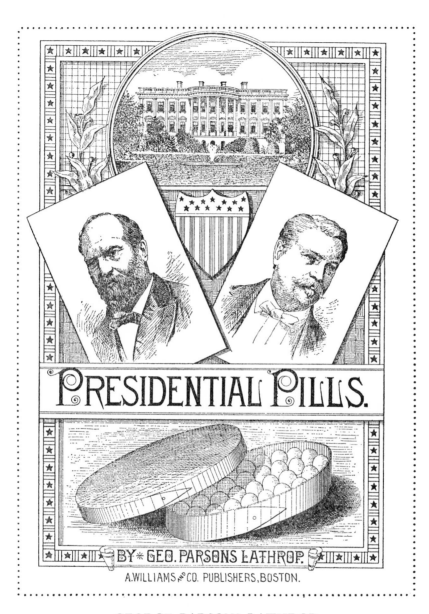

GEORGE PARSONS LATHROP
Entry No. 11427 Front of Wrapper
(Yale University Library)

Feb. 24–March 24, 1882. A copy in BA received March 7, 1882. Deposited March 9, 1882. Noted as *just issued* PW March 11, 1882. Listed PW March 18, 1882.

AAS   B   Y

11432. AN ECHO OF PASSION ...

BOSTON   HOUGHTON,   MIFFLIN   AND   COMPANY
NEW YORK: 11 EAST SEVENTEENTH STREET   THE
RIVERSIDE PRESS, CAMBRIDGE   1882

⟨1⟩-230; plus: publisher's catalog, pp. ⟨1⟩-16. Laid paper. 7⅛″ x 4¹¹⁄₁₆″.

⟨1⟩-14⁸, 15¹, ⟨16⟩²; plus: ⟨17⟩⁸.

S cloth: golden yellow, stamped in white. S cloth: green-gray, stamped in gold. White end papers printed in gray with a floral pattern. Laid paper flyleaf at back of some copies.

According to the publisher's records, 1560 copies printed April 5, 1882. Bound April 20, 1882–Feb. 15, 1883. Noted for *this week* PW April 29, 1882. A copy at BA received May 3, 1882. Listed PW May 6, 1882. Deposited May 11, 1882. The English (Hamilton, Adams; Douglas) edition advertised *in the press* Ath July 26, 1884; listed PC Sept. 15, 1884.

AAS   H   LC   Y

11433. The Cambridge Book of Poetry and Song ... by Charlotte Fiske Bates ...

New York: Thomas Y. Crowell & Co., No. 13 Astor Place. ⟨1882⟩

Reprint save for "To My Son," p. 334. Collected as "The Child's Wish Granted" in *Dreams and Days*, 1892.

Reissued as a two-volume work, not before 1890, with the imprint: *New York: 46 East 14th Street ... Boston: 100 Purchase Street* ⟨1882⟩.

For further comment see entry No. 7887.

11434. Harper's Christmas Pictures & Papers ... Done by the Tile Club & Its Literary Friends

Published by Harper & Brothers   Franklin Square, New York ⟨1882⟩

"Oley Grow's Daughter," p. 19. Collected in *Two Sides of a Story* ... ⟨1889⟩.

H copy received Nov. 14, 1882. For fuller comment see entry No. 3405.

11435. One Hundred Choice Selections No. 21 ...

Published by P. Garrett & Co., 708 Chestnut Street, Philadelphia, Pa., and 130 E. Adams Street, Chicago, Ill. 1882.

"Keenan's Charge ... Chancellorsville, May, 1863," pp. 198-200. Collected in *Dreams and Days*, 1892.

For comment see entry No. 2486.

11436. ⟨Writings of Nathaniel Hawthorne. Riverside Edition⟩

Boston   Houghton, Mifflin and Company New York: 11 East Seventeenth Street   The Riverside Press, Cambridge   1883

12 Vols. Edited by Lathrop. For fuller entry see BAL No. 7643. Additional volumes were not edited by Lathrop. The many later reprintings have been ignored.

1: *Twice-Told Tales.*

"Introductory Note," pp. ⟨7⟩-12.

2: *Mosses from an Old Manse.*

"Introductory Note," pp. ⟨7⟩-10.

3: *The House of the Seven Gables ... The Snow Image and other Twice-Told Tales.*

"Introductory Note⟨s⟩," pp. ⟨7⟩-12, ⟨381⟩-383.

4: *A Wonder-Book   Tanglewood Tales ... Grandfather's Chair.*

"Introductory Note⟨s⟩," pp. ⟨9⟩-11, ⟨201⟩-203, ⟨425⟩-428.

5: *The Scarlet Letter ... The Blithedale Romance.*

"Introductory Note⟨s⟩," pp. ⟨9⟩-14, ⟨315⟩-320.

6: *The Marble Faun.*

"Introductory Note," pp. ⟨7⟩-12.

7-8: *Our Old Home ... English Note-Books.*

"Introductory Note⟨s⟩," pp. ⟨9⟩-12, ⟨407⟩-409, Vol. 7.

9: *Passages from the American Note-Books.*

"Introductory Note," pp. ⟨5⟩-11.

10: *Passages from the French and Italian Note-Books.*

"Introductory Note," pp. ⟨5⟩-7.

11: *The Dolliver Romance   Fanshawe ... Septimius Felton ... Ancestral Footstep.*

"Introductory Note⟨s⟩," pp. ⟨9⟩-13, ⟨221⟩-226, ⟨433⟩-436.

12: *Tales, Sketches and Other Papers.*

"Introductory Note," pp. ⟨7⟩-10. "Biographical Sketch of Nathaniel Hawthorne," pp. ⟨441⟩-569.

11437. Concord Lectures on Philosophy . . .

Cambridge, Mass. Moses King, Publisher Harvard Square. ⟨1883⟩

"The Symbolism of Color," pp. 149-151.

For comment see entry No. 129.

11438. SPANISH VISTAS . . .

NEW YORK   HARPER & BROTHERS, FRANKLIN SQUARE 1883

⟨i⟩-xii, ⟨1⟩-210, 2 pp. advertisements. Illustrated. 9" x 6⅝".

⟨-⟩⁶, 1-2⁸, 3⁴, 3*⁴, 4⁴, 4*⁴, 5⁸, 6⁴, ⟨6*⟩⁴, ⟨7⟩⁴, ⟨7*⟩⁴, 8⁴, 8*⁴, 9⁴, 9*⁴, 10-13⁸, 14². The signature marks 5* on p. 69 and 11* on p. 165 are superfluous.

Two bindings noted. The sequence is presumed correct.

A

S cloth: red. Front and spine stamped in gold, silver, and black. Covers bevelled. Brown-coated on white end papers. Olive-coated on white end papers. Flyleaves. Top edges gilt. A copyright copy thus; a copy in BA received May 17, 1883, thus.

B

T cloth: green. Front unstamped. Spine stamped in gold only. White wove end papers. Top edges plain. Remainder?

Deposited May 14, 1883. A copy at BA (Binding A) received May 17, 1883. Listed PW May 19, 1883.

AAS (A) BA (A) H (A) LC (both) UV (A) Y (A)

11439. Puck on Wheels. No. IV. For the Summer of 1883 . . .

New York: Published by Keppler & Schwarzmann, 1883.

"Plain Fact," p. ⟨84⟩.

For comment see entry No. 1888.

11440. PECONIC PARK   AN EXPLORATION OF LONG ISLAND . . .

NEW-YORK   PRINTED FOR PRIVATE CIRCULATION 1883.

⟨1⟩-40. Five folded inserts; other illustrations in text. 10" x 7⅞".

⟨1⟩-5⁴.

S cloth: tan. White end papers printed in ecru with a floral pattern. Flyleaves.

P R

11441. HISTORY OF THE UNION LEAGUE OF PHILADELPHIA, FROM ITS ORIGIN AND FOUNDATION TO THE YEAR 1882 . . .

PHILADELPHIA: J. B. LIPPINCOTT & CO. 1884.

⟨1⟩-170. 10¼" full x 7⅜".

⟨1⟩-21⁴, 22¹.

S cloth: brown; brown-olive. Covers bevelled. Blue-coated on white end papers printed in black with a leafy pattern. Flyleaves. Top edges gilt.

Deposited Oct. 22, 1883.

B H

11442. NEWPORT . . .

NEW YORK   CHARLES SCRIBNER'S SONS   1884

Two printings noted:

1

⟨i-x⟩, ⟨1⟩-297; blank, p. ⟨298⟩; 6 pp. advertisements, 3 blank leaves. Pp. ⟨i-ii⟩ and final blank leaf excised or pasted under end papers. 6¾" x 4¾". Laid paper. Sheets bulk ⅞".

⟨1-20⁸⟩. Leaves ⟨1⟩₁ and ⟨20⟩₈ excised or pasted under end papers.

S cloth: blue; brown. V cloth: mustard; tan. Stamped in blue and gold; or, brown and gold. End papers printed in light brown or light gray-green with a floral pattern.

Note: The publisher's spine imprint noted in two forms. The sequence, if any, is not known; the designations are for identification only.

A: SCRIBNER'S

B: SCRIBNERS

Advertised for Feb. 13 PW Feb. 9, 1884. Published Feb. 13, 1884 (publisher's records). Listed PW Feb. 23, 1884. The London (Sampson Low) edition listed Ath April 12, 1884.

2

⟨i-iv⟩, ⟨1⟩-297; blank, p. ⟨298⟩; advertisements, pp. ⟨299-300⟩. Laid paper. 7⅛" x 4¹³⁄₁₆". Sheets bulk ⁹⁄₁₆".

⟨1-19⁸⟩.

Printed yellow paper wrapper. Presumably the *Summer Edition* advertised for June 26 PW June 21, 1884.

AAS (1st, binding A, binding B) BPL (1st, binding A) H (1st, binding B) LC (1st, binding B) NYPL (1st, binding B) UV (1st, binding A; 2nd) Y (1st, binding A, binding B)

11443. Stories by American Authors III . . .

New York   Charles Scribner's Sons   1884

"Two Purse-Companions," pp. ⟨62⟩-98.

Two bindings noted; for descriptions see entry No. 10567. For other comment see entry No. 2063. BA copy (rebound) received May 6, 1884.

11444. TRUE AND OTHER STORIES . . .

FUNK & WAGNALLS NEW YORK 1884 LONDON 10 AND 12 DEY STREET 44 FLEET STREET ALL RIGHTS RESERVED

In *Standard Library Series.*

Cloth

⟨i-ii⟩, ⟨i⟩-iv, ⟨5⟩-270. Laid paper. 7⅜" x 4¹⁵⁄₁₆".

⟨1-17⁸⟩.

V cloth: golden yellow. Covers bevelled; *but see note below.* Yellow end papers. Flyleaves.

Wrapper

⟨i-ii⟩,⟨i⟩-iv, ⟨5⟩-270. Laid paper. 7⅜" scant x 4⅞".

⟨1-8¹⁶, 9⁸⟩.

Printed tan paper wrapper. Issued under date Nov. 17, 1884, as No. 128 in the series.

Note: According to the advertisement on the inner front wrapper books in the series were issued in three formats: Printed paper wrapper; *standard cloth edition;* and, *cheap cloth edition.* It is probable that the *standard cloth edition* was issued with bevelled covers; *cheap cloth edition* with unbevelled covers. All copies in cloth examined by BAL have covers bevelled.

Deposited (wrapper) Dec. 1, 1884. Listed PW Dec. 20, 1884 as in cloth (at $1; otherwise unidentified); and in wrapper (at 25¢).

AAS (wrapper)   H (cloth)   LC (wrapper)   UV (cloth)   Y (wrapper)

11445. Some Noted Princes, Authors, and Statesmen of Our Time . . . Edited by James Parton.

New York: Thomas Y. Crowell & Co., 13 Astor Place. ⟨1885⟩

"Nathaniel Hawthorne's College Days," pp. 312-318.

For comment see entry No. 207.

11446. First Annual Meeting of the American Copyright League, Held at the Rooms of the Author's Club, 19 West 24th Street, New York City, November 7, 1885.

⟨New York, 1885⟩

Contains remarks by Lathrop.

For comment see entry No. 6544.

11447. Representative Poems of Living Poets American and English Selected by the Poets Themselves with an Introduction by George Parsons Lathrop

Cassell & Company, Limited   739 & 741 Broadway, New York 1886

"Introduction," pp. vii-xxvi.

Reprint save for:

"The Phoebe-Bird," pp. 388-389. Collected in *Dreams and Days,* 1892.

For comment see entry No. 436.

11448. June Edited by Oscar Fay Adams . . .

Boston   D. Lothrop and Company   Franklin and Hawley Streets   ⟨1886⟩

Reprint save for "O June, Sweet June," p. 101.

For comment see entry No. 64.

11449. "BEHIND TIME" . . .

CASSELL & COMPANY, LIMITED, 739 & 741 BROADWAY, NEW YORK. ⟨1886⟩

⟨i-iv⟩, ⟨1⟩-198, 6 pp. advertisements. Laid paper. Frontispiece and 6 plates inserted. 6⅝" full x 4½".

⟨1-13⁸⟩.

S cloth: blue; green; yellow. V cloth: blue. White end papers printed in ochre with a leafy pattern. Laid paper flyleaves.

Deposited Sept. 30, 1886. Listed (without name of publisher) Ath Oct. 9, 1886. Listed PW Dec. 29, 1888 ⟨sic⟩.

AAS   H   Y

11450. October Edited by Oscar Fay Adams . . .

Boston   D. Lothrop and Company   Franklin and Hawley Streets   ⟨1886⟩

Reprint save for "Days and Voices," p. 111.

For comment see entry No. 68.

11451. No. 14.   Standard Comic Recitations by Best Authors . . . Compiled . . . by Frances P. Sullivan . . . December, 1886 . . .

J. M. Ivers ⟨sic⟩ & Co., Publishers, 86 Nassau Street, N. Y. . . . ⟨1886⟩

Printed paper wrapper.

"One of the Pack," p. 20.

Deposited Dec. 6, 1886. Reprinted with the publisher's later address, 379 Pearl Street, in the imprint.

LC NYPL

11452. Ballads of Books Chosen by Brander Matthews

New York   George J. Coombes   275 Fifth Avenue   1887

"The Book Battalion," pp. 91-92, "written ... for the present collection."—p. ⟨xi⟩.

For comment see entry No. 1905.

11453. Appletons' Cyclopædia of American Biography Edited by James Grant Wilson and John Fiske ... Volume II ...

New York   D. Appleton and Company   1, 3 and 5 Bond Street   1887

"Richard Henry Dana," Vol. 2, pp. 70-72.

"Ralph Waldo Emerson," Vol. 2, pp. 343-348.

For comment see entry No. 6020.

11454. What American Authors Think about International Copyright

New-York   American Copyright League   1888

One-paragraph statement, p. 7.

For comment see entry No. 218.

11455. GETTYSBURG: A BATTLE ODE READ BEFORE THE SOCIETY OF THE ARMY OF THE POTOMAC, AT GETTYSBURG, ON THE TWENTY-FIFTH ANNIVERSARY OF THE BATTLE, JULY 3, 1888 ...

NEW-YORK   CHARLES SCRIBNER'S SONS   1888 THE DE VINNE PRESS

⟨i-iv⟩, ⟨1⟩-16. Laid paper. 8″ x 5¾″.

⟨-⟩10. Signed: ⟨-⟩2, 1A2, 1B6.

Two printings of the wrapper noted. The sequence, if any, is not known and the designations are for identification only.

A

Heavy white laid paper wrapper, printed in brown. Letterpress on front only. The designation Nathan Hale Edition not present. The surviving copyright deposit copy thus.

B

Heavy white laid paper wrapper, printed in blue. Designated on front: Nathan Hale Edition. On back wrapper: This edition is generously donated by Mr. Lathrop to the Society of the Sons of the Revolution ... It is limited to 300 copies.

Also appears in the following publication; date of publication not determined: The Society of the Army of the Potomac. Report of the Nineteenth Annual Re-Union, at Gettysburg, Pennsylvania, July 1st, 2d and 3d, 1888, New York, 1888; printed paper wrapper.

Collected in Dreams and Days, 1892.

Mr. G. P. Lathrop will publish this month ... —PW Aug. 18, 1888. Deposited Oct. 1, 1888.

AAS (B)   H (both)   LC (A)   Y (both)

11456. Authors at Home ... Edited by J. L. & J. B. Gilder

Cassell & Company, Limited   104 & 106 Fourth Avenue, New York   ⟨1888⟩

"George H. Boker in Philadelphia," pp. 31-38.

"George William Curtis at West New Brighton," pp. 75-82.

A copy at H received Feb. 13, 1889. Listed PW Feb. 23, 1889.

H NYPL

11457. TWO SIDES OF A STORY   OLEY GROW'S DAUGHTER.—MRS. WINTERROWD'S MUSICALE.—"UNFINISHED." —MARCH AND APRIL.—RAISING CAIN ...

CASSELL & COMPANY, LIMITED   104-106 FOURTH AVENUE, NEW YORK   ⟨1889⟩

⟨i-vi⟩, 1-238; 12 pp. advertisements. 7³⁄₁₆″ x 4¹³⁄₁₆″.

⟨1-16⟩8.

Note: The title-leaf may be a cancel.

For prior publication of "Oley Grow's Daughter" see Harper's Christmas ... , above, under ⟨1882⟩.

Printed paper wrapper. Issued under date Aug. 1, 1889, as Vol. 1, No. 33, of Cassell's Sunshine Series of Choice Fiction.

Noticed as at once PW June 1, 1889. Deposited July 12, 1889. Listed PW July 27, 1889.

LC

11458. WOULD YOU KILL HIM?   A NOVEL ...

NEW YORK   HARPER & BROTHERS, FRANKLIN SQUARE   1890

⟨i⟩-iv, ⟨1⟩-384. 7⅜″ scant x 4¹⁵⁄₁₆″.

⟨-⟩2, 1-1612.

S cloth: brown. Flyleaves.

Noted as *at once* PW Nov. 9, 1889. Deposited Nov. 12, 1889. Listed PW Nov. 16, 1889. The British edition (London & Edinburgh: Douglas; Hamilton, Adams) noted as *nearly ready* Ath Oct. 19, 1889; noted as though ready and with the statement *published simultaneously in Great Britain and United States*, Ath Nov. 16, 1889; listed Ath Nov. 23, 1889. The British printing not seen by BAL.

AAS BA NYPL

11459. Society of Sons of the Revolution ... New York ... Constitution, By-Laws, Membership.

New York: Exchange Printing Company, 47 Broad Street. 1890.

Printed paper boards, cloth shelfback.

"The Name of Washington," p. ⟨7⟩. Collected in *Dreams and Days*, 1892.

H (Received April 21, 1890)

11460. NATHANIEL HAWTHORNE.

PHILADELPHIA: J. B. LIPPINCOTT COMPANY. 1890.

Anonymous.

⟨1⟩-11. 7⅝" x 5⅛".

⟨-⟩⁶.

Printed mottled gray paper wrapper.

Note: Prepared for copyright purposes only. Published in *Chambers's Encyclopædia ... New Edition ...* , Vol. V, 1890.

Deposited April 25, 1890.

LC

11461. The Art of Authorship ... Compiled ... by George Bainton.

London: James Clarke & Co., 13 & 14, Fleet Street. 1890.

Contribution, pp. 339-346.

For comment see entry No. 1271. Also see next entry.

11462. The Art of Authorship ... Compiled ... by George Bainton

New York D. Appleton and Company 1890

Contribution, pp. 339-346.

For comment see entry No. 1272. See also preceding entry.

11463. THE LETTER OF CREDIT A NOVEL BY GEORGE PARSONS LATHROP AND WILLIAM H. RIDEING.

COPYRIGHTED, 1890. NEW YORK. P. F. COLLIER, PUBLISHER, 65 WARREN STREET. 1890.

⟨i-iv⟩, 1-118, 6 pp. advertisements and cartoons. 7" x 5⅜".

⟨1-4⟩¹⁶.

Printed white paper wrapper. Issued under date Aug. 25, 1890, as Vol. 1, No. 26, in Collier's *Once a Week Library*.

Two states of the wrapper noted. In all likelihood issued simultaneously. The designations are for identification only.

A

Inner front imprinted with: *Agents Wanted Everywhere* ...

B

Inner front blank.

AAS (wrapper B) NYPL (wrapper A)

11464. Occasional Addresses Edited by Laurence Hutton and William Carey

New-York The Dunlap Society 1890

"An Address," pp. 124-125.

"Prologue to The Wife," pp. 137-138.

For comment see entry No. 5655.

11465. Records and Papers of the New London County Historical Society. Part I. Volume I. Arranged by the Secretary.

Published by the Society: New London, Connecticut. 1890.

Printed paper wrapper.

"Description of the Public Library at New London ... ," pp. 90-91. Reprinted from *Harper's Weekly*, July 27, 1889.

AAS

11466. Gold of Pleasure ...

Philadelphia: J. B. Lippincott Company. ⟨1891⟩

Boards, cloth shelfback.

The June, 1891, issue of *Lippincott's Monthly Magazine*, with title-page as above. See under 1892 for formal publication.

H NYPL

11467. Shoemaker's Best Selections for Readings and Recitations Number 19 Compiled by Mrs. Anna Randall-Diehl

Philadelphia The Penn Publishing Company 1891

"The Wedding of the Moon," pp. 175-176.

For comment see entry No. 5562.

11468. Werner's Readings and Recitations No. 4 Compiled . . . by Elsie M. Wilbor

Edgar S. Werner Publishing & Supply Company (Inc.) New York Copyright, 1891 . . .

"Marthy Virginia's Hand," pp. 33-35. Collected in *Dreams and Days*, 1892.

For comment see entry No. 2509.

11469. . . . REASONS FOR ACCEPTING THE AUTHORITY OF THE CHURCH. A LETTER . . .

⟨At head of title:⟩ PUBLISHED BY THE WORCESTER CONFERENCE OF THE CATHOLIC TRUTH SOCIETY OF AMERICA. ⟨n.d., 1891?⟩

Single cut sheet folded to make four pages. The above at head of p. ⟨2⟩. Text on pp. ⟨2-3⟩; pp. ⟨1⟩ and ⟨4⟩ blank. Page: 7¾" x 4¹¹⁄₁₆".

Lathrop's letter, New London, Conn., March 24 ⟨1891?⟩, addressed to J. J. Roche, editor of *The Boston Pilot*.

AAS

11470. DREAMS AND DAYS POEMS . . .

NEW-YORK CHARLES SCRIBNER'S SONS 1892

⟨i-iv⟩, ⟨i⟩-⟨x⟩, ⟨3⟩-188. 7¾" x 5".

⟨1-10⁸, 11⁴, 12-13⁸⟩.

V cloth: blue; gray-blue; green. Top edges gilded.

Published May 7, 1892, in an edition of 750 copies, of which 230 were destroyed (publisher's records). Deposited May 7, 1892. Noted as *just ready* PW May 7, 1892. A copy at BA received May 11, 1892. Listed PW May 14, 1892.

B H NYPL

11471. GOLD OF PLEASURE . . .

PHILADELPHIA: J. B. LIPPINCOTT COMPANY. 1892.

For prior publication see above under 1891.

⟨1⟩-140, 4 pp. advertisements. Frontispiece inserted. Laid paper. 7⅛" x 4⅝".

⟨1⟩-12⁶. *Signed:* ⟨a⟩-i⁸. *Also signed:* ⟨A⟩-F¹².

V cloth: gray. White end papers printed in green with a leafy pattern. Laid paper flyleaves.

Listed PW Oct. 15, 1892.

N

11472. Christmas Number 1892 New York Sunday Mercury

William Cauldwell Proprietor Copyright 1892

Printed paper wrapper.

"The Rich Relation," pp. 11-15.

EM

11473. Wide Awake Pleasure Book Gems of Literature and Art by American Authors and Artists

Boston D Lothrop Company Washington Street opposite Bromfield ⟨1892⟩

Pictorial boards. Unpaged.

Contains "Puck and Puppypult."

Not to be confused with the earlier *Wide Awake Pleasure Book* series, concerning which see BAL, Vol. 1, p. 73.

H

11474. The First Book of the Authors Club Liber Scriptorum . . .

New York Published by the Authors Club M DCCC XCIII

"Elsewhere," pp. ⟨351⟩-363.

For comment see entry No. 1283.

11475. A STORY OF COURAGE ANNALS OF THE GEORGETOWN CONVENT OF THE VISITATION OF THE BLESSED VIRGIN MARY FROM THE MANUSCRIPT RECORDS BY GEORGE PARSONS LATHROP AND ROSE HAWTHORNE LATHROP

Trade Edition

BOSTON AND NEW YORK HOUGHTON, MIFFLIN AND COMPANY THE RIVERSIDE PRESS, CAMBRIDGE 1894

Title-page printed in black.

⟨i-ii⟩, ⟨i⟩-⟨xiv⟩, ⟨1⟩-380, blank leaf. Frontispiece, 4 plates, and one 2-page facsimile inserted. 7⅝" x 5".

⟨1⁶, 2⁵, 3-25⁸, 26⁴⟩. Leaf ⟨2⟩₂ inserted.

V cloth: blue. Blue-black-coated on white end papers. Top edges gilt.

Edition de Luxe

CAMBRIDGE PRINTED AT THE RIVERSIDE PRESS M DCCC XCV ⟨*i.e.*, 1894⟩

Title-page printed in black and red.

⟨i-ii⟩, ⟨i⟩-⟨xiv⟩, ⟨1⟩-380, blank leaf. Laid paper. Watermarked: *The Riverside Press.* 8¾" x 5⅛". Inserted: Frontispiece and 9 plates, each with printed protective tissue; 1 two-page facsimile.

⟨1², 2⁹, 3-25⁸, 26⁴⟩. Leaf ⟨2⟩₆ inserted. ⟨1⟩ is printed on paper other than bookstock and is appreciably heavier.

V cloth: white. Flyleaf at front. Top edges gilt.

On copyright page: *Two Hundred and Fifty Copies Printed Number* . . .

Announced PW Aug. 11, 1894. Trade edition printed Oct. 26, 1894, 1012 copies. Limited edition printed Nov. 10, 1894, 257 copies. Noted as *nearly ready* PW Nov. 10, 1894. Limited edition bound during the period Nov. 14–Dec. 20, 1894. Trade edition bound during the period Nov. 14, 1894–Sept. 12, 1901. Deposited (limited) Nov. 16, 1894. Trade format advertised as *new* PW Dec. 1, 1894. Listed (both formats) PW Dec. 15, 1894.

B (trade)   H (limited)   LC (limited)

11476. Camera Mosaics A Portfolio of National Photography   Being a Collection of Many Hundred Pictures . . . Introduction . . . by Murat Halstead . . . Text . . . by a Corps of Brilliant Writers Including Hjalmar Hjorth Boyesen . . . George Parsons Lathrop . . . ⟨and Others⟩

New York . . . Harry C. Jones 92, 94 and 96 Fifth Avenue 1894

Authorship of the individual passages of the text not given.

Y

A Story of Courage . . .

Cambridge . . . M DCCC XCV

See above under 1894.

11477. THE SCARLET LETTER DRAMATIC POEM . . . MUSIC BY WALTER DAMROSCH

⟨BOSTON, 1895⟩

". . . A Dramatic Poem . . . on the theme of Hawthorne's *Scarlet Letter* . . . "—p. ⟨3⟩.

⟨1⟩-40. 9¹/₁₆" x 5¹³/₁₆".

⟨1², 2-3⁸, 4²⟩.

Printed blue laid paper wrapper.

Copyright notice on wrapper dated 1894. "Introductory Note" dated *January, 1895.* Deposited Feb. 4, 1896 ⟨*sic*⟩. Reprinted under the title: *The Scarlet Letter A Dramatic Composition . . . for Music by Walter Damrosch,* New York & London: Transatlantic Publishing Co., 1896; deposited March 6, 1896; noted as *at once* PW March 7, 1896.

AAS B H LC NYPL Y

11478. Library of the World's Best Literature Ancient and Modern Charles Dudley Warner Editor . . . Thirty Volumes . . .

New York R. S. Peale and J. A. Hill Publishers ⟨1896–1899⟩

"William Cullen Bryant," Vol. 5, pp. 2623-2627. Deposited Feb. 15, 1897.

"Thomas Gray," Vol. 11, pp. 6623-6625. Deposited May 29, 1897.

Lathrop's contribution to Vol. 28 is reprint.

For comment see entry No. 10624.

11479. YADDO: AN AUTUMN MASQUE. IN HONOUR OF KATRINA TRASKE ⟨*sic*⟩ . . .

⟨n.p.⟩ OCTOBER, 1897.

⟨i-v⟩, ⟨1⟩-26; 5 blank leaves. Laid paper. 5¹⁵/₁₆" x 4¼". *Caution:* Pagination statement tentative.

Signature collation: The only copy located has been rebound; statement of signature collation impractical.

Printed brown laid paper wrapper.

On inner front of wrapper: *Privately Printed. Not Published.*

NYPL

Library of the World's Best Literature Ancient and Modern . . .

New York . . . ⟨1898⟩

See entry 11478.

11480. Nugae Illiteratae Sodalitatis "Lusuum Naturae" sive "Freaks" ex Ipsis Veterum Fontibus Scriptorum Collatae. Recensuerunt atque ad Socios Dedicaverunt Fredericus de Clot et Kenneth Gulielmus Millican

Imprimatur: Franciscus P. Foster, Praeses.— MDCCCXCIX.

A collection of pseudonymous humorous verse. G. P. Lathrop is listed herein as one of the "Freaks" and so, presumably, was the author of one of the contributions.

150 copies only.

AAS   B

11481. The Casket of Opals . . .

Portland Maine Privately Printed M D CCCC

Vellum binding, tape ties. Printed throughout on vellum.

Reprinted from *Dreams and Days,* 1892, with textual variations.

". . . 15 copies and no more are done on pure vellum . . . printed . . . May, M D CCCC . . . This is Number"—Certificate of issue.

Y

11482. The Masterpieces of Catholic Literature, Oratory and Art . . . Choice Selections by the Most Celebrated Writers . . . Edited by Hyacinthe Ringrose . . . Volume III.

1901. Published by E. J. Sweeney & Co., 1022 Market Street, Philadelphia, Pa., U.S.A. All Rights Reserved.

Cloth?

"Catholicity and the American Mind," pp. ⟨745⟩-756.

Deposited May 16, 1901.

LC

REPRINTS

The following publications contain material by Lathrop reprinted from earlier books.

Poems of Places Edited by Henry W. Longfellow . . . New England. Vol. I.

Boston . . . 1879.

For comment see entry No. 12208.

Harper's Cyclopædia of British and American Poetry Edited by Epes Sargent

New York . . . 1881

For comment see entry No. 4336.

Poems of American Patriotism Chosen by J. Brander Matthews

New-York . . . 1882

For comment see in Lanier, *Section IV.*

The Poets' Tributes to Garfield . . . ⟨Second Edition⟩

Cambridge . . . 1882

For comment see entry No. 1248.

Surf and Wave: The Sea as Sung by the Poets. Edited by Anna L. Ward . . .

New York: Thomas Y. Crowell & Co. 13 Astor Place. ⟨1883⟩

An Old Scrap-Book. With Additions . . .

⟨Cambridge⟩ February 8, 1884.

For comment see entry No. 7763.

December Edited by Oscar Fay Adams . . .

Boston . . . ⟨1885⟩

For comment see entry No. 57.

Bugle-Echoes . . . Edited by Francis F. Browne

New York . . . MDCCCLXXXVI

For comment see BAL, Vol. 1, p. 75.

April Edited by Oscar Fay Adams . . .

Boston . . . ⟨1886⟩

For comment see entry No. 61.

American War Ballads and Lyrics . . . Edited by George Cary Eggleston . . .

New York and London G. P. Putnam's Sons The Knickerbocker Press ⟨1889⟩

2 Vols. Printed paper boards, cloth shelfback. Listed, as in two volumes, PW Dec. 7, 1889. Reprinted, two volumes in one, not before 1895; see *Supplement to Brief Catalogue and Trade Order List of the Publications of G. P. Putnam's Sons . . . from July, 1895, to October, 1896.*

No. 29. Standard Recitations by Best Authors . . . Compiled . . . by Frances P. Sullivan . . . September, 1890 . . .

. . . N. Y. . . . ⟨1890⟩

For fuller entry see No. 9026.

The Poets' Year . . . Edited by Oscar Fay Adams . . .

Boston . . . ⟨1890⟩

For comment see entry No. 80.

American Sonnets Selected . . . by T. W. Higginson and E. H. Bigelow

Boston . . . 1890

For comment see entry No. 8373.

Representative Sonnets by American Poets . . . by Charles H. Crandall

Boston . . . 1890

For comment see entry No. 8374.

Local and National Poets of America ... Edited ... <by> Thos. W. Herringshaw ...

Chicago ... 1890.

For fuller entry see BAL, Vol. 2, p. 391.

Songs of Three Centuries Edited by John Greenleaf Whittier ...

Boston and New York Houghton, Mifflin and Company The Riverside Press, Cambridge 1890

Younger American Poets 1830–1890 Edited by Douglas Sladen ...

... London ... 1891

For comment see entry No. 6557. All Lathrop material herein reprinted from earlier books. "Gettysburg," p. 287, extracted from *Gettysburg: A Battle Ode*, 1888.

Younger American Poets 1830–1890 Edited by Douglas Sladen ...

... New York 1891

For comment see entry No. 6558. Also see preceding entry.

Werner's Readings and Recitations. No. 5 ... Compiled ... by Sara Sigourney Rice.

New York ... 1891.

"The Cavalry Charge," pp. 74-75, is a partial printing of "Keenan's Charge," which had prior publication in *One Hundred Choice Selections No. 21* ..., 1882; see above. For comment see entry No. 3433.

The Lover's Year-Book of Poetry <Second Series> ... Married-Life and Child-Life <Compiled> by Horace Parker Chandler ...

Boston ... 1893

For comment see entry No. 10903.

Book-Song An Anthology ... Edited by Gleeson White ...

London ... 1893

For comment see entry No. 717.

One Winter Day ...

Boston ... <1895>

For comment see BAL, Vol. 3, p. 243.

Martial Recitations Heroic, Pathetic, and Humorous for the Veterans' Camp-Fire Collected ... by James Henry Brownlee ...

Chicago New York The Werner Company <1896>

Printed paper wrapper.

The Treasury of American Sacred Song ... Edited by W. Garrett Horder ...

London ... 1896

For fuller entry see in Lucy Larcom, *Section III*.

Poems of American Patriotism 1776–1898 Selected by R. L. Paget

Boston ... MDCCCXCVIII

For comment see BAL, Vol. 1, p. 249.

Book Lovers' Verse ... Compiled ... by Howard S. Ruddy ...

Indianapolis ... <1899>

For comment see entry No. 745.

Songs of Nature Edited by John Burroughs

New York ... MCMI ...

For comment see entry No. 2169.

Lothrop's Annual ...

Boston ... <1904>

For comment see BAL, Vol. 1, p. 260.

Short Story Classics (American) ... Edited by William Patten ...

... New York <1905>

5 Vols. For comment see entry No. 6378.

Dreams and Images An Anthology ... Edited by Joyce Kilmer

... New York 1917

For comment see entry No. 11115.

The Catholic Anthology by Thomas Walsh ...

New York The Macmillan Company 1927 ...

Deposited Sept. 14, 1927.

Youth's Companion Edited by Lovell Thompson ...

... Boston ... 1954

For comment see entry No. 10927.

REFERENCES AND ANA

Elaine, by Alfred, Lord Tennyson.

"... In 1887 <Lathrop> had seen his dramatization of Tennyson's *Elaine*, written in collaboration with Henry Edwards, presented in Madison Square Theatre, New York. Later in 1887 the play was presented in Boston and Chicago . . ."—DAB

Presumably unpublished. No entry found in the copyright records under either Lathrop or Edwards.

A Romance of the Future of Electricity.

An abandoned project, in collaboration with Thomas A. Edison. Announced by Heine-mann PC Oct. 1, 1890: "will be published serially through the McClure syndicate." Other comments appeared in PC April 11, 1891; Ath Sept. 5, 1891, Sept. 26, 1891; PC Oct. 3, 1891. For a comment see *Edison,* by Matthew Josephson, N. Y. ⟨1959⟩, pp. 380-381.

Prometheus Bound, by Aeschylus.

Ath March 25, 1893, reported Lathrop "has adapted a verse translation ⟨by another hand?⟩ . . . for the Theatre of Arts and Letters of New York." Presumably unpublished.

EMMA LAZARUS

1 8 4 9 – 1 8 8 7

11483. POEMS AND TRANSLATIONS...
WRITTEN BETWEEN THE AGES OF
FOURTEEN AND SIXTEEN...

NEW YORK: PRINTED FOR PRIVATE CIRCULATION.
1866.

⟨i⟩-⟨viii⟩, ⟨1⟩-207. 7¹¹⁄₁₆″ x 5″.

⟨-⟩⁴, 1-13⁸.

C cloth; blue; green. HC cloth: purple; rose.
Buff-coated on white end papers. Flyleaves. Top
edges gilded. Covers bevelled.

Note: No copyright notice on verso of title-page.
A slip with the copyright notice is pasted in
some copies.

A copy in AAS inscribed by Lazarus May, 1866.

AAS NYPL UV Y

11484. POEMS AND TRANSLATIONS...
WRITTEN BETWEEN THE AGES OF
FOURTEEN AND SEVENTEEN...

NEW YORK: PUBLISHED BY HURD AND HOUGHTON,
459 BROOME STREET. 1867.

⟨i⟩-viii, ⟨1⟩-297, blank leaf. Laid paper. 7¾″
scant x 5¹⁄₁₆″.

⟨-⟩⁴, 1-18⁸, 19⁶.

C cloth: green. Coarse P cloth: purple-brown.
Covers bevelled. Yellow-coated on white end
papers. Laid paper flyleaves. Top edges gilded.
An errata slip present in some copies.

The following poems here first collected:

"Aphrodite"

"Clytie"

"Drifted"

"Elfrida"

"Met Again"

"Penelope's Choice"

"The Prussian's Story"

"Recollections of Shakspeare"

"Song," beginning: *It is late, love, late* ...

"A Spring Morning"

Deposited Dec. 27, 1866. Listed ALG Jan. 1, 1867.

AAS B H Y

11485. ADMETUS AND OTHER POEMS...

NEW YORK: PUBLISHED BY HURD AND HOUGHTON.
CAMBRIDGE: RIVERSIDE PRESS. 1871.

⟨i⟩-⟨viii⟩, ⟨1⟩-⟨230⟩, blank leaf. Laid paper.
7⅝″ x 5″ full.

⟨-⟩⁴, 1-14⁸, 15⁴.

C cloth: green; purple; terra-cotta. Covers bevelled. Yellow-coated on white end papers. Top
edges gilded.

500 copies printed (publisher's records). A copy
at UV inscribed by Lazarus April 26, 1871. Listed
PW May 15, 1871.

AAS B NYPL UV Y

11486. ALIDE: AN EPISODE OF GOETHE'S
LIFE...

PHILADELPHIA: J. B. LIPPINCOTT & CO. 1874.

⟨1⟩-214; 2 pp. of *Opinions of the Press.* 7″ x
4⅞″.

⟨1⟩⁴, 2-17⁶, 18⁸.

C cloth: orange. FL cloth: purple. S cloth:
green; purple; rust. Brown-coated on white end
papers. Flyleaves.

Note: Also occurs in the following variant (remainder?) forms:

Variant A

Printed paper wrapper. Cancel title-leaf imprinted: *Philadelphia: J. B. Lippincott & Co.*
⟨1874⟩

Variant B

Cloth. Cancel title-leaf imprinted: *Philadelphia:
J. B. Lippincott & Co.* ⟨1874⟩

*

[handwritten inscription]

THE SPAGNOLETTO,

A Play,

IN 5 ACTS,

BY

EMMA LAZARUS.

COPYRIGHTED, 1876.

UNPUBLISHED MANUSCRIPT.

Listed PW Feb. 21, 1874. Reviewed Ath April 18, 1874, as though issued jointly by Lippincott and Trübner.

AAS (1st) B (1st) H (1st; *Variant B*) Y (1st; *Variant A*)

11487. . . . THE SPAGNOLETTO . . .

⟨n.p.⟩ 1876.

At head of title: [UNPUBLISHED MANUSCRIPT.]

⟨1⟩-56. 7⅝″ x 4⁹⁄₁₆″.

⟨1-2¹², 3⁴⟩. Leaves ⟨2⟩₃.₁₀ are single inserted leaves (one or both a cancel?).

Printed pale tan paper wrapper.

A copy at Y inscribed by Lazarus Sept. 1876.

AAS H UV Y

11488. Poems and Ballads of Heinrich Heine. Translated by Emma Lazarus. To Which Is Prefixed a Biographical Sketch of Heine.

New York: R. Worthington, 770 Broadway. 1881.

⟨i⟩-xxiv, ⟨1⟩-224. Laid paper. 7⅜″ x 4⅞″.

A copy at H inscribed by Lazarus *June, 1881*. Listed PW July 2, 1881. Reprinted and reissued with the imprint: *New York: Hurst & Co., Publishers, 122 Nassau St.* ⟨n.d., not before 1882⟩

B H UV Y

11489. SONGS OF A SEMITE: THE DANCE TO DEATH, AND OTHER POEMS . . .

NEW YORK: OFFICE OF "THE AMERICAN HEBREW," 498-500 THIRD AVENUE. 1882.

⟨i-iv⟩, ⟨1⟩-80; plus: 2 pp. advertisements. 9⁹⁄₁₆″ x 6¹⁄₁₆″.

⟨1-21²; plus: 22¹⟩.

S cloth: green; mustard; terra-cotta. White wove end papers. White end papers printed in green with a floral pattern. Laid paper flyleaves in some copies. Also issued in printed tan paper wrapper.

Listed (cloth and wrapper) PW Oct. 14, 1882. Deposited Dec. 30, 1882.

AAS (wrapper) B (wrapper) H (cloth) NYPL (wrapper) Y (both)

11490. The Cambridge Book of Poetry and Song . . . by Charlotte Fiske Bates . . .

New York: Thomas Y. Crowell & Co., No. 13 Astor Place. ⟨1882⟩

Reprint save for:

"Pleasant Prospect. [From Scenes in the Wood. Suggested by Robert Schumann.]," pp. 336-337.

"Night. [From Scenes in the Wood. Suggested by Robert Schumann.]," p. 337.

The above otherwise unlocated save in *Lippincott's Magazine,* Aug. 1875.

"A March Violet," pp. 337-338. Otherwise unlocated save in *Lippincott's Magazine,* April, 1875.

Reprinted and reissued as a 2-volume work, not before 1890, with the imprint: *New York: 46 East 14th Street . . . Boston: 100 Purchase Street* ⟨1882; i.e., not before 1890⟩

For further comment see entry No. 7887.

11491. Ralph Waldo Emerson His Life, Genius, and Writings . . . by Alexander Ireland Second Edition . . .

London: Simpkin, Marshall, & Co. 1882 . . .

Extract from Lazarus's article, "Emerson's Personality," pp. 294-296. The article was first published in *The Century Magazine* (New York), July, 1882. See *Friendship and Character by Ralph Waldo Emerson* . . . , 1906, below, for publication of the article in full.

For comment see BAL, Vol. 1, p. 25.

H

11492. Catalogue of the Pedestal Fund Art Loan Exhibition, at the National Academy of Design . . .

⟨New York: Theo. L. De Vinne & Co.⟩ December, 1883.

Printed paper wrapper.

"The New Colossus," p. ⟨9⟩.

At head of poem: (*Written for the* PORTFOLIO *of the* ART LOAN COLLECTION *in aid of the* PEDESTAL FUND.) The *Portfolio* was not a printed publication but a collection of ". . . literary matter . . . specimen pages of the MSS. of various authors . . . poems written for the occasion by Emma Lazarus . . . autographs . . ." sold during the exhibition for the benefit of the Bartholdi Pedestal Fund.

The exhibition opened Dec. 3, 1883; see the *New York Tribune,* Dec. 4, 1883, p. 2, column 4.

Note: Collected in *Poems,* 1889. BAL has disregarded other printings of the poem published 1884 and later, save for the separate printing of 1949, the earliest such printing noted.

BPL NYPL

11493. The Genius and Character of Emerson
Lectures at the Concord School of Philosophy
Edited by F. B. Sanborn

Boston   James R. Osgood and Company
1885

"Sonnet of 1884 ... to R.W.E.," p. 215.

For comment see entry No. 131.

11494. January Edited by Oscar Fay Adams ...

Boston   D. Lothrop and Company   Franklin
and Hawley Streets   ‹1885›

"Winter Night," pp. 65-66. Elsewhere unlocated
save for *Lippincott's Magazine* (Phila.) March,
1878.

For comment see entry No. 58.

11495. February Edited by Oscar Fay Adams ...

Boston   D. Lothrop and Company   Franklin
and Hawley Streets   ‹1886›

"Expectation," p. 110. Extracted from "Expectation," *Lippincott's Magazine* (Phila.) Nov. 1872.
For another extract from the same poem see
entry No. 11498. Otherwise unlocated.

For comment see entry No. 59.

11496. April Edited by Oscar Fay Adams ...

Boston   D. Lothrop and Company   Franklin
and Hawley Streets   ‹1886›

"Spring Joy," pp. 22-23. Otherwise unlocated
save for *Lippincott's Magazine* (Phila.) May
1875.

For comment see entry No. 61.

11497. Representative Poems of Living Poets
American and English Selected by the Poets
Themselves with an Introduction by George
Parsons Lathrop

Cassell & Company, Limited   739 & 741
Broadway, New York   1886

"Off Rough Point," p. 393.

"The World's Justice," pp. 394-395.

Both collected in *Poems*, 1889.

For comment see entry No. 436.

11498. May Edited by Oscar Fay Adams ...

Boston   D. Lothrop and Company   Franklin
and Hawley Streets   ‹1886›

"Expectation," pp. 24-25. Extracted from "Expectation," *Lippincott's Magazine* (Phila.) Nov.
1872. For another extract from the same poem
see entry No. 11495. Otherwise unlocated.

For comment see entry No. 63.

11499. June Edited by Oscar Fay Adams ...

Boston   D. Lothrop and Company   Franklin
and Hawley Streets   ‹1886›

"A June Night," pp. 91-93. Collected in *Poems*,
1889.

For comment see entry No. 64.

11500. September Edited by Oscar Fay Adams ...

Boston   D. Lothrop and Company   Franklin
and Hawley Streets   ‹1886›

"Harvest," pp. 34-36. Elsewhere unlocated save
for *Lippincott's Magazine* (Phila.) Nov. 1873.

For comment see entry No. 67.

11501. Hymns and Anthems Adapted for Jewish
Worship. Selected and Arranged by Dr. Gustav Gottheil ...

New York. 1886.

Reprint save for "Admonition," p. 67. Collected
in *Poems*, 1889.

"Meditation on Death," pp. 178-179 is otherwise
"Meditations" in *Songs of a Semite*, 1882.

Title entered for copyright July 17, 1886; no
record of book deposit.

UV

11502. Mother Songs Selected by Esther T.
Housh ...

Brattleboro, Vt.: Frank E. Housh & Co., Publishers. 1888.

Printed paper wrapper.

"Mater Amabilis," pp. 4-6. Collected in *Poems*,
1889.

Title entered for copyright Nov. 30, 1887; no
record of book deposit.

B

11503. THE POEMS OF EMMA LAZARUS IN
TWO VOLUMES ...

BOSTON AND NEW YORK   HOUGHTON, MIFFLIN
AND COMPANY   THE RIVERSIDE PRESS, CAMBRIDGE
1889

2 Vols.

1: ... NARRATIVE, LYRIC, AND DRAMATIC

2: ... JEWISH POEMS: TRANSLATIONS

1: ‹i-ii›, ‹i›-‹vi›, ‹1›-342, blank leaf. Laid paper. Frontispiece inserted. 6$^{15}/_{16}$" x 4⅝".

2: ⟨i-ii⟩, ⟨1⟩-⟨6⟩, ⟨1⟩-257, blank leaf.

1: ⟨1⁴, 2-22⁸, 23⁴⟩.

2: ⟨1⁴, 2-16⁸, 17⁶, 18⁴⟩.

V cloth: green. White laid end papers. Top edges gilded.

1012 copies, of both vols., printed Dec. 10, 1888 (publisher's records). Bound Dec. 12, 1888–Feb. 28, 1894 (publisher's records). Deposited Dec. 14, 1888. Listed PW Dec. 29, 1888. A copy at H received Jan. 16, 1889. Reviewed Bkr Feb. 1889. Reprinted under date ⟨1888⟩.

AAS   B   BA   H   NYPL

11504. American Sonnets. Selected ... by William Sharp.

London   Walter Scott, 24 Warwick Lane New York and Toronto: W. J. Gage & Co. ⟨n.d., 1889⟩

Reprint save for "The Taming of the Falcon," p. 126; elsewhere unlocated save in *Scribner's Monthly* (New York) Dec. 1879.

Lazarus's poems on pp. 129-133, here separately titled, are reprinted from "Symphonic Studies," *Poems*, 1889.

For comment see BAL, Vol. 3, p. 101.

H

11505. Later American Poems Edited by J. E. Wetherell ...

Toronto: The Copp, Clark Company, Limited. 1896.

Reprint save for "Among the Thousand Islands;" elsewhere unlocated save in *The Century Magazine* (New York) Dec. 1881.

JH

11506. The Banner of the Jew.

New York: The Critic Co.   1898.

Not seen. Issued as *Critic Leaflet*, No. 5. 2 pp.?

Presumably reprinted from *Songs of a Semite*, 1882.

Advertised *The Critic* (New York), March 26, 1898. Listed PW April 30, 1898.

For description of another title in this series see entry No. 7781B.

11507. ... AN EPISTLE TO THE HEBREWS ...

MARCH, 1900   NEW YORK   PRESS OF PHILIP COWEN, 213-215 EAST 44TH STREET

At head of title: PUBLICATIONS OF THE FEDERATION OF AMERICAN ZIONISTS NO. 6

⟨i⟩-⟨viii⟩, ⟨7⟩-80. 9¹⁄₁₆″ x 5⅞″ scant. Frontispiece inserted. Laid paper. Also occurs on mixed papers, both laid and wove.

⟨1⁹, 2-5⁸⟩. ⟨1⟩₃ inserted.

Printed gray paper wrapper.

"... First appeared in ... *The American Hebrew*, between November 10, 1882, and February, 1883."—p. ⟨vi⟩.

LC   Y

11508. Friendship and Character by Ralph Waldo Emerson with an Essay on Emerson's Personality by Emma Lazarus

New York   The Century Co.   1906

"Emerson's Personality," pp. ⟨vii⟩-xxvii. For a partial printing of this essay see above *Ralph Waldo Emerson* ... , 1882.

AAS

11509. Emma Lazarus   Selections from Her Poetry and Prose Edited, with an Introduction, by Morris U. Schappes ...

Published by Cooperative Book League Jewish-American Section, International Workers Order   New York   ⟨1944⟩

Printed paper wrapper.

Reprint save for the following:

"Was the Earl of Beaconsfield a Representative Jew?" pp. 60-62.

"Russian Christianity Versus Modern Judaism," pp. 63-67. *Note:* CHAL, Vol. 3, p. 122, suggests that this was issued as a separate; no separate publication found. For original publication see *The Century Magazine* (New York), May 1882.

"The Jewish Problem," pp. 68-73.

"The Poet Heine," pp. 90-92.

"A Day in Surrey with William Morris," pp. 92-95.

"M. Renan and the Jews," pp. 96-97.

"Henry Wadsworth Longfellow," pp. 97-98.

"The Last National Revolt of the Jews," pp. 99-102.

Deposited April 1, 1944. For an extended edition see next entry.

LC   NYPL

11510. Emma Lazarus   Selections from Her Poetry and Prose Edited ... by Morris U. Schappes ... Revised and Enlarged Edition

Book League   Jewish People's Fraternal
Order of the International Workers Order,
New York   1947

Printed paper wrapper.

For first edition see preceding entry.

Extended by the addition of the following:

"The New Ezekiel," p. 53.

"Letter from Emma Lazarus to Henry George,
Oct. 17, 1881," pp. 103-104.

BPL   Y

11511. Heinrich Heine   Poems & Ballads Translated by Emma Lazarus ...

Hartsdale House   New York   ⟨1947⟩

Reprint.

Deposited Oct. 22, 1948. Reprinted and reissued
by Perma Giants, New York ⟨1950⟩; printed
paper boards.

LC   Y

11512. THE LETTERS OF EMMA LAZARUS
1868–1885   EDITED, WITH AN INTRO-
DUCTION, BY MORRIS U. SCHAPPES ...

NEW YORK   THE NEW YORK PUBLIC LIBRARY
1949

⟨i-ii⟩, ⟨1⟩-56; ⟨iii-iv⟩; 57-68; blank, pp. ⟨69-72⟩.
Note: The frontispiece (here considered pp.
⟨i-ii⟩) and its blank conjugate (here considered
pp. ⟨71-72⟩) are printed on coated paper;
otherwise printed on uncalendered wove paper
throughout. P. ⟨iii⟩ imprinted with a facsimile
title-page; p. ⟨iv⟩ blank. 10″ scant x 7″.

⟨-⟩³⁸. *Signed* (pp. ⟨i-ii⟩, ⟨71-72⟩ disregarded):
⟨1⟩⁴, 2-5⁸. The signature marks appear on the
fold and were designed to be concealed in
binding.

Printed pale buff paper wrapper.

According to the printer's code on the reverse
of the title-page 300 copies printed Oct. 10,
1949.

UV

11513. The New Colossus ...

⟨n.p. n.d., New York: Philip and Fanny
Duschnes, December, 1949⟩

Single cut sheet. Wove paper watermarked:
Beckett. 12¾″ x 9″. Printed on recto. Anon.

Issued with a printed slip: *This poem ... is
sent with the warmest Holiday Greetings to
the friends of Philip and Fanny Duschnes, December Mcmxlix. 500 copies   decorated and
printed by hand by Valenti Angelo ...*

Earliest located separate printing. For prior
publication see *Catalogue of the Pedestal
Fund ...* , 1883; and *Poems,* 1889.

H

REPRINTS

The following publications contain material by
Lazarus reprinted from earlier books.

March Edited by Oscar Fay Adams ...

Boston ... ⟨1886⟩

For comment see entry No. 60.

No. 11. Standard Recitations by Best Authors
... Compiled ... by Frances P. Sullivan ...
March, 1886 ...

... N. Y. ... ⟨1886⟩

Reprinted with the publisher's later address:
379 Pearl Street, N. Y. For fuller comment
see entry No. 4624.

The Poets' Year ... Edited by Oscar Fay
Adams ...

Boston ... ⟨1890⟩

For comment see entry No. 80.

American Sonnets Selected ... by T. W. Higginson and E. H. Bigelow

Boston ... 1890

For comment see entry No. 8373.

Representative Sonnets by American Poets ...
by Charles H. Crandall

Boston ... 1890

For comment see entry No. 8374.

Local and National Poets of America ...
Edited ... ⟨by⟩ Thos. W. Herringshaw ...

Chicago ... 1890.

For fuller entry see BAL, Vol. 2, p. 391.

Songs of Three Centuries Edited by John
Greenleaf Whittier ...

Boston ... 1890

For comment see entry No. 11384.

Younger American Poets   1830–1890   Edited
by Douglas Sladen ...

... London ... 1891

For comment see entry No. 6557.

Younger American Poets   1830–1890   Edited
by Douglas Sladen ...

... New York   1891

For comment see entry No. 6558.

Werner's Readings and Recitations. No. 5 . . . Compiled . . . by Sara Sigourney Rice.

New York . . . 1891.

For comment see entry No. 3433.

Souvenir Book of the Fair in Aid of the Educational Alliance, and Hebrew Technical Institute.

⟨New York⟩ Copyrighted, 1895, by Frederick Spiegelberg.

Three Minute Readings for College Girls Selected and Edited by Harry Cassell Davis . . .

Copyright, 1897 . . . Hinds & Noble, Publishers 4-5-13-14 Cooper Institute New York City

Library of the World's Best Literature Ancient and Modern Charles Dudley Warner Editor . . . Thirty Volumes Vol. XXVIII

New York . . . ⟨1898⟩

For comment see entry No. 10624. Deposited Feb. 23, 1898.

The International Library of Famous Literature . . . Compiled . . . by Nathan Haskell Dole, Forrest Morgan and Caroline Ticknor . . .

New York Merrill and Baker Publishers ⟨1898⟩

For fuller entry see in Sarah Orne Jewett reprints.

The International Library of Famous Literature . . . Edited by Dr. Richard Garnett . . . in Twenty Volumes . . .

London Issued by The Standard 1899

For comment see entry No. 10638.

REFERENCES AND ANA

Letters to Emma Lazarus in the Columbia University Library Edited by Ralph L. Rusk . . .

New York: Morningside Heights Columbia University Press 1939

Deposited May 13, 1939

. . . The World of Emma Lazarus

Schocken Books New York ⟨1949⟩

At head of title: H. E. Jacob

. . . Emma Lazarus Woman with a Torch

New York The Citadel Press ⟨1956⟩

At head of title: Eve Merriam

Printed paper boards, cloth shelfback. On copyright page: *First edition.*

The Link between Heinrich Heine and Emma Lazarus by Aaron Kramer

⟨Reprinted from: Publication of the American Jewish Historical Society Vol. XLV, No. 4 (June, 1956)⟩

Caption-title. Imprint on front wrapper.

Printed paper wrapper.

CHARLES GODFREY LELAND

(Hans Breitmann, Meister Karl)

1 8 2 4 - 1 9 0 3

11514. The Opal: A Pure Gift for the Holy Days. MDCCCXLVIII. Edited by Mrs. Sarah J. Hale.

New York: J. C. Riker, 129 Fulton Street. 1848.

"The Carnival at Rome," pp. ⟨303⟩-313. Collected in *Meister Karl's Sketch-Book,* 1855.

For comment see entry No. 1030.

11515. The May Breezes Words Translated from the German by Charles G. Leland . . . Composed . . . by Maximilian Zorer . . .

New York Published by Firth, Pond & Co. 1 Franklin Sq. . . . 1849 . . .

Sheet music. Cover-title. Plate number: 409.

Issued with piano; and, guitar accompaniment.

Note: Jackson dates this piece ⟨1842⟩ although his reproduction (a poor one) seems to show an 1849 date. BAL has been unable to trace Jackson's copy in order to confirm that he was in error. In 1842 the publisher's firm name was *Firth & Hall,* not *Firth, Pond & Co.*

Deposited June 15, 1849.

H NYPL

11516. Agatha . . . Translated from the German by Charles G. Leland . . . Music . . . by F. Abt Arranged for the Piano Forte by Max Zorer . . .

New York . . . Firth, Pond & Co. 1 Franklin Sq. . . . 1849 . . .

Not seen. Title and imprint postulated. Entry on the basis of a printing with the publisher's later (1856–1863) address: *547 Broadway.*

Sheet music. Cover-title. Plate number: 465.

At head of p. 3: *Agathe* for *Agatha.* A copy in B (with variant text) appears to be a quite late printing; plate number 5517; *Agatha* correctly spelled at head of p. ⟨3⟩.

Deposited Sept. 24, 1849.

Y

11517. The Sons of Temperance Offering: For 1850 . . . Edited by T. S. Arthur.

New York: Published by Nafis & Cornish. ⟨1849⟩

Leather.

"The Campo Santo," pp. 113-115.

No record of copyright deposit.

H

11518. . . . The Bird and the Snare . . . Translated from the German, by Charles G. Leland . . . Composed by Max Zorer . . .

New York Firth, Pond & Co., 1 Franklin Sq. . . . 1850 . . .

Sheet music. Cover-title. At head of title: To Miss Mary Taylor. Plate number: 610.

Deposited Feb. 19, 1850.

LC

11519. The Memorial: Written by Friends of the Late Mrs. Osgood and Edited by Mary E. Hewitt . . .

New-York: George P. Putnam, 155 Broadway. 1851.

"The South of France," pp. 277-282. Collected, with revisions, as part of the chapter "Our Diligence and Arles" in *Meister Karl's Sketch-Book,* 1855.

For comment see entry No. 1187.

11520. The Christmas Tribute, and New-Year's Gift: A Souvenir for MDCCCLI.

Philadelphia: Published by E. H. Butler & Co. 1851.

Cloth?

"Window-Love," pp. ⟨253⟩-263. Collected in *Meister Karl's Sketch-Book,* 1855.

No copyright information found. Also issued without date according to Thompson.

NYPL

11521. The Snow-Flake: A Christmas, New-Year, and Birthday Gift, for MDCCCLII.

   Philadelphia: Published by E. H. Butler & Co. 1852.

Cloth; and, leather.

"Dorothea. The Breeze and the Stream," p. ⟨287⟩.

Listed LW and NLA Sept. 15, 1851. Advertised by Chapman, as an importation, Ath Dec. 6, 1851. Noticed by LG Dec. 27, 1851.

NYPL

11522. Memorial of James Fenimore Cooper

   New York   G P Putnam   1852

Letter, pp. 38-39.

For comment see entry No. 1650.

11523. The Knickerbocker Gallery: A Testimonial to the Editor of the Knickerbocker Magazine from Its Contributors ...

   New-York: Samuel Hueston, 348 Broadway. MDCCCLV.

"The Wedding-Trip of Jarl Alvar Rafn," pp. ⟨323⟩-327. Collected in *Meister Karl's Sketch-Book,* 1855.

For comment see entry No. 1033.

11524. Pictures of Travel. Translated from the German of Henry Heine. By Charles G. Leland.

   Philadelphia: John Weik, No. 195 Chestnut Street. 1855.

Five paper-covered parts.

1

⟨1⟩-96. 7¹⁵⁄₁₆″ x 5⅛″. "Translator's Preface," pp. 3-8, dated at end *May 15, 1855.*

2

97-192. 7¹⁵⁄₁₆″ x 5″.

3

193-288. 8⅜″ x 5⅛″.

4

289-384. 8⅜″ x 5⅛″.

5

Not seen. Not located.

385-471.

"A single number .. of about one hundred pages, will appear once a month ..."—From the prospectus.

Part 1 reviewed LG Oct. 13, 1855. Parts 1-2 advertised Ath Nov. 10, 1855. Part 3 advertised Ath Dec. 1, 1855. Part 4 advertised Ath March 29, 1856.

Also issued in cloth: Pp. ⟨1⟩-471. Frontispiece inserted. 7⁵⁄₁₆″ x 4⅞″ scant. Inserted at front: *Notices of the Press,* pp. ⟨i-viii⟩; publisher's catalog, pp. ⟨1⟩-8, inserted at back of some copies.

The "notices" are based on the issue in parts and are variously dated July 14, 1855 to Feb. 1856.

Title deposited July 7, 1855. Listed Ath Aug. 16, 1856. Noticed and advertised as *now published* Ath Aug. 30, 1856. A copy in AAS inscribed by early owner Sept. 21, 1856. No listings found for the work either in parts or as a single cloth-bound volume, APC June, 1855–Dec. 1856.

A *Fourth Revised Edition* was issued in Philadelphia and London, 1863. A cursory comparison indicates no alterations of consequence save for an extended footnote, p. 309. Did this alteration appear in an earlier printing?

AAS (cloth)   B (Part 1; cloth)   PHS (Parts 1-4)

11525. MEISTER KARL'S SKETCH-BOOK ...

   PHILADELPHIA: PARRY & McMILLAN, SUCCESSORS TO A. HART, LATE CAREY & HART. 1855.

⟨3⟩-338. 7½″ full x 5″.

⟨1⟩⁴, 2-28⁶, 29².

A cloth: blue; plum. A-like cloth: green-gray. T cloth: black; brown; green. TZ cloth: purple. Brown-coated on white end papers. Flyleaves. Inserted at back is a publisher's catalog, 1-⟨32⟩, dated *August, 1855;* or undated.

Note: In all examined copies "How Ladies Are Always Borrowing Pens and Ink" is erroneously listed in the table of contents as beginning on p. 29.

Also note: A letter Nov. 26, 1855, Leland to Rufus W. Griswold (published in *Passages from the Correspondence and Other Papers of Rufus W. Griswold,* Cambridge, Mass., 1898, p. 301) suggests that when first printed the book contained a dedication addressed to Griswold; and that on Griswold's insistence, the dedication was removed. No copy examined has a dedication. Without denying the possibility that copies with a dedication may yet be found, BAL theorizes that Leland sent Griswold a set of proofs and that the dedication was removed before the book went to press. Consideration of the date of the letter and of publication date permits such a conclusion.

Advertised as *nearly ready* APC Nov. 3, 1855. Listed APC Dec. 22, 1855. A copy in FLP inscribed by early owner *Christmas, 1855.* Deposited Dec. 29, 1855. Listed PC Jan. 16, 1856. Advertised Ath Jan. 26, 1856; reviewed LG Jan. 26, 1856. See under 1872 for revised edition.

AAS   FLP   H   NYPL

11526. Ornaments of Memory; or, Beauties of History, Romance, and Poetry ...

New York: D. Appleton and Company, 346 & 348 Broadway. M D C C C L V.

Cloth; and, leather.

The following four contributions are by Leland and are credited to him herein; for comment on other possible contributions see note below.

"The Knight of Sayn and the Gnomes," pp. ⟨9⟩-12.

"The Game of Chess," pp. ⟨35⟩-42.

"The Knight's Death," pp. ⟨63⟩-67.

"First Love," pp. ⟨93⟩-96, credited to *Meister Karl.*

"If Leland did not edit this beautiful gift volume, there are evidences that he contributed at least half of its contents, some of the articles being ascribed to *Anonymous* ..."—Jackson, p. 18. Jackson, p. 19, lists four poems which he believes to be by Leland: "The War-Song of the Kipchak," "The False Lesson," "The Image Breaker" and "The Maiden and the Fairy King."

LCP

11527. The Poetry and Mystery of Dreams. ⟨Compiled⟩ by Charles G. Leland ...

Philadelphia: Published by E. H. Butler & Co. M.DCCC.LVI.

⟨1⟩-⟨271⟩; blank, p. ⟨272⟩; advertisements, pp. ⟨273-288⟩. 7¾" x 4¹³⁄₁₆".

"Preface," pp. 5-vii ⟨sic⟩.

"Introduction," pp. 9-xi ⟨sic⟩.

"Anvil," pp. 28-29.

"Beer and Ale," pp. 38-40.

"Bohemian Beer Song," pp. 40-41, translated from the Bohemian.

"The Bridge and the Brook," pp. 60-61.

"Chess or Dice," pp. 68-69.

"Deer," pp. 91-92, translated from the German of Uhland.

"The Dream Angel," pp. 13-16.

"The Dream of Odenwald," p. 251, translated from the German.

"Eating," pp. 102-103, "imitated from the Russian by ... Leland."

"Entertainments," pp. 106-108.

"House Burning," pp. 147-148, translated from the Swedish of Tykeson.

"Love," pp. 172-174.

"Mirror," pp. 180-181.

"Nightingale," pp. 193-194, translated from the German.

"Nun," pp. 195-196, translated from the German.

"Old Age," p. 200, translated from the German of Uhland.

"Painting," pp. 202-203, translated from the German of Simrock.

"Roses," pp. 219-220, translated from the Swedish of Signil.

"Sailing," pp. 222-223.

"Swallows," pp. 242-243.

In addition to the above, also contains on the following pages, untitled verses, some being translations by Leland: 20, 27, 31-32, 36, 165-166, 229, 246, 248, 257.

It is probable that certain of the unattributed pieces herein were also done by Leland.

Two formats issued; sequence, if any, not known:

A: *Cloth gilt.* Both sides lettered in gold *Poetry and Mystery of Dreams;* sides otherwise stamped in blind; edges plain.

B: *Cloth extra-gilt.* Sides unlettered but stamped in gold with an ornate decoration within a triple-rule frame; edges gilt.

Advertised for Sept. 1 in APC Sept. 1, 1855. Deposited Sept. 3, 1855. Listed APC Sept. 15, 1855. Reviewed K Nov. 1855.

AAS   B   BA   H   UV   Y

11528. The New American Cyclopædia: A Popular Dictionary of General Knowledge. Edited by George Ripley and Charles A Dana ...

New York: D. Appleton and Company, 346 & 348 Broadway. London: 16 Little Britain. M.DCCC.LVIII. ⟨–M.DCCC.LXIII.⟩

"Altogether, I wrote about two hundred articles, great and small, for the Cyclopædia."—Leland's *Memoirs* (1893), p. 232. The list of contributors in Vol. 16 identifies some of Leland's contributions.

For comment see entry No. 3715.

11529. A Budget of Humorous Poetry. Comprising Specimens of the Best and Most Humorous Productions of the Popular American and Foreign Poetical Writers of the Day. By the Author of The "Book of Anecdotes and Budget of Fun."

Philadelphia: G. G. Evans, Publisher, No. 439 Chestnut Street. 1859.

Reprint save for "The Locked Out," pp. 166-168.

"A Legend of Salem," pp. 276-278 is an extract from "Yankee Stories" in *Meister Karl's Sketch-Book,* 1855.

HM

11530. Folk Songs Selected and Edited by John Williamson Palmer . . .

New York: Charles Scribner, 124 Grand Street. London: Sampson Low, Son and Company. M DCCC LXI.

Reprint save for "The Landlady's Daughter," pp. 30-32, by Uhland, translated by Leland and Palmer.

For comment see entry No. 11312.

11531. The Rebellion Record: A Diary of American Events . . . Edited by Frank Moore . . . First Volume . . .

New York: G. P. Putnam. C. T. Evans, General Agent. 1861.

Originally issued in seventy-three paper parts and a supplement but see notes below.

Note: Advertised APC Dec. 5, 1861, as available in weekly parts; monthly parts; and, cloth. Noted only in monthly parts; and, cloth. *Printed on wove paper.* Leaf: 9⅜″ x 6⁷⁄₁₆″.

Also note: "Charles T. Evans . . . announces a large-paper edition . . . for purposes of illustration. The size will be small folio, and the number of copies limited to one hundred, at ten dollars in sheets."—APC June 1, 1863. Advertised APC June 15, 1863: ". . . Large-Paper Edition, Small Folio, on Handsome Laid ⟨sic⟩

Paper . . . One hundred copies only . . . will be published in small folio, 13 by 9½ inches. Folded and collated, $10.00 a volume, or in half Roxburghe, $12.00." Further information wanting.

Pagination as given below refers to the sections "Poetry and Incidents."

Vol. 1 (Parts 1-6)

"The Fight at Sumter," p. ⟨1⟩.

"The Battle of Morris' Island, a Cheerful Tragedy," pp. 2-3.

"Northmen, Come Out!," p. 5.

"Out and Fight," p. 15.

Title-page as above.

Part 1 advertised APC April 27, 1861, as *will be issued immediately;* noticed APC May 25, 1861. Part 2 noticed APC June 29, 1861. Vol. 1 advertised APC Aug. 17, 1861, for *the 1st October.* Part 6 noticed as *issued* APC Oct. 14, 1861. Vol. 1 noticed as *will be issued in a few days complete* APC Oct. 14, 1861. Part 6 listed APC Oct. 14, 1861. Vol. 1 listed APC Nov. 15, 1861.

Vol. 2 (Parts 7-12)

. . . Second Volume . . .

New York: G. P. Putnam. C. T. Evans, General Agent. 1862.

"Cavalry Song," p. 50. Collected in *The Music-Lesson . . .* , 1872.

Part 7 noticed as *issued* APC Oct. 14, 1861; listed APC Oct. 14, 1861. Part 9 advertised as *now ready* APC Dec. 5, 1861. Part 10 advertised for *next week* APC Dec. 5, 1861. Parts 9-10 noticed APC Jan. 1862. Part 11 noticed APC Feb. 1862. Vols. 1-2 advertised as *now ready* APC Feb. 1862 as in cloth; sheep; half morocco; half calf; advertisement repeated APC March, 1862. Part 12 noticed APC March, 1862.

Vol. 3 (Parts 13-18)

. . . Third Volume . . .

New York: G. P. Putnam. Chas. T. Evans, General Agent. 1862.

Part 13 noticed APC March, 1862. Part 14 noticed APC April, 1862. Part 16 noticed APC May, 1862. Part 18 noticed APC June, 1862. Vols. 1-3 advertised APC Sept. 1, 1862, as in cloth extra; sheep extra; half calf, antique; half morocco, extra.

Vol. 4 (Parts 19-24)

. . . Fourth Volume . . .

New York: G. P. Putnam, 532 Broadway. Chas. T. Evans, 448 Broadway. 1862.

Part 19 noticed APC July, 1862. Part 20 noticed APC Sept. 1, 1862. Part 22 noticed APC Oct. 1, 1862. Part 23 noticed APC Nov. 1, 1862. Part 24 advertised as *ready November 1* APC Nov. 1, 1862. Vol. 4 advertised as *ready November 1* APC Nov. 1, 1862. Part 24 noticed APC Dec. 1, 1862. Vols. 1-4 advertised as *now complete* APC Dec. 1, 1862.

Vol. 5 (Parts 25-31)

... Fifth Volume ...

New York: G. P. Putnam, 441 Broadway. Chas. T. Evans, 448 Broadway. 1863.

Part 26 noticed APC Feb. 2, 1863. Vol. 5 advertised as *ready in May* APC May 1, 1863. Vol. 5 listed APC June 1, 1863. Vols. 1-5 advertised as though published APC June 15, 1863.

Vol. 6 (Parts 32-38)

... Sixth Volume ...

New-York: G. P. Putnam, 441 Broadway, C. T. Evans, 448 Broadway. 1863.

Vols. 1-6 advertised as *now ready* and Vol. 6 listed ALG Dec. 1, 1863. Vol. 6 again listed ALG Jan. 15, 1864. *Query:* Was the Dec. 1, 1863, listing of Vol. 6 premature? *Note:* Engraving opposite p. 19 miscaptioned *Brig. Gen. Godfrey Weitzel* (for *Gen. G. F. Shepley*); all thus?

Vol. 7 (Parts 39-45)

... Seventh Volume ...

New-York: D. Van Nostrand, Publisher, 192 Broadway. 1864.

Part 39 advertised as *ready* ALG Jan. 15, 1864. Part 43 listed ALG Aug. 15, 1864. Vol. 7 listed ALG Jan. 16, 1865.

Vol. 8 (Parts 46-52)

... Eighth Volume ...

New York: D. Van Nostrand, Publisher, No. 192 Broadway. 1865.

Vol. 8 listed ALG Jan. 1, 1866.

Vol. 9 (Parts 53-59?)

... Ninth Volume ...

New York: D. Van Nostrand, 192 Broadway. 1866.

Publication information wanting.

Vol. 10 (Parts 60-66?)

... Tenth Volume ...

New York: D. Van Nostrand, 192 Broadway. 1867.

Publication information wanting.

Vol. 11 (Parts 67-73)

... Eleventh Volume ...

New York: D. Van Nostrand, 192 Broadway. 1868.

Publication information wanting.

SUPPLEMENT

... Supplement—First Volume ...

New-York: G. P. Putnam. Henry Holt. Publication Office, 441 Broadway. 1864.

All published? Listed ALG June 15, 1864.

H

The Rebellion Record: A Diary of American Events ... Edited by Frank Moore ... Second Volume ...

New York: G. P. Putnam. C. T. Evans, General Agent. 1862.

"Cavalry Song," p. 50. Collected in *The Music-Lesson* ... , 1872.

For comment see preceding entry.

11532. War-Songs for Freemen. Dedicated to the Army of the United States ... ⟨Edited by Francis J. Child⟩

Boston: Ticknor and Fields. 1862 ...

Reprint save for:

"We're at War," pp. 12-13.

"Shall Freedom Droop and Die," p. 16.

"Sharpshooter's Song," pp. 22-23.

For comment see entry No. 8818. Also see *Fourth Edition* of this collection, 1863, below.

11533. SUNSHINE IN THOUGHT ...

NEW YORK: CHARLES T. EVANS, 448 BROADWAY. 1862.

⟨1⟩-197; blank, p. ⟨198⟩; advertisements, pp. ⟨199-203⟩. 6⅞" scant x 4¹⁵⁄₁₆".

⟨1⟩-8¹², 9⁶.

TR cloth: lavender. Z cloth: green; purplish-blue; purplish-brown. Covers bevelled. Brown-coated on white end papers. Flyleaves. Top edges gilded.

Title deposited Nov. 26, 1862; no record of book deposit. Noticed APC May 1, 1863. Advertised APC May 1, 1863: *Second Edition, Now Ready;* dated 1863? Listed PC May 15, 1863.

AAS   H

11534. ... O WE'RE NOT TIRED OF FIGHTING YET! ...

⟨n.p., n.d., BOSTON, 1863⟩

The above on p. ⟨2⟩. At head of p. ⟨2⟩: ⟨*Page number*⟩ *56 No. 30*. At head of p. ⟨3⟩: *No. 30*. ⟨*Page number*⟩ *57* Text and music on p. ⟨2⟩. Text on p. ⟨3⟩. Pp. ⟨1⟩ and ⟨4⟩ blank.

Single cut sheet folded to make four pages. Page: 6¾″ scant x 4⁵⁄₁₆″.

Offprint (preprint?) from *War-Songs for Freemen ... Fourth Edition*, Boston, 1863. See next entry.

The inscription of a copy in BPL indicates this was issued on March 5, 1863, by the New England Loyal Publication Society. A copy in B inscribed by F. J. Child, editor of *War-Songs for Freemen*: "From the 4th edition of *War Songs for Freemen*. (2000 copies of this printed to circulate as a broadside.)" A copy of *War-Songs for Freemen ... Fourth Edition*, in H, presented by the editor April 7, 1863.

B   BPL   PHS   Y

11535. War-Songs for Freemen. Dedicated to the Army of the United States. Fourth Edition. ⟨Edited by Francis J. Child⟩

Boston: Ticknor and Fields. 1863 ...

Printed paper wrapper. For first edition see above under 1862.

Reprint with the possible exception of "O We're Not Tired of Fighting Yet!," pp. 56-57. See preceding entry.

A copy in H inscribed by the editor April 7, 1863.

H

11536. ⟨New England Loyal Publication Society⟩ [No. 71.] Peace that Shall Be Peace ...

⟨n.p., n.d., Boston, New England Loyal Publication Society, May 29, 1863⟩

Single sheet. Text in three columns.

Contains "The Interest of Foreigners to Sustain the Union."

BPL

11537. YE BOOK OF COPPERHEADS

PHILADELPHIA: FREDERICK LEYPOLDT. 1863.

Anonymous. Written in collaboration with H. P. Leland and others. See Pennell, Vol. 1, p. 254. Leland commented on the collaboration in a letter to Edward McPherson, Dec. ⟨?⟩ 19, 1865 (original in LC): "... If De Kay says

or said that he ever contributed *one line* of writing or drawing to the Book of Copperheads he is a liar ... This is the true account of the book. I drew *all* the pictures except No 24, which was drawn by my brother H. P. Leland. I wrote all the verses except four by Frank Wells and four by G. H. Boker (in the Checker Boarders &c) and three by E. S. Rand Rand ⟨*sic*⟩ Jr. in the Modern Heathen-ians ... I trust there has been some mistake as to De Kay's claiming the authorship of my poor little squib of a brochure ..."

⟨i-ii⟩, 1-⟨30⟩. Illustrated. 5¼″ full x 9¼″.

⟨-⟩¹⁶.

Printed tan paper wrapper.

Note: One copy at P and four at PHS are of unknown status. Printed on one side of leaf only. Leaf: 5⅝″ x 9⅞″. The copy at P is apparently George H. Boker's personal copy and inscribed by him Oct. 1863. On the title-page *No. 39* inscribed (by Boker?); which inscription is struck out and the statement *No. 24* inserted. The copies at PHS do not have a number on the title-page. A special printing for Leland and others?

Title deposited June 25, 1863. Listed APC July 15, 1863. Reprinted and reissued Indianapolis, 1864; copy in LC. Leland refers to the Indianapolis printing in his letter to McPherson: "... The Copperhead Book was republished in Indianapolis as a campaign document during the Presidential fight between Lincoln and the Little Mackerel ..."

BA   H   MHS   NYPL   Y

11538. CENTRALIZATION, OR "STATES RIGHTS." ...

C. T. EVANS, PUBLISHER, 448 BROADWAY, NEW-YORK. ⟨n.d., 1863⟩

Cover-title.

⟨i-ii⟩, ⟨1⟩-14. 9¼″ x 5¹¹⁄₁₆″.

⟨-⟩⁸.

Printed self-wrapper.

AAS   BA   LC   PHS   Y

11539. Heine's Book of Songs. Translated by Charles G. Leland ...

Philadelphia: Frederick Leypoldt. New York: F. W. Christern. 1864.

⟨i-ii⟩, ⟨i⟩-xiv, 1-239, blank leaf. 6⅝″ x 4⅜″. *Note:* The final blank leaf is excised or pasted under the end paper in some copies.

Cloth, paper label on spine printed in red; or, black.

Two states (printings?) noted; the sequence has not been determined and the designations are for identification only.

A: The device on the title-page is within a wreath; the word *Finis* is present at foot of p. 239.

B: The device on the title-page is not within a wreath; the word *Finis* is not present at foot of p. 239.

Advertised as *in preparation* APC May 1, 1863. Advertised as *ready this week* ALG Nov. 2, 1863. A copy at P inscribed by the author to Boker Nov. 21, 1863. Listed ALG Dec. 1, 1863. Advertised Bkr Jan. 30, 1864. Reviewed Ath May 14, 1864.

Note: Many of the poems herein appear in Leland's translation of Heine's *Pictures of Travel,* 1855. There are many alterations in the translations.

AAS (A)   B (A)   H (A)   P (A, B)

11540. Mother Goose from Germany . . .

Philadelphia: Frederick Leypoldt. New York: F. W. Christern. 1864.

Anonymous translation by Leland; see his *Memoirs,* 1893, p. 251 and Jackson p. 46.

⟨1⟩-72. Illustrated. 8⅜″ x 6¹¹⁄₁₆″. Pictorial boards, cloth shelfback.

Advertised *ready by the 20th of December* ALG Dec. 12, 1863. Listed ALG Jan. 1, 1864.

H

11541. LEGENDS OF THE BIRDS . . .

PHILADELPHIA 1864. FREDERICK LEYPOLDT . . .

25 leaves as follows: Title-leaf; 12 leaves of text (irregularly paged); 12 pictorial divisional title-pages, in colors, each with a pasted down picture of a bird in chromolithograph. 8½″ x 6¹¹⁄₁₆″.

Pale blue paper boards sides, printed in black, the front heightened in gold; green T cloth shelfback. Brown-coated on white end papers. Flyleaves.

Also occurs in a variant (remainder?) binding: White paper boards sides printed in dull gold; red-orange T cloth shelfback. Pasted to the front is a large label which repeats the printing of the title-page. Brown-coated on white end papers. Flyleaves.

Announced ALG Nov. 16, 1863. Advertised in ALG Dec. 15, 1863, for Dec. 20 publication. Listed ALG Jan. 15, 1864. Listed PC March 1, 1864. Unsold sheets were issued with the cancel

title-leaf of Henry Holt & Co., New York, 1874; copy in LC.

B   FLP   P (variant)   Y (both)

11542. MOTHER PITCHER'S POEMS FOR LITTLE PEOPLE

PHILADELPHIA: FREDERICK LEYPOLDT. NEW YORK: F. W. CHRISTERN. 1864.

Anonymous. See Leland's *Memoirs,* 1893, p. 251.

⟨1⟩-54, blank leaf. Illustrated. 8½″ scant x 6¹³⁄₁₆″.

⟨1⁴, 2-4⁸⟩.

Printed white paper boards sides, orange A cloth; or, tan V cloth shelfback. Yellow end papers.

Advertised for the *beginning of December* ALG Nov. 16, 1863. Deposited Dec. 30, 1863. Listed ALG Jan. 15, 1864.

LC

11543. Letters to a Lady by Wilhelm von Humboldt. From the German. With an Introduction by Charles Godfrey Leland.

Philadelphia: Frederick Leypoldt. New York: F. W. Christern. 1864.

Cloth, printed paper label on spine.

Edited, not translated, by Leland. Translator not known to BAL. "The history of this work— a partial English translation from which I have been requested to edit for the first time for the American public . . ."—p. vii.

"Introduction," pp. iii-viii.

Advertised as *just ready* ALG Feb. 15, 1864. Listed ALG March 1, 1864. Listed PC April 1, 1864.

AAS   FLP   LCP   UV   Y

11544. Great Central Fair, to Be Held in Philadelphia, June 1864 . . .

⟨n.p., n.d., Philadelphia, 1864.⟩

Single cut sheet folded to make four pages. The above at head of p. ⟨1⟩. A letter, signed by Leland and others, on p. ⟨1⟩. P. ⟨2⟩ blank. Executive Committee's letter on pp. ⟨3-4⟩, dated March 1, 1864.

"The Executive Committee of the Sanitary Commission having decided that A Newspaper should be published, during the Great Fair, which is to be held in Philadelphia, in June next, we would respectfully solicit your aid, as contributor to the publication . . ." The newspaper was *Our Daily Fare;* see below under 1864.

NYPL   Y

11545. The Spirit of the Fair . . .

New York . . . 1864.

"Ever Free," No. 17, p. 200. Collected with revisions in *The Music-Lesson of Confucius* . . . , 1872.

For comment see entry No. 11186.

11546. Our Daily Fare . . .

Philadelphia . . . June 8 . . . June 21. 1864.

An occasional newspaper published by the Great Central Sanitary Fair, Philadelphia. Complete in 13 numbers, June 8, 1864 to June 21, 1864; a final number (No. 13) issued under date Sept. 11, 1865. Not issued June 12, 19, 1864. Ground plan inserted in No. 1 as a supplement.

"Our subscription list was originally very large, and has increased daily; so much, in fact, as to require several of our earlier numbers to be reprinted."—No. 12, June 21, 1864, p. 92. BAL has made no attempt to distinguish the first from the later printings.

As chairman of the Editorial Committee, Leland probably contributed some material; but nothing is signed by him. Jackson, p. 53, lists several pieces which he attributes to Leland.

H (12 numbers)   Y (13 numbers)

11547. An Artist's Poems.   Written and Illustrated by Carl Heinrich Schmolze. Translated by Charles Godfrey Leland . . . Published Exclusively for the Benefit of the Great Central Fair for the United States Sanitary Commission . . .

Philadelphia: Frederick Leypoldt. 1864.

Unpaged. 8 leaves, printed on recto only; and, 7 photographic reproductions. 12⅞" x 10". Issued in a portfolio.

"Translator's Preface," on leaf 2.

Listed ALG Oct. 1, 1864. Deposited Oct. 6, 1864.

H   LC   Y

11548. THE ART OF CONVERSATION, WITH DIRECTIONS FOR SELF EDUCATION.

NEW YORK: CARLETON, PUBLISHER, 413 BROADWAY. M DCCC LXIV.

Anonymous.

⟨i⟩-vi, ⟨7⟩-234; advertisements, pp. ⟨3⟩-8. Laid paper. 7⁵⁄₁₆" x 4¹⁵⁄₁₆".

⟨1⟩-9, ⟨10⟩¹². *Note:* Signature mark 5 is present as a vestige.

Three forms (printings?) noted. The following variations are sufficient for immediate identification:

1

Pagination and collation as above.

On p. ⟨ii⟩ *The Habits of Good Society* is priced $1.50.

Terminal advertisements:

P. ⟨3⟩: *The Art of Conversation* priced $1.25.

P. 4: *Darkness and Daylight* described as *In press.*

P. 6: *Out in the World* described as *In press.*

TR cloth: brown. Z cloth: dull green. Sides bordered by a Greek fret rule. Blue paper end papers. Laid; or, wove paper flyleaves. Spine device occurs ⅝" scant or ⅝" full wide.

1A

Pagination and collation as above. Extensive battering of the plates suggests a late run, possibly a reprint. See, for example, the lower right corner of p. 232.

TR cloth: purple-brown. The frame on the sides is composed of simple rules and an arrangement of small triangular units. Green end papers. Wove paper flyleaves. Spine device ⅝" full wide.

2

Pagination as above. Printed on wove paper.

⟨1-20⟩⁶. *Signed:* ⟨1⟩-9, ⟨10⟩¹². *Note:* Signature mark 5 present as a vestige.

P. ⟨ii⟩: *The Habits of Good Society* priced $1.50.

Terminal advertisements:

P. ⟨3⟩: *The Art of Conversation* priced $1.25.

P. 4: *Darkness and Daylight* described as *Just published.*

P. 5: *Out in the World* described as *In press.*

BD cloth: green. The frame on the sides is composed of simple rules and an arrangement of small triangular units. Green end papers. Flyleaves. Spine device ½" wide.

3

Pagination as above. Printed on wove paper.

⟨1⟩-9, ⟨10⟩¹². *Note:* Signature mark 5 present as a vestige.

CHARLES GODFREY LELAND
Entry No. 11540
Reduced
(Harvard University Library)

P. ⟨ii⟩: *The Habits of Good Society* priced $1.75.

Terminal advertisements:

P. ⟨3⟩: *The Art of Conversation* priced $1.50.

P. 4: *Darkness and Daylight* described as *Just published*.

P. 5: *Out in the World* is priced $1.50; the *In press* statement absent.

TR cloth: brown; dull green. The frame on the sides is composed of simple rules and an arrangement of small triangular units. Green end papers. Off-white end papers. Flyleaves. Spine device ½″ wide.

Note: All examined copies, all forms of the book, have the error CONFIDFNCE for CONFIDENCE in the running head, p. 33; and, an erroneous signature mark 3* on p. 33. The errors are also present in the reprint of 1870.

Advertised as though ready ALG March 1, 1864, at $1.25. Listed ALG March 15, 1864, at $1.25. Frequent later advertisements at $1.25. Deposited Aug. 25, 1864. After Sept. 15, 1864, Carleton appears to have discontinued advertising the book; hence, no record found of when the price advanced to $1.50.

AAS (1) H (3) LC (1; 1A; 2, being a deposit copy) LCP (1) Y (1; 1A)

11549. The Boatswain's Whistle. Published at the National Sailors' Fair . . .

Boston, November 9-19, 1864.

"The Beginning of the End," No. 2, p. 11. Collected in *The Music-Lesson of Confucius . . .*, 1872.

A certificate regarding a special printing of the Emancipation Proclamation, No. 8, p. 60.

For comment see entry No. 1416.

11550. . . . Ma Foi! . . .

New York . . . Wm. A. Pond & Co.   547 Broadway . . . 1864 . . .

Sheet music. Cover-title. At head of title: Parlor Flowers by Louis Selle . . .

Translated from the German by Leland.

No copyright record found.

B

11551. Memoirs of a Good-for-Nothing. From the German of Joseph von Eichendorff, by Charles Godfrey Leland . . .

New York: Leypoldt & Holt, 1866.

⟨1⟩-192. Laid paper. Cloth, covers bevelled; top edges gilded. 7″ x 4⁷⁄₁₆″. *Also:* Printed paper wrapper, top edges plain. 6⅝″ x 4¼″.

"Memoir of the Author," pp. 5-16.

Reviewed ALG May 15, 1866. Listed and advertised ALG May 15, 1866, as in cloth. Deposited Aug. 2, 1866. Listed PC Oct. 1, 1866.

AAS H PHS UV

11552. THE UNION PACIFIC RAILWAY, EASTERN DIVISION, OR, THREE THOUSAND MILES IN A RAILWAY CAR . . .

PHILADELPHIA: RINGWALT & BROWN, STEAM-POWER BOOK AND JOB PRINTERS, NOS. 111 AND 113 SOUTH FOURTH STREET. 1867.

Note: In some copies the comma after *Printers* is lacking.

⟨1⟩-95. 9¾″ x 5⅞″.

⟨1⟩-6⁸. *Note:* Some copies lack signature mark 2 on p. 17.

Printed green; or, terra-cotta paper wrapper. Some copies contain an inserted slip asking for copies of notices or reviews.

Note: The erroneous reading, p. 10, line 7 up, *. . . would be went . . .* is present in all examined copies.

Also note: Appletons' Cyclopædia of American Biography, revised edition, Vol. 3, 1898, p. 683, lists "a pamphlet describing a journey to the far west," titled *To Kansas and Back* (1866). Not seen by BAL. Ghost? Erroneous entry for *The Union Pacific Railway*? Leland's "Preface" to *The Union Pacific Railway . . .* indicates that it is a "record of a journey . . . from Philadelphia to Kansas and back, during the month of November, 1866 . . ." Leland's *Memoirs*, 1893, pp. 334-335 records that the letters appeared, prior to pamphlet publication, in *Forney's Weekly Press* (Philadelphia).

Listed ALG March 15, 1867. A copy at Y contains an inserted presentation slip dated March 27, 1867.

AAS BA PHS Y

11553. The Sayings of Dr. Bushwhacker, and Other Learned Men, by Fred'c S. Cozzens . . .

New York: A. Simpson & Co 1867.

"Dainty Hints for Epicurean Smokers," pp. ⟨143⟩-145.

For comment see entry No. 4008.

THE BREITMANN BALLADS

Publication sequence for the London editions (Trübner; and, Hotten) has not been firmly established.

The Hotten and the Trübner editions came out very nearly simultaneously in the early months of 1869. It is possible that *Hans Breitmann as a Politician* (Trübner) and *Hans Breitmann in Politics* (Hotten) were issued simultaneously. The rivalry of the competing publishers is amply demonstrated in letters published in the British trade periodicals and particularly in Leland's *The Breitmann Ballads. An Appeal ...* , London, n.d., 1869, described below.

Trübner was Leland's authorized British publisher; Leland furnished him with unpublished ballads, and extended and revised others, which permitted Trübner to obtain British copyrights.

Hotten took his text from books and periodicals published in United States; the texts vary from those issued by Trübner. Leland makes clear in his *Breitmann Ballads. An Appeal* that Hotten introduced certain alterations for which he, Leland, was not responsible: "... ⟨Hotten⟩ has ... taken many unwarrantable liberties in altering the spelling, going so far as to change the sense and point of a word ..."

The glossaries in Trübner's London editions were compiled by the publisher. See Leland's statement in the London, 1889, edition of *The Breitmann Ballads,* p. ⟨295⟩.

The tremendous popularity of the *Ballads* in Great Britain is indicated by the extraordinarily large number of notices, advertisements and listings devoted to them. Certain London editions contain added matter and are described in the present list. BAL suspects however that other extended editions may have escaped notice.

11554. HANS BREITMANN'S PARTY. WITH OTHER BALLADS.

PHILADELPHIA: T. B. PETERSON & BROTHERS; 306 CHESTNUT STREET. ⟨1868⟩

⟨1⟩-32. 8½" x 5¾".

⟨1-4⟩⁴.

Printed white paper wrapper. Printed in black and green; or, black and red.

Listed ALG July 15, 1868. Advertised (by Trübner as an importation) Bkr Sept. 1, 1868. Deposited Oct. 29, 1868.

BA   H   LC   P   UP   UV   Y

11555. Hans Breitmann's Party. With Other Ballads ...

London: Trübner & Co., 60 Paternoster Row. 1868.

Printed paper wrapper. Also printed paper boards? Also cloth? Pp. 64.

Basically a reprint of *Hans Breitmann's Party,*

Philadelphia ⟨1868⟩ (see preceding entry), but with some minor alterations (by Leland?) and the addition of a "Preface to the English Edition" (not by Leland) and a "Glossary" written by Nicholas Trübner. On p. 54 appears a translation into English (by Leland?) of the final eight lines of "How Breitmann Cut Him Out," which are in German only in the Philadelphia edition.

Two states (probably printings) noted:

1

Imprint as above.

Last entry, p. ⟨63⟩: *Knasterbart.*

2

To the imprint has been added: [*All rights reserved.*]

The glossary extended by the addition of three entries; the last entry on p. ⟨63⟩ being: *Kop.*

According to contemporary trade notices (see Bkr Sept. 1, 1868) the Philadelphia edition was imported into Great Britain and distributed by Trübner. The *Trübner* edition (pp. 64; as above) noted as *in a few days* Ath Oct. 24, 1868; again announced (as in boards; cloth; paper) Bkr Nov. 2, 1868; listed (paper only) Ath Nov. 7, 1868; reviewed Ath Nov. 14, 1868; reviewed Bkr Dec. 12, 1868, in which review it is stated that the vocabulary (*i.e.,* the glossary) was contributed by the English editor. A *Truelove* (error for Trübner?) edition, pp. 74 (error for 64?) listed PC Dec. 10, 1868; no Truelove edition otherwise reported.

BPL (1st)   P (2nd)   PHS (2nd)

11556. Hans Breitmann's Party. With Other Ballads. By Charles G. Leland. New and Enlarged Edition.

Philadelphia: T. B. Peterson & Brothers; 306 Chestnut Street. ⟨1869⟩

Printed paper wrapper.

Reprint save for:

"Hans Breitmann's Christmas," pp. 33-40.

"Schnitzerl's Philosopede," pp. 41-42. Part 1 only. For Part 2 see *Hans Breitmann's Christmas* (London: Trübner & Co., 1869) and *Hans Breitmann und His Philosopede* (New York: Jesse Haney & Co., 1869).

"Der Freischuetz," pp. 43-48.

Note: A reprint adds to the title-page: *Author of "Hans Breitmann in Church, with Other New Ballads," "Hans Breitmann about Town," Etc., Etc.;* issued not before 1870.

Listed ALG March 1, 1869. A copy at PHS presented by Leland April 16, 1869.

AAS B BPL PHS UV

11557. Hans Breitmann's Christmas. With Other Ballads ...

London: Trübner & Co., 60 Paternoster Row. 1869. [All Rights Reserved.]

Printed paper wrapper.

Reprint save for:

"Hans Breitmann about Town"

"Wein Geist"

For first American book publication of these see *Hans Breitmann about Town,* Philadelphia: Peterson ⟨1869⟩, below.

"Schnitzerl's Philosopede," Part 2. For Part 1 see preceding entry. For first American book publication see below under *Hans Breitmann und His Philosopede,* New York: Haney, 1869.

"The text ... has been revised and corrected ... with the sanction and approval of Mr. Leland. The present collection comprises ballads now published for the first time; moreover, to the ballads previously published, and which have been carefully revised, new matter has been added by the author himself."—P. ⟨5⟩.

Advertised as *in the press* Ath March 6, 1869. Advertised for *this day* Ath March 13, 1869. Noted as *ready* PC March 15, 1869. Advertised as though published Ath March 20, 1869. Listed Ath March 27, 1869. Listed PC April 1, 1869. Reviewed Ath April 3, 1869.

FLP Y

11558. HANS BREITMANN AS A POLITICIAN ...

LONDON: TRÜBNER & CO., 60 PATERNOSTER ROW. 1869. [ALL RIGHTS RESERVED.]

For possible simultaneous publication of the first three sections see the next two entries. For first American edition see *Hans Breitmann in Politics,* Philadelphia: Lippincott, 1869.

⟨i⟩-⟨xiv⟩, ⟨15⟩-72. 5¾″ x 4½″.

⟨A⟩-I⁴.

Printed white paper wrapper. On a slip of lavender paper inserted at front: *Notice. On the point of going to press ... we are informed that a London Publisher* ⟨presumably Hotten⟩ *has also announced this Poem. In order that the Public may not be led into error, we beg to state that this Poem consists of Three Parts, only the first of which can be issued by any*

other house than our own, as Parts Two and Three are Copyright, having been printed from the Author's Original MS ..."

Contains eight sections of the poem in three parts. "... Only the first part ... has hitherto been published; so that the second and third parts ... appear ⟨here⟩ in print for the first time ..."—p. ⟨iii⟩.

Advertised for *early next week* Ath March 13, 1869. Noted as *ready next week* PC March 15, 1869. Advertised *in the press* Ath March 20, 1869. Listed Ath March 27, 1869; PC April 1, 1869. Reviewed Ath April 3, 1869. Second edition listed PC June 1, 1869.

H

11559. HANS BREITMANN IN POLITICS ... A SECOND SERIES OF THE BREITMANN BALLADS. WITH A FEW EXPLANATORY NOTES BY J.C.H. AND H.L.W.

LONDON: JOHN CAMDEN HOTTEN, PICCADILLY. 1869. [ALL RIGHTS RESERVED.]

See preceding entry; see next entry. For first American edition see below: *Hans Breitmann in Politics,* Philadelphia: Lippincott, 1869.

⟨i-ii⟩, ⟨i⟩-⟨xii⟩, ⟨13⟩-54; 4 pp. advertisements paged: ⟨9⟩-10, 13, 21. 6³⁄₁₆″ x 4⅝″.

⟨A⟩⁶, B-D⁸. Leaf ⟨A⟩₁, printed on verso with publisher's advertisements, used as pastedown.

Printed cream paper wrapper. Inserted at back: Publisher's *Special List for 1869,* pp. 1-9, 15-20; p. 20 used as pastedown.

Contains three sections only, not eight, as in the preceding entry. Also contains a poem, "Piet Breitmann in Cincinnati"; not written by Leland.

Ath April 24, 1869, published the following letter from Leland, dated *Philadelphia, April 6, 1869:* "... I have supplied Mr. Trübner with such alterations and additions to my *Breitmann Ballads* as will make his future editions of them the only complete ones, and that, in fact, the series which he now publishes contain several entire poems first published and copyrighted in England. This is especially the case with the volume entitled *Breitmann As a Politician,* which is altogether imperfect and incomplete in any shape save that issued by Mr. Trübner. The original American publication ⟨*Lippincott's Magazine,* March, 1869⟩ of *Breitmann As a Politician,* having been issued in haste, is extremely faulty; and it is this which is now issued in reprint to the English public by Mr. John Camden Hotten ..."

Advertised as *now ready* and listed PC April 1, 1869.

FLP H

11560. HANS BREITMANN'S BALLADS. FIRST & SECOND SERIES

⟨LONDON: JOHN CAMDEN HOTTEN, 1869⟩

Cover-title; thus on cloth copies. See binding note below.

An omnibus volume made up of the sheets of:

Hans Breitmann's Barty, London: Hotten, 1869; see in *Section II*.

Hans Breitmann in Politics, London: Hotten, 1869; see preceding entry.

The single volumes, and the omnibus volume, appear to have been published simultaneously.

Cloth; and, printed paper wrapper. The wrapper imprinted on front: ... *Hans Breitmann's Ballads* ... *Both Series Complete* ...

Deposited BMU March 30, 1869. Advertised as *now ready* Bkr April 1, 1869; PC April 1, 1869. Listed as in cloth and paper Bkr April 1, 1869; PC April 1, 1869.

AAS (cloth) LCP (wrapper) PHS (wrapper) UMi (wrapper)

11561. HANS BREITMANN UND HIS PHI-LOSOPEDE ...

NEW YORK: JESSE HANEY & CO., PUBLISHERS. 1869.

⟨1⟩-22, 2 pp. advertisements. Illustrated. 7⅛″ x 4⅞″.

⟨-⟩12.

Printed lavender-coated paper wrapper.

"Brolock" (*i.e.,* Part 1 of *Hans Breitmann und His Philosopede*) appeared earlier in *Hans Breitmann's Party. With Other Ballads ... New and Enlarged Edition,* Philadelphia ⟨1869⟩, above. Both parts also appeared (simultaneously?) in *Hans Breitmann's Christmas ...* , London: Trübner & Co., 1869.

A copy in P presented by Leland to G. H. Boker, March 31, 1869. Listed ALG April 1, 1869.

AAS B NYPL P Y

11562. HANS BREITMANN IN POLITICS ... [REPRINTED FROM LIPPINCOTT'S MAGAZINE.]

PHILADELPHIA J. B. LIPPINCOTT AND CO. 1869.

First American edition. For prior publication see *Hans Breitmann as a Politician,* London:

Trübner, 1869; and, *Hans Breitmann in Politics,* London: Hotten, 1869.

⟨i-ii⟩, ⟨1⟩-13. Frontispiece inserted. 8¾″ x 5¾″. ⟨-⟩8.

Printed brown; or, orange paper wrapper.

Deposited April 29, 1869. Listed ALG May 15, 1869.

AAS NYPL UV

11563. Hans Breitmann's Christmas. With Other Ballads ... Second Edition.

London: Trübner & Co., 60 Paternoster Row. 1869. [All Rights Reserved.]

Printed paper wrapper.

Reprint save for "Advertisement," p. ⟨5⟩: "I hereby beg to state that Messrs Trübner & Co. of London are the sole authorised publishers in England of my Ballads. Their Editions contain additional verses and alterations made by me to nearly all of the several poems, and which at this time have not appeared in any American or other editions ... Philadelphia, 2d April 1869." For presumed simultaneous publication see next entry.

Listed PC May 15, 1869.

P

11564. Hans Breitmann's Party. With Other Ballads ... Eighth Edition, Enlarged.

London: Trübner & Co., 60 Paternoster Row. 1869. [All Rights Reserved.]

Printed paper wrapper.

Reprint save for:

"Advertisement," p. ⟨ix⟩: "I hereby beg to state that Messrs Trübner & Co. of London are the sole authorised publishers in England of my Ballads. Their Editions contain additional verses and alterations made by me to nearly all of the several poems, and which at this time have not appeared in any American or other editions ... Philadelphia, 2d April 1869."

The "Advertisement" also appears in *Hans Breitmann's Christmas. Second Edition,* London, Trübner, 1869; see preceding entry. Does it also appear in an earlier Trübner publication? PC May 15, 1869: "*Hans Breitmann's Party* ... has arrived at the eighth edition, and the second and third series ⟨*Hans Breitmann's Christmas* and *Hans Breitmann As a Politician*⟩ have been comparatively as successful. To these editions ⟨all three?⟩ *a note of hand,* by the author ... is attached, authorising Messrs. Trübner to act as his sole publishers in England ..."

"A Ballad apout de Rowdies," pp. ⟨69⟩-72. For first American book publication see next entry.

Noticed by PC May 15, 1869.

LC LCP P

11565. Hans Breitmann about Town. And Other New Ballads ... Second Series of the Breitmann Ballads.

Philadelphia: T. B. Peterson & Brothers; 306 Chestnut Street. ⟨1869⟩

Printed paper wrapper printed in black and green; or, black and red.

First American edition for the following:

"Hans Breitmann about Town"

"Wein Geist"

Both the above had prior publication in *Hans Breitmann's Christmas,* London: Trübner, 1869, above.

"A Ballad apout de Rowdies." For prior publication see preceding entry.

Title deposited May 4, 1869. Listed ALG June 1, 1869.

AAS BA H NYPL UV

11566. THE BREITMANN BALLADS. AN APPEAL BY CHARLES GODFREY LELAND, OF PHILADELPHIA, TO HIS COLLEAGUES OF THE PRESS IN ENGLAND.

⟨n.p., LONDON⟩ PRINTED FOR PRIVATE CIRCULATION. ⟨n.d., 1869⟩

Cover-title.

⟨1⟩-22; advertisements, pp. ⟨1⟩-2. 5⅜″ x 4⅜″.

⟨A⟩-C⁴.

Printed self-wrapper.

A letter, dated Philadelphia, April 17, 1869, regarding Hotten's unauthorized publication of the Breitmann ballads.

H

11567. HANS BREITMANN IN CHURCH. WITH OTHER BALLADS ...

LONDON: TRÜBNER & CO., 60 PATERNOSTER ROW. 1870. [ALL RIGHTS RESERVED.]

For first American edition see next entry.

Two printings noted. The sequence has not been established and the designations are for identification only.

A

⟨i-iv⟩, ⟨i⟩-⟨viii⟩, ⟨9⟩-79; blank, p. ⟨80⟩; plus: advertisement, p. ⟨81⟩; blank, pp. ⟨82-84⟩. 5⁷⁄₁₆″ scant x 4⅜″.

⟨A⟩⁶, B-I, K⁴, plus: ⟨L⟩². Leaves ⟨A⟩₁ and ⟨L⟩₂ used as pastedowns.

Printed tan paper wrapper.

B

⟨i-iv⟩, ⟨i⟩-⟨viii⟩, ⟨9⟩-79; blank, p. ⟨80⟩; advertisement, p. ⟨81⟩; blank, pp. ⟨82-84⟩.

⟨-⟩², ⟨A⟩-E⁸, ⟨F⟩². Leaves ⟨-⟩₁ and ⟨F⟩₂ used as pastedowns.

Printed cream white paper wrapper.

Advertised as *in press* Ath Jan. 29, 1870. Reviewed Ath Feb. 12, 1870. Listed Ath Feb. 12, 1870; PC Feb. 15, 1870; Bkr March 1, 1870.

AAS (A) Y (B)

11568. HANS BREITMANN IN CHURCH. WITH OTHER NEW BALLADS ... THIRD SERIES OF THE BREITMANN BALLADS.

PHILADELPHIA: T. B. PETERSON & BROTHERS; 306 CHESTNUT STREET. ⟨1870⟩

For prior London publication see preceding entry.

⟨1⟩-8, 107-154. 8½″ x 5¹¹⁄₁₆″.

⟨1⟩-7⁴. Also signed: ⟨14⟩⁷, 15-18⁴, 19⁵.

Printed white paper wrapper. *Two states of the wrapper noted:*

1: Outer back: *Hans Breitmann's Ballads ... 3 Volumes ...* A copy thus at H from the library of James Russell Lowell marked (in pen and ink) *Advance Copy.* A copy at BA received March 2, 1870.

2: Outer back: *Hans Breitmann's Ballads ... Four Volumes ...*

Deposited Feb. 25, 1870. Listed ALG March 1, 1870. A copy at BA received March 2, 1870.

BA (1st) H (1st) NYPL (1st, 2nd) Y (1st)

11569. Tom Hood's Comic Annual for 1871 ...

London: Published at the Fun Office, 80 Fleet Street, E. C. ⟨n.d., 1870⟩

Printed paper wrapper.

"An American Cock-Tale," pp. 90-92. Collected in *Brand-New Ballads,* 1885.

Advertised as *shortly* in *Fun* (London), Oct. 8, 1870; for Oct. 27, *ibid.,* Oct. 22, 1870; as *now ready, ibid.,* Nov. 5, 1870. A second printing was advertised in *Fun,* Dec. 10, 1870, as *by the end of the week;* and was advertised as *ready, ibid.,* Dec. 24, 1870.

LC

11570. FRANCE, ALSACE, AND LOR-
RAINE . . .

> LONDON: TRÜBNER & CO., 60 PATERNOSTER ROW. 1870. PRICE ONE SHILLING.

Anonymous.

Cover-title.

⟨1⟩-23. 8½″ x 5⁹⁄₁₆″.

⟨-⟩¹².

Printed self-wrapper.

". . . Mr. Trübner was very anxious to have me write a pamphlet vindicating the claim of Germany to Alsace and Lorraine, and I offered to do it gladly . . . The result of this was the *brochure* . . . which had a great success. It at once reappeared in America, and even in Spanish in South America . . ."—Leland's *Memoirs,* New York, 1893, p. 403. The American edition has not been located.

Advertised as *new* Ath Dec. 17, 24, 1870; Jan. 7, 1871; Feb. 4, 1871.

H

11571. Hans Breitmann as a Politician . . .
Third Edition.

> London: Trübner & Co., 60 Paternoster Row. 1870. [All Rights Reserved.]

Printed paper wrapper.

Reprint save for:

Two stanzas added to "The Nomination" which appears here in ten 4-line stanzas.

One stanza added to "Mr. Twine Explains . . . ," here given in fifteen 4-line stanzas.

One stanza added to "Breitmann's Great Speech" which appears here in 19 stanzas.

For first American appearance of the added stanzas see entry No. 11577.

Query: Do these added stanzas appear in a Trübner *Second Edition* (unlocated by BAL)?

AAS

Tom Hood's Comic Annual for 1871 . . .

> London . . . ⟨n.d.⟩

See entry No. 11569.

11572. BREITMANN AS AN UHLAN . . .

> LONDON: TRÜBNER & CO., 60 PATERNOSTER ROW. 1871 [ALL RIGHTS RESERVED.]

⟨i⟩-⟨xvi⟩, ⟨17⟩-70; blank leaf. 5¾″ x 4⁷⁄₁₆″.

⟨-⟩², ⟨A⟩², B-H⁴, I², ⟨J⟩². ⟨-⟩₁ and ⟨J⟩₂ used as pastedowns.

Printed off-white paper wrapper.

With some slight variations the text is the same as that in the American edition; see next entry.

Advertised for *next week* Ath Dec. 10, 1870; Dec. 17, 1870. Advertised as though published Ath Dec. 24, 1870. Listed Ath Dec. 24, 1870; PC Dec. 31, 1870; Bkr Jan. 4, 1871.

AAS   UV   Y

11573. HANS BREITMANN AS AN UHLAN. WITH OTHER NEW BALLADS . . . FOURTH SERIES OF THE BREITMANN BALLADS.

> PHILADELPHIA: T. B. PETERSON & BROTHERS; 306 CHESTNUT STREET. ⟨1871⟩

First American edition. For prior London publication see preceding entry.

⟨1⟩-47. 8⅜″ full x 5⅞″.

⟨1⟩-6⁴.

Printed white paper wrapper.

Published this Day! January 25th, 1871 . . . -- publisher's circular at Y. A copy at BA received Jan. 26, 1871. Listed ALG Feb. 1, 1871.

AAS   BA   H   PHS   UP   UV   Y

11574. The Breitmann Ballads . . . Complete Edition.

> London: Trübner & Co., 60 Paternoster Row. 1871. [All Rights Reserved.]

About two thirds of the pieces herein reprinted from earlier books. The following here first:

"Preface," pp. ⟨vii⟩-xi, dated at end: *London, 1871.* For first American appearance see *Hans Breitmann's Ballads . . . Complete Edition . . .* Philadelphia: Peterson ⟨1871⟩.

"The Picnic"

"Breitmann in la Sorbonne"

"Breitmann in Belgium" in three parts

"Breitmann in Paris"; see note below

"Breitmann in Forty-Eight"

"Breitmann in Holland" in four parts

"Germany" in five parts

"Italy" in three parts

For first American book publication of the preceding pieces see next entry.

Note: "Hans Breitmann in Paris" was advertised by Trübner, as a separate collection, in Ath June 5, 1869; no further advertisements seen. The collection was described as *the fourth series* of the *Ballads* and was to be issued *shortly.* Since Trübner applied the term *fourth series* to his edition of *Hans Breitmann in Church,* 1870, and since this last contains nothing that can be considered *Hans Breitmann in Paris,* it appears that the project was abandoned.

Announced Bkr May 1, 1871. Advertised as *shortly* Bkr May 1, 1871. Listed Ath May 20, 1871. Noticed Ath May 27, 1871. Described as *new* Bkr June 2, 1871; Ath June 3, 1871. Listed PC June 15, 1871. Described as *new* Bkr July 3, 1871. Listed Bkr July 3, 1871.

P Y

11575. Hans Breitmann's Ballads ... Volume Two ...

Philadelphia: T. B. Peterson & Brothers; 306 Chestnut Street. ⟨1871⟩

For Vol. 1 see entry No. 11713.

Reprint save for:

"Hans Breitmann in Europe" in three parts

"Hans Breitmann in Belgium" in three parts

"Hans Breitmann in Holland" in four parts

"Hans Breitmann in Germany" in five parts

"Hans Breitmann in Italy" in three parts

"Hans Breitmann at a Picnic"

For prior publication of the above see preceding entry.

"Hans Breitmann as a Trumpeter"

A copy in H inscribed by early owner June, 1871. Listed ALG July 15, 1871.

AAS B FLP H NYPL P PHS Y

11576. Tom Hood's Comic Annual for 1872 ...

London: Printed at the Fun Office, 80 Fleet Street, E. C. ⟨n.d., 1871⟩

Printed paper wrapper.

"Judge Wyman: A Rural Yankee Legend," pp. 98-99. Collected in *Brand-New Ballads,* 1885.

Advertised in *Fun* (London), Nov. 4, 1871, as *now ready.*

NYPL

11577. Hans Breitmann's Ballads ... Complete Edition in One Volume.

Philadelphia: T. B. Peterson & Brothers; 306 Chestnut Street. ⟨1871⟩

Two editions noted:

1

⟨i-ii⟩, ⟨1⟩-46, ⟨1⟩-62, ⟨1⟩-8, 107-148, ⟨1⟩-⟨46⟩, ⟨1⟩-4, 209-312.

Reprint.

2

⟨1⟩-312.

Extended edition. First American book appearance of the following:

"Preface," pp. 3-8, undated. Also appears in *Breitmann Ballads ... , Complete Edition,* London: Trübner, 1871, where it is dated at end: *London, 1871. Note:* It is presumed, but presumed only, that the London edition was issued prior to the American.

Two stanzas added to "The Nomination" which appears here in ten stanzas.

One stanza added to "Mr. Twine Explains ..." which appears here in fifteen stanzas.

One stanza added to "Breitmann's Great Speech" which appears here in nineteen stanzas.

The added stanzas had prior publication in *Hans Breitmann as a Politician, Third Edition,* London: Trübner, 1870, above.

H (2nd) P (1st) PHS (2nd)

Tom Hood's Comic Annual for 1872 ...

London ... ⟨n.d.⟩

See entry No. 11576.

11578. THE MUSIC-LESSON OF CONFUCIUS, AND OTHER POEMS ...

LONDON: TRÜBNER & CO., 8 & 60, PATERNOSTER ROW. 1872. [ALL RIGHTS RESERVED.]

Title-page in black and red.

For first American edition see next entry.

⟨i⟩-viii, ⟨1⟩-168. 6″ x 4″.

⟨-⟩⁴, 1-10⁸, 11⁴.

Two bindings noted. The sequence is not known, and the designations are for identification only.

A

V cloth: blue; green. Covers bevelled. Front blackstamped save as noted: ⟨rule⟩ / ⟨boxed fillet⟩ / ⟨ornament⟩ / ⟨goldstamped circular device⟩ / ⟨ornament⟩ / ⟨boxed fillet⟩ / ⟨rule⟩ / ⟨all of the preceding within a single rule box⟩ / Blue-coated on white end papers. Greenish-black-coated on white end papers.

B

V cloth: blue. Covers bevelled. Front black-stamped save as noted: ⟨horizontal filigree, not in a box⟩ / ⟨triangular filigree⟩ / ⟨goldstamped circular ornament⟩ / ⟨triangular filigree⟩ / ⟨horizontal filigree, not in a box⟩ / ⟨all the preceding in a single rule frame⟩ / Blue-black-coated on white end papers.

Advertised as *in preparation* Ath Sept. 16, 1871; Ath Oct. 7, 1871; as *shortly* Ath Oct. 28, 1871; advertised as *shortly* Ath Nov. 11, 1871; Ath Nov. 18, 1871. Advertised (prematurely? erroneously?) as *now ready* Ath Nov. 25, 1871. Listed Ath Dec. 16, 1871. Advertised for Dec. 18 Ath Dec. 16, 1871; as *now ready* Ath Dec. 23, 1871. Listed PC Dec. 30, 1871. Reviewed Ath Dec. 30, 1871.

AAS (B)   B (A)   PHS (A)

11579. THE MUSIC-LESSON OF CONFUCIUS, AND OTHER POEMS …

BOSTON: JAMES R. OSGOOD AND COMPANY, LATE TICKNOR AND FIELDS, AND FIELDS, OSGOOD, AND CO. 1872.

Title-page in black and red.

First American edition. For prior publication see preceding entry.

⟨i⟩-viii, ⟨1⟩-168. 6¹⁄₁₆″ x 4¹⁄₁₆″.

⟨-⟩⁴, 1-10⁸, 11⁴.

V cloth: green; orange; terra-cotta. Covers bevelled. Brown-coated on white end papers. Fly-leaves.

Two issues of the binding noted:

1: No publisher's imprint on spine.

2: Spine imprint: HOUGHTON MIFFLIN & CO

According to the publisher's records, 1,500 sets of the English sheets imported in Dec. 1871. 500 copies bound Dec. 29 and 30, 1871. A copy at BPL received Jan. 6, 1872. A copy at BA received Jan. 8, 1872. Listed ALG Jan. 15, 1872. 29 copies bound March 11 and 13, 1886. Sept. 13, 1890, 430 sets of sheets were pulped. Information regarding the remaining sheets is lacking.

AAS (1st)   B (1st)   BA (1st)   BPL (1st)   H (1st)   UP (2nd)

11580. Gaudeamus! Humorous Poems Translated from the German of Joseph Victor Scheffel and Others. By Charles G. Leland.

London: Trübner & Co., 8 & 60, Paternoster Row. 1872 …

For American edition see below under 1872.

⟨i⟩-⟨xx⟩, ⟨1⟩-154, blank leaf. 5¹⁄₁₆″ x 3¹⁵⁄₁₆″. Errata slip inserted in the front matter.

"Translator's Preface," pp. ⟨v⟩-viii.

"Joseph Victor Scheffel. An Introductory Memoir," pp. ⟨ix⟩-xix; unsigned; presumably by Leland.

Advertised as *in preparation* Ath Sept. 16; Oct. 7, 1871. Listed Ath Jan. 20, 1872. Noted as *ready* Ath Jan. 27, 1872.

FLP

11581. Meister Karl's Sketch-Book …

Philadelphia: T. B. Peterson & Brothers. London: Trübner & Co., 60 Paternoster Row. ⟨1872⟩

For first edition see under 1855.

"Preface," pp. 21-25.

A revised edition; certain of the original 1855 pieces dropped and others added.

Noted for Jan. 20 WTC Jan. 18, 1872. A copy at BA received Jan. 22, 1872. Listed Ath May 4, 1872.

BA   NYPL   UV   Y

11582. Gaudeamus! Humorous Poems Translated from the German of Joseph Victor Scheffel and Others. By Charles G. Leland.

Boston: James R. Osgood and Company, Late Ticknor and Fields, and Fields, Osgood, and Co. 1872.

First American edition. For prior publication see above under 1872.

⟨i⟩-⟨xx⟩, ⟨1⟩-154, blank leaf. 5″ x 3⅞″. In some copies the final blank leaf is excised. Errata slip inserted in some copies.

"Translator's Preface," pp. ⟨v⟩-viii.

"Joseph Victor Scheffel. An Introductory Memoir," pp. ⟨ix⟩-xix; unsigned; presumably by Leland.

Noted for future publication WTC Jan. 18, 1872. The publisher's records indicate that 500 sets of sheets of the English printing were imported in Jan. 1872. Bound Jan. 26–May 16, 1872. Listed WTC Feb. 15, 1872.

AAS   B   FLP   NYPL   PHS

11583. Tom Hood's Comic Annual for 1873 …

London: Published at the Fun Office, 80 Fleet Street, E. C. ⟨n.d., 1872⟩

"Fritzerl Schnall," pp. 66-67. Collected in *Brand-New Ballads*, 1885.

For comment see entry No. 1095.

11584. THE EGYPTIAN SKETCH-BOOK . . .

STRAHAN & CO. AND TRÜBNER & CO. LUDGATE HILL, LONDON. 1873. [ALL RIGHTS RESERVED.]

For American edition see below under 1874.

⟨i⟩-viii, ⟨1⟩-316. 7½″ scant x 4⅞″.

⟨-⟩⁴, A-I, K-T⁸, U⁴, X².

C cloth: blue. Yellow-coated on white end papers. Errata slip inserted in the front matter.

Noted as *shortly* Ath May 24, 1873; *in the press* PC June 2, 1873; PC June 17, 1873; *immediately* Ath and PC Aug. 16, 1873; *now ready* Ath Aug. 30, 1873. Listed Ath Aug. 30, 1873. Reviewed Ath Sept. 13, 1873. Listed PC Sept. 16, 1873. Noted as *recent* and *new* PC Oct. 1, 1873; Ath Oct. 25, 1873.

LCP Y

11585. THE ENGLISH GIPSIES AND THEIR LANGUAGE . . .

LONDON TRÜBNER & CO., 57 & 59 LUDGATE HILL 1873 [ALL RIGHTS RESERVED]

For American edition see next entry.

⟨i⟩-⟨xvi⟩, ⟨1⟩-259. 7³⁄₁₆″ x 4⅞″.

⟨-⟩⁸, A-I, K-Q⁸, R².

Issued in cloth according to Jackson, p. 80.

Noted as *in press* Ath March 29, 1873; PC April 17, 1873; *shortly* Ath May 24, 1873, June 14, 1873, July 5, 1873. Advertised for Oct. 15 in Ath Oct. 11, 1873. Noted as *now ready* Ath Oct. 18, 1873. Listed Ath Oct. 25, 1873; PC Nov. 1, 1873. A copy in BA received Nov. 6, 1873.

BA (rebound)

11586. THE ENGLISH GIPSIES AND THEIR LANGUAGE . . .

NEW YORK PUBLISHED BY HURD AND HOUGHTON CAMBRIDGE: THE RIVERSIDE PRESS 1873

First American edition. For prior publication see preceding entry.

⟨i⟩-⟨xvi⟩, ⟨1⟩-259. 7¼″ x 4¾″. Pp. ⟨i-ii⟩ excised.

⟨-⟩⁸, A-I, K-Q⁸, ⟨R⟩². Leaf ⟨-⟩₁ excised.

C cloth: brown. Blue-green-coated on white end papers. Flyleaves. Edges stained red.

Note: Made up of the sheets of the London printing save for the title-leaf which, in the American issue, is a cancel; and, pp. 257-259. According to the records of the Riverside Press, Cambridge, Mass., 250 copies of pp. 257-259 (comprising the final gathering) were printed Nov. 13, 1873; no information found regarding the number of copies imported. In the New York issue, therefore, the title-leaf and pp. 257-259 are printed on paper unlike that used in the body of the book; pp. 257-259 printed from a face other than that used by the London publisher. All copies of the New York issue examined by BAL exhibit these variations. The two printings of pp. 257-259 may be readily identified by examination of p. 259:

London issue: Ballantyne imprint present.

New York issue: Ballantyne imprint not present.

Under the title *The Gipsies in England* listed PW Nov. 22, 1873. Advertised as *published this day, Saturday, 22d November* PW Nov. 22, 1873. A copy at AAS received by early owner Nov. 26, 1873.

AAS Y

11587. THE EGYPTIAN SKETCH BOOK . . .

NEW YORK: PUBLISHED BY HURD AND HOUGHTON. THE RIVERSIDE PRESS, CAMBRIDGE. 1874.

First American edition. For prior publication see above under 1873.

⟨i-ii⟩, ⟨i⟩-⟨x⟩, ⟨1⟩-331. Laid paper. 7³⁄₁₆″ x 4⅞″.

⟨1-28⁶, 29⁴⟩. *Signed:* ⟨-⟩⁶, 1-20⁸, 21⁶.

C cloth: brown; green; terra-cotta. Brown-coated on white end papers. Flyleaves have been noted as follows: laid paper; wove paper; laid paper flyleaf at back only.

Advertised as *published this day, Saturday, 22d November* PW Nov. 22, 1873. Listed PW Nov. 22, 1873.

H NYPL Y

11588. Tom Hood's Comic Annual for 1874 . . .

London: Published at the Fun Office, 80 Fleet Street, E. C. ⟨n.d., 1873⟩

"Miss Miles, the Telegraph Girl," pp. 106-107. Collected in *Brand-New Ballads*, 1885.

For comment see entry No. 1098.

11589. Fusang or the Discovery of America by Chinese Buddhist Priests in the Fifth Century . . .

London: Trübner & Co., Ludgate Hill. 1875 . . .

For American edition see next entry.

⟨i⟩-⟨xx⟩, ⟨1⟩-212. 7½″ x 5″.

"The original document on which the Chinese historians based their account of Fusang was the report of a Buddhist monk or missionary . . .

In 1841 Carl Friedrich Neumann ... published the original narrative ... This little work I translated into English, under the supervision of Professor Neumann, and with his aid ..."— pp. ⟨v⟩-vi.

Listed Ath April 17, 1875.

BA H Y

11590. Fusang or the Discovery of America by Chinese Buddhist Priests in the Fifth Century ...

New York: J. W. Bouton, 706 Broadway. 1875.

First American edition. For prior publication see preceding entry.

⟨i⟩-⟨xx⟩, ⟨1⟩-212. 7⅛″ full x 4¾″.

Both the New York and the London editions printed from the same plates at the Ballantyne Press, Edinburgh and London.

Listed PW May 8, 1875.

PHS Y

11591. English-Gipsy Songs. In Rommany with Metrical English Translations. By Charles G. Leland, Professor E. H. Palmer, and Janet Tuckey.

London: Trübner & Co., Ludgate Hill. 1875. [All Rights Reserved.]

For American edition see next entry.

⟨i⟩-xii, ⟨1⟩-276. 7″ x 4¹¹⁄₁₆″.

S cloth: blue. Covers bevelled. *Trübner & Co.* imprint on spine. Brown-coated on white end papers. Also occurs in a variant (later?) binding: S cloth: purple-red. Covers not bevelled. Publisher's imprint not on spine. Leaf: 6¹³⁄₁₆″ x 4⅝″.

Noted as *preparing* Ath April 18, 1874. Noted as *shortly* Ath Nov. 7, 1874; Bkr Dec. 1, 1874. Noted as *shortly* Ath March 13 and April 10, 1875. Listed Ath May 29, 1875; PC June 16, 1875. Reviewed Bkr Ath June 19, 1875.

BA (variant) FLP NYPL

11592. English-Gipsy Songs. In Rommany with Metrical English Translations. By Charles G. Leland, Professor E. H. Palmer, and Janet Tuckey.

Philadelphia: J. B. Lippincott & Co. 1875.

First American edition. For prior publication see preceding entry.

⟨i⟩-xii, ⟨1⟩-276. 6¹³⁄₁₆″ x 4⁹⁄₁₆″.

Ballantyne (Edinburgh and London) imprint at foot of p. 276.

Listed PW June 26, 1875. Advertised as *just published* PW Sept. 4, 1875. Advertised as *recently published* PW Sept. 25, 1875.

LCP PHS Y

11593. The Illustrated Family Christian Almanac for ... 1876 ...

American Tract Society, 150 Nassau Street, New York. Sold by Booksellers and Traders. ⟨n.d., 1875⟩

Printed paper wrapper.

"The Farmer Feedeth All," p. 34.

A copy in H received Oct. 26, 1875.

H

11594. ... Lost Dreams ... Music by Virginia Gabriel ...

New York. C. H. Ditson & Co. 711 Broadway ... ⟨n.d., ca. 1875⟩

Sheet music. Cover-title. At head of title: Written expressly for and sung by Mr. J. E. Perkins. Plate number: 28537.

Also in *The Music-Lesson of Confucius,* 1872.

B

11595. Johnson's New Universal Cyclopædia: A Scientific and Popular Treasury of Useful Knowledge ... Editors-in-Chief. Frederick A. P. Barnard ... Arnold Guyot ... Assistant Editors ... Charles G. Leland ...

A. J. Johnson & Son ... New York ... MDCCC-LXXV. ⟨Should be MDCCCLXXIV?⟩

Caution: Entry tentative.

4 Vols. Presumably issued in a variety of custom bindings. The imprints vary and are dated: MDCCCLXXV, MDCCCLXXVI, MDCCCLXXVII, MDCCC-LXXVIII, respectively.

Leland contributed no less than 15 pieces to this work. *Note:* Leland's name appears on the title-page of Vol. 1 only as one of the assistant editors.

H NYPL

11596. PIDGIN-ENGLISH SING-SONG OR SONGS AND STORIES IN THE CHINA-ENGLISH DIALECT. WITH A VOCABULARY ...

LONDON: TRÜBNER & CO., LUDGATE HILL. 1876. [ALL RIGHTS RESERVED.]

For American edition see next entry.

⟨i⟩-viii, ⟨1⟩-139, blank, p. ⟨140⟩; advertisements, pp. ⟨1⟩-3. 6⅝″ x 4½″ full.

⟨-⟩⁴, A-I⁸.

V cloth: yellow. Cream-coated on white end papers.

Listed Ath June 17; PC July 1, 1876. A copy at BA received July 20, 1876.

AAS   BA   NYPL

11597. PIDGIN-ENGLISH SING-SONG OR SONGS AND STORIES IN THE CHINA-ENGLISH DIALECT. WITH A VOCABULARY ...

PHILADELPHIA: J. B. LIPPINCOTT & CO. 1876.

First American edition. For prior publication see preceding entry.

⟨iii⟩-viii, ⟨1⟩-139; 2 leaves excised. 6⅝″ x 4½″.

⟨-⟩³, A-I⁸. ⟨-⟩₂ is an insert. Leaves I₇₋₈ (advertisements?) excised.

V cloth: yellow. Cream-coated on white end papers.

Note: A variant, deposited in LC June 27, 1876, now rebound but probably collating as above, is imprinted: PHILADELPHIA: / 1876. Publisher's name not present. Prepared for copyright purposes only?

Deposited (with Lippincott imprint) July 24, 1876. Listed PW July 29, 1876.

AAS   B   H   LC

11598. JOHNNYKIN AND THE GOBLINS ...

LONDON   MACMILLAN & CO. 1877. ⟨*i.e.,* 1876⟩ ALL RIGHTS RESERVED

For American edition see next entry.

⟨i⟩-⟨viii⟩, ⟨9⟩-212; 4 pp. advertisements. Illustrated. 7³⁄₁₆″ scant x 4¹³⁄₁₆″.

⟨A⟩-I, K-N⁸, O⁴.

Two states noted:

1: P. ⟨215⟩ is headed: ... BOOKS FOR THE YUNG.

2: P. ⟨215⟩ is headed: ... BOOKS FOR THE YOUNG.

V cloth: blue. All edges gilt. Brown-coated on white end papers.

Announced PC Oct. 2, 1876; Ath Oct. 14, 1876. Noted as *immediately* PC Oct. 17, 1876. Listed Ath Oct. 28; PC Nov. 2, 1876. Reviewed PC Nov. 2, 1876. Noted as *this day* PC Nov. 2; Ath Nov. 4, 1876.

P (1st)   PHS (2nd)   UV (2nd)

11599. JOHNNYKIN AND THE GOBLINS
...

NEW YORK   MACMILLAN & CO. 1876   ALL RIGHTS RESERVED

First American edition. For prior publication see preceding entry.

⟨i⟩-⟨viii⟩, ⟨9⟩-212, 4 pp. advertisements. Illustrated. 7³⁄₁₆″ x 4⅞″.

⟨A⟩-I, K-N⁸, O⁴.

C cloth: blue. Brown-coated on white end papers.

A copy at BA received Nov. 7, 1876. Listed PW Dec. 2, 1876.

AAS   B   NYPL   UP

Johnnykin and the Goblins ...

London ... 1877 ⟨*i.e.,* 1876⟩

See above under 1876 (Oct.).

11600. Hood's Comic Annual for 1879 ...
⟨Edited by the Brothers Dalziel⟩

London: Published for the Proprietors at the Fun Office, 153 Fleet Street, E. C. ⟨1878⟩

Printed paper wrapper. Publisher's preface dated *October, 1878*.

"In the Wrong Box," pp. ⟨14⟩-15. Collected in *Brand-New Ballads,* 1885.

Advertised as *ready on the 15th, Fun* (London) Oct. 7, 1878. Advertised as *now ready, Fun* (London) Oct. 14, 1878. Listed Bkr Nov. 5; PC Nov. 16, 1878.

BPL

11601. ABRAHAM LINCOLN ...

LONDON: MARCUS WARD & CO., 67, 68, CHANDOS STREET AND ROYAL ULSTER WORKS, BELFAST 1879

For American edition see next entry.

⟨1⟩-246, 2 pp. advertisements. Portrait frontispiece inserted. 6¹³⁄₁₆″ x 4¹³⁄₁₆″.

⟨A⟩-I, K-P⁸, Q⁴.

V cloth: black. Buff-coated on white end papers printed in red-brown with a pattern of mazes and rosettes.

Announced as No. 4 in the *New Plutarch* series PC March 1, 1879. Announced as *the next* ⟨*volume*⟩ *published* PC June 17, 1879, July 1, 1879, Aug. 1, 1879. Noted for *early in September* Ath Aug. 16, 1879. Noted as though ready PC Sept. 1, 1879; as *now ready* PC Oct. 2, 1879. Listed Ath Sept. 6, 1879; PC Sept. 16, 1879. A copy in B inscribed by Leland Sept. 29, 1879. Reviewed Ath Oct. 11, 1879.

Also noted with the imprint: *London: Marcus Ward & Co., 67, 68, Chandos Street and at Belfast and New York* ⟨n.d., not before 1882⟩

Reissued in 1894 as a volume in Marcus Ward's *Heroes of History* series; see Ath Feb. 24, 1894.

Note: The following entry taken from Foley: *Life of Abraham Lincoln, 12mo. London, 1863.* No other record of such publication found; presumably an erroneous entry for the present work.

AAS   B   LC

11602. ABRAHAM LINCOLN AND THE ABOLITION OF SLAVERY IN THE UNITED STATES ...

NEW YORK   G. P. PUTNAM'S SONS   182 FIFTH AVENUE 1879

First American edition. For prior publication see preceding entry. See below under 1879 for the second edition. In *The New Plutarch* series.

⟨1⟩-246; advertisements, pp. ⟨247-252⟩; blank leaf; leaf excised or pasted under end paper. Portrait frontispiece inserted. $6\frac{13}{16}$" x $4\frac{13}{16}$".

⟨A⟩-I, K-Q⁸. Leaf Q_8 excised or pasted under end paper.

V cloth: white. Buff end papers. Flyleaf at front.

Listed PW Oct. 4, 1879.

AAS   H   Y

11603. Hood's Comic Annual for 1880 ... ⟨Edited by the Brothers Dalziel⟩

London: Published for the Proprietors at the Fun Office, 153 Fleet Street, E. C. ⟨1879⟩

Printed paper wrapper. Publisher's preface dated *October, 1879.*

"Zion Jersey Boggs. An American Legend," pp. ⟨28⟩-30. Collected in *Brand-New Ballads,* 1885.

Advertised as *ready on the 16th, Fun* (London) Oct. 8, 1879. Advertised as *now ready, Fun* (London) Oct. 15, 1879. Listed PC Nov. 3, 1879; Bkr Nov. 5, 1879.

AAS

11604. Abraham Lincoln and the Abolition of Slavery in the United States ...

New York   G. P. Putnam's Sons   182 Fifth Avenue 1879

For first edition see above under 1879.

"In issuing this second edition ... the publishers have taken occasion to correct a few errors in dates and proper names, and in citations from documents, that had crept into the first edition ..."—*Publisher's Note,* p. ⟨3⟩. Also contains an appendix (added).

Reprinted and reissued by Putnam in 1881 and 1883. The earliest of the 1881 reprints carry the publisher's address: *182 Fifth Avenue;* the later 1881 printings: *27-29 West 23 Street.*

Reprints were also issued by H. M. Caldwell Company, New York, n.d., 1896; and by Merrill & Baker, New York ⟨1879; i.e., not before 1894⟩. The Caldwell printing listed PW Oct. 24, 1896.

B

Hood's Comic Annual for 1880 ...

London ... ⟨1879⟩

See entry No. 11603.

11605. EYE-MEMORY, A LECTURE DELIVERED BEFORE THE FRANKLIN INSTITUTE, MARCH 29, 1880 ...

PHILADELPHIA, 1880

Not seen. Not located. Entry from Jackson, p. 89.

Presumably an offprint from *The Journal of the Franklin Institute,* May, 1880, pp. 327-336; June, 1880, pp. 391-399.

Jackson locates a copy in Historical Society of Pennsylvania. The Society reports no copy in its collections (June 24, 1964).

11606. THE MINOR ARTS. PORCELAIN PAINTING, WOOD-CARVING, STENCILLING, MODELLING, MOSAIC WORK ...

LONDON: MACMILLAN AND CO. 1880. THE RIGHT OF TRANSLATION AND REPRODUCTION IS RESERVED.

In the *Art at Home Series.*

⟨i⟩-⟨xx⟩, ⟨1⟩-148; plus: 1 page advertisements. Illustrated. $7\frac{1}{8}$" x $4\frac{7}{8}$".

⟨A⟩⁸, b², B-I, K⁸, L²; plus: ⟨M⟩¹.

Mottled blue flexible S cloth. Brown-coated on white end papers.

Noted as *nearly ready* Ath Nov. 15, 1879. Advertised as *shortly* PC July 15, 1880; *immediately* PC Aug. 2, 1880; *next week* Ath Aug. 7, 1880. Listed Ath Aug. 14, 1880; PC Sept. 1, 1880; PW Sept. 25, 1880. Reviewed PC Oct. 1, 1880.

UV   Y

The section on wood carving was issued as follows:

A Manual of Wood Carving. By Charles G. Leland ... Revised by John J. Holtzapffel ...

London: Whittaker and Co., Paternoster Square. Sold Also by Holtzapffel and Co., 64, Charing Cross. 1890.

The publisher's prefatory note is somewhat ambiguous when read in the light of the title-page. It is not clear whether the revisions were done wholly by Holtzapffel or in collaboration with Leland.

Advertised as *new and forthcoming* PC Oct. 1, 1890. Listed Ath Oct. 4, 1890 (as in boards); PC Oct. 15, 1890; Bkr Nov. 1890 (as in cloth).

Location: BPL

Wood Carving ... Revised by John J. Holtzapffel ... Second Edition Revised.

London: Whittaker and Co., Paternoster Square. Sold Also by Holtzapffel and Co., 64, Charing Cross. 1891.

Printed paper boards. Did Leland have a hand in the revisions? A so-called *Third Edition* was issued under date 1894.

Advertised Ath July 25, 1891; Ath Aug. 1, 1891; PC Aug. 15, 1891.

Locations: NYPL (*Second Edition*) P (*Third Edition*)

A Manual of Wood Carving ... Revised by John J. Holtzapffel ...

New York   Charles Scribner's Sons   1891

Printed paper boards.

Noted as *just ready* PW March 14, 1891. Deposited March 16, 1891. A copy in BPL received March 18, 1891.

Locations: AAS BPL H Y

11607. Hood's Comic Annual for 1881 ...

London: Published for the Proprietors at the Fun Office, 153 Fleet Street, E. C. ⟨1880⟩

Printed paper wrapper. Publisher's preface dated *October, 1880.*

"American Legends," pp. ⟨28⟩-30, in two parts: "The Ballad of the Green Old Man" and "Carrying Coals." Collected in *Brand-New Ballads,* 1885.

Advertised for *October 14th, Fun* (London) Oct. 13, 1880. Advertised as *now ready, Fun* (London) Oct. 20, 1880.

BPL

11608. ... INDUSTRIAL AND DECORATIVE ART IN PUBLIC SCHOOLS. READ AT A MEETING OF THE ASSOCIATION, OCTOBER 21ST, 1880 ...

PUBLISHED BY THE PHILADELPHIA SOCIAL SCIENCE ASSOCIATION, 720 LOCUST STREET, PHILADELPHIA. ⟨n.d., 1880?⟩

Cover-title. At head of title: PHILADELPHIA SOCIAL SCIENCE ASSOCIATION.

⟨1⟩-17. 9⅜″ x 6⅛″.

⟨1⁸, 2¹⟩

Printed self-wrapper.

Note: Not the same as *Industrial Art in Schools,* 1882.

BPL H LC

Hood's Comic Annual for 1881 ...

London ... ⟨1880⟩

See entry No. 11607.

11609. Atti del IV Congresso Internazionale degli Orientalisti Tenuto in Firenze nel Settembre 1878. Volume Secondo ...

Firenze. Coi Tipi dei Successori Le Monnier. 1881.

Printed paper wrapper.

"On the English Gipsy or Rommani Language," pp. 31-37.

H

11609A. Hood's Comic Annual for 1882 ...

London: Published for the Proprietors at the Fun Office, 153 Fleet Street, E. C. ⟨1881⟩

Printed paper wrapper. Publisher's preface dated *October, 1881.*

"Carey, of Carson," pp. 73-74. Collected in *Brand-New Ballads,* 1885.

BPL

11610. Recreations of the Rabelais Club. 1880–1881 ...

⟨London⟩ Printed for the Members ... ⟨n.d., 1881?⟩

Cloth; and, vellum.

"*The Tempest* and *The Storm;* or, Shakespeare and Rabelais," pp. ⟨117⟩-127.

100 numbered copies only.

On pp. ⟨ii⟩ and ⟨174⟩: Imprint of Billing and Sons, Guildford.

H

11611. The Art Work Manuals

1881–1882

Edited by Leland. Twelve parts. Illustrated (in part) by a series of inserted, folded, diagrams and designs. A full suite probably comprises 114 plates, but the figure is not certain.

No. 1

Art Work Manuals Edited by Charles G Leland Ceramic Painting . . .

New York: The Art Interchange Publishing Co., 140 Nassau Street . . .

Printed paper wrapper. Cover-title. Issued under date *October, 1881.*

⟨1⟩-29; advertisements, pp. ⟨30-32⟩. Illustrated. 10⅚₆″ x 8⅛″.

No. 2

. . . Tapestry or Dye Painting . . .

New York: The Art Interchange Publishing Co., 140 Nassau Street . . .

Printed paper wrapper. Cover-title. Issued under date *November, 1881.*

⟨i-ii⟩, ⟨1⟩-12; advertisements, pp. ⟨13-14⟩.

No. 3

. . . Wood Carving . . .

New York: The Art Interchange Publishing Co., 140 Nassau Street . . .

Printed paper wrapper. Cover-title. Issued under date *December, 1881.*

⟨1⟩-19. Illustrated.

No. 4

. . . Art Needlework. Part I. Outline Embroidery . . .

New York. The Art Interchange Publishing Company, No. 140 Nassau Street.

Note: With publication of this part the publishers altered the format slightly to permit issuance with a true title-page.

Printed paper wrapper. Issued under date *January, 1882.*

⟨1⟩-21; advertisements, pp. 22-24. Illustrated.

No. 5

. . . Leather Work . . .

New York: The Art Interchange Publishing Company, No. 140 Nassau Street.

Printed paper wrapper. Issued under date *February, 1882.*

⟨1⟩-18; advertisements, pp. 19-20. Illustrated.

No. 6

. . . Decorative Oil Painting . . .

New York: The Art Interchange Publishing Company, No. 140 Nassau Street.

Printed paper wrapper. Issued under date *March, 1882.*

⟨1⟩-11; advertisement, p. 12. At end of text: *J. Liberty Tadd.*

No. 7

. . . Art Needlework. Part II. Filled-in Embroidery. By Elizabeth Robins . . .

New York. The Art Interchange Publishing Company, No. 140 Nassau Street.

Printed paper wrapper. Issued under date *April, 1882.*

⟨1⟩-22, blank leaf. At end of text: *Elizabeth Robins.*

No. 8

. . . Repoussé Work, or, Embossing on Sheet Brass . . .

New York. The Art Interchange Publishing Company, No. 140 Nassau Street.

Printed paper wrapper. Issued under date *May, 1882.*

⟨1⟩-12. Illustrated.

No. 9

. . . Stencilling . . .

New York. The Art Interchange Publishing Company, No. 140 Nassau Street.

Printed paper wrapper. Issued under date *June, 1882.*

⟨1⟩-14, blank leaf. Illustrated.

No. 10

. . . Drawing and Decorative Design . . .

New York. The Art Interchange Publishing Company, No. 140 Nassau Street. July, 1882.

Printed paper wrapper.

⟨1⟩-18. Illustrated.

Note: A copy in PHS does not have the date in the imprint. Reprint?

No. 11

. . . Papier-Mache . . .

New York. The Art Interchange Publishing Company, No. 140 Nassau Street. August, 1882.

Printed paper wrapper.

⟨1⟩-12. Illustrated.

Note: A copy in PHS does not have the date in the imprint; and, has the acute accent mark in *Papier-Maché.* Reprint?

No. 12

... Modeling in Clay, and, Underglase ⟨sic⟩ Faience Decoration ...

New York. The Art Interchange Publishing Company, No. 140 Nassau Street, September, 1882.

Printed paper wrapper.

⟨1⟩-14. Illustrated. Signed at end of text: *J. Liberty Tadd.*

Note: Issues of this series with the publisher's later address, 37 & 39 West 22nd Street, New York, were published not before 1885.

AAS (No. 8) BPL (Nos. 2-12) PHS (Nos. 1-3, 5-6, 8-11)

11612. A MEMOIR OF CHAPMAN BIDDLE, READ BEFORE THE HISTORICAL SOCIETY OF PENNSYLVANIA, MARCH 13, 1882 ...

PHILADELPHIA: COLLINS, PRINTER, 705 JAYNE STREET. 1882.

⟨1⟩-24. Portrait frontispiece inserted. Laid paper. 9¾″ x 6½″.

⟨1⟩⁸, 2⁴.

Printed light gray-green paper wrapper. Double flyleaves of bookstock at front and back of some copies.

A copy at PHS presented to the Society by Walter L. C. Biddle Oct. 19, 1882.

AAS BA Y

Hood's Comic Annual for 1882 ...

London ... ⟨1881⟩

See entry No. 11609A.

11613. ... RESULT OF INDUSTRIAL ART EDUCATION IN SCHOOLS. READ AT A MEETING OF THE ASSOCIATION, MARCH 23D, 1882 ...

PUBLISHED BY THE PHILADELPHIA SOCIAL SCIENCE ASSOCIATION. 720 LOCUST STREET, PHILADELPHIA. ⟨n.d., 1882?⟩

Cover-title. At head of title: PHILADELPHIA SOCIAL SCIENCE ASSOCIATION.

⟨1⟩-18. 8¹³⁄₁₆″ x 5¾″ scant.

⟨1⁸, 2¹⟩.

Printed self-wrapper.

Note: Not the same as *Industrial Art in Schools,* 1882.

H LCP

11614. THE GYPSIES ...

BOSTON HOUGHTON, MIFFLIN AND COMPANY NEW YORK: 11 EAST SEVENTEENTH STREET THE RIVERSIDE PRESS, CAMBRIDGE 1882

⟨i⟩-viii, ⟨9⟩-372. 7¹¹⁄₁₆″ x 5″.

⟨1-15¹², 16⁶⟩. Signed: ⟨1⟩-⟨7⟩, 8-23⁸, 24².

S cloth: dark blackish-brown; red-brown. Gray-green-coated on white end papers. Flyleaves. Inserted at front is a single leaf imprinted on verso with advertisements. Top edges stained red.

The printing history from the publisher's records is as follows:

May 2, 1882, 1st printing, 1022 copies. 15½ signatures.

May 4, 1882, the advertising page (inserted at front) composed and printed, 1000 copies.

May 10, 1882, 491 copies bound. All copies bound by June 27, 1882.

June 1, 1882, 1000 copies of "cancel ... pp 103 &c" printed; *i.e.,* pp. 103-104 and conjugate pp. 113-114. *Is this entry postdated?* No textual variations have been noted by BAL. Were all copies, including those bound on May 10, issued with the cancel?

Aug. 16, 1882. Second printing. 284 copies. 16½ signatures.

March 12, 1883. Third printing. 270 copies. 16½ signatures. Issued under date 1883.

BAL has been unable to distinguish the first from the second printing. According to the publisher's records the second printing consisted of 16½ signatures (the first printing consisted of 15½ signatures). The third printing (dated 1883) has an integral terminal catalog. Is an integral terminal catalog present in the second printing? A copy dated 1882 (in FLP) has a terminal catalog, but the volume has been rebound and short of taking the book apart it cannot be determined whether the catalog is integral or inserted.

Advertised for May 10, PW May 6, 1882. A copy in BPL received May 15, 1882. Deposited May 16, 1882. Listed PW May 20, 1882. The London (Trübner) edition, 261 sets of American sheets, with cancel title-page, shipped to England June 9, 1882. Listed Ath and PC July 15, 1882.

AAS BPL Y

11615. Hood's Comic Annual for 1883 ...

London: Published for the Proprietors at the Fun Office, 153 Fleet Street, E. C. ⟨1882⟩

Printed paper wrapper. Publisher's preface dated *October, 1882.*

"Josephi in Benicia," pp. 99-100. Collected in *Brand-New Ballads,* 1885.

Advertised as *ready Thursday October 19th, Fun* (London) Oct. 18, 1882. Advertised as *just out, Fun* (London) Oct. 25, 1882. Listed PC Nov. 1, 1882; Bkr Nov. 6, 1882.

BPL

11616. INTERESTING LETTER AND GEN-EROUS PROPOSAL. (FROM THE MES-SENGER.) PHILADELPHIA, OCT. 20, 1882 ...

⟨n.p., n.d., PHILADELPHIA, 1882⟩

Proof printing. Issued thus?

Single cut sheet printed on recto only. 17¾" x 4½" (approximate).

A letter to Rev. P. S. Davis regarding the intro-duction of the study of art work and handicrafts into the public schools.

Y

11617. ... INDUSTRIAL ART IN SCHOOLS ...

WASHINGTON: GOVERNMENT PRINTING OFFICE. 1882 ...

At head of title: CIRCULARS OF INFORMATION OF THE BUREAU OF EDUCATION. NO. 4—1882.

⟨1⟩-37; blank, p. ⟨38⟩; blank leaf. 9⅛" x 5¾" full. Also paged: 209-245; blank, p. ⟨246⟩; blank leaf.

⟨1⟩-2⁸, 3⁴.

Printed drab; or, green paper wrapper.

Note: The earliest examined printing has at foot of title-page the number *4940.* Reprints have been seen with either of the following numbers at foot of title-page: *5734; 10212.*

Printed after Nov. 20, 1882. For an amplifica-tion of this paper see *Practical Education,* 1888.

Y

Hood's Comic Annual for 1883 ...

London ... ⟨1882⟩

See entry No. 11615.

11618. The Song of the Bees ...

⟨n.p., n.d., 1883⟩

Title on p. ⟨3⟩.

Single cut sheet folded to make four pages. Page: 5" x 4½". Wove paper; some copies water-marked: *Diamond Mills First Class.*

Unpaged. On p. ⟨2⟩: *Amwes-winto-wagen* ... ; a poem in Amerindian, written, according to the text of the poem, by Peter John Gabriel. On p. ⟨3⟩: *The Song of the Bees* ... , dated at end: *Campobello, N. B., Aug. 12th, 1883,* being an anonymous translation of the poem on p. ⟨2⟩. Pp. ⟨1⟩ and ⟨4⟩ blank.

That Leland was the translator is indicated by a letter by F. Max Müller, Nov. 30, 1883, in Ath Dec. 8, 1883: "... The following is a speci-men of Red Indian poetry, got up to sell at a fair to raise funds for a rectory house, and trans-lated by Mr. Leland ... I never saw a more eloquent appeal for building a parsonage. If others think the same I can give them Mr. Charles Leland's address."

PHS   UV

11619. The Life and Achievements of Edward Henry Palmer ... by Walter Besant ...

London   John Murray, Albemarle Street 1883 ...

For American edition see next entry.

"Miro Pal," p. 420; in Romany; by Leland. Le-land's translation into English, p. 421, as "My Brother."

A copy in BPL received June 12, 1883.

BA

11620. The Life and Achievements of Edward Henry Palmer ... by Walter Besant ...

New York   E. P. Dutton and Company   1883

First American edition. For prior publication see preceding entry.

"Miro Pal," p. 420; in Romany, by Leland. Translated into English by Leland as "My Brother," p. 421.

Listed PW Sept. 29, 1883.

H

11621. Hood's Comic Annual for 1884 ...

London: Published for the Proprietors at the Fun Office, 153 Fleet Street, E. C. ⟨1884; *i.e.,* 1883⟩

Printed paper wrapper. Publisher's preface dated *October, 1884;* should be *October, 1883.*

"The Ballad of Charity," p. ⟨100⟩. Collected in *Brand-New Ballads,* 1885.

Advertised as *ready October 18th, Fun* (London) Oct. 17, 1883. Advertised as *just out, Fun* (London) Oct. 24, 1883. Listed Bkr Nov. 3, 1883; PC Nov. 15, 1883.

BPL

11622. Repoussé Designs . . . Part I. ⟨II⟩ ⟨III⟩ General Directions. Copyright, 1884, by William Whitlock . . .

The Art Interchange Company, 140 Nassau St., New York . . .

Single sheets imprinted as above (on recto only) with heading, directions, etc. At end: Charles G. Leland. The sheets vary in size, the largest noted being 16½″ x 21½″.

According to the PW listing, Jan. 24, 1885, issued as three separate paper-covered parts. Was each part issued in a printed paper wrapper? Perhaps the whole in a portfolio?

Part 1: A sheet as described above with 11 (12?) numbered plates. Deposited Feb. 8, 1884.

Part 2: A sheet as described above with 12 numbered plates. Deposited April 17, 1884; or, June 9, 1884; the records are not clear.

Part 3: A sheet as described above with 12 numbered plates. Deposited April 17, 1884; or, June 9, 1884; the records are not clear.

LC

11623. THE ALGONQUIN LEGENDS OF NEW ENGLAND OR MYTHS AND FOLK LORE OF THE MICMAC, PASSAMA-QUODDY, AND PENOBSCOT TRIBES . . .

BOSTON   HOUGHTON, MIFFLIN AND COMPANY NEW YORK: 11 EAST SEVENTEENTH STREET   THE RIVERSIDE PRESS, CAMBRIDGE   1884

⟨i⟩-⟨xviii⟩, ⟨1⟩-379; blank, p. ⟨380⟩; plus: advertisements, pp. ⟨381-392⟩. Frontispiece and 11 plates inserted. Laid paper. $7^{11}/_{16}$″ x $4^{15}/_{16}$″. ⟨1⁸, 2¹, 3-17¹², 18¹⁰; plus: 19⁴, 20²⟩. *Signed:* ⟨a⟩¹, ⟨b⟩¹⁶, ⟨1⟩-23⁸, 24¹².

S cloth: black; red-brown. Green-gray-coated on white end papers. Laid paper flyleaves. Top edges stained terra-cotta.

According to the publisher's records, 1000 copies printed Sept. 3, 1884. On Sept. 11, 1884, 1000 copies of the list of illustrations and 275 cancel title-leaves with the Sampson Low imprint printed. Sept. 12, 1884, 262 copies shipped in sheets to Sampson Low. Bound Sept. 22–Dec. 22, 1884. Deposited Sept. 25, 1884. Advertised for Oct. 4 and listed PW Oct. 4, 1884. A copy at BA received Oct. 7, 1884. The London (Sampson Low, Marston, Searle & Rivington) edition an-

nounced PC Oct. 1, 1884; listed Ath Nov. 1; PC Nov. 15; Bkr Dec. 13, 1884. See under 1885 for the second edition.

AAS   BA   BPL   H

Hood's Comic Annual for 1884 . . .

London . . . ⟨1884; *i.e.*, 1883⟩

See entry No. 11621.

11624. Hood's Comic Annual for 1885 . . .

London: Published for the Proprietors at the Fun Office. 153 Fleet Street, E. C. ⟨1884⟩

Printed paper wrapper. Publisher's preface dated *October, 1884*.

"Est Modus in Rebus. A Narrative of New York," p. ⟨71⟩. Collected in *Brand-New Ballads,* 1885.

Advertised as *ready October 22nd, Fun* (London) Oct. 15, 1884. Advertised as *now ready, Fun* (London) Oct. 22, 1884. Listed Bkr Nov. 6, 1884; PC Dec. 6, 1884.

BPL

11625. ART AND HAND WORK FOR THE PEOPLE BEING THREE PAPERS READ BEFORE THE SOCIAL SCIENCE CONGRESS SEPTEMBER 1884 BY REV. W. TUCKWELL   CHARLES GODFREY LELAND AND WALTER BESANT

PUBLISHED BY PERMISSION OF THE COUNCIL OF THE NATIONAL ASSOCIATION FOR THE PROMOTION OF SOCIAL SCIENCE   1884

⟨1⟩-32. 8¼″ x $5^{5}/_{16}$″.

Signed: ⟨A⟩-B⁸.

Printed mottled blue-gray paper wrapper.

"Ought Elementary Instruction in Drawing to Be Made an Essential Part of the National Education?," pp. 10-18.

FLP   LCP

Hood's Comic Annual for 1885 . . .

London . . . ⟨1884⟩

See entry No. 11624.

11626. The Algonquin Legends of New England . . . Second Edition

Boston   Houghton, Mifflin and Company New York: 11 East Seventeenth Street   The Riverside Press, Cambridge   1885

For first edition see under 1884.

Contains a few revisions. According to the publisher's records on Dec. 23, 1884, 3½ hours were spent in composition of corrections and 14 hours in altering the plates. Dec. 29, 1884, date altered, edition statement inserted and 270 copies printed.

H

11627. Clover Leaves. A Commemorative Volume.

Published by the Clover Club. Philadelphia: 1885

"The Town of Rock an' Rye," pp. ⟨47⟩-55.

Deposited Aug. 22, 1885. For comment see entry No. 1229.

11628. BRAND-NEW BALLADS . . .

LONDON: "FUN" OFFICE, 153 FLEET STREET, E. C ⟨sic⟩ 1885.

⟨i-ii⟩, ⟨i⟩-vi, ⟨1⟩-149; printer's device, p. ⟨150⟩; advertisement, p. ⟨151⟩. Illustrated. 7¹⁄₁₆" x 4⅞" scant.

⟨-⟩⁴, 1-9⁸, 10⁴. Leaves ⟨-⟩₁ and 10₄ used as pastedowns.

Printed stiff paper wrapper. *Two states of the wrapper noted.* The sequence, if any, has not been determined and the designations are for identification only.

A

Front wrapper imprint: "FUN" OFFICE: 153 Fleet Street, E. C. Note presence of quotation marks. Outer back wrapper unprinted save for decorative areas in imitation of three-quarters binding.

B

Front wrapper imprint: 'FUN" OFFICE: 153 Fleet Street, E. C. Note single and double quotation marks. Outer back wrapper decorated as above but also imprinted with an advertisement for *Jack and Jill.*

Advertised as *just out, Fun* (London) Sept. 2, 1885. Advertised as *just out, Fun* (London) Sept. 9, 1885, with quotation from a review. *Second Edition* noticed Ath May 22, 1886.

AAS (wrapper B)   FLP (wrapper A)   Y (wrapper B)

11629. SNOOPING . . . COMIC ANECDOTES ABOUT PEOPLE WHO PEEP OVER OTHER PEOPLE'S SHOULDERS.

LONDON: "FUN" OFFICE, 153 FLEET STREET, E. C. ⟨n.d., 1885⟩

⟨i-viii⟩, ⟨1⟩-166; advertisement, p. ⟨167⟩. 7¼" scant x 4¹³⁄₁₆". Illustrated.

⟨1⟩-11⁸. Leaves ⟨1⟩₁ and 11₈ used as pastedowns.

Printed white paper wrapper.

Advertised *Fun* (London) Sept. 30, 1885.

PHS   Y

11630. Hood's Comic Annual for 1886 . . .

London: Published for the Proprietors at the Fun Office. 153 Fleet Street, E. C. ⟨1885⟩

Printed paper wrapper. Publisher's preface dated *October, 1885.*

"The Men of Homerton," pp. 84-85.

Advertised for Oct. 21, *Fun* (London) Oct. 14, 1885. Advertised as *now ready, Fun* (London) Oct. 21, 1885. Listed PC Nov. 2, 1885; Bkr Nov. 6, 1885.

BPL

11631. Transactions of the National Association for the Promotion of Social Science. Birmingham Meeting, 1884.

London: Longmans, Green, and Co. 1885.

"On the Same," *i.e.,* "Elementary Instruction on Drawing," pp. 689-698.

LC

Hood's Comic Annual for 1886 . . .

London . . . ⟨1885⟩

See entry No. 11630.

11632. EXTRAORDINARY COINCIDENCE . . .

⟨n.p., n.d., 1886⟩

Single leaf. Printed on recto only. 4" x 5⁷⁄₁₆". Proof only.

"In *Snooping* ⟨n.d., 1885⟩ there is a story of a certain John, arrested by gendarmes, in France, on suspicion of having sketched a fortress . . ." The paragraph was inspired by publication in *St. James's Gazette,* June 25, 1886, of the "arrest of English artists in France." Leland's paragraph probably appeared in *Fun* (London).

PHS

11633. Hood's Comic Annual for 1887 . . .

London: Published for the Proprietors at the Fun Office. 153 Fleet Street, E. C. ⟨1886⟩

Printed paper wrapper. Publisher's preface dated *October, 1886.*

"Three Gipsy Songs," pp. ⟨65⟩-67.

Advertised for Oct. 22, *Fun* (London) Oct. 20, 1886. Advertised as *just out, Fun* (London) Oct. 27, 1886. Listed Bkr Nov. 6, 1886.

BPL

11634. Two Pilgrims' Progress by Joseph and Elizabeth Robins Pennell . . .

Boston Roberts Brothers London Seeley & Co. 1887

"A Friend's Apology for this Booke," pp. ⟨v⟩-viii.

Deposited Nov. 20, 1886. Listed PW Dec. 4, 1886.

H NYPL

11635. THE MYTHOLOGY, LEGENDS, AND FOLK-LORE OF THE ALGONKINS . . .

REPRINTED FROM THE TRANSACTIONS OF THE ROYAL SOCIETY OF LITERATURE, VOL. XIV—PART I, 1887. ⟨n.p., n.d., LONDON, 1887⟩

Cover-title.

⟨1⟩-24. 8⅜″ x 5¼″ scant.

a⁸, b⁴.

Printed green paper wrapper.

The paper was read June 23, 1886. Appears also in *Transactions of the Royal Society of Literature, Second Series, Vol. XIV, Part I* ⟨n.p., n.d., London, 1887⟩ pp. ⟨68⟩-91.

UP (Inscribed by Leland Dec. 3, 1887)

11636. Hood's Comic Annual for 1888 . . .

London: Published for the Proprietors at the Fun Office. 153 Fleet Street, E. C. ⟨1887⟩

Printed paper wrapper. Publisher's preface dated *October, 1887.*

"How Ah-Chung Got His Start in Life," pp. ⟨52⟩-55.

BPL

11637. Practical Education. Treating of the Development of Memory, the Increasing Quickness of Perception, and Training the Constructive Faculty . . .

London: Whittaker and Co., Paternoster Square, E. C. 1888. [All Rights Reserved.]

An amplification of Leland's *Industrial Art in Schools,* 1882.

Two binding issues noted:

A

Leaf ⟨-⟩₁ is devoted to an advertisement for *Technical School and College Buildings.*

B

Leaf ⟨-⟩₁ (as described above) is removed and inserted at the back.

Note: All examined copies (save one) have an inserted 12 page terminal catalog. A rebound copy at LC has a 28 page catalog at back; leaf ⟨-⟩₁ at back.

Listed Ath Feb. 11, 1888. Two copies (Binding A) in PHS inscribed by Leland Feb. 12, 1888. Advertised as *just published* Ath Feb. 25, 1888. Listed PC March 1, 1888. No American printing found. The *third edition* listed (but as not seen) PW Jan. 18, 1890, with the D. Van Nostrand, New York, imprint. Presumably imported by Van Nostrand. The *third edition,* London, 1889, has a slightly extended appendix.

BA (Binding B)   PHS (Binding A)

11638. What American Authors Think about International Copyright

New-York   American Copyright League   1888

One-paragraph statement, p. 7.

For comment see entry No. 218.

11639. . . . DRAWING AND DESIGNING: IN A SERIES OF LESSONS . . .

LONDON: WHITTAKER AND CO., PATERNOSTER SQUARE, E. C. 1888. [ALL RIGHTS RESERVED.]

At head of title: MINOR ARTS AND INDUSTRIES.

For American edition see under 1889. For *Third Edition* see under 1897.

⟨i⟩-viii, ⟨1⟩-79; Chiswick Press device, p. ⟨80⟩. Illustrated. 7¹¹⁄₁₆″ x 6⅛″.

A⁴, B-F⁸.

Printed tan paper wrapper.

Listed PC July 16, 1888, as in *cloth,* pp. 78, at 1/-. Again listed PC Aug. 1, 1888, as in *paper,* at 1/-, pp. 80. Was the July entry erroneous?

FLP

11640. Hood's Comic Annual for 1889 . . .

London   Published for the Proprietors at the Fun Office. 153 Fleet Street, E. C. ⟨1888⟩

Printed paper wrapper. Publisher's preface dated *18th October, 1888.*

"A New Breitmann Ballad," pp. ⟨50⟩-52. Collected as "The Magic Shoes" in *The Breitmann Ballads . . . a New Edition,* 1889.

Reviewed PC Dec. 6, 1888.

BPL   LCP

11641. Verhandlungen des VII. Internationalen Orientalisten-Congresses Gehalten in Wien im Jahre 1886. Arische Section . . .

Wien, 1888. Alfred Hölder K. K. Hof- und Universitäts-Buchhändler. 1., Rothenthurm-strasse 15.

Printed paper wrapper.

"The Original Gypsies and Their Language," pp. ⟨149⟩-156.

Note: According to BMU also issued as a separate, 10 pp., by Alfred Hölder, Vienna, 1888. Not seen by BAL.

H

11642. Recreations of the Rabelais Club. 1885–1888 . . . Printed for the Members.

⟨London⟩ For Private Circulation Only. [All Rights Reserved.] ⟨n.d., 1888?⟩

"The Gipsy Lover," pp. ⟨35⟩-36. Also in (reprinted from?) *The Breitmann Ballads . . . a New Edition*, 1889.

100 copies only. On p. ⟨ii⟩: Imprint of Billing and Sons, Guildford.

H

Hood's Comic Annual for 1889 . . .

London . . . ⟨1888⟩

See entry No. 11640.

11643. The Breitmann Ballads . . . a New Edition.

London: Trübner & Co., Ludgate Hill. 1889. [All Rights Reserved.]

In *The Lotos Series.*

Reprint save for the following:

"Preface to the Edition of 1889," pp. ⟨ix⟩-xii.

"The Gypsy Lover." Here first collected. Also in (reprinted from?) *Recreations of the Rabelais Club* ⟨n.d., 1888?⟩, above.

"Dornenlieder."

"Breitmann's Sleigh-Ride."

"The Magic Shoes." Previously in *Hood's Comic Annual for 1889*, above.

Three formats issued. Presumably simultaneous.

LARGE PAPER

101 numbered copies. Printed on laid Van Gelder. Printed paper wrapper. Leaf: 7⁷⁄₁₆" x 5⅝".

CLOTH

Unwatermarked wove paper. Blue V cloth stamped in blue, gold, red. All edges gilded. Leaf: 6⅛" x 4¹⁄₁₆".

HALF CLOTH

Unwatermarked wove paper. Blue V cloth, white imitation vellum shelfback, stamped in gold and brown. Top edges gilded, otherwise untrimmed. Leaf: 6⁵⁄₁₆" x 4⁵⁄₁₆".

Noticed editorially as in preparation Ath Sept. 1, 1888. Advertised as *nearly ready* Ath Oct. 13, 1888. Announced as No. 1 of *The Lotos Series* Bkr Jan. 1889; as No. 2 for *May* PC Feb. 15, 1889. All three formats advertised for *May* Bkr March 1889. Advertised as *now ready* Ath May 4, 1889. Listed Ath May 11; PC May 15. Reviewed (both small paper and large paper) Ath June 15, 1889.

BA (cloth) H (cloth) P (half cloth) Y (large paper; half cloth)

11644. . . . DRAWING AND DESIGNING IN A SERIES OF LESSONS . . .

CHICAGO AND NEW YORK: RAND, MCNALLY & COMPANY, PUBLISHERS. 1889.

At head of title: KENSINGTON ART SERIES.

First American edition. For prior publication see above under 1888. For *Third Edition* see under 1897.

⟨i⟩-viii, 1-80; plus: blank, p. ⟨81⟩; advertisements, pp. ⟨82-84⟩. Illustrated. Printed on mixed wove papers, both white and toned white. *Note:* It could be that what is now taken for toning may in fact be oxidation and that originally the whole work was printed on two grades of equally white paper. 7⁷⁄₁₆" x 5⁵⁄₁₆".

⟨1-5⁸, 6⁴; plus: 7²⟩. *Signed:* ⟨A⟩⁴, ⟨B⟩-D⁸, ⟨E⟩⁸, F¹⁰. Leaves ⟨1⟩₁₋₂ excised; the title-leaf and conjugate full-page plate pasted to the stubs.

S cloth: blue. White end papers printed in blue with a floral pattern. Flyleaves.

Deposited Dec. 2, 1889.

LC

11645. The Smoker's Garland . . . Part I.

Liverpool: At the Office of "Cope's Tobacco Plant." 1889.

Printed paper wrapper.

Cope's Smoke Room Booklets, No. 2.

"Breitmann's Rauch-Lied," pp. 49-51, dated at end: *London, March 16, 1871.*

H

11646. A Dictionary of Slang, Jargon & Cant Embracing English, American and Anglo-Indian Slang   Pidgin English, Tinkers' Jargon and Other Irregular Phraseology Compiled and Edited by Albert Barrère . . . and Charles G. Leland . . .

Printed for Subscribers Only at the Ballantyne Press MDCCCLXXXIX ⟨-MDCCCXC⟩

2 Vols. Vol. 1 dated MDCCCLXXXIX; Vol. 2 dated MDCCCXC.

For revised edition see under 1897.

1: ⟨i⟩-⟨xxiv⟩, ⟨1⟩-528. Van Gelder. 8⅝″ full x 7″.

2: ⟨i-iv⟩, ⟨1⟩-428.

Printed paper wrapper folded over boards; and, cloth, leather shelfback. Loosely inserted is a *Notice to Subscribers* . . .

Limited to 675 numbered copies.

Advertised Ath April 21, 1888; PC May 1, 1888. Advertised PW May 26, 1888, as *shortly*. Vol. 1 received at H Sept. 9, 1889; Vol. 2 received at H Oct. 28, 1890. Reviewed Ath Feb. 14, 1891.

AAS   PHS   Y

11647. Hood's Comic Annual for 1891 . . .

London: Published for the Proprietors at the Fun Office, 153 Fleet Street, E. C. ⟨1890⟩

Printed paper wrapper. Publisher's preface dated *October, 1890.*

"The Witch's Box," p. ⟨118⟩. Collected in *Songs of the Sea,* 1895.

Advertised as *ready Thursday October 16th, Fun* (London) Oct. 15, 1890. Advertised as *now ready, Fun* (London) Oct. 22, 1890. Listed PC Nov. 1, 1890; Bkr Nov. 6, 1890.

BPL

11648. . . . The Mastery of Memorizing . . .

James P. Downs, Publisher. Harrisburg, Pa., and 243 Broadway, New York. ⟨1890⟩

At head of title: Vol. I. November–December, 1890. No. 1. The Memory Library . . . a Bi-Monthly Publication . . . The Memory and Thought Series . . .

Printed paper wrapper.

"Development of the Memory," pp. ⟨5⟩-64.

Deposited Dec. 9, 1890. Listed PW Dec. 13, 1890. For the second part in this series see under 1891.

H   LC   Y

A Manual of Wood Carving . . .

London . . . 1890.

See *The Minor Arts* . . . , 1880, above.

Hood's Comic Annual for 1891 . . .

London . . . ⟨1890⟩

See entry No. 11647.

11649. GYPSY SORCERY AND FORTUNE TELLING ILLUSTRATED BY NUMEROUS INCANTATIONS, SPECIMENS OF MEDICAL MAGIC, ANECDOTES AND TALES . . .

NEW YORK   CHARLES SCRIBNER'S SONS   MDCCCXCI

⟨i⟩-xvi, ⟨1⟩-271. 10⅝″ x 7⅝″ scant. Illustrated.

⟨1⟩⁴, 1*⁴, 2-29, 31-36⁴.

V cloth: tan.

Listed PW Dec. 13, 1890. Issued in London by T. Fisher Unwin. After several premature announcements the Unwin edition was finally advertised as *shortly* in Ath and PC, Jan. 24, 1891; and, PC Feb. 7, 1891; listed Ath Feb. 7, 1891; PC Feb. 14, 1891.

AAS   H

11650. . . . Quickness of Perception.

James P. Downs, Publisher, Harrisburg, Pa., and 243 Broadway, New York. ⟨1891⟩

At head of title: Vol. I. January–February. No. 2. The Memory Library . . . a Bi-Monthly Publication . . . The Memory and Thought Series . . .

Printed paper wrapper.

"Quickness of Perception," pp. 11-70.

Deposited Feb. 7, 1891. Listed PW Feb. 14, 1891. For the first part of this series see under 1890.

H   LC   Y

11651. The Works of Heinrich Heine Translated from the German by Charles Godfrey Leland . . .

London   William Heinemann . . . ⟨*See dates below*⟩

12 Vols. Vols. 1-8 translated by Leland. "I was able in 1890 to persuade the late Charles Godfrey Leland to undertake the translation of the complete works of Heinrich Heine. The plan was to divide them into twelve volumes, and he did actually accomplish the work of translating the first eight volumes . . . The last four volumes he did not live to finish . . ."—from the "Publisher's Note," Vol. 11, 1905.

See next entry.

1: Florentine Nights The Memoirs of Herr von Schnabelewopski The Rabbi of Bacharach and Shakespeare's Maidens and Women. *Dated 1891*. "Introductory Note," pp. ⟨v⟩-ix; in the 1892 reprint signed *R.G.;* apparently not by Leland. "Translator's Preface" to *Shakespeare's Maidens and Women*, pp. ⟨243⟩-247. Announced PC Oct. 1, 1890. *Nearly ready*—Ath April 18, 1891; PC May 23, 1891. *Ready shortly*—Ath July 4, 1891. *Next week*—Ath July 18, 1891. Listed Ath July 25, 1891.

2: Pictures of Travel ... Volume I. 1823–1826. *Dated 1891*. "Translator's Preface," pp. v-xix; a revised and extended version of the preface to *Pictures of Travel*, 1855. *Nearly ready*—PC Sept. 26, 1891. *Early in November*—Ath Oct. 24, 1891. Listed Ath Nov. 7, 1891; PC Nov. 28, 1891. Reviewed PC Nov. 28, 1891.

3: Pictures of Travel ... Volume II. 1828. *Dated 1891*. For publication notes see preceding.

4: The Salon or Letters on Art, Music, Popular Life and Politics. *Dated 1893*. "Translator's Preface," pp. v-xii, dated at end: *October 14, 1892*. After a series of premature notices, some with the erroneous title *Book of Songs,* the volume was issued 1893 under the title *The Salon.* The earliest announcement observed appeared in Ath Feb. 20, 1892 ⟨*sic*⟩. Listed Ath Aug. 5, 1893; PC Aug. 12, 1893.

5: Germany ... Volume I. *Dated 1892*. "Translator's Preface," pp. ⟨v⟩-xix, dated at end: *July 1891. Shortly*—Ath Feb. 20, 1892. *Now ready*—Ath April 9, 1892. Listed Ath April 9, 1892; PC April 23, 1892.

6: Germany ... Volume II. *Dated 1892*. For publication notes see preceding.

7: French Affairs Letters from Paris ... Volume I. 1832. *Dated 1893*. "Translator's Preface," pp. ⟨v⟩-xii, dated at end: *August 15, 1892*. Advertised as though published Ath Feb. 18, 1893. Listed Ath Feb. 18, 1893; PC April 4, 1893.

8: French Affairs Letters from Paris ... Volume II. Lutetia. *Dated 1893*. For publication notes see preceding.

The 8 volumes above were distributed in the United States by Scribner; listed PW May 14, 1898.

9: The Book of Songs, translated by Thomas Brooksbank. *Dated 1904*.

10: New Poems, translated by Margaret Armour. *Dated 1904*.

11: Germany, Romancero I & II, translated by Margaret Armour. *Dated 1905*.

12: Romancero III, Last Poems, translated by Margaret Armour. *Dated 1905*.

The complete set of 12 volumes was distributed in the United States with cancel title-pages imprinted: *New York: E. P. Dutton and Company London: William Heinemann 1906*

Note: A large paper edition was issued in 1893. Advertised as *in preparation* Ath April 1, 15, 1893, with volumes 1-3 described as *now ready*. According to the advertisements the large paper edition was limited to 100 sets. Not seen by BAL.

At a time unknown to BAL the set was reprinted by Heinemann in twenty volumes for publication in the United States by Croscup & Sterling, New York. The only Croscup & Sterling set examined by BAL was issued without date. According to a prospectus for the set (in H) the work was published in a limited edition: 325 copies on Dutch hand made paper; and, 1000 copies on English deckle-edge paper; available in a variety of cloth; and, leather bindings.

H (Vols. 2-12)   LCP (Vols. 1-8)   Y (Vols. 1-8)

11652. The Works of Heinrich Heine ...

New York John W. Lovell Company 150 Worth Street ... ⟨*See dates below*⟩

First American edition. For prior publication see preceding entry.

Vols. 1-3, 5-6. Translated by Leland. Vol. 4 appears not to have been issued by Lovell.

1: Florentine Nights The Memoirs of Herr von Schnabelewopski The Rabbi of Bacharach and Shakespeare's Maidens and Women. Vol. 1 of the set although not so identified. *Dated 1891*. "Introductory Note," pp. ⟨v⟩-ix; in the British reprint of 1892 signed *R.G.;* apparently not by Leland. "Translator's Preface" to *Shakespeare's Maidens and Women*, pp. ⟨243⟩-247. Listed PW Oct. 10, 1891.

2: Pictures of Travel ... Volume I. 1823–1826. *Dated 1891*. "Translator's Preface," pp. v-xix, is a revised and extended version of the preface to *Pictures of Travel*, 1855. Listed PW Dec. 26, 1891. Advertised as *now ready* PW March 12, 1892. Reprinted and reissued by Lovell, Coryell & Company, n.d., *ca.* 1894–1895.

3: Pictures of Travel ... Volume II. 1828. *Dated 1891*. For publication notes see preceding.

4: The Salon. Lovell appears not to have published this volume.

5: Germany ... Volume I. *Dated 1892*. "Translator's Preface," pp. ⟨v⟩-xix, dated at end: *Geneva, July 1891*. Listed PW July 2, 1892.

6: Germany . . . Volume II. *Dated 1892*. Listed PW July 2, 1892. A copy in BPL received July 6, 1892.

Note: Vol. 2 was reprinted and reissued by Lovell, Coryell & Co., New York, n.d., *ca.* 1894–1895. Were the other volumes similarly reissued?

BPL (Vols. 2,6) H (Vols. 1,3) P (Vols. 5,6) UV (Vol. 1)

11653. Hood's Comic Annual for 1892 . . .

London: Published for the Proprietors at the Fun Office, 153 Fleet Street, E. C. ⟨1891⟩

Printed paper wrapper. Publisher's preface dated *October, 1891.*

"The Story of Samuel Jackson," pp. ⟨38⟩-40. Collected in *Songs of the Sea,* 1895.

Advertised for Oct. 22, *Fun* (London) Oct. 21, 1891. Advertised as *just out, Fun* (London) Oct. 28, 1891.

BPL

11654. Congrès International des Traditions Populaires Première Session   Paris 1889 Compte Rendu des Séances

Paris Bibliothèque des Annales Économiques Société d'Éditions Scientifiques   4, Rue Antoine-Dubois, 4   Place de l'École-de-Médecine 1891

Cover-title. Printed self-wrapper.

"Rapports des Tziganes de l'Europe avec les Traditions Populaires," pp. 52-59.

H

11655. THE SALAGRAMA, OR HOLY STONE . . .

⟨n.p., n.d., LONDON, 1891⟩

Caption-title. The above at head of p. ⟨1⟩.

⟨1⟩-9. 9 9/16″ x 5 7/8″.

Issued thus? Extracted from a larger work? Offprinted from a larger work?

Printed self-wrapper.

A paper read before the Ninth International Congress of Orientalists on the 2nd of September, 1891.

NYPL

A Manual of Wood Carving . . .

New York . . . 1891

See *The Minor Arts . . .* , 1880, above.

Wood Carving . . . Second Edition . . .

London . . . 1891.

See *The Minor Arts . . .* , 1880, above.

Hood's Comic Annual for 1892 . . .

London . . . ⟨1891⟩

See entry No. 11653.

11656. LEATHER WORK. A PRACTICAL MANUAL FOR LEARNERS . . .

LONDON: WHITTAKER & CO. NEW YORK AGENTS: MACMILLAN & CO. 1892.

⟨i-ii⟩, ⟨i⟩-⟨xiv⟩, ⟨1⟩-96. Illustrated. 8 7/16″ x 6 3/4″. A-G⁸.

Two states noted; sequence, if any, not determined. The designations are for identification only.

A

Imprint as above. *Prepared thus for American publication?*

Front cover lettered: Leather / Work / by / C. G. Leland.

Bound in green paper boards stamped in imitation of leather.

B

Imprint: LONDON: WHITTAKER AND CO., PATERNOSTER SQUARE. SOLD ALSO BY HOLTZAPFFEL AND CO., 64, CHARING CROSS. 1892.

Front cover lettered: Leather / Work / by / C G Leland. / London / Whittaker / & Co. *Prepared thus for British publication?*

Bound in green paper boards stamped in imitation of leather.

Announced PC Oct. 3, 1891. Advertised as *immediately* Bkr April, May, June, 1892; Ath May 28, 1892. Listed Ath June 25, 1892; PC July 9, 1892. No PW listing found, 1892–1893.

AAS (A)   B (A)   PHS (B)   Y (B)

11657. Hood's Comic Annual for 1893 . . .

Dalziel Brothers, "Fun" Office, 153 Fleet Street, London, E.C. ⟨1892⟩

Not seen. Entry on the basis of a photographic copy.

Printed paper wrapper.

"The Merman," pp. ⟨34⟩-36. Collected in *Songs of the Sea,* 1895.

Listed PC Oct. 29, 1892.

11658. ETRUSCAN ROMAN REMAINS IN POPULAR TRADITION ...

LONDON   T. FISHER   UNWIN   PATERNOSTER SQUARE   MDCCCXCII

For first American edition see below under 1892.

Trade Edition

⟨i⟩-viii, 1-385; blank, p. ⟨386⟩; printer's imprint, p. ⟨387⟩. Frontispiece inserted; other illustrations in text. 10⅝″ x 7½″.

⟨1⟩-49⁴, 50².

V cloth: terra-cotta. Off-white wove end papers.

Limited Edition

⟨i⟩-viii, 1-385; printer's imprint, p. ⟨386⟩. Laid paper watermarked Van Gelder Zonen. Certificate of issue inserted before p. ⟨i⟩. Original drawing inserted following inserted printed frontispiece. Other illustrations in text. 11½″ x 9″. *Note:* In Y copy the final leaf is printed on paper watermarked Whatman.

⟨-⟩¹, ⟨1⟩-49⁴, 50¹.

V cloth: terra-cotta. Off-white laid end papers. Top edges gilded.

"... Fine Edition, One Hundred in number ... This is Number ..."—Certificate of issue, signed by Leland.

Both formats announced PC Oct. 15, 1892; Ath and PC Nov. 12, 1892. Listed Ath Nov. 5, 1892; PC Nov. 19, 1892.

AAS (trade)   B (both)   H (trade)   Y (limited)

11659. THE HUNDRED RIDDLES OF THE FAIRY BELLARIA ...

LONDON   T. FISHER   UNWIN   PATERNOSTER SQUARE   MDCCCXCII

Trade Edition

⟨i⟩-xii, ⟨1⟩-149; blank, p. ⟨150⟩; Gresham Press imprint, p. ⟨151⟩. Illustrated. 6½″ x 5¼″.

⟨-⟩², ⟨1⟩⁴, 2-10⁸, 11⁴.

V cloth: green, stamped in black and green. V cloth: pink, stamped in black and red. Pale yellow-coated end papers. Also: Printed white paper wrapper.

Limited Edition

⟨i⟩-xii, ⟨1⟩-149; blank, p. ⟨150⟩; Gresham Press imprint, p. ⟨151⟩. Wove paper watermarked: UNBLEACHED ARNOLD 1892. Illustrated. 7″ full x 5¹³⁄₁₆″.

⟨1⟩⁶, 2-10⁸, 11⁴.

Inserts: An original pen and ink drawing by Leland inserted as a frontispiece; and, at front

end paper, printed in red, a certificate of issue: *This is a copy of the fine edition ... limited to 100 copies.*

V cloth: greenish-gray. Printed paper label on spine. White wove end papers.

All three formats (trade, cloth; trade, paper; limited) advertised PC Oct. 15, 1892; Ath Nov. 12, 1892. Deposited BMU Nov. 12, 1892. Reviewed Ath Dec. 3, 1892.

AAS (trade, cloth; limited)   B (trade, cloth)   BA (trade, paper; limited)   FLP (trade, cloth)

11660. ETRUSCAN ROMAN REMAINS IN POPULAR TRADITION ...

NEW YORK   CHARLES SCRIBNER'S SONS   1892

First American edition. For prior publication see above under 1892.

⟨i⟩-viii, 1-385, blank leaf. Frontispiece inserted; other illustrations in text. 10⁹⁄₁₆″ x 7⁹⁄₁₆″.

⟨1⟩-49⁴, 50².

V cloth: brown-orange.

Advertised PW *Christmas Bookshelf*, 1892, as a Scribner importation. A copy at BA received Dec. 5, 1892. Listed PW Dec. 10, 1892.

BA   UV

11661. Actes du Huitième Congrès International des Orientalistes, Tenu en 1889 à Stockholm et à Christiania. Quatrième Partie. Sections III: Africaine; IV: De l'Asie Centrale et de l'Extrême Orient; V: De la Malaisie et de la Polynésie ...

Leide, E. J. Brill. 1892.

Cover-title. Printed self-wrapper.

"Pidgin-English und Sein Verhältniss zu Anderen Mischsprachen," Section de l'Asie Centrale et de l'Extrême Orient, Part IV, pp. ⟨97⟩-103.

H (received Feb. 14, 1893)

11662. ETRUSCO-ROMAN REMAINS IN MODERN TUSCAN TRADITION ...

⟨LONDON: D. NUTT, 1892⟩

The above on p. ⟨185⟩; caption-title. Imprint taken from front of wrapper.

⟨185⟩-201. 8⅝″ scant x 5⁷⁄₁₆″.

Signed: ⟨N⟩⁴, O⁵.

Printed gray wove paper wrapper.

Offprinted from: *The International Folk-Lore Congress 1891. Papers and Transactions. Edited by Joseph Jacobs and Alfred Nutt* ... , Published for the Organising Committee by David Nutt, 270-271 Strand, London, 1892.

Note: Not to be confused with Leland's *Etruscan Roman Remains in Popular Tradition,* 1892.

P

11663. SLANG.

PHILADELPHIA: J. B. LIPPINCOTT COMPANY, 1892.

Not seen. Entry from LC catalog. Not found at LC Dec. 1963.

8 pp. Probably uniform with BAL No. 9020.

Presumably prepared for copyright purposes prior to publication in *Chambers's Encyclopædia ... New Edition,* 1892, Vol. 9, pp. 495-497.

11664. The Life and Adventures of James P. Beckwourth ... Written from His Own Dictation by T. D. Bonner New Edition. Edited, with Preface, by Charles G. Leland ...

London: T. Fisher Unwin Paternoster Square. MDCCCXCII

"Preface to the New English Edition," pp. ⟨5⟩-15.

Also issued with the imprint (probably for distribution in United States): *London: T. Fisher Unwin. New York: Macmillan & Co.* MDCCCXCII A copy thus in AAS.

Noted for *the end of the year* Ath Oct. 10, 1891. Announced Ath March 19, 1892; PC Oct. 15, 1892. No listings or reviews found in any 1892 publications. Again announced Ath March 25, 1893. Announced as a *new issue* in the *Adventure Series* Ath and PC Sept. 16, 1893. Listed Ath Sept. 23, 1893; PC Oct. 7, 1893. Reviewed Bkr Oct. 10, 1893.

H   Y

Hood's Comic Annual for 1893 ...

... London ... ⟨1892⟩

See entry No. 11657.

11665. Old Rabbit the Voodoo and Other Sorcerers by Mary Alicia Owen Introduction by Charles Godfrey Leland ...

London   T. Fisher Unwin   Paternoster Square   MDCCCXCIII

For American edition see below, *Voodoo Tales,* 1893.

"Introduction," pp. v-ix.

Advertised Ath Jan. 28, 1893. Listed Ath Feb. 11, 1893. Advertised PC Feb. 18, 1893. Listed

PC Feb. 25, 1893. Reviewed PC March 4, 1893.

H

11666. The Family Life of Heinrich Heine Illustrated by One Hundred and Twenty-Two Hitherto Unpublished Letters Addressed by Him to Different Members of His Family Edited by His Nephew Baron Ludwig von Embden and Translated by Charles Godfrey Leland ...

London   William Heinemann   1893   [All Rights Reserved]

⟨i-ii⟩, ⟨i⟩-xviii, ⟨1⟩-276. Laid paper. Frontispiece and 3 plates inserted; each with inserted printed protective tissue. 8¼" x 5⅜". Inserted at back: Publisher's catalog, pp. ⟨1⟩-16, dated on p. ⟨1⟩: *November 1892.*

Advertised as *just published* Ath March 11, 1893. Listed Ath March 18, 1893; PC March 25, 1893. Advertised with extract from a review Ath April 1, 1893. A *Cheap Edition,* in the *Great Lives and Events* series, listed PC July 25, 1896. Sheets of the first printing occur with cancel title-leaf dated 1896; in this form the book is not in the *Great Lives and Events* series.

Y

11667. Voodoo Tales As Told among the Negroes of the Southwest Collected from Original Sources by Mary Alicia Owen Introduction by Charles Godfrey Leland ...

G. P. Putnam's Sons   New York   London 27 West Twenty-Third Street   24 Bedford Street, Strand   The Knickerbocker Press   1893

First American edition. For prior publication see *Old Rabbit the Voodoo,* 1893.

"Introduction," pp. v-ix.

Listed PW April 8, 1893. Deposited April 10, 1893. Reissued as *Ole Rabbit's Plantation Stories,* Philadelphia, 1898.

AAS   H   UV

11668. MEMOIRS ... IN TWO VOLUMES ...

LONDON   WILLIAM HEINEMANN   1893   [ALL RIGHTS RESERVED]

For first American edition see next entry.

1: ⟨i⟩-⟨xvi⟩, ⟨1⟩-307. Portrait frontispiece inserted. 8¾" x 5⅝".

2: ⟨i-viii⟩, ⟨1⟩-306, blank leaf. *Note:* In some copies the final blank leaf is excised. Portrait frontispiece inserted.

1: ⟨-⟩⁸, A-I, K-T⁸, U².

2: ⟨-⟩⁴, A-I, K-T⁸, U². *Note:* In some copies leaf U₂ is excised.

H cloth: blue-green. Covers bevelled. Publisher's catalog, dated *September 1893,* inserted at back of some copies of Vol. 2.

Announced Ath Sept. 23, 1893. Noted as *just published* Ath Oct. 14, 1893. Listed Ath Oct. 14, 1893; PC Oct. 21, 1893. The *Second Edition* (printed from the same setting as the American edition) listed PC March 31, 1894.

AAS   BA   NYPL

11669. MEMOIRS ...

NEW YORK   D. APPLETON AND COMPANY   1893

First American edition. For prior publication see preceding entry.

⟨i⟩-⟨xii⟩, ⟨1⟩-439; blank, p. ⟨440⟩; 4 pp. advertisements. Portrait frontispiece inserted. 7⅛″ x 5¹⁄₁₆″ full.

⟨1⟩-19¹².

S cloth: light green. Green-coated on white end papers. Flyleaves. Top edges gilded.

Advertised PW Nov. 4, 1893. A copy at H received Nov. 8, 1893. Listed PW Nov. 11, 1893. Deposited April 2, 1894.

AAS   B   H   NYPL

11670. Hood's Comic Annual for 1894. Conducted by Charles Dalziel ...

London: Frederick Warne and Co., Bedford Street, Strand. ⟨1893⟩

Not seen. Entry on the basis of a photographic copy of the British Museum copy. Presumably issued in printed paper wrapper.

"The Transformation," p. 29.

Listed Bkr Nov. 1893.

11671. ELEMENTARY METAL WORK   A PRACTICAL MANUAL FOR AMATEURS AND FOR USE IN SCHOOLS ...

LONDON   WHITTAKER AND CO., PATERNOSTER SQUARE   SOLD ALSO BY BARKENTIN AND KRALL, 291 AND 289, ⟨*sic*⟩ REGENT STREET   1894

⟨i⟩-xvi, ⟨1⟩-111. Illustrated. 8⅜″ x 6¾″.

⟨A⟩-H⁸.

Printed tan paper boards, terra-cotta V cloth shelfback. Cream end papers.

Originally advertised under the title *Hammered Metal Work.* Advertised as *in the press* Bkr's Christmas issue, 1892 ⟨*sic*⟩. Noted as *ready in*

a few weeks Bkr's Christmas issue, 1893. Listed Ath Feb. 24, 1894; PC March 17, 1894.

American Issue

Sheets of the above with cancel title-leaf imprinted: NEW YORK   MACMILLAN AND CO., 66, FIFTH AVENUE LONDON: WHITTAKER AND CO. 1894

Listed PW April 7, 1894.

P (American)   UV (American)   Y (London)

11672. SONGS OF THE SEA AND LAYS OF THE LAND ...

LONDON   ADAM AND CHARLES BLACK   1895

⟨i⟩-⟨xvi⟩, ⟨1⟩-278; 2 pp. advertisements. Laid paper. 8″ full x 5¾″.

⟨-⟩⁸, 1-17⁸, 18⁴.

Green linen. Also: Unbleached linen. White laid end papers. Top edges gilded.

Two forms of the binding noted. The sequence, if any, is not known, and the designations are for identification only.

A: Spine stamped in white. At foot of spine: LONDON

B: Spine stamped in green. At foot of spine: A & C ⟨dot⟩ BLACK

Advertised as *now ready* PC March 2, 1895; Ath March 9, 1895. Listed Ath March 2, 1895; PC March 16, 1895. Listed PW April 6, 1895, as though published by Macmillan, New York; perhaps issued with cancel title-leaf bearing the Macmillan imprint? A *cheap edition* titled *Songs of the Sea and Land* listed PC Sept. 18, 1897; unlocated.

AAS (A)   B (A)   BA (A)   H (B)   UP (B)   UV (B)   Y (A)

11673. HANS BREITMANN IN GERMANY TYROL ...

LONDON   T FISHER UNWIN ⟨n.d., 1895⟩

Title-page in black and red.

⟨i-iv⟩, ⟨1⟩-168. 6¹⁵⁄₁₆″ x 4⅜″.

⟨-⟩², ⟨A⟩-I, K⁸, L⁴.

V cloth: buff. Laid end papers.

Note: Copies intended for distribution in the United States have the Lippincott imprint on spine; copies distributed in Great Britain have the T. Fisher Unwin imprint on spine.

Announced PC March 2, 1895. Under the title *Hans Breitmann's Book of Travel* advertised without comment as a new volume in the *Cameo Series,* Bkr May, 1895; not issued thus.

Listed Ath June 1, 1895 (prematurely?). Announced Ath Aug. 17, 1895. Listed PC Sept. 7, 1895. Advertised Ath Sept. 14, 1895. Reviewed PC Sept. 14, 1895. A copy in PHS (Unwin binding) inscribed by Leland Sept. 17, 1895. A copy in BPL (Lippincott binding) received Sept. 21, 1895. Listed (Lippincott) PW Oct. 26, 1895.

B (Unwin) BA (Lippincott) BPL (Lippincott) H (Lippincott) PHS (Unwin) Y (Unwin)

11674. LEGENDS OF FLORENCE COLLECTED FROM THE PEOPLE AND RETOLD BY CHARLES GODFREY LELAND ... FIRST SERIES

LONDON: DAVID NUTT 270-71 STRAND 1895

For first American edition see next entry. For second edition and *Second Series* see below under 1896.

⟨i-ii⟩, ⟨i⟩-xiv, ⟨1⟩-271; printer's imprint, p. ⟨272⟩; plus: publisher's catalog, pp. ⟨1⟩-4. Laid paper. 7½″ x 5″ full.

⟨-⟩8, A-I, K-R8; plus: S2.

White linen. Covers bevelled. White laid end papers. Top edges gilded.

Advertised as *in the press*, for May publication, Ath May 11, 1895. Listed Ath June 1, 1895; PC June 8, 1895. A copy at BA received June 24, 1895. Reviewed Ath Oct. 26, 1895.

BA LC

11675. LEGENDS OF FLORENCE COLLECTED FROM THE PEOPLE AND RETOLD BY CHARLES GODFREY LELAND ... FIRST SERIES

NEW YORK MACMILLAN AND CO 1895

First American edition. For prior publication see preceding entry. For second edition and *Second Series* see below under 1896.

⟨i-ii⟩, ⟨i⟩-xiv, ⟨1⟩-271; printer's imprint, p. ⟨272⟩. Laid paper. 7⁹⁄₁₆″ x 5³⁄₁₆″.

⟨-⟩8, A-I, K-R8.

V cloth: white (pale tan?). Covers bevelled. White laid end papers. Top edges gilded.

A copy at H received July 10, 1895. Listed PW Aug. 17, 1895.

AAS B H Y

11676. LEGENDS OF FLORENCE COLLECTED FROM THE PEOPLE AND RETOLD BY CHARLES GODFREY LELAND ... SECOND SERIES

LONDON: DAVID NUTT 270-71 STRAND 1896

For first American edition see below under 1896. For *First Series* see under 1895.

⟨i⟩-⟨viii⟩, ⟨1⟩-278; advertisements, p. ⟨279⟩. Laid paper. 7⁹⁄₁₆″ x 5″.

⟨-⟩4, A-I, K-R8, S4.

V cloth: mottled white-green. White laid end papers. Top edges gilded.

Note: Also issued with the imprint: LONDON: DAVID NUTT 270-71 STRAND FLORENCE: B. SEEBER 20 VIA TORNABUONI 1896 A copy thus at H inscribed by early owner June 1, 1896.

Listed Ath April 18, 1896; PC April 25, 1896.

BA (Nutt imprint) H (Nutt and Seeber imprint)

11677. Legends of Florence Collected from the People ... First Series Second Edition, Revised and Enlarged

London: David Nutt 270-71 Strand 1896

For first edition see above under 1895.

Cloth; and, printed paper wrapper.

"The Second Edition has been carefully revised throughout, and an Appendix and Index have been added. Florence, March 1896."—p. xii.

Copies in cloth noted in three forms. The sequence, if any, is not known, and the designations are for identification only.

A

Title-page imprinted: *London: David Nutt 270-71 Strand 1896* Bound in mottled blue-green cloth. Covers not bevelled. Nutt imprint on spine.

B

Title-page imprinted: *London: David Nutt 270-71 Strand Florence: B. Seeber 20 Via Tornabuoni 1896* Bound in mottled blue-gray cloth. Covers not bevelled. Nutt imprint on spine.

C

Title-page imprinted: *London: David Nutt 270-71 Strand 1896* Bound in green cloth. Covers bevelled. Seeber imprint on spine.

Listed PC April 25, 1896.

B (wrapper) JH (B) NYPL (A) P (C)

11678. LEGENDS OF FLORENCE COLLECTED FROM THE PEOPLE AND RETOLD BY CHARLES GODFREY LELAND ... SECOND SERIES

NEW YORK MACMILLAN AND CO. 66 FIFTH AVENUE 1896

First American edition. For prior publication see above under 1896. For *First Series* see above under 1895.

⟨i⟩-⟨viii⟩, ⟨1⟩-278; advertisement, p. ⟨279⟩. Laid paper. 7⁹⁄₁₆″ x 5¹⁄₁₆″.

⟨-⟩⁴, A-I, K-R⁸, S⁴.

V cloth: mottled gray-blue; mottled gray-green. White laid end papers. Top edges gilded.

Listed PW May 23, 1896.

AAS   H   Y

11679. A MANUAL OF MENDING & RE-PAIRING ...

LONDON   CHATTO & WINDUS, PICCADILLY   1896

Title-page in black and orange.

For first American edition see next entry.

⟨i-ii⟩, ⟨i⟩-xxii, ⟨1⟩-263. 7¼″ x 4⅞″. Illustrated.

⟨a⟩⁴, b⁸, A-I, K-Q⁸, R⁴.

Black cloth grained with a leather-like pattern. Green-coated on white end papers. Inserted at back: Publisher's catalog, pp. ⟨1⟩-32, dated *March, 1896. Note:* A copy in FLP has an inserted terminal catalog of *ca.* 1909; the March 1896 catalog is not present.

Advertised as *shortly* PC April 4 and May 2, 1896; Ath April 11 and 18, 1896. Advertised for May publication Ath May 2, 1896; as *in the press* PC May 16, 1896. Advertised for June 11 in Ath and PC June 6, 1896. Advertised as though published Ath June 13, 1896. Listed Ath June 20, 1896; PC June 27, 1896. A copy at BPL received July 7, 1896. Scribner importation listed PW Aug. 29, 1896.

AAS   BA   FLP   Y

11680. A MANUAL OF MENDING AND RE-PAIRING ...

NEW YORK   DODD, MEAD AND COMPANY   1896

First American edition. For prior publication see preceding entry.

⟨i⟩-⟨xxii⟩, ⟨1⟩-264, blank leaf. Illustrated. 7¾″ scant x 5¹⁄₁₆″.

⟨1-18⟩⁸. *Note:* In all examined copies a superfluous signature mark R on p. 257.

Two bindings noted. The order is probable.

A

V cloth: tan. Stamped in gold and green. Top edges gilt. White laid end papers. Issued with an erratum slip at pp. 162-163?

B

V cloth: green. Stamped in green only. Top edges plain. White wove end papers. Erratum slip inserted at pp. 162-163.

The erratum slip reads: ERRATUM. | *The last line on page 162 should be read as if at* | *the bottom of page 163.* | The error thus noted is present in all examined copies of the book.

Deposited June 11, 1896. Listed PW Oct. 17, 1896.

NYPL (B)   PHS (A)   UV (A)   Y (B)

11681. A Dictionary of Slang, Jargon & Cant ... Compiled and Edited by Albert Barrère ... and Charles G. Leland ...

London   George Bell & Sons   1897

For first edition see under 1889.

2 Vols. On verso of title-leaf: *Revised Edition 1897*

Noted as *in preparation* PC Feb. 13, 1897. Advertised Ath March 6, 1897; PC March 13, 1897. Listed PC March 20, 1897.

P   PHS

11682. Drawing and Designing in a Series of Lessons ... Third Edition with Additional Designs

London   Whittaker and Co., Paternoster Square, E. C. and 66, Fifth Avenue, New York   1897 ...

For earlier editions see under 1888 and 1889.

The statement *Third Edition* suggests a *Second Edition* but no printing so designated has been located. Did the publisher consider the New York, 1889, edition, the second edition?

Listed PC Dec. 11, 1897.

H   HSP

11683. Library of the World's Best Literature Ancient and Modern Charles Dudley Warner Editor ... Thirty Volumes Vol. XXVIII

New York   R. S. Peale and J. A. Hill Publishers ⟨1898⟩

Reprint save for the following which are here in their earliest located American book publication; all had prior publication in *Songs of the Sea,* London, 1895.

"The Old Tavern," pp. 16545-16546.

"El Capitan-General," pp. 16546-16548.

"One, Two, Three," pp. 16548-16549.

"The Beautiful Witch," pp. 16549-16550.

"Time for Us to Go," pp. 16550-16551.

"The Lover to the Sailor," p. 16551.

Vol. 28 deposited Feb. 23, 1898. For comment see entry No. 10624.

11684. Lyra Nicotiana ... Edited ... by William G. Hutchison ...

London Walter Scott, Limited Paternoster Square ⟨n.d., 1898⟩

Cloth, paper label on spine.

Reprint save for:

"J'ai du Bon Tabac," pp. 36-38.

"Tobacco et Baccho," pp. 148-149.

Noticed Ath Sept. 24, 1898.

H NYPL

11685. HAVE YOU A STRONG WILL? OR HOW TO DEVELOPE ⟨sic⟩ WILL-POWER, OR ANY OTHER FACULTY OR ATTRIBUTE OF THE MIND, AND RENDER IT HABITUAL BY THE EASY PROCESS OF SELF-HYPNOTISM ...

LONDON GEORGE REDWAY 1899

⟨i⟩-xxxii, ⟨1⟩-235; blank, p. ⟨236⟩; advertisements, pp. ⟨237-240⟩. Laid paper. 7⅜″ scant x 4¹⁵⁄₁₆″.

⟨a⟩-b⁸, B-I, K-Q⁸.

T cloth: red.

Noted *is to appear* Ath Jan. 28, 1899. Advertised Ath May 6, 1899; advertised as though published Ath June 10, 1899; Ath Aug. 5, 1899. No listings found.

AAS PHS

Other editions and printings noted:

Have You a Strong Will ...

New York: Drummond, 1899

A 20 pp. copyright printing, being a version of Chap. XI of the *Second and Enlarged Edition,* London, 1902. See full entry below under 1899.

Have You a Strong Will ... Second and Enlarged Edition

London: Wellby, 1902

Enlarged edition. For full entry see below under 1902.

Have You a Strong Will ... Enlarged ⟨i.e., Third⟩ Edition

London: Wellby, 1903

Enlarged edition. For full entry see below under 1903.

The Mystic Will ...

Chicago: Atkinson, 1907

First American edition of the preceding save for the omission of Chap. XI. For description see entry No. 11701.

Have You a Strong Will ... Fourth Edition

London: Wellby, 1907

Reprint.

Have You a Strong Will ...

New York: Brentano's ⟨1919⟩

Reprint.

11686. ARADIA OR THE GOSPEL OF THE WITCHES ...

LONDON DAVID NUTT, 270-71 STRAND 1899

⟨i⟩-⟨xvi⟩, ⟨1⟩-133; advertisements, pp. ⟨1⟩-3. Laid paper. 7½″ x 5⅛″.

⟨-⟩⁸, A-H⁸, I⁴.

V cloth: green. Front whitestamped. Top edges gilt. White laid end papers.

Note: Also noted in a variant (remainder? thus bound for American publication?) binding: Front cover wholly unstamped; top edges gilt; white laid end papers.

Announced PC Sept. 30, 1899. Advertised for Oct. 2 Ath Sept. 23, 1899. Advertised as *now ready* and listed Ath Oct. 7, 1899. A copy (front whitestamped) at NYPL received Nov. 2, 1899. Scribner importation listed PW Dec. 2, 1899.

AAS H LC (variant) NYPL Y

11687. The Unpublished Legends of Virgil. Collected by Charles Godfrey Leland.

New York: The Macmillan Company. 1900 ⟨i.e., 1899⟩

Published simultaneously with the London edition? See next entry.

⟨i⟩-xx, ⟨1⟩-208. Frontispiece. 7¹³⁄₁₆″ x 5⁵⁄₁₆″.

A copy at H received Nov. 22, 1899. Listed PW Dec. 16, 1899. A copy at AAS inscribed by early owner Dec. 19, 1899.

AAS BPL FLP Y

11688. The Unpublished Legends of Virgil. Collected by Charles Godfrey Leland.

London: Elliot Stock, 62, Paternoster Row, E. C. 1899

Issued simultaneously with the New York edition? See preceding entry.

⟨i⟩-xx, ⟨1⟩-208. Frontispiece. 7¾″ x 5³⁄₁₆″.

Advertised as *shortly* Ath Sept. 2, 1899. Advertised as a *new work* Bkr Oct. 1899. Listed Ath Nov. 25, 1899. A copy at PHS inscribed by Leland Dec. 5, 1899.

BA   NYPL   PHS

11689. HAVE YOU A STRONG WILL? . . .

NEW YORK   ROBERT DRUMMOND   1899

Cover-title.

For comment see *Have You a Strong Will* . . . , 1899, above.

⟨1⟩-20. 7¼″ x 5″ scant.

⟨-⟩¹⁰.

Printed self-wrapper.

Prepared for copyright purposes only. This is a version of Chapter XI as published in the *Second and Enlarged* London edition, 1902.

Deposited Dec. 9, 1899.

LC

The Unpublished Legends of Virgil . . .

New York . . . 1900 ⟨*i.e.,* 1899⟩

See above under 1899.

11690. Useful Arts and Handicrafts Planned by Charles Godfrey Leland . . . Edited by H. Snowden Ward . . .

London   Dawbarn & Ward, Limited   1900 ⟨–1902⟩ ⟨*i.e.,* 1899–1902⟩

4 Vols.

1: *Comprising parts 1 to 13 inclusive.* Imprint: As above.

2: *Comprising parts 14 to 26 inclusive.* Imprint: As above.

3: *Comprising parts 27 to 39 inclusive.* Imprint: *London   Dawbarn & Ward, Limited   1901*

4: *Comprising parts 40 to 52 inclusive.* Imprint: *London   Dawbarn & Ward, Limited   1902*

"Introductory to the Series," Vol. 1, pp. 3-8.

"This series of Essays was planned by Mr Charles Godfrey Leland for publication in one large volume, to be called *One Hundred Minor Arts.* The publishers have thought, however, that the widest publicity might be obtained by issuing them in the form of a series of small hand-books, especially in view of the author's desire to make his work accessible to students and to poor people who could hardly afford a large book. At the same time, it has been ar-

ranged to issue ample indices and handsome cloth binding cases without any charge to those who purchase a series of the small volumes and who may wish to have them bound. For this purpose two distinct paginations are provided, one re-commencing with each book, the other (at foot of page) running through the series which will form a volume."—From the "Editor's Introduction," Vol. 1, p. 1.

As the above indicates the work is made up of a series of fifty-two booklets. On the basis of somewhat meagre evidence it appears that the London issues were printed on *laid paper;* the American issues on *wove paper.* The London and American issues were done from totally different settings. *See below for a description of the parts.* The bound volumes were made up of the original parts with the wrappers and advertisements removed.

In *A Manual of Mending & Repairing,* London, 1896, is an announcement of a work to be titled *One Hundred Profitable Arts,* presumably an early title for the *Useful Arts and Handicrafts* series.

The following are representative of the parts.

American Issue

No. 1. Price, 25c. $10.00 a Year. Designing and Drawing for Beginners by Charles Godfrey Leland . . . Edited by F. Dundas Todd.

Chicago: The Photo-Beacon Co., Tribune Building. London: Dawbarn and Ward, Ltd. Entered at the Postoffice at Chicago as Second-Class Mail Matter. Copyright, 1899 . . . November 30, 1899.

Cover-title. Printed in blue and blue-gray.

i-ii, 1-24, iii-iv. Wove paper. 7¹¹⁄₁₆″ x 6⅞″. Frontispiece and 5 plates inserted; other illustrations in text.

1¹⁴.

Printed white paper wrapper.

British Issue

No. 3. Price 6d. net. Post Free, 7d. Picture Frames by Novel Methods by Charles Godfrey Leland . . . and Thos. Bolas . . . Edited by H. Snowden Ward.

London: Dawbarn and Ward, Ltd. 6 Farringdon Avenue, E. C. Chicago: F. Dundas Todd, Tribune Building   All Rights of Translation and Reproduction Reserved by Dawbarn & Ward, Ltd., and in the United States by F. Dundas Todd, Chicago. ⟨1899⟩

Cover-title. Printed in blue and brown.

⟨1⟩-24; advertisements, pp. i-viii. Laid paper. 7″ full x 6⅛″. Frontispiece and 5 plates inserted;

other illustrations in text. Also paged: 49-72, i-viii.

C¹², ⟨-⟩⁴.

Printed mottled blue-gray paper wrapper.

According to a statement on the inner front wrapper, issued Dec. 1899.

Of the 52 parts comprising the whole, Leland appears to have written, either as sole author or as collaborator, the following parts only:

No. 1. *Designing and Drawing for Beginners;* see description above. Deposited (U.S.) Dec. 18, 1899. The London issue listed Bkr Dec. 1899. A copy of the American issue is in LC.

No. 2. *Wood-Carving.* Not located. Noted as *on our table* Ath Dec. 2, 1899. The American issue listed (belatedly) PW May 12, 1900.

No. 3. *Picture Frames by Novel Methods;* see description above. In collaboration with Thomas Bolas. American issue not located. London issue in LC. Issued *ca.* Dec. 1899.

No. 4 (erroneously numbered 2). *Dyes, Stains, Inks, Lacquers, Varnishes and Polishes.* According to the cover-title written in collaboration with Thomas Bolas; according to the caption-title written by Bolas only. Deposited (U.S.) Dec. 18, 1899. Listed (belatedly) PW May 12, 1900. London issue unlocated. American issue in LC.

No. 5. *Decorated Wood-Work by Carving, Colouring, Wire-Inlaying, &c.* Not located. In collaboration with Charles E. Dawson.

No. 6. *Gouge-Work and Indented Wood-Work.* In collaboration with F. C. Lambert. Not located. The American issue listed PW May 12, 1900.

No. 7. *Wood-Engraving and Placard Cutting.* In collaboration with Thomas Bolas. A copy of the London issue in BPL inscribed by early owner May 29, 1900. American issue unlocated.

No. 8. *Bent Iron or Strip-Work.* In collaboration with George Day. Issued *ca.* March, 1900. A copy of the London issue in NYPL. American issue not located.

No. 11. *Artificial Wood and Shavings in Decoration.* Not located. In collaboration with F. C. Lambert.

No. 12. *Marquetry and Inlaying by Charles J. Lock. With a Note on Venetian Marquetry by Charles Godfrey Leland.* Not located.

No. 16. *Fret-Cutting.* Not located. In collaboration with "Jack Plane."

No. 17. *Repoussé and Metal-Chasing.* Not located.

No. 18. *Tools and Their Uses.* Not located. In collaboration with Thomas Bolas.

No. 27. *Adornment of the Home.* Unlocated.

No. 30. *Woven Fabrics: Their Decoration, Cleaning, and Repair.* Not located. In collaboration with F. C. Lambert.

No. 32. *Glue, Gum, Paste, and Other Adhesives.* Not located. In collaboration with Thomas Bolas.

No. 33. *Perfumes and Cosmetics.* Unlocated. In collaboration with Thomas Bolas. The London issue listed Bkr June, 1901.

No. 46. *Miscellaneous Minor Arts (Part I.) Including Bone and Horn, Shells, Beads and Wampum, Coral, Amber, Egg-Shells and Water-Glass. Condensed from the Ms. of Charles Godfrey Leland ... by Aaron Briggs.* Not located. The London issue listed Bkr July, 1902.

No. 47. *Miscellaneous Minor Arts (Part II.) Including Stone Mosaic, Scagliola, Ceresa, Imitation Mosaic, Nail-and-Scale Work, Bead-Inlay, and the Making of Wooden Tankards. Condensed from the Notes of Charles Godfrey Leland ... by Aaron Briggs.* Not located. The London issue listed Bkr Aug. 1902.

Publication as a four-volume work: *Vol. 1:* Listed Ath March 17, 1900; PC March 24, 1900. *Vol. 2:* Listed Ath Oct. 27, 1900; PC Oct. 27, 1900. *Vol. 3:* Listed Ath Dec. 7, 1901. *Vol. 4:* Listed Ath Dec. 13, 1902.

LC (4 Vols. format)

11691. **The Lawyer's Alcove Poems by the Lawyer ... and about the Lawyer Edited by Ina Russelle Warren ...**

New York Doubleday, Page & Company 1900

"Judge Wyman. A Rural Yankee Legend," pp. 89-92. Earliest located American book publication. Previously in *Tom Hood's Comic Annual for 1872,* London ⟨1871⟩; and, *Brand-New Ballads,* London, 1885.

For comment see entry No. 7785.

Modern Eloquence ...

   ... Philadelphia ⟨1900; *i.e.,* 1901⟩

See below under 1901.

Useful Arts and Handicrafts ...

   London ... 1900

See entry No. 11690.

11692. **Modern Eloquence ... ⟨Edited by⟩ Thomas B. Reed ...**

John D. Morris and Company   Philadelphia ⟨1900; *i.e.,* 1901⟩

"Hans Breitmann's Return," Vol. 2, pp. 717-719; delivered at a Lotos Club dinner in Leland's honor, Jan. 31, 1880.

Vol. 2 deposited April 19, 1901. Listed PW June 8, 1901, as with the imprint of the University Society.

For further comment see entry No. 3467.

Useful Arts and Handicrafts . . .

London . . . 1901

See entry No. 11690.

11693. Have You a Strong Will? Or How to Develope ⟨*sic*⟩ and Strengthen Will-Power, Memory, or Any Other Faculty or Attribute of the Mind, by the Easy Process of Self-Hypnotism . . . Second and Enlarged Edition.

    Philip Wellby   6 Henrietta Street, Covent Garden   London, W. C. 1902

Revised and extended. See under 1899 for first edition. For an earlier printing of Chapter XI see entry No. 11689.

Listed Bkr March 1902.

H   HSP

11694. The Breitmann Ballads Selected by Charles G. Leland   A New Edition

    London   Kegan Paul, Trench, Trübner & Co. Ltd. Paternoster House, Charing Cross Road 1902

Reprint save for "Preface to the New Edition," pp. ix-x, dated at end: *Florence, Dec. 4, 1901.*

Listed Bkr April 1902, as in cloth; and, leather.

UI

11695. FLAXIUS   LEAVES FROM THE LIFE OF AN IMMORTAL . . .

    LONDON   PHILIP WELLBY   6 HENRIETTA STREET, COVENT GARDEN 1902

⟨i-ii⟩, ⟨i⟩-x, ⟨1⟩-320; plus: advertisements, pp. ⟨321-324⟩. Laid paper. $7\frac{7}{16}$″ x $5\frac{1}{16}$″.

⟨-⟩⁶, A-I, K-U⁸; plus: ⟨*⟩².

V cloth: gray-blue. White wove; and, laid end papers.

Advertised as *forthcoming* Ath April 19, 1902. Listed Ath Aug. 16, 1902. Reviewed Ath Sept. 6, 1902.

PHS has a set of proofs for this work which contains a short (5 pp.) chapter omitted from the published book. The omitted chapter is titled "Flaxius and Piovano Arlotto."

BA   H   Y

11696. Kulóskap the Master and Other Algonkin Poems Translated Metrically by Charles Godfrey Leland . . . and John Dyneley Prince . . .

    Funk & Wagnalls Company   New York and London   1902

⟨1⟩-370; advertisements, pp. ⟨371-373⟩; blank leaf. Frontispiece with printed tissue and 7 plates inserted; other illustrations in text. $7\frac{7}{16}$″ x $5\frac{3}{16}$″.

"Preface," pp. ⟨11⟩-18.

On copyright page: *Published November, 1902.* Deposited Nov. 11, 1902. Listed PW Nov. 15, 1902; Ath Dec. 13, 1902.

AAS   B   FLP   H   LC   PHS   UV   Y

Useful Arts and Handicrafts . . .

London . . . 1902

See entry No. 11690.

11697. Have You a Strong Will? Or How to Develop and Strengthen Will-Power, Memory, or Any Other Faculty or Attribute of the Mind, by the Easy Process of Self-Hypnotism . . . Enlarged Memorial Edition (With Additiona ⟨*sic*⟩ Chapter on Paracelsus).

    Philip Wellby   6 Henrietta Street, Covent Garden   London, W. C. 1903

Extended edition; chapter 12 added. For first edition see under 1899.

B   FLP   H

11698. . . . THE ALTERNATE SEX . . .

    COPYRIGHTED 1904 BY PHILIP WELLBY.   SHURMER SIBTHORP, PUBLISHER, NEW YORK.

Cover-title. At head of title: HAPPY THOUGHT LIBRARY.

⟨i-ii⟩, ⟨1⟩-13. $7\frac{1}{2}$″ scant x $4\frac{15}{16}$″.

⟨-⟩⁸.

Printed self-wrapper.

Presumably prepared for copyright purposes only. Deposited Feb. 1, 1904. For published editions see next two entries.

LC

11699. THE ALTERNATE SEX OR THE FE-
MALE INTELLECT IN MAN, AND THE
MASCULINE IN WOMAN . . .

LONDON   PHILIP WELLBY, COVENT GARDEN, W.C.
1904

For presumed copyright printing see preceding
entry. For first published American edition see
next entry.

⟨i⟩-⟨viii⟩, ⟨1⟩-134; advertisements, pp. ⟨135-
136⟩. 7¼″ scant x 4¾″.

⟨-⟩⁴, 1-8⁸, 9⁴.

Red V cloth sides, tan buckram shelfback.

Listed Ath Feb. 13, 1904; Bkr March 10, 1904.
Reprinted and reissued with the imprint: *London: William Rider & Son, Ltd. 164, Aldersgate
Street, E. C.* ⟨1904; *i.e.,* 1910⟩; listed Bkr July 1,
1910.

NLM

11700. THE ALTERNATE SEX OR THE
FEMALE INTELLECT IN MAN, AND
THE MASCULINE IN WOMAN . . .

NEW YORK   FUNK & WAGNALLS COMPANY   1904

First published American edition. See preceding
two entries.

⟨i⟩-⟨viii⟩, ⟨1⟩-134, blank leaf. 7½″ full x 5³⁄₁₆″.

⟨1-9⟩⁸. *Signed:* ⟨-⟩⁴, 1-8⁸, 9⁴.

T cloth: brown.

". . . Completed only a few months before Mr.
Leland's death . . . presented . . . without the
benefit of the author's revision and correction.
Mrs. Joseph Pennell . . . has kindly seen the
book through the press."—p. ⟨iv⟩.

Listed PW June 11, 1904.

AAS   BA   H   Y

The Works of Heinrich Heine Translated from
the German by Charles Godfrey Leland . . .

New York: E. P. Dutton and Company
London: William Heinemann 1906

For comment see above under 1891, *The Works
of Heinrich Heine* . . .

11701. THE MYSTIC WILL   A METHOD
OF DEVELOPING AND STRENGTHEN-
ING THE FACULTIES OF THE MIND,
THROUGH THE AWAKENED WILL, BY
A SIMPLE, SCIENTIFIC PROCESS POS-
SIBLE TO ANY PERSON OF ORDINARY
INTELLIGENCE . . . AMERICAN EDI-
TION

PUBLISHED BY WILLIAM WALKER ATKINSON   MA-
SONIC TEMPLE CHICAGO, ILL. 1907

See *Have You a Strong Will?*, 1899, above.

⟨1⟩-119. 7⅝″ x 5³⁄₁₆″.

⟨1-7⁸, 8⁴⟩.

T cloth: gray-blue.

Three printings noted:

1

As above.

2

Issued with the joint imprint of The Progress
Company, 515-519 Rand McNally Building, Chi-
cago, Illinois; L. N. Fowler & Co., 7, Imperial
Arcade, Ludgate Circus, London, E. C. ⟨n.d.⟩.
On the basis of the terminal advertisements
issued not before 1908. Copy in BA.

3

Issued with the joint imprint of Yogi Publica-
tion Society, Chicago, Illinois; and L. N.
Fowler & Co., 7, Imperial Arcade, Ludgate
Circus, London, E. C. ⟨n.d.⟩. Copy in AAS.

AAS   H

11702. St. Nicholas Book of Verse Edited by
Mary Budd Skinner and Joseph Osmun Skinner . . .

Published by The Century Co. New York and
London MCMXXIII

"The Flower Girl," pp. 118-119.

For comment see entry No. 818.

Reprints of Leland's own books; books with Leland's name on the title-page containing reprinted Leland material; musical settings of poems reprinted from Leland's own books.

11703. Heinrich Heine's Pictures of Travel. Translated from the German, by Charles Godfrey Leland ... Fourth Revised Edition.

Philadelphia: Frederick Leypoldt, London: Trübner & Co. 1863.

Advertised as *nearly ready* LG and PC May 1, 1863. Noticed LG June 1, 1863. Listed LG July 15, 1863. Contains at least one minor revision; see note under entry 11524.

11704. . . . Faithless . . . by Ambrose Davenport . . .

Boston. Henry Tolman & Co. 291 Washington St. . . . 1866 . . .

Sheet music. Cover-title. Plate number: 5215. At head of title: *Tone-Poems* . . . Reprint of a translation of an untitled poem in *Heine's Book of Songs*, 1864.

11705. . . . Thou Art Like a Lovely Flow'ret . . . by Ambrose Davenport . . .

Boston. Henry Tolman & Co. 291 Washington St. . . . 1866 . . .

Sheet music. Cover-title. Plate number: 5216. At head of title: *Tone-Poems* . . . Reprint of a translation of an untitled poem in *Pictures of Travel*, 1855.

11706. Heine's Book of Songs. Translated by Charles G. Leland . . . Third Edition.

New York: Leypoldt & Holt. 1868.

11707. Hans Breitmann's Barty and Other Ballads . . . with a Few Explanatory Notes by J.C.H. and H.L.W.

London: John Camden Hotten, 74 & 75 Piccadilly. 1869 . . .

Printed paper wrapper. Advertised as *now ready* and listed PC April 1, 1869. (See next entry.)

11708. . . . Hans Breitmann's Ballads. The Complete Work . . .

London: John Camden Hotten, 74 & 75, Piccadilly. ⟨1869⟩

Printed paper wrapper. Cover-title. At head of title: *Author's New Enlarged Edition* . . . Also issued in cloth according to statement on front wrapper. An omnibus volume printed from the plates of the following, with title-page for each present:

Hans Breitmann's Barty and Other Ballads . . . , London: John Camden Hotten, 74 & 75 Piccadilly. 1869 . . . (See preceding entry.)

Hans Breitmann. 1: Christmas 2: In Politics and Other Ballads . . . , London: John Camden Hotten, 74 & 75 Piccadilly. 1869 . . . (See next entry.)

Advertised (this volume?) Ath May 1, 1869. Issued after March 27, 1869; *Spectator* of this date specifically states that "Christmas" is in "none of Mr. Hotten's issues."

11709. Hans Breitmann . . . Christmas . . . In Politics and Other Ballads . . .

London: John Camden Hotten, 74 & 75 Piccadilly. 1869 . . .

Printed paper wrapper. *Note:* Not seen save as part of an omnibus volume; see preceding entry. As a separate listed PC June 1, 1869; PC (again) June 15, 1869.

11710. Hans Breitmann's Ballads . . . Complete in One Volume.

Philadelphia: T. B. Peterson & Brothers; 306 Chestnut Street. ⟨1869⟩

A copy at H received June 25, 1869. Listed ALG July 1, 1869. The Trübner importation listed PC Aug. 2, 1869.

11711. Hans Breitmann's Party. With Other Ballads . . . Ninth Edition.

London: Trübner & Co., 60 Paternoster Row. 1869 . . .

Printed paper wrapper.

Hans Breitmann's Party. With Other Ballads ... First Series ...

Philadelphia ... ⟨1869⟩

See entry No. 11716.

11712. The Breitmann Ballads. Four Series Complete.

London: Trübner & Co., 60 Paternoster Row. 1870 ...

Issued in cloth according to PC's listing of March 15, 1870. An omnibus volume containing four previously published books. The rebound copy at BPL (the only copy located) suggests the book was made up of unsold sheets and reissued with a new, inserted, title-leaf for the whole. Listed Ath Feb. 12, 1870; PC March 15, 1870.

11713. Hans Breitmann's Ballads ... New, Enlarged and Complete Edition.

Philadelphia: T. B. Peterson & Brothers, 306 Chestnut Street. ⟨1870⟩

On binding: *Complete Edition* Although not so marked this is Vol. 1 of the *Ballads.* For Vol. 2 see entry No. 11575. Listed ALG April 1, 1870.

11714. Hans Breitmann's Barty and Other Ballads ... First Series of the Breitmann Ballads.

Toronto: M. Shewan, St. Lawrence Arcade. 1870.

Probably issued in printed paper wrapper.

11715. Hans Breitmann's Christmas. With Other Ballads ... Fourth Edition.

London: Trübner & Co., 60 Paternoster Row. 1870 ...

Printed paper wrapper.

11716. Hans Breitmann's Party. With Other Ballads. By Charles G. Leland. Author of "Hans Breitmann in Church ... First Series of the Breitmann Ballads.

Philadelphia: T. B. Peterson & Brothers, 306 Chestnut Street. ⟨1869; *i.e., not before* 1870⟩

Printed paper wrapper.

11717. Hans Breitmann's Party. With Other Ballads ... Tenth Edition.

London: Trübner & Co., 60 Paternoster Row. 1870 ...

Printed paper wrapper. Reprint in spite of the statement on front wrapper: *Tenth Edition, Enlarged.*

11718. Hans Breitmann in Europe. With Other New Ballads ...

Philadelphia: T. B. Peterson & Brothers; 306 Chestnut Street. ⟨1871⟩

Printed paper wrapper. Listed ALG Aug. 1, 1871.

11719. The Breitmann Ballads. Four Series Complete.

London: Trübner & Co., 60 Paternoster Row. 1871 ...

An omnibus volume containing four previously published books. The book is apparently made up of unsold sheets with a new, inserted, title-page for the whole.

11720. Heine's Book of Songs. Translated by Charles G. Leland ...

New York   Holt & Williams   1871.

11721. ... O Were My Love a Sugar Bowl ... Music by A. Waldauer ...

New York   Wm. A. Pond & Co. 547 Broadway. & 39 Union Square ... 1871 ...

Sheet music. Cover-title. Plate number: 8118. At head of title: *To Miss "Lotta."* Otherwise "Love Song," *Hans Breitmann in Church* ⟨1870⟩.

11722. The Breitmann Ballads ... Complete Edition.

London: Trübner & Co., 60 Paternoster Row. 1872 ...

Cloth?

11723. The Breitmann Ballads ... Complete Edition.

London: Trübner & Co., Ludgate Hill. 1876 ...

11724. Hans Breitmann's Ballads.

London: George Routledge and Sons, 1876.

Not located. Title and imprint postulated. *Reprint?* Entry from listing in PC June 16, 1876. 96 pp. Printed paper wrapper.

11725. Hans Breitmann's Barty and Other Ballads ...

London: Ward, Lock, & Co., Warwick House, Dorset Buildings, Salisbury Square, E. C. ⟨n.d., 1877⟩

Pictorial paper wrapper. Advertised PC Sept. 1, 1877. A copy at LCP inscribed by early owner Sept. 27, 1877. Listed PC Oct. 2, 1877.

11726. Heinrich Heine's Pictures of Travel. Translated from the German, by Charles Godfrey Leland . . . Eighth Revised Edition.

Philadelphia: Published by Schaefer & Koradi. 1879.

Cloth?

11727. The Breitmann Ballads . . . Complete Edition.

London: Trübner & Co., Ludgate Hill. 1881 . . .

11728. Hans Breitmann's Ballads . . . Complete Edition in One Volume.

Philadelphia: T. B. Peterson & Brothers; 306 Chestnut Street. ⟨1884⟩

Cloth, unstamped, printed paper label on spine; also, cloth, goldstamped, all edges gilded. Probably reprinted several times without alteration of the title-page. A quite late printing has an inserted portrait of Leland. Advertised for *this day* PW Jan. 19, 1884. Listed PW March 22, 1884. Deposited March 26, 1884.

11729. Brand-New Ballads . . . Second Edition.

London: "Fun ⟨*sic*⟩ Office, 153 Fleet Street, E. C. 1885.

Printed paper wrapper. Noticed Ath May 22, 1886.

11730. . . . The Mermaid, Song, Words from the Breitmann Ballads. Music by Franz Hamel.

Paterson & Sons . . . 27, George St. . . . The Words . . . Taken from the "Breitmann Ballads by George ⟨*sic*⟩ Leland with . . . Permission of Messrs. Trubner & Co. London. ⟨n.d., ca. 1885⟩

Sheet music. Cover-title. At head of title: To the Members of the Crighton Club, London. Otherwise "Ballad," (*Der noble Ritter Hugo*), *Hans Breitmann's Party*, Philadelphia ⟨1868⟩.

11731. Pidgin-English Sing-Song or Songs and Stories in the China-English Dialect. With a Vocabulary . . . Second Edition.

London: Trübner & Co., Ludgate Hill. 1887 . . .

Listed PC Aug. 15, 1888.

11732. The Breitmann Ballads . . . a New Edition.

London: Trübner & Co., Ludgate Hill. 1890 . . .

11733. Ole Rabbit's Plantation Stories as Told among the Negroes of the Southwest Collected from Original Sources by Mary Alicia Owen Introduction by Charles Godfrey Leland . . .

Philadelphia George W. Jacobs & Co. 103 South 15th Street 1898

Reprint of *Voodoo Tales* . . . , 1893. Advertised among *New Publications* PW Nov. 27, 1897. Listed PW Dec. 11, 1897.

11734. The Breitmann Ballads . . . a New Edition.

London: Kegan Paul, Trench, Trübner, & Co. Ltd Paternoster House, Charing Cross Road. 1895.

Cloth, imitation vellum shelfback.

11735. Hans Breitmann's Ballads . . . Complete Edition

Philadelphia David McKay, Publisher 1022 Market Street ⟨1897⟩

Reprinted from the plates of the Peterson ⟨1884⟩ edition. Reprinted with the publisher's later address: 610 South Washington Square.

11736. Pictures of Travel by Heinrich Heine Translated by Charles Godfrey Leland with a Critical and Biographical Introduction by Charles Harvey Genung . . .

New York D. Appleton and Company 1898

Cloth, printed paper label on spine. Probably issued in a variety of custom bindings. A truncated edition of *Pictures of Travel*, 1855. Deposited April 27, 1898.

11737. The Breitmann Ballads . . . a New Edition.

London: Kegan Paul, Trench, Trübner, & Co. Ltd Paternoster House, Charing Cross Road. 1898.

11738. The Breitmann Ballads . . . a New Edition.

London: Kegan Paul, Trench, Trübner, & Co. Ltd Paternoster House, Charing Cross Road. 1901.

On spine: *Lotos Series*

11739. A Manual of Mending and Repairing with Diagrams ...

New York   Dodd, Mead and Company   1907

Described as a *new edition* in PW May 11, 1907. A cursory examination indicates that this is nothing more than a new printing, from the original plates, of the 1896 work. The transposition, pp. 162-163, present in the original printing, is here corrected.

11740. Have You a Strong Will? ... Fourth Edition

Philip Wellby   6 Henrietta Street, Covent Garden   London, W. C. 1907 ...

11740A. Hans Breitmann's Ballads ... with an Introduction by Elizabeth Robins Pennell

Boston and New York   Houghton Mifflin Company   The Riverside Press   Cambridge 1914

Printed boards, paper label on spine. 350 numbered copies only. Deposited Nov. 2, 1914.

11741. Have You a Strong Will? ... Introduction by John Herman Randall

New York   Brentano's Publishers   ⟨1919⟩

Printed paper boards. Deposited Dec. 1, 1919.

11742. Florentine Nights by Heinrich Heine from the Translation by Charles Godfrey Leland ...

Methuen & Co. Ltd. 36 Essex Street W. C. London ⟨1927⟩

In THIS SECTION are listed books by authors other than Leland which contain material by him reprinted from earlier books. See *Section II* for a list of reprints issued under Leland's name.

Laurel Leaves ... Edited by Mary E. Hewitt ...

New York ... 1854.

For comment see BAL, Vol. 2, p. 496.

The Household Book of Poetry ... Edited by Charles A. Dana.

New York ... 1858.

For comment see entry No. 12120.

The Atlantic Souvenir, for 1859 ...

New York: Derby & Jackson, 119 Nassau Street. 1859.

Noted only in publisher's leather.

... Lyrics of the War

Published by David Scattergood, No. 304 Chestnut Street Philadelphia. ⟨n.d., 1862⟩

Cover-title. Printed paper wrapper. At head of title: [*Price, 20 Cents* ... Deposited July 10, 1862.

War-Songs for Freemen ... Second Edition.

Boston ... 1863 ...

For comment see BAL Vol. 4, p. 380.

Lyrics of Loyalty ... Edited by Frank Moore

New York ... 1864

For comment see entry No. 1203.

... Soldiers' and Sailors' Patriotic Songs. New York, May, 1864.

New York ... 1864.

For comment see BAL, Vol. 3, p. 156.

Songs of the Soldiers ... Edited by Frank Moore

New York ... 1864

For comment see entry No. 261.

... Ballads of the War.

New York ... ⟨1864⟩

For comment see BAL, Vol. 1, p. 248.

... Lyrics of the War ⟨First Number⟩

Philadelphia ... 1864 ...

For comment see entry No. 1194E.

Pearls from Heine ...

Philadelphia: Frederick Leypoldt. 1865.

Pictorial wrapper.

Folk Songs ... Edited by John Williamson Palmer ... a New Edition ...

New York ... M DCCC LXVII.

For comment see BAL, Vol. 4, p. 443.

More Yankee Drolleries ...

London ... ⟨n.d., 1869⟩

For comment see entry No. 1547.

The Lady's Almanac, for the Year 1871

Boston, Issued by George Coolidge 289 Washington Street ⟨1870⟩

Songs of Life Selected from Many Sources ...

New York: Charles Scribner & Company. 1870.

The Poets and Poetry of Europe ... by Henry Wadsworth Longfellow ... Revised and Enlarged ...

Philadelphia ... 1871.

For comment see entry No. 9554.

Songs of Home Selected from Many Sources ...

New York: Charles Scribner and Company. 1871.

Humorous Poems ... Edited by William Michael Rossetti ...

London ... ⟨n.d., 1872⟩

For comment see BAL, Vol. 1, p. 207.

... Lady's Almanac for 1873

... Boston. ⟨1872⟩

For comment see entry No. 424.

The Poets and Poetry of America. By Rufus Wilmot Griswold ... Revised ...

New York ... 1873.

All Leland material herein reprinted from earlier books. "The Two Friends," *The Music-Lesson of Confucius,* 1872, appears herein (somewhat altered) under the title "The Three Friends." For fuller entry see No. 9565.

Illustrated Library of Favorite Song ... Edited by J. G. Holland ...

New York ... ⟨1873⟩

For comment see entry No. 2853.

The Muses of Mayfair ... by H. Cholmondeley-Pennell ...

London ... 1874

"There's a Time to Be Jolly," pp. ⟨188⟩-189; otherwise "Manes" in *Meister Karl's Sketch-Book,* 1855. For comment see entry No. 279.

The Reading Club and Handy Speaker ... Edited by George M. Baker. No. 1.

Boston ... ⟨1874⟩

For comment see BAL, Vol. 2, p. 247.

Vers de Société Selected ... by Charles H. Jones ...

New York ... 1875

For comment see BAL, Vol. 1, p. 73.

More Yankee Drolleries: A Second Series ...

London ... 1875.

For fuller entry see BAL, Vol. 4, p. 329.

The Comic Poets of the Nineteenth Century ... by W. Davenport Adams ...

London ... ⟨n.d., 1875⟩

For comment see BAL, Vol. 3, p. 471.

Songs of Three Centuries. Edited by John Greenleaf Whittier.

Boston ... 1876.

For comment see entry No. 11341.

Yankee Drolleries Second Series ...

London ... ⟨n.d., 1876⟩

For comment see entry No. 1553.

Poems of Places Edited by Henry W. Longfellow ... Spain. Vol. I.

Boston ... 1877.

For comment see entry No. 12187.

Poems of Places Edited by Henry W. Longfellow ... Switzerland and Austria.

Boston ... 1877.

"Water of Hungary," pp. 214-216; otherwise "Eau de Cologne" in *The Music-Lesson of Confucius,* 1872. For comment see entry No. 12190.

Poems of Places Edited by Henry W. Longfellow ... Germany. Vol. I.

Boston ... 1877.

For comment see entry No. 12192.

Poems of Places Edited by Henry W. Longfellow ... Germany. Vol. II.

Boston ... 1877.

For comment see entry No. 12193.

Poems of Places Edited by Henry W. Longfellow ... Asia. Asia Minor, Mesopotamia ...

Boston ... 1878.

For comment see entry No. 12203.

Poems of Places Edited by Henry W. Longfellow ... Asia. Persia ...

Boston ... 1878.

For comment see entry No. 12204.

A Collection of Humorous, Dramatic, and Dialect Selections, Edited ... by Alfred P. Burbank ...

New York: Dick & Fitzgerald, Publishers. ⟨1878⟩

Printed paper wrapper.

Poetry of America ... ⟨Edited⟩ by W. J. Linton.

London ... 1878.

For comment see entry No. 7872.

Merry Thoughts. By Tom Hood and Other Authors ...

London: Published at the "Fun" Office, 153 Fleet Street, E. C. ⟨n.d., not before 1878⟩

Unsold copies of *Tom Hood's Comic Annual* (for 1874, BAL No. 1098; for 1875, BAL No. 1102; for 1879, BAL No. 11600), stripped of wrappers, terminal advertisements and front matter; and, issued as a cloth-bound volume with inserted title-page as above.

Dick's Recitations and Readings No. 9 . . . Edited by Wm. B. Dick . . .

New York . . . ⟨1879⟩

For comment see entry No. 5537.

Home Life in Song with the Poets of To-Day . . .

New York . . . ⟨1879⟩

For comment see entry No. 432.

Dialect Recitations of Acland von Boyle . . . Arranged by Himself.

Boston: George M. Baker and Company. 1879.

The Princeton Poets, Compiled by S. Miller Hageman.

. . . Princeton . . . 1879.

All Leland material herein reprinted from earlier books. "Eyes," p. ⟨20⟩, is extracted from "A Spark in the Ashes," *The Music-Lesson of Confucius*, 1872. For comment see BAL, Vol. 1, p. 249.

Harper's Cyclopædia of British and American Poetry Edited by Epes Sargent

New York . . . 1881

For comment see entry No. 4336.

Selections in Verse . . .

Philadelphia . . . 1881.

All Leland material herein reprinted from earlier books. "Voices of Spring," pp. 16-17, extracted from "A New Spring," *Pictures of Travel*, 1855. For fuller entry see in Helen Hunt Jackson list, *Section III*.

The Cambridge Book of Poetry and Song . . . by Charlotte Fiske Bates . . .

New York . . . ⟨1882⟩

For comment see entry No. 7887.

Brilliant Diamonds of Poetry and Prose . . . ⟨Compiled by⟩ Rev. O. H. Tiffany . . .

Published for the Trade. ⟨n.p., 1883⟩

Gems for the Fireside . . . ⟨Compiled by⟩ Rev. O. H. Tiffany . . .

Springfield, Mass. . . . ⟨1883⟩

For comment see in Longfellow, *Section IV*.

Surf and Wave: The Sea as Sung by the Poets. Edited by Anna L. Ward . . .

New York: Thomas Y. Crowell & Co. 13 Astor Place. ⟨1883⟩

Representative Poems of Living Poets . . .

. . . New York 1886

For comment see entry No. 436.

Humorous Masterpieces from American Literature Edited by Edward T. Mason

New York . . . 1886

For comment see entry No. 4624A.

No. 14. Standard Comic Recitations . . . Compiled . . . by Frances P. Sullivan . . . December, 1886 . . .

. . . N. Y. . . . ⟨1886⟩

For comment see entry No. 11451.

The Prose Writings of Heinrich Heine: Edited, with an Introduction, by Havelock Ellis.

Walter Scott   London: 24 Warwick Lane Paternoster Row   1887

Cloth?

Mark Twain's Library of Humor . . .

New York . . . 1888

For comment see entry No. 9636.

Prosperity or Pauperism? Physical, Industrial, and Technical Training. Edited by the Earl of Meath, (Lord Brabazon.)

London: Longmans, Green, and Co. And New York: 15 East 16th Street. 1888. All Rights Reserved.

A copy at BA received May 22, 1888.

No. 21. Standard Comic Recitations . . . Compiled . . . by Frances P. Sullivan . . . September, 1888 . . .

. . . N. Y. . . . ⟨1888⟩

For comment see in Joseph Kirkland list of reprints.

Half-Hours with the Best Humorous Authors. Selected . . . by Charles Morris . . . American.

Philadelphia . . . 1889.

For comment see entry No. 3813.

Local and National Poets of America ... Edited ... ⟨by⟩ Thos. W. Herringshaw ...

Chicago ... 1890.

For fuller entry see BAL, Vol. 2, p. 391.

Out of the Heart   Poems ... Selected by John White Chadwick ... and Annie Hathaway Chadwick ...

Troy, N. Y. ... 1891

For comment see in Jackson, *Section III.*

Cope the Universal Soother

Printed and Published at the Office of "Cope's Tobacco Plant." ⟨Liverpool, n.d., 1893⟩

Cover-title. Printed paper wrapper.

No. 42. Standard Comic Recitations ... Compiled ... by Frances P. Sullivan ...

... N. Y. ... 1895 ...

For comment see entry No. 724.

... American Humorous Poetry ...

⟨London⟩ "Review of Reviews" Office ... ⟨n.d., 1897?⟩

For comment see entry No. 7828A.

... Masterpieces of Wit and Humor with ... Introduction by Robert J. Burdette ...

⟨n.p.⟩ Copyright, 1902, by E. J. Long

For comment see entry No. 2013.

Stories of Humor in Two Parts ...

New York ... ⟨1908⟩

For comment see BAL, Vol. 4, p. 62.

Poems of Country Life ... ⟨Edited⟩ by George S. Bryan ...

New York ... 1912

For comment see entry No. 7906.

The German Classics of the Nineteenth and Twentieth Centuries Masterpieces of German Literature Translated into English ... ⟨Edited by⟩ Kuno Francke ... ⟨and⟩ William Guild Howard ... ⟨Vol. 6⟩

The German Publication Society   New York ⟨1913⟩

20 Vols. Probably issued in a variety of bindings and with varying imprints.

The Joy of Life   An Anthology ... ⟨Edited⟩ by E. V. Lucas ...

... London ⟨1927⟩

For comment see in Kilmer reprints.

REFERENCES AND ANA

Pipps among the Wide-Awakes   How He Was Joined unto Them, and How He Was Unjoined. How He Fit Bled and Died, and How He Got over It. Showing the Correct and Entire Method of Being Wide Awake, Awoke, and Awaken ...

New-York: Wevill & Chapin. 1860.

Anonymous. Printed paper wrapper.

"The only copy seen by ⟨Jackson⟩ ... is the one in the Leland Papers in the Historical Society of Pennsylvania. On the title page of this copy, is the inscription in the author's handwriting: *Written by Charles G. Leland."* —Jackson, p. 35. HSP denies that the handwriting is Leland's. Authorship questionable.

Vanity Fair Railroad and Steamboat Library. Volume One ...

New-York: Published at the Office of Vanity Fair, No. 113 Nassau Street. ⟨1860⟩

All published? Printed paper wrapper. According to Jackson, pp. 35-36, the following were contributed by Leland: "Counter-Jumps. A Poemettina—After Walt Whitman," p. 6; "Opening-Day. (After Tennyson.)," p. 65; "Nice Men Milliners," pp. 67-68; "Counter-Jumper. A Melody," p. 73; "The Counter-Jumper Swell. The Poem of a Very Little Life that Was a Great Deal Too Long. An Humble Imitation of the Author of *Babie Bell,"* pp. 77-79.

According to Leland's *Memoirs,* 1893, and Pennell, Leland was co-editor of *Vanity Fair* where these productions appeared anonymously.

Walter Ashwood. A Love Story. By Paul Siogvolk ...

New York: Rudd & Carleton, 130 Grand Street, M DCCC LX.

Sometimes misattributed to Leland. The author was Albert Mathews. Deposited April 11, 1860.

⟨Reply to an autograph collector⟩

⟨*ca.* 1860⟩

Not seen. "There was some 'genius of freedom'—*i.e.,* one who takes liberties—who collected autographs, and had not even the politeness to send a written request. He forwarded to me this printed circular:

" 'Dear Sir: As I am collecting the autographs of distinguished Americans, I would be much obliged to you for your signature. Yours truly, ———— ————.'

"While I was editing *Vanity Fair* I received one of these circulars. I at once wrote:—

" 'Dear Sir: It gives me great pleasure to comply with your request. Charles G. Leland.'

"I called the foreman, and said, 'Mr. Chapin, please to set this up and pull half-a-dozen proofs.' It was done, and I sent one to the autograph-chaser. He was angry, and answered impertinently. Others I sent to Holmes and Lowell. The latter thought that the applicant was a great fool not to understand that such a printed document was far more of a curiosity than a mere signature ..." —*Memoirs,* New York, 1893, p. 247.

Life of Abraham Lincoln.

London, 1863.

Not seen. No copy located. Entry from Foley. Presumably a ghost. See under 1879 in *Section I* of this list.

Ye Sneak Yclepid Copperhead. A Satirical Poem ...

Philadelphia: A. Winch, 505 Chestnut St.; Willis P. Hazard, 724 Chestnut St.; F. Leypoldt, 1323 Chestnut St. 1863.

Anonymous. Printed paper wrapper. *Note:* Not the same as *Ye Book of Copperheads,* 1863. "Although this work was issued anonymously, it is not only known that Leland was its author, but the copy in the library of the Historical Society of Pennsylvania, bears an autographic inscription from him, presenting it to the institution."—Jackson, p. 42. The Society denies possession of any such copy. BAL has found no evidence to support Jackson's attribution. The Copyright Office reports that copyright was issued to one Rev. I. J. Stine who, in his application, stated that he was the author.

... Brightly Beaming Golden Star ... by Ambrose Davenport ...

Boston. Henry Tolman & Co. 291 Washington St. ... 1866 ...

Sheet music. Cover-title. At head of title: *Tone-Poems* ... Plate number: 5218. Translated by Leland? Translator's name not present. Possibly a revision ⟨by Leland?⟩ of Leland's translation of the same poem in *Heine's Book of Songs,* 1864. See in *Section II* under 1866 for two other pieces in the same suite translated by Leland.

The Iron Worker and King Solomon. By Joseph Harrison, Jr. With a Memoir and an Appendix ... Printed for Private Circulation.

Philadelphia: J. B. Lippincott & Co. 1868.

"The Blacksmith," by Leland, pp. 55-56. Reprinted from *Poetry and Mystery of Dreams,* 1856.

Also contains a prose piece titled "The Blacksmith and King Solomon. A Rabbinical Legend," pp. 51-53. *By Leland?* Harrison's prefatory note is somewhat ambiguous and appears to suggest that Leland was the author.

Some Notes on America to Be Rewritten: Suggested, with Respect, to Charles Dickens, Esq.

Printed for the Author. Philadelphia: Sherman & Co., Printers 1868.

Anonymous. Printed paper wrapper. Jackson, p. 55, attributes this publication to Leland. BAL has found no evidence to support the attribution.

"Topside Galah!" Long-Piecee-Man Hab Makee W'Litee ... a Pidgin-English Translation of Longfellow's "Excelsior," Altered from the "China Magazine," the Illustrations Drawn by an Officer of the U. S. Navy ⟨Lt. R. C. Hooker⟩.

Shanghae ⟨sic⟩, 1869.

Single leaf. Printed on recto only. $9^{15}/_{16}$" x $8^{5}/_{16}$". Text of translation, illustrated, on three photographic reproductions pasted to leaf.

Translated by Lt. Hooker? Sometimes credited to Leland but the translation, under the title "Excelsior," and varying somewhat textually, appears in Leland's *Pidgin-English Sing-Song* ... , 1876, with the following note: *This anonymous ⟨sic⟩ parody ... was introduced to the reading public in "Macmillan's Magazine" and Mr Sim⟨p⟩son's entertaining work "Meeting the Sun."* (*Meeting the Sun* ... , by William Simpson, London, 1874, pp. 279-280, under the title "Topside-Galow!," the text varying from both the Shanghai and the 1876 versions.) Willis Thornton, in *The Nine Lives of Citizen Train,* 1948, pp. 64-66, reports that George Francis Train credited the translation to Augustine Heard; and that while Heard had the ability to do the translation Thornton thought Leland "the more likely author."

Ramequins! No. 1. De Gospel According to Saint Breitmann! His Holy War, and de Acts of His Apostles ... by Cullen Morfe ⟨pseud? *Call 'em off?* Or is the *f* meant to be a long *s*?⟩

Wimborne: Printed and Published by J. N. Wood, King Street. ⟨1871⟩

Printed paper wrapper.

The May Flower.

Sentinel Printing Co., Printers, Keene. ⟨N.H., 1873⟩

Cover-title. Printed paper wrapper.

An occasional publication; all published. Issued under date May 1, 1873, for the benefit of the Invalids' Home, Keene, N. H. A copy in AAS.

"A Dutchman's Love Letter: Or 'Declaration of—'Dependence'," pp. 18-19. At end: *Hans B.* By Leland? Otherwise unlocated.

Letter, Leland to Ath, Sept. 16, 1871, from Baden-Baden, Sept. 8, 1871, stating that he has no connection whatever with the "comic weekly," *Hans Breitmann,* and has never written a line for it; "I have been severely handled during the past year at different times as the author of several pamphlets, and quite a number of poems and prose articles, written in German-English, and bearing the name of Hans Breitmann, none of which were by me ... I would state that the only writings of the kind for which I hold myself responsible are contained in the complete edition of the ... *Ballads,* published by ... Trübner."

Industrial and Decorative Art in Schools. Abstract of Lecture on Industrial and Decorative Art in Schools. Delivered by Charles G. Leland, before the Philadelphia Social Science Association, October 21st, 1880.

⟨n.p., n.d., Philadelphia, 1880?⟩

Single cut sheet. Printed on recto only. Galley proof only? Prepared as a press release? The lecture referred to is *Industrial and Decorative Art in Public Schools ...* , Philadelphia Social Science Association ⟨1880⟩ *q.v.* Is this abstract by Leland?

⟨Phi Beta Kappa poem delivered at Harvard in 1881.⟩

Never published according to Pennell, Vol. 2, p. 116; and, Clark Sutherland Northup, *A Bibliography of the Phi Beta Kappa Society,* New York, 1928, p. 116.

... Home Arts & Industries Association. Brief Elementary Instructions for Class-Holders ... Intended as Guides ... ⟨By M.C.K. McCallum⟩

⟨n.p., n.d., probably London, 1881–1882⟩

Cover-title. Printed self-wrapper. At head of title: *No. 1. ...* A series of pamphlets designed as aids in the teaching of Leland's art work theories. See *The Art Work Manuals* in *Section I,* under 1881–1882.

A Collection of Letters of Thackeray 1847–1855 ...

New York   Charles Scribner's Sons MDCCCLXXXVII

PC May 1, 1885, reported Leland "will probably edit in America" a collection of letters of Thackeray to "a college friend." No further evidence found associating Leland with the book. "In this final arrangement of the letters, and in some additional annotation, the publishers have enjoyed the privilege of advice and assistance from Mr. James Russell Lowell ...".— p. ⟨v⟩.

Songs of the Great Dominion ... Selected and Edited by William Douw Lighthall ...

London: Walter Scott, 24 Warwick Lane, Paternoster Row. 1889.

Cloth? Translations are attributed to Leland in the body of the book, but an erratum slip inserted between pp. ⟨436-437⟩ attributes them to Mrs. Wallace Brown.

Magonia: A Poem

Noted as *forthcoming* Ath Sept. 26, 1891; PC Oct. 3, 1891. Announced by Heinemann in the autumn of 1891; *in the press* in Heinemann's lists dated March and October, 1892; not present in the Heinemann list issued for the autumn of 1893. Pennell, Vol. 2, p. 348, states: "... A long poem in blank verse, *Magonia,* never published."

Album of Designs for Sheet Metal Work

1896?

Title taken from an advertisement in Leland's *A Manual of Mending and Repairing,* London, 1896.

No work of this title located. Perhaps related to entries 11622 or 11671.

Charles Godfrey Leland   A Biography by Elizabeth Robins Pennell ...

Boston and New York   Houghton, Mifflin and Company   The Riverside Press, Cambridge 1906

2 Vols. On copyright page: *Published September 1906* Also a limited edition, cloth, printed paper label on spine; on copyright

page: *Of This First Edition 150 Copies Have Been Bound Entirely Uncut, With Paper Label* Deposited Sept. 4, 1906. Listed PW Oct. 6, 1906. The London (Constable) edition, printed at The Riverside Press, Cambridge, Mass., from the original metal, listed Ath Oct. 20, 1906.

A Bibliography of the Works of Charles Godfrey Leland by Joseph Jackson

Reprinted from the Pennsylvania Magazine of History and Biography ‹n.p., n.d., Philadelphia, 1927?›

Cover-title. Printed paper wrapper.

Sunshine in Thought ... by Charles Godfrey Leland   A Facsimile Reproduction with an Introduction by Benjamin T. Spencer ...

Gainesville, Florida   Scholars' Facsimiles & Reprints   1959

ALFRED HENRY LEWIS

1 8 5 7 - 1 9 1 4

Note: Lewis's birth date has been assigned on the basis of a letter from Lucile M. Morsch, Chief, Descriptive Cataloging Division of the Library of Congress, Nov. 4, 1964: "Our authority card for Lewis shows that nine different sources give five different dates. The date 1857 was chosen as the most authentic because of a notice received from the New York Public Library in October 1919 indicating that that date was based on information from A. H. Lewis' brother. The authority card also mentions a letter from Axel Moth, New York Public Library, dated June 1921 to Charles Martel which confirms the dates as 1857–1914 . . ."

Also note: Do not confuse the subject of this list with Abram Herbert Lewis, 1836–1908, author of a series of theological works including *A Critical History of Sunday Legislation* . . . , 1888; *A Critical History of the Sabbath and the Sunday in the Christian Church* . . . , 1886; *Paganism Surviving in Christianity,* 1892; *Spiritual Sabbathism* . . . , 1910. Nor is our author to be confused with a Canadian of the same name, Alfred Henry Lewis, born 1869 and author of *South Vancouver Past and Present* . . . , Vancouver ⟨1920⟩.

11743. WOLFVILLE . . .

NEW YORK   FREDERICK A. STOKES COMPANY PUBLISHERS ⟨1897⟩

⟨i-xii⟩, ⟨1⟩-337, blank leaf. Frontispiece and 11 plates inserted. Other illustrations in text. *Note:* The plate used as the frontispiece is listed as appearing at p. 115. 7⅜" full x 4⅞".

⟨1-22⟩⁸.

V cloth: orange; red; yellow.

Note: Swann Galleries (New York), Sale No. 408, April 21, 1955, in describing this book states: "First issue, with no printer's credit line on copyright page." No such line present in any copy examined by BAL, including copies marked *Third Edition* and *Tenth Edition.*

Noted *will publish in June* PW May 1, 1897. Listed PW Aug. 14, 1897. Second edition noted

PW Aug. 28, 1897. The London (Lawrence & Bullen) edition listed Ath Oct. 9, 1897.

AAS   H   UV   Y

. . . A Wolfville Thanksgiving . . .

New York . . . ⟨1897⟩

See below under 1901.

11744. SANDBURRS . . .

NEW YORK   FREDERICK A. STOKES COMPANY PUBLISHERS ⟨1900⟩

Title-page in black and red.

⟨i-iv⟩, ⟨1⟩-6, ⟨1⟩-318. Laid paper. Frontispiece and 15 plates inserted. 7⅜" x 4¹⁵⁄₁₆".

⟨1⁴, 2⁸, 3⁴, 4-19⁸, 20⁴, 21-22⁸⟩. *Signed:* ⟨-⟩⁵, ⟨1⟩-14, ⟨15-16⟩, 17-19⁸, 20⁷.

T cloth: brown; red. White laid end papers.

Listed PW April 7, 1900.

AAS   NYPL   Y

11745. RICHARD CROKER . . .

NEW YORK   LIFE PUBLISHING COMPANY   1901

⟨iii⟩-⟨xvi⟩, ⟨1⟩-372. Laid paper. Frontispiece and 15 plates inserted. 8" x 5¼".

⟨1-24⁸, 25¹⟩.

V cloth: green. Top edges tinted pale green.

Two issues noted:

1

Text of final paragraph, p. 26, garbled due to transposed line of text. Page ends: . . . *denunciatory of savagery; so*

2

Text of final paragraph, p. 26, corrected. Page ends: . . . *and define the* The leaf is a cancel.

Title deposited June 12, 1901. Listed PW Aug. 10, 1901. Deposited Aug. 31, 1901.

AAS (2nd)   BA (2nd)   H (1st)   NYPL (1st)   UV (both)

11746. ... A Wolfville Thanksgiving ...

New York   Frederick A. Stokes Company Publishers ⟨1897; i.e., 1901⟩

At head of title: Half Hour Classics by Modern Masters of Fiction

Reprinted from *Wolfville* ⟨1897⟩.

Advertised in publisher's catalog dated July 1901. Advertised PW Sept. 28, 1901, in Stokes's *Fall Announcement* list.

NYPL   UV

11747. WOLFVILLE DAYS ...

NEW YORK   FREDERICK A. STOKES COMPANY PUBLISHERS ⟨1902⟩

Title-page in black, red and gray.

⟨i⟩-⟨xii⟩, ⟨1⟩-311. Laid paper. Frontispiece inserted. 7¼″ x 4⅞″ full.

⟨1², 2-21⁸⟩.

T cloth: red.

Listed PW Feb. 22, 1902. A copy at BA received Feb. 25, 1902. The London (Isbister) edition advertised as though published Ath March 7, 1903; issued according to *English Catalogue* in Feb. 1903.

AAS   NYPL

11748. WOLFVILLE NIGHTS ...

NEW YORK. FREDERICK A. STOKES COMPANY. PUBLISHERS ⟨1902⟩

Title-page in black, gray and orange.

⟨i-vi⟩, ⟨1⟩-326, 3 blank leaves. The last leaf used as a pastedown. Laid paper. Frontispiece inserted. 7¼″ x 4⅞″.

Note: The frontispiece occurs as follows; sequence, if any, not determined:

A: Printed in sepia. Noted only in the first printing.

B: Printed in black. Noted thus in both the first and the second printings.

⟨1⁹, 2-21⁸⟩. ⟨1⟩₂ (the title-leaf) inserted. ⟨21⟩₈ used as pastedown.

V cloth: blue-black. Stamped in gold, blue and white. White wove end paper at front; leaf ⟨21⟩₈ used as terminal pastedown.

On copyright page: *Published, September, 1902.*

Two printings noted:

1

As above.

2

Title-page printed in black only.

⟨i-vi⟩, ⟨1⟩-326, 2 blank leaves. Wove paper. Frontispiece inserted.

⟨1-10¹⁶, 11⁸⟩.

The statement *Published, September, 1902,* not present on copyright page.

V cloth: blue-black. Stamped in orange and blue.

Listed PW Oct. 11, 1902.

AAS (1st)   NYPL (1st)   UV (1st)   Y (2nd)

11749. THE BLACK LION INN ...

NEW YORK   R. H. RUSSELL   1903

Title-page in black and red.

⟨i-ii⟩, ⟨i⟩-⟨vi⟩, 1-⟨381⟩; blank, p. ⟨382⟩, 2 pp. advertisements. Frontispiece and 15 plates inserted. 7⅜″ x 4¹⁵⁄₁₆″.

⟨-⟩⁴, 1-24⁸.

V cloth: tan. White laid end papers.

On copyright page: *Published, May, 1903.* Advertised for May PW April 25, 1903. Advertised as *brought out this week* PW May 9, 1903. Listed PW May 16, 1903.

AAS   Y

11750. PEGGY O'NEAL ...

DREXEL BIDDLE PUBLISHER   PHILADELPHIA ⟨1903⟩

Title-page in black and orange.

⟨i-ii⟩, ⟨1⟩-494, blank leaf. Two frontispieces and three plates inserted. 7¾″ x 5¼″.

⟨1⁵, 2-16¹⁶, 17⁴⟩. Leaf ⟨1⟩₂ (the title-leaf) inserted. Signature marks 2 on p. 17, 3 on p. 33; otherwise unsigned.

Two printings noted:

1

Title-page, pagination, collation as above.

Fore and bottom edges untrimmed.

P. 96, line 6: ... *held* ...

P. 474, line 16: ... *coat* ...

2

Title-page printed in black only.

⟨i-ii⟩, ⟨1⟩-494, blank leaf. Two frontispieces and three plates inserted.

⟨1⁵, 2-31⁸, 32⁴⟩. Leaf ⟨1⟩₂ (the title-leaf) inserted.

All edges trimmed.

P. 96, line 6: ... *hold* ...

P. 474, line 16: ... *cloak* ...

On copyright page: *Published, May, 1903.* Noted for May 23 PW May 9, 1903. Listed PW June 6, 1903. A copy at AAS inscribed by early owner June 17, 1903. Reprinted and reissued by The American News Company ⟨1903; *i.e.,* 1904⟩; advertised as *will be issued as No. 39 The People's Library* PW Feb. 20, 1904; advertised as though published PW March 19, 1904. Reprinted and reissued by Fenno, who succeeded to Drexel Biddle in Feb. 1904.

AAS (1st)   UV (2nd)   Y (both)

11751. THE BOSS AND HOW HE CAME TO RULE NEW YORK ...

NEW YORK   A. S. BARNES & COMPANY   MDCCCCIII

⟨i⟩-⟨xiv⟩, ⟨1⟩-409; blank, p. ⟨410⟩, 6 pp. advertisements, blank leaf. Frontispiece and 9 plates inserted. 7⁵⁄₁₆″ x 4¹⁵⁄₁₆″.

⟨1-27⟩⁸.

T cloth: green.

On copyright page: *October* Deposited Oct. 26, 1903. Advertised as *ready October 30,* PW Oct. 24, 1903. Listed PW Oct. 31, 1903. The London (Gay & Bird) edition listed Ath May 20, 1905.

AAS   BA   H   NYPL

11752. THE PRESIDENT A NOVEL ...

NEW YORK   A. S. BARNES AND COMPANY   MDCCCCIV

⟨i⟩-⟨x⟩, ⟨1⟩-514; blank, p. ⟨515⟩; advertisements, pp. ⟨516-518⟩. Frontispiece and 7 plates inserted. 7⁵⁄₁₆″ x 4¹⁵⁄₁₆″.

⟨1-33⟩⁸.

T cloth: blue. Blue ribbon marker, imprinted with an advertisement, bound in some copies.

On copyright page: *September* Announced for *early autumn* PW July 23, 1904; Aug. 27, 1904. Deposited Sept. 7, 1904. Noted as *just ready* and advertised as *just published* PW Sept. 10, 1904. Listed PW Sept. 17, 1904. The London (Gay & Bird) edition listed Ath May 20, 1905.

AAS   NYPL   Y

11753. The Mormon Menace Being the Confession of John Doyle Lee ... Introduction by Alfred Henry Lewis ...

New York Home Protection Publishing Co. 156 Fifth Avenue ⟨1905⟩

"The Mormon Purpose," pp. vii-xxii.

Two issues noted; the order is probable:

1

The list of illustrations leaf is an integral part of its gathering; 5 plates (including frontispiece) listed.

2

The list of illustrations leaf is a cancel; 4 plates (including frontispiece) listed.

Listed PW Feb. 4, 1905.

H (1)   NYPL (1)   UV (1)   Y (both)

11754. THE SUNSET TRAIL ...

NEW YORK   A. S. BARNES & CO.   1905

⟨i⟩-⟨xvi⟩, 1-393; blank, p. ⟨394⟩; advertisements, pp. ⟨395-400⟩. Frontispiece and 7 plates inserted. 7³⁄₁₆″ full x 4¹⁵⁄₁₆″.

⟨1-26⟩⁸.

T cloth: maroon.

On copyright page: *Published April, 1905* Advertised for May 1, PW March 18, 1905. Noted as *shortly* PW April 1, 1905. Deposited April 21, 1905. Noted for *this week* PW April 22, 1905. Listed PW May 13, 1905. PW July 15, 1905, reported that the publishers had arranged *large Australian editions. A second edition* advertised PW Nov. 25, 1905. The London (Brown, Langham & Co.) edition advertised for *early next week* Ath Feb. 24, 1906; listed Ath March 10, 1906.

Note: In all examined copies the third title in the advertisements on p. ⟨400⟩ is listed as by *Richard Henry Shoddard* ⟨*sic*⟩.

AAS   Y

11755. THE THROWBACK A ROMANCE OF THE SOUTHWEST ...

NEW YORK   THE OUTING PUBLISHING COMPANY   1906

⟨i⟩-⟨viii⟩, 1-347; blank, p. ⟨348⟩, 2 pp. advertisements, blank leaf. Laid paper. Frontispiece and 3 plates inserted. 7⁵⁄₁₆″ x 5″.

⟨1⁴, 2-23⁸⟩.

V cloth: green.

Note: Unsold sheets were issued by A. L. Burt Company, New York, with their imprint on the spine; leaves ⟨23⟩₇₋₈ excised.

Announced for *early spring* PW Jan. 27, 1906. Noted for March PW March 17, 1906. Listed PW April 14, 1906. The London (Cassell) edition listed Ath Sept. 7, 1907.

AAS H Y

11756. THE STORY OF PAUL JONES   AN HISTORICAL ROMANCE ...

G. W. DILLINGHAM COMPANY PUBLISHERS   NEW YORK ⟨1906⟩

⟨1⟩-308. Frontispiece and 7 plates inserted. *Note:* The plate listed as opposite p. 98 is inserted opposite p. 90. 7¼″ x 4⅞″.

⟨1⟩-2, ⟨3-19⁸, 20²⟩.

V cloth: green. Stamped in white, gold and dark blackish-green.

Two printings noted:

1

As above.

2

⟨1⟩-308; advertisements, pp. ⟨309-314⟩; blank leaf. Frontispiece and 7 plates inserted.

⟨1⟩-2, ⟨3-19⁸, 20⁶⟩.

V cloth: yellow-green. Stamped in brown and green.

Printed not before 1907.

On copyright page: *Issued May, 1906* Noted as *in preparation* PW March 10, 1906. Deposited May 12, 1906. Noted as *just issued* PW May 19, 1906. Advertised as *published May 18* PW May 19, 1906. Listed PW June 2, 1906.

AAS (2nd)   NYPL (1st)   UV (1st)   Y (1st)

11757. CONFESSIONS OF A DETECTIVE ...

NEW YORK   A. S. BARNES & COMPANY   MDCCCCVI

⟨i-xii⟩, 1-280. Frontispiece and 7 plates inserted. *Note:* The plate listed as at p. 28 is used as the frontispiece. 7¼″ x 5″.

⟨1², 2⁴, 3-19⁸, 20⁴⟩.

T cloth: red.

On copyright page: *October* Advertised as *ready in October* PW Sept. 29, 1906. Listed PW Nov. 3, 1906. Deposited Feb. 9, 1907. Reprinted and reissued in printed paper wrapper as *Log Cabin Series Number 5*, New York, Log Cabin Press ⟨1921⟩; copy in UV.

AAS H

11758. ... A Compilation of the Messages and Speeches of Theodore Roosevelt 1901–1905 Edited by Alfred Henry Lewis ...

Published by Bureau of National Literature and Art 1906

At head of title: [Supplemental]

Supplement to *A Supplement to a Compilation of the Messages and Papers of the Presidents 1789–1902, by James D. Richardson,* compiled by George Raywood Devitt ⟨Washington, D. C.⟩, 1902.

2 Vols. Continuous pagination. Noted only in three-quarters morocco, marbled boards sides, but probably issued in a variety of custom bindings.

"Introduction," Vol. 1, pp. ⟨i⟩-xv. For a truncated version of this "Introduction" see next entry.

H LC NYPL

11759. Roosevelt

Lewis's sketch of Theodore Roosevelt occurs in two forms: In full (see preceding entry); and, in highly truncated form. *Publication sequence of the two forms has not been determined.* The truncated text has been noted in the publications listed below.

Since the following were issued by subscription publishers it is entirely possible that they occur in a variety of bindings, perhaps with varying imprints.

A

The Presidents ⟨Compiled by George Raywood Devitt⟩

1906   The Gravure Company of America New York and Washington

Divisional title-page: *The White House Gallery of Official Portraits of the Presidents*

The only copy located is in a typical subscription binding; perhaps originally issued as a series of portfolios. The copy here described carries a certificate of issue identifying it as *The Executive Edition,* copy No. 1721. Also contains an inserted registration of ownership, also numbered 1721, dated Nov. 1, 1906. 19½″ x 16″.

Unpaged. Lewis's sketch (in truncated form) appears on a single page.

An earlier edition does not contain the Lewis contribution.

B

Supplement to the Messages and Papers of the Presidents Covering the Presidential Terms of

Theodore Roosevelt September 14, 1901, to March 4, 1909 ...

Published by Bureau of National Literature (Inc.) New York ⟨n.d., but after March 4, 1909⟩

The truncated text, pp. 6636c-6636D, is altered to the extent that the tense is changed from the present to the past.

Presumably added to editions of *A Compilation of the Messages and Papers of the Presidents* issued 1909 and later.

C

The White House Gallery of Official Portraits of the Presidents Copyright, 1901 ... 1912 ...

Prepared for Publication by the Bureau of National Literature for the Syndicate Publishing Company 12 and 14 West 32d Street New York City

Portfolio. 14⅛" x 9⅞". *Reprint.*

D

A Compilation of the Messages and Papers of the Presidents ... Volume XIV

Published by Bureau of National Literature, Inc. New York ⟨n.d., not before Jan. 6, 1919, the date of Theodore Roosevelt's death, which fact is here recorded on p. 6638.⟩

Reprint.

H (A,B,C,D)

11760. WHEN MEN GREW TALL OR THE STORY OF ANDREW JACKSON ...

D. APPLETON AND COMPANY   NEW YORK   1907

Title-page in black and orange.

⟨i⟩-⟨x⟩, ⟨1⟩-⟨331⟩; blank, p. ⟨332⟩; 10 pp. advertisements. Frontispiece and 15 plates inserted. 7¹¹⁄₁₆" x 5³⁄₁₆".

⟨1⟩-22⁸.

T cloth: red. Top edges gilded. Illustration pasted to front.

Below text, p. ⟨331⟩, is the symbol (1); indicating: *First Printing.*

On copyright page: *Published November, 1907* Noted for Nov. 1 PW Oct. 26, 1907. Deposited Oct. 30, 1907. Listed PW Dec. 21, 1907.

AAS   B   H

11761. AN AMERICAN PATRICIAN OR THE STORY OF AARON BURR ...

D. APPLETON AND COMPANY   NEW YORK   1908

Title-page in black and orange.

⟨i-ii⟩, ⟨i⟩-⟨x⟩, 1-⟨336⟩. Frontispiece and 15 plates inserted. 7⅝" x 5⅛".

⟨1⟩⁶, 2-22⁸.

T cloth: maroon. Top edges gilded. Illustration pasted to front.

Below text, p. ⟨336⟩, is the symbol (1); indicating: *First Printing.*

On copyright page: *Published February, 1908* Noted for Feb. 14 PW Feb. 8, 1908. Deposited Feb. 14, 1908. A copy at NYPL received Feb. 15, 1908. A copy at BA received Feb. 18, 1908. Listed PW March 7, 1908.

AAS   BA   H

11762. WOLFVILLE FOLKS ...

NEW YORK   D. APPLETON AND COMPANY   1908

⟨i⟩-viii, 1-⟨322⟩; blank leaf, 4 pp. advertisements. Frontispiece inserted. 7⅜" full x 4¹⁵⁄₁₆".

⟨1⟩-21⁸.

V cloth: orange-brown.

Below text, p. ⟨322⟩, is the symbol (1); indicating: *First Printing.*

On copyright page: *Published May, 1908*

Have postponed until May 15, PW May 2, 1908. Deposited May 15, 1908. Listed PW May 16, 1908.

AAS   NYPL   Y

11763. THE APACHES OF NEW YORK ...

G. W. DILLINGHAM COMPANY PUBLISHERS   NEW YORK   ⟨1912⟩

⟨1⟩-272. Frontispiece and 10 plates inserted. 7¼" x 4⅞".

⟨1-17⟩⁸.

T cloth: red. Stamped in gold.

Note: Also occurs in red V cloth, stamped in black only. Inserted at front is a leaf in facsimile of Lewis's handwriting: *For V. J. O'Farrell— From whom, with the exception of Bow Kum, I got the stories ... Mar 20, 1912 ...* Such copies were issued with the *compliments of The Val O'Farrell Detective Agency ... New York ...*

Noted as *just issued* PW April 6, 1912. Listed PW April 13, 1912.

AAS   UV (variant)   Y

11764. FARO NELL AND HER FRIENDS WOLFVILLE STORIES ...

G. W. DILLINGHAM COMPANY PUBLISHERS   NEW YORK   ⟨1913⟩

⟨1⟩-348, 4 pp. advertisements. Frontispiece and 11 plates inserted. 7¼" x 4¹³⁄₁₆".

⟨1-22⟩⁸.

T cloth: red.

Two states (printings?) noted. The sequence has not been established and the designations are for identification only. The following variation is sufficient for recognition:

A

P. ⟨349⟩: *Seven Splendid Novels by William MacLeod Raine* . . .

B

P. ⟨349⟩: *Three Splendid Books by Alfred Henry Lewis* . . .

Listed PW April 5, 1913. A copy in BA received April 8, 1913.

AAS (B)   BA (A)   NYPL (B)   Y (B)

11765. NATION-FAMOUS NEW YORK MURDERS . . .

G. W. DILLINGHAM COMPANY PUBLISHERS NEW YORK ⟨1914⟩

⟨1⟩-315; advertisements, pp. ⟨316-320⟩. 7⅜" x 4⅞" full.

⟨1-20⟩⁸.

T cloth: maroon.

Deposited July 2, 1914. Listed PW July 18, 1914: *320 pp*. Listed PW Aug. 8, 1914: *315 pp*.

AAS H UV Y

11766. Familiar Stories for Children by Mary Hartwell Catherwood   Alfred Henry Lewis . . . Etc. Etc.

New York   Hurst & Company Publishers ⟨1914⟩

"A Wolfville Thanksgiving," pp. ⟨96⟩-108; reprinted from *Wolfville* ⟨1897⟩.

For comment see entry No. 2985.

11767. The Dismissal of Silver Phil . . .

. . . 1914 . . . The Winthrop Press   New York

Pictorial paper wrapper. A miniature book, 2⅞" x 2¼". Issued as a premium by the manufacturers of Egyptienne Straights and other cigarettes.

Reprinted from *Wolfville Nights* ⟨1902⟩.

H

11768. The Ghost of the Bar-B-8 . . .

. . . 1914   The Winthrop Press   New York

Uniform with the preceding entry. Noted with, and without, advertising on the outer back wrapper.

Reprinted from *Wolfville Nights* ⟨1902⟩.

UV

REPRINTS

The following publications contain material by Lewis reprinted from earlier books.

Short Story Classics (American) . . . Edited by William Patten . . .

. . . New York ⟨1905⟩

5 Vols. For comment see entry No. 6378.

International Short Stories Edited by William Patten . . . American

. . . New York ⟨1910⟩

For comment see entry No. 782.

ANA

Pearls and Swine

On the title-page of *Wolfville Days* ⟨1902⟩ Lewis is described as *Author of "Wolfville," "Sandburrs," "Pearls and Swine," Etc.* BAL has found no book or story of this title by Lewis.

Wolfville   A Drama of the South West by Clyde Fitch & Willis Steell (From Alfred Henry Lewis's Book of the Same Name)

⟨n.p., n.d.⟩

Typescript (in UP). No record of publication found.

GEORGE LIPPARD

1 8 2 2 – 1 8 5 4

NOTE: In the preparation of this list BAL has relied heavily on Roger Butterfield, a constant and willing aid who permitted us to draw freely on his work (both published and unpublished) and on his time.

ALSO NOTE: The present list is broken down into five sections as follows:

I: Lippard's books (first and extended editions); books containing contributions by him.

II: Reprints of Lippard's own books.

III: Books containing reprinted Lippard material.

IV: Misattributions, ghosts, ana. Alphabetically arranged by title.

V: References

SECTION I

Lippard's books (first and extended editions), books containing contributions by him.

11769. ADRIAN, THE NEOPHYTE . . .

PHILADELPHIA: I. R. & A. H. DILLER, PUBLISHERS. 1843

Cover-title? *Pagination and signature collation in doubt.*

⟨1⟩-13. 8⁹⁄₁₆″ x 5½″.

⟨1¹, 2-4²⟩.

Printed paper wrapper? Self-wrapper?

UV

11770. . . . THE BATTLE-DAY OF GERMAN-TOWN . . .

PHILADELPHIA: A. H. DILLER, PUBLISHER. 1843

At head of title: ORIGINAL REVOLUTIONARY CHRONICLE.

⟨i-viii⟩, ⟨1⟩-34, blank leaf. Frontispiece. 8⅞″ x 5¹³⁄₁₆″.

⟨-⟩⁴, A-B⁴, 3-4⁴, 5².

Printed pink paper wrapper.

Reported for sale in *Boston Evening Transcript*, Nov. 28, 1843. Listed NAR Jan. 1844.

NYPL UV

11771. THE LADYE ANNABEL; OR, THE DOOM OF THE POISONER. A ROMANCE BY AN UNKNOWN AUTHOR . . .

PHILADELPHIA: R. G. BERFORD, PUBLISHER. 1844.

⟨i⟩-⟨viii⟩, ⟨1⟩-133, blank leaf. 8¾″ full x 5⅝″ full.

⟨-⟩⁴, A-H⁸, I⁴.

Printed salmon paper wrapper.

Noted as *out a week* in *Citizen Soldier* (Phila.), Feb. 14, 1844. Listed as an April publication in WPLNL May, 1844, with authorship credited to Lippard.

See under 1845 for *Third Edition.* See under 1849 for an extended edition. Reprinted and reissued under the following titles: *The Ladye of Albarone; or, the Poison Goblet* . . . ⟨1859⟩; and, *The Mysteries of Florence* . . . ⟨1864⟩, ⟨1876⟩.

HSP

11772. HERBERT TRACY, OR THE LEGEND OF THE BLACK RANGERS. A ROMANCE OF THE BATTLE-FIELD OF GERMANTOWN . . .

PHILADELPHIA: R. G. BERFORD, PUBLISHER. BARRETT AND JONES, PRINTERS, NO. 33 CARTER'S ALLEY. 1844.

⟨i⟩-vi, ⟨7⟩-168. 7½″ x 4½″.

⟨1⟩-7¹².

Printed tan paper wrapper.

Note: Butterfield (p. 303) reports a 166-page printing; this has been proved a ghost.

Published after Feb. 18, 1844, a letter from Poe, so dated, on pp. 167-168. Advertised in *Boston Daily Advertiser* as though ready, March 22, 1844.

H

11773. THE QUAKER CITY; OR, THE MONKS OF MONK-HALL. A ROMANCE OF PHILADELPHIA LIFE, MYSTERY AND CRIME.

PHILADELPHIA: G. B. ZIEBER AND CO. 1844.

Anonymous.

Issued in ten paper-covered parts. *No complete set in parts has been located; the present entry is tentative.* It is probable that the first four(?) parts were issued in 1844 and the remaining parts in 1845. For a further comment on the publication of this book see under the 1845 edition; also see under 1849.

⟨1⟩-206; ⟨i-ii⟩; 207-494. Vignette title-page inserted. 8⁷⁄₁₆″ x 5½″.

⟨1-31⁸⟩. *Signed:* ⟨1⟩-⟨26⟩, 27-32⁴.

Publisher's "Advertisement," p. ⟨4⟩, dated *September 28, 1844. Part 1* advertised *Boston Daily Advertiser,* Oct. 8, 1844; listed as an October publication in WPLNL Nov. 1844. *Part 3* advertised *Daily Evening Transcript* (Boston), Nov. 9, 1844.

HSP

11774. The Ladye Annabel: A Romance of the Alembic, the Altar, aud ⟨sic⟩ the Throne ... Third Edition.

Philadelphia: G. B. Zieber & Co. Printed by B. E. Smith, S. E. Corner of Second and Market Sts. 1845.

Cloth, printed paper label on spine.

For first edition see under 1844; also see under 1849.

"Preface to the Third Edition," pp. ⟨iii⟩-viii, dated at end: Jan. 8, 1845.

Note: Presence of the statement *Third Edition* suggests publication of a *second edition* but no printing so marked has been reported or found. Lippard probably considered periodical appearance the first edition; the 1844 separate (the

first book publication) the second edition; and this 1845 publication the third edition. For an indication of Lippard's thinking in the matter see *Herbert Tracy,* 1844, p. vi.

FLP Pennsylvania State Teachers College, West Chester, Penna.

11775. The Quaker City; or, the Monks of Monk-Hall. A Romance of Philadelphia Life, Mystery, and Crime ...

Philadelphia: Published by the Author, and for Sale by All Booksellers. 1845.

10 paper-covered parts (according to Lippard; see note below).

For first edition see under 1844; also see under 1849.

Reprint with the exception of the dedication to Charles Brockden Brown, dated at end: *Monday May 5, 1845,* pp. 3-4. The dedication in the first edition (1844) is to A.J.H. Duganne and is a brief seven lines.

"It ⟨this book⟩ was commenced on the 5th of September 1844, and published in ten numbers, with a success, almost without parallel ... Since its first publication, near 40,000 numbers of the book have been sold ... I now present the work to the public in complete form, after nine editions in numbers, have met with a rapid sale ... On the night, November Eleventh, 1844, a play taken from this book, was withdrawn by the Managers of the Chesnut Street Theatre, because the same Mob who with characteristic cowardice, threatened to murder the Author, declared their intention to destroy or burn the building in case the piece was played ..."—p. 4.

Reissued by T. B. Peterson, Philadelphia ⟨1845; *i.e.,* not before 1858⟩; 2 Vols., printed paper wrapper. On the wrapper: *The Author's Revised Edition.* Cursory examination indicates that the text is of the 1845 edition.

Note: Butterfield informs BAL that the title *The Quaker City, a Romance of the Rich and Poor ... ,* (Butterfield, p. 303) appears to have been used only in advertisements; no copy of the book so titled has been seen or reported.

Noted by BJl June 7, 1845.

AAS   B   N   P   Y

The Quaker City ... in Two Volumes ... ⟨27th edition⟩

Philadelphia: Published by the Author. And for Sale by All Booksellers. ⟨1845; *i.e.,* 1849⟩

See below under 1849.

11776. THE NAZARENE; OR, THE LAST OF THE WASHINGTONS, A REVELATION OF PHILADELPHIA, NEW YORK, AND WASHINGTON, IN THE YEAR 1844 ...

PHILADELPHIA: G. LIPPARD AND CO., PUBLISHERS. FOR SALE BY ALL THE BOOKSELLERS AND PERIODICAL AGENTS, THROUGHOUT THE UNION. 1846.

Printed yellow paper wrappers. Issued in 5 parts:

1

⟨1⟩-4, v-⟨viii⟩, 9-48. $10\frac{3}{16}''$ x $6\frac{3}{8}''$.

⟨1-2⁴, 3-4⁸⟩. *Signed:* ⟨1⟩-4, ⟨5⟩-6⁴.

2

49-96.

⟨1-3⁸⟩. *Signed:* 7-12⁴. Superfluous signature mark 3 on p. 85; this feature present also in the 1854 reprint.

3

97-144.

⟨1-4⁶⟩. *Signed:* 13-18⁴. *Note:* Also occurs in a second printing: ⟨1-3⁸⟩, *signed* 13-18⁴.

4

145-192.

⟨1-3⁸⟩. *Signed:* 19-24⁴.

5

193-240.

⟨1-3⁸⟩. *Signed:* 25-30⁴.

The wrapper imprint varies as follows:

1-3

Philadelphia: Published by the National Publishing Company, for George Lippard and Co. ...

4

Philadelphia: Published by John A. Bell, (Agent,) No. 7 Arcade, for George Lippard and Co. ...

5

Philadelphia: G. B. Zeiber ⟨*sic*⟩ & Co. For George Lippard and Co. ...

Advertised as *now in press* in *The New Popular Magazine* (Phila.), Oct. 31, 1846.

HSP (Part 1) NYPL (Parts 1-5, Part 3 being 1st printing) Y (Part 3, being 2nd printing)

11777. BLANCHE OF BRANDYWINE; OR, SEPTEMBER THE ELEVENTH, 1777. A ROMANCE, COMBINING THE POETRY, LEGEND, AND HISTORY OF THE BATTLE OF BRANDYWINE ...

PHILADELPHIA: G. B. ZIEBER & CO. 1846.

Printed drab paper wrappers; issued in three parts.

1

⟨i⟩-viii, 9-128. $9\frac{13}{16}''$ x $6\frac{1}{8}''$. Frontispiece inserted.

⟨1-8⁸⟩. *Signed:* ⟨1⟩-5, ⟨6⟩-16⁴.

2

129-240.

⟨1-7⁸⟩. *Signed:* 17-30⁴.

3

241-351.

⟨1-7⁸⟩. *Signed:* 31-44⁴.

Advertised for *September* NYM Aug. 29, 1846. Advertised as *complete in three parts* NYM Sept. 8, 1846.

On the basis of a single located copy (in Y) imprinted: *Philadelphia: G. B. Zieber & Co. 1847,* BAL theorizes that such copies may be made up of sheets of the first printing, stripped of the original wrappers, and offered as a single volume with cancel title-leaf.

There were three or more reprints issued by T. B. Peterson, Philadelphia, under date ⟨1846⟩.

Y

11778. WASHINGTON AND HIS GENERALS: OR, LEGENDS OF THE REVOLUTION ...

PHILADELPHIA: G. B. ZIEBER AND CO. 1847.

Issued 4 parts in 3.

1

⟨i⟩-iv, 25-132. $9\frac{11}{16}''$ x $6\frac{1}{16}''$. *Note:* The biographical sketch of the author by Rev. C. Chauncey Burr (called for by the title-page) is not present which accounts for the hiatus in the pagination. P. iii paged 3.

⟨1-7⁸⟩. *Signed:* ⟨1⟩-14⁴.

2

133-244.

⟨1-7⁸⟩. *Signed:* 15-16, ⟨17⟩-28⁴.

3&4

Issued as a single part.

245-538, blank leaf.

⟨1-17⁸, 18-20⁴⟩. *Signed:* ⟨29⟩-46, ⟨47⟩-65⁴. Superfluous signature mark 57 on p. 483.

Printed terra-cotta paper wrappers.

Advertised as *in press, The Popular Magazine* (Phila.) Oct. 1846. *Part 1* noted as *issued, Saturday Courier* (Phila.), April 3, 1847. *Part 1* listed as an April publication LW April 24, 1847. Reviewed (Part 1 only?) NYM May 29, 1847. *Part 2* listed LW June 5, 1847. *Part 3-4* advertised for *week ending Aug. 28th* NYM Aug. 28, 1847; noted as *issued, Saturday Courier* (Phila.), Aug. 28, 1847; listed LW Sept. 4, 1847.

Another printing (in 12's) was issued with the imprint: *Philadelphia. G. B. Zieber and Co. 1847.;* paged: ⟨i-ii⟩, ⟨i⟩-⟨xxviii⟩, 3-iv, 25-538, 3 blank leaves. Issued in two paper-covered parts? Contains the biographical sketch by Burr; see comment above. This printing reviewed by *Massachusetts Quarterly Review* (Boston), Dec. 1847. For a separate printing of the Burr sketch see below under *References and Ana.*

At least two reprintings were issued by T. B. Peterson, Philadelphia, under date ⟨1847⟩.

H (lacking *Part 2*)   NYPL

11779. Semi-Annual Pictorial Saturday Courier
    Andrew McMakin.   July Fourth 1847   Philadelphia.

Special issue. Page: 31¾" x 22¼". 8 pp.

Contains "The Rose of Wissahikon," pp. ⟨1-3⟩.

For formal book publication see next entry.

HSP

11780. THE ROSE OF WISSAHIKON, OR, THE FOURTH OF JULY, 1776. A ROMANCE, EMBRACING THE SECRET HISTORY OF THE DECLARATION OF INDEPENDENCE ...

    PHILADELPHIA: G. B. ZIEBER & CO., 3 LEDGER BUILDING. 1847.

See preceding entry.

⟨1⟩-70, blank leaf. 6⅞" scant x 4⅜" scant.

⟨1⟩-3¹².

Printed paper wrapper.

Note: The wrapper has been noted in the following states; sequence, if any, has not been determined and the designations are for identification only.

Wrapper A

Outer front, line 14: *"Washington, and his*

Generals ... ⟨Note presence of comma.⟩   Colors noted: brown, green, orange, yellow. *All examined copies lack back of wrapper.*

Wrapper B

Outer front, line 14: *"Washington and his Generals ...* ⟨Note absence of comma.⟩

Inner back: *... New Publications on the Cheap Plan ...*

Outer back: *New Juvenile Publications ...*

Colors noted: blue, brown, green.

Wrapper C

Outer front, line 14: *"Washington and his Generals ...* ⟨Note absence of comma.⟩

Inner back: *Mrs. Hale's Cook-Book ...*

Outer back: *New Juvenile Publications ...*

Colors noted: yellow.

Title deposited May 25, 1847. Advertised for the week ending Aug. 28 NYM Aug. 28, 1847. Listed LW Sept. 4, 1847. Advertisements in Lippard's weekly paper, *Quaker City,* during the period Nov.–Dec. 1849, indicate that the book may have been republished under a revised title: *The Fourth of July, 1776; or, the Declaration and the Signers.* Same as entry No. 11801?

AAS (A)   BPL (B)   LC (C)   LCP (B)   NYPL (A)   UV (A,B)   Y (A)

11781. LEGENDS OF MEXICO, BY GEORGE LIPPARD ...

    PHILADELPHIA: T. B. PETERSON, 98 CHESNUT STREET. 1847.

⟨9⟩-136. 9⅝" x 5⅞".

⟨1-8⁸⟩. *Signed:* ⟨1⟩-16⁴.

Printed brown paper wrapper.

Title deposited for copyright Sept. 1, 1847. Listed LW Sept. 11, 1847. Reviewed by *Godey's Magazine and Lady's Book,* Nov. 1847.

Note: Several Peterson reprints were issued; each published under date ⟨1847⟩.

Under the title *Legends of Mexico; or, the Battles of Old Rough and Ready,* reprinted and reissued under date ⟨1847; i.e., 1848⟩; reviewed *Saturday Courier* (Philadelphia), Nov. 11, 1848; misdated ⟨1848⟩ by Butterfield, p. 305. Lippard's weekly paper, *The Quaker City* (Philadelphia), June 30, 1849, noted a London & Glasgow (Tegg, Griffin) printing.

Y

11782. Semi-Annual Pictorial Saturday Courier
    Philadelphia: December, 1847

Not seen. Entry from Jackson, p. 143. For another issue in this series see above under July, 1847.

Contains "Washington's Christmas, a Legend of Valley Forge." Collected in *Washington and His Men* . . . , Philadelphia ⟨1849⟩.

11783. 'BEL OF PRAIRIE EDEN. A RO-MANCE OF MEXICO . . .

BOSTON: PUBLISHED BY HOTCHKISS & CO., 13, COURT-STREET. 1848.

⟨5⟩-88. 10¼″ x 6¾″.

⟨1-5⁸, 6²⟩.

Printed tan paper wrapper.

Listed LW March 4, 1848.

Note: Sabin (in note under entry No. 41399) lists an 1845 edition under the title *Belle of Prairie Eden.* An obvious error since the action of the story takes place during the Mexican War.

HSP LC P UV

11784. PAUL ARDENHEIM, THE MONK OF WISSAHIKON . . .

PHILADELPHIA: T. B. PETERSON, NO. 98 CHESNUT STREET, ONE DOOR ABOVE THIRD. ⟨1848⟩

⟨1⟩-536. 9⅛″ scant x 5⅝″. Vignette title-page inserted.

⟨1⟩-32⁸, 33⁴, ⟨-⟩⁴, 34⁴. Superfluous signature mark 31 on p. 421.

Contemporary notices indicate the book was issued in two paper-covered parts. Examination of the rebound copy at P supports the indication.

Vol. 1 listed LW Nov. 25, 1848. Advertised as in two volumes *Saturday Courier* (Phila.), Nov. 25, 1848. Vol. 1 listed *Saturday Evening Post* (Phila.), Nov. 25, 1848. Reviewed *Godey's Magazine and Lady's Book,* Jan. 1849.

Reprints noted:

A: Publisher's address in imprint: *102 Chesnut Street;* dated: ⟨1848; *i.e.,* not before 1854⟩.

B: Publisher's address in imprint: *306 Chesnut Street;* dated ⟨1848; *i.e.,* not before 1858⟩.

Note: Wright (entry No. 1687) calls for a printing issued under the imprint: *Wissahikon, Penn. 1848.* This may be dismissed as a ghost. The entry was made on the basis of a single copy (Y) made up of a set of Peterson sheets with a fabricated title-leaf.

AAS H OS P

11785. Ladye Annabel; or, the Child of Aldarin

Philadelphia, 1849

An extended version of *The Ladye Annabel* . . . , 1844, 1845.

Not seen. Entry on the basis of notices in Lippard's weekly paper, *The Quaker City,* Jan. 27, 1849; March 17, 1849; March 31, 1849: "It is in many respects, an entirely new work . . . rewritten . . ."

See in *Section II* under ⟨1859⟩ for what is presumed to be a reprint of this revised text.

11786. The Quaker City; or, the Monks of Monk-Hall. A Romance of Philadelphia Life, Mystery, and Crime . . . in Two Volumes . . . ⟨27th Edition⟩

Philadelphia: Published by the Author. And for Sale by All Booksellers. ⟨1845; *i.e.,* 1849⟩

Probably issued in two paper-covered parts. See above under 1844 and 1845 for earlier editions.

Inserted between the title-leaf and p. 3 of some copies is a single leaf imprinted with Lippard's "Preface to the Twenty-Seventh American Edition." Dated at end *Philadelphia, February 22, 1849.*

Reprinted and reissued by T. B. Peterson, Philadelphia, under date ⟨1845⟩; and (later) under date ⟨1876⟩. The Peterson plates were used in the still later printing issued by Leary, Stuart & Company, Philadelphia.

AAS ("Preface" present) P ("Preface" not present)

11787. MEMOIRS OF A PREACHER, A REVELATION OF THE CHURCH AND THE HOME . . .

PHILADELPHIA: JOS. SEVERNS AND COMPANY, 72 CHESNUT STREET, BETWEEN SECOND AND THIRD. ⟨1849⟩

⟨i⟩-viii, ⟨9⟩-94; ⟨leaf, lacking in only examined copy⟩. Frontispiece and vignette title-page inserted. 1 illustration in text. 10⁹⁄₁₆″ x 6⅝″ full. P. 93 paged 9; all thus?

⟨1-6⁸⟩. *Signed:* ⟨1⟩-12⁴. *Note:* Signature mark *10* appears incorrectly as *01*.

Printed tan paper wrapper. *Note:* The only located copy has the statement *Second Edition* on the front wrapper. All thus? It is probable that Lippard considered original periodical publication the first edition; and, the first book appearance the second edition. For evidence of Lippard's thinking in the matter see *Herbert Tracy,* 1844, p. vi.

Noted as *ready* by Lippard's weekly paper, *The Quaker City,* May 12, 1849. Reviewed *Godey's Magazine and Lady's Book,* July, 1849.

UV

11788. THE EMPIRE CITY OR NEW YORK BY NIGHT AND DAY ... ⟨PART 1⟩

PHILADELPHIA, 1849.

Not seen; not located. Entry on the basis of a notice in Lippard's paper, *The Quaker City*, May 19, 1849, offering subscribers *The Empire City* "as far as published in this paper. 100 pages." For earliest located edition see below under 1850.

11789. THE MAN WITH THE MASK; A SEQUEL TO THE MEMOIRS OF A PREACHER ...

PHILADELPHIA: JOS. SEVERNS AND COMPANY, NO. 72 CHESNUT STREET, BETWEEN SECOND AND THIRD. ⟨n.d., 1849⟩

⟨1⟩-⟨107⟩; 4 pp. advertisements. 10⅞" x 6¹³⁄₁₆".

⟨1-7⁸⟩. *Signed:* ⟨1⟩-14⁴. Signature *10* erroneously signed *01*.

Printed tan paper wrapper.

Noted in Lippard's weekly paper *Quaker City*, June 2, 1849, as though published.

UV

11790. THE ENTRANCED; OR, THE WANDERER OF EIGHTEEN CENTURIES ...

PHILADELPHIA: JOSEPH SEVERNS AND COMPANY, 1849.

Not seen; not located. Entry on the basis of Butterfield (No. 15); examination of Mr. Butterfield's incomplete copy of the work; and correspondence with Mr. Butterfield.

Pp. 92. 9" x 5⅝".

Probably issued in printed paper wrapper.

Contents:

"The Entranced"; reprinted in *The White Banner*, 1851, *q.v.*, with slight revisions as "Adonai, the Pilgrim of Eternity."

"Adrian, the Neophyte"; see above under 1843.

"Jesus and the Poor"

"The Heart-Broken"

Advertised for Nov. 3 in Lippard's weekly paper, *Quaker City*, Nov. and Dec. 1849; mentioned in *Quaker City* Jan. 12, 1850, as though published some time previously.

11791. WASHINGTON AND HIS MEN: A NEW SERIES OF LEGENDS OF THE REVOLUTION ...

PHILADELPHIA: JOS. SEVERNS AND COMPANY, 72 CHESNUT STREET, BETWEEN SECOND AND THIRD. ⟨1849⟩

⟨i⟩-⟨x⟩, ⟨11⟩-70; 2 pp. advertisements. Frontispiece. 10½" x 6⅞".

⟨1-4⁸, 5⁴⟩. A fragment of signature mark 3 on p. 17.

Printed brown paper wrapper.

Contains 12 numbered legends, the 11th being misnumbered 10; all thus?

Advertised in Lippard's weekly paper, *The Quaker City*, Nov.–Dec., 1849. For a comment on an extended edition see below under 1850 in the section of reprints (Lippard's own books).

UV

11792. THE EMPIRE CITY OR NEW YORK BY NIGHT AND DAY ...

NEW YORK: STRINGER & TOWNSEND, 222 BROADWAY. 1850.

2 Vols. See above under 1849 for what appears to be prior partial publication.

1: ⟨i⟩-vi, ⟨7⟩-100. 9¾" full x 6³⁄₁₆".

2: ⟨i-iv⟩, ⟨101⟩-203.

1: ⟨1-2⟩, 3-6⁸, ⟨7⟩².

2: ⟨-⟩², ⟨7⟩-8, ⟨9⟩-11, ⟨12⟩⁸, ⟨13⟩⁴.

Note: The title-page for each volume was printed from the same setting; each has the error QUAKEB *for* QUAKER in the list of titles credited to Lippard.

Printed off-white paper wrapper. The wrapper for *Part One* has been noted in two forms; sequence (if any) has not been determined and the designations are for identification only; the following features are sufficient for recognition:

A

Inner front wrapper: *Opinions Of The Press* ...

Outer back wrapper: *Now is the time to Subscribe!!! Lippard's Newspaper. The Quaker City ... New Volume commencing January, 1850* ...

B

Inner front wrapper blank.

Outer back wrapper: *To The Travelling Public. The American Railway Guide ... April, 1850* ...

Advertised LW July 13, 1850. Advertised as *ready* LW Oct. 26, 1850.

AAS (*Part 1* in wrapper A) UP (*Parts 1-2*, lacking wrappers) Y (*Part 1* in wrapper B)

11793. THE KILLERS. A NARRATIVE OF REAL LIFE IN PHILADELPHIA ... BY A MEMBER OF THE PHILADELPHIA BAR.

GEORGE LIPPARD
Entry No. 11784
Reduced
(Harvard University Library)

PHILADELPHIA: PUBLISHED BY HANKINSON AND BARTHOLOMEW. 1850.

Cover-title? Anonymous.

⟨3⟩-50. 9½″ x 6⅛″.

⟨1⟩-3⁸.

Printed paper wrapper? Self-wrapper?

Reissued, with Lippard's name present as author, as *The Bank Director's Son, a Real and Intensely Interesting Revelation of City Life,* Philadelphia, 1851.

HSP UV

11794. The Robbers: By Frederick Schiller, Translated from the German, Chiefly by Henry G. Bohn ... with a Preface by George Lippard.

New York: Stringer & Townsend, 222 Broadway. 1850.

Printed paper wrapper.

"Preface," pp. ⟨v⟩-vi.

UV

11795. The White Banner ... George Lippard, Editor. (Published Quarterly.) Vol. I.

Philadelphia: George Lippard, Publisher, on Behalf of the Shareholders. 1851.

Printed paper wrapper; and, cloth.

A projected periodical. All published.

Also contains a title-page for *Adonai the Pilgrim of Eternity,* Philadelphia: Published by the Author. 1851.

Pp. ⟨1⟩-152, ⟨1⟩-24.

Contents:

"Adonai, the Pilgrim of Eternity." Jackson (p. 148) states "also issued separately"; no such separate has been seen and its existence is doubted. For another version see *The Entranced,* 1849, above.

"The Coming Time"

"Legends of Every Day," comprising 12 pieces.

"Brotherhood versus Atheistic Sectarism," comprising 8 pieces.

"Editorial Department"

"H. F. Constitution of ——— Circle of the Brotherhood of the Union ... ," separately paged: ⟨1⟩-24. Signature mark 20 on p. ⟨1⟩.

Reviewed in *Sartain's Union Magazine of Literature and Art* (Phila.), Sept. 1851.

B HSP UV

11796. NEW YORK: ITS UPPER TEN AND LOWER MILLION ...

CINCINNATI: H. M. RULISON, QUEEN CITY PUBLISHING HOUSE, 278 WESTERN ROW. 1853.

⟨iii⟩-xvi, 21-284, 10 pp. advertisements. 9⅛″ x 5¾″ scant.

⟨1⟩-18⁸.

A cloth: purple; red. Yellow end papers. Flyleaves. Inserted in some copies is a printed slip (6⅛″ x 4⁷⁄₁₆″): *Map Establishment ... E. Mendenhall ... Maps of all other Publishers.*

Deposited Nov. 26, 1853. Advertised in *Daily Cincinnati Gazette,* Nov. 29, 1853, as *just published.*

H NYPL UV

11797. THE MIDNIGHT QUEEN; OR, LEAVES FROM NEW-YORK LIFE ...

NEW-YORK: GARRETT & CO., PUBLISHERS, 18 ANN STREET. ⟨1853⟩

⟨1⟩-110; ⟨2 pp. advertisements?⟩. 9³⁄₁₆″ x 5¾″.

⟨1⟩-7⁸. *Collation in doubt;* 7₈ excised in all copies?

Printed pink paper wrapper.

Two states (printings?) noted:

1: As above. Copyright notice dated 1853 present.

2: As above but does not contain a copyright notice; issued without date. Quite probably a second printing; the only located copy has been tightly rebound and signature collation is not readily ascertainable.

Reprinted and reissued by Dick & Fitzgerald, New York, n.d., not before 1858; copies in AAS, UV.

FLP (dated) **H** (dated) **LC** (dated) **UV** (undated)

11798. Thomas Paine   Author-Soldier of the American Revolution ... Philadelphia, January 25th, 1852 ⟨Edited by James B. Elliott⟩ ...

⟨n.p., n.d., Philadelphia, 1894?⟩

Cover-title. ⟨1⟩-16. 8⁹⁄₁₆″ x 5⅝″. Printed paper wrapper.

Editor's "Biographical Sketch of George Lippard" dated at end: *Philadelphia, Pa., Nov. 15, 1894.*

Lippard gave at least three public lectures on Thomas Paine: Jan. 26, 1846, at the Julianna Street Church, Philadelphia (reported, with extracts, in *Saturday Courier,* Feb. 7, 1846); Jan.

29, 1850, at Arch Street Hall, Philadelphia (text printed in full in Lippard's weekly paper, *Quaker City*, Feb. 9, 1850); and, Jan. 25, 1852, at the Chinese Museum, Philadelphia, before the City Institute.

Elliott (p. ⟨1⟩ of the 1894 publication here collated) identifies the text as that of the 1852 delivery and further states (p. ⟨14⟩) that the text is taken from "the *New Era*, a weekly newspaper published in Philadelphia in 1852." No copy of the *New Era* has been located. The version published in the *New Era* (on the basis of Elliott's 1894 text) varies only slightly from that printed in Lippard's *Quaker City*, Feb. 9, 1850.

Elliott (p. ⟨14⟩) also states that a "portion" of the text was published in Thomas Paine's *The Age of Reason*, Boston (Mendum), 1859. The 1859 copy of the Paine at Yale does not contain the "portion"; it does appear in Mendum's 1860 printing of the book. The Mendum text of Lippard's sketch has also been noted in: *Testimonials to the Merits of Thomas Paine . . . ,*

compiled by Joseph N. Moreau, Boston, 1874, an enlarged edition of an 1861 printing in which the Lippard text does not appear. And in: *A Brief Biography of the Patriot Thomas Paine*, n.p., n.d., *ca.* 1890; title at head of first page of text. The only examined copy of this last (imperfect; hence the title is postulated) is in unprinted paper wrapper; the *Biography* is on pp. ⟨1⟩-5; "Paine's Last Moments" and "Dr. Ladd" are on p. 6; followed by Lippard's sketch (slightly altered) paged ⟨1⟩-6.

All examined texts vary from one another.

The earliest located book appearance of Lippard's comments on Paine is in his *Washington and His Generals*, 1847, pp. 425-448.

According to a card in the Library of Congress catalog there was a printing of Lippard's sketch, *n.p., n.d., 18—, 8 pp.,* under the title *The Author Hero of the American Revolution.* The pamphlet is reported "not found" and is presumed lost.

H   LC

SECTION II

Reprints of Lippard's own books issued under altered titles, altered dates, or both. Obvious reprints omitted.

11799. Dora Livingstone, the Adulteress: Or, the Quaker City ...

London: Published by G. Purkess, Compton Street, Soho; E. Lloyd, 12, Salisbury Square, Fleet-Street; and Sold by All Booksellers. ⟨n.d., 1848⟩

Not seen. Reprint of *The Quaker City* ... , 1844.

11800. Legends of the American Revolution; or, Washington and His Generals ...

Philadelphia: T. B. Peterson and Brothers, 306 Chestnut Street. ⟨1847; *i.e.,* not before 1858⟩

Reprint of *Washington and His Generals* ... , 1847. Printed paper wrapper?

11801. The Fourth of July, 1776, and Herbert Tracy: Two Legends of the Revolution ...

Philadelphia: Jos. Severns and Company, No. 72 Chestnut Street for Sale by Booksellers Generally throughout the United States. ⟨n.d., 1849⟩

Printed tan paper wrapper. Reprint of (respectively) *The Rose of Wissahikon,* 1847; and, *Herbert Tracy,* 1844. Advertised in Lippard's weekly paper, *The Quaker City* (Philadelphia), Nov.–Dec., 1849.

11802. Washington and His Men: A New Series of Legends of the Revolution ...

New York: Stringer & Townsend, 222 Broadway. 1850.

Reprint of the 1849 edition with the addition of two legends, these being *Rose of Wissahikon,* 1847; and, *Herbert Tracy,* 1844, herein titled (respectively) "Legend Thirteenth ..." and "Legend Fourteenth ..."

Printed paper wrapper. Advertised as *now ready* LW Oct. 26, 1850.

11803. The Bank Director's Son, a Real and Intensely Interesting Revelation of City Life ...

Philadelphia; Published by E. E. Barclay and A. R. Orton. 1851.

Printed paper wrapper. Reprint of *The Killers,* 1850.

11804. Mysteries of the Pulpit: Or, a Revelation of the Church and the Home ...

Philadelphia; E. E. Barclay, 283 Market Street. 1851.

Printed paper wrapper? Reprint of *The Memoirs of a Preacher* ... ⟨1849⟩. For reference to another work of the same title (*Mysteries of the Pulpit*), not written by Lippard, see Butterfield, p. 303.

11805. The Nazarene; or, the Last of the Washingtons. A Revelation of Philadelphia, New York, and Washington, in the Year 1844 ...

Philadelphia: T. B. Peterson. No. 102 Chestnut Street. ⟨1854⟩

Printed paper wrapper? Reprint of the 1846 publication. Reprinted and reissued with the publisher's later address in the imprint: *306 Chestnut Street.*

11806. The Ladye of Albarone; or, the Poison Goblet. A Romance of the Dark Ages ...

Philadelphia: T. B. Peterson and Brothers, 306 Chestnut Street ⟨1859⟩

Probably issued as a single volume in cloth; and, two parts in printed paper wrapper. Presumably a reprint of the unlocated *Ladye Annabel* ... , 1849.

11807. The Empire City; or, New York by Night and Day ...

Philadelphia: T. B. Peterson & Brothers, 306 Chestnut Street. ⟨1864⟩

Printed paper wrapper. Advertised as *in press, and nearly ready* APC Sept. 15, 1863.

11808. The Memoirs of a Preacher; or, the Mysteries of the Pulpit ...

413

Philadelphia: T. B. Peterson & Brothers, 306 Chestnut Street. ‹1864›

Reprint of *Memoirs of a Preacher* . . . ‹1849›; and, *Man with the Mask* . . . ‹n.d., 1849›. Printed paper wrapper. Advertised as *in press, and nearly ready* APC Sept. 15, 1863.

11809. The Mysteries of Florence . . .

Philadelphia: T. B. Peterson & Brothers, 306 Chestnut Street. ‹1864›

Cloth; and, printed paper wrapper. Reprint of *The Ladye of Albarone* . . . ‹1859›. Listed ALG Dec. 15, 1864. Reprinted under date ‹1876›. *Note:* DAB erroneously titles this publication *Legends of Florence.*

11810. 'Bel of Prairie Eden. A Romance of Mexico . . .

New-York: Robert M. De Witt, Publisher, No. 33 Rose Street . . . 1870 . . .

Printed paper wrapper. No. 58 in *De Witt's Ten Cent Romances.* See under 1848 for first printing.

11811. The Legends of the American Revolution. "1776." Or, Washington and His Generals . . .

Philadelphia: T. B. Peterson & Brothers; 306 Chestnut Street. ‹1876›

Cloth; and, printed paper wrapper. Reprint of *Washington and His Generals* . . . , 1847. Reprinted and reissued under date ‹1876› by Leary, Stuart & Company, Philadelphia.

11812. Blanche of Brandywine or, September the Eighth to Eleventh, 1777 . . .

Philadelphia: T. B. Peterson & Brothers; 306 Chestnut Street. ‹1876›

Cloth; and, printed paper wrapper. Reprint of *Blanche of Brandywine* . . . , 1846.

11813. The Quaker City; or, the Monks of Monk Hall . . .

Philadelphia: T. B. Peterson & Brothers; 306 Chestnut Street. ‹1876›

Cloth; and (?), printed paper wrapper. Reprint of the *27th Edition* (see under 1849); the "Preface" in this reprint is truncated. Reprinted and reissued under date ‹1876› by Leary, Stuart & Company, Philadelphia.

11814. Washington and His Men. Being the "Second Series" of the Legends of the American Revolution, of "1776." . . .

Philadelphia: T. B. Peterson & Brothers; 306 Chestnut Street. ‹1876›

Cloth; and, printed paper wrapper. Reprint of *Washington and His Men: A New Series* . . . , 1850.

GEORGE LIPPARD

SECTION III

In this section are listed books by authors other than Lippard which contain material by him reprinted from earlier books. See *Section II* for reprints issued under Lippard's name.

One Hundred Choice Selections ... No. 2 ... Compiled ... by Phineas Garrett.

... Philadelphia ... 1869.

"Death-Bed of Benedict Arnold," pp. 107-110. Reprinted from *Washington and His Generals* ... , 1847, pp. 294-296. For fuller description see entry No. 2910.

One Hundred Choice Selections No. 17 ...

... Philadelphia ... 1879.

"Arnold, the Traitor," pp. 161-164. Reprinted from *Washington and His Generals* ... , 1847, pp. 284-286. For fuller description see BAL, Vol. 2, pp. 248-249.

One Hundred Choice Selections No. 19 ...

... Philadelphia ... 1881.

"Heroes of the Land of Penn," pp. 28-31. Reprinted from *Washington and His Generals* ... , 1847, pp. 299-301. For fuller description see entry No. 3392.

Excelsior Recitations and Readings No. 3 ...

New York ... ⟨1884⟩

"The Black Horse and His Rider," pp. 58-60. Reprinted from *Washington and His Generals* ... , 1847, pp. 176-182. For fuller description see BAL, Vol. 2, p. 472.

One Hundred Choice Selections No. 25 ...

... Philadelphia ... 1886.

"The Hero Woman," pp. 110-115. Reprinted from *Washington and His Generals* ... , 1847, pp. 116-119. For fuller description see BAL, Vol. 2, p. 274.

Misattributions, ghosts, ana. Arranged alphabetically by title.

Adventures of the Texas Rangers in the Mexican War, and of the Rancheros under Father Jaranta.

New York, 1849.

No copy traced by BAL and extended search and appropriate inquiry have failed to produce any information. No record in Library of Congress under Lippard's name, under title, or otherwise. Appears as entry No. L-367 in *U.S.Iana (1650–1950) . . .*, compiled by Wright Howes, New York, 1962.

Black Hubert, the Robber of Grasslinn: A Legend of England.

1846.

Advertised in *Public Ledger* (Phila.), Dec. 12, 1846, but no copy traced.

. . . Blanche of Brandywine. An American Patriotic Spectacle. Dramatised for, and Originally Performed at Laura Keene's Theatre, Thursday Evening, April 22, 1858 . . .

. . . 1858 . . . J. G. Burnett . . . New York. New York T. H. French . . . 28 West 23d Street London   Samuel French Publisher   89 Strand

At head of title: French's Standard Drama The Acting Edition. No. CCVI.

Printed paper wrapper. The above is not the earliest printing and is here listed for the record only.

Brotherhood of the Union.

"In 1850 he ⟨Lippard⟩ organized the Brotherhood of the Union, of which he constituted himself the *Supreme Washington,* or head. This organization was an effort to carry into effect his idea of a brotherhood of man, and at the time of his death there were circles, or lodges, of the order in twenty-three states . . ."
—DAB

Lippard was responsible for much of the printed material issued by the order: Notices of meetings, reports, etc., etc., including a prospectus of the order's periodical, *The White Banner.* BAL has made no attempt to describe this ephemeral material, a small collection of which has been preserved in the archives of The Brotherhood of America.

Representative of the material prepared for the order's use is the anonymous *Dedication, Festival and Funeral Ceremonies* ⟨n.p., n.d.⟩; cover-title; pp. 16; printed self-wrapper. A copy is in The Edgar Allan Poe House, Philadelphia.

The Buttonwoods or the Refugees of the Revolution. A Historical Sketch . . . by the Author of "Legends of Revolution." The "Forest Inn," &c. &c.

Philadelphia: Martin E. Harmstead, Publisher & Bookseller, No. 64 North Fifth Street. 1849

Probably issued in printed paper wrapper. Sometimes credited to Lippard. Authorship not known.

Coro, the Priest Robber.

A "play . . . which was not printed; but the story appears in the posthumous volume, *Legends of Florence* (1864)."—DAB. See *Legends of Florence,* below. No story positively identifiable as *Coro . . .* found in *The Mysteries of Florence.*

. . . The Dime Speaker . . . by Louis Legrand, M. D.

New York . . . ⟨1859⟩

"The Glass Railroad," pp. 44-46. *By Lippard?* Published in Lippard's weekly paper, *The Quaker City,* Nov. 3, 1849, with other anecdotes related to Lippard by John Lofland who had recently died. The story is told in the first person, as though by Lofland, who told Lippard it was a "vision" he had while suffering from *delirium tremens.*

For fuller description see entry No. 1523A.

Eleanor; or, Slave Catching in Philadelphia.

1854.

Listed in DAB as though published in book form. No copy traced by BAL. The story appeared serially in *Sunday Mercury* (Phila.), Jan. 29–March 12, 1854.

Legends of Florence.

1864.

A "posthumous volume" according to DAB. An erroneous entry for *The Mysteries of Florence*.

Legends of the Revolution. By Darppil.

1847.

Entry from *Initials and Pseudonyms; a Dictionary of Literary Disguises,* by William Cushing, New York, 1885, p. 78. BAL has found no evidence that Lippard ever used the pseudonym *Darppil. Query:* Is *Darppil* an erroneous transcription of *Drappil?*

Life and Adventures of Charles Anderson Chester, the Notorious Leader of the Philadelphia "Killers." Who Was Murdered, While Engaged in the Destruction of the California House, on Election Night, October 11, 1849.

Printed for the Publishers. Philadelphia. 1850.

Printed paper wrapper. Anonymous. Sometimes attributed to Lippard but Butterfield (interviewed Oct. 22, 1964) asserted "not by Lippard." Possibly based on Lippard's *The Killers . . . ,* 1850, portions of which appear herein.

One Hundred Choice Selections No. 14 . . .

. . . Philadelphia . . . 1877.

"The Glass Railroad," pp. 25-27. See *The Dime Speaker,* above.

For fuller description see BAL, Vol. 2, p. 104.

Posy, or, the Pilgrimage of St. George.

ca. 1846.

Not located as a book. Listed on the title-page of *Blanche of Brandywine,* 1846, as one of Lippard's titles.

The Quaker Soldier: Or, the British in Philadelphia. An Historical Novel . . .

Philadelphia: T. B. Peterson and Brothers, 306 Chestnut Street. ⟨1858⟩

Erroneously attributed to Lippard by Sabin. The author was John Richter Jones.

Three Minute Readings for College Girls Selected and Edited by Harry Cassell Davis . . .

Copyright, 1897 . . . Hinds & Noble, Publishers 4-5-13-14 Cooper Institute New York City

"The Battle of Germantown," pp. 364-367; the first portion extracted from *The Battle-Day of Germantown,* 1843, *Part the Fifth;* the final portion, not found in Lippard's writings, was probably written by the editor of the compilation.

REFERENCES

An Essay on the Writings and Genius of George Lippard. By Rev. C. Chauncey Burr . . .

Philadelphia: George B. Zieber & Co. 1847.

Printed paper wrapper. Appears also in reprints of Lippard's *Washington and His Generals . . . ,* 1847.

"This Essay . . . was furnished . . . as an Introductory Essay to . . . *Washington and His Generals . . .* It has been deemed proper to publish it in the present form, not only as an eloquent and searching vindication of the writings and genius of Mr. Lippard, but as an original work possessing the greatest interest for the general reader . . ."—p. ⟨iv⟩.

The Life and Choice Writings of George Lippard. With a Portrait, and Fac-Simile of a Portion of a Letter Written in the Early Part of His Illness . . .

New York: Published by H. H. Randall, 50 Ann Street. 1855.

Cloth; and, printed paper wrapper. Deposited July 5, 1855.

Anonymous. Possibly by John Bell Bouton.

The Historical Life of Jesus of Nazareth, and Extracts from the Apostolic Age. Given by Themselves through the Inspiration of Olive G. Pettis . . . Volume I.

Providence: A. Crawford Greene, Book and Job Printer, Railroad Halls, 1870.

Binder's title: *Jesus and the Apostolic Age.*

Noted only bound with the following entry.

"Preface," p. ⟨4⟩, "by" George Lippard.

"Sentence by sentence ⟨this book⟩ . . . has been printed before me in bright electric letters ere I consigned ⟨it⟩ . . . to paper . . ." —from the medium's "Introductory."

Errata slip inserted at end.

Further Communications Concerning the Historical Life of Jesus of Nazareth, and Extracts from the Apostolic Age. Given by Themselves through the Inspiration of Olive G. Pettis . . . Volume II.

> Providence: A. Crawford Greene, Book and Job Printer, Railroad Halls. 1871.

> See preceding entry. "The Last Inscription Bearing upon the Age That Brought Light into the World," "by" George Lippard, p. 142.

Fiftieth Annual Session of the Supreme Circle, Brotherhood of the Union, Philadelphia, October 7–11, 1900.

> Published under the Auspices of the Anniversary Committee. ⟨Philadelphia, 1900⟩

> Printed paper wrapper. "George Lippard," by O.W.C. Whinna, pp. 11-23. "Recollections of George Lippard," by J.M.W. Geist, pp. 25-28.

A Bibliography of the Works of George Lippard by Joseph Jackson Reprinted from the Pennsylvania Magazine of History and Biography April, 1930

> Published by the Historical Society of Pennsylvania ⟨Philadelphia, 1930⟩

> Printed paper wrapper. Cover-title.

The Brotherhood of the Rosy Cross The First World Parliament and Meeting of the Council of Seven The Consecration of Washington the Deliverer Fulfilment of the Prophecy

> Published by the Rosicrucian Foundation (Registered) Beverly Hall Quakertown, Pa. ⟨1935⟩

> Edited by R. Swinburne Clymer.

> Contains extracts from *Paul Ardenheim* . . . ⟨1848⟩; and, *Washington and His Generals* . . . , 1847.

George Lippard and His Secret Brotherhood by Roger Butterfield

> Offprint from The Pennsylvania Magazine of History and Biography, Volume LXXIX, Number 3, July, 1955

> Printed paper wrapper. Cover-title. Contains a "Check List of the Separately Published Works of George Lippard."

DAVID ROSS LOCKE

(Petroleum Vesuvius Nasby)

1 8 3 3 – 1 8 8 8

11815. THE NASBY PAPERS. LETTERS AND SERMONS CONTAINING THE VIEWS ON THE TOPICS OF THE DAY, OF PETROLEUM V. NASBY . . .

INDIANAPOLIS, IND.: C. O. PERRINE & CO., PUBLISHERS. 1864.

⟨1⟩-64. 8½″ x 5¼″.

⟨1⟩-4⁸.

Printed paper wrapper; both ecru and yellow noted.

The wrapper has been noted in a variety of forms; probably altered to accommodate individual distributors. The designations are not to be interpreted as suggesting a sequence although it appears safe to assume that *Wrapper A* preceded *Wrapper Aa*.

A

Outer front imprinted: *C. O. Perrine & Co., Indianaolis,* ⟨sic⟩ *Ind.*

Aa

Outer front imprinted: *C. O. Perrine & Co., Indianapolis, Ind.*

B

Outer front imprinted: *T. R. Dawley, New York.*

C

Outer front imprinted: *Randal & Aston, Columbus, O.*

It is entirely probable that the publication was issued with yet other imprints on the wrapper.

Note: A copy of unknown status in LC (not a deposit copy) has been trimmed to 7¾″ scant x 5¹⁄₁₆″. Examination indicates that a buff paper wrapper was once present; and that this original wrapper was replaced by an ecru paper wrapper

imprinted: *Indianapolis, Ind.: C. O. Perrine & Co., Publishers. 1864.* Perhaps a copy (one of many) recalled by the publisher from an agent and offered with a substitute wrapper?

Listed ALG Nov. 1, 1864.

AAS (A, B)   BA (Aa)   H (A)   UV (C)   Y (Aa)

11816. [No. 293.] New England Loyal Publication Society. Office, No. 8 Studio Building, Boston. November 2, 1865 . . .

Single sheet. Printed on recto only.

Contains "Mr. Nasby's Appeal to the Democracy of the North. Saint's Rest . . . Oct. 4, 1865." Collected in *Nasby. Divers Views . . .* , 1866.

BPL   MHS

11817. NASBY. DIVERS VIEWS, OPINIONS, AND PROPHECIES OF YOORS TROOLY PETROLEUM V NASBY . . .

CINCINNATI: R. W. CARROLL & CO., PUBLISHERS, JOS. L. TOPHAM & CO., GENERAL AGENTS, (OPERAHOUSE BUILDING.) 1866.

⟨i⟩-⟨xvi⟩, ⟨25⟩ ⟨sic⟩-424; plus: Publisher's advertisements, paged ⟨1-2⟩, 69-70, 116, 206, 227, 90, 89, 247, 82, 18, 172, 171, unpaged leaf. Illustrated. 8″ x 5⁵⁄₁₆″ (cloth). 7⅞″ x 5″ (leather).

⟨1⟩-26⁸; plus: ⟨-⟩⁸.

C cloth: brownish-purple; purple. Brown-coated on white end papers. Double flyleaves at front and back. Also issued in leather.

Note: Most of the material herein was reprinted in *The Struggles . . .* , 1872, with annotations.

Title deposited Nov. 16, 1865. Listed ALG Jan. 15, 1866. Listed PC March 1, 1866; Bkr March 31, 1866.

NYPL   UV

11818. [No. 312.] New England Loyal Publication Society. Office, No. 8 Studio Building, Boston. May 11, 1866 ...

Single sheet. Printed on recto only.

Contains "Mr. Nasby Sees a Gleam of Light"; a Nasby letter dated April, 1866. Collected in *Swingin round the Cirkle*, 1867.

BPL   H

11819. SWINGING ROUND THE CIRCLE; OR, ANDY'S TRIP TO THE WEST, TOGETHER WITH A LIFE OF ITS HERO. BY PETROLEUM V. NASBY ...

     ... 1866 ... J. C. HANEY & CO. ... THE AMERICAN NEWS COMPANY, AGENTS, 119 & 121 NASSAU STREET. N.Y.

Cover-title.

⟨i-ii⟩, ⟨1⟩-38, 8 pp. advertisements. Illustrated. 7⁹⁄₁₆" x 4½".

⟨-⟩²⁴.

Printed self-wrapper.

P. ⟨13⟩ is a supplementary title-page as follows: ANDROO JOHNSON, HIS LIFE, INCLUDIN' HIS INFANCY, HIS BOYHOOD, AND HIS DIMOCRISY AND ABOLITIONISM, SEPARATE AND MIXED. BY PETROLEUM V. NASBY ... 1866, BY J. C. HANEY & CO. ...

Examination of a large number of copies indicates that this publication was reprinted several (perhaps many) times. Known later printings were issued under the revised title, *Andy's Trip to the West* ... BAL theorizes that the alteration was made in order to prevent confusion with Locke's *Swingin round the Cirkle* ... , Boston: Lee and Shepard, 1867; both were listed in the same issue of ALG: Jan. 15, 1867. For the purposes of this entry copies issued under the known later title (*Andy's Trip to the West*) have been ignored.

Two printings with the title *Swinging round the Circle* have been noted. The designations are for identification only and are not intended to suggest a sequence:

A

Cover-title within a triple-rule box.

The illustration, p. ⟨39⟩ captioned: *The Tragic End.*

B

Cover-title within a double-rule box.

The illustration, p. ⟨39⟩ captioned: *Secrets Worth Knowing* ...

Warning: Another purported printing, with the divisional title-page used as cover-title, has been seen. It was produced by stripping off the original outer leaves (⟨-⟩₁, ₂₄), the remaining leaves refolded to cause the divisional title-page to appear as the cover-title. In this fabricated form the pagination is: ⟨13⟩-38; advertisements, pp. ⟨39-44⟩; illustrations, pp. ⟨45-56⟩.

AAS (B)   H (B)   UV (A)   Y (B)

11820. "SWINGIN ROUND THE CIRKLE." BY PETROLEUM V. NASBY ... HIS IDEAS OF MEN, POLITICS, AND THINGS, AS SET FORTH IN HIS LETTERS TO THE PUBLIC PRESS, DURING THE YEAR 1866 ...

BOSTON: LEE AND SHEPARD. 1867.

⟨1⟩-299. Frontispiece and 7 plates inserted. 7½" x 4⅞".

⟨1-11¹², 12-14⁶⟩. *Signed:* ⟨1⟩-18⁸, 19⁶.

C cloth: green; purple; terra-cotta. Yellow end papers. Flyleaves.

A copy at BA received Dec. 24, 1866. Deposited Jan. 1, 1867. Listed ALG Jan. 15, 1867.

AAS   H   NYPL

11821. EKKOES FROM KENTUCKY. BY PETROLEUM V. NASBY ... BEIN A PERFECT RECORD UV THE UPS, DOWNS, AND EXPERIENCES UV THE DIMOCRISY, DOORIN THE EVENTFUL YEAR 1867, EZ SEEN BY A NATURALIZED KENTUCKIAN ...

BOSTON: LEE AND SHEPARD. 1868.

⟨1⟩-324. Frontispiece and 7 plates inserted. 7½" x 4¾".

⟨1-11¹², 12⁶, 13-14¹²⟩. *Signed:* ⟨1⟩-19, ⟨20⟩⁸, 21².

C cloth: green. RH cloth: purple. Yellow end papers. Flyleaves.

Noted for *December* ALG Nov. 1, 1867. A copy in H inscribed by early owner Dec. 25, 1867. Listed ALG Jan. 15, 1868. Advertised and listed Bkr April 1, 1868. Listed PC April 15, 1868. Deposited April 21, 1868.

AAS   H   NYPL   Y

11822. ... THE IMPENDIN CRISIS UV THE DIMOCRACY ... BY PETROLEUM V. NASBY ...

TOLEDO, OHIO: MILLER, LOCKE & CO., 1868.

Cover-title. *Note:* It is probable that copies first printed have the following at head of title: *Price 10 Cents—A Liberal Discount to the Trade.* Copies occur without the statement.

⟨1⟩-23; advertisements, p. ⟨24⟩. 7¾″ x 4¹³⁄₁₆″.
⟨-⟩¹².

Printed self-wrapper.

Note: Also occurs with the imprint: *American News Co., 119 & 121 Nassau Street, New York.* Also issued with the imprint of other distributors?

Issued not before Aug. 10, 1868, the date of the author's dedication, p. ⟨2⟩.

LC MHS

11823. NASBY ON DIXON. MR. NASBY GOES TO CONNECTICUT TO ASSIST ONE OF A. JOHNSON'S ESPECIAL FRIENDS, VIZ., DIXON—HE ESSAYS A SPEECH, OF WHICH ONLY A SMALL PORTION IS DELIVERED . . .

⟨n.p., n.d., 1869?⟩

Caption-title. The above at head of text.

Single cut sheet. Printed on recto only. 11¹⁵⁄₁₆″ x 8¹⁵⁄₁₆″.

At head of first column: *Confedrit X Roads . . . March 9, 1869.*

AAS   Union College (Schenectady, N.Y.)

11824. Th: Nast's Illustrated Almanac for 1872 . . .

. . . 1871 . . . Harper & Brothers . . . ⟨New York⟩

"The Early Training of Nasby," p. 40. This is another version of a story told in *"In Search of the Man of Sin; a Lecture Delivered in Music Hall, Boston, Dec. 29, 1870"* in *The Struggles . . . ,* 1872.

For fuller entry see No. 3332.

11825. LYCEUM MAGAZINE. OCTOBER, 1871.] BOSTON LYCEUM BUREAU. [EXTRA LEAF. D. R. LOCKE. (NASBY.) WE RECEIVE FROM OUR CORRESPONDENTS FREQUENT INQUIRIES AS TO NASBY'S NEW LECTURE:—"THE MISSION OF SKINENOYH." . . .

REDPATH & FALL, BOSTON LYCEUM BUREAU, 36 BROMFIELD ST., BOSTON.

Single leaf. Printed on recto only. 10¹⁄₁₆″ x 6¼″ scant.

Contains a synopsis of the lecture divided into twelve numbered parts. The introductory statement indicates that the synopsis was written by Locke: "We have repeatedly asked our famous client to furnish us with a syllabus . . . or to

loan us the manuscript . . . Wearied out by our importunities, the Postmaster ⟨*i.e.,* Locke⟩ has at last sent us the following sketch of it . . ."

Note: There is every likelihood that this is representative of other similar promotional pieces issued by Locke's lecture agents.

AAS

11826. THE STRUGGLES (SOCIAL, FINANCIAL AND POLITICAL) OF PETROLEUM V. NASBY . . . EMBRACING HIS TRIALS AND TROUBLES, UPS AND DOWNS, REJOICINGS AND WAILINGS; LIKEWISE HIS VIEWS OF MEN AND THINGS. TOGETHER WITH THE LECTURES "CUSSID BE CANAAN," "THE STRUGGLES OF A CONSERVATIVE WITH THE WOMAN QUESTION," AND "IN SEARCH OF THE MAN OF SIN." . . .

BOSTON: I. N. RICHARDSON AND COMPANY. 1872.

⟨1⟩-720; plus: advertisements, pp. 721-727. Portrait frontispiece, presentation leaf, and 23 plates inserted. 8¾″ x 5⅞″.

⟨-⟩⁴, ⟨1⟩⁴, 2-45⁸; plus: ⟨46⟩⁴.

FL cloth: green. Brown-coated end papers. Fly-leaves.

Two printings noted:

1

Collation as above.

Frontispiece does not have imprint: *Daniels, Pr. Boston.*

Title on spine: THE STRUGGLES OF / ⟨etc., etc.⟩

2

⟨1⟩-45⁸; plus: ⟨46⟩⁴.

On frontispiece: *Daniels, Pr. Boston.*

Title on spine: STRUGGLES / OF / ⟨etc., etc.⟩

In addition to much added material, reprints with commentary, most of the text of *Divers Views . . . ,* 1866.

Deposited June 1, 1872. A copy at B (1st printing) inscribed by early owner June 19, 1872.

B (1st)   H (1st)   Y (2nd)

11827. That Convention; or, Five Days a Politician. By F.G.W.—et als . . .

New York and Chicago: F. G. Welch & Co., Publishers. Agents for Supplying the Trade: American News Company . . . New England News Co. . . . Western News Co. . . . 1872.

Cloth; and, printed paper wrapper.

"Rev. Petroleum V. Nasby Converts the 'Corners' to the 'Cabbage Candidate'," pp. <159>-165. Dated *Confedrit X Roads ... May 8, 1872.*

Note: The F.G.W. given as editor is probably the F. G. Welch of the imprint, but further information is wanting. The copyright records do not disclose F.G.W.'s identity.

Deposited July 2, 1872.

H (wrapper)   NYPL (cloth)   UV (cloth)

11828. EASTERN FRUIT ON WESTERN DISHES BY PETROLEUM V. NASBY ...

LONDON   GEORGE ROUTLEDGE AND SONS   THE BROADWAY, LUDGATE <1875>

For American edition see next entry.

<1>-157; printer's imprint, p. <158>; 2 pp. advertisements. 6⅜" full x 4¹⁄₁₆".

<A>-I, K⁸.

Printed yellow boards. White end papers printed with advertisements.

Listed Ath April 3, 1875; PC April 16, 1875. Noticed Ath April 24, 1875.

UV

11829. EASTERN FRUIT ON WESTERN DISHES. THE MORALS OF ABOU BEN ADHEM. EDITED BY D. R. LOCKE ...

BOSTON: LEE AND SHEPARD, PUBLISHERS. NEW YORK: LEE, SHEPARD, AND DILLINGHAM. 1875.

First American edition. For prior publication see preceding entry.

<i>-viii, <9>-231; blank, p. <232>; 7 pp. advertisements. 7½" x 4⅞". Noted on laid paper; and, on wove paper. On the basis of type wear copies on laid paper appear to have been first printed. Do the two types of paper represent two printings? The surviving deposit copy is on laid paper; a copy in H, received May 10, 1875, is also on laid paper.

<1-10>¹². *Signed:* <1-2>, 3-5, <6-11>, 12-15⁸.

C cloth: brown; green; red-orange; terra-cotta. Brown-coated end papers. Flyleaves.

Note: The following errors are present in all examined copies, including a reprint issued under date <1875; *i.e.,* not before 1885>:

P. 69, line 10: *... as as he ...*

P. 123, line 8 up: *a kopack ...* for *a kopeck ...*

A copy at H (laid paper) received May 10, 1875. Deposited (laid paper) May 20, 1875. Listed PW May 22, 1875. A copy at BA (laid paper) received June 11, 1875.

AAS (laid)   BA (laid)   H (both)   LC (laid)   NYPL (wove)   Y (wove)

11830. Lotos Leaves . . . Edited by John Brougham and John Elderkin . . .

Boston: William F. Gill and Company, Late Shepard and Gill, 151 Washington Street. 1875.

"The Truthful Resolver," pp. <159>-167.

For comment see entry No. 3363.

11831. INFLATION AT THE CROSS ROADS, BEING A HISTORY OF THE RISE AND FALL OF THE ONLIMITED TRUST AND CONFIDENCE COMPANY, OF CONFEDRIT X ROADS. IN A SERIES OF FIVE LETTERS, BY PETROLEUM V. NASBY ...

NEW YORK: AMERICAN NEWS COMPANY. 1875. PRICE, TEN CENTS.

Cover-title.

<1>-24. Illustrated. 7⁷⁄₁₆" x 5".

<->¹².

Printed paper wrapper: blue; green; mauve; salmon; yellow.

Deposited Nov. 23, 1875. See next entry for an extended edition.

AAS   H   LC   UV   Y

11832. . . . Nasby on Inflation.   A New Comic Book . . .

Philadelphia: Published by Barclay & Co., No. 21 North Seventh Street. <1875>

At head of title: Deep-Seated Mirth Holds a Place in Every Line.

An edition of *Inflation at the Cross Roads* (see preceding entry), extended by the addition of a preliminary and a terminal letter.

Printed paper wrapper.

Deposited Jan. 24, 1876.

AAS   Y

11832A. PETROLEUM V. NASBY'S "FOUNTIN UV YOUTH," AS DISCOVERED BY HIM IN NEW YORK CITY.

MIRROR PRESS, MANCHESTER, N.H. <n.d., *ca.* 1875>

The above on p. <1>.

Single cut sheet folded to four pages.

<1-4>. 4⁵⁄₁₆" full x 2¾".

Lyceum Magazine.

OCTOBER, 1871.]   BOSTON LYCEUM BUREAU.   [EXTRA LEAF.

D. R. LOCKE.

(NASBY.)

We receive from our correspondents frequent inquiries as to NASBY's new lecture: — "THE MISSION OF SKINENOYH."

We have repeatedly asked our famous client to furnish us with a syllabus of it, or to loan us the manuscript, so that we might speak of it from our own knowledge. Wearied out by our importunities, the Postmaster has at last sent us the following sketch of it, which may probably be of interest to our correspondents: —

THE MISSION OF SKINENOYH.

I.—A short account of the Indian mode of life, by one best fitted to give it, as he knows nothing about it.

II.—Skinenoyh, a noble red man, desirous to see for himself the superiority of the white men, determines to go among them.

III.—The way the Comanches raised funds to send him, viz: — Fairs, Tableaux, Entertainments, &c.

IV.—He strikes civilization at Kansas, and gets some ideas from land agents.

V.—He investigates grain gambling at Chicago.

VI.—Business in New York.

VII.—Politics in the rural districts.

VIII.—Society in general.

IX.—A comparison of the Comanche girl and the pale-face girl.

X.—A general comparison of the merits of the two peoples.

XI.—He balances accounts, and decides that instead of endeavoring to make the Comanche like the white man, it would be better to make the white man like the Comanche, and goes home a wiser and sadder Indian.

XII.—Moral reflections!

It will be seen that this lecture affords to "Nasby" the finest opportunities for the exercise of his great genius for exposing, with an ironical, but ever-genial pen, the shams and humbugs of politics and social life. While we cannot speak of the lecture as a whole, it is safe to say that the conception is much happier than that of any of his previous efforts, and no one who is familiar with his published writings can doubt that the execution will be worthy of the plan. Indeed, from scattered passages of it, we have no hesitation in predicting that it will be vastly superior, both as a literary production and for humor, to any of his other lectures.

As Mr. Locke can not give so large a portion of his time to lecturing this season, our correspondents who wish to secure him will very greatly oblige us by sending in their applications and fixing their dates at once.

Terms, from $110 to $150.

Address,   REDPATH & FALL,
                              BOSTON LYCEUM BUREAU,
                                36 BROMFIELD ST., BOSTON.

Issued as an advertisement for *Barrett's Hair Restorative,* a hair dye.

H

11833. Salt River Guide Pictorial ...

⟨n.p., n.d., New York, 1876⟩

Cover-title. Printed self-wrapper. An anti-Tammany news sheet.

A Nasby letter, dated Sept. 22, 1876, pp. 24-25.

AAS

11834. THE PRESIDENT'S POLICY BEING AN EXPOSITION OF THE SAME FROM THE STAND-POINT OF THE CONFEDRIT X ROADS, IN THE FORM OF SIX LETTERS FROM THE PEN OF THE PHILOSOPHICAL PETROLEUM V. NASBY ...

TOLEDO, O.: BLADE COMPANY. 1877.

Cover-title.

⟨1⟩-23. 8″ x 5⅜″.

⟨-⟩¹².

Printed gray paper wrapper.

Nasby's letter dated *Jooly 20, 1877.*

UMi

11835. ... FINANCE AND COMMUNISM. THE BROADSIDE EXTRA ...

⟨n.p., 1878?⟩

At head of title: PETROLEUM V. NASBY

Single sheet. Printed on recto only. 24⅛″ x 18⅝″.

Prints seven Nasby letters: *Jooly 1, 1878; Jooly 16, 1878; Jooly 29, 1878; August 12, 1878; August 19, 1878; Sept. 1, 1878; Sept. 15, 1878.* All but the Aug. 12, 1878 letter are collected in *The Nasby Letters* ⟨1893⟩.

AAS H Y

11836. The Broadside ... Vol. 1. October 23, 1878. No. 21 ...

⟨n.p., 1878⟩

Single sheet. Printed on recto only. Printed in 7 columns, newspaper fashion.

Contains "Mr. Nasby's Last Experience with Fiat Money," dated Oct. 15, 1878. Collected in *The Nasby Letters* ⟨1893⟩.

AAS

11837. A PAPER CITY ...

BOSTON: LEE AND SHEPARD, PUBLISHERS. NEW YORK CHARLES T. DILLINGHAM. 1879.

⟨1⟩-431. 7½″ x 5″.

⟨1-18⟩¹². *Signed:* ⟨1⟩-27⁸.

C cloth: brown; red-orange. P cloth: green. S cloth: blue-gray; brown; green; mauve. Brown-coated end papers. Cream end papers. Flyleaves.

Listed PW Dec. 21, 1878.

AAS H NYPL

11838. Dick's Recitations and Readings No. 10 ... Edited by Wm. B. Dick ...

New York: Dick & Fitzgerald, Publishers, No. 18 Ann Street ⟨1879⟩

"Hannah Jane," pp. 175-178. For formal publication see under 1882.

For comment see entry No. 5538.

11839. THE DEMOCRATIC JOHN BUNYAN BEING ELEVEN DREAMS BY REV. PETROLEUM V. NASBY. SHOWING WHAT IS VERY LIKELY TO HAPPEN IN THE EVENT OF THE ELECTION OF HANCOCK AND ENGLISH.

TOLEDO, OHIO: TOLEDO BLADE COMPANY, 1880.

⟨1⟩-24. Illustrated. 7¾″ x 5³⁄₁₆″ full.

⟨-⟩¹².

Printed blue-gray paper wrapper.

AAS LC Y

11840. THE DIARY OF AN OFFICE SEEKER BEING A RECORD OF THE EXPERIENCE OF THOMAS JEFFERSON WATKINS, (WHO WANTED AN OFFICE, AND LABORED FOR ONE, BUT DIDN'T GET IT,) IN THE FIELD OF POLITICS. EDITED BY D. R. LOCKE ...

TOLEDO, OHIO: BLADE COMPANY, PUBLISHERS. 1881.

⟨i⟩-viii, 9-31, advertisement, p. 32. 6⅞″ scant x 5⅝″.

⟨-⟩¹⁶. *Signed:* ⟨1⟩-2⁸.

Printed blue-gray paper wrapper.

Deposited March 28, 1881.

LC

11841. HANNAH JANE ...

BOSTON LEE AND SHEPARD PUBLISHERS NEW YORK CHARLES T. DILLINGHAM 1882

For prior publication see *Dick's Recitations and Readings No. 10 . . .* ⟨1879⟩.

⟨1-31⟩; advertisements, p. ⟨32⟩. Illustrated. 8″ x 6⅜″.

⟨1-4⟩⁴.

P cloth: brown; green; mustard; olive; red; yellow. Covers bevelled. White end papers printed in brown; or gray, with a floral design. Double flyleaves. Edges gilded.

Note: Reprinted under date ⟨1881⟩.

Deposited Oct. 12, 1881. Listed PW Nov. 12, 1881.

AAS H LC UV

11842. NASBY IN EXILE: OR, SIX MONTHS OF TRAVEL IN ENGLAND, IRELAND, SCOTLAND, FRANCE, GERMANY, SWITZERLAND AND BELGIUM, WITH MANY THINGS NOT OF TRAVEL . . .

TOLEDO AND BOSTON: LOCKE PUBLISHING COMPANY. 1882.

⟨i⟩-⟨xvi⟩, ⟨17⟩-672. Illustrated. 8⅝″ x 5⅞″.

⟨1⟩-42⁸.

C cloth: brown. P cloth: brown. Brown-coated end papers. Flyleaves. Also issued in leather according to PW listing July 1, 1882.

Two styles of binding noted; simultaneously issued? The following variation is sufficient for ready recognition. The designations are for identification only and are not intended to suggest a sequence:

A: Front stamped in black and gold.

B: Front stamped in blind only.

Two editions noted:

1

As above.

2

⟨i-iv⟩, ⟨17⟩-⟨370⟩, 461-672; blank leaf. Illustrated. 8″ x 5″.

⟨1², 2-18¹⁶, 19⁸, 20⁴⟩. Irregularly signed in 8.

The hiatus in the pagination caused by the omission of Chaps. 25-29, a section devoted to an intemperate criticism of royalty, of English treatment of Ireland, etc.

V cloth: green-yellow. Sides trimmed to size of leaf. Front stamped in black, binding otherwise unstamped. Leaves ⟨1⟩₁ and ⟨20⟩₄ used as pastedowns.

Issued simultaneously with the first edition? Or, perhaps, some years later? The "new edition" listed in PW April 28, 1888, with Lee & Shepard,

Boston, given as publisher, is priced at $2.50 which price suggests a book far more elaborate than the second edition.

Listed PW July 1, 1882. Deposited April 5, 1883.

BA H JB (second edition) NYPL UV

11843. Wit and Humor of the Age . . . by Mark Twain, Robt. J. Burdette, Josh Billings, Alex. Sweet, Eli Perkins. With the Philosophy of Wit and Humor, ⟨Edited⟩ by Melville D. Landon . . .

Chicago: Western Publishing House. 1883.

"Nasby on Temperance," pp. 478-479.

"Nasby's Love Story," pp. 702-703.

For comment see entry No. 11220.

11844. BEER AND THE BODY. TESTIMONY OF PHYSICIANS AGAINST THIS GREAT EVIL   FROM THE TOLEDO BLADE . . .

NEW YORK: THE NATIONAL TEMPERANCE SOCIETY AND PUBLICATION HOUSE 58 READE STREET. 1884.

Cover-title.

⟨1⟩-24. 7⅜″ x 4⅞″.

⟨-⟩¹².

Printed pale faun paper wrapper.

AAS H

11845. What the Temperance Century Has Made Certain . . . with a Symposium of Suggestions, for the New Century. By Rev. Wilbur Fisk Crafts . . .

Funk & Wagnalls. New York: 18 and 20 Astor Place. London: 44 Fleet Street. Copyright, 1885.

Cloth; and, printed paper wrapper.

Letter on temperance, in reply to a circular letter, p. 171.

NYPL

11846. Reminiscences of Abraham Lincoln . . . Collected and Edited by Allen Thorndike Rice . . .

New York North American Publishing Company 30 Lafayette Place 1886

Cloth; sheep; half morocco; and, full morocco.

"David R. Locke," *i.e.,* Locke's reminiscences, pp. ⟨439⟩-453.

Listed PW June 26, 1886.

H NYPL

11847. PROHIBITION.

Two printings noted. The sequence not known and the designations are for identification only. Locke's article first appeared in the *North American Review,* October, 1886.

Printing A

PROHIBITION ... REPRINTED BY SPE-CIAL PERMISSION FROM THE "NORTH AMERICAN REVIEW."

NEW YORK: THE NATIONAL TEMPERANCE SOCIETY AND PUBLICATION HOUSE, 58 READE STREET. 1886.

⟨1⟩-22, 2 pp. advertisements. 6¹⁵⁄₁₆″ x 4⅝″.

⟨-⟩¹².

Printed peach paper wrapper.

Printing B

PETROLEUM V. NASBY,—ON—PROHIBI-TION (FROM NORTH AMERICAN RE-VIEW.) ...

⟨n.p., n.d., 1886?⟩

Caption-title. The above at head of p. ⟨1⟩.

Single cut sheet folded to make 4 pages. Un-paged. Page: 11⅞″ x 9⁹⁄₁₆″.

Note: Not to be confused with the next entry.

AAS (B)   NYPL (A)

11848.   NO. 274.   HIGH LICENSE DOES NOT DIMINISH THE EVIL. [EXTRACT FROM AN ARTICLE IN THE NORTH AMERICAN REVIEW ...

⟨NEW YORK: NATIONAL TEMPERANCE SOCIETY AND PUBLICATION HOUSE, NO. 58 READE STREET, NEW YORK, n.d., 1887?⟩

Caption-title. The above at head of p. ⟨1⟩; im-print at foot of p. ⟨4⟩.

Single cut sheet folded to make 4 pages. Paged: ⟨1⟩-4. Leaf: 7⅜″ x 4½″.

A partial printing of Locke's article in NAR Sept. 1887. Not to be confused with the preceding en-try.

H (received April 8, 1889)

11849. THE DEMAGOGUE   A POLITICAL NOVEL ...

BOSTON   1891   LEE AND SHEPARD PUBLISHERS 10 MILK ST., NEXT "THE OLD SOUTH MEETING HOUSE"   NEW YORK   CHARLES T. DILLINGHAM 718 AND 720 BROADWAY

⟨i-ii⟩, ⟨i⟩-iv, ⟨1⟩-465; blank, p. ⟨466⟩, 8 pp. advertisements. 7⁵⁄₁₆″ x 5″.

⟨1-30⟩⁸.

BF cloth: brown. H cloth: brown; red; P cloth: blue. S cloth: olive. Wove paper flyleaves; also, laid paper flyleaf at front, wove paper flyleaf at back. Tan end papers printed in tan with a floral pattern.

Deposited Oct. 31, 1890. Advertised PW Nov. 22/29, 1890. Listed PW Dec. 6, 1890.

LC   UV

11850. The Temperance Platform ... Compiled by Miss L. Penney ...

New York: The National Temperance Society and Publication House, No. 58 Reade Street. 1892.

Printed paper wrapper.

"Pulverize the Rum Power," pp. 47-48.

NYPL

11851. THE NASBY LETTERS. BEING THE ORIGINAL NASBY LETTERS, AS WRITTEN DURING HIS LIFETIME ...

TOLEDO, OHIO: THE TOLEDO BLADE CO.   ⟨1893⟩

Three printings noted:

1

⟨1⟩-512. Facsimile, p. ⟨16⟩; portrait of Locke, p. ⟨508⟩. 8¹⁄₁₆″ x 5″ scant.

⟨1-16⟩¹⁶.

V cloth: tan, mounted on boards, trimmed to size of leaf.

2

⟨1⟩-510; pp. ⟨511-512⟩ used as terminal paste-down. Portrait of Locke inserted as frontispiece; facsimile, p. ⟨16⟩.

⟨1-16⟩¹⁶. ⟨16⟩₁₆ used as pastedown.

V cloth: green-yellow; tan.

3

⟨i-ii⟩, ⟨1⟩-510. Portrait of Locke, p. ⟨ii⟩; fac-simile, p. ⟨16⟩. *Note:* The portrait is printed on an integral leaf.

⟨1-16⟩¹⁶.

V cloth: blue-green.

A selection of letters previously in book form together with "those of later years, up to the final one ever written."—p. ⟨2⟩.

AAS (2nd)   H (2nd)   UV (1st; 3rd)

11852. Voigtländer and I in Pursuit of Shadow Catching ... by James F. Ryder

Cleveland, O.: The Cleveland Printing & Pub-lishing Co. The Imperial Press   1902

Letter to J. F. Ryder, dated January 8, 1866, pp. 243-244.

Deposited Oct. 28, 1902. Listed PW Dec. 6, 1902.

H

11853. ... Masterpieces of Wit and Humor with Stories and an Introduction by Robert J. Burdette ...

⟨n.p.⟩ Copyright, 1902, by E. J. Long

"Nasby Makes a Mistake," pp. 105-106 is a version of "Mr. Nasby Regulates a School," in *The Struggles* ... , 1872.

"Discussing the Woman Question," pp. 226-229 is extracted from "The Struggles of a Conservative with the Woman Question" in *The Struggles* ... , 1872.

"Did Not Want Much," p. 413. Elsewhere unlocated.

"Don't Know Enough to Vote," p. 423. Elsewhere unlocated in Locke's works. *By Locke?* For another version, with a different cast of characters, see "Ignorant Women," anonymous, in Melville D. Landon, *Wit and Humor of the Age,* 1883, pp. 442-443.

For comment see entry No. 2013.

11854. ... Civil War Letters of Petroleum V. Nasby Compiled, with an Introduction, by Harvey S. Ford

Ohio State University Press for the Ohio Historical Society ⟨1962⟩

At head of title: Ohio Civil War Centennial Commission

Printed paper wrapper.

Publications of the Ohio Civil War Centennial Commission, No. 8.

Contains a selection of letters reprinted from *The Struggles* ... , 1872; and, first located book appearance of "Secession in a New Spot," pp. 7-9. According to the editor this last "first appeared in the *Bucyrus Journal,* December 13, 1860." In revised form it appeared in *Divers Views,* 1866, under the title "Wingert's Corners Secedes."

BPL   H

DAVID ROSS LOCKE

SECTION II

Reprints of Locke's own books; and, books containing reprinted Locke material but with Locke's name on the title-page. For a list of books by authors other than Locke containing reprinted Locke material see *Section III*.

11855. The Nasby Papers. By Petroleum V. Nasby ...

London: Frederick Warne and Co., Bedford Street, Covent Garden. 1865.

Pictorial wrapper. Publisher's "Preface" dated Aug. 1865. Listed PC Sept. 15, 1865; Bkr Sept. 30, 1865.

11856. The Nasby Papers. By Petroleum V. Nasby ...

London: S. O. Beeton, 248, Strand, W. C. 1865.

Printed paper wrapper. On back wrapper is an extract from Ath of Oct. 21, 1865. Reviewed Bkr Oct. 31, 1865.

11857. The Nasby Papers by Petroleum V. Nasby ... with an Introduction by George Augustus Sala   Original Stereotyped Edition

London   Ward, Lock, and Tyler   158 Fleet Street   MDCCCLXV

Printed paper wrapper. Issued in the *Sixpenny Volume Library*. Listed PC Nov. 15, 1865; again, with added note regarding Sala's introduction, Dec. 8, 1865.

11858. The Nasby Papers by Petroleum V. Nasby ... with an Introduction by George Augustus Sala ...

London   Ward, Lock, and Tyler   158 Fleet Street   MDCCCLXVI

Listed PC March 15, 1866; Bkr March 31, 1866; as in printed paper wrapper in the *Sixpenny Volume Library* series.

11859. *Entry cancelled.*

Nasby's Life of Andy Jonsun ...

New York ... ⟨1866; *i.e.*, 1869⟩

See below under ⟨1869⟩.

11860. The Nasby Papers. (Southern Humour.) By Petroleum V. Nasby ... Author's Unabridged Edition

London: George Routledge and Sons, The Broadway, Ludgate ⟨n.d., 1868⟩

Two printings noted:

1: As above. Imprint of *Levey and Co., Printers* on reverse of the title-leaf and at foot of p. 88. Probably issued in printed paper wrapper.

2: As above. Imprint of *George Levey* on reverse of title-leaf and at foot of p. 88. Noted in printed paper wrapper.

Listed Bkr July 1, 1868.

11861. Nasby's Life of Andy Jonsun ... by Petroleum V. Nasby ...

New York: Jesse Haney & Co., Publishers, No. 119 Nassau Street. ⟨1866; *i.e.*, 1869⟩

Cover-title. Printed paper wrapper. *Note:* Another printing has no imprint on the front of wrapper and varies in other features; sequence not determined. Reprint of *Swinging round the Circle; or, Andy's Trip to the West* ... , 1866.

11862. The Moral History of America's Life-Struggle ... Sold Only by Subscription ...

Boston, Mass.: I. N. Richardson and Company. St. Louis, Mo.: Etna Publishing Co. ⟨1874⟩

Cloth; and, leather. "Three editions of this work were issued under the title of *The Struggles of Petroleum V. Nasby*, and a fourth was nearly ready, when the fire-fiend, so active of late in this city, ⟨Boston⟩ consumed it. In re-issuing the work, after its baptism of fire, a new title has been adopted, more suggestive of its true import and contents ..."—from the "Publishers' Preface," p. ⟨4⟩.

11863. Nasby as a Banker   Inflation at the Cross Roads ... by Petroleum V. Nasby ...

Toledo: Toledo Blade Co., 1880 ...

Cover-title. Printed paper wrapper. Reprint of *Inflation at the Cross Roads*, 1875.

11864. ... The Nasby Papers   Southern Humour.

London: George Routledge & Sons. ⟨n.d., 1888⟩

Cover-title. At head: *Price Sixpence, Complete.* Pictorial paper wrapper. *Note:* The only located copy lacks the title-page.

11865. ... Kings of the Platform and Pulpit by Melville D. Landon ... and Lectures of ... Nasby ...

Chicago   F. C. Smedley & Co., Publishers. 1890

"Nasby's Lecture on the Woman Question," pp. 100-120; extracted from "The Struggles of a Conservative with the Woman Question," in *The Struggles* ... , 1872.

"Nasby's Best Story," pp. 120-122; a version of "Mr. Nasby Regulates a School," in *The Struggles* ... , 1872.

For comment see BAL, Vol. 2, p. 249.

11866. Present Problems ... December 15, 1896 ... Petroleum V. Nasby on Silver ...

Present Problems Publ. Co. 57 Park Place, New York City ...

Cover-title. Printed paper wrapper. Vol. 1, No. 10 of the series. Reprinted from *The Nasby Letters* ⟨1893⟩.

11867. American Lecturers and Humorists by Melville D. Landon ... and Lectures of ... Nasby ... and Others ...

The Saalfield Publishing Company   Akron, Ohio   New York ⟨1906⟩

For comment see entry No. 11240.

11868. ... Let's Laugh ⟨by⟩ Petroleum V. Nasby Edited ... by Lloyd E. Smith

Haldeman-Julius Company   Girard, Kansas ⟨1924⟩

At head of title: *Little Blue Book No. 20 Edited by E. Haldeman-Julius* Printed paper wrapper. "The present volume is a selection from the various newspaper letters ... These letters were afterwards collected and published in volumes bearing various titles ..."—p. 4. Deposited Jan. 24, 1925.

Note: Another printing (with the editor's name and prefatory note not present) was issued as *Ten Cent Pocket Series*, No. 20; Haldeman-Julius Company, Girard, Kansas ⟨n.d.⟩; sequence not determined. A copy in H received in 1932.

DAVID ROSS LOCKE

SECTION III

In this section are listed books by authors other than Locke which contain material by him reprinted from earlier books. See *Section II* for a list of collections of reprinted material issued under Locke's name.

Yankee Drolleries . . .

> London . . . 1866.
>
> For comment see entry No. 1542.

Yankee Drolleries . . . Complete Editions, with Introductions by George Augustus Sala.

> London: John Camden Hotten, 74, Piccadilly. ‹n.d., 1868›
>
> An omnibus volume made up of earlier separate publications, each with its own title-page. Contains *The Nasby Papers* ‹n.d., 1868›; see above in *Section II*. Listed Bkr April 1, 1868; advertised as though published PC April 1, 1868.

The Treasure-Trove Series. (The Choicest Humor by the Great Writers.) Story . . .

> Boston: William F. Gill and Company. 1875.
>
> Cloth? A copy in BA received Dec. 1, 1875.

Yankee Drolleries. The Most Celebrated Works of the Best American Humourists . . . with Introductions by George Augustus Sala.

> London: Chatto and Windus, Piccadilly. 1876.

Fenno's Favorites . . . ‹Compiled› by Frank H. Fenno . . . ‹No. 1›

> Philadelphia . . . ‹1884›
>
> For comment see entry No. 11193.

Half-Hours with Best Humorous Authors. Selected . . . by Charles Morris . . . American.

> Philadelphia . . . 1889.
>
> For comment see entry No. 3813.

American Lecturers and Humorists by Melville D. Landon . . .

> . . . Akron . . . ‹1893; *i.e., ca.* 1898›
>
> For comment see entry No. 11228.

Platform Pearls for Temperance Workers and Other Reformers A Collection of Recitations . . . Compiled by Lilian M. Heath

> New York Funk & Wagnalls Company London and Toronto 1896

. . . Gems of Modern Wit and Humor with . . . Introduction by Robert J. Burdette . . .

> ‹n.p., n.d., 1903›
>
> For comment see entry No. 2013.

Masters of Mirth and Eloquence by Melville D. Landon . . .

> The Golden West Publishing Company Seattle, Washington ‹1906›

REFERENCES AND ANA

Swinging Round the Circle Wigwam Junction. By the Very Dickens! . . .

> American News Co., 121 Nassau Street, New York. ‹n.d., 1867›
>
> Printed self-wrapper. Cover-title. Presumably not by Locke. Authorship attributed to *L. A. Hunt and others* by Cushing.

Happy New Year. To the Patrons of the Toledo Blade the Carriers Respectfully Dedicate This Annual New Year's Address. January 1, 1869.

> ‹Toledo, Ohio, Jan. 1, 1869›
>
> Cover-title. Anonymous. *By Locke?* 4 pp. Printed on pale green laid paper. Printed yellow-coated paper wrapper. Copy in Y.

One Hundred Choice Selections No. 4 . . . by Phineas Garrett . . .

> . . . Philadelphia . . . 1871.
>
> "Betsy Destroys the Paper," pp. 151-154, herein credited to Locke. *Not by Locke.* The poem was written by Mrs. Helen Louisa (Barron) Bostwick, 1826–1907, and appears in her *Four-o'Clocks* . . . , Philadelphia, 1880.
>
> For comment see entry No. 2461.

Standard Recitations by Best Authors . . . Compiled . . . by Frances P. Sullivan.

> M. J. Ivers & Co., Publishers, 86 Nassau Street, N. Y. ‹1883›

Printed paper wrapper. Deposited April 20, 1883. The earliest printing (printings?) does not have present a statement identifying the publication as No. 1 of the series.

"Betsy Destroys the Paper," pp. 39-41. See preceding entry.

Some American Humorists by Napier Wilt . . .

Thomas Nelson and Sons   New York   1929

Petroleum Vesuvius Nasby by Cyril Clemens . . .

1936   International Mark Twain Society
Webster Groves, Missouri

The Struggles of Petroleum V. Nasby by David Ross Locke . . . Abridged Edition.   Selected, Edited and with an Introduction by Joseph Jones. Notes to the Chapters by Gunther Barth.

Beacon Press   Boston   ‹1963›

Printed paper wrapper.

JACK LONDON

1 8 7 6 – 1 9 1 6

"He was ... known successively as John Griffith London and Jack London ..."—*Jack London ...*, by Richard O'Connor ⟨1964⟩, p. 9.

Certain of London's novels (*e.g., White Fang*, 1905) were printed in prepublication form for copyright purposes. The prepublication printings seen are here described but others, unknown to BAL, may have been printed.

⟨Facsimile letter dated Oakland, Calif., Jan. 31, 1900⟩

> For a comment on this publication see below in section of *References and Ana* under *Sailor on Horseback*, 1938.

11869. THE SON OF THE WOLF   TALES OF THE FAR NORTH ...

BOSTON AND NEW YORK   HOUGHTON, MIFFLIN AND COMPANY   THE RIVERSIDE PRESS, CAMBRIDGE 1900

According to the publisher's records there were three printings without alteration of the title-page; these are:

First Printing

⟨i-viii⟩, ⟨1⟩-251; printer's imprint, p. ⟨252⟩. Frontispiece inserted. 7¹¹⁄₁₆″ x 5″ scant.

⟨1⁴, 2-22⁶⟩.

V cloth: gray. Stamped in silver. White laid end papers. Flyleaf at back.

2028 copies printed March 21, 1900. Between March 23–April 6, 1900, 19 copies were bound in paper; *prepared for review?* Copies in cloth were bound March 27–July 18, 1900.

NOTE

The following, presumably trial bindings, have been seen on first printing sheets only; no sequence is known and the designations are for identification only:

Trial Binding A: Unfinished (rough) grass-green V cloth. Stamped in silver. White laid end papers. Flyleaf at back. Noted only on a surviving copyright deposit copy in LC.

Trial Binding B: Greenish-black V cloth. Stamped in silver. White laid end papers. Flyleaf at back.

Trial Binding C: White buckram stamped in red only. White laid end papers. Flyleaf at back.

For a pictorial binding see below under *Third Printing*.

ALSO NOTE

The earliest bindings have the spine imprint in the following style: HOUGHTON / MIFFLIN & CO. A copy of the third printing (in silver-stamped gray V) has been seen with the spine imprint in the following style: HOUGHTON / MIFFLIN ⟨dot⟩ & ⟨dot⟩ CO

Second Printing

⟨i-vi⟩, ⟨1⟩-251; printer's imprint, p. ⟨252⟩, blank leaf. Frontispiece inserted.

⟨1-6⁸, 7-19⁶, 20⁴⟩.

V cloth: gray. Stamped in silver. White laid end papers. Flyleaf at front probable.

1010 copies printed July 13, 1900. Bound July 24–Sept. 7, 1900.

Third Printing

⟨i-vi⟩, ⟨1⟩-251; printer's imprint, p. ⟨252⟩, blank leaf. Frontispiece inserted.

⟨1-21⁶, 22⁴⟩.

V cloth: gray. Stamped in silver. White laid end papers. Flyleaf at front. Also occurs in a pictorial binding; see note below.

1004 copies printed Sept. 25, 1900. Bound Oct. 4–Nov. 18, 1900. 241 copies bound Nov. 16–18 in a *new style* binding; *i.e.*, green V cloth, stamped in white and red, with (on front cover) an illustration of a man in far northern dress; this feature is not present in the earlier bindings and has been noted on the third and later printings only.

Deposited March 28, 1900. A copy of the first printing in BA received April 17, 1900. Listed

PW April 21, 1900. The London (Isbister) edition listed Ath Oct. 11, 1902. *Note:* The publisher's records show that on March 30, 1900, six copies of the first printing were prepared with cancel title-leaf bearing the London imprint of A. P. Watt & Son; further information wanting. The London (Everett) edition listed PC April 26, 1913. Issued by Mills & Boon (London) under the title *An Odyssey of the North;* listed PC May 15, 1915.

EM (2nd in silver-stamped gray V)   H (1st in silver-stamped gray V)   HEH (1st in silver-stamped gray V; 3rd in silver-stamped gray V; 3rd in pictorial green V)   LC (being a deposit copy, 1st in silver-stamped unfinished rough grass-green V)   NYPL (1st in silver-stamped greenish-black V; 3rd in silver-stamped gray V)   UV (1st in red-stamped white buckram)   Y (1st in silver-stamped gray V; 3rd in pictorial green V)

11870. THE GOD OF HIS FATHERS & OTHER STORIES ...

NEW YORK   McCLURE, PHILLIPS & COMPANY MCMI

⟨i-xii⟩, 1-299. 7⁹⁄₁₆″ x 5³⁄₁₆″.

⟨-⟩⁶, 1-14, ⟨15⟩, 16-18⁸, 19⁶.

T cloth: blue.

Deposited May 15, 1901. A copy at BA received May 17, 1901. Advertised PW May 18, 1901. Listed PW June 1, 1901. The London (Isbister) edition listed Ath Feb. 8, 1902. The London (Mills & Boon) edition listed PC Oct. 16, 1915.

AAS BA H NYPL UV Y

11871. CHILDREN OF THE FROST ...

NEW YORK   THE MACMILLAN COMPANY   LONDON: MACMILLAN & CO., LTD. 1902 ALL RIGHTS RESERVED

Printed for copyright purposes only; for published edition see below under 1902.

⟨i-iv⟩, ⟨1⟩-263. Wove paper. 7⅛″ scant x 4⅞″.

⟨1², 2-34⁴⟩. *Signed:* ⟨A⟩², ⟨B⟩, C-D, ⟨E⟩, F, ⟨G⟩, H-I, K-L, ⟨M⟩, N-R⁸, S⁴.

Printed white laid paper wrapper.

Note: The text varies somewhat from the published edition deposited Sept. 27, 1902.

Deposited May 28, 1902. On copyright page: *Set up and electrotyped June, 1902.*

LC

11872. ... THE CRUISE OF THE DAZZLER ...

NEW YORK THE CENTURY CO MCMII

Title-page in black and blue. At head of title: ST NICHOLAS BOOKS

⟨i-iv⟩, ⟨i⟩-⟨viii⟩, ⟨1⟩-250, blank leaf. Illustrated. 7⅜″ x 4¹⁵⁄₁₆″.

⟨-⟩⁶, ⟨1⟩-15⁸, 16⁶.

V cloth: ecru.

On copyright page: *Published October, 1902* Deposited Sept. 16, 1902. Listed PW Oct. 11, 1902. The London (Hodder & Stoughton) edition listed Ath Sept. 29, 1906. The Mills & Boon (London) edition listed PC Nov. 20, 1915.

AAS H NYPL UV Y

11873. CHILDREN OF THE FROST ...

NEW YORK   THE MACMILLAN COMPANY   LONDON: MACMILLAN & CO., LTD. 1902 ALL RIGHTS RESERVED

First published edition. For a copyright printing see above under 1902.

⟨i⟩-⟨viii⟩, ⟨1⟩-261; blank, p. ⟨262⟩; 2 pp. advertisements; plus: 1 p. advertisements. Laid paper. Frontispiece and 7 plates inserted. 7½″ x 5⅛″.

⟨1-17⁸; plus: 18¹⟩. ⟨1⟩₄₋₅ inserted. *Signed:* ⟨A⟩⁴, ⟨B⟩-F, ⟨G⟩-I, K-L, ⟨M⟩-R⁸, S⁴; plus: ⟨T⟩¹.

V cloth (smooth, semi-polished): blue-gray; a copy thus in NYPL inscribed by London Oct. 15, 1902. Also noted in a variant binding of relatively rough V cloth, not semi-polished: blue-gray; a copy thus in NYPL inscribed by London Nov. 16, 1902.

On copyright page: *Set up and electrotyped September, 1902.* Noted as *in preparation* PW Sept. 13, 1902. Deposited Sept. 27, 1902. A copy (smooth, semi-polished cloth) in NYPL inscribed by London Oct. 15, 1902. The London (Macmillan) edition listed Ath Nov. 8, 1902. The London (Mills & Boon) edition listed PC July 31, 1915.

AAS H NYPL UV Y

11874. A DAUGHTER OF THE SNOWS ...

PHILADELPHIA J. B. LIPPINCOTT COMPANY MCMII

⟨1⟩-334, 2 pp. advertisements. Frontispiece and 3 plates inserted. 7⅜″ x 5″.

⟨1⟩-21⁸.

V cloth: red.

On copyright page: *Published October, 1902* Deposited Oct. 11, 1902. A copy at NYPL presented by the author to George Sterling, Nov.

20, 1902. Listed PW Nov. 22, 1902. The London (Isbister) edition listed Ath July 16, 1904.

AAS   H   NYPL   UV   Y

11875. THE KEMPTON-WACE LETTERS ...

NEW YORK   THE MACMILLAN COMPANY   LONDON: MACMILLAN & CO., LTD. 1903   ALL RIGHTS RESERVED

Anonymous. Written in collaboration with Anna Strunsky.

⟨i-vi⟩, 1-256, 3 pp. advertisements, blank leaf. 7⅜″ x 5″.

⟨1-16⁸, 17⁶⟩. *Signed:* ⟨A⟩³, B-I, K-O, ⟨P⟩-R⁸, ⟨S⟩³.

V cloth: grayish-blue. Top edges gilded.

On copyright page: *Set up and electrotyped May, 1903.* Deposited May 5, 1903. A copy in UV inscribed by Simeon Strunsky *May, 1903.* Listed PW June 6, 1903. The London (Isbister) edition listed Ath Oct. 10, 1903. According to *English Catalogue* the London (Mills & Boon) edition (n.d.) was issued in 1921.

AAS   H   NYPL   UV   Y

11876. ... THE CALL OF THE WILD ...

NEW YORK   THE MACMILLAN COMPANY   LONDON: MACMILLAN & CO., LTD. 1903   ALL RIGHTS RESERVED ...

Title-page printed in black and blue.

At head of title: ILLUSTRATED BY PHILIP R. GOODWIN AND CHARLES LIVINGSTON BULL

⟨5⟩(*sic*)-231; blank, p. ⟨232⟩; advertisements, pp. 1-2. Frontispiece inserted; and, 10 inserted plates reckoned in the printed pagination. Other illustrations in text. 7⁹⁄₁₆″ x 5⅛″.

⟨1-12⁸, 13⁴⟩; plus: 1 leaf inserted in ⟨3⟩, ⟨4⟩, ⟨11⟩; 2 leaves inserted in ⟨8⟩. *Signed (insertions here ignored):* ⟨A⟩⁶, B⁷, C⁶, D⁸, ⟨E⟩-F⁶, G⁸, H⁷, I⁶, K-L⁷, M⁸, N-O⁷, P⁴.

T cloth: green. White end papers printed in blue with dog-team and mountain scene. Top edges gilded.

On copyright page: *Set up, electrotyped, and published July, 1903.* Advertised for *early in the summer* PW May 9, 1903. Advertised as *just published* PW July 18, 1903. A copy at NYPL presented by the author to George Sterling July 23, 1903. Listed PW Aug. 1, 1903. The London (Heinemann) edition listed Ath Aug. 22, 1903.

Note: On March 28, 1903, the Copyright Office received two copies in *paper,* presumably an advance copyright printing; for an example of

such see *Children of the Frost,* under 1902, above. Further information wanting. No copyright deposits recorded for the period July–Aug. 1903.

AAS   H   NYPL   UV   Y

11877. THE PEOPLE OF THE ABYSS ...

NEW YORK   THE MACMILLAN COMPANY   LONDON: MACMILLAN & CO., LTD. 1903   ALL RIGHTS RESERVED

⟨i⟩-⟨xiv⟩, 1-319; plus: advertisements, pp. 1-3. Frontispiece and 9 plates inserted; also: 9 full-page plates, each an integral part of its gathering, but not reckoned in the printed pagination. Other illustrations in text. 8¼″ x 5⅞″.

⟨1-22⁸; plus: 23²⟩. *Signed:* ⟨A⟩⁷, B-E⁸, F⁹, G-H⁸, I¹², K-L⁸, ⟨M⟩⁹, N-O⁸, P¹⁰, Q⁹, R-U⁸, X⁸; plus: ⟨Y⟩².

T cloth: gray-blue. Stamped in black and gold. Top edges gilt. *Note:* Woodbridge, London & Tweney (p. 50) report "a copy ... in plain slate gray cloth with no decorations at all ... front cover is lettered in black ..."

On copyright page: *... published October, 1903.* Deposited Oct. 20, 1903. A copy in H received Oct. 28, 1903. Listed PW Nov. 7, 1903. The London (Isbister) edition listed Ath Nov. 7, 1903. Also issued (simultaneously?) with the imprint: *Toronto   George N. Morang & Company, Limited 1903;* printed in U.S.A. from the same setting as the New York edition; copies in UV, Y.

H   NYPL   UV   Y

11878. THE FAITH OF MEN AND OTHER STORIES ...

NEW YORK   THE MACMILLAN COMPANY   LONDON: MACMILLAN & CO., LTD. 1904   ALL RIGHTS RESERVED

⟨i⟩-⟨vi⟩, ⟨1⟩-286; advertisements, pp. 1-2; blank leaf. Laid paper. 7½″ x 5¹⁄₁₆″.

⟨1-18⁸, 19⁴⟩. *Signed:* ⟨A⟩³, ⟨B⟩-I, K-T⁸, ⟨U⟩¹.

T cloth: blue. Lettering on front stamped in black. Top edges gilt. *Note:* Jack London's personal copy (in HEH) has the front lettered in silver; presumably an experimental binding.

On copyright page: *... published April, 1904.* Advertised as though published PW April 16, 1904. A copy at BA received May 10, 1904. Listed PW June 4, 1904. The London (Heinemann) edition advertised for May 9 in Ath April 30, 1904; listed Ath May 14, 1904.

AAS   HEH (variant)   NYPL   UV

11879. THE BANKS OF THE SACRAMENTO ... PRICE ONE PENNY.

"DAILY MAIL" PUBLISHING OFFICE, CARMELITE HOUSE, CARMELITE STREET, LONDON, E.C. COPYRIGHT IN THE UNITED STATES OF AMERICA BY PERRY MASON CO., 1904.

Not seen. Entry on the basis of a photographic copy and correspondence.

Cover-title.

Prepared for copyright purposes only.

12 leaves. 7½" x 4½".

Deposited in BMU March 17, 1904. Originally in *The Youth's Companion* (Boston), March 17, 1904. For formal book publication see in *Dutch Courage*, 1922; and, *Stories of Ships and the Sea* ⟨1922⟩.

11880. ... THE TRAMP ...

WILSHIRE'S MAGAZINE, 125 EAST 23D STREET, NEW YORK ... ⟨n.d., 1904⟩

Cover-title. At head of title: WILSHIRE LEAFLET NO. 8 ...

⟨1⟩-8. 9½" x 6⅜".

⟨-⟩⁴.

Printed self-wrapper.

Note: The footnote on p. ⟨2⟩ cites *The Saturday Evening Post* of Nov. 23, 1904. The date is incorrect and should read Nov. 23, 1901.

Advertised as *just out,* in *Wilshire's Magazine,* Sept. 1904. Reprinted and reissued with the publisher's later address: 200 William Street, New York ⟨n.d., not before 1905⟩. Reprinted (at least twice) as an undated pamphlet by Charles H. Kerr & Co., Chicago; advertised as *just added ... to our Pocket Library of Socialism* in *International Socialist Review,* Chicago, June, 1911.

UCB

11881. Prosit   A Book of Toasts Compiled by Clotho ...

Paul Elder and Company   San Francisco and New York ⟨1904⟩

A toast, p. 56. In slightly altered form also appears in *The Loving Cup   Original Toasts by Original Folks,* edited by Wilbur D. Nesbit, Chicago ⟨1909⟩.

For fuller comment see entry No. 1123.

11882. THE SEA-WOLF ...

NEW YORK   THE MACMILLAN COMPANY   LONDON: MACMILLAN & CO., LTD. 1904   ALL RIGHTS RESERVED

⟨i⟩-⟨viii⟩, 1-366; advertisements, pp. ⟨367-369⟩; blank, p. ⟨370⟩; blank leaf. Laid paper. Frontispiece and 5 plates inserted. 7⁷⁄₁₆" x 5¹⁄₁₆".

⟨1-23⟩⁸, 24⁶. *Signed:* ⟨A⟩⁴, B-I, K-O, ⟨P⟩-U, X-Z, 2A⁸, ⟨2B⟩².

Two issues noted:

1

Title-leaf is not a cancel. Copyright notices dated 1904. *Issued thus?* The only example located (in HEH) is London's personal copy.

2

Title-leaf is a cancel. Copyright notices dated 1903 and 1904.

T cloth: blue. Top edges gilded.

Two forms of the binding noted; the sequence, if any, is not known, and the designations are for identification only.

A: Spine goldstamped.

B: Spine whitestamped.

On copyright page: ... *Published October, 1904.* Published Nov. 9, 1904 according to *The American Catalogue.* Noted for *next week* PW Nov. 12, 1904. Listed PW Nov. 19, 1904. *Third edition advertised* PW Dec. 17, 1904. The London (Heinemann) edition advertised as though published Ath Nov. 26, 1904; listed Ath Dec. 3, 1904.

AAS (2nd, both bindings)   HEH (1st, binding A) NYPL (2nd, binding B)

11883. In Many Wars by Many War-Correspondents.

Printed by the Tokyo Printing Company ⟨Tokyo, 1904⟩

"A Camera and a Journey," pp. 123-129.

For comment see entry No. 6253.

11884. ... THE SCAB ... (REPRINTED FROM THE ATLANTIC MONTHLY) ...

PUBLISHED BY CHARLES H. KERR & COMPANY (COOPERATIVE) 56 FIFTH AVENUE CHICAGO ⟨n.d., 1905⟩

Cover-title. At head of title: PRICE 5 CENTS

Issued as No. 44 of the *Pocket Library of Socialism.*

⟨1⟩-25; advertisements, pp. ⟨26-32⟩. 5¹³⁄₁₆" x 3½" scant.

⟨-⟩¹⁶.

Printed self-wrapper.

Advertised as though published *Appeal to Reason* (Girard, Kansas), March 11, 1905. Reviewed in *The International Socialist Review* (Chicago), April, 1905.

Note: Reprinted several, probably many, times. Known reprints have the publisher's later address on the title-page, in the advertisements; either or both; some reprints were issued without street address on the title-page. Kerr's chronology is as follows: 1900–1905: *56 Fifth Avenue;* 1905–1908: *East Kinzie Street;* 1908–1912: *West Kinzie Street;* 1912–1917: *East Ohio Street, Chicago,* and, *74 Beekman Street, New York.*

Collected in *The War of the Classes,* 1905.

Y

11885. WAR OF THE CLASSES ...

NEW YORK   THE MACMILLAN COMPANY   LONDON: MACMILLAN & CO., LTD.   1905   ALL RIGHTS RESERVED

⟨i⟩-⟨xx⟩, ⟨1⟩-278; advertisements, pp. ⟨279-281⟩; blank leaf. 7⅚″ x 4¹⁵⁄₁₆″.

⟨1-19⟩⁸. Signed: ⟨-⟩², ⟨A-B⟩, C-I, K-S⁸, T⁶.

T cloth: maroon.

On copyright page: ... *Published April, 1905.* Deposited April 11, 1905. Listed (as in cloth) PW April 22, 1905; listed (as in paper) PW July 22, 1905. Paper format advertised in *Appeal to Reason* (Girard, Kansas) July 22, 1905. "When the *Appeal* offered London's *War of the Classes* ... in paper ... the orders ... swamped the New York publisher ... The orders piled up so that enough books could not be printed to supply the first rush, but the publisher writes me that he has now filled the back orders and has a supply on hand ..."—*Appeal to Reason,* Nov. 4, 1905. The London (Heinemann) edition listed Ath Sept. 16, 1905. Reissued by Mills & Boon, London under date ⟨1905⟩; listed in *English Catalogue* as published in February, 1920.

BA   H   NYPL   UV   Y

11886. THE GAME ...

NEW YORK   THE MACMILLAN COMPANY   LONDON: MACMILLAN & CO., LTD.   1905   ALL RIGHTS RESERVED

Title-page in black and brown.

⟨i-xiv⟩, 15-182; advertisements, pp. ⟨183-188⟩. Frontispiece and 5 plates inserted, all reckoned in the printed pagination; other illustrations in text. 7½″ x 5⅛″.

⟨1-11⟩⁸. Signed: ⟨A⟩⁷, B-H⁷·⁸, ⟨I⟩⁸, K-L⁷·⁸, M⁶.

T cloth: green. White end papers printed in brown with wrestling figures, pugilist, cupid, garland, skull, hourglasses. Top edges gilded.

On copyright page: ... *Published June, 1905.* Announced PW April 22, 1905. Advertised PW May 6, 1905. Advertised for *June* PW May 27, 1905. Advertised for *next week* and noted as *will not be published until the 7th inst., the very large advance demand having interfered with its publication* PW June 3, 1905. A copy in BA received June 13, 1905. Advertised for *next week* PW June 17, 1905. Listed PW June 17, 1905. The London (Heinemann) edition (American-printed) advertised for July 5, in Ath June 24, 1905; listed Ath July 15, 1905.

Note: Some copies have present on the copyright page a rubber-stamped notice reading: *Copyright, 1905, by the Metropolitan Magazine Co.* The notice occurs in two forms of unknown sequence if any:

A: Stamped from types ¹⁄₁₆″ tall.

B: Stamped from types ³⁄₃₂″ tall.

Note: Woodbridge, London & Tweney (p. 59) report a 102-page printing, in printed paper wrapper, with the statement *Published May, 1905* on the copyright page. Copyright printing?

AAS   BA   H   NYPL

11887. TALES OF THE FISH PATROL ...

NEW YORK   THE MACMILLAN COMPANY   LONDON: MACMILLAN & CO., LTD.   1905   ALL RIGHTS RESERVED

⟨1⟩-243; blank, p. ⟨244⟩; advertisements, pp. ⟨245-247⟩. Frontispiece and 6 plates inserted; 1 full-page map an integral part of its gathering. 7½″ x 5⅛″.

⟨A⟩-I, K-N, ⟨O⟩-P⁸, Q⁴.

V cloth: blue. Top edges gilded. "Two states of binding; no established priority."—Johnson (1942); further information wanting.

On copyright page: ... *Published September, 1905.* Listed PW Oct. 14, 1905. A copy at BA received Oct. 17, 1905. The London (Heinemann) edition listed Ath Feb. 17, 1906.

BA   H   NYPL   UV   Y

11888. WHITE FANG ...

NEW YORK   THE MACMILLAN COMPANY   LONDON: MACMILLAN & CO., LTD.   1905   ALL RIGHTS RESERVED

Printed for copyright purposes only; for published edition see below under 1906.

⟨i-ii⟩, ⟨i⟩-vi, ⟨1⟩-327. Laid paper. 7¼″ x 5″.

⟨A⟩⁴, ⟨B⟩-I, ⟨K⟩-⟨O⟩, P-⟨U⟩, X⁸, Y⁴.

Printed gray paper wrapper.

On copyright page: *Set up and electrotyped. Published ⟨space⟩, 1905.* Deposited Nov. 15, 1905.

UV

11889. The California Society of the Friends of Russian Freedom Statement . . .

⟨San Francisco, n.d., 1905⟩

Caption-title. 4pp? 6pp?

An appeal for members and contributions. Signed at end by Jack London, George Sterling, and others.

"We believe that the people of Russia must themselves solve the problems of their political and social life . . ."

HEH

11890. Inter-Collegiate Socialist Society . . . Call for Organization Meeting . . . Minutes of Meeting . . . September 12, 1905.

⟨New York, n.d., 1905⟩

Single cut sheet folded to four pages. The above on p. ⟨1⟩. Text preceded by a note signed by London, Thomas Wentworth Higginson and others.

Note: The above is representative of the printed material issued by this organization; the same note appears in other like publications. London was the first president of the society and his name is probably attached to other similar productions.

HEH

11891. . . . WHAT COMMUNITIES LOSE BY THE COMPETITIVE SYSTEM . . .

THE TWENTIETH CENTURY PRESS, LIMITED (TRADE UNION AND 48 HOURS), 37A, CLERKENWELL GREEN, LONDON, E. C. ⟨n.d., 1906⟩

Cover-title. At head of title: ONE PENNY.

⟨1⟩-15; advertisements, p. ⟨16⟩. 8%₁₆″ x 5⅜″.

⟨-⟩⁸.

Printed self-wrapper.

Reprinted from *Cosmopolitan*, New York, Nov. 1900. Pamphlet advertised in *Social Democrat*, London, March 15, 1906–Dec. 15, 1906. Collected in Foner ⟨1947⟩.

DU

11892. ⟨UPTON SINCLAIR'S *THE JUNGLE*⟩

1906

An open letter urging support of Upton Sinclair's book, *The Jungle*, 1906. First published in *Appeal to Reason* (Girard, Kansas), Nov. 18, 1905; collected in Foner ⟨1947⟩, pp. 80-82. In addition to the open letter, London wrote what appears to be a private letter to Sinclair; both letters were used to promote the sale of *The Jungle*, the private letter in part only, and are here designated *Open Letter* and *Private Letter*. The following printings have been seen.

Open Letter A (B?)

CIRCULATE "THE JUNGLE." DEAR COMRADES: HERE IT IS AT LAST! THE BOOK WE HAVE BEEN WAITING FOR . . .

YOURS FOR THE REVOLUTION—JACK LONDON. ⟨5-line note: Prices, etc., ending:⟩ THE JUNGLE PUBLISHING COMPANY, P. O. BOX 2064, NEW YORK. (PUBLISHED FEBRUARY 15TH, 1906.) ⟨Union label, New York, N.Y., shop No. 20⟩

Single leaf. White wove paper. Printed on recto only. 6″ x 3½″. The date at end refers to publication of *The Jungle*, not to the leaflet.

Open Letter B (A?)

The Books of Upton Sinclair . . .

The Jungle Publishing Co., P. O. Box 2064, New York ⟨n.d., 1906?⟩

Single cut sheet folded to eight pages. Pale yellow paper. Paged ⟨1⟩-8. P. ⟨1⟩ as above. Page: 6%₁₆″ x 4½″.

Text of the letter (in full) on p. 3. On p. 4 is a one-line comment referring to Sinclair's novel, *Manassas*.

Open Letter C

A Terrible Book . . . The Jungle . . .

For Sale by Appeal to Reason, Girard, Kan. ⟨not before March, 1906⟩

Single cut sheet folded to six pages. Unpaged. White wove paper. Page: 5⅞″ x 3%₁₆″. P. ⟨1⟩ as above.

Text of letter (in full) on p. ⟨4⟩.

Open Letter D

The Jungle . . .

⟨The Jungle Publishing Co., New York, n.d., 1906?⟩

Single cut sheet folded to four pages. Unpaged. Page: 6¼″ x 3½″. White wove paper. Caption-title. Imprint at foot of p. ⟨4⟩. A one-line extract from the open letter on p. ⟨1⟩.

Issued after publication of *The Jungle*.

WHITE FANG

BY

JACK LONDON

AUTHOR OF "THE CALL OF THE WILD," "CHILDREN
OF THE FROST," ETC., ETC.

New York
THE MACMILLAN COMPANY
LONDON: MACMILLAN & CO., Ltd.
1905

JACK LONDON
Entry No. 11888
Front of wrapper, copyright printing
(University of Virginia, Barrett Collection)

Two printings noted: 1: On p. ⟨4⟩ the price of *The Jungle* is given as *$1.35;* 2: On p. ⟨4⟩ the price of *The Jungle* is given as *$1.20.*

Open Letter E

A New Edition of The Jungle . . .

⟨Pasadena, Cal., Upton Sinclair, n.d., *ca.* 1920⟩

Single cut sheet folded to four pages. Unpaged. Page: 6¹¹⁄₁₆″ x 4½″. Brown paper. Caption-title. Text of letter (in full) on p. ⟨4⟩; or, on pp. ⟨3-4⟩; see below.

Two printings of unknown sequence noted:

a: London's letter on p. ⟨4⟩; imprint on p. ⟨3⟩.

b: London's letter on pp. ⟨3-4⟩; imprint on p. ⟨4⟩.

Open Letter F

A New Edition of the Jungle . . .

⟨Pasadena, Cal., Upton Sinclair, n.d., *ca.* 1920⟩

Single cut sheet folded to four pages. Unpaged. Page: 6¾″ x 4⁷⁄₁₆″. Brown paper. Caption-title. Text of letter (in full) on pp. ⟨2-3⟩. Imprint on p. ⟨4⟩.

Note: A brief extract from the open letter, much revised (by an editor?) appears in a four-page circular issued by Doubleday, Page & Co., New York, in (presumably) 1906. Copy in IU.

The letter also appears on the front wrapper of the London (Heinemann) edition of *The Jungle,* 1907. Also in: *Upton Sinclair Biographical and Critical Opinions . . .* ⟨Pasadena, Cal., n.d., 1923?⟩; printed paper wrapper. This last went into two or more printings; the earliest noted by BAL has on the outer back a list of ten titles by Sinclair; a later printing has on the outer back a list of *Books . . . in . . . Print . . . 1931 . . .*

Private Letter

"*The Jungle* is going splendidly. The way it picks up and keeps picking up is tremendous . . ."

Two printings of the private letter have been seen. The sequence has not been determined and the following designations are arbitrary.

A

The Jungle . . .

The Jungle Publishing Company, Princeton, N. J. ⟨n.d., 1906?⟩

Single leaf. White wove paper. Printed on recto only. 5¹³⁄₁₆″ x 3⁷⁄₁₆″.

B

The Jungle . . .

The Jungle Publishing Company, P. O. Box 2064, New York. (Published February 15th, 1906.) ⟨Union label, New York, N.Y., shop No. 20⟩

Single leaf. White wove paper. Printed on recto only. 5¾″ x 3⁹⁄₁₆″.

IU (all of the above)   UV (Open letter A)

11893. Argonaut Stories . Selected from the Argonaut   Jerome Hart, Editor

San Francisco: Payot, Upham & Company   Agents for Pacific Coast   1906

Printed paper wrapper.

"Moon-Face," pp. 3-10. Collected in *Moon-Face,* 1906.

Johnson (1942), p. 320, states: "First edition does not contain press notices." The reference is, presumably, to the inner back wrapper. Further information wanting; all copies examined by BAL are imprinted on the inner back wrapper with *Opinions of the Press.*

Title entered for copyright Jan. 11, 1906. No further copyright record found. Listed PW April 21, 1906.

HEH   LC   Y

11894. MOON-FACE AND OTHER STORIES . . .

NEW YORK   THE MACMILLAN COMPANY   LONDON: MACMILLAN & CO., LTD. 1906   ALL RIGHTS RESERVED

Printed for copyright purposes only; for published edition see entry No. 11895.

⟨i⟩-⟨vi⟩, ⟨1⟩-273. Laid paper. 7¼″ x 4⅞″.

⟨1⁴, 2-18⁸⟩. Signed: ⟨A⟩³, ⟨B⟩-I, K-S⁸, T¹.

Printed tan paper wrapper.

Note: Pasted to pp. 3, 59, 89, 117, and 149 are copyright notices.

On copyright page: . . . *Published* ⟨space⟩, *1906.* Deposited April 27, 1906.

Note: The text varies somewhat from the published edition.

LC   NYPL   Y

11894A. LOVE OF LIFE AND OTHER STORIES . . .

NEW YORK   THE MACMILLAN COMPANY   LONDON: MACMILLAN & CO., LTD. 1906   ALL RIGHTS RESERVED

Prepared for copyright only. For published edition see entry No. 11904.

⟨i⟩-⟨vi⟩, ⟨1⟩-265. Laid paper. 7⅜" x 5".

⟨1⁴, 2-17⁸, 18⁴⟩. *Signed:* ⟨A⟩³, ⟨B⟩-I, K-R⁸, S⁵.

Printed tan paper wrapper.

On copyright page: ... *Published* ⟨*space*⟩, *1906.*

Deposited May 9, 1906.

Y

11894B. BEFORE ADAM ...

NEW YORK   THE MACMILLAN COMPANY   LONDON: MACMILLAN & CO., LTD. 1906   ALL RIGHTS RESERVED

Prepared for copyright only. For published edition see entry No. 11903.

⟨i-viii⟩, 1-215. 7⅜" x 5".

⟨1⁴, 2-14⁸, 15⁴⟩.

Printed tan laid paper wrapper.

On copyright page: ... *Published* ⟨*space*⟩, *1906.*

Deposited June 30, 1906. *Note:* Stone proofs of the first two installments as published in *Everybody's Magazine* (New York), pp. 445-455, 844-852, were deposited on, respectively, Aug. 22, 1906; Oct. 9, 1906; in LC.

Y

11895. MOON-FACE AND OTHER STORIES ...

NEW YORK   THE MACMILLAN COMPANY   LONDON: MACMILLAN & CO., LTD. 1906   ALL RIGHTS RESERVED

First published edition; for a copyright printing see entry No. 11894.

⟨i⟩-⟨vi⟩, ⟨1⟩-273; blank, p. ⟨274⟩; advertisements, pp. ⟨275-278⟩; 2 blank leaves. Laid paper. 7½" x 5⅛".

⟨1-18⟩⁸. *Signed:* ⟨A⟩³, ⟨B⟩-I, K-S⁸, T⁵.

V cloth: blue. Top edges gilded.

On copyright page: ... *Published September, 1906.* A copy at BA received Sept. 6, 1906. Deposited Sept. 11, 1906. Noted for *this week* PW Sept. 15, 1906. Listed PW Sept. 22, 1906. The London (Heinemann) edition advertised and listed Ath Oct. 6, 1906. Reprinted and reissued by The Regent Press, New York ⟨1906; *i.e., ca.* 1915⟩.

AAS   H   NYPL   Y

11896. WHITE FANG ...

NEW YORK   THE MACMILLAN COMPANY   LONDON: MACMILLAN & CO., LTD. 1906   ALL RIGHTS RESERVED

First published edition; for a copyright printing see above under year 1905.

⟨i⟩-⟨viii⟩, ⟨1⟩-327; blank, p. ⟨328⟩; plus: 4 pp. advertisements. Printed on laid paper but see note below. Frontispiece, 7 plates, 5 divisional plates (printed in brown-orange) inserted. 7½" scant x 5⁵⁄₁₆".

⟨1-21⁸; plus: 22²⟩. *Signed:* ⟨A⟩⁴, ⟨B⟩-I, K-S, ⟨T⟩-U, X⁸, Y⁴; plus: ⟨Z⟩².

Note: Copies occur with a cancel title-leaf printed on either wove or on laid paper. Copies also occur with the title-leaf printed (on laid paper) as an integral part of the gathering. The significance has not been determined; the following possibility is suggested:

1: *Postulated:* With an erroneous title-leaf.

2: Error (if such there was) corrected by means of a singleton cancel. Copies already in binding corrected thus?

3: Error (if such there was) corrected by means of a two-leaf cancel; *i.e.,* leaf ⟨1⟩₂ and its conjugate. Copies in sheets corrected thus?

T cloth: gray. White laid end papers printed in brown-orange with mountain scenes.

On copyright page: *Set up and electrotyped. Published October, 1906.* Noted as *in preparation* PW July 21, 1906. Advertised for *October* PW Sept. 15, 1906. Advertised PW Sept. 29, 1906. Deposited Oct. 2, 1906. A copy in NYPL (cancel title-leaf) inscribed by London Oct. 30, 1906. Listed PW Nov. 3, 1906. The London (Methuen) edition announced Ath Jan. 19, 1907; listed Ath Feb. 9, 1907.

AAS (integral) H (cancel) NYPL (cancel) UV (cancel)   Y (cancel)

11897. THE APOSTATE   A PARABLE OF CHILD LABOR ...

1906   THE APPEAL TO REASON   GIRARD, KANSAS

Cover-title.

⟨1⟩-15; extract from James Russell Lowell, p. ⟨16⟩. 7½" scant x 5⅜".

⟨-⟩⁸.

Printed salmon paper wrapper.

No record of copyright deposit found; the pamphlet carries no copyright notice. Advertised in *Appeal to Reason* (Girard, Kansas), Oct. 27, 1906. First published in *Woman's Home Companion* (Springfield, O.) Sept. 1906. Reprinted in *International Socialist Review* (Chicago), June 1909. Collected in *When God Laughs,* 1911. There were many reprints; the earliest (probably not before 1912), was issued by Charles H. Kerr & Company Co-Operative, Chicago, n.d. Reprinted as No. 640 in *The Little Blue Book* series, Haldeman-Julius Co., Girard, Kansas, n.d.; according to the publisher this was issued Dec. 20, 1924, but BAL has reason to believe that publication dates furnished by this publisher may not be wholly reliable. Under the title *He Renounced the Faith,* issued as *People's Pocket Series,* No. 47, Girard, Kansas, n.d., 1920; advertised in *Appeal to Reason,* Oct. 30, 1920.

H   NYU

11898. SCORN OF WOMEN IN THREE ACTS ...

NEW YORK   THE MACMILLAN COMPANY   LONDON: MACMILLAN & CO., LTD.   1906   ALL RIGHTS RESERVED

⟨i⟩-x, ⟨1⟩-256; advertisements, pp. ⟨257-259⟩; blank, p. ⟨260⟩; blank leaf. Laid paper. 6⅞" full x 4¾" full.

⟨1⁶, 2-16⁸, 17², 18⁸⟩. *Signed:* ⟨A⟩⁵, ⟨B⟩-I, K-M, ⟨N⟩-R⁸, ⟨S⟩³.

Maroon T cloth sides, white V cloth shelfback. Top edges gilded. Imprint on spine: THE MAC-MILLAN COMPANY

Note: Also issued in a variant (remainder?) binding: top edges plain; spine imprint: MAC-MILLAN

On copyright page: ... *Published November, 1906.* Deposited Nov. 15, 1906. A copy at NYPL received Nov. 17, 1906. The London (Macmillan) edition advertised as though published and listed Ath Jan. 19, 1907.

AAS (variant)   BA   H (both)   NYPL   UV   Y (both)

11899. Fifty-Two Pioneer Stories All round the Compass. Stories of Travellers ... Edited by Alfred H. Miles ...

London: Hutchinson & Co., 34, Paternoster Row. ⟨1906⟩

Not seen.

"The King of Mazy May," pp. 155-163. First published in *The Youth's Companion* (Boston) Nov. 30, 1899.

BMU (received Nov. 23, 1906).

11900. WHAT LIFE MEANS TO ME ...

⟨THE INTERCOLLEGIATE SOCIALIST SOCIETY, PRINCETON, N. J., n.d., 1906⟩

Cover-title. Imprint from p. ⟨2⟩. On p. ⟨4⟩ is the imprint of Appeal to Reason Press, Girard, Kansas.

⟨1⟩-15. 5¾" scant x 3⁷⁄₁₆".

⟨-⟩⁸.

Printed self-wrapper.

No record of copyright deposit found. First published in *Cosmopolitan Magazine* (New York), March, 1906. Advertised as though published, *Appeal to Reason* (Girard, Kansas), Sept. 8, 1906; Oct. 27, 1906. An announcement issued for *London Night,* Piedmont Club House, Friday, Nov. 9, 1906, states that *What Life Means to Me* was first published in *Cosmopolitan Magazine* and also published as a tract by *The Intercollegiate Socialist Society,* New York.

Collected in *Revolution and Other Essays,* New York, 1910.

REPRINTS

There were many reprints. The following have been noted by BAL.

Reprint A

What Life Means to Me ...

Chicago   Charles H. Kerr & Company Co-Operative ⟨n.d., not before 1912⟩

Cover-title. Printed self-wrapper. *Two printings noted:* 1, with the imprint of *John F. Higgins* on p. ⟨2⟩; 2, p. ⟨2⟩ blank. Other variations are present but the preceding is sufficient for ready recognition.

Reprint B

Jack London's "What Life Means to Me" Memorial Edition   San Francisco December 3, 1916 ..

⟨San Francisco, 1916⟩

Cover-title. Printed self-wrapper.

Reprint C

... The Dream of Debs ... What Life Means to Me ...

People's Press   Girard, Kansas ⟨n.d., 1919⟩

At head of title: *The Appeal's Pocket Series No. 30 First Edition* Printed paper wrapper. Advertised in *Appeal to Reason* (Girard, Kansas), Sept. 27, 1919.

Reprint D (E?)

What Life Means to Me.

Appeal to Reason, Girard, Kansas, 1921.

Not seen; not located. Entry on the basis of an advertisement in *Appeal to Reason* (Girard, Kansas), March 26, 1921, where this title (apparently as a separate; *i.e.*, without *The Dream of Debs*) is described as No. 30 in *The Appeal's Pocket Series*.

Reprint E (D?)

... The Dream of Debs ... What Life Means to Me ...

Appeal to Reason, Girard, Kans. ⟨n.d., 1920?⟩

At head of title: *People's Pocket Series No. 30* Printed paper wrapper. According to a letter from the publisher this printing was published Sept. 18, 1920, but BAL has found that such statements from this publisher are not wholly reliable. A copy of this printing was in the possession of the late E. Walter Latendorf, New York City, in Nov. 1948.

Reprint F

... What Life Means to Me ...

Haldeman-Julius Company   Girard, Kansas ⟨1924⟩

At head of title: *Little Blue Book No. 30* ... Printed paper wrapper.

Reprint G

... What Life Means to Me ...

Haldeman-Julius Company   Girard, Kansas ⟨n.d., not before 1924⟩

At head of title: *Little Blue Book No. 30* ... Printed paper wrapper.

A reprint, date routed from the plate, of *Reprint F*.

UCB (Reprints C, G)   USC (Reprint F)   UV (1st; Reprints A2, B, F)   Y (1st; Reprints A1, B)

11901. London Night in Honor of Mr. and Mrs. Jack London

Ruskin Club   Oakland, Calif. ⟨1906⟩

Not seen. Entry from Woodbridge, London & Tweney, pp. 263-264. Issued as a menu.

"Contains the conclusion of London's speech to the students of the University of California ... March 20, 1905 ..."

The Plan of Laughing Land ... by W. Costley

(Copyrighted 1906) ⟨*i.e.*, not before 1917⟩

See below under 1917.

11902. THE IRON HEEL ...

NEW YORK   THE MACMILLAN COMPANY   LONDON: MACMILLAN & CO., LTD.   1907   ALL RIGHTS RESERVED

Prepared for copyright purposes only. For published edition see entry No. 11908.

⟨i-ii⟩, ⟨i⟩-xiv, 1-354. Laid paper. 7⅜" x 5" scant. ⟨A⟩-⟨D⟩, E-I, K-U, X-Z⁸, 2A¹.

Printed tan paper wrapper.

On copyright page: ... *Published* ⟨*space*⟩, *1907*. Deposited Jan. 5, 1907.

LC (incomplete)   Y

11903. BEFORE ADAM ...

NEW YORK   THE MACMILLAN COMPANY   LONDON: MACMILLAN & CO., LTD.   1907   ALL RIGHTS RESERVED

For a copyright printing see entry No. 11894B.

⟨i⟩-⟨viii⟩, 1-242; advertisements, pp. ⟨243-246⟩. Frontispiece, 7 full-page plates and a 2-page map inserted; other illustrations in text. The 7 full-page plates are reckoned in the printed pagination. 7⁹⁄₁₆" x 5³⁄₁₆".

⟨1-15⟩⁸. *Signed:* ⟨A⟩⁴, B⁸, C⁷, D-E⁸, F-H⁷, I⁸, K⁷, L⁸, M⁷, N-P⁸, Q⁷, R³.

Light-brown rough buckram. Top edges stained light tan.

On copyright page: *Published February, 1907.* Noted for spring publication PW Feb. 9, 1907. Noted for *this week* PW Feb. 23, 1907. A copy at BA received Feb. 27, 1907. Listed PW March 2, 1907. The London (Werner Laurie) edition listed Ath May 9, 1908.

AAS   BA   H   NYPL   Y

11904. LOVE OF LIFE AND OTHER STORIES ...

NEW YORK   THE MACMILLAN COMPANY   LONDON: MACMILLAN & CO., LTD.   1907   ALL RIGHTS RESERVED

For a copyright printing see entry No. 11894A.

⟨i⟩-⟨vi⟩, ⟨1⟩-265; blank, p. ⟨266⟩; plus: 4 pp. advertisements. 7½" x 5¹⁄₁₆".

⟨1-17⟩⁸; plus: 18²⟩. ⟨1⟩₂ (title-leaf) is a cancel. *Signed:* ⟨A⟩³, ⟨B⟩-I, K-R⁸, S⁵; plus: ⟨T⟩².

V cloth: blue.

On copyright page: *Published September, 1907.* Noted *will publish in the fall* PW July 20, 1907. Advertised for Sept. 25, PW Sept. 28, 1907. A copy at BA received Oct. 1, 1907. Listed PW Oct. 5, 1907. The London (Everett & Co.) edition listed Ath Feb. 22, 1908. The Mills & Boon edition listed PC May 27, 1916.

AAS   H   NYPL   Y

11905. Sea Stories Retold from St. Nicholas

New York   The Century Co.   1907

"To Repel Boarders," pp. 3-16. Collected in *Dutch Courage . . .* , 1922.

Listed PW Oct. 5, 1907.

USC

11906. THE ROAD . . .

NEW YORK   THE MACMILLAN COMPANY   1907
ALL RIGHTS RESERVED

⟨i⟩-⟨xiv⟩, 1-224; advertisements, pp. ⟨225-226⟩; plus: 2 pp. advertisements. Frontispiece and 47 plates inserted. 8″ full x 5⅝″ full.

⟨1-15⁸; plus: 16¹⟩. *Signed:* ⟨A⟩⁷, B-I, K-P⁸, ⟨Q⟩¹; plus: ⟨R⟩¹.

V cloth: gray. Stamped in gold and black. Top edges gilded.

Note: Also occurs in a variant (remainder?) binding: Stamped in black only; top edges plain; ⟨16⟩ (advertisements) not present.

On copyright page: . . . *Published November, 1907.* Noted as *shortly* PW Nov. 16, 1907. Deposited Nov. 29, 1907. Advertised PW Nov. 30, 1907. A copy in UV inscribed by early owner Dec. 6, 1907. Noted as *just . . . out* PW Dec. 7, 1907. Listed PW Dec. 14, 1907. The London (Mills & Boon) edition listed Ath March 21, 1914.

NYPL   UV (both bindings)   Y

11907. Fifty-Two Excelsior Stories for Boys . . . Edited by Alfred H. Miles . . .

London: Hutchinson & Co., 34, Paternoster Row. ⟨1907⟩

Not seen.

"Dutch Courage," pp. 302-312. Reprinted from *The Youth's Companion* (Boston) Nov. 1, 1900. Collected in *Dutch Courage . . .* , 1922.

BMU (Received Nov. 19, 1907)

11908. THE IRON HEEL . . .

NEW YORK   THE MACMILLAN COMPANY   LON-
DON: MACMILLAN & CO., LTD. 1908   ALL RIGHTS
RESERVED

First published edition; for a copyright printing see above under 1907.

⟨i⟩-⟨xvi⟩, 1-354; advertisements, pp. ⟨355-358⟩; blank leaf. Laid paper. 7½″ x 5⅛″.

⟨A⟩-I, K-U, X-Z⁸, 2A⁴.

V cloth: blue.

On copyright page: . . . *Published February, 1908.* Advertised as *ready next week* PW Feb. 15, 1908. Listed PW Feb. 29, 1908. The London (Everett) edition listed Ath Nov. 21, 1908. What

is supposedly this book was advertised without title by T. Fisher Unwin as *in preparation* Bkr Jan. 1908; with title given advertised Bkr Aug. 1908; no further word seen of an Unwin printing; not published? The Everett (London) edition listed PC Nov. 21, 1908. The Mills & Boon (London) edition listed PC Jan. 15, 1916.

AAS   H   NYPL   Y

11909. MARTIN EDEN . . .

NEW YORK   THE MACMILLAN COMPANY   1908
ALL RIGHTS RESERVED

Printed for copyright purposes only; for published edition see below under 1909.

⟨i-iv⟩, 1-411. Wove paper. 7¼″ full x 5″ full.

⟨1-52⟩⁴. *Signed:* ⟨A⟩², B-E, ⟨F-G⟩, H-I, ⟨K⟩, L-T, ⟨U⟩, X-⟨Y⟩, Z, 2A-2C⁸, 2D⁶.

Printed pale tan laid paper wrapper.

On copyright page: . . . *Published ⟨space⟩, 1908.* Deposited May 23, 1908.

LC   Y

11910. Life, Battles and Career of Battling Nelson Lightweight Champion of the World by Himself . . . ⟨Oscar Matthew Nelson⟩

Hegewisch, Ill.   1908

Pictorial wrapper; and, cloth.

"How Different People View Fighters. Brain Beaten by Brute Force . . . ," pp. 178-183. Originally in *San Francisco Examiner,* Sept. 10, 1905.

HEH   UCB   USC

11911. A BRIEF EXPLANATION

⟨Hobart, Tasmania, 1909?⟩

Not seen. Entry on the basis of a description in *The Mystery of Jack London . . .* , by Georgia Loring Bamford, Oakland ⟨1931⟩, pp. 221-223.

A mimeographed statement explaining why London was abandoning his cruise on the *Snark.* Mrs. Bamford reports that the statement was prepared for the information of London's friends; BAL suspects it was also prepared as a press release.

Issued not after Jan. 21, 1909.

11912. MARTIN EDEN . . .

NEW YORK   THE MACMILLAN COMPANY   1909
ALL RIGHTS RESERVED

First published edition. For a copyright printing see above under 1908.

⟨i-vi⟩, 1-411; advertisements, pp. ⟨413-422⟩; 2 blank leaves. Laid paper. Frontispiece inserted. 7½″ x 5⅛″.

⟨1-27⟩⁸. *Signed:* ⟨A⟩³, B-I, K-U, X-Z, 2A-2D⁸, ⟨2E⟩⁵.

V cloth: blue.

On copyright page: ... *Published September, 1909.* Advertised and noted for publication *during September* PW Sept. 11, 1909. Advertised as *ready Sept. 22,* PW Sept. 25, 1909. Noted as *just ready* PW Oct. 2, 1909. Listed PW Oct. 9, 1909. A copy in NYPL inscribed by London Nov. 27, 1909. The London (Heinemann) edition advertised for *next week* Ath July 2, 1910; listed Ath July 9, 1910.

AAS   NYPL   UV

11913. REVOLUTION ...

    CHICAGO   CHARLES H. KERR & COMPANY CO-OPERATIVE   ⟨1909⟩

Cover-title. Date on basis of publisher's prefatory note.

⟨1⟩-31; advertisements, p. ⟨32⟩. 5¹¹⁄₁₆″ x 3½″ scant.

⟨-⟩¹⁶.

Printed self-wrapper.

Collected in *Revolution and Other Essays,* 1910.

Four printings noted; the order is tentative.

A

Advertisements, p. ⟨32⟩ headed: *A Socialist Success*

Publisher's address in terminal advertisements: *118 Kinzie Street*

B

Advertisements, p. ⟨32⟩ headed: *Pocket Library of Socialism*

Publisher's address in terminal advertisements: *118 W. Kinzie Street*

C

Advertisements, p. ⟨32⟩ headed: *Study Socialism*

Publisher's address in terminal advertisements: *118 W. Kinzie Street*

D

Advertisements, p. ⟨32⟩ headed: *Socialist Literature*

Publisher's address in terminal advertisements: *118 W. Kinzie Street*

Advertised in *The International Socialist Review* (Chicago), Oct. 1909. Listed PW Nov. 6, 1909.

"Jack London delivered this address before the students of Yale University in 1905. A leading review in London published it a year or so after its delivery, but Americans had to wait ... until the *International Socialist Review* ... grew big enough to use it. We published it by special arrangement with Jack London in August, 1909. Since then a hundred thousand copies have been circulated in booklet form ..."—From the "Publishers' Note to the Hundredth Thousand," issued n.d., 1914.

"A new edition from new plates, large clear type, extra book paper, artistic cover" advertised in *The International Socialist Review* (Chicago), April, 1914, as *just published.*

AAS (B)   HEH (D)   USC (A, B)   Y (C)

11914. ... GLEN ELLEN, SONOMA CO., CAL., DEC. 31, 1909. MR. G. J. GRIFFITH, DEAR SIR:—⟨text, 14 lines, beginning: I have just finished reading *Crime and Criminals,* and I write to congratulate you ...⟩

    ⟨LOS ANGELES, JAN. 4, 1910⟩

Single leaf. Printed on recto only. 8⁷⁄₁₆″ x 5½″.

Printed letter. On the letterhead of the Prison Reform League, Los Angeles, Cal. At head of letter is a prefatory note dated Jan. 4, 1910: *Jack London ... was the second person to subscribe to* Crime and Criminals, *the book just issued by the Prison Reform League. The following letter was received from him today:*

HEH

11915. LOST FACE ...

    NEW YORK   THE MACMILLAN COMPANY   1910   ALL RIGHTS RESERVED

⟨i⟩-⟨viii⟩, ⟨1⟩-240; advertisements, pp. ⟨241-244⟩; 2 blank leaves. Frontispiece and 5 plates inserted. 7⁷⁄₁₆″ x 5⅛″ full.

⟨1-16⟩⁸. *Signed:* ⟨A⟩⁴, ⟨B⟩-I, K-Q⁸, ⟨R⟩⁴.

V cloth: blue.

On copyright page: ... *Published March, 1910.* Noted for *this month* PW Feb. 5, 1910. Listed PW March 12, 1910. A copy at NYPL inscribed by London March 23, 1910. The London (Mills & Boon) edition listed Bkr Nov. 1915.

NYPL   UV

11916. REVOLUTION AND OTHER ESSAYS ...

    NEW YORK   THE MACMILLAN COMPANY   1910   ALL RIGHTS RESERVED

⟨i⟩-⟨x⟩, ⟨1⟩-309; blank, p. ⟨310⟩; plus: 4 pp. advertisements. 7⅜" x 5".

⟨1-20⁸; plus: 21²⟩. *Signed:* ⟨A⟩⁵, ⟨B⟩-I, K-M, ⟨N⟩-U⁸, X⁵.

T cloth: maroon. Stamped in gold and in blind. The publisher's spine imprint occurs in two forms; the following sequence is probably correct:

1: THE MACMILLAN COMPANY ⟨Deposit copies thus⟩

2: MACMILLAN

Note: Also noted in a variant (remainder?) binding: V cloth: brown; blackstamped; no terminal advertisements; spine imprint: MAC-MILLAN.

On copyright page: ... *Published March, 1910.* Deposited April 14, 1910. A copy in NYPL (spine imprint THE MACMILLAN COMPANY) inscribed by London April 24, 1910. Listed PW April 30, 1910. The London (Mills & Boon) edition listed Ath June 4, 1920.

AAS (variant) H (1, 2) LC (1) NYPL (1) UV (2) Y (1)

11917. ... To-Day's Problems and Their Solution by 150 Able Writers

Trade Union Book Concern Chicago, Ills. Price 5 Cents in Chicago—outside 10 Cts ⟨1910⟩

Cover-title. At head of title ⟨all copies thus?⟩: Chicago Edition 500,000

Printed pale green paper wrapper.

P. ⟨1⟩: ... *150 Messages of Hope and Cheer by 150 Able Writers ... A pocket manual to induce right thinking for the common good. The most valuable collection of heart-to-heart talks ever published in any language* ... ⟨*Chicago*⟩ *Copyrighted 1910, by Henry E. Allen.*

"The Right, Nothing More nor Less," p. 10.

Reviewed in *The San Francisco Examiner*, Aug. 6, 1910.

NYU

11918. BURNING DAYLIGHT ...

NEW YORK THE MACMILLAN COMPANY 1910 ALL RIGHTS RESERVED

⟨i⟩-⟨viii⟩, 1-361; blank, p. ⟨362⟩; advertisements, pp. ⟨363-365⟩; blank, p. ⟨366⟩; advertisements, pp. ⟨367-374⟩; blank leaf. Frontispiece and 7 plates inserted. 7½" x 5⅛".

⟨1-24⟩⁸. *Signed:* ⟨A⟩⁴, B-I, K-U, X-Z, 2A⁸, ⟨2B⟩⁴.

Two printings noted:

First Printing

As above. A copy thus in NYPL inscribed by London Oct. 15, 1910.

Second Printing

⟨i⟩-⟨viii⟩, 1-361; blank, p. ⟨362⟩; advertisements, pp. ⟨363-365⟩; blank, p. ⟨366⟩; advertisements, pp. ⟨367-374⟩; 3 blank leaves. Frontispiece and 7 plates inserted. 7½" x 5⅛".

⟨1-23⁸, 24¹⁰⟩. Leaves ⟨24⟩₂₋₃ inserted.

Query: Does the *first printing* described above represent an advance printing?

V cloth: blue.

Note: All examined copies, both printings, have the publisher's spine imprint set in a single line thus: MACMILLAN Johnson reports copies with the imprint reading *The / Macmillan / Company;* no copy thus traced by BAL.

On copyright page: *Published October, 1910.* Advertised as *ready* Oct. 5 PW Sept. 10; Sept. 24, 1910. Announced for fall publication PW Sept. 24, 1910. Listed PW Oct. 15, 1910. A copy of the first printing in NYPL inscribed by London Oct. 15, 1910. The London (Heinemann) edition advertised as *just published* Ath May 6, 1911; listed Bkr May 12, 1911.

AAS (2nd) H (2nd) NYPL (both) Y (2nd)

11919. THEFT A PLAY IN FOUR ACTS ...

NEW YORK THE MACMILLAN COMPANY LONDON: MACMILLAN & CO. LTD. 1910 ALL RIGHTS RESERVED

⟨i⟩-⟨xiv⟩, ⟨1⟩-272, blank leaf. 6¹⁵⁄₁₆" x 4¹¹⁄₁₆".

⟨1-18⟩⁸. *Signed:* ⟨-⟩⁷, ⟨1⟩-17⁸, ⟨18⟩¹.

Maroon T cloth sides, white V cloth shelfback. Front stamped in white. Top edges gilded.

Note: Also issued in a variant (remainder?) binding: V cloth: olive; red. Top edges plain. Front unstamped.

On copyright page: ... *Published November, 1910* Deposited Nov. 17, 1910. A copy at NYPL received Nov. 19, 1910. Listed PW Dec. 3, 1910.

AAS H HEH (variant) NYPL USC (variant) Y

11920. ⟨Advertisement for *An Interview* by Daniel W. Church.⟩

⟨Issued by the Berlin Carey Company, Chicago, 1910⟩

Single cut sheet folded to make four pages. Unpaged. White calendered paper. 6⅞" x 4¾".

On p. ⟨3⟩ is a letter from London, May 5, 1910, addressed to D. W. Church.

USC

11921. "A Book of Verses"

Published by P. C. : A. C. 1910 ⟨Oakland, Cal., Carruth & Carruth Co.⟩

Printed paper wrapper. Unpaged.

Contains "The Worker and the Tramp." Woodbridge, London & Tweney (p. 249) report a separate printing of the poem issued by the Jack London Amateur Press Club.

USC UV

11922. ... BUNCHES OF KNUCKLES ...

⟨Paris, 1910⟩

Caption-title. The above at head of p. 3. At head of title: The New York Herald, Paris, Sunday, December 18, 1910—Christmas Supplement.

Pp. 1-6? Pp. 3-6? 16″ x 11⁷⁄₁₆″.

Collected in *The Night Born,* 1913.

HEH

11923. The Poems of Sappho by John Myers O'Hara

Smith & Sale   Portland   Maine   Publishers ⟨n.d., 1910⟩

Cover-title. Printed self-wrapper. Issued as a prospectus. 8 pp.

Testimonial, p. ⟨7⟩.

HEH

11924. Francisco Ferrer   His Life, Work and Martyrdom with Messages Written Especially for This Brochure by Ernst Haeckel ... Jack London and Others ...

Published by Francisco Ferrer Association, 241 Fifth Avenue, New York. ⟨n.d., 1910⟩

Printed paper wrapper. Cover-title.

Edited by Leonard D. Abbott.

Tribute, p. 77.

AAS   H

11925. About Fagots of Cedar by Ivan Swift ...

Sheehan & Co. ... ⟨1910⟩

Not seen. Entry from Woodbridge, London & Tweney, p. 268.

Single leaf. Contains a brief statement by London.

11926. WHEN GOD LAUGHS AND OTHER STORIES ...

NEW YORK   THE MACMILLAN COMPANY   1911 ALL RIGHTS RESERVED

⟨i⟩-⟨x⟩, ⟨1⟩-319; blank, p. ⟨320⟩; advertisements, pp. ⟨321-324⟩; blank leaf. Frontispiece and 5 plates inserted. 7¼″ x 4¾″ full.

⟨1-21⟩⁸. *Signed:* ⟨A⟩⁵, ⟨B⟩-I, ⟨K⟩-U, P⟨*sic*⟩⁸, ⟨X⟩³.

Note: In all examined copies leaf ⟨1⟩₂ (the title-leaf) is a cancel.

V cloth: green.

On copyright page: ... *Published January, 1911.* Deposited Jan. 26, 1911. Noted as *ready this week* PW Feb. 4, 1911. Listed PW Feb. 4, 1911. The London (Mills & Boon) edition listed Bkr March 15, 1912.

H NYPL Y

11927. ADVENTURE ...

THOMAS NELSON AND SONS LONDON, EDINBURGH, DUBLIN, LEEDS, AND NEW YORK   LEIPZIG: 35-37 KÖNIGSTRASSE. PARIS: 61, RUE DES SAINTS-PÈRES. ⟨1911⟩

For American edition see next entry.

⟨i⟩-vi, ⟨7⟩-376; publisher's catalog, pp. ⟨I⟩-VIII. Frontispiece inserted. 7³⁄₁₆″ scant x 4¾″.

⟨1⟩-12¹⁶.

Printed green paper boards, grained in imitation of linen. White end papers printed in green with wreaths enclosing the letter *N,* eighteenth-century figures, garlands.

On verso of title-page: *First published in 1911.* Advertised as *just ready* Bkr Jan. 18, 1911. Listed Bkr Feb. 24, 1911; Ath Feb. 25, 1911. Reviewed Ath March 18, 1911. The Mills & Boon (London) edition listed PC Oct. 28, 1916.

B

11928. ADVENTURE ...

NEW YORK   THE MACMILLAN COMPANY   1911 ALL RIGHTS RESERVED

First American edition. For prior publication see preceding entry.

⟨i⟩-⟨x⟩, 1-405; blank, p. ⟨406⟩; plus: 8 pp. catalog. Laid paper. 7⅜″ x 5″.

⟨1-26⟩⁸; plus: 27⁴. *Signed:* ⟨A⟩⁵, B-I, K-U, X-Z, 2A-2C⁸, 2D³; plus: ⟨2E⟩⁴.

V cloth: blue. Stamped in white, blue, intaglio. A principal feature of the front cover is an illustration: Palm trees, sea, boat, etc.

Also noted in a variant (remainder?) binding: V cloth: red. Stamped in white only. The illustration described above not present. On the front the principal decoration is the Macmillan monogram.

On copyright page: *Published March, 1911.* Deposited March 9, 1911. A copy in BA received March 14, 1911. Listed PW March 18, 1911.

AAS (variant)   NYPL   UV   Y

11929. THE CRUISE OF THE SNARK ...

NEW YORK   THE MACMILLAN COMPANY   1911
ALL RIGHTS RESERVED

⟨i⟩-xiv, 1-340; 6 pp. advertisements. Frontispiece inserted. Also, 1 plate inserted between pp. 270-271, not included in list of illustrations. Other illustrations in text. 7¾″ x 5¼″.

⟨1-22⁸, 23⁴⟩. *Signed:* ⟨A⟩⁷, B-I, K-U, X-Y⁸, Z⁵.

Note: In all examined copies leaf ⟨1⟩₂ (the title-leaf) is a cancel.

T cloth: blue. Top edges gilded. Color print pasted to front cover.

On copyright page: ... *Published June, 1911.* Listed PW June 24, 1911. The London (Mills & Boon) edition listed Bkr Sept. 19, 1913.

BA   H   NYPL   UV   Y

11930. The Red-Hot Dollar and Other Stories from The Black Cat by H. D. Umbstaetter with an Introduction by Jack London

L. C. Page & Company   Boston   MDCCCXI

"Introduction," pp. v-ix, dated March 25, 1911.

On copyright page: *First Impression, July, 1911.* Deposited July 28, 1911. Listed PW Aug. 5, 1911.

HEH   NYPL   UV   Y

11931. THE STRENGTH OF THE STRONG ...

CHICAGO   CHARLES H, ⟨*sic*⟩ KERR & COMPANY
CO-OPERATIVE ⟨1911⟩

⟨1⟩-30; advertisements, pp. ⟨31-32⟩. Illustrated. 6¹³⁄₁₆″ x 4¹⁵⁄₁₆″.

⟨-⟩¹⁶.

White paper wrapper, printed in blue.

Publisher's address in advertisements: 118 West Kinzie Street, Chicago.

Advertised as *ready by July 15, The International Socialist Review* (Chicago), July, 1911. Advertised as though published, *ibid.,* Aug. 1911. Deposited Aug. 1, 1911. Listed PW Sept. 2, 1911.

Note: Reprinted several times by Charles H. Kerr. The reprints may be identified by the presence of one or more of the following features: Imprint dated 1912; publisher's address in the advertisements given as 341-349 E. Ohio St.; text ends on p. 29.

Other reprints noted:

As No. 148 in *People's Pocket Series,* Appeal to Reason, Girard, Kansas, n.d., 1920? According to the publisher (letter to BAL) published Dec. 1, 1920. Advertised in *Appeal to Reason* (Girard, Kansas), Feb. 12, 1921. A copy was in the possession of the late E. Walter Latendorf, New York City, Nov. 1948.

As No. 148 in *Ten Cent Pocket Series,* Girard, Kansas, n.d., 192-?. Copy in H.

As No. 148 in *Little Blue Book Series,* Haldeman-Julius Co., Girard, Kansas ⟨1924⟩. Copies in UCB, UV.

Collected in *The Strength of the Strong,* New York, 1914.

LC (being a deposit copy)   USC

11932. SOUTH SEA TALES ...

NEW YORK   THE MACMILLAN COMPANY   1911
ALL RIGHTS RESERVED

⟨i-ii⟩, ⟨i⟩-⟨vi⟩, ⟨1⟩-327; plus: 8 pp. advertisements; 4 blank leaves. Frontispiece inserted. 7½″ full x 5⅛″.

⟨1-21⁸; plus: 22⁸⟩. *Signed:* ⟨A⟩⁴, ⟨B⟩-F, ⟨G⟩-I, K-R, ⟨S⟩-U, X⁸, Y⁴; plus: ⟨Z⟩⁸.

V cloth: blue.

On copyright page: ... *Published October, 1911.* A copy at BA received Oct. 10, 1911. Listed PW Oct. 28, 1911. Mentioned under the title *South Sea Stories* Bkr March 11, 1911, as *shortly* to be published by Heinemann; no other mention found. The London (Mills & Boon) edition listed Bkr Nov. 22, 1912.

AAS   BA   H   NYPL

11933. Burning Daylight ... Copyright, 1910

Reprinted by Land's End Eucalyptus Forest Site by Express Permission of the Author ⟨Chicago, 1911⟩

Cover-title. Printed self-wrapper.

A synopsis and reprint of portions of the novel. Issued as an advertisement for the Land's End Eucalyptus Forest Site, Chicago. On p. ⟨16⟩ is a letter from London to "Dear Comrade Buck," May 31, 1911, granting permission to publish.

USC

11934. NORTH OF BAY COUNTIES CALIFORNIA ...

⟨n.p., n.d., *ca.* 1911⟩

Caption-title. The above on p. 1.

1-16. 9⅜″ x 6½″. Illustrated.

⟨-⟩⁸.

Printed self-wrapper.

"Jack London ... recently drove a coach and four through this territory and describes his adventures in his unique way in an article for *Sunset, The Pacific Monthly,* entitled, 'Navigating Four Horses North of the Bay'. Parts of this interesting article are re-printed in this booklet together with brief outlines of the resources and possibilities to be found in the North of Bay Counties."—p. 1. The article appeared in *Sunset* Sept. 1911. Collected in *The Human Drift,* 1917.

Y

11935. ⟨A printed letter addressed to guests. The first page is headed:⟩ JACK LONDON GLEN ELLEN SONOMA CO., CALIFORNIA U.S.A. ...

⟨n.d., 1911?⟩

Single cut sheet folded to make four pages. Printed on pp. ⟨1⟩ and ⟨3⟩ only; otherwise blank. Printed in blue on blue-gray wove paper watermarked MAIL ORDER BOND Page: 6⁵⁄₁₆″ x 3½″.

Directions for getting to Glen Ellen; comment on accommodations, etc.

UCB   USC   UV

11936. THE HOUSE OF PRIDE AND OTHER TALES OF HAWAII ...

NEW YORK   THE MACMILLAN COMPANY   1912 ALL RIGHTS RESERVED

⟨i⟩-⟨vi⟩, ⟨1⟩-232; advertisements, pp. ⟨233-234⟩; plus: 6 pp. advertisements, 3 blank leaves. Frontispiece inserted. 7⁹⁄₁₆″ x 5⅛″.

⟨1-15⁸; plus: 16⁶⟩. *Signed:* ⟨A⟩³, ⟨B⟩-I, K-Q⁸, ⟨R⟩³.

V cloth: green.

On copyright page: ... *Published March, 1912.* Advertised for *March or April* PW March 2, 1912. Deposited March 21, 1912. A copy at BA received March 27, 1912. Listed PW April 13, 1912. The London (Mills & Boon) edition listed Bkr April 3, 1914.

AAS   BA   NYPL   UV

11937. A SON OF THE SUN ...

GARDEN CITY   NEW YORK   DOUBLEDAY, PAGE & COMPANY   1912

⟨i-viii⟩, ⟨1⟩-333; printer's imprint, p. ⟨334⟩; blank leaf. Frontispiece and 3 plates inserted. 7⅜″ x 5″.

⟨1-21⁸, 22⁴⟩.

V cloth: blue.

A copy at BA received May 22, 1912. Advertised PW May 25, 1912. Listed PW June 1, 1912. The London (Mills & Boon) edition listed Bkr March 7, 1913.

NYPL   UV   Y

11938. WONDER OF WOMAN   A "SMOKE BELLEW" STORY (IN TWO PARTS) ...

INTERNATIONAL MAGAZINE CO.   NEW YORK ⟨1912⟩

⟨1⟩-32. 8¹³⁄₁₆″ x 5¹⁵⁄₁₆″. Paper watermarked: Olde Style.

⟨-⟩¹⁶.

White paper wrapper printed in blue and gold.

First published in *Cosmopolitan Magazine* (New York), May–June, 1912. The text is that of the magazine appearance, not the slightly altered text of the book appearance (*Smoke Bellew,* 1912). Presumably issued prior to *Smoke Bellew;* see next entry.

UCB   USC   UV   Y

11939. SMOKE BELLEW ...

NEW YORK   THE CENTURY CO   1912

⟨i-viii⟩, ⟨1⟩-385; blank leaf; blank leaf used as pastedown. Frontispiece inserted; and, 7 inserted plates reckoned in the printed pagination. 7½″ x 5⅛″.

⟨1⁴, 2-24⁸, 25⁴⟩.

V cloth: blue-gray. Stamped in black, gray, yellowish-white; decorated with moon and mountain scene, Alaskan grotesque. Johnson (1942), p. 319, reports "a copy ... in plain grey-blue cloth; status unknown"; further information wanting.

On copyright page: *Published, October, 1912* Noted for Sept. 24 PW Sept. 21, 1912; advertised in same issue for Sept. 28. A copy in NYPL inscribed by London Oct. 3, 1912. Listed PW Oct. 5, 1912. The London (Mills & Boon) edition listed Bkr June 11, 1913.

AAS   H   NYPL   Y

11940. THE SCARLET PLAGUE ...

PAUL R. REYNOLDS   NEW YORK   1912

Presumably prepared for copyright purposes although no record found in the Copyright Office; for published edition see under 1915.

⟨1⟩-51. 8³⁄₁₆″ x 5⁹⁄₁₆″.

⟨-⟩²⁶.

Printed blue paper wrapper.

UV

11941. THE DREAM OF DEBS

This story went into several (many?) printings.
A positive sequence has not been determined.
The present entry is tentative, although there is
reason to believe the following sequence is correct. It must be noted that each of the following
may represent one or more printings.

A(?)

THE DREAM OF DEBS A STORY OF IN-
DUSTRIAL REVOLT BY JACK LONDON

CHICAGO   CHARLES H. KERR & COMPANY CO-
OPERATIVE ⟨n.d., not before 1912⟩

⟨1⟩-32. 7¼″ x 5″.

⟨-⟩¹⁶.

Glazed white paper wrapper, printed in blue.
Front: THE / DREAM OF DEBS / ⟨half tone portrait of Debs⟩ / BY JACK LONDON / 10 CENTS
Outer back: *History of The Supreme Court of
the United States by Gustavus Myers* ... Inner
wrapper unprinted.

B (?)

THE DREAM OF DEBS BY JACK LONDON

CHICAGO   CHARLES H. KERR & COMPANY CO-
OPERATIVE ⟨n.d., not before 1912⟩

⟨1⟩-31; p. ⟨32⟩ blank. 6¹³⁄₁₆″ x 5⅛″.

⟨-⟩¹⁶.

Glazed white paper wrapper, printed in blue.
Front: THE / DREAM OF DEBS / BY JACK LONDON /
⟨half tone portrait of Debs⟩ / PRICE / 10 CENTS
Outer back: *Books by Jack London* ... Inner
wrapper unprinted.

Note: An undoubted later printing, issued not
before 1914, varies from the above as follows:
P. ⟨32⟩ imprinted with publisher's advertisements; front wrapper lacks the word PRICE; outer
back wrapper headed: STUDY SOCIALISM. On
known reprints the sub-title, *A Story of Industrial Revolt,* is not present.

First published in *The International Socialist
Review* (Chicago), Jan.–Feb. 1909. Collected in
(reprinted from?) The Strength of the Strong,
1914. Reprinted, with London's *What Life
Means to Me,* as *The Appeal's Pocket Series,*
No. 30, People's Press, Girard, Kansas, n.d.,
1919; advertised in *Appeal to Reason* (Girard,
Kansas), Sept. 27, 1919.

Reprinted, with *What Life Means to Me,* as No.
30 in *The People's Pocket Series,* Appeal to Reason, Girard, Kansas, n.d., 1920?.

LC (B)   NYU (B)   UCB (A)   UV (A)   Y (A)

11942. THE NIGHT-BORN AND ALSO THE
MADNESS OF JOHN HARNED, WHEN
THE WORLD WAS YOUNG, THE BENE-
FIT OF THE DOUBT, WINGED BLACK-
MAIL, BUNCHES OF KNUCKLES, WAR,
UNDER THE DECK AWNINGS, TO KILL
A MAN, THE MEXICAN ...

NEW YORK   THE CENTURY CO. 1913

⟨i-vi⟩, ⟨1⟩-290; blank, p. ⟨291⟩; advertisements,
p. ⟨292⟩; blank leaf. Frontispiece inserted. 7⁷⁄₁₆″
x 5⅛″.

⟨1-18⁸, 19⁶⟩.

Polished V cloth: gray-blue. Goldstamped save
for blackstamped totem poles on front and
spine.

Two printings noted. The order is presumed
correct.

1

As above.

2

⟨i-viii⟩, ⟨1⟩-290; blank, p. ⟨291⟩; advertisements, p. ⟨292⟩; 2 blank leaves.

⟨1⁴, 2-19⁸, 20⁴⟩.

Unpolished V cloth: blue-gray. Stamped in blue
save for blindstamped totem poles on front and
spine.

On copyright page: *Published, February, 1913*
Advertised PW Feb. 22, 1913. Deposited Feb.
26, 1913. A copy (1st printing) received by BA
March 4, 1913. Listed PW March 11, 1913. The
Toronto (Bell & Cockburn) edition (in Y) has
on the copyright page: *Published, February,
1913;* printed from the setting of the New York
edition; issued simultaneously with the New
York edition? The London (Mills & Boon) edition listed Bkr Aug. 1916.

AAS (1st)   BA (1st)   H (1st)   NYPL (1st)   SG (2nd)
Y (1st)

11943. HOW WILL YOUR VOTE EFFECT
⟨*sic*⟩ THIS BOY? ...

⟨FRESNO, CAL., n.d., 1913⟩

Cover-title. Place taken from union device at
foot of p. ⟨4⟩.

Single cut sheet folded to make 4 pages. 8½″ x
5½″.

*John Barleycorn by Jack London (Taken from
Story in Saturday Evening Post, March 15, 1913)*
—p. ⟨2⟩.

A truncated version of the first installment of
John Barleycorn as published in *The Saturday
Evening Post,* March 15, 1913. Presumably is-

sued soon thereafter and prior to publication of the book which was issued in Aug. 1913.

HEH

11944. THE VALLEY OF THE MOON ... REPRINTED FROM COSMOPOLITAN MAGAZINE FOR APRIL, 1913

NEW YORK: 1913

Not located. Entry on the basis of a fragment pasted in Vol. 12, Jack London scrapbook, in HEH. For publication of the full novel see below under 1913 (Oct.–Nov.).

"This pamphlet contains the first installment of Jack London's new novel, *The Valley of the Moon.* The remainder of the story will appear in the next eight issues of *Cosmopolitan Magazine* ... This pamphlet is presented with the compliments of the publishers ..."

11945. THE ABYSMAL BRUTE ...

NEW YORK   THE CENTURY CO.   1913

⟨i-iv⟩, ⟨1⟩-169; advertisements, p. ⟨170⟩; blank leaf. Frontispiece inserted. 6¹³⁄₁₆″ x 4½″.

⟨1-11⟩⁸.

Smooth V cloth: olive-green. Stamped in black (deep green?) and yellow.

Note: Also noted in a variant binding, status unknown, of rough V cloth (green) stamped in black and green.

Also note: Johnson (1942) reports a "later binding ... stamped in black"; no copy stamped in black only has been traced by BAL.

On copyright page: *Published, May, 1913* Advertised for *May 24* PW May 17, 1913. A copy in NYPL inscribed by London May 27, 1913. Listed PW May 31, 1913.

AAS   H   NYPL   UV (variant)   Y

11946. JOHN BARLEYCORN ...

NEW YORK   THE CENTURY CO.   1913

For prior partial printing see above under 1913: *How Will Your Vote Effect* ⟨sic⟩ *This Boy?*

Two printings noted:

1

⟨i-viii⟩, ⟨1⟩-343, blank leaf. Frontispiece inserted; and, 7 inserted plates reckoned in the printed pagination. 7½″ scant x 5³⁄₁₆″.

⟨1⁴, 2-21⁸, 22⁶⟩.

2

⟨i-viii⟩, ⟨1⟩-343, 3 blank leaves. Frontispiece inserted; and, 7 inserted plates reckoned in the printed pagination.

⟨1⁴, 2-22⁸⟩.

V cloth: blackish-green.

On copyright page: *Published, August, 1913* Advertised for Aug. 15, PW Aug. 16, 1913. Deposited Aug. 19, 1913. A first printing in NYPL inscribed by London Aug. 22, 1913. Listed PW Aug. 23, 1913. The London (Mills & Boon) edition listed Bkr July 24, 1914.

AAS (1st)   BA (1st)   H (1st)   NYPL (1st)   UV (1st, 2nd)

11947. THE VALLEY OF THE MOON ...

NEW YORK   THE MACMILLAN COMPANY   1913

For prior partial publication see above under 1913 (April).

⟨i-vi⟩, ⟨1⟩-530; advertisements, pp. ⟨531-536⟩; blank leaf. Frontispiece inserted. 7½″ scant x 5⅛″.

⟨1-34⟩⁸.

V cloth: orange.

On copyright page: ... *Published October, 1913* Announced for Oct. 29, PW Oct. 4, 1913. Listed PW Nov. 15, 1913. The London (Mills & Boon) edition listed Bkr Dec. 26, 1913.

NYPL   UV   Y

11948. JACK LONDON BY HIMSELF ...

PUBLISHERS   THE MACMILLAN COMPANY   64-66 FIFTH AVENUE   NEW YORK   ⟨n.d., 1913⟩

Cover-title, printed in black and red.

⟨1-7⟩; advertisements, p. ⟨8⟩. Illustrated. Cream-white paper. 7¼″ x 5⁵⁄₁₆″.

⟨-⟩⁴.

Printed self-wrapper.

Issued as an advertisement, primarily for *The Valley of the Moon* (Oct. 1913). Mills & Boon, Ltd., London, issued a printing as an advertisement primarily for their edition of *The Valley of the Moon* (Dec. 1913). Mills & Boon reprinted and reissued the sketch in 1915, with emphasis on *The Mutiny of the Elsinore* (issued in London Jan. 1915). Collected in *The Star Rover* ... ⟨1963⟩.

HEH (New York)   UV (New York; both London printings)

11948A. ... The World's Great Events ... by Great Historians Edited by Esther Singleton ... Volume Eight from A.D. 1899 to A.D. 1906

P. F. Collier & Son   New York ⟨1913⟩

At head of title: New Standard Edition

"The San Francisco Disaster," pp. 2687-2698. Originally in *Collier's* (New York), May 5, 1906, under the title "The Story of an Eye-Witness."

Query: Was this preceded by a 1908 edition?

Deposited Feb. 20, 1913.

UV

11948B. JACK LONDON SAYS:

⟨LONDON: THE HELLIER DENSELOW STUDIO, 40 GUNNERSBURY LANE, 1913⟩

Single leaf of laid paper folded to make four pages. Page: 5⁷⁄₁₆″ x 3¹¹⁄₁₆″. P. ⟨1⟩ as above; imprint at foot of p. ⟨2⟩.

Issued as an advertisement. On p. ⟨2⟩ is an extract from a letter, Jack London to the studio, "expressing his opinion of the Bookplate we designed for him."

A copy was in the collection of the late George S. MacManus, Philadelphia, April, 1967.

11949. Education for Socialism   What Twenty-Four Well Known Party Members Say about the Rand School of Social Science ...

... Rand School of Social Science, 140 East 19th St., New York. ⟨n.d., 1913?⟩

Caption-title. Single cut sheet of pale buff paper. Printed on recto only. A watermark is present, but the only located example is pasted down; hence, watermark not readily readable. 8″ x 5″. Size postulated.

Dear Comrades: In the rapid growth of the Socialist movement today there is a certain menace to its strength and success ...

An endorsement of the Rand School of Social Science, New York City, signed at end by London and others.

HEH

11950. Extracts from John Barleycorn ... (by Permission) for the Campaign for Statewide Prohibition in California ...

⟨Woman's Christian Temperance Union of California, San Francisco, n.d., 1913?⟩

4-page leaflet. Caption-title. The above at head of p. ⟨1⟩.

Reprint? Extracted from the book? Issued **prior** to the book? See above under 1913.

HEH

11951. A LETTER FROM JACK LONDON GLEN ELLEN, SONOMA COUNTY, CALIFORNIA, APRIL 15th, 1913 ...

⟨n.p., n.d., 1913?⟩

Single cut sheet. A trimmed example measures 8³⁄₁₆″ x 7⅛″.

Testimonial for an antiseptic.

I am glad to say a good word for so good a thing as Chinosol ...

HEH

11952. No Drunkard Plan

⟨n.p., n.d., *ca.* 1913⟩

Not seen. Entry from Woodbridge, London & Tweney, p. 259. Pamphlet.

Contains a letter from Jack London, May 15, 1913.

11953. Sabotage   Its History, Philosophy & Function ⟨by⟩ Walker C. Smith

⟨I.W.W. Publishing Bureau, 1001 W. Madison St., Chicago, 1913(?)⟩

Cover-title. Printed paper wrapper.

Letter, Dec. 5, 1913, from London to "Dear Comrade Smith:—Just a line to tell you that I have finished reading your pamphlet *Sabotage*. ... Yours for the Revolution, Jack London."

UV

11954. Anecdotes of the Hour by Famous Men As Told by Winston Churchill ⟨American novelist, 1871–1947⟩ ... Jack London ... and about 100 Other Notable Men ...

New York   Hearst's International Library Co. 1914

Anecdote, p. 11.

Deposited April 13, 1914.

H

11955. THE STRENGTH OF THE STRONG ...

NEW YORK   THE MACMILLAN COMPANY   1914

⟨i⟩-⟨viii⟩, 1-257; blank, p. ⟨258⟩; advertisements, pp. ⟨259-264⟩. Frontispiece inserted. 7½″ x 5″.

⟨1-17⟩⁸.

V cloth: blue.

For prior publication of the title-story see above under 1911.

On copyright page: ... *Published May, 1914* Advertised as *ready shortly* PW May 16, 23, 1914. A copy at BA received June 2, 1914. Listed PW June 20, 1914. The London (Mills & Boon) edition listed Ath Feb. 1917.

BA NYPL UV Y

11956. THE MUTINY OF THE ELSINORE ...

NEW YORK THE MACMILLAN COMPANY 1914

⟨i-vi⟩, 1-378; plus: 8 pp. advertisements. Frontispiece inserted. 7½″ x 5⅛″ scant.

⟨1-24⁸; plus: 25⁴⟩.

V cloth: orange.

On copyright page: ... *Published September, 1914* Deposited Sept. 10, 1914. Advertised as *just published* and listed PW Oct. 3, 1914. The London (Mills & Boon) edition listed Ath Jan. 16, 1915. The Nelson (London) edition received by BMu Dec. 5, 1916.

AAS NYPL UV Y

11957. *Entry cancelled.*

11958. King Albert's Book A Tribute to the Belgian King and People from Representative Men and Women throughout the World ⟨Edited by Hall Caine⟩

The Daily Telegraph ⟨London⟩ in Conjunction with The Daily Sketch The Glasgow Herald and Hodder and Stoughton ⟨1914⟩

Contribution, p. 122. For American edition see next entry.

For comment see entry No. 9830A.

11959. King Albert's Book A Tribute to the Belgian King and People from Representative Men and Women throughout the World ⟨Edited by Hall Caine⟩

New York Hearst's International Library Co ⟨1914; *i.e.*, 1915⟩

Contribution, p. 122. See preceding entry.

For comment see entry No. 9831A.

11960. THE SCARLET PLAGUE ...

NEW YORK THE MACMILLAN COMPANY 1915 ALL RIGHTS RESERVED

First published edition. For a copyright printing see above under 1912.

⟨1⟩-181; blank, p. ⟨182⟩; advertisements, pp. ⟨183-188⟩; 2 blank leaves. Illustrated. 7⁹⁄₁₆″ x 5⅛″.

⟨1-12⟩⁸. *Signed:* ⟨B⟩-I, K-L, ⟨M⟩-N⁸.

V cloth: plum. White end papers printed in orange with a dotted field on which is the illustration appearing at p. 128.

On copyright page: ... *Published May, 1915.* Advertised for *this month* PW April 10, 1915. A copy at BA received May 11, 1915. Listed PW May 15, 1915. The London (Mills & Boon) edition listed PC Dec. 4, 1915.

BA H NYPL

11961. The Cry for Justice An Anthology of the Literature of Social Protest ... Edited by Upton Sinclair ... with an Introduction by Jack London ...

Philadelphia The John C. Winston Company Publishers ⟨1915⟩

Cloth. Also limp black morocco, edges stained red. "The John C. Winston Company was at this time one of the foremost publishers of Bibles. When it published this *Socialists' Bible,* a small number were issued with this distinctively *Bible* binding and edge treatment."—*A Catalogue of Books, Manuscripts, and Other Materials from the Upton Sinclair Archives,* Bloomington, The Lilly Library, Indiana University ⟨n.d., 1963⟩; the morocco binding not seen by BAL.

"Introduction," pp. 3-5. Otherwise reprint, save for 4 lines on p. 519.

Listed PW July 17, 1915. Deposited July 29, 1915.

H Y

11962. THE JACKET (THE STAR ROVER) ...

MILLS & BOON, LIMITED 49 RUPERT STREET LONDON, W. ⟨1915⟩

Not seen. Entry on the basis of a photographic copy of the title-leaf of the copy in BMu. For American edition see next entry.

Pp. 333. On reverse of title-leaf: *Published 1915*

Listed and reviewed Ath July 31, 1915. Deposited in BMu Aug. 4, 1915. Listed and reviewed Bkr Aug. 6, 1915. Advertised as *ready* Ath Aug. 7, 1915. Listed PC Aug. 7, 1915. Reissued 1916, 320 pp., in *Mills & Boon's Shilling Library.*

11963. THE STAR ROVER ...

NEW YORK THE MACMILLAN COMPANY 1915

First American edition. For prior publication see preceding entry.

⟨i-vi⟩, 1-329; *Printed in the United States of America*, p. ⟨330⟩; plus: 10 pp. advertisements, blank leaf. Frontispiece inserted. 7½″ x 5¹⁄₁₆″.

⟨1-21⁸; plus: 22⁶⟩.

V cloth: blue.

On copyright page: *Published October, 1915* A copy at BA received Oct. 14, 1915. Listed PW Oct. 23, 1915.

H   UV

THE LITTLE LADY OF THE BIG HOUSE ...

NEW YORK ... 1915 ...

See this title below under 1916 (April).

11964. THE ACORN-PLANTER A CALIFORNIA FOREST PLAY PLANNED TO BE SUNG BY EFFICIENT SINGERS ACCOMPANIED BY A CAPABLE ORCHESTRA ...

NEW YORK   THE MACMILLAN COMPANY   1916 ALL RIGHTS RESERVED

⟨i⟩-vi, ⟨1⟩-84; publisher's advertisements, 6 pp. 6¹⁵⁄₁₆″ x 4¾″.

⟨1-6⟩⁸. *Signed:* ⟨A⟩³, ⟨B⟩-F⁸, G⁵.

Maroon T cloth sides, white V cloth shelfback. Three forms of the binding noted; the sequence is uncertain and the designations are for identification only:

A: Spine lettered: THE / ACORN / PLANTER / JACK / LONDON / THE / MACMILLAN / COMPANY Top edges gilded. Deposit copies thus.

B: Spine lettered: THE / ACORN / PLANTER / JACK / LONDON Top edges gilded. Note absence of publisher's spine imprint. *Query:* Was the spine imprint originally present? And now worn away?

C: Spine lettered: THE / ACORN / PLANTER / ⟨3 dots⟩ / JACK / LONDON / THE / MACMILLAN / COMPANY Top edges gilded.

Note: Johnson (1942) states: "First state of binding has white spine." All copies examined by BAL are thus.

On copyright page: *Published February, 1916.* Deposited Feb. 24, 1916. Listed PW March 11, 1916. American sheets distributed in London with cancel title-leaf of *Mills & Boon, Limited 49 Rupert Street London, W.* ⟨1916; probably issued 1917⟩.

AAS (A) BA (A) H (A) LC (A) NYPL (A,C) UV (A,B)

11965. THE RESIGNATION OF JACK LONDON   DEAR COMRADES: ⟨text of London's resignation from the Socialist Party⟩ ...

⟨n.p., n.d., 1916⟩

Single cut sheet. Watermarked: RAILROAD BOND ... Done in imitation of a typewritten letter. 11″ scant x 8½″.

Foner (pp. 122-123) states that the letter was dictated as early as Jan. 1916, but not mailed until March 7, 1916; Foner dates the letter *Honolulu, March 7, 1916.* O'Connor (p. ⟨383⟩) states that London *began* the letter on March 7, 1916. It is probable the letter was also published as a separate in forms other than the one here described.

H   HEH

11966. THE LITTLE LADY OF THE BIG HOUSE ...

NEW YORK   THE MACMILLAN COMPANY   1916 ALL RIGHTS RESERVED

⟨i-vi⟩, 1-392; title-leaf for catalog, pp. ⟨393-394⟩; plus: 4 pp. advertisements. Frontispiece inserted. 7½″ full x 5³⁄₁₆″.

⟨1-25⁸; plus: 26²⟩.

The copyright notices read: Copyright, 1915 / BY JACK LONDON / ⟨rule⟩ / Copyright, 1916 / BY JACK LONDON / Set up and electrotyped. Published April, 1916 / ⟨rule⟩ / Copyrighted in Great Britain

V cloth: blue.

Note: A variant of unknown status has been seen; it varies from the above as follows:

Imprint dated *1915* (not *1916*).

Copyright notices read: Copyright, 1915 and 1916 / BY JACK LONDON / ⟨rule⟩ / Copyright, 1916 / BY JACK LONDON / Set up and electrotyped. Published April, 1916 / ⟨rule⟩ / Copyrighted in Great Britain

On copyright page: ... *Published April, 1916* Advertised as *ready April 5* PW Jan. 8, 1916. Advertised as *published April 5* PW April 8, 1916. Noted as *published last Wednesday* ⟨i.e., April 5⟩ PW April 8, 1916. BA copy received April 11, 1916. Listed PW April 15, 1916. The London (Mills & Boon) edition listed PC April 15, 1916; issued simultaneously with the New York edition? The Nelson (London) edition received at BMu Nov. 12, 1917.

H   NYPL   Y (both)

11967. AN OLD LIE FINALLY NAILED ⟨11-line notice beginning *The authorship of the letter* ...⟩

⟨n.d., 1916⟩

Cover-title. Single cut sheet folded to make 4 pages. 7¹⁄₁₆" x 4".

P. ⟨2⟩: *Young Men: The lowest aim in your life is to become a soldier* . . .

P. ⟨3⟩ prints a letter from London, dated Aug. 5, 1916, addressed to Lieutenant James D. Willson, denying authorship of the *lowest aim* statement.

P. ⟨4⟩: A statement urging enlistment in the United States Navy.

At USC is a letter from Lt. Willson to Jack London, September 12, 1916, which indicates that the Navy probably issued the denial leaflet during the late summer of 1916.

NYPL   USC   UV

NOTE

An Old Lie Finally Nailed (collated above) is Jack London's denial of authorship of an appeal to young men not to join the military, issued under Jack London's name, and published under various titles, the following among them: *The Good Soldier; Why Be a Soldier; Open Letter to a Young Man; Advice to the Young Soldier; Advice to Young Soldiers; The Military Ideal.* The appeal declared (among other things) that a young man's "lowest aim . . . is to become a soldier" and similar antimilitaristic sentiments. The earliest dated appearance BAL has found is in *The International Socialist Review* (Chicago), Oct. 1913, where it is prominently displayed under Jack London's name. However, Jack London's denial (printed in essence but not verbatim in *Army and Navy Journal* for May 2, 1914) implies that the appeal is of earlier date: "Some years ago . . . some printed cards were scattered . . . which gave *Advice to Young Soldiers*. In order to impress the readers with the terrors of war, he ⟨sic⟩ was referred to a description in one of London's books of a ⟨fictional⟩ battle supposed to take place in Chicago, in 1929. ⟨The description is in London's *The Iron Heel*, 1908.⟩ A news despatch was sent out giving London not as a writer whose description of a battle was referred to, but giving London as the actual author of the carded 'advice'."

In the 1916 denial collated above London states that "as far as I can trace the history . . . ⟨the advice⟩ was originally published and circulated in Germany, and later on was brought over to the United States, translated and circulated with my name attached . . ." BAL has found no German printing, either in German or in English. It may be that London had in mind a printing of January 1914, reported in *Army and Navy Journal* (April 17, 1915) as an "effusion . . . laid to a German printer in London named Valentine Freitag" under the title *The Military Ideal*.

A printing of the advice in HEH bears a notation in Charmian London's hand: *Jack did not write this.*

The circumstances of the 1914 denial may be significant. *Army and Navy Journal* for May 2, 1914, reports on them: "The hostile feeling which Jack London encountered on the transport *Kilpatrick* when he went on board at Galveston, preparatory to its sailing for Mexico, caused him to break his silence regarding the much quoted *Advice to Young Soldiers* . . . This he did in a statement, issued for publication, as he leaned over the railing of the *Kilpatrick* . . . Four other correspondents sailed, but London could not get aboard except after a special plea and a telegram to Washington, according to the *Houston Chronicle* . . . We have yet to learn that London has made any protest to labor organizations against the use of his name in connection with it . . ." BAL has found no denial of authorship in *The International Socialist Review*.

It must be observed that the sentiments set forth in the advice are indeed not contrary to London's beliefs, his denials notwithstanding.

In his book *Wobbly* (Chicago ⟨1948⟩, p. 206), Ralph Chaplin attributes authorship to Jack London. In a private letter (in NYPL) written in response to an inquiry regarding the authorship, Chaplin (Nov. 4, 1948) stated: ". . . For a long time, before World War I, I published *Why be a Soldier* . . . and similar items over Jack London's by-line *without any protest by him*. That was the J. L. who delighted in shocking the bourgeois world with the thunderous verbal threats of *The Iron Heel* and *The Dream of Debs* . . . I doubt if you can prove Jack wrote them. I am in no position to do so . . ."

Philip S. Foner (*Jack London* ⟨1947⟩, pp. 115–116) comes to the same conclusion: "Whether or not Jack London actually wrote *The Good Soldier* will never be known since other articles were published in his name which he did not write. Yet it is difficult to believe that *The International Socialist Review* would have published the article under his name unless they had reasonable assurance that it expressed London's sentiments; nor did he protest the publication when it appeared. Again, parts of the article are reminiscent of his descriptions of the guards at the coronation of King Edward in *The People of the Abyss: Myriads of men, splendid men, the pick of the people, whose sole function in life is to blindly obey, and blindly to kill and destroy and stamp out life.*"

11968. THE TURTLES OF TASMAN . . .

NEW YORK   THE MACMILLAN COMPANY   1916
ALL RIGHTS RESERVED

‹i-vi›, 1-268; 7 pp. advertisements, 3 blank leaves. 7½″ x 5⅛″.

‹1-18›⁸.

V cloth: mauve.

On copyright page: . . . *Published, September, 1916.* Deposited Sept. 28, 1916. Listed PW Oct. 21, 1916. A copy in H received Nov. 2, 1916. The London (Mills & Boon) edition listed Bkr July 1917.

BA H NYPL Y

11969. Letters and Opinions of the Western Press of "The Heart of the Hills" and Other Poems . . .

‹Ukiah, Cal., Northern Crown Publishing Co., 1916›

Cover-title. Single cut sheet folded to make 4 pages. Issued as an advertisement for *Heart of the Hills* by Grover C. McGimsey.

London's letter, dated Nov. 6, 1916, p. ‹2›.

USC

11970. General Types of Superior Men   A Philosophico-Psychological Study of Genius, Talent and Philistinism in Their Bearings upon Human Society and Its Struggle for a Better Social Order by Osias L. Schwarz with a Preface by Jack London . . .

Boston: Richard G. Badger   Toronto: The Copp Clark Co., Limited ‹1916›

"Preface," pp. 5-6, dated at end *August 19, 1915.*

Announced PW Sept. 23, 1916. Deposited Jan. 6, 1917. Listed PW Jan. 13, 1917.

H

11971. "What Do You Know about a Horse?" By Francis A. Cox . . . with Foreword by Jack London . . .

London: G. Bell and Sons Ltd.   York House, Portugal Street, W. C.   1916

Not seen. Entry on the basis of a photographic copy of the BMU copy (in H).

Printed paper boards.

"Foreword," pp. xi-xvi, dated at end *Honolulu, Hawaii, 8th June 1915.*

Note: A proof printing with 1915 ‹sic› imprint (in HEH) does not contain the London foreword.

Listed Ath and Bkr Feb. 1917.

11972. THE HUMAN DRIFT . . .

NEW YORK   THE MACMILLAN COMPANY   1917

‹i-viii›, 1-184; plus: 8 pp. advertisements. Portrait frontispiece inserted. 7½″ x 5⅛″.

‹1-12⁸; plus: 13⁴›.

V cloth: red-brown. Front and spine gold-stamped save for a blindstamped border on front. Also noted in a variant (remainder?) binding: Smooth red linen; front unstamped; spine stamped in black; copy in Y.

On copyright page: . . . *Published, February, 1917.* Deposited Feb. 23, 1917. A copy at H received March 1, 1917. Listed PW March 10, 1917. The London (Mills & Boon) edition listed Bkr Nov. 1919.

AAS BA H NYPL

11973. JERRY OF THE ISLANDS . . .

NEW YORK   THE MACMILLAN COMPANY   1917
ALL RIGHTS RESERVED

‹i›-‹x›, 1-337; blank, p. ‹338›; advertisements, pp. ‹339-342›; plus: Advertisements, pp. ‹343-346›. Frontispiece inserted. 7½″ x 5¹⁄₁₆″.

‹1-22⁸; plus: 23²›.

V cloth: red.

Note: A copy in HEH has certain leaves of Sig. ‹1› present as singletons; status not known. Repaired?

On copyright page: . . . *Published, April, 1917.* A copy at BA received April 24, 1917. Listed PW April 28, 1917. The London (Mills & Boon) edition listed Bkr Aug. 1917.

AAS BA H NYPL UV Y

11974. MICHAEL BROTHER OF JERRY . . .

NEW YORK   THE MACMILLAN COMPANY   1917
ALL RIGHTS RESERVED

‹i›-‹x›, 1-344; 10 pp. advertisements; 2 blank leaves. Frontispiece inserted. 7½″ x 5⅛″.

‹1-23›⁸.

V cloth: red.

On copyright page: . . . *Published, November, 1917.* Deposited Nov. 8, 1917. A copy at BA received Nov. 13, 1917. Listed PW Nov. 24, 1917.

BA NYPL UV Y

11975. EIGHT GREAT FACTORS OF LITERARY SUCCESS . . .

‹n.p., n.d., 1917›

Single cut sheet. Printed on recto only. 8⅞₁₆″ x 6″.

This is a partial printing of "Eight Factors of Literary Success" which was published in *The Silhouette, a Quarterly Magazine of Stories in Profile* (Oakland, Cal.) Feb. 1917. In the periodical appears the statement: *Written for The Silhouette.*

Note: Not to be confused with a similar production, *Jack London by Himself;* see entry No. 11948.

A copy in PSU was sent to Fred Lewis Pattee by Charmian London on April 29, 1917.

UCB   USC   UV

11976. The Plan of Laughing Land ... by W. Costley

(Copyrighted 1906)   ⟨San Francisco: New Mission Press, not before 1917⟩

Printed paper wrapper. On wrapper: Revised Edition

On inner front wrapper: "What London Said of Laughing Land," a letter beginning: "Dear Comrade Costley: Just a line to tell you how much I like your *Laughing Land* ..."

UV

11977. THE RED ONE ...

NEW YORK   THE MACMILLAN COMPANY   1918 ALL RIGHTS RESERVED

⟨i-vi⟩, 1-193; blank, p. ⟨194⟩; advertisements, pp. ⟨195-200⟩; blank leaf. Frontispiece inserted. 7½″ x 5″ full.

⟨1-13⟩⁸.

Printed brown paper boards.

On copyright page: ... *Published, October, 1918* Advertised for Oct. 22 PW Sept. 28, 1918. Deposited Oct. 24, 1918. A copy in H received Oct. 31, 1918. Listed PW Nov. 9, 1918. The London (Mills & Boon) edition listed Ath Aug. 15, 1919.

AAS   BA   NYPL

11978. HEARTS OF THREE ...

MILLS & BOON, LIMITED   49 RUPERT STREET LONDON, W.   ⟨n.d., 1918⟩

For American publication see below under 1920.

⟨i-ii⟩, ⟨i⟩-xii, ⟨1⟩-292; 10 pp. advertisements, 2 blank leaves. 7⅜₁₆″ x 4¾″.

⟨1-10⟩¹⁶. Leaves ⟨1⟩₁ and ⟨10⟩₁₆ used as pastedowns.

Printed gray-blue paper boards, grained in imitation of coarse V cloth.

Reviewed TLS Oct. 31, 1918. Listed Ath Nov. 1918; Bkr Dec. 1918.

H

11979. Literary California Poetry Prose and Portraits Gathered by Ella Sterling Mighels ...

Harr Wagner Publishing Co.   San Francisco, California 1918

Reprint save for "The Way of War," pp. 202-203.

For comment see BAL, Vol. 1, p. 226.

H   NYPL

11980. The Way into Print

James Knapp Reeve   Franklin, Ohio   ⟨n.d., not before Nov. 11, 1918⟩

Printed paper wrapper. Cover-title.

"Getting into Print," pp. 2-6. Reprinted from *The Editor* (New York) March, 1903.

Gd

11981. ON THE MAKALOA MAT ...

NEW YORK   THE MACMILLAN COMPANY   1919 ALL RIGHTS RESERVED

⟨i-vi⟩, 1-229, 2 blank leaves. 7⅜″ x 5₁₆¹″.

⟨1-15⟩⁸.

V cloth: blue.

On copyright page: ... *Published, September, 1919* Deposited Oct. 22, 1919. A copy at BA received Nov. 4, 1919. Listed PW Nov. 8, 1919. Issued in London ⟨1920⟩ as *Island Tales.*

AAS   BA   H   NYPL

11982. HEARTS OF THREE ...

NEW YORK   THE MACMILLAN COMPANY   1920 ALL RIGHTS RESERVED

First American edition. For prior publication see above under 1918.

⟨i⟩-⟨x⟩, 1-373. 7⅜″ x 5₁₆¹″.

⟨1-24⟩⁸.

S cloth: maroon.

On copyright page: *Published, September, 1920* Deposited Oct. 14, 1920. A copy at BA received Oct. 26, 1920. Listed PW Oct. 30, 1920.

AAS   BA   Y

11983. Jack London by Charmian London ...

Mills & Boon, Limited   49 Rupert Street London, W. 1 ⟨1921⟩

2 Vols. Issued in the United States as *The Book of Jack London,* 1921.

The text varies somewhat from the American edition; see in list of *References and Ana.* The most notable variation is the inclusion herein of "Jack London's First Story," Vol. 1, pp. 142-148, which incorporates for the first time in a book London's "Story of a Typhoon off the Coast of Japan." This last collected in *Dutch Courage and Other Stories,* New York, 1922, *q.v.*

Listed Bkr Dec. 1921.

H

11984. Our Hawaii (Islands and Islanders) by Charmian London ... New and Revised Edition

New York   The Macmillan Company   1922 All Rights Reserved

"My Hawaiian Aloha," pp. 1-33.

"The present volume is a revision of ... ⟨the 1917 edition⟩, from which I have eliminated the bulk of personal memoirs, by now incorporated into my book *Book of Jack London,* a thoroughgoing biography ... Also, instead of making an independent work out of Jack London's three articles, written in 1916, entitled, *My Hawaiian Aloha,* I am making them a part of my book ..."—p. vii.

On copyright page: *New and Revised Edition; February, 1922*   Issued in London ⟨1923⟩ as *The New Hawaii.*

H

11985. DUTCH COURAGE AND OTHER STORIES ...

NEW YORK   THE MACMILLAN COMPANY   1922 ALL RIGHTS RESERVED

⟨i⟩-⟨xvi⟩, 1-180. Frontispiece and 7 plates inserted. 7⅜" x 5" scant.

⟨1-12⁸, 13²⟩.

Coarse B cloth: maroon.

On copyright page: *Published September, 1922.* Deposited Oct. 4, 1922. A copy in BA received Oct. 17, 1922. Listed PW Nov. 11, 1922. The London (Mills & Boon) edition listed N&A Oct. 27, 1923; reviewed N&A Nov. 10, 1923. *See next entry.*

AAS   BA   Y

11986. ... STORIES OF SHIPS AND THE SEA ...

HALDEMAN-JULIUS COMPANY   GIRARD, KANSAS ⟨1922⟩

At head of title: LITTLE BLUE BOOK NO. 1169 EDITED BY E. HALDEMAN-JULIUS

Reprint? See note below.

⟨1⟩-64. 5" full x 3⅜" scant.

⟨-⟩³².

Printed blue paper wrapper.

Contents:

"Chris Farrington: Able Seaman." Also in preceding entry.

"Typhoon off the Coast of Japan." Also in preceding entry; and, *Jack London,* by Charmian London, London ⟨1921⟩.

"The Lost Poacher." Also in preceding entry.

"The Banks of the Sacramento." Also in preceding entry. For a separate printing see above under year 1904.

"In Yeddo Bay." Also in preceding entry.

In all likelihood there were many printings of this booklet. The first printing (printings?) has the date *1922* present in the copyright notice; later printings (printing?) have the date absent.

Note: Precise date of publication not known. If issued after *Dutch Courage and Other Stories* (preceding entry), the book is a complete reprint.

EM (reprint)   UCB (with date present)

11987. The Mystery of Jack London   Some of His Friends   Also a Few Letters   A Reminiscence by Georgia Loring Bamford ...

Published by Georgia Loring Bamford   1428 Castro Street   Oakland, California ⟨1931⟩

Cloth, paper labels.

Reprint save for:

Inscriptions in Bamford's books, pp. ⟨174⟩-178.

Letters, pp. 181-225.

H

11988. The Omnibus of Sport Edited by Grantland Rice and Harford Powel ...

Harper & Brothers Publishers   New York and London   1932

Reprint save for "The Story of a Smile," pp. 505-513, the final article in a series of eleven published in *New York Herald* (and other papers) June 24–July 5, 1910. "The Story of a Smile" appeared in the *Herald* under the title "Jack Johnson v. Jim Jeffries."

On copyright page: *First Edition;* and, code letters *E-G* (signifying *printed May, 1932*). Deposited July 20, 1932.

LC

11989. THE SEA SPRITE AND THE SHOOT-ING STAR ...

⟨PRIVATELY PRINTED, NOVEMBER, 1932.⟩

Single cut sheet folded to 4 pages. Cover-title. Text on pp. ⟨2-3⟩. Imprint at end. Cream-white paper, embossed with an irregular pattern. Page: 10¾″ x 5¾″.

First published in "The Letter Box" of *The San Francisco Call* in 1899. A proof printing of the original appearance is in the London archive at HEH.

A copy at B received Dec. 10, 1932.

Note: Woodbridge, London & Tweney (p. 275) report a reprint of unknown date issued by the Jack London Amateur Press Club.

AAS   B   HEH   NYPL   UCLA

11990. THE LETTERS OF WESTERN AU-THORS NUMBER 12, DECEMBER 1935 JACK LONDON WITH COMMENT BY CHARMIAN KITTREDGE LONDON

PUBLISHED FOR ITS MEMBERS BY THE BOOK CLUB OF CALIFORNIA ⟨SAN FRANCISCO, 1935⟩

Cover-title (printed in black and red). Single cut sheet of heavy white laid paper folded to 4 pages. Page: 9¹⁵⁄₁₆″ x 8¼″.

Pasted to p. ⟨3⟩ is an envelope containing a facsimile Jack London letter addressed to *Dear Cloudesley,* dated *Papeete, Tahiti, Feb. 17 / 08.* The letter is printed on 5 leaves.

Issued as part of *The Letters of Western Authors A Series of Letters, Reproduced in Facsimile, of Twelve Distinguished Pacific Coast Authors.*

H   LC

11991. The New Junior Classics Edited by Mabel Williams and Marcia Dalphin ... Volume Nine Sport and Adventure

⟨n.p., New York⟩ P. F. Collier & Son Corporation ⟨1938⟩

"Chased by the Trail," pp. 138-150.

Deposited June 16, 1938.

LC

11992. Jack London's First by Wm. McDevitt ... Limited to 500 Copies

Recorder-Sunset Press   San Francisco   1946

Printed paper wrapper. Cover-title.

"Two Gold Bricks," pp. 12-17.

H   LC   UV

11993. Jack London American Rebel A Collection of His Social Writings together with an Extensive Study of the Man and His Times, Edited by Philip S. Foner

The Citadel Press   New York   ⟨1947⟩

Contains some material here first collected from periodicals.

Deposited Dec. 4, 1947.

AAS   H   LC   NYPL   Y

11994. Jack London's Tales of Adventure Edited by Irving Shepard

Hanover House, Garden City, New York ⟨1956⟩

In addition to the two pieces noted below ("The Run Across" and "Bonin Islands") the first section of this book ("The Young Man") consists of extracts from Jack London's writings. Certain of these extracts appear here for the first time in book form. "Typhoon off the Coast of Japan" had prior book publication in Mrs. London's *Jack London,* London ⟨1921⟩; and, *Dutch Courage ...,* New York, 1922.

"While it is not my intent to comment on each of the selections to be found in this volume, there are a number that do merit special notice. One of these is 'Typhoon off the Coast of Japan,' the first article Jack London wrote for publication ... Other unusual pieces are 'The Run Across' and 'Bonin Islands,' both of which appeared in 1895 in the Oakland High School magazine, *The Aegis.* They are based on his experiences aboard the *Sophie Sutherland.* These two articles, as well as the Russo-Japanese War dispatches, the Johnson-Jeffries fight, 'Through the Rapids on the Way to Klondike,' and 'From Dawson to the Sea' have never before appeared in book form."—p. xi. See *The Omnibus of Sport,* 1932, above.

On copyright page: *First Edition* Deposited Nov. 9, 1956.

LC

11995. ... The Call of the Wild The Cruise of the Dazzler and Other Stories of Adventure with the Author's Special Report: Gold Hunters of the North

Platt & Munk, Publishers New York ⟨1960⟩

At head of title: Jack London

Reprint save for "Fuzziness of Hoockla-Heen."

Deposited Aug. 29, 1960.

LC

11996. Creator and Critic A Controversy between Jack London and Philo M. Buck, Jr. Edited ... by King Hendricks ...

Utah State University Press   Logan, Utah Monograph Series Volume VIII March, 1961 Number 2

Printed paper wrapper.

Correspondence between Jack London and Philo M. Buck, Jr., Nov. 5, 1912 to July 19, 1913, pp. 30-44.

H UV Y

11997. ... THE ASSASSINATION BUREAU, LTD.

McGRAW-HILL BOOK COMPANY, INC. NEW YORK TORONTO LONDON ⟨1963⟩

At head of title: JACK LONDON   COMPLETED BY ROBERT L. FISH FROM NOTES BY JACK LONDON

Jack London stops and Mr. Fish begins on page 122—p. 179.

Printed Veined Brown Paper Boards

⟨i-vi⟩, 1-184, blank leaf. 8″ x 5¼″.

⟨1-6⟩[16].

Pictorial Paper Wrapper

⟨i-vi⟩, 1-184, blank leaf. 7¹⁵⁄₁₆″ x 5⅜″ scant.

So-called perfect binding.

On copyright page: *First Edition* and, code number *38655.*

Deposited Nov. 12, 1963. Listed PW Dec. 30, 1963, as in boards; and, paper.

LC (boards) UV (paper)

11998. LETTERS FROM JACK LONDON CONTAINING AN UNPUBLISHED CORRESPONDENCE BETWEEN LONDON AND SINCLAIR LEWIS EDITED BY KING HENDRICKS AND IRVING SHEPARD

PUBLISHED BY THE ODYSSEY PRESS, NEW YORK ⟨1965⟩

⟨i⟩-⟨x⟩, ⟨1⟩-502. A gathering of 8 leaves of illustrations inserted. 9¼″ scant x 6⅛″.

⟨1-16⟩[16].

Stamped rough-toothed drab paper boards sides, green V cloth shelfback. Top edges stained orange. Rough-toothed red-brown end papers.

"... In selecting the letters we have tried to choose those that are most representative of London. We began our series with his first letter to an editor when he was twenty-two years old ... We know that there are earlier ones but we have not had access to any worthy of inclusion ..." pp. vii-viii.

H

Reprints of London's own books; and, books containing reprinted London material but with London's name on the title-page. For a list of books by authors other than London containing reprinted London material see *Section III*.

11999. The Spinners' Book of Fiction by ‹16 authors› . . . with a Dedicatory Poem by George Sterling . . .

Paul Elder and Company San Francisco and New York ‹1907›

Noted in four bindings. The following order is probable:

A

Blue-black and white tweed-like cloth. Stamped in orange and brown. Oval color-print pasted to front cover. Top edges gilded. The PW listing (Nov. 23, 1907) states: "bound in blue homespun linen."

B

Coarse unbleached linen. Stamped in green. Oval color-print pasted to front cover. Top edges gilded.

C

Coarse brown buckram. Stamped in green. Oval color-print pasted to front cover. Top edges stained brown.

D

Coarse brown buckram. Stamped in green. Oval color-print pasted to front cover. Top edges plain.

Deposited Oct. 8, 1907. Listed PW Nov. 23, 1907.

11999A. The Chinago and Other Stories . . .

Leslie-Judge Company New York ‹1911; *i.e.*, 19—›

Reprinted from *When God Laughs* . . . , 1911, pp. 155-319.

12000. . . . A Souvenir Chapter of . . . A Son of the Sun . . .

Mills & Boon Ltd. 49 Rupert St. London, W. ‹1913›

Cover-title. At head of title: *With Mills & Boon's Compliments.* Printed paper wrapper. The text comprises pp. 1-8 of the novel.

12001. 300 Latest Stories by 300 Famous Story Tellers as Told by . . . O. Henry Jack London . . . ‹and Others›

Star Library Company New York ‹1914; *i.e.*, not before 1915›

Printed paper wrapper. Issued as *Star Fiction Library,* No. 3. An omnibus volume printed from the plates of *Anecdotes of the Hour by Famous Men* . . . , New York: Hearst's International Library Co., 1914; and of another (unlocated, unidentified) book.

Also issued in cloth with spine imprint H.I.L.CO ‹*i.e.*, Hearst's International Library Company›. In this cloth format not identified as part of the *Star Fiction Library.*

12002. An Odyssey of the North . . .

Mills & Boon, Limited 49 Rupert Street. London, W. ‹n.d., 1915›

Reprint of *The Son of the Wolf,* 1900. Listed PC May 15, 1915.

12003. ‹Works›

New York: The Review of Reviews Company, 1917.

Printed from the original Macmillan plates. *Imprint postulated.* No complete set located.

12004. ‹Novels and Tales. The Sonoma Edition›

New York The Macmillan Company London: Macmillan & Co., Ltd. . . . ‹1917–1921?›

Note: The imprint varies in certain of the volumes. Printed from the original Macmillan plates.

The volumes were offered as separates, not as a set, with the first volumes published in 1917. Certain volumes printed from the plates of two separate works with the folios altered to present continuous pagination. 21 Vols.?

12005. ... Foreword ⟨to *Michael Brother of Jerry,* N. Y., 1917⟩

⟨Boston: The Massachusetts Society for the Prevention of Cruelty to Animals and The American Humane Education Society, 1917; *i.e.,* 1918⟩

Caption-title. At head of title: *If you ever loved a dog read this "Foreword" from Jack London's "Michael Brother of Jerry."* ...

Pp. i-iv. Single cut sheet folded to four pages.

There were at least two printings of this separate:

1: Folio *i* present. No footnote on p. i. Copies in UCB and H.

2: Folio *i* not present. Footnote on p. ⟨i⟩ stating that The Jack London Club has 160,000 members. Copy in HEH.

Issued as promotion for The Jack London Club.

"... First printed by our two Societies in October, 1918 ..."—Letter, Massachusetts Society for the Prevention of Cruelty to Animals, March 22, 1965, to BAL.

12006. Smoke and Shorty ...

Mills & Boon, Limited   49 Rupert Street London, W. 1 ⟨1920⟩

On copyright page: *Published 1920* The only examined copy has a rubber-stamped notice on the title-page: *Colonial Library*

Listed Ath Jan. 30, 1920; PC Jan. 31, 1920.

12007. Island Tales ...

Mills & Boon, Limited   49 Rupert Street London, W. 1 ⟨1920⟩

Issued in the United States as *On the Makaloa Mat,* 1919. Listed Ath Aug. 6, 1920; PC Aug. 14, 1920. *Not seen.*

12008. ... He Renounced the Faith

Appeal to Reason   Girard, Kansas   ⟨n.d., 1920⟩

Printed paper wrapper. At head of title: *People's Pocket Series No. 47.* Advertised *Appeal to Reason* (Girard, Kansas) Oct. 30, 1920. Otherwise *The Apostate;* see in *Section I* under 1906.

12009. Brown Wolf and Other Jack London Stories as Chosen by Franklin K. Mathiews ...

New York   The Macmillan Company 1920 ...

Deposited Dec. 11, 1920.

12010. ... An Odyssey of the North ...

Haldeman-Julius Company   Girard, Kansas ⟨1920⟩

Printed paper wrapper. At head of title: *Little Blue Book No. 1022 Edited by E. Haldeman-Julius* Reprint of *The Son of the Wolf;* for earlier publication under this title see in *Section II* under 1915.

12011. ... The Son of the Wolf ...

Haldeman-Julius Company   Girard, Kansas ⟨1920⟩

Printed paper wrapper. At head of title: *Little Blue Book No. 152 Edited by E. Haldeman-Julius* Also issued without date.

12012. ... Tales of the Far North ...

Haldeman-Julius Company   Girard, Kansas ⟨1920⟩

Printed paper wrapper. At head of title: *Little Blue Book No. 288 Edited by E. Haldeman-Julius* Also issued without date.

12013. The New Hawaii by Charmian London ... Containing My Hawaiian Aloha by Jack London

Mills & Boon, Limited   49 Rupert Street London, W. 1 ⟨1923⟩

Note: In all examined copies the table of contents leaf is a cancel. Otherwise *Our Hawaii ...,* by Charmian London; see in *Section I* under 1922. Listed PC Nov. 3, 1923.

12014. ... Tales of the White Silence ...

Haldeman-Julius Company   Girard, Kansas ⟨n.d., 1926?⟩

Printed paper wrapper. At head of title: *Little Blue Book No. 1024 Edited by E. Haldeman-Julius*   Published June 8, 1926.*

12015. ... The Wife of a King ...

Haldeman-Julius Company   Girard, Kansas ⟨n.d., 1926?⟩

Printed paper wrapper. At head of title: *Little Blue Book No. 223 Edited by E. Haldeman-Julius*   Published July 13, 1926.*

* Date on the basis of information supplied by the publisher. It is necessary to emphasize that such information supplied by this publisher is not invariably accurate; date in doubt. *All examined copies printed from plates from which the date has been removed.* Status of this publication uncertain. Reprint?

12016. The Call of the Wild and Other Stories ... with an Introduction by Frank Luther Mott ...

The Macmillan Company Publishers   New York MCMXXVI The Modern Readers' Series

Cloth, leather shelfback.

12017. London's Essays of Revolt ... Edited ... by Leonard D. Abbott

New York Vanguard Press MCMXXVI

Editor's introduction dated at end: *June, 1926.*

12018. ... Stories of Adventure ...

Haldeman-Julius Publications Girard, Kansas ‹n.d., 1927?›

Printed paper wrapper. At head of title: *Little Blue Book No. 1168 Edited by E. Haldeman-Julius* Published Feb. 17, 1927.*

12019. Selected Stories of Jack London

Published for Three Pay Sales Corporation ... New York City by the World Syndicate Publishing Company Cleveland New York 1930 ...

Cloth?

12020. Jack London's Stories for Boys ...

Cupples & Leon Company Publishers New York ‹1936›

12021. Best Short Stories of Jack London

The Sun Dial Press Garden City, New York ‹1945›

Cloth; and, paper boards. Deposited April 7, 1945.

12022. Love of Life and Other Stories ... Introduction by George Orwell

Paul Elek   Thirty Eight Hatton Garden London ‹1946›

12023. South Sea Tales ...

Cleveland New York The World Publishing Company ‹1946›

On copyright page: *First Printing March 1946*

* Date on the basis of information supplied by the publisher. It is necessary to emphasize that such information supplied by this publisher is not invariably accurate; date in doubt. *All examined copies printed from plates from which the date has been removed.* Status of this publication uncertain. Reprint?

12024. Four Short Stories ... Edited ... by K.R.H. Ewing ...

Longmans, Green & Co. London New York Toronto ‹1949›

Printed paper wrapper.

12025. The Sun-Dog Trail and Other Stories ...

The World Publishing Company Cleveland and New York ‹1951›

On copyright page: *First Edition* Deposited Sept. 17, 1951.

12026. The Adventures of Captain Grief ...

The World Publishing Company Cleveland and New York ‹1954›

A reprint, under altered title, of *A Son of the Sun,* 1912. The "Prologue" is extracted from pp. 25-29 of "A Son of the Sun" in *A Son of the Sun,* 1912.

12027. The Call of the Wild and Other Stories by Jack London ... ‹Edited› by Louis B. Salomon

New York Dodd, Mead & Company ‹1960›

Deposited March 1, 1960.

12028. ... Short Stories Edited ... by Maxwell Geismar

American Century Series   Hill and Wang New York ‹1960›

Printed paper wrapper. At head of title: Jack London:

12029. The Bodley Head Jack London Edited ... by Arthur Calder-Marshall

The Bodley Head London ‹1963›

12030. The Star Rover ... Autobiographical Introduction Epilogue by Gardner Murphy ...

The Macmillan Company, New York Collier-Macmillan Ltd., London ‹1963›

The "Autobiographical Introduction" had prior publication in 1913 under the title *Jack London by Himself.* See above in *Section One.*

12031. White Fang and Other Stories ...

New York Dodd, Mead & Company ‹1963›

12032. ... The Sea-Wolf and Selected Stories with an Afterword by Franklin Walker

A Signet Classic   Published by The New American Library ⟨New York, 1964⟩

At head of title: *Jack London*   Printed paper wrapper. On copyright page: *First Printing, April, 1964*   Received at Library of Congress May 25, 1964.

12033. Stories of Hawaii by Jack London Edited by A. Grove Day

Appleton-Century   New York ⟨1965⟩

Printed paper boards, cloth shelfback. On copyright page: *First edition.*

12034. Great Short Works of Jack London Edited . . . by Earle Labor . . .

Harper & Row, Publishers   New York ⟨1965⟩

Deposited March 7, 1966.

JACK LONDON

SECTION III

IN THIS SECTION are listed books by authors other than London which contain material by him reprinted from other books. See *Section Two* for reprints issued under London's name. No attempt has been made to record all the reprint appearances of London's most anthologized story, "To Build a Fire," first collected in *Lost Face,* 1910.

Short Story Classics (American) ... Edited by William Patten ...

    ... New York ⟨1905⟩

5 Vols. For comment see entry No. 6378.

The Loving Cup   Original Toasts by Original Folks Edited by Wilbur D. Nesbit

    Published by P. F. Volland & Company Chicago ⟨1909⟩

    Printed paper wrapper. "Here's to a Pard," p. 21, is a slightly altered version of a toast published in *Prosit* ... ⟨1904⟩, above.

Pathway to Western Literature ⟨Edited⟩ by Nettie S. Gaines ...

    Stockton, California   Nettie S. Gaines   All Rights Reserved ⟨1910⟩

The Great Events by Famous Historians A Comprehensive and Readable Account of the World's History ... Edited by Charles F. Horne ... Volume XX

    The National Alumni ⟨n.p., 1914⟩

    A subscription book and as such probably issued in a variety of bindings with varying imprints. Deposited Nov. 27, 1914.

Modern Short-Stories Edited ... by Margaret Ashmun ...

    New York   The Macmillan Company   1914

West Winds   California's Book of Fiction Written by California Authors ... Edited by Herman Whitaker

    Paul Elder and Company Publishers   San Francisco ⟨1914⟩

    Cloth, print pasted to front cover.

... The Socialist Appeal   Prose Passages Which Voice the Call for a New Social Order

    ... 1916 ... Appeal to Reason   Girard, Kansas

    Printed paper wrapper. At head of title: Appeal Socialist Classics Edited by W. J. Ghent No. 11

Modern Short Stories ... by Frederick Houk Law ...

    New York ... 1918

    For comment see BAL, Vol. 2, p. 427.

The Best Psychic Stories Edited ... by Joseph Lewis French ...

    Boni & Liveright   New York ⟨1920⟩

    Listed PW June 12, 1920.

Masterpieces of Adventure in Four Volumes ... Edited by Nella Braddy

    Garden City   New York   Doubleday, Page & Company   1921

    BA copy received Feb. 15, 1921. Deposited March 21, 1921. Listed PW March 5, 1921.

The Windmill: Stories, Essays, Poems & Pictures ... Edited by L. Callender

    London: William Heinemann Ltd. MCMXXIII

    Boards, cloth shelfback.

A Book of American Literature ... Edited by Franklyn B. Snyder ... and Edward D. Snyder ...

    New York   The Macmillan Company   1927 ...

Songs and Stories Selected ... by Edwin Markham ...

    Powell Publishing Company   San Francisco   Los Angeles   Chicago ⟨1931⟩

The Social Revolt   American Literature from 1888 to 1914 Edited by Oscar Cargill ...

    New York   The Macmillan Company   1933

American Poetry and Prose Edited by Norman
Foerster . . . Revised and Enlarged Edition

Houghton Mifflin Company   Boston . . .
⟨1934⟩

Golden Tales of the Far West Selected . . . by
May Lamberton Becker . . .

New York   Dodd, Mead & Company   1935

The Bedside Book of Famous American Stories
Edited by Angus Burrell . . . and Bennett A.
Cerf . . .

Random House Publishers New York ⟨1936⟩

Twenty-Two Short Stories of America Selected
. . . by Edith Mirrielees . . .

D. C. Heath and Company . . . Boston . . .
⟨1937⟩
Deposited April 28, 1937.

War or Peace Edited by Alfred Brant . . . and
Frederick Houk Law . . .

Harper & Brothers Publishers New York and
London 1938

Our Literary Heritage Literature We Like
⟨Edited by⟩ Russell Blankenship . . . Winifred
H. Nash . . .

Charles Scribner's Sons, New York . . . ⟨1939⟩
Code letter *A* on copyright page of first printing. Deposited April 29, 1939.

Tellers of Tales 100 Short Stories . . . Selected
. . . by W. Somerset Maugham

Doubleday, Doran & Company, Inc. New
York 1939
On copyright page: First Edition

For Men Only A Collection of Short Stories
Edited . . . by James M. Cain

Cleveland and New York The World Publishing Company ⟨1944⟩

Modern American Short Stories Edited . . . by
Bennett Cerf

Published in Cleveland and New York The
World Publishing Company ⟨1945⟩
On copyright page: First Printing July 1945

The American West A Treasury of Stories . . .
Edited . . . by William Targ

The World Publishing Company Cleveland
and New York ⟨1946⟩

On copyright page: First Published April
1946

The Golden Argosy A Collection of . . . Short
Stories . . . Edited . . . by Charles Grayson and
Van H. Cartmell

The Dial Press New York, 1947

Golden Book of Dog Stories Edited by Era
Zistel

Ziff-Davis Publishing Company   Chicago
⟨1947⟩

A Treasury of Short Stories . . . Edited by
Bernardine Kielty

Simon and Schuster New York 1947

Our Lives American Labor Stories Edited by
Joseph Gaer

Boni and Gaer New York ⟨1948⟩
Deposited Oct. 18, 1948.

A Treasure Chest of Sea Stories Compiled by
Max J. Herzberg

Julian Messner, Inc. New York ⟨1948⟩
Deposited Oct. 28, 1948.

The St. Nicholas Anthology Edited by Henry
Steele Commager . . .

Random House New York ⟨1948⟩
Listed PW Nov. 20, 1948.

The Spell of the Pacific An Anthology of Its
Literature . . . Edited by Carl Stroven and A.
Grove Day . . .

1949 The Macmillan Company New York

A Treasury of Great Reporting . . . Edited by
Louis L. Snyder . . . and Richard B. Morris . . .

1949 Simon and Schuster New York

Read up on Life The Holt Literature Series
. . . Edited by Harold H. Wagenheim Elizabeth
Voris Brattig Rudolf Flesch . . .

Henry Holt and Company New York, 1952

The World's Greatest Boxing Stories Edited . . .
by Harold U. Ribalow

New York: Twayne Publishers, Inc. ⟨1952⟩

Flights in Friendship Beacon Lights of Literature by Georgia Gantt Winn . . . ⟨and Others⟩

Iroquois Publishing Company, Inc. . . . Syracuse, New York . . . ⟨1953⟩
Deposited June 10, 1953.

An Anthology of Famous American Stories Edited by Angus Burrell and Bennett Cerf

The Modern Library New York ‹1953›

Youth's Companion Edited by Lovell Thompson . . .

   . . . Boston . . . 1954

For comment see entry No. 10927.

The Saturday Evening Post Treasury Selected . . . by Roger Butterfield and the Editors of the Saturday Evening Post

Simon and Schuster New York ‹1954›

Printed paper boards, cloth shelfback. On copyright page: *First Printing*

Out West An Anthology of Stories Edited by Jack Schaefer

Boston Houghton Mifflin Company 19 . . . 55

. . . Exploring Life . . . Edited by Harold H. Wagenheim . . . ‹and Others›

New York Henry Holt and Company ‹1956›

At head of title: *Our Reading Heritage* Deposited Jan. 9, 1956.

. . . Ourselves and Others . . . Edited by Harold H. Wagenheim . . . ‹and Others›

New York Henry Holt and Company ‹1956›

At head of title: *Our Reading Heritage* Deposited Jan. 12, 1956.

. . . This Is America . . . Edited by Harold H. Wagenheim . . . ‹and Others›

New York Henry Holt and Company ‹1956›

At head of title: *Our Reading Heritage* Deposited April 3, 1956.

. . . Great Stories from the World of Sport Edited by Peter Schwed and Herbert Warren Wind

1958 Simon and Schuster New York

At head of title: *Volume I ‹II› ‹III›* On copyright pages: First Printing Deposited Nov. 10, 1958.

A Cavalcade of Collier's Edited by Kenneth McArdle

A. S. Barnes & Company, Inc. New York ‹1959›

What Was Naturalism? Materials for an Answer Edited by Edward Stone . . .

Appleton-Century-Crofts, Inc. New York ‹1959›

Printed paper wrapper.

The Great Quotations Compiled by George Seldes . . .

A Caesar-Stuart Book: Lyle Stuart, New York ‹1960›

The Short Story Reader Revised Edition Edited by Rodney A. Kimball . . .

The Odyssey Press New York ‹1961›

On copyright page: *First Printing* A copy in LC received May 19, 1961.

The Californians: Writings of Their Past and Present Edited by Robert Pearsall ‹and› Ursula Spier Erickson . . .

San Francisco Hesperian House ‹1961›

2 Vols. Reprint with the possible exception of a 14-line extract, Vol. 1, p. 451. The extract otherwise unlocated by BAL.

The Fireside Book of Boxing Edited by W. C. Heinz

Simon and Schuster New York 1961

Printed paper boards, cloth shelfback. On copyright page: *First Printing*

My First Publication Edited . . . by James D. Hart . . .

‹San Francisco› The Book Club of California 1961

Printed paper boards, cloth shelfback, printed paper label on spine.

The Old West in Fiction Edited by Irwin R. Blacker

Ivan Obolensky, Inc. New York ‹1961›

Boards, cloth shelfback.

Years of Conscience The Muckrakers An Anthology . . . Edited . . . by Harvey Swados

Meridian Books The World Publishing Company Cleveland and New York ‹1962›

Meridian Books, No. M 129. Printed paper wrapper. On copyright page: *First printing February 1962*

The Trail of Ninety-Eight Edited by Lowell Thomas, Jr.

Duell, Sloan and Pearce New York ‹1962›

On copyright page: *First Edition* A copy in LC received April 19, 1962.

Ellery Queen's 1963 Anthology Edited by Ellery Queen ‹*i.e.*, Frederic Dannay and Manfred B. Lee›

  Davis Publications, Inc. 505 Park Avenue New York 22, New York ‹1962›

  Printed paper wrapper. On copyright page: *First Printing*   A copy in LC received Aug. 20, 1962.

The Saturday Evening Post Reader of Sea Stories Edited by Day Edgar

  Doubleday & Company, Inc.   Garden City, New York   1962

  Printed paper boards. A copy in LC received Aug. 28, 1962. Listed PW Sept. 24, 1962.

The Fabulous Country   An Anthology ‹Edited by› Charles Laughton

  New York ... McGraw-Hill Book Company, Inc. ‹1962›

  Printed paper boards.

. . . Adventures in Appreciation   Volume I Short Stories ‹Edited by› Walter Loban ‹and› Rosalind A. Olmsted ...

  Harcourt, Brace & World, Inc.   New York ... ‹1963›

  At head of title: Laureate Edition

The Art of Short Fiction ‹Edited by› Barbara Pannwitt ...

  Ginn and Company   Boston ... ‹1964›

  Printed paper wrapper.

REFERENCES AND ANA

Little Pilgrimages among the Men Who Have Written Famous Books   Second Series by E. F. Harkins ...

  Boston   L. C. Page & Company   MDCCCIII

Jack London   A Sketch of His Life and Work ...

  The Macmillan Company   66 Fifth Avenue, New York   1905

  Printed paper wrapper. Issued with varying imprints on the wrapper.

The Great Interrogation. A Play in One Act by Jack London and Lee Bascom (Mrs. G. H. Marsden).

  Presumably unpublished. Performed at The Alcazar Theatre, San Francisco, Aug. 21, 1905. The Copyright Office reports no record of deposit.

Jack London at Yale   Edited by the State Secretary of the Socialist Party of Connecticut ‹James C. Irvine›

  Published by the Connecticut State Committee & Printed at the Ariel Press, Westwood, Mass. ‹n.d., 1906›

  Printed paper wrapper. An account of London's lecture on socialism, "The Coming Crisis," at Woolsey Hall, Yale University, Jan. 26, 1906.

. . . Jack London   Who He Is and What He Has Done

  The Macmillan Company   64-66 Fifth Avenue, New York   ‹n.d., 1908?›

  Printed paper wrapper. At head of title: "About me are the great natural forces ..."

The Works of Jack London   Full Descriptive List of His Novels and Economic Writings ...

  The New York Call   409-415 Pearl St. New York   ‹n.d., not before 1910›

  A single cut sheet folded (stretcher fashion) to 12 pages. Printed throughout in red.

Socialist Dialogues and Recitations   Compiled by Josephine R. Cole and Grace Silver

  Chicago   Charles H. Kerr & Company   1913

  Printed paper wrapper. "The Machine Breakers," pp. ‹5›-11. "Condensed from Act II, scene II, of *The Iron Heel,* dramatized by W. G. Henry, by permission, from Jack London's novel of the same name." The Copyright Office reports no record of deposit.

Through the South Seas with Jack London by Martin Johnson ...

  New York   Dodd, Mead and Company   1913

  On copyright page: *Published, November, 1913*   The London (Werner Laurie) edition announced Bkr March 6, 1914.

‹An open letter urging young men not to enlist›

  Ca. 1914.

  Anti-militarist propaganda, printed many times and in many forms. For comment see *An Old Lie Finally Nailed* in *Section 1,* above, under the year 1916.

On the Face of the Earth (You are One)   Lyric by Jack London Music by Hassack Kubanoff and Jos. Riseman.

  New York, Phila. Melodious Music Co. Boston Mass. ... ‹1915›

Sheet music. Cover-title. Jack Neiburg (Boston bookseller and song-writer) identifies Jack London as a Boston song-writer; not the subject of this list.

Our Hawaii by Charmian Kittredge London . . .

New York The Macmillan Company 1917 All Rights Reserved

Also issued with cancel title-leaf imprinted *Patten Company, Ltd. Honolulu, Hawaii* ‹1917›. See in *Section 1* for revised edition of 1922 which contains first book publication of Jack London's "My Hawaiian Aloha."

From Coast to Coast with Jack London by A No 1 the Famous Tramp . . . First Edition . . .

1917 . . . The A No 1 . . . Publishing Company Erie, Penn'a, U.S.A.

Printed paper wrapper.

Jack London and Hawaii by Charmian Kittredge London . . .

Mills & Boon, Limited 49 Rupert Street London, W. 1 ‹1918›

Otherwise *Our Hawaii,* New York, 1917.

The Book of Jack London by Charmian London . . .

New York The Century Co. 1921

2 Vols. Listed PW Oct. 8, 1921. For the English edition, with textual variations, see *Jack London* ‹1921›, in *Section 1* above.

Jack London by Charmian London . . .

. . . London . . . ‹1921›

For fuller entry see in *Section 1* above.

Our Hawaii . . . by Charmian London . . . New and Revised Edition

New York . . . 1922 . . .

For fuller entry see in *Section 1* above.

The Twenty-Fifth Man The Strange Story of Ed. Morrell, the Hero of Jack London's "Star Rover" by Ed. Morrell . . .

New Era Publishing Co. Montclair, N. J. ‹1924›

Two printings noted. The following sequence is probable.

A: Leaf 8″ scant x 5⅜″. Top edges gilt. A copy thus (in UV) inscribed by the author July 20, 1924.

B: Leaf 7¼″ x 4¹⁵⁄₁₆″. Top edges plain. A copy thus (in UV) in the dust jacket, the jacket imprinted with extracts from reviews.

The Soul of Jack London by Edward Biron Payne Edited by Felicia R. Scatcherd

London: Rider & Co. Paternoster Row, E. C. 4 ‹1926›

The Mystery of Jack London . . . by Georgia Loring Bamford . . .

. . . Oakland, California ‹1931›

For fuller entry see in *Section 1* above.

. . . Jack London Bibliography and Biographical Data Abstract from the SERA Project . . . California Literary Research

‹San Francisco, State Emergency Relief Administration, n.d., 1935?›

At head of title: *Monograph #1 Edited by Joseph Gaer.* Mimeographed. 37 pp. A second edition (marked *Revised* on the title-page) is extended to 45 pp. by the addition of an index; contains a few minor revisions.

. . . Sailor on Horseback The Biography of Jack London . . .

Houghton Mifflin Company The Riverside Press Cambridge 1938

At head of title: *By Irving Stone* In addition to the trade edition, there was a *special gift edition* with the following notice on the front end paper: Included with this special gift edition . . . is a facsimile of an autobiographical letter written to Houghton Mifflin Company by Jack London in connection with the publication of his first book, *The Son of the Wolf.*

The letter, a 4-page facsimile of the original, dated Jan. 31, 1900, is inserted in a pocket on the front pastedown.

An entry in the publisher's records dated May 31, 1900, indicates that a biographical sketch of Jack London was printed; apparently a leaflet measuring 3″ wide. Further information wanting; perhaps a promotional piece based on London's letter of Jan. 31, 1900?

Jack London and His Times An Unconventional Biography by Joan London

Doubleday, Doran & Company, Inc. New York 1939

On copyright page: *First Edition*

Footloose in Arcadia A Personal Record of Jack London, George Sterling, Ambrose Bierce by Joseph Noel

Carrick & Evans, Inc. New York ⟨1940⟩

Jack London American Rebel ... by Philip S. Foner

    The Citadel Press New York ⟨1947⟩

    For fuller entry and comment see in *Section 1* of this list. Also see below under 1964.

Jack London as Poet and as Platform Man Did Jack London Commit Suicide? By Wm. McDevitt ...

    Recorder-Sunset Press San Francisco 1947

    Printed paper wrapper. *Limited to 500 Copies*—Certificate of issue.

Creator and Critic A Controversy between Jack London and Philo M. Buck, Jr. Edited ... by King Hendricks ...

    ... Logan, Utah ... 1961

    For fuller entry see in *Section I* above.

Jack London American Rebel ⟨by⟩ Philip S. Foner

    The Citadel Press New York ⟨1964⟩

    Printed paper wrapper. A reprint, with supplementary biographical material, of Foner's biographical sketch first published in *Jack London American Rebel* ... ⟨1947⟩.

Jack London A Biography ⟨by⟩ Richard O'Connor ...

    Little, Brown and Company Boston Toronto ⟨1964⟩

    On copyright page: *First Edition*

Jack London: A Bibliography Compiled by Hensley C. Woodbridge ... John London ... George H. Tweney ...

    The Talisman Press Georgetown, California 1966

HENRY WADSWORTH LONGFELLOW

1 8 0 7 – 1 8 8 2

This list is presented in six sections as follows:

Section One: Primary books in first or revised edition; books containing first book publication, including contributions to the works of others; musical settings of poems provided the text thus published is prior to book publication.

CAUTION: Many of the collected editions published in Great Britain, often unauthorized, were issued without date and frequently publication information is lacking. Consequently all entries for such publications (*e.g., The Poetical Works,* London, 1877, entry No. 12195) must be considered tentative. Further, BAL has been unable to locate an estimated 100 British printings advertised or otherwise noted in British trade periodicals.

Where publication information has been found, it has been recorded, but it has not always been possible to relate such information with complete certainty. This comment does not apply to authorized publications.

Section Two: Dated reprints of Longfellow's own books.

Section Three: Undated reprints of Longfellow's own books.

Section Four: Books by authors other than Longfellow containing material by Longfellow reprinted from earlier books.

Section Five: Sheet music, the text being reprinted from books.

Section Six: References and ana.

INDEX TO CERTAIN UNDATED PUBLICATIONS

The following selected publications were issued without date and are here listed alphabetically by title as a convenience. Unless otherwise noted these contain first edition material and are listed in *Section One.*

Alarm-Bell of Atri, The. See entry No. 12156.

Ballad of the French Fleet, A. See entry No. 12194.

Book of Beauty, The. See in *Section Six* under year 1879.

Gleanings from the English Poets, edited by Robert Inglis. See entry No. 12130.

Longfellow's First Poem. See in *Section Six* under year 1900.

. . . Maiden and Weathercock. See entry No. 12220.

Poems: Lyrical and Dramatic . . . , London: William Tegg. See entry No. 12093.

Poetical Works, The. Edinburgh: Gall & Inglis; London: Houlston & Wright. See entry No. 12142.

. . . The Poetical Works . . . (Including Recent Poems.). London: Warne. In the *Chandos Classics* series. See entry No. 12162.

. . . The Poetical Works . . . Reprinted from the Best Editions. London: Warne. In the *Lansdowne Poets* series. See comment in entry No. 12162.

Poetical Works, The. London and New York: Ward, Lock. See entry No. 12224.

Prose Works, The. Edited by the Author of "Tennysoniana." London: Chatto & Windus. See entry No. 12165.

Prose Writers of America, The. See in *Section Six* under year 1879.

. . . Song & Story for the Homestead in Every Land and Clime. See *There Was a Little Girl,* under year 1883.

Via Solitaria. See in *Section Six* under year 1890.

Village Blacksmith, The. See entry No. 12650.

Windmill, The. See entry No. 12218.

Wrong Side Up, a Poem. See *There Was a Little Girl,* under year 1883.

SECTION I

Primary books in first or revised edition; books containing first book publication, including contributions to the works of others; musical settings of poems provided the text thus published is prior to book publication.

12035. Catalogue of the Library of the Peucinian Society, Bowdoin College

Hallowell: Goodale, Glazier & Co Printers. 1823.

Cover-title. ⟨1⟩-26. 6⅞″ scant x 4⅜″ scant. Printed self-wrapper, the stitching concealed by a shelfback of unprinted blue paper.

The following notes are extracted from the manuscript *Records of the Peucinian Society* . . . , Bowdoin College, Vol. 3, 1819–1831:

"July 18. ⟨1823⟩ . . . Ayer, Badger, Cheever, Longfellow and Shepley, were chosen a Committee to prepare a catalogue of the Books belonging to this Society and get it printed . . ."

"Dec. 5. ⟨1823⟩ . . . Voted, That, after deducting from the number in the hands of the Committe ⟨sic⟩ those already subscribed for, the remaining catalogues of the Library of this Society, be paid for by and become the property of the Society."

BD

12036. Boston Prize Poems, and Other Specimens of Dramatic Poetry.

Boston: Published by Joseph T. Buckingham, at the Office of the New England Galaxy. 1824.

Noted in both printed paper boards; and, unprinted paper boards. Also noted in ⟨publisher's?⟩ leather. Marbled paper boards, leather shelfback and corners; issued thus?

Untitled ode, pp. 27-32, by Longfellow, here published anonymously. Uncollected.

For a comment on this publication see "An Inquiry into the Importance of *Boston Prize Poems*," by Lawrance Thompson, in *The Colophon, New Graphic Series,* Vol. 1, No. 4, 1940, pp. ⟨55-62⟩.

Listed USLG April 1, 1824.

B   BA   UV   Y

12037. Miscellaneous Poems Selected from the United States Literary Gazette.

Boston: Cummings, Hilliard and Company, and Harrison Gray. 1826.

e "The Angler's Song," pp. 75-76.

c "An April Day," pp. 96-97. Begins: *When the warm sun, that brings* . . . Collected under the title "An April Day" in *Voices of the Night,* 1839. Under the title "April" reprinted in *The National Reader* . . . , London, 1829. Confusion has been caused by the altered title; and by a poem by Caroline Anne Bowles Southey titled "April Day" which also appears in *The National Reader.* Mrs. Southey's poem (which begins *All day the low-hung clouds have dropped*), under the title "April" appears, erroneously credited to Longfellow, in *Garden Walks with the Poets,* edited by Mrs. C. M. Kirkland, New York, 1852. Mrs. Southey's poem also appears, anonymously, in *The Waif,* 1845, under the title "April."

c "Autumn," pp. 102-103.

a "Autumnal Nightfall," pp. 106-108.

a "Dirge over a Nameless Grave," pp. 12-13.

c "Hymn of the Moravian Nuns at the Consecration of Pulaski's Banner," pp. 58-60.

d "The Indian Hunter," pp. 64-65.

a "Italian Scenery," pp. 148-151.

d "The Sea Diver," pp. 168-169.

a "A Song of Savoy," pp. 113-114.

c "Sunrise on the Hills," pp. 53-54.

b "Thanksgiving," pp. 47-49.

a "The Venetian Gondolier," pp. 155-156.

c "Woods in Winter," pp. 111-113. Eight stanzas; seven stanzas only in *Voices of the Night,* 1839.

KEY

a—Collected in *Early Poems,* London, 1878; *Works,* Boston, 1886.
b—Collected in *Poems,* London (Tegg, n.d., 1848); *Works,* Boston, 1886.
c—Collected in *Voices of the Night,* Cambridge, 1839.
d—Collected in *Poems,* London (Tegg, n.d., 1848); *Poetical Works,* Boston, 1868.
e—Collected in *Works,* Boston, 1886. Also in: Samuel Longfellow's *Life of . . . Longfellow . . .* 1886.

For fuller entry see No. 1591.

12038. The Atlantic Souvenir; a Christmas and New Year's Offering. 1827.

Philadelphia: H. C. Carey & I. Lea. ⟨1826⟩

"Burial of the Minnisink," pp. 200-201. Collected in *Voices of the Night,* 1839.

"The Song of the Birds," pp. 113-114. Collected in *Works,* Boston, 1886.

For fuller entry see No. 614.

12039. The Atlantic Souvenir; a Christmas and New Year's Offering. 1828.

Philadelphia: Carey, Lea & Carey. Sold in Boston by Hilliard, Gray, & Co. <1827>

"The Spirit of Poetry," pp. 38-39. Collected in *Voices of the Night,* 1839.

For comment see entry No. 10122.

12040. Manuel de Proverbes Dramatiques … <Preliminary Edition>

Samuel Colman: Portland. Griffin's Press: Brunswick. 1830

Edited anonymously by Longfellow.

"Avis de l'Éditeur," pp. <3>-7.

<i-iv>, <1>-156. 7¹³⁄₁₆″ x 4⅝″.

Almost certainly issued in cloth with printed paper label on spine; Livingston (p. 7) describes the Chamberlain-Wakeman copy thus. That same copy, the example here described, has been rebacked since examination by Livingston and no trace of the label can be seen.

Contains seven *proverbes dramatiques.*

Certain errata are common to both this preliminary edition and the first edition; see next entry. However, the error *La Diette* for *La Diète,* pp. <25>-54, occurs only in the preliminary edition.

" … I am engaged in the publication of another book, which I intend to make one of my text-books in teaching french <sic>. It is a collection of small comedies in french, such as are performed in the Soirées of Paris. I hardly know what name I shall give it: perhaps 'Manuel de Proverbes Dramatiques'; as 'proverbes dramatiques' is the title of the whole collection from which I make the choise <sic>. What think you? —I shall send you the 'première livraison' with the grammar: for from necessity I Shall be obliged to publish the work in parts, wanting it for immediate use in one of my classes … "— Longfellow to Alexander Slidel <sic>, Brunswick, Maine, Jan. 7, 1830; original in MHS.

" … J'ai puisé ce recueil dans une collection de pièces du même genre, publiée à Paris, entre les années 1768 et 1782, sous le titre … *Proverbes Dramatiques.* La collection complète consiste en huit volumes in-douze, contenant cent trois pièces … "—P. 4.

For other editions see next entry and under 1832. The edition of 1840, the so-called *Troisième Édition,* contains no new matter.

BPL

12041. Manuel de Proverbes Dramatiques … <First Edition>

Samuel Colman: Portland. Griffin's Press: Brunswick. 1830.

See preceding entry. For a second edition see under 1832.

Edited anonymously by Longfellow.

<i-iv>, <1>-288. 7¹³⁄₁₆″ x 4⅝″. Cloth, printed paper label on spine. *Also:* Printed paper boards, cloth shelfback.

Contains the seven *proverbes dramatiques* of the *Preliminary Edition* (preceding entry) and seven others.

Note: All examined copies have the following errors: P. 278 mispaged 178; p. 288 mispaged 188.

BPL copy presented by Longfellow to George Ticknor, June 1, 1830. H copy received from Longfellow July, 1830. Listed NAR Oct. 1830.

AAS   BD   BPL   H   NYPL   UV   Y

12042. Elements of French Grammar; by M. Lhomond … Translated from the French, with Notes, and Such Illustrations as Were Thought Necessary for the American Pupil. For the Use of Schools. By an Instructer.

Samuel Colman: Portland. Griffin's Press; Brunswick. 1830.

<i>-viii, <3>-108. P. vi mispaged iv. 7¾″ x 4⅝″. Noted in: Purple muslin, printed paper label on spine; and, tan paper boards, green muslin shelfback, printed paper label on spine. Erratum slips inserted between pp. 34-35, 38-39, 60-61, 72-73, 78-79. *Note:* The erratum slips occur either with or without page numbers; sequence, if any, not determined.

See note relating to this publication under the next entry.

Copies occur with and without signature mark 1* on p. 5; sequence not determined.

For second and third editions see below under 1831, 1834. BAL has made no effort to locate or describe editions issued after the third edition, 1834.

Letter (original in H), Oct. 15, 1829, Longfellow to his father: " … I shall publish my grammar soon. An edition of 500 Copies will cost about $72.00 … "

Letter (original in H), Oct. 15, 1829, Longfellow to Alexander Slidell <sic>: " … I am also very busy in translating an elementary grammar from the French—intended for my own use as instructer here—and for the use of Schools. It is already in a state of forwardness—and I shall put it to press without delay … "

CATALOGUE

OF THE

LIBRARY

OF THE

PEUCINIAN SOCIETY,

BOWDOIN COLLEGE

———◆———

HALLOWELL:

GOODALE, GLAZIER & CO.....PRINTERS.

· · · · ·

1823.

HENRY WADSWORTH LONGFELLOW
Entry No. 12035
(Bowdoin College Library)

Letter (original in H), Oct. 24, 1829, Longfellow to his father: "... With regard to my book, I do not think your view of the subject correct. In the first place, it is not a work of my own compiling; but a grammar, which has long been in universal use throughout France as a schoolbook—and which has been recommended by Mr. Gallatin as the best grammar in use. So that in regard to reputation, I risk nothing, for the work is a translation—and what notes I myself shall add will be only some principles taken from other grammars, to supply what is wanting in mine in order to adapt it to the understanding of the American pupil ... The book is now ready for the press: and after taking into consideration what I have stated above, I think you will not object to proceeding with it ..."

Letter (original in H), Dec. 20, 1829, Longfellow to his father, indicates that Longfellow was still correcting proof on the book; letter, Longfellow to Slidel ⟨sic⟩, Jan. 7, 1830, (original in MHS): "... My Grammar is printed, and will soon be published ..."

Listed NAR July, 1830. H copy received from Longfellow July, 1830.

AAS   B   BA   H   UV

12043. French Exercises: Selected Chiefly from Wanostrocht and Adapted to the Elements of French Grammar, by M. Lhomond ... by an Instructer.

Samuel Colman: Portland. Griffin's Press: Brunswick. 1830.

⟨i-iv⟩, ⟨1⟩-102, blank leaf. 7⅝″ x 4⁵⁄₁₆″ (trimmed). 7¾″ x 4⅝″ (untrimmed). Purple muslin, printed paper label on spine. Erratum slips inserted between pp. 20-21, 38-39.

Note: Copies of the above are found bound together with *Elements of French Grammar* (preceding entry). A "letter (Colman to Longfellow, July 31, 1830) shows that the separate bindings of these two French textbooks precede the binding together in one volume." Original not located by BAL; text extracted from Wilson, Vol. 1, p. 179.

Letter (original in H), April 10, 1830, Longfellow to his sister Mary: "... The Exercises to my Grammar will soon be published—and so will the Book of Comédies. I shall send you and Ellen—a copy of each, as soon as they are finished. I am waiting for the purple cotton to bind the Grammars in. Pray get it for me soon ..."

Listed NAR Oct. 1830.

AAS   UV   Y

12044. Novelas Españolas. El Serrano de las Alpujarras; y el Cuadro Misterioso.

Brunswick: Imprenta de Griffin. Se Halla de Venta en la Libreria de Colman—Portland. 1830.

Anonymous.

⟨1⟩-80. 7⅜″ x 4¾″. Marbled paper boards, black T cloth shelfback. Also: Marbled paper boards.

Supposedly occurs in two issues:

1

The *Al Lector* leaf (pp. ⟨3-4⟩) is an integral leaf. P. ⟨3⟩, last line, reads: *dar á la estampa esta nueva edicion. /* Noted only thus by BAL.

2

The *Al Lector* leaf (pp. ⟨3-4⟩) is a cancel. P. ⟨3⟩, last line, reads: *nueva edicion. /* Not seen by BAL. Information from Livingston, p. 9. The reading thus (*nueva edicion./*) is present in the 1831 printing of the book. *Query:* Did Livingston have before him a copy made of sheets of the 1830, 1831 printings?

Edited by Longfellow, with a dedication (p. ⟨2⟩) and a preface (p. ⟨3⟩) by Longfellow. The text is selected from George Washington Montgomery's *Tareas de un Solitario ó Nueva Coleccion de Novelas,* Madrid, 1829. According to the preface the two stories contained herein are Spanish versions of Washington Irving's "Rip Van Winkle" and "The Young Italian."

The 1831 printing is from a somewhat altered setting of the first printing and contains corrections. The following is a partial list of the alterations:

1830	*1831*
	P. ⟨2⟩
Dedication present	The page is blank
	P. ⟨3⟩, last line
dar á la estampa esta nueva edicion. /	*nueva edicion. /*
	P. ⟨5⟩, line 6 up
... Aun saben /	*... Aun saben se- /*
	P. 6, last line
... de aquel- /	*... de aque- /*
	P. 7, line 1
los pueblos ...	*llos pueblos ...*
	P. 8, line 4 up
cacion ...	*aplicacion ...*
	P. 10, line 8
... pertene- /	*... pertenecian /*
	P. 11, last line
posicion ...	*te posicion ...*

P. 12, line 2

prender . . .   *prehender* . . .

P. 13, line 3 up

. . . *las mon-/*   . . . *las monta-* /

P. 14, line 12

. . . *pusilán-* /   . . . *pusilá-* /

Note: The above notes will be found useful in checking salvage copies made up of mixed sheets, wherein the publisher used both the 1830 and 1831 printings. Copies thus are in BD and in H.

Letter, Longfellow to George Washington Greene, Oct. 20, 1830 (original in H): ". . . The one ⟨textbook⟩ I commence with . . . is a little thing I have published for my own use, entitled *Novelas Españolas*. It consists of two stories paraphrased from Washington Irving, and published with other tales at Madrid about two years ago. I will send it to you . . ." See this title under the year 1845 in *Section Two* of this list.

AAS   BD   H   UV

12045. Elements of French Grammar; by M. Lhomond . . . Translated . . . by H. W. Longfellow . . . Second Edition.

Boston: Gray and Bowen. 1831.

The first title-page to carry Longfellow's name. For first edition see under 1830; for third edition see under 1834.

"Note to the Second Edition," p. iv.

Not seen as a separate book; located only bound together with *French Exercises . . . Second Edition*, 1831. Paper boards, cloth shelfback, printed paper label on spine.

Letter, Gray & Bowen to Longfellow, Aug. 19, 1831 (original in H), reports the book as "just out."

H   UV

12046. Le Ministre de Wakefield. Traduction Nouvelle, précédée d'un Essai sur la Vie et les Écrits d'Olivier Goldsmith, par M. Hennequin . . .

Boston: Gray et Bowen, Libraires-Éditeurs. M DCCC XXXI.

Paper boards, cloth shelfback, printed paper label on spine.

Edited by Longfellow, not translated by him. The work is a reprint of the translation by T.F.G. Hennequin, Paris, 1825, with some inconsequential editorial revisions by Longfellow.

Note: All examined copies lack the terminal word *il*, p. 73, line 5, although one copy examined (BD) has the letter *i* present.

Letter, Gray & Bowen to Longfellow (original in H), Oct. 15, 1831, reports that copies are being sent to Longfellow; excuses are made for delay in completing the book.

Listed NAR Jan. 1832.

AAS   B   BD   BPL   H   UV

12047. The Token; a Christmas and New Year's Present. Edited by S. G. Goodrich . . .

Boston. Published by Gray and Bowen. MDCCCXXXII.

"La Doncella," from the Spanish, p. ⟨280⟩. Signed: *L******. Collected in *Outre-Mer,* 1835.

"The Indian Summer," pp. ⟨24⟩-35. Signed: *L.* Collected in *Works,* New York ⟨1909⟩.

For comment see entry No. 3256.

12048. Syllabus de la Grammaire Italienne. Par H. W. Longfellow, Professeur de Langues Modernes à Bowdoin-College. À l'Usage de Ceux Qui Possèdent la Langue Française.

Boston: Gray et Bowen: M DCCC XXXII.

Two states of the title-page have been noted; sequence not determined; the order of presentation is almost wholly arbitrary:

Title-Page A

Does not have a rule below the line: *à Bowdoin-College.*

Title-Page B

A rule is present below the line: *à Bowdoin-College.*

⟨i-iv⟩, ⟨1⟩-104. The leaf size varies as follows: 7¾″ x 4¾″ (*Binding A*). 7⅛″ x 4½″ (*Binding B*). 7⁷⁄₁₆″ x 4⁷⁄₁₆″ (*Binding C*). 7⁷⁄₁₆″ x 4⁷⁄₁₆″ (*Binding D*).

Signature collation: ⟨-⟩², 1-8⁶, 9⁴.

Two issues of Sig. ⟨-⟩ *noted:*

1

⟨-⟩₂ is not a cancel. P. ⟨iii⟩ (*i.e.,* ⟨-⟩₂ᵣ), line 2 from bottom, reads: . . . *dans la traité de* /

2

⟨-⟩₂ is a cancel. P. ⟨iii⟩, line 2 from bottom, reads: . . . *dans le traité de* /

Note on the Cancel

The cancel comprises pp. ⟨iii-iv⟩. Occurs in two states and almost certainly printed simultaneously from two settings. No sequence may be claimed if, in fact, the leaves were printed simultaneously: The following designations are for identification only:

Cancel A

The heading on p. <iii>: AVERTISSEMENT. (including the period) is set 1 $\frac{13}{16}$″ wide.

Cancel B

The heading on p. <iii>: AVERTISSEMENT. (including the period) is set 1 $\frac{15}{16}$″ wide.

Note: Many other variations are present but the above is sufficient for immediate identification.

The Errata Slip

Inserted at the back of some copies is an errata slip. The slip occurs in two states, printed from two different settings. In all likelihood the slips were printed simultaneously. If, in fact, the slips were simultaneously printed, no sequence may be claimed for either. The following designations are presented arbitrarily with only sufficient description to make ready identification:

Errata Slip A

In the correction for p. 34 the word *et* lines up left of the word *le* which is immediately below.

Errata Slip B

In the correction for p. 34 the word *et* is set flush above the word *le*.

BINDING

Noted in the following bindings. The designations are for identification only, and since no sequence has been established the order of presentation is all but purely arbitrary.

Binding A

Purple muslin. Printed paper label on spine, the lettering from a face $\frac{1}{8}$″ scant high and set between horizontal rules. White wove end papers. Flyleaves.

Binding B

Black T cloth. Printed paper label on spine, the lettering from a face $\frac{1}{8}$″ full high and set between horizontal rules. White wove end papers. Flyleaves.

Note: Since labels were customarily printed from multiple settings there is small likelihood a sequence (A *vs* B) is here involved. Indeed, it may be that other variants of the label exist. *Also note:* The label usually reads up the spine; a copy in NYPL has two labels present, one concealing the other. Examination indicates that the label first pasted to the spine was inverted which causes the lettering to read down the spine; the covering label corrects the faulty positioning. A like copy with two labels (JB), from which the upper label was removed by

JB, supports this statement. Examination of a like copy in BD further supports the observation.

Binding C

Black T cloth. Spine lettered up in gold: GRAMMAIRE ITALIENNE—LONGFELLOW Yellow end papers. Flyleaves.

Binding D

Black A cloth. Leather shelfback. Spine gold-stamped: GRAMMAIRE / ITALIENNE Spine embossed in blind with an arrangement of rococo designs. Yellow end papers. Flyleaves.

Note: All examined copies have the following error in the sixth line of the "Publishers' Notice," p. <ii>: ... *in order to an* /

The book has been seen in the following forms; sequence (if any) has not been determined and the designations are for identification only. BAL presumes that other forms exist.

A

Binding: A

Title-page: A

<->$_2$: Integral leaf; error present.

Errata slip: None

Locations: AAS   BD   H   NYPL

B

Binding: A

Title-page: B

<->$_2$: Integral leaf; error present.

Errata slip: B

Locations: BA

C

Binding: B

Title-page: A

<->$_2$: Integral leaf; error present.

Errata slip: None

Locations: H   UV   Y

D

Binding: B

Title-page: B

<->$_2$: Integral leaf; error present.

Errata slip: None

Locations: NYPL

E

Binding: C

Title-page: B
⟨-⟩₂: Integral leaf; error present.
Errata slip: None
Locations: UV

F

Binding: D
Title-page: A
⟨-⟩₂: Integral leaf; error present.
Errata slip: None
Locations: BPL

G

Binding: D
Title-page: B
⟨-⟩₂: Integral leaf; error present.
Errata slip: None.
Locations: BA

H

Binding: A
Title-page: A
⟨-⟩₂: Cancel, State A
Errata slip: State A
Locations: H

I

Binding: A
Title-page: A
⟨-⟩₂: Cancel, State A
Errata slip: State B
Locations: H UV

J

Binding: A
Title-page: A
⟨-⟩₂: Cancel, State B
Errata slip: State B
Locations: B

K

Binding: A
Title-page: B
⟨-⟩₂: Cancel, State A
Errata slip: State B
Locations: B

L

Binding: A
Title-page: B
⟨-⟩₂: Cancel, State B
Errata slip: State B
Locations: H UV

Deposited March 2, 1832. Noted for *February* AMR March, 1832. Listed NAR April, 1832.

12049. Saggi de' Novellieri Italiani d' Ogni Secolo: Tratti da' Più Celebri Scrittori, con Brevi Notizie intorno alla Vita di Ciascheduno. Da H. W. Longfellow ...

Boston: Presso Gray e Bowen. M DCCC XXXII.

⟨i⟩-⟨viii⟩, ⟨1⟩-168. 7⅜″ x 4¾″. Muslin, printed paper label on spine. List of errata, p. ⟨vii⟩; see below.

Note: In all examined copies the leaves of signature 1 are singletons. Error in imposition corrected thus?

The following errata listed, p. ⟨vii⟩. The errors are of two kinds: *Textual;* and, *Typographic.*

TEXTUAL ERRORS

All examined copies have these textual *errors present.*

P. 3, line 5: *buóno* for *buóna*
P. 24, line 8: *attegiamento* for *atteggiamento*
P. 44, line 15: *can* for *con*
P. 53, line 4 up: *contenterla* for *contentarla*

TYPOGRAPHIC ERRORS

Caused by dropped types or by faulty make-ready. These variations present in only some copies.

P. 39, line 7 up: ... *ven va,* / or ... *veniva,* /
P. 80, line 2 up: *il vero* ... or *È il vero* ...
P. 80, last line: *fferto* ... or *sofferto* ...
P. 92, line 9: *ella* ... or *della* ...

Note: In addition to the above the folio on p. 116 occurs either with or without the numeral 6. In some copies folio 80 is not present.

The following notes indicate that as in the case of Longfellow's *Manuel de Proverbes Dramatiques* ..., 1830, preliminary truncated copies were prepared for Longfellow's private use; no copy located. Letter*, Longfellow to Charles Folsom, March 3, 1832: "I am going to trouble

* *Original letter in* BPL *and here reprinted by courtesy of the Trustees of the Boston Public Library.*

you with a word or two concerning the *Saggi de' Novellieri*. The sheets sent reached me safely, and I have been using them for a week. Of course, as I go over them with new-beginners, it is difficult for an error to escape our scrutiny. I have accordingly picked up one or two ...

"I think it will be necessary to *reprint* the first *two pages* ... I think it best ... to strike out the words '*l'autore di questa Novella*' ...

"Be kind enough to send me also a proof of the Title-page and Introduction ...

"I intend to prepare a Vocabulary of the antiquated words ... which must go in on the last signature. In order to prepare this, I must have the sheets of the work before me. Will you be good enough to send them to me as soon as you can ... You may send those already struck off *now,* if you please; and so continue them as they come out of press ..."

Letter*, Longfellow to Gray & Bowen, March 29, 1832: "... I have now a class of 8 or 10—who have finished what was sent in sheets—and in about ten days shall commence with another class of about 30!—What is to be done?—Would it not be well to do up 40 or 50 copies in paper—and then when the remainder is finished all can be bound up together. Please write me on this point ..."

Noted as *in press* AMR March, 1832. Letter, Gray & Bowen to Longfellow, April 7, 1832 (original in H): "... We have sent a bundle ... containing 40 copies of the Italian Reading Book ..." Letter, Gray & Bowen to Longfellow, April 16, 1832 (original in H): "... All the copy we now have of the Italian Reader will make about 108 pages. The work should extend to about 150 pages we think ..." Letter, Longfellow to George W. Greene, July 6, 1832, (photostat in CH) Longfellow reports that the book "paraître incessamment." A copy in BD inscribed by early owner *July.* Listed NAR Oct. 1832.

AAS B BA BD BPL H NYPL UV Y

12050. Manuel de Proverbes Dramatiques ... Seconde Édition.

Boston: Gray et Bowen. 1832.

Boards, cloth shelfback, printed paper label on spine.

See above under 1830 for two earlier editions.

Edited anonymously by Longfellow. "Advertisement," p. ⟨5⟩, dated and signed at end: *H.W.L. Bowdoin College, October 3, 1832.*

* *Original letter in* BPL *and here reprinted by courtesy of the Trustees of the Boston Public Library.*

Contains eight *proverbes dramatiques* not present in the earlier editions.

Cours de Langue Francaise. Course of Study in the French Language ... Volume II. Proverbes Dramatiques.—General title-page.

Noted as *in press* AMR April, 1832. Listed NAR Jan. 1833.

AAS H UV Y

12051. The Token and Atlantic Souvenir. A Christmas and New Year's Present. Edited by S. G. Goodrich.

Boston. Published by Gray and Bowen. MDCCCXXXIII.

"An Evening in Autumn," signed *H.W.L.*, pp. ⟨150⟩-152. Collected in *Works,* New York ⟨1909⟩.

"The Bald Eagle," pp. ⟨74⟩-89. Anonymous. Sometimes misattributed to Nathaniel Hawthorne. For evidence of Longfellow's authorship see letter (original in H), Longfellow to George Washington Greene, March 9, 1833. Collected in *Works,* New York ⟨1909⟩.

For fuller entry see No. 6126.

12052. A Grammatical Text-Book, in Which the Several Moods are Clearly Illustrated by Diagrams ... Being an Abstract of a Practical Grammar, &c. Designed for the Use of Schools. By Roscoe G. Greene.

Boston: Lilly, Wait, Colman and Holden. 1833.

Printed paper boards, leather shelfback.

"Art and Nature," p. 30. Translated from the Spanish of Medrano. Collected in *Coplas ...,* Boston, 1833.

"Sunset after Rain," p. 59. Uncollected. Greene, letter to Longfellow, Oct. 24, 1832 (original in H) wrote requesting an "extract"; the lines are extracted from Longfellow's PBK poem, 1832, and are here in their earliest located book appearance.

"The Two Harvests," p. 30. Translated from the Spanish of Medrano. Collected in *Coplas ...,* Boston, 1833.

CH copy inscribed by Longfellow *May 1833.*

CH

12053. OUTRE-MER; A PILGRIMAGE BEYOND THE SEA. N°. I ...

BOSTON: HILLIARD, GRAY, & CO. M DCCC XXXIII.

Anonymous. For *Part II* see below under 1834. For extended editions see under 1835, 1846.

⟨i⟩-⟨vi⟩, ⟨3⟩-107. 9⅝" x 5⅞".

⟨A⟩², B⁴, 1-12⁴, 13².

Printed marbled paper wrapper. Double fly-leaves.

Title-page: Publisher's name present.

Copyright page: Publisher's name present.

P. ⟨iii⟩: The heading is set in two lines, thus: THE / EPISTLE DEDICATORY

Published in the above form. The front matter also occurs in a preliminary printing; hence:

PRELIMINARY PRINTING

Title-page: Publisher's name not present.

Copyright page: Publisher's name not present.

P. ⟨iii⟩: The heading is in one line, thus: EPISTLE DEDICATORY

THE WRAPPER

The wrapper has been noted in three forms; the following sequence is probable:

WRAPPER A

Five-line quotation present. Imprint in two lines, publisher's name not present.

WRAPPER B

Five-line quotation present. Imprint in three lines; publisher's name present.

WRAPPER C

Five-line quotation is not present. Imprint in three lines; publisher's name present.

VARIANT BINDINGS

Also noted in the following variant bindings. In each both *Part 1* and *Part 2* are present. Sequence, if any, not known.

Variant Binding A

Purple muslin, printed paper label on spine. Sig. ⟨-⟩, being the front matter of *Part 2*, is not present. A copy thus in NYPL inscribed by Longfellow May 14, 1834.

Variant Binding B

Brown L-like cloth, goldstamped leather label on spine. Sig. ⟨-⟩, being the front matter of *Part 2*, is present.

Letter,* Longfellow to Hilliard, Gray & Co.,

* Original in the Henry W. and Albert A. Berg Collection of The New York Public Library with whose kind permission this extract is here published.

June 30, 1833: "500 copies have been printed. 425 I shall send you; 25 of which are for gratuitous distribution; 25 more, I shall myself distribute; and 50 copies will remain in Mr. Griffin's ⟨the printer⟩ hands for the market here ⟨Brunswick, Maine⟩ and in Portland."

Letter,† Longfellow to Charles Folsom, July 7, 1833: "I herewith send you No 1 of the sketches of Europe ... The publication has been delayed from day to day ... But ... is at length completed, and will *appear incessantly;—il paraîtra incessamment ...*"

Deposited July 9, 1833. Noted by *Boston Daily Atlas,* July 12, 1833, as received, with Hilliard, Gray & Co., given as publisher. *Note:* The *Daily Atlas* citation is from a scrapbook kept by Longfellow (in H) with date and name of paper present in Longfellow's hand. Reviewed AMR Aug. 1833, with the statement "bears the imprint of J. Griffin, Brunswick, Me." (The Griffin imprint, as printer, is on the copyright page of all examined copies.) Noted for July AMR Aug. 1833. Listed NAR Aug. 1833.

Locations

Preliminary printing, Wrapper A: PDH

Sheets in Wrapper B: H   IU   NYPL   UV   Y

Sheets in Wrapper C: IU   NYPL   PDH   Philip H. and A.S.W. Rosenbach Foundation Museum and Library, Philadelphia.

Variant Binding A: NYPL   UV

Variant Binding B: H   UV

12054. Coplas de Don Jorge Manrique, Translated from the Spanish; with an Introductory Essay on the Moral and Devotional Poetry of Spain. By Henry W. Longfellow ...

Boston: Allen and Ticknor. 1833.

⟨i⟩-⟨viii⟩, ⟨1⟩-89; 3 blank leaves. 7¼" scant x 4¹¹⁄₁₆". Cloth, printed paper label on spine.

Note: The final 3 blank leaves (8_{4-6}) have been noted in the following forms; sequence, if any, not known:

Binding Variant A

8_4 present as a blank; 8_5 used as a pastedown; 8_6 excised or pasted under 8_5.

Binding Variant B

8_{4-6} present as blank leaves; true binder's end paper at back.

† Original in BPL and here reprinted by courtesy of the Trustees of the Boston Public Library.

Binding Variant C

8₄ used as a pastedown; 8₅₋₆ excised or pasted under 8₄.

"Preface," pp. ⟨iii⟩-vi. "Introductory Essay on the Moral and Devotional Poetry of Spain," pp. ⟨1⟩-27.

A copy in H inscribed by Longfellow Sept. 19, 1833. Noted for *September* AMR Oct. 1833. Noted by K Oct. 1833. Advertised by Kennett as an American book, BMLA March, 1836.

AAS H NYPL UV Y

12055. The Token and Atlantic Souvenir. A Christmas and New Year's Present. Edited by S. G. Goodrich.

Boston. Published by Charles Bowen. MDCCC-XXXIV.

Leather.

"The Convent of the Paular. Translated from a Spanish Manuscript," pp. ⟨79⟩-98. At end of text: *L.* Not found in Longfellow's works. NAR Jan. 1834 says "probably" by Longfellow. For a discussion of Longfellow's probable authorship see Ralph Thompson's "Additions to Longfellow Bibliography . . . ," in *American Literature,* Nov. 1931; and Lawrance Thompson's *Young Longfellow . . . ,* 1938, p. 389.

"To a Dying Child," pp. ⟨170⟩-171; and "A Troubador Lay of War," pp. ⟨172⟩-174; both signed at end: *L***.* These are sometimes attributed to Longfellow. BAL has found no evidence to support the attribution.

Deposited Oct. 1, 1833. Reviewed Ath Nov. 9, 1833; NEM Nov. 1833; NAR Jan. 1834.

CH

12056. OUTRE-MER; A PILGRIMAGE BEYOND THE SEA. Nº. II . . .

BOSTON: LILLY, WAIT, AND COMPANY. M DCCC XXXIV.

For *Part I* see above under 1833. Anonymous.

⟨i-iv⟩, ⟨109⟩-208. 9⅞" x 6" scant.

⟨-⟩², 14-25⁴, 26².

Printed blue paper wrapper. Two flyleaves at back. Also noted in the following variant bindings of unknown status:

Variant Binding A

Brown paper boards, brown muslin shelfback, spine lettered in gold.

Variant Binding B

Green paper boards, green paper shelfback, printed paper label on spine.

Variant Binding C

Blue paper boards, blue paper shelfback. Issued with spine label?

For a comment on other variant bindings, with both parts bound as a single volume, see under entry for *Part I, 1833.*

Noted as *October* AMR Nov. 1833.

AAS (Variant C) B (Variant B) H IU (Variant B) NYPL Philip H. and A.S.W. Rosenbach Foundation Museum and Library UV (also Variant A) Y

12057. Elements of French Grammar: By M. L'Homond . . . Translated . . . by H. W. Longfellow . . . Third Edition.

Boston: Published by Charles Bowen. 1834.

For first edition see under 1830; for second edition see under 1831.

Revised.

Not seen as a separate book; located only bound together with *French Exercises . . . Third Edition,* 1834. Paper boards, cloth shelfback, printed paper label on spine reading FRENCH GRAMMAR.

H

12058. The Token and Atlantic Souvenir. A Christmas and New Year's Present. Edited by S. G. Goodrich.

Boston. Published by Charles Bowen. MDCCC-XXXV.

"The Youth of Mary Stuart," credited to *L,* pp. ⟨65⟩-75. Includes two poems as follows:

On pp. 72-73, poem beginning *In accents sad and low . . . ;* under the title "On the Death of Her Husband, Francis the Second," collected in *Poets and Poetry of Europe,* 1845, p. 452.

On pp. 74-75, poem beginning *Farewell, beloved France . . . ;* under the title "Farewell to France," collected in *Poets and Poetry of Europe,* 1845, p. 452.

"Good Night," from the German of Körner, translation credited to *L,* p. ⟨64⟩. This translation was not collected in *Poets and Poetry of Europe,* 1845, in which Longfellow published a translation by Richardson. Probably translated by Longfellow.

For fuller entry see No. 6799.

12059. OUTRE-MER; A PILGRIMAGE BEYOND THE SEA . . . IN TWO VOLUMES
. . .

NEW-YORK: PUBLISHED BY HARPER & BROTHERS, NO. 82 CLIFF-STREET. 1835.

Anonymous. For first edition see under 1833, 1834. See next entry. Also see under 1846.

Vol. 1 is a reprint of the earlier publication with the addition of "Spain" and "A Tailor's Drawer." Vol. 2 is composed of material here first in book form with the exception of "Coplas de Manrique" which had been published in *Coplas . . .* , 1833.

1: ⟨i-viii⟩, ⟨1⟩-226, blank leaf. 7⁵⁄₁₆" x 4½".

2: ⟨i-iv⟩, ⟨1⟩-252.

1: ⟨-⟩⁴, A-I, K-T⁶.

2: ⟨-⟩², A-I, K-U, X⁶.

Two states of Vol. 2 noted:

1

P. ⟨175⟩, line 5: . . . *crown it, encircles* /

2

P. ⟨175⟩, line 5: . . . *crown, it encircles* /

Noted in various types of cloth. Flyleaves. Publisher's catalog (*see below*) inserted at front of Vol. 1. The following designations are for identification only; no sequence is suggested:

Cloth 1

Coarse-grained H cloth: blue; brown; green.

Cloth 2

Purple muslin embossed with a maze-like pattern.

Cloth 3

Coarse-grained P cloth: green.

Cloth 4

P-like cloth: blue; green; purple.

Cloth 5

S cloth: purple. Damasked with a floral pattern.

Cloth 6

S cloth: purple. Damasked with a wood-grain pattern.

Note: The catalog (inserted at front of Vol. 1) has been noted in two printings; the following sequence is probably correct:

Catalog A

A single gathering in 12 paged ⟨3⟩-11, 14-28.

Catalog B

A single gathering in 8 paged ⟨3⟩-18.

P. ⟨i⟩, Vol. 1, dated *May, 1835*. Noted *will publish* K Jan. 1835. Noted as *in the press* NYLG Feb. 7, 1835. Reviewed AMM May, 1835; K May, 1835. A copy in AAS inscribed by early owner June, 1835 (first state of Vol. 2). Listed NAR July, 1835.

AAS (1st state)   BD (1st state)   BPL (1st state)   H (both states)   NYPL (1st state)   UV (both states)   Y (1st state)

12060. Outre-Mer: Or, a Pilgrimage to the Old World. By an American . . . in Two Volumes . . .

London: Richard Bentley, New Burlington Street. 1835.

See preceding entry.

Boards, cloth shelfback, printed paper label on spine.

Reprint save for "Old English Prose Romances," Vol. 1, pp. ⟨101⟩-159. Not otherwise located in Longfellow's works.

Advertised as *just published* LG June 20, 1835; Ath June 20, 1835. Published June 22, 1835 (Bentley's 1835 list). Reviewed LG June 27, 1835. Reviewed (again) LG July 25, 1835, where the author's name is guessed as *Longbody*. Listed BMLA July, 1835.

H   UV

12061. The Boston Book. Being Specimens of Metropolitan Literature, Occasional and Periodical.

Boston: Light and Horton. 1836.

"The Notary," pp. ⟨76⟩-83; here reprinted.

"Truth," p. ⟨106⟩; *Oh holy and eternal Truth! Thou art . . . ;* here in its earliest located book appearance. Stanzas 1-3, 5, extracted from Longfellow's PBK poem, 1833; source of stanza 4 not known. Collected in *Works,* New York ⟨1909⟩. Not to be confused with an aphorism of the same title, "Truth," in *Belfry of Bruges,* 1846.

Reviewed NEM Oct. 1835.

BA   BD   H   UV

12062. The Origin of the Danish, and an Abstract of Scandinavian Literature, with Short Chronological Specimens of the Old Danish, Icelandic, Norwegian, Swedish, and a Notice of the Dalecarlian and Ferroe Dialects. By the Rev. J. Bosworth . . .

London: Published by Longman, Rees, Orme, Brown, and Green. MDCCCXXXVI.

Cloth, printed paper label on front.

"King Christian," translated from the Danish by Longfellow, p. 24. Collected in *Voices of the Night,* 1839.

"Dialect of the Dalecarlia," p. 27.

CH

12063. Anglo-Saxon Language. Dear Sir, I beg leave to call your attention to a valuable work which has lately appeared in England entitled, "A Dictionary of the Anglo-Saxon Language ... by the Rev. J. Bosworth ...

... Charles Little & Co., Boston ... ⟨1837?⟩

Issued as a prospectus. Single leaf. 9⅜" x 7½". Printed on recto only. Signed at end (in pen and ink) by Longfellow.

Query: Written by Longfellow? Or was he but one of several sponsors who signed the prospectus in recommendation?

Y

12064. HYPERION, A ROMANCE. BY THE AUTHOR OF "OUTRE-MER." ...

NEW YORK: PUBLISHED BY SAMUEL COLMAN, 8, ASTOR HOUSE. 1839.

2 Vols. See under 1845 for a note on revised editions.

1: ⟨i-iv⟩, ⟨1⟩-213, blank leaf. 7¹⁵⁄₁₆" x 4¹⁵⁄₁₆".

2: ⟨i-iv⟩, ⟨1⟩-226, blank leaf.

1: ⟨-⟩², 1-9¹².

2: ⟨-⟩², 1-9¹², 10⁶.

NOTE

Sig. ⟨-⟩ (pp. ⟨i-iv⟩) of each volume was produced by multiple setting. Since these were simultaneously printed no priority may be claimed for either. The designations are for identification only.

Setting A

Title-page, Vol. 1. A period (not a comma) is present at end of second line in the imprint.

Title-page, Vol. 2. The letterpress is 5⁵⁄₁₆" scant deep.

Setting B

Title-page, Vol. 1. A comma (not a period) is present at end of second line in the imprint.

Title-page, Vol. 2. The letterpress is 5¼" scant deep.

Tan paper boards, printed paper label on spine. White wove end papers. *Note:* Also occurs with brown wove end papers pasted to the underlying white paper pastedown which gives to the free portion of the white end paper the ap-

pearance of a flyleaf. On the basis of dated inscriptions the book appears to have been first issued with the white, not the brown, end papers.

Remainder Bindings

On Feb. 27, 1845, James Munroe & Co., Boston, wrote to Longfellow (original letter in H): "Some 12 months since we bo⟨ugh⟩t the bal-⟨an⟩ce of the Edition of *Hyperion* 2 Vols & have had the sale of say 350 Copies ..." Munroe issued the sheets in black T cloth as follows:

2 Vols. In some copies of Vol. 1 there is inserted a 4-page Munroe advertisement. A copy has been seen inscribed by early owner *Aug. 1844.*

2 Vols., bound in one.

Note: A copy has been seen (NYPL) bound in green C-like cloth, edges marbled. Status unknown but BAL suspects the binding was done considerably later than the 1840's, perhaps in Germany or France.

Noted as *in press* NYR July, 1839. BA copy (now rebound) received Aug. 24, 1839. A copy (white end papers) in UV inscribed by Longfellow Aug. 1839. Reviewed K Sept. 1839.

B (brown end papers) H (white end papers; also, remainder) MHS (brown end papers) NYPL (white end papers; brown end papers; remainder) UV (white end papers; remainder)

12065. VOICES OF THE NIGHT ...

CAMBRIDGE: PUBLISHED BY JOHN OWEN. M DCCC XXXIX.

⟨i⟩-⟨xvi⟩, ⟨1⟩-144. 7" x 4⅜".

⟨-⟩⁸, 1-9⁸.

Note: The following textual alterations (done during the course of the first printing?) have been noted. No copy examined has all of the original readings present, but such copies may exist.

Original Reading	*Altered Reading*
P. ⟨v⟩	
Prelude listed as at p. v	*Prelude* listed as at p. vii
P. 18, line 10	
... *flowers a part* /	... *flowers, a part* /
P. 23, line 11	
... *rose and fell,* /	... *rose and fell* /
P. 78, line 10	
His, Hector's arm ...	*The arm of Hector* ...

Note: It has been pointed out that the error, *v* for *vii*, also occurs in the 1840 printing (marked *Second Edition* on the title-page). However, since the *Second Edition* is from a new setting, presence of the error in no way negates the sequence presented above. The *Third Edition* (1840), so marked on the title-page, is from yet another setting.

Tan paper boards, printed paper label on spine.

A copy in PDH inscribed by Longfellow Dec. 8, 1839. Deposited Dec. 9, 1839. Reviewed Ath June 13, 1840.

The present entry made on the basis of copies (some being imperfect) in:

AAS   B   BA   BD   BPL   H   NYPL   UV   Y

12066. The Boston Book. Being Specimens of Metropolitan Literature.

Boston: George W. Light, 1 Cornhill. 1841.

Reprint save for:

"Wreck of the Hesperus," pp. ⟨74⟩-77. Collected in *Ballads,* 1842.

"Life in Sweden," pp. ⟨193⟩-201. See note under *Prose Works,* 1857, below, relating to "Frithiof's Saga."

For comment see entry No. 631.

12067. The Token and Atlantic Souvenir, an Offering for Christmas and the New Year.

Boston: Published by David H. Williams ... 1842.

"The Two Locks of Hair," from the German of Pfizer, pp. ⟨22⟩-23. Collected in *Ballads,* 1842.

For comment see entry No. 1005.

12068. POEMS ON SLAVERY ...

CAMBRIDGE: PUBLISHED BY JOHN OWEN. M DCCC XLII.

⟨1⟩-31; plus: Publisher's catalog, 7 pp. 7¼″ full x 4¾″.

⟨1⟩-2⁸; plus: ⟨3⟩⁴.

Printed glazed cream-yellow paper wrapper.

Deposited Dec. 24, 1842. Listed NAR Jan. 1843. For a comment on the undated reprint issued by the New England Anti-Slavery Tract Association see below, under title, in *Section III.*

AAS   H   MHS   NYPL   UV   Y

12069. The Poets of America ... Edited by John Keese. [Volume Second of the Series.]

New York: Published by Samuel Colman ... 1842.

Reprint with the possible exception of "The Village Blacksmith," pp. ⟨35⟩-37. Also in (reprinted from?) *Ballads,* 1842.

For comment see entry No. 3280.

12070. BALLADS AND OTHER POEMS ...

CAMBRIDGE: PUBLISHED BY JOHN OWEN. M DCCC XLII.

⟨i⟩-⟨xxvi⟩, ⟨27⟩-132. 7⅛″ x 4⁹⁄₁₆″ full.

⟨1⟩-8⁸, 9². *Also signed:* ⟨A⟩-P⁴, Q².

Cream-yellow paper boards, printed paper label on spine. Cream-yellow glazed end papers. Triple flyleaves.

Note: All examined copies of the first printing (*i.e.,* copies without the statement SECOND ⟨or later⟩ EDITION on the title-page) have the following features:

P. 34, line 1: ... *grew,"* / The quotation marks are superfluous. In some copies they have been removed from the printed page by erasure.

P. 88, last line: *teacher* ... Note use of lower case initial.

Also note: All examined copies, including known reprints, have below the text on p. 132 the bald statement: END. In one known copy (UV) the statement reads: THE END. The status of this copy is not known. The publisher's usual style is: END.

Reprints

On the title-page of known reprints appears the statement SECOND ⟨or later⟩ EDITION

P. 34, line 1: ... *grew,* / The quotation marks (as above) are not present; removed at the press.

P. 88, last line: *Teacher* ... Note use of capital initial.

Intermediates marked SECOND EDITION have been seen as follows; BAL has not determined whether these were caused by the use of mixed sheets or by alterations during the run of the SECOND EDITION. The designations are for identification only and no sequence is either suggested or implied.

Intermediate A

On title-page: SECOND EDITION

P. 34, line 1: ... *grew,"* /

P. 88, last line: *Teacher* ...

Copy in EM (Aug. 1965).

Intermediate B

On title-page: SECOND EDITION

P. 34, line 1: *. . . grew, /*

P. 88, last line: *teacher . . .*

Copy in UV.

A copy in NYPL inscribed by early owner Dec. 25, 1841. A copy of the *Second Edition* (in H) inscribed by Longfellow Dec. 25, 1841. Deposited Jan. 4, 1842. Noted as *in press* ⟨sic⟩ USDR Jan. 1842. Reviewed NYR Jan. 1842.

B H NYPL UV Y

12071. THE SPANISH STUDENT. A PLAY, IN THREE ACTS . . .

CAMBRIDGE: PUBLISHED BY JOHN OWEN. M DCCC XLIII.

⟨i⟩-⟨viii⟩, ⟨9⟩-183. 7″ full x 4¹³⁄₁₆″.

⟨1⟩-11⁸, 12⁴. *Also signed:* ⟨A⟩-W⁴.

Cream-yellow glazed paper boards. Printed paper label on spine. Flyleaves. Cream-yellow glazed end papers.

A copy in H inscribed by Longfellow June 21, 1843. Deposited July 19, 1843. A copy in NYPL inscribed by Longfellow July, 1843. Listed WPLNL Aug. 1843; ALB Aug. 1843.

NYPL UV

12072. Voices of the True-Hearted . . .

Philadelphia . . . J. Miller M'Kim, No. 31 North Fifth Street . . .

Cover-title. 18 paper-covered parts in 13(?). The imprint on some parts varies from the above.

1: Wrapper dated 1844. Pp. ⟨1⟩-16. Two printings noted:

   1: Present is a prefatory note dated *Philadelphia, 11th mo. 8th, 1844.*

   2: The prefatory note is not present. Not located as a single part; seen only in the 1846, 1-volume, clothbound, issue; see below. Text extended by the addition of three poems by Longfellow: "The Arrow and the Song," "Endymion" and "The Light of Stars." For a comment on the Longfellow poems see below.

2: Wrapper dated *Eleventh month, 1844.* Pp. ⟨17⟩-32.

3: Wrapper dated *First month, 1845.* Pp. ⟨33⟩-48.

4: Wrapper dated *Second month, 1845.* Pp. ⟨49⟩-64.

5: Wrapper dated *Third month, 1845.* Pp. ⟨65⟩-80.

6: Wrapper dated *Fourth month, 1845.* Pp. ⟨81⟩-96.

7: Wrapper dated *Fifth month, 1845.* Pp. ⟨97⟩-112.

8: Wrapper dated *Sixth month, 1845.* Pp. ⟨113⟩-128.

9: Wrapper dated *Seventh month, 1845.* Pp. ⟨129⟩-144.

10: Wrapper undated. Issued Aug. 1845? Pp. ⟨145⟩-160.

11-12: Issued as a single part. Wrapper undated. Sept. 1845? Oct. 1845? Pp. ⟨161⟩-192. On p. ⟨177⟩: *No. 12.*

13-14: Issued as a single part. Wrapper undated. Oct. 1845? Nov. 1845? Dec. 1845? Pp. ⟨193⟩-224. On p. ⟨209⟩: *No. 14.*

15-18: Issued as a single part? At head of front wrapper of *Parts 13-14* is the statement: *The next issue . . . will be our last.* Pp. ⟨225⟩-288. On pp. ⟨225⟩, ⟨241⟩, ⟨257⟩, ⟨273⟩, respectively, appear: *No. 15; No. 16; No. 17; No. 18.* If issued as singles No. 17 could not have been published prior to Feb. 2, 1846.

Note: Sheets of the publication were issued in cloth with an index and a general title-page imprinted: *Philadelphia . . . J. Miller M'Kim . . . 1846.*

All the Longfellow poems in this publication are reprints with the possible exception of:

"The Arrow and the Song," *Part 1,* second printing, p. 1. The poem also appears in *The Belfry of Bruges . . . ,* 1846 (*i.e.,* Dec. 1845). Precise publication date of *Part 1* (second printing) not known.

"The Arsenal at Springfield," *Part 14,* p. 215. The poem also appears in *Poems,* 1845, which was deposited for copyright Nov. 25, 1845. Precise publication date for *Part 14* not known.

The present entry based on examination of copies in:

BPL G H HA NYPL PDH S UV

12073. Youth's Keepsake, a Christmas and New Year's Gift for Young People . . .

Boston: T. H. Carter and Company. 118½ Washington Street. ⟨1845⟩

Fly-title-page: *Youth's Keepsake for 1845.*

"Childhood," pp. ⟨111⟩-112. Translated from the Danish of Baggesen. Collected in *Poets and Poetry of Europe,* 1845 (June).

Advertised by Briggs's Bookstore, *Daily Evening Transcript* (Boston), Nov. 18, 1844.

BA BD

12074. The Gift: A Christmas, New Year, and Birthday Present. MDCCCXLV.

Philadelphia: Carey and Hart. 1845.

Cloth; and, leather.

"A Gleam of Sunshine," pp. ⟨7⟩-9. Collected in *Poems*, 1845, below.

"The Hemlock Tree," translated from the German, p. ⟨276⟩. Collected in *Poets and Poetry of Europe*, 1845, below.

For comment see entry No. 4024.

12075. The Waif: A Collection of Poems . . .

Cambridge: Published by John Owen. 1845.

Edited by Longfellow.

"Proem," pp. ⟨ix⟩-xi. Collected in *Poems,* 1845, as "The Day is Done."

For a comment on the anonymous poem herein, "April," see above under *Miscellaneous Poems . . .* , Boston, 1826.

Illuminated paper wrapper; illuminated paper boards; cream paper boards, printed paper label on spine; cream paper wrapper, printed paper label on spine. Also noted in several types of cloth, edges gilt.

Note: "The . . . early form ⟨of the label⟩ carries the date *1845,* and does not mention Longfellow's name."—Wilson, p. 217.

Deposited Dec. 27, 1844. A copy in H inscribed by Longfellow Jan. 1, 1845. Reviewed NYM Jan. 25, 1845. Listed as a January publication in ALB Feb. 1845. Listed PC May 1, 1845. A Clarke (London) edition listed PC March 1, 1849.

AAS   H   NYPL   UV

12076. The Liberty Bell. By Friends of Freedom . . .

Boston: Massachusetts Anti-Slavery Fair. MDCCCXLV.

Cloth; and, printed paper boards.

"The Norman Baron," pp. 31-35. Collected in *Poems*, 1845.

Issued at The Ladies' Annual Anti-Slavery Fair, which opened in Boston, Dec. 17, 1844. A copy at CH inscribed by early owner Jan. 1, 1845.

H   NYPL

12077. The Knickerbocker Sketch-Book . . . Edited by Lewis Gaylord Clark . . .

New-York: Burgess, Stringer and Company. 1845.

"The Blank Book of a Country Schoolmaster," pp. ⟨33⟩-46. Collected in *Works*, 1886. *Note:*

Part 4 of this piece, "The Happy Man and the Lucky Dog," is a revised version of a passage in *Hyperion*, 1839, Vol. 2, pp. 125-127.

"Saga of the Skeleton in Armor," pp. ⟨87⟩-90. Reprint save for the marginal notes.

For comment see entry No. 10162.

12078. The Poets and Poetry of Europe. With Introductions and Biographical Notices. By Henry Wadsworth Longfellow . . .

Philadelphia: Carey and Hart, Chestnut Street. M DCCC XLV.

Cloth; and, leather.

Two printings noted:

1: On copyright page, imprint of *Metcalf And Company*

2: On copyright page, imprint of *T. K. & P. G. Collins*

". . . In the preparation of this work I have been assisted by Mr. C. C. Felton, who has furnished me with a large portion of the biographical sketches prefixed to the translations . . ."—P. vi.

In addition to the editorial notes, this publication contains a number of translations by Longfellow. Of these (with the exceptions noted) the following are here in their earliest located book appearances; others, not here listed, had prior publication in one or more of Longfellow's earlier books. It is entirely probable that the book contains other translations by Longfellow which have passed unrecognized as his. See, for example, the anonymous translation from Richard Cœur-de-Lion, p. 437, and compare it with Longfellow's translation of part of the same poem in Samuel Longfellow's *Life of . . . Longfellow,* Boston, 1886, Vol. 1, p. 162.

"Annie of Tharaw," by Dach, p. 240.

"Beowulf's Expedition to Heort," pp. ⟨8⟩-9.

"Blessed are the Dead," by Dach, p. 240.

"The Brave Man," by Bürger, pp. 277-278.

"Childhood," by Baggesen, p. 90. Previously in *Youth's Keepsake,* 1845, above.

"Christmas Carol," (*When Christ was born* . . .), from the Neapolitan, p. 619.

"Death of Archbishop Turpin," from *Chanson de Roland,* p. ⟨414⟩.

"Duke William at Rouen," from *Roman du Rou,* pp. 415-416. Translated by Longfellow? Appears also in *Outre-Mer,* London (Routledge), 1851.

"Elegy. Written in the Ruins of an Old Castle," by Matthisson, p. 318.

"Farewell to France," by Marie Stuart, p. 452. Previously in *The Token*, 1835, as part of "The Youth of Mary Stuart."

"Friar Lubin," by Marot, p. 445.

"Frithiof's Homestead," by Tegnér, p. 156.

"Frithiof's Temptation," by Tegnér, pp. 163-169.

"From the Fuggitiva of Tommaso Grossi," p. 620.

"From the Milagros de Nuestra Señora . . . ," by Berceo, pp. 635-636.

"From the Tancia of Michel Angelo," p. 620.

"The Hemlock Tree," from the German, p. 238. Previously in *The Gift*, 1845, above.

"The Legend of the Crossbill," by Mosen, p. 356.

"Let Me Go Warm," by Góngora, p. 695.

"The Nature of Love," by Guinicelli, p. ‹511›.

"On the Death of Her Husband, Francis the Second," by Marie Stuart, p. 452. Previously in *The Token*, 1835, as part of "The Youth of Mary Stuart."

"Popular Song," Calabrian dialect, p. 619.

"Praise of Little Women," by Hita, p. 640.

"Richard's Escape," from *Roman du Rou*, p. 416. Translated by Longfellow? Appears also in *Outre-Mer*, London (Routledge), 1851.

"Rondel," by d'Orléans, p. 440.

"Rondel," by Froissart, p. 438.

"The Sea Hath its Pearls," by Heine, p. 351.

"Silent Love," from the German, p. 238.

"A Sledge-Ride on the Ice," by Tegnér; p. 152; here untitled.

"Soldier's Song," Neapolitan dialect, pp. 619-620.

"Song," Neapolitan dialect, *One morning, on the seashore as I strayed* . . . , p. 620.

"Song," by Casero, *Whenever a fresh, mild, and pleasant breeze* . . . , p. 620.

"The Soul's Complaint against the Body," from the Anglo-Saxon, p. 28.

"The Spring Evening," by Matthisson, pp. 318-319. A note in the *ms* of *Poets and Poetry of Europe* (in H) suggests that Longfellow was the translator of this piece.

"The Statue over the Cathedral Door," by Mosen, pp. 355-356.

Noted for *March* NYM Feb. 15, 1845. Title deposited May 10, 1845. A copy in UV inscribed by

Longfellow June 17, 1845. Listed as a June publication WPLNL July, 1845; ALB July, 1845. Reviewed Ath Oct. 4, 1845; LG Oct. 25, 1845. Listed (as an importation) PC Nov. 1, 1845.

AAS (1st)　　BD (1st)　　H (1st, 2nd)　　UV (1st)

12079. Poems . . .

Philadelphia: Carey and Hart, Chesnut St. MDCCCXLV.

Cloth; and, various styles of leather.

Reprint save for the following poems:

a "Afternoon in February"

a "The Arsenal at Springfield." Also in (previously?) *Voices of the True-Hearted*, 1844–1846; see above.

a "The Belfry of Bruges"

a "The Bridge"

a "Carillon"

a "Curfew"

d "The Day is Done"

b "A Gleam of Sunshine"

c "The Norman Baron"

a "Nuremberg"

a "The Occultation of Orion"

a "Rain in Summer"

a "Sea-Weed"

a "To the Driving Cloud"

a "Walter von der Vogelweide"

KEY

a—Earliest located book publication.
b—Previously in *The Gift* . . . , Philadelphia, 1845, *i.e.*, Oct. 1844.
c—Previously in *The Liberty Bell* . . . , Boston, 1845, *i.e.*, Dec. 1844.
d—Previously in *The Waif* . . . , Cambridge, 1845, *i.e.*, Dec. 1844.

Under date Nov. 24, 1845, Longfellow, writing to the publishers, acknowledged receipt of a copy "on ‹last› Saturday"; letter in The Olin Library, Wesleyan University, Middletown, Conn. Deposited Nov. 25, 1845. AAS copy inscribed by early owner Nov. 30, 1845. Listed WPLNL Dec. 1845. Distributed in London by Wiley & Putnam: Advertised as *now ready* Ath Dec. 27, 1845; listed Ath Dec. 27, 1845; LG Dec. 27, 1845; PC Jan. 1, 1846; reviewed Ath Jan. 10, 1846.

AAS　BA　BPL　NYHS　NYPL

12080. Hyperion, a Romance ... Second Edition.

Cambridge: Published by John Owen. 1845.

For first edition see under 1839. Also see under 1869.

Revised. BAL has not compared the texts of all editions, hence the following list is incomplete. However, further revisions are present in the *Seventh Edition*, 1850; *Ninth Edition*, 1851; *Tenth Edition*, 1851 (a minor alteration); *Fourteenth Edition*, 1854; *Revised Edition*, 1869. In the 1869 edition the untitled poem (pp. 198-200) beginning *Come, golden evening* ... , is identified as by James Montgomery.

Reviewed NYM Dec. 27, 1845. Deposited Dec. 29, 1845.

BPL   H   Y

12081. The Happiest Land ... Music ... by Charles F. Heuberer ...

Boston, Published by Henry Prentiss 33 Court St. ... 1845 ...

Sheet music. Cover-title. Plate number 511.

"The Happiest Land" reprinted from *Voices of the Night*, 1839.

Reprint save for a brief testimonial by Longfellow on the front cover.

Other settings (testimonial not present) noted:

Music by M. W. Balfe: London: Boosey & Co., n.d., 1856?

Music by W. H. Jude: Boston: Oliver Ditson Co., 1896.

Music by J. Ernest Perring: New York: William A. Pond & Co., 1870.

B   BPL   UV

12082. The Parlor Annual and Christian Family Casket. 1846. Edited by an Association of Clergymen.

Published by J.E.D. Comstock, 126 Nassau-Street. N-York ⟨1845? 1846?⟩

Sheets of *The Christian Family Annual*, Vol. 4, Nos. 1-12, bound in cloth and issued with a title-page as above.

"Eternity. Extract from an Unpublished Poem," p. 219. Consists of four stanzas, the first two are extracted from the version of Longfellow's PBK poem which he read in Cambridge in 1833; the third and fourth stanzas are in the PBK poem read in Brunswick, 1832; and, in Cambridge, 1833.

UV

12083. THE BELFRY OF BRUGES AND OTHER POEMS ...

CAMBRIDGE: PUBLISHED BY JOHN OWEN. 1846.

⟨i⟩-⟨viii⟩, ⟨1⟩-151. $7\frac{1}{8}$" x $4\frac{3}{4}$" scant (in wrapper). 7" full x $4\frac{5}{8}$" (in boards).

⟨-⟩⁴, 1-9⁸, 10⁴. *Also signed:* ⟨A⟩-T⁴.

White paper wrapper lithographed in gold; double flyleaves at front and at back; also, double flyleaves at front only. White paper boards lithographed in gold; flyleaves; top edges either plain, or gilded.

Reprint with the exception of:

"The Arrow and the Song." Also in (previously?) *Voices of the True-Hearted*, 1844–1846, above.

"Autumn." *Thou comest, Autumn, heralded by rain* ...

"Dante"

"Drinking Song"

"The Evening Star." *Lo! in the painted oriel* ...

"The Old Clock on the Stairs"

"Poetic Aphorisms"

"To a Child"

"To an Old Danish Song-Book"

Daily Evening Transcript (Boston), Dec. 23, 1845: *Published this morning.* NYPL copy inscribed by Duyckinck Dec. 24, 1845. A copy in H received from the publisher Dec. 25, 1845. Deposited Dec. 29, 1845. Reviewed Ath March 14, 1846.

AAS   H   NYPL   UV

12084. The Liberty Bell. By Friends of Freedom ...

Boston: Massachusetts Anti-Slavery Fair. MDCCCXLVI.

"The Poet of Miletus," pp. 25-26. Collected in *Works*, New York ⟨1909⟩.

" ... This twelfth Anti-Slavery Bazaar will commence on Tuesday, Dec. 23d ... *The Liberty Bell* will be published on the first morning of the Bazaar ..."—*Daily Evening Transcript* (Boston) Dec. 23, 1845. Contemporary inscriptions also indicate that the book was issued Dec. 23, 1845.

For fuller entry see No. 6495.

12085. Outre-Mer, a Pilgrimage beyond the Sea ... Second Edition.

Boston: William D. Ticknor & Co. 1846.

Revised. For earlier editions see above under 1833, 1834, 1835.

Title deposited June 2, 1846. According to the publisher's records paper sufficient for 600 copies was shipped to the printer on July 16, 1846. Listed as an August publication WPLNL Sept. 1846.

AAS   B   BPL   LC   NYPL   Y

12086. Reports of the Committees Appointed to Prepare, in a Tabular Form, an Arrangement of Studies for the Whole College Course; First, on the Plan of Requiring All the Studies; Secondly, on the Elective System, with Such Modifications of the Existing Plan as the Committee Have Thought Expedient. Printed Privately for the Use of the Faculty ...

⟨Cambridge, Mass., 1846⟩

Caption-title. The above at head of p. ⟨1⟩. 8 pp.

7-line postscript by Longfellow, p. 7.

Consists of two reports dated, respectively, Nov. 6, 1846; Nov. 16, 1846.

H

A Book of Hymns for Public and Private Devotion.

Cambridge ... 1846.

See in *Section Six*.

Voices of the True-Hearted ...

Philadelphia ... 1846.

See above under 1844.

12087. The Opal: A Pure Gift for the Holydays. MDCCCXLVII. Edited by John Keese ...

New-York: J. C. Riker, 129 Fulton-Street. 1847.

"Birds of Passage," pp. ⟨11⟩-12. Collected in *The Seaside and the Fireside*, 1850.

For comment see entry No. 6853.

12088. The Estray: A Collection of Poems ...

Boston: William D. Ticknor & Co. 1847.

Edited by Longfellow.

"Proem," pp. ⟨xi⟩-xiv. Collected in *The Seaside and the Fireside*, 1850, as "Pegasus in Pound."

Cream paper boards, printed paper label on spine; T cloth: brown, cream; illuminated paper wrapper; blue silk.

According to the publisher's records 1150 copies were printed; and, published Dec. 22, 1846. "*The Estray* is published"—Longfellow's journal, Dec. 22, 1846. Deposited Dec. 30, 1846. Listed as a December, 1846, publication ALB Jan. 1847; WPLNL Jan. 1847. Copies have been seen (AAS, BA, UV) inscribed by Longfellow Jan. 1, 1847.

AAS   BPL   H   NYHS   NYPL   UV   Y

12089. EVANGELINE, A TALE OF ACADIE ...

BOSTON: WILLIAM D. TICKNOR & COMPANY. 1847.

⟨1⟩-163. 7³⁄₁₆″ x 4¹¹⁄₁₆″.

⟨1⟩-10⁸, 11².

Brownish-gray paper boards, printed paper label on spine, white end papers, flyleaves. Glazed yellow paper boards, printed paper label on spine, yellow-coated end papers, flyleaves. Inserted at the front of some copies is a publisher's catalog, pp. ⟨1⟩-4, dated *October 1, 1847*. BAL has seen no copy of the first printing in cloth.

Note: Copies first *printed* (not necessarily the copies first *published*), p. 61, line 1, read: *Long* ... Examination indicates that during the run of the first printing the reading became *Lo* ... , due to an unknown, accidental, cause. The faulty reading is present in all examined copies of the *Second, Third* (but see note below) and *Fourth Editions;* and in some copies of the *Fifth Edition.* The repair appears to have been made during the printing of the *Fifth Edition* but it may be argued with equal force that copies of the *Fifth Edition* with the *Lo* reading were made up of mixed sheets; *i.e.,* sheets of the *Fifth Edition* and an earlier printing.

Note: A curious hybrid (in FM) has been seen; title-page dated 1848 and marked *Third Edition; Long* reading present on p. 61 (examination of type wear indicates that the gathering is of the first printing); publisher's inserted catalog dated *January 1, 1846*. BAL finds no evidence of restoration and supposes it a salvage copy made up of mixed sheets.

Also note: Forgeries of the title-page have been seen.

Paper sufficient for 2100 copies sent to the printer Oct. 2, 1847. Printed October, 1847. Copies have been seen (NYPL, UV) inscribed by Longfellow Oct. 30, 1847. Published Nov. 1, 1847 (publisher's records). A copy in H inscribed by Longfellow Nov. 1, 1847. No record of a *second printing* found but copies marked *Second Edition* are dated 1848. The *Third Edition* (so marked), dated 1848, 1100 copies, was

printed Nov. 17, 1847 (publisher's records).
Listed LW Nov. 20, 1847. Deposited Dec. 19,
1847.

H NYHS NYPL UV

British Publication

The following notes are on the basis of trade
periodical listings and advertisements; not on
the basis of examination of the books. The arrangement is alphabetical by publisher. Also
see in *Section II* and *Section III* of this list.
Place of publication is London unless otherwise
stated.

Aylott & Jones: Listed PC Dec. 15, 1848.

Bell & Daldy: Listed Bkr Oct. 31, 1866; PC Nov.
1, 1866.

Blackie: Listed Bkr Dec. 2, 1878; PC Dec. 6,
1878.

Bogue: Listed LG Dec. 29, 1849; PC Jan. 15,
1850.

H. G. Clarke: Listed PC July 1, 1848.

Kent & Richards: Listed Ath June 24, 1848.

Knight & Son: Listed Ath June 11, 1853; PC
July 1, 1853.

Longmans: Published? Advertised Ath Jan. 1,
1876, as one in a series of "annotated poems" of
English ⟨sic⟩ authors.

Milner & Sowerby (Halifax): Advertised PC Dec.
1, 1856.

Routledge: Several printings or editions: Listed
Ath April 9, 1853. *Another* listed Ath Nov. 15,
1856; PC Dec. 1, 1856. *Another* listed PC Feb.
16, 1878.

George Slater: Listed Ath June 30, 1849; PC
July 16, 1849.

Tegg: Listed PC Dec. 15, 1848.

Theobald: Listed LG Oct. 11, 1851; PC Nov. 1,
1851.

The Ladies' Casket ... 1848.

... New York. ⟨n.d., 1847?⟩

See in Section Six.

12090. The Opal: A Pure Gift for the Holy
Days. MDCCCXLVIII. Edited by Mrs. Sarah J.
Hale.

New York: J. C. Riker, 129 Fulton Street.
1848.

"By the Sea-Side," pp. ⟨13⟩-14. Collected in
The Seaside and the Fireside, 1850, as "Twilight."

For comment see entry No. 1030.

12091. Proceedings of the American Academy of
Arts and Sciences. Vol. I. From May, 1846, to
May, 1848. Selected from the Records.

Boston and Cambridge: Metcalf and Company. 1848.

Cloth?

Report of the committee of the American Academy of Arts and Sciences appointed to consider
the proposed plan for the organization of the
Smithsonian Institution, pp. 185-194. Signed at
end by Longfellow and others.

Originally issued in four (paper-covered?) parts:
Pp. 1-48, 1847; pp. 49-160, 1847; pp. 161-296,
1848; pp. 297-366, 1848.

H copy of Part 3 received Feb. 15, 1848.

H

12092. ... The (Old) Farmer's Almanack ...
for the Year of Our Lord 1849 ... by Robert
B. Thomas ...

Boston: Published and Sold by Jenks, Palmer
& Co. ... 1848 ...

Printed paper wrapper. At head of title: Number Fifty-Seven.

"The Builders," p. 40; being a 4-stanza extract
from the complete poem. Here reprinted? *See
next two entries.*

Deposited Oct. 18, 1848.

H NYPL

12093. Poems: Lyrical and Dramatic ... a New
Edition, Complete in One Volume.

London: William Tegg & Co.; Aylott &
Jones; Partridge & Oakey; H. Washbourne.
Glasgow: W. Collins; Griffin & Co. Edin-
burgh: J. Johnstone. ⟨n.d., 1848⟩

Pp. xvi, 460.

Issued in the *London Domestic Library* according to the terminal advertisements and contemporary trade notices; see below.

Reprint save for:

"Earth with Her Thousand Voices Praises God,"
otherwise "Thanksgiving." Previously in *Miscellaneous Poems Selected from the United States
Literary Gazette,* Boston, 1826. For first collected American appearance see *Works,* 1886.

"The Builders." *See preceding entry; see next
entry.* Here first collected. Here first in book
form?

"The Indian Hunter," previously in *Miscellaneous Poems Selected from the United States Literary Gazette,* Boston, 1826. For first collected

American appearance see *Poetical Works,* Boston, 1868.

"The Sea Diver," same note as preceding.

Advertised as a volume in the *London Domestic Library* Ath Nov. 25, 1848. Listed Ath Nov. 25, 1848. Supposedly the same edition is advertised as No. 3 in the series Ath July 21, 1849; and as No. 4 in the series Ath Oct. 27, 1849.

CH

12094. Golden Leaflets: A Selection of Poetry ... Edited by J. M. Fletcher ...

　　Boston: Published by J. Buffum. ⟨1848⟩

Reprint save for "The Builders," pp. 14-15. Earliest located appearance of the complete poem in an American book. *See preceding two entries.* For first collected appearance in U.S. see *The Seaside and the Fireside,* 1850.

Publication information wanting. No record of copyright deposit found. Copyright notice dated 1848.

CH

12095. The Modern Pulpit. A Sermon Preached at the Ordination of Samuel Longfellow, at Fall River, Mass., February 16th, 1848. By John Weiss ...

　　Fall River: Printed by Henry Pratt. 1848.

Printed paper wrapper.

Hymn, *Christ to the young man said* ..., p. 36. Collected in *The Seaside and the Fireside,* 1850, as "Hymn for My Brother's Ordination."

The hymn "was reprinted the same year in the fifth edition of the collection of Unitarian Hymns edited by Samuel Longfellow and Samuel Johnson, *A Book of Hymns for Public and Private Devotion,* 1848."—Livingston, p. 50. Not seen by BAL.

BA   NYPL   UV   Y

12096. KAVANAGH, A TALE ...

　　BOSTON: TICKNOR, REED, AND FIELDS. M DCCC XLIX.

⟨i-iv⟩, ⟨1⟩-188. 7³⁄₁₆″ x 4⅝″.

⟨-⟩², ⟨1⟩-11⁸, 12⁶.

FIRST PRINTING, FIRST STATE

According to the publisher's records the first printing was completed by May 12, 1849, on which date the first printing (5100 copies) was put on sale.

Pagination and collation as above.

P. 25, line 12: ... *Cartwright's* ...

P. 96, line 14: ... *Arian;* /

P. 132, line 2: ... *yellow* /

P. 173, last line: ... *left. At* ...

P. 177, line 11: *hte* ...

P. 180, line 6: ... *now only* ...

P. 188: The word END is not present at end of text.

T cloth: brown; purple. Peach end papers. Flyleaves. Sides stamped in blind only; the floret at each inner corner of the sides enclosed by an arc. Not seen in extra-gilt but possibly so issued. See note below for a comment on the inserted catalog.

FIRST PRINTING, ALTERED STATES

On the evidence of dated inscriptions four alterations were made during the first printing. Copies exhibit one or more of the following alterations.

P. 173, last line: ... *left him* ...

P. 177, line 11: *the* ...

P. 180, line 6: ... *less than* ...

P. 188: The word END is present at end of text.

H cloth: purple. T cloth: black; brown; purple. Peach end papers. Flyleaves. Sides stamped in blind only, the floret at each inner corner of the sides enclosed by an arc. Not seen in extra-gilt but possibly so issued. See note below for a comment on inserted catalog.

SECOND PRINTING

According to the publisher's records the second printing (500 copies) was done in Sept. 1849.

Pagination and collation as above.

P. 25, line 12: ... *Wainwright's* ...

P. 96, line 14: ... *Arius;*/

P. 132, line 2: ... *golden*/

P. 173, last line: ... *left him* ...

P. 177, line 11: *the* ...

P. 180, line 6: ... *less than* ...

P. 188: The word END is present at end of text.

T cloth: brown. Yellow or tan end papers. Sides stamped in blind only, the florets at each inner corner of the sides not enclosed by arcs. Also noted in extra-gilt binding, a principal feature being gilded edges. See note below for a comment on inserted catalog.

THE CATALOG

Some copies have an inserted publisher's catalog dated *May 1, 1849.* The catalog occurs in two printings; sequence, if any, not known. The following designations are for identification only. Other variations are present but the following is sufficient for recognition:

A: P. 2: The entry for Motherwell's *Minstrelsy* reads: ... *Minstrelsy, An-* /

B: P. 2: The entry reads: ... *Minstrelsy, Ancient* /

Note: Livingston, p. 51, states that the error *wonld* for *would,* p. 172, was corrected, and places the error in line 2. The error does not occur in line 2, but in line 11. ⟨*Query:* Did Livingston misread his hand-written 11 for II?⟩ All copies examined by BAL, including a reprint of 1863, have the error present.

A copy of the first printing (first state) in H presented by Longfellow to his wife, May 10, 1849; another (in UV) inscribed by early owner May 11, 1849. Published (5100 copies) May 12, 1849. Second printing (500 copies) printed Sept. 20, 1849. Third printing (500 copies) published Nov. 20, 1850; postdated *1851? London publication:* Advertised PC June 1, 1849, as an importation, *ready for sale June 4;* listed Ath June 9, 1849.

BD (1st printing 1st state)   BPL (1st printing altered state; 2nd printing)   H (1st printing 1st state; 1st printing altered state)   LC (1st printing altered state)   NYPL (1st printing altered state)   UV (1st printing 1st state; 1st printing altered state; 2nd printing)   Y (1st printing 1st state; 1st printing altered state; 2nd printing)

12097. Echoes of Infant Voices ... ⟨Edited by M.A.H.⟩

   Boston: Wm. Crosby and H. P. Nichols, 111 Washington Street. 1849.

Reprint save for "Resignation," pp. 141-144. Collected in *The Seaside and the Fireside,* 1850.

Title deposited May 25, 1849. Book deposited June 8, 1849. Listed NAR July, 1849.

H

12098. The Boston Book. Being Specimens of Metropolitan Literature.

   Boston: Ticknor, Reed, and Fields. MDCCCL.

Reprint save for "Footprints of Angels," pp. ⟨357⟩-364, an altered extract from *Hyperion,* 1839.

For comment see entry No. 5929.

12099. THE SEASIDE AND THE FIRESIDE ...

   BOSTON: TICKNOR, REED, AND FIELDS. M DCCC L.

See next entry.

The trade edition was available in four styles; see advertisement in LW Dec. 15, 1849. The designations are those of the publisher.

⟨i-ii⟩, ⟨i⟩-⟨vi⟩, ⟨1⟩-141, blank leaf. 7³⁄₁₆″ x 4⁹⁄₁₆″.

⟨-⟩⁴, 1-9⁸.

Cloth

T cloth: brown. Sides blindstamped. Edges plain. Yellow end papers. Flyleaves. The publisher's spine imprint stamped from two varying brasses; sequence, if any, not known; the designations are for identification only:

   A: The ampersand is a vertical character.

   B: The upper portion of the ampersand inclines to the right.

Boards

Tan paper boards, printed paper label on spine. Pale tan end papers. Edges plain. Noted with: Single flyleaves; single flyleaf at front; triple flyleaves.

Note: Copies of the trade format have been reported in glazed yellow paper boards, printed paper label on spine. No copy thus traced by BAL which suspects the report in error.

Cloth, Gilt

T cloth: blue; green; purple; red; slate. In some copies leaf 9₈ is either excised or pasted under the terminal pastedown. Sides stamped in blind and gold. Edges gilded. Flyleaf at front; flyleaves. Leaf: 7″ x 4⁷⁄₁₆″.

Cloth, Gilt-Extra

T cloth: blue; green; purple; red; slate. In some copies leaf 9₈ is either excised or pasted under the terminal pastedown. Sides stamped in gold. Edges gilded. Flyleaves. Leaf 7″ x 4⁷⁄₁₆″.

Inserted Catalogs

Catalogs are inserted in some copies of the *cloth* and the *boards* formats; not seen in either the *gilt* or the *gilt-extra* formats. The catalogs are variously dated October, 1849; November, 1849; December, 1849.

Note: Not to be confused with Vol. VI of the large paper edition of Longfellow's *Poems* which has on the title-page: VOL. VI. THE SEASIDE AND THE FIRESIDE.

⟨i-ii⟩, ⟨i⟩-⟨vi⟩, ⟨1⟩-141, blank leaf. 9¹⁵⁄₁₆″ x 6¹³⁄₁₆″.

⟨1-19⟩⁴. *Signed:* ⟨-⟩⁴, 1-9⁸.

Yellow glazed paper boards, printed paper label on spine. Glazed yellow on white end papers. Flyleaves.

Livingston (p. 53) states: "Probably in January, 1850, some copies were printed off on large paper"; the implication being that trade copies were first printed and published. BAL has seen two copies of the large paper edition (in H, UV) each inscribed by Longfellow Jan. 1, 1850, which suggests that large paper copies were printed in December, 1849, not in January, 1850. The exact status of large paper copies remains in doubt; no mention of large paper copies found in the publisher's records.

Trade format: 5000 copies printed in Dec. 1849 (publisher's records). Advertised for Dec. 22, in LW Dec. 15, 1849. *Daily Evening Transcript,* Boston, Dec. 20, 1849, noted the book as *just given to the public.* A copy in NYPL inscribed by Longfellow Dec. 20, 1849. Reviewed LW Dec. 22, 1849. Deposited Dec. 29, 1849. *Large paper copies* have been seen inscribed by Longfellow Jan. 1, 1850. A note in PC Dec. 15, 1849, reports that the book was to be imported by John Chapman. David Davidson advertised the book as a recent importation, Ath Jan. 19, 1850; PC Feb. 1, 1850. Listed LG Jan. 26, 1850.

AAS BA H (also large paper) LC (large paper) NYHS NYPL UV (also large paper) Y

12100. THE SEASIDE AND THE FIRE-SIDE ...

LIVERPOOL: JOHN WALKER, 7, CLAYTON SQUARE. LONDON: DAVID BOGUE; HAMILTON, ADAMS, AND CO.; JOHN JOHNSTONE. EDINBURGH: OLIVER & BOYD; JOHN JOHNSTONE. DUBLIN: J. M'GLASHAN. ⟨n.d., 1849⟩

Title-page in black and red. Issued simultaneously with the Boston edition? See preceding entry.

Contains the same poems as those in the Boston edition save for "The Builders" which is not here present.

⟨i-iv⟩, ⟨1⟩-75. 6¼" x 4⁷⁄₁₆". *Note:* Pagination postulated.

⟨-⟩², 1-4⁸, 5⁶.

Printed gray paper wrapper.

The publishers (PC Dec. 1, 1849) announced that by arrangement with Longfellow they would be able "to supply it first to the British public." What appears to be this edition listed Ath Dec. 22, 1849; LG Dec. 22, 1849; PC Jan. 1, 1850.

Y

Other British Editions Announced

H. G. Clarke: Announced for Jan. 1, 1850, in PC Dec. 1, 1849, as No. 6 ⟨sic⟩ in *The Cabinet Library.* Announced for Jan. 1, 1850, Ath Dec. 8, 1849; and, PC Dec. 15, 1849, as No. 4 ⟨sic⟩ in *The Cabinet Library.* No further comment found; project abandoned?

Bentley: Advertised as *just ready* in Ath Nov. 24, 1849. Advertised for *December* Ath Dec. 1, 8, 15, 22, 1849. No further comment found; project abandoned?

George Slater: Advertised as *just ready,* as No. 14 in the *Shilling Series,* PC March 15, 1850. No further comment found; project abandoned?

Query: Were Clarke, Bentley and Slater prevented from publishing because of copyright? And if so, is this indication that the Walker edition was published prior to, or simultaneously with, the Boston edition? The announcement in PC Dec. 1, 1849, states that the Walker edition "alone" had "the advantage of" Longfellow's "supervision." Correspondence in the Longfellow archive (in H) indicates that the Walker edition was authorized and published by arrangement with Longfellow.

12101. Outre-Mer: A Pilgrimage beyond the Sea ... to Which Are Added, the Latest Poems of the Author ...

London: George Routledge & Co., Soho Square. M DCCC LI.

Reprint save for:

"The Ladder of St. Augustine"

"The Phantom Ship"

Both of the above in *The Courtship of Miles Standish,* 1858.

Also contains "Duke William at Rouen" and "Richard's Escape" both of which had prior publication in *The Poets and Poetry of Europe,* 1845; by Longfellow?

Two printings noted; type-wear indicates the following sequence:

A: Leaf 5¹⁄₁₆" x 3¼". Text not enclosed by rules boxes.

B: Leaf 6¹¹⁄₁₆" x 4³⁄₁₆". Text enclosed by rules boxes.

An edition (this?) listed PC March 15, 1851.

BD (both)   BPL (A)   UV (B)

12102. THE GOLDEN LEGEND ...

BOSTON: TICKNOR, REED, AND FIELDS. M DCCC LI.

See next entry.

⟨i-iv⟩, ⟨1⟩-301, blank leaf. 7¹⁄₁₆″ x 4⁹⁄₁₆″ (cloth, gilt). 6¹⁵⁄₁₆″ x 4⅜″ (cloth, extra-gilt).

⟨-⟩², 1-19⁸.

Cloth, Gilt

T cloth: brown. Sides blindstamped. Flyleaves. Edges plain. Inserted at front of some copies is a publisher's catalog, pp. ⟨1⟩-4, dated *October, 1851;* or, *January, 1852.* Yellow end papers.

Cloth, Extra-Gilt

T cloth: blue; green. Sides stamped in gold and blind. Flyleaves. Edges gilded. Yellow end papers.

Query: Also issued in brown paper boards, printed paper label on spine?

Note: The publisher's records and date of deposit indicate that during the course of first printing the imprint date was altered from M DCCC LI to M DCCC LII. The record is as follows:

Sept. 16, 1851: Paper shipped to the printer.

Oct. 16, 1851: A second shipment of paper sent to the printer. This and the earlier shipment combined to produce 3600 copies, some dated M DCCC LI, others dated M DCCC LII.

Nov. 25, 1851: A copy (dated M DCCC LI) in CH bears this date in Longfellow's hand.

Nov. 29, 1851: Published this date.

Dec. 4, 1851: On this date a copy dated M DCCC LII deposited for copyright. Bound in tan paper boards, printed paper label on spine.

Dec. 1851: Paper sufficient for 888 copies sent to the printer. Published Dec. 27, 1851.

BAL is indebted to Mr. James E. Walsh for the notes relating to textual alterations. For a discussion of the publication of *The Golden Legend* see Mr. Walsh's "American Printings of Longfellow's *The Golden Legend, 1851–1855,*" in *The Papers of the Bibliographical Society of America,* Vol. 57, 1963, pp. 81-88.

First Printing

The copies first printed dated M DCCC LI. Date altered to M DCCC LII during the course of printing.

P. 5, line 6 up: *Fulgora* . . .

P. 6, line 7: . . . *wardens* . . .

P. 11, line 3: *and restless.* |

P. 14, last line: . . . *have heard* . . .

P. 21, line 4 up: . . . *such books,* |

P. 31, line 4: . . *glow* . . .

P. 32, line 6: . . . *wardens* . . .

P. 139, line 11: ANACHIEL. |

P. 169, line 2 up: . . . *Ahr* |

P. 176, line 7: *King René* . . .

P. 275, line 15: . . . *it,* |

P. 291, line 1: *That* . . .

Second Printing

Title-page dated M DCCC LII.

P. 5, line 6 up: *Fulgora* . . .

P. 6, line 7: . . . *warders* . . .

P. 11, line 3: *and restless. Midnight.* |

P. 14, last line: . . . *hear* . . .

P. 21, line 4 up: . . . *your books,* |

P. 31, line 4: . . . *grow* . . .

P. 32, line 6: . . . *warders* . . .

P. 139, line 11: ORIFEL. |

P. 169, line 2 up: . . . *Ahr.* |

P. 176, line 7: *King René* . . .

P. 275, line 15: . . . *believe,* |

P. 291, line 1: *Which* . . .

Third Printing

Title-page dated M DCCC LII.

P. 5, line 6 up: *Fulgura* . . .

P. 6, line 7: . . . *warders* . . .

P. 11, line 3: *and restless. Midnight.* |

P. 14, last line: . . . *hear* . . .

P. 21, line 4 up: . . . *your books,* |

P. 31, line 4: . . . *grow* . . .

P. 32, line 6: . . . *warders* . . .

P. 139, line 11: ORIFEL. |

P. 169, line 2 up: . . . *Ahr.* |

P. 176, line 7: *King René* . . .

P. 275, line 15: . . . *believe,* |

P. 291, line 1: *Which* . . .

Fourth Printing

Title-page dated M DCCC LIII.

Readings as in the *Third Printing,* above.

Fifth Printing

Title-page dated M DCCC LIV.

Readings as in the *Third Printing,* above. However, pp. 193, 194, 205, show extensive revisions. The following is sufficient for identification:

Printings 1-4   5th Printing

P. 193, last line

eyes!| ... Vandals?|

P. 194, line 4

To cross ...   To crosier ...

P. 205, line 12

Put on your disguise! | And what is the won-
der! |

Note: In this printing Longfellow's "Notes" (revised) first appear in an American book, pp. ⟨305⟩-326. For a comment see *The Golden Legend*, London (Bogue), 1854, below.

Sixth Printing

Title-page dated M DCCC LV.

The text appears to be the same as that of the *Fifth Printing* save for a single alteration. In all earlier printings p. 176, line 7, reads *King René ... ;* in the *Sixth Printing* the reading is: *Saint Ulric ...*

Note: A cursory examination of the text as printed in *Christus*, 1872, indicates that save for some minor alterations in punctuation, the reading is the same as that in the *Sixth Printing.*

The first printing was advertised for Nov. 29, 1851, in LW Nov. 15, 1851. A copy in CH inscribed by Longfellow Nov. 25, 1851. Listed LW Nov. 29, 1851. Published Nov. 29, 1851 (publisher's records). A copy of the first printing, dated M DCCC LII, deposited for copyright Dec. 4, 1851.

Note: Intermediates may exist. This statement is made on the basis of a letter (in H) from the publisher to the printer, Feb. 3, 1852, reporting forty incomplete copies of the "first edition" in stock; and requesting sheets for the purpose of perfecting these. The letter lists the needed signatures. Since the request was made well after the printing of the first printing, the printer may have supplied sheets printed from altered plates which would have produced intermediates. However, no such intermediates have been traced.

AAS (1st, dated M DCCC LI)   BA (1st, dated M DCCC LI; 4th)   BD (1st, dated M DCCC LII; 3rd)   BPL (5th)   H (1st dated M DCCC LI; 1st dated M DCCC LII; 2nd; 3rd; 6th)   NYPL (1st, dated M DCCC LI)   Y (5th)

12103. THE GOLDEN LEGEND ...

LONDON: DAVID BOGUE, FLEET STREET. M.DCCC.LI.

Issued simultaneously with the Boston edition; see preceding entry. The text varies from the first Boston printing. For a discussion of the textual variations see James E. Walsh's "American Printings of Longfellow's *The Golden Legend*, 1851–1855," in *The Papers of the Bibliographical Society of America*, Vol. 57, 1963, pp. 81-88.

⟨i-iv⟩, ⟨1⟩-294; pp. ⟨295-296⟩ excised; ⟨289⟩-295. 6¾" x 4³⁄₁₆".

⟨A⟩², B-I, K-T⁸, T*⁴, U⁴. Leaf T*₄ excised.

A letter in H from the publisher to Longfellow, Dec. 23, 1851, explains both the faulty pagination and the excision of leaf T*₄. The pertinent portion of the letter reads: "I duly received the additional scene ⟨*i.e.,* "The Epilogue"⟩ just in time to include it in all the copies of the work ..."

It is possible that the text of the added matter (Sig. U) was printed from two settings; but this is theory only and further study is indicated. The printer appears to have run out of book stock; hence copies of Sig. U occur on stock 5/1000" thick; and, on stock measuring 4/1000" plus thick.

Signature T* was printed (presumably simultaneously) from two settings; hence typographic variations are present. It is probable that the settings were inserted by the binders *ad. lib.,* and that one or the other may occur in either state of the book; see below. The following variations are sufficient for identification of Sig. T*:

Sig. T*, Setting A

P. 289: The rule is ⅜" full.

P. 291, line 2: ... *ring, drawn ...*

Sig. T*, Setting B

P. 289: The rule is 9⁄₁₆" full.

P. 291, line 2: ... *ring drawn ...*

Two printings of the book have been seen:

First Printing

Pagination and signature collation as above.

P. ⟨ii⟩: Imprint of G. Barclay.

Two states of the first printing noted; the following order is suggested:

First Printing, State A   *First Printing, State B*

Page 145 (Sig. L)

Mispaged 541   Paged 145

Page 241 (Sig. R)

Signature mark R present.   Signature mark not present.

Page 242, line 1 (Sig. R)

Of a truth ... The *O* lacking

Note: A binder's variant (in BD) has been seen: Sig. L, state A; Sig. R, state B.

Second Printing

The second printing is in large part reset. The following variations are sufficient for ready identification:

⟨i-iv⟩, ⟨1⟩-300; p. ⟨301⟩ (mispaged 295); leaf excised.

⟨A⟩², B-I, K-U⁸. Leaf U₈ excised.

P. ⟨iv⟩: Imprint of G. Barclay.

TZ cloth: rose-purple; noted on first printing, state A; also noted on the intermediate in BD. H cloth: rose-purple; noted on first printing, state B. TB cloth: green; noted on a second printing. Yellow-coated end papers. Inserted at front: A single leaf printed on both sides headed *Professor Longfellow's Works.* Inserted at back: Publisher's catalog, pp. ⟨1⟩-24, dated on p. ⟨1⟩ *November 1851.* Copies of the second printing have been seen in rose-purple A cloth; one of these with publisher's catalog dated *January, 1850* ⟨sic⟩; the other with catalog dated *November 1851.* Also issued in morocco according to an advertisement in Ath Dec. 27, 1851.

Advertised as *in a few days* PC Nov. 15, 1851. Advertised for Nov. 29 Ath Nov. 15, 1851. Advertised for Nov. 22 ⟨error for Nov. 29?⟩ Ath Nov. 22, 1851. Advertised as *now ready* Ath Nov. 29, 1851. Listed Ath Nov. 29, 1851; LG Nov. 29, 1851. "... Issued simultaneously in England and the U.S., securing its copyright in both countries, in conformity with the provisions of the late judgment ... by Lord Campbell ..."—PC Dec. 1, 1851. Listed PC Dec. 1, 1851. Reviewed LG Dec. 6, 1851; Ath Dec. 13, 1851. Letter (in H) publisher to Longfellow, Dec. 23, 1851: "... I am glad to hear you have been so successful with it ⟨i.e., *The Golden Legend*⟩ there. Here I printed 2000 & the last of them are now in the binders hands. This is much better than I expected ..." Letter (in H) publisher to Longfellow, Oct. 8, 1852: "... *The Golden Legend* continues to move. I have about 850 left out of 4000 printed ..." A *second edition* listed Ath Oct. 16, 1852; LG Oct. 16, 1852; PC Nov. 1, 1852; these preceding described as pp. 352; illustrated edition? A *Routledge* printing listed Ath Sept. 23, 1854; LG Sept. 23, 1854; PC Oct. 16, 1854. A *Knight & Son* printing listed PC March 15, 1856. Knight & Son also issued *The Golden Legend* bound together with *The Song of Hiawatha;* listed PC March 15, 1856.

BA (2nd printing) BD (intermediate; 2nd printing) BPL (1st printing, state B) CH (2nd printing) H (1st printing, state A)

12104. Reports from Committees: Thirteen Volumes. 7. Manchester and Salford Education. Session 3 February—1 July 1852. Vol. XI.

⟨London: The House of Commons, Select Committee on Manchester and Salford Education⟩ 1852.

Boards, cloth shelfback, printed paper label on spine.

Answers to "Questions Respecting the Common Schools of New England," p. 499.

Reprinted in *Evidence as to the Religious Working of the Common Schools in the State of Massachusetts, with a Preface by the Hon. Edward Twisleton* ... , London, 1854.

H

12105. Autumn Leaves. Original Pieces in Prose and Verse ...

Cambridge: John Bartlett. 1853.

Edited by Anne Wales Abbot.

"In the Churchyard at Cambridge. A Legend of Lady Lee," pp. ⟨11⟩-12. Collected in *The Courtship of Miles Standish* ... , 1858.

BA copy inscribed by early owner Oct. 10, 1853.

BA BD H UV Y

12106. The Golden Legend ...

London: David Bogue, 86, Fleet Street. MDCCCLIV.

For first edition see above under 1851. Also see below under 1855. Issued in both cloth; and, morocco according to trade notices.

"Notes," written for this edition, pp. ⟨211⟩-224. For a revision of these notes see comment on the *Fifth Printing* (American) under *The Golden Legend,* Boston, 1851.

Examination of the several printings of *The Golden Legend* and original correspondence in H produces the following note:

Longfellow prepared a series of notes for the above edition. Under date Nov. 11, 1853, Bogue acknowledged receipt of Longfellow's manuscript of the notes.

A *revision* of the preceding notes published in the *Fifth Printing* (American) of *The Golden Legend.* See above under *The Golden Legend,* Boston, 1851. The *Fifth Printing* of the Boston edition was done in May, 1854.

Bogue's edition published Nov. 1854. The notes are in the original, unrevised, text.

Bogue's edition distributed in United States with cancel title-leaf imprinted: *Boston: Ticknor and Fields. MDCCCLV.* See below under year 1855.

Advertised as *in preparation* Ath Oct. 28, 1854; PC Nov. 1, 1854. Listed Ath Nov. 18, 1854; LG Nov. 18, 1854. Reviewed LG Nov. 25, 1854. Listed PC Dec. 6, 1854.

AAS MHS Y

12107. The Native Poets of Maine. By S. Herbert Lancey ...

Bangor: David Bugbee & Co. 1854.

Reprint with the possible exception of "Phantoms," pp. 20-21. *See next entry.* Otherwise "Haunted Houses." Collected in *The Courtship of Miles Standish,* 1858.

Deposited Nov. 21, 1854.

NYPL

12108. ... The Unitarian Congregational Register, for the Year 1855.

Boston: Published by the Executive Committee of the American Unitarian Association, 21 Bromfield Street. ⟨n.d., 1854⟩

Printed paper wrapper. At head of title: Annual Series. No. 5.

"Phantoms," pp. 49-50. *See preceding entry.* Here reprinted? Here prior to appearance in preceding entry?

Precise date of publication not known. Listed in *Christian Register,* Boston, Dec. 2, 1854, as a publication "received ⟨prior⟩ to Nov. 30, 1854." Reviewed in *Christian Register* Dec. 9, 1854.

NYPL

12109. The Golden Legend ... Illustrated with Fifty Engravings on Wood, from Designs by Birket Foster and Jane E. Hay.

Boston: Ticknor and Fields. MDCCCLV.

Not to be confused with the unillustrated edition.

Sheets of the London (Bogue), MDCCCLIV, printing with cancel title-page as above. First American publication of the notes prepared by Longfellow for Bogue. See above: *The Golden Legend,* London: David Bogue ... , MDCCCLIV, for comment.

The following notes are taken from the publisher's records: 500 copies were received from Bogue on Oct. 16, 1854. According to the order given on Aug. 29, 1854, the copies were to be bound as follows: 250 in cloth; 100 in antique morocco; and 150 copies were to be sent in sheets.

A copy in CH inscribed by Longfellow Jan. 1, 1855.

BPL H MHS

12110. The Knickerbocker Gallery: A Testimonial to the Editor of the Knickerbocker Magazine from Its Contributors ...

New-York: Samuel Hueston, 348 Broadway. MDCCCLV.

"The Emperor's Bird's Nests," pp. ⟨247⟩-248. Collected in *The Courtship of Miles Standish,* 1858.

For fuller comment see entry No. 1033.

12111. THE SONG OF HIAWATHA ...

LONDON: DAVID BOGUE, FLEET STREET. MDCCCLV.

For first American printing see next entry.

Simultaneously issued in two formats: Cloth; and, printed paper wrapper.

Cloth

⟨i⟩-⟨iv⟩, ⟨1⟩-316. 6¾″ x 4¼″.

⟨A⟩², B-I, K-U⁸, X⁶.

A cloth: green; purple. H cloth: blue. Yellow-coated end papers. Inserted at back: Publisher's catalog, pp. ⟨1⟩-24, dated *March 1855.*

Note: All examined copies save one (a copy in UV) have the sides blindstamped with a frame composed principally of straight rules and boxes. The exception, in green A cloth, has the sides blindstamped with a straight rules frame enclosing a leafy frame; status not known.

Printed Paper Wrapper

⟨i⟩-iv, ⟨1⟩-176. 6¹¹⁄₁₆″ x 4¼″.

⟨A⟩², B-I, K-M⁸.

Printed tan stiff paper wrapper. Inserted at back: Publisher's catalog, pp. ⟨1⟩-24, dated *March 1855.*

Printed from the same setting as the cloth-bound edition (above) but with the leading removed; and, some slight revision of the text. See, for example, p. 100, lines 9-11 (cloth) and compare with the reading on p. 54 of the printing in paper wrapper. The Boston printing follows that of the revised London edition.

Noted as *in a few days* Ath Oct. 27, 1855. Both printings advertised as *now ready* PC Nov. 1,

1855. Advertised, cloth only, as *published this day* Ath Nov. 3, 1855. Listed, both printings, Ath Nov. 3, 1855. Both printings advertised as *just ready* Ath Nov. 10, 1855. Reviewed Ath Nov. 10, 1855; LG Nov. 10, 1855. Listed PC, both cloth and paper, Nov. 15, 1855.

BA (cloth)   BD (cloth)   H (cloth; wrapper) NYPL (cloth; wrapper)   UV (wrapper; cloth variant)   Y (cloth)

12112. THE SONG OF HIAWATHA ...

BOSTON: TICKNOR AND FIELDS. M DCCC LV.

For prior publication see preceding entry.

⟨i⟩-iv, ⟨1⟩-316. 7³⁄₁₆″ x 4½″ (cloth, gilt). 6⅞″ x 4⁷⁄₁₆″ (cloth, gilt extra).

⟨-⟩², 1-19⁸, 20⁶.

Cloth, Gilt

T cloth: brown. Sides blindstamped. Edges plain. Yellow end papers. Flyleaves. Inserted in some copies is a publisher's catalog, pp. 1-⟨12⟩, dated either *October, 1855;* or *November, 1855.*

Cloth, Gilt Extra

T cloth: gray-green; red. Sides stamped in gold and blind. Edges gilded. Yellow-coated on white end papers. Flyleaves. No copy noted with inserted advertisements; extra gilt bindings were normally issued without such insertions.

Cloth, Super-gilt Extra

The publisher's records indicate that a few copies were done in super-gilt extra. In all likelihood the sides are stamped wholly in gold (not blind and gold), edges gilded.

Note: According to the publisher's records there were three printings issued under the date M DCCC LV. Dates of printing and publication taken from the publisher's records and other sources; see publication notes below. The following notes are sufficient for identification of the three printings.

Also note: Binder's variants occur; *i.e.,* copies made up of mixed sheets which contain early readings in combination with later.

First Printing

Printed Oct. 2, 1855. 5250 copies. Published Nov. 10, 1855.

P. 27, line 9: ... *heron /*

P. 32, line 11: *In the Moon* ...

P. 39, line 11: *Wahonomin* ...

P. 96, line 7: *Dove* ...

P. 268, line 11: *"Wahonomin* ...

P. 268, line 14: *Wahonomin* ...

P. 278, line 4 up: *Cooed the Omemee* ...

Note: P. 279, line 5 up, the word *one* occurs with the letter *n* present or absent. Examination of many copies of first and later printings suggests that copies first printed may lack the letter *n;* and that the missing letter was added to the plate. The letter is present in all examined reprints.

Second Printing

Printed Nov. 22, 1855. 3000 copies. Published Nov. 26, 1855.

P. 27, line 9: ... *heron /*

P. 32, line 11: *To the melancholy* ...

P. 39, line 11: *Wahonowin* ...

P. 96, line 7: *Dived* ...

P. 268, line 11: *"Wahonowin* ...

P. 268, line 14: *Wahonowin* ...

P. 278, line 4 up: *Cooed the pigeon* ...

Third Printing

Printed Dec. 26, 1855. 3000 copies.

P. 27, line 9: ... *curlew /*

P. 32, line 11: *To the melancholy* ...

P. 39, line 11: *Wahonowin* ...

P. 96, line 7: *Dived* ...

P. 268, line 11: *"Wahonowin* ...

P. 268, line 14: *Wahonowin* ...

P. 278, line 4 up: *Cooed the pigeon* ...

Note: All the preceding issued under date M DCCC LV. All subsequent printings issued under altered date, most of which carry a statement of printing (*Thirteenth Thousand,* etc., etc.) on the copyright page. BAL has noted textual alterations in the following printings. No alterations noted in the fourth printing (*Thirteenth Thousand);* the fifth printing (issued in large paper format; 8¼″ x 5⁹⁄₁₆″; also marked *Thirteenth Thousand);* the sixth printing (*Fifteenth Thousand).*

Seventh Printing

On copyright page: *Twentieth Thousand.* Imprint dated M DCCC LVI. Printed March 1, 1856. 5000 copies. A single alteration noted but others may be present. Copy in DEV.

Eighth Printing

On copyright page: *Twenty-Fifth Thousand.* Imprint dated M DCCC LVI. Printed April 8, 1856. 5000 copies. Contains at least 34 alterations. Copy in H.

Ninth Printing

On copyright page: *Thirtieth Thousand.* Imprint dated M DCCC LVI. Printed April 8, 1856. 5000 copies. The reading on p. 77, line 10, reverts to the reading of all printings through the 7th; *i.e.,* the *Twentieth Thousand.* Copy in DEV.

Announced APC Sept. 1, 1855. Printed Oct. 2, 1855, 5250 copies (publisher's records). Advertised as *preparing* APC Oct. 20, 1855. Deposited Nov. 5, 1855, according to the Copyright Office records; but the only surviving deposit copy is of the *Thirtieth Thousand* (so marked on the copyright page) and is imprinted M DCCC LVI; received for copyright April 28, 1856. Advertised for Nov. 10 APC Oct. 27, 1855. Published Nov. 10, 1855; the date from the publisher's records, confirmed by an entry in Longfellow's journal. A copy in NYPL inscribed by James T. Fields Nov. 10, 1855. Listed APC Nov. 17, 1855.

BA (1st)   H (1st, 2nd, 3rd)   LC (1st)   NYPL (1st, 2nd, 3rd)   UV (1st, 2nd, 3rd)   Y (1st, 2nd, 3rd)

12112A. Cyclopædia of American Literature; Embracing Personal and Critical Notices of Authors . . . by Evert A. Duyckinck and George L. Duyckinck. In Two Volumes . . .

New York: Charles Scribner. 1855.

Reprint save for:

"The Jewish Cemetery at Newport," Vol. 2, pp. 447-448. Collected in *The Courtship of Miles Standish,* 1858.

"The Two Angels," Vol. 2, p. 661. Collected in *Voices of the Night,* London, 1857; *The Courtship of Miles Standish,* Boston, 1858.

For comment see entry No. 11092A.

12113. Pictures and Readings from American Authors, Being the Choice Volume of Putnam's Magazine.

New York: Leavitt and Allen. 1855.

"Galgano. A Tale of Giovanni Fiorentino," pp. 512-516.

". . . Longfellow intended to use ⟨it⟩ for *Tales of a Wayside Inn,* but never did . . ."—Wilson, Vol. 1, p. 243.

For comment see entry No. 11179.

12114. An Appeal to the People of the United States in Behalf of Lamartine . . .

⟨New York: D. Appleton & Co., 1856⟩

Caption-title. The above at head of p. ⟨1⟩. 4 pp.

Signed by Longfellow and others.

For comment see entry No. 10193.

12115. Sweet Home; or, Friendship's Golden Altar. Edited by Frances E. Percival . . .

Boston: L. P. Crown & Co., 61 Cornhill. Philadelphia: J. W. Bradley, 48 North Fourth Street. 1856.

"My Lost Youth," pp. 31-35. Collected in *The Courtship of Miles Standish,* 1858.

H copy inscribed by early owner Sept. 5, 1856. Title-page deposited Dec. 31, 1856 (although the printed copyright notice is dated 1855). No record of deposit of book.

H

12116. Prose Works . . . in Two Volumes . . .

Boston: Ticknor and Fields. M DCCC LVII.

Blue and Gold Edition.

Two printings of Vol. 1 noted:

Vol. 1, First Printing

P. ⟨ii⟩ lists *Longfellow's Poems* and no other title.

Vol. 1, Second Printing

P. ⟨ii⟩ lists ten titles.

BAL has been unable to differentiate between the first and the second printings of Vol. 2.

Reprint save for the following material in Vol. 1:

"Frithiof's Saga," pp. ⟨321⟩-371. The publication history of this is as follows:

1: Under the title "Tegnér's Frithiof's Saga" published NAR July, 1837.

2: A portion of the above, under the title "Life in Sweden," published in *The Boston Book* . . . , 1841; see above under 1841.

3: The immediate preceding, in somewhat revised form, collected in *Ballads,* 1842, as the preface to "The Children of the Lord's Supper."

4: Under the title "Esaias Tegnér" an abbreviated version of the original periodical text was published in *Poets and Poetry of Europe,* 1845.

5: Under the title "Frithiof's Saga," which is a revision of the original periodical text, collected in *Prose Works,* 1857.

"Hawthorne's Twice-Told Tales," pp. ⟨372⟩-378.

"The Great Metropolis," pp. ⟨379⟩-383.

"Anglo-Saxon Literature," pp. <384>-411. A version of "Anglo-Saxon Language and Poetry," in *Poets and Poetry of Europe,* 1845.

"Paris in the Seventeenth Century," pp. <412>-418.

"Dante," pp. <419>-433. An altered version of "Dante Alighieri" in *Poets and Poetry of Europe,* 1845.

"The Divina Commedia," pp. <434>-449.

"Table-Talk," pp. <450>-455.

First printing: 3000 copies printed March 20, 1857. Published March 28, 1857. Deposited March 28, 1857. *Second Printing:* 2000 copies printed Sept. 22, 1857. See *Drift-Wood . . . ,* 1852, in *Section Six.*

AAS (2nd) B (2nd) BA (1st) BD (2nd) H (1st, 2nd) MHS (1st) UV (1st) Y (1st)

12117. *Entry cancelled.*

The Fiftieth Birthday of Agassiz. May 28, 1857 . . .

    <n.p., n.d.>

Single leaf. Printed on recto only. See *Harvard Musical Association. Seventh Symphony Concert . . . Boston Music Hall . . . ,* under year 1874, in *Section Four.*

12118. The Voices of the Night, Ballads, and Other Poems . . . with Illustrations by John Gilbert . . .

    London: George Routledge & Co. Farringdon Street. 1857.

Pp. 118.

Reprint save for:

"The Two Angels," here first collected. See entry No. 12112A.

"The Rope Walk" and "The Warden of the Cinque Ports." Here in their earliest located book appearance. First collected American book publication: *The Courtship of Miles Standish,* Boston, 1858. See below: *The Household Book of Poetry . . . ,* New York, 1858.

Listed PC Oct. 16, 1857.

B BPL

12119. The Poetical Works of Henry Wadsworth Longfellow. A Complete Edition, Including The Song of Hiawatha. With Illustrations by John Gilbert, and an Engraved Portrait by Lawrence.

    London: G. Routledge & Co., Farringdon Street. New York: 18, Beekman Street. 1858.

Two printings have been seen; both from the same plates, but with variant title-pages.

First Printing

Title-page as above.

Second Printing

The Poetical Works of Henry Wadsworth Longfellow. A New Complete Edition. With Illustrations by John Gilbert.

    London: George Routledge and Co. Farringdon Street. 1858.

Contains in the front matter a single cut sheet folded to make four pages, paged <ix>-xii; being an "Introductory Preface. Abridged from *Allibone's Dictionary . . .*"; this feature is not present in the first printing.

Reprint save for "Santa Filomena"; first collected American publication: *The Courtship of Miles Standish,* Boston, 1858.

First printing listed PC April 15, 1858. Second printing listed PC Dec. 1, 1858.

B (1st, 2nd)

12120. The Household Book of Poetry. Collected and Edited by Charles A. Dana.

    New York: D. Appleton and Company, 346 & 348 Broadway. London: 16 Little Britain. 1858.

Cloth, leather shelfback.

Reprint save for "The Warden of the Cinque Ports," p. 515, here in its earliest located American book appearance. See above *The Voices of the Night . . . ,* London, 1857.

Deposited Aug. 18, 1858.

H

12121. THE COURTSHIP OF MILES STANDISH, AND OTHER POEMS . . .

    LONDON: W. KENT & CO. (LATE D. BOGUE), 86, FLEET STREET, AND PATERNOSTER ROW. MDCCCLVIII.

For first American edition see next entry.

Issued in two formats as follows:

Paper

<i>-viii, <1>-135; plus: Publisher's catalog, pp. <1>-4. 6¹¹⁄₁₆″ x 4³⁄₁₆″. Not illustrated.

<A>⁴, B-I⁸, K⁴, plus: <L>².

Printed brown paper wrapper.

Cloth

<i>-xii, <1>-227. Frontispiece. 6¾″ scant x 4³⁄₁₆″.

⟨A⟩⁶, B-I, K-P⁸, Q².

A cloth: blue; blue-gray; brown; green. T cloth: blue; green; purple. TZ cloth: blue. Publisher's catalog, pp. ⟨1⟩-40, inserted at back; both *January, 1858* and *October, 1858* noted. Yellow-coated end papers. Also issued in morocco according to contemporary notices.

With the exception of the front matter, both formats were printed from the same setting. Examination of typewear indicates that the 135-page printing was done first; and, by leading out, the 227-page printing (in cloth) was printed second.

The "Preface" was supplied by the English publisher in order to secure British copyright; see letter to Longfellow, from Kent & Co., Sept. 10, 1858; original in H. The "Preface" was slightly revised for the 227-page printing.

In both printings the text reads *ruddy,* not *treacherous;* for a comment on this alteration see note in next entry. Letter, publisher to Longfellow (original in H), Sept. 15, 1858: "Your favour of the 30th August we have duly to hand and for which we have to thank you. We have received also by the same mail from Mr Field ⟨sic⟩ the sheets of the Poem and will attend to the alteration you wish of the word *treacherous* substituting *ruddy.* Mr Field ⟨sic⟩ also communicates that he will not publish your Poem in America until the 16th Octr ..."

Advertised Ath Aug. 14, 1858; the advertisement states: *Two editions, at 5s and 1s will be issued simultaneously.* Advertised for *Sept. 22* in Ath Sept. 18, 1858. Both cloth and paper listed Bkr Sept. 24, 1858; Ath Sept. 25, 1858; LG Sept. 25, 1858. Reviewed Ath Sept. 25, 1858; format not mentioned. Reviewed LG Sept. 25, 1858; format not mentioned. Both cloth and paper listed PC Oct. 1, 1858. A *second edition* in paper listed PC Oct. 15, 1858. *Note:* No copy marked *second edition* located by BAL; does this mean that the book was issued without such notice? and that BAL has failed to identify two printings in paper? A copy in cloth received at BMu Dec. 3, 1858.

Illustrated Edition

Also issued in an *Illustrated Edition* with illustrations by John Absolon, Birket Foster and M. Morgan. Advertised as *now ready* PC Dec. 15, 1858. Listed LG Dec. 18, 1858; Bkr Dec. 24, 1858; PC Jan. 17, 1859.

Other London Editions

Routledge: Listed Ath Nov. 6, 1858; PC Nov. 15, 1858.

Bohn: Listed PC July 17, 1860.

BPL (cloth) H (paper) NYPL (cloth, paper) UV (cloth, paper)

12122. THE COURTSHIP OF MILES STANDISH, AND OTHER POEMS ...

BOSTON: TICKNOR AND FIELDS. M DCCC LVIII.

For prior publication see preceding entry.

⟨i⟩-⟨vi⟩, ⟨7⟩-215. 7¼" x 4⁹⁄₁₆" (cloth, gilt). 7¹⁄₁₆" x 4⁷⁄₁₆" (extra-gilt bindings).

⟨1-18⟩⁶. Signed: ⟨1⟩-13⁸, 14⁴.

Cloth, Gilt

T cloth: brown. Sides wholly blindstamped. Edges plain. Brown-coated end papers. Purple-coated end papers. Flyleaves. Inserted at front of some copies is a single leaf advertisement for the *Waverley Novels.* Publisher's catalog inserted at back, pp. ⟨1⟩-⟨12⟩, dated *October, 1858.*

Cloth, Gilt Extra

A cloth: blue; purple; salmon. Sides stamped in gold and blind. Edges gilt. Brown-coated end papers. Rose-coated end papers. Flyleaves. No copy noted with inserted advertisements; extra-gilt bindings were normally issued without such insertions.

Cloth, Full Gilt

A cloth: blue; purple-rose. Sides stamped in gold. Edges gilt. Brown-coated end papers. Rose-coated end papers. Flyleaves. No copy noted with inserted advertisements; extra-gilt bindings were normally issued without such insertions.

Note: All examined copies dated M DCCC LVIII have the reading ... *treacherous* ... , p. 124, line 3. All examined copies dated M DCCC LIX, or later, have the reading altered to *ruddy.*

According to the publisher's records (see below) there were four printings in 1858. The first and later printings may be identified by the following features.

First Printing

Title-page dated M DCCC LVIII.

P. 119, last line: *Cry of pain on crags Caucasian. /*

P. 124, line 3: *The revel of the treacherous wine, /*

Second (also Third?) Printing

Title-page dated M DCCC LIX.

P. 119, last line: *Cry of pain on crags Caucasian. /*

P. 124, line 3: *The revel of the ruddy wine, /*

Fourth (also Third?) Printing

Title-page dated M DCCC LIX.

P. ⟨119⟩, last line: *Born of heavenward aspiration,* |

P. 124, line 3: *The revel of the ruddy wine,* |

Fifth Printing

Title-page dated M DCCC LIX.

P. ⟨119⟩, last line: *Born of heavenward aspiration,* |

P. 124, line 3: *The revel of the ruddy wine,* |

On copyright page: TWENTY-SEVENTH THOUSAND. (Such identification not present in the earlier printings.)

The following publication notes are based in part on the publisher's records and notices in trade periodicals.

First Printing

Paper sufficient for 5280 copies sent to the printer during August, 1858. Date of printing not known. Livingston (p. 60) quotes an unlocated letter, Longfellow to Osgood, Aug. 19, 1858, directing alteration of the reading *treacherous* to *ruddy*. On Sept. 7, 1858, the publishers ordered a 12-page catalog for insertion. On Sept. 15, 1858, the London publishers (W. Kent & Co.) wrote Longfellow (letter in H) acknowledging receipt of "the sheets of the Poem." Listed BM Oct. 1, 1858. Noted as *just appeared* BM Oct. 1, 1858. On Oct. 3, 1858, the publishers sent paper for additional copies of a 12-page catalog. An extra-gilt copy in Y inscribed by early owner Oct. 12, 1858. Deposited Oct. 14, 1858. Published Oct. 16, 1858. On Oct. 16, 1858, the publisher ordered the printing of a 16-page catalog.

Second Printing

Paper sufficient for 5000 copies sent to the printer Sept. 25, 1858. Printed Oct. 2, 1858. A copy of the second printing presented to H by the publisher Oct. 19, 1858.

Third Printing

10,000 copies printed Oct. 15-20, 1858. The twentieth thousand (*i.e.,* the third printing) advertised BM Nov. 1, 1858.

Fourth Printing

Paper sufficient for 5000 copies sent to the printer Oct. 20, 1858. Printed Nov. 8, 1858.

Fifth Printing

Printed not before Jan. 1859. On Jan. 6, 1859, the publisher sent to the printer paper sufficient for 2434 copies.

AAS (trade) BA (trade) H (trade) BPL (full gilt) NYHS (trade) NYPL (trade; gilt extra) UV (trade; full gilt) Y (trade; gilt extra; full gilt)

12123. Gifts of Genius: A Miscellany of Prose and Poetry, by American Authors.

New York: Printed for C. A. Davenport. ⟨1859⟩

"My Secret," translated from the French, pp. 42-43. Collected in *Poetical Works* ... , London ⟨n.d., May, 1872⟩; *Works,* Boston, 1886.

For comment see entry No. 3717.

12124. To the Literature of the Language What a Dictionary of Words Is to the Language Itself. Allibone's Dictionary of Authors ...

Childs & Peterson, 602 Arch Street, Philadelphia. ⟨1859⟩

Printed self-wrapper. Cover-title.

Letter, Dec. 28, 1858, p. 3.

NYPL

12125. Irvingiana: A Memorial of Washington Irving ...

New York: Charles B. Richardson. 1860.

"Mr. Longfellow's Address," pp. xxxvi-xxxvii.

Collected in:

Prose Works, London (Chatto & Windus), n.d., 1874, under the title "Washington Irving."

Works, New York ⟨1909⟩, under the title "Washington Irving."

For fuller entry see No. 656.

12126. The Children's Hour ... Music ... by J. Gaspard Maeder ...

New York ... Firth, Pond & Co 547 Broadway ... 1860 ...

Sheet music. Cover-title. Plate number 4983.

On the front cover is a four-line note from Longfellow to the composer, Nahaut ⟨sic⟩, Sept. 8, 1860, granting permission to set the poem to music.

Collected in *Tales of a Wayside Inn,* 1863.

Deposited Nov. 8, 1860.

H UV

12127. THE NEW ENGLAND TRAGEDY.

BOSTON: TICKNOR AND FIELDS. M DCCC LX.

Anonymous.

A set of page-proofs. Paged: ⟨i-iv⟩, ⟨1⟩-130,

blank leaf. The internal blank leaves disregarded in the printed pagination. $7^{13}\!/_{16}''$ x $4\frac{3}{4}''$.

‹-›², 1⁸, 2⁴, 3⁸, 4-5², 6⁸, 7², 8-9⁸, 10⁴, 11⁸, 12⁶.

Said to be printed for private distribution but more probably prepared for the author's use only. Prose; wholly rewritten in verse as "John Endicott" and published in *The New England Tragedies*, 1868. The H copy is accompanied by a fragment of paper wrapper inscribed by Longfellow: *The first New England Tragedy in Prose. Rough sketch privately printed.* The running heads read: *Wenlock Christison.*

H   PDH

12128. Proceedings in Behalf of the Morton Testimonial.

Boston: Printed by Geo. C. Rand & Avery, No. 3 Cornhill 1861.

Printed paper wrapper.

"The Boston Appeal," pp. ‹33›-34; signed by Longfellow and others.

H   NYPL

12129. ‹Printed letter urging defeat of House of Representatives "A Bill to Amend the Act Respecting Copyrights."›

New York . . . April 25, 1862.

4 pp. An open letter, signed by Longfellow and others.

H

12130. Gleanings from the English Poets, Chaucer to Tennyson, with Biographical Notices of the Authors by Robert Inglis . . .

Edinburgh: Gall & Inglis, 6 George Street. London: Houlston & Wright. ‹n.d., 1862›

Noted in leather. Also issued in cloth according to advertisement cited below.

Reprint save for "The Children's Hour," pp. 502-503. Earliest located book appearance. For prior publication as sheet music see above under 1860. Collected in *Tales of a Wayside Inn*, 1863.

Listed PC Dec. 8, 1862. Advertised in same issue as in cloth; and, morocco.

BD

12131. . . . The Cumberland . . . Music by F. Boott . . .

Boston . . . Oliver Ditson & Co. 277 Washington St. . . . 1863 . . .

Sheet music. Cover-title. At head of title: *To Miss Charlotte Cushman* Plate number 21839.

For earliest located book publication see next entry. Collected in *Tales of a Wayside Inn*, 1863.

Two states noted:

1: With price on the front cover given as 2½, i.e., 25¢. A deposit copy thus.

2: With the 2½ erased and the figure 3 inserted.

Deposited June 9, 1863.

B (1st, 2nd)   LC (1st)

12132. Songs of the War . . .

Albany: J. Munsell, 78 State Street. 1863.

"The Cumberland," pp. 56-57. Earliest located book publication. See preceding entry.

For fuller comment see entry No. 259.

12133. The Sixth Reader; Consisting of Extracts in Prose and Verse . . . for the Use of Advanced Classes in Public and Private Schools. By G. S. Hillard . . .

Boston: Brewer and Tileston. Philadelphia: Martin and Randall. 1863.

Cloth, leather shelfback.

Reprint with the exception of "Paul Revere's Ride," pp. 187-191. Earliest located book publication. Collected in *Tales of a Wayside Inn*, 1863.

Reprinted and reissued with the imprint of *Brewer and Tileston* ‹1863›.

Deposited Aug. 29, 1863.

CH

12134. Poetical Pen-Pictures of the War: Selected from Our Union Poets. By J. Henry Hayward . . .

New York: Published by the Editor. 13 Park Row. 1863.

Reprint save for:

"The Two Sharpshooters," credited to W. H. Longfellow ‹*sic*›, p. 204. Otherwise unlocated save for publication in Livingston, 1908, pp. 126-127. By Longfellow?

"Death of His Son," pp. 231-232, credited to W. Henry Longfellow; otherwise "The Cumberland" and here reprinted.

For comment see entry No. 1037.

12135. TALES OF A WAYSIDE INN . . .

LONDON: ROUTLEDGE, WARNE, AND ROUTLEDGE, FARRINGDON STREET. 1864. ‹*i.e.*, 1863›

For first American edition see next entry.

⟨i-ii⟩, ⟨i⟩-⟨vi⟩, ⟨1⟩-244; advertisements, pp. ⟨245-248⟩, paged ⟨1⟩-4. Frontispiece portrait inserted. 6⅝″ x 4³⁄₁₆″.

⟨-⟩², ⟨A⟩², B-I, K-Q⁸, R⁴.

Noted in the following states:

1

P. v, the poem listed as at p. 239: *A Day in June*

P. 239, the poem is titled: *A Day in June*

P. 242, verse 1: *Till at length it is or seems*

P. ⟨245⟩: The first title listed is *Tennyson's Poems*

2 (3?)

P. v, the poem listed as at p. 239: *A Day of Sunshine*

P. 239, the poem is titled: *A Day of Sunshine*

P. 242, verse 1: *Till at length it is or seems*

P. ⟨245⟩: The first title listed is: *Tennyson's Poems*

3 (2?)

P. v, the poem listed as at p. 239: *A Day in June*

P. 239, the poem is titled: *A Day in June*

P. 242, verse 1: *Till at length our burden seems*

P. ⟨245⟩: The first title listed is: *Robinson Crusoe*

4

P. v, the poem listed as at p. 239: *A Day of Sunshine*

P. 239, the poem is titled: *A Day of Sunshine*

P. 242, verse 1: *Till at length the burden seems*

P. ⟨245⟩: The first title listed is *Robinson Crusoe*

Note: It is wholly probable that 2 and 3 above were caused in part at the bindery; and that other binding variants exist.

V cloth: green. P cloth: red. Brown-coated end papers.

Advertised without comment Ath Oct. 24, 1863. Advertised for Nov. 6 in Ath Oct. 31, 1863. Listed Ath Nov. 7, 1863. Reviewed Ath Nov. 14, 1863. Listed PC Nov. 16, 1863. For *Author's Edition* see in *Section II.*

BD (1st, 2nd)   BPL (4th)   H (1st)   UV (3rd)

12136. TALES OF A WAYSIDE INN . . .

BOSTON: TICKNOR AND FIELDS. 1863.

For prior publication see preceding entry.

⟨i⟩-⟨viii⟩, ⟨1⟩-225, blank leaf. Vignette title-page inserted. Laid paper. 7¹⁄₁₆″ x 4⅝″.

⟨-⟩⁴, 1-9¹², 10⁶.

Cloth Binding

BD cloth: purple; terra-cotta. HC cloth: blue-black; green; purple; red; slate. HT cloth: green; purple. L cloth: purple; slate. LI cloth: purple. P cloth: purple. PD cloth: green; purple. TR cloth: blue-black; green; greenish-black; purple; red; salmon; slate. Z cloth: blue-green; green. Covers bevelled. Brown-coated end papers. Laid or wove flyleaves. Top edges gilt. In the preceding the title of the book is stamped on the spine in a rustic face. Copies have been seen in brown T cloth with the title stamped from a roman face; the precise status of such copies has not been established but contemporary inscriptions, and the fact that this style appears on 1864 (and later) printings, may be significant.

Inserted at back of most copies is a publisher's catalog dated *November, 1863.* There were two printings of the catalog, a distinguishing feature being:

A: On p. 11 *Tales of a Wayside Inn* is unpriced and described as *Nearly ready.*

B: On p. 11 *Tales of a Wayside Inn* is priced $1.25.

On the basis of contemporary dated inscriptions it appears safe to assume that copies first shipped had *Catalog A* inserted.

Leather Binding

Copies have been seen in leather and are presumed original publisher's bindings. The designations are for identification only.

A: Brown morocco. Sides blindstamped with a border; at center an upright ornament measuring 2¾″ x 2″. Edges gilded. Copy in FM.

B: Brown morocco. Sides blindstamped with a border; at center an upright ornament measuring 2⅝″ x 1½″. Edges gilded. Copy in H.

C: Brown calf. Sides blindstamped with a border, a small rosette at each corner. Edges marbled. Copy in H.

NOTE ON THE FIRST PRINTING

The title-page of the first printing is dated *1863.* The following readings are present:

P. 125, verse 3: *Whistled, saying . . .*

P. 174, verse 4 up: *His only pastime . . .*

NOTE ON THE SECOND AND LATER PRINTINGS

The following alterations were made for the second printing:

Date on the title-page altered to *1864.*

P. 125, verse 3: *Whistling, said* . . .

P. 174, verse 4 up: *His sole diversion* . . .

On the basis of over fifty copies examined BAL concludes that the alterations did not occur during the run of the first printing (finished by Nov. 24, 1863); that the alterations first appeared in the second printing (finished by Feb. 1, 1864) which was issued under the date 1864. Intermediates have been seen. Examination indicates that such intermediates were caused at the bindery by use of mixed sheets and are not the result of alterations during printing.

Paper for the first printing sent to the printer Nov. 6, 1863. The first printing consisted of 15,000 copies. Advertised for *November* APC Sept. 15, 1863. First copies bound Nov. 17, 1863; by Jan. 29, 1864, 14,828 copies were in binding. A copy in H inscribed by Longfellow Nov. 21, 1863. According to the publisher's records the book was published Nov. 25, 1863. Noted by ALG Dec. 1, 1863. Advertised ALG Dec. 1, 1863. The Ticknor & Fields and the Routledge editions listed ALG Dec. 15, 1863. Deposited Jan. 13, 1864. Listed (Ticknor & Fields) PC Jan. 16, 1864. Second printing, Feb. 1, 1864, 5020 copies; bound Feb. 4, 1864 to Nov. 12, 1873 <sic>.

AAS   BA   BD   H   NYPL   UV   Y

TALES OF A WAYSIDE INN . . .

LONDON . . . 1864 <i.e., 1863>

See above under 1863 (November).

12137. NOËL . . .

CAMBRIDGE 1864

Cover-title. Anonymous. In French.

<1>-8. Laid paper. 7" scant x 4½".

<->⁴.

Printed self-wrapper.

Printed for private distribution on Christmas Day, 1864. Reissued, together with translation into English by John E. Norcross <Philadelphia, 1867>. Collected in *Flower-de-Luce*, 1867.

H (1864)   NYPL (1867)   UV (both)

12138. The High Tide, by Jean Ingelow, with Notices of Her Poems.

Boston: Roberts Brothers, Publishers, 143 Washington Street. 1864.

Issued as an advertisement. Printed paper wrapper. Three-line comment, p. 3.

EM

12139. The Divine Comedy of Dante Alighieri Translated by Henry Wadsworth Longfellow . . .

Boston   Ticknor and Fields 1865 <1866> <1867>

3 Vols. Vol. 1 dated 1865; Vol. 2 dated 1866; Vol. 3 dated 1867. See below under 1867 for the revised published edition.

Privately printed for Longfellow's use. 10 copies? 12 copies?

1: <i-iv>, <1>-216. Laid paper. 10" scant x 7".

2: <i-iv>, <1>-219.

3: <i-iv>, <1>-223.

Three-quarters red morocco, marbled paper boards sides, top edges either plain or gilded.

Contemporary inscriptions indicate that the volumes were in Longfellow's hands not later than: Vol. 1, Feb. 27, 1865; Vol. 2, March 30, 1866; Vol. 3: Feb. 27, 1867.

AAS   H   UV

12140. Household Poems . . .

Boston: Ticknor and Fields. 1865.

Printed paper wrapper; but see below.

Reprint save for "The Bridge of Cloud," "Christmas Bells" and "Palingenesis."

The first printing, May 29, 1865, consisted of 20,100 copies. 15,000 copies bound in paper by June 6, 1865. The remaining sheets were bound during the period Oct. 13, 1865 to Nov. 16, 1870, the records indicating that some were bound in cloth. Some of the copies in cloth show evidence that they were originally in paper wrapper. Copies in cloth contain an inserted portrait frontispiece, a feature not present in wrappered copies. BAL has not been able to determine how many sets of sheets were used in producing *The Companion Poets*, which see in *Section II* under 1866 and 1867.

Advertised as *in press* ALG May 15, 1865. Deposited June 5, 1865. Listed ALG June 15, 1865; PC Aug. 1, 1865; both listings, on the basis of price, for the wrappered format.

Note: A copy in NYPL has a printed notice tipped in at the front, apparently intended for the guidance of reviewers.

AAS   H   NYPL   UV   Y

12141. The Complete Works, Revised Edition 1866

Limited Edition

Paper boards, green C cloth shelfback, printed paper label on spine. Certificate of issue: *One hundred copies printed* ... Copyright notice dated 1866. Sold as a set, 7 volumes.

1

The Complete Works of Henry Wadsworth Longfellow Revised Edition Vol. I. Outre-Mer

Boston Ticknor and Fields 1866

Reprint.

2

The Complete Works of Henry Wadsworth Longfellow Revised Edition Vol. II. Hyperion

Boston Ticknor and Fields 1866

Reprint.

3

The Complete Works of Henry Wadsworth Longfellow Revised Edition Vol. III Kavanagh. Drift-Wood

Boston Ticknor and Fields 1866

Reprint save for "Ancient French Romances from the French of Paulin Paris," pp. ⟨191⟩-240. Embodied in the translation is a poem, "The Death of Archbishop Turpin," which had prior publication in *The Poets and Poetry of Europe,* 1845, above.

4

The Complete Works of Henry Wadsworth Longfellow Revised Edition Vol. IV. Voices of the Night. Ballads and Other Poems. Poems on Slavery. The Spanish Student.

Boston Ticknor and Fields 1866

Reprint.

5

The Complete Works of Henry Wadsworth Longfellow Revised Edition Vol. V. The Belfry of Bruges and Other Poems. Evangeline. The Seaside and the Fireside.

Boston Ticknor and Fields 1866

Reprint.

6

The Complete Works of Henry Wadsworth Longfellow Revised Edition Vol. VI. The Golden Legend. The Courtship of Miles Standish. Birds of Passage.

Boston Ticknor and Fields 1866

Reprint.

7

The Complete Works of Henry Wadsworth Longfellow Revised Edition Vol. VII. The

Song of Hiawatha. Tales of a Wayside Inn. Birds of Passage.

Boston Ticknor and Fields 1866

Reprint.

Trade Edition

Cloth. Also leather? The copies first bound have the spine imprint of *Ticknor & Co.;* later bindings have the spine imprint of *James R. Osgood & Co.* Sold as two sets; *i.e., Prose Works,* 3 Vols.; *Poetical Works,* 4 Vols.; see title-pages below. The *Limited Edition* was printed and bound prior to the printing of *Trade Edition* but precise publication information is wanting. Were the two formats issued simultaneously?

Prose Works, Vol. 1

The Prose Works of Henry Wadsworth Longfellow Revised Edition Vol. I. Outre-Mer.

Boston Ticknor and Fields 1866

Reprint. Copyright notice dated 1865.

Prose Works, Vol. 2

The Prose Works of Henry Wadsworth Longfellow Revised Edition Vol. II. Hyperion.

Boston Ticknor and Fields 1866

Reprint. Copyright notice dated 1865.

Prose Works, Vol. 3

The Prose Works of Henry Wadsworth Longfellow Revised Edition Vol. III. Kavanagh. Drift-Wood.

Boston Ticknor and Fields 1866

"Ancient French Romances from the French of Paulin Paris," pp. ⟨191⟩-240. See note under Vol. 3, *Limited Edition,* above. Copyright notice dated 1865.

Poetical Works, Vol. 1

The Poetical Works of Henry Wadsworth Longfellow Revised Edition Vol. I. Voices of the Night. Ballads and Other Poems. Poems on Slavery. The Spanish Student.

Boston Ticknor and Fields 1866

Reprint. Copyright notice dated 1865.

Poetical Works, Vol. 2

The Poetical Works of Henry Wadsworth Longfellow Revised Edition Vol. II. The Belfry of Bruges and Other Poems. Evangeline. The Seaside and the Fireside.

Boston Ticknor and Fields 1866

Reprint. Copyright notice dated 1866.

Poetical Works, Vol. 3

The Poetical Works of Henry Wadsworth Long-
fellow Revised Edition Vol. III. The Golden
Legend. The Courtship of Miles Standish.
Birds of Passage.

Boston Ticknor and Fields 1866

Reprint. Copyright notice dated 1866.

Poetical Works, Vol. 4

The Poetical Works of Henry Wadsworth Long-
fellow Revised Edition Vol. IV. The Song of
Hiawatha. Tales of a Wayside Inn. Birds of
Passage.

Boston Ticknor and Fields 1866

Reprint. Copyright notice dated 1866.

Limited edition printed April 20, 1866; bound
Sept. 20, 1866. Trade edition printed during the
period Sept. 27–Oct. 16, 1866. *Poetical Works*
(*i.e.,* trade edition, Vols. 4-7) advertised ALG
Nov. 1, 1866. Trade edition listed ALG Nov. 15,
1866.

Entry on the basis of sets (limited) in: B, BPL,
H, LC, NYPL, Y. Trade edition (some sets being
incomplete) in: AAS, BD, H, UV, Y.

12142. The Poetical Works . . . with Prefatory
Notice Eight Engravings on Steel.

Edinburgh: Gall & Inglis, 6 George Street.
London: Houlston & Wright. ⟨n.d., possibly
(but not probably) as early as Oct. 1866; but
before June, 1868⟩

Pp. 698.

Reprint with the possible exception of the following poems, all of which appear also in
Flower-de-Luce, 1867 (Nov. 1866):

"The Bells of Lynn"

"Concord" (Later titled "Hawthorne")

"Giotto's Tower"

"The Kalif of Baldacca" (Otherwise "Kambalu")

"Killed at the Ford"

"On Translating the Divina Commedia," a series of four sonnets:

*How strange the sculptures that adorn these
towers . . .*

I enter, and see thee in the gloom . . .

I lift mine eyes, and all the windows blaze . . .

Oft have I seen at some cathedral door . . .

"To-Morrow"

"The Wind over the Chimney"

FM

12143. FLOWER-DE-LUCE . . .

LONDON: GEORGE ROUTLEDGE AND SONS, THE
BROADWAY, LUDGATE. 1867.

For first American edition see next entry.

⟨1⟩-63. 6¹⁄₁₆″ x 4½″.

⟨A⟩-D⁸.

Printed blue paper wrapper.

Listed Ath Nov. 10, 1866; PC Nov. 15, 1866. Reviewed Ath Nov. 17, 1866. Listed Bkr Dec. 31,
1866.

BD UV Y

12144. FLOWER-DE-LUCE . . .

BOSTON: TICKNOR AND FIELDS. 1867.

For prior publication see preceding entry.

⟨1⟩-72. Frontispiece and 4 plates inserted. 6⅝″ x
4¹⁵⁄₁₆″ (cloth). 6⁹⁄₁₆″ x 4⅞″ full (leather).

⟨1⟩-4⁸, 5⁴.

Note: The publisher's records show three printings during the period 1866–1867, and a fourth
printing in Jan. 1868; see below. It is probable that the first two printings (also the third?)
were dated 1867. Presumably the fourth printing was dated 1868. If reprints were in fact
dated 1867 BAL has been unable to distinguish
the first printing from the later.

C cloth: green; purple; terra-cotta. Covers bevelled. Brown-coated end papers. Edges gilt.
Wove paper flyleaves. A copy has been seen
with a laid paper flyleaf at front, a wove paper
flyleaf at back. *Also:* Brown morocco, marbled
end papers, flyleaves, edges gilt.

Advertised for *November* ALG Sept. 15, 1866.
First printing, Nov. 2, 1866, 5950 copies; bound
Nov. 13, 1866–Dec. 29, 1866. H copy received
from the publisher Nov. 16, 1866. A copy in
UV inscribed by Longfellow Nov. 17, 1866. Reviewed ALG Dec. 1, 1866. Deposited Jan. 25,
1867. *Second printing,* 520 copies, Feb. 1, 1867;
bound Feb. 13, 1867–Nov. 14, 1867. *Third printing,* 520 copies, Dec. 27, 1867; dated 1868?;
bound Jan. 16, 1868–Feb. 26, 1869 (*sic*). *Fourth
Printing,* 500 copies, Jan. 14, 1868; bound Aug.
25–27, 1868.

AAS BA H LC NYHS NYPL UV

12145. . . . The Poetical Works . . . (Including
Recent Poems.) With Steel Portrait . . .

London: Frederick Warne and Co. Bedford
Street, Covent Garden. 1867.

At head of title: The Chandos Poets.

Issued in cloth according to contemporary notices.

Two editions noted:

First Edition

Text ends on p. 627.

The portrait frontispiece is captioned in facsimile: *Henry W. Longfellow;* not, *Yours truly / Henry W. Longfellow.* For a comment on this see below under *The Frontispiece.*

Earliest located book publication of "Three Cantos of Dante's Paradiso," being cantos 23, 24, 25, reprinted from *The Atlantic Monthly,* Jan. 1864. The text varies from both the privately printed and the published editions of *The Divine Comedy of Dante Alighieri,* Vol. 3, Boston, 1867.

From the publisher's "Preface": "This edition contains ... three cantos of his ⟨*i.e.,* Longfellow's⟩ forthcoming translation of the Divina Commedia of Dante."

Listings and advertisements in British trade periodicals (see below) indicate that this Warne edition was issued in Dec. 1866. The records of the American publisher show that no separate printing of *The Divine Comedy,* Vol. 3, could have issued prior to Jan. 31, 1867.

Second Edition

Text ends on p. 628.

Imprint dated 1867. An undated printing was issued prior to Dec. 25, 1870.

The portrait frontispiece is captioned in facsimile: *Yours truly / Henry W. Longfellow* not simply *Henry W. Longfellow.* For a comment on this see Warne's letter quoted below.

This second edition was extended by the addition of a few poems but contains no material here first in book form. Listed PC June 1, 1867.

The Frontispiece

Longfellow wrote a complaining letter (location unknown) to Warne, stating that the facsimile autograph used as caption for the frontispiece was unsatisfactory; this on the basis of Warne's letter to Longfellow (in H), March 29, 1867: "Your favour of March 9th we duly received, and it affords us pleasure to have the opportunity of having the Autograph to your portrait correct in a second Edition of your Poems, which we shall shortly issue ..."

First and Second Editions

Noted as *new* Bkr Oct. 31, 1866. Advertised as *now ready* Ath Nov. 17, 1866. Listed PC Dec. 8, 1866; Bkr Dec. 31, 1866 (as a November publication). The extended edition listed PC June 1, 1867.

Later Printings

A new printing noted by PC July 1, 1868, as "being reprinted from the" plates of the Chandos Poets edition; listed Ath July 4, 1868; PC July 15, 1868; Bkr Aug. 1, 1868. *Another edition* listed PC Dec. 10, 1868. A *new edition* listed Ath May 25, 1872; PC June 17, 1872.

H (1st, 2nd)

12146. THE DIVINE COMEDY OF DANTE

See above under 1865–1867 for a privately printed version. The published edition, presented below, is revised and contains material not present in the privately printed version.

BOSTON EDITION

The Divine Comedy of Dante Alighieri Translated by Henry Wadsworth Longfellow ... Vol. I.

Boston   Ticknor and Fields   1867

Note: According to the publisher's records there were four printings in 1867.

Vol. 1, First Printing

⟨i⟩-⟨xii⟩, ⟨1⟩-413, blank leaf. Laid paper. 9¾" x 6⅞".

⟨a⟩², ⟨b⟩⁴, 1-52⁴.

P. 223, note 116: ... *Di quegli antichi spiriti dolenti.*

Vol. 1, Second (also Third?) Printing

⟨i-ii⟩(excised), ⟨iii-iv⟩, ⟨i⟩-⟨xii⟩, ⟨1⟩-413, blank leaf. Laid paper.

⟨a-b⟩⁴, 1-52⁴. ⟨a⟩₁ excised.

P. 223, note 116: ... *Vedrai gli antichi spiriti dolenti.*

Vol. 1, Extended Edition

Third Printing? Third and Fourth Printings? Fourth Printing only?

Text extended by the insertion of matter in Lowell's "The Posthumous Dante," pp. 356-360. The Lowell material (abbreviated) appears on pp. 356-359 of the earlier printings.

⟨i⟩-⟨xii⟩, ⟨1⟩-414, blank leaf. Laid paper.

⟨a⟩², ⟨b⟩⁴, 1-52⁴.

C cloth: green. Covers bevelled. White laid end papers. Top edges gilt. Bound without flyleaves. For comment on flyleaves in Vols. 2-3 see below.

First printing: April 13, 1867; 1000 copies; bound during the period April 23–May 27, 1867. Advertised for April ALG April 15, 1867. *Second printing:* April 22, 1867; 506 copies;

bound during the period May 23, 1867–Sept. 28, 1867. Deposited April 23, 1867. A first printing in H received from the publisher April 24, 1867. A first printing in H inscribed by Longfellow April 27, 1867. A first printing in NYPL inscribed by Longfellow May 1, 1867. Listed ALG May 1, 1867. *Third printing:* May 16, 1867; 510 copies; bound during the period May 18, 1867–June 22, 1867. *Fourth printing:* Aug. 9, 1867; 500 copies; bound during the period Aug. 22–27, 1867.

AAS (2nd ⟨3rd?⟩)   B (1st)   H (1st)   LC (1st, being a deposit copy)   MHS (extended)   NYPL (1st; 2nd ⟨3rd?⟩; extended)   UV (1st)   Y (1st)

Vol. 2

The Divine Comedy of Dante Alighieri Translated by Henry Wadsworth Longfellow ... Vol. II.

Boston   Ticknor and Fields   1867

Note: According to the publisher's records there were four printings in 1867; BAL has been unable to identify these. The variations noted below may have been produced in binding and that possibility should be considered before attempting to relate them to the four printings.

The only textual alteration found identifies the earliest printings (printing?):

First (and Second?) Printing

P. 350, note 32 reads: *It will be noted that Dante |*

Third and Fourth Printings (also Second?)

P. 350, note 32 reads: *It will be observed that Dante |*

On June 10, 1867, Longfellow wrote * Routledge regarding the alteration. Since, by that date, the first two printings had been done, and the third printing was not done until June 20, 1867, it is reasonable to theorize that the alteration may have been done for the third and later printings. In the letter cited Longfellow states that p. 350 had been reprinted; which suggests that the alteration was probably done in copies already printed by cancelling pp. 350-351 and conjugate pp. 347-348.

Vol. 2, Variant A

⟨i-ii⟩, ⟨i⟩-⟨x⟩, ⟨1⟩-410, blank leaf. Laid paper.

⟨a⟩², ⟨b⟩⁴, 1-51⁴, 52².

---

* Letter in the possession of Adeline Roberts, 1940, an autograph dealer in New York City; a copy of the letter in CH; location of original not known.

Noted only with the original reading, p. 350. Bound with a laid paper flyleaf at front and at back.

Vol. 2, Variant B

⟨i-ii⟩, ⟨i⟩-⟨x⟩, ⟨1⟩-410, 2 blank leaves; leaf pasted under the end paper. 9¾" x 7" scant. Laid paper.

⟨a⟩², ⟨b⟩⁴, 1-52⁴. Leaf 52₄ pasted under the end paper. Note presence of blank leaves 52₂₋₃.

Noted only with the original reading, p. 350. Bound with a laid paper flyleaf at front.

Vol. 2, Variant C

⟨i-ii⟩ (pasted under the end paper), ⟨iii-vi⟩, ⟨i⟩-⟨x⟩, ⟨1⟩-410, 2 blank leaves; leaf pasted under the end paper. Laid paper.

⟨a-b⟩⁴, 1-52⁴. Leaves ⟨a⟩₁ and 52₄ pasted under the end paper. Note presence of blank leaves 52₂₋₃.

Noted with both readings, p. 350. Bound without flyleaves.

Advertised for *May* ALG April 15, 1867. *First printing:* May 17, 1867 ⟨sic⟩; 1012 (962?) copies; bound during the period May 16, 1867 ⟨sic⟩ to June 3, 1867. Deposited (variant A) May 21, 1867. A copy in H (variant A) received from the publisher May 22, 1867. *Second printing:* May 28, 1867; 506 copies; bound during the period June 3, 1867 to Sept. 21, 1867. Listed ALG June 1, 1867. *Third printing:* June 20, 1867; 562 copies; bound during the period July 3-23, 1867. *Fourth printing:* Aug. 30, 1867; 512 copies; bound during the period Sept. 30, 1867 to March 11, 1869.

AAS (B)   B (C)   H (A, B, C)   NYPL (A, B, C)   Y (C)

Vol. 3

The Divine Comedy of Dante Alighieri Translated by Henry Wadsworth Longfellow ... Vol. III.

Boston   Ticknor and Fields   1867

⟨i-ii⟩ (pasted under the end paper), ⟨iii-vi⟩, ⟨i⟩-⟨x⟩, ⟨1⟩-452. Laid paper. 9¾" x 7" scant.

⟨a-b⟩⁴, 1-28, ⟨29⟩-56⁴, 57². Leaf ⟨a⟩₁ pasted under the end paper.

Note: According to the publisher's records there were four printings in 1867. BAL has been unable to identify these.

The copyright notice occurs in two forms; sequence, if any, not known; the designations are all but arbitrary. Reference is to the second line of the notice (HENRY WADSWORTH LONGFELLOW,):

A: The H in HENRY is set beneath the first *c* in *according*

B: The H in HENRY is set beneath the *a* in *according*

Note: Laid paper flyleaf at back.

Advertised for *June* ALG April 15, 1867. *First printing:* June 12, 1867; 1004 copies; bound during the period June 14–25, 1867. Deposited June 25, 1867. A copy in H received from the publisher June 25, 1867. *Second printing:* June 26, 1867; 564 copies; bound during the period July 16–23, 1867. A copy in BA received July 2, 1867. *Third printing:* July 3, 1867; 514 copies bound during the period July 10, 1867–Oct. 1, 1867. Listed ALG July 15, 1867. *Fourth printing* (dated 1868?): Sept. 27, 1867; 500 copies; bound during the period Feb. 15, 1868–March 11, 1869.

AAS   B   H   NYPL   UV   Y

LONDON ISSUES

A portion of the translation had publication in entry No. 12145 above.

Sheets of the American printing of the three-volume set were issued in London with the following imprint: *London   George Routledge and Sons   The Broadway, Ludgate   1867* Vol. 1 is of the unexpanded (pp. 413) text. Vol. 2 is of the altered text, p. 350. Issued after May 6, 1867, on which date the American publisher recorded printing of the London title-pages. More precise publication date wanting. Copies in H, UV.

British-Printed Edition

There appears to be some overlapping of publication dates; *i.e.,* Vol. 1 may have appeared in London a few days prior to publication in Boston; but the record is not certain.

The Divine Comedy of Dante Alighieri. Translated by Henry Wadsworth Longfellow . . . Inferno. ⟨Purgatorio.⟩ ⟨Paradiso.⟩

London: George Routledge & Sons, The Broadway, Ludgate. New York: 416, Broome Street. 1867.

1

⟨i⟩-⟨viii⟩, ⟨1⟩-246; publisher's note, p. ⟨247⟩; advertisement, p. ⟨248⟩. 7½″ scant x 4¹⁵⁄₁₆″.

Two states noted:

First State

P. 118, note 116: . . . *Di quegli antichi* . . .

Second State

P. 118, note 116: . . . *Vedrai gli antichi* . . .

Note: In some copies signature mark *R**, p. 245, is not present; significance undetermined.

2

⟨i⟩-⟨x⟩, ⟨249⟩-489; blank, p. ⟨490⟩; plus: 4 pp. advertisements.

3

⟨i⟩-viii, ⟨491⟩-760; advertisements, pp. ⟨761-762⟩; plus: 8 pp. advertisements.

A cursory examination indicates that Vol. 1 is of a text earlier than that of the Boston, 1867, edition. The texts of Vols. 2-3 appear to be the same in both the Boston and the London editions. The variations in Vol. 1 are minor.

Vol. 1: Listed Ath April 20, 1867. Advertised as *now ready* Ath April 27, 1867. Listed PC May 1, 1867. Advertised as *now ready* Ath May 11, 1867. Reviewed Ath May 18, 1867.

Vol. 2: Listed Ath May 25, 1867. Listed PC June 1, 1867. Advertised as *ready* Ath June 8, 1867. Reviewed Ath June 29, 1867.

Vol. 3: Advertised for *the 29th* Ath June 8, 1867; again Ath June 15, 1867. Listed Ath June 29, 1867; PC July 15, 1867. Reviewed Ath Aug. 10, 1867.

CH (1st, 2nd)

Later British Editions

Routledge: A 1-volume edition listed by PC Aug. 15, 1867.

Routledge: In the *Excelsior Series*. First appeared in this series *ca.* 1875; reissued in same series 1877, 1886.

Routledge: Advertised as a "new volume in Routledge's Standard Library" Ath Feb. 3, 1877.

Routledge: Listed PC May 1, 1880. Presumably a 3-volume set.

12147. ⟨Open letter:⟩ Boston, Dec. 4, 1867. J. K. Paine, Esq. Dear Sir, We have heard with much pleasure of the approbation with which your Mass was received by the severely critical audience of the Berlin Sing-Academie . . .

Boston, Jan. 1, 1868 . . .

Single leaf. Printed on recto only. 8″ scant x 5¹⁄₁₆″. Signed by Longfellow and others.

Issued as an advertisement for Paine's announced concert to be held at Boston Music Hall, April 12, 1868.

H

12148. THE NEW ENGLAND TRAGEDIES. I. WENLOCK CHRISTISON. II. GILES COREY OF THE SALEM FARMS.

‹CAMBRIDGE, MASS.› PRIVATELY PRINTED. 1868.

Anonymous.

In verse. For a prose version see *The New England Tragedy,* above, 1860. For published edition see entry 12150.

‹1›-‹180›. Laid paper. 7¾" x 5¹⁄₁₆".

‹1›-22⁴, 23².

Marbled paper boards sides, green morocco shelfback and corners. Marbled end papers. Flyleaves. Top edges gilt.

Certificate of issue: Only Ten copies printed. / No. / UNIVERSITY PRESS: WELCH, BIGELOW, & CO., / CAMBRIDGE.

Letters in the Longfellow archive in H suggest, but do not precisely state, that this printing was prepared for the use of Routledge (London) and Tauchnitz (Leipzig).

Ready for distribution May 5, 1868, or before. A copy in NYPL presented by Longfellow to James T. Fields, May 5, 1868; a copy in H presented by Longfellow to Charles Sumner, May 6, 1868.

H NYPL UV

12149. The Poetical Works of Henry Wadsworth Longfellow Illustrated by John Gilbert Complete Edition

Boston Ticknor and Fields 1868

Paged: xxi, 414, *415-*421, ‹413›-436. At foot of p. 436: *Printed by R. Clark, Edinburgh.*

See below for comment on binding.

Reprint save for "The Indian Hunter" and "The Sea Diver," both here in their earliest collected American appearance. Both had prior publication in *Miscellaneous Poems Selected from the United States Literary Gazette,* 1826, above; and, *Poems,* London (Tegg), n.d., 1848, above.

Advertised PW Sept. 1, 1868, as "to be published before November 15." Listed PW Oct. 1, 1868, as in cloth; half calf; morocco.

Y

12150. THE NEW ENGLAND TRAGEDIES

Issued Oct. 10, 1868, simultaneously in Boston (Ticknor & Fields), London (Routledge) and Leipzig (Tauchnitz). See above under 1868 (May) for prior printing for private distribution.

Letter, Longfellow to Fields, Aug. 23, 1868: "... Please publish the *New England Tragedies* on Saturday, October 10. That is the day I have agreed upon with Routledge, with whom I have made a very good arrangement. Tauchnitz will publish on the same day ..."—*Final Memorials ...* , 1887, pp. 111-112.

BOSTON EDITION

THE NEW-ENGLAND TRAGEDIES ... I. JOHN ENDICOTT. II. GILES COREY OF THE SALEM FARMS.

BOSTON: TICKNOR AND FIELDS. 1868.

‹1›-179. Laid paper. 6⅞" x 4½". See below under leather bindings regarding leaf size.

‹1›-7¹², 8⁶. *Also signed:* ‹A›-K⁸, L².

C cloth: green; purple; terra-cotta. Brown-coated end papers. Laid paper flyleaves. The copies first bound have at the foot of the spine the TF device which occurs in two forms as follows; the order is presumed correct:

A: The pendants in the device are more or less solid lozenges.

B: The pendants in the device are hollow outline.

Quite late bindings (not before Oct. 29, 1868) display the spine imprint: *Fields, Osgood & Co.* It is probable that this later form of the stamping was first used on copies of the fourth printing.

Leather Bindings

Also issued in brown morocco. Sequence, if any, not known; the following designations are for identification only:

A: Brown morocco. Sides blindstamped, a principal feature of the stamping being a four-ringed ornament measuring 3⅝" tall x 2⅝" wide. Leaf: 6⅞" x 4⁷⁄₁₆". Edges gilded. Marbled end papers. Flyleaves.

B: Brown morocco. Sides blindstamped, a principal feature of the stamping being a filigree measuring 2⅛" tall x 1⅜" wide. Leaf: 6¾" scant x 4⁷⁄₁₆". Edges gilded. Brown-coated end papers. Flyleaves.

C: Brown morocco. Sides blindstamped, a principal feature of the stamping being a strapwork ornament measuring 2⅜" tall x 2¼" wide. Leaf: 6¹³⁄₁₆" x 4½" scant. Edges gilded. Marbled end papers. Laid paper flyleaves.

FOUR PRINTINGS

First printing, Sept. 30, 1868, 10,000 copies; bound by Welch & Co., Oct. 1-15, 1868. A copy in H received from the publisher Oct. 8, 1868. Deposited Oct. 12, 1868. Listed ALG Oct.

15, 1868. *Second printing*, Oct. 19, 1868, 2022 copies; bound by Welch & Co., Oct. 21–24, 1868. *Third printing*, Oct. 23, 1868, 2016 copies; bound by Sanborn & Co., Oct. 27–31, 1868. *Fourth printing*, Nov. 3, 1868, 1540 copies; bound by Sanborn & Co., Nov. 14, 1868–Aug. 18, 1869. Listed PC Dec. 10, 1868. Advertised by Trübner as an importation Bkr Dec. 12, 1868. So far as known the first four printings were issued under date 1868.

BAL has been unable to discover any alterations that might distinguish the first from the succeeding three printings. However, the following features may assist in such determination:

Some battering of the plates occurred during the course of the four printings and the following defects are significant:

P. 12, line 19: In the earliest printing (printings?) the name *Isaiah* is printed from unbattered metal.

P. 71, line 4 from bottom: In the earliest printing (printings?) the name *Upsall* is printed from unbattered metal.

The present entry made on the basis of copies in: AAS, BA, CH, DeV, H, NYHS, NYPL, UV, Y.

LONDON EDITION

THE NEW ENGLAND TRAGEDIES …

> LONDON: GEORGE ROUTLEDGE AND SONS, THE BROADWAY, LUDGATE. 1868.

⟨i⟩-⟨viii⟩, ⟨1⟩-⟨222⟩; printer's imprint, p. ⟨223⟩; blank, p. ⟨224⟩; plus: Publisher's catalog, pp. ⟨1⟩-8. 6¹¹⁄₁₆″ x 4³⁄₁₆″.

⟨A⟩⁴, B-I, K-P⁸; plus: ⟨Q⟩⁴.

Two printings noted; the sequence has not been firmly established and the designations are for identification only.

A

The title-page reads: THE NEW ENGLAND / TRAGEDIES. / ⟨etc., etc.⟩

P. 179 paged 17.

B

The title-page reads: THE / NEW ENGLAND TRAGEDIES. / ⟨etc., etc.⟩

P. 179 so paged.

Letter, Longfellow to *My Dear Sir* ⟨i.e., George Routledge⟩, Oct. 23, 1868; original in P: "… On page 130 of the *Tragedies* there is an error, which please correct. Four lines ⟨i.e., of text⟩ from bottom of the page, for *The house of Jacob*, read *The house of Job* … In the Dram. Part, p. vii the *r* is broken in *Governor.*"

The error is present in both Routledge printings. Both the Boston and Leipzig editions read: *The house of Job.* The error does not occur in the private printing. As for the broken letter referred to by Longfellow, actually it is the *n* that is broken, not one of the *r*'s. All examined copies of *Printing A* have the broken letter; all examined copies of *Printing B* have the letter undamaged.

C cloth: blue; green. Brown-coated end papers.

Note: The text varies from both American editions.

PC and Bkr Oct. 1, 1868: "… Will be published in Boston this month … and ⟨in London⟩ on the 10th instant by Routledge." Advertised for Oct. 10 in Ath Oct. 3, 1868; for *this day* Ath Oct. 10, 1868. Listed Ath Oct. 10; PC Oct. 15, 1868. Reviewed Ath Oct. 17, 1868. A *second edition* advertised Ath Oct. 24, 1868. Listed ALG Nov. 2, 1868; Bkr Nov. 2, 1868. Reviewed Bkr Nov. 2, 1868.

BA (B)   BD (A)   H (A,B)   UV (A,B)   Y (A)

LEIPZIG EDITION

THE NEW-ENGLAND TRAGEDIES … AUTHORIZED EDITION. ENDICOTT. GILES COREY OF THE SALEM FARMS.

> LEIPZIG BERNHARD TAUCHNITZ 1868.

⟨i-iv⟩, ⟨1⟩-⟨259⟩; printer's imprint, p. ⟨260⟩. 5¹⁵⁄₁₆″ x 4³⁄₁₆″ (cloth). 6⁷⁄₁₆″ x 4⁹⁄₁₆″ (wrapper).

⟨-⟩², 1-16⁸, 17².

V cloth: purple. Edges gilt. Green-coated end papers. *Also:* Printed paper wrapper; and unlike the usual wrapper of this publisher, the wrapper is undated.

Issued as Vol. 982 of *Collection of British Authors* series.

Letter, Tauchnitz to Longfellow (in H), Leipzig, Sept. 15, 1868: "I have received your esteemed lines of Sept 6 as well as the two *Tragedies* ⟨the private printing⟩ and beg to thank you for both. I shall have much pleasure in publishing the *Tragedies* Oct. 10 …"

BD (wrapper)   H (cloth)

12151. Prang's Chromos. Fac-simile Reproductions of Water-Color Paintings. Testimonials from Eminent Artists and Distinguished Persons …

> L. Prang & Co., Fine Art Publishers, Boston. ⟨1869?⟩

Single leaf. Printed on recto only. A series of testimonials, some dated, the latest date being June 1, 1869.

Contains an undated three-line testimonial.

HM

12152. Hyperion ... Revised Edition ...

Boston Fields, Osgood, & Co. Successors to Ticknor and Fields 1869

Revised. See note under *Second Edition,* Cambridge, 1845, above.

According to the publisher's records 518 copies were printed June 23, 1869; bound June 30, 1869 to Oct. 22, 1870.

UV

12153. The Piccadilly Annual of Entertaining Literature ...

London: John Camden Hotten, 74 & 75, Piccadilly. ⟨1870⟩

"The Alarm-Bell of Atri," pp. 15-16. Collected in *Three Books of Song,* 1872. See *The Alarm-Bell of Atri,* below, under year 1871.

For fuller comment see entry No. 3323.

The Reveille ...

Salem ... Dec. 21, 1870 ...

See under *"There Was a Little Girl"* ... , 1883.

Wrong Side Up. A Poem ...

⟨n.p., n.d., *ca.* 1870⟩

See under *"There Was a Little Girl"* ... , 1883.

12154. The Works of Charles Sumner ...

Boston: Lee and Shepard. 1870. ⟨–1883.⟩

Cloth; and, three-quarters leather. Inserted in Vol. 1 of the latter is a page imprinted: *Subscriber's Copy* and signed by Charles Sumner.

15 volumes as follows:

Vols. 1-2 dated 1870

Vols. 3-4 dated 1871

Vols. 5-6 dated 1872

Vols. 7-8 dated 1873

Vols. 9-10 dated 1874

Vol. 11 dated 1875

Vol. 12 dated 1877

Vol. 13 dated 1880

Vols. 14-15 dated 1883

"George Nichols and John Owen did the editing and read the proofs but always with more or less assistance from Longfellow."—Livingston, p. 104.

"I have taken upon myself the whole responsibility of the three remaining volumes of Sumner. I am not sure that this is very wise; but it seemed the only way of getting the work completed. It was inconvenient to consult with the two busy lawyers in town, and I hope that we shall now go on more speedily."—Letter, Longfellow to G. W. Greene, Jan. 25, 1879; original letter in H.

"A year ago Owen was engaged to make an Index to Sumner. At the last accounts he had completed six pages of the first volume. At this rate he will not finish his work before the middle of the next century. I am making the Index myself, and have already reached the tenth volume."—Letter, Longfellow to G. W. Greene, Sept. 26, 1881; original letter in H. Longfellow died before completing the index.

H

12155. The Poets and Poetry of Europe. With Introductions and Biographical Notices. By Henry Wadsworth Longfellow. A New Edition, Revised and Enlarged ...

Philadelphia: Porter and Coates, 822 Chestnut Street. 1871.

For first edition see under 1845.

The following translations are here first in book form:

"The Angel and the Child"

"Consolation"

"The Gleaner of Sapri"

"Remorse"

"Santa Teresa's Book-Mark"

"To Cardinal Richelieu"

"To Italy"

"Wanderer's Night-Songs"

Note: Livingston errs in stating that the "Epigrams" herein are here first in book form; each had prior publication in *The Belfry of Bruges,* 1846, under the heading "Poetic Aphorisms."

For comment see entry No. 9554.

Balloon Post ...

Boston ... 1871 ...

See under *"There Was a Little Girl"* ... , 1883.

12156. ... THE ALARM-BELL OF ATRI ...

⟨BOSTON, Dec. 5–16, 1871⟩

Caption-title. At head of title: *Fair for Our Dumb Animals, Boston, December, 1871* ...

Single cut sheet folded to four pages.

⟨1⟩-3; picture of horse, p. ⟨4⟩. 10⅛″ x 6″.

At end of text: [*Printed by permission, from the Atlantic Monthly of July, 1870.*]

For prior book publication see *The Piccadilly Annual* . . . , London ⟨1870⟩. Collected in *Three Books of Song*, 1872. The poem sometimes appears (in reprints) under the altered title "The Bell of Atri."

Reprinted in similar format with the following statement at the head of p. ⟨1⟩: (*Reprinted for the Fair of February, 1875.*) ; the picture of the horse does not appear on p. ⟨4⟩.

In the first printings of the poem the first line of the second stanza reads: *How happily the days* . . . About 1872 Longfellow revised the reading to: *How swift the happy days* . . . This alteration is sufficient to indicate the status of those several reprintings issued by The Massachusetts Society for the Prevention of Cruelty to Animals, The American Humane Education Society, and others.

B H UV

12157. THE DIVINE TRAGEDY . . .

BOSTON JAMES R. OSGOOD AND COMPANY 1871

Issued in both small and large paper formats, popularly designated *16mo* and *8vo*. For the purposes of this entry the terms *small paper* and *large paper* are used. It is commonly asserted that the small paper format was published prior to the large paper, but BAL has found no firm evidence on which to base the assertion. The publication notes (see below) support the thought that the two formats were simultaneously issued, even though there is documentary evidence which shows that the copies first received by Longfellow were of the small paper format.

SMALL PAPER FORMAT

In the publisher's records referred to as *The Farringford Edition* and the *16mo* edition.

⟨i⟩-iv, ⟨1⟩-150, blank leaf. Laid paper. 6⅞″ x 4½″ full.

⟨1², 2-7¹², 8⁴⟩. *Signed:* ⟨-⟩², 1-9⁸, 10⁴.

C cloth (both fine and coarse grained): green; purple; terra-cotta (both light and dark noted). Star-sprinkled C: purple (both light and dark noted). Covers bevelled. Brown-coated end papers. Flyleaves of either laid, or of wove, paper. Also morocco.

Note: There were two printings of the small paper format in 1871 (see notes below). Was the second printing dated 1872? If both printings

were dated 1871 BAL has been unable to distinguish the first from the second.

LARGE PAPER EDITION

In the publisher's records referred to as both *The Fine Edition* and the *8vo* edition.

⟨i-ii⟩, ⟨i⟩-⟨vi⟩, ⟨1⟩-313, blank leaf. Laid paper. 8¹/₁₆″ full x 5½″.

⟨1-40⁴, 41²⟩. *Signed:* ⟨-⟩⁴, ⟨1⟩-5⁸, 6¹², 7⁴, 8-16, ⟨17⟩-19⁸, 20⁶.

C cloth: green; purple; terra-cotta. Covers bevelled. Edges gilt. Brown-coated end papers. Wove paper flyleaves; also: Wove paper flyleaf at front, laid paper flyleaf at back. Also issued in morocco.

Publication Notes

Longfellow's journal, Nov. 17, 1871: "Two editions . . . will be published at the same time . . ."

Small Paper: Entry for the first printing, 8000 copies, dated Dec. 8, 1871. Bound Dec. 7 ⟨*sic*⟩, 1871–Jan. 16, 1872. A copy in BA received Dec. 8, 1871.

Large Paper: Bound Dec. 8, 1871–Jan. 4, 1872; but note that the publisher's records (delayed entry?) show that the large paper format, 2000 copies, was printed Dec. 22, 1871.

Longfellow's journal, Dec. 12, 1871: ". . . Published to-day."

Small Paper: Deposited Dec. 13, 1871. No record of deposit of *Large Paper*.

Small Paper: Letter, Longfellow to G. W. Greene, Dec. 14, 1871 (original not seen; taken from Livingston, p. 80): "I send you to-day . . . a copy of *The Divine Tragedy*. I am sorry it is of the small size; but the larger ones have not been sent to me. You shall have one of them when you come."

Small Paper: Letter, Longfellow to G. W. Greene, Dec. 17, 1871 (original in H): ". . . Ten thousand copies ⟨*i.e.*, 8000 *Small Paper*, 2000 *Large Paper*⟩ were published on Tuesday last ⟨Dec. 12⟩, and the printers are already at work on three thousand more . . ."

Small Paper: Second printing, 3500 copies, Dec. 22, 1871. Bound Dec. 27, 1871–Jan. 3, 1872. *Issued under date 1872?*

Both formats: Copies of both formats have been seen with inscriptions dated Dec. 25, 1871.

Both formats: Listed ALG Jan. 1, 1872.

Small Paper: Third printing, 1012 copies, Feb. 29, 1872. Presumably issued under date 1872.

AAS (both) BA (small) H (both) NYHS (small) NYPL (both) Y (small)

12158. The Pellet . . .

Boston: Published by the Fair. 1872 . . .

An occasional newspaper.

"Anæsthesia," No. 1, p. 7. Uncollected.

"Vox Populi," No. 5, p. 12. Collected in *Aftermath*, 1873.

For comment see entry No. 169.

12159. THREE BOOKS OF SONG . . .

BOSTON: JAMES R. OSGOOD AND COMPANY. 1872.

⟨i⟩-iv, ⟨1⟩-⟨204⟩. Laid paper. 6⅞″ x 4⁹⁄₁₆″.

⟨1², 2-9¹², 10⁶⟩. *Signed:* ⟨-⟩², ⟨1⟩-12⁸, 13⁶. Superfluous signature mark 12 on p. 165.

C cloth: green; purple; terra-cotta. Bevelled covers. Top edges gilt. Brown-coated end papers. White laid, or wove, flyleaves. Also: In some copies a wove paper flyleaf at front (or at back) and a laid paper flyleaf at back (or at front).

Note: A copy in H has blank leaves between pp. 196-197 and pp. ⟨200⟩-201. This was produced by the failure of the binder to remove the blanks before binding; not due to printer's error.

Note: Two printings are recorded in the publisher's records under date of May 20, 1872; one of 5000 copies, the other of 3000 copies. BAL has been unable to distinguish the first from the second.

Noted for *immediate publication* WTC May 9, 1872. Announced for the *25th* WTC May 23, 1872. Listed WTC May 23, 1872. A copy in UV inscribed by Longfellow May 25, 1872. The London (Routledge) edition advertised in Ath June 8, 1872; listed Ath June 8, 1872. The Routledge edition was issued in two formats: Cloth, 3/6; and, paper, 1/-.

AAS   BA   H   NYHS   NYPL   UV   Y

12160. Christus . . .

Boston . . . 1872

3 Vols.

According to the publisher's records 512 copies of each volume were printed Sept. 24, 1872. The set was advertised as *just ready* WTC Sept. 26, 1872. A set in H received Sept. 30, 1872; listed WTC Oct. 3, 1872.

Note: Livingston and Wilson err in stating that the set contains four added pieces. Longfellow added but three as here indicated. "Introitus," which appears in Vol. 1, had prior publication in *The Divine Tragedy*, 1871.

VOL. 1

Christus a Mystery . . . Part I.—The Divine Tragedy

Boston   James R. Osgood and Company   1872

Reprint save for "The Abbot Joachim," pp. ⟨153⟩-159.

For prior publication of *The Divine Tragedy* see above under 1871.

BA   BD   H   NYPL   Y

VOL. 2

Christus a Mystery . . . Part II.—The Golden Legend.

Boston   James R. Osgood and Company   1872

Reprint. For prior publication see *The Golden Legend*, 1851.

Note: The error, p. 171, line 20: . . . *set sail* . . . for . . . *sail set* . . . is present in all examined copies of the 1872 printing. The correction, . . . *sail set* . . . , appears to have been made for the 1873 printings.

BA   BD   H   NYPL   Y

VOL. 3

Christus a Mystery . . . Part III.—The New England Tragedies.

Boston   James R. Osgood and Company   1872

Reprint save for "Martin Luther," pp. ⟨ix⟩-xvi; and, "Finale. St. John," pp. ⟨183⟩-186.

For prior publication of *The New England Tragedies* see above under 1868.

BA   H   NYPL   Y

Cadenabbia . . .

Summer, 1872 . . .

See in *Section II*.

12161. Catalogue of the School of Modern Languages. Seventh Year, 1872–73.

⟨Cambridge, Mass.⟩   The Riverside Press. 1872.

Printed paper wrapper.

Testimonial, *Cambridge, May 15, 1872*, p. 24. The testimonial is repeated in the catalogs for 1873 and 1874.

BPL

12162. . . . The Poetical Works . . . (Including Recent Poems.)

London: Frederick Warne and Co., Bedford Street, Covent Garden. ⟨n.d., not before May, 1872⟩

Pp. 656. At head of title: The Chandos Classics.

Publisher's "Preface to the Fifth Edition" signed at end *May, 1872.*

Note: Also occurs with a cancel title-page reading: ... *The Poetical Works ... Reprinted from the Best Editions.* Imprint: *London: Frederick Warne and Co. Bedford Street, Covent Garden. New York: Scribner, Welford and Co.* At head of title: *The Lansdowne Poets.* Issued simultaneously?

Reprint with the possible exception of:

a "The Ballad of Carmilhan"

a "The Baron of St. Castine"

a "The Boy and the Brook"

a "The Fugitive"

a "Lady Wentworth"

b "My Secret"

KEY

a—Also in (reprinted from?) *Three Books of Song*, Boston, 1872.
b—Previously in *Gifts of Genius ...* , New York ⟨1859⟩. For collected American publication see *Works*, Boston, 1886.

LC (Lansdowne)   UV (Chandos)

12163. The Tonic ...

⟨Portland, Maine, 1873⟩

An occasional newspaper.

"Changed," issue of June 16, 1873. According to a note in the issue of June 14, 1873, the poem was written for this publication. However, an editorial note in *The Cambridge Edition of the Complete Poetical Works*, p. 296, states that the poem was written in 1858. Collected in *Aftermath*, 1873.

For comment see entry No. 8885.

12164. AFTERMATH

Apparently published simultaneously in Boston and London.

BOSTON EDITION

AFTERMATH ...

BOSTON: JAMES R. OSGOOD AND COMPANY, LATE TICKNOR & FIELDS, AND FIELDS, OSGOOD, & CO. 1873.

⟨i-ii⟩, ⟨i⟩-⟨vi⟩, ⟨1⟩-⟨144⟩. Frontispiece inserted. 6¹⁵⁄₁₆" scant x 4½".

⟨-⟩⁴, 1-6¹². *Also signed:* ⟨-⟩⁴, ⟨A⟩-I⁸.

Note: All examined copies dated 1873 have the following readings:

P. ⟨iii⟩, line 2 up: SCARDERBEG *for* SCANDERBEG

P. 54, verse 7: *Little cared ...*

All examined copies dated 1874 have the following readings:

P. ⟨iii⟩, line 2 up: SCANDERBEG

P. 54, verse 7: *Or for his ...*

There is a possibility that 1874 copies appear with the earlier readings but no such example has been traced. What appears to be an intermediate dated 1873 (made up of mixed sheets?) was offered as item No. 530 in *First Editions of Ten American Authors Collected by J. Chester Chamberlain, Part I*, New York: The Anderson Auction Company, 1909. In this catalog the copy offered is described as "second issue, with *Or* at page 54."

C cloth: green; purple. FL-like cloth: green; purple; terra-cotta. Covers bevelled. Brown-coated end papers. Flyleaves; or, flyleaf at back only.

First printing, Aug. 1873, 5000 copies. Letter, Longfellow to G. W. Greene, Aug. 17, 1873 (Livingston, p. 84) gives Sept. 6, 1873, as day of publication; the date is confirmed in Routledge's letter to Longfellow, July 9, 1873; letter from Routledge's agent to Longfellow, Sept. 2, 1873; for these letters see publication notes below under the London edition. BA copy received Sept. 8, 1873. Listed PW Sept. 13, 1873. Deposited Sept. 16, 1873. *Second printing*, dated 1874, 950 copies, Dec. 1873.

AAS   B   BA   H   NYHS   NYPL   UV   Y

LONDON EDITION

AFTERMATH ...

LONDON: GEORGE ROUTLEDGE AND SONS, THE BROADWAY, LUDGATE. 1873. [THIS WORK IS COPYRIGHT.]

⟨i⟩-⟨viii⟩, ⟨9⟩-⟨154⟩; advertisements, pp. ⟨1⟩-⟨6⟩. 6¼" x 4".

⟨B⟩-I, K-L⁸.

Two states (printings?) noted:

1

P. 64, verse 7: *Little cared for his Babes ...*

Noted only in green V cloth.

2

P. 64, verse 7: *Or for his Babes ...*

Noted in green S and green V cloths.

Common to both: P. ⟨6⟩ of the terminal advertisements, line 4: *te* for *to*.

S cloth: green. V cloth: green. *But see above.* Covers bevelled. Brown-coated end papers. Gray-brown-coated end papers.

Letter (in H), publisher to Longfellow, July 9, 1873: "... I found on my arrival at the Store to day a letter from Mr Osgood stating that your new book was to be published on Sept 6th. I wish it had been Oct 6th as it would have suited the sale in England much better ..." Announced Ath Aug. 9, 16, 30, 1873. Listed (prematurely; advance sheets?) Ath Aug. 30, 1873. Letter (in H), Joseph L. Blamire, Routledge's American agent, to Longfellow, Sept. 2, 1873: "Messrs Routledge have sent to me for signature by you the accompanying Memorandum of Agreement with reference to your book *Aftermath* which they are to publish in London on the 6th inst. ..." Noted as *ready* Ath Sept. 6, 1873. Reviewed Ath Sept. 6, 1873. Listed PC Sept. 16, 1873.

B (2nd)   BD (1st)   BPL (1st)   H (2nd)   UV (1st) Y (2nd)

12165. The Prose Works ... Edited, with an Introduction, by the Author of "Tennysoniana," ⟨*i.e.,* Richard Herne Shepherd⟩ ...

London: Chatto and Windus, Publishers. (Successors to John Camden Hotten.) ⟨n.d., 1874⟩

Reprint save for "Washington Irving," here first collected. See *Irvingiana* ... , New York, 1860.

Noted as *nearly ready* Ath Dec. 20, 1873; Jan. 3, 1874. Advertised as though ready Ath Feb. 21, 1874. Listed Ath Feb. 21, 1874; PC March 1, 1874.

Note: A copy in AAS has an inserted catalog dated *May, 1877.* Reprint? Later binding?

BA   P

12166. THE HANGING OF THE CRANE, 1874–1875

U. S. COPYRIGHT PRINTING

THE HANGING OF THE CRANE ...

BOSTON: JAMES R. OSGOOD AND COMPANY. 1874.

Cover-title.

⟨1⟩-16. Laid paper. 7¼" x 5¹⁄₁₆".

⟨-⟩⁸.

Printed self-wrapper.

Prepared for copyright purposes only. Noted in the following forms; the first two probably represent preliminary printings.

Copyright Printing A

P. ⟨3⟩, last line: *Into the endless* ...

P. 7, line 6: *I see the selfsame* ...

P. 15, line 12: ... Gold ₴ ... The letters *en* improperly set; not from the same font as the rest of the setting. Presumably inserted by the typesetter to indicate that he had run out of sorts.

P. 16: No acorn ornament at end.

Copyright Printing B

P. ⟨3⟩, last line: *Into the endless* ...

P. 7, line 6: *I see the selfsame* ...

P. 15, line 12: ... *Golden* ... Completely and properly set.

P. 16: Acorn ornament at end.

Copyright Printing C

P. ⟨3⟩, last line: *Into the boundless* ...

P. 7, line 6: *Appears the selfsame* ...

P. 15, line 12: ... *Golden* ... Completely and properly set.

P. 16: Acorn ornament at end.

On the basis of fair evidence Wilson (p. 263) states: "It was certainly done ⟨*i.e.,* printed⟩ by Jan. 21, ⟨1874⟩." The entry does not occur in the printer's records until Jan. 31, 1874, on which date there is a charge of $20.73 for setting sixteen pages, correcting and proving. Title-page deposited Feb. 27, 1874. There is no record of receipt of the finished pamphlet.

Locations: H (A,C)   UV (B)

BRITISH COPYRIGHT PRINTING

The Hanging of the Crane ...

London: George Routledge and Sons, The Broadway, Ludgate. 1874. [All Rights Reserved.]

Not seen. Entry on the basis of a photographic copy (in H) of the original in BMU.

16 pp. Pamphlet. Deposited for copyright in BMU May 6, 1874. *Not illustrated.*

Wilson (p. 263) states "printed by Feb. 12, 1874" but no evidence is given to support the assertion; but see Longfellow's letter to Osgood, Feb. 26, 1874, below. Reviewed Ath Feb. 21, 1874.

Letter (in H), Longfellow to G. W. Greene, Feb. 25, 1874: "... A paper from London this morning informs me that Routledge has already published *The Hanging of the Crane* ... the proofsheets ⟨of the privately printed Boston pamphlet, presumably⟩ were sent to him for the use of the artists, if he should wish to publish an illustrated edition ..."

Letter, Longfellow to Osgood, Feb. 26, 1874:

"... Routledge has published the book ... I sent Routledge a copy for the use of artists ... I did not authorize him to publish it in any shape ... ⟨Routledge's son⟩ wrote ⟨me⟩ on the 5th of Feb. and before the 12th the book was out ..."—Livingston, p. 86; location of original letter not known.

Letter (in H), Routledge to Longfellow, Feb. 28, 1874: "... It is not ⟨*sic*⟩ published and ... not one copy has been sold ... in my absence my son sent a copy ... to the Atheneum ⟨*sic*⟩ & one or two other papers—but these copies are going to be given up to us again. Only 12 were printed ... to secure a ⟨copy⟩right by entering at Stationers Hall ..." In the same letter Routledge describes the pamphlet as "being only 16 pages."

Locations: BMU (not seen)   H (Xerox copy)

FIRST AMERICAN PUBLICATION

The New York Ledger, March 28, 1874.

FORMAL BOOK PUBLICATION

Trade notices indicate that simultaneous publication was planned for both the London and the Boston editions but the dated notices suggest the London edition may have issued a day or so prior to the Boston edition.

FIRST BRITISH EDITION

THE HANGING OF THE CRANE ... WITH ILLUSTRATIONS

LONDON   GEORGE ROUTLEDGE AND SONS   THE BROADWAY, LUDGATE   1875

⟨i⟩-⟨xii⟩, ⟨13⟩-64. Illustrated. 8³⁄₁₆" x 6½" full.

⟨A⟩-H⁴.

Note: The book is printed on a fairly heavy grade of calendered wove paper with interleaving of relatively light-weight wove paper. The interleaving is disregarded in the pagination and signature collation here given.

S cloth: blue; terra-cotta. Covers bevelled. Yellow-coated end papers. Edges gilt.

Advertised for October in Ath Oct. 3, 1874. Listed (prematurely?) Ath Oct. 17, 1874. Advertised for Nov. 6 in Ath Oct. 31, 1874. Listed PC Nov. 16, 1874. Reviewed Ath Nov. 21, 1874. Listed Bkr Dec. 1, 1874. Advertised under *Christmas Books* Ath Dec. 5, 1874.

Locations: BD   H

FIRST AMERICAN EDITION

THE HANGING OF THE CRANE ... WITH ILLUSTRATIONS

BOSTON   JAMES R. OSGOOD AND COMPANY   LATE TICKNOR & FIELDS, AND FIELDS, OSGOOD, & CO. 1875

⟨iii⟩-x, ⟨11⟩-64, blank leaf. Illustrated. 8⁷⁄₁₆" full x 6".

32 single leaves of plate paper.

C cloth: terra-cotta. FL cloth: terra-cotta. FL-like cloth: green. S cloth: blue; green; mauve. T cloth: terra-cotta. T cloth (moiréd): blue; brown; green. Covers bevelled. Brown-coated end papers; green-coated end papers. Flyleaves. Edges gilt.

Note: Also issued in brown morocco. The binders appear to have been allowed some latitude in the selection of brasses and at least three different forms of the stamping have been seen. Copies in DEV, H, NYPL.

Also note: All examined copies have the following reading on p. 37, line 5: *A Princess from the Fairy Tales,* The same reading is present in printings done as late as 1902.

Note: There were at least three printings done with the date 1875 on the title-page; BAL has been unable to distinguish the first.

Paper sent to the printer Oct. 1, 1874. Letter (in H) Osgood to Longfellow, Nov. 13, 1874: "Owing to the advance orders we have postponed *The Crane* until Wednesday next ⟨*i.e.,* Nov. 18⟩. We send you copies by Sawin." Bound Nov. 12–Dec. 17, 1874. A copy in H (presumably one of those mentioned in Osgood's letter of Nov. 13) inscribed by Longfellow Nov. 15, 1874. Published Nov. 18, 1874; date confirmed by a letter (in H), Longfellow to G. W. Greene, Nov. 17, 1874. Precise date of printing not known but on Nov. 19, 1874, the publishers recorded that 5020 copies had been printed. A copy in BA received Nov. 19, 1874. Longfellow presented copies (in CH) to his daughters Nov. 20, 1874. Advertised for Nov. 28 in PW Nov. 21, 28, 1874. Cloth; and, morocco, listed PW Nov. 28, 1874. *Second printing,* 2010 copies, Dec. 17, 1874. *Third printing,* 1000 copies, Feb. 4, 1875. *Fourth printing,* 2040 copies, Sept. 28, 1875; date altered to 1876.

For another 1875 printing (pp. 47) see in *Section II* under 1875.

AAS   BA   H   LC   NYPL

12167. The Ark ...

  Boston ... 1875 ...

An occasional newspaper.

"A Nameless Grave," and an introductory letter, Feb. 15, 1875, in No. 1, p. ⟨1⟩. The poem collected in *Masque of Pandora,* 1875 (Oct.).

In No. 6 is a four-line extract, here reprinted, from "The Builders."

For comment see entry No. 281.

12168. MORITURI SALUTAMUS. POEM FOR THE FIFTIETH ANNIVERSARY OF THE CLASS OF 1825 IN BOWDOIN COLLEGE ...

PRIVATELY PRINTED. 1875.

Cover-title.

⟨1⟩-12. Laid paper. 9½″ full x 6¹³⁄₁₆″.

⟨-⟩⁶.

Only twenty copies printed. No. —p. ⟨2⟩.

Read at the ceremonies July 7, 1875. No record of copyright found.

Note on the Text

1st: Private printing as above. BAL suspects that the pamphlet was prepared for Longfellow's use in reading; and, for the use of *Harper's New Monthly Magazine,* in which the poem was first published Aug. 1875. The only located copy of the pamphlet is inscribed by George William Curtis (conductor of the magazine's *Easy Chair* department): *George William Curtis from H.W.L. with Longfellow's own corrections.*

2nd: As published in *Harper's.* Text revised. The revisions are those present in G. W. Curtis's copy of the pamphlet printing; see above.

3rd: As a pamphlet privately printed by James Harrison, New York City, not after July 26, 1875. Unauthorized. The text is that of the *Harper's* appearance. Longfellow's own copy (in H) has an inserted letter, Harrison to Longfellow, July 26, 1875: "Permit a stranger to thank you for your beautiful poem ... I wished for a copy in compact form for ready reference. Employing my leisure moments, I have set it up in its present dress, and have struck off 6 copies, one of which I take the liberty of enclosing for your acceptance as a tribute of my respectful regard." Obviously printed after publication of *Harper's New Monthly Magazine* for Aug. 1875.

4th: With further revisions the poem was collected in *Masque of Pandora,* 1875 (Oct.).

See next entry.

H (Harrison) UV (1st)

12169. ... The Poetical Works of Henry Wadsworth Longfellow. (Reprinted from the Revised American Edition, Including Recent Poems.) With Explanatory Notes, Portrait and Original Illustrations.

London: Frederick Warne and Co., Bedford Street, Strand. ⟨1875⟩

At head of title: The Chandos Poets.

Date taken from publisher's preface at end of which: *September, 1875.*

Reprint with the possible exception of "Morituri Salutamus," pp. 549-554. Here reprinted from *Harper's New Monthly Magazine,* Aug. 1875. *See preceding entry.* Presumably first book publication of the poem.

FM

12170. THE MASQUE OF PANDORA AND OTHER POEMS ...

BOSTON   JAMES R. OSGOOD AND COMPANY   LATE TICKNOR & FIELDS, AND FIELDS, OSGOOD, & CO. 1875

See next entry.

⟨i⟩-iv, ⟨1⟩-146, blank leaf. 6¹³⁄₁₆″ x 4½″.

⟨-⟩², 1-6¹², ⟨7⟩². *Also signed:* ⟨-⟩², A-I⁸, ⟨J⟩².

C cloth: green; terra-cotta. FL cloth: purple; terra-cotta. Bevelled covers. Flyleaf at front. Brown-coated end papers.

Note: The sale catalog of the Wakeman collection (American Art Association, Inc., N. Y., 1924, entry No. 756) quotes Wakeman's curious dictum that the earliest copies were issued with an 1876 *imprint* and further states "that when the plate with the copyright inscription was made, it, by mistake, bore the date *1876.* The 6 was cut out and a smaller 5 inserted in its place." Wilson (Vol. I, p. 268) dismisses the Wakeman statement by saying "Wakeman's attempt ... to puff a copy with an 1876 date ... is just plain inaccurate"; BAL concurs. All printings examined by BAL, issued under date 1875 and 1876, carry an 1875 copyright notice. If copies exist with an 1876 copyright notice they have not been seen by BAL.

There were six printings of the book during the period Oct. 11 to Dec. 31, 1875. The publisher's records show that the date on the title-page was altered from 1875 to 1876 in the second printing. All copies of the first printing were issued with the imprint dated 1875.

First Printing

Oct. 11, 1875. 3030 copies.

Imprint dated 1875. Copyright notice dated 1875.

P. ⟨iii⟩, line 2 up: CADENABRIA for CADENABBIA

P. 32, line 2: *Heard in* ...

P. 141, running head: SEA-TIDES.

Second Printing (also others?)

At some unknown time alterations were made to produce the following readings. The publisher's records show that the date on the title-page was altered with the second printing.

Second printing, Nov. 3, 1875, 1012 copies.

Imprint dated 1876. Copyright notice dated 1875.

P. ⟨iii⟩, line 2 up: Corrected to: CADENABBIA

P. 32, line 2: *Heard in* ...

P. 141, running head corrected to: THE TIDES.

Later Printings

Imprint dated 1876. Copyright notice dated 1875.

P. ⟨iii⟩, line 2 up: With the corrected reading: CADENABBIA

P. 32, line 2, with the revised reading: *Once heard in* ...

P. 141, running head: With the corrected reading: THE TIDES.

First printing: 3030 copies, Oct. 11, 1875. A copy of the first printing in UV inscribed by Longfellow Oct. 15, 1875. Noted for *this week* PW Oct. 23, 1875. Listed PW Oct. 30, 1875. *Second printing:* 1012 copies, Nov. 3, 1875. A copy of the second printing in CH inscribed by Longfellow Nov. 13, 1875. *Third printing:* 1020 copies, Nov. 15, 1875. *Fourth printing:* 566 copies, Dec. 3, 1875. *Fifth printing:* 804 copies, Dec. 17, 1875. *Sixth printing:* 1020 copies, Dec. 31, 1875. The Toronto (Belford) edition noted as *just issuing* CM Jan. 1876.

AAS (1st) BA (1st; reprint) BPL (1st; 2nd) H (1st; reprint) NYPL (1st; 2nd; reprint) UV (1st; reprint)

12171. THE MASQUE OF PANDORA AND OTHER POEMS ...

    LONDON GEORGE ROUTLEDGE AND SONS 1875 [COPYRIGHT]

See preceding entry; issued simultaneously with the Boston edition?

⟨1⟩-⟨152⟩; advertisements, pp. ⟨1⟩-⟨8⟩. 6⁵⁄₁₆″ x 4⅛″.

⟨B⟩-I, K-L⁸.

S cloth: orange. Covers bevelled. Brown-coated end papers.

P. ⟨5⟩: Erroneous reading, *Cadenabria,* present.

P. 38, line 2: The earlier reading, *Heard in* ... , present.

P. 147, running head: Erroneous reading, *Sea-Tides,* present.

Advertised as though ready Ath Oct. 23, 1875: "Published by special arrangement with the author." Advertised, with extracts from reviews Ath Oct. 30, 1875. Listed Ath Oct. 30; PC Nov. 1, 1875.

B BD NYPL Y

12172. Poems of Places Edited by Henry W. Longfellow ... England. Vol. I.

    Boston: James R. Osgood and Company, Late Ticknor & Fields, and Fields, Osgood, & Co. 1876.

Note: Each volume in this series, whether part of a multi-volume title or otherwise, is here entered as though a single, separately published, volume.

Reprint save for:

Preface, pp. ⟨i⟩-iv.

"Boston," pp. 74-75. Collected in *Kéramos,* 1878.

Note: Livingston (p. 93), in referring to the entire series states: "In addition to the poems from foreign writers which have at end *Tr. Anon.,* and which can be positively identified as having been translated by Longfellow, there are no less than eighty-six others signed in the same way. Some of these were perhaps translated by Longfellow, but which, if any, it seems now impossible to discover."

Two binding issues noted:

1: With the spine imprint of James R. Osgood & Co.

2: With the spine imprint of Houghton, Osgood & Co.

A copy in UV inscribed by Longfellow Sept. 9, 1876. Listed PW Sept. 9, 1876.

AAS (2nd) BD (1st) H (1st) NYPL (1st) UV (1st) Y (1st)

12173. Poems of Places Edited by Henry W. Longfellow ... England. Vol. II.

    Boston: James R. Osgood and Company, Late Ticknor & Fields, and Fields, Osgood, & Co. 1876.

Contains no material known to be by Longfellow. See *Note,* entry No. 12172.

Listed PW Sept. 23, 1876.

AAS BD H NYPL UV Y

12174. Poems of Places Edited by Henry W. Longfellow ... England. Vol. III.

    Boston: James R. Osgood and Company, Late Ticknor & Fields, and Fields, Osgood, & Co. 1876.

Contains no material known to be by Longfellow. See *Note,* entry No. 12172.

Listed PW Oct. 7, 1876.

AAS BD H NYPL UV Y

12175. Poems of Places Edited by Henry W. Longfellow ... England and Wales. Vol. IV.

Boston: James R. Osgood and Company, Late Ticknor & Fields, and Fields, Osgood, & Co. 1876.

Reprint save for "Woodstock Park," p. 93. Here published anonymously. Collected in *Kéramos*, 1878.

See *Note,* entry No. 12172.

Listed PW Oct. 21, 1876.

AAS   BD   H   NYPL   Y

12176. Poems of Places Edited by Henry W. Longfellow ... Ireland.

Boston: James R. Osgood and Company, Late Ticknor & Fields, and Fields, Osgood, & Co. 1876.

Contains no material known to be by Longfellow. See *Note,* entry No. 12172.

Two binding issues noted:

1: With the spine imprint of James R. Osgood & Co.

2: With the spine imprint of Houghton, Osgood & Co.

Listed PW Oct. 28, 1876.

AAS (1st)   BD (2nd)   H (1st)   NYPL (2nd)   UV (1st)   Y (1st)

12177. Poems of Places Edited by Henry W. Longfellow ... Scotland. Vol. I.

Boston: James R. Osgood and Company, Late Ticknor & Fields, and Fields, Osgood, & Co. 1876.

Contains no material known to be by Longfellow. See entry No. 12172 for a comment.

Two binding issues noted:

1: With the spine imprint of James R. Osgood & Co.

2: With the spine imprint of Houghton, Osgood & Co.

Listed PW Dec. 2, 1876.

AAS (1st)   BD (1st, 2nd)   H (1st)   NYPL (2nd) UV (1st)   Y (1st)

12178. Poems of Places Edited by Henry W. Longfellow ... Scotland. Vol. II.

Boston: James R. Osgood and Company, Late Ticknor & Fields, and Fields, Osgood, & Co. 1876.

Reprint save for "A Wraith in the Mist," pp. 69-70. Here published anonymously. Collected in *Kéramos*, 1878.

See *Note,* entry No. 12172.

Listed PW Dec. 2, 1876.

AAS   H   NYPL   UV   Y

12179. Poems of Places Edited by Henry W. Longfellow ... Scotland. Denmark, Iceland, Norway, Sweden. Vol. III.

Boston: James R. Osgood and Company, Late Ticknor & Fields, and Fields, Osgood, & Co. 1876.

Longfellow's poems herein reprinted from other, earlier, volumes. See comment under entry No. 12172.

Two binding issues noted:

1: With the spine imprint of James R. Osgood & Co.

2: With the spine imprint of Houghton, Osgood & Co.

Listed PW Dec. 23, 1876.

AAS (1st)   BD (1st, 2nd)   H (1st)   NYPL (1st)   UV (1st)   Y (1st)

12180. Centennial Records of the Women of Wisconsin ... Editing Committee: Anna B. Butler, Emma C. Bascom, Katharine F. Kerr.

Madison, Wis.: Atwood and Culver. 1876.

Inserted between pp. ⟨82-83⟩ are three leaves, printed on the rectos only, bearing in facsimile autograph Longfellow's "The Four Lakes of Madison." Also in *Poems of Places ... America. Western States,* 1879; collected in *In the Harbor,* 1882.

Issued after April 25, 1876.

UV   Y

12181. ⟨Prospectus for⟩ The Native Races of the Pacific States of North America. By Hubert Howe Bancroft.

New York: D. Appleton and Company, 549 & 551 Broadway. 1876.

Cover-title. Printed paper wrapper.

Letter, Sept. 21, 1874, p. ⟨14⟩.

H

12182. Poems of Places Edited by Henry W. Longfellow ... France. Vol. I.

Boston: James R. Osgood and Company, Late Ticknor & Fields, and Fields, Osgood, & Co. 1877.

Reprint save for the following translations:

c – "At la Chaudeau," pp. 220-221. Anonymous translation.

b – "The Banks of the Cher," pp. 134-137. Anonymous translation.

b – "Fontenay," pp. 181-183. Anonymous translation.

a – "On Returning from Baréges," pp. 51-52. Anonymous translation.

a – "On the Terrace of the Aigalades," pp. 21-23.

b – "To the Forest of Gastine," pp. 187-188. Anonymous translation.

c – "The Wine of Jurançon," pp. 203-204. Anonymous translation.

KEY

a – Collected in *Kéramos*, 1878.
b – Collected in *Works*, 1886.
c – Collected in *In the Harbor*, 1882.

Two binding issues noted:

1: With the spine imprint of James R. Osgood & Co.

2: With the spine imprint of Houghton, Osgood & Co.

For a comment see entry No. 12172.

A copy in uv inscribed by Longfellow Jan. 27, 1877. Listed pw Jan. 27, 1877.

AAS (1st)   BD (1st)   H (1st)   NYPL (2nd)   UV (1st)   Y (1st)

12183. Poems of Places Edited by Henry W. Longfellow ... France and Savoy. Vol. II.

Boston: James R. Osgood and Company, Late Ticknor & Fields, and Fields, Osgood, & Co. 1877.

Reprint save for:

a – "Pray for Me," pp. 3-4. Anonymous translation.

b – "To My Brooklet," pp. 196-197. Anonymous translation.

b – "To the River Rhone," p. 120.

b – "To the River Yvette," p. 210.

a – "Vire," pp. 202-204. Anonymous translation.

KEY

a – Collected in *Works*, 1886.
b – Collected in *Kéramos*, 1878.

See *Note*, entry No. 12172.

A copy in uv inscribed by Longfellow Jan. 27, 1877. Listed pw Jan. 27, 1877.

AAS   BD   H   NYHS   UV   Y

12184. Poems of Places Edited by Henry W. Longfellow ... Italy. Vol. I.

Boston: James R. Osgood and Company, Late Ticknor & Fields, and Fields, Osgood, & Co. 1877.

Reprint save for "Inarimé," pp. 185-186; collected under the title "Vittoria Colonna" in *Kéramos*, 1878. For a comment see entry No. 12172.

Two binding issues noted:

1: With the spine imprint of James R. Osgood & Co.

2: With the spine imprint of Houghton, Osgood & Co.

Listed pw April 28, 1877.

BD (2nd)   H (1st)   NYPL (2nd)   UV (1st)   Y (1st)

12185. Poems of Places Edited by Henry W. Longfellow ... Italy. Vol. II.

Boston: James R. Osgood and Company, Late Ticknor & Fields, and Fields, Osgood, & Co. 1877.

The only poem herein attributed to Longfellow is reprinted from an earlier book. For a comment see entry No. 12172.

Two binding issues noted:

1: With the spine imprint of James R. Osgood & Co.

2: With the spine imprint of Houghton, Osgood & Co.

Listed pw April 28, 1877.

AAS (1st)   BD (2nd)   H (1st)   NYPL (2nd)   UV (1st)   Y (1st)

12186. Poems of Places Edited by Henry W. Longfellow ... Italy. Vol. III.

Boston: James R. Osgood and Company, Late Ticknor & Fields, and Fields, Osgood, & Co. 1877.

"Venice," pp. 207-208. Collected in *Kéramos*, 1878. For a comment see entry No. 12172.

Two binding issues noted:

1: With the spine imprint of James R. Osgood & Co.

2: With the spine imprint of Houghton, Osgood & Co.

Listed pw April 28, 1877.

BD (2nd)   H (1st)   NYPL (2nd)   UV (1st)   Y (1st)

12187. Poems of Places Edited by Henry W. Longfellow ... Spain. Vol. I.

Boston: James R. Osgood and Company, Late Ticknor & Fields, and Fields, Osgood, & Co. 1877.

Reprint save for "Castles in Spain," pp. 25-28. Also in (previously?) *Poetical Works*, London (Warne) 1877; see below. Collected in *Kéramos*, 1878.

See *Note,* entry No. 12172.

Listed PW June 30, 1877.

AAS   BD   H   NYPL   UV   Y

12188. Poems of Places Edited by Henry W. Longfellow ... Spain, Portugal, Belgium, Holland. Vol. II.

Boston: James R. Osgood and Company, Late Ticknor & Fields, and Fields, Osgood, & Co. 1877.

Reprint save for:

"A Dutch Picture," pp. 256-258. Also in (previously?) *Poetical Works*, London (Warne), 1877; see below. Collected in *Kéramos*, 1878.

"The Emperor's Glove," pp. 171-172; anonymous. Collected in *Kéramos*, 1878.

See *Note,* entry No. 12172.

Listed PW June 30, 1877.

AAS   BD   H   NYPL   UV   Y

12189. KÉRAMOS ...

⟨n.p., n.d., CAMBRIDGE, 1877⟩

Caption-title. The above at head of p. ⟨1⟩.

⟨1⟩-12. Laid paper. 9″ x 5¹⁵⁄₁₆″.

⟨-⟩⁶.

Printed self-wrapper. Sewn.

At end of text, p. 12: *Henry W. Longfellow.*

Privately printed for Longfellow's use. It is generally believed that six copies only were printed, but BAL has been unable to substantiate the assertion.

Printed July, 1877? August, 1877? In a letter (in H), Aug. 6, 1877, James T. Fields asks Longfellow for a copy; the reference is, presumably, to the printed pamphlet. For first book publication see below under 1878.

H   UV

12190. Poems of Places Edited by Henry W. Longfellow ... Switzerland and Austria.

Boston: James R. Osgood and Company, Late Ticknor & Fields, and Fields, Osgood, & Co. 1877.

Longfellow poems herein reprinted from other, earlier, books.

See *Note,* entry No. 12172.

A copy in UV inscribed by Longfellow Sept. 3, 1877. Listed PW Sept. 8, 1877.

AAS   BD   H   NYPL   UV   Y

12191. Golden Songs of Great Poets ...

New York: Sarah H. Leggett, No. 1184 Broadway. 1877.

Unpaged.

Contains "The Poets." Collected in *Kéramos*, 1878.

For comment see entry No. 1760.

12192. Poems of Places Edited by Henry W. Longfellow ... Germany. Vol. I.

Boston: James R. Osgood and Company, Late Ticknor & Fields, and Fields, Osgood, & Co. 1877.

Longfellow poems herein reprinted from other, earlier, books.

See *Note,* entry No. 12172.

A copy in UV inscribed by Longfellow Dec. 8, 1877. Listed PW Dec. 15, 1877.

AAS   BD   H   NYPL   UV   Y

12193. Poems of Places Edited by Henry W. Longfellow ... Germany. Vol. II.

Boston: James R. Osgood and Company, Late Ticknor & Fields, and Fields, Osgood, & Co. 1877.

Longfellow poems herein reprinted from other, earlier, books.

See *Note,* entry No. 12172.

A copy in UV inscribed by Longfellow Dec. 8, 1877. Listed PW Dec. 15, 1877.

AAS   BD   H   NYPL   UV   Y

12194. A BALLAD OF THE FRENCH FLEET OCTOBER 1746

First published in *The Atlantic Monthly*, April, 1877. Also noted in the following publications of uncertain sequence. The order of presentation is arbitrary.

A

A BALLAD OF THE FRENCH FLEET OCTOBER 1746 ...

⟨BOSTON?⟩ HELIOTYPE. EDWARD DEWSON. DEL. ⟨n.d., 1877?⟩

Cover-title.

Six leaves of flexible cardboard, the sixth leaf being blank. Printing on rectos only. Text on leaves 2-5 inclusive, in facsimile autograph. 11⅞″ x 9⅞″. Tied with blue silk ribbon. Issued at The Old South Fair, Boston, Dec. 1877?

B

In: Poems of the "Old South" by Henry Wadsworth Longfellow, Oliver Wendell Holmes, John Greenleaf Whittier, Julia Ward Howe, Edward Everett Hale, and James Freeman Clarke. Illustrated

  Boston   William F. Gill & Co 1877

Advertised, as though published, in *The Dial of the Old South Clock,* an occasional newspaper, Dec. 6, 1877. BPL copy received Dec. 14, 1877. Listed PW Dec. 15, 1877.

The poem also appears in *History of the Old South Meeting-House in Boston,* by Everett W. Burdett, Boston, 1877; listed PW Jan. 12, 1878.

Also in *The Poetical Works,* London (Warne), 1877, below. Collected in *Kéramos,* 1878.

AAS (B)   BA (B)   BPL (B)   H (A,B)   NYPL (A,B) UV (A,B)   Y (A,B)

... Song & Story for the Homestead in Every Land and Clime ...

  ⟨New York, n.d., *ca.* 1877⟩

See under *"There Was a Little Girl"* ... , 1883.

12195. ... The Poetical Works of Henry Wadsworth Longfellow. (Reprinted from the Revised American Edition, Including Recent Poems.) With Explanatory Notes, &c. Portrait and Illustrations.

  London: Frederick Warne and Co., Bedford Street, Strand. ⟨1877⟩

At head of title: The Lansdowne Poets. Date from publisher's preface: *London, February, 1877.*

Precise date of publication not known; hence the following qualified statement. Reprint with the possible exception of:

*"Ballad of the French Fleet." See above under 1877.

*"Castles in Spain." Also in *Poems of Places ... Spain,* Vol. 1, Boston, 1877 (June).

*"A Dutch Picture." Also in *Poems of Places ... Spain,* Vol. 2, Boston, 1877 (June).

Published not before April, 1877; possibly as late as Nov. 1877. Advertised (this edition?) Bkr Nov. 5, 1877.

*Collected in *Kéramos,* 1878.

B   CH

12196. The Three Silences / ⟨sonnet beginning: *Three silences there are, the first of speech*⟩ / Oct. 28, 1877. / To J. G. Whittier / ⟨n.p., n.d., 1877?⟩

Facsimile of the original holograph. Single leaf of white bristol. Printed on recto only. 8¹⁄₁₆″ x 6⅜″.

Proof only? Collected in (previously in?) *Kéramos,* 1878.

Location: Old South Meeting House, Boston.

12197. Wapentake. / To Alfred Tennyson. / ⟨sonnet beginning: *Poet! I come to touch thy lance; with mine*⟩ / June 12, 1877. / ⟨n.p., n.d., 1877?⟩

Facsimile of the original holograph. Single leaf of white bristol. Printed on recto only. 8⅛″ x 6⁹⁄₁₆″.

Proof only? Collected in (previously in?) *Kéramos,* 1878.

A companion piece is a facsimile of a letter from Tennyson to Longfellow, dated *Dec / 77,* acknowledging receipt of the poem as "a Christmas greeting." Single leaf of white bristol. Printed on recto only. 6¾″ full x 5⅞″.

Location: Old South Meeting House, Boston.

12198. Poems of Places Edited by Henry W. Longfellow ... Greece, and Turkey in Europe.

  Boston: James R. Osgood and Company, Late Ticknor & Fields, and Fields, Osgood, & Co. 1878.

Longfellow poems herein reprinted from other, earlier, books. For a comment see entry No. 12172.

Two binding issues noted:

1: With the spine imprint of James R. Osgood & Co.

2: With the spine imprint of Houghton, Osgood & Co.

A copy in H received Feb. 2, 1878. A copy in UV inscribed by Longfellow Feb. 2, 1878. Listed PW Feb. 9, 1878.

AAS (2nd)   BD (1st)   H (1st)   UV (1st)   Y (1st)

12199. KÉRAMOS AND OTHER POEMS

The Boston and London editions appear to have been published simultaneously. See above under 1877 for a private printing of the title-poem.

BOSTON EDITION

KÉRAMOS AND OTHER POEMS ...

BOSTON   HOUGHTON,   OSGOOD & COMPANY   THE
RIVERSIDE PRESS, CAMBRIDGE.   1878

⟨i⟩-⟨viii⟩, ⟨1⟩-148. Laid paper. 7″ x 4½″.

⟨1⁴, 2-7¹², 8²⟩.

H cloth: green. S cloth: blue (two shades noted);
green (2 shades noted); mauve; purple; terra-
cotta. Covers bevelled. Brown-coated end papers.
Flyleaves.

Note: Two binding issues seen:

1: With the spine imprint: HOUGHTON, OSGOOD &
CO.

2: With the spine imprint: HOUGHTON, MIFFLIN &
CO.

3000 copies printed April 18, 1878. Bound April
19, 1878 to May 12, 1886. A copy in H received
April 27, 1878. A copy in NYPL inscribed by
Longfellow April 28, 1878. Deposited May 1,
1878. Listed PW May 4, 1878. On Nov. 6, 1897,
the remaining unbound copies, 665 in all, were
"ground up."

AAS (1st)   BA (1st)   H (1st)   NYPL (1st)   UV (1st,
2nd)   Y (1st)

LONDON EDITION

KÉRAMOS AND OTHER POEMS ...

LONDON   GEORGE ROUTLEDGE AND SONS   1878
[COPYRIGHT]

⟨1⟩-156; advertisements, pp. ⟨1⟩-4. 6⅜″ scant x
4¹⁄₁₆″ (trimmed). 6¹¹⁄₁₆″ x 4¼″ (untrimmed).

⟨B⟩-I, K-L⁸. *Note:* In some copies signature
mark F is not present.

BD cloth (fine-grained): purple. C cloth: purple.
TB cloth: purple. Covers bevelled. Brown-coated
end papers.

Noted as *immediately* Ath April 13, 1878; *now
ready* Ath April 20, 1878. Listed Ath April 27,
1878. Reviewed Ath April 27, 1878. A copy in
Y inscribed by early owner May 1, 1878. Listed
Bkr May 1, 1878; PC May 1, 1878. Advertised,
with extracts from reviews, Ath May 4, 1878.

AAS   BA   H   LC   Y

Note

The single poem, "Kéramos," also appears in
the following publication:

The Poetry of Pottery. Homer's Hymn ...
Longfellow's Poem, from Harper's New Monthly
Magazine. With Pottery Illustrations ... Published As Descriptive of a Pair of Vases Manu-
factured at the Royal Porcelain Works, Worcester, for the Paris Exhibition, 1878.

⟨The Gresham Press: Unwin Brothers, London and Chilworth, n.d., 1878?⟩

"Kéramos," pp. ⟨7⟩-26. Extracts from the poem
on pp. 28, 30, 32, 34.

Here reprinted? The exhibition opened May 1,
1878.

CH

12200. The Elocutionist's Annual Number 6
... Edited by J. W. Shoemaker ...

Philadelphia: J. W. Shoemaker & Co., Publishers. 1878.

Cloth; and, printed paper wrapper.

Precise date of publication not known. Hence
the following qualified statement:

Reprint with the possible exception of "Home
Song," p. 104; otherwise "Song," (*Stay, stay at
home, my heart, and rest*), *Kéramos,* 1878
(April).

Entered for copyright Dec. 6, 1880; received for
copyright Dec. 11, 1880. No. 5 of the series was
issued under date 1877; No. 7 of the series
issued under date 1880.

LC

12201. Poems of Places Edited by Henry W.
Longfellow ... Russia.

Boston: Houghton, Osgood and Company.
Cambridge: The Riverside Press. 1878.

Reprint with the possible exception of:

"Ovid in Exile ... ," translated from Ovid, pp.
233-241; and, "The White Czar," pp. ⟨218⟩-220.
Both also in *Kéramos,* 1878, above.

See *Note,* entry No. 12172.

A copy in UV inscribed by Longfellow April 27,
1878. Listed PW April 27, 1878. Deposited May
1, 1878.

BD   H   NYPL   UV   Y

12202. Poems of Places Edited by Henry W.
Longfellow ... Asia. Syria.

Boston: Houghton, Osgood and Company.
The Riverside Press, Cambridge. 1878.

Longfellow poems herein reprinted from other,
earlier, books.

See *Note,* entry No. 12172.

A copy in UV inscribed by Longfellow Aug. 7,
1878. Listed PW Aug. 10, 1878.

AAS   BD   H   NYPL   UV   Y

12203. Poems of Places Edited by Henry W. Longfellow ... Asia. Asia Minor, Mesopotamia, Arabia, Turkestan, Afghanistan.

Boston: Houghton, Osgood and Company. The Riverside Press, Cambridge. 1878.

Longfellow poems herein reprinted from other, earlier, books.

See *Note,* entry No. 12172.

A copy in UV inscribed by Longfellow Aug. 7, 1878. Listed PW Aug. 10, 1878.

AAS   BD   H   NYPL   UV   Y

12204. Poems of Places Edited by Henry W. Longfellow ... Asia. Persia, India, Chinese Empire, Japan.

Boston: Houghton, Osgood and Company. The Riverside Press, Cambridge. 1878.

Longfellow poems herein reprinted from other, earlier, books.

See *Note,* entry No. 12172.

A copy in UV inscribed by Longfellow Aug. 7, 1878. Listed PW Aug. 10, 1878.

AAS   BD   H   NYPL   UV   Y

12205. THE EARLY POEMS OF HENRY WADSWORTH LONGFELLOW NOW FIRST COLLECTED EDITED ... BY RICHARD HERNE SHEPHERD

LONDON   PICKERING AND CO.   196 PICCADILLY 1878

⟨i-iv⟩, ⟨i⟩-xii, ⟨1⟩-55. Laid paper. 6⅞" x 4¼".

⟨-⟩², ⟨A⟩-D⁸, E².

Two states of the binding noted; sequence, if any, not determined. The following designations are for identification only:

Binding A

Green V cloth. Spine lettered up: EARLY POEMS OF LONGFELLOW

Binding B

Green S cloth. Spine lettered up: LONGFELLOW'S EARLY POEMS

Contains twenty-one poems of which the following are here first collected; the remaining twelve had prior collected appearance.

a "Autumnal Nightfall"

a "Dirge over a Nameless Grave"

a "Italian Scenery"

b "Jeckoyva"

b "The Lunatic Girl"

b "Musings"

c "Song," (*Where from the eye of day* ...)

a "A Song of Savoy"

a "The Venetian Gondolier"

KEY

a—Previously in *Miscellaneous Poems Selected from the United States Literary Gazette,* Boston, 1826. Collected in *Works,* 1886.

b—Earliest located American book appearance: *Henry W. Longfellow* ..., by W. Sloane Kennedy, Cambridge, 1882. Collected in *Works,* 1886.

c—Earliest located American book appearance: *Henry W. Longfellow* ..., by W. Sloane Kennedy, Cambridge, 1882. Also in Samuel Longfellow's *Life of ... Longfellow,* Boston, 1886. Formally collected in *Works,* 1886.

Advertised as *immediately* Ath Aug. 31, 1878. Listed Ath Sept. 7, 1878. Reviewed Ath Sept. 14, 1878. Listed PC Sept. 16, 1878.

AAS (A)   B (B)   H (B)   LC (B)   NYHS (B)   UV (A)   Y (A,B)

12206. Poems of Places Edited by Henry W. Longfellow ... Africa.

Boston: Houghton, Osgood and Company. The Riverside Press, Cambridge. 1878.

Longfellow poems herein reprinted from other, earlier, books.

See *Note,* entry No. 12172.

A copy in UV inscribed by Longfellow Oct. 12, 1878. Listed PW Oct. 19, 1878.

AAS   H   NYPL   UV   Y

12207. The Children's Almanac. For 1879-80-81-82-83. Edited by Ella Farman.

Boston: D. Lothrop and Company, Franklin St., Corner of Hawley. ⟨1878⟩

Unpaged. Contains Longfellow's "January."

Livingston, pp. 99-101, states that "these verses seem never to have been collected." Livingston in error. The lines were collected in *In the Harbor,* 1882, where they appear as part of "The Poet's Calendar."

For fuller entry see No. 2471.

... Play-Day Poems ... Edited by Rossiter Johnson ...

New York ... 1878

See in Section Six.

12208. Poems of Places Edited by Henry W. Longfellow ... America. New England. Vol. I.

Boston: Houghton, Osgood and Company. The Riverside Press, Cambridge. 1879.

Longfellow poems herein reprinted from other, earlier, books.

See *Note,* entry No. 12172.

A copy in UV inscribed by Longfellow Dec. 15, 1878. Listed PW Dec. 21, 1878.

AAS   BD   H   NYPL   UV   Y

12209. Poems of Places Edited by Henry W. Longfellow ... America. New England. Vol. II.

Boston: Houghton, Osgood and Company. The Riverside Press, Cambridge. 1879.

Longfellow poems herein reprinted from other, earlier, books.

See *Note,* entry No. 12172.

A copy in UV inscribed by Longfellow Dec. 15, 1878. Listed PW Dec. 21, 1878.

AAS   BD   H   NYPL   UV   Y

12210. BAYARD TAYLOR ...

⟨n.p., n.d., CAMBRIDGE, 1879⟩

Caption-title. The above at head of p. ⟨1⟩.

⟨1-3⟩. Laid paper. 6¾″ x 4¹¹⁄₁₆″.

Single leaf folded to four pages.

Text on pp. ⟨1-3⟩; p. ⟨4⟩ blank.

Letter, Longfellow to G. W. Greene, Jan. 3, 1879*: "... There is to be a meeting at the Music Hall next week to commemorate the death of Bayard Taylor. I have written some verses for the occasion, which I hope you will like. I will send them to you in a few days ..."

Letter, Longfellow to G. W. Greene, Jan. 6, 1879*: "... There is to be a Memorial Meeting in memory of Bayard Taylor on Friday, but nobody seems to know anything about it, nor in whose hands the management is. My name appears in the list of speakers; but I certainly shall not speak, and expressly said so to the gentleman who called to see me on the subject ..."

Letter, Longfellow to Charlotte Fiske Bates, Jan. 7, 1879; original letter in HEH; transcript from a photostat in H: "... I send you with this the first copy of the lines on Bayard Taylor. No one has seen it yet but yourself and the printer. Please show it to no one till after Friday ..." (Here reprinted by permission of Henry E. Huntington Library and Art Gallery.)

Letter, Longfellow to G. W. Greene, Jan. 10, 1879*: "... I have sent my poem to be read by someone else, as you will see by the following notice. ⟨Newspaper clipping attached.⟩ How good a reader Holmes may be, I do not know; but hope everything will go off well." The clipping reports the arrangements for the meeting and states that Oliver Wendell Holmes had been selected to read the poem.

The earliest located book publication of the poem is in *The Life, Travels, and Literary Career of Bayard Taylor,* by Russell H. Conwell, Boston (B. B. Russell & Co.), 1879; listed PW May 17, 1879; issued in both cloth; and, half morocco.

Collected in *Ultima Thule,* 1880.

* Original in H.

AAS   H

12211. Poems of Places Edited by Henry W. Longfellow ... America. Middle States.

Boston: Houghton, Osgood and Company. The Riverside Press, Cambridge. 1879.

Longfellow poems herein reprinted from other, earlier, books.

See *Note,* entry No. 12172.

A copy in UV inscribed by Longfellow Feb. 27, 1879. Listed PW March 1, 1879.

AAS   BD   H   LC   NYPL   UV   Y

12212. FROM MY ARM-CHAIR

1879

"A very pleasant incident of the seventy-second birthday, in 1879, was the gift from the children of Cambridge of an arm-chair, which Mr. Longfellow found on coming into his study in the morning. It was made ... from the wood of the horse-chestnut tree under which the 'village smithy' of Cambridge had once stood ...

"There were some seven hundred children of the public schools who contributed their dimes ... Of the poem which was written in answer to this gift, the author gave a printed copy to every child who came to see and sit in the chair."—Samuel Longfellow's *Life,* 1886, Vol. 2, pp. 465-466.

Letter (in H), March 7, 1879, Longfellow to G. W. Greene: "... Of the birth-day chair, I hear nothing further, but shall hear soon, no doubt, and have written a poem in reply to anything that may come ..."

"... I send you some verses ⟨*the printed leaflet?*⟩ which I have written to the children by way of thanks for their present. Please do not show them to anyone out of your own house before the end of the week, as they are to appear first in the Cambridge papers, as is right and proper . . ."—Letter, Longfellow to Mrs. Annie Fields, March 12, 1879; original in HEH and here quoted with the permission of The Henry E. Huntington Library and Art Gallery. As indicated by Longfellow the poem appeared in the *Cambridge Tribune*, March 14, 1879; *Cambridge Press*, March 15, 1879; *Cambridge News*, March 29, 1879.

PROOF PRINTING

FROM MY ARM-CHAIR. / ⟨rule⟩ / TO THE CHILDREN OF CAMBRIDGE, / Who presented it to me on my Seventy-second Birthday, / FEBRUARY 27, 1879. / ⟨rule⟩ / ⟨text⟩

The above on p. ⟨1⟩ of a single leaf folded to four pages.

Pp. ⟨1-4⟩. 6¼″ x 5¹⁄₁₆″. Printed on unwatermarked wove paper.

Stanza 2, line 2: May it . . .

Stanza 11, line 3: . . . are wrought /

At end of text: HENRY W. LONGFELLOW. / FEBRUARY 27, 1879. ⟨set 1³⁄₁₆″ wide⟩

Location: UV

PUBLISHED EDITION

FROM MY ARM-CHAIR. / ⟨rule⟩ / TO THE CHILDREN OF CAMBRIDGE, / Who presented to me, on my Seventy-second Birthday, / February 27, 1879, this Chair, made from the Wood / of the Village Blacksmith's Chestnut Tree. / ⟨rule⟩ / ⟨text⟩

The above on p. ⟨1⟩ of a single leaf folded to four pages.

Pp. ⟨1-4⟩. Printed on laid paper. See below for page size.

All copies of the published edition have the following features:

Stanza 2, line 2: It may . . .

Stanza 11, line 3: . . . is wrought /

At end of text: *Henry Wadsworth Longfellow.* / FEBRUARY 27, 1879. ⟨set 1⅛″ scant wide⟩

Three forms (printings?) have been noted. BAL has been unable to establish a sequence, if sequence there is, and the following designations are for identification only. It will be noted that the *m* in *my*, stanza 1, line 1, in the proof printing is broken. This feature is reported in the following descriptions.

Published Edition A

The chain lines run horizontally.

Paper 4.5/1000″ thick to 5/1000″ thick.

Page: 7¹⁄₁₆″ x 5⅜″ scant.

The *m* in *my*, stanza 1, line 1, is broken.

A copy has been seen inscribed by Longfellow with the date *1879*.

Locations: B, H, NYPL, Y.

Published Edition B

The chain lines run vertically.

Paper 8/1000″ scant thick.

Page: 7⅛″ x 5⅜″.

The *m* in *my*, stanza 1, line 1, is broken.

A copy has been seen inscribed by Longfellow with the date *1879*.

Location: AAS

Published Edition C

The chain lines run vertically.

Paper 5/1000″ scant thick.

Page: 8¹⁄₁₆″ x 5⅜″ scant.

The *m* in *my*, stanza 1, line 1, is not broken.

A copy has been seen inscribed by Longfellow with the date *1879*.

Locations: H, NYPL, UV.

The poem has been noted in the following books issued under date 1880:

Papyrus Leaves, edited by William Fearing Gill, New York, 1880. Deposited Dec. 26, 1879. See entry No. 2477.

Selected Poetical Gems, for the Cottage, Palace and Platform, compiled by D. Gilbert Dexter, Cambridge, Mass., Tribune Publishing Co., 1880. Noted as *just issued* in the *Cambridge Tribune,* May 28, 1880.

Poems of Longfellow. Selected from the Best Editions . . . , London (Kent), 1880. Published June, 1880. See entry No. 12221.

Collected in *Ultima Thule,* 1880 (Sept.). See entry No. 12223.

12213. Poems of Places Edited by Henry W. Longfellow . . . America. Southern States.

Boston: Houghton, Osgood and Company. The Riverside Press, Cambridge. 1879.

Longfellow poems herein reprinted from other, earlier, books.

See *Note,* entry No. 12172.

A copy in UV inscribed by Longfellow March 31, 1879. Listed PW April 5, 1879.

BD   H   LC   NYPL   UV   Y

12214. Poems of Places Edited by Henry W. Longfellow ... America. Western States.

Boston: Houghton, Osgood and Company. The Riverside Press, Cambridge. 1879.

Reprint save for "The Four Lakes of Madison," which is here first located in a Longfellow book. For prior book publication see *Centennial Records* ... , 1876, above. Collected in *In the Harbor*, 1882.

See *Note,* entry No. 12172.

A copy in H received April 12, 1879. Listed PW April 19, 1879.

BD   H   LC   NYPL   UV

12215. Poems of Places Edited by Henry W Longfellow ... America. British America.-Danish America.-Mexico. Central America.-South America. West Indies.

Boston: Houghton, Osgood and Company. The Riverside Press, Cambridge. 1879.

Longfellow poems herein reprinted from other, earlier, books.

See *Note,* entry No. 12172.

A copy in UV inscribed by Longfellow May 17, 1879. A copy in H received May 17, 1879. Listed PW May 24, 1879.

BD   H   LC   NYPL   UV   Y

12216. Poems of Places Edited by Henry W. Longfellow ... Oceanica. Australasia, Polynesia, and Miscellaneous Seas and Islands.

Boston: Houghton, Osgood and Company. The Riverside Press, Cambridge. 1879.

Longfellow poems herein reprinted from other, earlier, books.

See *Note,* entry No. 12172.

A copy in UV inscribed by Longfellow May 17, 1879. Listed PW May 24, 1879.

BD   H   NYPL   UV   Y

12217. Essays from the North American Review. Edited by Allen Thorndike Rice.

New York: D. Appleton and Company, 549 and 551 Broadway. 1879.

"Defense of Poetry," pp. ⟨303⟩-333. Reprinted from NAR Jan. 1832; Rice erroneously gives July, 1832. Collected in *Works* ⟨1909⟩. A revised version appeared in *Outre-Mer*, 1835.

For comment see entry No. 679.

The Old Fashioned Mother Goose' Melodies Complete with Magic Colored Pictures ...

G. W. Carleton & Co. ... 1879.

See under *"There Was a Little Girl"* ... , 1883.

The Book of Beauty ...

... New York. ⟨n.d., 1879?⟩

See in *Section Six.*

The Prose Writers of America ...

New York ... ⟨n.d., 1879?⟩

See in *Section Six.*

12218. ... THE WINDMILL ...

⟨n.p., n.d., BOSTON, 1880⟩

Not seen; entry on the basis of Wilson, Vol. 1, p. 277.

Single leaf. Printed on recto only. 7 7/16″ x 4″. Proof printing. At head of title: *For the Companion.*

First published in *The Youth's Companion,* April 15, 1880. Collected in *Ultima Thule,* 1880 (September). A copy mailed by Longfellow to John L. Hayes, Cambridge, Mass., in an envelope postmarked April 18 ⟨1880⟩.

In the Wilson collection (Wilson, Vol. 1, p. 277) is a letter, presumably addressed to *The Youth's Companion,* March 30, 1880: "I hereby acknowledge the receipt of your cheque for $200, in payment of *The Windmill* and *Maiden and Weathercock.* When they are set up, will you do me the favor to have the lines leaded, and to send me duplicate proofs ..."

For the companion piece see entry No. 12220.

12219. Tales of the Chesapeake by Geo. Alfred Townsend ...

New York: American News Company, 39 and 41 Chambers Street. 1880.

Contains, on an inserted leaf, testimonial by Longfellow and others.

For fuller description see entry No. 8945.

12220. ... MAIDEN AND WEATHERCOCK ...

⟨n.p., n.d., BOSTON, 1880⟩

Single leaf. Printed on recto only. 6¾″ x 4⅞″. Proof printing. At head of title: *For the Companion.*

First published in *The Youth's Companion,* May 27, 1880. Collected in *Ultima Thule,* 1880.

See entry No. 12218 for a comment on the production of this printing. For publication as sheet music see in *Section Five.*

HEH

12221. Poems of Longfellow. Selected from the Best Editions. In Two Volumes ...

London: W. Kent & Co., Paternoster Row. MDCCCLXXX.

2 Vols.

Reprint with the exception of "The Chamber over the Gate"; collected in *Ultima Thule*, 1880 (Sept.). Also in *The Poetical Works ...*, London (Ward, Lock, and Co.); see entry No. 12224.

Issued as Vols. 5-6 of *The Miniature Library of the Poets* although not so identified within the volumes or on the binding. Issued in cloth; and, leather, according to contemporary notices. The review in PC of July 1, 1880, describes the format as "semi-limp red cloth, gilt edges, in a case." Noted only in conventional blue S cloth over stiff boards.

Advertised for *early in June* PC June 1, 1880. Listed Ath June 19, 1880. Reviewed PC July 1, 1880. Listed PC July 1, 1880.

WUL

12222. ULTIMA THULE ...

LONDON   GEORGE ROUTLEDGE AND SONS   BROAD-WAY, LUDGATE HILL   1880 [COPYRIGHT.]

Issued simultaneously with the American edition? See next entry.

⟨i⟩-vi, ⟨7⟩-63. 6⅝" x 4⅜".

⟨B⟩-E⁸.

Printed tan paper wrapper. In some copies: White end papers.

Note: In this edition the first two lines, p. 29, read: *But still the burden of his song | Is love of right, disdain of wrong;|* In the Boston edition (p. 27) the reading is revised: *But still the music of his song | Rises o'er all elate and strong; |*

Letter (in H) from Routledge to Longfellow, May 27, 1880: "... We shall issue it on the 11th of September ..." Noted for Sept. 11 Ath Sept. 4, 1880. Noted as *now ready* Ath Sept. 18, 1880. A copy in CH inscribed by early owner Sept. 30, 1880. Listed PC Oct. 1, 1880.

CH   H

12223. ULTIMA THULE ...

BOSTON: HOUGHTON, MIFFLIN AND COMPANY. THE RIVERSIDE PRESS, CAMBRIDGE. 1880.

See preceding entry.

⟨i⟩-⟨vi⟩, ⟨7⟩-61, blank leaf. Portrait frontispiece inserted. Laid paper. 6¾" x 4¼".

⟨1-8⟩⁴.

S cloth: blue; brown; gray. V cloth: blue; gray. White laid end papers. Laid paper flyleaves. Top edges gilt.

Printed Sept. 2, 1880, 2000 copies (publisher's records). Longfellow's journal, Sept. 15, 1880, states: *Ultima Thule published.* A copy in MHS inscribed by Longfellow Sept. 18, 1880. Listed PW Sept. 18, 1880. A second printing of 500 copies was done in Nov. 1880 (publisher's records), with an alteration on the title-page; the alteration, presumably, was change of date from 1880 to 1881.

AAS   BA   H   MHS   NYPL   UV   Y

12224. The Poetical Works of Henry W. Longfellow.

Ward, Lock, and Co., London: Warwick House, Salisbury Square, E. C. New York: Bond Street. ⟨n.d., not before June, 1880.⟩

Reprint with the possible exception of the following, all of which appear also in *Ultima Thule*, 1880:

"The Chamber over the Gate." Also in *Poems*, London (Kent), 1880 (June).

"Helen of Tyre"

"The Iron Pen"

"The Poet and His Songs"

"The Sifting of Peter"

CH

12225. The Masque of Pandora. By Henry W. Longfellow. Music by Alfred Cellier. Arranged for the Stage by Bolton Rowe, with the Permission of the Author. Produced for the First Time at The Boston Theatre, by The Blanche Roosevelt English Opera Company, 10th January, 1881.

⟨The Riverside Press, Cambridge, 1881⟩

Printed paper wrapper.

For first edition of Longfellow's original text see under 1875.

Deposited Jan. 19, 1881.

... The adaptation for the stage has been done with a due regard for the beauty of Longfellow's words, and, with a few trifling exceptions, the poem is retained intact. Where lines have been needed in the construction of the stage version, Prof. Longfellow has supplied them, but the production of the work in its operatic form has been intrusted entirely to Bolton Rowe and Alfred Cellier ... The characters in the poem have been retained, but the economies of the stage have necessitated the omission of some of the choruses. The "Workmen of Hephaestus," "The Celestial Chorus of Women's Voices," "The Guests of Epimetheus" and the "Ballet of Dreams" take the place of "The Chorus of Birds," "The Chorus of Reeds," the "Choruses of the Eumenides" and others. The scenes in the "Masque" are eight in number but in the opera they are reduced to four ... and the scenes in Olympus and in the air are omitted. For the rest the librettist has found words for his choruses—with two exceptions—in the poem ...—*Boston Sunday Herald*, Jan. 9, 1881.

H UV

12226. The Dante Society, of Cambridge, Massachusetts, proposes to print the hitherto inedited Latin Comment on the Divine Comedy by Benvenuto da Imola ...

Cambridge, Mass., June, 1881.

Single leaf. 10" x 7¹⁵⁄₁₆". Printed on recto only.

Signed at end by Longfellow and others. See entry No. 12232.

The above was accompanied by a printed letter, signed at end by Longfellow and others, addressed *To the Members of the Dante Society,* dated at end *Cambridge, Mass., June, 1881,* reading in part: *The accompanying circular concerning the printing of the Comment of Benvenuto da Imola* ... Single leaf. 9¹⁵⁄₁₆" x 7¹⁵⁄₁₆", printed on recto only.

H

12227. Exercises in Celebrating the Two Hundred and Fiftieth Anniversary of the Settlement of Cambridge Held December 28, 1880 ...

Cambridge University Press: John Wilson and Son 1881

Reprint save for "Remarks," pp. 29-30, *i.e.,* Longfellow's address to the children of Cambridge.

For comment see entry No. 8957.

12228. "The City and the Sea," with Other Cambridge Contributions, in Aid of the Hospital Fund ...

Cambridge: John Wilson and Son, University Press. 1881.

"The City and the Sea," p. ⟨11⟩. Collected in *In the Harbor,* 1882.

For comment see entry No. 8325.

12229. In Memoriam. Gems of Poetry and Song on James A. Garfield. With Portrait and Eulogy ...

Columbus, O⟨hio⟩. J. C. McClenahan & Company. 1881.

"President Garfield," p. 27. Collected in *In the Harbor,* 1882.

For comment see entry No. 122.

12230. James T. Fields Biographical Notes and Personal Sketches with Unpublished Fragments and Tributes from Men and Women of Letters

Boston   Houghton, Mifflin and Company The Riverside Press, Cambridge 1881

"Auf Wiedersehen," pp. 274-275. Collected in: *In the Harbor,* 1882; also in: *Poetical Works* ..., London (Warne), ⟨n.d., 1882?⟩, entry No. 12246.

For fuller entry see No. 5987.

12231. On account of illness, Mr. Longfellow / finds it impossible to answer any letters at / present. / He can only acknowledge their receipt, and / regret his inability to do more./ Cambridge, Mass. ⟨n.d., 1881⟩

⟨1-4⟩. Laid paper. 7" x 4⅜".

Single cut sheet folded to make four pages.

Text on p. ⟨1⟩, otherwise blank.

Livingston (p. 108) states: "... In November, 1881, ... ⟨Longfellow⟩ had this printed sheet prepared ..."

PDH

12232. In a Circular issued in June last, the Dante Society of Cambridge, Massachusetts, announced its intention of publishing the hitherto inedited Comment on the Divine Comedy by Benvenuto da Imola, provided that a sufficient number of subscribers could be ...

Cambridge, Mass., December, 1881.

Single leaf. 10" x 7¹⁵⁄₁₆". Printed on recto only.

Signed at end by Longfellow and others. Announcing withdrawal of the proposal. See entry No. 12226.

H

12233. ⟨Advertisement for⟩ Mr. ⟨John James⟩ Piatt's Poems ... Extracts from Letters ...

⟨n.p., n.d., after Sept. 19, 1881⟩

Four-page leaflet. Issued as an advertisement for Piatt's poems. The above at head of p. ⟨1⟩.

Comment, p. ⟨1⟩.

WMG

12234. Henry W. Longfellow. A Memoir by Richard H. Stoddard ... Including His Latest Poem, "Hermes Trismegistus."

London: Frederick Warne and Co., Bedford Street, Strand. ⟨n.d., 1882⟩

Not to be confused with Stoddard's *Henry Wadsworth Longfellow, a Medley in Prose and Verse*, New York, 1882.

Cloth; and, printed paper wrapper.

Is "Hermes Trismegistus" herein reprinted? Also appears in:

Longfellow's Poetical Works ..., London (Routledge), 1882 (April? August?).

Henry W. Longfellow ..., by W. S. Kennedy, Cambridge, 1882 (May 27, 1882).

In the Harbor, 1882 (June).

Advertised as though ready Ath April 8, 1882. Listed PC April 15, 1882.

BD

12235. ... Longfellow's Poetical Works With Illustrations by Sir John Gilbert, R. A.

London George Routledge and Sons Broadway, Ludgate Hill New York: 9 Lafayette Place 1882.

At head of title: Author's Complete Copyright Edition

Cloth?

Reprint with the possible exception of:

"Hermes Trismegistus," p. 612. *See preceding entry.*

"Mad River," p. 613. Also appears in:

Henry W. Longfellow ..., by W. S. Kennedy, Cambridge, 1882 (May 27, 1882).

In the Harbor, 1882 (June).

Wayside Gleanings ..., 1882; *see below.*

Precise date of publication not established. An edition (this?) listed in *The English Catalogue of Books* as an April, 1882, publication. Deposited BMU Aug. 4, 1882.

NYPL

12236. Henry W. Longfellow Biography Anecdote, Letters, Criticism by W. Sloane Kennedy ...

Cambridge, Mass. Moses King, Publisher Harvard Square 1882

Contains letters, here in their earliest located book publication. Also contains a group of poems all of which had prior American book publication except the following:

a "Hermes Trismegistus"

b "Jeckoyva"

b "The Lunatic Girl"

c "Mad River"

b "Musings"

d "Song," (*Where from the eye of day ...*)

KEY

a—Also in *Henry W. Longfellow ...*, by R. H. Stoddard, London ⟨n.d., April, 1882⟩, see above. *Longfellow's Poetical Works ...*, London (Routledge), 1882 (April? August?), see above. *In the Harbor,* 1882 (June).

b—Also in *Early Poems*, 1878; *Works*, 1886.

c—*Longfellow's Poetical Works ...*, London (Routledge), 1882 (April? August?), see above. *In the Harbor,* 1882 (June). *Wayside Gleanings*, 1882, see below.

d—Also in *Early Poems*, 1878; Samuel Longfellow's *Life of ... Longfellow*, 1886. Formally collected in *Works*, Boston, 1886.

A copy in H received May 23, 1882. Listed PW May 27, 1882. Deposited June 2, 1882.

NYPL UV

12237. Henry Wadsworth Longfellow. A Medley in Prose and Verse. By Richard Henry Stoddard.

New York: George W. Harlan & Co., Publishers, 44 West 23d Street. 1882.

Not to be confused with Stoddard's *Henry W. Longfellow. A Memoir ...*, London ⟨n.d., 1882⟩, above.

Contains some Longfellow letters here in their earliest located book appearance. The poems, pp. 19-39, had prior American book publication. The following poems may have some claim to primacy:

"The Soul. An Extract from an Unpublished Poem," pp. 56-57, is here in its earliest located American book publication. Appears also in *The Poetical Works*, London (Warne), n.d., *i.e.,* entry 12246. "The Soul" is extracted from Longfellow's partially unpublished PBK poem, 1832. For another version see "The Warning," in *Poems on Slavery,* 1842.

Six lines of verse, untitled, p. 169. First published in *Century Magazine*, June, 1882. Collected under the title "Inscription on the Shanklin Fountain"; also appears in:

Poetical Works ..., London (Warne) ⟨n.d., 1882?⟩, *i.e.,* entry No. 12246.

Complete Poetical Works, Cambridge ⟨1893⟩.

Note: Livingston errs in stating that the six lines were collected in *In the Harbor,* 1882.

Deposited June 12, 1882. Listed PW June 17, 1882.

BD H NYPL UV

12238. Henry Wadsworth Longfellow. Seventy-Fifth Birthday. Proceedings of the Maine Historical Society, February 27, 1882.

    Portland: Hoyt, Fogg and Donham, 193 Middle Street. ⟨1882⟩

Letter, Feb. 12, 1882, p. ⟨9⟩.

Telegram, Feb. 27, 1882, p. 13.

"Ode," otherwise "Lovewell's Fight," pp. 152-154. Originally in the Portland *Advertiser,* May 24, 1825. Reprinted in *The Illustrated Fryeburg Webster Memorial,* Fryeburg, Maine, 1882 (deposited Aug. 9, 1882). Collected in *Works,* 1886.

Copies occur with top edges plain; and, gilded.

A copy in H received June 14, 1882. Deposited June 17, 1882.

BD BPL H NYPL UV Y

12239. IN THE HARBOR   ULTIMA THULE.—PART II ...

BOSTON   HOUGHTON, MIFFLIN AND COMPANY NEW YORK: 11 EAST SEVENTEENTH STREET   THE RIVERSIDE PRESS, CAMBRIDGE 1882

See next entry.

⟨i⟩-⟨viii⟩, ⟨9⟩-88. Frontispiece inserted. Laid paper. $6\frac{11}{16}$″ x $4\frac{3}{16}$″.

⟨1-2⟩, 3-4, ⟨5⟩⁸, 6⁴. Signature mark 2 on p. 21.

Three issues noted:

1

P. 27, line 2 up: *I can longer* ...

Leaf ⟨2⟩₆ is not a cancel.

2

P. 27, line 2 up: *I can no longer* ...

Leaf ⟨2⟩₆ is a cancel.

3

P. 27, line 2 up: *I can no longer* ...

The correction done by reprinting conjugate leaves ⟨2⟩₃.₆.

The publisher's records indicate that the error was discovered after some copies of the book had been bound which accounts for the variation distinguishing the 2nd from the 3rd issue. Copies in binding had the correction done by cancelling a single leaf; copies in sheets were corrected more neatly (and more simply) by removing conjugates ⟨2⟩₃.₆ and inserting reprinted (corrected) leaves.

S cloth: blue; brown; green. White laid end papers. Laid paper flyleaves. Top edges gilt. Also issued in flexible calf?

3000 copies printed June 22, 1882. Binding commenced June 26, 1882. A copy in CH inscribed by Ernest Longfellow June 28, 1882. On June 30, 1882, 1500 cancels were printed. Deposited July 3, 1882. On July 8, 1882, 1300 cancels were printed. Listed PW July 8, 1882. By May 12, 1886, 2827 copies had been bound. On Nov. 6, 1897, the remaining 159 copies in sheets were pulped.

AAS (2nd)   BA (3rd)   CH (1st, 2nd)   H (1st, 2nd, 3rd)   NYPL (1st, 2nd, 3rd)   UV (1st)   Y (1st, 2nd)

12240. IN THE HARBOR ...

    LONDON   GEORGE ROUTLEDGE AND SONS   BROADWAY, LUDGATE HILL   NEW YORK: 9, LAFAYETTE PLACE 1882 [COPYRIGHT]

Issued simultaneously with the Boston edition? See preceding entry.

⟨i⟩-⟨viii⟩, 9-88, 8 pp. advertisements. $6\frac{1}{2}$″ full x $4\frac{1}{4}$″.

⟨B⟩-G⁸.

S cloth: blue. Cream end papers. Top edges gilt.

Noted as *about to be published* Ath June 17, 1882. Listed Ath July 1, 1882; PC July 15, 1882.

B CH NYPL

12241. ⟨Facsimile letter addressed to Mr L. Reich, 13 West 11 St., New York⟩ Cambridge March 13, / 1882. / My Dear Sir, / Another case of your / Tokayer Ausbruch of 1868 / has reached me safely, / ⟨etc., etc.⟩

    ⟨New York, 1882?⟩

Single cut sheet folded to make 4 pp. Page: $6\frac{15}{16}$″ x $4\frac{1}{2}$″. P. ⟨4⟩ blank.

Presumably issued by Lorenz Reich as an advertisement. Copies also occur with a tipped-on label printed in red: (*Longfellow's Last Letter*)

H

12242. Charles River Railway V.S. Union & Camb. Railroads State House 1882 ...

    ⟨n.p., n.d., probably Boston, 1882⟩

Cover-title. 2 Vols. Issued without title-pages.

Six-line note, Cambridge, Feb. 25, 1882, Vol. 2, p. 490.

MSL

12243. Henry Wadsworth Longfellow a Memory by Rev. P. Murphy ...

Routledge and Sons, London. Edward Howell, Liverpool. 1882.

Inserted as a frontispiece is a facsimile Longfellow letter addressed to the author.

UV

12244. Longfellow's Poetical Works With 83 Illustrations by Sir John Gilbert, R.A and other Artists ...

London George Routledge and Sons Broadway, Ludgate Hill New York: 9 Lafayette Place ⟨n.d., after July 6, 1882⟩

Pp. 564. On p. ⟨vi⟩: *The Author's Copyright Edition . . . contains . . . 86 Copyright Poems . . .*

On the basis of internal evidence this edition was issued after July 6, 1882, but before March 1, 1883. Further publication information wanting.

Another edition (which *"contains 125 poems which can only be found here"*) was listed PC March 1, 1883.

Reprint with the possible exception of:

"Columbus." Also in *The Poetical Works . . .*, London (Warne), n.d., after July 6, 1882; *i.e.,* entry No. 12247. "Columbus," translated from the German of Schiller, was first published in *The Independent* (N.Y.), July 6, 1882. For earliest located American book publication see entry No. 12251.

FM

12245. ⟨Facsimile letter⟩ Nahant, Aug 20. / 1881. / Dear Sir, / It will give me pleasure / to comply with your request. / I will sign any copies you / may send me of Marshall's / portrait, not to exceed one / thousand in all. / Yours truly / Henry W. Longfellow. / Mr George Barrie / ⟨n.p., n.d., Philadelphia, *ca.* 1882⟩

Single cut sheet folded to four pages. Wove paper watermarked: *Caslon Bond.* The above on p. ⟨1⟩, otherwise blank. Page: 6$\frac{15}{16}$" x 4$\frac{5}{8}$".

Issued with the engraved portrait of Longfellow by William Edgar Marshall published by George Barrie, Philadelphia.

PDH

12246. ... The Poetical Works of Longfellow. Including Recent Poems. With Explanatory Notes, etc.

London: Frederick Warne and Co., Bedford Street, Strand. ⟨n.d., not before June, 1882⟩

At head of title: The "Chandos Classics."

Pp. 632.

If issued after June 28, 1882, this book is a complete reprint. If issued prior to that date the book is possibly first edition for:

a "Auf Wiedersehen"

b "The Bells of San Blas"

b "Decoration Day"

c "Inscription on the Shanklin Fountain"

KEY

a—Also in *James T. Fields Biographical Notes . . .*, 1881, above; *In the Harbor,* 1882, above.

b—Also in *In the Harbor,* 1882, above.

c—See under *Henry Wadsworth Longfellow. A Medley . . .*, 1882, above.

Note: Also contains "The Soul ...''; for a comment on this see entry No. 12237.

BD

12247. The Poetical Works of Longfellow. Including Recent Poems. With Explanatory Notes, etc.

London: Frederick Warne & Co Bedford Street, Strand. ⟨n.d., after July 6, 1882⟩

Pp. 664. *Chandos Classics* series; so identified on the binding.

Printed from the plates of the *Chandos Classics* printing (632 pp.), above, with added material.

In all likelihood there were several printings from the same plates, the earliest having signature mark B present, p. ⟨1⟩. Noted in cloth with *Chandos Classics* at foot of spine; and, padded leather, the statement *Chandos Classics* not present.

Reprint with the possible exception of:

"Apostrophe to Time" *By Longfellow?* Dated *Avon, May, 1835.* According to Longfellow's journal the poet was in England in May, 1835, and could have visited Avon but precise information is wanting. The poem appears also in *Poetical Works . . .*, London (Griffith & Farran), n.d., 1883.

"Columbus." See note relating to this, entry No. 12244.

"The Golden Sunset" herein is not by Henry W. Longfellow but by Samuel Longfellow. Collected in Samuel Longfellow's *Hymns and Verses*, 1894.

B   H

12248. Wayside Gleanings for Leisure Moments. Printed for Private Circulation.

⟨University Press: John Wilson and Son, Cambridge⟩ 1882.

Reprint with the possible exception of "Longfellow's Last Poem," p. 124; otherwise "Mad River." For a record of other contemporary appearances see above: *Henry W. Longfellow . . . ,* by W. Sloane Kennedy, 1882 (May).

"Longfellow's First Poem . . . Mr. Finney's Turnip," p. 122. Not by Longfellow. See in *Section Six* under year 1900.

Precise date of publication not known.

H

12249. Flower-de-Luce . . . Reproduced in Fac Simile from the Original MS. Illustrated by Isaac Sprague

Boston   S. E. Cassino, Publisher   1883

Flexible illuminated paper boards. Advertised in PW Nov. 25, 1882: "The leaflets are fastened together by white silk ribbon and put up in a heavy manila envelope, ready for mailing, $1.25; with fringe, $1.50." A surviving copyright deposit copy is in the fringed binding.

The poem appears herein in an early, 9-stanza version; and, also, in the later, revised, 8-stanza version as collected in *Flower-de-Luce*, 1867.

Two issues noted:

1: With the imprint reading as above.

2: With the publisher's later style: *S. E. Cassino & Co., Publishers, 1883.*

Reprinted and reissued, Boston, n.d., by Estes & Lauriat.

BD   LC   NYPL   Y

12250. MICHAEL ANGELO

The publication sequence of this poem is somewhat involved as the following notes indicate. It has been thought best to present all known early printings as a single entry. The descriptions in both Livingston and in Wilson of the copyright printing are erroneous, both authorities being misled by the incomplete, and misbound, Foote-Chamberlain-University of Texas copy.

Copyright Printing, Part 1

MICHAEL ANGELO . . . ⟨Part 1⟩

LONDON: GEORGE ROUTLEDGE AND SONS, BROADWAY, LUDGATE HILL. 1882 . . .

Cover-title.

⟨i-ii⟩, ⟨1⟩-35. 9⅜″ x 6¹⁄₁₆″.
⟨1¹, 2-3⁸, 4²⟩.

Printed self-wrapper.

Running heads undated.

Printed from altered setting used in *Atlantic Monthly,* Jan. 1883.

Not seen.

According to the records 40 copies were printed Dec. 1, 1882, at The Riverside Press, Cambridge, Mass. Received at The Bodleian Library, Feb. 8, 1883.

H (a microfilm of the Bodleian copy)   UT (incomplete)

Copyright Printing, Part 2

MICHAEL ANGELO . . . ⟨Part 2⟩

LONDON: GEORGE ROUTLEDGE AND SONS, BROADWAY, LUDGATE HILL. 1882 . . .

Cover-title.

⟨i-ii⟩, ⟨37⟩-62; 2 blank leaves. 9⅜″ x 6¹⁄₁₆″.
⟨-⟩¹⁶.

Printed self-wrapper.

The date *February, 1883.* is present in the running heads.

Printed from the altered setting used in *Atlantic Monthly,* Feb. 1883.

According to the records thirty (thirty-seven?) copies were printed at The Riverside Press, Cambridge, Mass., Dec. 18, 1882.

H (a microfilm of the Bodleian copy)   UV

Copyright Printing, Part 3

MICHAEL ANGELO . . . ⟨Part 3⟩

LONDON: GEORGE ROUTLEDGE AND SONS, BROADWAY, LUDGATE HILL. 1883 . . .

Cover-title.

⟨i-ii⟩, ⟨63⟩-93. 9⅜″ x 6¹⁄₁₆″.
⟨1¹⁶, 2¹⟩.

Printed self-wrapper.

The running heads are undated.

Printed from the altered setting used in *Atlantic Monthly,* March, 1883.

Not seen.

According to the records thirty (forty-two?) copies were printed at The Riverside Press, Cambridge, Mass., Jan. 22, 1883.

H (a microfilm of the Bodleian copy) UT (incomplete)

PUBLISHED EDITIONS

The poem appears in the following (simultaneously issued?) editions, here designated A-D. The designations are almost wholly arbitrary. During this period Longfellow's popularity (measured in terms of sales) was at its peak, with sales averaging over 1000 volumes a week. Consequently, the following printings (A,B,C,D) may represent not one printing each but two or more. In the copies first printed Michael Angelo's 24th speech, Part 2, Sc. 4, reads: ... *His worth is scattered* ... ; in later printings the reading is: ... *His wealth is scattered* ... The charge for alteration of the plates was entered in the publisher's records July 5, 1883.

Published Edition A

The Poetical Works ... Diamond Edition.

> Boston: Houghton, Mifflin and Company. The Riverside Press, Cambridge. 1883.

Pp. 519.

"Michael Angelo," pp. 442-502.

No record of copyright deposit found.

The following information is from the publisher's records:

May 17, 1883. The cost books show record of composition and electrotyping for additions to this edition. The entry specifically names "In the Harbor" and "Michael Angelo" as the material added.

May 18, 1883: 10,043 copies of this edition printed.

May 29, 1883: 1075 copies of this edition bound. The binding continued during the period May 29, 1883 to Oct. 1, 1883. By Oct. 1, 1883, a total of 9748 copies had been bound. The binding record indicates that copies were done in cloth; morocco; tree calf.

A copy of the above is in CH.

The following is a reprint of the above:

The Poetical Works of Henry Wadsworth Longfellow

> *Boston and New York Houghton, Mifflin and Company The Riverside Press, Cambridge ‹1883; i.e., not before 1886›*

Pp. 519.

Published Edition B

Poems ... New Revised Edition. With Numerous Illustrations.

> Boston: Houghton, Mifflin and Company. The Riverside Press, Cambridge. 1883.

Pp. 492.

Each page decorated with a red rule frame.

"Michael Angelo," pp. 415-467.

The following information is from the publisher's records:

April 21, 1883: 72 pages of added matter composed. (This same setting was used in the production of the *Household Edition;* see *Published Edition C.*)

May 23, 1883: 276 sets of sheets of the added matter ("Michael Angelo," etc.) printed.

June 2, 1883: By or on this date 90 copies of the extended (pp. 492) edition were bound. This was made up of sheets of an earlier printing (pp. 426) bound with sheets of the added matter.

July 13, 1883: By this date all copies bound.

July 16, 1883: 976 additional copies of the complete work printed.

Nov. 13, 1883: 1018 additional copies of the complete work printed. Postdated?

A copy of the above is in H.

Published Edition C

The Poetical Works ... Household Edition.

> Boston: Houghton, Mifflin and Company. The Riverside Press, Cambridge. 1883.

Pp. 492.

"Michael Angelo," pp. 415-467.

The following information is from the publisher's records:

April 21, 1883: 72 pages of added matter composed. (This same setting was used in the production of the *red line* edition; see *Published Edition B.*)

May 1, 1883: Entry in the cost books for alteration of table of contents.

June 9, 1883: 10,158 copies printed.

June 14, 1883: First copies bound by this date. 90 copies.

Sept. 14, 1883: During the period June 14, 1883 to Sept. 14, 1883, in small lots, 9720 copies bound. The record indicates that copies were bound in cloth; morocco; tree calf.

In addition to the above printing there were two other printings in 1883: Sept. 14, 2594 copies; Sept. 29, 5034 copies. It is presumed that these have the altered reading, p. 443; see above for comment on this alteration.

Copies in BD, DEV, H.

Published Edition D

The Complete Poetical Works ... with Numerous Illustrations.

> Boston: Houghton, Mifflin and Company. The Riverside Press, Cambridge. 1883.

Not seen. Entry postulated.

Family Edition although not so marked. Printed in two columns. Reprint? Contains an estimated 340 pages, the final pages given over to "Michael Angelo" and to notes. An earlier printing, pp. 305, does not contain "Michael Angelo."

Printed June 14, 1883. 3584 copies. Bound June 23–Aug. 14, 1883. Reprinted (postdated?) Aug. 15, 1883, 10,092 copies.

REPRINTS

Reprint A

The Poetical Works ... in Four Volumes ...

> Boston   Houghton, Mifflin and Company The Riverside Press, Cambridge   1883

4 Vols. *Cambridge Edition.*

Printed during the period June 4, 1883–July 12, 1883. Vol. 4, which contains the added "Michael Angelo," printed July 12, 1883, 510 copies.

Reprint B

The Complete Prose Works ... with ... Later Poems ... with a Biographical Sketch by Octavius B. Frothingham

> Boston   Houghton, Mifflin and Company New York: 11 East Seventeenth Street   The Riverside Press, Cambridge ⟨1883⟩

Uniform with *The Poetical Works,* 1879–1880; for a comment see in *Section II.* First issued in paper parts (*i.e., Parts 31-45* of the set). The parts were printed during the period July 31–Nov. 30, 1883. As a single volume available in cloth; and, several styles of leather. The first printing of each part comprised 5000 copies.

Reprint C

Michael Angelo   A Dramatic Poem ...

> Boston   Houghton, Mifflin and Company New York: 11 East Seventeenth Street   The Riverside Press, Cambridge   1884

Pp. 184. Cloth. Bound Japanese fashion with maroon cord. Also issued in leather.

Nov. 5, 1883: 3472 copies printed, of which 514 were shipped to London; see *Reprint D.*

Nov. 9, 1883: Binding commenced. The binding continued through Dec. 3, 1884.

Nov. 24, 1883: Copies deposited for copyright.

Dec. 8, 1883: Listed PW of this date.

Reprint D

Michael Angelo   A Dramatic Poem ...

> London   George Routledge & Sons   Broadway, Ludgate Hill ⟨n.d., 1883⟩

American-printed sheets.

Announced Ath Sept. 29, 1883; PC Oct. 1, 1883; Bkr Oct. 1, 1883. Advertised as though published Ath Nov. 24, 1883. Listed Ath Nov. 24, 1883. For further details see publication notes under *Reprint C.*

12251. Henry Wadsworth Longfellow   His Life, His Works, His Friendships by George Lowell Austin ...

> Boston   Lee and Shepard, Publishers   1883

Cloth; and, leather.

"Columbus," translated from Schiller, printed in facsimile on an inserted leaf facing p. 368. See entry No. 12244 for prior book (London) publication.

"The Dead," pp. 248-249. Extracted from Longfellow's PBK poem, 1832, first published in K Dec. 1834. Not to be confused with "The Dead" (*Voices of the Night,* 1839), a translation from Klopstock.

Listed PW April 7, 1883.

H   UV

12252. "There Was a Little Girl" ... Illustrated by Bertha M. Schaeffer

> New York (Copyright 1883) R. Worthington 770 Broadway. Julius Bien & Co. Lith. N. Y.

Fringed flexible pictorial boards, tied with cord. Also pictorial boards, cloth shelfback.

Listed PW Nov. 24, 1883, as "fringed". Advertisements noted in PW (Dec. 6, 1884; *Christmas Issue,* 1886) mention the fringe.

Copies in: B   BPL   NYPL   UV   Y

By Longfellow? Doubt exists as to how much, if any, of this nursery rhyme was written by Longfellow. Authorship is ascribed to him in the above (unauthorized?) publication. Longfellow's son, Ernest Wadsworth Longfellow, in his *Random Memories,* 1922, pp. 15-16, unequivocally ascribes the first stanza to his father. It is also ascribed to him by Blanche Roosevelt

Tucker-Macchetta in her *The Home Life of Henry W. Longfellow* ... , 1882. For a discussion of the authorship and a record of early appearances of the rhyme see "There Was a Little Girl: Its First Printings, Its Authorship, Its Variants," by Sidney Kramer, in *The Papers of the Bibliographical Society of America*, Vol. 40, Fourth Quarter, 1946.

The versions of the rhyme are almost as many as its appearances. BAL has made no attempt to record the textual variations. The following is a list of those appearances seen by BAL issued prior to publication of the 1883 publication above.

A

In: *The Reveille*. Anonymous. An occasional newspaper published at the Grand Army Fair, Salem, Mass., issue of Dec. 21, 1870. The earliest located dated appearance. A copy is in The Essex Institute, Salem, Mass.

B

Wrong Side Up. / A POEM. / ⟨text⟩ / ⟨n.p., n.d., *ca.* 1870⟩

Single leaf. Printed on recto only. Anonymous.

A copy in UV is accompanied by a letter from Mrs. Louis Mansfield Ogden, Tuxedo Park, New York, Oct. 24, 1936: "The poem about the Little Girl ... was found in a tin box containing letters received by my father, William Gilbert Davies, ranging in date from 1857 to 1870. So I imagine that it must have been printed at about that period."

Copies in NYPL, UV

C

Balloon Post ...

   Boston, Mass., April ... 1871 ...

Edited by Susan Hale. An occasional newspaper published at the Fair in Aid of the Destitute People of France. Issued April 11–17, 1871. Not issued on Sunday, April 16. Complete in 6 numbers.

"There Was a Little Girl," No. 1, pp. ⟨8-9⟩. Anonymous.

Copies in H, NYPL, UV

D

In: *The American Publisher*, Hartford, June, 1871. p. 5. The first six lines only. Untitled. Anonymous.

LC

E

... Marjorie Daw and Other People ...

   Boston ... 1873

At head of title: Thomas Bailey Aldrich

Three lines quoted at p. 37. Anonymous.

For fuller description see entry No. 276.

F

... Song & Story for the Homestead in Every Land and Clime ...

   ⟨Lyon Manufacturing Co., Manufacturing Chemists, 53 Park Place, New York, n.d., *ca.* 1877⟩

Cover-title. At head of title: *Vol. 2.* Printed paper wrapper.

First stanza, p. 9. Anonymous.

Issued as an advertisement and probably published with varying imprints on the back wrapper. The only copy examined is imprinted on back wrapper: *F. M. Weatherbee, 635 Washington Street, Boston.*

UV

G

Illustrated National Nursery Songs and Games Selected and Arranged, in an Easy and Pleasing Manner, by A. H. Rosewig.

   ⟨Philadelphia: W. F. Shaw, 1879⟩

Pictorial paper wrapper. Unpaged.

"The Girl with the Curl." Anonymous.

Deposited for copyright in either March or November, 1880; the month is uncertain.

Copy in LC

H

The Old Fashioned Mother Goose' ⟨sic⟩ Melodies Complete with Magic Colored Pictures.

   G. W. Carleton & Co., Publishers; Donaldson Brothers, Designers & Printers; M.D.CCC. L.XX.IX. Copyrighted by Donaldson Brothers, 1879.

A transformation book so printed to present altered pictures when the leaves are turned one way or the other. Unpaged.

Contains a version of the rhyme. Anonymous.

Deposit date not known.

Copy in UV

I

The Home Life of Henry W. Longfellow. Reminiscences of Many Visits at Cambridge and Nahant, during the Years 1880, 1881 and 1882. By Blanche Roosevelt Tucker-Macchetta.

   New York: Copyright, 1882, by G. W. Carleton & Co., Publishers. London: S. Low, Son & Co. MDCCCLXXXII.

"There Was a Little Girl," p. 90. Here credited to Longfellow.

For comment on this book see *Section Six*.

Copies in BD, NYPL, UV, Y

For a comment on publication in sheet-music form see "Songe of ye Nurserie," *Section Five*.

12253. ... The Poetical Works ... Including Recent Poems. With Explanatory Notes, &c. Portrait and Original Illustrations.

>   Griffith and Farran, at the Sign of the "Bible and Sun," West Corner of St. Paul's Churchyard, London ⟨n.d., 1883⟩

At head of title: The Lansdowne Poets.

Leather.

Reprint with the possible exception of "Apostrophe to Time," p. 586. By Longfellow? See *The Poetical Works of Longfellow ...*, entry No. 12247.

P. 632 dated *7/6/83*.

NYPL

12254. FROM THE LATE GREAT AND GOOD POET / Prof. Henry W. Longfellow. / ENCOURAGEMENT CAME IN THE FOLLOWING LINES,— / "NAHANT AUGUST 26, 1880. / PROF. GEO. VAUGHAN. / Dear Sir. / ⟨text in 6 lines⟩ / Yours very truly / HENRY. W. LONGFELLOW." / ⟨n.p., n.d., 1883?⟩

Single leaf. Printed on recto only. 7⁵⁄₁₆" x 5⁷⁄₁₆".

Possibly issued as an advertisement for Vaughan's *Progressive Religious and Social Poems,* second edition, 1883.

CAW

12255. Suwanee River Tales by Sherwood Bonner ⟨pseud. for Katherine Sherwood Bonner McDowell⟩ ...

>   Boston   Roberts Brothers   1884

Untitled poem, 15 lines, in French, pp. 106-107: *Qu'elle est belle la marquise* ...

"... The dainty French poem ... is from Longfellow's hand ... published ... with his consent, but, at his request, without acknowledgment ..." **—p. vii.**

H   UV

12256. Fourth Annual Report of the Dante Society. May 19, 1885. With an Appendix, Containing Additional Notes to the Divine Comedy, by Henry Wadsworth Longfellow.

>   Cambridge: John Wilson and Son. University Press. 1885.

Printed paper wrapper.

"Additional Notes on the Divine Comedy," pp. ⟨17⟩-31. Collected in *Works,* 1886.

AAS   UV   Y

12257. Eminent Opinions on Woman Suffrage ...

>   Office "Woman's Journal," 5 Park Street, Boston ... American Woman Suffrage Association. ⟨n.d., 1885?⟩

Single leaf. Title at head of p. ⟨1⟩. Imprint at foot of p. 2.

Three-line statement, p. ⟨1⟩.

H   NYPL

History of the Ordination of Caleb D. Bradlee ...

>   Boston ... 1885.

See in *Section Six*.

12258. LIFE OF HENRY WADSWORTH LONGFELLOW WITH EXTRACTS FROM HIS JOURNALS AND CORRESPONDENCE EDITED BY SAMUEL LONGFELLOW ...

>   BOSTON   TICKNOR AND COMPANY   1886

2 Vols. Title-pages printed in black only.

1: ⟨i⟩-⟨xii⟩, ⟨1⟩-433, blank leaf. Frontispiece and 7 plates inserted; other illustrations in text. 8⁵⁄₁₆" x 5⁵⁄₁₆". Printed on laid paper save for the title-leaf and its conjugate which are printed on wove paper.

2: ⟨i⟩-⟨viii⟩, ⟨1⟩-481, blank leaf. Frontispiece and 4 plates inserted. Printed on laid paper save for the title-leaf and its conjugate which are printed on wove paper.

1: ⟨a², b⁴⟩, 1-27⁸, 28².

2: ⟨a-b⟩², 1-30⁸, 31².

V cloth: blue; green; maroon. White laid end papers. Top edges gilt.

Contains, in addition to "extracts from ... ⟨Longfellow's⟩ journals and correspondence," the following poems:

a "The Angler's Song"

b "The Battle of Lovell's Pond"

b "The Cross of Snow"

b ⟨"Fragments"⟩. Comprising four untitled pieces:

Neglected record of a mind neglected; Vol. 1, p. 299.

O faithful, indefatigable tides; Vol. 2, p. 92.

So from the bosom of darkness . . . ; Vol. 2, p. 286.

Soft through the silent air . . . ; Vol. 2, p. 103.

b "Mezzo Cammin"

c "Song," (*Where from the eye of day . . .*)

b "To Ianthe"

KEY

a—Previously in *Miscellaneous Poems Selected from the United States Literary Gazette,* 1826. For formal collection see *Works,* 1886.
b—Formally collected in *Works,* 1886.
c—Previously in *Early Poems,* London, 1878; and, *Henry W. Longfellow . . . ,* by W. Sloane Kennedy, 1882. Formally collected in *Works,* 1886.

Note: Also a large paper printing limited to 300 numbered copies. Title-pages printed in black and red. Imprint: *Boston Ticknor and Company MDCCCLXXXVI* Paper boards, printed paper label on spine; reprint; see publication notes below.

Note: Vol. 1, first printing, p. 332, line 2 from bottom, reads: *. . . Tamerlane./* In the large paper printing, and in the second printing (marked *Second Edition* on verso of title-leaf), the reading is corrected to *Tamlane.* Vol. 2, first printing, p. 84, line 11 from bottom, the reading is *. . . Paige's . . ./*; p. 85, line 4, the reading is *. . . Paige. /* In the large paper printing and in the *Second Edition* the reading is, respectively, *Page's* and *Page.*

4016 copies (trade format) printed Feb. 27, 1886, of which 1012 copies in sheets were shipped to London for distribution by Kegan Paul. A few copies of the trade printing were put in binding March 1, 1886; the remaining copies were bound March 4–April 15, 1886. A copy of the trade printing received by H March 12, 1886. Deposited (trade format) March 13, 1886. Both formats listed PW March 20, 1886, but the large paper listing was on the basis of publisher's information, not by actual receipt. *Large paper:* 315 copies printed April 14, 1886; bound April 20–22, 1886. Second printing of the trade format, 1128 copies, April 28, 1886.

London Edition

Distributed in London (American sheets) by Kegan Paul. Prematurely announced for *early autumn* Ath April 18, 1885; PC May 1, 1885. Again announced PC Oct. 1, 1885. 1012 sets of sheets received by Kegan Paul sometime after

Feb. 27, 1886. Listed Ath March 27, 1886. Reviewed Ath April 17, 1886. Twenty-five copies of large paper format shipped to Kegan Paul April 20, 1886.

H (both formats) NYPL (trade) UV (large paper)

12259. Works

1886

11 Vols. Edited by Horace E. Scudder.

"The present edition . . . includes all the prose and poetry which the author admitted into the latest edition of his works, together with those pieces which have appeared since his death . . . The text is the last revised by the author . . ."—From the publisher's preliminary "Advertisement."

Large Paper Edition

Imprint: Cambridge Printed at the Riverside Press 1886

Limited to 500 numbered copies. Boards, cloth shelfback and corners, printed paper label on spine.

Riverside Edition

Imprint: Boston and New York Houghton, Mifflin and Company The Riverside Press, Cambridge M DCCC LXXXVI

1500 copies printed according to the publisher's records.

Outre-Mer and Drift-Wood

Large Paper Edition, Vol. 1. Printed Aug. 28, 1886. Bound Sept. 10, 1886.

Riverside Edition, The Prose Works, Vol. 1. Printed Aug. 13, 1886. Bound Aug. 30, 1886 and later. Deposited (*Riverside Edition*) Sept. 20, 1886.

Reprint save for "The Blank Book of a Country Schoolmaster," pp. ⟨411⟩-424, a series of eighteen short pieces. Twelve of the pieces had prior book publication in *The Knickerbocker Sketch-Book,* 1845, *q.v.* The following six pieces are here first located: "An Old Saying," "A Passage from Dante," "History," "A Wise Saw," "Autumn," "Death of the Young."

Hyperion and Kavanagh

Large Paper Edition, Vol. 2. Printed Aug. 30. 1886. Bound Sept. 10, 1886.

Riverside Edition, The Prose Works, Vol. 2 Printed Aug. 24, 1886. Bound Sept. 7, 1886 and later. Deposited (*Riverside Edition*) Sept. 20, 1886.

Reprint.

Voices of the Night, Etc.

Large Paper Edition, Vol. 3. Printed Sept. 18, 1886. Bound Oct. 5–6, 1886.

Riverside Edition, The Poetical Works, Vol. 1. Printed Sept. 24, 1886. Bound Oct. 5, 1886 and later. A copy in H received Oct. 8, 1886. Deposited (*Riverside Edition*) Oct. 9, 1886.

Reprint save for:

a "The Angler's Song"

b "Autumnal Nightfall"

c "Battle of Lovell's Pond"

b "Dirge over a Nameless Grave"

b "Italian Scenery"

e "Jeckoyva"

g "Lover's Rock"

e "The Lunatic Girl"

c "Mezzo Cammin"

e "Musings"

h "Ode ... Lovewell's Fight"

i "Song," (*Where from the eye of day ...*)

b "A Song of Savoy"

f "Song of the Birds"

d "Thanksgiving"

c "To Ianthe"

b "The Venetian Gondolier"

KEY

a—Previously in *Miscellaneous Poems Selected from the United States Literary Gazette*, 1826; Samuel Longfellow's *Life of ... Longfellow*, 1886.

b—Previously in *Miscellaneous Poems Selected from the United States Literary Gazette*, 1826; *Early Poems*, London, 1878.

c—Previously in Samuel Longfellow's *Life of ... Longfellow*, 1886.

d—Previously in *Miscellaneous Poems Selected from the United States Literary Gazette*, 1826; *Poems*, London (Tegg), n.d., 1848.

e—Previously in *Early Poems*, London, 1878; *Henry W. Longfellow ...*, by W. Sloane Kennedy, Cambridge, 1882.

f—Previously in *The Atlantic Souvenir ... 1827*, Philadelphia ⟨1826⟩.

g—Earliest located book appearance here.

h—Previously in *Henry Wadsworth Longfellow. Seventy-Fifth Birthday ...*, Portland ⟨1882⟩.

i—Previously in *Early Poems*, London, 1878; *Henry W. Longfellow ...*, by W. Sloane Kennedy, Cambridge, 1882; Samuel Longfellow's *Life of ... Longfellow*, 1886.

Evangeline ... Hiawatha ... Courtship of Miles Standish

Large Paper Edition, Vol. 4. Printed Sept. 23, 1886. Bound Oct. 5–6, 1886.

Riverside Edition, The Poetical Works, Vol. 2. Printed Oct. 2, 1886. Bound Oct. 5, 1886 and later. A copy in H received Oct. 8, 1886. Deposited (*Riverside Edition*) Oct. 9, 1886.

Reprint.

Birds of Passage

Large Paper Edition, Vol. 5. Printed Oct. 19, 1886. Bound Nov. 3, 1886.

Riverside Edition, The Poetical Works, Vol. 3. Printed Oct. 22, 1886. Bound Oct. 30, 1886 and later. Deposited (*Riverside Edition*) Nov. 5, 1886. A copy in H received Nov. 9, 1886.

Reprint save for "The Cross of Snow" and "Fragments," both here first formally collected. Both had prior publication in Samuel Longfellow's *Life of ... Longfellow*, Cambridge, 1886.

Tales of a Wayside Inn

Large Paper Edition, Vol. 6. Printed Oct. 25, 1886. Bound Nov. 3, 1886.

Riverside Edition, The Poetical Works, Vol. 4. Printed Oct. 28, 1886. Bound Nov. 2, 1886 and later. Deposited (*Riverside Edition*) Nov. 5, 1886. A copy in H received Nov. 9, 1886.

Reprint.

Christus: A Mystery

Large Paper Edition, Vol. 7. Printed Nov. 11, 1886. Bound Dec. 21, 1886.

Riverside Edition, The Poetical Works, Vol. 5. Printed Nov. 19, 1886. Bound Dec. 7, 1886 and later. Deposited (*Riverside Edition*) Dec. 20, 1886. A copy in H received Dec. 20, 1886.

Reprint.

Judas Maccabæus, Michael Angelo, Translations

Large Paper Edition, Vol. 8. Printed Dec. 17, 1886. Bound Dec. 21, 1886.

Riverside Edition, The Poetical Works, Vol. 6. Printed Dec. 13, 1886. Bound Dec. 15, 1886 and later. Deposited (*Riverside Edition*) Dec. 20, 1886. A copy in H received Dec. 20, 1886.

Reprint save for the following:

a "The Assumption of the Virgin"

b "The Banks of the Cher"

a "Clear Honor of the Liquid Element"

a "The Disembodied Spirit"

b "Fontenay"

a "Ideal Beauty"

a "The Lover's Complaint"

c "My Secret"

a "The Nativity of Christ"

d "Pray for Me"

a "Scenes Omitted from Michael Angelo"

a "Sicilian Canzonet"

"Song of the Rhine," here first formally collected. Previously in (untitled) *The Knickerbocker Sketch-Book* ... , 1845; and, Vol. 1 of the present entry; in both the poem appears as part of "The Blank Book of a Country Schoolmaster."

a "The Stars"

a "Tell me, tell me, thou pretty bee ..."

b "To the Forest of Gastine"

d "Vire"

KEY

a—Earliest located book appearance.
b—Here first collected. Previously in *Poems of Places, France,* Vol. 1, 1877.
c—Here first collected. Previously in *Gifts of Genius,* New York ⟨1859⟩. Also in *Poetical Works,* London (Warne), n.d., 1872.
d—Here first collected. Previously in *Poems of Places, France,* Vol. 2, 1877.

The Divine Comedy, Inferno *

Large Paper Edition, Vol. 9. Printed Nov. 30, 1886. Bound Dec. 18, 1886.

Riverside Edition, The Translation of Dante's Divina Commedia ... , Vol. 1. Printed Nov. 27, 1886. Bound Dec. 2, 1886 and later.

The Divine Comedy, Purgatorio *

Large Paper Edition, Vol. 10. Printed Nov. 5, 1886. Bound Dec. 18, 1886.

Riverside Edition, The Translation of Dante's Divina Commedia ... , Vol. 2. Printed Nov. 6, 1886. Bound Nov. 29, 1886 and later. Deposited *(Riverside Edition)* Dec. 8, 1886.

The Divine Comedy, Paradiso *

Large Paper Edition, Vol. 11. Printed Dec. 13, 1886. Bound Dec. 18, 1886.

Riverside Edition, The Translation of Dante's Divina Commedia ... , Vol. 3. Printed Dec. 3,

* Reprint save for the insertion of additional notes; for prior publication of the notes see *Fourth Annual Report of the Dante Society* ... , 1885.

1886. Bound Dec. 4, 1886 and later. Deposited *(Riverside Edition)* Dec. 8, 1886.

BPL *(Large Paper)*   H (both)

12260. FINAL MEMORIALS OF HENRY WADSWORTH LONGFELLOW EDITED BY SAMUEL LONGFELLOW ...

BOSTON   TICKNOR AND COMPANY   1887

Title-page printed in black.

⟨i-iv⟩, ⟨i⟩-⟨viii⟩, ⟨1⟩-447. Laid paper. 8⅜" x 5½". Frontispiece and 9 plates inserted.

⟨-⟩⁶, 1-28⁸.

V cloth: blue; maroon. Top edges gilt. According to trade notices (see below) also issued in half leather.

In addition to the trade edition (above) there were printed 300 numbered copies imprinted: *Boston Ticknor and Company MDCCCL-XXXVII;* title-page printed in red and black; paper boards, printed paper label on spine. See publication notes below.

Note: This, together with the *Life,* 1886, rearranged to give a chronological sequence, reissued in three volumes, Boston and New York, 1891, as *Life of Henry Wadsworth Longfellow.*

Trade edition: 2610 copies printed April 23, 1887. Bound May 2, 1887 and later. Noted for *May 7* in PW May 7, 1887. Deposited May 9, 1887. Listed PW May 14, 1887. Advertised PW May 28, 1887, as in cloth; half calf; half morocco.

Limited edition: Printed April 22, 1887. Advertised in PW May 14, 1887, as *ready about May 25th.* Bound May 24, 1887.

London (Kegan Paul): 260 sets of sheets (trade printing) shipped by the American publisher on April 27, 1887. Listed Ath May 7, 1887. Advertised as though ready Ath May 7, 1887.

H (trade, limited)   UV (limited)

12261. The Cross and the Grail. By Lucy Larcom. With Selections from the Poets   Shakespeare, Longfellow ...

1887. Woman's Temperance Pub'n Association   Chicago.

Unpaged.

Contains six extracts from Longfellow, four of which have been traced and are herein reprinted. The following two have not been located in Longfellow's works; by Longfellow? And if by Longfellow, herein reprinted?

He who drinks beer thinks beer. | And he who drinks wine thinks wine. |

Pray for the living in whose heart, | The strug-
gle between right and wrong, | Is raging terrible
and strong. | As when good angels war with
devils. |

For fuller entry see No. 11378.

12262. What American Authors Think about
International Copyright

New-York American Copyright League 1888

Facsimile of a portion of a letter, p. ⟨2⟩; reprinted from *The Century Magazine*, March,
1888.

For comment see entry No. 218.

Longfellow's Latest Poems   Copyright

London . . . 1890

See in *Section Six*.

12263. The Complete Poetical Works . . . Cambridge Edition

Boston and New York Houghton, Mifflin
and Company The Riverside Press, Cambridge ⟨1893⟩

Edited by Horace E. Scudder.

Pp. 689.

Reprint with the exception of:

"Inscription on the Shanklin Fountain," p. 359.
Earliest located collected publication in an
American book. See note under *Henry Wads-*
worth Longfellow. A Medley . . . , by Richard
Henry Stoddard, 1882.

AAS BA H

12264. Voices of the Night Ballads and Other
Poems . . .

New York New York Publishing Company,
26 City Hall Place, 1895.

On binding: *Empire Edition*

Reprinted from the plates of two unlocated earlier publications; probable titles: *Voices of the*
Night, Ballads, and Other Poems, pp. 130; and,
The Spanish Student, and Other Poems, pp.
106.

The first part of the volume (*i.e., Voices of the*
Night . . .) is a complete reprint. The second
part of the book (*i.e., The Spanish Student* . . .)
is also a complete reprint, but it contains the
first *dated* American book appearance of the
following material:

"The Good George Campbell," from the German of O.L.B. Wolf, pp. 66-67. Also contains a
letter (pp. 101-103) from Longfellow, Feb. 19,
1845, addressed to the editor of *Graham's Maga-*
zine, in which Longfellow defends himself from

a charge of plagiarism. Longfellow (in the letter) explains that he translated the poem from
the German of Wolf, wholly unaware that Wolf
had translated the original ballad, "Bonnie
George Campbell" (William Motherwell's *Min-*
strelsy . . . , Glasgow, 1827). In brief: "Bonnie
George Campbell," a Scots ballad, had been
translated into German by Wolf, and "The
Good George Campbell" is Longfellow's translation of the German translation. Both the letter
and Longfellow's translation have been seen in
several undated British and American publications of uncertain date.

BD

12265. Thoughts and Experiences in and out of
School by John B. Peaslee . . . accompanied by
Letters from Longfellow, Whittier, Holmes,
and Other American Authors

Printed for the Author by Curts & Jennings,
Cincinnati, Ohio 1900

Letters, Dec. 25, 1879, p. 284; Feb. 23, 1880, p.
286.

Here included only because Longfellow's name
appears on the title-page. The letters are inconsequential and are here in their earliest
located book publication. ("*Books containing*
letters . . . unless obviously intended for publica-
tion, are disregarded in these lists."—BAL, Vol.
1, p. xvii).

Deposited Dec. 22, 1899. A copy in H received
Jan. 30, 1900. Listed PW March 31, 1900.

H

Longfellow's First Poem.

⟨n.p., n.d., *ca.* 1900⟩

See in *Section Six*.

. . . Fifth Year Book The Bibliophile Society . . .

⟨Boston, 1906⟩

See in *Section Six*.

12266. ORIGIN AND GROWTH OF THE
LANGUAGES OF SOUTHERN EUROPE
AND OF THEIR LITERATURE AN IN-
AUGURAL ADDRESS BY HENRY WADS-
WORTH LONGFELLOW . . . DELIVERED
SEPTEMBER 2, 1830

BOWDOIN COLLEGE LIBRARY BRUNSWICK, MAINE
1907

⟨i⟩-⟨xiv⟩, ⟨1⟩-125; printer's imprint, p. ⟨126⟩,
2 blank leaves. Wove paper watermarked *Strath-*
more USA. 6½" x 4" (wrapper). 6⅜" full x 4"
(leather). 6⅜" x 3¹⁵⁄₁₆" (cloth).

⟨1-18⟩⁴.

Printed gray-green paper wrapper folded over flexible boards, printed paper label on spine, 4 flyleaves of bookstock at front and at back. *Also:* Olive-brown sheep, green-coated end papers, double flyleaves of bookstock at front, top edges gilt. *Also:* Olive S cloth, white end papers printed in green with a wood-grain pattern, double flyleaves of bookstock at front, top edges gilt.

Certificate of issue, p. ⟨iv⟩: *Only 250 copies printed This is No. . . .*

Deposited Feb. 18, 1907. A copy in AAS inscribed by early owner Feb. 27, 1907. A copy in H received Feb. 27, 1907. According to the publisher's prospectus (a copy in B) the book was to be published Feb. 27, 1907, and available in the three bindings described above.

AAS (wrapper) B (wrapper) BA (cloth) H (wrapper, leather) LC (leather, being a deposit copy) UV (wrapper) Y (wrapper)

12267. The Wadsworth-Longfellow House Longfellow's Old Home Portland, Maine Its History and Its Occupants by Nathan Goold

⟨n.p., probably Portland, Maine⟩ Lakeside Printing Company 1908

Printed paper wrapper.

Reprint save for: "Old Parish Church," pp. 14-15. Originally in the *Portland Advertiser*, Sept. 25, 1824. Collected in *Longfellow's Boyhood Poems*, 1925.

Note: The poem does not appear in the 1905 edition.

CH

12268. The Works of Longfellow ⟨Binder's Title⟩

The Davos Press New York ⟨1909⟩

A subscription book and as such probably issued in a variety of formats with varying imprints. Noted in the *Edition de Luxe* (10 Vols.); and, *Aldus Edition de Luxe* (3 Vols., being the text of *Edition de Luxe*, Vols. 1-6 only; complete thus?), with the imprint of *National Library Company, New York*. Each of these limited to 1000 numbered sets.

Edited by Charles Welsh.

Vol. 1

Prose Works. Outre-Mer. Defense of Poesy.

Reprint save for "The Defense of Poesy," here first collected. For prior book publication see *Essays from the North American Review*, 1879, above, where it appears as "Defense of Poetry."

Vol. 2

Prose Works. Hyperion. The Lay Monastery.

Reprint save for the following:

"The Author," "Winter Months," "The Literary Spirit of Our Country," "Poets and Common-Sense Men," "Valentine Writing." These five pieces, "the first two published under the title of *The Lay Monastery*, and signed *The Lay Monk*, the last three bearing the latter, both as title and signature, appeared in *The United States Literary Gazette* on March 1, March 15, April 1, June 1, and October 1, 1825, and have not apparently been reprinted . . . Longfellow wrote to his mother on March 2, 1825, as follows:—*If you choose to read some of my prose writing, look into the U. S. Literary Gazette for March 1, No. 22, under the title of The Lay Monastery, and you will find the first number of a series of essays, which I am writing occasionally, for your amusement and my own profit."* —P. ⟨349⟩. The letter also appears in Samuel Longfellow's *Life*, 1886, Vol. 1, pp. 61-62.

"Washington Irving." Previously in *Irvingiana . . .* , New York, 1860, *q.v.*, above.

Vol. 3

Prose Works. Kavanagh. The Indian Summer. The Bald Eagle. Drift-Wood.

Reprint save for:

"The Bald Eagle." Here first collected. See *The Token . . .* , Boston, 1833, above.

"The Indian Summer." Here first collected. See *The Token . . .* , Boston, 1832, above.

Vol. 4

Poetical Works. Earlier Poems. Translations. The Spanish Student and Other Poems.

Reprint save for:

"An Evening in Autumn." Here first collected. See *The Token . . .* , Boston, 1833, above.

"Truth." Here first collected. See *The Boston Book . . .* , Boston, 1836, above.

"The Poet of Miletus." Here first collected. See *The Liberty Bell*, 1846, above.

Vol. 5

Poetical Works. Evangeline. The Golden Legend. Miles Standish and Other Poems.

Reprint.

Vol. 6

Poetical Works. Hiawatha. Birds of Passage. Tales of a Wayside Inn and Other Poems.

Reprint.

Vols. 7-10

The Divine Comedy of Dante Alighieri.

Reprint.

BD

12269. LONGFELLOW'S BOYHOOD POEMS A PAPER BY THE LATE GEORGE THOMAS LITTLE ... TOGETHER WITH THE TEXT OF HITHERTO UN-COLLECTED EARLY POEMS AND BIBLI-OGRAPHY EDITED BY RAY W. PET-TENGILL ...

SARATOGA SPRINGS, N. Y.   R. W. PETTENGILL 1925

⟨i-ii⟩, ⟨i⟩-vi, ⟨1⟩-62, blank leaf. Laid paper. 8½″ scant x 5¾″.

⟨1-4⁸, 5⁴⟩.

V cloth: blue. Printed paper label on spine.

"This first edition is limited to five hundred copies"—P. ⟨iv⟩.

Deposited June 1, 1925.

AAS   H   NYHS   NYPL   UV

12270. AN UNKNOWN PROSE TALE BY LONGFELLOW BY JAMES TAFT HAT-FIELD REPRINTED FROM AMERICAN LITERATURE, VOL. III, NO. 2, MAY, 1931

⟨DURHAM, N. C., 1931⟩

Cover-title.

⟨i-ii⟩, 135-148. Wove paper watermarked *Louvain Book.* 9″ x 5⅞″.

Leaves extracted from *American Literature* and issued in printed paper wrapper.

The "unknown prose tale" is Longfellow's "The Wondrous Tale of a Little Man in Gosling Green." For another comment on this story see Thompson's *Young Longfellow,* pp. 391-392.

BD

12271. ... The Longfellow-Freiligrath Corre-spondence ⟨Edited by⟩ James Taft Hatfield

Published by the Modern Language Associa-tion of America   100 Washington Square East New York ⟨1933⟩

Cover-title. Printed paper wrapper. At head of title: Reprinted from PMLA Publications of The Modern Language Association of Amer-ica ... Volume XLVIII December, 1933 Num-ber 4

Pp. 1223-1293. Laid paper. 9½″ x 6⁵⁄₁₆″.

Certain of the letters herein had prior publi-cation in Samuel Longfellow's *Life of ... Long-fellow,* 1886.

H

12271A. Characters in Tales of a Wayside Inn by John van Schaick, Jr. ...

Boston   The Universalist Publishing House 16 Beacon Street ⟨1939⟩

"Some New Longfellow Letters," pp. ⟨161⟩-172.

BA

12272. A Gift to Bowdoin College by Henry W. Longfellow

Brunswick, Maine: Bowdoin College Library, 1963

Cover-title. Printed paper wrapper. Edited by Herbert Brown.

Text of Longfellow's letter to *My Dear Mr Packard, Cambridge Nov 8 1869.* Illustrated with a 4-page facsimile of the original letter.

BD   H

IN THIS SECTION are listed collections of *dated* reprints issued under Longfellow's name (or pseudonym); and, separate editions, *i.e.*, separate printings of poems extracted from collections issued by the author. Poems issued in sheet music form, the poems being reprinted from Longfellow's books, are listed in *Section V*. For *undated* reprints see *Section III*. See *Section IV* for books by others containing material by Longfellow reprinted from earlier books.

Note: The text of the books included in this section has not been collated against earlier printings and certain of these reprints may contain revisions. Similarly, publishers of some of the books listed in this section used original periodical text rather than the revised text of the authorized editions. No attempt has been made to indicate which of the texts occurs in the reprints.

Arrangement

The books are listed in order of their publication (*i.e.*, by month or by closer date) if such information has been determined. All books issued (for example) under date 1876, are grouped in the 1876 section. Postdated books (*e.g.*, a book dated 1876 but in fact issued late in 1875) are placed according to the date in the imprint or (lacking dated imprint) by date of copyright notice or other ascertainable date. Books for which the precise date of publication has not been determined, but for which the year of publication is known or assumed, are arranged alphabetically by title following the known chronology. In this group books issued by two or more publishers under the same title (*Poems* or *Poetical Works*, etc.) are listed alphabetically by place of publication; hence *Poems ...*, *Boston*, precedes *Poems ...*, *London.* If two or more books were issued by two or more publishers at the same place, the entries are arranged by publisher, hence *Poems, London ... Bohn*, precedes *Poems, London ... Routledge*, and both precede *Poems, London ... Walker.*

While preparing this list of reprints it became apparent that anything resembling completion is a virtual impossibility. To test this belief the Houghton, Mifflin & Company records

were checked for the representative years 1880 to 1889 inclusive; and so far as could be readily determined there were 159 printings of Longfellow's collected works during the period. Only volumes titled *Complete Poetical Works, Early Poems, Poems, Poetical Works, Prose Works, Works*, were considered in the survey. Printings of separate works (*The Song of Hiawatha, Outre-Mer*, etc.), or volumes issued under titles such as *Twenty Poems, Selections, Longfellow Birthday-Book*, etc., were ignored.

The 159 printings totalled nearly 525,000 volumes, with multi-volume sets counted as single volumes only. The figure represents, roughly, a sale of 1000 volumes per week during the period considered.

In some entries given below BAL has noted recognition of two or more printings; *e.g., The Poetical Works ... Household Edition with Illustrations*, Boston, 1886. But since BAL has located only an estimated half of the recorded 159 Houghton, Mifflin & Company printings, it is obvious that a like note may well apply to other entries. Further, and closer, study of both the books and of the publisher's records will doubtless identify other printings. Such identification will require assembling an inestimable number of volumes and an incalculable number of years.

For a study of Longfellow's incredible popularity as measured by sales see William Charvat's "Longfellow's Income from His Writings, 1840–1852," in *The Papers of the Bibliographical Society of America*, Vol. 38, First Quarter, 1944, pp. 9-21.

12273. French Exercises: Selected Chiefly from Wanostrocht, and Adapted to the Elements of French Grammar, by M. Lhomond ... by an Instructer. Second Edition.

Boston: Gray and Bowen. 1831.

Paper boards, cloth shelfback, printed paper label on spine. Noted only bound together with Longfellow's *Elements of French Grammar ... , Second Edition*, 1831.

12274. French Exercises ... by M. Lhomond, Third Edition.

Boston: Published by Charles Bowen. 1834.

Paper boards, cloth shelfback, printed paper label on spine. Noted only bound together with Longfellow's *Elements of French Grammar . . . , Third Edition,* 1834.

12275. Manuel de Proverbes Dramatiques. Troisième Édition.

Boston; Munroe et Compagnie 1840.

Cloth, printed paper label on spine. Deposited June 26, 1840.

12276. Voices of the Night . . . Second Edition.

Cambridge: Published by John Owen. M DCCC XL.

Paper boards, printed paper label on spine.

12277. Voices of the Night . . . Third Edition.

Cambridge: Published by John Owen. M DCCC XL.

Paper boards, printed paper label on spine. Noted only in large paper state: 10⅛″ x 6½″.

12278. Voices of the Night . . . Fourth Edition.

Cambridge: Published by John Owen. M DCCC XL.

Probably issued in paper boards, printed paper label on spine.

12279. Voices of the Night . . . Fifth Edition.

Cambridge: Published by John Owen. M DCCC XLI.

Paper boards, probably with printed paper label on spine.

12280. Poems on Slavery . . . Second Edition.

Cambridge: Published by John Owen. M DCCC XLII.

Printed paper wrapper. Deposited Dec. 24, 1842.

12281. Ballads and Other Poems . . . Second Edition.

Cambridge: Published by John Owen. M DCCC XLII.

Paper boards, probably printed paper label on spine.

12282. Ballads and Other Poems . . . Third Edition.

Cambridge: Published by John Owen. M DCCC XLII.

Paper boards, printed paper label on spine. Only large paper copies noted. Leaf: 10″ full x 6¼″.

12283. Ballads and Other Poems . . . Fourth Edition.

Cambridge: Published by John Owen. M DCCC XLII.

Paper boards, printed paper label on spine.

12284. Poems . . .

Cambridge Published by John Owen M DCCC XLII

2 Vols. Issued in boards, printed paper label on spine? Vol. 2 has been noted in what is probably publisher's leather.

12285. Voices of the Night . . . Sixth Edition.

Cambridge: Published by John Owen. M DCCC XLII.

Paper boards, printed paper label on spine.

12286. Voices of the Night, and Other Poems . . .

London: H. G. Clarke and Co., 66, Old Bailey. 1843.

Illuminated paper wrapper. Issued as Vol. 1 in *Clarke's English Helicon, American Series.* Listed PC Dec. 1, 1843.

12287. Ballads and Other Poems . . .

London: Edward Moxon, Dover Street. M DCCC XLIII.

Cloth; and, paper boards. Listed LG Dec. 9, 1843; PC Jan. 1, 1844.

12288. The Spanish Student . . .

London: Edward Moxon, Dover Street. M DCCC XLIII.

Paper boards, printed paper label on spine. Printed (probably in the United States) from the American setting. Listed LG Dec. 9, 1843; PC Jan. 1, 1844.

12289. Voices of the Night . . .

London: Edward Moxon, Dover Street. M DCCC XLIII.

Not seen as a separate. Located only as part of an omnibus volume bound together with Moxon's printing of *Ballads and Other Poems,* 1843; and, *The Spanish Student,* 1843. Binder's title *Longfellow's Ballads Poems & Drama.* The separate volume, *Voices of the Night,* listed PC Jan. 1, 1844.

12290. Ballads and Other Poems ... Fifth Edition.

Cambridge: Published by John Owen. M DCCC XLIII.

Probably issued in paper boards, printed paper label on spine.

12291. Longfellow's Ballads Poems & Drama

⟨London: Edward Moxon, 1843⟩

Cover-title. An omnibus volume made up of the sheets of *Ballads and Other Poems, Voices of the Night,* and *The Spanish Student;* see above under 1843.

12292. Poems on Slavery ... Third Edition.

Cambridge: Published by John Owen. M DCCC XLIII.

Issued in paper boards, printed paper label on spine? Only large paper copies noted. Leaf: 9⅞" x 6⅛".

12293. Voices of the Night ... Eighth Edition.

Cambridge: Published by John Owen. M DCCC XLIII.

Paper boards, printed paper label on spine.

12294. Ballads and Other Poems ... Seventh Edition.

Cambridge: Published by John Owen. M DCCC XLIV.

Paper boards, printed paper label on spine.

12295. Ballads and Other Poems ... Eighth Edition.

Cambridge: Published by John Owen. M DCCC XLIV.

Illuminated paper wrapper.

12296. Voices of the Night ... Ninth Edition.

Cambridge: Published by John Owen. M DCCC XLIV.

Paper boards, printed paper label on spine.

12297. Voices of the Night ... Tenth Edition.

Cambridge: Published by John Owen. M DCCC XLIV.

Illuminated paper wrapper.

12298. Voices of the Night, and Other Poems ...

London: H. G. Clarke and Co., 66, Old Bailey. 1844.

Illuminated paper wrapper. Issued in *Clarke's*

English Helicon, American Series. See above under 1843 for the first Clarke printing. Unsold sheets issued in cloth by George Slater, London, with his catalog inserted at back; quite probably the issue listed LG Jan. 3, 1852.

12299. Ballads and Other Poems ... Ninth Edition.

Cambridge: Published by John Owen. M DCCC XLV.

Illuminated paper wrapper; and, paper boards, printed paper label on spine.

12300. Novelas Españolas: Y Coplas de Manrique; con Algunos Pasages de Don Quijote, etc.

Por J. Griffin Brunswick ... J. Munroe, Boston ... Wiley y Putnam, N. York y Londres. M DCCC XLV.

Anonymous. Reprint of Longfellow's *Novelas Españolas,* 1830; and, *Coplas de Don Jorge Manrique,* 1833; with added material by another hand.

12301. The Poetical Works ... Complete Edition.

London: T. Allman, 42, Holborn Hill. 1845.

12302. Voices of the Night ...

Boston: Redding and Company. 1845.

Printed paper wrapper.

12303. Poems ... Second Edition.

Philadelphia: Carey and Hart. 1846.

Cloth; and, leather. "We have the pleasure to inform you that we have issued a Second Edition of Five Hundred Copies ..."—Letter, Carey & Hart, to Longfellow, Jan. 16, 1846; letter in H.

12304. Poems ... Third Edition.

Philadelphia: Carey and Hart. 1846.

Cloth? Leather? "... Prospect of a third edition being required in less than 8 or 10 weeks ..."—Letter, Carey & Hart, to Longfellow, Feb. 10, 1846; letter in H.

12305. The Poems of Henry Wadsworth Longfellow. Complete in One Volume.

New York: Harper and Brothers. 1846.

Printed paper wrapper. Deposited May 26, 1846. Listed WPLNL July 1846.

12306. Poems ... Fourth Edition.

Philadelphia: Carey and Hart. 1846.

Cloth; and, leather. "We have just printed & published a fourth illustrated Ed of your Poems ..."—Letter, Carey & Hart to Longfellow, Dec. 21, 1846; letter in H.

12307. The Belfry of Bruges and Other Poems ... Second Edition.

Cambridge: Published by John Owen. 1846.

12308. The Belfry of Bruges and Other Poems ... Third Edition.

Cambridge: Published by John Owen. 1846.

12309. The Belfry of Bruges ... Fourth Edition.

Cambridge: Published by John Owen. 1846.

Paper boards, printed paper label on spine. Only large paper copies noted. Leaf: 9½" scant x 6¼".

12310. Hyperion, a Romance ... Third Edition.

Cambridge: Published by John Owen. 1846.

12311. *Entry cancelled.*

12312. The Poems ... Complete in One Volume   Second Edition.

New York: Harper and Brothers. 1846.

Printed paper wrapper.

12313. A Psalm of Life.

London: Harvey and Darton. 1846.

Not seen. Entry on the basis of an advertisement in PC June 15, 1846, p. 181; offered as one of a series of poems by Longfellow and others. The series was offered under the descriptive: "Select Poetical Pieces, by various Authors, adapted for sticking or hanging on the walls of Schools, Mechanics' Institutes, &c; with Notes and Illustrative Extracts. By H. G. Adams ..."

12314. The Poems ... Complete in One Volume   Third Edition.

New York: Harper & Brothers. 1847.

Printed paper wrapper.

12315. The Poems ... Complete in One Volume   Fourth Edition.

New York: Harper and Brothers. 1847.

Printed paper wrapper.

12316. Poems ... with Illustrations by D. Huntington ... Fifth Edition.

Philadelphia: Carey and Hart. 1847.

Leather. Also cloth?

12317. Voices of the Night; and Other Poems ...

London: H. G. Clarke & Co., 278, Strand. 1848.

Probably issued in illuminated paper wrapper in *Clarke's English Helicon, American Series.* Listed Ath Oct. 28; PC Nov. 1, 1848.

12318. Poems ...

London: Kent & Richards, Paternoster Row. 1848.

Listed Ath Oct. 7; PC Nov. 1, 1848.

12319. Ballads and Other Poems ... Tenth Edition.

Boston: William D. Ticknor & Co. 1848.

Cloth; and, paper boards, printed paper label on spine.

12320. The Belfry of Bruges and Other Poems ...

London: H. G. Clarke and Co., 278, Strand. 1848.

Probably issued in illuminated paper wrapper in *Clarke's English Helicon, American Series.*

12321. Evangeline, a Tale of Acadie ...

Boston: William D. Ticknor & Company. 1848.

Large paper edition. 9⅝" x 6⅜".

12322. Outre-Mer, a Pilgrimage beyond the Sea ... Third Edition.

Boston: William D. Ticknor & Co. 1848.

12323. The Poems ... Fifth Edition.

New York: Harper and Brothers. 1848.

Printed paper wrapper.

12324. Voices of the Night ... Twelfth Edition.

Boston: William D. Ticknor & Co. 1848.

12325. Hyperion ...

London: George Slater, 252, Strand. 1849.

Advertised as in cloth. Issued in Slater's *Shilling Series.* Listed Ath May 26; PC June 1, 1849.

12326. Evangeline: A Tale of Acadie . . .

London: George Slater, 252, Strand. 1849

Pictorial paper wrapper. Also advertised and listed as in cloth. Issued as No. 4 of Slater's *Shilling Series*. Listed Ath June 30; PC July 16, 1849. Also issued ⟨n.d.⟩.

12327. The Belfry of Bruges and Other Poems . . .

London: George Slater, 252, Strand 1849

Cloth; and, pictorial paper wrapper. Issued in Slater's *Shilling Series*. Listed Ath Oct. 6; PC Oct. 15, 1849.

12328. Kavanagh, a Tale . . .

London: George Slater, 252, Strand. 1849.

Cloth; and, pictorial paper wrapper. Issued in Slater's *Shilling Series*. Listed PC Oct. 15, 1849.

12329. The Poems . . . Complete in One Volume.

New York: Harper and Brothers. 1849.

Printed paper wrapper.

12330. Poems . . . Seventh Edition.

Philadelphia: Carey and Hart. 1849.

12331. Evangeline . . .

London: David Bogue, 86, Fleet Street. MDCCCL.

Pictorial paper boards; and, leather. Listed Ath and LG Dec. 29, 1849. Distributed in United States with the imprint of Ticknor, Reed, and Fields, MDCCCL.

12332. Poems . . .

Boston: Ticknor, Reed, and Fields. M DCCC L.

6 Vols. Large paper edition. Probably issued in a variety of custom bindings. Noted as follows:

Unbound sheets. Wholly untrimmed. Leaf 10⅛" x 7³⁄₁₆".

Marbled boards sides, green leather shelfback and corners, edges marbled.

Roxburghe. Purple paper boards, leather shelfback and corners.

Note: Vol. 6 is not to be confused with the large paper printing of the first edition of *The Seaside and the Fireside*, 1850, q.v. As issued in this six-volume set the title-page reads: *Poems . . . A New Edition, Vol. VI. The Seaside and the Fireside . . .*

12333. The Poetical Works . . .

London: H. G. Clarke and Co., 4, Exeter Change. 1850.

Issued as No. 4 of *Clarke's Cabinet Library*. Listed PC Feb. 1, 1850.

12334. Voices of the Night; and Other Poems . . .

London: George Slater, 252, Strand. 1850.

Cloth; and, printed paper wrapper. Issued in Slater's *Shilling Series*. Listed Ath Feb. 2; PC Feb. 15, 1850.

12335. The Poetical Works . . .

London: George Routledge & Co., Soho Square M DCCC L.

An edition at 2/- listed LG Jan. 26, 1850; advertised as *now ready* Ath Feb. 9, 1850, described as in cloth, gilt edges. The preceding is presumed to be the format described above; leaf: 5³⁄₁₆" x 3¼". An edition at 4/-, described as *Library Edition*, offered in Ath March 9, 1850; listed PC March 15, 1850. Copies in leather offered for sale Ath Dec. 6, 1851.

12336. Poems . . . A New Edition.

Boston: Ticknor, Reed, and Fields. M DCCC L.

2 Vols. Cloth; leather; paper boards, printed paper label on spine. A Boston letter dated April 11 in LW April 20, 1850, states that "Messrs. Ticknor, Reed & Fields, are just upon the point of publishing Longfellow's *complete* poetical works, in two volumes duodecimo, with the last revisions of the author . . ." Advertised for April 20, LW May 4, 1850. The London (John Chapman) importation listed PC Dec. 16, 1850.

12337. Hyperion . . . Seventh Edition.

Boston: William D. Ticknor & Co. M DCCC L.

12338. Hyperion . . . Eighth Edition.

Boston: William D. Ticknor & Co. M DCCC L.

Another *"Eighth Edition"* was issued with the imprint of Ticknor, Reed & Fields, 1850.

12339. Outre-Mer, a Pilgrimage beyond the Sea . . . Fourth Edition.

Boston: Ticknor, Reed, and Fields. M DCCC L.

12340. Outre-Mer, a Pilgrimage beyond the Sea . . .

London: H. G. Clarke & Co., 4, Exeter Change 1850.

12341. Poems, Lyrical and Dramatic. Including the Seaside and the Fireside . . . with an Introductory Essay . . . by George Gilfillan . . . Second Edition.

Liverpool: John Walker, 7, Clayton Square. London: David Bogue; Hamilton, Adams, and Co.; John Johnstone. Edinburgh: Oliver & Boyd; John Johnstone. Dublin: J. M'Glashan. 1850.

Cloth?

12342. Voices of the Night, and Other Poems . . .

London: Charles Gilpin, 5, Bishopsgate Street. Edinburgh:—J. Menzies. MDCCCL.

Printed paper boards.

12343. Voices of the Night . . . with Illustrations by a Lady. ⟨Mrs. Lees⟩

⟨London⟩ Dickinson Bros, 114 New Bond Stt. ⟨sic⟩ MDCCCL.

Printed paper boards.

12344. The Prose Works . . .

London: David Bogue, Fleet Street. MDCCCLI.

Cloth. Also advertised as in leather. Listed Ath and LG May 10, 1851.

12345. The Poetical Works . . .

London: David Bogue, Fleet Street. MDCCCLI.

Cloth; and, leather. Listed PC Dec. 15, 1851.

12346. Hyperion, and Kavanagh . . .

London: George Routledge & Co., Soho Square. 1851.

12347. Outre-Mer, a Pilgrimage beyond the Sea . . . Second Edition.

London: Whittaker and Co.; Hamilton, Adams, & Co.; Henry Washbourne. Edinburgh: Adam & Charles Black. Liverpool: Edward Howell. 1851.

12348. Poems . . . in Two Volumes . . . a New Edition.

Boston: Ticknor, Reed, and Fields. M DCCC LI.

12349. Poems, Lyrical and Dramatic. Including The Seaside and The Fireside . . . with an Introductory Essay . . . by George Gilfillan . . . Third Edition.

London: Whittaker and Co.; Johnstone and Hunter; Hamilton, Adams, and Co.; David Bogue; Henry Washbourne. Edinburgh: Johnstone and Hunter; Oliver and Boyd. Dublin: J. M'Glashan. Liverpool: Edward Howell. 1851.

12350. Poems . . . with Illustrations by D. Huntington . . . Ninth Edition.

Philadelphia: Henry C. Baird, (Successor to E. L. Carey,) S. E. Cor. Market & Fifth Streets. 1851.

Leather. Also cloth?

12351. The Poetical Works . . .

London: George Routledge & Co., Soho Square M DCCC LI

Two formats issued: *Illustrated edition.* Leaf: $6\frac{7}{16}$" x $3\frac{15}{16}$". Noted only in what appears to be publisher's leather. Imprint of *Savill and Edwards* on reverse of title. *Unillustrated edition.* Leaf: $5\frac{1}{4}$" x $3\frac{1}{4}$". Noted only in what appears to be publisher's leather. Imprint of *Savill and Edwards* on p. ⟨400⟩.

12352. The Poetical Works . . . with Numerous Original Illustrations.

London: Published for J. Walker, 61 Conduit Street, Late of Liverpool, by David Bogue, 86, Fleet Street. 1851.

Cloth?

12353. The Poetical Works . . . with Numerous Original Illustrations.

London: J. Walker, 61, Conduit Street, Regent Street, Late of Liverpool. 1851.

12354. Poems . . . Illustrated . . . by Jane E. Benham, Birket Foster . . .

London: David Bogue, 86, Fleet Street. MDCCCLII.

Listed Ath and LG Nov. 29, 1851, in cloth; and, morocco. A *New Edition* listed Ath and LG March 27, 1852; PC April 1, 1852, as in cloth; and, morocco.

12355. Outre-Mer . . . Fifth Edition.

Boston: Ticknor, Reed, and Fields. M DCCC LII.

12356. Poems . . . Illustrated with Upwards of One Hundred Engravings on Wood, from Designs by Jane E. Benham, Birket Foster, etc.

Boston: Ticknor, Reed, and Fields. MDCCCLII

Cloth; and, leather.

12357. The Poetical Works ...

London: T. Nelson and Sons, Paternoster Row, and Edinburgh. MDCCCLII.

Listed PC July 16, 1852.

12358. Hyperion: A Romance ... a New Edition, Revised by the Author.

London: Printed and Published by Knight & Son, 11, Clerkenwell Close. 1852.

12359. Hyperion, and Kavanagh ...

London: George Routledge and Co., 2 & 3, Farringdon Street. 1852.

12360. Poems ... in Two Volumes ... a New Edition.

Boston: Ticknor, Reed, and Fields. M DCCC LII.

12361. The Poetical Works and Translations ...

London: H. G. Bohn, York Street, Covent Garden. 1852.

Two volumes in one; pp. 317, 312. Cloth?

12362. The Poetical Works ... with Illustrations by John Gilbert.

London: George Routledge & Co. Farringdon Street. 1852.

12363. The Poetical Works ... with Numerous Original Illustrations.

London: Published for J. Walker, 61, Conduit Street, by George Routledge & Co., Farringdon Street. 1852.

Also issued with the imprint: London: John Walker, 61, Conduit Street, Regent Street; Hamilton, Adams, & Co.; Simpkin, Marshall, & Co.; Robert Theobald; H. Washbourne; Routledge and Co., Farringdon Street. 1852.

12364. The Prose Works ... Hyperion, Outre-Mer, and Kavanagh.

London: H. G. Bohn, York Street, Covent Garden. 1852.

Three volumes in one; pp. 267, 309, 153.

12365. The Prose Works ... Complete in One Volume.

London: George Routledge and Co., Farringdon Street. 1852.

Two volumes in one; pp. 359, 268.

12366. The Prose Works ... Hyperion ... Kavanagh.

London: John Walker, 61, Conduit Street, Regent Street; Hamilton, Adams, & Co.; Simpkin, Marshall, & Co.; Robert Theobald; H. Washbourne; Routledge and Co., Farringdon Street. 1852.

12367. The Seaside and the Fireside: With Other Poems ...

Halifax: Milner and Sowerby. 1852.

12368. Voices of the Night; and Other Poems ... Illustrated with Sixty-Four Engravings on Wood ...

Boston: Ticknor, Reed, and Fields. MDCCCLII.

Cloth; and, leather.

12369. Voices of the Night; The Seaside and the Fireside; and Other Poems ... Illustrated with Sixty-Four Engravings on Wood ...

London: David Bogue, 86, Fleet Street. MDCCCLII.

12370. Hyperion: A Romance ... Illustrated .. by Birket Foster.

London: David Bogue, 86, Fleet Street. MDCCCLIII.

Listed Ath and LG Jan. 29; PC Feb. 16, 1853.

12371. The Poetical Works, Lyrical and Dramatic ... Introductory Essay by the Rev. G. Gilfillan ... Fourth Edition.

London: John Walker, 61, Conduit Street, Regent Street; Hamilton, Adams and Co.; Simpkin and Co.; R. Theobald; H. Washbourne. Edinburgh: Oliver and Boyd. Dublin: M'Glashan. Liverpool: E. Howell, Church Street. 1853.

According to contemporary notices issued in both cloth; and, leather. Listed LG Jan. 29; PC Feb. 16, 1853. Other contemporary notices suggest that the sheets may have been issued with the single Liverpool (Howell) imprint; see Ath Aug. 20, 1853.

12372. The Prose Works ... Complete in One Volume.

London: George Routledge and Co., Farringdon Street. 1853.

Two volumes in one; pp. 359, 268. Listed Ath Jan. 29, 1853; PC Feb. 1, 1853.

12373. Poems on Slavery, by Longfellow, Whittier, Southey, H. B. Stowe . . .

London: Clarke, Beeton, & Co., 148, Fleet Street. MDCCCLIII.

Cloth? Listed Ath March 26; PC April 15, 1853. Reviewed LG June 25, 1853.

12374. Evangeline . . . to Which Are Added Poems on Slavery, Voices of the Night, The Children of the Lord's Supper, and Other Poems . . .

London: Printed and Published by Knight and Son, Clerkenwell Close, and Sold by All Booksellers. ⟨n.d., 1853⟩

Listed PC Nov. 1, 1853, as in boards.

12375. Hyperion: A Romance . . . Illustrated . . . by Birket Foster.

Boston: Ticknor, Reed, and Fields. MDCCCLIII.

Sheets of the London (Bogue, 1853) printing with cancel title-leaf.

12376. Hyperion . . . Illustrated with Nearly One Hundred Engravings . . . from Drawings by Birket Foster. Second Edition.

London: David Bogue, 86, Fleet Street. ⟨1853⟩

12377. Outre-Mer: A Pilgrimage beyond the Sea . . . to Which Are Added, Essays on the Italian and French Languages and Poetry . . .

London: G. Routledge & Co., Farringdon Street. MDCCCLIII.

Cloth; and, printed paper boards. The added essays had prior publication in *The Poets and Poetry of Europe*, 1845.

12378. Poems . . . in Two Volumes . . . a New Edition.

Boston: Ticknor, Reed, and Fields. M DCCC LIII.

Cloth; and, leather.

12379. Poems . . . with Illustrations by D. Huntington . . . Tenth Edition.

Philadelphia: Henry C. Baird, (Successor to E. L. Carey,) No. 7 Hart's Buildings, Sixth Street above Chestnut. 1853.

12380. The Poetical Works . . .

Halifax: Milner and Sowerby. 1853.

The vignette title-page is dated 1852.

12381. The Poetical Works . . .

London: G. Routledge & Co., Farringdon Street. MDCCCLIII.

12382. The Prose Works . . . Complete in One Volume . . .

London: George Routledge and Co. Farringdon Street. 1853.

12383. The Poetical Works . . . Complete Edition, with "The Seaside and the Fireside."

London: Knight and Son, Clerkenwell Close. 1854.

Listed LG March 4; PC March 15, 1854.

12384. Poems . . . Illustrated with Upwards of One Hundred Engravings on Wood, from Designs by Jane E. Benham, Birket Foster, etc.

London: David Bogue, 86, Fleet Street. MDCCCLIV.

A copy in BA inscribed by early owner May 21, 1854.

12385. Evangeline, Voices of the Night, Ballads, and Poems on Slavery . . . the Fourth Thousand. Illustrated Edition.

London: George Routledge & Co. Farringdon Street. 1854.

Cloth; and, printed paper boards.

12386. . . . Hyperion. Authorized Edition.

Dessau: Katz Brothers. 1854 . . .

At head of title: *The Works of Henry W. Longfellow. Vol. III.* Probably issued in printed paper wrapper. Issued as *Standard American Authors,* Vol. 6.

12387. Poems . . . in Two Volumes . . . a New Edition.

Boston: Ticknor, Reed, and Fields. M DCCC LIV.

12388. Poems . . . in Two Volumes . . . a New Edition.

Boston: Ticknor and Fields. M DCCC LIV.

12389. . . . Poems. Authorized Edition.

Dessau: Katz Brothers. 1854 . . .

At head of title: *The Works of Henry W. Longfellow. Vol. I.* Probably issued in printed paper wrapper. Issued as *Standard American Authors,* Vol. 4.

12390. Poems . . . New Edition.

London: David Bogue, Fleet Street. MDCCCLIV.

12391. Poems . . . with Illustrations by D. Hunt-ington . . . Tenth Edition.

Philadelphia: Henry Carey Baird, (Successor to E. L. Carey,) No. 7 Hart's Buildings, Sixth Street, above Chestnut. 1854.

Cloth? See above under 1853 for another "tenth edition."

12392. The Poetical Works . . .

London: T. Nelson and Sons, Paternoster Row; and Edinburgh. MDCCCLIV.

Cloth?

12393. . . . The Spanish Student. Evangeline. The Golden Legend. Authorized Edition.

Dessau: Katz Brothers. 1854 . . .

At head of title: *The Works of Henry W. Longfellow. Vol. II.* Printed paper wrapper. Is-sued as *Standard American Authors,* Vol. 5.

12394. Poems . . . Illustrated with Upwards of One Hundred Engravings on Wood, from Designs by Jane E. Benham, Birket Foster, etc.

Boston: Ticknor and Fields. MDCCCLV.

Made up of sheets of the London (Bogue, 1854) printing with cancel title-leaf.

12395. Poems . . . in Two Volumes . . . a New Edition.

Boston: Ticknor and Fields. M DCCC LV.

12396. Poems . . . Illustrated with Upwards of One Hundred Engravings, Designed by John Gilbert, Engraved by Dalziel Brothers. A New Edition.

London: George Routledge & Co. Farringdon Street. MDCCCLV.

The above (a singleton title-leaf) is bound to-gether with gatherings B-I, K-U, X-Z, AA-II, KK-UU, xx; and, duplicate gatherings C-I, K-L, of *The Poetical Works . . . ,* London, Routledge, MDCCC-LVI, printing. The title-leaf is presumed to be a trial printing; the accompanying gather-ings surplus sheets. Bound in unstamped cloth. On the front pastedown is the following in-scription in ink: *Imperfect Copy—wanting Por-trait—and all after page 344 George Routledge & Co.* ‹and, the following added in pencil:› *duplicate of pp. 9-80.* The only located example is in H. Here listed for the record only.

12397. Poems . . . with Illustrations by D. Hunt-ington, Engraved by American Artists. Tenth Edition.

Philadelphia: Henry Carey Baird, (Successor to E. L. Carey,) No. 7 Hart's Buildings, Sixth Street, above Chestnut. 1855.

See above under 1853 and 1854 for other print-ings identified as *Tenth Edition.*

12398. The Poetical Works . . .

T. Nelson and Sons, London; Edinburgh; and New York. MDCCCLV.

Cloth; and, printed paper boards. The boards binding has been noted in two forms; sequence, if any, unknown. A: No inserted catalog; end papers imprinted with advertisements. B: In-serted terminal catalog dated 1854; yellow end papers. Also issued in printed paper boards bound together with Nelson's printing of *The Song of Hiawatha,* London, 1855.

12399. The Poetical Works . . . with Illustra-tions by John Gilbert

London: George Routledge & Co. Farringdon Street. 1855.

Cloth? *Not seen.* Entry on basis of photostats.

12400. The Song of Hiawatha . . .

T. Nelson and Sons, London; Edinburgh; and New York. MDCCCLV.

Probably issued as a separate volume in cloth. Noted only bound together with Nelson's edi-tion of *The Poetical Works . . . ,* 1855.

12401. The Song of Hiawatha . . .

London: G. Routledge and Co., Farringdon Street. 1856.

Advertised as in paper boards; and, cloth. Listed LG Dec. 8; PC Dec. 17, 1855.

12402. The Poetical Works . . . a New Edition, Illustrated . . . by John Gilbert . . .

Boston: Ticknor and Fields. M.DCCC.LVI.

Cloth; and, leather. Printed in England. De-posited Dec. 24, 1855.

12403. The Poetical Works . . . a New Edition, Illustrated . . .

London: George Routledge & Co. Farringdon Street. M.DCCC.LVI.

Cloth; and, leather. Listed (this edition?) PC Jan. 16, 1856.

12404. The Poetical Works . . . a New Complete Edition, Including the Song of Hiawatha. With Illustrations by John Gilbert.

London: George Routledge and Co. Farringdon Street. 1856.

Listed (this edition?) PC Jan. 16, 1856. A copy in DEV inscribed by early owner April 23, 1856.

12405. The Prose Works . . . Hyperion . . . Kavanagh.

London: Bickers and Bush, Leicester Square. MDCCCLVI.

Listed Ath Dec. 6; PC Dec. 15, 1856.

12406. Poems . . . New and Complete Edition.

London: David Bogue, Fleet Street. MDCCCLVI.

Noted in leather only. Listed (this printing?) PC Feb. 2, 1857.

12407. Hyperion: A Romance . . . a New Edition, Revised by the Author.

London: Printed and Published by Knight & Son, 11, Clerkenwell Close. 1856.

12408. Outre-Mer . . . Eighth Edition.

Boston: Ticknor and Fields. M DCCC LVI.

12409. Poems . . . in Two Volumes . . . a New Edition.

Boston: Ticknor and Fields. M DCCC LVI.

12410. Poems . . . Authorized Edition.

Leipzig: Alphons Dürr . . . 1856.

Printed paper wrapper. *Dürr's Collection of Standard American Authors*, Vol. 4. Issued as *The Works of . . . Longfellow*, Vol. 1.

Note: The full set comprises seven volumes as follows:

1: *Poems*, 1856. Issued as Vol. 4 of the series.

2: *The Spanish Student* . . . , 1856. Issued as Vol. 5 of the series.

3: *Hyperion*, 1856. Issued as Vol. 6 of the series.

4: *Kavanagh* . . . , 1858. Issued as Vol. 7 of the series.

5: *The Song of Hiawatha*, 1856. Issued as Vol. 17 of the series.

6: *The Courtship of Miles Standish* . . . , 1859. Issued as Vol. 39 of the series. Not identified as the sixth volume in the set but listed as such on the wrapper of Dürr's printing of *Tales of a Wayside Inn*, 1864.

7: *Tales of a Wayside Inn* . . . , 1864. Issued as Vol. 66 of the series. Not identified as the seventh volume in the set.

12411. Poems . . . Tenth Edition.

Philadelphia: Henry Carey Baird, (Successor to E. L. Carey,) No. 7 Hart's Buildings, Sixth Street, above Chestnut. 1856.

Leather. Also cloth? See above under 1853, 1854, and 1855, for other printings identified as the *Tenth Edition*.

12412. The Poetical Works . . . with Prefatory Notice. Eight Engravings on Steel.

Edinburgh: Gall & Inglis, 38 North Bridge. ⟨1856⟩

Cloth? Date from end of prefatory note.

12413. The Poetical Works . . . Authorized Edition. In Two Volumes . . .

Leipzig Bernhard Tauchnitz 1856.

Printed paper wrapper. Issued as Nos. 347, 348, in *Collection of British Authors*. See No. 12464. Two printings of unknown sequence noted; the order is arbitrary. A: As above. With the statement *In Two Volumes* on the title-pages. B: As above but without the statement *In Two Volumes* on the title-pages.

12414. Poetical Works . . . Illustrated with Upwards of One Hundred and Sixty Engravings on Wood, from Designs by Jane E. Benham, Birket Foster, Etc.

London: David Bogue, 86, Fleet Street. MDCCCLVI.

Noted only in publisher's leather.

12415. The Poetical Works . . . Complete Edition, with "The Seaside and the Fireside."

London: Knight and Son, Clerkenwell Close. 1856.

12416. The Song of Hiawatha . . .

Boston: Ticknor and Fields. M DCCC LVI.

On copyright page: *Thirteenth Thousand.* Large paper edition. Leaf: 8¼" x 5⁹⁄₁₆".

12417. The Song of Hiawatha . . .

Leipzig: Alphons Dürr. 1856 . . .

Printed paper wrapper. *Dürr's Collection of Standard American Authors*, Vol. 17. Issued as *The Works of . . . Longfellow*, Vol. 5. See *Poems* . . . , Leipzig, 1856, above, for a list of volumes in the set.

12418. The Song of Hiawatha . . . New Edition, with the Author's Latest Corrections.

London: David Bogue, Fleet Street. MDCCCLVI.

Basically a reprint. Contains, however, certain of the textual alterations described in the entry for the first edition. Precise publication date not known; hence exact status in doubt.

12419. The Spanish Student. Evangeline. The Golden Legend . . . Authorized Edition.

Leipzig: Alphons Dürr . . . 1856.

Printed paper wrapper. *Dürr's Collection of Standard American Authors*, Vol. 5. Issued as *The Works of . . . Longfellow*, Vol. 2. See *Poems . . .* , Leipzig, 1856, above, for a list of volumes in the set.

12420. Poems . . . Complete in Two Volumes . . .

Boston: Ticknor and Fields. M DCCC LVII.

Issued in the *Blue and Gold* series. Deposited Dec. 15, 1856.

12421. The Prose Works . . .

London: David Bogue, Fleet Street. MD.CCC.LVII.

Issued in cloth according to listing in PC Feb. 2, 1857. *Note:* In June, 1857, Kent & Company took over the Bogue firm, after Bogue's death in 1856.

12422. Outre-Mer . . . to Which Are Added, Essays . . .

London: G. Routledge & Co., Farringdon Street. 1857.

The essays are reprinted from *Poets and Poetry of Europe*, 1845.

12423. A Pilgrimage beyond the Sea; (A Book for a Quiet Hour) . . .

Liverpool: Edward Howell, Church Street. 1857.

Printed paper boards. Reprint of *Outre-Mer.*

12424. Poems . . . in Two Volumes . . . a New Edition.

Boston: Ticknor and Fields. M DCCC LVII.

12425. The Poetical Works . . . a New Edition, Illustrated . . . by John Gilbert . . .

London: George Routledge & Co. Farringdon Street. M.DCCC.LVII.

Leather.

12426. The Poetical Works . . . New Edition.

London: G. Routledge & Co., Farringdon Street. MDCCCLVII.

12427. Kavanagh . . .

London: W. Kent and Co. (Late D. Bogue), 86, Fleet Street. MDCCCLVIII.

Cloth. Also issued in leather according to contemporary notices. Listed Ath and LG Nov. 14; PC Nov. 16, 1857.

12428. Kavanagh. Outre-Mer . . . Authorized Edition.

Leipzig: Alphons Dürr . . . 1858.

Printed paper wrapper. *Dürr's Collection of Standard American Authors*, Vol. 7. Issued as *The Works of . . . Longfellow,* Vol. 4. See *Poems . . .* , Leipzig, 1856, above, for a list of the volumes in the set.

12429. Poems . . . Complete in Two Volumes . . .

Boston: Ticknor and Fields. M DCCC LVIII.

Issued in the *Blue and Gold* series. *Note:* Some copies lack the period following *Fields* in the imprint.

12430. The Poetical Works . . .

London: T. Nelson and Sons, Paternoster Row; Edinburgh; and New York. MDCCCLVIII.

Cloth?

12431. The Voices of the Night, Ballads, and Other Poems . . . with Illustrations by John Gilbert, Engraved by the Brothers Dalziel.

London: George Routledge & Co. Farringdon Street. 1858.

12432. The Poetical Works . . . a New Complete Edition Including Miles Standish and Other Poems. With Illustrations by John Gilbert, ⟨sic⟩

London: Routledge, Warnes, and Routledge, Farringdon Street. 1859.

Not seen. Entry on the basis of photostats. Listed Ath and LG Nov. 27; PC Dec. 1, 1858.

12433. The Courtship of Miles Standish and Other Poems . . . with Twenty-Five Illustrations by John Gilbert, Engraved by the Brothers Dalziel.

Boston: Ticknor and Fields. MDCCCLIX.

Noted only in leather. Also issued in cloth?

12434. The Courtship of Miles Standish, and Other Poems ... Authorized Edition.

Leipzig: Alphons Dürr ... 1859.

Printed paper wrapper. *Dürr's Collection of Standard American Authors*, Vol. 39. Not identified as the sixth volume of *The Works of ... Longfellow*, but listed as such on the wrapper of Dürr's printing of *Tales of a Wayside Inn*, 1864. See *Poems ...*, Leipzig, 1856, for a list of the volumes in the set.

12435. The Courtship of Miles Standish, and Other Poems ... Illustrated from Designs by John Absolon, Birket Foster, and Matthew S. Morgan ...

London: W. Kent & Co. (Late D. Bogue), 86, Fleet Street. MDCCCLIX.

12436. The Courtship of Miles Standish, and Other Poems ... with Illustrations by John Gilbert.

London: G. Routledge & Co. Farringdon Street. 1859.

Printed paper wrapper?

12437. The Courtship of Miles Standish, and Other Poems ... with Twenty-Five Illustrations by John Gilbert ...

London: Routledge, Warnes, & Routledge, Farringdon Street. 1859.

12438. Outre-Mer ... Ninth Edition.

Boston: Ticknor and Fields. M DCCC LIX.

12439. Poems ... Complete in Two Volumes ...

Boston: Ticknor and Fields. M DCCC LIX.

Blue and Gold edition. *Note:* Some copies lack the period after *Fields* in the imprint of Vol. 2.

12440. Poems ... in Two Volumes ... a New Edition.

Boston: Ticknor and Fields. M DCCC LIX.

12441. Poems ... New and Complete Edition.

Edinburgh: William P. Nimmo, 2 St⟨sic⟩ David Street. M.DCCC.LIX.

Red line edition.

12442. The Poetical Works ...

London: T. Nelson and Sons, Paternoster Row; Edinburgh; and New York. MDCCCLIX.

12443. Poems ... New and Complete Edition.

London: W. Kent & Co. (Late D ⟨sic⟩ Bogue), Fleet Street. MDCCCLX.

Issued in cloth according to contemporary listings. Listed LG Nov. 5; PC Nov. 15, 1859.

12444. Poems ... Complete in Two Volumes ...

Boston: Ticknor and Fields. M DCCC LX.

Blue and Gold edition.

12445. Poems ... in Two Volumes ... a New Edition.

Boston: Ticknor and Fields. M DCCC LX.

12446. The Poetical Works ... New Edition.

London: Routledge, Warne, and Routledge, Farringdon Street. 1861.

Listed (this edition presumably) PC March 1, 1861.

12447. The Poetical Works ... Including ... Translations and Notes. Illustrated with Above Two Hundred Engravings on Wood, from Designs by Birket Foster, John Gilbert, G. H. Thomas, John Absolon, etc.

London: Henry G. Bohn, York Street, Covent Garden. 1861.

Noted only in leather. A copy (at H) presented to Longfellow by the publisher Sept. 23, 1861.

12448. Poems ... Complete in Two Volumes ...

Boston: Ticknor and Fields. M DCCC LXI.

Blue and Gold edition.

12449. Poems ... in Two Volumes ... a New Edition.

Boston: Ticknor and Fields. M DCCC LXI.

12450. The Poetical Works ... a New Edition, Illustrated with Upwards of One Hundred Designs, Drawn by John Gilbert ...

London: Routledge, Warne, & Routledge, Farringdon Street. M.DCCC.LXI.

Cloth?

12451. Prose Works ... Complete in Two Volumes ...

Boston: Ticknor and Fields. M DCCC LXI.

Blue and Gold edition.

12452. The Poems ...

London: Bell and Daldy, 186, Fleet Street, and Sampson Low, Son, and Co. 47, Ludgate Hill. 1862.

According to contemporary notices issued in wrapper; cloth; "superior binding for presents and prizes"; and several styles of leather. Listed (cloth; and, paper) PC Nov. 15, 1861.

12453. The Poetical Works ... Eight Engravings on Steel.

Halifax: Milner and Sowerby. 1862.

Listed PC Dec. 31, 1862; Ath Jan. 3, 1863.

12454. Poems ... Complete in Two Volumes ...

Boston: Ticknor and Fields. M DCCC LXII.

Blue and Gold edition. Vol. 1: pp. 375; Vol. 2: pp. 405.

12455. Poems ... Complete in Two Volumes ...

Boston: Ticknor and Fields. M DCCC LXII.

Blue and Gold edition. Vol. 1: pp. 420; Vol. 2: pp. 467.

12456. Poems ... Complete in Two Volumes ...

Boston: Ticknor and Fields. M DCCC LXII.

Polished V cloth: green and purple noted. Front cover dated *1862;* or, *1863.*

12457. The Poetical Works ... Complete Edition. With Illustrations by John Gilbert.

London: Routledge, Warne, and Routledge, Farringdon Street. 1862.

Cloth?

12458. The Poetical Works ...

London: T. Nelson and Sons, Paternoster Row; Edinburgh; and New York. MDCCCLXII.

12459. In the Woods with Bryant, Longfellow, and Halleck ...

New York: James G. Gregory, Publisher. MDCCCLXIII.

"When Woods Were Green;" otherwise, "Prelude" to *Voices of the Night,* 1839. For comment see entry No. 1675.

12460. The Ship of State. Issued by the Loyal National League at the Sumter Mass Meeting, April 11, 1863, at Union Square ...

Issued from the Offices of the Rebellion Record, 441 and 448 Broadway, New-York. ⟨1863⟩

Single leaf. Printed on recto only. Extract from "The Building of the Ship" in *The Seaside and the Fireside,* 1850.

12461. Poems ... Complete in Two Volumes ...

Boston: Ticknor and Fields. M DCCC LXIII.

Blue and Gold edition.

12462. Poems ... Complete in Two Volumes ...

Boston: Ticknor and Fields. M DCCC LXIII.

Printed from the altered plates of the *Blue and Gold* edition.

12463. Poems ... in Two Volumes ... a New Edition.

Boston: Ticknor and Fields. M DCCC LXIII.

12464. The Poetical Works ... Authorized Edition. Vol. III.

Leipzig Bernhard Tauchnitz 1863.

Printed paper wrapper. Issued as No. 687 of the *Coll. of British Authors.* See entry 12413. Letter, Tauchnitz to Longfellow (original in H), Jan. 8, 1864: "... Thank you ... for the sheets of *Tales of a Wayside* ⟨sic⟩. According to your wish I have formed a small volume from this poem, *The Courtship of Miles Standish* and adding *Birds of Passage.* It will give me great pleasure of sending you copies of my edition by the first opportunity ..."

12465. The Poetical Works ... Complete Edition. With Illustrations by John Gilbert.

London: Routledge, Warne, and Routledge, Farringdon Street. 1863.

12466. Tales of a Wayside Inn ... ⟨Author's Edition⟩

London: Routledge, Warne, and Routledge, Farringdon Street. 1864.

Printed paper wrapper. Pp. 140. Terminal catalog dated *November, 1863.* On front: *Author's Edition.* Announced as *ready* Ath Nov. 28, 1863. Listed Ath Dec. 5; PC Dec. 8, 1863.

12467. Forest Scenes by William Cullen Bryant, Henry Wadsworth Longfellow, Fitz-Greene Halleck, Alfred B. Street, Illustrated by John A. Hows ...

New York: Published by Hurd and Houghton. The Riverside Press: Cambridge. ⟨1864⟩

Reprinted and reissued not before 1880 imprinted: Boston: Houghton, Mifflin and Company. The Riverside Press, Cambridge. ⟨1864⟩

"When Woods Were Green," pp. ⟨46⟩-56; otherwise "Prelude" to *Voices of the Night,* 1839.

12468. Poems ... Complete in Two Volumes

Boston: Ticknor and Fields. M DCCC LXIV.

Blue and Gold edition.

12469. Poems ... Complete in Two Volumes ...

Boston: Ticknor and Fields. M DCCC LXIV.

On binding: *1863*

12470. Poems ... in Two Volumes ... a New Edition.

Boston: Ticknor and Fields. M DCCC LXIV.

Cloth?

12471. The Poetical Works ...

Edinburgh: William P. Nimmo. 1864.

Noted only in publisher's leather.

12472. The Poetical Works ... Eight Engravings on Steel.

Halifax: Milner and Sowerby. 1864.

12473. The Poetical Works ... Complete Edition. With Illustrations by John Gilbert, etc.

London: Routledge, Warne, and Routledge, Farringdon Street. 1864.

12474. Prose Works ... Complete in Two Volumes ...

Boston: Ticknor and Fields. M DCCC LXIV.

Blue and Gold edition.

12475. Prose Works ... Complete in Two Volumes ...

Boston: Ticknor and Fields. M DCCC LXIV.

On binding: *Longfellow's Prose 1865*

12476. The Prose Works ... Illustrated by John Gilbert. A New Edition.

London: Routledge, Warne, and Routledge, Farringdon Street. 1864.

12477. Tales of a Wayside Inn ... Authorized Edition.

Leipzig: Alphons Dürr. 1864.

Printed paper wrapper. Issued as *Dürr's Collection of Standard American and British Authors,* Vol. 66. Not identified as Vol. 7 of *The Works of ... Longfellow.* See *Poems ... ,* Leipzig, 1856.

12478. The Poetical Works ... Complete Edition.

London: George Routledge and Sons, Broadway, Ludgate Hill. 1865.

Issued in two styles: cloth; and, cloth, leather shelfback. Also issued (later) in calf; morocco; boards. Listed (prematurely?) in Bkr March 31, 1865, as in cloth; and, cloth, leather shelfback. Listed PC July 1, 1865, cloth; cloth, leather shelfback. Listed Ath July 1, 1865, cloth. Listed Bkr July 31, 1865, cloth; cloth, leather shelfback. Listed PC Aug. 1, 1865, cloth; cloth, leather shelfback. Advertised as *in calf and morocco* Ath Aug. 19, 1865. Listed as in boards PC Nov. 15, 1865. Listed PC Dec. 18, 1865, cloth; cloth, leather shelfback; boards.

12479. Hyperion ...

London: Alfred William Bennett, 5, Bishopsgate Without. MDCCCLXV.

Cloth. Also morocco according to advertisements. Listed Ath Nov. 5; Bkr Dec. 10; PC Dec. 15, 1864.

12480. Poems ... Complete in Two Volumes ·•·•·•·

Boston: Ticknor and Fields. M DCCC LXV.

Blue and Gold edition.

12481. The Poems of Henry Wadsworth Longfellow.

London: Bell and Daldy, 186, Fleet Street. 1865.

Cloth?

12482. The Poetical Works ... a New Edition, Illustrated with One Hundred and Forty-Nine Designs, Drawn by John Gilbert, Engraved by the Brothers Dalziel.

London: Routledge, Warne, and Routledge, Broadway, Ludgate Hill. M.DCCC.LXV.

12483. Prose Works ... Complete in Two Volumes ...

Boston: Ticknor and Fields. M DCCC LXVI.

On binding: *1865*

12484. Companion Poets ... Longfellow's Household Poems. Tennyson's Songs for All Seasons. Browning's Lyrics of Life.

Boston: Ticknor and Fields. 1866.

Cloth; and, leather. An omnibus volume made up of the sheets of Longfellow's *Household Poems*, 1865; Tennyson's *Songs for All Seasons*, Boston, 1865; Robert Browning's *Lyrics of Life*, Boston, 1865.

12485. The Poetical Works ... Complete Edition. With Illustrations by John Gilbert.

London: George Routledge and Sons, Broadway, Ludgate Hill. 1866.

Issued in cloth according to contemporary notices. Listed PC April 16; Bkr April 30, 1866.

12486. Longfellow's Poetical Works ⟨cover-title⟩

Boston Ticknor and Fields 1866

4 Vols., as follows:

1: The Poetical Works ... Revised Edition ... Voices of the Night. Ballads and Other Poems. Poems on Slavery. The Spanish Student.

2: The Poetical Works ... Revised Edition ... The Belfry of Bruges and Other Poems. Evangeline. The Seaside and the Fireside.

3: The Poetical Works ... Revised Edition ... The Golden Legend. The Courtship of Miles Standish. Birds of Passage.

4: The Poetical Works ... Revised Edition ... The Song of Hiawatha. Tales of a Wayside Inn. Birds of Passage.

12487. Poems ... Complete in Two Volumes

⟨• • •⟩

Boston: Ticknor and Fields. M DCCC LXVI.

Blue and Gold edition.

12488. The Poetical Works ... Complete Edition.

London: George Routledge and Sons, Broadway, Ludgate Hill. 1866.

Probably issued in cloth.

12489. Tales of a Wayside Inn ... with Illustrations by John Gilbert.

Boston: Ticknor and Fields. 1866.

Cloth; and, leather.

12490. Companion Poets ... Longfellow's Household Poems. Tennyson's Songs for All Seasons. Browning's Lyrics of Life.

Boston: Ticknor and Fields. 1867.

Cloth. Also leather? An omnibus volume made up of the sheets of Longfellow's *Household Poems*, 1865; Tennyson's *Songs for All Seasons*, Boston, 1865; Browning's *Lyrics of Life*, Boston, 1866.

A copy in H inscribed by early owner *Christmas, 1866.*

12491. The Poetical Works ... Complete Edition.

Boston: Ticknor and Fields. 1867.

Issued in cloth; *Diamond Edition* stamped on binding. Also issued in leather without the identifying statement, *Diamond Edition,* on binding. A copy at H received from the publisher April 18, 1867.

12492. ... The Poetical Works ... (Including Recent Poems.) With Steel Portrait ...

London: Frederick Warne and Co. Bedford Street, Covent Garden. 1867.

Pp. 628. At head of title: The Chandos Poets. For a comment on this reprint see entry 12145.

12493. The Divine Comedy of Dante Alighieri. Translated by Henry Wadsworth Longfellow ...

London: George Routledge & Sons, The Broadway, Ludgate, 1867.

Three volumes in one. See in *Section I* for prior publication in three volumes. Listed PC Aug. 15, 1867.

12494. Noël.

⟨Philadelphia: Ringwalt & Brown, Printers, 111 and 113 South Fourth Street, 1867⟩

Printed paper wrapper. Fifty numbered copies only. Contains the text of Longfellow's poem (in French) together with English translation by John E. Norcross. A copy in H has a covering presentation letter from Norcross to Charles Sumner dated Aug. 30, 1867. For an earlier separate printing see in *Section I* under 1864.

12495. The Divine Comedy of Dante Alighieri ... Authorized Edition ...

Leipzig Bernhard Tauchnitz 1867.

Printed paper wrapper. 3 Vols. Nos. 901-903 in *Collection of British Authors* series.

Vol. 1 listed *Börsenblatt für den deutschen Buchhandel* (Leipzig) May 7, 1867; Vol. 2 listed June 18, 1867. Vol. 3 issued after July 12, 1867. "... I hope that the sheets of vol. 3, which you have been kind enough to send to Messrs Leypoldt & Holt will soon reach me ...''—Letter, Tauchnitz to Longfellow, July 12, 1867 (letter in H).

12496. Evangeline, a Tale of Acadie ... with Illustrations by F.O.C. Darley.

Boston: Ticknor and Fields. 1867.

12497. Poems ... Complete in Two Volumes ...

Boston: Ticknor and Fields. M DCCC LXVII

Blue and Gold edition. Noted only in publisher's(?) leather.

12498. The Poetical Works ... a New Edition, Illustrated with One Hundred and Seventy-Four Designs, Drawn by John Gilbert ...

London: George Routledge and Sons, the Broadway, Ludgate. 1867.

Advertised (this edition?) PC Dec. 8, 1866, as *new*. Possibly the edition listed in *English Catalogue* as a March, 1867, publication.

12499. The Poetical Works ... Illustrated by John Gilbert Complete Edition

London George Routledge and Sons The Broadway, Ludgate 1867

Cloth; and, leather. Red line edition.

12500. The Poetical Works ... Complete Edition, Containing "Flower de Luce," etc. With Illustrations by John Gilbert.

London: George Routledge and Sons, the Broadway, Ludgate. 1867.

Noted only in publisher's leather.

12501. The Works ... Vol. II. The Spanish Student. Evangeline. The Golden Legend. Authorized Edition.

Leipzig: Alphons Dürr. 1867.

Printed paper wrapper. *Dürr's Collection of Standard American and British Authors*, Vol. 5. For the first Dürr printing of this volume see under 1856.

12502. The Poetical Works ... Complete Edition.

Boston: Ticknor and Fields. 1868.

Issued in cloth with binding stamped: *Diamond Edition*. Also issued in leather without *Diamond Edition* stamped on binding. A copy (cloth) in H inscribed by Longfellow Feb. 27, 1868.

12503. The Poetical Works ... Edited and Prefaced by Robert Buchanan ...

London: Edward Moxon and Co. 44, Dover Street, W. 1868 <–1869>

2 Vols.

Vol. 1: Narrative Poems, and Ballads. 1868.

Vol. 2: Dramas, Moralities, Songs, &c., &c. 1869.

Vol. 1 listed Ath Oct. 17; PC Nov. 16, 1868. Vol. 2 listed Ath June 5, 1869.

12504. The Poetical Works ... Including ... Translations and Notes. Illustrated with Nearly Two Hundred and Fifty Engravings ...

Boston: Ticknor and Fields. 1868.

Noted only in leather.

12505. The Poetical Works ... Illustrated by F. Gilbert.

London: John Dicks, 313, Strand; and All Booksellers. 1868.

Cloth. Also printed paper wrapper?

12506. The Poetical Works ... Complete Edition, Containing "Flower de Luce," etc. With Illustrations by John Gilbert.

London: George Routledge and Sons, the Broadway, Ludgate. 1868.

12507. Poems ... Complete in Two Volumes ...

Boston: Fields, Osgood, & Co., Successors to Ticknor and Fields. 1869.

Blue and Gold edition.

12508. The Poems ...

London: Bell and Daldy, York Street, Covent Garden. 1869.

12509. The Poetical Works ... Complete Edition.

Boston: Fields, Osgood, & Co., Successors to Ticknor and Fields. 1869.

Diamond Edition.

12510. The Poetical Works ... Complete Edition, with Illustrations.

Boston: Fields, Osgood, & Co. Successors to Ticknor and Fields. 1870.

Red line edition. Listed (presumably this edition) PC Nov. 1, 1869. Advertised by Trübner as an importation Bkr Dec. 13, 1869.

12511. The Building of the Ship . . .

Boston: Fields, Osgood, & Co. 1870.

Cloth; and, leather. First complete, separate edition; reprinted from *The Seaside and the Fireside,* 1850. Advertised for Nov. 10, ALG Nov. 1, 1869. Deposited Nov. 9, 1869. Listed ALG Dec. 1, 1869; PC Feb. 1, 1870. Issued, not before 1880, with the Houghton, Mifflin and Co. monogram on the front cover and spine. Reprinted by Houghton, Mifflin and Co. under date ⟨1869; *i.e.,* not before 1880⟩.

12512. The Complete Works of Henry Wadsworth Longfellow Revised Edition . . .

Boston: Fields, Osgood, & Co., Successors to Ticknor and Fields. 1870.

4 Vols. Binding dated 1866 ⟨sic⟩.

1: Voices of the Night. Ballads and Other Poems. Poems on Slavery. The Spanish Student.

2: The Belfry of Bruges and Other Poems. Evangeline. The Seaside and the Fireside.

3: The Golden Legend. The Courtship of Miles Standish. Birds of Passage.

4: The Song of Hiawatha. Tales of a Wayside Inn. Birds of Passage.

12513. The Poetical Works . . . Edited . . . by William Michael Rossetti. Illustrated by Wilfred Lawson.

London: E. Moxon, Son, & Co., Dover Street. 1870.

12514. The Poetical Works . . . Edited . . . by Wlliam ⟨sic⟩ Michael Rossetti. Illustrated by . . . Edwin Edwards.

London: E. Moxon, Son, & Co., Dover Street. ⟨1871⟩

Vignette title-page dated 1871. Listed Ath Oct. 29, 1870; PC Dec. 8, 1870. Reviewed Bkr Dec. 8, 1870; Ath Dec. 24, 1870.

12515. The Complete Poetical Works . . . Illustrated with One Hundred and Seventy-Eight Designs, Drawn by John Gilbert, Engraved by the Brothers Dalziel. Author's Edition.

London: George Routledge & Sons, the Broadway, Ludgate. 1871.

12516. Forest Scenes Drawn by John A. Hows

⟨New York: Hurd and Houghton. Cambridge: Riverside Press. 1871⟩

Binder's title. For comment see BAL, Vol. 1, p. 377.

12517. The Poetical Works . . . Complete Edition.

Boston: James R. Osgood and Company, Late Ticknor & Fields, and Fields, Osgood, & Co. 1871.

Diamond Edition.

12518. The Divine Tragedy . . .

London: George Routledge and Sons, the Broadway, Ludgate. 1872 . . .

Reviewed Ath Dec. 23, 1871. Listed PC Dec. 30, 1871.

12519. Three Books of Song. London, 1872.

Issued in two formats:

Cloth

Three Books of Song . . .

London: George Routledge and Sons, the Broadway, Ludgate. 1872. [This Work Is Copyright.]

Pp. 204.

Paper

Three Books of Song . . .

London: George Routledge and Sons, the Broadway, Ludgate. 1872.

Pp. 128.

Note: Both the above printed from the same setting, the leading removed (inserted?) which accounts for the variation in the pagination.

Listed (pp. 204, cloth) PC June 17, 1872; (pp. 128, paper wrapper) PC July 1, 1872.

12520. The Divine Tragedy . . . Authorized Edition.

Leipzig Bernhard Tauchnitz 1872.

Presumably issued in printed paper wrapper.

Collection of British Authors, Vol. 1208. "I am much obliged for your esteemed letter of Nov. 22 and for the sheets of *The Divine Tragedy* . . . I am publishing *The Divine Tragedy* separately . . ."—Letter, Tauchnitz to Longfellow, Jan. 26, 1872; letter in H.

12521. Excelsior . . . with Twelve Illustrations by Fred. T. Vance.

New York: The Excelsior Life Insurance Company, 68 and 70 William Street. 1872.

Cloth; and, printed paper wrapper.

12522. Kavanagh and Other Pieces . . .

Boston James R. Osgood and Company 1872

12523. Longfellow's Poetical Works ⟨Cover-title⟩

Boston: James R. Osgood and Company, Late Ticknor & Fields, and Fields, Osgood, & Co. 1872.

4 Vols. For a list of the volumes in the set see *The Complete Works . . . Revised Edition*, Boston, 1870, above.

12524. The Poetical Works . . . Complete Edition . . .

Boston: James R. Osgood and Company, Late Ticknor & Fields, and Fields, Osgood, & Co. 1872.

Red line edition. Pp. 504.

12525. The Poetical Works . . . Complete Edition.

Boston: James R. Osgood and Company, Late Ticknor & Fields, and Fields, Osgood, & Co. 1872.

Diamond Edition. Pp. 363.

12526. The Poetical Works . . . Complete Edition. With Illustrations.

Boston: James R. Osgood and Company, Late Ticknor & Fields, and Fields, Osgood, & Co. 1872

Red line edition. Pp. 363.

12527. Cadenabbia . . .

Summer 1872. H. W. Longfellow ⟨probably Italy, *ca.* 1875⟩

Lithographed leaf, $4\frac{7}{8}$" x $2\frac{15}{16}$", pasted to the verso of a card; on recto of card is a photograph captioned: *81. Gran Hôtel Belle Vue Cadenabbia Lago di Como* Issued thus?

A typical sepia photo-souvenir prepared for tourists. According to *Works*, 1886, the poem was written at Nahant, Mass., Aug. 8, 1874. The condition of the lithographed leaf suggests that it was removed from a scrapbook (or like repository) and mounted on the card here described.

The date 1872 is erroneous. The poem was first published in *The Atlantic Monthly*, Dec. 1874. Collected in *Masque of Pandora*, 1875.

The only copy located is in UV.

12528. Christus: A Mystery . . . in Three Parts.

Boston: James R. Osgood and Company. 1873.

Blue and Gold edition.

12529. Christus: A Mystery . . . in Three Parts . . .

Boston: James R. Osgood and Company, Late Ticknor & Fields, and Fields, Osgood, & Co. 1873.

Red line edition.

12530. Christus A Mystery . . . in Three Parts

Boston James R. Osgood and Company 1873

Issued in three formats. The sequence has not been established and the designations are for identification only.

A: Leaf: 8" x $5\frac{3}{8}$" scant. On front: *Christus: A Mystery* . . .

B: Leaf: $6\frac{7}{16}$" x $4\frac{1}{16}$". On front: *Longfellow's Christus*

C: Leaf: $5\frac{7}{16}$" x 4". Imprint: *Boston: James R. Osgood and Company, Late Ticknor & Fields, and Fields, Osgood, & Co. 1873*. On front: *Diamond Edition*

Note: The punctuation of the three title-pages varies.

12531. Flower-de-Luce and Three Books of Song . . . Authorized Edition.

Leipzig Bernhard Tauchnitz 1873.

Printed wrapper. *Collection of British Authors*, No. 1360. "I am very much obliged by your kind letter of February 28, and the communications contained therein about the title etc. of my volume *Flower de Luce etc*. Everything you wish shall be attended to, with the utmost care. I hope to publish the volume in no far time . . ."—Letter, publisher to Longfellow, March 24, 1873; letter in H.

12532. Longfellow's Poetical Works ⟨Postulated cover-title⟩

Boston: James R. Osgood and Company, Late Ticknor & Fields, and Fields, Osgood, & Co. 1873.

4 Vols. *Note:* Minor variations in punctuation in the imprint are present.

1: The Complete Works . . . Revised Edition . . . Voices of the Night. Ballads and Other Poems. Poems on Slavery. The Spanish Student.

2: The Complete Works . . . Revised Edition . . . The Belfry of Bruges and Other Poems. Evangeline. The Seaside and the Fireside.

3: The Poetical Works . . . Revised Edition . . . The Courtship of Miles Standish. Birds of Passage. The Song of Hiawatha.

4: The Poetical Works ... Revised Edition ... Tales of a Wayside Inn. Birds of Passage. Flower-de-Luce. Three Books of Song.

12533. The Poetical Works ... Complete Edition.

Boston: James R. Osgood and Company, Late Ticknor & Fields, and Fields, Osgood, & Co. 1873.

Diamond Edition.

12534. The Poetical Works ... Revised Edition Four Volumes in Two ...

Boston   James R. Osgood and Company Late Ticknor & Fields, and Fields, Osgood, & Co. 1873

12535. The Poetical Works ... Complete Edition.

Boston: James R. Osgood and Company, Late Ticknor & Fields, and Fields, Osgood, & Co. 1874.

Diamond Edition.

12536. The Poetical Works ... Household Edition.

Boston: James R. Osgood and Company, Late Ticknor & Fields, and Fields, Osgood, & Co. 1874.

12537. The Poetical Works of H. W. Longfellow. Illustrated by F. Gilbert.

London: John Dicks, 313, Strand; and All Booksellers. 1874.

Cloth; and, printed paper wrapper.

12538. The Hanging of the Crane ... with Illustrations

Boston   James R. Osgood and Company Late Ticknor & Fields, and Fields, Osgood, & Co. 1875

Pp. 47. Leaf: 6⅞" x 4½" full. Printed on one side of leaf only. Jan. 20, 1875, composed and electrotyped (publisher's records). Jan. 28, 1875, 4500 copies printed (publisher's records). A copy in the possession of DEV inscribed by early owner Feb. 1, 1875. Listed PW Feb. 6, 1875. A copy at AAS inscribed by early owner Feb. 8, 1875. For prior publication see in *Section I* under 1874–1875.

12539. The Masque of Pandora and Other Poems ... Authorized Edition.

Leipzig   Bernhard Tauchnitz   1875

Printed wrapper. *Collection of British Authors,* No. 1546. Wrapper dated *December 1875.* Inserted terminal catalog dated *November 1875.* A letter (in H) from the publisher to Longfellow, Nov. 25, 1875, clearly indicates that the Tauchnitz edition was issued well after the Boston edition; that the Tauchnitz edition, in part, was set up from sheets of the Boston edition forwarded from Boston Oct. 11, 1875.

12540. The Poetical Works ... Complete Edition. With Illustrations.

Boston: James R. Osgood and Company, Late Ticknor & Fields, and Fields, Osgood, & Co. 1875.

Red line edition.

12541. The Poetical Works ... Household Edition.

Boston: James R. Osgood and Company, Late Ticknor & Fields, and Fields, Osgood, & Co. 1875.

12542. The Complete Poetical Works ... with Numerous Illustrations.

Boston: James R. Osgood and Company, Late Ticknor & Fields, and Fields, Osgood & Co. 1876.

Cloth; and, printed paper wrapper. Printed in two columns. On front of wrapper: *Centennial Edition...* Printings from these plates were issued *ca.* 1880 and later as the *Family Edition* although not so marked.

12543. Longfellow's Poetical Works ⟨Cover-title⟩

Boston: James R. Osgood and Company, Late Ticknor & Fields, and Fields, Osgood, & Co. 1876.

4 Vols. *Note:* Minor variations in punctuation in the imprint are present. For a list of the volumes in the set see *Longfellow's Poetical Works,* Boston, 1873.

12544. The New Poems of Jean Ingelow. John Greenleaf Whittier. Henry Wadsworth Longfellow.

Toronto: Belford Brothers. 1876.

12545. The Poetical Works ... Household Edition.

Boston: James R. Osgood and Company, Late Ticknor & Fields, and Fields, Osgood, & Co. 1876.

12546. The Poetical Works of Henry Wadsworth Longfellow.

William P. Nimmo: London: 14 King William Street, Strand; and Edinburgh. 1876.

12547. Prose Works ... Complete in Two Volumes ...

Boston: James R. Osgood and Company, Late Ticknor & Fields, and Fields, Osgood, & Co. 1876.

12548. Poems of Places Edited by Henry W. Longfellow ... England ⟨England and Wales⟩ ...

London Macmillan and Co. 1877

2 Vols. *Golden Treasury Series.* Advertised for *next week* Ath June 9; *this day* PC June 16, 1877. Listed Ath June 16; PC July 1, 1877. Reviewed PC July 17, 1877. A copy in BPL received July 18, 1877. A one-volume edition, advertised Ath July 7, 1877, as the *third and cheaper edition.*

12549. The Poetical Works ... Household Edition.

Boston: James R. Osgood and Company, Late Ticknor & Fields, and Fields, Osgood, & Co. 1877.

A copy at H inscribed by early owner Oct. 22, 1877.

12550. The Skeleton in Armor ... with Illustrations

Boston James R. Osgood & Co. 1877.

Cloth; and, leather. Oct. 22, 1876, 8000 copies printed (publisher's records). A copy at BPL received Nov. 7, 1876. Listed PW Nov. 11, 1876. Advertised PC Dec. 18, 1876.

12551. Poems ... New Revised Edition. With Numerous Illustrations.

Boston: James R. Osgood and Company, Late Ticknor & Fields, and Fields, Osgood, & Co. 1877.

Cloth. Also leather? Red line edition. A copy at H received Nov. 25, 1876.

12552. The Poetical Works ... Complete Edition.

Boston: James R. Osgood and Company, Late Ticknor & Fields, and Fields, Osgood, & Co. 1877.

Diamond Edition. A copy at BD inscribed by early owner Christmas, 1876.

12553. King Robert of Sicily and The Birds of Killingworth.

Hull: Brown; London: Simpkin Marshall, 1877.

Not seen. Entry from PC listing, June 16, 1877. Wrapper. Pp. 32.

12554. Favorite Poems ...

Boston: James R. Osgood and Company, Late Ticknor & Fields, and Fields, Osgood, & Co. 1877.

Vest-Pocket Series.

12555. The Poetical Works ... Complete Edition. With Illustrations.

Boston: James R. Osgood and Company, Late Ticknor & Fields, and Fields, Osgood, & Co. 1877.

Red line edition.

12556. The Poetical Works ... New and Revised Edition ...

Boston: James R. Osgood and Company, Late Ticknor & Fields, and Fields, Osgood, & Co. 1877.

Red line edition.

12557. The Poetical Works ...

William P. Nimmo: London: 14 King William Street, Strand; and Edinburgh. 1877.

12558. The Poetical Works ... Illustrated with One Hundred and Eighty Designs by Sir John Gilbert, R. A., Engraved by the Brothers Dalziel. Author's Edition.

London: George Routledge & Sons, the Broadway, Ludgate. 1877.

12559. The Prose Works ... Revised Edition ...

Boston: James R. Osgood and Company, Late Ticknor & Fields, and Fields, Osgood, & Co. 1877.

3 Vols. *Note:* Minor variations are present in the punctuation in the imprint.

12560. The Poetical Works ... Complete Edition. With Illustrations.

Boston: James R. Osgood and Company, Late Ticknor & Fields, and Fields, Osgood, & Co. 1878.

Red line edition. A copy at H inscribed by early owner Sept. 12, 1878.

12561. ... Longfellow's Poetical Works ...

London   George Routledge and Sons   Broadway, Ludgate Hill 1878

At head of title: *The Author's Pocket-Volume Edition.* 11 Vols. Boxed. According to contemporary notices issued in both cloth; and, in printed paper wrapper.

1: Voices of the Night and Earlier Poems, &c. Listed PC June 1, 1878.

2: Evangeline and Miles Standish. Listed PC July 2, 1878.

3: The Song of Hiawatha. Listed PC Aug. 2, 1878.

4: The Spanish Student and Judas Maccabæus. Listed PC Aug. 16, 1878.

5: Translations, Songs, and Sonnets. Listed PC Sept. 2, 1878.

6: Tales of a Wayside Inn. Listed PC Oct. 2, 1878.

7: The Divine Tragedy. Listed PC Oct. 2, 1878.

8: The Golden Legend. Listed PC Oct. 16, 1878.

9: The New England Tragedies.

10: Birds of Passage.

11: Flower-de-Luce, Masque of Pandora, &c.

The complete set, boxed, listed PC Nov. 2, 1878.

12562. Excelsior ... with Illustrations

Boston   James R. Osgood and Company   Late Ticknor & Fields, and Fields, Osgood, & Co. 1878

Issued in cloth; antique morocco; tree calf. Listed PW Nov. 17, 1877. The London (George Routledge & Sons) printing, n.d., was done from the same setting. For first separate edition see under 1872.

12563. Favorite Poems ... Illustrated by Sir John Gilbert ...

London: George Routledge and Sons, the Broadway, Ludgate. 1878.

Issued in *The Emerald Series.*

12564. Poems ... New Revised Edition. With Numerous Illustrations.

Boston: James R. Osgood and Company, Late Ticknor & Fields, and Fields, Osgood, & Co. 1878.

Cloth? Red line edition.

12565. Poems ... New Revised Edition. With Numerous Illustrations.

Boston: Houghton, Osgood and Company, Cambridge: The Riverside Press. 1878.

Red line edition.

12566. The Poetical Works ... Household Edition.

Boston: James R. Osgood and Company, Late Ticknor & Fields, and Fields, Osgood, & Co. 1878.

Noted only in publisher's leather.

12567. The Poetical Works ... Household Edition.

Boston: Houghton, Osgood and Company, The Riverside Press, Cambridge. 1878.

12568. 1. A Psalm of Life ...

⟨Satara, Printed on the "Columbian Press" Jan. 1878⟩

Caption-title. The above at head of p. 1; imprint at foot of p. 4.

Longfellow's poem, p. 1; translation into Marathi by Mrs. H. J. Bruce of the Marathi Mission, p. 2; on p. 3: text of the poem in translation but "written in English characters, according to the Jonesian system"; on p. 4: the poem "literally re-translated from the Marathi, to show the variation of sentiment and idiom."

12569. Poems ... New Revised Edition. With Numerous Illustrations.

Boston: Houghton, Osgood and Company, Cambridge: The Riverside Press. 1879.

Red line edition. A copy at H inscribed by early owner Christmas, 1878.

12570. The Poetical Works ... Complete Edition. With Illustrations.

Boston: Houghton, Osgood and Company. The Riverside Press, Cambridge. 1879.

Red line edition. A copy in DEV inscribed by early owner Dec. 25, 1878.

12571. American Poems   Longfellow: Whittier: Bryant: Holmes: Lowell: Emerson   With Biographical Sketches and Notes

Boston   Houghton, Osgood and Company   The Riverside Press,   Cambridge   1879

12572. Christus   A Mystery ... in Three Parts   Household Edition with Illustrations

Boston   Houghton, Mifflin and Company   New York: 11 East Seventeenth Street ⟨1879; *i.e.*, not before 1880⟩

12573. . . . Longfellow's Poetical Works

London   George Routledge and Sons   Broadway, Ludgate Hill 1879

At head of title: *Author's Complete Copyright Edition*   Issued in two styles of binding; sequence, if any, not known. The designations are for identification only.

A

S cloth: terra-cotta. Front lettered: LONGFELLOW'S POETICAL WORKS / COMPLETE / ‹circular device› / COPYRIGHT EDITION / STANDARD LIBRARY

B

S cloth: olive. Front lettered: LONGFELLOW'S WORKS / Henry W. Longfellow ‹facsimile autograph› / AUTHOR'S EDITION

12574. The Poetical Works . . . Household Edition.

Boston: Houghton, Osgood and Company, The Riverside Press, Cambridge. 1879.

12575. The Poetical Works . . . New and Revised Edition, with More Than Two Hundred and Fifty Illustrations.

Boston: Houghton, Osgood and Company. The Riverside Press, Cambridge. 1879.

Cloth; and, leather. Red line edition.

12576. The Poetical Works . . . Complete Edition.

Boston: Houghton, Osgood and Company. The Riverside Press, Cambridge. 1879.

Diamond Edition.

12577. Selections from American Authors. A Reading Book for School and Homes. Franklin, Adams, Cooper, Longfellow. Edited by Samuel Eliot . . .

New York: Taintor Brothers, Merrill & Co. 758 Broadway. ‹1879›

12578. The Poetical Works . . . Illustrated . . .

Vol. 1: Boston   Houghton, Osgood and Company   The Riverside Press, Cambridge   1879

Vol. 2: Boston   Houghton, Mifflin and Company   The Riverside Press, Cambridge   1880

Cloth; leather; and, 30 paper-covered parts. Parts 1-20 of the early printings have the copyright notice in the name of Houghton, Osgood and Company; Parts 21-30 in the name of Houghton, Mifflin & Co. Later printings of Parts 1-20 have the copyright notice in the name

of Houghton, Mifflin & Co. Listed (as a 2-volume work) PW Dec. 18, 1880.

Note: Leaf 12″ x 9¼″.

For Vol. 3 see *The Complete Prose Works* ‹1883›.

According to a prospectus, the three volumes were designated the *Subscription Edition* and issued in 45 paper-covered parts. Purchasers were offered a binding service as follows: 3 Vols., cloth; 3 Vols., half morocco; 3 Vols., full turkey morocco; 6 Vols., "Soft Flexible Morocco . . . Plain gold border line and the single word LONGFELLOW in plain gold letters stamped on cover. Full gilt edges, extra fine quality throughout"; 6 Vols., cloth, "Identical with the six volumes Soft Flexible Morocco, except that muslin is used instead of leather. May be had with gilt top and uncut edges if preferred."

No attempt has been made to establish a sequence for the numerous reprintings.

12579. American Prose   Hawthorne   Irving Longfellow Whittier Holmes Lowell Thoreau Emerson   With Introductions and Notes by the Editor of "American Poems" ‹Horace E. Scudder›

Boston   Houghton, Osgood and Company The Riverside Press, Cambridge   1880

12580. The Complete Poetical Works . . . with Numerous Illustrations.

Boston: Houghton, Osgood and Company. The Riverside Press, Cambridge. 1880.

12581. The Poetical Works . . . Complete Edition.

Boston: Houghton, Osgood and Company. The Riverside Press, Cambridge. 1880.

Diamond Edition. Pp. 407.

12582. The Poetical Works . . . Complete Edition.

Boston: Houghton, Osgood and Company. The Riverside Press, Cambridge. 1880.

Diamond Edition. Pp. 435.

12583. The Poetical Works . . . Household Edition.

Boston: Houghton, Osgood and Company, The Riverside Press, Cambridge. 1880.

12584. The Poetical Works . . . Revised Edition Four Volumes in Two . . .

Boston   Houghton, Osgood and Company The Riverside Press, Cambridge. 1880

12585. The Complete Poetical Works ... with Numerous Illustrations.

Boston: Houghton, Mifflin and Company. James R. Osgood and Company. 1880.

12586. ... Evangeline. Courtship of Miles Standish. Favorite Poems ...

Boston: Houghton, Mifflin and Company. The Riverside Press, Cambridge. 1880.

At head of title: *Modern Classics.* An omnibus volume.

12587. The Poetical Works ... Complete Edition.

Boston: Houghton, Mifflin and Company. The Riverside Press, Cambridge. 1880.

12588. The Poetical Works ... Complete Edition. With Illustrations.

Boston: Houghton, Mifflin and Company. The Riverside Press, Cambridge. 1880.

Red line edition.

12589. The Poetical Works ... Household Edition.

Boston: Houghton, Mifflin and Company. The Riverside Press, Cambridge. 1880.

Noted only in three-quarters leather.

12590. The Poetical Works ... in Four Volumes ...

Boston   Houghton, Mifflin and Company The Riverside Press, Cambridge   1880

Cambridge Edition. Entry tentative; Vol. 2 unlocated.

The Poetical Works ... Illustrated ...

Boston   Houghton, Mifflin and Company ... ⟨1880; *i.e., ca.* 1885⟩

Issued in 30 paper-covered parts. See below under *ca.* 1885.

12591. The Poetical Works ...

London: T. Nelson and Sons, Paternoster Row; Edinburgh; and New York. 1880.

Red line edition.

12592. The Prose Works ... in Two Volumes ...

Boston   Houghton, Mifflin and Company The Riverside Press, Cambridge   1880

Cambridge Edition.

12593. The Longfellow Birthday-Book. Arranged by Charlotte Fiske Bates ...

Boston: Houghton, Mifflin and Company. The Riverside Press, Cambridge. 1881.

According to contemporary notices, issued in cloth; limp morocco; calf; sealskin. A copy at BA received March 1, 1881. Listed PW March 5, 1881. Reprinted under date ⟨1881⟩ by Houghton, Mifflin & Co. Reprinted under date ⟨1881; *i.e.,* not before 1908⟩ by Houghton Mifflin Company.

12594. Leaflets from Standard Authors. Longfellow. Poems and Prose Passages from the Works ... Compiled by Josephine E. Hodgdon. Illustrated.

Boston: Houghton, Mifflin and Company. The Riverside Press, Cambridge. 1881.

Printed paper wrapper. Also issued as a set of single leaves in printed paper box. Advertised for June 18, PW June 11, 1881. Deposited June 23, 1881 (as loose leaves; and, in wrapper). Listed PW June 25, 1881.

12595. Poems ... with Notes ...

London: W. Mack, 4, Paternoster Square, and 38, Park Street, Bristol. ⟨1881⟩

Flexible leather; and, vellum. Preface dated *Oct., 1881.*

12596. The Complete Poetical Works ...

Boston: Houghton, Mifflin and Company. James R. Osgood and Company. 1881.

12597. Poems ... New Revised Edition. With Numerous Illustrations.

Boston: Houghton, Mifflin and Company. The Riverside Press, Cambridge. 1881.

Red line edition.

12598. The Poetical Works ... Complete Edition.

Boston: Houghton, Mifflin and Company. The Riverside Press, Cambridge. 1881.

Cloth; and, flexible leather. On cloth binding: *Diamond Edition.*

12599. The Poetical Works ... Complete Edition. With Illustrations.

Boston: Houghton, Mifflin and Company. The Riverside Press, Cambridge. 1881.

Red line edition.

12600. The Poetical Works ... Household Edition

Boston: Houghton, Mifflin and Company. The Riverside Press, Cambridge. 1881.

12601. The Poetical Works ... Illustrated ...

Boston   Houghton, Mifflin and Company The Riverside Press, Cambridge   1881 ⟨–1882⟩

2 Vols. Noted only in publisher's leather. For fuller comment on this set see above under 1879 *The Poetical Works ... Illustrated.*

12602. The Poetical Works ... in Four Volumes ...

Boston   Houghton, Mifflin and Company The Riverside Press, Cambridge   1881

Cambridge Edition.

12603. Poetical Works ... Including ... Translations and Notes. Illustrated with Twenty-Four Engravings on Wood from Designs by Birket Foster, John Gilbert, G. H. Thomas, John Absolon, etc.

London: George Bell & Sons, York Street, Covent Garden. 1881.

Cloth? *Note:* "Alpine Ode," pp. 274-275, is by James Montgomery, not by Longfellow; see the Boston, 1869, edition of *Hyperion,* pp. 198-200.

12604. Seven Voices of Sympathy, from the Writings of Henry Wadsworth Longfellow. Edited by Charlotte Fiske Bates.

Boston: Houghton, Mifflin and Company. New York: 11 East Seventeenth Street. The Riverside Press, Cambridge. 1882.

Deposited Dec. 9, 1881. Listed PW Dec. 24, 1881.

12605. Poets and Etchers ...

Boston   James R. Osgood and Company   1882

Listed PW Dec. 10, 1881. Also a "China-paper Edition," limited to 100 numbered copies.

12606. American Classics for Schools   Longfellow

Boston   Houghton, Mifflin and Company New York: 11 East Seventeenth Street   The Riverside Press, Cambridge   1882

Advertised for Feb. 18, PW Feb. 11, 1882. Deposited Feb. 22, 1882. Listed PW Feb. 25, 1882.

12607. *Entry cancelled.*

12608. Hyperion ...

Boston   Houghton, Mifflin and Company The Riverside Press, Cambridge   1882

Printed paper wrapper. On front: *Revised Copyright Edition.* Advertised for *this day* PW April 15, 1882. Listed PW April 22, 1882.

12609. Outre-Mer ... Revised Edition ...

Boston   Houghton, Mifflin and Company The Riverside Press, Cambridge   1882

Cloth; and, printed paper wrapper. Advertised for *this day* PW April 15, 1882. Listed PW April 22, 1882.

12610. The Poems of Goethe Translated ... by H. W. Longfellow ... ⟨and others⟩

New York: Thomas Y. Crowell & Co. No. 13 Astor Place. ⟨1882⟩

Cloth; and, boards, leather shelfback. The copyright notice is in the name of S. E. Cassino and is dated 1882. Advertised by Crowell as though published PW May 27, 1882.

12611. The Poets and Poetry of Europe. With Introductions and Biographical Notices. By Henry Wadsworth Longfellow. A New Edition, Revised and Enlarged ...

Boston: Houghton, Mifflin and Company. The Riverside Press, Cambridge. 1882. ⟨Copyright notice dated 1870⟩

Advertised PW June 10, 1882 as "carefully revised by Mr. Longfellow during the last weeks of his life ..." The statement appears to be nothing more than a publisher's blurb. Cursory examination indicates that the 1882 printing is the same as the 1871 save for the transfer of pp. xxiii-xxvii (of the 1871 printing) to the back of the 1882 printing where they appear as pp. 917-921. Listed PW June 24, 1882.

12612. Selections from the Poems of Henry W. Longfellow ... Made by the Special and Very Kind Permission of Messrs. Houghton, Mifflin & Co. ...

Published by the Massachusetts Society for the Prevention of Cruelty to Animals, No. 96 Tremont Street, Boston, Mass. 1882.

Cover-title. Printed self-wrapper. The preface is dated July 1, 1882.

12613. Old St. David's at Radnor ...

Bradford, Aug. 12, 1882.

Single leaf. 8½" scant x 3½" scant. Wove paper watermarked *Superior Mills.* Printed on recto only. For another printing see No. 12870.

12614. Poems of America Edited by Henry Wadsworth Longfellow ...

Boston   Houghton, Mifflin and Company
New York: 11 East Seventeenth Street   The
Riverside Press, Cambridge   1882

3 Vols. Advertised for Oct. 14 PW Oct. 7, 1882. Deposited Oct. 20, 1882. Listed (cloth and half calf) PW Oct. 21, 1882.

12615. The Complete Poetical Works ... with Numerous Illustrations.

Boston: Houghton, Mifflin and Company. The Riverside Press, Cambridge. 1882.

12616. ... Evangeline and the Building of the Ship ... with Notes and a Biographical Sketch.   Selected from "American Poems."

Boston: Houghton, Mifflin and Company. New York: 11 East Seventeenth Street.   The Riverside Press, Cambridge. 1882.

At head of title: American Authors.—No. 1.

Printed paper wrapper.

12617. Life and Works of Henry W. Longfellow. Cambridge Edition.

Cambridge: Tribune Publishing Company, 1882.

Cloth; printed paper wrapper; printed paper boards, cloth shelfback. *Note:* "The Golden Sunset," pp. 64-65, is not by Henry W. Longfellow, but by Samuel Longfellow; collected in Samuel Longfellow's *Hymns and Verses,* 1894.

12618. The Longfellow Calendar with Selections for Every Day in the Year ...

Houghton, Mifflin & Company   Boston ⟨1882⟩

Single card, 11⅞″ x 8⅜″, lithographed in colors as above, decorated with portrait of Longfellow, Priscilla, Evangeline, etc., etc. At foot: Copyright 1882 by Houghton, Mifflin & Co. Armstrong & Co. Lith. The Riverside Press. On reverse of card, printed in green-gray, calendar for 1883, and Jan.–April 1884; the whole decorated. Affixed to the card: 365 slips, one for each day of the year, each with an extract from one of Longfellow's productions. *Note:* BAL has not checked the text and presumes that no first edition material appears herein.

12619. Poems and Fragments Selected from the Works of H. W. Longfellow by Urda.

Joh. G. Stemler Cz. Amsterdam. 1882.

12620. Poems ... New Revised Edition. With Numerous Illustrations.

Boston: Houghton, Mifflin and Company. The Riverside Press, Cambridge. 1882.

Cloth; and, leather. Red line edition. *Two printings noted;* sequence not known; the designations are for identification only.

A: Copyright notices dated 1848–1878.

B: Copyright notices dated 1841–1880.

12621. The Poetical Works ... Complete Edition.

Boston: Houghton, Mifflin and Company. The Riverside Press, Cambridge. 1882.

12622. The Poetical Works ... Diamond Edition.

Boston: Houghton, Mifflin and Company. The Riverside Press, Cambridge. 1882.

12623. The Poetical Works ... Household Edition.

Boston: Houghton, Mifflin and Company. The Riverside Press, Cambridge. 1882.

12624. The Poetical Works ... in Four Volumes ...

Boston   Houghton, Mifflin and Company   The Riverside Press, Cambridge   1882

Three-quarters morocco, marbled paper boards sides. Also, cloth, printed paper label on spine, which designates the set the *Riverside Edition.*

12625. The Poetical Works ... New and Revised Edition, with More Than Two Hundred and Fifty Illustrations.

Boston   Houghton, Mifflin and Company   New York: 11 East Seventeenth Street   The Riverside Press, Cambridge   1882

Red line edition.

12626. The Poetical Works ... with a Biographical Sketch. Very Fully Illustrated.

Boston: Houghton, Mifflin and Company. New York: 11 East Seventeenth Street. The Riverside Press, Cambridge. 1882.

Red line edition.

12627. The Prose Works ... in Two Volumes ...

Boston   Houghton, Mifflin and Company   The Riverside Press, Cambridge   1882

On binding: *Cambridge Edition* Also issued in cloth, printed paper label on spine, the designation *Riverside Edition* on the label.

12628. ... Amalfi con la Versione Italiana di Giulio Minervini

Napoli R. Stabilimento del Comm. G. de Angelis e Figlio Portamedina alla Pignasecca, 44 1883.

Cover-title. Printed self-wrapper. At head of title: *E. G. <sic> Longfellow*. This poem went into many separate printings (in Italy). An 1890 printing, issued in Palermo, has also been seen.

12629. The Complete Poetical Works ... with Numerous Illustrations.

Boston: Houghton, Mifflin and Company. The Riverside Press, Cambridge. 1883.

Family Edition (although not so marked). Pp. 305. For the extended edition (pp. 340?) see above in *Section I* under *Michael Angelo*, 1882–1883.

12630. The Complete Prose Works ... with ... Later Poems ... with a Biographical Sketch by Octavius B. Frothingham

Boston Houghton, Mifflin and Company New York: 11 East Seventeenth Street The Riverside Press, Cambridge <1883>

Issued with the *Poetical Works*, 1879–1880, in 45 parts; see above in *Section II*, under 1879–1880, for comment. For another comment see *Michael Angelo*, 1882–1883, in *Section I*.

12631. Longfellow's Poetical Works The Memorial Edition

London George Routledge and Sons Broadway, Ludgate Hill New York: 9, Lafayette Place 1883

12632. Poems ... New Revised Edition. With Numerous Illustrations.

Boston: Houghton, Mifflin and Company. The Riverside Press, Cambridge. 1883.

Pp. 426. Red line edition.

12633. The Poetical Works ... Diamond Edition.

Boston: Houghton, Mifflin and Company. The Riverside Press, Cambridge. 1883.

Pp. 445.

12634. The Poetical Works ... Household Edition.

Boston: Houghton, Mifflin and Company. The Riverside Press, Cambridge. 1883.

Pp. 426.

12635. The Poetical Works ... in Four Volumes ...

Boston Houghton, Mifflin and Company The Riverside Press, Cambridge 1883

Cambridge Edition.

The Poetical Works of Henry Wadsworth Longfellow

Boston and New York Houghton, Mifflin and Company The Riverside Press, Cambridge <1883; *i.e.*, not before 1886>

Pp. 519. For comment see below under 1886.

12636. The Prose Works ... in Two Volumes ...

Boston Houghton, Mifflin and Company The Riverside Press, Cambridge 1883

Three-quarters leather. Also cloth, printed paper label on spine, the designation *Riverside Edition* on the label. Also in cloth with *Cambridge Edition* on the spine.

12637. Twenty Poems from Henry Wadsworth Longfellow Illustrated from Paintings by His Son Ernest W. Longfellow

Boston Houghton, Mifflin and Company New York: 11 East Seventeenth Street The Riverside Press, Cambridge 1884

Cloth; morocco; and, tree calf. May 31, 1883, 3000 copies printed (publisher's records). Advertised for Sept. 15, PW Sept. 8, 1883. A copy at H received Sept. 19, 1883. Oct. 31, 1883, 2000 copies printed (issued under date <1883>?). Listed PW Dec. 15, 1883.

12638. Michael Angelo A Dramatic Poem ...

Boston Houghton, Mifflin and Company New York: 11 East Seventeenth Street The Riverside Press, Cambridge 1884

For comment see *Michael Angelo*, 1882–1883, in *Section I*.

12639. The Poetical Works ... with a Prefatory Notice ... by Eva Hope.

London: Walter Scott, 14 Paternoster Square, and Newcastle-on-Tyne. 1884.

Issued in *The Canterbury Poets* series. Listed PC Dec. 6, 1884.

12640. The Complete Poetical Works ... with Numerous Illustrations.

Boston: Houghton, Mifflin and Company. The Riverside Press, Cambridge. 1884.

12641. Flower-de-Luce ... Reproduced in Fac Simile from the Original Ms. Illustrated by Isaac Sprague

Troy, N.Y. H. B. Nims and Company 1884 Reprinted by Permission of Houghton, Mifflin, & Co.

Pictorial stiff paper wrapper.

12642. Leaflets from Standard Authors. Longfellow. Poems and Prose Passages ... Compiled by Josephine E. Hodgdon ... Eighth Edition.

Boston: Houghton, Mifflin and Company, 11 East Seventeenth Street, New York. The Riverside Press, Cambridge. 1884.

Printed paper wrapper. Probably also issued as a set of loose leaves in a box.

12643. Poems ... New Revised Edition. With Numerous Illustrations.

Boston: Houghton, Mifflin and Company. The Riverside Press, Cambridge. 1884.

Red line edition.

12644. The Poetical Works ... in Four Volumes ...

Boston Houghton, Mifflin and Company The Riverside Press, Cambridge 1884

Vols. 1 and 4 not seen. On binding: *Cambridge Edition*

12645. The Poetical Works ... Household Edition.

Boston: Houghton, Mifflin and Company. The Riverside Press, Cambridge. 1884.

12646. The Poetical Works ... Diamond Edition.

Boston: Houghton, Mifflin and Company. The Riverside Press, Cambridge. 1884.

12647. The Poetical Works ...

Edinburgh: W. P. Nimmo, Hay, & Mitchell (William P. Nimmo and Co.), 1884.

Cloth?

12648. The Early Poems of Henry Wadsworth Longfellow ...

Boston Houghton, Mifflin and Company New York: 11 East Seventeenth Street The Riverside Press, Cambridge 1885

Issued with the imprint of various publishers on the spine. The following have been noted:

Houghton, Mifflin & Co.; Belford, Clarke & Co.; T. Y. Crowell & Co.; Hurst & Company. Deposited Oct. 22, 1884.

12649. The Prose Works ... in Two Volumes ...

Boston Houghton, Mifflin and Company New York: 11 East Seventeenth Street The Riverside Press, Cambridge 1885

Vol. 2 not seen. Vol. 1 deposited March 28, 1885.

12650. The Village Blacksmith ...

New York E. P. Dutton & Company 31 West Twenty-Third Street ⟨1885⟩

Two printings noted:

1: Pictorial imprint of *Rockwell & Churchill* ⟨*sic*⟩ on copyright page. Inserted notice (on a slip: 2⁷⁄₁₆″ x 5⁷⁄₁₆″) reading: *This Edition Published By Special Arrangement* ... Noted in cloth. Also publisher's leather? Deposited Oct. 3, 1885.

2: Typographic imprint of *Rockwell and Churchill* ⟨*sic*⟩ on copyright page. The notice cited above printed on p. ⟨viii⟩. Noted in printed paper boards; and, printed paper boards, cloth shelfback.

Note: The following undated separate reprints have been seen; no attempt at a sequence has been made. Order of presentation is absolutely arbitrary.

A: Imprinted: *Providence Shepard and Company ... Westminster Street* Pictorial paper wrapper. Illustrated with the altered engravings of the ⟨1885⟩ Dutton edition.

B: Imprinted: *London Pictorial Literature Society Churchill Road* Pictorial paper wrapper. Illustrated with the altered engravings of the ⟨1885⟩ Dutton edition.

C: Imprinted: *London, John Walker & Co. Farringdon House, Warwick Lane, E. C. Designed in London & Printed in Holland.* Pictorial paper wrapper. Printed throughout in brown and sepia. A copy in B inscribed by early owner Dec. 25, 1890.

D: Imprinted: *Raphael Tuck & Sons, Ltd ... London, Paris, New York.* Illustrated by Harold Copping and others. Pictorial paper wrapper, scalloped edges.

E: Imprinted: *Castell Brothers. London. New York E* ⟨*sic*⟩ *& J. B. Young & Co. Printed in Bavaria.* Pictorial paper boards sides, cloth shelfback.

F: Imprinted: *New York: E. P. Dutton & Co. 31 West 23rd Street [Designed in England]*

[*Printed in Germany*] Pictorial paper wrapper. Illustrated with lithographs in brown adapted from the engravings of the ⟨1885⟩ Dutton edition.

G: Imprinted: *London: Ernest Nister   New York: E. P. Dutton & Co. Printed in Bavaria* ...   Pictorial paper wrapper, scalloped edges.

H: Imprinted: *Cupples & Leon   New York Published by Permission of E. P. Dutton & Co.* Pictorial paper boards.

I: Imprinted: *H. J. Wehman, Song Publisher, 50 Chatham St., New York.* Single leaf. 9⁵⁄₁₆″ x 6³⁄₁₆″. Printed on recto only. Issued as No. 533 of a series.

J: Imprinted: *Griffith, Farran, Okeden & Welsh ... London* ...   A copy at BD inscribed by early owner 1885.

K: Imprinted: *Hartford   G. Fox and Company 406, 408 & 410 Main Street*   Pictorial paper wrapper.

L: Printed with the *Marseilleis* ⟨sic⟩ *Hymn.* Imprinted: *Printed at the "Catnach Press" (Est. 1813.) by W. S. Fortey, ⟨S⟩even Dials London* ...   Issued not before 1860. Single leaf. 10″ scant x 7⁷⁄₁₆″. Printed in two columns on recto only.

12651. The Poetical Works ... Household Edition with Illustrations

Boston and New York   Houghton, Mifflin and Company   The Riverside Press, Cambridge   1885

12652. The Poetical Works ... Household Edition with Illustrations

Boston   Houghton, Mifflin and Company New York: 11 East Seventeenth Street   The Riverside Press, Cambridge   1885

12653. The Poetical Works ... with Numerous Illustrations.

Boston: Houghton, Mifflin and Company. New York: 11 East Seventeenth Street. The Riverside Press, Cambridge. 1885.

12654. The Poetical Works ... in Four Volumes ...

Boston   Houghton, Mifflin and Company New York: 11 East Seventeenth Street   The Riverside Press, Cambridge   1885

Printed from the plates of the *Cambridge Edition.* Noted only in three-quarters leather. Do copies in cloth bear the statement *Cambridge*

Edition on the spine? Also issued in cloth, printed paper label on spine with the designation *Riverside Edition?* Note: Imprint of Vol. 3 lacks the line: *New York: 11 East Seventeenth Street*

12655. The Poetical Works ... Illustrated ...

Boston   Houghton, Mifflin and Company The Riverside Press, Cambridge ⟨1880; *i.e.*, not before *ca.* 1885⟩

Issued in 30 parts.

12656. The Skeleton in Armour ...

Location of J. & P. Coats' Exhibit, F to G, Column 7 to 9, at the Cotton Centennial Exposition, New Orleans, 1885.

The above printed on the reverse of a card; the recto imprinted in colors with a picture of the Old Stone Mill at Newport, done in petit-point. 5³⁄₄″ x 4¹⁄₈″.

12657. Voices of the Night   Ballads and Other Poems ...

New York   James B. Millar & Co., Publisher 1885

12658. Voices of the Night   Ballads and Other Poems ...

New York: R. Worthington, Publisher. 1885

12659. The Early Poems ...

Boston   Houghton, Mifflin and Company New York: 11 East Seventeenth Street   The Riverside Press, Cambridge   1886

A copy at H inscribed by early owner May 15, 1886.

12660. ... The Children's Hour and Twenty Other Selections ... with Notes and a Biographical Sketch

Houghton, Mifflin and Company   Boston: 4 Park Street   New York: 11 East Seventeenth Street   The Riverside Press, Cambridge   1886

At head of title: The Riverside Literature Series

Issued in printed paper wrapper as No. 11 of the series under date May 26, 1886.

12661. The Poetical Works ... Household Edition with Illustrations

Boston and New York   Houghton, Mifflin and Company   The Riverside Press, Cambridge   1886

Deposited July 31, 1886.

12662. The Wreck of the Hesperus.

London: Griffith, Farran, Okeden & Welsh, 1886.

Not seen. Not located. Entry on the basis of listings: Ath Sept. 4, 1886; PC Oct. 1, 1886.

12663. ... Poems, by H. W. Longfellow ... ⟨Caption-title⟩

⟨At head of title:⟩ ... The Leisure Hour Library ... F. M. Lupton ... September 11, 1886 ... New York ...

Printed self-wrapper. Issued as No. 111, *New Series, Vol. I.* Caution: Entry on the basis of a printing marked *Fourth Edition.*

12664. Poems ... New Revised Edition. With Numerous Illustrations.

Boston: Houghton, Mifflin and Company. The Riverside Press, Cambridge. ⟨1886⟩

Red line edition.

12665. The Poetical Works of Henry Wadsworth Longfellow

Boston and New York Houghton, Mifflin and Company The Riverside Press, Cambridge ⟨1883; *i.e.,* not before 1886⟩

Printed from the plates of the extended *Diamond Edition,* 1883. For a comment see *Michael Angelo,* 1882–1883, in *Section I.*

12666. The Poetical Works ...

Boston and New York Houghton, Mifflin and Company The Riverside Press, Cambridge 1886

12667. The Poetical Works ...

Boston and New York Houghton, Mifflin and Company The Riverside Press, Cambridge ⟨1886⟩

12668. The Poetical Works ... Diamond Edition.

Boston: Houghton, Mifflin and Company. New York: 11 East Seventeenth Street. The Riverside Press, Cambridge. 1886.

12669. The Poetical Works ... Illustrated ...

Boston Houghton, Mifflin and Company The Riverside Press, Cambridge ⟨1886⟩

2 Vols. Reprint of the 1879–1880 edition. Presumably issued in a variety of bindings. For a comment on the bindings see entry 12578.

12670. The Poetical Works ... Household Edition with Illustrations

Boston and New York Houghton, Mifflin and Company The Riverside Press, Cambridge 1886

Pp. 492.

12671. The Poetical Works ... Household Edition with Illustrations

Boston and New York Houghton, Mifflin and Company The Riverside Press, Cambridge ⟨1886⟩

Pp. 492. There were several printings from the same plates with no alteration of the title-leaf; these may be distinguished by variations in the advertisements. No attempt has been made to record the variations.

12672. The Poetical Works ... Household Edition with Illustrations

Boston and New York Houghton, Mifflin and Company The Riverside Press, Cambridge ⟨1886; *i.e.,* not before 1887⟩

Pp. 496.

12673. The Poetical Works ... with a Prefatory Notice, Biographical and Critical. By Eva Hope.

London: Walter Scott, 24 Warwick Lane, Paternoster Row, and Newcastle-on-Tyne. 1886.

Probably issued in cloth, printed paper label on spine.

12674. The Poetical Works ... with Photographic Illustrations by Payne Jennings.

London: Suttaby & Co., Amen Corner. MDCCCLXXXVI.

Noted only in limp leather. "Publisher's Preface" dated at end *July 1882;* the only example located is almost surely a reprint of an unlocated (1882?) printing.

⟨Standard Library Edition⟩

Boston ... ⟨1886 ...⟩

See below under 1891.

12675. The Poetical Works ... with Numerous Illustrations.

Boston: Houghton, Mifflin and Company. New York: 11 East Seventeenth Street. The Riverside Press, Cambridge. 1887.

A copy at Y inscribed by early owner Dec. 25, 1886.

12676. ... The Golden Legend ... with Notes by Samuel Arthur Bent ...

Houghton, Mifflin and Company Boston: 4 Park Street; New York: 11 East Seventeenth Street The Riverside Press, Cambridge 1887

At head of title: The Riverside Literature Series

Printed boards, cloth shelfback. Issued as *Numbers 25 and 26* of the series. Deposited Feb. 2, 1887.

12677. Longfellow's "Hyperion," "Kavanagh," and "The Trouvères" with an Introduction by William Tirebuck

London Walter Scott, 24 Warwick Lane Paternoster Row 1887

Cloth, printed paper label on spine. Issued in *The Camelot Classics*. Listed PC March 1, 1887.

12678. Sunrise on the Hills ...

New York Thomas Y. Crowell & Co. ⟨1887⟩

Pictorial paper boards. According to contemporary notices issued in paper; cloth; and, celluloid. Listed PW Oct. 29, 1887.

12679. Maidenhood: A Poem. Illustrated by Stanley. Printed by Kaufman of Baden.

London: Sampson Low, 1887? 1888?

Not seen. Not located. Entry from trade notices. Listed Ath Nov. 19; PC Dec. 6, 1887. Reviewed PC Dec. 6, 1887.

12680. The Wreck of the Hesperus ...

New York E. P. Dutton and Company 31 West Twenty-Third Street 1887

A copy at BD inscribed by early owner Christmas 1887.

12681. The Early Poems ...

Boston and New York Houghton, Mifflin and Company The Riverside Press, Cambridge 1887

Red line edition.

12682. Nuremberg ...

Nuremberg Joh. Leonh. Schrag 1887.

Cloth over flexible boards.

12683. The Poetical Works ...

Boston and New York Houghton, Mifflin and Company The Riverside Press, Cambridge 1887

12684. The Poetical Works ... Household Edition with Illustrations

Boston and New York Houghton, Mifflin and Company The Riverside Press, Cambridge 1887

12685. The Poetical Works ... with a Prefatory Notice, Biographical and Critical. By Eva Hope.

London: Walter Scott, 24 Warwick Lane, Paternoster Row, and Newcastle-on-Tyne. 1887.

Cloth, printed paper label on spine.

12686. ... The Poetical Works of Longfellow Including Recent Poems. With Explanatory Notes, etc. Portrait and Original Illustrations.

London: Frederick Warne and Co., Bedford Street, Strand. 1887.

At head of title: The Lansdowne Poets.

12687. Voices of the Night Ballads and Other Poems ...

New York John B. Alden, Publisher 1887.

12688. Voices of the Night Ballads and Other Poems ...

New York: Worthington Co., 747 Broadway. 1887.

Franklin Edition.

12689. Longfellow's Days The Longfellow Prose Birthday Book Extracts from the Journals and Letters of H. W. Longfellow Edited by Laura Winthrop Johnson ...

Boston Ticknor and Company 1888

BAL has not checked the text and presumes that no first edition material appears herein. Deposited Oct. 3, 1887.

12690. ... A Longfellow Night A Short Sketch of the Poet's Life, with Songs and Recitations from His Works for the Use of Catholic Schools and Catholic Literary Societies by Katharine A. O'Keeffe

Boston Houghton, Mifflin and Company New York: 11 East Seventeenth Street The Riverside Press, Cambridge 1888

At head of title: *The Riverside Literature Series.* Printed paper wrapper. Issued under date *April 1888,* as an extra number in the series. Deposited April 18, 1888.

12691. Nuremberg. Illustrated with Twenty-Eight Photogravures by the Gebbie & Husson Company. Illuminated and Arranged by Mary and Amy Comegys.

London: Sampson Low, 1888.

Not seen. Not located. Entry on the basis of trade notices. Announced Ath Sept. 29; PC Oct. 1, 1888. Listed PC Oct. 15, 1888.

12692. ... The Building of the Ship and Other Poems ...

Houghton, Mifflin and Company Boston: 4 Park Street; New York: 11 East Seventeenth Street The Riverside Press, Cambridge 1888

At head of title: *The Riverside Literature Series* Printed paper wrapper. Issued as No. 38 of the series under the date *Nov. 1888.* Deposited Nov. 10, 1888. Reprinted and reissued under date ⟨1888⟩.

12693. Nuremberg ... Illustrated with Twenty-Eight Photogravures ... Illuminated and Arranged by Mary E. and Amy Comegys

Philadelphia Gebbie & Co., Publishers 1888

Cloth; and, leather. Advertised for fall publication PW May 19, 1888, as in cloth gilt; and, a limited edition on India paper. Copy in BA received Nov. 13, 1888. Listed PW Dec. 29, 1888 (as in parchment and morocco). Deposited July 10, 1889 ⟨sic⟩.

12694. The Story of the Luck of Edenhall by Amanda B Harris ... Longfellow's ... "The Luck of Edenhall" ... "Edenhall" by Susan Coolidge ...

Boston D Lothrop Company Franklin and Hawley Streets ⟨1888⟩

Printed paper wrapper. Deposited Dec. 12, 1888.

12695. The Early Poems ...

Boston and New York Houghton, Mifflin and Company The Riverside Press, Cambridge 1888

Red line edition.

12696. Poems and Ballads ... Illustrated

New York Worthington Co., 747 Broadway 1888

12697. The Poetical Works ... [Selected.] With a Prefatory Notice, Biographical and Critical, by Eva Hope

London Walter Scott, 24 Warwick Lane Paternoster Row 1888

Cloth, printed paper label on spine. *The Canterbury Poets* series.

12698. Woods in Winter ...

⟨Boston: L. Prang & Co., 1888⟩

Tied with ribbon. Unprinted stiff paper wrapper. Christmas card pasted to front.

12699. Ballads, Lyrics and Sonnets from the Poetic Works of Henry Wadsworth Longfellow

Boston and New York Houghton, Mifflin and Company The Riverside Press, Cambridge M DCCC LXXXIX

Cloth; half morocco; and, half levant. Deposited Oct. 3, 1889. Listed PW Oct. 12, 1889.

12700. Longfellow Gems Illustrated by W. Goodrich Beal

Boston Samuel E. Cassino 196 Summer Street ⟨1889⟩

Deposited Nov. 16, 1889. Reprinted with the imprint: *Boston: Samuel E. Cassino, Exchange Building.* ⟨1889⟩

12701. Ballads, Lyrics & Sonnets ...

London Macmillan and Co. 1889

12702. The Early Poems ...

Boston and New York Houghton, Mifflin and Company The Riverside Press, Cambridge 1889

12703. The Poetical Works ... with Numerous Illustrations.

Boston: Houghton, Mifflin and Company. New York: 11 East Seventeenth Street. The Riverside Press, Cambridge. 1889.

12704. The Prose Works ...

London: George Bell & Sons, York Street Covent Garden. 1889.

Cloth?

12705. King Robert of Sicily.

Manchester: Ledsham; London: Simpkin Marshall, 1890.

Not seen. Not located. Entry from PC listing July 1, 1890. Wrapper? Pp. 14.

12706. Ballads, Lyrics and Sonnets from the Poetic Works of Henry Wadsworth Longfellow

Boston and New York   Houghton, Mifflin and Company   The Riverside Press, Cambridge   M DCCC XC

12707. The Early Poems . . .

Boston and New York   Houghton, Mifflin and Company   The Riverside Press, Cambridge 1890

Marbled boards, leather shelfback. Catalogue of T. Y. Crowell & Co., New York, inserted at back. Occurs with the Crowell imprint at foot of spine; and, foot of spine unstamped.

12708. Longfellow's Latest Poems Copyright

London   George Routledge and Sons, Limited   Broadway, Ludgate Hill   Glasgow, Manchester, and New York   1890

Reprint? For comment see in *Section Six.*

12709. Poems and Ballads . . . Illustrated.

New York: Worthington Co., 747 Broadway. 1890.

12710. The Poetical Works . . . with Numerous Illustrations.

Boston: Houghton, Mifflin and Company. New York: 11 East Seventeenth Street. The Riverside Press, Cambridge. 1890.

The Complete Poetical Works . . .

New York   Grosset & Dunlap Publishers ⟨1891; *i.e.,* not before 1905⟩

See below under 1905.

12711. . . . Longfellow Leaflets   Poems and Prose Passages from the Works of Henry Wadsworth Longfellow . . . Compiled by Josephine E. Hodgdon   Illustrated

Houghton, Mifflin and Company   Boston: 4 Park Street; New York: 85 Fifth Avenue   Chicago: 378-388 Wabash Avenue   The Riverside Press, Cambridge   ⟨1891⟩

At head of title: Riverside Literature Series

Cloth; and, printed paper wrapper. On wrapper: Issued Monthly   No. 42, Extra (Double No. F) April, 1889 ⟨*sic*⟩   On cloth binding: Extra Double Number F

Caution: The only located example (and here described) was issued not before May, 1901. Was there a printing issued with the earlier New York address *11 East Seventeenth Street?*

For prior publication under a variant title see entry No. 12594.

12712. . . . Longfellow's Poetical Works   New Edition . . .

London   George Routledge and Sons, Limited   Broadway, Ludgate Hill   Glasgow, Manchester, and New York   1891

At head of title: Author's Complete Copyright Edition

12713. Outre-Mer: A Pilgrimage beyond the Sea . . . Revised Edition.

Philadelphia: David McKay, Publisher, 23 South Ninth Street. 1891.

12714. Poems . . . New Revised Edition. With Numerous Illustrations.

Boston: Houghton, Mifflin and Company. The Riverside Press, Cambridge. ⟨1891⟩

Cloth? Red line edition.

12715. Poems and Ballads . . . Illustrated.

New York   Worthington Co., 747 Broadway   1891

12716. The Poetical Works . . . with Numerous Illustrations.

Boston: Houghton, Mifflin and Company. New York: 11 East Seventeenth Street. The Riverside Press, Cambridge. 1891.

Reprinted under date ⟨1891⟩.

12717. The Poetical Works . . .

Boston and New York   Houghton, Mifflin and Company   The Riverside Press, Cambridge   ⟨1891⟩

Cabinet Edition.

12718. The Poetical Works . . . Household Edition with Illustrations

Boston and New York   Houghton, Mifflin and Company   The Riverside Press, Cambridge   ⟨1891⟩

12719. ⟨Standard Library Edition⟩

Boston and New York   Houghton, Mifflin and Company   The Riverside Press, Cambridge

Vols. 1-11 dated ⟨1886; *i.e.,* 1891⟩. Vols. 12-14 dated ⟨1891⟩.

12720. The Song of Hiawatha . . . with Illustrations from Designs by Frederic Remington

Boston and New York   Houghton, Mifflin and Company   The Riverside Press, Cambridge   M DCCC XCI

Cloth; suède; and, 250 numbered copies in vellum.

12721. Woods in Winter. Sunrise on the Hills ...

Boston: Samuel E. Cassino. Copyright 1892.

Printed pictorial wrapper.

Deposited July 14, 1892.

12722. Kavanagh and Other Pieces ... Nineteenth Edition

Boston   Houghton, Mifflin and Company   New York: 11 East Seventeenth Street   The Riverside Press, Cambridge   1892

Cloth?

12723. Poems ... Illustrated by Louis K. Harlow ... ⟨and others⟩

Boston   Samuel E. Cassino   Exchange Building ⟨1892⟩

On pp. 58-81 appear twelve poems which, according to the editor, "have not been included in any volume of Mr. Longfellow's poems." The statement is erroneous; the poems had prior publication in several of Longfellow's works.

12724. The Early Poems of Henry Wadsworth Longfellow with Biographical Sketch by N. H. Dole.

New York: 46 East 14th Street. Thomas Y. Crowell & Co. Boston: 100 Purchase Street. ⟨1893⟩

Deposited Aug. 7, 1893.

12725. Poems ... Vignette Edition. With One Hundred New Illustrations by Charles Howard Johnson

New York   Frederick A. Stokes Company Publishers ⟨1893⟩

Three quarters cloth, floral or marbled paper boards sides. Deposited Sept. 13, 1893.

12726. The Complete Poetical Works ... Handy Volume Edition ...

Boston and New York   Houghton, Mifflin and Company   The Riverside Press, Cambridge   1893

5 Vols. Deposited Nov. 22, 1893.

12727. ... The Poetical Works ...

London   Henry Frowde   Oxford University Press Warehouse Amen Corner, E. C.   1893

At head of title: Complete Copyright Edition.

Issued on ordinary paper and India paper. Issued in cloth and leather according to contemporary notices. Listed PC Dec. 9; Bkr Dec. 15, 1893.

12728. The Belfry of Bruges, The Seaside and the Fireside and Other Poems ...

Boston   Samuel E. Cassino   1893

Celluloid binding. Pagination: ⟨i-vi⟩, 229-⟨352⟩.

12729. Choicest Poems of Henry W. Longfellow with Photogravure Illustrations

New York   Geo. M. Allen Company   Broadway, Cor. 21st Street   1893

12730. The Complete Poetical Works ... Cambridge Edition

Boston and New York   Houghton, Mifflin and Company   The Riverside Press, Cambridge   1893

12731. The Early Poems ... with Biographical Sketch by Nathan Haskell Dole.

New York: 46 East 14th Street. Thomas Y. Crowell & Co. Boston: 100 Purchase Street. ⟨1893⟩

12732. The Hanging of the Crane and Other Poems of the Home ...

London   Longmans, Green, and Co. 1893 ...

On verso of title page: The Riverside Press, Cambridge, Mass., U.S.A. Printed by H. O. Houghton & Company.

12733. Poems ... with Biographical Sketch by Nathan Haskell Dole

Boston: 100 Purchase Street   Thomas Y. Crowell & Company New York: 46 East 14th Street ⟨1893⟩

12734. Poems Selections ...

H M Caldwell Co   New York & Boston ⟨1893⟩

Cloth label on cover.

12735. Three Noted Poems ...

New York   E. P. Dutton & Company   31 West Twenty-Third Street   1893

12736. Voices of the Night and Other Poems ... with Biographical Sketch by N. H. Dole

New York: 46 East Fourteenth Street   Thomas Y. Crowell & Company   Boston: 100 Purchase Street ⟨1893⟩

Cloth; printed wood veneer boards, cloth shelf-back; flowered paper boards sides, cloth shelf-back.

12737. The Hanging of the Crane and Other Poems of the Home . . .

Boston and New York   Houghton, Mifflin and Company   The Riverside Press, Cambridge M DCCC XCIV

Deposited Oct. 18, 1893.

12738. The Poetical Works . . . Household Edition with Illustrations

Boston and New York   Houghton, Mifflin and Company   The Riverside Press, Cambridge ⟨1894⟩

Deposited July 14, 1894.

12739. . . . Paul Revere's Ride and Other Poems . . . with Explanatory Notes

Houghton, Mifflin and Company Boston: 4 Park Street; New York: 11 East Seventeenth Street Chicago: 28 Lakeside Building The Riverside Press, Cambridge ⟨1894⟩

At head of title: The Riverside Literature Series

Printed paper wrapper. Issued as No. 63 of the series under date *Sept. 5, 1894.* Deposited Sept. 19, 1894.

12740. The Children's Hour and Other Poems Paul Revere's Ride and Other Poems . . .

Houghton Mifflin Company Boston . . . New York . . . Chicago . . . The Riverside Press Cambridge ⟨1894; *i.e.,* not before 1908⟩

At head of title: The Riverside Literature Series

Query: Previously issued by Houghton, Mifflin & Company?

12741. The Complete Poetical Works . . . Household Edition with Illustrations

Boston and New York   Houghton, Mifflin and Company   The Riverside Press, Cambridge ⟨1894⟩

12742. Poems . . . New Revised Edition. With Numerous Illustrations.

Boston: Houghton, Mifflin and Company. The Riverside Press, Cambridge. ⟨1894⟩

Red line edition.

12743. . . . The Poetical Works . . . (Reprinted from the Revised American Edition, Including Recent Poems.) With Explanatory Notes.

London: Frederick Warne and Co., Bedford Street, Strand. 1894.

At head of title: The "Albion" Edition.

12744. The Belfry of Bruges The Seaside and the Fireside and Other Poems . . .

Philadelphia Henry Altemus 1895

12745. The Courtship of Miles Standish . . . Illustrations . . . by Boughton, Merrill, Reinhart Perkins, Hitchcock, Shapleigh, and Others

Boston and New York   Houghton, Mifflin and Company   The Riverside Press, Cambridge M DCCC XCVI

Deposited Oct. 10, 1895.

12746. Selections from Longfellow's Poems Including Evangeline Edited . . . by M. T. Quinn . . .

London   George Bell & Sons   And Bombay 1896

In *Bell's English Classics* series.

12747. The Works . . . Poems and Prose . . . with Life of Longfellow by Robert Cochrane . . .

Edinburgh   W. P. Nimmo, Hay, & Mitchell 1897

Cloth?

12748. . . . Selections from Longfellow.

Educational Publishing Company, 50 Bromfield St., Boston . . . New York . . . Chicago . . . San Francisco . . . 1898.

Cover-title. At head of title: Published Weekly. Vol. V. Sept. 12, 1898. No. 126 . . . Young Folk's Library of Choice Literature.

Printed paper wrapper.

12749. Christus . . . in Three Parts

Boston and New York   Houghton, Mifflin and Company   The Riverside Press, Cambridge ⟨1899⟩

Deposited June 15, 1899.

12750. The Complete Poetical Works . . . Handy Volume Edition . . .

Boston and New York   Houghton, Mifflin and Company   The Riverside Press, Cambridge 1899

3 Vols. Other volumes issued? See above under 1893.

12751. The Complete Poetical Works ... Household Edition with Illustrations

Boston and New York   Houghton, Mifflin and Company   The Riverside Press, Cambridge 1899

12752. Voices of the Night and Other Poems ... with Biographical Sketch by N. H. Dole

New York   Thomas Y. Crowell & Company Publishers ‹1899›

12753. The Complete Poetical Works ... Library Edition Illustrated with Photogravures

Boston and New York   Houghton, Mifflin and Company   The Riverside Press, Cambridge MDCCCC

Cloth? Deposited June 8, 1900.

12754. Evangeline ‹and Other Poems› ... with Notes and Biographical Sketch by Henry Ketcham

New York   A. L. Burt, Publisher ‹1900›

Deposited June 27, 1900.

12755. Poems ...

Chicago   W. B. Conkey Company Publishers ‹1900›

Deposited Aug. 20, 1900.

12756. The Courtship of Miles Standish and Other Poems ... with an Introduction by Richard Burton

New York   Thomas Y. Crowell & Co. Publishers ‹1900›

Cloth. Also printed paper boards, cloth shelfback. Deposited Oct. 11, 1900. *Note:* Several printings were done from the same plates without alteration; a copyright deposit copy is imprinted as above. A reprint was issued with the imprint: *New York   Thomas Y. Crowell and Company Publishers ‹1900›.*

12757. ... Giles Corey of the Salem Farms ...

Houghton, Mifflin and Company   Boston: 4 Park Street; New York: 11 East Seventeenth Street   Chicago: 378-388 Wabash Avenue   The Riverside Press, Cambridge ‹1900›

At head of title: The Riverside Literature Series

Printed paper wrapper. Issued as No. 146 of the series. Deposited Dec. 29, 1900.

12758. The Complete Poetical Works ... Household Edition with Illustrations

Boston and New York   Houghton, Mifflin and Company   The Riverside Press, Cambridge 1900

12759. Beautiful Thoughts from Henry Wadsworth Longfellow Arranged by F.W.H.

New York James Pott & Company MCMI.

Cloth, portrait pasted to front; and, flexible leather. Deposited Aug. 20, 1901. *Note:* BAL has not checked the text and presumes that no first edition material appears herein.

12760. The Complete Poetical Works ... Household Edition with Illustrations

Boston and New York   Houghton, Mifflin and Company   The Riverside Press, Cambridge ‹1901›

Presumably issued in cloth. Deposited Sept. 7, 1901.

12761. Poems ... with Biographical Sketch by Nathan Haskell Dole

New York   Thomas Y. Crowell & Co. Publishers ‹1901›

Deposited Dec. 24, 1901. *Three formats noted;* sequence, if any, not determined:

A: Maroon T cloth. On binding: *Astor Edition.* Leaf: 7¼" scant x 4⅞".

B: Green T cloth. Series not identified on binding. Leaf: 8¼" x 5⅝".

C: Padded skiver. Corners rounded; edges gilt over red. Leaf: 7⅛" x 4¾".

12762. The Complete Poetical Works ... Cabinet Edition

Boston and New York   Houghton, Mifflin and Company   The Riverside Press, Cambridge 1901

12763. The Courtship of Miles Standish and Other Poems ... with Biographical Sketch and Explanatory Notes by Henry Ketcham

New York A. L. Burt, Publisher ‹1901›

12764. Poems ... Selected and Arranged for Use in Schools by E. E. Speight ...

London   Adam and Charles Black   1901

Printed flexible cloth.

12765. Poems ... Including Evangeline   The Song of Hiawatha and the Courtship of Miles Standish with Biographical Sketch and Explanatory Notes by Henry Ketcham

New York A. L. Burt, Publisher ‹1901›

12766. Poems of Henry Wadsworth Longfellow with Illustrations from the Original Paintings . . .

A. L. Burt Company, Publishers 52-58 Duane Street, New York ⟨1901⟩

12767. Poems . . . Including Evangeline The Song of Hiawatha and the Courtship of Miles Standish with Biographical Sketch and Explanatory Notes by Henry Ketcham

A. L. Burt Company, Publishers, 52-58 Duane Street, New York ⟨1901⟩

Pp. 347.

12768. Poems . . . Including Evangeline The Song of Hiawatha The Courtship of Miles Standish and Tales of a Wayside Inn with Biographical Sketch and Explanatory Notes by Henry Ketcham

A. L. Burt Company, Publishers New York ⟨1901⟩

Issued in cloth, with the designation, *The Home Library,* on binding. Also issued in flexible leather without designation of series on binding.

Pp. 399.

12769. Poems . . . Vignette Edition. With One Hundred New Illustrations by Charles Howard Johnson

New York James Pott Co. MCMI

Flexible leather.

. . . Longfellow Leaflets . . .

Houghton, Mifflin and Company Boston . . . New York: 85 Fifth Avenue . . . ⟨1891, *i.e.,* not before May, 1901⟩

See entry No. 12711.

12770. Poems . . . with Biographical Sketch by Nathan Haskell Dole

New York Thomas Y. Crowell Company Publishers ⟨1901; *i.e.,* not before 1911⟩

Astor Edition.

12771. The Poems . . . with a Biographical Sketch by Nathan Haskell Dole

New York Thomas Y. Crowell Company Publishers ⟨1901; *i.e.,* not before 1911⟩

12772. The Complete Poetical Works . . . Cambridge Edition

Boston and New York Houghton, Mifflin and Company The Riverside Press, Cambridge ⟨1902⟩

12773. The Complete Poetical Works . . . Household Edition . . .

Boston and New York Houghton, Mifflin and Company The Riverside Press, Cambridge M DCCCC II

Reprinted under date ⟨1902⟩.

12774. . . . H. W. Longfellow and W. C. Bryant with an Introduction to Longfellow by Edwin Markham . . .

P. F. Collier & Son New York City ⟨1902⟩

At head of title: A Library of Poetical Literature in Thirty-Two Volumes

Pp. 347, ⟨368⟩.

12775. Poems . . .

Chicago Homewood Publishing Company Publishers ⟨1902⟩

12776. The Complete Poetical Works . . . Cambridge Edition

Boston and New York Houghton, Mifflin and Company The Riverside Press, Cambridge ⟨1903⟩

12777. The Complete Poetical Works . . . Household Edition with Two Hundred and Seventy Illustrations

Boston and New York Houghton, Mifflin and Company The Riverside Press, Cambridge ⟨1903⟩

Cloth?

12778. The Complete Poetical Works . . . Library Edition . . .

Boston and New York Houghton, Mifflin and Company The Riverside Press, Cambridge MDCCCCIII

12779. The Poetical Works . . . with Explanatory Notes . . . Vol. I

London Grant Richards 48 Leicester Square 1903

All issued? *The World's Classics,* Vol. 39.

12780. Selections from the Poems of H. W. Longfellow with an Introduction by Lilian M. Faithfull . . .

London   Methuen & Co. 36 Essex Street, W.C. MDCCCCIII

12781. ... The Complete Writings ... in Eleven Volumes ... ⟨Fly-title-page⟩

Boston and New York   Houghton, Mifflin and Company   The Riverside Press, Cambridge MCMIV

At head: *Edition de Luxe.* Linen; and, buckram, printed paper label on spine. Limited to 750 numbered copies.

Deposited Nov. 17, 1904; listed PW Feb. 11, 1905.

12782. ... The Complete Writings ... in Eleven Volumes ... ⟨Fly-title-page⟩

Boston and New York   Houghton, Mifflin and Company   The Riverside Press, Cambridge ⟨1904⟩

At head: Craigie Edition. *Note:* Entry based on a mixed set; *i.e.,* certain volumes are reprints with the imprint of Houghton Mifflin Company.

12783. The Complete Poetical Works ... Illustrated

New York   Grosset & Dunlap Publishers ⟨1891; *i.e.,* not before *ca.* 1905⟩

12784. ... Selected Poems   Longfellow, Macaulay, Lowell ... with Introductions and Notes ...

Houghton, Mifflin and Company   Boston ... New York ... Chicago ... The Riverside Press, Cambridge ⟨1905⟩

At head of title: The Riverside Literature Series

12785. The Complete Poetical Works ... Household Edition with Two Hundred and Seventy Illustrations

Boston and New York   Houghton, Mifflin and Company   The Riverside Press, Cambridge ⟨1906⟩

Cloth? Deposited April 9, 1906.

12786. A Longfellow Calendar Edited by Anna Harris Smith

New York   Thomas Y. Crowell & Co. Publishers ⟨1906⟩

On copyright page: *Published, September, 1906*

Listed PW Oct. 13, 1906. Reissued with a cancel title-page: *London   George G. Harrap & Company 15 York Street, Covent Garden* ⟨n.d., 1906⟩. Reissued as *Longfellow Day by Day,* New York: Crowell ⟨1906; *i.e.,* 1908⟩; see below.

Note: BAL has not checked the text and presumes that no first edition material appears herein.

12787. ... The Building of the Ship and Other Poems ...

Houghton, Mifflin and Company   Boston ... New York ... Chicago ... The Riverside Press, Cambridge ⟨1906⟩

At head of title: The Riverside Literature Series

Printed paper wrapper. Issued as No. 38 of the series.

Longfellow Day by Day Edited by Anna H Smith

New York ... ⟨1906⟩

See below under 1908.

12788. The Sonnets of Henry Wadsworth Longfellow Arranged with an Introduction by Ferris Greenslet

Boston and New York   Houghton Mifflin & Company MDCCCCVII

Printed paper boards; leaf: 6″ x 4″. Also a large paper edition, paper boards, paper label on spine, limited to 275 numbered copies; leaf: 7¾″ x 5⅛″. Large paper copies deposited Nov. 6, 1907.

12789. The Children of the Lord's Supper. By Esaias Tegnér. Translated by H. W. Longfellow.

Manchester: H. Rawson and Co., Printers, New Brown Street. 1907.

Printed paper wrapper folded over flexible boards.

12790. Greetings from Longfellow

Copyright 1907   Cupples & Leon Co. New York

Cover-title. Pictorial paper wrapper. *Note:* Several printings have been noted, including one without date. No attempt has been made to establish a sequence.

12791. ... The Poetical Works of Longfellow

Henry Frowde   Oxford University Press London, New York, and Toronto   1907

At head of title: Oxford Complete Copyright Edition

12792. ... The Complete Poetical Works ...

Boston and New York Houghton Mifflin Company The Riverside Press Cambridge ⟨1908⟩

At head of title: Autograph Poets

12793. The Complete Poetical Works ... Cambridge Edition

Boston and New York Houghton Mifflin Company The Riverside Press, Cambridge ⟨1908⟩

12794. Longfellow Day by Day Edited by Anna H Smith

New York T Y Crowell & Co Publishers ⟨1906; *i.e.,* 1908⟩

Cloth; and, leather. On copyright page: *Published, September, 1906* Listed PW Oct. 8, 1908. A reissue of *A Longfellow Calendar* ⟨1906⟩, see above. Reprinted and reissued with the imprint: *New York Thomas Y Crowell Company Publishers* ⟨1906; *i.e.,* not before 1911⟩

12795. Poems of New England Edited by Henry Wadsworth Longfellow

Boston and New York Houghton Mifflin Company The Riverside Press Cambridge 1908

Flexible leather; and, paper boards, cloth shelfback, printed paper label on front.

12796. The Poems of Henry Wadsworth Longfellow 1823–1866

London: Published by J M Dent & Co And in New York by E P Dutton & Co ⟨1909⟩

"Introduction," dated at end 1909, by Katharine Tynan. *Everyman's Library* series.

12797. From Day to Day with Longfellow Compiled by Olive Van Buren

New York Barse & Hopkins Publishers ⟨1910⟩

Deposited July 21, 1910. Listed PW Aug. 20, 1910.

12798. Christmas Bells ...

Buffalo New York The Hayes Lithographing Co. ⟨1910⟩

Pictorial paper boards. *The Best Wishes Series.*

12799. ... The Complete Poetical Works ...

Boston and New York Houghton Mifflin Company The Riverside Press Cambridge 1910

At head of title: Autograph Poets

12800. The Poetical Works ...

London: Henry Frowde Oxford University Press, Amen Corner, E.C. New York: 35 West 32nd Street Toronto: 25-27 Richmond Street West Melbourne: Cathedral Buildings 1912

Cloth?

12801. ... The Complete Poetical Works ...

Boston and New York Houghton Mifflin Company The Riverside Press Cambridge ⟨1913⟩

At head of title: Autograph Poets

12802. Poems by Tegnér The Children of the Lord's Supper Translated ... by Henry Wadsworth Longfellow ...

New York The American-Scandinavian Foundation 1914

Deposited Oct. 21, 1914. Issued as Vol. 2 of *Scandinavian Classics.*

12803. The Complete Poetical Works ... Cambridge Edition

Boston and New York Houghton Mifflin Company The Riverside Press, Cambridge ⟨1914⟩

12804. ... The Poetical Works ...

Humphrey Milford Oxford University Press London ... New York ... 1921

Padded leather. At head of title: Oxford Edition

12805. The Three Kings ...

⟨New York, 1922⟩

Boards. "Four hundred copies ... printed ... by William Edwin Rudge ... Christmas MCMXXII"

12806. Sonnets Preceding the Inferno, Purgatorio, and Paradiso of the Comedy of Dante Alighieri ...

San Francisco: Printed for Aurelia Henry Reinhardt by John Henry Nash MDCCCCXXV

Paper wrapper, printed paper label on front. 400 copies only.

12807. The Liberty Bell of Louvain Poems by Henry Wadsworth Longfellow and Johann Christoph Friedrich von Schiller ...

Privately Printed for Edward Dean Adams Chairman of the Committee on War Memorial to American Engineers 1928 ⟨New York⟩

Printed paper boards. "A souvenir of Louvain July fourth, 1928 ..."—p. ⟨3⟩.

12808. The Leap of Roushan Beg ... a Complete Facsimile Edited with an Introduction and Notes by Arthur Christy

New York William Edwin Rudge 1931

500 copies only. Deposited May 26, 1931.

12809. Selected Poems ...

Walter J. Black, Inc. New York ⟨1932⟩

Flexible leather, label on spine and on front.

12810. *Entry cancelled.*

12811. Henry Wadsworth Longfellow Representative Selections, with Introduction, Bibliography, and Notes by Odell Shepard ...

American Book Company New York Cincinnati Chicago Boston Atlanta ⟨1934⟩

On copyright page of first printing: *W.P.1.*

12812. The Poems of Longfellow ...

Illustrated Modern Library New York ⟨1944⟩

Printed paper boards, cloth shelfback. Deposited Dec. 9, 1944.

12813. Favorite Poems of ⟨*i.e.,* by⟩ Henry Wadsworth Longfellow with an Introduction by Henry Seidel Canby and Illustrations by Edward A. Wilson

Garden City, New York Doubleday & Company, Inc. MCMXLVII

12814. The Continental Tales of Henry Wadsworth Longfellow ⟨Edited by J. I. Rodale⟩ ...

The Story Classics Allentown Pennsylvania 1948

Printed boards sides, cloth shelfback. On copyright page: *First Story Classics Edition.* Deposited May 14, 1948.

12815. Best Loved Poems ... with Twelve Original Illustrations by Paul Hamlin

Peoples Book Club Chicago ⟨1949⟩

IN THIS SECTION are listed collections of *undated* reprints issued under the author's name; and, separate editions, *i.e.*, separate printings of poems extracted from collections issued by the author. For *dated* reprints see in *Section II*. See *Section IV* for books by others containing material by Longfellow reprinted from earlier books.

Note: The text of the books included in this section has not been collated against earlier printings and certain of these reprints may contain revisions. Similarly, publishers of some of the books listed in this section used original periodical text rather than the revised text of the authorized editions. No attempt has been made to indicate which of the texts occurs in the reprints.

ARRANGEMENT

Entries in this section are arranged alphabetically by first principal word in the title. Publications with the same title (*Poems* or *Poetical Works,* etc.) are further broken down alphabetically by place of publication; hence, *The Poems . . . , Boston,* precedes *The Poems . . . , London;* etc. Two or more printings of the same title published by two or more publishers at the same place are arranged by publisher; hence, *London: Bohn* precedes *London: Routledge* and both precede *London: Walker.*

Warning: BAL has been unable to establish precise publication dates for certain of the books listed in the following section; entries for such publications must be considered tentative.

Amalfi

See *Longfellow's . . . ,* below.

12815A. ⟨The Arrow and the Song⟩

⟨Cambridge, Mass., after March 24, 1882, before Dec. 12, 1882⟩

Single cut sheet folded to make 4 pages. Pp. ⟨1⟩ and ⟨4⟩ blank.

P. ⟨2⟩: *From the Longfellow Memorial Association of Cambridge, Mass. to the Children of America . . .*

P. ⟨3⟩: ⟨Wood engraving captioned:⟩ *View of Mr. Longfellow's Home . . .* ⟨in facsimile:

The Arrow and the Song, twelve lines of text⟩ . . .

Page: 7⅛″ full x 4½″ scant.

12816. The Arrow and the Song . . .

⟨n.p., n.d., New York, 1939⟩

Cover-title. 435 copies only. A Christmas token issued by Mr. and Mrs. George Arents.

12817. Ballads and Poems . . .

H M Caldwell Co   New York & Boston ⟨n.d., not before 1897⟩

Printed paper boards, cloth shelfback, print pasted to front cover.

12818. The Belfry of Bruges   The Seaside and the Fireside and Other Poems . . .

Boston   Samuel E. Cassino ⟨n.d., ca. 1880⟩

Probably issued in pictorial paper wrapper.

12819. The Birds of Killingworth

⟨Boston: American Humane Education Society, n.d., not before 1889⟩

Printed self-wrapper.

The Book of Beauty . . . Edited by Henry Wordsworth ⟨sic⟩ Longfellow.

. . . New York. ⟨n.d., 1879?⟩

See in *Section Six.*

12820. . . . The Bridge . . .

A. W. Auner's Card and Job Printing Rooms, Philadelphia, Pa. ⟨n.d., not before 1871⟩

Anonymous. At head of title: *A. W. Auner . . . Philadelphia, Pa.* Single leaf. Printed on recto only. Issued as an advertisement for the sheet music issued by Harding, New York. 8″ x 4⅝″.

12821. Brilliants from Longfellow

Buffalo   New York   The Hayes Lithographing Co. ⟨n.d., not before 1901⟩

12822. Christmas Bells Longfellow

⟨n.p., n.d., probably after 1910⟩

Pictorial paper boards. Printed throughout in colors. Apparently issued as a Christmas booklet. Printed from the stones of the Hayes Lithographing Company's ⟨1910⟩ edition; see in *Section II.*

12823. The Courtship of Miles Standish ⟨and Other Poems⟩ . . .

Chicago W. B. Conkey Company ⟨n.d., not before 1894⟩

Oxford Series. Text, pp. 208; notes, pp. 209-255.

12824. The Courtship of Miles Standish ⟨and Other Poems⟩ . . .

Chicago W. B. Conkey Company ⟨n.d., not before 1894⟩

Limp leather. Pp. 208.

12825. The Courtship of Miles Standish ⟨and Other Poems⟩ . . .

Chicago and New York The Henneberry Company ⟨n.d., not before 1900⟩

12826. . . . The Courtship of Miles Standish and Other Poems . . .

London: "Review of Reviews" Office. Price One Penny. ⟨n.d., 1896?⟩

At head of title: *The Masterpiece Library* . . . Issued as No. 46 of the series. Printed paper wrapper.

12827. The Courtship of Miles Standish ⟨and Other Poems⟩ . . .

New York Barse & Hopkins Publishers ⟨n.d., not before 1910⟩

Limp suède.

12828. The Courtship of Miles Standish ⟨and Other Poems⟩ . . .

H M Caldwell Co New York & Boston ⟨n.d., not before 1897⟩

Printed paper boards, cloth shelfback, print pasted to front.

12829. The Courtship of Miles Standish ⟨and Other Poems⟩ . . .

New York Hurst & Company Publishers ⟨n.d., *ca.* 1900-1912⟩

Noted in the following bindings: Padded leather; cloth, stamped in gold; cloth, print pasted to front cover; cloth, sides unstamped, spine stamped in gold and blind; suède. At least four printings, with variations in the imprint, were issued *ca.* 1900-1912.

12830. The Courtship of Miles Standish and Other Poems . . .

New York The Mershon Company Publishers ⟨n.d., *ca.* 1900⟩

12831. . . . The Courtship of Miles Standish and Other Poems Illustrated

Philadelphia Henry Altemus Company ⟨n.d., *ca.* 1901⟩

At head of title: Henry Wadsworth Longfellow

Cloth, print pasted to front cover.

12832. . . . The Cross of Snow . . . July 10, 1879 . . .

⟨n.p., n.d., not before May 7, 1887⟩

Heavy pink card. Printed on recto only. 8¼″ x 4″. Edges bevelled and gilded. At head is an extract from *Life of Henry W. Longfellow.*

12833. The Day Is Done . . .

London: Ernest Nister 24 St. Bride Street E. C. Printed by E Nister at Nuremberg (Bavaria.) New York: E. P. Dutton & Co. 31 West Twenty Third Street. ⟨n.d., *ca.* 1885⟩

12834. The Divine Comedy of Dante Alighieri. Translated by Henry Wadsworth Longfellow . . . Inferno.

London George Routledge and Sons Broadway, Ludgate Hill New York: 416 Broome Street ⟨n.d., 1880?⟩

Issued in the *Excelsior Series.*

12835. The Earlier Poems of Henry Wadsworth Longfellow.

New York: The Bridge Pub. Co. ⟨n.d., *ca.* 1895⟩

Cloth?

12836. The Earlier Poems of Henry Wadsworth Longfellow.

New York: A. L. Burt, Publisher. ⟨n.d., *ca.* 1898⟩

Cloth? A copy in possession of ʙᴇᴠ inscribed by early owner April 1, 1898.

12837. Earlier Poems . . .

⟨New York⟩ The F. M. Lupton Publishing Company ⟨n.d., not before 1892⟩

In the *White Series.*

12838. Evangeline: A Tale of Acadie. With an Introduction, Historical and Explanatory. By H. W. Longfellow.

London: Kent and Richards, Paternoster Row. ⟨n.d., 1848⟩

Cloth? Paper boards? Date on the basis of the introduction which is dated at end: *June, 1848. Note:* The title-page is ambiguous and suggests that Longfellow wrote the "introduction, historical and explanatory"; reading indicates that Longfellow did not write the introduction.

12839. Evangeline A Tale of Acadie . . . Illustrated by Arthur Dixon.

London: Ernest Nister New York: E. P. Dutton & Co 1856. ⟨*i.e.,* n.d., *ca.* 19—⟩

Note: The *1856* below the imprint is a plate number, not a date.

12840. Evangeline ⟨and Other Poems⟩ . . .

Philadelphia Henry Altemus ⟨n.d., *ca.* 1895⟩

A copy at H inscribed by early owner Dec. 25, 1897.

12841. . . . Evangeline and Other Poems

Philadelphia Henry Altemus Company ⟨n.d., *ca.* 1903⟩

At head of title: *Henry W. Longfellow* Cloth, stamped in gold, two prints pasted to front cover. *Note:* On the basis of the terminal advertisements issued not before 1903.

12842. Evangeline and Other Poems . . .

The Mershon Company Rahway, N. J. New York ⟨n.d., *ca.* 1900⟩

Padded paper boards.

12843. Forget-Me-Not . . . Illustrated by Bessie Simpson . . .

Raphael Tuck & Sons, Ltd. . . . London, Paris, New York. ⟨n.d., 19—?⟩

Pictorial paper boards; cover scalloped and embossed; tied. Cover also cut with a lace-like effect to set off imprinted ivy leaves. Otherwise "Flowers," *Voices of the Night,* 1839.

12844. Gleanings from Nature from Bryant Longfellow & Whittier. Illustrated by David L. Munro.

⟨Lith. & Printed by Charles Hart & Sons, 36 Vesey St., N. Y., n.d., 1890?⟩

Cover-title. Pictorial paper wrapper. Unpaged. A copy in B inscribed by early owner Christmas, 1890.

12845. The Golden Legend . . .

London: Published by Knight and Son, 11, Clerkenwell Close. ⟨n.d., not before 1855⟩

12846. Harvard College During the War. By Capt. Nathan Appleton. Harvard Memorial Poems, by Emerson, Longfellow, Holmes, Lowell and S. F. Smith. Reproduced from the New England Magazine.

⟨The New England Magazine, Boston, n.d., 1891⟩

Printed paper wrapper. Cover-title.

12847. Henry W. Longfellow

Chicago: M. A. Donohue & Co 407-429 Dearborn St. ⟨n.d., *ca.* 1905⟩

Binder's title: *Longfellow's Poems*

12848. Hiawatha's Wooing . . .

⟨A. Henderson, Printer, 109 Fulton Street, N. Y., n.d., *ca.* 1869⟩

Cover-title. Printed paper wrapper. Issued as an advertisement for a painting by Jerome Thompson, "Hiawatha's Wooing," on exhibition at Gurney's Gallery, New York City.

12849. Household Poems . . .

The Happy Hour Library, Inc. New York, N. Y. ⟨n.d., 19—⟩

Cloth?

12850. Hyperion: A Romance . . . a New Edition, Revised by the Author.

London: William Tegg & Co.; Aylott & Jones; Partridge & Oakey; H. Washbourne. Glasgow: W. Collins; Griffin & Co. Edinburgh: J. Johnstone. ⟨n.d., not before 1847⟩

12851. Kavanagh, a Tale . . .

Liverpool: John Walker, 97, Bold Street. London: David Bogue, John Johnstone, Hamilton, Adams, and Co. Edinburgh: John Johnstone, Oliver and Boyd. Dublin: J. M'Glashan. ⟨n.d., 1849⟩

Advertised as *nearly ready* PC June 1, 1849; listed Ath June 23, 1849. Reprinted and reissued, not later than 1850, with the imprint: *Liverpool: John Walker, 7, Clayton Square* ...

12852. Kavanagh: A Tale ...

London: Printed and Published by Knight and Son, Clerkenwell Close; and Sold by All Booksellers. ⟨n.d., 1857⟩

12853. Kavanagh: A Tale ...

London: William Tegg & Co.; Aylott & Jones; Partridge & Oakey; H. Washbourne. Glasgow: W. Collins; Griffin & Co. Edinburgh: J. Johnstone. ⟨n.d., 1849⟩

12854. ... King Alfred and Othere (the Discoverer of the North Cape.)

Published by W. P. Nimmo. Edinburgh Marcus Ward & Co. ⟨n.d., 1872⟩

Cover-title. At head of title: *Price One Shilling.* Pictorial wrapper. Issued in *Marcus Ward's Royal Illuminated Legends* series. Listed PC Nov. 16, 1872.

12855. King Robert of Sicily ... Illustrated by Jane Willis Grey.

Raphael Tuck & Sons, London-Paris-New York ... ⟨n.d., 1894⟩

In the *Artistic Series*. Listed Bkr Dec. 14, 1894.

12856. The Legend Beautiful ...

Raphael Tuck & Sons, London, Paris, and New York ⟨n.d., 1889⟩

Cover-title. Self-wrapper. Listed PC Aug. 15, 1889.

12857. Longfellow

M. A. Donohue & Co. Chicago ⟨n.d., ca. 1905⟩

Padded leather.

12858. Longfellow's Flowers Illustrated by Ada Hanbury and Cloëte Brown.

London Sockl & Nathan. ⟨n.d., ca. 1885⟩

Pictorial boards, cloth shelfback.

12859. Longfellow's Poem of Amalfi

Souvenir de l'Hôtel Marine Rivière Italy Amalfi ⟨n.d., after June 1890⟩

Printed paper wrapper. Issued as an advertisement. Also issued by other establishments; several variant printings have been seen. BAL sus-

pects that no hotel in Amalfi failed to issue its own printing.

12860. Longfellow's Poems

Chicago M. A. Donohue & Company ⟨n.d., ca. 1905⟩

Cloth?

12861. Longfellow's Poems

Chicago M. A. Donohue & Co. 407-429 Dearborn St. ⟨n.d., ca. 1905⟩

Cloth, print pasted to front cover.

12862. Longfellow's Poetical Works Introduction and Notes by Walter Jerrold Copyright Edition

The John C. Winston Company Chicago Philadelphia Toronto ⟨n.d., not before 1900⟩

Flexible leather. At foot of p. 444: London and Glasgow: Collins' Clear-Type Press.

12863. Maidenhood a Poem ...

Boston: Estes & Lauriat, Washington Street. ⟨n.d., 1888⟩

Printed paper wrapper. Listed PW Dec. 29, 1888.

12864. Maidenhood ... Illustrated by J. Stanley.

Sampson Low, Marston, Searle & Rivington St. Dunstan's House, Fetter Lane, Fleet St., London ⟨n.d., not before 1875⟩

Printed paper wrapper.

12865. Michael Angelo A Dramatic Poem ...

London George Routledge & Sons Broadway, Ludgate Hill ⟨n.d., 1883⟩

For comment see *Michael Angelo,* 1882–1883, in *Section I.*

12866. Mixed Sweets from Routledge's Annual. By Mrs. Henry Wood ... H. W. Longfellow. With Illustrations.

London: George Routledge and Sons, the Broadway, Ludgate. ⟨n.d., 1867⟩

Printed paper wrapper. The only examined copy lacks the wrapper; was the wrapper dated? Listed in *English Catalogue* as a June, 1867, publication.

12867. Nature and the Child. (To Agassiz.) ...

⟨n.p., n.d., 19—⟩

Single leaf. Printed on recto only. Salmon-colored wove paper, probably of twentieth century manufacture. $5^{15}/_{16}$″ full x $3^{1}/_{8}$″ full. Otherwise "On the 50th Birthday of Agassiz." The title suggests an early printing; but the text is that of the collected appearance in *The Courtship* . . . , 1858.

12868. Nature Poems . . . Illustrated by Paul de Longpré

London: Ward, Lock & Bowden, Limited Warwick House, Salisbury Square, E. C. ⟨n.d., not before 1879⟩

12869. The Old Clock on the Stairs

Cowell's Anastatic Press   Ipswich ⟨England⟩ ⟨n.d., *ca.* 1875⟩

Flexible cloth.

12870. Old St. David's at Radnor.

⟨n.p., n.d., *ca.* 1880⟩

Cover-title. Two gray-blue cards, 6″ x 7″, hinged with cloth. On p. ⟨2⟩: Text of "Old St. David's at Radnor." On p. ⟨3⟩: A pasted photograph captioned: *Old St. David's Church, Radnor* . . . Probably prepared for sale at St. David's Church, Radnor. Reprint? In *Ultima Thule,* 1880. For another printing see No. 12613.

12871. Outre-Mer   A Pilgrimage beyond the Sea . . .

New York   United States Book Company   5 and 7 East Sixteenth Street. Chicago: 266 & 268 Wabash Ave. ⟨n.d., 1892–1894⟩

12872. Poems . . .

Chicago   W. B. Conkey Company ⟨n.d., not before 1894⟩

Also occurs with the imprint: *Chicago   W. B. Conkey Company Publishers* ⟨n.d.⟩; noted thus in leather only.

12873. Poems . . .

Chicago: Donohue, Henneberry & Co., 407-429 Dearborn Street. ⟨n.d., *ca.* 1895⟩

Reprinted and reissued by M. A. Donohue & Co.

12874. Poems . . . with an Introduction by the Right Rev. W. Boyd Carpenter . . .

The Gresham Publishing Company   34 Southampton Street Strand   London ⟨n.d., *ca.* 1900⟩

12875. Poems . . .

London: Kent & Richards, Paternoster Row. ⟨n.d., 1846–1848⟩

Cloth; and, printed paper wrapper. BMU copy received Aug. 22, 1848.

12876. Poems . . . with a Prefatory Note by Eva Hope.

London: Walter Scott, Limited, Paternoster Square. ⟨n.d., not before 1882⟩

12877. . . . Poems . . . The World's Popular Classics

Books, Inc. Publishers   New York   Boston ⟨n.d., *ca.* 1940⟩

At head of title: *Art-Type Edition.* Imitation leather.

12878. The Poems . . . Including the Song of Hiawatha

A. L. Burt Company, Publishers, 52-58 Duane Street, New York ⟨n.d., not before 1902⟩

12879. Poems . . .

H. M. Caldwell Company   New York ⟨n.d., not before 1896⟩

12880. Poems   Selections . . .

H M Caldwell Co   New York & Boston ⟨n.d., not before 1897⟩

Limp leather.

12881. Poems   Selections . . .

H. M. Caldwell Co., Publishers   New York and Boston ⟨n.d., not before 1897⟩

12882. . . . Poems by Henry Wadsworth Longfellow and William Cullen Bryant with Frontispiece

New York   P. F. Collier & Son . . . ⟨n.d., not before 1900⟩

Not seen. Entry on basis of photostats. At head of title: *American Authors in Prose and Poetry in Twelve Volumes*   Cloth?

12883. Poems . . .

New York   Home Book Company   45 Vesey Street ⟨n.d., 1893–1896⟩

On front: *Dresden Edition.* Also occurs with *New Beverly Edition* at foot of spine.

12884. Poems . . .

New York   Hurst & Company Publishers
⟨n.d., not before 1886⟩

Limp leather. Pp. 240.

12885. Poems . . .

New York   Hurst and Company Publishers
⟨n.d., *ca.* 1890⟩

Pp. 433.

12886. Poems . . .

New York   Hurst & Company Publishers
⟨n.d., *ca.* 1890–1900⟩

Pictorial boards, cloth shelfback. Pp. 489.

12887. Poems . . .

New York   Hurst & Company Publishers
⟨n.d., not before 1892⟩

Pp. 722.

12888. Poems . . .

New York: Hurst & Company, Publishers.
⟨n.d., not before 1892⟩

Three quarters leather. Pp. 780.

12889. Poems . . .

New York: The F. M. Lupton Publishing
Company. ⟨n.d., not before 1892⟩

12890. Poems . . .

New York   The Mershon Company Publishers ⟨n.d., not before *ca.* 1897⟩

12891. Poems . . .

Philadelphia   Henry Altemus ⟨n.d., *ca.* 1899⟩

2 Vols. A copy of Vol. 1 (only) at H has inserted
frontispiece dated 1899. *Note:* There were at
least two reprintings issued by *Henry Altemus
Company,* n.d.

12892. Poems and Ballads . . .

New York: The F. M. Lupton Publishing
Company. Nos. 72-76 Walker Street. ⟨n.d.,
not before 1893⟩

Another printing has been noted with the imprint: *New York: The F. M. Lupton Publishing
Company,* ⟨sic⟩ ⟨n.d.⟩

12893. Poems, Lyrical and Dramatic . . . with an
Introductory Essay, on the Genius & Writings
of the Author, by George Gilfillan . . .

Liverpool: John Walker, 97, Bold Street, Lon-
don: John Johnstone, Hamilton, Adams, and
Co., David Bogue. Edinburgh: Oliver &
Boyd, and John Johnstone. ⟨n.d., 1848⟩

Also noted with the imprint:

Liverpool: John Walker, 97, Bold Street, Lon-
don: Hamilton, Adams, and Co., David
Bogue, John Johnstone. Edinburgh: Oliver &
Boyd, and John Johnstone. Dublin: J.
M'Glashan. ⟨n.d., 1848⟩

"I embrace the earliest opportunity of thanking
you for your kind & polite letter of the 17th
April. I am glad to find that my edition ⟨pp.
358⟩ of your works has met with your favour
and in subsequent editions I will take care to
omit the pieces you mention . . ."—Letter from
John Walker to Longfellow, Liverpool, May 5,
1849 (letter in H). At least one such "subsequent" edition has been seen; text ends on p.
352.

Listed LG (cloth only) Dec. 30, 1848. There is a
possibility that the book was also issued in
printed paper boards.

12894. . . . Poems on Slavery . . .

⟨Boston: J. W. Alden, Publishing Agent, New
England Anti-Slavery Tract Association, n.d.,
1843⟩

Caption-title as above at head of p. 1. At head
of title: *Tract No. 1.* Imprint at foot of p. 8.
Self-wrapper. Advertised in the *Emancipator
and Free American* (Boston) Nov. 30, 1843:
"The two first of the new series of tracts, (the
regular publication of which will commence the
first of January next,) will be published in advance of that date. They are being stereotyped,
and will be ready for delivery early in December."

12895. The Poetical Works . . . with Prefatory
Notice   Eight Engravings on Steel.

Edinburgh: Gall & Inglis, 6 George Street.
London: Houlston & Wright. ⟨n.d., after
Jan. 1865⟩

Pp. 684.

12896. The Poetical Works . . . with Prefatory
Notice. Six Engravings on Steel.

Gall & Inglis. London: 25 Paternoster Sqr.
Edinburgh: 6 George Street. ⟨n.d., not before 1874⟩

12897. The Poetical Works . . . with Prefatory
Notice. Engravings on Steel.

Gall & Inglis. Edinburgh: Bernard Terrace.
London: 25 Paternoster Sqr. ⟨n.d., not before 1878⟩

12898. The Poetical Works ...

Edinburgh: William P. Nimmo. ⟨n.d., 1867⟩

Cloth? Pp. 599, 584*-598*, ⟨601⟩-619. Date assigned on the basis of the terminal advertisements. The first page of advertisements is dated 5.67. ⟨*i.e.,* May 1867⟩; the third page of advertisements is headed: ... *In Preparation for Christmas 1867.*

12899. The Poetical Works ...

Edinburgh: William P. Nimmo. ⟨n.d., 1868⟩

Pp. 633. Among *books received* PC July 1, 1868, this is described as in the "new style of binding, morocco elegant, with inlaid ivory side, illuminated in various colours and design." The above is so bound. Also noted with inserted terminal catalog *New Work for Christmas 1867.*

12900. The Poetical Works ...

Glasgow: Cameron and Ferguson, 88 and 94 West Nile Street. ⟨n.d., 1868⟩

Cloth. Also paper boards, cloth shelfback and corners. Also printed paper wrapper. Listed Bkr March 2; PC April 1, 1868, as the *People's Edition.* Advertised, with Pitman added to the imprint, Bkr Aug. 1, 1868.

12901. The Poetical Works ... Including His Translations and Notes ...

London: Bell & Daldy, 6, York Street, Covent Garden, and 186, Fleet Street. ⟨n.d., not before July 1867⟩

Publisher's leather. Also cloth?

12902. The Poetical Works ... with Illustrations.

London: James Blackwood & Co., Lovell's Court, Paternoster Row. ⟨n.d., not before 1869⟩

Date on basis of terminal advertisements.

12903. The Poetical Works ... Illustrated.

Cassell, Petter, Galpin & Co.: London, Paris & New York. [All Rights Reserved.] ⟨n.d., 1881⟩

Although not so identified this is the *Fine Art Edition.* Listed Ath March 5; PC April 1, 1881. *Note:* This was originally issued in paper-covered parts, 1879–18⟨80?⟩.

12904. The Poetical Works ... Edited, with a Critical Memoir, by William Michael Rossetti. Illustrated by Thomas Seccombe.

William Collins, Sons, & Co., Limited, London, Glasgow, and Edinburgh. ⟨n.d., not before 1880⟩

12905. ... The Poetical Works ... Edited, with a Critical Memoir, by William Michael Rossetti. Illustrated by Thomas Seccombe.

William Collins, Sons, & Co., Limited, London, Glasgow, and Edinburgh. ⟨n.d., after March 24, 1882⟩

At head of title: *The Grosvenor Poets.*

12906. The Poetical Works ...

London: Derry & Toms, Kensington. ⟨n.d., 188-?⟩

12907. The Poetical Works ... Complete. Illustrated by F. Gilbert.

London: John Dicks, 313, Strand; and All Booksellers. ⟨n.d., 1870⟩

Printed paper wrapper. Listed PC July 15; Bkr Aug. 3, 1870.

12908. Poetical Works of Longfellow

Eyre and Spottiswoode (Bible Warehouse), Ltd. 33, Paternoster Row, London, E.C. Edinburgh and New York ⟨n.d., 1906?⟩

Leather; silver embossed portrait of Longfellow on front cover.

12909. The Poetical Works of Longfellow Including Recent Poems

London: Griffith Farran & Co., Newbery House, 39, Charing Cross Road. ⟨n.d., 1889–1891⟩

The Newbery Classics.

12910. The Poetical Works ...

London: Milner and Sowerby. Paternoster Row. ⟨n.d., not before Sept. 1871⟩

12911. The Poetical Works ... Edited, with a Critical Memoir, by William Michael Rossetti. Illustrated by Wilfred Lawson.

London: E. Moxon, Son, & Co., Dover Street. ⟨n.d., 1870⟩

Listed Ath July 16; PC Aug. 15; Bkr Sept. 1, 1870. Reviewed Ath Aug. 20; Bkr Sept. 1, 1870. *Note:* The preceding relate to the small paper edition (7" x 4$\frac{11}{16}$") at 3/6. A large paper edition at 7/6 is first advertised in PC Oct. 1; listed Ath Oct. 8; PC Nov. 15, 1870. In PC Dec. 8, 1870, Moxon gives these forms: Cloth, 3/6;

morocco antique, 7/6; morocco extra, 10/6; large paper edition, 7/6.

12912. The Poetical Works ... Author's Complete Edition. With ⟨6⟩ Illustrations by Sir John Gilbert ...

London: George Routledge and Sons, the Broadway, Ludgate. ⟨n.d., 1879?⟩

Pp. viii, 726. Is this *The Five-Shilling Poet Edition* advertised Ath May 24, 1879? See next entry. *Two formats noted;* sequence, if any, not determined.

A: On front cover: LONGFELLOW / ILLUSTRATED

B: On front cover: LONGFELLOW /

12913. The Poetical Works ... Author's Copyright Edition with ⟨6⟩ Illustrations by Sir John Gilbert ...

London George Routledge and Sons Broadway, Ludgate Hill New York: 416 Broome Street ⟨n.d., 1879?⟩

Red line edition. Pp. viii, 726. Is this *The Five-Shilling Poet Edition* advertised Ath May 24, 1879? See preceding entry.

12914. The Poetical Works ... Edited, with a Critical Memoir, by William Michael Rossetti. Illustrated by Thomas Seccombe.

London: John Walker & Company, Farringdon House, Warwick Lane, E. C. ⟨n.d., after March 24, 1882⟩

Not seen. Entry on basis of photostats.

12915. The Poetical Works of Henry W. Longfellow.

London: Ward, Lock, & Co., Warwick House, Dorset Buildings, Salisbury Square, E. C. ⟨n.d., after Sept. 1878, before Sept. 1891⟩

12916. The Poetical Works ... Edited, with a Critical Memoir, by William Michael Rossetti. Illustrated by Thomas Seccombe.

London: Ward, Lock, & Co., Warwick House, Dorset Buildings, Salisbury Square, E. C. ⟨n.d., not before 1880⟩

Cloth? Leather? Red line edition.

12917. ... The Poetical Works ... (Including Recent Poems.) With Steel Portrait, and Illustrations by Cooper, Small, and Houghton.

London: Frederick Warne and Co. Bedford Street, Covent Garden. ⟨n.d., after March 29, 1867, before Dec. 25, 1870⟩

At head of title: *The Chandos Poets.* Noted only in publisher's leather.

12918. The Poetical Works ... (Reprinted from the Revised American Edition) with Explanatory Notes The "Albion" Edition

London Frederick Warne and Co. And New York ⟨n.d., 1882⟩

Listed PC Aug. 15, 1882.

12919. The Poetical Works ... (Comprising His Poems from 1839 to 1849.)

New York: Wm. L. Allison Company, Publishers. ⟨n.d., not before 1894⟩

12920. The Poetical Works ... (Comprising His Poems from 1839 to 1847.)

New York: The F. M. Lupton Publishing Company, Nos. 72-76 Walker Street. ⟨n.d., not before 1893⟩

Not seen. Entry on basis of photostats.

12921. The Poetical Works ...

Philadelphia The John C. Winston Co. Publishers ⟨n.d., not before 1891⟩

Flexible leather. Also cloth? At foot of p. 544: Collins' Clear-Type Press, London and Glasgow.

12922. The Prose Works ... Outre-Mer, Hyperion, and Kavanagh.

Cassell & Company, Limited: London, Paris, New York & Melbourne. ⟨n.d., 1891?⟩

Front end paper imprinted with advertisements dated *5.91.* Inserted advertisements at back dated *6.91.*

12923. The Prose Works ... Illustrated by Sir John Gilbert, R. A. Author's Edition

London George Routledge and Sons The Broadway, Ludgate New York: 416 Broome Street ⟨n.d., ca. 1875⟩

On the last page of terminal advertisements is an advertisement for *The Little Wide-Awake for 1876.* On binding: *Standard Library* Another printing (sequence not known) does not carry the statement *Standard Library* on the spine; the advertisements vary but support the *ca.* 1875 date.

The Prose Writers of America ... by Henry Wordsworth ⟨*sic*⟩ Longfellow.

New York ... ⟨n.d., 1879?⟩

See in Section Six.

12924. ... The Quadroon Girl ...

Sold by W. and F. G. Cash, 5, Bishopsgate Street, London; and by Jane Jowett Friends' Meeting Yard, Leeds, at 7d. per 100. ⟨n.d., 1852⟩

Single leaf. Printed on both sides. 7″ x 4⁵⁄₁₆″ scant. At head of title: Leeds Anti-slavery Series. No. 50.

12925. Resignation ...

⟨n.p., n.d., 1895?⟩

Cover-title. Single leaf folded to make four pages. Wove paper watermarked *Old Berkshire Mills 1895* Text on pp. ⟨2-3⟩. At foot of p. ⟨3⟩: *Printed by permission of Houghton, Mifflin & Co.* Immediately below text, p. ⟨3⟩: *From H. H. Dayton.*

12926. Resignation, and Other Poems ...

London Birn Brothers 27 Finsbury Street. Printed in Germany. ⟨n.d., 1889⟩

Printed stiff paper wrapper grained in imitation of leather. Listed PC Aug. 15, 1889.

12927. The Seaside and the Fireside ... Second Edition.

Liverpool: John Walker, 7, Clayton Square. London: Johnstone and Hunter; David Bogue; Hamilton, Adams, and Co.; Edinburgh: Johnstone and Hunter; Oliver and Boyd. Dublin: J. M'Glashan. ⟨n.d., not before 1850⟩

12928. Select Extracts from the Poetical Works ... Including Evangeline, and the Seaside and the Fireside.

London: J. Walker, 61, Conduit Street, Regent Street; Robert Theobald, 26, Paternoster Row, Late Johnstone and Hunter. ⟨n.d., 1851⟩

Listed Ath and LG Oct. 11; PC Nov. 1, 1851.

12929. A Selection from the Works of Henry Wadsworth Longfellow Edited and Prefaced by H. W. Dulcken ...

London: Ward, Lock & Co., Limited. ⟨n.d., not before 1896⟩

Flexible leather. On binding: *Gems from the Poets*

12930. The Singers ... with Etchings by Arthur Robertson

London: Elkin Mathews, Vigo Street, W. ⟨n.d., 1898⟩

Printed paper boards.

12931. The Song of Hiawatha ...

Educational Publishing Company   Boston   New York   Chicago   San Francisco   ⟨n.d., ca. 1900⟩

12932. Song of the Silent Land

⟨n.p., n.d., Boston, 1888?⟩

Cover-title. Single cut sheet folded to make four pages. Text on p. ⟨3⟩. Printed on flexible board. The only examined copy is inscribed: *Boston 1888.*

12933. Songs and Sonnets from Longfellow Illustrated by Henry Sandham.

London: Ernest Nister. New York: E. P. Dutton ... ⟨n.d., 1906⟩

Printed paper boards.

12934. Sonnets from the Spanish Including Torquemada ...

New York   A. L. Chatterton Company ⟨n.d., not before 1910⟩

Printed paper boards. "Torquemada" is a reprint of "The Theologian's Tale," in *Tales of a Wayside Inn,* 1863.

12935. The Spanish Student ...

London: John Dicks, 313, Strand; and All Booksellers. ⟨n.d., not before 1858⟩

Printed paper wrapper. Issued as No. 198 of *Dicks' Standard Plays.*

There Was a Little Girl

For all appearances of this jingle see under year 1883 in *Section I.*

12935A. Through the Year With Longfellow ...

Boston   DeWolfe, Fiske & Co. ⟨n.d., 1902–1905⟩

The Village Blacksmith

For a comment on the separate printings of this poem see in *Section II* under the year 1885.

12936. Voices of the Night; The Seaside and the Fireside; and Other Poems ... Illustrated with Sixty-Four Engravings on Wood ... Second Edition.

London: David Bogue, 86, Fleet Street. ⟨n.d., 1850⟩

Listed Ath Feb. 23, 1850.

12937. Voices of the Night   Ballads and Other Poems . . .

New York   Thomas Y. Crowell & Co. 46 East Fourteenth Street ⟨n.d., not before 1890⟩

Marbled paper boards, leather shelfback; also padded leather; also cloth.

12938. Voices of the Night   Ballads and Other Poems . . .

New York: Hurst & Co., Publishers, No. 122 Nassau Street. ⟨n.d., not before 1886⟩

Pp. 295. Occurs both with and without *Arlington Edition* on the binding. Another printing, with imprint in varying form, is paged 130, 106. Copies with the publisher's later address, *134-136 Grand Street,* were issued not before 1890. Quite late printings add *Evangeline.*

12939. Voices of the Night   Ballads and Other Poems . . .

Siegel-Cooper Co. New York Chicago ⟨n.d., not before 1896⟩

12940. Voices of the Night   Ballads and Other Poems . . .

Syndicate Trading Company, New York ⟨n.d., not before 1886⟩

Pp. 130, 77, 106.

12941. Voices of the Night   Ballads and Other Poems . . .

New York: R. Worthington, ⟨*sic*⟩ ⟨n.d., after 1885⟩

At foot of spine: *Household Edition*

12942. The White Czar; and Other Poems . . .

London: Ward, Lock, & Co., Warwick House, Dorset Buildings, Salisbury Square, E. C. ⟨n.d., 1878⟩

Printed paper boards. Listed PC Aug. 2, 1878.

12943. . . . The Witnesses . . .

Sold by W. and F. G. Cash, 5, Bishopsgate Street, London; and by Jane Jowett, Friends' Meeting Yard, Leeds, at 6*d.* per 100. ⟨n.d., 1853⟩

Anonymous. Single leaf. Printed on the verso of a single leaf. 7″ x 4⁵⁄₁₆″. At head of title: *Leeds Anti-slavery Series. No. 78.* On recto: *Leeds Anti-slavery Series. No. 77. Phoebe Morel* . . .

Two printings noted:

1: Stanza 2, line 3: *Float ships, with all their crews,* / Comma present at end of first line of imprint.

2: Stanza 2, line 3: *Float ships with all their crews,* / Comma not present at end of first line of imprint.

Note: A copy of the second printing has been seen in a bound volume made up of the *Leeds Anti-slavery Series* tracts; issued under the title: *Five Hundred Thousand Strokes for Freedom. A Series of Anti-Slavery Tracts* . . . , *London: W. & F. Cash* . . . *1853* . . .

HENRY WADSWORTH LONGFELLOW

SECTION IV

IN THIS SECTION are listed books by authors other than Longfellow containing material by him reprinted from earlier books. See *Section II* for dated reprints of Longfellow's own books; see *Section III* for undated reprints of Longfellow's own books.

The Classical Reader ... by Rev. F.W.P. Greenwood and G. B. Emerson ...

Boston ... 1826.

For fuller entry see BAL, Vol. 4, p. 187.

The Class Book of American Literature ... by John Frost.

Boston ... 1826.

For comment see BAL, Vol. 1, p. 136.

The National Reader ... ⟨Edited⟩ by John Pierpont ...

Boston ... 1827.

"April," p. 152; otherwise "An April Day." See note under *Miscellaneous Poems Selected from the United States Literary Gazette,* under year 1826, in *Section I.*

Specimens of American Poetry ... in Three Volumes. By Samuel Kettell ...

Boston ... MDCCCXXIX.

For comment see entry No. 3251.

The National Reader: A Selection of Exercises in Reading and Speaking ... by John Pierpont ... Re-Edited by E. H. Barker ...

London: Longman, Rees, Orme, Brown, and Green. Price Four Shillings and Six-Pence, Bound. 1829.

Publisher's leather. "April," p. 144; otherwise "An April Day." See note under *Miscellaneous Poems Selected from the United States Literary Gazette,* under year 1826, in *Section I.*

The Lyre. Fugitive Poetry of the XIXth Century.

London ... M DCCC XXX.

For comment see BAL, Vol. 3, p. 362.

Studies in Poetry ... a Copious Selection of Elegant Extracts ... and Translations from the Sacred Poets ... ⟨Compiled⟩ by George B. Cheever.

Boston: Carter and Hendee: M DCCC XXX.

Cloth? Title entered Dec. 31, 1829.

The American Common-Place Book of Poetry ... by George B. Cheever.

Boston ... 1831.

For comment see entry No. 1330. "Earth with Her Thousand Voices Praises God," pp. 332-334; otherwise "Thanksgiving," in *Miscellaneous Poems ...* , 1826.

Studies in Poetry and Prose ... by A. B. Cleveland ...

Baltimore: William and Joseph Neal. 1832.

Leather. Preface dated Aug. 1832.

Readings in Poetry ...

London ... MDCCCXXXIII.

For comment see BAL, Vol. 1, p. 370.

The First-Class Reader: A Selection for Exercises in Reading, from Standard British and American Authors, in Prose and Verse. For the Use of Schools in the United States. By B. D. Emerson ...

Boston: Russell, Odiorne, and Metcalf ... 1833.

Leather. Also noted with the imprint: *Philadelphia: Published by Hogan and Thompson ... 1833.* Deposited Jan. 1, 1834.

Selections from the American Poets ...

Dublin ... 1834.

For comment see BAL, Vol. 2, p. 397.

The Columbian Bard: A Selection of American Poetry; with Biographical Notices of the Most Popular Authors. By the Editor of "The Bard," etc.

London: Hamilton, Adams, and Co., Paternoster-Row; and J. Shillito, York. 1835.

The Gift; a Poetical Remembrancer ...

> Concord, N. H. Currier and Hall and Asa M'Farland. 1835.

> Leather; also, cloth, leather label on spine. Reprints "The Indian Hunter," pp. 311-312. Also contains "A Shetland Widow" which the late C. A. Wilson suspected may have been by Longfellow.

A Practical Grammar of the English Language ... Fourth Edition, Improved. By Roscoe G. Greene.

> Portland: Published by William Hyde, for Z. Hyde. 1835.

> Paper boards, leather shelfback.

The Young Lady's Book of Elegant Poetry ...

> Philadelphia ... 1835.

> For comment see BAL, Vol. 1, p. 206.

The Young Man's Book of Elegant Poetry ...

> Philadelphia ... 1835.

> For fuller entry see No. 1156.

The Laurel ...

> Boston ... 1836.

> For comment see entry No. 984.

The Portland Sketch Book. Edited by Mrs. Ann S. Stephens.

> Portland: Colman & Chisholm. Arthur Shirley, Printer. 1836.

> Deposited Nov. 23, 1836.

Gems from American Poets.

> London ... M DCCC XXXVI.

> "Earth with Her Thousand Voices Praises God," pp. 118-120, is a reprint of "Thanksgiving" in *Miscellaneous Poems* ... , 1826.

> For comment see BAL, Vol. 2, p. 397.

A Dictionary of the Anglo-Saxon Language ... by the Rev. J. Bosworth ...

> London: Longman, Rees, Orme, Brown, Green, and Longman; Talboys, Oxford; Stevenson, Cambridge. MDCCCVIII. ⟨*i.e.,* 1838⟩

> *Two states noted:* 1: Misdated as above. 2: Dated: MDCCCXXXVIII.

The Southern First Class Book ... Selected ... by M. M. Mason ...

Macon ... 1839.

> For comment see BAL, Vol. 1, p. 371.

The Poets of America ... Edited by John Keese.

> New York ... 1840.

> For comment see BAL, Vol. 1, pp. 232-233.

Selections from the American Poets. By William Cullen Bryant.

> New-York ... 1840.

> For comment see entry No. 1617.

The Bowdoin Poets. Edited by Edward P. Weston ...

> Brunswick: Published by Joseph Griffin. M DCCC XL.

> A copy in H inscribed by early owner Aug. 28, 1840. Reviewed NAR Oct. 1840.

> *Note:* Usually seen (and probably so first issued) with a one-page frontispiece: *E. Ruggles, del. Thayer, successor to Moore, Boston. Bowdoin College, Brunswick, Me.* Signed on the stone: *Bufford.* Copies also occur with a folded frontispiece: *Lane & Scott's Lith Tremont Temple, Boston. Published by J. Griffin. Bowdoin College Brunswick, Me.* Contemporary inscriptions suggest that the folded frontispiece may be later than the single page frontispiece.

> Noted in the following bindings. Sequence, if any, not known; the designations are for identification only.

> A: Sides blindstamped with an ornate frame, a goldstamped rose at center, all edges gilt. 1-page frontispiece.

> B: Sides blindstamped with an ornate frame, a goldstamped rose at center, edges plain. 1-page frontispiece.

> C: Sides stamped in blind only, edges plain. 1-page frontispiece.

> D: Sides blindstamped with a rules frame; a goldstamped lyre at center of front; blindstamped lyre at center of back. All edges gilt. This occurs with the folded frontispiece.

American Melodies ... Compiled by George P. Morris ...

> New-York ... 1841.

> For comment see entry No. 997.

Every Body's Book ... First Series.

> New-York ... 1841.

> For comment see in Irving list, *Section III.*

Songs and Ballads; Translated from ... German Lyric Poets. With Notes. By Charles T. Brooks.

Boston ... 1842.

A copy at BA received Sept. 20, 1842. For fuller comment see entry No. 1358.

Gems from American Poets ...

New-York ... ⟨1842⟩

For comment see entry No. 5193.

Readings in American Poetry. By Rufus W. Griswold ...

New-York ... 1843.

For comment see entry No. 6647.

Anti-Slavery Melodies: For the Friends of Freedom. Prepared for the Hingham Anti-Slavery Society, by Jairus Lincoln.

Hingham ⟨Mass.⟩: Published by Elijah B. Gill. Price 25 Cents. ⟨1843⟩

Printed paper wrapper.

The American Anti-Slavery Almanac, for 1844 ... Compiled by D. L. Child.

New York: Published by the American Anti-Slavery Society, 143 Nassau Street; 25 Cornhill, Boston; and 31 North Fifth St., Philadelphia. ⟨n.d., 1843⟩

Printed paper wrapper. Cover-title. Also issued with variant texts and imprints for various parts of the United States.

The Poetry of Love. Edited by Rufus W. Griswold ...

Boston ... 1844.

"Love Woman's Chief Attraction," p. 86, is extracted from *The Spanish Student*, 1843.

For comment see entry No. 1017.

The Poetry of Flowers ... Edited by Rufus W. Griswold.

Philadelphia ... 1844.

For comment see entry No. 4023. "The Language of Flowers," pp. 52-54; otherwise "Flowers," *Voices of the Night*, 1839.

The Mourner's Chaplet ... Selected ... by John Keese ...

Boston ... 1844.

For comment see entry No. 8548.

The Illustrated Book of Christian Ballads ... Edited by Rev. Rufus W. Griswold.

Philadelphia ... ⟨1844⟩

For comment see entry No. 6656.

The Book of Poetry Prepared for the Presbyterian Board of Publication.

Philadelphia Paul T. Jones Publishing Agent. 1844 ...

Cloth?

The Christian Family Annual. Vol. 3. Edited ... by Rev. Daniel Newell.

New York: No. 126 Nassau-Street ... ⟨n.d., 1844⟩

A periodical bound as an annual. Cloth? "Innocence," p. 252 is an altered extract from "Maidenhood," *Ballads*, 1842.

Gems from the American Poets ... by Rufus W. Griswold.

Philadelphia ... 1844.

For comment see entry No. 6657.

The Liberty Minstrel ... by Geo. W. Clark.

New-York: Leavitt & Alden ⟨*sic*⟩, 7 Cornhill, Boston: Saxton & Miles, 205 Broadway, N. Y.: Myron Finch, 120 Nassau St., N. Y.: Jackson & Chaplin, 38 Dean St., Albany, N. Y.: Jackson & Chaplin, Corner Genessee and Main St., Utica, N. Y. 1844.

"The Quadroon Maiden," pp. 29-31; otherwise "The Quadroon Girl," *Poems on Slavery*, 1842.

The Mourner Consoled; Containing the Cypress Wreath; by Rev. R. W. Griswold. The Mourner's Chaplet; by John Keese.

Boston: Gould, Kendall & Lincoln, 59 Washington Street. ⟨1844; *i.e.*, probably after 1844, but definitely prior to Nov. 1850⟩

Songs of Home and Happiness ...

Thomas Nelson, Edinburgh, and VIII Paternoster Row, London. MDCCCXLV.

All Longfellow material herein reprinted from other books. "The Silent Land," translated from the German, had prior publication in *Hyperion*, 1839, under the title "Song of the Silent Land." "The Ferry-Boat," translated from the German, had prior publication in *Hyperion*, 1839, under the title "Many a Year Is in Its Grave"; translated by Longfellow?

The District School Reader ... by William D. Swan ...

> Boston ... 1845.

> For fuller entry see in Irving, *Section Three.*

The Bridal Wreath, a Wedding Souvenir. Edited by Percy Bryant.

> Boston: William J. Reynolds, 1845.

The Forest Legendary ... Edited by John Keese. No. 1 ...

> New York ... 1845.

> For fuller entry see BAL, Vol. 4, p. 200.

The Poetry of the Passions. Edited by Rufus W. Griswold ...

> Philadelphia ... 1845.

> For comment see entry No. 1021. All Longfellow material herein is reprint. "The Poet's Dream of Fame," pp. 30-32; and, "Forgetfulness," p. 234, extracted from *The Spanish Student,* 1843.

The Poet's Gift ... Edited by John Keese.

> Boston ... 1845.

> For fuller entry see BAL, Vol. 1, p. 206.

The Southern Warbler: A New Collection of ... Old, and New Songs ...

> Charleston ⟨South Carolina⟩. Published by Babcock & Co. 1845.

Scenes in the Lives of the Apostles. Edited by H. Hastings Weld ...

> Philadelphia: Lindsay & Blakiston. ⟨1846⟩

> Leather. Listed WPLNL Oct. 1845.

Scenes in the Life of the Saviour ... Edited by Rufus W. Griswold ...

> Philadelphia ... 1846.

> For comment see entry No. 6672.

The Ladies' Casket ... by J. Wesley Hanson ...

> Lowell ... 1846.

> For comment see entry No. 9294A.

Dew-Drops of the Nineteenth Century ... by Seba Smith ...

> New York ... 1846.

> For comment see entry No. 1631.

A Book of Hymns for Public and Private Devotion.

> Cambridge ... 1846.

> For comment see this title in *Section Six.*

The Floral Gift, from Nature and the Heart Edited by Mary Chauncey.

> Worcester: Published by Jonathan Grout, Jr. 203 Main Street. 1846

> *Two printings noted;* the order is probable.

> 1: Imprinted: Worcester: Published by Jonathan Grout, Jr. 203 Main Street. 1846

> 2: Imprinted: Worcester: Published by Jonathan Grout, Jr. 201 Main Street. ⟨1846⟩

The Odd Fellow's Token: Devoted to Friendship, Love and Truth. Edited by Kate Barclay.

> Geneva: Published by Geo. H. Derby & Co. Cincinnati: H. W. Derby and Co. Auburn: J. C. Derby and Co. 1846.

> The untitled lines p. 119 are extracted from "Curfew," *Poems,* 1845.

Sibylline Verses; or, the Mirror of Fate. ⟨Compiled⟩ by Miss H. J. Woodman ...

> Boston: Published by Abel Tompkins, 38 Cornhill. 1846.

The Granite Songster. Containing the Poetry As Sung by the Hutchinson Family, at Their Concerts.

> Boston: Published by A. B. Hutchinson. W. L. Bradbury, Printer. 1847.

> Printed paper wrapper.

The Granite Songster; Comprising the Songs of the Hutchinson Family, without the Music.

> Boston: A. B. Hutchinson. New-York: Charles Holt, Jr. Music Publisher, 156 Fulton Street, 2d Door from Broadway. 1847.

The Ladies' Wreath ... Edited by Mrs. S. T. Martyn.

> New York ... 1847.

> Cloth; and, leather. Listed LW April 10, 1847. For further comment see BAL, Vol. 3, p. 273.

Pearls of American Poetry

> ... New York ... ⟨n.d., 1847⟩

> For comment see BAL, Vol. 3, p. 363.

Dempster's Original Ballad Soirees.

> Boston: Printed by Dutton & Wentworth, 37, Congress Street. 1847.

> Issued in three parts. Printed paper wrappers marked, respectively, *First Series, Second Series, Third Series.*

Flora's Album, Containing the Language of Flowers Poetically Expressed. Edited by John S. Adams ...

> Boston: Published by Elias Howe. 1847.

The Golden Gift: A Token for All Seasons. Edited by J. M. Fletcher.

> Nashua, N. H. Published by J. Buffum, Main Street. 1847.

> All Longfellow material herein is reprint. "The Will," p. 44, is extracted from "The Light of Stars," *Voices of the Night,* 1839.

> Reprinted *ca.* 1850 imprinted: *Boston: Published by J. Buffum.* ⟨*1846*⟩

The Olive Wreath, or Friendship's Gift ...

> Lowell: Nathaniel L. Dayton. 1847.

> "Sympathy," p. ⟨90⟩ extracted from "Shadows on the Wall," a chapter in *Hyperion,* 1839.

The Prose Writers of America ... by Rufus Wilmot Griswold ...

> Philadelphia ... 1847.

> For comment see entry No. 6676.

The Young American's Magazine of Self-Improvement ... Edited by George W. Light ... First Volume.

> Boston: Charles H. Peirce, 3 Cornhill. 1847.

> All published. Issued originally in six periodical numbers. With added front matter, issued as a cloth-bound book. "Postscript" to the editor's "Advertisement" pasted to p. 4.

> The issues that make up this publication are dated January to December, 1847. On p. 361 of the December issue is a note on Longfellow's *Evangeline:* "This poem has obtained a remarkable popularity, running through an edition every week ..." Hence, (see publication information on *Evangeline* in *Section I,* under 1847) the December issue of *The Young American's Magazine,* could not have been issued prior to Nov. 17, 1847.

The Ladies' Casket ... by Miss A. T. Wilbur. 1848.

... New York. ⟨n.d., 1847?⟩

> For comment see in *Section Six.*

The Free Soil Minstrel ...

> New York: Martyn & Ely, 162 Nassau St. 1848.

Friendship's Gift: A Souvenir for MDCCCXLVIII. Edited by Walter Percival.

> Boston ... 1848.

> For comment see BAL, Vol. 3, p. 109. "Jacqueline," pp. ⟨45⟩-52, extracted from *Outre-Mer,* 1835.

The Keepsake, or Token of Remembrance for 1848. Dew Drops of the Nineteenth Century ... Edited by Seba Smith.

> New York: John Levison, 196 Chatham Square. ⟨n.d., 1848⟩

The Lady's Token: Or Gift of Friendship. Edited by Cotesworth Pinckney.

> Nashua ... 1848.

> For comment see entry No. 6522.

The Lover's Gift; or Tributes to the Beautiful. American Series. Edited by Mrs. E. Oakes Smith ...

> Hartford: Henry S. Parsons. 1848.

Order of Services at the Ordination of Mr. Augustus Woodbury, As Pastor of the Second Congregational Church and Society in Concord, N. H. Wednesday, August 1, 1849.

> Concord: Printed by Morrill & Silsby, Ag'ts. 1849.

> 4-page program.

The Bowdoin Poets: Edited by Edward P. Weston ... Second Edition.

> Brunswick: Published by Joseph Griffin, from His Press, M DCCC XLIX.

The Canzonet, a Selection of Poems in Two Parts. By Bennett Palmer.

> Montpelier: Scott & Thompson, Printers. 1849.

> Printed paper wrapper? Self-wrapper? Cover-title?

Friendship's Forget-Me-Not ...

> London: Thomas Nelson, Paternoster Row; and Edinburgh. MDCCCXLIX.

> Cloth?

The Golden Present ... Edited by Mrs. J. Thayer.

Nashua 1849.

Contains seven pieces by Longfellow, here reprinted from earlier books. Included in the seven are the following extracts: "Night," pp. 9-10, otherwise "Hymn to the Night," *Voices of the Night*, 1839. "Woman," p. 24, extracted from *The Spanish Student*, 1843. "Evening," p. 53, extracted from "The Occultation of Orion," *Poems*, 1845. "Song," p. 64; otherwise "The Arrow and the Song," *Belfry of Bruges*, 1845. For fuller entry see BAL, Vol. 4, p. 201.

The Rosemary, a Collection of Sacred and Religious Poetry ...

Philadelphia: Lindsay and Blakiston. ‹1849›

Dempster's Original Ballad Soirees. Third Series.

Boston: Printed by Dutton & Wentworth, 37, Congress Street 1850.

Printed paper wrapper. Cover-title.

Gems from the Spirit Mine, Illustrative of Peace, Brotherhood, and Progress ...

London: Published for the League of Universal Brotherhood, by C. Gilpin, Bishopsgate Without. MDCCCL.

Printed paper boards.

... The (Old) Farmer's Almanack ... for the Year ... 1851 ... by Robert B. Thomas ...

Boston: Published and Sold by Jenks, Palmer & Co. ... 1850 ...

Printed paper wrapper. At head of title: *Number Fifty-Nine*. "The American Union," p. 40; extracted from "The Building of the Ship," *The Seaside and the Fireside*, 1850.

The Present, or a Gift for the Times. Edited by F. A. Moore ...

Manchester, N. H. Robert Moore. 1850.

The Irving Offering: A Token of Affection, for 1851.

New-York ... 1851.

For comment see entry No. 3171.

Memory and Hope.

Boston: Ticknor, Reed, and Fields. MDCCCLI.

Cloth; and, leather. Noticed LW Jan. 18, 1851.

The Controversy Touching the Old Stone Mill, in the Town of Newport, Rhode-Island ...

Newport ... MDCCCLI.

For fuller entry see No. 1374.

Love's Whisper. A Token from the Heart.

New York ... 1851.

For comment see note under entry No. 1021.

The Spirit Harp: A Gift, Presenting the Poetical Beauties of the Harmonial Philosophy. Compiled by Maria F. Chandler ...

Springfield, Mass.: Published by R. P. Ambler. Geo. W. Wilson, Printer. MDCCCLI.

Cloth?

... The Unitarian Congregational Register, for the Year 1852. Printed for the American Unitarian Association.

Boston: Wm. Crosby and H. P. Nichols, 111 Washington Street ... ‹n.d., 1851›

Printed paper wrapper. At head of title: Annual Series. No. 2.

The Young Ladies' Oasis: Or, Gems of Prose and Poetry. Edited by N. L. Fergurson ‹sic› ...

Lowell: Nathaniel L. Dayton. 1851.

"Ladies of Long Ago," p. 69, credited to *Longfellow's Col.*, is a translation, by Costello, from Villon; reprinted from *The Poets and Poetry of Europe*, 1845. "A Sentiment," p. 202, credited to *Longfellow's Col.*, is a translation from Camoens by Strangford; reprinted from *The Poets and Poetry of Europe*, 1845. "Woman," p. 214, is extracted from *The Spanish Student*, 1843.

The Young Ladies' Oasis: Or, Gems of Prose and Poetry. Edited by N. L. Fergurson ‹sic› ... Second Edition.

Lowell: Nathaniel L. Dayton, 1851.

Leather. Also cloth? See preceding entry.

The Young Ladies' Oasis: Or, Gems of Prose and Poetry. Edited by N. L. Fergurson ‹sic› ... Third Edition.

Lowell: Nathaniel L. Dayton. 1851.

Cloth. Also leather? See preceding two entries.

The Youth's Poetical Instructor, Part II ...

Belfast ... 1851.

For fuller entry see BAL, Vol. 1, p. 373.

Lotos-Eating . . . by George William Curtis . . .

London . . . 1852.

For comment see entry No. 4262. Untitled poem, pp. 142-143, extracted from "Seaweed," *Poems*, 1845.

The Silver Cup of Sparkling Drops . . . Edited by Miss C. B. Porter . . .

Buffalo . . . 1852.

Entered for copyright July 18, 1851. For fuller entry see No. 2887.

Lotus-Eating . . . by George William Curtis . . .

New York . . . 1852.

For comment see entry No. 4263. Untitled poem, p. 153, is extracted from "Seaweed," *Poems*, 1845.

The Dew-Drop . . . for MDCCCLII.

Philadelphia . . . 1852.

For comment see entry No. 1188.

Garden Walks with the Poets. By Mrs. C. M. Kirkland.

New-York . . . 1852.

For comment see entry No. 1379.

The Christian Parlor Book: Devoted to Science, Literature, and Religion.

New-York: Published by George Pratt, No. 116 Nassau Street. 1852.

The Oasis: Or, Golden Leaves of Friendship. Edited by N. L. Ferguson . . .

Lowell: Nathaniel L. Dayton. 1852.

The String of Diamonds . . . by a Gem Fancier.

Hartford . . . 1852.

For fuller entry see No. 1190.

The Rose, Thistle and Shamrock. A Selection of English Poetry, Chiefly Modern. By Ferdinand Freiligrath.

Stuttgart. Edward Hallberger. 1853.

A copy at CH inscribed by the editor March 1853.

Thalatta: A Book for the Sea-Side . . .

Boston . . . MDCCCLIII.

For comment see entry No. 1380.

The Crystal Gem. Edited by J.S.A. . . .

Boston: J. Buffum, 11 Cornhill. ⟨1853⟩

Five Hundred Thousand Strokes for Freedom. A Series of Anti-Slavery Tracts . . .

London. W. & F. Cash . . . 1853 . . .

A bound book made up of a collection of *Leeds Anti-Slavery Tracts*. See *The Witnesses* in *Section III*.

. . . The Garland of Freedom . . . by a Friend of the Negro. Part II. ⟨III.⟩ . . .

London . . . MDCCCLIII.

For fuller entry see BAL, Vol. 1, p. 373; Vol. 2, p. 155.

Gift of Love. A Token of Friendship for 1853. Edited by Rufus W. Griswold . . .

New-York: Leavitt & Allen, 27 Dey Street. M.DCCC.LIII.

Leather. For comment see note under entry No. 1021.

The Oasis: Or, Golden Leaves of Friendship. Edited by N. L. Ferguson . . .

Boston: Dayton and Wentworth, 86 Washington Street. 1853.

The Pilot . . .

Cambridge: Printed by John Ford and Company. 1853.

Printed flexible boards. "Architects of Fate," pp. 15-16. Otherwise "The Builders," *The Seaside and the Fireside*, 1850.

The Wheat-Sheaf . . .

Philadelphia . . . 1853.

For comment see entry No. 3176.

The White Veil . . . Edited by Mrs. Sarah Josepha Hale . . .

Philadelphia . . . 1854.

For comment see entry No. 6883. "Faithfulness," p. 150, is extracted from "Annie of Tharaw," *Poems*, 1845. "Affection," p. 228, is extracted from *The Spanish Student*, 1843.

Davidson's Temperance Melodist . . .

London: F. Pitman, 20, Paternoster Row, E. C. ⟨n.d., 1854⟩

Printed paper wrapper.

Euphonia; a Collection of Glees and Part Songs ... for the Use of Musical Conventions, Teacher's Institutes, and Singing Clubs. By the Professors Charles F. Heuberer & H. Perabeau.

> Boston ... John P. Jewett & Co., and B. B. Mussey & Co. Cleveland, Ohio: Jewett, Proctor & Worthington. 1854.

> Printed paper boards, cloth shelfback. Contains fifteen pieces credited to Longfellow, twelve being reprinted from earlier books. The remaining three pieces ("Forget Not Me," "Mary, Arise" and "Boat Song") have not been located in Longfellow's works. BAL presumes they are not by Longfellow and are here misattributed to him. BAL has too much respect for Longfellow to charge him with the authorship of these three songs.

Evidence As to the Religious Working of the Common Schools in the State of Massachusetts, with a Preface by the Hon. Edward Twisleton ...

> London: James Ridgway, Piccadilly. 1854.

> Printed paper wrapper.

Gift of Love. A Token of Friendship for 1854. Edited by Rufus W. Griswold ...

> New-York: Leavitt & Allen, 27 Dey Street. M.DCCC.LIV.

> Leather. For comment see note under entry No. 1021.

The Oasis: Or, Golden Leaves of Friendship. Edited by N. L. Ferguson ...

> Boston: Dayton and Wentworth, 86 Washington Street. 1854.

Poetry of the Year Passages from the Poets Descriptive of the Seasons ...

> New York: D. Appleton and Co. MDCCCLIV.

> Leather.

The Wedding Dress. Edited by a Lady ...

> Boston: Thos. O. Walker. 1854.

> "What I Most Prize," p. 121, extracted from *The Spanish Student*, 1843.

The Young Lady's Cabinet of Gems: A Choice Collection of ... Poetry and Prose. ⟨Edited⟩ by Virginia De Forrest.

> Boston: Kelley & Brother. 1854.

> Longfellow material herein reprinted from other books. "October," p. 62, is extracted from "Autumn," *Voices of the Night*, 1839.

Lilies and Violets ... by Rosalie Bell ...

> New York ... 1855.

> For comment see entry No. 1658.

Gems of Spanish Poetry. ⟨Compiled by Francisco Javier Vingut⟩

> New-York. F. J. Vingut & Co. For Sale by Stringer & Townsend 222 Broadway. 1855.

> Also contains a title-page in Spanish. "Noon," pp. 92-94 and "The Alhambra," pp. 78-79 are credited to Longfellow. Both appeared previously in *The Poets and Poetry of Europe*, 1845, but without any indication there that they were translated by Longfellow.

... Lady's Almanac, for 1856.

> By Damrell & Moore & G. Coolidge Boston John P. Jewett & Co. Cleveland, Ohio Jewett, Proctor & Worthington ... 1854 ... ⟨*i.e.*, 1855⟩

> At head of title: *Number 3*. The untitled 9 lines of poetry, p. 89, are extracted from *The Golden Legend*, 1851.

The Oasis: Or, Golden Leaves of Friendship. Edited by N. L. Ferguson ...

> Boston: Dayton and Wentworth, 86 Washington Street. 1855.

> Also issued with the imprint: *New York: Dayton and Wentworth, 27 Beekman Street. 1855.*

> Unsold sheets were issued with a cancel titleleaf imprinted: *Boston: Wentworth & Co., 86 Washington St., 1855.*

... The (Old) Farmer's Almanack ... for the Year ... 1856 ... by Robert B. Thomas ...

> Boston: Published by Hickling, Swan & Brown ... 1855 ...

> Printed paper wrapper. At head of title: *Number Sixty-Four*. "Nature," p. 39, is extracted from "Sunrise on the Hills," *Voices of the Night*, 1839.

The Wide-Awake Gift: A Know-Nothing Token for 1855. Edited by "One of 'Em." ...

> New York: J. C. Derby, 119 Nassau Street. Boston: Phillips, Sampson & Co. Cincinnati: H. W. Derby. 1855.

> *Note:* It is probable that copies first printed, not necessarily first published, have on the title-page: *"One of 'Em."* Later copies: *"One of 'Em.'*

> *Two formats issued:*

Gilt: Edges plain; front stamped in gold and blind; back stamped in blind.

Extra gilt: Both sides stamped in gold only; edges gilt.

Reissued as *The American Gift Book,* 1856.

Sabbath Bells Chimed by the Poets . . .

New York: D. Appleton and Co. Broadway. 1856.

At foot of p. ⟨112⟩: Chiswick Press imprint. Also issued with British imprint? A copy in H inscribed by early owner Feb. 26, 1856.

The Preacher: A Sermon Preached at the Ordination of Frederick Frothingham . . . Wednesday, April 9, 1856. By Oliver Stearns . . .

Portland: Published by George R. Davis. 1856.

Printed paper wrapper.

The Harp of Freedom . . . by Geo. W. Clark . . .

New-York: Miller, Orton & Mulligan, 25 Park Row. Boston . . . Rochester, N. Y. 1856.

The Poetry and Mystery of Dreams. By Charles G. Leland . . .

Philadelphia . . . M.DCCC.LVI.

For comment see entry No. 11527. The untitled lines on pp. 18, 21, 33, 60, 264-265, 267-268, are extracted from *The Golden Legend,* 1851. The untitled translation from Uhland, pp. 63-65, is reprinted from *Hyperion,* 1839. The untitled lines, p. 211, are extracted from "Rain in Summer," *Poems,* 1845.

The Gift Book of Gems . . .

Bangor David Bugbee & Co. ⟨1856⟩

"A Passing Thought," p. 24, is extracted from "Autumn," *Voices of the Night,* 1839. Also contains other reprinted Longfellow material.

The Rural Poetry of the English Language . . . Topically Paragraphed . . . by Joseph William Jenks . . .

Boston: Published by John P. Jewett and Company. Cleveland, Ohio: Jewett, Proctor, and Worthington. New York: Sheldon, Blakeman, & Co. 1856.

Cloth?

Selections from the Best Spanish Poets. ⟨Edited by Gertrúdis F. de Vingut.⟩

New York. F. J. Vingut. For Sale by Roe Lockwood & Son. Broadway, No 411. 1856.

The Wheat-Sheaf; a Suggestive Reader, Containing Gems of Pure and Noble Thoughts for the Youthful Mind . . .

Philadelphia: Willis P. Hazard, 724 Chestnut Street ⟨1856⟩

"Preface to Third Edition," dated at end *10th month, 1856.* For first edition of this compilation see *The Wheat-Sheaf; or, Gleanings for the Wayside and Fireside . . . ,* above under the year 1853.

The Angel Visitor . . . Edited by Frances E. Percival . . .

Boston . . . 1857.

For fuller entry see in Washington Irving list, *Section Three.* Contains "Spirit Voices," otherwise "Footsteps of Angels," *Voices of the Night,* 1839.

The Harp and the Cross: A Collection of Religious Poetry, Compiled by Stephen G. Bulfinch . . .

Boston: American Unitarian Association, 21 Bromfield Street. 1857.

Devotional Library, Vol. 4. Listed *Christian Register* (Boston), April 18, 1857; reviewed *ibid.,* April 25, 1857.

The Christian's Gift. Edited by Rev. Rufus W. Clark.

Boston: Published by John P. Jewett and Company . . . 1857.

Poetry of the Age of Fable Collected by Thomas Bulfinch

Boston . . . ⟨1857⟩

See below under 1863.

Poetry of the Woods: Passages from the Poets Descriptive of Forest Scenes . . .

Philadelphia: Published by E. H. Butler & Co. 1857.

Reissued with the imprint: *New York: Leavitt & Allen Brothers. 1874.*

The Psalms of Life . . . ⟨Compiled⟩ by John S. Adams . . .

Boston . . . ⟨1857⟩

All Longfellow material herein reprinted from earlier books. "She Is Not Dead," p. 241, is extracted from "Resignation," *The Seaside and the Fireside,* 1850. For fuller entry see No. 11306.

Rhymes and Roundelayes in Praise of a Country Life . . .

London: David Bogue, 86, Fleet Street. MDCCCLVII.

Leather? Imprint of Richard Clay, London, on verso of title-leaf and at foot of last page of text. See next entry.

Rhymes and Roundelayes in Praise of a Country Life . . .

New York: D. Appleton and Co. Broadway. M DCCC LVII.

Leather. Imprint of Richard Clay, London, on verso of title-leaf and at foot of last page of text.

The Teachings of the Dead: By Rev. Thomas Smyth . . .

Columbia, S. C. Steam Power Press of E. H. Britton. 1857.

Printed paper wrapper. Cover-title. "The Speaking Dead," pp. ⟨1⟩-2, otherwise "Footsteps of Angels," *Voices of the Night,* 1839.

Lady's Almanac, for the Year 1859.

Boston. Damrell & Moore, & G. Coolidge. Published by Shepard, Clark & Brown Boston, Mass. ⟨1854; *i.e.,* 1858⟩

No copyright information found, 1857–1859. Advertised *Boston Evening Transcript,* Dec. 29, 1858, as though published.

Poetry of the Bells Collected by Samuel Batchelder, Jr

Riverside Press Printed in Aid of the Cambridge Chime by H. O. Houghton and Company 1858

The Poets of the Nineteenth Century . . . Edited by . . . Rev. Robert Aris Willmott . . .

New York . . . 1858.

For comment see entry No. 1663.

. . . The Constellation.

New York, 1859 . . .

For fuller description see entry No. 1034.

Hymns of the Ages. Being Selections from Lyra Catholica, Germanica, Apostolica, and Other Sources. With an Introduction by Rev. F. D. Huntington . . .

Boston: Phillips, Sampson, and Company. M DCCC LIX.

Two formats noted:

Small paper edition: 7⅝″ full x 5⁵⁄₁₆″.

Large paper edition: 8½″ scant x 5⅞″.

Announced BM Oct. 1, 1858.

The Atlantic Souvenir, for 1859 . . .

New York: Derby & Jackson, 119 Nassau Street. 1859.

Leather.

A Gallery of Famous English and American Poets. With an Introductory Essay, by Henry Coppée . . .

Philadelphia: Published by E. H. Butler & Co. 1859.

Leather.

Poetry for Repetition. Edited by the Rev. Henry Twells . . .

London: Longman, Brown, Green, Longmans, & Roberts. 1859.

The Poets of the West . . .

London . . . 1859.

For comment see BAL, Vol. 1, p. 101.

Proceedings of the Pennsylvania Yearly Meeting of Progressive Friends . . . 1859 . . .

New York: John F. Trow, Printer, 377 & 379 Broadway, Corner of White Street. 1859.

Printed paper wrapper.

Tribute to the Memory of Charles F. Hovey, Esq. [From "The Liberator," May 6, 1859.]

⟨n.p., Boston, 1859?⟩

The above at head of p. ⟨1⟩. Printed self-wrapper. "There Is No Death!", p. 24; extracted from "Resignation," *The Seaside and the Fireside,* 1850.

Order of Services at the Ordination of Mr. Charles Noyes, As Pastor of the First Congregational Church and Society in Brighton, Wednesday, January 4, 1860.

⟨n.p., probably Brighton, Mass., 1860⟩

Cover-title. Single leaf folded to make four pages. Issued as a program.

Proceedings of the Massachusetts Historical Society. 1858–1860 . . .

Boston: Printed for the Society. M.DCCC.LX.

H copy received April 28, 1860.

Washington Irving. Mr. Bryant's Address on His Life and Genius ...

New York ... 1860.

For comment see note under entry No. 8796.

Pearls from the Poets. Specimens of the Works of Celebrated Writers. Selected ... by H. W. Dulcken ...

London: Ward and Lock, 158 Fleet Street. ⟨1860⟩

Date from preface. Preface dated at end *October 2, 1860*.

A Book of Favourite Modern Ballads Illustrated with Fifty Engravings, from Drawings by the First Artists.

New York: D. Appleton and Co., 346 & 348, Broadway. 1860.

Leather. Imprint of Edmund Evans, London, on verso of title-leaf. Also issued with London imprint?

Gems from the Poets. Illustrated. The Designs by F. A. Lydon ...

London: Groombridge and Sons, 5, Paternoster-Row. MDCCCLX.

Not seen.

The Poets of the West ...

London ... New York ... 1860.

For fuller entry see BAL, Vol. 1, p. 374.

Proceedings of the Pennsylvania Yearly Meeting of Progressive Friends ... 1860 ...

New York: John F. Trow, Printer, 48 & 50 Greene Street. 1860.

Printed paper wrapper. Reprints "Haunted Houses." "Deeds and Words," p. 64; otherwise "Santa Filomena," *The Courtship of Miles Standish*, 1858.

Folk Songs ... Edited by John Williamson Palmer ...

New York ... M DCCC LXI.

For comment see entry No. 11312.

The Bentley Ballads. Containing the Choice Ballads, Songs and Poems Contributed to "Bentley's Miscellany."

London: Richard Bentley, New Burlington Street. 1861.

The Bouquet ... ⟨Edited⟩ by Benjamin Todd. ... Battle Creek, Mich. 1861.

For fuller entry see BAL, Vol. 3, p. 338.

Favorite Authors. A Companion-Book of Prose and Poetry ...

Boston ... M DCCC LXI.

For comment see entry No. 5943. "The Monk Felix," pp. ⟨211⟩-215, is extracted from *The Golden Legend*, 1851.

The Mosaic. Edited by J.H.B.

Buffalo: Breed, Butler & Co. 1861.

A collection of extracts. Those on pp. ⟨3⟩, 44, are from *Hyperion*, 1839; pp. 22-24, 32, are from *Outre-Mer*, 1835; pp. 53-54, 63, are from *Kavanagh*, 1849; pp. 57-59, 66-67, are from "Frithiof's Saga," *Prose Works*, 1857.

... The (Old) Farmer's Almanack .. for the Year ... 1862 ... by Robert B. Thomas ...

Boston: Published by Swan, Brewer & Tileston ... 1861 ...

Printed paper wrapper. At head of title: *Number Seventy*. "Gain by Toil," p. 40, extracted from "The Ladder of St. Augustine," *The Courtship of Miles Standish*, 1858.

Poems of Infancy ...

Boston: George Coolidge, 13 Tremont Row. 1861.

Sunshine in the Country. A Book of Rural Poetry ...

London: Richard Griffin and Company, 10, Stationers' Hall Court. 1861.

Reprints five poems, two of them under changed titles. "Woods," pp. 16-17; otherwise "The Spirit of Poetry," *Voices of the Night*, 1839. "Summer," pp. 135-136; otherwise "Sunrise on the Hills," *Voices of the Night*, 1839.

The Union Memorial ...

Boston: Published by Abel Tompkins, 38 & 40 Cornhill. 1861.

Printed paper wrapper. A copy at H received from the publisher July 13, 1861.

Jewels from the Quarry of the Mind ... Edited by James H. Head ...

Boston ... 1862.

For comment see entry No. 1036.

... Lyrics of the War

   ... Philadelphia. ⟨n.d., 1862⟩

For comment see entry No. 11531.

The American Tract Society's Almanac for the Year ... 1863 ...

   Published by the American Tract Society, 28 Cornhill, Boston. ⟨1862⟩

   Printed paper wrapper.

The Children's Garland from the Best Poets Selected and Arranged by Coventry Patmore

   Macmillan and Co. London and Cambridge 1862

Choice Poems and Lyrics ...

   London   Whittaker & Co., Ave Maria Lane 1862

   Cloth?

Poems of Religious Sorrow   Comfort   Counsel and Aspiration ...

   New York ... 1863

For comment see entry No. 1406.

Poetry of the Age of Fable Collected by Thomas Bulfinch

   Boston   J. E. Tilton. & Co.   ⟨1863; i.e., 1864?⟩

   Two printings noted:

1

Dated ⟨1863⟩. A copy thus deposited for copyright May 21, 1864. Listed ALG June 1, 1864.

2

Dated ⟨1857⟩. The date is erroneous. The publisher, J. E. Tilton & Co., first appears in the Boston directory for 1859.

"The Triumph of Bacchus," pp. 62-63, extracted from "Drinking Song." "The Lyre Invented by Pythagoras," p. 199, extracted from "To a Child;" both in *The Belfry of Bruges,* 1845. "Ajax," p. 155, extracted from "The Goblet of Life," *Ballads ...* , 1842. "The Death of Baldur," pp. 241-243; otherwise "Tegnér's Drapa," *The Seaside and the Fireside,* 1850. Also contains other reprinted Longfellow material.

... The (Old) Farmer's Almanack ... for the Year ... 1864 ... by Robert B. Thomas ...

   Boston: Published by Brewer & Tileston ... 1863 ...

Printed paper wrapper. At head of title: *Number Seventy-Two.* Reprints "Retribution." The four lines of verse on the title-page are extracted from the "Dedication" to *The Seaside and the Fireside,* 1850.

... Opinions of Prominent Men Concerning the Great Questions of the Times ...

   New York: C. S. Westcott & Co., Printers, No. 79 John Street. 1863.

   Printed paper wrapper. At head of title: The Loyal National League.

Snow-Flakes; a Chapter from the Book of Nature ...

   Published by the American Tract Society, No. 28 Cornhill, Boston. ⟨1863⟩

   "Peboan," p. 20, and "Winter," pp. 118-119, are extracted from *The Song of Hiawatha,* 1855.

Cloud Crystals; a Snow-Flake Album ... Edited by a Lady ...

   New York ... 1864.

For fuller entry see BAL, Vol. 1, p. 295.

Flowers from My Garden. Sketched and Painted from Nature by Laura Gordon Munson ...

   New York ... 1864.

For fuller entry see BAL, Vol. 3, p. 338. "The Stars of Earth;" otherwise "Flowers," *Voices of the Night,* 1839.

The School-Girl's Garland ... by Mrs. C. M. Kirkland. First Series ...

   New York ... 1864.

For comment see entry No. 4837.

Lyrics of Loyalty ... Edited by Frank Moore

   New York ... 1864

For comment see entry No. 1203.

The School-Girl's Garland ... by Mrs. C. M. Kirkland. Second Series ...

   New York ... 1864.

For comment see entry No. 6994.

Jewels Gathered from Painter & Poet. A Selection of Poems ...

   London: Cassell, Petter, and Galpin, La Belle Sauvage Yard, Ludgate Hill, E. C. ⟨n.d., 1864⟩

   Listed Bkr Oct. 31, 1864.

Patriotism in Poetry and Prose ... Selected ... by James E. Murdoch ...

Philadelphia ... 1864.

For fuller entry see BAL, Vol. 1, p. 248.

Christmas Poems and Pictures ...

New York: James G. Gregory, 46, Walker Street. MDCCCLXIV.

Declamation for the Million ... by R. G. Hibbard ...

Chicago ... 1864.

For fuller entry see No. 1041.

Life-Lights of Song. Songs of God and Nature. Edited by David Page ...

Edinburgh: William P. Nimmo, 1864.

"The Stars of Earth," pp. 89-92; otherwise "Flowers," *Voices of the Night*, 1839. Also contains other reprinted Longfellow material.

Life-Lights of Song. Songs of Love & Brotherhood. Edited by David Page ...

Edinburgh: William P. Nimmo. 1864.

... Lyrics of the War

Philadelphia ... 1864 ...

For fuller entry see No. 1194E. "Faith in the Union," p. 11, extracted from "The Building of the Ship," *The Seaside and the Fireside*, 1850.

... The (Old) Farmer's Almanack ... for the Year ... 1865 ... by Robert B. Thomas ...

Boston: Published by Brewer & Tileston ... 1864 ...

Printed paper wrapper. At head of title: *Number Seventy-Three*. In addition to one reprinted poem contains "A September Morning," p. 41; extracted from "The Student's Tale. The Falcon of Ser Federigo," *Tales of a Wayside Inn*, 1863.

Hymns of the Ages. Third Series.

Boston ... 1865.

For comment see entry No. 415. "Outside the Church," pp. <316>-318, extracted from the "Interlude" of "The Musician's Tale," *Tales of a Wayside Inn*, 1863.

Lyra Americana ... Selected ... by the Rev. George T. Rider ...

New York ... 1865.

For comment see entry No. 2827.

Home Ballads by Our Home Poets ...

New York ... 1865.

For comment see BAL, Vol. 1, p. 248.

Lyra Americana: Hymns of Praise and Faith, from American Poets.

London ... 1865.

For comment see BAL, Vol. 2, p. 93.

Golden Leaves from the American Poets Collected by John W. S. Hows

New York   James G. Gregory   540 Broadway   M DCCC LXV

Reprinted and reissued with the imprint: *New York   Bunce and Huntington*   M DCCC LXV

Machpelah: A Book for the Cemetery ...

New York: Anson D. F. Randolph, 770 Broadway, Corner of Ninth Street. 1865.

Cloth?

Pearls from Heine ...

Philadelphia: Frederick Leypoldt. 1865.

Pictorial wrapper.

Selection of English Poems Translated from the English into German by Hermann Simon. With the English Text. Third Volume.

Leipzig, Published by Arnold. 1865.

The Sunday Book of Poetry Selected and Arranged by C. F. Alexander ...

Cambridge   Sever and Francis   1865

Reissued with the imprint: *Sever, Francis, & Co. Boston and Cambridge. 1869.*

The Book of Rubies ...

New York ... 1866.

For comment see entry No. 5522.

The Flower of Liberty. Edited ... by Julia A. M. Furbish.

Boston ... 1866.

For comment see entry No. 1424.

Poetry Lyrical, Narrative, and Satirical of the Civil War ... Edited by Richard Grant White

New York ... 1866

For comment see entry No. 4604.

Patriotic Eloquence ... Compiled ... by Mrs. C. M. Kirkland.

New York ... 1866.

For comment see entry No. 11187. "Hymn at the Consecration of Pulaski's Banner, 1779," pp. 116-117; otherwise "Hymn of the Moravian Nuns of Bethlehem," *Voices of the Night,* 1839. "The Ship of State," pp. 208-209; otherwise "The Building of the Ship," *The Seaside and the Fireside,* 1850.

Anecdotes, Poetry and Incidents of the War ... Arranged by Frank Moore ...

New York ... 1866.

For comment see entry No. 3202.

Good Company for Every Day in the Year ...

Boston ... 1866.

For comment see entry No. 5950.

... The Lady's Almanac, for ... 1867.

Boston ... ⟨1865; *i.e.,* 1866⟩

Listed ALG Dec. 1, 1866. Deposited Feb. 18, 1867. For fuller entry see No. 2905.

One Hundred Choice Selections ... by Nathaniel K. Richardson ...

Philadelphia ... 1866.

For comment see entry No. 1425.

... The (Old) Farmer's Almanack ... for the Year ... 1867 ... by Robert B. Thomas ...

Boston: Published by Brewer & Tileston ... 1866 ...

Printed paper wrapper. At head of title: *Number Seventy-Five.*

Routledge's Christmas Annual for 1867; an Entertaining Volume of Christmas Literature by the Best Authors of the Day. Edited by Edmund Routledge ...

London: George Routledge and Sons, the Broadway, Ludgate. ⟨1866⟩

Not seen.

Songs of Praise and Poems of Devotion in the Christian Centuries. With an Introduction by Henry Coppée ...

Philadelphia: Published by E. H. Butler & Co. 1866.

Leather. Also cloth?

The Book of the Sonnet Edited by Leigh Hunt and S. Adams Lee ...

Boston ... 1867

Prepared for the press and partially edited by George Henry Boker. For comment see entry No. 1218.

Christ and the Twelve ... Edited by J. G. Holland ...

Springfield ... 1867.

For comment see entry No. 8604.

Later Lyrics of the Christian Church

London. Hamilton Adams & Co. ⟨n.d., 1867⟩

Edited anonymously by Lucy Fletcher Massey. All Longfellow material reprinted from other books with the possible (but unlikely) exception of "To-Morrow," p. 35, which also appears in *Flower-de-Luce,* London, 1867 (Nov. 1866). No listings found. Reviewed Ath July 25, 1867.

Folk Songs ... Edited by John Williamson Palmer ... a New Edition ...

New York ... M DCCC LXVII.

For comment see BAL, Vol. 4, p. 443.

... The Lady's Almanac, for the year 1868.

Boston ... ⟨1867⟩

For comment see BAL, Vol. 2, p. 246.

The Atlantic Almanac 1868 Edited by Oliver Wendell Holmes and Donald G. Mitchell ...

Boston ... 1867 ...

For comment see entry No. 266.

Roses and Holly: A Gift-Book for All the Year ...

Philadelphia: J. B. Lippincott & Co. 1867.

Cloth?

Sabbath Bells Chimed by the Poets ...

Philadelphia: Published by E. H. Butler & Co. 1867.

Leather.

A Thousand and One Gems of English Poetry. Selected and Arranged by Charles Mackay ...

London: George Routledge and Sons, The Broadway, Ludgate. New York: 416, Broome Street. 1867.

Joseph L. Blamire, Routledge's New York agent, wrote Longfellow April 5, 1867 (letter in H) reporting dispatch of a copy to Longfellow. Also occurs ⟨n.d.⟩; copies thus in H inscribed by early owners May, 1874; Christmas, 1876.

Christian Lyrics: Chiefly Selected from Modern Authors ...

London: Sampson Low, Son, and Marston, Milton House, Ludgate Hill. 1868.

Noted only in leather (publisher's?). Listed PC Nov. 1, 1867.

Chimes for Childhood ... ⟨Edited by Dana Estes⟩

Boston ... ⟨1868⟩

For comment see entry No. 11325.

The Golden Gift   A Book for the Young ...

Edinburgh ... ⟨1868⟩

For comment see entry No. 4257.

Christian Lyrics: Chiefly Selected from Modern Authors ...

New York: Scribner, Welford, and Co. 1868.

The Golden Gift   A Book for the Young ...

New York ... ⟨1868⟩

For comment see entry No. 4258.

Lyra Sacra Americana: Or, Gems from American Sacred Poetry. Selected ... by Charles Dexter Cleveland ...

New York: Charles Scribner and Company. London: Sampson Low, Son, and Marston. 1868.

The Sunday-School Speaker ... Arranged by O. Augusta Cheney.

... Boston. ⟨1869⟩

For comment see entry No. 1433A. "The Shadows of Twilight," pp. 68-69, extracted from *The Golden Legend,* 1851.

Tom Hood's Comic Readings in Prose and Verse ...

London ... ⟨n.d., 1869⟩

For comment see entry No. 1546.

The Bentley Ballads ... ⟨Edited⟩ by John Sheehan ... New Edition.

London: Richard Bentley, New Burlington Street ... 1869.

One Hundred Choice Selections ... No. 2 ... Compiled ... by Phineas Garrett.

... Philadelphia ... 1869.

For comment see entry No. 2910.

Light at Eventide. A Compilation of Choice Religious Hymns and Poems. By the Editor of "Chimes for Childhood," "Echoes from Home," etc. ⟨*i.e.,* Dana Estes⟩

Boston: Lee and Shepard, Publishers. New York: Lee, Shepard and Dillingham. ⟨1870⟩

Songs of Life Selected from Many Sources ...

New York: Charles Scribner & Company. 1870.

Songs for the People ...

⟨n.p., n.d., *ca.* 1870⟩

Single leaf. Printed on recto only. All poems anonymous.

Poems of Home Life ... ⟨Compiled by Mrs. Helen P. Warner⟩

American Tract Society, 150 Nassau-Street, New York. ⟨n.d., 1871⟩

Two printings noted: 1, in 8's; 2, in 4's. Listed ALG Jan. 2, 1871.

Winter Poems by Favorite American Poets ...

Boston ... 1871

For comment see BAL, Vol. 1, p. 377.

Public and Parlor Readings ... Humorous. Edited by Lewis B. Monroe.

Boston ... 1871.

Contains "Praise of Little Women," pp. 32-33, here reprinted. Also contains "The Widow," pp. 151-154, translated from Gellert by C. T. Brooks; the translation here erroneously credited to Longfellow. For fuller entry see No. 1550.

Good Selections ... by W. M. Jelliffe ...

New York ... 1871.

For comment see entry No. 3330.

One Hundred Choice Selections No. 4 ... by Phineas Garrett ...

... Philadelphia ... 1871.

For comment see entry No. 2461.

Declamations and Dialogues for the Sunday-School. By Prof. J. H. Gilmore . . .

Boston . . . ⟨1871⟩

For comment see in Larcom, *Section III.*

Songs of Home Selected from Many Sources . . .

New York: Charles Scribner and Company. 1871.

Child Life: A Collection of Poems, Edited by John Greenleaf Whittier . . .

Boston . . . 1872.

For comment see entry No. 11332.

The Garland of Poetry and Prose by Celebrated Authors . . .

Boston   D. Lothrop and Co.   Dover, N. H.: G. T. Day & Co.   1872

Good Selections, in Prose and Poetry . . . by W. M. Jelliffe . . .

New York: J. W. Schermerhorn & Co. 1872.

"The Son of the Evening Star," pp. 13-20, is extracted from *The Song of Hiawatha,* 1855.

Hymns for Mothers and Children. Second Series . . .

Boston . . . 1872.

For fuller entry see BAL, Vol. 4, p. 215.

. . . Lady's Almanac for 1873

. . . Boston. ⟨1872⟩

For comment see entry No. 424. "Commune with Nature," p. 31, is extracted from "Sunrise on the Hills," *Voices of the Night,* 1839.

A Mother's Souvenir. Compiled from the Writings of Some of the Most Distinguished Poets and Poetesses of the Day. By Mrs. H.W.T. Sayers . . .

Pittsburgh: A. A. Anderson & Sons, Book and Job Printers, No. 67 Fifth Ave. 1872.

The Poets of the Nineteenth Century . . . Edited by . . . Robert Aris Willmott . . .

New York . . . 1872.

For comment see in Larcom, *Section III.*

Public and Parlor Readings . . . Edited by Lewis B. Monroe.

Boston . . . 1872.

For fuller entry see in Larcom, *Section III.*

The Royal Illuminated Book of Legends . . . ⟨Edited⟩ by Marcus Ward . . . Second Series.

Edinburgh: William P. Nimmo. ⟨n.d., 1872⟩

Cloth, paper labels on front cover. Listed Bkr Dec. 3, 1872.

The Poets and Poetry of America. By Rufus Wilmot Griswold . . .

New York . . . 1873.

For comment see BAL, Vol. 4, p. 60.

Songs of Nature . . .

New York . . . 1873.

For comment see entry No. 4760.

Illustrated Library of Favorite Song . . . Edited by J. G. Holland . . .

New York . . . ⟨1873⟩

For comment see entry No. 2853.

Centennial Tea Party. Academy of Music. Wednesday Evening, December 17th, 1873 . . .

⟨Philadelphia: Rowley & Chew, 1873⟩

4 pp. Issued as a program.

The Atlantic Almanac 1874 . . .

Boston: James R. Osgood and Company. Late Ticknor & Fields, and Fields, Osgood, & Co. . . . 1873 . . .

Printed paper wrapper. A copy at H received Dec. 18, 1873.

The Poet's Gift of Consolation to Sorrowing Mothers.

A. S. Barnes & Co. New York. ⟨n.d., 1873⟩

Cloth?

Sacred Poems   Being a Selection from the Poets   Devotional & Moral

Boston   Lee & Shepard, Publishers   New York   Lee, Shepard, & Dillingham   1873

Query: Also issued with a British imprint? Ballantyne and Co., Edinburgh and London, imprint on verso of title-leaf.

Little People of God and What the Poets Have Said of Them Edited by Mrs George L Austin

Boston   Shepard and Gill   1874

Listed PW Dec. 20, 1873.

Harvard Musical Association. Seventh Symphony Concert ... Boston Music Hall ... Jan. 29, 1874 ...

<n.p., Boston, 1874>

4 pp. Wove paper. Page: 8⅞″ x 5½″. Program. P. <1> as above. Program on p. <2>. On p. <3>: THE FIFTIETH BIRTHDAY OF AGASSIZ. / MAY 28, 1857. / <rule> / [The following lines, by LONGFELLOW, were read among friends at a / birthday dinner, which they will long keep in fresh remembrance.] / <text of poem: Eight 4-line stanzas> P. <4> blank.

Here described in some detail since pp. <3-4> separated from pp. <1-2> may be erroneously considered a separate printing. The poem had prior publication in *The Courtship of Miles Standish*, 1858.

Sea and Shore ...

Boston ... 1874.

For comment see entry No. 4043.

Allman's English Classics for Elementary Schools. No. 5.

London, 1874.

Not seen. Entry from *British Museum Catalogue*. Contains "Rural Life in Sweden," otherwise the preface to *Ballads*, 1842.

American Sacred Songs Translated into the Armenian Language.

St. Lazarus Venice 1874

Printed paper wrapper. English and Armenian on opposing pages.

Beecher's Recitations and Readings ... Edited by Alvah C. Beecher, <sic>

New York ... <1874>

For comment see entry No. 3361.

Free Congregational Society of Florence. Programme of Dedicatory Exercises of Cosmian Hall, Beginning Wednesday Evening, March 25th ...

<n.p., n.d., Florence, Mass., 1874>

Caption-title. The above at head of p. <1>. 4 pp.

Half Hours with the Poets ...

New York ... 1874.

For comment see entry No. 5529.

... The Lady's Almanac, for 1875.

... Boston ... <1874>

For fuller entry see No. 5600.

Poetry of the Year: Passages from the Poets Descriptive of the Seasons ...

New York: Leavitt & Allen Brothers. 1874.

"A Winter Walk," pp. 122-123; otherwise "Woods in Winter," *Voices of the Night*, 1839.

The Rose, Thistle and Shamrock. A Book of English Poetry .. Selected and Arranged by Ferdinand Freiligrath. Fifth Edition ...

Stuttgart. Edward Hallberger. <1874>

Date from editor's "Prefatory Note." A copy at CH inscribed by the editor Christmas, 1874.

Vers de Société Selected ... by Charles H. Jones ...

New York ... 1875

For comment see BAL, Vol. 1, p. 73.

Parnassus Edited by Ralph Waldo Emerson ...

Boston ... 1875.

For comment see entry No. 5269. "Life," p. 149 is extracted from "Psalm of Life," *Voices of the Night*, 1839.

... Little Classics. Edited by Rossiter Johnson. Poems Narrative ...

Boston: James R. Osgood and Company, Late Ticknor & Fields, and Fields, Osgood, & Co. 1875.

At head of title: *Thirteenth Volume*. A copy at BA received June 22, 1875.

The Elocutionist's Annual Number 2 ... Edited by J. W. Shoemaker ...

Philadelphia ... 1875.

For comment see BAL, Vol. 2, p. 247. "The Ghosts," pp. 40-45, is extracted from *The Song of Hiawatha*, 1855.

The Elocutionist's Annual Number 3 ... Edited by J. W. Shoemaker ...

J. W. Daughaday & Co., Publishers, Philadelphia. 1875.

Cloth; and, printed paper wrapper. Deposited June 28, 1875. "The Famine," pp. 98-103, is extracted from *The Song of Hiawatha*, 1855.

One Hundred Choice Selections No. 11 ...

... Philadelphia ... 1875.

For comment see entry No. 4046.

The Illustrated Family Christian Almanac for ... 1876 ...

... New York ... ⟨n.d., 1875⟩

For fuller entry see No. 11593. "The New Household," p. 22, is extracted from *The Hanging of the Crane*, 1875.

... Little Classics. Edited by Rossiter Johnson. Minor Poems ...

Boston: James R. Osgood and Company, Late Ticknor & Fields, and Fields, Osgood, & Co. 1875.

At head of title: *Fifteenth Volume.* A copy at BA received Nov. 22, 1875.

Folk Songs. Translated from the German and Printed for the Fair in Aid of the Massachusetts Infant Asylum, December, 1875.

Boston: Press of John Wilson and Son. 1875.

Cover-title? Issued in printed wrapper?

Wide Awake Pleasure Book. ⟨Vol. 1⟩

Boston ... ⟨1875⟩

For comment see BAL, Vol. 1, p. 73. "King Baby," p. 238, is extracted from *The Hanging of the Crane*, 1875.

Christmas in Song and Story ...

New York   James Cockcroft & Company ⟨1875⟩

Leather.

Singers and Songs of the Liberal Faith; Being Selections of Hymns and Other Sacred Poems of the Liberal Church in America ... ⟨Compiled⟩ by Alfred P. Putnam.

Boston: Roberts Brothers. 1875.

Ballads of the War

⟨n.p., Boston⟩ Heliotype ⟨n.d., *ca.* 1875⟩

For comment see BAL, Vol. 4, p. 329.

Songs of Three Centuries. Edited by John Greenleaf Whittier.

Boston ... 1876.

For comment see entry No. 11341.

Laurel Leaves. Original Poems, Stories, and Essays ...

Boston ... 1876.

For comment see entry No. 116.

Theatrum Majorum. The Cambridge of 1776 ... Edited ... by A. G. ...

Cambridge ... M D CCC LXX VI.

For fuller entry see No. 11417. Extract from "To a Child," p. 31, *Belfry of Bruges*, 1845; extract from "Paul Revere's Ride," p. 66, *Tales of a Wayside Inn*, 1863.

One Hundred Choice Selections No. 12 ... Compiled ... by Phineas Garrett ...

... Philadelphia ... 1876.

For comment see entry No. 5530.

The Mountains ...

Boston ... 1876.

For comment see entry No. 1239.

Roadside Poems for Summer Travellers. Edited by Lucy Larcom.

Boston ... 1876.

For comment see entry No. 11343.

Poetic Localities of Cambridge. Edited by W. J. Stillman ...

Boston: James R. Osgood and Company, Late Ticknor & Fields, and Fields, Osgood, & Co. 1876.

Autumn Leaves. ⟨Edited by L. R. Swain?⟩

⟨n.p., n.d., 1876?⟩

All Longfellow material herein reprinted from earlier books. The untitled lines, p. 41, are extracted from "Haunted Houses," *The Courtship of Miles Standish*, 1858.

The Reading Club and Handy Speaker ... Edited by George M. Baker. No. 4.

Boston ... 1877.

For comment see entry No. 8303.

... The Quarterly Elocutionist ... Edited ... by Mrs. Anna Randall-Diehl ... April, 1877 ...

... New York ...

For comment see entry No. 290.

Hillside and Seaside in Poetry ... Edited by Lucy Larcom

Boston ... 1877

For comment see entry No. 11345.

Dick's Recitations and Readings No. 5 . . .

New York . . . ‹1877›

For comment see entry No. 5531. "Monk Felix," pp. 48-51, is extracted from *The Golden Legend*, 1851.

One Hundred Choice Selections No. 14 . . .

. . . Philadelphia . . . 1877.

For comment see BAL, Vol. 2, p. 104.

The Elocutionist's Annual Number 5 . . .

Philadelphia . . . 1877.

For comment see BAL, Vol. 2, p. 463.

History of the Old South Meeting-House in Boston. By Everett W. Burdett.

Boston: B. B. Russell. 1877.

Printed paper wrapper. Listed PW Jan. 12, 1878.

Poems of the Life Beyond and Within . . . Edited . . . by Giles B. Stebbins . . .

Boston . . . 1877.

For comment see entry No. 9451.

Star Selections, 1876 . . . ‹Edited› by Professor J. E. Goodrich.

New York . . . 1877.

For comment see BAL, Vol. 3, p. 471.

Christmastide Containing Four Famous Poems . . .

Boston . . . 1878

For comment see BAL, Vol. 1, p. 74.

Latter-Day Lyrics . . . Selected . . . by W. Davenport Adams . . .

London . . . 1878 . . .

For comment see BAL, Vol. 1, p. 74.

One Hundred Choice Selections No. 15 . . .

. . . Philadelphia . . . 1878.

For comment see entry No. 5534.

West Point Tic Tacs . . .

. . . New York. 1878.

Deposited June 25, 1878. For fuller entry see No. 7299.

Golden Thoughts . . . Introduction by Rev. Theo. L. Cuyler . . .

New-York . . . ‹1878›

All Longfellow material herein reprinted from earlier books. "The Little Children," p. 291; otherwise "Weariness," *Tales of a Wayside Inn*, 1863. For fuller entry see BAL, Vol. 2, p. 104.

Dick's Recitations and Readings No. 8 . . .

New York . . . ‹1878›

For comment see entry No. 8626.

Our Children's Songs . . .

New York . . . 1878.

All Longfellow material herein reprinted from earlier books. "Introductory Song," p. ‹13›; otherwise "Children," *The Courtship of Miles Standish*, 1858. For comment see BAL, Vol. 3, p. 471.

Poetry of America . . . ‹Edited› by W. J. Linton.

London . . . 1878.

For fuller entry see No. 7872.

Tears for the Little Ones. A Collection of Poems and Passages Inspired by the Loss of Children. Edited by Helen Kendrick Johnson . . .

Boston: James R. Osgood and Company, Late Ticknor & Fields and Fields, Osgood, & Co. 1878.

The Carnival Transcript . . .

Boston . . . 1879 . . .

For comment see entry No. 4053.

One Hundred Choice Selections No. 17 . . .

. . . Philadelphia . . . 1879.

For comment see BAL, Vol. 2, pp. 248-249.

Home Life in Song with the Poets of To-Day . . .

New York . . . ‹1879›

For comment see entry No. 432.

The Children's Book of Poetry: Carefully Selected . . . by Henry T. Coates . . .

Porter & Coates. Philadelphia. ‹1879›

The Christmas Bell . . .

New York: Anson D. F. Randolph & Company, 900 Broadway, Cor. 20th St. ⟨1879⟩

A novelty booklet cut in the outline of a bell. Illuminated paper wrapper.

Poetry for Children Edited by Samuel Eliot . . .

Authorized for Use in the Boston Public Schools 1879

Scrap-Book Recitation Series, No. 1 . . . Compiled by H. M. Soper . . .

Chicago . . . ⟨1879⟩

For comment see entry No. 2476.

As Time Glides On The Months in Picture and Poem Arranged by G. Thompson Hutchinson . . . ⟨and Others⟩

New York A. C. Armstrong & Son ⟨n.d., not before 1879⟩

Pictorial paper wrapper. Unpaged. Contains an extract from *Evangeline* here titled "September."

Apollo Club ⟨Program⟩

⟨Boston, Nov. 26, 1880⟩

Cover-title. Printed paper wrapper. "The Nun of Nidaros," pp. ⟨7-8⟩, reprinted from *Tales of a Wayside Inn*, 1863.

Papyrus Leaves . . . Edited by William Fearing Gill . . .

New York . . . 1880.

Deposited Dec. 26, 1879. For comment see entry No. 2477.

Bohemian Days Three American Tales by Geo. Alfred Townsend . . .

H. Campbell & Co., Publishers, No. 21 Park Row, New York. ⟨1880⟩

Printed paper wrapper. Listed PW Jan. 29, 1881.

Ballads and Lyrics. Selected . . . by Henry Cabot Lodge.

Boston: Houghton, Osgood and Company. The Riverside Press, Cambridge. 1880.

Birthplace Commemorative Services of the 100th Anniversary of the Birth of William Ellery Channing, Newport, R. I., April 7th, 1880.

⟨Newport, 1880⟩

Program. 4 pp.

Selected Poetical Gems, for the Cottage, Palace and Platform. Compiled by D. Gilbert Dexter.

Cambridge, Mass., Tribune Publishing Company. 1880.

Noted as "just issued," *Cambridge Tribune*, May 28, 1880.

Flower Songs for Flower Lovers. Compiled by Rose Porter . . .

New York: Anson D. F. Randolph & Company, 900 Broadway, Cor. 20th Street. ⟨1880⟩

Harper's Cyclopædia of British and American Poetry Edited by Epes Sargent

New York . . . 1881

For comment see entry No. 4336.

Selections in Verse . . .

Philadelphia . . . 1881.

For comment see in Helen Hunt Jackson, *Section Three.*

The Autograph Birthday Book . . . Edited by Amanda B. Harris . . .

Boston . . . ⟨1881⟩

For comment see BAL, Vol. 1, p. 74.

In Memoriam. James A. Garfield . . . Compiled by Henry J. Cookinham . . .

Utica, N. Y. . . . MDCCCLXXXI.

For comment see entry No. 10448.

Gems for the Fireside Comprising the Most Unique, Touching, Pithy, and Beautiful Literary Treasures . . . ⟨Compiled by⟩ Rev. O. H. Tiffany . . .

Boston, Mass., B. A. Fowler & Co., Publishers. 1881.

This publication has the appearance of a subscription book; if so, then quite probably issued with varying imprints and in various styles of binding.

Indian Summer Autumn Poems and Sketches ⟨Compiled by⟩ L. Clarkson . . .

New York . . . 1881 . . .

For comment see entry No. 10449.

Favorite Poems, Selected from English and American Authors.

New York . . . ⟨n.d., after May 1, 1881⟩

For comment see in Larcom, *Section Three.*

The Poets' Tributes to Garfield ... ‹Second Edition›

Cambridge ... 1882

For comment see entry No. 1248.

Dick's Recitations and Readings No. 14 ...

New York ... ‹1882›

For comment see BAL, Vol. 3, p. 472.

The Illustrated Fryeburg Webster Memorial.

Fryeburg, Me.: A. F. & C. W. Lewis. 1882.

Printed paper wrapper. Deposited Aug. 9, 1882.

The Cambridge Book of Poetry and Song ... by Charlotte Fiske Bates ...

New York ... ‹1882›

For comment see entry No. 7887.

Poems of American Patriotism Chosen by J. Brander Matthews

New-York ... 1882

A copy at H received Nov. 25, 1882. For fuller entry see BAL, Vol. 1, p. 74.

In the Saddle   A Collection of Poems on Horseback-Riding ‹Edited by Annie Allegra Longfellow› ...

Boston   Houghton, Mifflin and Company New York: 11 East Seventeenth Street   The Riverside Press, Cambridge   1882

All Longfellow material herein reprinted from other books. "Irmingard's Escape," pp. 37-42, extracted from *The Golden Legend*, 1851.

... Selections for School Exhibitions and Private Reading ... Nos. 1, 2, 3 ...

Boston ... 1882.

For comment see BAL, Vol. 2, p. 472.

Tender and True. Poems of Love ...

Boston ... 1882.

For fuller entry see in Jackson list, *Section Three.*

A Handful of Blossoms ... by Susie B. Skelding

New York ... 1883

For comment see in Jackson list, *Section Three.*

The Elocutionist's Annual Number 11 ...

Philadelphia ... 1883.

All Longfellow material herein reprinted from other books. "Finished," p. 94, extracted from "The Abbot Joachim," *Christus*, 1872.

For comment see entry No. 3413.

Flowers from Hill and Dale   Poems Arranged ... by Susie Barstow Skelding ...

New York ... 1883

For comment see entry No. 11363.

Brilliant Diamonds of Poetry and Prose ... ‹Compiled by› Rev. O. H. Tiffany ...

Published for the Trade. ‹n.p., 1883›

1884 The Independent Almanac

‹New York: The Independent, 1883›

Printed paper wrapper. Cover-title.

Fifty Perfect Poems. Selected and Edited by Charles A. Dana and Rossiter Johnson ...

New York: D. Appleton and Company, 1, 3, and 5 Bond Street. 1883.

Gems for the Fireside Comprising the Most Unique, Touching, Pithy, and Beautiful Literary Treasures ... ‹Compiled by› Rev. O. H. Tiffany ...

Springfield, Mass. Bay State Publishing Company. ‹1883›

A subscription book; in all likelihood issued in various styles of binding and with varying imprints.

Two editions noted; the order is probable.

1: As above. Paged ‹3›-727.

2: Imprinted: *Boston, Mass.: Russell & Henderson, Publishers.* ‹1883› Paged ‹5›-‹864›; p. ‹864› mispaged 912.

Picturesque American Scenery ... with Text by N. P. Willis and Others ...

Boston: Estes and Lauriat, Publishers. 1883.

Surf and Wave: The Sea As Sung by the Poets. Edited by Anna L. Ward ...

New York: Thomas Y. Crowell & Co. 13 Astor Place. ‹1883›

Flowers from Glade and Garden   Poems Arranged ... by Susie Barstow Skelding ...

New York ... 1884

For comment see BAL, Vol. 2, p. 39.

Young People's Scrap-Book: Containing Choice Selections ... Illustrated Poems ... ⟨Compiled by Daniel Curry⟩

    Cincinnati: Walden and Stowe. New York: Phillips and Hunt. 1884.

    Printed paper boards, cloth shelfback. Deposited Dec. 8, 1883. Reissued with cancel title-leaf imprinted: *Cranston & Stowe, Cincinnati, O.; Chicago, Ills.; St. Louis, Mo.* ⟨n.d., 1884–1892⟩

An Old Scrap-Book. With Additions ...

    ⟨Cambridge⟩ February 8, 1884.

    For comment see entry No. 7763.

No. 4. Standard Recitations ... Compiled ... by ... Frances P. Sullivan ... June, 1884 ...

    ... N. Y. ... ⟨1884⟩

    For comment see BAL, Vol. 4, p. 60.

The Elocutionist's Annual Number 12 ... Compiled by Mrs. J. W. Shoemaker.

    ... Philadelphia. 1884.

    For comment see entry No. 10454. "The Legend of the Beautiful," pp. 9-13; otherwise "The Legend Beautiful," *Tales of a Wayside Inn*, 1863.

Belford's Chatterbox. December, 1884. Edited by Elmo ...

    Chicago ... 1884.

    For comment see in Larcom, *Section III.* "Grandpapa's Pets," p. 18, extracted from "Children," *The Courtship of Miles Standish*, 1858. "How *Excelsior* Was Written," p. 73, (being a letter from Longfellow to C. K. Tuckerman) previously in W. Sloane Kennedy, *Henry W. Longfellow* (Cambridge, 1882).

Excelsior Recitations and Readings No. 3 ...

    New York ... ⟨1884⟩

    For fuller entry see BAL, Vol. 2, p. 472.

Fenno's Favorites ... ⟨Compiled⟩ by Frank H. Fenno ... ⟨No. 1⟩

    Philadelphia ... ⟨1884⟩

    For comment see entry No. 11193.

Midsummer Flowers ... Poems ... Arranged ... by Susie Barstow Skelding ...

    New York ... 1885

    For comment see in Lucy Larcom list, *Section III.*

December Edited by Oscar Fay Adams ...

    Boston ... ⟨1885⟩

    All Longfellow material herein reprinted from other books. "Winter," p. 44, extracted from *The Song of Hiawatha*, 1855. For comment see entry No. 57.

January Edited by Oscar Fay Adams ...

    Boston ... ⟨1885⟩

    For comment see entry No. 58.

Flowers from Here and There Poems Arranged and Illustrated by Susie Barstow Skelding ...

    New York White, Stokes, & Allen 1885

From Moor and Glen ... Poems ... Arranged ... by Susie B. Skelding ...

    New York White, Stokes, & Allen 1885

    Unpaged. Cloth, pictorial label pasted to front. Tied.

February Edited by Oscar Fay Adams ...

    Boston ... ⟨1886⟩

    For comment see entry No. 59.

March Edited by Oscar Fay Adams ...

    Boston ... ⟨1886⟩

    For comment see entry No. 60.

April Edited by Oscar Fay Adams ...

    Boston ... ⟨1886⟩

    For comment see entry No. 61.

Bugle-Echoes ... Edited by Francis F. Browne

    New York ... MDCCCLXXXVI

    For comment see BAL, Vol. 1, p. 75.

The Poets' Birthday Book ... Edited by Amanda B. Harris ...

    Boston ... ⟨1886⟩

    For comment see BAL, Vol. 1, p. 75.

June Edited by Oscar Fay Adams ...

    Boston ... ⟨1886⟩

    For comment see entry No. 64.

Hymns and Anthems Adapted for Jewish Worship. Selected and Arranged by Dr. Gustav Gottheil ...

    New York. 1886.

July Edited by Oscar Fay Adams ...

Boston ... ⟨1886⟩

For comment see entry No. 65.

August Edited by Oscar Fay Adams ...

Boston ... ⟨1886⟩

For comment see entry No. 66.

Wayside Flowers ... Poems Arranged by Ellen E. Dickinson ...

New York ... 1886

For comment see entry No. 7899.

Actors and Actresses of Great Britain and the United States ... Edited by Brander Matthews and Laurence Hutton ...

... New York ⟨1886⟩

For comment see entry No. 1904. The sonnet on Frances Ann Kemble, p. 240, is otherwise "Sonnet on Mrs. Kemble's Reading of Shakespeare," *The Seaside and the Fireside*, 1850.

September Edited by Oscar Fay Adams ...

Boston ... ⟨1886⟩

All Longfellow material herein reprinted from other books. "In September," p. 118, extracted from *Evangeline*, 1847. For comment see entry No. 67.

Belford's Annual 1886–7. Edited by Thomas W. Handford ...

Chicago ... ⟨1886⟩

All Longfellow material herein reprinted from earlier books. "Night's Soothing Power," p. 156, extracted from "Hymn to the Night," *Voices of the Night*, 1839. For comment see entry No. 10467.

Belford's Chatterbox December, 1886. Edited by Thomas W. Handford ...

Chicago ... ⟨1886⟩

All Longfellow material herein reprinted from earlier books. "Night's Soothing Power," p. 156, extracted from "Hymn to the Night," *Voices of the Night*, 1839. For comment see entry No. 10468.

October Edited by Oscar Fay Adams ...

Boston ... ⟨1886⟩

For comment see entry No. 68.

November Edited by Oscar Fay Adams ...

Boston ... ⟨1886⟩

For comment see entry No. 69.

The Children of the Poets An Anthology ... Edited ... by Eric S. Robertson.

London: Walter Scott, 24 Warwick Lane, Paternoster Row, and Newcastle-on-Tyne. 1886.

Cloth, printed paper label on spine.

The Sonnets of Europe A Volume of Translations Selected ... by Samuel Waddington ...

London: Walter Scott, 24 Warwick Lane, Paternoster Row, and Newcastle-on-Tyne. 1886.

Probably issued in cloth, printed paper label on spine.

The Two Voices Poems ... Selected by John W. Chadwick ...

Troy, N. Y. ... 1886

All Longfellow material herein reprinted from other books. "If Thou Art Worn," p. 176, extracted from "Sunrise on the Hills," *Voices of the Night*, 1839. For fuller entry see in Lucy Larcom, *Section III*.

Ballads of Books Chosen by Brander Matthews

New York ... 1887

For comment see entry No. 1905.

No. 16. Standard Recitations ... Compiled ... by Frances P. Sullivan ... June 1887 ...

... N. Y. ... ⟨1887⟩

For comment see BAL, Vol. 2, p. 391.

The Pictorial Budget of Wonders and Fun ...

The Juvenile Publishing Company. ⟨1887⟩

For comment see entry No. 3756.

Camp-Fire Sketches and Battle-Field Echoes of the Rebellion. Compiled by W. C. King, and W. P. Derby ...

W. C. King & Co., Publishers, Springfield, Mass. 1887.

Noted only in leather; probably issued in a variety of bindings. Preface dated *June, 1887*. Reissued under date 1888 titled *Camp-Fire Sketches and Battle-Field Echoes of 61–65*.

"Mustered Out," p. 605; otherwise "A Nameless Grave," *The Masque of Pandora*, 1875.

The Elocutionist's Annual Number 15 ... Compiled by Mrs. J. W. Shoemaker.

Publication Department, the National School of Elocution and Oratory. Philadelphia: 1887.

The Illustrated Family Christian Almanac for ... 1888 ...

American Tract Society, 150 Nassau Street, New York. Sold by Booksellers and Traders. ‹1887›

Printed paper wrapper. "The Pilgrim Fathers' Church," p. 19, extracted from *The Courtship of Miles Standish*, 1858.

The Poets of Maine ... Compiled by George Bancroft Griffith

Portland ... 1888

For comment see BAL, Vol. 1, p. 87.

Belford's Annual. 1888-9. Edited by Thomas W. Handford ...

Chicago ... ‹1888›

All Longfellow material herein reprinted from other books. "Go to the Woods and Hills," p. 200, extracted from "Sunrise on the Hills," *Voices of the Night*, 1839. For comment see entry No. 5735.

The Bugle Song and Other Poems ...

Boston Estes and Lauriat, Publishers ‹1888›

Golden Milestones ...

... Boston ... 1888 ...

Contains four untitled lines extracted from "The Golden Mile-Stone," *The Courtship of Miles Standish*, 1858. For fuller entry see in Lucy Larcom, *Section III*.

No. 23. Standard Recitations ... Compiled ... by Frances P. Sullivan ... March, 1889 ...

... N. Y. ... ‹1889›

For comment see entry No. 5558.

American Sonnets. Selected ... by William Sharp.

London ... ‹n.d., 1889›

For comment see BAL, Vol. 3, p. 101.

American War Ballads and Lyrics ... Edited by George Cary Eggleston ...

New York ... ‹1889›

For fuller entry see in G. P. Lathrop list of reprints.

... Harper's Fifth Reader American Authors

New York ... 1889

For comment see entry No. 7917.

The Elocutionist's Annual Number 17 ... Compiled by Mrs. J. W. Shoemaker

Philadelphia ... 1889

For comment see entry No. 1270.

Half-Hours with the Best Humorous Authors. Selected ... by Charles Morris ... American.

Philadelphia ... 1889.

For comment see entry No. 3813. "The Happy Man and the Lucky Dog," Vol. 1, pp. 365-366; extracted from "The Blank Book of a Country Schoolmaster," *Works*, 1886.

No. 26. Standard Recitations ... Compiled ... by Frances P. Sullivan ... December, 1889 ...

... N. Y. ... ‹1890›

For comment see entry No. 134.

The Poets' Year ... Edited by Oscar Fay Adams ...

Boston ... ‹1890›

For comment see entry No. 80.

American Sonnets Selected ... by T. W. Higginson and E. H. Bigelow

Boston ... 1890

For comment see entry No. 8373.

Representative Sonnets by American Poets ... by Charles H. Crandall

Boston ... 1890

For comment see entry No. 8374.

Fenno's Favorites, No. 9. 100 Choice Pieces for Reading and Speaking ... ‹Compiled› by Frank H. Fenno ...

Philadelphia: John E. Potter & Company, 1111 and 1113 Market Street. ‹1890›

Printed paper wrapper. All Longfellow material herein reprinted from other books. "Glimpses into Cloudland," pp. 147-148, extracted from *Hyperion*, 1839.

Out of the Heart Poems ... Selected by John White Chadwick ... and Annie Hathaway Chadwick ...

Troy ... 1891

For comment see in Helen Hunt Jackson list, *Section III*.

No. 38. Standard Recitations ... Compiled ... by Frances P. Sullivan ... December 1892 ...

... N. Y. ... 1893

For comment see entry No. 364.

Random Rhymes. ⟨Edited by Roland R. Conklin⟩

⟨n.p., Kansas City, Mo., 1893⟩

No. 39. Standard Recitations ... Compiled ... by Frances P. Sullivan ... March 1893

... N. Y. ... 1893

For comment see BAL, Vol. 3, p. 139.

The Lover's Year-Book of Poetry ⟨Second Series⟩ ... Married-Life and Child-Life ⟨Compiled⟩ by Horace Parker Chandler ...

Boston ... 1893

All Longfellow material herein reprinted from other books. The untitled lines, Vol. 1, p. ⟨204⟩, extracted from "The Poet's Calendar," *In the Harbor*, 1882. For fuller entry see No. 10903.

American Lecturers and Humorists by Melville D. Landon ...

... Akron ... ⟨1893⟩

See below under ⟨1893; *i.e.*, *ca.* 1898⟩

Quaker Poems A Collection of Verse Relating to the Society of Friends. Compiled by Charles Francis Jenkins.

Philadelphia: John C. Winston & Co. 1893.

Werner's Readings and Recitations Number Twelve Compiled and Arranged by Elsie M. Wilbor

Edgar S. Werner & Company New York Copyright, 1893 ...

Cloth?

A Symphony of the Spirit Compiled by George S. Merriam

Boston and New York Houghton, Mifflin and Company The Riverside Press, Cambridge 1894

Listed PW Feb. 3, 1894.

Childhood's Sunny Days ... ⟨by⟩ Lucy Larcom ... and Others ...

... 1895 ... Chicago ...

For comment see entry No. 4747.

The World of Wit and Humour ... ⟨New and Enlarged Edition⟩

... London ... 1895 ⟨–1896⟩ ...

For comment see BAL, Vol. 3, p. 400.

No. 44. Standard Recitations ... Compiled .. by Frances P. Sullivan ... June 1894 ...

... N. Y. ... 1896

For comment see BAL, Vol. 3, p. 139.

No. 45. Standard Recitations ... Compiled ... by Frances P. Sullivan ... September 1894 ...

... N. Y. ... 1896 ...

For comment see entry No. 2632.

The Lover's Year-Book of Poetry A Collection of Love Poems for Every Day in the Year The Other Life by Horace Parker Chandler Vol. I. January to June

Boston Roberts Brothers 1896

Martial Recitations ... Collected ... by James Henry Brownlee ...

Chicago ... ⟨1896⟩

For fuller entry see in G. P. Lathrop reprints.

Platform Pearls for Temperance Workers and Other Reformers A Collection of Recitations ... Compiled by Lilian M. Heath

New York Funk & Wagnalls Company London and Toronto 1896

The Treasury of American Sacred Song ... Edited by W. Garrett Horder ...

London ... 1896

For fuller entry see under Lucy Larcom, *Section III*.

Library of the World's Best Literature Ancient and Modern Charles Dudley Warner Editor ... Thirty Volumes Vol. XVI

New York R. S. Peale and J. A. Hill Publishers ⟨1897⟩

For comment see entry No. 10624. Deposited Aug. 9, 1897.

Voices of Doubt and Trust Selected by Volney Streamer

New York Brentano's 1897

Deposited Sept. 2, 1897.

Three Minute Readings for College Girls Selected and Edited by Harry Cassell Davis ...

Copyright, 1897 ... Hinds & Noble, Publishers 4-5-13-14 Cooper Institute New York City

Poems of American Patriotism 1776–1898 Selected by R. L. Paget

Boston ... MDCCCXCVIII

For comment see BAL, Vol. 1, p. 249.

Dew Drops and Diamonds ... for Boys and Girls ...

... 1898 ... Chicago ...

For comment see BAL, Vol. 1, p. 77.

American Lecturers and Humorists by Melville D. Landon ...

The Saalfield Publishing Company   Akron, Ohio   New York ⟨1893; i.e., ca. 1898⟩

For comment see entry No. 11228.

Glad Gleams across Life's Path. Illustrated by Emily T. Harding & E. W. Andrews.

Boston, A. D. Maclachlan   214 Clarendon Street. ⟨n.d., ca. 1900⟩

Pictorial wrapper. Unpaged. "Whitsuntide;" otherwise "The Children of the Lord's Supper," Ballads ... , 1842.

Modern Eloquence ... ⟨Edited by⟩ Thomas B. Reed ...

... Philadelphia ⟨1900; i.e., 1901⟩

For comment see entry No. 3467.

Songs of Nature Edited by John Burroughs

New York ... MCMI ...

For comment see entry No. 2169.

Masters of Mirth and Eloquence by Melville D. Landon ...

The Golden West Publishing Company   Seattle, Washington   ⟨1906⟩

Through Italy with the Poets Compiled by Robert Haven Schauffler ...

New York ... 1908

For comment see BAL, Vol. 4, p. 446.

International Short Stories Edited by William Patten ... American

... New York ⟨1910⟩

For comment see entry No. 782.

Impressions in and about Portland, Maine   Selected by Carrie Thompson Lowell

Published by Abner W. Lowell   608 Congress Street, Portland, Maine ⟨1910⟩

Printed paper wrapper.

A Roycroft Anthology Selected and Edited by John T. Hoyle ...

The Roycrofters   East Aurora, N. Y.   MCMXVII

Marbled boards, leather shelfback and corners.

The Poetry of Peace Selected by R. M. Leonard

Humphrey Milford   Oxford University Press   London ... New York ... 1918

St. Nicholas Book of Verse Edited by Mary Budd Skinner and Joseph Osmun Skinner ...

... New York ... MCMXXIII

For comment see entry No. 818.

American Mystical Verse   An Anthology Selected by Irene Hunter ...

D. Appleton and Company   New York MCMXXV

The St. Nicholas Anthology Edited by Henry Steele Commager ...

Random House   New York ⟨1948⟩

Listed PW Nov. 20, 1948.

Youth's Companion   Edited by Lovell Thompson with Three Former Companion Editors ...

... Boston ... 1954

For comment see entry No. 10927.

Gentlemen, Scholars and Scoundrels   A Treasury of the Best of Harper's Magazine from 1850 to the Present Edited by Horace Knowles

Harper & Brothers   New York   ⟨1959⟩

HENRY WADSWORTH LONGFELLOW

SECTION V

SHEET MUSIC

As originally projected this section was to include both American and British publication of Longfellow's poems in sheet music form. But after expenditure of much time and effort BAL was obliged, reluctantly, to abandon that plan and to include *dated* American sheet music only. The decision was made when it became apparent that BAL, even with the assistance of competent British authorities, could not compile a satisfactory list. One such authority comments:

"For most of the dating I have to rely on the accession stamps of the British Museum, and on the whole these will give a reliable ⟨albeit approximate⟩ date. But there are . . . snags. For instance there is a collection of thirty settings . . . by John Blockley. The first sixteen bear the reception date 11 May, 1855. This looks as though the composer suddenly realized he had not sent any copyright issues to the British Museum and sent them all in a batch. All one can say is, therefore, that they are not later than 1855. The dates for the remaining fourteen compositions, which range from 1856 to 1859, are *probably* accurate.

"In some cases there is no copy of the song required in the British Museum . . . the Music Department thinks that quite a number may have been destroyed in those days when music was the Cinderella of the British Museum and was left lying about in heaps.

". . . ⟨Certain of⟩ the publishers . . . who might have been able to give . . . information . . . have gone out of business . . .

". . . The copyright libraries were not so keen on enforcing the delivery of music, and probably a great deal never reached them from the publishers.

"I . . . point out that in only a single case ⟨of several hundred⟩ did I find a date printed on the music itself. In all other cases I have had to take the entry dates stamped on the music by the libraries. Thus it well may be that music stamped, for example, 14 January 1855, was published in 1854. Also it is quite likely that some publishers waited until they had a batch of music to send in . . ."

As an example of the problem: BAL has seen, or has notes on, thirteen British appearances of Longfellow's "Excelsior" by ten different composers, issued by twelve different publishers; each is undated and no certain publication information is available. BAL has notes on approximately four hundred British appearances of Longfellow in sheet music form, none issued with date; and after exhaustive search, to only a few can more than an approximate date be assigned.

The problem applies equally to the undated, uncopyrighted, pieces of sheet music issued in the United States. Virtually all of these are reprints of British publications.

Section Five, therefore contains, with a few exceptions, only *dated* American issues; all are reprints of the text, the text having had prior book publication. But: The texts have not been collated and some may be unrevised periodical readings. Those pieces of sheet music that are first publication outside of periodicals are described in *Section One*.

Also excluded are sheet music publications issued under date 1900 or later; and, all continental printings.

All settings noted by BAL are listed, but obvious reprints of such settings (obvious on the basis of date or of publisher's later imprint) are ignored.

Unless otherwise stated the title appears on the front cover.

For a comment on BAL and sheet music see BAL, Vol. 1, pp. xxi-xxii.

THE ARRANGEMENT IS ALPHABETICAL BY TITLE

Aftermath . . . Music by F. Boott . . .

Boston   Oliver Ditson & Co. 277 Washington St. . . . 1873 . . .

Plate number 27971. Title deposited Nov. 20, 1873. Copies deposited Nov. 28, 1873. Previously in *Aftermath*, 1873 (Sept.). A setting by C. Josie Maree, was published in Boston, 1874.

. . . Album of Twelve Songs . . . ⟨Music by Frederic H. Cowen⟩

New-York: G. Schirmer, 35 Union Square. ⟨n.d., after 1879⟩

"Thy Remembrance," pp. 1-3; otherwise "Delia," *Kéramos*, 1878. "Snow-Flakes," pp. 4-7, not by Longfellow but by Mary Mapes Dodge.

... Allah ... Music by G. W. Chadwick ...

Boston: Arthur P. Schmidt & Co., 13 and 15 West Street ... 1887 ...

Plate number 1552 (alto, baritone); 1553 (soprano, tenor). Reprinted from *Kéramos*, 1878. Under the title "The Bedouin's Prayer," music by Jules Jordan, published by Arthur P. Schmidt, 1890.

The Angel and the Child ... Music by Virginia Gabriel ...

New York. C. H. Ditson & Co. 711 Broadway. Boston, O. Ditson & Co. ... ⟨n.d., not before 1870⟩

Reprint? Plate number 27469. The poem was first published in *The Atlantic Monthly*, Sept. 1870. Collected in *Three Books of Song*, 1872.

The Arrow and the Song ... Music by M. W. Balfe ...

Boston ... Oliver Ditson & Co. 277 Washington St ... ⟨n.d., 1858–1876⟩

Plate number 22578. Reprinted from *The Belfry of Bruges*, 1845.

Other settings and printings noted; the order is alphabetical under name of composer:

Coerne, Louis Adolphe: Boston: Everett E. Truette & Co., 1894.

Elliot, C. S.: Boston: G. D. Russell, 1880.

Gounod, Charles: ⟨n.p., Philadelphia⟩ W. F. Shaw, 1884.

Hawley, C. B.: New York: Wm. A. Pond & Co., 1883.

Henschel, George, under the title *"I Shot an Arrow in the Air."* New York: G. Schirmer, 1880.

Mulligan, Wm. Ed.: New York: Edward Schuberth & Co., 1887.

Pinsuti: Boston: Oliver Ditson & Co., n.d., after 1877.

————: Boston: W. A. Evans, n.d., not before 1881.

————: Brooklyn, N.Y.: M. Franklin Jones, 1898.

————: New York: S. T. Gordon & Son, n.d., not before 1873.

————: New York: William A. Pond & Co., n.d., not before 1877.

————: New York: Richard A. Saalfield, n.d., *ca.* 1875. Two printings noted, a principal variation being the misspelling of the composer's name; in one printing: *Pinsuit;* in the other: *Pinsuti.*

————: Philadelphia: J. E. Ditson & Co., n.d., *ca.* 1875.

————: Philadelphia: W. F. Shaw, n.d., not before 1870.

... Auf Wiederseh'n ... Music by Hope Temple ...

Boosey & Co. 3 East Fourteenth Street, New York ... 1893 ...

Plate number 98-5. Reprinted from *In the Harbor*, 1882.

... The Ballad of Carmilhan ... Music ... by Archibald Davidson Arnott ...

London & New York Novello, Ewer and Co. ... 1894 ...

Plate number 9910. Reprinted from *Three Books of Song*, 1872.

The Bedouin's Prayer

See "Allah"

Beggar Dance

See "Hiawatha"

... The Bells ... Music by J. L. Hatton ...

Boston. Oliver Ditson & Co. 277 Washington St. ... ⟨n.d., after 1869⟩

Otherwise "Christmas Bells," *Household Poems*, 1865.

The Bells of San Blas Quartet for Equal Voices ... Music by F. Boott ...

Boston ... 1882 ... Olivep ⟨*sic*⟩ Ditson & Co. 451 Washington St. ...

Plate number 49112. Deposited July 21, 1882. Reprinted from *In the Harbor*, 1882 (deposited July 2, 1882).

Beware

See "I Knew a Maiden Fair"

... The Black Knight ... Cantata for Chorus and Orchestra The Poem by Uhland (Translated by Longfellow) ... Music ... by Edward Elgar ...

London & New York   Novello, Ewer and Co. ... 1893 ...

Plate number 8179. Reprinted from *Hyperion*, 1839.

The Blind Girl of Castèl-Cuillè ... Arranged by Marguerite W. Morton ...

New York   Edgar S. Werner ... 1892 ...

Deposited Dec. 3, 1892. Reprinted from *The Seaside and the Fireside*, 1850.

The Bridge ... Music ... by Agnes Landon ...

Boston ... Oliver Ditson   115 Washington St. ... ⟨n.d., not before 1854⟩

Plate number 8461. Reprinted from *Poems*, 1845.

Other settings and printings noted; the order is alphabetical under name of composer; under composer alphabetically by place.

Bucalossi, P., under the title "The Midnight Hour." Boston: Oliver Ditson & Co., n.d., not before 1881.

Carew, Lady: Boston: Oliver Ditson & Co., n.d., after 1875.

————: Boston: F. Trifet, 1899.

————: New York: J. L. Peters, n.d., *ca.* 1870.

————: New York: Richard A. Saalfield, n.d., *ca.* 1875.

————: Philadelphia: Thos. Hunter, n.d., *ca.* 1870–1880.

————: Philadelphia: M. D. Swisher, n.d., not before 1882.

Lindsay: Boston: W. H. Cundy, n.d., after 1877.

————: Boston: Oliver Ditson & Co., n.d., after 1867.

————: Boston: W. A. Evans & Bro., n.d., *ca.* 1881–1885.

————: Boston: Perry Mason & Co., n.d., after 1872.

————: Boston: G. D. Russell & Co., n.d., *ca.* 1865.

————: Boston: White, Smith & Co., 1876.

————: Chicago: National Music Co., n.d., after 1880.

————: Cincinnati: The John Church Co., n.d., after 1884.

————: Detroit: C. J. Whitney & Co., n.d., not before 1873.

————: Louisville, Kentucky: D. P. Faulds, n.d., not before 1865, under the title "I Stood on the Bridge at Midnight."

————: Milwaukee: H. N. Hempsted, n.d., *ca.* 1870.

————: New York: W. A. Evans & Bro., n.d., *ca.* 1885.

————: New York: S. T. Gordon, n.d., *ca.* 1865.

————: New York: William Hall & Son, n.d., *ca.* 1860.

————: New York: William A. Pond & Co., n.d., *ca.* 1865.

————: Norristown, Penna.: Thos. O'Neill, n.d., *ca.* 1870.

————: Philadelphia: Lee & Walker, n.d., 1856?

Smallwood, Samuel: Philadelphia: F. A. North & Co., n.d., not before 1872.

The Brook and the Wave ... Music by James L. Molloy.

Boston. Oliver Ditson & Co. 277 Washington St. ... ⟨n.d., not before 1858, not after 1876⟩

Reprint? Plate number 28311. According to Longfellow's *Works*, 1886, the poem was written in Oct. 1849. The Copyright Office reports no record of deposit 1870–1898. Collected in *Aftermath*, 1873. Reprint of an English publication?

A setting by Charles P. Scott was published by Arthur P. Schmidt, Boston, 1897.

See next entry.

The Brooklet ... Music by F. Boott.

Boston. Oliver Ditson & Co. 277 Washington St. ... 1874 ...

Plate number 28540. Otherwise "The Brook and the Wave"; see preceding entry.

Canoe Building Song

See "Hiawatha"

... The Castle by the Sea ... by Uhland. Translated by Longfellow, Music by Frederick Brandeis ...

New-York ... Wm. A. Pond & Co. 547 Broadway ... 1864 ...

No plate number. Reprinted from *Hyperion*, 1839.

... Catawba Wine ... Music by Wm. R. Dempster ...

Boston ... Oliver Ditson & Co 277 Washington St. ... 1858 ...

Plate number 18980. Deposited Dec. 31, 1858. Reprinted from *The Courtship of Miles Standish,* 1858 (Oct. 1858).

The Challenge of Thor ... Music by Alfred H. West ...

London & Leipzig Pitt & Hatzfeld. Boston. H. B. Stevens & Co. ... 1891 ...

Plate number P.&H.368. Otherwise "The Musician's Tale," *Tales of a Wayside Inn,* 1863.

Changed ... Music by F. Boott ...

Boston. Oliver Ditson & Co. ... 1873 ...

Plate number 27970. Deposited Dec. 23, 1873. Previously in *Aftermath,* 1873 (Sept.).

Chibiabo's Love Song

See "Hiawatha"

Children ... Music by William R. Dempster ...

Boston ... Oliver Ditson & Co 277 Washington St. ... 1859 ...

Plate number 19316. Reprinted from *The Courtship of Miles Standish,* 1858.

Other settings noted; the order is chronological:

Music by Sir Arthur Sullivan. Under the title "Living Poems." Philadelphia: W. H. Boner & Co., n.d., after 1864.

Music by Louis Selle. Under the title "Come to Me O Ye Children." New York: Horace Waters, 1868.

Music by George Baker. Galt, Canada, 1878.

Music by J. M. Driver. Under the title "Longfellow's Work Song." Boston: Oliver Ditson & Co., 1886.

Come to Me O Ye Children

See preceding entry.

Cradle Song

See "Hiawatha"

The Cumberland

See in *Section One* under year 1863.

Curfew

See next entry.

... Curfew Bell ... ‹Music by H. Perabeau›

Boston ... Oliver Ditson 115 Washington St. ... ‹n.d., 1844–1857›

Reprint? Plate number 6301. Also in *Poems,* 1845.

Other settings noted; the order is alphabetical under name of composer; under composer alphabetically by place.

Blockley, John: Baltimore: Miller & Beacham, n.d., not before 1854.

———: Boston: Oliver Ditson, n.d., not before 1855.

Finck, E. J.: Boston: Oliver Ditson & Co., n.d., not before 1867.

Glover, Stephen: Chicago: National Music Co., n.d., after 1880.

———: New York: Benjamin W. Hitchcock, n.d., *ca.* 1890.

Gow, G. C., in *A Group of Songs,* Boston, 1896, under the title "Curfew."

Hatton, John L.: Boston: White, Smith, & Perry, 1869.

Seward, Theo. F.: Rochester, N. Y., 1862, under the title "The Curfew."

The Day Is Cold ...

See "The Rainy Day"

The Day Is Dark ...

See "The Rainy Day"

The Day Is Done ... Music ... by M. W. Balfe ...

Philadelphia Lee & Walker 722 Chesnut St New York Jas. Couenhoven 856 Broadway ‹n.d., not before 1856›

Plate number 8158.9 Reprinted from *Poems,* 1845.

Other printings and settings noted; the order is alphabetical under name of composer; under composer alphabetically by place.

Balfe, M. W.: Boston: Oliver Ditson & Co., n.d., not before 1858.

———: Boston: Perry Mason & Co., n.d., not before 1873.

———: Detroit: C. J. Whitney & Co., n.d., 1875?

———: New York: William A. Pond & Co., n.d., not before 1863.

Davis, L. S.: San Francisco: Bancroft, Knight & Co., 1875. Probably a reprint of an A. E. Blackmar printing.

Kinney, John J.: New York: William A. Pond & Co., 1878.

Loud, Annie F.: Boston: Oliver Ditson & Co., 1882. Also issued without date.

Neidlinger, W. H.: Brooklyn: F. H. Chandler, 1879. Under the title "Resting."

Day Is Ending . . . Music by Rudolph Zabel . . .

Published by H. N. Hempsted, Milwaukee, Wis. 408, 410 and 412 Broadway, (*sic*) ‹1875›

Otherwise "An Afternoon in February," *Poems*, 1845.

Daybreak . . . Music by M. W. Balfe . . .

Boston   Published by Oliver Ditson & Co 277 Washington St . . . ‹n.d., 1858–1876›

Plate number 19167. Also in (reprinted from?) *The Courtship of Miles Standish*, 1858.

Other printings and settings noted; the order is alphabetical under name of composer; under composer alphabetically by place.

Balfe, M. W.: Boston: G. D. Russell & Co., n.d., 1863–1877.

————: Boston: A. P. Schmidt & Co., 1884.

————: New York: T. B. Harms & Co., n.d., not before 1883.

————: Philadelphia: Lee & Walker, n.d., not before 1872.

Braunschiedl, Johannes: Under the title "A Wind Came up out of the Sea." New York: C. H. Ditson & Co., 1883.

Lindsay: Boston: Oliver Ditson & Co., n.d., 1858–1876. On the basis of the plate number published after the Balfe setting.

————: Milwaukee: H. N. Hempsted & Co., n.d., ca. 1870–1873.

Malmene, Waldemar: Danbury, Conn.: Hoyt's Up-Stairs Music Store, 1873.

————: New York: R. A. Saalfield, 1873.

Marston, G. W.: New York: G. Schirmer, 1877.

Peuret, O.: Boston: A. P. Schmidt & Co., 1884.

The Death of Minnehaha . . . Music by Ch. C. Converse . . .

Boston . . . Oliver Ditson   115 Washington St. . . . ‹n.d., not before 1855›

Plate number 8422. Reprinted from *The Song of Hiawatha*, 1855. No record of copyright deposit found through the year 1857.

Other printings and settings noted; the order is alphabetical under name of composer; under composer alphabetically by place.

Coleridge-Taylor, S.: London: Novello & Co., Ltd., New York: The H. W. Gray Co., 1899.

Converse, Ch. C.: Cincinnati: W. C. Peters & Sons, n.d., not before 1859.

————: Cleveland: S. Brainard & Sons, n.d., not before 1866.

————: New York: John L. Peters, 1869.

Stoepel, Robert: New York: William Hall & Son, 1863. *See* "Hiawatha," below.

The Dreary Day

See "The Rainy Day"

Endymion . . . Music by Liza Lehmann.

The John Church Company. Cincinnati . . . ‹1899›

Plate number 13153-14. Reprinted from *Ballads*, 1842.

. . . Evangeline   Written ‹*i.e.*, adapted› by Charlotte Young   Composed by John Blockley . . .

Boston . . . Oliver Ditson   Washington St . . . ‹n.d., after 1854›

Evening Song

See "Footsteps of Angels"

. . . Excelsior . . . ‹Music by The Hutchinson Family›

New York . . . Firth & Hall   1 Franklin Sq. and J. L. Hewitt & Co. 239 Broadway. ‹1843›

Reprinted from *Ballads*, 1842. The earliest printing (printings?) is imprinted as above; no plate numbers. Later printings have one or more of the following features present: Added imprint of Firth, Hall & Pond; plate numbers present.

Carroll A. Wilson, in *First Appearance in Print of Some Four Hundred Familiar Quotations*, Middletown, Conn., 1935, reports a Hutchinson Family setting dated 1842; no copy so dated has been traced by BAL and extensive inquiry suggests that Wilson was in error. Significantly the date 1843 is given in Wilson's *Thirteen Author Collections . . .*, 1950. Merle Johnson in his *You Know These Lines!*, 1935, also gives an 1842 date, but Johnson relied heavily on Wilson for notes relating to Longfellow and probably repeated Wilson's error.

Other printings and settings noted; arranged alphabetically by composer; under composer alphabetically by place.

Balfe, M. W.: Boston: Oliver Ditson & Co., n.d., not before 1858.

Berger, Francesco: Boston: Oliver Ditson & Co., n.d., not before 1877.

Bird, Joseph: Issued without place or date. A copy in CH inscribed by A. W. Longfellow *Sept. 1847.* Further information wanting. *Reprint?*

Glover, S.: Boston: Oliver Ditson, n.d., 1844–1857.

Goldbeck, Robert: n.p., 1885.

Lindsay: Boston: Oliver Ditson, n.d., 1844–1857.

Peabody, George: Boston: Oliver Ditson & Co., 1884.

Composer's name not present: Boston: Oliver Ditson & Co., 1884.

With textual liberties issued:

Upidee A College Song and Chorus As Sung by the Students of Harvard College Arranged by H. G. Spaulding . . .

Boston . . . Oliver Ditson & Co 277 Washington St . . . 1859 . . .

Plate numbers 20210, 20220.

. . . Eyes, So Wistful . . .

Boston . . . MDCCCXCII . . . Oliver Ditson Company . . .

Plate number 36-55613-3. Reprinted from *Aftermath,* 1873. At foot of first page of text and music the copyright notice is dated MDCCCXCIII.

. . . The Farewell of Hiawatha ⟨Music by⟩ Arthur Foote . . .

Boston Arthur P. Schmidt & Co. 13 & 15 West St. ⟨1886⟩

Plate number 773-13. Reprinted from *The Song of Hiawatha,* 1855.

The Fisherman's Cottage . . . Music by W. H. Weiss.

Boston E. H. Wade 197 Washington St. ⟨n.d., 1845–1860⟩

Reprint? No plate number. Otherwise "Twilight" which appears in *The Seaside and the Fireside,* 1850; and, *The Opal . . . ,* 1848 (*i.e.,* Oct. 1847). Under the title "Twilight," setting by Geo. W. Morgan, published "free

with the New York Family Story Paper, No. 257" ⟨1878⟩.

Footprints on the Sands of Time

See "Tell Me Not in Mournful Numbers"

Footsteps of Angels . . . Music . . . by William R. Dempster . . .

Boston . . . Oliver Ditson 115 Washington St. . . . 1848 . . .

Plate number 1542. Reprinted from *Voices of the Night,* 1839.

Other settings noted:

Baer, Frank: New York: William Hall & Son, n.d., not before 1848.

Fletcher, Alfred M.: Under the title "Evening Song" published by Chicago Music Co., Chicago, 1881.

. . . The Fox Song & Chorus A Celebrated Student Song, Translated from the German by Longfellow . . .

Troy, N. Y. . . . E. P. Jones . . . 1859 . . .

Reprinted from *Hyperion,* 1839.

. . . Gathering Flowers in Heaven . . .

New York . . . 1878 . . .

See in *Section Six.*

. . . A Gleam of Sunshine . . . Music by Louis Campbell-Tipton . . .

White-Smith Music Publishing Co., Boston . . . ⟨1893⟩

Plate number 8868-3. Reprinted from *Poems,* 1845.

. . . Golden Legend

See "Scenes from Longfellow's . . ."

Good Night, Beloved . . . Composed by Dolores . . .

New York . . . William J. Hall & Son, No. 239 Broadway . . . ⟨n.d., not before 1848⟩

Plate number 3014. Reprinted from *The Spanish Student,* 1843.

Other settings or printings noted; arranged alphabetically by composer; under composer alphabetically by place.

Balfe, M. W.: Boston: Oliver Ditson & Co., n.d., not before 1858.

———: Cleveland: S. Brainard & Co., n.d., not before 1856.

————: New York: Firth, Pond & Co., n.d., not before 1856.

————: New York: S. T. Gordon, n.d., not before 1858.

————: New York: William Hall & Son, n.d., not before 1859.

Barnard, J. G.: New York: William A. Pond, 1870.

Denza, Luigi: Boston: Oliver Ditson & Co., n.d., not before 1883.

————: Boston: White-Smith Music Publishing Co., n.d., *ca.* 1891.

————: New York: T. B. Harms & Co., n.d., *ca.* 1883–1884.

Gilder, Frank: Under title "To Be Near Thee." Boston: Oliver Ditson & Co., 1879.

Glover: Philadelphia: Lee & Walker, n.d., not before 1856.

Graham, W. H. J.: New York: William A. Pond & Co., 1864.

Kimball, E. S.: Washington, D.C.: John F. Ellis & Co., 1885.

Moir, Frank L.: Boston: Oliver Ditson & Co., n.d., not before 1858.

Nevin, Ethelbert: Under the title "Serenade." New York: G. Schirmer, 1888.

Perabeau, H.: Under the title "Serenade." Boston: Oliver Ditson, n.d., not before 1853.

Philp, Elizabeth: Boston: Oliver Ditson, n.d., not before 1855.

Protheroe, D.: Scranton, Penna.: Lyric Music Co., 1894.

Silsby, Mae: Bangor, Maine: George S. Silsby, n.d., not before 1880.

Sullivan, Thomas D.: New York: John J. Daly, 1859.

Terschak, A.: Cincinnati: John Church & Co., 1880.

The Great Spirit's Allocution

See "Hiawatha"

The Green Trees Whispered Low & Mild ... Composed by J. Blockley ...

Boston ... Oliver Ditson & Co. 277 Washington St. ... ⟨n.d., not before 1858⟩

Otherwise "Prelude," *Voices of the Night,* 1839. Also set to music by M. W. Balfe and published: *Boston ... Oliver Ditson & Co 277 Washington St. ... ⟨n.d., not before 1858⟩.*

The Happiest Land

See under year 1845 in *Section One.*

The Harvest

See "Hiawatha"

He Said He Came to Find Me ...

See this title in *Section Six.*

... The Hemlock Tree ... Music by B. A. Whaples ...

New York ... Blelock & Co. 110 William St. 1864 ...

Reprinted from *Poems,* 1845.

... Hiawatha ... Music ... by Robert Stoepel ... Cradle Song ...

New-York ... Wm. Hall & Son, 543 Broadway ... 1863 ...

Plate number 4867. Reprinted from *The Song of Hiawatha,* 1855. According to a list on the front cover the full suite consists of the following separate pieces: "Beggar Dance"; "Canoe Building Song"; "Chibiabo's Love Song"; "Cradle Song"; "Death of Minnehaha"; "The Great Spirit's Allocution"; "The Harvest"; "Hiawatha's Birth"; "Hiawatha's Wooing"; "Magic Corn-Field Dance"; "The Ravens"; "Spring and Summer"; "War Song"; "(Winter) Ghosts, Famine and Fever."

Also see "Death of Minnehaha" above.

Hiawatha's Birth

See "Hiawatha"

... Hiawatha's Wedding-Feast ... Music ... by S. Coleridge-Taylor ...

London: Novello and Company, Limited. New York: The H. W. Gray Co. ... 1898 ...

Title-page as above. Printed paper wrapper. Reprinted from *The Song of Hiawatha,* 1855.

Hiawatha's Wooing

See "Hiawatha"

... The Holy Dead ... Words Translated from Klopstock ... Music by Faustina Hasse Hodges ...

New York. Firth, Pond & Co. 1 Franklin Square. Troy. J. W. Kinnicutt. ⟨n.d., 1848–1853⟩

Plate number 1612. Otherwise "The Dead," *Voices of the Night,* 1839.

Home Song

See "Stay at Home"

Hymn of the Moravian Nuns at the Consecration of the Banner of Pulaski ... Music by Miss M. Lindsay.

New York. Wm. A. Pond & Co. 547 Broadway. & 39 Union Sq. ... ⟨n.d., 1863–1877⟩

Plate number 8450. Reprinted from *Voices of the Night*, 1839.

... Hymn of the Night ... ⟨Music by Stephen Glover⟩

New York ... Firth, Pond & Co. 547 Broadway ... ⟨n.d., 1856–1862⟩

Plate number 3814. Otherwise "Hymn to the Night," *Voices of the Night*, 1839. See next entry.

... I Heard the Trailing Garments of the Night ... Music by Clarence T. Steele ...

New York   Hamilton S. Gordon   13 East 14th St. ... 1892 ...

Otherwise "Hymn to the Night," *Voices of the Night*, 1839. See preceding entry.

I Knew a Maiden Fair ... ⟨Music⟩ by C. S. T.

New York, Firth & Hall, 1, Franklin Square ... 1842 ...

No plate number. Deposited Jan. 26, 1842. Reprinted from *Voices of the Night*, 1839.

Other settings noted; the order is alphabetical under name of composer; under composer alphabetically by place.

Balfe, M. W.: Boston: Oliver Ditson & Co., n.d., not before 1864. Under the title "Trust Her Not."

———: New Orleans: A. E. Blackmar, n.d., not before 1865. Under the title "Trust Her Not."

———: New York: Firth, Pond & Co., n.d., not before 1856. Under the title "Trust Her Not."

———: New York: S. T. Gordon & Son, n.d., not before 1873. Under the title "Trust Her Not."

Dow, Howard M.: Boston: Oliver Ditson & Co., 1876. Under the title "Beware."

Elliot, C. S.: Boston: G. D. Russell, 1880. Under the title "Beware."

Gilbert, B. F.: Boston: Oliver Ditson & Co., 1876. Under the title "Beware."

Gounod, Charles: New York: William A. Pond & Co., n.d., not before 1863. Under the title "Beware."

Heuberer, Charles F.: Boston: H. Prentiss, 1845. Under the title "Beware."

Merz, Karl: New York: C. M. Tremaine, 1866. Under the title "Beware."

Moulton, Charles: New York: Beer & Schirmer, 1865. Under the title "Beware."

Perring, James Ernest: New York: William A. Pond & Co., 1864. Under the title "Beware."

R., F. W.: Richmond, Virginia: George Dunn & Co., 1863. Under the title "I Know a Maiden Fair to See."

Schaide, M.: Boston: Oliver Ditson, 1851. Under the title "Beware."

Sudds, W. F.: Boston: Thompson & Odell, 1882. Under the title "Trust Her Not."

Thayer, Arthur W.: Boston: Arthur P. Schmidt & Co., 1886. Under the title "Beware."

Whittlesey, Orramel: New York: Gould & Berry, 1852. Under the title "Take Care." Reprinted and reissued by S. T. Gordon, New York.

I Know a Maiden Fair to See

See "I Knew a Maiden Fair to See"

I Shot an Arrow in the Air

See "The Arrow and the Song"

I Stood on the Bridge at Midnight

See "The Bridge"

I Would Tell Her I Love Her ...

Memphis ... 1864 ...

See in *Section Six*.

... In the Woods ... ⟨Music⟩ by Dudley Buck, Jr. ...

New-York. Beer & Schirmer, 701 Broadway ... 1866 ...

An instrumental composition. At head of p. 3 is an extract from Longfellow's "Prelude," *Voices of the Night*, 1839.

Into the Silent Land ...

See "Music Sung ..."

... It Is Not Always May ... Music by Miss L. E. Stoddard ...

Cleveland ... S. Brainard & Sons, 203 Superior Street ... 1866 ...

Plate number 2633.-3. Reprinted from *Ballads*, 1842.

Other settings noted; the order is alphabetical under name of composer.

Cowen, Frederic H.: Boston: Oliver Ditson Company, 1892.

Gounod, Charles: Boston: Oliver Ditson Company, n.d., not before 1889.

————: Philadelphia: Lee & Walker, n.d., not before 1872.

Pinsuti: Boston: Oliver Ditson & Co., n.d., not before 1877.

Reiff, Anthony: New York: William A. Pond & Co., 1887.

... King Olaf's Christmas ... from Longfellow's "Saga of King Olaf." Composed for Male Chorus and Baritone and Tenor Solos ... by Dudley Buck ...

New York G. Schirmer. 35 Union Square ... 1881 ...

Plate number 2628. Reprinted from *Tales of a Wayside Inn*, 1863.

King Robert of Sicily ... Musical Accompaniment ... by John J. Wootton ...

Copyright 1888 by Edgar S. Werner. ‹New York›

The above on p. 2. Reprinted from *Tales of a Wayside Inn*, 1863.

... Kyrie Eleison ... ‹Music by F. Boott›

Boston ... Oliver Ditson & Co. Washington St. ... 1857 ...

Reprinted from *The Golden Legend*, 1851.

... The Legend of the Crossbill ... Music by le Chevalier Lemmens ...

Boston   G. D. Russell & Company   126 Tremont St. ... 1874 ...

Plate number 3036-5. Reprinted from *Poems*, 1845.

Other and later printings noted:

Boston: Oliver Ditson & Co., without alteration of the original copyright date. Issued not before 1877.

Boston: A. P. Schmidt & Co., 1884.

New York & Chicago: Richard A. Saalfield, n.d., *ca.* 1875.

Providence, R. I.: E. G. Billings, n.d., not before 1882.

Life Is Not an Empty Dream
    See "Tell Me Not in Mournful Numbers"

... The Light of Stars ... Music by John Horn.

Cincinnati. The John Church Co. 74 W. Fourth St. ... ‹1887›

Plate number 4997-4. Reprinted from *Voices of the Night*, 1839.

Living Poems
    See "Children"

Longfellow's Work Song
    See "Children"

... Love, What Wilt Thou with This Heart ... ‹Music by Frederic H. Cowen›

Boston ... MDCCCXCII ... Oliver Ditson Company ...

Plate number 36-55610-5. Otherwise "Rondel," by Froissart, which had several book appearances prior to formal publication in *Poetical Works*, Boston, 1868.

Magic Corn-Field Dance
    See "Hiawatha"

... Maiden and the Weathercock, ‹Music by› W‹alter›. Austin ...

New York: William A. Pond & Co., 25 Union Square ... ‹n.d., not before 1880 nor after 1896›

Reprint? Plate number 11145. See this title under the year 1880 in *Section One*. Reprint of a British publication?

... Maidenhood ... Music by Homer N. Bartlett ...

New-York, William A. Pond & Co. 25 Union Square ... 1881 ...

Plate number 10450. Reprinted from *Ballads*, 1842.

... The Meeting ... ‹Music by J. L. Hatton›

‹n.p., n.d., *ca.* 1876–1878›

Plate number 1874-4. Reprinted from *Aftermath*, 1873.

The Midnight Hour
    See "The Bridge"

... Morning Song ... ⟨Music⟩ by Vincenzo Cirillo ...

Boston   G. D. Russell & Company   126 Tremont St. ... 1876 ...

Plate number 3996-3. Reprinted from *The Spanish Student*, 1843.

A setting by Luigi Caracciola under the title "A Muleteer Song" issued by Oliver Ditson & Co., Boston, n.d., not before 1877.

A Muleteer Song

See preceding entry.

... The Murmuring Wind ...

Boston ... 1877 ...

See in Section Six.

The Music of the Sea ... Music by Benj. W. Loveland ...

New York. C. H. Ditson & Co. ... 1887 ...

Reprinted from *The Golden Legend,* 1851.

Music Sung by the Alumni at the Two Hundred and Fiftieth Anniversary of the Foundation of Harvard University November Seventh ... 1886.

Boston: Arthur P Schmidt ... 1886.

"Into the Silent Land," pp. 33-37, set to music by Arthur Foote. Otherwise "The Song of the Silent Land," *Hyperion*, 1839.

... My Algonquin   Song from ... Hiawatha Music ... by Ch. C. Converse.

Boston. Published by Oliver Ditson   Washington St. ... 1856 ...

Plate number 8268. Reprinted from *The Song of Hiawatha,* 1855.

... My Arm Chair ... Music by T. L. Jephson ...

Boston ... 1880 ... Oliver Ditson & Co. ...

Otherwise "From My Arm-Chair," 1879; see in *Section One.* Deposited May 27, 1880.

My Heart and the Sea ...

See "The Sea Hath Its Pearls"

My Lady Sleeps

See "Stars of the Summer Night"

... My Redeemer and My Lord ... ⟨Music by Dudley Buck⟩

... The John Church Company. Cincinnati ... ⟨1880⟩

Reprinted from *The Golden Legend,* 1851.

... The Nun of Nidaros ... from ... "Saga of King Olaf." ... ⟨Music⟩ by Dudley Buck ...

New-York: G. Schirmer ... 1879 ...

Plate number 2251. Reprinted from *Tales of a Wayside Inn,* 1863.

... O Holy Night ... Music by S. G. Pratt.

Cincinnati, John Church & Co. ... ⟨1883⟩

Plate number 3980-6. Otherwise "Hymn to the Night," *Voices of the Night,* 1839.

O Little Feet! ... Music by Wm. R. Dempster ...

New York   Published by S. T. Gordon   706 Broadway ... 1866 ...

Plate number 3957-4. Otherwise "Weariness," *Tales of a Wayside Inn,* 1863.

The Old Clock on the Stairs ... Music ... by T. Bricher ...

Boston ... C. Bradlee & Co. 184 Washington St. ... 1846 ...

Reprinted from *The Belfry of Bruges,* 1845.

Other settings noted; the order is alphabetical by composer.

Boott, F.: Boston: Oliver Ditson & Co., 1886.

Dolores: Boston: Oliver Ditson, n.d., not before 1854.

Marshall, L.: Boston: Oliver Ditson & Co., n.d., after 1857. Under the title: "The Old Timepiece on the Stairs."

Marston, G. W.: Boston: Arthur P. Schmidt, 1881.

Pease, Frederic H.: Detroit: C. J. Whitney & Co., 1876.

The Old Timepiece on the Stairs

See preceding entry.

Onaway! ... Music ... by Ch. C. Converse ...

Boston ... Oliver Ditson   Washington St. ... 1856 ...

Plate number 8414. Reprinted from *The Song of Hiawatha,* 1855.

Other settings noted:

Cowen, Frederic H.: Boston: Oliver Ditson Co., 1892.

Selle, Louis: Boston: Oliver Ditson & Co., n.d., not before 1858. Under the title "Serenade from Hiawatha."

Once As I Told in Glee, or the Viking's Bride Taken from ... Skeleton in Armor Music by M.C.Z.

Boston   Published by Oliver Ditson   115 Washington St. ... 1852 ...

Plate number 5015. Reprinted from *Ballads,* 1842. Under the title "The Tale of the Viking" issued 1881, music by George E. Whiting; in 1892, with music by Arthur Foote.

... Over the Cathedral Door ... Music by Frank H. Brackett ...

Boston   Oliver Ditson & Co. ... 1882 ...

Otherwise "The Statue over the Cathedral Door," *Poems,* 1845. A setting by Charles S. Hamlin, under the title "The Statue over the Cathedral Door," issued by Oliver Ditson & Co., Boston, 1884.

... Paul Revere's Ride ... Cantata for Men's Voices ... Music by Dudley Buck ...

New York   G. Schirmer ... 1898 ...

Plate number 14099. Reprinted from *Tales of a Wayside Inn,* 1863.

A Psalm of Life

See "Tell Me Not in Mournful Numbers"

The Rainy Day ... Music by William R. Dempster ...

Boston ... Oliver Ditson   115 Washington St. ... 1847 ...

Plate number 1398. Reprinted from *Ballads,* 1842.

Other settings and printings noted; arranged alphabetically by composer.

Behrend, A. H.: New York: Charles H. Ditson & Co., 1878.

Bischoff, J. W.: Cincinnati: The John Church Co., 1886.

Blockley, John: Boston: Oliver Ditson & Co., n.d., not before 1858. Under the title "The Day Is Cold, and Dark and Dreary."

Camille: Boston: G. D. Russell & Co., 1873. Under the title "The Day is Dark and Dreary."

Cheney, Amy Marcy: Boston: Oliver Ditson & Co., 1883.

Cowen, F. H.: New York: T. B. Harms & Co., n.d., not before 1881.

Dempster, W. R.: Boston: Oliver Ditson & Co., n.d., after 1880.

Hatton, John L.: New York: Beer & Schirmer, n.d., not after 1866. Reprinted and reissued by G. Schirmer, New York; and, by White, Smith & Co., Boston, not before 1873 but with copyright notice dated 1869.

Hodges, Faustina Hasse: New York: C. Breusing, 1860, under the title "The Dreary Day." Reprinted and reissued by Beer & Schirmer, New York, n.d., not before 1861.

Pratt, S. G.: Chicago: F. S. Chandler & Co., 1872.

Rudersdorff, Erminia: Boston: G. D. Russell & Co., 1873.

Wiebé, Edward: Boston: Henry Tolman & Co., 1867.

The Ravens

See "Hiawatha"

The Reaper and the Flowers ... Music ... by J. R. Thomas ...

Boston ... Oliver Ditson & Co   277 Washington St ... 1861 ...

Plate number 20938. Reprinted from *Voices of the Night,* 1839.

Other settings noted:

Balfe, M. W.: Boston: Oliver Ditson & Co., n.d., not before 1858.

Cowen, Frederic: Boston: Oliver Ditson & Co., n.d., not before 1877. Reissued 1884 by S. Brainard Sons, Cleveland and Chicago.

Resignation ... Music ... by ... J. Edgar Gould.

Boston   Published by Oliver Ditson   115 Washington St. ... 1850 ...

Plate number 1914. Reprinted from *The Seaside and the Fireside,* 1850.

Resting

See "The Day Is Done"

... Robert of Sicily   Cantata for Soli, Chorus and Orchestra ... Music by F. Kilvington Hattersley ...

London & New York   Novello, Ewer and Co. ... 1894 ...

Plate number 9782. Reprinted from *Tales of a Wayside Inn,* 1863.

Sad Heart, O Take Thy Rest ... Music by Virginia Gabriel ...

Boston. Oliver Ditson & Co. 277 Washington St. ... ⟨n.d., after 1857⟩

Reprinted, with textual liberties, from *Evangeline*, 1847.

... Saga of King Olaf

See "Scenes from the Saga of King Olaf"

... Scenes from Longfellow's Golden Legend. Symphonic Cantata for Solos, Chorus and Orchestra. By ⟨Dudley Buck⟩ *(sic)*

Cincinnati, Published by John Church & Co., 66 West Fourth St. for the Cincinnati Musical Festival Association ... 1880 ...

Title-page as above. Issued in printed paper wrapper. It is probable that the copies first printed do not have the composer's name on either title-page or wrapper; merely the statement: *By*

Selections from the above were issued by the John Church Co., under date 1880; *i.e.*, not prior to 1885.

... Scenes from the Saga of King Olaf ... Set to Music ... by Edward Elgar ...

London: Novello and Company, Limited. New York: The H. W. Gray Co. ... 1896 ...

Text reprinted from *Tales of a Wayside Inn*, 1863, with alterations by H. A. Acworth.

The Sculptor ... Music by Wentworth Bennett ...

London & New York Novello, Ewer & Co. ... ⟨n.d., 1887⟩

Plate number 7437. Otherwise "Gaspar Becerra," *The Seaside and the Fireside*, 1850.

... The Sea Hath Its Pearls ...

Boston ... Oliver Ditson Washington St ... ⟨n.d., after 1856⟩

Music by Elizabeth Philp.

Reprinted from *The Belfry of Bruges*, 1845.

Other settings noted; arranged alphabetically by name of composer.

Anonymous composer: Boston: Davenport Brothers, 1877. Reprinted by White-Smith Music Publishing Co., Boston, n.d.

Biermann, W.: Cleveland: S. Brainard's Sons, 1875.

Braunschiedl, Johannes: New York: C. H. Ditson & Co., 1883.

Cowen, Frederic H.: Boston: Oliver Ditson Co., 1892.

Gounod, Charles: Boston: G. D. Russell & Co., 1872.

Henry, Bertram C.: Boston: Arthur P. Schmidt & Co., 1889.

Morrill, Osma C.: Washington, D. C.: John F. Ellis & Co., 1892. Under the title "My Heart and the Sea and the Heaven."

O'Shea, John A.: Boston: Miles & Thompson, 1890.

Pinsuti: Boston: Oliver Ditson & Co., n.d., after 1869.

————: Philadelphia: Lee & Walker, n.d., not before 1876.

Radecki, Olga v.: Boston: Arthur P. Schmidt, 1882.

Tours, Berthold: Boston: Oliver Ditson & Co., n.d., not before 1864.

White, Maude Valérie: In: *Maude Valérie White's Album of German Songs*, Boston: Oliver Ditson & Co., n.d., after 1876.

Serenade (Good night! good night! Beloved)

See "Good Night, Beloved"

Serenade (Stars of the Summer Night)

See "Stars of the Summer Night"

Serenade from Hiawatha

See "Onaway"

She Sleeps! My Lady Sleeps!

See "Stars of the Summer Night"

... "Ships that Pass in the Night" ... Music by Ethel Harraden ...

Forsyth Brothers 267, Regent Street, London ... E. Schuberth & Co. 23, Union Square, New York ... 1894 ...

Reprinted from "The Theologian's Tale," *Tales of a Wayside Inn*, 1863.

... Slumber Song ...

Saint Louis ... ⟨1870⟩

See in *Section Six*.

Snow-Flakes

See "Album of Twelve Songs"

Song of Home

See "Stay at Home"

Song of the Silent Land ... Music ... by Herrmann Strachauer ...

Boston ... Oliver Ditson & Co ... 1860 ...

Reprinted from *Hyperion*, 1839.

Other settings noted:

Fanning, Eaton: London: Novello and Company, Ltd.; and, Novello, Ewer and Co., New York, 1896.

Pease, Frederic H.: Detroit: C. J. Whitney, 1882.

Songe of ye Nurserie ... Composed by John S. Hiller ...

Published by The John Church Company. Cincinnati, New York, Chicago. ‹1895›

Plate number 10827-3-L. See *There Was a Little Girl*, 1883, in *Section One*. Longfellow's name not present.

Spanish Serenade

See "Stars of the Summer Night"

Spring and Summer

See "Hiawatha"

Stars of the Summer Night! A Serenade from the Spanish Student ... Music by O. W. Withington.

Boston ... Geo. P. Reed, No. 17 Tremont Row ... 1843 ...

Printed on pp. ‹2-3› of an otherwise unprinted sheet. Title and imprint on p. ‹2›. Plate number 347. Reprinted from *The Spanish Student*, 1843.

Other settings and printings noted; arranged alphabetically by composer; under composer alphabetically by place of publication.

Anonymous composer: Boston: Nathan Richardson, 1856. Under the title "Serenade."

Baker, B. F.: Boston: G. P. Reed, 1844.

————: Boston: Henry Tolman & Co., 1865.

————: Cleveland: S. Brainard's Sons, 1865.

Boott, F.: Boston: Oliver Ditson & Co., 1857.

Compton, C. H.: Boston: Oliver Ditson, n.d., not after 1857. Presumably a reprint of the London edition which was listed in Ath Dec. 30, 1854.

Cowen, Frederic H.: Boston: Oliver Ditson Company, 1892. Under the title "My Lady Sleeps."

Cutler, Ellen Gifford: Buffalo, N. Y.: Blodgett & Bradford, n.d., *ca.* 1858.

Foerster, Ad. M.: Philadelphia: W. F. Shaw, 1879. Under the title "Serenade."

Glover, Stephen: New York: Firth, Pond & Co., n.d., not before 1856. Presumably a reprint of the London edition which was noted by Ath June 14, 1856.

————: New York: New York Musical World Print, n.d. Presumably a reprint of the preceding.

Hatton, J. L.: Boston: Oliver Ditson & Co., n.d., after 1876. Under the title "The Students Serenade."

Heuser, Carl: New York: C. Heuser, 1873. Under the title "Serenade."

Johns, D. G.: Boston: Oliver Ditson & Co., 1883. Under the title "My Lady Sleeps."

Kleber, H.: Philadelphia: Lee & Walker, 1846.

Marston, G. W.: Boston: G. D. Russell & Co., 1877. Under the title "My Lady Sleeps."

Merz, Charles J.: Boston: Oliver Ditson & Co., 1857.

Nevin, Ethelbert: Boston: Oliver Ditson & Co., 1887.

Pease, Alfred H.: New York: G. Schirmer, 1865. Originally issued by Beer & Schirmer?

Rivarde, P. A.: New York: Beer & Schirmer, 1867.

Sandford, Lucy A.: New York: William Hall & Son, 1849.

Shepperd, Frank N.: New York: William A. Pond & Co., 1888.

Tours, Berthold: Boston: Oliver Ditson & Co., n.d., *ca.* 1880.

————: Philadelphia: William H. Boner & Co., n.d., not before 1872.

van Gelder, Martinus: Philadelphia: Philadelphia Musical Academy, 1882. Under the title "Spanish Serenade."

Webster, Mrs. E. L.: Boston: Published by the Author and E. H. Wade, 1849. Under the title "My Lady Sleeps."

Weil, Oscar: San Francisco: M. Gray, 1874.

Wellings, Milton: n.p., n.d., *ca.* 1880. Front cover lithograph signed *Thornburn, N. Y.*

White, Otis R.: Chicago: National Music Co., 1892. Under the title "A Summer Night Serenade."

Y., F. G.: New York, n.d. Under the title "She Sleeps! My Lady Sleeps!" On front cover: "Words from the Spanish Student."

Yale Glee Club, as Sung by. New York: William A. Pond & Co., 1866.

The Statue over the Cathedral Door

See "Over the Cathedral Door"

Stay at Home ... Music by John Barnett ...

Boston, Carl Prüfer 30 West St. ‹n.d., *ca.* 1878›

Reprint? Also in *Kéramos,* 1878, under the title "Song." Not found in the copyright records, 1870–1897.

Other settings noted, arranged alphabetically by name of composer.

Brown, Mrs. A. Swan: New York: Spear & Dehnhoff, 1885.

Cirillo, V.: Boston: G. D. Russell & Co., 1878. Under the title "To Stay at Home Is Best."

Coerne, Louis Adolphe: Boston: Everett E. Truette & Co., 1894.

Cowen, Frederic H.: Boston: Oliver Ditson Company, 1892.

Cutter, Jr., E.: Boston: E. Cutter, Jr., 1891. Under the title "Song of Home."

Liddle, S.: London & New York: Boosey & Co., 1896. Under the title "Home Song."

Wadsworth, W.: Newburgh, N. Y.: Estey Organ Co., 1879.

The Students Serenade

See "Stars of the Summer Night"

A Summer Night Serenade

See "Stars of the Summer Night"

... Sundown ... ‹Music by Frederic H. Cowen› ...

Boston ... MDCCCXCII ... Oliver Ditson Company ...

Plate number 36-55612-3. Copyright notice on p. 3 dated MDCCCXCIII. Reprinted from *In the Harbor,* 1882.

Sweet and Low

See "Slumber Song," *Section Six,* under year 1870.

Sweet Remembrance ... Music by J. W. Bischoff.

Cincinnati ... John Church Co. ... ‹1890›

Otherwise "Delia," *Kéramos,* 1878.

Take Care

See "I Knew a Maiden Fair"

Tale of the Viking

See "Once As I Told in Glee"

... "Tell Me Not in Mournful Numbers" ... Adapted ‹from a melody by Franz Schubert› by L. O. Emerson ...

Boston ... Oliver Ditson 115 Washington St. ... 1854 ...

Otherwise "A Psalm of Life," *Voices of the Night,* 1839.

Other settings; arranged alphabetically by name of composer.

Blockley, John: Boston: Oliver Ditson & Co., n.d., not before 1858. Under the title "A Psalm of Life."

Hewitt, G. W.: Philadelphia: Lee & Walker, 1869. Under the title "A Psalm of Life."

Miller, C. C.: Cleveland: S. Brainard's Sons, n.d., not before 1866. Under the title "A Psalm of Life."

Römele, J. M.: Louisville, Ky.: Henry Knöfel, 1882. Under the title "A Psalm of Life."

Tepé, Frank A.: Baltimore: Henry McCaffrey, 1855. Under the title "Life Is Not an Empty Dream."

Titus, Amanda Welsh: Philadelphia: Lee & Walker, 1873 ‹1879?›. Under the title "Footprints on the Sands of Time."

Wood, Albert H.: New York: Beer & Schirmer, 1862. Under the title "A Psalm of Life."

... Three Friends of Mine ... Music by F. Boott ...

Boston: Oliver Ditson & Co. ... ‹1882›

Plate number 48989. Deposited May 26, 1882. Reprinted from *The Masque of Pandora,* 1875.

... The Three Singers ... Music by Berthold Tours ...

Boston. Oliver Ditson & Co. 451 Washington St. ... ‹n.d., after 1876›

Plate number 47749. Otherwise "The Singers," *The Seaside and the Fireside,* 1850.

Thy Remembrance

See "Album of Twelve Songs"

... The Tide Rises the Tide Falls ... Music by J. C. Meininger ...

St. Louis, Mo. Balmer & Weber ... 1886 ...

Plate number 4600-5. Reprinted from *Ultima Thule*, 1880.

To Be Near Thee

See "Good Night, Beloved."

To Stay at Home Is Best

See "Stay at Home"

... Too Late, Too Late ⟨Music by Miss C.⟩ Lindsay ...

... New York ... ⟨n.d.⟩

See in *Section Six* under year 1860.

Trust Her Not

See "I Knew a Maiden Fair"

Twilight ...

See "The Fisherman's Cottage"

Upidee

See "Excelsior"

"The Village Blacksmith." ... Music ... by Charles F. Heuberer ...

Boston ... A & J. P. Ordway 339 Washington St. ... 1848 ...

Plate number 30-10. Reviewed in H Aug. 5, 1848. Reprinted from *Ballads*, 1842.

Other printings and settings noted; the arrangement is alphabetical by composer's name; under composer by place of publication.

Buck, Dudley: Boston: Arthur P. Schmidt, 1893.

Heuberer, Charles F.: Boston: E. H. Wade, 1848; i.e., not before 1848, not after 1860.

Jephson, T. L.: Milwaukee: H. N. Hempsted & Co., n.d., ca. 1870.

Noyes, Charles F.: Boston: Oliver Ditson Company, 1898.

Peabody, George: Boston: Oliver Ditson Company, 1890.

Warden, David A.: Philadelphia: Lee & Walker, 1867; i.e., ca. 1872.

————: Philadelphia: David A. Warden, 1867.

Weiss, W. H.: Boston: Oliver Ditson & Co., n.d., after 1857.

————: Philadelphia: F. A. North & Co., n.d., not before 1872.

... The Voice of Christ ... ⟨Music by David A. Warden⟩

Philadelphia: Lee & Walker, 722 Chestnut Street, Wm. H. Boner & Co., 1102 Chestnut Street. ⟨1862⟩

Plate number 8702.3. Extracted from "The Arsenal at Springfield," *Poems*, 1845.

War Song

See "Hiawatha"

... Weariness ... ⟨Music by Henry Pontet⟩

Boston: Oliver Ditson & Co. ... ⟨n.d., ca. 1883⟩

Plate number 50270. Reprinted from *Tales of a Wayside Inn*, 1863.

Whither? ... Music by Karl P. Harrington ..

Boston ... 1883 ... Oliver Ditson & Co. ...

Reprinted from *Hyperion*, 1839.

A Wind Came up out of the Sea

See "Daybreak"

The Windmill ... Music ... by Gustavus Tuckerman ...

Boston Arthur P. Schmidt & Co. ... 1885 ...

Plate number APS&Co. 493-6.

See in *Section One* under year 1880.

... Winter ... Music by Fred D. Bates.

Boston Louis H. Ross & Co. 3 West St. ... 1885 ...

Plate number 30-2. Otherwise "Woods in Winter," *Voices of the Night*, 1839.

(Winter). Ghosts, Famine and Fever

See "Hiawatha"

Wreck of the Hesperus ... Music by ... Hatton.

Boston ... Oliver Ditson & Co 277 Washington St. ... ⟨n.d., after 1867⟩

Plate number 46164. Reprinted from *Ballads*, 1842.

Other settings noted; the order is alphabetical by name of composer.

Anderton, Thomas: Boston: Carl Prüfer, n.d., 1882; deposited Jan. 20, 1882. Reissued: Boston: Oliver Ditson Company, n.d., after 1888.

Blockley: Boston: Oliver Ditson Company, n.d., not before 1889.

Burr, Jr., Willard: Boston: Oliver Ditson & Co., 1889.

————: New York: G. Schirmer, 1889.

Hullah, J.: Philadelphia: Lee & Walker, n.d., not before 1872.

Wareing, Herbert W.: London & New York: Novello, Ewer & Co., 1895.

REFERENCES AND ANA

New Year's Address for 1822

Portland, Maine: The Portland Gazette, Jan. 1, 1822

No copy located. Title and imprint postulated.

Longfellow was a competitor for the prize offered by *The Portland Gazette* for the best new year's address for 1822. "... The editor ... found himself not only fully supplied with poems, but also in great perplexity as to which should be awarded the premium. As a compromise he awarded the prize to one, printed another for the carrier, and gave his readers three of them in successive issues of his journal. They are unsigned, and a careful reading has not yet enabled me to decide which is Longfellow's ..."—George Thomas Little: *Longfellow's Boyhood Poems* ... , 1925, p. 16.

"I have studied these unsigned pieces and can discover no basis for conclusive identification of any one as by Longfellow."—Lawrance Thompson: *Young Longfellow* ... , 1938, p. 350.

Pioneer Carrier's Address to His Friends—Jan. 1, 1834 ... Remembrance of the Poor.

⟨n.p., n.d., probably issued by *The Family Pioneer and Juvenile Key,* Brunswick, Me., 1834⟩

Single sheet. Sometimes attributed to Longfellow but the authorship is not known. The probable author was one of Joseph Griffin's children. Anonymous. Copy in NYPL.

A Sketch of the History of Newbury. By Joshua Coffin [Henry Wadsworth Longfellow].

Boston, 1845.

Thus Halkett & Laing, Vol. 5, p. 283. BAL has found no evidence to support Halkett & Laing's attribution.

A Book of Hymns for Public and Private Devotion.

Cambridge: Metcalf and Company, Printers to the University. 1846.

For comment see entry No. 1630. Reprints one poem and also "Peace on Earth," No.

421, which is extracted from "The Arsenal at Springfield," *Poems,* 1845.

"The Departed," No. 354. "... Probably not ... by Longfellow as in the fifth edition of the *Book of Hymns* ... the authorship is given *Anonymous.*"—Livingston, p. 45.

"Ordination Hymn," No. 384. Not by Henry Wadsworth Longfellow but by Samuel Longfellow. Higginson's copy of this book (at H) has *S. Longfellow,* in Higginson's hand, pencilled in. Collected in Samuel Longfellow's *Hymns and Verses,* as "Hymn for the Ordination of Edward Everett Hale."

"Ordination," No. 385. Higginson's copy of this book has *J. A. Swan* inserted in Higginson's hand. Not by Henry Wadsworth Longfellow.

The Ladies' Casket, a Gift of Friendship for the Young, by Miss A. T. Wilbur. 1848.

Edward A. Rice, Publisher, No. 162 Nassau Street. New York. ⟨n.d., 1847?⟩

Cloth? Not a book but a periodical bound as an annual. Bound in at the back are leaves extracted from a monthly magazine, *The Magnolia* (Boston?), on pp. 129-130 of which insertion appears Longfellow's "Flowers," reprinted from *Voices of the Night,* 1839. *Query:* Were all copies of *The Ladies' Casket* issued with the leaves extracted from *The Magnolia?*

He Said He Came to Find Me Do You Really Think He Did? ... ⟨Music⟩ by John C. Andrews ...

Boston ... W. H. Oakes ... Sold by E. H. Wade 197 Washington Str. ... 1849 ...

Sheet music. Cover-title. Plate number 375-4. Deposited Dec. 14, 1849.

By Longfellow? Not elsewhere located.

A reprint has been noted lacking the name *W. H. Oakes* in the imprint.

I waited till the twilight, | And yet he did not come, | I strayed along the brookside, | And slowly wandered home, | When who should come behind me, | But him I would have chid, | He said he came to find me ...

Night's Revealings; from the Ancient Sclavonian of Hans Hammergaffstein. By H. W. L. [Henry Wadsworth Longfellow].

Boston, 1850.

Thus Halkett & Laing, Vol. 4, p. 188. BAL has been unable to find either the book or evidence that Longfellow produced such a translation.

The Book of Poetry

Presbyterian Board of Publication, *ca.* 1850.

Not seen. "About 1850 there was published by the Presbyterian Board of Publication, a collection of religious verse under the title *The Book of Poetry,* and containing a poem 'Hymn of the Churchyard,' *Ah me! this is a sad and silent city,* by 'Longfellow.' The authorship is, however, attributed, in other collections, to John Bethune, a Scotch poet."— Livingston, p. 54. The poem is in *Poems by the Late John Bethune* . . . , Edinburgh, 1840.

Drift-Wood. A Collection of Essays and Reviews.

1852

". . . I am . . . thinking about a volume of old matters collected from corners of reviews and magazines, to be called *Drift-Wood.* Write a short Preface for the same."—Longfellow's Journal, Dec. 2, 1852.

Samuel Longfellow in *Life of Henry Wadsworth Longfellow,* Boston, 1886, Vol. 2, p. 229, states: "This was partially printed but never published. Some parts of it, under the same title, are printed in the Complete Works."

The plan to issue the material separately was abandoned; the text survived only as a section which appeared for the first time in *Prose Works,* 1857, *q.v.* No further reference is made to it in the journal of this period.

Eighth Annual Report of the Board of Regents of the Smithsonian Institution . . .

Two printings noted; sequence has not been determined.

A

Imprinted: *Washington: Beverley Tucker, Senate Printer. 1854.*

Issued as a Senate document; at head of p. ⟨3⟩: *33d Congress, 1st Session.* [Senate.] *Mis. Doc. No. 73.* 10,000 copies printed, of which 500 were for the use of The Smithsonian Institution.

B

Imprinted: *Washington: A. O. P. Nicholson, Public Printer. 1854.*

Issued as a House of Representatives document; at head of p. ⟨3⟩: *33d Congress, 1st Session.* [Ho. of Reps.] *Miscellaneous, No. 97.* 10,000 copies printed.

Note: The wording of the certificate of issue in each of the above suggests a printing earlier than either, but search has failed to produce such a printing.

Contains a report signed by Longfellow and others; pp. 148-155, *Printing A;* pp. 140-147, *Printing B.*

Anglo Ab-Original Sleighing Song, in Five Canters. Written after Longfellow. Air—Highwaythere. Dedicated to the Marshals and Their Neigh-Bors.

New Haven: T. J. Stafford, Printer. 1856.

Printed paper wrapper. *Anonymous.*

. . . Hiawatha: Or, Ardent Spirits and Laughing Water. A Musical Extravaganza, in Two Acts. By Charles M. Walcot . . .

New York: Samuel French, 121 Nassau-Street. ⟨1856⟩

Probably issued in printed paper wrapper. At head of title: *The Minor Drama. No. CIX.* Date taken from dedication. A burlesque of Longfellow.

Illustrations of Longfellow's Courtship of Miles Standish. By John W. Ehninger. Photographed from the Original Drawings by Brady.

New York: Rudd & Carleton, 310 Broadway. M.DCCC.LIX.

Leather.

. . . Too Late, Too Late ⟨Music by Miss C.⟩ Lindsay . . .

. . . S. T. Gordon, 706 Broadway, New York . . . ⟨n.d., 1860–1870⟩

Sheet music. Cover-title. Probably a reprint of a British publication.

Not by Longfellow. The text was written by Tennyson, here miscredited to Longfellow.

⟨Printed letter urging defeat of House of Representatives "A Bill to amend the Act respecting Copyrights."⟩

New York ⟨etc.⟩ April 25, 1862.

4 pp. An open letter signed by Longfellow and others. For fuller entry see BAL, Vol. 4, p. 33.

I Would Tell Her I Love Her ... Music by S. Schlesinger ...

Memphis Tenn. Published by F. Katzenbach 317 Main St. ... 1864 ...

Sheet music. Cover-title. Plate number 5845.

Copyright notice in the name of K. Katzenbach. A presumed reprint issued with the imprint of E. A. Benson, St. Louis, Missouri.

Almost surely not by Longfellow. But whether by Longfellow or not this is a reprint of a piece of sheet music issued by Kretschmar & Nunns, Philadelphia, 1834. In the 1834 printing the name of the lyricist is not given.

I would tell her I love her | Did I know but the way | Could my lips but discover ...

Noël

‹Philadelphia: Ringwalt & Brown, Printers, 111 and 113 South Fourth Street, 1867›

Printed paper wrapper. A translation into English by John E. Norcross of Longfellow's poem in French. Longfellow's French original collected in *Flower-de-Luce,* 1867. 50 copies printed. Issued not after Aug. 30, 1867. See under 1864 in *Section One.*

The New-England Tragedies in Prose. By Rowland H. Allen ...

Boston: Nichols and Noyes. 1869.

"Topside Galah!" Long-Piecee-Man Hab Makee W'Litee ...

Shanghae ‹sic›, 1869.

Single leaf. A translation into pidgin-English of "Excelsior."

For comment see under year 1869 in the *References and Ana* list, Charles Godfrey Leland.

... Slumber Song Sweet and Low Lullaby ... Music by N. Ravnkilde.

Saint Louis ... Balmer & Weber, 206 North Fifth St. ... ‹1870›

Sheet music. Cover-title. Plate number 2509-3. At head of title: *To Mrs. C. A. Spencer.* Not by Longfellow; text by Tennyson.

"Ad Tres Familiares."

Cantabrigiae Neo-Anglorum ... Winlock & Lane. MDCCCLXXVI.

Printed paper wrapper. Cover-title. A translation into Latin of "Three Friends of Mine," *The Masque of Pandora,* 1875. The

translator has not been identified save for the initials *D.D.D.*

A Paraphrase of Henry Wadsworth Longfellow's ... The Courtship of Miles Standish, by Ariel Standish Thurston ...

R. M. Watts' Lake-St. Publishing House. Elmira, N. Y. 1876.

The Threshing Floor.

"Last month we mentioned that the American papers declared that Mr. Longfellow was going to bring out a new volume of poems, called *The Threshing Floor.* Mr. Longfellow now writes to Messrs. Routledge that this statement of the American journals is erroneous. 'I have no volume of poems,' he says, 'in the press, or in preparation, except so far as the patient accumulation of pieces may be called preparation. The title of *The Threshing Floor* never entered my head. As soon as I have anything ready I will notify to ‹sic› you.' "—Ath March 31, 1877, p. 420.

... The Murmuring Wind ... Music by Vincenzo Cirillo ...

Boston, Arthur P. Schmidt 40 Winter St. ... 1877 ...

Sheet music. Cover-title. Plate number A.P.S.5. Reprinted after 1878 with the publisher's later address: *146 Tremont Street.* By Longfellow? Not found in the works.

Wind so gently, gently blowing, | Thou to her must give repose ...

... Gathering Flowers in Heaven ... Music by C. P. Longley ...

New York ... Wm. A. Pond & Co. 25 Union Sq. ... 1878 ...

Sheet music. Cover-title. Plate number 9515.

By Longfellow? Not located in the works.

Long ago I loved her! Well the angels know, | How my soul grew rich and strong, many years ago. | How a voice of music, tender sweet and low, | Thro' my soul went murmuring, long ah! long ago ...

... Play-Day Poems ... Edited by Rossiter Johnson ...

New York Henry Holt and Company 1878

At head of title: *Leisure Hour Series.—No. 97* "Topside Galah!," pp. 147-148; a translation into pidgin-English of Longfellow's "Excelsior." See "Topside Galah!," in the

Charles Godfrey Leland list of *References and Ana* under year 1869.

The Book of Beauty   A Souvenir. Edited by Henry Wordsworth ⟨*sic*⟩ Longfellow.

Manhattan Publishing Company, 37 Dey Street, New York. ⟨n.d., 1879?⟩

Not, in spite of the title-page, edited by Longfellow. This publication appears to be made up of the sheets of an early reprinting (Hartford: Andrus, *ca.* 1848) of *The American Book of Beauty*, edited by *A Lady*, New York: Wilson and Company, 1845, with the cancel title-leaf of the Manhattan Publishing Company.

The Prose Writers of America ... by Henry Wordsworth ⟨*sic*⟩ Longfellow.

New York: Manhattan Publishing Company, 37 Dey Street. ⟨n.d., 1879?⟩

Not, in spite of the title-page, edited by Longfellow. A reprint of *The American Common-Place Book of Prose,* edited by George B. Cheever, Boston, 1828.

... Longfellow Portfolio, Being a Selection of Seventy-Five Artist-Proofs from the Original Wood-Cuts Illustrating the New Subscription Edition of Longfellow's Poetical Works ...

Boston: Published by Houghton, Mifflin and Company. New York: 11 East Seventeenth Street. The Riverside Press, Cambridge. ⟨1881⟩

At head of title: *Edition De Luxe.* Portfolio. Seventy-five engravings, each on a separate leaf, together with four leaves of front matter. Certificate of issue pasted to inner side of portfolio. 500 numbered sets.

A Royal Amour. A Novel. In Two Volumes. By R. Davey ...

London: Remington and Co., New Bond Street, W. 1882. [All Rights Reserved.] Entered According to Act of Congress at Washington, U.S.A.

"... I cannot forbear ... mentioning Mr. Henry W. Longfellow in a special manner, since, with his usual goodness, he read the story chapter by chapter with great care and attention, and afforded me his invaluable advice."—From "The Preface." Deposited in Library of Congress (Copyright Office) June 5, 1882.

Henry Wadsworth Longfellow   A Biographical Sketch by Francis H. Underwood ...

Boston   James R. Osgood and Company 1882

Also issued as *The Life of Henry Wadsworth Longfellow with Critical and Descriptive Sketches of His Writings,* Boston: B. B. Russell, 1882. Both printed from the same plates. According to the J. R. Osgood records, 5310 copies printed May 18, 1882, of which 3010 had the Russell imprint. Also bound in half morocco according to the Osgood records. Listed (Osgood imprint) pw June 10, 1882.

Laus Laureati. Henry Wadsworth Longfellow. February 27, 1882 ... by James P. Baxter.

Portland: Stephen Berry, Printer. 1882.

Printed paper wrapper. Cover-title.

The Home Life of Henry W. Longfellow. Reminiscences of Many Visits at Cambridge and Nahant, During the Years 1880, 1881 and 1882. By Blanche Roosevelt Tucker-Macchetta.

New York: Copyright, 1882, by G. W. Carleton & Co., Publishers. London: S. Low, Son & Co. MDCCCLXXXII.

Noted in two styles of binding; sequence, if any, not determined.

A: Stamped in blind and gold only.

B: Stamped in black, gold, and blind.

Facsimile letter inserted at front. "There Was a Little Girl," p. 90; for comment see *There Was a Little Girl,* 1883, in *Section One.*

Deposited (*Binding A*) May 13, 1882.

Life and Works of Henry W. Longfellow. Cambridge Edition.

Cambridge: Tribune Publishing Company, 1882.

For fuller entry see in *Section Two.*

Longfellow Memorial Address, before the Alumni of Bowdoin College, July 12, 1882. By Rev. Daniel R. Goodwin ...

Portland: Stephen Berry, Printer. 1882.

Printed paper wrapper.

Memorial Addresses in Honor of Henry Wadsworth Longfellow, by Mr. Richard H. Stoddard, Mr. Edwin P. Whipple, and Prof. Felix Adler, Delivered before the Society for Ethical Culture on Sunday, April 2d, 1882, at Chickering Hall.

New York: Lehmaier & Bro. Print, 95, 97, Fulton St. 1882

Printed paper wrapper. Inserted at front of some copies is a slip imprinted: *Sold for the*

Benefit of the Workingman's School and Free Kindergarten. Price, 25 cents.

Tributes to Longfellow and Emerson by the Massachusetts Historical Society ...

Boston ... 1882.

Large paper copies noted only in cloth. Small paper copies noted in cloth; and, printed paper boards. For fuller entry see BAL, Vol. 3, p. 64.

Henry Wadsworth Longfellow His Life, His Works, His Friendships by George Lowell Austin ...

Boston   Lee and Shepard, Publishers   1883

Cloth; and, leather.

The Genius and Life-Work of Longfellow. A Paper Read before the Literary and Historical Society of Quebec, 7th March, 1883, by Geo. Stewart ... (Fifty Copies.)

Quebec: Printed at the "Morning Chronicle" Office. 1883.

Printed paper wrapper.

Henry Wadsworth Longfellow. Seventy-Eighth Birthday. Proceedings of the Maine Historical Society, February 27, 1885.

Portland: Hoyt, Fogg & Donham, 193 Middle Street. ⟨1885⟩

Printed paper wrapper.

History of the Ordination of Caleb D. Bradlee. Also History of the Thirtieth Anniversary of His Ordination ...

Boston: Printed for the Author. D. Clapp & Son, Printers. 1885.

Printed paper wrapper. The hymn, p. 7 is not by Henry Wadsworth Longfellow. For comment see note under "Ordination Hymn," No. 384, in *A Book of Hymns* ... , 1846, in *References and Ana,* above.

The Longfellow Collectors' Hand-Book   A Bibliography ⟨Compiled by Beverly Chew⟩ ...

New York   William Evarts Benjamin   744 Broadway 1885

Printed paper boards, white vellum shelfback. 250 copies only.

"Mr. Chew's first published writing is *The Longfellow Collector's Handbook* ⟨sic⟩, which appeared in 1885 ..."—*Essays & Verses about Books,* by Beverly Chew, edited by Ruth Shepard Granniss, New York, 1926, p. vii.

Life of Henry Wadsworth Longfellow by Eric S. Robertson

London   Walter Scott   24 Warwick Lane, Paternoster Row 1887

Issued in two formats: Large paper: 8⅜" x 5½". Small paper: 6⅞" x 4¾". In the *Great Writers* series.

Longfellow's Latest Poems   Copyright

London   George Routledge and Sons, Limited   Broadway, Ludgate Hill   Glasgow, Manchester, and New York   1890

Paper boards, cloth shelfback. Reprint with the exception of "Two Offerings," pp. 317-318, dated at end: *Cambridge, April 10, 1838.*

"The following poem, says the *New York World,* was written by Henry W. Longfellow while a Professor at Harvard College many years ago, and presented to Mrs. Margaret Brewster, who was at that time visiting at the house of a Mrs. Craigie, where the poet then had lodgings. Careful investigations made by the *World* leave little doubt as to the genuineness of the poem."

By Longfellow? The poem is dated at end *Cambridge, April 10, 1838,* but according to Longfellow's journal (in H) the poet was in Maine on that date.

Published April, 1890, according to *English Catalogue.* See next entry.

No. 27. Standard Recitations by Best Authors ... March, 1890 ...

... N. Y. ... ⟨1890⟩

"Two Offerings," pp. 6-7; see preceding entry. For fuller entry see No. 4161.

Via Solitaria. An Unpublished Poem, by Henry W. Longfellow ...

⟨n.p., n.d., *ca.* 1890⟩

The above at head of a card, 4⁹⁄₁₆" x 3⁹⁄₁₆". Three cards, printed on one side only, laced together by white ribbons.

Not by Longfellow. By Obadiah Milton Conover of Madison, Wisconsin. See Wm. Sloane Kennedy, *Henry W. Longfellow* ... , Cambridge, 1882, pp. 204-207.

... Snow Flakes ...

Boston   Oliver Ditson Company ... ⟨n.d., 1891?⟩

Sheet music. Cover-title. At head of title: Frederic H. Cowen's Album of Twelve Songs ...   Plate number: 54972-4. *Not by Longfellow* but by Mary Mapes Dodge.

Longfellow's First Poem.

⟨n.p., n.d., *ca.* 1900⟩

Caption-title. Single cut sheet folded to make four pages. P. ⟨1⟩ as above. Pp. ⟨2⟩ and ⟨4⟩ blank. On p. ⟨3⟩: Prefatory note by an editor; and, text of the poem, "Mr. Finney's Turnip."

Not by Longfellow. See *Henry W. Longfellow* ..., by Wm. Sloane Kennedy, 1882, pp. 223-225. *Note:* "Mr. Finney's Turnip" is also in *Wayside Gleanings* ..., 1882; see above in *Section One.*

Henry Wadsworth Longfellow by George Rice Carpenter

Boston   Small, Maynard & Company   MD-CCCCI

... Henry Wadsworth Longfellow by Thomas Wentworth Higginson

Boston ... 1902

For fuller description see entry No. 8448.

Contains material by Longfellow, including his commencement address at Bowdoin, 1825, pp. 30-36, "Our Native Writers."

... Fifth Year Book   The Bibliophile Society Printed for Members Only

⟨Boston, 1906⟩

At head of title: *1906*   Boards, printed paper label on spine. 500 copies only.

"The Last of the Household," pp. 19-20; with reproduction of the original manuscript. Not by Longfellow but by Grenville Mellen whose name (as the reproduction shows) has been incompletely erased from the original manuscript.

Boyhood Poems of Henry Wadsworth Longfellow Not Included in His Collected Works.

Privately Printed, Brunswick, Maine, 1906.

A ghost? Entry from CHAL, Vol. 2, p. 429.

"... *Longfellow's Boyhood Poems* ... was written for delivery ⟨by Geo. Thomas Little⟩ before some Portland society, but thus far the editor has not been able to learn either the name of the society or the date. Clearly it was written after Mr. Little collected these early poems, about 1906, and the manuscript suggests a date between 1910 and his death in 1915.   ... Following Dr. Little's paper, I have reprinted the full text of all identified poems of this first period which have not been included in the collected works ..."—

Longfellow's Boyhood Poems, a Paper by the Late George Thomas Little ..., edited by Ray W. Pettengill, Saratoga Springs, 1925, pp. ⟨v⟩-vi. See entry in *Section One* under year 1925.

Henry Wadsworth Longfellow A Sketch of His Life by Charles Eliot Norton

This work occurs as follows:

Limited Edition

Henry Wadsworth Longfellow   A Sketch of His Life by Charles Eliot Norton together with Longfellow's Chief Autobiographical Poems

Boston and New York   Houghton, Mifflin and Company MDCCCCVII

Two issues noted; the following is sufficient for ready identification:

1: Page 121 so paged. P. ⟨122⟩: *The Riverside Press | Electrotyped and printed by H. O. Houghton & Co. | Cambridge, Mass., U.S.A. |* On p. ⟨v⟩ the editorial note reads: *The proposed commemoration* ...

2: Page 121 is unpaged. P. ⟨122⟩: FOUR HUNDRED COPIES PRINTED AT | THE RIVERSIDE PRESS CAMBRIDGE | MASSACHUSETTS IN DECEMBER 1906 | On p. ⟨v⟩ the editorial note reads: *The proposed commemoration* ...

410 copies printed Dec. 28, 1906. Bound during the period Dec. 31, 1906–Jan. 23, 1907.

A copy of the first issue deposited for copyright Jan. 2, 1907.

Goldstamped V cloth. Leaf: 8¾" tall.

Riverside Literature Series

Not located. Issued as No. 167 of the series. Jan. 4, 1907, 2040 copies printed; bound in cloth. Jan. 7, 1907, 1530 copies printed, bound in printed paper wrapper.

Trade Edition

Henry Wadsworth Longfellow   A Sketch of His Life by Charles Eliot Norton together with Longfellow's Chief Autobiographical Poems

Boston and New York   Houghton, Mifflin and Company MDCCCCVII

According to the publisher's records there were three printings in 1907; BAL has been unable to distinguish the first from the later printings. *First printing:* Feb. 9, 1907, 514 copies, bound Feb. 16-21, 1907. *Second printing:* March 19, 1907, 521 copies. *Third printing:* May 25, 1907, 262 copies. *Note:* The whole of the third printing was shipped to Constable (London).

On p. ⟨v⟩ the editorial note reads: *The commemoration* ...

S cloth: Stamped in gold and blind. Leaf: 7¼"
tall.

Subscription Edition

Henry Wadsworth Longfellow   A Sketch of
His Life by Charles Eliot Norton

Boston and New York   Houghton, Mifflin
and Company   MDCCCVII

Probably prepared for purchasers of the *Complete Writings* in eleven volumes, 1904.

Contains a certificate of issue: *Copy No. ⟨space
for number⟩ Presented To ⟨space for recipient's name⟩ With The Compliments Of
Houghton, Mifflin And Company ... February
27, 1907*

Printed Feb. 13, 1907, 820 copies; spine label
printed Feb. 21, 1907.

Paper boards, linen shelfback, printed paper
label on spine. Leaf: 8¾" tall.

... A Bibliography of the First Editions in
Book Form of the Writings of Henry Wads-
worth Longfellow Compiled Largely from the
Collection Formed by the Late Jacob Chester
Chamberlain with Assistance from His Notes
and Memoranda by Luther S. Livingston

New York   Privately Printed   1908

At head of title: *The Chamberlain Bibliographies*   Printed paper boards, leather label
on spine. "Five Hundred ⟨numbered⟩ Copies
Printed On Old Stratford Paper And Fifty
Copies On Van Gelder"—Certificate of issue.

Contains, pp. 121-127, the following poems;
all but one (as noted) being by Longfellow:

"An Evening in Autumn," pp. 121-122. Previously in *The Token* ... , 1833. Also in
The Works ... , New York ⟨1909⟩.

"The Soul," p. 123. Previously in *Henry
Wadsworth Longfellow. A Medley* ... , by
Stoddard, 1882.

"Truth," p. 124. Previously in *The Boston
Book*, 1836. Also in *The Works* ... , New
York ⟨1909⟩.

"The Poet of Miletus," pp. 124-125. Previously in *The Liberty Bell*, 1846. Also in
The Works ... , New York ⟨1909⟩.

"April," pp. 125-126 (*All day the low-hung
clouds have dropped* ...). Not by Longfellow. See note under *Miscellaneous Poems
Selected from the United States Literary
Gazette*, 1826, in, *Section One*.

"The Two Sharpshooters," pp. 126-127. Previously in *Poetical Pen-Pictures of the War*,
1863, *q. v.*

"January," p. 127. Previously in *The Children's Almanac* ... , Boston ⟨1878⟩; and, as
part of "The Poet's Calendar," *In the Harbor*, 1882.

A copy at H received Nov. 16, 1908. Noted as
has just been privately printed PW Nov. 21,
1908. Listed PW Dec. 5, 1908.

Random Memories by Ernest Wadsworth Longfellow ...

Boston and New York   Houghton Mifflin
Company   The Riverside Press   Cambridge
1922

A Victorian American   Henry Wadsworth Longfellow by Herbert S. Gorman

New York   George H. Doran Company
⟨1926⟩

Longfellow and Spain by Iris Lilian Whitman ...

Instituto de las Españas en los Estados Unidos
New York   1927

Printed paper wrapper.

Twilight   A Poem by Rudyard Kipling

⟨New York: The Harvard Press, n.d., 1932⟩

Cover-title. Single cut sheet folded to make
four pages. "Fifty copies have been privately
printed by the Harvard Press for Harvey
Taylor." Not by Kipling. A reprint of five
lines from Longfellow's "The Discoverer of
the North Cape."

New Light on Longfellow with Special Reference to His Relations to Germany by James
Taft Hatfield ...

Boston and New York   Houghton Mifflin
Company   The Riverside Press   Cambridge
1933

Young Longfellow (1807–1843) by Lawrance
Thompson ...

New York   The Macmillan Company   1938

Professor Longfellow of Harvard by Carl L.
Johnson ...

University of Oregon   Eugene, Oregon.
Printed at the University Press. 1944.

Printed paper wrapper.

Longfellow and Scandinavia   A Study of the
Poet's Relationship with the Northern Languages and Literature by Andrew Hilen

New Haven   Yale University Press ... 1947

"Longfellow's Scandinavian Journal, June 16–September 24, 1835," pp. ⟨113⟩-148, "is the first complete transcription of the poet's Scandinavian journal ..."

Longfellow   His Life and Work ⟨by⟩ Newton Arvin

An Atlantic Monthly Press Book   Little, Brown and Company   Boston   Toronto ⟨1963⟩

Henry Wadsworth Longfellow by Cecil B. Williams ...

Twayne Publishers, Inc.   New York ⟨1964⟩

Henry Wadsworth Longfellow   Portrait of an American Humanist ⟨by⟩ Edward Wagenknecht ...

New York   Oxford University Press   1966

Initials, Pseudonyms, and Anonyms for Volume V

Address of the Friends of Domestic Industry ... October 26, 1831 ... *By John Pendleton Kennedy and others*

Afterglow. *By George Parsons Lathrop*

Agapida, Fray Antonio. *Pseud. for Washington Irving*

Ambrose, Mr. *Pseud. for John Pendleton Kennedy*

Ambrose, Paul. *Pseud. for John Pendleton Kennedy*

American, An. *Pseud. for Henry Wadsworth Longfellow on* Outre-Mer ..., *London, 1835*

American Gentleman, An. *See entry No. 10096*

Art of Conversation, The. *By Charles Godfrey Leland*

Author of *Knickerbocker's History of New York.* Washington Irving

——— *Margaret, a Tale of the Real and Ideal.* Sylvester Judd

——— *Mercy Philbrick's Choice.* Helen Hunt Jackson

——— *A New Home.* Caroline M. Kirkland

——— *Outre-Mer.* Henry Wadsworth Longfellow

——— *Philo.* Sylvester Judd

——— *The Sketch Book.* Washington Irving

———*Swallow Barn.* John Pendleton Kennedy

——— *Wild Western Scenes.* John Beauchamp Jones

Baltimore Long Ago. *By John Pendleton Kennedy*

Battles of Joshua, The. *See in list of S. B. H. Judah attributions*

Book of Copperheads, Ye. *By Charles Godfrey Leland*

Book of Visions, The. *By John Beauchamp Jones*

Border States, The, Their Power and Duty. *By John Pendleton Kennedy*

Breitmann, Hans. *Pseud. for Charles Godfrey Leland*

Carrier's Address. Evening Bulletin (Phila.) 1877. *See in Thomas A. Janvier list of ana*

Citizen of Maryland, A. *Pseud. for John Pendleton Kennedy*

Clavers, Mrs. Mary. *Pseud. for Caroline Matilda Kirkland*

Clerke of Oxenforde, The. *Pseud. for Pendleton Kennedy; sometimes erroneously identified as John Pendleton Kennedy*

Crayon, Geoffrey. *Pseud. for Washington Irving*

David and Uriah. A Drama ... *See in S. B. H. Judah list of attributions*

Defence of Fort M'Henry. *By Francis Scott Key*

Devil and Tom Walker, The. *By Washington Irving*

Diedrich Knickerbocker. *Pseud. for Washington Irving*

Eldest Grandson, The. *Pseud. for Sidney Lanier*

Eli Perkins. *Pseud. for Melville D. Landon*

Falkland, Lucius. *Pseudonym? Sometimes identified as John Pendleton Kennedy; BAL has found no evidence to support the attribution*

Fragment of a Journal of a Sentimental Philosopher ..., 1809. *For a comment see in the Washington Irving list of references and ana*

France, Alsace, and Lorraine ..., 1870. *By Charles Godfrey Leland*

Gentleman in Black, The. *By Washington Irving*

Gentleman of New-York, A. *Pseud. for Washington Irving, entry No. 10099*

Geoffrey Crayon. *Pseud. for Washington Irving*

Gotham and the Gothamites. *By S. B. H. Judah*

Green Bowl, The. *By Sarah Orne Jewett*

H. H. *Helen Hunt Jackson*

H. W. L. *Henry Wadsworth Longfellow*

Hans Breitmann. *Pseud. for Charles Godfrey Leland*

History of Rip Van Winkle, The. *By Washington Irving*

Holm, Saxe. *Pseud. for Helen Hunt Jackson*

Instructer, An. *Pseud. used by Henry Wadsworth Longfellow on his* Elements of French Grammar, *1830; and,* French Exercises, *1830*

Jonathan Oldstyle. *Pseud. for Washington Irving*

Kempton-Wace Letters, The. *By Jack London and Anna Strunsky*

Knickerbocker, Diedrich. *Pseud. for Washington Irving*

L., H. W. *Henry Wadsworth Longfellow*

Lan. *Pseud. for Melville D. Landon*

Langstaff, Launcelot. *Pseud. for Washington Irving*

Launcelot Langstaff. *Pseud. for Washington Irving*

Layman, A. *See in Washington Irving list of references and ana under the year 1811*

Leila among the Mountains. *By Lucy Larcom? See entry No. 11314*

Letters from a Cat. *See entry No. 10438*

Letters of a Man of the Times, to the Citizens of Baltimore . . . *Presumably by John Pendleton Kennedy*

Life and Adventures of Charles Anderson Chester . . . *See in the George Lippard list, Section IV*

Literary Picture Gallery . . . , The, Ballston-Spa, 1808. *See in the Washington Irving list of references and ana*

Littleton, Mark. *Pseud. for John Pendleton Kennedy*

Lottie's Thought-Book. *By Lucy Larcom*

Lucius Falkland. *Pseudonym? Sometimes attributed to J. P. Kennedy; BAL has found no evidence to support the attribution*

Luke Shortfield. *Pseud. for John Beauchamp Jones*

Maid of Midian, The, a Tragedy . . . *See in the S. B. H. Judah list of attributions*

Man of the Times, A. *Pseud. for John Pendleton Kennedy*

Manuel de Proverbes Dramatiques. *See entry No. 12040*

Margaret. A Tale of the Real and Ideal . . . *By Sylvester Judd*

Mark Littleton. *Pseud. for John Pendleton Kennedy*

Mary Clavers, Mrs. *Pseud. for Caroline Matilda Kirkland*

Member of the Committee of Safety of 1908, A. *Pseud. for Thomas A. Janvier*

Member of the Philadelphia Bar, A. *Pseud. for George Lippard*

Member of the Twenty-Seventh Congress, A. *Pseud. for John Pendleton Kennedy*

Mephistopheles. *Pseud. for John Pendleton Kennedy*

Mercy Philbrick's Choice. *By Helen Hunt Jackson*

Mother Goose from Germany, Philadelphia, 1864. *Translated by Charles Godfrey Leland*

Mother Pitcher's Poems for Little People. *By Charles Godfrey Leland*

Mystical Craft, The, the Most Crafty of All Crafts . . . *See in the S. B. H. Judah list of attributions*

Nasby, Petroleum V. *Pseud. for David Ross Locke*

Nathaniel Hawthorne, Philadelphia, 1890. *By George Parsons Lathrop*

New England Tragedies . . . , The, Privately Printed, 1868. *By Henry Wadsworth Longfellow*

New England Tragedy, The, Boston, 1860. *By Henry Wadsworth Longfellow*

Noël, Cambridge, 1864. *By Henry Wadsworth Longfellow*

Novelas Españolas. El Serrano de las Alpujarras ... *See entry No. 12044; edited by Henry Wadsworth Longfellow*

Oldstyle, Jonathan. *Pseud. for Washington Irving*

Outre-Mer; a Pilgrimage beyond the Sea. *By Henry Wadsworth Longfellow*

Paul Ambrose. *Pseud. for John Pendleton Kennedy*

Perch, Philemon. *Pseud. for Richard Malcolm Johnston*

Perkins, Eli. *Pseud. for Melville D. Landon*

Petroleum V. Nasby. *Pseud. for David Ross Locke*

Philemon Perch. *Pseud. for Richard Malcolm Johnston*

Phlogobombos, Terentius. *Pseud. for S. B. H. Judah*

Pious Lawyer, A. *Pseud. for Francis Scott Key*

Pipps among the Wide-Awakes ... *See in the Charles Godfrey Leland list of references and ana*

Privilege of the Writ of Habeas Corpus under the Constitution, The. *By John Pendleton Kennedy*

Quaker City, The, or, the Monks of Monk-Hall. *By George Lippard*

Quest of the Holy Grail, The. *See entry No. 10612*

Red Book, The. *By John Pendleton Kennedy and Peter Hoffman Cruse*

Richelieu: A Domestic Tragedy. *See in the S. B. H. Judah list of attributions*

Rip Van Winkle, The History of. *By Washington Irving*

Saxe Holm. *Pseud. for Helen Hunt Jackson*

Secession, Coercion, and Civil War. The Story of 1861 ... *By John Beauchamp Jones*

Secondthoughts, Solomon. *Pseud. for John Pendleton Kennedy*

Shortfield, Luke. *Pseud. for John Beauchamp Jones*

Sneak Yclepid Copperhead, Ye ... *See in the Charles Godfrey Leland list of references and ana*

Solomon Secondthoughts. *Pseud. for John Pendleton Kennedy*

Some Notes on America to Be Rewritten ... *See in the Charles Godfrey Leland list of references and ana*

Song of the Bees, The. *See entry No. 11618*

Southern Man, A. *Pseud. for John Pendleton Kennedy*

Spirit of Fanaticism ... *See in the S. B. H. Judah list of attributions*

Squatter, A. *Pseud. for John Beauchamp Jones*

Swallow Barn, or a Sojourn in the Old Dominion. *By John Pendleton Kennedy*

Terentius Phlogobombos. *Pseud. for S. B. H. Judah*

Unknown Author, An. *Pseud. for George Lippard*

Witnesses, The. *By Henry Wadsworth Longfellow*

Word in Season, A, by a Layman, New-York, 1811. *See in Washington Irving list of references and ana*

Wrong Side Up. A Poem. *See under entry No. 12252*

Young Man's Account of His Conversion from Calvinism, A. *By Sylvester Judd*